Make Instruction Needs-Based

- Identify where your students are struggling and customize your instruction to address their needs.
- Gauge how your entire class or individual students are doing by viewing the easy to use grade book.
- Ensure your students are getting the additional reinforcement and direction they need between class meetings.

Getting Started is as EASY as 1, 2, 3 . . . 4!

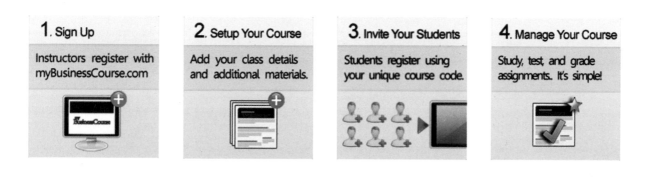

1. Sign Up
Instructors register with myBusinessCourse.com

2. Setup Your Course
Add your class details and additional materials.

3. Invite Your Students
Students register using your unique course code.

4. Manage Your Course
Study, test, and grade assignments. It's simple!

Provide Instruction and Practice 24/7

- Assign homework from your Cambridge Business Publishers textbook and have myBusinessCourse grade it for you automatically.
- With our eLectures, your students can revisit accounting topics as often as they like or until they master the topic.
- Guided Examples show students how to solve select problems.
- Make homework due before class to ensure students enter your classroom prepared.
- Upgrade to include the eBook and you have all the tools needed for an online course.

Want to learn more about myBusinessCourse?

Contact your sales representative or visit **www.mybusinesscourse.com**.

STUDENTS: Find your access code on the myBusinessCourse insert on the following pages. If you have a used copy of this textbook, you can purchase access online at **www.mybusinesscourse.com**.

Cambridge Business Publishers Series in Accounting

Financial Accounting

- **Financial Accounting for Undergraduates, 2e** by Ferris, Wallace, and Christensen
- **Financial Accounting, 4e** by Dyckman, Magee, and Pfeiffer
- **Financial Accounting for MBAs, 5e** by Easton, Wild, Halsey, and McAnally
- **Financial Accounting for Executives & MBAs, 3e** by Simko, Ferris, and Wallace
- **Cases in Financial Reporting, 7e** by Engel, Hirst, and McAnally

Managerial Accounting

- **Managerial Accounting, 6e** by Hartgraves & Morse
- **Cases in Managerial and Cost Accounting, 1e** by Allen, Brownlee, Haskins, and Lynch

Combined Financial & Managerial Accounting

- **Financial & Managerial Accounting for MBAs, 3e** by Easton, Halsey, McAnally, Hartgraves, and Morse

Intermediate Accounting

- **Cases in Financial Reporting, 7e** by Engel, Hirst, and McAnally

Cost Accounting

- **Cases in Managerial and Cost Accounting, 1e** by Allen, Brownlee, Haskins, and Lynch

Financial Statement Analysis & Valuation

- **Financial Statement Analysis & Valuation, 3e** by Easton, McAnally, Sommers, and Zhang
- **Cases in Financial Reporting, 7e** by Engel, Hirst, and McAnally

Advanced Accounting

- **Advanced Accounting, 2e** by Hamlen, Huefner, and Largay
- **Advaced Accounting, 2e** by Halsey & Hopkins

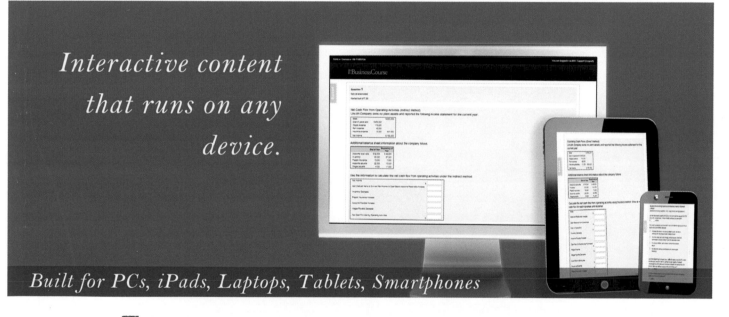

Financial Accounting
for Undergraduates

Second Edition

Kenneth R. Ferris
W.P. Carey School of Business
Arizona State University

James S. Wallace
The Peter F. Drucker and Masatoshi Ito
Graduate School of Management
Claremont Graduate University

Theodore E. Christensen
The Marriott School of Management
Brigham Young University

FINANCIAL ACCOUNTING FOR UNDERGRADUATES, Second Edition, by Kenneth Ferris, James Wallace, and Theodore Christensen.

ISBN 978-1-61853-040-0

Bookstores & Faculty: To order this book, contact the company via email **customerservice@cambridgepub.com** or call 800-619-6473.

Students & Retail Customers: To order this book, please visit the book's Website and order directly online.

Printed in the United States of America.
10 9 8 7 6 5 4 3 2 1

About the Authors

KENNETH R. FERRIS is a Professor in the W.P. Carey School of Business at Arizona State University. He received a B.B.A. and an M.B.A. from The George Washington University and an M.A. and a Ph.D. from The Ohio State University. He previously served on the faculties of Northwestern University, The Claremont Graduate University, Southern Methodist University, and Thunderbird School of Global Management, In addition, he has taught at numerous academic institutions in Australia, Hong Kong, Japan, and New Zealand. Professor Ferris is the author or co-author of eleven books, over fifty academic and professional publications, and over eighty case studies. He previously served as a director of several NYSE listed companies and is active in executive education programs around the world.

JAMES S. WALLACE is an Associate Professor at The Peter F. Drucker and Masatoshi Ito Graduate School of Management at The Claremont Graduate University. He received his B.A. from the University of California, Santa Barbara, his M.B.A. from the University of California, Davis, and his Ph.D. from the University of Washington. Professor Wallace also holds a CPA certification from the state of California. He previously served on the faculty of the University of California, Irvine and has served as a visiting professor at the University of California, San Diego. Professor Wallace's work has appeared in leading academic journals including the *Journal of Accounting and Economics*, the *Journal of Corporate Finance*, and *Information Systems Research*, along with leading applied journals such as the *Journal of Applied Corporate Finance*, the *Journal of Accountancy*, *Issues in Accounting Education* and *Accounting Horizons*. Prior to his career in academics, Professor Wallace worked in public accounting and in industry with a Fortune 500 company. He has done consulting work with numerous companies in multiple industries.

THEODORE E. CHRISTENSEN has been a faculty member at Brigham Young University since 2000. Prior to coming to BYU, he was on the faculty at Case Western Reserve University for five years. He received a B.S. degree in accounting at San Jose State University, a M.Acc. degree in tax at Brigham Young University, and a Ph.D. in accounting from the University of Georgia. Professor Christensen has authored and coauthored articles published in many journals including *The Accounting Review, Journal of Accounting and Economics, Journal of Accounting Research, Review of Accounting Studies, Contemporary Accounting Research, Accounting Organizations and Society,* the *Journal of Business Finance & Accounting, Accounting Horizons,* and *Issues in Accounting Education.* He is also the author of an advanced financial accounting textbook. Professor Christensen has taught financial accounting at all levels, financial statement analysis, business valuation, both introductory and intermediate managerial accounting, and corporate taxation. He is the recipient of numerous awards for both teaching and research. He has been active in serving on various committees of the American Accounting Association and is a CPA.

Preface

Welcome to the Second Edition of *Financial Accounting for Undergraduates*. We wrote this book to satisfy the needs of students taking their first financial accounting course by providing a **high quality, contemporary, and engaging textbook at an affordable price**. *Financial Accounting for Undergraduates* is written for students who want to understand how financial statements are prepared and how the information in published financial reports is used. The *Second Edition* has benefited from extensive feedback from adopters of the first edition and suggestions from focus groups, market surveys, manuscript reviews, and interviews with faculty from across the country.

TARGET AUDIENCE

Financial Accounting for Undergraduates is intended for use in the first financial accounting course at the undergraduate level; one that balances the preparation of financial statements with their interpretation and use. This book teaches students how to read, analyze, and interpret financial accounting data to make informed business decisions.

We believe students become more engaged in the course when they see how the content pertains to their everyday lives. Once engaged in the course, students perform much better and enjoy the class more. Furthermore, we believe accounting is a discipline best learned by doing. Unlike some other disciplines, accounting needs to be practiced. Consequently, we took great care to incorporate a number of pedagogical devices and real examples that show students the relevance of financial accounting to their lives and that help students succeed in the course.

RELEVANCE

"Why do I need to study financial accounting?"

Students frequently ask this or similar questions. The extent to which they feel accounting is relevant to their daily lives will often determine how much effort they put into the course. The following features are used throughout the book to convey the relevance of accounting to their lives and society.

Real Data and Examples

Today's students must be skilled in using real financial statements to make business decisions. Through their exposure to various financial statements, students will learn that, while financial statements do not all look the same, they can readily understand and interpret them to make business decisions. In each chapter, we incorporate a wide range of examples using real companies that students know. In addition, the **Extending Your Knowledge** section in the assignments of each chapter requires students to use the financial statements of **Columbia Sportswear Company** and **Under Armour Corporation**..

COLUMBIA
SPORTSWEAR
COMPANY

UNDER ARMOUR,
INC.

EYK4-2. Comparative Analysis Problem: Columbia Sportswear Company vs. Under Armour, Inc. The financial statements for **Columbia Sportswear** can be found in Appendix A and **Under Armour**'s financial statements can be found in Appendix B at the end of this textbook.

Required

a. Calculate for each company the following ratios for 2011:
  1. Current ratio
  2. Debt-to-total-assets ratio
  3. Return on sales ratio
b. Comment on the companies' relative profitability, liquidity, and solvency.

Accounting in Practice

These boxed inserts help bridge the gap between the classroom and what students encounter in the real world. **Accounting In Practice** illustrations document situations a reader is likely to encounter and present the choices that companies make in reporting financial results.

	ACCOUNTING IN PRACTICE
Bond Risk Ratings	

The relative riskiness of different bonds may vary considerably. Bond investors who want to know the relative quality of a particular bond issue can consult a bond-rating service. Two major firms that rate the riskiness of bonds are **Standard & Poor's Corporation** (S&P) and **Moody's Investors Service** (Moody's). The rating categories used by these firms are similar. The schedule below shows the relationship between the ratings and the degree of risk using Standard & Poor's rating system:

Low Risk							High Risk
AAA	AA	A	BBB	BB	B	CCC	D

I- - - - - - - - - Investment Grade Bonds - - - - - - - -I- - - - - - - - Junk Bonds - - - - - - - -I

Investment grade bonds are highly-rated bonds with little risk that the issuing company will fail to pay interest as scheduled or fail to repay the principal at a bond's maturity. Junk bonds, on the other hand, are low-quality, high-yield bonds. In the S&P rating system, junk bonds are any bond rated BB and lower. Generally, bonds with poor credit ratings must offer higher interest rates than highly-rated bonds to attract potential buyers.

A.K.A. Junk bonds are often referred to as *high-yield bonds* because of the higher yield rates that typically accompany this type of debt investment.

Forensic Accounting

Forensic Accounting is the one of the fastest growing areas in the practice of accounting. These boxed inserts help students understand how financial accounting knowledge can be used to aid in the prevention of financial accounting errors and the detection of fraud.

	FORENSIC ACCOUNTING
Accountant as Detective—Cash Fraud Schemes	

Frauds involving cash are the most common frauds, and are more common than corruption or fraudulent financial statements. The more common cash schemes include (1) skimming, where an employee accepts cash from a customer but does not record a sales transaction, (2) cash larceny, where an employee steals cash from the daily receipts before they are deposited in a bank, (3) check tampering, where an employee steals blank company checks and makes them out to themselves or an accomplice, and (4) cash register disbursement, where an employee fraudulently voids a sale on his or her cash register and steals the cash.

Corporate Social Responsibility

Increasingly, companies have found that "doing good" leads to a more successful, profitable enterprise. These boxed inserts help students understand how corporate social responsibility is being embraced by forward-thinking enterprises as part of their long-term business models.

	CORPORATE SOCIAL RESPONSIBILITY
Reporting on Triple Bottom Line	

Companies worldwide are focused on more than just the bottom line. Research shows that financial responsibility goes hand in hand with social responsibility. This is labeled a "virtuous cycle" because financial success provides the means to act socially responsible, and acting socially responsible increases a company's financial performance. Financial statements are not well suited for measuring social performance. To aid in the pursuit of socially responsible behavior, accountants have developed a **triple bottom line** framework in which the single bottom line of financial performance is supplemented with a social bottom line and an environmental bottom line. The triple bottom line standard for urban and community accounting has been ratified by the United Nations and has become widely used in public sector accounting.

SUCCESS

Financial accounting can be challenging—especially for students lacking business experience or previous exposure to business courses. To help students succeed in the course, we include many features that provide direction to students and require them to recall and apply the financial accounting techniques and concepts described in each chapter.

Putting each chapter in context

Often, students lose sight of the big picture. The Past/Present/Future feature provides students with an overview of where the chapter fits within the whole course.

PAST

Chapter 2 explained how we analyze and record transactions (the first two steps in the *accounting cycle*), including the system of debits and credits.

PRESENT

This chapter completes our examination of the final three steps in the five-step accounting cycle: adjust, report, and close.

FUTURE

Chapter 4 examines the balance sheet and income statement more closely and introduces techniques for analyzing and interpreting financial statements.

Mapping each chapter

Each chapter begins with an overview that visually depicts the layout of the chapter.

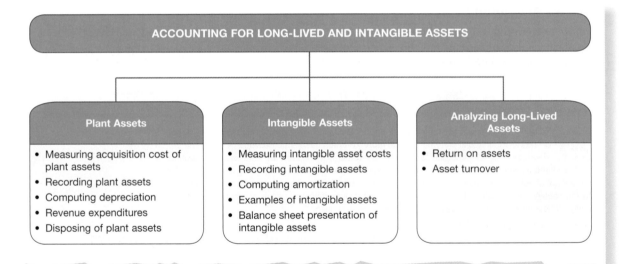

ACCOUNTING FOR LONG-LIVED AND INTANGIBLE ASSETS

Plant Assets
- Measuring acquisition cost of plant assets
- Recording plant assets
- Computing depreciation
- Revenue expenditures
- Disposing of plant assets

Intangible Assets
- Measuring intangible asset costs
- Recording intangible assets
- Computing amortization
- Examples of intangible assets
- Balance sheet presentation of intangible assets

Analyzing Long-Lived Assets
- Return on assets
- Asset turnover

Your Turn!

Your Turn boxes are integrated throughout each chapter as a means of reinforcing the material just presented. Solutions are provided at the end of the chapter so students can check their work.

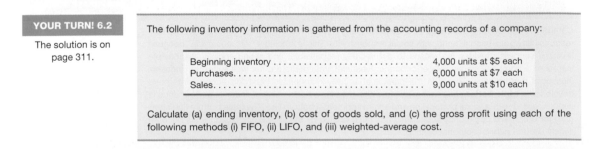

YOUR TURN! 6.2

The solution is on page 311.

The following inventory information is gathered from the accounting records of a company:

Beginning inventory	4,000 units at $5 each
Purchases	6,000 units at $7 each
Sales	9,000 units at $10 each

Calculate (a) ending inventory, (b) cost of goods sold, and (c) the gross profit using each of the following methods (i) FIFO, (ii) LIFO, and (iii) weighted-average cost.

A.K.A. Boxes

A.K.A. (Also Known As) boxes inform students of commonly used alternative terms that they may encounter.

> Accounts receivable includes only those amounts relating to credit sales of goods or services. Other amounts due, such as from advances to employees or loans to affiliated companies, should be included with the Other Receivables account on the balance sheet. Other Receivables may be either a current asset or a noncurrent asset.

A.K.A. Accounts receivable are also sometimes referred to as *trade receivables*.

Hints

Helpful suggestions are inserted in the margin as **Hints** to help students understand difficult concepts.

to the required amount—$1,560, as shown below.

Allowance for Doubtful Accounts

400	Beg.
1,160	Dec. 31
1,560	Bal.

Hint: In contrast to the percentage of net sales method, the accounts receivable aging method takes into account the beginning balance for doubtful accounts.

It is also possible to have a debit balance in the allowance account before the year-end adjustment, implying an underestimation expense in the prior period. This would...

Takeaways

These in chapter summaries ensure that students grasp key concepts before proceeding to the next topic.

Concept	Method	Assessment	TAKEAWAY 4.1
Can a company meet its short-term obligations?	Current assets and current liabilities from the balance sheet. $$\text{Current ratio} = \frac{\text{Current assets}}{\text{Current liabilities}}$$	A larger current ratio implies greater liquidity and a greater ability to pay short-term obligations.	

ETHICS

In today's post-Sarbanes-Oxley world, ethical decision making has never been more pertinent to business and students studying accounting. We discuss ethics where appropriate in the text, and we have included at least one assignment in each chapter that raises an ethical issue. Assignments involving ethics are identified by the icon in the margin.

Ethics and Accounting

Ethics deals with the values, rules, and justifications that govern one's way of life. Although fundamental ethical concepts such as right and wrong, good and evil, justice and morality are abstract, many issues in our daily lives have ethical dimensions. The way that we respond to these issues defines our ethical profile. In both our personal and professional lives, our goal is to act ethically and responsibly.

Ethical behavior has not always been the rule in business. Business history reveals unethical activities such as price gouging of customers, using inside information for per-

INTERNATIONAL FINANCIAL REPORTING STANDARDS (IFRS)

The convergence of U.S. GAAP and International Financial Reporting Standards (IFRS) is in process. Our introductory students should be prepared for this eventuality with a basic understanding of the similarities and differences in the current reporting requirements and methods under U.S. GAAP and IFRS. Consequently, we incorporate discussions that examine these similarities and differences where appropriate throughout the book in IFRS Alert! boxes. In addition, the financial statements for Tesco, PLC are included in Appendix C at the end of the book. Each chapter includes an IFRS assignment related to Tesco. The IFRS icon identifies those assignments.

IFRS ALERT!

Under IFRS, LIFO is *not* generally accepted. Further, under U.S. GAAP inventory may not be revalued above its acquisition cost. IFRS permits inventory to be revalued upwards if the inventory's fair value appreciates above acquisition cost. When inventory is revalued upward under IFRS a parallel increase is made to an equity account called Asset Revaluation Reserve. To illustrate, assume that Tesco's ending inventory at year-end is valued on its books at 2,669 million British pounds. Also assume that a review by management concluded that the fair value of its inventory had appreciated to 3,000 million British pounds. Under IFRS, we make the following journal entry to revalue inventory:

A = L + SE
+331   +331

Inventories	331	
Asset revaluation reserve		331
To write up inventory to its fair market value.		

Appendix C at the end of this book presents the IFRS financial statements of Tesco. Tesco's asset revaluation reserve is in the equity section of its balance sheet.

Thinking Globally

In addition to **IFRS Alert!** boxes, these **Thinking Globally** inserts emphasize the similarities and differences between the United States and other countries that are not necessarily related to reporting standards.

THINKING GLOBALLY

While U.S. corporations principally distribute cash and/or stock dividends, property dividend distributions are common among Japanese corporations. For example, **McDonald's Holding Company of Japan** annually distributes to its stockholders coupons for a free Big Mac as a property dividend. And, **DyDo Drinco, Inc.**, distributes to its stockholders samples of its beverage products as a property dividend. Companies that distribute their products or coupons for their products to stockholders as a property dividend believe that by making stockholders more familiar with the company's products, they will retain the investment commitment of their stockholders on a longer term basis than would otherwise be the case.

NEW TO THIS EDITION

- **myBusinessCourse:** This complete learning and assessment program is free with new copies of the textbook. myBusinessCourse includes a complete learning path for students. Students will be able to watch eLectures, and see how representative problems are solved before proceeding to their homework. As the instructor, you can select assignments from the textbook or test bank and have students' responses automatically graded. You also have access to a robust grade book that provides many course management and diagnostic tools. Whether you teach a complete online course or just want to provide your students with additional resources to master the content, myBusinessCourse will prove to be an invaluable resource for you and your students.

- **Chapter 1 has been streamlined:** The opening chapter has been rewritten to better motivate the subject. A section on careers in accounting has been added and the financial statements of **Columbia Sportswear** are used to underscore the important role accounting plays in businesses familiar to students.

- **Under Armour replaces Timberland:** Under Armour replaces Timberland as the comparison company to Columbia Sportswear. Assignments and 10-K excerpts have been updated to reflect this change.

- **Change in chapter sequence:** In response to adopter and reviewer feedback, the "Understanding Financial Statements" chapter has been moved from Chapter 2 in the first edition to Chapter 4 in the new edition. This placement creates the more logical progression from transaction analysis and financial statement preparation to financial statement interpretation and use for decision making.

- **Refinement of the accounting cycle chapters:** The highly touted accounting cycle chapters (Chapters 1-3) have been refined further to make better use of design and pedagogy to help students grasp more easily the transaction analysis and adjustment process.
- **Single-step and multi-step income statements:** Chapter 4 now includes a detailed discussion of single-step and multi-step income statements to better prepare students for the merchandising and inventory chapters that follow.
- **Chapter 5 and chapter 6 have been streamlined:** Chapters 5 and 6 have been revised to eliminate redundancy between the chapters.
- **Direct write-off method moved to appendix:** Under US GAAP, the direct write-off method is only permissible when the amount of the credit losses is immaterial. Consequently, the direct write-off method has been moved from the body of Chapter 8 (Receivables) to an appendix at the end of the chapter to reflect the limited use of this method in practice.
- **Leases moved to appendix:** In response to reviewer feedback, the discussion of leases in Chapter 10 (Liabilities) has been moved from the body of the chapter and placed in an appendix at the end of the chapter.
- **Expanded IFRS and global accounting:** In response to the ever changing worldwide accounting environment, the authors have expanded their discussion of IFRS and other global accounting issues as appropriate.

SUPPLEMENT PACKAGE

For Instructors

Instructor CD-ROM: This convenient supplement provides the text's ancillary materials on a portable CD-ROM. All the faculty supplements that accompany the textbook are available, including Power-Point, Solutions Manual, Test Bank, and Computerized Test Bank.

Solutions Manual: Created by the authors, the *Solutions Manual* contains complete solutions to all the assignment material in the text.

PowerPoint: The PowerPoint slides outline key elements of each chapter.

Test Bank: The test bank includes multiple-choice items, matching questions, short essay questions, and problems.

Excel Templates: We provide Excel spreadsheets for assignments. These spreadsheets will save time in data entry and allow students to dedicate additional time to learning the material. The Excel spreadsheets are identified by the Excel icon.

Website: All instructor materials are accessible via the book's Website (password protected) along with other useful links and marketing information. **www.cambridgepub.com**

myBusinessCourse: A web-based learning and assessment program intended to complement your textbook and classroom instruction. This easy-to-use course management system grades homework automatically and provide students with additional help when you are not available. In addition, detailed diagnostic tools assess class and individual performance. myBusinessCourse is ideal for online courses or traditional face-to-face courses for which you want to offer students more resources to succeed. Assignments with the ✅ in the margin are available in myBusinessCourse.

For Students

Excel Templates: We provide Excel spreadsheets for assignments. These spreadsheets will save students' time in data entry and allow them to dedicate additional time to learning the material. The Excel spreadsheets are identified by the Excel icon.

Website: Practice quizzes and other useful links are available to students free of charge on the book's Website.

myBusinessCourse: A web-based learning and assessment program intended to complement your textbook and faculty instruction. This easy-to-use program grades homework automatically and provides you with additional help when your instructor is not available. Assignments with the ✅ in the margin are available in myBusinessCourse. Access is free with new copies of this textbook (look for page containing the access code towards the front of the book) If you buy a used copy of the book, you can purchase access at **www.mybusinesscourse.com**.

ACKNOWLEDGMENTS

The First and Second Editions of this book benefited greatly from the valuable feedback of focus group attendees, reviewers, students, and colleagues. We are extremely grateful to them for their help in making this project a success.

Markus Ahrens *St. Louis Community College*
David Ambrosini *Cabrillo College*
Matthew Anderson *Michigan State University*
James Bannister *University of Hartford*
Debbie Benson *Kennesaw State University*
Lydia Botsford *DeAnza College*
Rada Brooks *University of California—Berkeley*
Marilyn Brooks-Lewis *Warren County Community College*
Amy Browning *Ivy Tech Community College*
Sandra Byrd *Missouri State University*
Jeffrey Byrne *Indiana University—Southeast*
Mike Campbell *Montana State University*
Tommy Carnes *Berry College*
Betty Chavis *California State University—Fullerton*
Alan Cherry *Loyola Marymount University*
Leslie Cohen *University of Arizona*
Nancy Coster *Loyola Marymount University*
John Coulter *Western New England College*
Rosemond Desir *Colorado State University*
Cole Engel *Fort Hayes State University*
Alan Falcon *Loyola Marymount University*
Julie Finnegan *Mendocino College*
Carolyn Galantine *Pepperdine University*
Lisa Gillespie *Loyola University*
Bruce Gunning *Kent State University*
Bob Hartman *University of Iowa*
Rosemary Hayward *Cabrillo College*
Haihong He *California State University—Los Angeles*
Cynthia Hollenbach *University of Denver*
Steven Hornik *Central Florida University*
Marsha Huber *Youngstown State University*

Stephen Jablonsky *Colorado State University*
Marianne James *California State University—Los Angeles*
Ching-Lih Jan *California State University—Northridge*
Catherine Jeppson *California State University—Northridge*
Gene Johnson *University of Hawaii*
Randy Johnston *University of Colorado*
Thomas Kam *Hawaii Pacific University*
Kathryn Kapka *University of Texas—Tyler*
Jocelyn Kauffunger *University of Pittsburgh*
Christine Kloezeman *Glendale Community College*
John Koeplin *University of San Francisco*
Christopher Kwak *De Anza College*
Cathy Larson *Middlesex Community College*
Doug Larson *Salem State University*
Greg Lauer *North Iowa Area Community College*
Ron Lazer *University of Houston*
Elliott Levy *Bentley College*
Zining Li *Southern Methodist University*
Siyi Li *University of Illinois*
Christine Li *College of Marin*
Lihong Liang *Syracuse University*
Emily Lindsay *American University*
Nancy Lynch *West Virginia University*
Joe Manzo *Lehigh University*
Ariel Markelevich *Suffolk University*
Dawn Massey *Fairfield University*
Michele Matherly *Xavier University*
Allison McLeod *University of North Texas*
Jeff McMillan *Clemson University*
Sara Melendy *Gonzaga University*
Michael Meyer *University of Notre Dame*
Michelle Moshier *SUNY—Albany*
Tracie Nobles *Austin Community College*
Sarah Nutter *George Mason University*
Ken O'Brien *Farmingdale State University*

Mary Pearson *Southern Utah University*
Kimberly Perkins *Austin Community College*
Marietta Peytcheva *Lehigh University*
Gary Pieroni *University of California—Berkeley*
Ronald Premuroso *University of Montana*
Allan Rabinowitz *Pace University*
Paul Recupero *Newbury College*
Maria Roxas *Central Connecticut State University*
Albert Schepanski *University of Iowa*
Arnold Schneider *Georgia Tech University*
Steve Sefcik *University of Washington*
Cathy Sevigny *Bridgewater State University*
Ray Shaffer *Youngstown State University*
Carol Shaver *Louisiana Tech University*
John Shon *Fordham University*
Gregory Sinclair *San Francisco State University*
Ken Sinclair *Lehigh University*
Eric Slayter *Cal Poly—San Luis Obispo*
Gene Smith *Eastern New Mexico University*
Nancy Snow *University of Toledo*
John Suckow *Lansing Community College*
Ted Takamura *Eastern Oregon University*
Diane Tanner *University of North Florida*
Linda Tarrago *Hillsborough Community College*
Sheri Trumpfheller *University of Colorado—Colorado Springs*
Joan Van Hise *Fairfield University*
Marcia Viet *University of Central Florida*
George Violette *University of Southern Maine*
Robert Walsh *University of Dallas*
Daryl Woolley *University of Idaho*
Susan Wright *DeKalb Technical College*
Rong Yang *SUNY—Brockport*
Kathryn Yarbrough *University of North Carolina—Charlotte*

In addition, we are extremely grateful to George Werthman, Jill Fischer, Linda Lange, Jocelyn Mousel, Rich Kolasa, Debbie Golden, Terry McQuade, and the entire team at Cambridge Business Publishers for their encouragement, enthusiasm, and guidance. Feedback is always welcome. Please feel free contact us with your suggestions or questions.

Ken Ferris   Jim Wallace   Ted Christensen

Brief Contents

Contents

CHAPTER **3**

Accrual Basis of Accounting   116

CHAPTER **4**

Understanding Financial Statements   178

CHAPTER 5

Accounting for
Merchandising
Operations **220**

CHAPTER 6

Accounting for Inventory **260**

CHAPTER 7

Internal Control and Cash 312

CHAPTER 8

Accounting for Receivables 360

CHAPTER 9

Accounting for Long-Lived and Intangible Assets   404

CHAPTER 10

Accounting for Liabilities   448

CHAPTER 11

Stockholders' Equity 502

CHAPTER 12

Statement of Cash Flows 548

CHAPTER 13

Analysis and Interpretation of Financial Statements   598

APPENDIX A

Columbia Sportswear Company: Annual Report and Social Responsibility Report   A-1

APPENDIX **B**

Financial Statements for Under Armour   B-1

APPENDIX **C**

Financial Statements for Tesco PLC   C-1

APPENDIX **D**

Accounting for Investments and Consolidated Financial Statements   D-1

APPENDIX **E**

Accounting and the Time Value of Money   E-1

1

Financial Accounting and Business Decisions

PRESENT

This chapter explains business formation, the use and users of accounting, the types of activities companies pursue, and financial statements that report on business.

FUTURE

The next chapters more fully explain financial statements, including how they are prepared, constructed, analyzed, and interpreted.

LEARNING OBJECTIVES

1. **Explain** business organization and its three forms. *(p. 4)*

2. **Describe** business activities. *(p. 5)*

3. **Indicate** who uses accounting information. *(p. 6)*

4. **Explain** the accounting process and generally accepted accounting principles. *(p. 10)*

5. **Describe** the accounting equation and each financial statement. *(p. 12)*

6. **Explain** additional disclosures that accompany financial statements. *(p. 19)*

7. **Describe** careers in accounting. *(p. 21)*

8. Appendix 1A: **Discuss** FASB's conceptual framework. *(p. 25)*

WHAT THE NUMBERS MEAN

If it's true that accounting is the language of business, then this textbook is crucial to your future livelihood. All of us confront accounting issues in our daily lives. We must control our cash and other assets; we must monitor our paychecks and our expenses; we must purchase items that fit within our budgets; and we must use accounting data in making business decisions.

It is no surprise then that accounting knowledge ranks near the top of what employers look for when hiring new workers. It is also no surprise that students with accounting knowledge perform better than those that do not understand the basics of accounting. This book provides fundamental financial accounting knowledge for future success in business and life.

Columbia Sportswear Company (Columbia.com), a maker of clothing for dedicated lovers of the greater outdoors, must also rely upon accounting for its success. It uses financial reports to judge its performance and that of its managers. It uses accounting controls to monitor its inventory. It uses accounting data to assess the wisdom of payments, and their amounts, to shareholders. Consequently, accounting not only impacts our lives, but also the business activities of all companies worldwide. We even witness national and international politicians using accounting data to justify or reject key economic and governmental policies.

This first chapter introduces us to many basic relations and principles underlying financial accounting reports. It also identifies many key users of accounting information and how that information is useful in businesses globally.

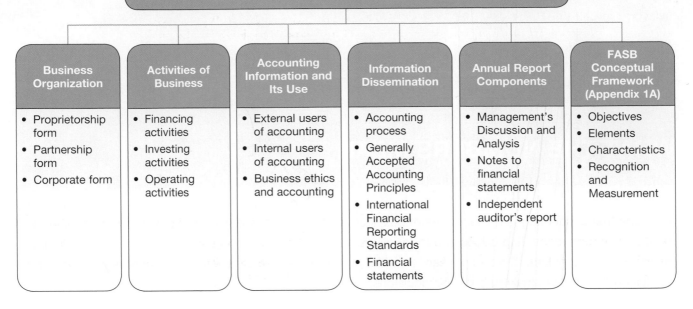

BUSINESS ORGANIZATION

LO1 **Explain** business organization and its three forms.

The three principal forms of business organization are the sole proprietorship, the partnership, and the corporation. Although each of these organizational forms is treated as an accounting entity, only the corporation is viewed under the law as a legal entity separate and distinct from its owners.

A **sole proprietorship** is a business owned by one person; it is the most common of the three forms of business organization. The primary advantage of the sole proprietorship is its ease of formation. As the only owner, the sole proprietor makes all of the decisions affecting the business. This organizational form also enjoys certain income tax advantages relative to a corporation in that the income of that business is not taxed; instead, its income is included as part of the owner's income that is reported to the taxation authorities.

A **partnership** is a voluntary association of two or more persons for the purpose of conducting a business. Partnerships and sole proprietorships differ principally with respect to the number of owners. Partnerships are also easy to establish. Because a partnership involves multiple owners, the partners should establish the rights and obligations of each partner to avoid any misunderstandings that might lead to disputes and lawsuits. An advantage of the partnership form over the sole proprietorship is the broader skill set that multiple partners can bring to a business. Partnerships also enjoy the same income tax advantage as sole proprietorships.

A **corporation**, on the other hand, is a legal entity created under the laws of a state or the federal government. The owners of a corporation receive shares of stock as evidence of their ownership interest in the business, and consequently, they are referred to as **stockholders** (or *shareholders*). Since corporations are a separate legal entity, they must pay income taxes on any earned profits. This leads to a situation of double taxation because the income of the corporation is taxed and stockholders also pay taxes on dividends they receive from the corporation. The corporation is the dominant organizational form in terms of the volume of business activity conducted in the United States and worldwide.

While most businesses start off as either a sole proprietorship or as a partnership, some outgrow these organizational forms and convert to the corporate form. For example, the **Columbia Sportswear Company** was incorporated in 1961 after beginning as a sole proprietorship in 1938. Two primary reasons for converting a sole proprietorship or a partnership to the corporate form of business are the ease of raising capital to grow the business and the protection afforded to stockholders against personal liability. A third advantage of the corporate form is the relative ease of selling ownership shares. Stock exchanges, such as the **New York Stock Exchange (NYSE)**, exist to enable stockholders to readily buy and sell their ownership shares. No such exchanges exist for sole proprietors or partners, and thus, selling an ownership interest in a sole proprietorship or a partnership is a more difficult, time-consuming event.

Proprietorship

- One owner controlled
- Business not taxed, but owner taxed
- Not legal entity
- Limited life

Partnership

- Shared owner control
- Business not taxed, but owners taxed
- Not legal entity
- Limited life

Corporation

- All types of owner control
- Business taxed **and** owners taxed
- Separate legal entity
- Unlimited life

Identify two characteristics for each of the three principal forms of business organizations.

1. sole proprietorship
2. partnership
3. corporation

YOUR TURN! 1.1

The solution is on page 54.

ACTIVITIES OF A BUSINESS

Every business, regardless of its organizational form, its industry, or its size, is involved in three types of business activities—financing, investing, and operating.

LO2   Describe business activities.

Financing Activities

Before a company can begin operations, a company must acquire money to support its operations. Employees need to be hired, buildings constructed, raw materials purchased, and machinery put in place. Companies can obtain the necessary funds to undertake these activities in several ways. These **financing activities** are generally categorized as either debt financing or equity financing.

Debt financing involves borrowing money from sources such as a bank by signing a note payable or directly from investors by issuing bonds payable. The individuals or financial institutions that lend money to companies are called their **creditors**. Debt financing involves an obligation to repay a creditor both the amount initially borrowed, called the **principal**, and an interest fee for the use of the funds.

Equity financing involves selling shares of stock to investors. In contrast to creditors who lend money to a business and expect to receive that money back with interest, investors that purchase shares of stock are actually buying an ownership interest in the company. Investors hope that their stock will increase in value so that they can earn a profit when the stocks are sold. The owners of a company's stock may also receive dividend payments when the company decides to distribute some of its net income.

Investing Activities

For a company to undertake its business, it needs to purchase certain long-term resources necessary to conduct its business, such as a printing press purchased by a printing company. The purchase of these resources is known as **investing activities**. Companies can obtain the money needed to make an investment in such items as land, buildings, and equipment from either the financing activities discussed above or from any excess cash accumulated from running the business profitably.

Investing activities involve acquisition and disposition of items such as factories, office furniture, computer and data systems, and delivery vehicles, to carry out the business plans. These items are referred to as *assets*. Investing decisions regarding these assets are known as *asset management*.

Operating Activities

The day-to-day activities of producing and selling a product or providing a service are referred to as **operating activities**. Operating activities are critical for a business because if a company is unable to generate income from its operations it is very likely that the business will fail. If creditors and stockholders do not believe that a company will be able to generate a profit, they are unlikely to provide the financing needed to start, or maintain, its operations.

Exhibit 1-1 provides a summary of the three types of business activities. Arrows are pointing both toward, and away from, operating activities. This is because financing and investing activities are necessary to carry out a company's operating activities; however, if a company's operating activities generate excess cash, then the excess cash can be used to either finance additional investments or repay the company's creditors.

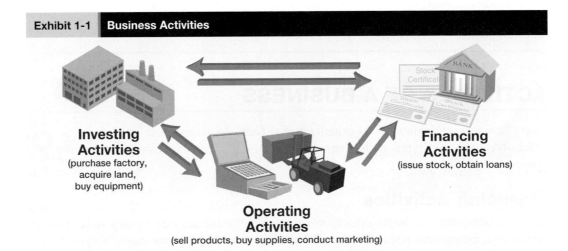

Exhibit 1-1   Business Activities

Investing Activities
(purchase factory, acquire land, buy equipment)

Financing Activities
(issue stock, obtain loans)

Operating Activities
(sell products, buy supplies, conduct marketing)

YOUR TURN! 1.2

The solution is on page 54.

Classify each of the following activities as a financing, investing, or operating activity.

1. Receiving a loan from a bank.
2. Selling merchandise online.
3. Purchasing a delivery truck.
4. Purchasing merchandise for resale to customers.
5. Issuing shares of stock in exchange for cash.
6. Paying employee salaries.

ACCOUNTING INFORMATION AND ITS USE

LO3 Indicate who uses accounting information.

In today's society, many individuals and agencies are involved in the economic life of a business. The information needs of these parties are fulfilled, in part, by accounting information. Information users are classified by their relation to a business as either *external users* or *internal users*.

External Users of Accounting

An important function of the accounting process is to accumulate and report accounting information that details a business's results of operations, cash flows, and financial position. By U.S. law, publicly owned businesses must publish financial statements annually and quarterly. The subset of accounting that produces these publicly available financial statements is referred to as **financial accounting**.

Financial accounting information serves a variety of users. Potential investors and investment professionals need financial data to compare prospective investments to determine which, if any, should be invested in, and at what price. Creditors must consider the financial strength of a business before lending it funds, and stockholders must evaluate whether to remain invested in a business, buy more shares, or sell their existing shares of stock.

The financial statements issued by a company are the main source of financial information for these external users. Because financial statements are often used to evaluate the management team running the business, their objectivity is sometimes called into question because the reports are prepared by the management team itself. To establish the validity of financial statements, most businesses have their financial data audited by an independent public accountant. The independent public accountant, or independent auditor, examines the financial statements and recommends any changes or improvements that are warranted. The independent auditor then expresses a professional opinion as to whether the financial statements are fairly presented "in conformity with generally accepted accounting principles." External users have greater confidence in financial statements that have been audited by an independent, certified public accountant.

The Big Four	ACCOUNTING IN PRACTICE

Independent auditors are licensed by the state in which they do their auditing work and are identified as **certified public accountants (CPAs)**. To qualify as a CPA, an individual must pass a rigorous examination that is administered nationally and must meet the educational and work experience requirements set by each state to ensure high standards of accounting and auditing performance. The four largest U.S. public accounting firms, referred to as the *Big Four*, have offices located throughout the world and employ thousands of auditors. These firms are **PricewaterhouseCoopers**, **Deloitte and Touche**, **Ernst & Young**, and **KPMG, LLP**.

There are many other external users of a company's accounting information. For example, a business's customers may want information to help them determine if a company like **Whirlpool** will be able to honor its product warranties. Labor unions require information to determine the level of pay raises that they can demand from companies like **United Parcel Service**. Exhibit 1-2 illustrates the kind of accounting information that is required by a company's external users.

Exhibit 1-2	Accounting Information Needs of External Users
User Group	**Accounting Information Needed to Answer Questions such as:**
Potential investors and stockholders	How does the profitability of **Target** compare to that of **WalMart**? How does **Bank of America Corporation** compare with **Wells Fargo & Company** in terms of firm size?
Creditors and lenders	Will **Delta Airlines** be able to repay its creditors in a timely fashion? Is it safe to provide a bank loan to the **Federal Express Corporation**?
Taxation authorities and regulators	Is **Time Warner Inc.** reporting the proper amount of taxable income? Is **Duke Energy**'s rate hike justified by its operating costs?

Internal Users of Accounting

A major function of accounting is to provide the internal management of a company with the data needed for decision making and the efficient management of the business. While managers have an interest in the information reported to external users, managers also require various other types of information, such as the cost of its products, estimates of the income to be earned from a sales campaign, cost comparisons of alternative courses of action, and long-range budgets. Because of the strategic nature of much of this information, it is usually only available to a company's top-level management. The process of generating and analyzing such data is referred to as **managerial accounting**. Exhibit 1-3 illustrates the various types of accounting information that are required by a company's internal users.

Exhibit 1-3	Accounting Information Needs of Internal Users
User Group	**Accounting Information Needed to Address Questions such as:**
Marketing Department	What is the optimal price to sell the **Samsung** Galaxy phone to maximize the company's sales revenue?
	Was the promotional campaign by **Paramount Pictures** successful in promoting the company's film "The Avengers"?
Management Team	How much is the Olive Garden restaurant chain contributing to the overall profitability of its parent company, the **Darden Restaurant Group**?
	What is the projected profitability of the **General Motors'** Chevrolet brand for the coming year?
Finance Department	Is there sufficient cash available for **Hewlett Packard** to buy back a large amount of its outstanding common stock?
	Will **General Electric** have sufficient cash flow to pay its short-term expenses?

YOUR TURN! 1.3

The solution is on page 54.

1. Are financial statements the primary output of managerial or financial accounting? Explain.
2. Identify at least two internal users and explain why they need accounting information.
3. Identify at least two external users and explain why they need accounting information.

Ethics and Accounting

Ethics deals with the values, rules, and justifications that govern one's way of life. Although fundamental ethical concepts such as right and wrong, good and evil, justice and morality are abstract, many issues in our daily lives have ethical dimensions. The way that we respond to these issues defines our ethical profile. In both our personal and professional lives, our goal is to act ethically and responsibly.

Ethical behavior has not always been the rule in business. Business history reveals unethical activities such as price gouging of customers, using inside information for personal gain, paying bribes to government officials for favors, ignoring health and safety regulations, selling arms and military equipment to aggressor governments, polluting the environment, and issuing misleading financial information. Recent accounting scandals at such companies as **Enron**, **WorldCom**, and **AIG** have again brought ethics to the forefront.

Increasingly, business managers recognize the importance and value of ethical behavior by their employees. It is now commonplace for businesses to develop a written code of ethics to help guide the behavior of employees. Similarly, professional organizations of accountants have written ethics codes. The **American Institute of Certified Public Accountants** (AICPA), for example, has a professional code of ethics to guide the conduct of its member CPAs. Similarly, the **Institute of Management Accountants** (IMA) has written standards of ethical conduct for accountants employed in the private sector.

Unethical behavior that results in misleading financial statements such as those at Enron and WorldCom has the potential to erode public confidence and trust in accounting information. In response to this decline in public confidence, the U.S. Congress passed the **Sarbanes-Oxley Act** in 2002 with the goal of restoring investor trust by reducing the likelihood of future accounting scandals. Among the many changes required by this legislation is that a company's top management must certify in writing the accuracy of its reported financial statement information, and these executives risk criminal prosecution for fraudulent certification. In addition, companies must now report on the internal controls put into place to help deter errors in the financial reporting process and to detect them should they occur.

A.K.A. The *Sarbanes-Oxley Act* of 2002 is often referred to as SarBox or SOX.

FORENSIC ACCOUNTING

Accountant as Detective—CSI in Real Life

Law enforcement personnel are not the only people who perform criminal investigations. A branch of accounting known as **forensic accounting** is vitally important in many types of criminal investigations, from financial statement fraud, to money laundering, to massive investment frauds such as the one perpetrated by Bernard Madoff (who is currently serving a 150-year prison sentence). Unlike law enforcement personnel, forensic accountants are involved both before and after the commission of a crime.

Accountants face several unique ethical dimensions as a result of their work. These dimensions include the following:

1. The output produced by accountants has financial implications for individuals, as well as businesses. These situations generate considerable pressure on the accountant to "improve" the reported results. The amount of income taxes to be paid by an individual or business, the amount of a bonus to be received by an employee, the price to be paid by a customer, and the amount of money to be distributed to a business's owners are examples of situations in which the financial implications can lead to efforts to influence the outcome. *Ethical behavior mandates that accountants ignore these pressures.*

2. Accountants have access to confidential, sensitive information. Tax returns, salary data, details of financial arrangements, planned acquisitions, and proposed price changes illustrate this type of information. *Ethical behavior mandates that accountants respect the confidentiality of information.*

3. A criticism of U.S. business practices is that they are too "bottom-line" (that is, short-term profit) oriented. This orientation can lead to unethical actions by management to increase reported short-term profits. Because accountants measure and report a firm's profit, they must be particularly concerned about these ethical breakdowns. *Both accountants and management must recognize the importance of a long-run perspective.* Studies indicate that, over the long term, successful companies and ethical practices go hand in hand.

YOUR TURN! 1.4

The solution is on page 54.

As an accountant for the Madoff Corporation, you are responsible for measuring and reporting the company's net income. It appears that actual results are going to be less than was expected by Wall Street analysts. Your supervisor has asked that you report some of next period's sales revenue early so that the current period's net income will be in line with analyst expectations. You know that reporting revenue like this represents a violation of generally accepted accounting principles. He states that you will not really be doing anything wrong because the sales revenues are real—the company will just be reporting the revenue earlier than accounting guidelines allow. What should you do?

THE ACCOUNTING PROCESS

LO4 **Explain** the accounting process and generally accepted accounting principles.

Accounting is *the process of measuring economic activity of an entity in monetary terms and communicating results to users.* The accounting process consists of two principal activities—measurement and communication.

The measurement process must (1) identify the relevant economic activities of a business, (2) quantify these economic activities, and (3) record the resulting measures in a systematic manner. Measurement is done in monetary terms. In the United States, measurements are stated in U.S. dollars. In other countries, measurements are expressed in the local currency. In Mexico, for example, measurements are stated in pesos, and in most European countries, they are stated in euros.

The purpose of accounting is to provide useful financial information, and the communication process is extremely important. Accordingly, the accounting process (1) prepares financial reports to meet the needs of the user and (2) helps interpret the financial results for that user. To provide reports that serve users effectively, managers must be aware of how these users are likely to apply the reports. The needs of the various users differ; as such, there are different types of accounting reports. Managers employ various techniques to help users interpret the content of reports. These techniques include the way the report is formatted, the use of charts and graphs to highlight trends, and the calculation of ratios to emphasize important financial relations.

THINKING GLOBALLY

Companies measure their operating performance using the currency of their principal place of business. The **Johnson & Johnson Company**, a well-known maker of baby shampoo and Band-Aids, is headquartered in New Jersey, and reports its financial results using the U.S. dollar. On the other hand, **Moet Hennessy Louis Vuitton**, the luxury goods manufacturer, is headquartered in Paris, France, and reports its financial results using the euro. Some companies prepare "convenience translations" of their financial statements in the currency and language of other countries so that potential foreign investors can more readily understand the company's financial performance and condition.

Generally Accepted Accounting Principles

It is important that financial statements be prepared under a set of rules that is understood by the users of reports. Imagine if every business were free to determine exactly how it measured and communicated its financial health and operating performance. How would a user of this information be able to compare one company's results to another if each played by a different set of rules? Financial statement users who rely on accounting data expect that all companies will follow the same standards and procedures when preparing their statements. These standards and procedures are called **generally accepted accounting principles**.

A.K.A. *Generally accepted accounting principles* are often referred to as GAAP (pronounced like the clothing store "Gap").

Generally accepted accounting principles (GAAP) are guides to action that can (and do) change over time. Sometimes specific accounting principles must be altered or new principles formulated to fit a changing set of economic circumstances or changes in business practices. For instance, there existed no generally accepted accounting principles to account for the emerging dot.com companies; and consequently, the business community had to create a set of guidelines for companies such as **Amazon.com** and **eBay** to measure and communicate their financial results.

Financial Accounting Oversight

Organizations such as the **Financial Accounting Standards Board** (FASB), the American Institute of Certified Public Accountants (AICPA), and the **U.S. Securities and Exchange Commission** (SEC) have been instrumental in the development of generally accepted accounting principles in the United States. As a federal agency, the SEC's primary focus is to regulate the interstate sale of stocks and bonds. The SEC requires companies under its jurisdiction to submit audited annual financial statements to the agency which it then makes available to the general public. The SEC has the power to set the accounting principles used by these companies, but the agency has largely delegated that principle-setting responsibility to the FASB (and earlier, the AICPA).

The FASB is a nongovernmental entity whose pronouncements establish U.S. GAAP (see the appendix to this chapter for additional information on the conceptual framework the FASB has developed to formulate accounting standards). The FASB[1] consists of a seven-member board and follows a process that allows for input from interested parties as it considers a new or changed accounting principle. A new or changed principle requires the support of at least a majority of the board members. More recently, the **Public Company Accounting Oversight Board** (PCAOB) was established. The PCAOB is empowered to approve auditing standards, known as **generally accepted auditing standards** (GAAS), and monitor the quality of financial statements and audits.

Exhibit 1-4	Financial Accounting Oversight

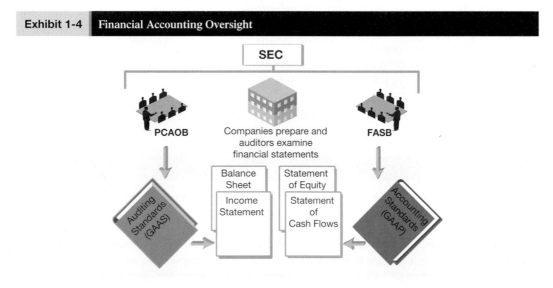

Accounting principles, however, do differ among countries of the world. Energized by the continuing growth of international business, efforts are underway to create greater uniformity in worldwide accounting principles. The FASB completed a major restructuring, called the FASB Accounting Standards Codification, in 2009 concerning how GAAP is organized and communicated. This codification represents the authoritative U.S. GAAP for non-governmental entities and is easily researched through an online database maintained by the FASB. A major justification for the codification project was to ease the convergence of U.S. GAAP and international standards.

---

[1] Paralleling the FASB structure, the Governmental Accounting Standards Board (GASB) was organized in 1984 to formulate the generally accepted accounting principles for state and local governments.

International Financial Reporting Standards

The past few decades have witnessed a steady acceptance for the need for international financial reporting standards. This acceptance coincides with the increasing globalization of business. Although several organizations are working to increase international harmonization in accounting, the organization that has taken the lead in formulating international accounting principles is the **International Accounting Standards Board** (IASB). The accounting standards formulated by the IASB are referred to as the **International Financial Reporting Standards** (IFRS). Approximately 120 nations or reporting jurisdictions either require or permit the use of IFRS. This includes the European Union, Australia, New Zealand, Israel, and Canada. Other large economies including the United States, Japan, China, India, and Russia are working hard to converge their national standards with IFRS.

A.K.A. *International financial reporting standards are often referred to as IFRS (pronounced "eye furs").*

The SEC has assumed a leadership role, dating back several decades, in the development of a strong set of international reporting standards. In 1988 the SEC issued a policy statement supporting the establishment of international accounting standards. In 2002 the SEC announced support for the FASB and the IASB to work toward the convergence of U.S. GAAP and IFRS. In 2007 the SEC voted to accept foreign issuers of financial statements prepared using IFRS to file in the United States without reconciliation to U.S. GAAP. In 2008 the SEC proposed a roadmap for moving U.S. companies to IFRS. In 2009, the SEC approved 110 U.S. firms as potential early adopters of IFRS. The SEC, however, has not made a final decision as of the writing of this textbook in 2012 as to whether to allow, or require, all U.S. firms to adopt IFRS.

The arguments for the need for international financial reporting standards revolve around the increase in companies raising capital in more than one country and the high cost of complying with multiple accounting standards. A common set of standards like IFRS will aid investors in comparing the financial performance of companies from different countries. Multinational companies with subsidiaries in multiple countries could lower their reporting costs by using a common set of accounting standards companywide. An additional benefit of a common set of international accounting standards would be the increased mobility for accounting professionals. A solid knowledge of IFRS would allow an accounting professional to work in many different parts of the world without requiring him or her to learn a whole different set of accounting standards.

IFRS ALERT!

How do you get a German, an Italian, and a Spaniard to communicate in the same language? When it comes to communicating financial information, that decision has already been made—the language is called "IFRS." IFRS refers to *International Financial Reporting Standards* as established by the International Accounting Standards Board (IASB). While accounting standards have traditionally been established on a country-by-country basis, making the comparability of financial information across national borders difficult, the IASB was established to "harmonize" global accounting practices. Many countries have now replaced their national GAAP with the International Financial Reporting Standards (IFRS) issued by the IASB.

FINANCIAL STATEMENTS

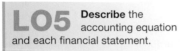
Describe the accounting equation and each financial statement.

There are four basic financial statements: the balance sheet, the income statement, the statement of stockholders' equity, and the statement of cash flows. Each financial statement begins with a heading. The heading provides the name of the company, the name of the financial statement, and the date or time period of the statement.

Balance Sheet

The **balance sheet** is a listing of a firm's assets, liabilities, and stockholders' equity as of a given date, usually the end of an accounting period. The balance sheet depicts a framework called the **accounting equation**. The accounting equation states that the sum of a business's economic resources must equal the sum of any claims on those resources. That is, a business obtains resources that it utilizes in its operations from outside sources, principally creditors and stockholders, who maintain claims on those resources. Consequently, the accounting equation can be written as:

A.K.A. The *balance sheet* is also referred to as the statement of financial position.

A.K.A. The *accounting equation* is also called the balance sheet equation.

$$\text{Resources of a company} = \text{Claims on resources}$$

Assets refer to a company's resources, liabilities refer to creditor claims on those resources, and stockholders' equity refers to owner claims on those resources. Using these terms, the accounting equation can be reformulated as:

$$\text{Assets} = \text{Liabilities} + \text{Stockholders' equity}$$

This equation states that the firm's assets equals the sum of its liabilities plus its stockholders' equity—see Exhibit 1-5. Throughout the accounting process, the accounting equation must always remain in balance.

Exhibit 1-5	Accounting Equation for a Business				
Economic Terms	Resources	=	Creditor claims on resources	+	Stockholder (owner) claims on resources
Business Terms	Assets	=	Liabilities	+	Stockholders' equity

Assets are the economic resources of a business that can be expressed in monetary terms. Assets take many forms. Cash is an asset, as are claims to receive cash payments from customers for goods or services provided, called accounts receivable. Other types of assets include inventory, supplies, land, buildings, and equipment. The key characteristic of any asset is that it represents a probable future economic benefit to a business.

Liabilities are the obligations or debts that a business must pay in cash or in goods and services at some future time as a consequence of past transactions or events. For example, a business can borrow money and sign a promissory note agreeing to repay the borrowed amount in six months. The business reports this obligation as a liability called notes payable. Similarly, if a business owes money to various suppliers for goods or services already provided, it is called accounts payable, or if it owes wages to its employees for work already performed, it is called wages payable. The business reports these obligations on its balance sheet.

Hint: Only resources that can be expressed in monetary terms are included among the assets reported on the balance sheet. There exist some assets that cannot be expressed in monetary terms, such as the value of a company's workforce, and, therefore, are not reported on a balance sheet.

Stockholders' equity refers to the ownership (stockholder) claims on the assets of the business. Stockholders' equity represents a *residual claim* on a business's assets; that is, it is a claim on the assets of a business that remain after all liabilities to creditors have been satisfied. For this reason, stockholders' equity is sometimes referred to as a business's **net assets**, where net assets equal the difference between the total assets and total liabilities. In equation format,

$$\text{Assets} - \text{Liabilities} = \text{Stockholders' equity}$$

and,

$$\text{Net assets} = \text{Stockholders' equity}$$

Columbia's balance sheet is shown in Exhibit 1-6 and reports the company's assets, liabilities, and stockholders' equity. (All Columbia Sportswear amounts are in thousands of dollars.) Columbia's assets totaled $1,382,542 at year-end 2011, with the largest asset being inventories of $365,199. Total assets ($1,382,542) are equal to the sum of liabilities ($307,997) and stockholders' equity ($1,074,545). This equality must always exist as required by the accounting equation.

Columbia's balance sheet indicates that the company principally depends on stockholders' equity to finance its operations since liabilities totaled only $307,997 at 2011 year-end, or approximately 22 percent of total assets. Columbia has been quite profitable in the past and its board of directors has chosen not to distribute much of its net income.

Hint: Final totals in the financial statements are double underlined. Follow this format whenever asked to prepare a financial statement.

Exhibit 1-6	Columbia Sportswear Balance Sheet

COLUMBIA SPORTSWEAR COMPANY
Balance Sheet
December 31, 2011
(In thousands)

Assets

Cash.	$ 241,034
Investments	2,878
Accounts receivable.	351,538
Inventories	365,199
Prepaid expenses and other current assets.	36,392
Property, plant, and equipment, net	250,910
Other assets.	134,591
Total assets	$1,382,542

Liabilities and Stockholders' Equity

Liabilities

Accounts payable.	$ 148,973
Income taxes payable.	27,968
Other liabilities	131,056
Total liabilities.	307,997
Stockholders' Equity	
Common stock.	3,037
Retained earnings.	1,071,508
Total stockholders' equity.	1,074,545
Total liabilities and stockholders' equity	$1,382,542

TAKEAWAY 1.1	Concept	Method	Assessment
	What mix of financing does a company use?	The balance sheet provides information regarding the various forms of financing, both debt financing and equity financing.	A higher ratio of liabilities to equity implies a higher use of creditor financing, and vice versa. Creditor financing is viewed by users as more risky.
		Compare the amount of liabilities appearing on the balance sheet to the amount of equity appearing on the balance sheet.	

Income Statement

A.K.A. The *income statement* is also called the statement of operations, the statement of income, and the earnings statement.

A.K.A. *Sales revenue* is also referred to as revenue, sales, net sales, or net revenue.

The **income statement** reports the results of operations for a business for a given time period, usually a quarter or a year. The income statement lists the revenues and expenses of the business. **Sales revenue** are increases to a company's resources that result when goods or services are provided to customers. The amount of sales revenue earned is measured by the value of the assets received in exchange for the goods or services delivered.

Expenses are decreases in a company's resources from generating revenue. Expenses are generally measured by the value of the assets used up or exchanged as a result of a business's operating activities. Common examples of expenses include the cost of the items sold, referred to as cost of goods sold, selling expenses, marketing expenses, administrative expenses, interest expense, and income taxes. When total revenue exceeds total expenses, the resulting amount is called **net income**; when total expenses exceed sales revenue, the resulting amount is called a **net loss**.

A.K.A. *Net income* is also referred to as net earnings or net profit.

Columbia's income statement is presented in Exhibit 1-7. The statement begins with the business's name, statement title, and time period to which the statement applies. For Columbia, total revenue in 2011 is reported to be $1,711,015 (remember amounts are rounded to the nearest $1,000). Next, Columbia subtracts a series of expenses totaling $1,607,536, yielding net income of $103,479.

Exhibit 1-7	Columbia Sportswear Income Statement

COLUMBIA SPORTSWEAR COMPANY
Income Statement
For Year Ended December 31, 2011
(In thousands)

Revenue	
Sales.	$1,693,985
Other revenue.	17,030
Total revenue.	1,711,015
Expenses	
Cost of sales.	958,677
Selling, general, and administrative expense.	614,658
Income tax expense	34,201
Total expenses	1,607,536
Net income.	$ 103,479

Concept ➝	Method ➝	Assessment	TAKEAWAY 1.2
Is a company profitable?	The income statement reports a company's performance for a given period of time. Compare reported sales revenue to reported expenses.	Sales revenue in excess of expenses yields net income, implying a profitable company. If expenses exceed revenue, the company has a net loss.	

Reporting on Triple Bottom Line	CORPORATE SOCIAL RESPONSIBILITY

Companies worldwide are focused on more than just the bottom line. Research shows that financial responsibility goes hand in hand with social responsibility. This is labeled a "virtuous cycle" because financial success provides the means to act socially responsible, and acting socially responsible increases a company's financial performance. Financial statements are not well suited for measuring social performance. To aid in the pursuit of socially responsible behavior, accountants have developed a **triple bottom line** framework in which the single bottom line of financial performance is supplemented with a social bottom line and an environmental bottom line. The triple bottom line standard for urban and community accounting has been ratified by the United Nations and has become widely used in public sector accounting.

Statement of Stockholders' Equity

The **statement of stockholders' equity** reports the events causing an increase or decrease in a business's stockholders' equity during a given time period, including both the changes in a company's common stock and changes in its retained earnings. The statement of stockholders' equity consists of two parts—contributed capital and earned capital. **Contributed capital** is a measure of the capital contributed by the stockholders of a company when they purchase ownership shares in the company. Ownership shares are called *common shares* or *common stock*. **Earned capital** is a measure of the capital that is earned by the company, reinvested in the business, and not distributed to its stockholders—that is, its *retained earnings*.

Retained earnings are increased when operations produce net income and decreased when operations produce a net loss. Retained earnings also decrease when a company pays a dividend to its stockholders. A company's retained earnings for a period is determined as follows (sometimes called *statement of retained earnings*):

Note: According to a 2011 survey of 500 companies, nearly 98% (489 out of 500) of the companies surveyed issue a Statement of Stockholders' Equity, while only 1% issue a separate Statement of Retained Earnings. Source: Accounting Trends & Techniques, 2011.

Retained earnings, beginning of period.	$ 996,922
Add: Net income (loss).	103,479
Less: Dividends and other.	(28,893)
Retained earnings, end of period.	$1,071,508

Columbia's statement of stockholders' equity appears in Exhibit 1-8. We focus here on Columbia's retained earnings from its statement of stockholders' equity to emphasize two important concepts: (1) the relation between the income statement and the balance sheet and (2) the components of retained earnings. Columbia's statement of stockholders' equity in Exhibit 1-8 begins with its ending retained earnings from 2010 of $996,922. Its net income of $103,479 from 2011 is added. Can you find this amount on Columbia's income statement in Exhibit 1-7? Next, the portion of these earnings that was distributed to Columbia's stockholders in 2011 as a dividend ($28,893) is subtracted to yield an ending retained earnings balance of $1,071,508 as of December 31, 2011. Can you find this amount on Columbia's balance sheet in Exhibit 1-6?

Exhibit 1-8	Columbia Sportswear Statement of Stockholders' Equity

COLUMBIA SPORTSWEAR COMPANY
Statement of Stockholders' Equity
For Year Ended December 31, 2011

(In thousands)	Common Stock	Retained Earnings	Total
Balance, December 31, 2010.	$ 5,052	$ 996,922	$1,001,974
Add: Common stock issued.	17,985		17,985
Net income.		103,479	103,479
Less: Common stock repurchased	(20,000)		(20,000)
Dividends and other.		(28,893)	(28,893)
Balance, December 31, 2011.	$ 3,037	$1,071,508	$1,074,545

TAKEAWAY 1.3	Concept ⟶	Method ⟶	Assessment
	What portion of a company's current period net income is distributed to its stockholders, and what portion is retained?	The statement of stockholders' equity reports both a company's net income and the amount of dividends distributed to stockholders. Compare the company's dividends to its net income.	A higher ratio of dividends to net income implies that a company is distributing more of its net income to its stockholders, whereas a lower ratio implies it is retaining more of its income for purposes, such as growing its business.

Statement of Cash Flows

The **statement of cash flows** reports a business's cash inflows and cash outflows during a given period of time. The cash flows are grouped into the three business activities of operating, investing, and financing. The cash flow from operating activities reveals the cash spent on operating expenses and the cash received from the sale of goods or services. The cash flow from investing activities includes the cash payments and receipts when a business buys and sells certain assets that it uses in its operations. The cash flow from financing activities reports the issuances and repurchases of shares in a business and the amounts borrowed and repaid to creditors.

Columbia's statement of cash flows is in Exhibit 1-9. This statement shows that Columbia's cash balance increased during 2011 by $6,777 from $234,257 on December 31, 2010, to $241,034 on December 31, 2011. Can you find the ending cash balance on Columbia's balance sheet in Exhibit 1-6?

The statement of cash flows reveals how Columbia acquired its cash and how it was used. We see that its day-to-day operations generated $63,796 of cash. So if Columbia's operations generated all this cash, why did its cash balance only go up by $6,777? The statement reveals that uses of cash included $78,236 for capital expenditures along with several other large cash disbursements. We devote considerable time to understanding and analyzing financial statements such as those of Columbia's in later chapters.

Exhibit 1-9	Columbia Sportswear Statement of Cash Flows

COLUMBIA SPORTSWEAR COMPANY
Statement of Cash Flows
For Year Ended December 31, 2011
(In thousands)

Cash flows from operating activities	
Cash receipts	$1,642,628
Cash disbursements	1,578,832
Cash provided by operating activities	63,796
Cash flows from investing activities	
Net sales (purchases) of investment securities	65,721
Net capital expenditures	(78,236)
Cash used by investing activities	(12,515)
Cash flows from financing activities	
Repurchase of common stock	(20,000)
Cash dividends paid, exchange rate changes, and other	24,504
Cash used in financing activities	(44,504)
Net increase in cash	6,777
Cash at beginning of year	234,257
Cash at end of year	$ 241,034

Concept →	Method →	Assessment	TAKEAWAY 1.4
What are the major sources and uses of a company's cash?	The statement of cash flows reports a company's sources and uses of cash separated into three activities: operating, investing, and financing. Identify a company's sources and uses of cash as reported in the statement of cash flows.	Sources of cash are reported as positive numbers and uses of cash as negative numbers. Larger positive numbers represent major cash sources and larger negative numbers represent major cash uses.	

Relations Among the Financial Statements

The income statement, the statement of stockholders' equity, the balance sheet, and the statement of cash flows are linked to one another. That is, the financial statements *articulate*. To illustrate the linkages, refer to the financial statements of Columbia Sportswear in Exhibit 1-11. Observe that **Ⓐ**, the company's net income (or net loss) for a period is an input to the statement of stockholders' equity, and that **Ⓑ**, the ending common stock, retained earnings, and total equity are inputs to the balance sheet. The statement of cash flows **Ⓒ** explains the change in the cash balance on the balance sheet for a period.

When financial statements are prepared, the sequence suggested by these relations is customarily followed; that is, (1) the income statement is first prepared, followed by (2) the statement of stockholders' equity, then (3) the balance sheet, and finally (4) the statement of cash flows.

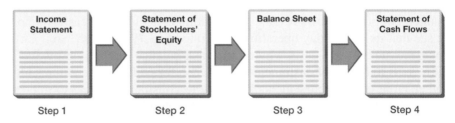

Three of these financial statements present information covering a specific period of time: the income statement, the statement of stockholders' equity, and the statement of cash flows. For this reason, these financial statements are referred to as **period-in-time statements**. In contrast, the balance sheet reports information as of a specific date. The balance sheet, therefore, is referred to as a **point-in-time statement**.

Exhibit 1-10	Financial Statement Links Across Time

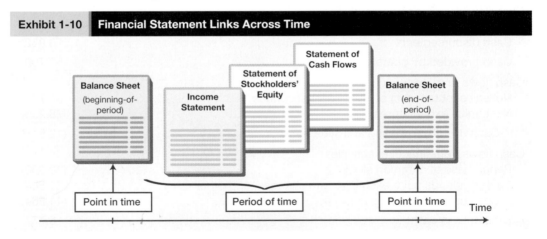

YOUR TURN! 1.5

The solution is on pages 54–55.

Kanzu Corporation started business on January 1, 2013. The following information was compiled by Kanzu as of December 31, 2013.

Sales revenue	$20,000	Accounts payable	$ 4,000
Expenses	12,000	Notes payable	33,000
Dividends	3,000	Common stock	20,000
Cash	1,500	Retained earnings	?
Accounts receivable	2,500	Cash flow from operating activities	6,500
Inventory	3,000	Cash flow from investing activities	(55,000)
Equipment	15,000	Cash flow from financing activities	50,000
Building	40,000		

Prepare the company's year-end financial statements: an income statement, a statement of stockholders' equity, a balance sheet, and a statement of cash flows.

Exhibit 1-11	**Financial Statements for Columbia Sportswear Company**

Columbia Sportswear Company
Income Statement
For Year Ended December 31, 2011

Revenue

Sales..................	$1,693,985
Other revenue..........	17,030
Total revenue	1,711,015

Expenses

Cost of sales............	958,677
Selling, general, and administrative..........	614,658
Income tax expense......	34,201
Total expenses..........	1,607,536
Net income.............	$ 103,479

Ⓐ

Columbia Sportswear Company
Statement of Stockholders' Equity
For Year Ended December 31, 2011

	Common Stock	Retained Earnings	Total
Balance, December 31, 2010..	$ 5,052	$ 996,922	$1,001,974
Add: Common stock issued .	17,985		17,985
Net income		103,479	103,479
Less: Common stock repurchased	(20,000)		(20,000)
Dividends and other ...		(28,893)	(28,893)
Balance, December 31, 2011..	$ 3,037	$1,071,508	$1,074,545

Ⓑ

Columbia Sportswear Company
Balance Sheet
December 31, 2011

Assets

		Liabilities	
Cash	$ 241,034	Accounts payable....................	$ 148,973
Investments	2,878	Income taxes payable	27,968
Accounts receivable....................	351,538	Other liabilities	131,056
Inventories	365,199	Total liabilities......................	307,997
Prepaid expenses and other current assets..	36,392	**Stockholders' Equity** Common stock + retained earnings	
Property, plant, and equipment, net	250,910	Common stock......................	3,037
Other assets............................	134,591	Retained earnings	1,071,508
		Total stockholders' equity	1,074,545
Total assets	$1,382,542	Total liabilities and stockholders' equity .	$1,382,542

Ⓒ

Columbia Sportswear Company
Statement of Cash Flows
For Year Ended December 31, 2011

Cash flows from operating activities	
Cash provided by operating activities	$ 63,796
Cash flows from investing activities	
Cash used by investing activities..	(12,515)
Cash flows from financing activities	
Cash used in financing activities	(44,504)
Net increase in cash...	6,777
Cash at beginning of year	234,257
Cash at end of year	$241,034

ADDITIONAL INFORMATION

Columbia Sportswear Company, like all publicly traded companies in the United States, must file an **annual report** called a Form **10-K** with the U.S. Securities and Exchange Commission (SEC). Some companies also mail a less detailed version of their annual report to their stockholders. The four

LO6 Explain additional disclosures that accompany financial statements.

financial statements explained in this chapter are essential components of this report. Additional components of the annual report are the Management Discussion and Analysis, the notes to the financial statements, and the auditor's report.

Management Discussion and Analysis

The **Management Discussion and Analysis**, or MD&A, contains management's interpretation of the company's recent performance and financial condition. This interpretation helps financial statement users gain a context within which to place their own analysis and interpretation of the numbers that appear in the financial statements.

The MD&A is also where a company's management provides its opinion regarding what the future holds for its business. Discussions of future opportunities and risks are called "forward-looking" and are helpful to any financial statement user interested in learning about such things as potential new markets for the company's products or potential new competitors. Obviously these forward-looking statements are subjective in nature, and the statement users must do an independent analysis of the financial statements.

The following is a short excerpt from Columbia's MD&A.

Strategy and Outlook

Our business, like other branded consumer product companies, is heavily dependent upon discretionary consumer spending patterns. Our net sales volumes have been negatively affected by the volatility of the global economy and its impact on consumer purchasing behavior, and retailers' behavior related to advance orders, order cancellations, and seasonal reorders. The current macro-economic environment has caused tightening of credit for some of our wholesale customers, independent distributors, and consumers and a significant slowing of retail sales. This has resulted in, and could continue to cause, a more cautious approach by many of our wholesale customers and independent distributors when placing advance orders for seasonal products and reducing, delaying delivery of, or cancelling advance orders placed in earlier periods. We expect our retail revenues to partially offset some of this anticipated wholesale revenue decline.

Notes to Financial Statements

A skilled financial statement user wants to know more than just the bare numbers reported in financial statements. That user also wants to know assumptions and estimates that were used in preparing the statements, the measurement procedures that were followed, and the details behind certain summary numbers. **Notes to the financial statements**, which are both quantitative as well as qualitative, provide a great deal more information than just the numbers alone. For example, notes usually contain a description regarding how the company determined the value of its inventory, a detailed chart to explain the property, plant, and equipment account, and a description of any pending lawsuits. No analysis of the annual report is complete without a careful reading of the notes to the financial statements. The following is a short excerpt from Columbia's notes:

Accounts receivable Accounts receivable have been reduced by an allowance for doubtful accounts. The Company makes ongoing estimates of the collectability of accounts receivable and maintains an allowance for estimated losses resulting from the inability of the Company's customers to make required payments. The allowance for doubtful accounts was $7,545,000 and $7,098,000 at December 31, 2011 and 2010, respectively.

Auditor's Report

The report of the independent auditor, commonly referred to as the **auditor's report**, describes the activities undertaken by a company's independent auditor and reports that auditor's opinion regarding whether the financial statements fairly present the results of the company's operations and financial health. A short excerpt from the auditor's report included with Columbia Sportswear's annual report follows. **Deloitte & Touche**, which is Columbia's independent auditor, reports that the financial statements of Columbia are, in its opinion, fairly presented. The independent auditor has intentionally avoided using language such as the statements are "correctly presented" or are "exactly correct." As we will see in subsequent chapters, the financial statements are prepared only after the management team makes a number of assumptions, estimates, and accounting policy decisions. As a consequence, it is inappropriate to describe the statements as being right or wrong since the reported numbers are dependent on the accounting policies selected and the assumptions and estimates made by management.

Report of Independent Registered Public Accounting Firm

In our opinion, such consolidated financial statements present fairly, in all material respects, the financial position of Columbia Sportswear Company and subsidiaries as of December 31, 2011 and 2010, and the results of their operations and their cash flows for each of the three years in the period ended December 31, 2011, in conformity with accounting principles generally accepted in the United States of America. Also, in our opinion, such a financial statement schedule, when considered in relation to the basic consolidated financial statements taken as a whole, presents fairly, in all material respects, the information set forth therein.

DELOITTE & TOUCHE LLP

Match each of the items in the left column with the appropriate annual report component where we would find that item, from the right column.

1. An opinion regarding the fair presentation of financial statements.
2. Information regarding the procedures followed to value a company's assets.
3. A discussion of new markets that a company plans to enter.

a. Management Discussion and Analysis
b. Notes to the Financial Statements
c. Auditor's report

YOUR TURN! 1.6

The solution is on page 55.

CAREERS IN ACCOUNTING

Without a doubt one of the primary considerations students have when selecting a major are the job prospects after graduation. The good news for accounting majors is that the present is very good and the future looks even brighter. According to a 2011 American Institute of Certified Public Accountants survey of the demand for public accounting recruits, "Newly minted accountants have some of the brightest job prospects in the nation." A June 2011 *Journal of Accountancy* article noted that hiring of accountants slowed a bit during the economic downturn of 2008 and 2009, but has since picked up. A March 31, 2011 *Fortune* article titled "Bean Counters Wanted: Why the Big 4 are in a hiring frenzy," further supports the great prospects for accounting graduates.

LO7 **Describe** careers in accounting.

Accounting opportunities are present in multiple areas. Exhibit 1-12 lists some typical job titles and major employers in (1) private accounting; (2) public accounting; and (3) government. Accountants working in the private sector work for a particular company, whereas an accountant working in public accounting spends most of their time working for clients of their employer.

Accounting professionals are not just in high demand, they are also held in high regard by the public. Accounting professionals often earn various certificates in order to further distinguish themselves. The most sought after certification is the Certified Public Accountant (CPA) certificate. This certification requires both education and professional experience, passing an examination, and the highest ethical standards. Three other important certifications are the Certified Management Accountant (CMA), the Certified Internal Auditor (CIA), and the Certified Fraud Examiner (CFE) certificates.

Exhibit 1-12	Careers in Accounting		
	Private Accounting	**Public Accounting**	**Government Accounting**
Typical Positions	Internal audit Tax Financial reporting Analyst Budgeting Cost accounting	Auditor Tax Consulting Strategy	Auditor Tax Budgeting Criminal investigation

One of the reasons that accounting graduates find great opportunities upon graduation is because the accounting courses provide specific skills that can be applied immediately on the job. In contrast, courses in the humanities, and even the sciences and general management courses do not train students for a particular occupation. It is therefore quite apparent that when one compares the advantages and disadvantages of an accounting career, the positive job outlook and the high salaries are often listed. Accountants also have a great deal of mobility and upward advancement potential.

According to the U.S. Bureau of Labor Statistics, the 2010 median pay for the 1.2 million accounting jobs in their database was $61,690. Exhibit 1-13 compares the 2012 salaries of starting accountants, accountants with a couple years of experience, and more senior accountants in both public accounting and in large corporations.

Exhibit 1-13	Accounting Salaries	
Area of Employment	**Position and Experience**	**Typical Salary Range**
Private Accounting	Bookkeeper	$33,250–$43,750
	Financial Analyst < 1 year	$42,500–$53,750
	Financial Analyst 1–3 years	$51,750–$69,500
	Financial Analyst Manager	$84,250–$114,500
	Corporate Controller.	$142,750–$199,000
	Chief Financial Officer	$275,000–$411,000
Public Accounting	Junior Accountant < 1 year	$51,500–$63,500
	Senior Accountant	$72,000–$94,250
	Senior Manager	$109,750–$175,000

Source: Robert Half 2012 Salary Guide

	Accounting Career Resources	**ACCOUNTING IN PRACTICE**

Careers in accounting are both numerous and varied. You can learn more about accounting careers by visiting the following Websites:

The American Institute of Certified Public Accountants (AICPA) www.aicpa.org
The American Association of Finance & Accounting (AAFA) www.aafa.com
The National Society of Accountants (NSA) www.nsacct.org
The Accounting Degree Guide www.myaccountingdegree.org
Accounting Coach www.accountingcoach.com
Robert Half www.roberthalf.com

COMPREHENSIVE PROBLEM

You have been approached by Janet Jones about helping her assemble a set of December 31 financial statements for her new business. Janet began the operations of her bakery shop on January 1, 2013. Janet decided that she did not want to risk any personal liability resulting from operating the business; consequently, she organized the bakery, called Sweet Pleasures, as a corporation.

Required

Use the format of Exhibits 1-6 through 1-9 to prepare an income statement, statement of stockholders' equity, balance sheet, and statement of cash flows for Sweet Pleasures as of December 31, 2013. Use the account titles and balances provided below. Be sure to use proper underlining and double underlining.

Sales of goods	$200,000	Dividends	$ 10,000
Cash	99,000	Bank loan payable	20,000
Rent expense	16,000	Accounts receivable	40,000
Interest payable	1,600	Cash received from operating activities	160,000
Cash received from issuance of common stock	50,000	Cash payments for operating activities	94,000
Insurance expense	20,000	Salary expense	40,000
Purchase of equipment	27,000	Cash received from borrowing from bank	20,000
Equipment	27,000	Interest expense	1,600
Common stock	50,000	Administrative expense	18,000
Cash dividends paid	10,000		

Solution

SWEET PLEASURES CORPORATION
Income Statement
For Year Ended December 31, 2013

Revenue		
Sales of goods		$200,000
Expenses		
Rent expense	$16,000	
Insurance expense	20,000	
Salary expense	40,000	
Administrative expense	18,000	
Interest expense	1,600	
Total expenses		95,600
Net income		$104,400

SWEET PLEASURES CORPORATION
Statement of Stockholders' Equity
For Year Ended December 31, 2013

	Common Stock	Retained Earnings	Total
Balance, January 1, 2013..................................	$ 0	$ 0	$ 0
Add: Common stock issued	50,000		50,000
Net income		104,400	104,400
Less: Dividends		(10,000)	(10,000)
Balance, December 31, 2013..............................	$50,000	$ 94,400	$144,400

SWEET PLEASURES CORPORATION
Balance Sheet
December 31, 2013

Assets		Liabilities	
Cash...................	$ 99,000	Bank loan payable	$ 20,000
Accounts receivable.......	40,000	Interest payable	1,600
Equipment	27,000	Total liabilities.............................	21,600
		Stockholders' Equity	
		Common stock.............................	50,000
		Retained earnings	94,400
		Total stockholders' equity	144,400
Total assets	$166,000	Total liabilities and stockholders' equity	$166,000

SWEET PLEASURES CORPORATION
Statement of Cash Flows
For Year Ended December 31, 2013

Cash flow from operating activities		
Cash received from operating activities.....................................	$160,000	
Cash payments for operating activities	(94,000)	
Cash provided by operating activities.....................................		$66,000
Cash flow from investing activities		
Purchase of equipment.......................................	(27,000)	
Cash used by investing activities		(27,000)
Cash flow from financing activities		
Borrowing from bank	20,000	
Issuance of common stock...	50,000	
Cash dividends paid...	(10,000)	
Cash provided by financing activities.....................................		60,000
Net increase of cash..		99,000
Cash at January 1, 2013		0
Cash at December 31, 2013		$99,000

APPENDIX 1A: FASB's Conceptual Framework

The FASB has developed a conceptual framework, in coordination with the International Accounting Standards Board, to guide the formulation of U.S. generally accepted accounting principles. The **conceptual framework** is a cohesive set of interrelated objectives and fundamentals for external financial reporting. This framework, outlined in Exhibit 1A-1, consists of (1) financial reporting objectives, (2) financial statement elements, (3) qualitative characteristics of accounting information, and (4) recognition and measurement criteria for financial statements. A recurrent theme in the conceptual framework is the importance of providing information that is useful to financial statement users.

LO8 Appendix 1A: **Discuss** FASB's conceptual framework.

Exhibit 1A-1	Summary of Conceptual Framework

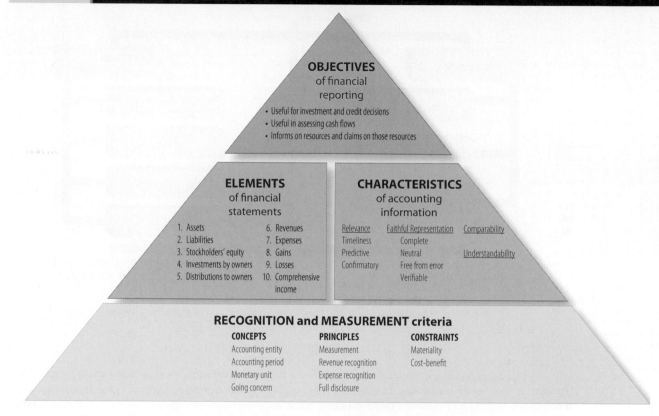

Financial Reporting Objectives

The **financial reporting objectives** of the conceptual framework focus on information useful to investors and creditors. Accordingly, financial statements have the principal objective of providing information that is (1) useful in making investment, credit, and similar decisions and (2) helpful in assessing the ability of enterprises to generate future cash flows. Financial statements should also (3) contain information about a company's economic resources, the claims on those resources, and the effects of events that change those resources and claims. This helps to identify a company's financial strengths and weaknesses, predict future performance, and evaluate earlier expectations.

Financial Statement Elements

The **financial statement elements** of the conceptual framework are the components of financial statements. These elements include assets, liabilities, stockholders' equity, investments by owners, distributions to owners, revenues, expenses, gains, losses, and comprehensive income.

Qualitative Characteristics

The **qualitative characteristics of accounting information** are depicted in Exhibit 1A-2. These qualities are intended to contribute to decision usefulness. The two primary qualities are **relevance** and **faithful representation**. To be relevant, accounting information must make a difference in a user's decisions.

Relevant information must be timely and contribute to the predictive and evaluative decisions made by investors and creditors. Faithful representation has the characteristics of being complete, neutral, free from error, and verifiable.

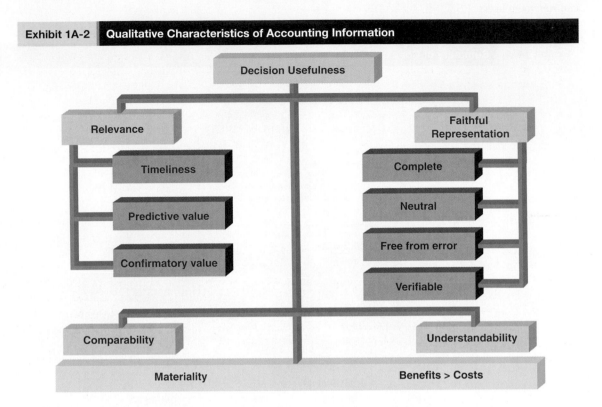

Exhibit 1A-2   **Qualitative Characteristics of Accounting Information**

Additional enhancing qualitative characteristics of accounting information are comparability, verifiability, timeliness, and understandability. In order to enable users to most effectively compare financial results across companies, U.S. GAAP requires that companies disclose in the notes to financial statements the accounting policy choices they elected to use in the preparation of their financial statements. **Comparability** aids users to understand similarities and differences among items. Related to comparability is **consistency**, although they are not the same. Comparability relates to making comparisons among more than one item, whereas consistency relates to a single item and means the same accounting methods are used from one accounting period to the next. U.S. GAAP requires that when a firm changes a method of reporting its financial results that the financial impact of the method change be revealed in its notes to financial statements.

Verifiability means that different individuals could reach the same conclusion regarding financial data, and therefore helps assure that the financial data is being faithfully represented. **Timeliness** means that the decision maker has the information available when it is needed to make their decision. **Understandability** is enhanced if information is classified, characterized, and presented clearly and concisely.

Recognition and Measurement Criteria

The **recognition and measurement criteria** of the framework specify the conditions that must be satisfied before a particular asset, liability, revenue, or expense can be recorded in the financial records. An item under consideration must meet the definition of an element and be measurable, and information about the item must achieve the primary qualitative characteristics of accounting information. The recognition and measurement criteria consist of four concepts, four principles, and two constraints.

Concepts

A fundamental concept in accounting is the entity. An **accounting entity** is an economic unit with identifiable boundaries for which we accumulate and report financial information. Before we can analyze and report activities, we must identify the particular entity. Each sole proprietorship, partnership, and corporation is an entity, and separate accounting records must be maintained for each unit. In accumulating financial information, we maintain a record of the activities of the accounting entity separately from the economic and personal activities of its owners. The operations of most businesses are virtually continuous. Yet, the economic life of a company can be divided into specific periods of time, known as the **accounting period**, which is typically one year for purposes of preparing financial statements. Although the division of the total life of a business into segments based on annual periods is artificial, the concept of the accounting period is useful for financial reporting. The **monetary unit concept** specifies that a monetary unit (the dollar in the United States and the euro in the European Union) is to be used to measure and record an entity's economic activity. Only items that can be expressed in these monetary units are included in the financial statements. When all assets, liabilities, and stockholders' equity are stated in monetary terms, they can be added or subtracted to prepare financial statements. Also, relations among financial statement components can be calculated and presented to help interpret the statements. In the absence of evidence to the contrary, a business is assumed to have an indefinite life. The **going concern concept** presumes that an enterprise will continue to operate indefinitely and will not be sold or otherwise liquidated.

Principles

Four principles frame financial accounting information: measurement, revenue recognition, expense recognition, and full disclosure. U.S. GAAP is a mixed measurement system. It is primarily founded on the **cost principle**, meaning assets and liabilities are initially recorded at the amount paid or obligated to pay. Historical acquisition cost is considered the proper initial measurement because, for example, at the time an asset is acquired, it represents the fair value of the asset as agreed upon by both the buyer and seller. However, the fair value principle is sometimes applied after acquisition, which is a "market-based" measurement system for assets and liabilities. The **revenue recognition principle** states that sales revenue should be recorded when services are performed or goods are sold. The revenue recognition principle requires two conditions to exist before sales revenue is recorded on the income statement: (1) the revenue must be earned and (2) it must be realized or realizable. Normally, both conditions are not met until services are performed or goods are sold. To the extent feasible, all expenses related to a company's earned sales revenue should be recognized (matched) with, or deducted from, that revenue in the determination of net income. The **expense recognition (matching) principle** states that net income is determined by linking any expenses incurred with the related earned sales revenues. Thus, expenses are recorded in the period that they help to generate the revenues.

Together, the revenue recognition principle and the expense recognition principle define the accrual basis of accounting. Under the **accrual basis of accounting**, sales revenue is recognized when it is both earned and realized (revenue recognition principle) and expenses are recorded in the period in which they help to generate the earned revenue (expense recognition principle). It is important to observe that recording revenues and expenses do not depend upon the receipt or payment of cash. The accrual basis of accounting is widely used. Under the **cash basis of accounting**, revenues are recorded when cash is received from operating activities and expenses are recorded when cash payments are made for operating activities. Net income, therefore, becomes the difference between operating cash receipts and operating cash payments. The cash basis is not considered generally accepted.

All information necessary for a user's understanding of financial statements should be disclosed in a company's annual report. The purpose of accounting is to provide useful information to those parties interested in a firm's financial health. Sometimes, facts or conditions exist that, although not specifically part of the data in the accounting system, have considerable influence on a full understanding and interpretation of financial statements. To properly inform financial statement users, the **full disclosure principle** requires that a business disclose all significant financial facts and circumstances.

Constraints

Two factors constrain the qualitative characteristics of accounting information: materiality and cost-benefit. Applying accounting procedures requires effort and costs money. When amounts involved are too small to affect the financial picture, the application of theoretically correct accounting procedures is hardly worth its cost. The concept of **materiality** permits a firm to expense the cost of such assets as small tools, office equipment, and furniture when acquired because their cost is "immaterial" in amount. The **cost-benefit constraint** requires that the benefit derived from the information outweighs the cost of providing it.

SUMMARY OF LEARNING OBJECTIVES

LO1   Explain business organization and its three forms. (p. 4)

■   There are three primary organizational forms that a business can take. They are the sole proprietorship, the partnership, and the corporation.

■   A sole proprietorship consists of a single owner. It is the most common form of business and the easiest to establish.

■   A partnership is similar to a sole proprietorship except that there is more than one owner. Partnerships are also relatively easy to establish. An advantage of the partnership form over the sole proprietorship is the broader set of skills and resources that multiple partners can bring to an enterprise.

■   A corporation is the most complex of the three organizational forms. The advantages of the corporate form of business include the ease of transferring ownership interests and the ease of raising funds. Another advantage is the limited liability protection it offers its owners. A disadvantage of the corporate form is the possibility of double taxation of the company's net income.

LO2   Describe business activities. (p. 5)

■   Companies engage in three types of business activities: operating, investing, and financing.

■   Operating activities consist of selling products or providing services to generate sales revenue and using economic resources to manufacture goods or provide services.

■   Investing activities consist of those activities needed to provide the infrastructure to run a company's operations. Also included in this activity category are investments of excess cash.

■   Financing activities consist of both debt financing and equity financing. Debt financing involves the procurement of a bank loan, whereas equity financing involves the sale of shares of stock to investors.

LO3   Indicate who uses accounting information. (p. 6)

■   Accounting information is important to both internal and external users.

■   The process of generating and analyzing data for internal management use is referred to as managerial accounting.

■   Business leaders recognize the importance of ethical behavior.

■   Financial accounting produces publicly available financial statements for external users including investors, creditors, taxation authorities, regulatory agencies, labor unions, and customers.

LO4   Explain the accounting process and generally accepted accounting principles. (p. 10)

■   Accounting is the process of measuring the economic activities of an enterprise in money terms and communicating the results to interested parties.

■   The basic purpose of accounting is to provide financial information that is useful in making economic decisions.

■   The Financial Accounting Standards Board (FASB) is an organization in the private sector that has responsibility for formulating generally accepted accounting principles in the United States.

■   Generally accepted accounting principles (GAAP) are the standards and procedures that guide the preparation of financial statements.

■   The International Accounting Standards Board (IASB) has taken the lead role in formulating International Accounting Reporting Standards (IFRS).

■   The SEC has strongly supported the establishment of international accounting standards.

■   A common set of standards such as the IFRS benefit multinational companies, investors, and accounting professionals.

LO5   Describe the accounting equation and each financial statement. (p. 12)

■   The accounting equation, Assets = Liabilities + Stockholders' Equity, is the fundamental framework within which accounting analysis takes place.

•   Assets are the economic resources of a business that can be expressed in money terms.

•   Liabilities are the obligations that a business must pay in money or services in the future as a consequence of past transactions or events.

•   Stockholders' equity is the residual interest of the owners in the assets of a business.

- *Income statement:* Presents a company's sales revenues and expenses for a period of time.
- *Statement of stockholders' equity:* Reports the financial events causing a change in stockholders' equity during a period of time, and includes retained earnings and common stock.
- *Balance sheet:* Presents a company's assets, liabilities, and stockholders' equity as of a given date.
- *Statement of cash flows:* Reports a company's cash inflows and outflows during a period of time.

Explain additional disclosures that accompany financial statements. (p. 19)   LO6

In addition to the basic financial statements, the annual report includes Management Discussion and Analysis, notes to the financial statements, and an auditor's report.

- The Management Discussion and Analysis (MD&A) provides management with an opportunity to both analyze past performance and discuss future opportunities and concerns involving a company.
- The notes to the financial statements provide both a quantitative and a qualitative description of a company's financial statements and explain the numbers reported in those financial statements.
- The auditor's report, issued by an independent auditor, provides a degree of assurance that a company's financial statements are presented fairly and can be relied upon for decision-making purposes.

Describe careers in accounting. (p. 21)   LO7

- Accounting graduates are in high demand and can anticipate bright employment prospects.
- Accountants can find jobs in public accounting, private corporations, and the government.
- One must balance the high salaries and favorable job prospects of an accounting career with the hard work and often long hours associated with accounting careers.

Appendix 1A: Discuss FASB's conceptual framework. (p. 25)   LO8

- The conceptual framework provides a guide to the formulation of U.S. generally accepted accounting principles.
- The framework consists of interrelated objectives, elements, characteristics, and recognition and measurement criteria.
- The financial reporting objectives of the conceptual framework focus on information useful to investors and creditors.
- The financial statement elements of the conceptual framework are the components of financial statements.
- The qualitative characteristics of accounting information are intended to contribute to decision usefulness.
- The recognition and measurement criteria of the framework specify the conditions that must be satisfied before a particular asset, liability, revenue, or expense can be recorded in the financial records.

Concept ⟶	Method ⟶	Assessment	SUMMARY
What form of financing does a company use?	The balance sheet provides information regarding the various forms of financing, both debt financing and equity financing. Compare the amount of liabilities appearing on the balance sheet to the amount of equity appearing on the balance sheet.	A higher ratio of liabilities to stockholders' equity implies a higher use of creditor financing, and vice versa. Creditor financing is viewed by users as more risky.	TAKEAWAY 1.1
Is a company profitable?	The income statement reports a company's performance for a given period of time. Compare reported sales revenue to reported expenses.	Sales revenue in excess of expenses yields net income, implying a profitable company. If expenses exceed revenue, the company has at a net loss.	TAKEAWAY 1.2

continued

SUMMARY	Concept	Method	Assessment
TAKEAWAY 1.3	What portion of a company's current period net income is distributed to its stockholders, and what portion is retained?	The statement of stockholders' equity reports both a company's net income and the amount of dividends distributed to stockholders. Compare the company's dividends to its net income.	A higher ratio of dividends to net income implies that a company is distributing more of its net income to it stockholders, whereas a lower ratio implies that it is retaining more of its income for purposes, such as growing its business.
TAKEAWAY 1.4	What are the major sources and uses of a company's cash?	The statement of cash flows reports a company's sources and uses of cash separated into three activities: operating, investing, and financing. Identify a company's sources and uses of cash as reported in the statement of cash flows.	Sources of cash are reported as positive numbers and uses of cash as negative numbers. Larger positive numbers represent major cash sources and larger negative numbers represent major cash uses.

KEY TERMS

10-K (p. 19)

Accounting (p. 10)

Accounting entity (p. 26)

Accounting equation (p. 13)

Accounting period (p. 27)

Accrual basis of accounting (p. 27)

American Institute of Certified Public Accountants (AICPA) (p. 9)

Annual report (p. 19)

Assets (p. 13)

Auditor's report (p. 21)

Balance sheet (p. 13)

Cash basis of accounting (p. 27)

Certified public accountants (CPAs) (p. 7)

Comparability (p. 26)

Conceptual framework (p. 24)

Consistency (p. 26)

Contributed capital (p. 16)

Corporate Social Responsibility (p. 15)

Corporation (p. 4)

Cost-benefit constraint (p. 27)

Cost principle (p. 27)

Creditors (p. 5)

Debt financing (p. 5)

Earned capital (p. 16)

Equity financing (p. 5)

Ethics (p. 8)

Expense recognition (matching) principle (p. 27)

Expenses (p. 14)

Faithful representation (p. 25)

Financial accounting (p. 7)

Financial Accounting Standards Board (FASB) (p. 11)

Financial reporting objectives (p. 25)

Financial statement elements (p. 25)

Financing activities (p. 5)

Forensic accounting (p. 9)

Full disclosure principle (p. 27)

Generally accepted accounting principles (GAAP) (p. 10)

Generally accepted auditing standards (GAAS) (p. 11)

Going concern concept (p. 27)

Income statement (p. 14)

Institute of Management Accountants (p. 9)

International Accounting Standards Board (IASB) (p. 12)

International Financial Reporting Standards (IFRS) (p. 12)

Investing activities (p. 6)

Liabilities (p. 13)

Management Discussion and Analysis (MD&A) (p. 20)

Managerial accounting (p. 8)

Materiality (p. 27)

Monetary unit concept (p. 27)

Net assets (p. 13)

Net income (p. 15)

Net loss (p. 15)

New York Stock Exchange (NYSE) (p. 5)

Notes to the financial statements (p. 20)

Operating activities (p. 6)

Partnership (p. 4)

Period-in-time statements (p. 18)

Point-in-time statement (p. 18)

Principal (p. 5)

**Public Company Accounting
  Oversight Board
  (PCAOB)** (p. 11)
**Qualitative characteristics
  of accounting
  information** (p. 25)
**Recognition and measurement
  criteria** (p. 26)
Relevance (p. 25)

Retained earnings (p. 16)
**Revenue recognition
  principle** (p. 27)
Sales revenue (p. 14)
Sarbanes-Oxley Act (p. 9)
Sole proprietorship (p. 4)
Statement of cash flows (p. 17)
**Statement of stockholders'
  equity** (p. 15)

Stockholders (p. 4)
Stockholders' equity (p. 13)
Timeliness (p. 26)
Triple bottom line (p. 15)
Understandability (p. 26)
**U.S. Securities and Exchange
  Commission (SEC)** (p. 11)
Verifiability (p. 26)

SELF-STUDY QUESTIONS

(Answers to Self-Study Questions are at the end of this chapter.)

1. **Which form of business organization is characterized by limited liability?** **LO1**
   a. Sole proprietorship
   b. Partnership
   c. Corporation
   d. Both sole proprietorship and partnership

2. **Which of the following processes best defines accounting?** **LO4**
   a. Measuring economic activities
   b. Communicating results to interested parties
   c. Preventing fraud
   d. Both a and b.

3. **Generally accepted accounting principles are:** **LO4**
   a. A set of guidelines to aid in the financial reporting process
   b. A set of laws to prevent financial fraud
   c. A set of standards for ethical conduct
   d. A set of voluntary "best business practices"

4. **To which area of accounting are generally accepted accounting principles primarily relevant?** **LO3**
   a. Managerial accounting
   b. Financial accounting
   c. Tax accounting
   d. Financial reporting to all regulatory agencies

5. **Which of the following is not one of the three types of business activities?** **LO2**
   a. Investing
   b. Financing
   c. Marketing
   d. Operating

6. **If assets total $70,000 and liabilities total $40,000, how much are net assets?** **LO5**
   a. $30,000
   b. $40,000
   c. $70,000
   d. $110,000

7. **What are increases in resources that a firm earns by providing goods or services to its customers?** **LO5**
   a. Assets
   b. Revenues
   c. Expenses
   d. Liabilities

8. **Which of the following items is not required to be included as part of a company's annual report?** **LO6**
   a. Notes to the financial statements
   b. Management discussion and analysis
   c. Detailed history of the company
   d. Auditor's report

LO3   9. **Which of the following situations presents ethical challenges to accountants?**
   a. Pressure by superiors to produce a "good" number
   b. Avoiding the disclosure of confidential information
   c. An emphasis on short-term results
   d. All the above present ethical challenges to accountants

LO1   10. **Match the following organizational attributes in the left column with the organizational form in the right column that the attribute is most often associated with.**

   1. Tax advantages   a. Sole proprietorship
   2. Unlimited liability   b. Partnership
   3. Shared control   c. Corporation
   4. Most complex to set up
   5. Easiest to raise a large amount of funds
   6. Single owner

LO5   11. **The financial statements of Bower Company contain the following. How much is its net income?**

Accounts payable.	$10,000
Revenues	17,000
Accounts receivable.	12,000
Expenses	9,000
Cash.	5,000

   a. $15,000   c. $17,000
   b. $8,000   d. $7,000

LO5   12. **If Ross Company reports its year-end total liabilities to be $75,000, and its year-end stockholders' equity to be $85,000, how much is Ross Company's year-end total assets?**
   a. $10,000
   b. $160,000
   c. $85,000
   d. Cannot be determined from the given information

LO5   13. **Huff Company began the year with a retained earnings balance of $20,000, reported net income for the year of $60,000, and reported ending retained earnings of $70,000. How much dividends did Huff Company report for the year?**
   a. $150,000   c. $10,000
   b. $20,000   d. $30,000

QUESTIONS

1. Define *accounting*. What is the basic purpose of accounting?
2. What is the distinction between *financial* accounting and *managerial* accounting?
3. Who are some of the outside groups that may be interested in a company's financial data and what are their particular interests?
4. What are *generally accepted accounting principles* and what organization has primary responsibility for their formulation in the United States?
5. What are the main advantages and disadvantages of the corporate form of business?
6. What role does financial accounting play in the allocation of society's financial resources?
7. What is the accounting equation? Define *assets, liabilities,* and *stockholders' equity.*
8. What are the three principal business activities and how do they differ?
9. What is meant by corporate social responsibility?
10. What is the difference between generally accepted accounting principles (GAAP) and international financial reporting standards (IFRS)?
11. What are *revenues* and *expenses*?
12. What is the purpose of an income statement? The statement of stockholders' equity? The balance sheet? The statement of cash flows?

13. What is a *period-in-time statement*? Give three examples.

14. What is a *point-in-time statement*? Give one example.

15. On December 31, the Miller Company had $700,000 in total assets and owed $220,000 to creditors. If the corporation's common stock amounted to $300,000, what amount of retained earnings should appear on its December 31 balance sheet?

16. What are three aspects of the accounting environment that may create ethical pressure on an accountant?

17. What type of information might you find in the Management Discussion and Analysis (MD&A) section of the annual report?

18. What is the purpose of having the financial statements audited by an independent auditor?

19. Determine whether the following statements are true or false and explain why:

   a. The accounting process is only interested in communicating economic activity.
   b. There are few potential users of accounting information.
   c. Financial accounting is primarily used to communicate to outside users.
   d. Auditors ensure the validity of a company's financial statements.

20. Why did the FASB develop a conceptual framework?

21. What are two primary qualities of accounting information that contribute to decision usefulness?

22. How would you describe, in one sentence, each of the following accounting principles, concepts and constraints?

Accounting entity	Consistency
Accounting period	Revenue recognition
Monetary unit	Expense recognition (matching)
Cost-benefit	Materiality
Going concern	Full disclosure

23. All of the following are primary qualitative characteristics of accounting information except:
   a. Relevance
   b. Faithful representation
   c. Comparability
   d. All of the above are important characteristics.

SHORT EXERCISES

SE1-1. **Forms of Business Organization** Match the following forms of business organization with the set of attributes that best describes that form of business: sole proprietorship, partnership, or corporation.   **LO1**

   a. Shared control, unlimited liability, tax advantages, increased skills and resources
   b. Best for raising large amounts of funds, double taxation, limited liability, easiest to transfer ownership interests
   c. Sole ownership, easiest to establish, tax advantages, unlimited liability

SE1-2. **Accounting Processes** Identify the following processes as either measuring or communicating.   **LO4**

   a. Prepare financial statements for the entity
   b. Identify relevant economic activities of the entity
   c. Record relevant economic activities of the entity
   d. Interpret financial results of the entity
   e. Quantify relevant economic activities of the entity

SE1-3. **Types of Statements** Match the following type of report with the most likely statement user: management, taxation authority, regulatory agency, or investor.   **LO3**

   a. Financial statements
   b. Tax return
   c. Annual budget
   d. Special report on a bank's financial health

LO4   **SE1-4.**   **Accounting Organizations**   Match the following organizations with the set of accounting guidelines: Financial Accounting Standards Board (FASB), International Accounting Standards Board (IASB).

   a.   Generally accepted accounting principles (GAAP)
   b.   International financial reporting standards (IFRS)

LO2   **SE1-5.**   **Business Activities**   Match the following activities with the type of activity: Operating, Investing, Financing.

   a.   Day-to-day business activities
   b.   Purchase of land for a new warehouse
   c.   Sale of merchandise inventory
   d.   Obtain a new bank loan
   e.   Payment of dividends
   f.   Invest excess cash
   g.   Purchase office supplies
   h.   Sell old equipment that is no longer needed

LO5   **SE1-6.**   **Financial Statement Items**   Identify the financial statement in which each of the following items would appear: income statement (IS), statement of retained earnings (SRE), balance sheet (BS), or statement of cash flows (SCF).

   a.   Assets
   b.   Revenues
   c.   Cash flow from investing activities
   d.   Stockholders' equity
   e.   Expenses
   f.   Net change in cash
   g.   Net income
   h.   Liabilities

LO6   **SE1-7.**   **Annual Report Components**   Which of the following would not be part of the notes to the financial statements in a company's annual report?

   a.   Qualitative information about potential lawsuits
   b.   Additional information about the reported total of notes payable
   c.   Details about potential new products to be introduced during the next year
   d.   Details of estimates used to compute the expected amount of warranty expense

LO3   **SE1-8.**   **Sarbanes-Oxley Act**   The Sarbanes-Oxley Act of 2002 was enacted to help restore confidence in financial reporting. Which of the following was not part of the legislation?

   a.   Severe penalties for fraudulent reporting
   b.   A requirement for certification of the financial statements by top management
   c.   A new statement of social responsibility
   d.   A report on controls to help prevent and detect errors in the reporting process

LO4   **SE1-9.**   **Financial Accounting and Generally Accepted Accounting Principles**   Answer the following multiple-choice questions:

   1.   What is not a primary function of financial accounting in society?
      a.   Provide comedy material for late-night talk shows.
      b.   Aid in the proper allocation of financial resources in a free enterprise economic system.
      c.   Aid users to make better investing decisions.

   2.   IFRS refers to:
      a.   A random set of letters.
      b.   A set of standards and procedures that form guidelines for international financial accounting.
      c.   A set of standards and procedures that form guidelines for international managerial accounting.

   3.   GAAP:
      a.   Is the distance between two objects.
      b.   Is a set of guidelines for preparing managerial reports in the United States.
      c.   Is a set of guidelines for preparing financial reports in the United States.

SE1-10. Cash Flow Activity Classification Classify each activity as financing, investing, or operating: **LO2**

1. Repay a loan from a bank.
2. Sell merchandise from a storefront operation.
3. Dispose of an old delivery truck.
4. Pay rent on a company warehouse.
5. Repurchase shares of stock from stockholders.
6. Pay utilities.

SE1-11. Using the Basic Accounting Equation Use the basic accounting equation to answer the following: **LO5**

a. Kendrick Company has total assets of $100,000 and total liabilities of $60,000. How much is the company's total stockholders' equity?
b. Gassol Company has total liabilities of $80,000 and total stockholders' equity of $75,000. How much total assets does the company have?
c. If Brown Company's total assets increased by $15,000 during the year, and its total liabilities decreased during the same year by $10,000, what was the change in the company's total stockholders' equity?

SE1-12. Using the Basic Accounting Equation Henderson Company had beginning-of-the-year total assets **LO5** of $200,000 and total liabilities of $120,000.

a. If during the year total assets increased by $25,000 and total liabilities increased by $30,000, what is the end-of-year total stockholders' equity?
b. If during the year total assets increased by $50,000 and total liabilities decreased by $10,000, what is the end-of-year total stockholders' equity?
c. If during the year total liabilities increased by $20,000 and total stockholders' equity increased by $30,000, what are the end-of-year total assets?

SE1-13. Financial Statements Indicate which statement you would examine to locate the following items: **LO5** balance sheet (BS), income statement (IS), statement of stockholders' equity (SE), or statement of cash flows (CF).

a. Expenses for the period
b. Cash at year-end
c. Cash used to purchase new equipment
d. Dividends for the period

SE1-14. Financial Statements Indicate which statement you would examine to locate the following items: **LO5** balance sheet (BS), income statement (IS), statement of retained earnings (RE), or statement of cash flows (CF).

a. Revenues for the period
b. Cash at year-end
c. Cash used to pay back borrowings
d. Dividends for the period

SE1-15. Principles of Accounting Which of the following accounting principles applies to the statement of **LO8** cash flows? **(Appendix 1A)**

a. Materiality
b. Conservatism
c. Accrual basis of accounting
d. Cash basis of accounting

SE1-16. Generally Accepted Accounting Principles Select the best answer to each of the following **LO8** questions: **(Appendix 1A)**

1. Accounting rules are developed to provide:
   a. Simplicity
   b. Useful information
   c. Complexity
   d. Ability to change over time

2. The conceptual framework consists of each of the following except:
   a. Financial reporting objectives
   b. Financial statement elements
   c. Ratio analysis guidelines for analysts
   d. Recognition criteria for financial statement items

3. Which of the following is a financial statement element?
   a. Income statement
   b. Liabilities
   c. Balance sheet
   d. Statement of cash flows

LO8
(Appendix 1A)   **SE1-17. Basic Accounting Principles** Match the following list of accounting concepts, principles, and assumptions with the definitions below:

Accounting period concept	Consistency	Cost principle
Going concern concept	Materiality constraint	Full disclosure principle
	Comparability	

1. Ability to compare the financial performance of different companies.
2. Assumption that a company will continue to operate beyond the current period.
3. Only items large enough to make a difference to a user must be disclosed in the financial statements.
4. Prepare financial statements at set time intervals.
5. Record assets on the balance sheet at an amount equal to what was paid for them.
6. A company prepares its financial statements using the same methods used in prior periods.
7. All items of importance to the users of financial statements should be disclosed in the annual report.

LO8
(Appendix 1A)   **SE1-18. FASB Codification** A major reason for the codification project completed by the FASB in 2009 was to:

   a. ease the convergence between financial and managerial accounting
   b. ease the convergence between U.S. GAAP and IFRS
   c. ease the convergence between financial and tax accounting
   d. ease the convergence between U.S. GAAP and GASB

LO8
(Appendix 1A)   **SE1-19. Basic Accounting Principles** Which of the following is not considered a qualitative characteristic of accounting information?

   a. free from error
   b. consistency
   c. assets must equal liabilities and stockholders' equity
   d. timeliness

Assignments with the ✅ logo in the margin are available in BusinessCourse.
See the Preface of the book for details.

EXERCISES—SET A

LO1   **E1-1A. Forms of Business Organization** Match the following organizational attributes in the left column with the organizational form in the right column. More than one organizational form may be associated with a given attribute.

1. Unlimited liability	a. Sole proprietorship
2. Full control	b. Partnership
3. Business income combined with owner(s) income for income tax purposes	c. Corporation
4. Relatively more difficult to establish	
5. Easier to raise funds	

LO4   **E1-2A. Accounting Process** Establish the correct sequence of steps in the accounting measurement process.

   a. Record in a systematic fashion
   b. Identify relevant economic activity
   c. Quantify economic activity

E1-3A. **Types of Accounting** Identify the type of accounting associated with each type of report: Managerial, Financial, Tax, combination as needed. **LO3**

    a. Budget for internal use by management
    b. Tax return for state income taxes
    c. Audited financial statements
    d. Special reports for regulators of a public utility

E1-4A. **Corporate Social Responsibility** Which of the following is not part of the triple bottom line reporting framework? **LO5**

    a. Economic bottom line
    b. Social bottom line
    c. Competitive bottom line
    d. Environmental bottom line

E1-5A. **Generally Accepted Accounting Principles** Identify whether the following statements are true or false: **LO4**

    a. U.S. GAAP is universally accepted in all countries in the world.
    b. U.S. GAAP is established by the IASB.
    c. Once established, U.S. GAAP is rarely, if ever, modified.
    d. The international counterpart to the FASB is the IASB.

E1-6A. **Business Activities** Identify each of the following activities as operating (O), investing (I), or financing (F): **LO2**

    a. Payment of employee salaries
    b. Repayment of a loan
    c. Issuance of common stock
    d. Purchase of equipment to manufacture a company's products
    e. Sale of merchandise inventory
    f. Investment of excess cash in the shares of another company

E1-7A. **The Accounting Equation** Determine the missing amount in each of the following cases: **LO5**

Assets	Liabilities	Stockholders' Equity
$200,000	$85,000	?
?	$32,000	$28,000
$93,000	?	$52,000

E1-8A. **Determining Net Income** The beginning and ending balances of retained earnings for the year were $30,000 and $35,000, respectively. If dividend payments from stockholders' equity exceed new capital contributions during the year by $3,000, determine the net income or net loss for the year. **LO5**

    a. $8,000 net loss
    b. $14,000 net income
    c. $2,000 net income
    d. $8,000 net income

E1-9A. **Determining Retained Earnings and Net Income** The following information appears in the records of Bock Corporation at year-end: **LO5**

Accounts receivable...........	$ 23,000	Retained earnings	$?
Accounts payable...............	11,000	Supplies	9,000
Cash..........................	8,000	Equipment, net.................	138,000
Common stock.................	110,000		

    a. Calculate the balance in retained earnings at year-end.
    b. If the amount of the retained earnings at the beginning of the year was $30,000, and $12,000 in dividends is paid during the year, calculate net income for the year.

LO5   **E1-10A. Determining Stockholders' Equity**   Determine the following:

    a.   The stockholders' equity of a corporation that has assets of $450,000 and liabilities of $326,000.

    b.   The assets of a corporation that has liabilities of $400,000, common stock of $200,000, and retained earnings of $185,000.

LO5   **E1-11A. Financial Statements**   Karl Flury operates a golf driving range. For each of the following financial items related to his business, indicate the financial statement (or statements) in which the item would be reported:

    a.   Accounts receivable
    b.   Cash received from the sale of land
    c.   Net income
    d.   Cash invested in the business by Flury
    e.   Notes payable
    f.   Supplies expense
    g.   Land
    h.   Supplies

LO5   **E1-12A. Omitted Financial Statement Data**   For the following four unrelated situations, A through D, calculate the unknown amounts appearing in each column:

	A	B	C	D
Beginning				
Assets....................................	$28,000	$12,000	$28,000	$?
Liabilities...............................	18,600	5,000	19,000	9,000
Ending				
Assets....................................	30,000	26,000	34,000	40,000
Liabilities...............................	17,300	?	15,000	19,000
During Year				
Sales revenue.........................	?	23,500	28,000	24,000
Expense	8,500	21,000	11,000	17,000
Dividends	3,000	1,500	?	3,000

LO6   **E1-13A. Other Components of the Annual Report**   Identify where the following items will appear in a company's annual report: Management Discussion and Analysis (MD&A), notes to the financial statements, or the auditor's report.

    a.   A comment that the financial statements appear to be fairly presented
    b.   A discussion about new competition likely to occur next year
    c.   A quantitative summary of notes payable appearing on the balance sheet
    d.   The "secret" ingredients in the company's special sauce

LO2   **E1-14A. Ethics**   In each of the following cases, (a) identify the aspect of the accounting environment primarily responsible for the ethical pressure on the accountant and (b) indicate the appropriate behavioral response for the accountant.

    1.   James Jehring, a tax accountant, is preparing an income tax return for a client. The client asks Jehring to take a sizable deduction on the tax return for business-related travel even though the client states that he has no documentation to support the deduction. "I don't think the IRS will audit my return," declares the client.

    2.   Willa English, an accountant for Dome Construction Company, has just finished putting the numbers together for a construction project on which the firm is going to submit a bid next month. At a social gathering that evening, a friend casually asks English what Dome's bid is going to be. Ms. English knows that the friend's brother works for a competitor of Dome.

    3.   The manager of Cross Department Store is ending his first year with the firm. December's business was slower than expected, and the firm's annual results are trailing last year's results. The manager instructs Kyle Tarpley, the store accountant, to include sales revenues from the first week of January in the December data. "This way, we'll show an increase over last year," declares the manager.

E1-15A. International Accounting Principles The worldwide acceptance of a global set of international accounting principles will provide certain benefits.

LO4

    a. Which group has taken the lead in developing a set of international accounting principles?

    b. Identify and briefly discuss two major benefits that would result from the adoption of a global set of international accounting principles.

E1-16A. International Accounting Principles Identify whether the following statements are true or false.

LO4

    1. One argument for IFRS is that companies raise capital in more than one country.

    2. IFRS is accepted as GAAP in every country of the world.

    3. The SEC allows foreign companies to file their annual reports using IFRS.

E1-17A. The Conceptual Accounting Framework The Financial Accounting Standards Board worked many years to develop a conceptual framework for U.S. GAAP.

LO8
(Appendix 1A)

    a. What is the purpose of a conceptual framework?

    b. Identify the financial reporting objectives that are specified in the conceptual framework.

E1-18A. Recognition and Measurement Criteria Indicate the accounting concepts, principles, or constraints that underlie each of the following independent situations:

LO8
(Appendix 1A)

    a. Dr. Kline is a practicing pediatrician. Over the years, she has accumulated a personal investment portfolio of securities, virtually all of which have been purchased from her earnings as a pediatrician. The investment portfolio is not reflected in the accounting records of her medical practice.

    b. A company purchases a desk tape dispenser for use by the office secretary. The tape dispenser cost $10 and has an estimated useful life of 15 years. The purchase is immediately expensed on the company's income statement.

    c. A company sells a product that has a two-year warranty covering parts and labor. In the same period that revenues from product sales are recorded, an estimate of future warranty costs is recorded on the company's income statement.

    d. A company is sued for $1 million by a customer claiming that a defective product caused an accident. The company believes that the lawsuit is without merit. Although the case will not be tried for a year, the company adds a note describing the lawsuit to its current financial statements.

E1-19A. Revenue Recognition Principle For each of the following situations, determine whether the criteria for revenue recognition have been met by December 31, 2012.

LO8
(Appendix 1A)

    a. A manufacturing company received $50,000 cash on December 31, 2012, as an advance payment on a special order for a piece of equipment. The equipment will be manufactured by March 31, 2013.

    b. A television dealer acquired six new high-definition television sets for $8,400 cash on December 31, 2012, and advertised their availability, at $2,000 each, in that evening's newspaper.

    c. A snow removal service signed a contract on November 15, 2012, with a shopping mall to clear its parking lot of all snowfalls over 1 inch during the months of December 2012 through March 2013. The cost is $600 per month and payment is due in two $1,200 installments: January 2, 2013, and February 1, 2013. By December 31, 2012, no snowfall over 1 inch had occurred.

E1-20A. Basic Accounting Principles Identify whether the following statements are true or false.

LO8
(Appendix 1A)

    1. Together the revenue recognition principle and the expense recognition (matching) principle define the accrual basis of accounting.

    2. The cash basis of accounting is only used in the preparation of the statement of cash flows.

    3. The accrual basis of accounting is used in the preparation of the income statement and the balance sheet.

EXERCISES—SET B

E1-1B. Forms of Business Organization Match the following organizational attributes in the left column with the organizational form in the right column. More than one organizational form may be associated with a given attribute.

LO1

1. Limited liability	*a.* Sole proprietorship
2. Shared control	*b.* Partnership
3. Double taxation	*c.* Corporation
4. Easiest to form	
5. Easier to transfer ownership	

LO4   **E1-2B.** **The Accounting Process** Establish the correct sequence of steps in the accounting measurement process.

    a. Quantify economic activity
    b. Identify relevant economic activity
    c. Record in a systematic fashion

LO3   **E1-3B.** **Types of Accounting** Identify the type of accounting associated with each type of report: Managerial, Financial, Tax, combination as needed.

    a. Cost report for a new product
    b. Tax return for federal income taxes
    c. Unaudited financial statements requested for a bank loan
    d. Special report for banking regulators

LO5   **E1-4B.** **Corporate Social Responsibility** Which of the following is not part of the triple bottom line reporting framework?

    a. Social bottom line
    b. Environmental bottom line
    c. Economic bottom line
    d. Efficiency bottom line

LO4   **E1-5B.** **Generally Accepted Accounting Principles** Identify whether the following statements are true or false.

    a. GAAP can differ from one country to another.
    b. U.S. GAAP is established by the FASB.
    c. U.S. GAAP is a guide to action that may change over time.
    d. At this time there is no international counterpart to the FASB.

LO2   **E1-6B.** **Business Activities** Identify each of the following activities as operating (O), investing (I), or financing (F).

    a. Payment of rent on the company headquarters
    b. Repurchase of the company's common stock
    c. Obtain a long-term bank loan
    d. Sale of an empty warehouse
    e. Delivery of consulting service
    f. Sale of short-term investments

LO5   **E1-7B.** **The Accounting Equation** Determine the missing amount in each of the following cases:

Assets	Liabilities	Stockholders' Equity
$300,000	?	$170,000
$ 80,000	$32,000	?
?	$40,000	$ 49,000

LO5   **E1-8B.** **Determining Net Income** The beginning and ending balances of retained earnings for the year were $45,000 and $52,500, respectively. If dividends paid from stockholders' equity exceed new capital contributions during the year by $4,500, determine the net income or net loss for the year:

    a. $12,000 net loss
    b. $21,000 net income
    c. $3,000 net income
    d. $12,000 net income

E1-9B. Determining Retained Earnings and Net Income The following information appears in the records of the Jones Corporation at year-end: **LO5** ✓

Accounts receivable..............	$ 40,000	Retained earnings	$?
Accounts payable................	19,000	Supplies	27,000
Cash.........................	17,000	Equipment, net..................	108,000
Common stock..................	210,000		

a. Calculate the amount of retained earnings at year-end.

b. If the amount of the retained earnings at the beginning of the year was $60,000, and $25,000 in dividends is paid during the year, calculate net income (net loss) for the year.

E1-10B. Determining Stockholders' Equity Determine the following: **LO5** ✓

a. The stockholders' equity of a sole proprietorship that has assets of $750,000 and liabilities of $300,000.

b. The assets of a corporation that has liabilities of $170,000, common stock of $85,000, and retained earnings of $74,000.

E1-11B. Financial Statements Kattie Klein operates a bakery. For each of the following financial statement items related to her business, indicate the financial statement (or statements) in which the item would be reported: **LO5**

a. Accounts payable

b. Cash received from the sale of equipment

c. Net loss

d. Cash invested in the business by Klein

e. Notes receivable

f. Rent expense

g. Building

h. Inventory

E1-12B. Omitted Financial Statement Data For the following four unrelated situations, A-D, calculate the unknown amounts appearing in each column: **LO5** ✓

	A	B	C	D
Beginning				
Assets...........................	$42,000	$18,000	$42,000	?
Liabilities.........................	27,900	7,500	28,500	13,500
Ending				
Assets...........................	45,000	39,000	51,000	60,000
Liabilities.........................	25,950	?	22,500	28,500
During Year				
Sales revenue.....................	?	35,250	36,000	36,000
Expense	12,750	31,500	16,500	25,500
Dividends	4,500	2,250	?	4,500

E1-13B. Other Components of the Annual Report Identify where the following items will appear in a company's annual report: Management Discussion and Analysis (MD&A), notes to the financial statements, the auditor's report, or not disclosed. **LO6**

a. A comment that the statements are presented in conformity with generally accepted accounting principles

b. A discussion about new products to be introduced next year

c. A quantitative summary of property, plant, and equipment appearing on the balance sheet

d. The salaries of every employee

E1-14B. Ethics In each of the following cases, (a) identify the aspect of the accounting environment primarily responsible for the ethical pressure on the accountant and (b) indicate the appropriate behavioral response for the accountant. **LO3**

1. Jenny Jones, a tax accountant, is preparing an income tax return for a client. The client asks Jones to omit some income she received for consulting services because the amount was paid in cash. "I don't think the IRS will audit my return," declares the client. "And even if they do, what are the chances they would catch this?"

2. Fred French, an accountant for Top Electronics Company, has just finished estimating the cost for a new iPod device that the company plans to introduce. Cost estimates help the company to determine the price they can charge for new products. At a social gathering that evening, a friend casually asks Fred what Top's cost for the iPod device came out to be. Fred knows that the friend's brother works for a competitor of Top Electronics.

3. The manager of Jazz Department Store is ending his first year with the firm. December's business was slower than expected, and the firm's annual results are below Wall Street's expectations. The manager instructs Chris Green, store accountant, to record some of December's expenses in the following year. "This way, we'll meet Wall Street's expectations," declares the manager.

LO4

E1-15B. International Accounting Principles Although there are obstacles to the worldwide acceptance of a global set of international accounting principles, the potential benefits appear significant.

Identify and briefly discuss three potential benefits to the worldwide acceptance of a global set of international accounting principles.

LO8
(Appendix 1A)

E1-16B. The Conceptual Framework The Financial Accounting Standards Board worked many years to develop a conceptual framework for U.S. GAAP.

a.   Identify the financial statement elements that are specified in the conceptual framework.

b.   Before a financial statement element may be recorded in the accounts, certain recognition criteria must be met. What are those recognition criteria?

LO8
(Appendix 1A)

E1-17B. Recognition and Measurement Criteria Indicate the accounting concepts, principles, or constraints that underlie each of the following independent situations:

a.   Ford Motor Company reports in its annual report to stockholders that revenues from automotive sales "are recorded by the company when products are shipped to dealers."

b.   The annual financial report of Chrysler Corporation and subsidiaries includes the financial data of its significant subsidiaries, including Chrysler Financial Corporation (which provides financing for dealers and customers), Chrysler Technologies Corporation (which manufactures high-technology electronic products), and Pentastar Transportation Group, Inc. (which includes Thrifty Rent-A-Car System, Inc., and Dollar Rent A Car Systems, Inc.).

c.   A company purchased a parcel of land several years ago for $65,000. The land's estimated current market value is $80,000. The Land account balance is not increased but remains at $65,000.

d.   A company has a calendar-year fiscal year-end. On January 8, 2013, a tornado destroyed its largest warehouse, causing a $1,800,000 loss. This information is reported in a footnote to the 2012 financial statements.

LO5, 8
(Appendix 1A)

E1-18B. Accrual Basis of Accounting versus Cash Basis of Accounting On December 31, Jayne Leigh completed her first year as a financial planner. The following data are available from her accounting records:

Fees billed to clients for services rendered	$97,000	Rent expense for year just ended	$10,800
Cash received from clients.	85,000	Utility expense incurred	2,500
Supplies purchased for cash	4,500	Utility bills paid	2,200
Supplies used during the year	3,300	Salary earned by assistant	30,000
Cash paid for rent (rent is paid through		Salary paid to assistant	27,500
Feb. of next year)	12,600		

a.   Compute Leigh's net income for the year just ended using the accrual basis of accounting.

b.   Compute Leigh's net income for the year just ended using the cash basis of accounting.

c.   Which net income amount is computed in accordance with generally accepted accounting principles?

E1-19B. Recognition and Measurement Criteria The following are unrelated accounting practices:

LO8
(Appendix 1A)

1. A recession has caused a slowing of business activity and lower profits for Balke Company. Consequently, the firm delays making its payments for December's rent and utilities until January and does not record either of these expenses in December.
2. Gail Derry, a consultant operating as a sole proprietorship, used her business car for a personal, month-long vacation. A full year's gas and oil expenditures on the car are charged to the firm's gas and oil expense account.
3. Vine Company purchased a new $18 snow shovel that is expected to last six years. The shovel is used to clear the firm's front steps during the winter months. The shovel's cost is recorded on the company's balance sheet as an asset.
4. Filene Corporation has been named as the defendant in a $40 million pollution lawsuit. Because the lawsuit will take several years to resolve and the outcome is uncertain, Filene's management decides not to mention the lawsuit in the current year financial statements.

Required
For each of the given practices, indicate which accounting concepts, principles, or constraints apply and whether they have been applied appropriately. For each inappropriate accounting practice, indicate the proper accounting procedure.

PROBLEMS—SET A

P1-1A. Forms of Business Organization Presented below are four independent situations:

LO1

a. Kali Kane, a senior in college looking for summer employment, decided to start a dog-walking business. Each morning and evening she picks up a group of dogs and walks them around the city park.
b. Brothers Joe and Jay Simmons each owned a separate electronics repair shop. They decided to combine their talents and resources in order to expand the amount of business they could undertake.
c. Three chemists at a large engineering company decided to start their own business based on an experimental chemical process they had developed outside the company. The process had the potential to be very successful; however, it was quite dangerous and could result in large legal problems.
d. Jack Prince ran a small, but successful holistic healing spa. The spa has gained a strong reputation beyond the community where it is located. Jack decided to open a chain of similar spas across the state to capitalize on his reputation. This will require a substantial investment in supplies and employee training. In addition, since Jack will not be able to closely supervise each location, he is worried about potential liability.

Required
Explain the form of organization that would be best in each situation—sole proprietorship, partnership, or corporation. Explain what factors you considered important in each situation.

P1-2A. Financial Statements While each of the financial statements is likely to aid in any business decision, it is often the case that a particular financial statement may be best suited to help in a particular decision. Consider each decision below independently:

LO5

a. You are trying to determine whether a particular firm is a good investment. You understand that share price increases are impacted heavily by a company's earnings potential.
b. You are employed in the lending department of a large bank. You are trying to determine if you should lend to a potential customer. If you do make the loan you are especially concerned that the company will have sufficient collateral in the event that it is unable to repay the loan.
c. You wish to invest in a firm that provides you with a steady source of income. You especially want a firm that pays out a large part of its net income as dividends.
d. You are trying to determine if a particular firm will have sufficient cash flow in order to keep expanding without relying too heavily on external sources of financing.

Required

Determine which of the financial statements contains the most useful information to help in your decision. Explain what information you used from each statement to help you make your decision.

LO5 ✔ **P1-3A.** **Balance Sheet** The following balance sheet data are for Normandy Catering Service, a corporation, at May 31, 2013:

Accounts receivable...........	$18,300	Accounts payable...........	5,200
Notes payable	20,000	Cash.....................	12,200
Equipment, net..............	55,000	Common stock............	42,500
Supplies	16,400	Retained earnings	?

Required

Prepare a balance sheet for Normandy as of May 31, 2013.

LO5 ✔ **P1-4A.** **Statement of Stockholders' Equity and Balance Sheet** The following is balance sheet information for Lynch Janitorial Service, Inc., at the end of 2013 and 2012:

	December 31, 2013	December 31, 2012
Accounts payable........................	$ 6,000	$ 9,000
Cash..............................	23,000	20,000
Accounts receivable.....................	42,000	33,000
Land.............................	40,000	40,000
Building, net.........................	250,000	260,000
Equipment, net.......................	43,000	45,000
Mortgage payable	90,000	100,000
Supplies	20,000	18,000
Common stock.......................	220,000	220,000
Dividends	10,000	0
Retained earnings	?	?

Required

a. Prepare a balance sheet as of December 31 of each year.

b. Prepare a statement of stockholders' equity for 2013. (*Hint:* The increase in retained earnings is equal to the net income less the dividend.)

LO5 ✔ **P1-5A.** **Statement of Retained Earnings and Balance Sheet** The following is balance sheet information for House Janitorial Service, Inc., at the end of 2013 and 2012:

	December 31, 2013	December 31, 2012
Accounts payable.......................	$ 12,000	$ 18,000
Cash..............................	46,000	40,000
Accounts receivable.....................	84,000	66,000
Land.............................	80,000	80,000
Building, net.........................	500,000	520,000
Equipment, net.......................	86,000	90,000
Mortgage payable	180,000	200,000
Supplies	40,000	36,000
Common stock.......................	440,000	440,000
Dividends	20,000	0
Retained earnings	?	?

Required

a. Prepare a balance sheet as of December 31 of each year.

b. Prepare a statement of retained earnings for 2013. (*Hint:* The increase in retained earnings is equal to the net income less the dividend.)

P1-6A. **Income Statement and Balance Sheet** On March 1, 2013, Amy Dart began Dart Delivery Service, which provides delivery of bulk mailings to the post office, neighborhood delivery of weekly newspapers, data delivery to computer service centers, and various other delivery services using leased vans. On February 28, Dart invested $15,000 of her own funds in the firm and borrowed $6,000 from her father on a six-month, non-interest-bearing note payable. The following information is available at March 31:

 LO5

Accounts receivable	$9,700	Delivery fees earned	$19,300
Rent expense	1,500	Cash	12,900
Advertising expense	900	Supplies	6,500
Supplies expense	2,700	Notes payable	6,000
Accounts payable	1,200	Insurance expense	800
Salaries expense	6,300	Common stock	15,000
Miscellaneous expense	200	Retained earnings	?

Required

a. Prepare an income statement for the month of March.

b. Prepare a balance sheet as of March 31, 2013.

P1-7A. **Statement of Cash Flows** Shown below is selected information from the financial records of Mantle Corporation as of December 31:

 LO5

Inventory	$ 72,000	Cash purchase of equipment	$ 27,000
Cash collected from customers	330,000	Buildings, net	440,000
Equipment, net	125,000	Sales revenue	475,000
Retained earnings	275,000	Cash paid for operating activities	210,000
Cash dividends paid	42,000	Principal payments on existing note payable	47,000
Salary expense	110,000	Common stock	155,000

Required

a. Determine which of the above items will appear on the statement of cash flows and then prepare the statement for Mantle Corporation for the year ended December 31, 2013.

b. Comment on the adequacy of Mantle's operations to provide cash for its investing and financing activities.

P1-8A. **Ethics** In each of the following cases, (a) identify the aspect of the accounting environment primarily responsible for the ethical pressure on the accountant and (b) indicate the appropriate behavioral response that the accountant should take.

LO3

1. Patricia Kelly, an accountant for Wooden Company, is reviewing the costs charged to a government contract that Wooden worked on this year. Wooden is manufacturing special parts for the government and is allowed to charge the government for its actual manufacturing costs plus a fixed fee. Kelly notes that $75,000 worth of art objects purchased for the president's office is buried among the miscellaneous costs charged to the contract. Upon inquiry, the firm's vice president replies, "This sort of thing is done all the time."

2. Barry Marklin, accountant for Smith & Wesson partnership, is working on the 2013 year-end financial data. The partnership agreement calls for Smith and Wesson to share the firm's 2013 net income equally. In 2014, the partners will share the net income 60 percent to Smith and 40 percent to Wesson. Wesson plans to cut back his involvement in the firm. Smith wants Marklin to delay recording sales revenue from work done at the end of 2013 until January 2014. "We haven't received the cash yet from those services," declares Smith.

3. The St. Louis Wheelers, a professional football franchise, just signed its first-round draft pick to a multiyear contract that is reported in the newspapers as a four-year, $20 million contract. Johanna Factor, the Wheelers' accountant, receives a call from an agent of another team's first-round pick. "Just calling to confirm the contract terms reported in the papers," states the agent. "My client should receive a similar contract, and I'm sure you don't want him to get shortchanged."

LO5 **P1-9A.** **Income Statement, Statement of Stockholders' Equity, and Balance Sheet** Napolean Corporation started business on January 1, 2013. The following information was compiled by Napolean's accountant on December 31, 2013:

Sales revenue	30,000	Building, net	60,000
Expenses	18,000	Accounts payable	6,000
Dividends	4,500	Notes payable	49,500
Cash	2,250	Common stock	30,000
Accounts receivable	3,750	Retained earnings	?
Inventory	4,500		
Equipment, net	22,500		

Required

a. You have been asked to assist the accountant for the Napolean Corporation in preparing year-end financial statements. Use the above information to prepare an income statement, statement of stockholders' equity, and a balance sheet as of December 31, 2013.

b. Comment on the decision to pay a $4,500 dividend.

LO3 **P1-10A.** **Ethics** As the accountant for Minkow Corporation, you are responsible for reporting the company's profit. It appears that the company's actual results are much better than was expected by Wall Street analysts. Your supervisor has requested that you report some of next period's expenses now so that this period's profits will be in line with analyst expectations. He states that you are not really doing anything wrong since the reported results will be more conservative. In addition, this will make it easier to make next year's numbers. What should you do?

LO8 **P1-11A.** **Recognition and Measurement Criteria** The following are unrelated accounting situations and the
(Appendix 1A) accounting treatment that was followed in each firm's records:

1. Martin Company mounts a $600,000 year-long advertising campaign on a national cable television network. The firm's annual accounting period is the calendar year. The television network required full payment in December at the beginning of the campaign. Accounting treatment is
      Increase Advertising Expense, $600,000
      Decrease Cash, $600,000

2. Because of a local bankruptcy, machinery worth $200,000 was acquired at a "bargain" purchase price of $180,000. Accounting treatment is
      Increase Machinery, $180,000
      Decrease Cash, $180,000

3. Tim Vagly, a consultant operating a sole proprietorship, withdrew $20,000 from the business and purchased stocks as an investment gift to his wife. Accounting treatment is
      Increase Investments, $20,000
      Decrease Cash, $20,000

4. Sioux Company received a firm offer of $96,000 for a parcel of land it owns that cost $68,000 two years ago. The offer was refused, but the indicated gain was recorded in the accounts. Accounting treatment is
      Increase Land, $28,000
      Increase Revenue from Change in Land Value, $28,000

Required

In each of the given situations, indicate which accounting concepts, principles or constraints apply and whether they have been applied appropriately. If you decide the accounting treatment is not generally accepted, discuss the effect of the departure on the balance sheet.

PROBLEMS—SET B

LO1 **P1-1B.** **Forms of Business Organization**
Presented below are four independent situations:

a. Dino Owens, a photography major in college, decided to start a photography business specializing in weddings and similar occasions. Dino is still able to go to school full-time as all of his jobs are on weekends or holidays.

b. Joe Thursday and Jay Lightfoot each owned a separate detective agency. They decided to combine their talents and resources in order to expand the amount of business they could undertake.

c. Three business school professors at a large university decided to start their own consulting business based on their combined talents. They feel that the insurance they can obtain will satisfy any possible legal issues they may face. They plan to use one professor's home office to meet clients, so start-up costs should be minimal.

d. Vera Gold runs a small, but successful beauty salon. The salon has gained a strong reputation beyond the community where it is located. Vera has decided to open a chain of similar salons across the state to capitalize on her reputation. This will require a substantial investment in facilities and supplies. In addition, since Vera will not be able to closely supervise each location, she is worried about potential liability.

Required
Explain the form of organization that would be best in each situation—sole proprietorship, partnership, or corporation. Explain what factors you considered important in each situation.

P1-2B. **Financial Statements** While each of the financial statements is likely to aid in any business decision, **LO5** it is often the case that a particular financial statement may be best suited to help in a particular decision. Consider each decision below independently:

a. You are trying to determine whether a particular firm is a good investment. You want to invest in a firm that has strong revenue growth.

b. You are employed as a financial analyst for a large investment firm. You are trying to assess the riskiness of a particular investment opportunity. You understand that the more debt a firm has relative to its stockholders' equity, the riskier the firm is.

c. You are trying to determine how much of a firm's net income it distributes to its stockholders.

d. You are trying to determine how a particular firm was able to finance its large expansion during the year.

Required
Determine which of the financial statements contains the most useful information to help in your decision. Explain what information you used from each statement to help you make your decision.

P1-3B. **Balance Sheet** The following balance sheet data are for Bettis Plumbing Contractors, Inc., as of June **LO5** 30, 2013:

Accounts payable.	$ 8,900	Common stock.	$100,000
Cash.	14,700	Retained earnings	?
Supplies.	30,500	Notes payable	30,000
Equipment, net.	98,000	Accounts receivable.	9,200
Land.	25,000		

Required
Prepare a balance sheet as of June 30, 2013.

P1-4B. **Statement of Stockholders' Equity and Balance Sheet** Balance sheet information for Jordan Packaging Service at the end of 2013 and 2012 is as follows: **LO5**

	December 31, 2013	December 31, 2012
Accounts receivable.	$22,800	$17,500
Accounts payable.	1,800	1,600
Cash.	10,000	8,000
Equipment, net.	32,000	27,000
Supplies.	4,700	4,200
Notes payable	25,000	25,000
Dividends.	12,000	0
Common stock.	5,000	5,000
Retained earnings	?	?

Required
a. Prepare a balance sheet as of December 31 of each year.
b. Prepare a statement of stockholders' equity for 2013. (*Hint:* The increase in retained earnings is equal to the net income less the dividend.)

ASSIGNMENTS

LO5 **P1-5B.** **Statement of Retained Earnings and Balance Sheet** Balance sheet information for Jackson Packaging Service at the end of 2013 and 2012 is as follows:

	December 31, 2013	December 31, 2012
Accounts receivable...............................	$45,600	$35,000
Accounts payable.................................	3,600	3,200
Cash..	20,000	16,000
Equipment	64,000	54,000
Supplies	9,400	8,400
Notes payable	50,000	50,000
Dividends	24,000	0
Common stock..................................	10,000	10,000
Retained earnings	?	?

Required

a. Prepare a balance sheet as of December 31 of each year.

b. Prepare a statement of retained earnings for 2013. (*Hint:* The increase in retained earnings is equal to the net income less the dividend.)

LO5 **P1-6B.** **Income Statement and Balance Sheet** The records of R. Levy, Interior Decorator, show the following information for the year-end December 31, 2013:

Notes payable	$ 4,000	Supplies	$ 6,100
Decorating fees earned	67,600	Cash...........................	4,200
Supplies expense.................	9,700	Accounts receivable..............	10,600
Insurance expense................	1,500	Advertising expense..............	1,700
Miscellaneous expense	200	Salaries expense	30,000
Common stock..................	11,600	Rent expense	7,500
Retained earnings	?	Accounts payable.................	1,800

Required

a. Prepare an income statement for the year.

b. Prepare a balance sheet as of December 31, 2013.

LO5 **P1-7B.** **Statement of Cash Flows** Shown below is selected information from the books of Mays Corporation as of December 31, 2013:

Inventory.............................	$144,000	Cash purchase of equipment.............	127,000
Cash collected from customers...........	660,000	Buildings, net	880,000
Equipment, net........................	250,000	Sales revenue.........................	950,000
Retained earnings	550,000	Cash paid for operating activities..........	420,000
		Principal payments on existing	
Cash dividends paid...................	84,000	note payable........................	127,000
Salary expense.......................	220,000	Common stock.......................	310,000

Required

a. Determine which of the above items will appear on the statement of cash flows and then prepare the statement for Mays Corporation for the year ended December 31, 2013.

b. Comment on the adequacy of Mays' operations to provide cash for its investing and financing activities.

LO3 **P1-8B.** **Ethics** In each of the following cases, (a) identify the aspect of the accounting environment primarily responsible for the ethical pressure on the accountant and (b) indicate the appropriate behavioral response that the accountant should take:

1. Kenneth Mills, an accountant for the Riley Company, is reviewing costs charged to a big government contract to supply logistical support. The contract specifies that Riley is entitled to its cost plus 10 percent extra for profit. Kenneth notices that gardening services at the home of the company president, Stu Riley, are included under miscellaneous expenses. The company's vice

president, Slick Lowe, tells you not to worry about this since the government expects a little bit of fancy accounting to be included in all of its contracts.

2. Sergio Salles, an accountant for the law partnership Dewy and Suem, is working on the year-end financial statements. Currently the two partners, Dewy and Suem, each receive one-half of the firm's net income. Next year the allocation will change to a two-thirds, one-third split since Suem will be taking considerable time off to do pro bono work, something Dewy never does. Dewy suggested to Salles that he delay booking a large partial settlement the partnership received in December until January of next year when they will receive the final cash payment. Dewy commented that it would be "cleaner" to keep it all together.

3. Pete Freely is the accountant for a large professional services firm. Part of his responsibility is to complete payroll tax reports based on the salaries paid to all the employees. Pete received a call from a friend at a search firm that specializes in personnel such as those employed at Pete's place of employment. Pete's friend casually asked how much certain employees were making, explaining he wanted to be able to calibrate market wages for work he was doing.

P1-9B.   **Financial Statements and Other Components**   Match each of the items in the left column with the appropriate annual report component from the right column:

LO5, 6

1.	The company's total assets	*a.*	Income Statement
2.	An opinion regarding whether the financial statements followed GAAP	*b.*	Statement of Stockholders' Equity
3.	Information regarding the estimates used in the financial statements	*c.* *d.*	Balance Sheet Statement of Cash Flows
4.	The use of cash during the period	*e.*	Management Discussion and Analysis (MD&A)
5.	The company's total expenses for the period	*f.*	Notes to the Financial Statements
6.	A discussion of potential risks that a company may encounter in the future	*g.*	Auditor's report
7.	The amount of a company's earnings that are distributed to the company's stockholders		

P1-10B.   **Recognition and Measurement Criteria**   The following are unrelated accounting situations and the accounting treatment that was followed in each firm's records:

LO8
(Appendix 1A)

1. The Baldwin Company mounts an $800,000 year-long advertising campaign on a new national cable television network. The firm's annual accounting period is the calendar year. The television network required full payment in December at the beginning of the campaign. Accounting treatment is

     Increase Advertising Expense, $800,000
     Decrease Cash, $800,000

2. Because of a local bankruptcy, machinery worth $300,000 was acquired at a "bargain" purchase price of $150,000. Accounting treatment is

     Increase Machinery, $150,000
     Decrease Cash, $150,000

3. J.P. Smith, a consultant operating a sole proprietorship, withdrew $40,000 from the business and purchased stocks as an investment gift to his wife. Accounting treatment is

     Increase Investments, $40,000
     Decrease Cash, $40,000

4. Morongo Company received a firm offer of $106,000 for a parcel of land it owns that cost $75,000 two years ago. The offer was refused, but the indicated gain was recorded in the accounts. Accounting treatment is

     Increase Land, $31,000
     Increase Revenue from Change in Land Value, $31,000

Required

In each of the given situations, indicate which accounting concepts, principles or constraints apply and whether they have been applied appropriately. If you decide the accounting treatment is not generally accepted, discuss the effect of the departure on the balance sheet.

SERIAL PROBLEM: KATE'S CARDS

SP1.   Kate Collins has always been good at putting together rhymes for any occasion. Recently, Kate's financial assistance for college was cut back due to budget problems in the state where she lives. Kate determined that the best way to raise enough money to stay in school and still have enough time for her studies was to start a greeting card business. She feels that this will not only help her to raise money, but it will supplement what she is learning at school as a business major.

Kate decided that she would start small and work out of her dorm room, designing the cards on a new Apple iMac that she was planning to purchase. Kate also decided to offer classes in greeting card design to other aspiring greeting card producers. After much thought, Kate decided to name her business "Kate's Cards."

Required

a.   What form of business—sole proprietorship, partnership, or corporation—should Kate choose? Discuss why the organizational form that you selected is most appropriate for Kate.

b.   What accounting information will Kate need to run her business?

c.   What balance sheet accounts—assets, liabilities, and stockholders' equity—and income statement accounts—revenues and expenses—will Kate likely need to use?

d.   Should Kate use her personal bank account or open a separate business bank account?

EXTENDING YOUR KNOWLEDGE

REPORTING AND ANALYSIS

COLUMBIA
SPORTSWEAR
COMPANY

EYK1-1.   **Financial Reporting Problem: Columbia Sportswear Company** Financial statements for the **Columbia Sportswear Company** are reported in Appendix A at the end of the textbook.

Required
Refer to Columbia Sportswear's financial statements to answer the following questions:

a.   How much did Columbia's total assets increase or decrease from December 31, 2010, to December 31, 2011?

b.   How much did Columbia's cash and cash equivalents increase or decrease from December 31, 2010, to December 31, 2011, and how much cash did Columbia report on its December 31, 2011, balance sheet?

c.   How much accounts receivable and accounts payable did Columbia report on December 31, 2011? Does it appear that Columbia is able to collect from its customers as well as pay its own bills?

d.   Did Columbia experience revenue growth in 2011?

e.   Was Columbia profitable in 2011? How does the company's 2011 profit compare to 2010?

COLUMBIA
SPORTSWEAR
COMPANY

UNDER ARMOUR

EYK1-2.   **Comparative Analysis Problem: Columbia Sportswear Company vs. Under Armour, Inc.** Simplified financial statements for the **Columbia Sportswear Company** are reported in Exhibit 1-11 and **Under Armour**'s financial statements are presented in Appendix B at the end of this book.

Required
1.   Based on the information in these financial statements, compare the following for each company as of December 31, 2011:
   a.   Total assets
   b.   Sales
   c.   Net income
   d.   Cash flow from operations
2.   From this information, what can you conclude about the relative size and operating performance of each company?

EYK1-3. **Business Decision Problem** Paul Seale, a friend of yours, is negotiating the purchase of an exterminating company called Total Pest Control. Seale has been employed by a national pest control service and knows the technical side of the business. However, he knows little about accounting, so he asks for your assistance. The owner of Total Pest Control, Greg Krey, provided Seale with income statements for the past three years, which showed an average net income of $72,000 per year. The latest balance sheet shows total assets of $285,000 and liabilities of $45,000. Seale brings the following matters to your attention:

1. Krey is asking $300,000 for the firm. He told Seale that because the firm has been earning a 30 percent return on stockholders' equity, the price should be higher than the net assets reported on the balance sheet. (Note: The return on stockholders' equity is calculated as net income divided by total stockholders' equity.)

2. Seale noticed that there was no salary expense reported for Krey on the income statements, even though he worked half-time in the business. Krey explained that, because he had other income, he withdrew only $18,000 each year from the firm for personal use. If he purchases the firm, Seale will hire a full-time manager to run the firm at an annual salary of $36,000.

3. Krey's tax returns for the past three years report a lower net income for the firm than the amounts shown in the financial statements. Seale is skeptical about the accounting principles used in preparing the company's financial statements.

Required

a. If Seale accepts Krey's average annual income figure of $72,000, what would Seale's percentage return on stockholders' equity be, assuming that the net income remained at the same level and that the firm was purchased for $300,000?

b. Should Krey's withdrawals of $18,000 per year affect the net income reported in the financial statements? What will Seale's percentage return be if he takes into consideration the $36,000 salary he plans to pay a full-time manager?

c. Could there be legitimate reasons for the difference between net income as shown in the financial statements and net income as reported on the tax returns, as mentioned in point 3? How might Seale obtain additional assurances about the propriety of the company's financial statements?

EYK1-4. **Financial Analysis Problem** Todd Jansen is deciding among several job offers. One job offer he is considering is in the marketing department at Columbia Sportswear. Before he makes his decision, he decides to review the financial reports of the company.

Required

Use the Columbia Sportswear annual report located in Appendix A at the end of this book to answer the following questions:

a. Were the financial statements of Columbia audited? If so, what firm performed the audit?

b. What was the amount of Columbia's 2011 net income? How does this compare with 2010 net income?

c. How much cash was provided or used for investing activities? What were the major sources and uses of cash from investing activities?

d. How much were accrued liabilities in 2011? What makes up this balance?

e. What are some of the more significant estimates used in the preparation of the company's financial statements?

f. To what amount are the financial statements rounded?

CRITICAL THINKING

EYK1-5. **Accounting Research Problem** Go to this book's Website and locate the annual report of General Mills, Inc. for the year ending May 29, 2011 (fiscal year 2011).

GENERAL MILLS, INC.

Required

a. Refer to the company's balance sheet.
  1. What form of business organization does General Mills use? What evidence supports your answer?
  2. What is the date of the most recent balance sheet?
  3. For the most recent balance sheet, what is the largest asset reported? the largest liability?

b. Refer to the company's income statement.
    1. What time period is covered by the most recent statement of earnings?
    2. What total amount of sales revenues did General Mills generate in the most recent period? What is the change in sales revenues from last year to the current report year?
    3. What is the net income (i.e., net earnings, including earnings attributable to noncontrolling interests) for the most recent period?
c. Refer to the company's statement of cash flows.
    1. For the most recent period, what is the amount and trend of the cash flow from operating activities?
    2. For the most recent period, what is the amount and trend of the cash flow from investing activities?
    3. For the most recent period, what is the amount and trend of the cash flow from financing activities?

EYK1-6.   **Accounting Communication Activity** Jasper Simmons is an intern for the Newby Company. He knows the company's balance sheet is supposed to balance, but he is not having much luck getting it to balance. Jasper knows that you are taking a course in accounting so he asks for your help. Jasper provides you with the following balance sheet that is currently out of balance:

NEWBY COMPANY			
Balance Sheet			
December 31, 2013			
Assets		**Liabilities**	
Cash......................	15,000	Inventory...........................	20,000
Accounts receivable...........	30,000	Notes payable	38,000
Equipment, net...............	28,000	**Stockholders' Equity**	
Accounts payable.............	(22,000)	Dividends	(11,000)
		Common stock......................	10,000
		Retained earnings, beginning of year......	10,000
Total	51,000	Total	67,000

In addition, Jasper provides you with a correct income statement that reports a net income for 2013 of $24,000.

Required
a. Prepare a corrected balance sheet for the Newby Company.
b. Write a memo to Jasper explaining what he did wrong.
c. In the memo explain the purpose of the balance sheet.

EYK1-7.   **Accounting Ethics Case** Jack Hardy, CPA, has a brother, Ted, in the retail clothing business. Ted ran the business as a sole proprietor for 10 years. During this 10-year period, Jack helped Ted with various accounting matters. For example, Jack designed the accounting system for the company, prepared Ted's personal income tax returns (which included financial data about the clothing business), and recommended various cost control procedures. Ted paid Jack for all of these services. A year ago, Ted expanded the business and incorporated. Ted is president of the corporation and also chairs the corporation's board of directors. The board of directors has overall responsibility for corporate affairs. When the corporation was formed, Ted asked Jack to serve on its board of directors. Jack accepted. In addition, Jack now prepares the corporation's income tax returns and continues to advise his brother on accounting matters.

Recently, the corporation applied for a large bank loan. The bank wants audited financial statements for the corporation before it will decide on the loan request. Ted asked Jack to perform the audit. Jack replied that he cannot do the audit because the code of ethics for CPAs requires that he be independent when providing audit services.

Required
Why is it important that a CPA be independent when providing audit services? Which of Jack's activities or relationships impair his independence?

EYK1-8. **Corporate Social Responsibility Problem** Go to the **Columbia Sportswear Company** Website and find the section on their commitment to corporate responsibility. This section can be found near the bottom of their home page under the section "About Us."

COLUMBIA SPORTSWEAR COMPANY

Required
Answer the following questions.

a. How does Columbia describe the company's efforts at corporate responsibility?
b. What is the stated purpose of Columbia's sustainability efforts?
c. What featured initiative has Columbia embarked upon?
d. Why do you think that Columbia makes these efforts to be a good corporate citizen? Why do you think they devote so much space on their Website to promote these efforts?

EYK1-9. **Forensic Accounting Problem** Go to the Association of Certified Fraud Examiners Website and find their description of a forensic accountant. This can be found under the Career tab, Career Paths, then click on Forensic Accountant.

Required
Answer the following questions.

a. What type of engagements do forensic accountants work on?
b. What are some of the useful skills that a forensic accountant should possess?
c. How might the knowledge learned from this course help you to become a forensic accountant?

EYK1-10. **Analyzing IFRS Financial Statements** Tesco PLC is the world's third largest retailer. Tesco is based in the United Kingdom but also maintains operations in the United States. Tesco's IFRS financial statements are presented in Appendix C at the end of this book. After reviewing the company's financial statements, consider the following questions:

a. What is Tesco's largest asset account on its 2011 balance sheet? What percentage of total assets does this asset represent?
b. Is Tesco principally debt financed or equity financed in 2011? What percentage of Tesco's assets is financed with debt?
c. Is Tesco profitable in 2011? What percentage of the company's sales revenue in 2011 is represented by its "profit for the year," or its net income?
d. How much is Tesco's cash flow from operating activities in 2011? How does Tesco's profit for the year (net income) compare with its cash flow from operating activities?

EYK1-11. **Working with the Takeaways** You have just learned that you inherited a large sum of money. You know that it is important to invest this money wisely, and you have decided to invest in the shares of several different companies. One of those companies is the Columbia Sportswear Company.

Required
Answer the following questions regarding your potential investment in Columbia Sportswear shares:

a. Should you request financial statements from the company, and if so, which ones?
b. Is it important that the financial statements be audited by an independent auditor? Explain.
c. What does each of the four financial statements tell you about Columbia's financial health or operating performance?

ANSWERS TO SELF-STUDY QUESTIONS:

1. c, (p. 5) 2. d, (p. 10) 3. a, (p. 10) 4. b, (p. 10) 5. c, (p. 9) 6. a, (p. 13) 7. b, (p. 14) 8. c, (p. 20)
9. d, (pp. 7–8) 10. (pp. 4–5)

    1. Sole proprietorship and partnership
    2. Sole proprietorship and partnership
    3. Partnership
    4. Corporation
    5. Corporation
    6. Sole proprietorship

11. b, (p. 14) 12. b, (p. 13) 13. c, (p. 15)

YOUR TURN! SOLUTIONS

Solution 1.1

Sole proprietorship: Easiest to set up, owner controlled, and tax advantages.

Partnership: Relatively easy to establish, larger skill set, and tax advantages.

Corporations: Easiest to raise capital, easiest to transfer ownership, and protection against personal liability.

Solution 1.2

1. Financing
2. Operating
3. Investing
4. Operating
5. Financing
6. Operating

Solution 1.3

1. The financial statements are the primary output of financial accounting. External users require information on a business's performance and financial position. This is the type of information provided by the financial statements.
2. Internal users include management, the marketing department, the human resources department, and the finance department, among others. Each of these groups require data for decision making.
3. External users include, among others, investors, lenders, and regulators. These external groups require accounting information to help them make decisions regarding a company's performance and financial position.

Solution 1.4

Your supervisor is asking you to participate in the preparation of fraudulent financial statements. This is not only unethical; it is also illegal and could subject you to criminal prosecution. By reporting the sales revenue early, the financial statements will mislead users into thinking the company is doing better than it actually is. This in turn may lead them to make erroneous investment decisions. You should not follow your supervisor's request. Instead you should explain to your supervisor why reporting sales revenue prior to when it is earned is unethical. If your supervisor continues to pressure you, you should report your supervisor's request to a higher level of management in the company.

Solution 1.5

KANZU CORPORATION Income Statement For Year Ended December 31, 2013	
Sales revenue.	$20,000
Expenses.	12,000
Net income.	$ 8,000

KANZU CORPORATION Statement of Stockholders' Equity For Year Ended December 31, 2013			
	Common Stock	Retained Earnings	Total
Balance, January 1, 2013.	$ 0	$ 0	$ 0
Add: Common stock issued.	20,000		20,000
Net income.		8,000	8,000
Less: Dividends		(3,000)	(3,000)
Balance, December 31, 2013.	$20,000	$5,000	$25,000

KANZU CORPORATION
Balance Sheet
December 31, 2013

Assets		Liabilities		
Cash....................	$ 1,500	Accounts payable....................	$ 4,000	
Accounts receivable..........	2,500	Notes payable	33,000	
Inventory..................	3,000	Total liabilities........................		$37,000
Building	40,000	**Stockholders' Equity**		
Equipment	15,000	Common stock.....................	20,000	
Total assets	$62,000	Retained earnings	5,000	
		Total stockholders' equity		25,000
		Total liabilities and stockholders' equity ...		$62,000

KANZU CORPORATION
Statement of Cash Flows
For Year Ended December 31, 2013

Cash flow from operating activities	$ 6,500
Cash flow from investing activities...	(55,000)
Cash flow from financing activities..	50,000
Net increase in cash...	1,500
Cash at January 1, 2011	0
Cash at December 31, 2011	$ 1,500

Solution 1.6

1. c
2. b
3. a

2

Processing Accounting Information

PAST

Chapter 1 described the environment of financial accounting. It also introduced the financial statements and basic analysis of them.

PRESENT

This chapter explains the accounting system, including transaction analysis, the system of debits and credits, and the journalizing of transactions.

FUTURE

Chapter 3 describes accounting adjustments, the construction of financial statements, and the period-end closing process.

LEARNING OBJECTIVES

1. **Identify** the five major steps in the accounting cycle. *(p. 58)*

2. **Analyze** and **record** transactions using the accounting equation. *(p. 59)*

3. **Explain** the nature, format, and purpose of an account. *(p. 65)*

4. **Describe** the system of debits and credits and its use in recording transactions. *(p. 66)*

5. **Explain** the process of journalizing and posting transactions. *(p. 67)*

6. **Describe** the trial balance. *(p. 75)*

(AC)COUNTING STARS

Many think accountants and movie stars have little in common. At least one night every year, however, they share the stage at the annual Academy Awards. The global accounting firm **PricewaterhouseCoopers** recently celebrated its 78th year counting and verifying the Oscar ballots to determine the Oscar winners.

Accounting firms such as PricewaterhouseCoopers, **Ernst and Young**, **KPMG**, and **Deloitte and Touche** have earned a reputation of honesty and ethical conduct—attributes critical to the accounting profession. Many consider ethics the most fundamental principle underlying financial accounting and the independent accounting firms.

The PricewaterhouseCoopers accountants at the Academy Awards work on the project from a top-secret location. One of the accountants involved explained: "We're proud of our track record and heritage of hand counting every ballot to deliver the utmost level of accuracy and reliability to the Academy."

Although all accounting work is not as glamorous as controlling Oscar ballots, that work is crucial to a successful, global capital market. Businesses as varied as **Disney**, **Lowes**, **Google**, and **McDonald's** all require financial statements for making good business decisions.

This chapter describes the details of the accounting system of debits and credits. That system is applied throughout the world in all business settings. This chapter also explains the process of journalizing and posting transactions so that financial statements can be prepared for both internal and external users of accounting information.

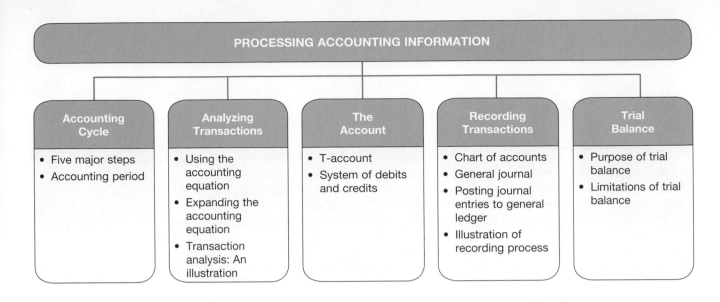

PROCESSING ACCOUNTING INFORMATION				
Accounting Cycle	**Analyzing Transactions**	**The Account**	**Recording Transactions**	**Trial Balance**
• Five major steps • Accounting period	• Using the accounting equation • Expanding the accounting equation • Transaction analysis: An illustration	• T-account • System of debits and credits	• Chart of accounts • General journal • Posting journal entries to general ledger • Illustration of recording process	• Purpose of trial balance • Limitations of trial balance

ACCOUNTING CYCLE

LO1 **Identify** the five major steps in the accounting cycle.

Businesses engage in economic activities. The role of accounting is to analyze these activities for their impact on a company's accounting equation, and then enter the results of that analysis in the company's accounting system. When a company's management team needs financial data for decision-making purposes and for reports to external parties, the company's financial statements are prepared and communicated. At the end of the accounting period, the "books are closed," a process that prepares the accounting records for the next accounting period. The accounting activities described constitute major steps in the **accounting cycle**—a sequence of activities undertaken by accountants to accumulate and report the financial information of a business. Stated succinctly, these steps are analyze, record, adjust, report, and close. Exhibit 2-1 shows the sequence of the major steps in the accounting cycle.

Exhibit 2-1	Five Major Steps in the Accounting Cycle

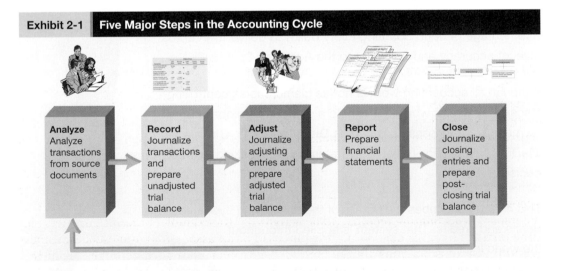

Analyze
Analyze transactions from source documents

Record
Journalize transactions and prepare unadjusted trial balance

Adjust
Journalize adjusting entries and prepare adjusted trial balance

Report
Prepare financial statements

Close
Journalize closing entries and prepare post-closing trial balance

The five steps in the accounting cycle do not occur with equal frequency. A business analyzes and records financial transactions daily during the accounting period. It adjusts and reports accumulated financial data whenever management needs financial information, usually at weekly, monthly, or quarterly intervals, but at least annually. Closing the books occurs just once, at the end of the accounting period. This chapter focuses on the first two steps of the accounting cycle—analyze and record. In Chapter 3, we examine the final three steps of the cycle.

It is important to know that the steps in the accounting cycle are undertaken whether a business uses a manual accounting system or a computer-based system. This chapter explains the accounting cycle using a manual system for WebWork, a Website development and consulting business launched on December 1, 2012.

Accounting Periods	ACCOUNTING IN PRACTICE

The annual accounting period is known as a **fiscal year**. Businesses with fiscal year-ends on December 31, are said to be on a **calendar year**. About 60 percent of U.S. businesses are on a calendar year. Many companies prefer to have their accounting year coincide with their "natural" year—that is, at a point in time when business activity is at a low point. For example, many retailers conclude their fiscal year when inventory quantities are low and easier to count, as year-end accounting procedures are more efficiently accomplished when there is less inventory. The "natural" year does not necessarily coincide with the calendar year. For example, Gap, a retailer, ends its fiscal year on the Friday nearest January 31. The company's busiest period is November through January, when its customers are holiday shopping. Similarly, the Boston Celtics, a professional basketball team, concludes its fiscal year on June 30, following completion of the NBA finals.

ANALYZING TRANSACTIONS

Many companies utilize a computer-based accounting system to record their financial transactions. You may have some personal experience using accounting software programs like QuickBooks by Intuit. While these computer-based accounting systems are not as sophisticated as the systems used by major corporations, they work in much the same way. Similarly, manual systems might lack the sophistication of large accounting systems utilized by companies like Ford Motor Company, but the basic process remains the same.

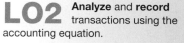 **LO2** **Analyze** and **record** transactions using the accounting equation.

The accounting equation is written as:

$$\text{Assets} = \text{Liabilities} + \text{Stockholders' equity}$$

This accounting equation provides a convenient way to analyze and summarize a company's financial transactions and data. The first step in the accounting cycle—analyze—is to determine just what information (if any) must be recorded in a company's accounting records. Recall from Appendix 1A that only items that can be expressed in monetary terms are recorded in financial statements. For example, the payment of wages to Tim Cook, the CEO of Apple, is recorded because it can be expressed in monetary terms.

An **accounting transaction** is an economic event that must be recorded in the company's accounting records. In general, any event that affects any of the elements of the accounting equation—assets, liabilities, or stockholders' equity—must be recorded in a company's accounting records. Some activities—for example, ordering supplies, bidding on a contract, or negotiating the purchase of an asset—may represent a business activity, but an accounting transaction does not occur until such activities result in a change in one or more amounts of an asset, liability, or stockholders' equity.

An accounting transaction impacts the accounting equation. However, that equation always remains in balance and at least two elements of the equation are always affected. This is where the term **double-entry accounting** comes from. For example, if an asset account such as Cash is increased, one of the following financial events must also occur to keep the accounting equation in balance:

a. Another asset, such as accounts receivable, must decrease; or

b. A liability, such as notes payable, must increase; or

c. Stockholders' equity, such as sales revenue, must increase.

IFRS ALERT!

Both the FASB in the United States and the FASB's international counterpart, the IASB, are working hard to "harmonize" remaining differences between U.S. GAAP and IFRS. One area that these organizations do not need to worry about is how double-entry accounting works. The same process that is described in this chapter, using debits and credits, is universally followed.

Accounting Equation Expanded

Stockholders' equity has two components—the amount invested by stockholders (common stock) and the cumulative net income of the business that has not yet been distributed to stockholders as a dividend (retained earnings). Common stock is increased when the company issues shares of stock, and retained earnings is increased by a company's net income (or decreased by a net loss) and decreased by a company's payment of dividends. Incorporating these two components into stockholders' equity, the *expanded accounting equation* is illustrated in Exhibit 2-2.

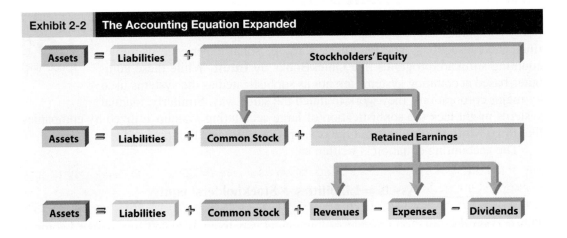

Exhibit 2-2   The Accounting Equation Expanded

Transactions and the Accounting Equation: An Illustration

We now consider the transactions of WebWork, Inc., a developer of web-based applications, to illustrate how various economic activities and events lead to financial statements.

Steve Gates first established WebWork on December 1, 2012. The company's transactions for December, the first month of operations, are analyzed on the following pages. The accounting equation for WebWork is shown after each transaction so that the financial effects of each transaction can be examined. The accounting equation remains in balance following each transaction. This is not a coincidence; it is the result of the fundamental structure of the accounting system.

The following pages illustrate eleven transactions that occurred during December 2012, at WebWork. Avoid the temptation to skip any of these transactions because each transaction is included to illustrate a particular concept or approach to recording an economic event utilizing the accounting equation.

Transaction 1. Issued Stock

On December 1, 2012, Steve Gates invested $30,000 cash in exchange for the company's common stock. This transaction increased the company's assets, Cash, by $30,000 and increased its stockholders' equity, Common Stock, by $30,000, as illustrated below using the accounting equation. (For each transaction that impacts stockholders' equity, we add a brief description—in this case "Issued stock.")

	Assets	=	Liabilities	+	Stockholders' Equity	
	Cash	=			Common Stock	
(1)	+30,000	=			+30,000	Issued stock
	$30,000				$30,000	

It is important to verify the equality of the accounting equation following each transaction. After the above transaction is recorded, both sides of the equation total $30,000.

Transaction 2. Paid Rent in Advance

On December 1, WebWork prepaid its office rent for the next six months, December 2012 through May 2013. WebWork's rent is $1,800 per month; meaning it paid a total of $10,800 cash (6 × $1,800). This transaction decreased Cash by $10,800 and increased Prepaid Rent by $10,800.

	Assets			=	Liabilities	+	Stockholders' Equity
	Cash	+	Prepaid Rent	=			Common Stock
	30,000						30,000
(2)	−10,800		+10,800				
	19,200	+	10,800				30,000
	$30,000			=			$30,000

The expenditure for prepaid rent is recorded as an asset because the advance payment is a future economic benefit to the company. This outlay of cash has value to the business beyond the current accounting period, but any rent that is used up in the current accounting period will be recorded as an expense for the month of December.

Transaction 3. Purchased Office Supplies on Account

On December 1, WebWork purchased office supplies on account totaling $2,850. Businesses often extend credit to their customers. Credit allows businesses to pay for goods or services at a later date. When credit is used to purchase goods or services, the purchase is said to be made *on account*. This transaction increased Office Supplies by $2,850 and it increased Accounts Payable by the same amount.

	Assets					=	Liabilities	+	Stockholders' Equity
	Cash	+	Office Supplies	+	Prepaid Rent	=	Accounts Payable	+	Common Stock
	19,200				10,800				30,000
(3)			+2,850				+2,850		
	19,200	+	2,850		+10,800	=	2,850	+	30,000
	$32,850					=			$32,850

Office supplies are recorded as an asset because they are expected to be used by the business in future periods beyond the current accounting period. Any supplies that are used up in the current accounting period will be recorded as an expense for the month of December. Following the purchase of office supplies, its assets total $32,850, which is equal to the sum of total liabilities of $2,850 plus stockholders' equity of $30,000.

Transaction 4. Signed Bank Note in Exchange for Cash

On December 1, WebWork obtained a two-year bank loan in the amount of $36,000, after signing a note payable. Annual interest charges on the note amount to 10 percent and are due each November 30. As a consequence of this loan, the company's Cash account increased by $36,000 and the Notes Payable account, a liability, is increased by $36,000.

		Assets				=	Liabilities			+	Stockholders' Equity
	Cash	+	Office Supplies	+	Prepaid Rent	=	Accounts Payable	+	Notes Payable	+	Common Stock
	19,200		2,850		10,800		2,850				30,000
(4)	+36,000								+36,000		
	55,200 +		2,850	+	10,800	=	2,850	+	36,000	+	30,000
			$68,850						$68,850		

Transaction 5. Purchased Equipment With Cash

On December 2, WebWork used cash to purchase office equipment costing $32,400. This transaction decreased Cash by $32,400 and it increased Office Equipment by the same amount. The accounting equation remains in balance because an equal amount, $32,400, is both added to and subtracted from total assets.

		Assets						=	Liabilities			+	Stockholders' Equity
	Cash	+	Office Supplies	+	Prepaid Rent	+	Equipment	=	Accounts Payable	+	Notes Payable	+	Common Stock
	55,200		2,850		10,800				2,850		36,000		30,000
(5)	−32,400						+32,400						
	22,800	+	2,850	+	10,800	+	32,400	=	2,850	+	36,000	+	30,000
			$68,850								$68,850		

Transaction 6. Received Customer Prepayment

On December 5, WebWork received a prepayment in the amount of $3,000 for services to be performed over the next few months. Because WebWork has not yet performed the services, and following the revenue recognition principle discussed in Appendix 1A, it does not record the $3,000 payment as revenue. Instead, a liability account, **Unearned Revenue**, is increased by $3,000, and the company's Cash account is increased by $3,000. Unearned revenue is a liability because the company accepted payment for goods or services that have not yet been provided and, therefore, the amount cannot be recorded as earned revenue.

A.K.A. Unearned revenue is also called *deferred revenue*.

		Assets								=	Liabilities					+	Stockholders' Equity
	Cash	+	Office Supplies	+	Prepaid Rent	+	Equip- ment	=	Accounts Payable	+	Unearned Revenue	+	Notes Payable	+	Common Stock			
	22,800		2,850		10,800		32,400		2,850				36,000		30,000			
(6)	+3,000										+3,000							
	25,800	+	2,850	+	10,800	+	32,400	=	2,850	+	3,000	+	36,000	+	30,000			
			$71,850								$71,850							

Transaction 7. Provided Services for Customers

On December 6, WebWork performed services for several customers and it was paid $13,510 cash. This transaction increased Cash by $13,510 and it increased Fee Revenue by the same amount.

	Assets			=	Liabilities			+	Stockholders' Equity				
Cash +	Office Supplies +	Prepaid Rent +	Equip-ment =		Accounts Payable +	Unearned Revenue +	Notes Payable +		Common Stock +	Retained Earnings			
										Rev.	– Exp.	– Div.	
25,800	2,850	10,800	32,400		2,850	3,000	36,000		30,000				
(7) +13,510										+13,510			Fee revenue
39,310 +	2,850 +	10,800 +	32,400 =		2,850 +	3,000 +	36,000 +		30,000 +	13,510			
	$85,360						$85,360						

Transaction 8. Performed Services for Both Cash and on Account

On December 8, WebWork performed $4,740 of services and received $1,000 in cash with the remaining $3,740 to be paid to WebWork by customers within 90 days. Businesses often extend credit to customers, allowing them to pay for goods or services at a later date. Under accrual accounting, revenue must be recorded when earned, regardless of when payment is received. Consequently, this transaction increased Cash by $1,000, it increased Accounts Receivable by $3,740, and it increased Fee Revenue by $4,740. The accounting equation remains in balance because both sides of the equation are increased by $4,740.

A.K.A. Delivering goods or services in advance of payment is referred to as providing goods or services "*on account*" or "on credit."

		Assets				=	Liabilities			+	Stockholders' Equity				
Cash +	Accounts Receivable +	Office Supplies +	Prepaid Rent +	Equip-ment =			Accounts Payable +	Unearned Revenue +	Notes Payable +		Common Stock +	Retained Earnings			
												Rev.	– Exp.	– Div.	
39,310		2,850	10,800	32,400			2,850	3,000	36,000		30,000	13,510			
(8) +1,000	+3,740											+4,740			Fee revenue
40,310 +	3,740 +	2,850 +	10,800 +	32,400 =			2,850 +	3,000 +	36,000 +		30,000 +	18,250			
		$90,100							$90,100						

Non-Accounting Transaction. Hired an Employee

On December 9, WebWork hired an employee to provide administrative help in the office. The employee will be paid $1,620 every two weeks and begins work Monday, December 12. At the time the employee is hired there is no immediate financial effect on the assets, liabilities, or stockholders' equity of the company. There is only an employment agreement between the employee and the company. The employee has not yet performed any work, nor has the employee received any wages.

Transaction 9. Paid Employee Wages

On December 23, WebWork paid the employee after she completed her first two weeks on the job. This transaction decreased Cash by $1,620, and it increased Wage Expense by $1,620. By definition, an increase in expenses decreases stockholders' equity.

		Assets				=	Liabilities			+	Stockholders' Equity				
Cash +	Accounts Receivable +	Office Supplies +	Prepaid Rent +	Equip-ment =			Accounts Payable +	Unearned Revenue +	Notes Payable +		Common Stock +	Retained Earnings			
												Rev.	– Exp.	– Div.	
40,310	3,740	2,850	10,800	32,400			2,850	3,000	36,000		30,000	18,250			
(9) −1,620													−1,620		Wage expense
38,690 +	3,740 +	2,850 +	10,800 +	32,400 =			2,850 +	3,000 +	36,000 +		30,000 +	18,250 −	1,620		
		$88,480							$88,480						

Transaction 10. Received Payment on Account from Customer

On December 27, WebWork received a payment of $2,400 cash from a customer that had previously received services performed on account (see Transaction 8). This transaction increased Cash by $2,400, and decreased Accounts Receivable by $2,400.

	Assets				=	Liabilities			+	Stockholders' Equity			
Cash	Accounts Receivable	Office Supplies	Prepaid Rent	Equip-ment	Accounts Payable	Unearned Revenue	Notes Payable	Common Stock	Retained Earnings		
										Rev.	Exp.	Div.
38,690	3,740	2,850	10,800	32,400	2,850	3,000	36,000	30,000	18,250	1,620	
(10) +2,400	−2,400										
41,090 +	1,340 +	2,850 +	10,800 +	32,400 =	2,850 +	3,000 +	36,000 +	30,000 +	18,250 −	1,620	

$88,480 $88,480

The balance in Accounts Receivable becomes $1,340. This represents the amount still owed to WebWork for services that were previously performed on account but remain unpaid.

Transaction 11. Paid Cash Dividend

On December 30, WebWork paid a cash dividend. Dividends are not a business expense, and are not included in the calculation of net income. Rather, dividends are a distribution of the company's accumulated net income to its stockholders. Payment of the dividend decreases Cash by $500 and increases Dividends by $500. (By definition, an increase in dividends causes a decrease in stockholders' equity.)

	Assets				=	Liabilities			+	Stockholders' Equity			
Cash	Accounts Receivable	Office Supplies	Prepaid Rent	Equip-ment	Accounts Payable	Unearned Revenue	Notes Payable	Common Stock	Retained Earnings		
										Rev.	Exp.	Div.
41,090	1,340	2,850	10,800	32,400	2,850	3,000	36,000	30,000	18,250	1,620	
(11) −500												−500 Dividends
40,590 +	1,340 +	2,850 +	10,800 +	32,400 =	2,850 +	3,000 +	36,000 +	30,000 +	18,250 −	1,620 −	500

$87,980 $87,980

Transaction Summary

Exhibit 2-3 provides a summary of the eleven accounting transactions for WebWork, for the month of December. The exhibit illustrates the financial effect of each transaction using the accounting equation. It is important that the accounting equation remains in balance at all times, and that the equality between total assets and the sum of total liabilities and stockholders' equity is maintained following each transaction.

Exhibit 2-3   Summary of December Transactions and Their Effect on the Expanded Accounting Equation

	Assets				=	Liabilities			+	Stockholders' Equity			
Cash	Accounts Receivable	Office Supplies	Prepaid Rent	Equip-ment	Accounts Payable	Unearned Revenue	Notes Payable	Common Stock	Retained Earnings		
										Rev.	Exp.	Div.
(1) +30,000									+30,000			
(2) −10,800			+10,800									
(3)		+2,850			+2,850							
(4) +36,000							+36,000					
(5) −32,400				+32,400								
(6) +3,000						+3,000						
(7) +13,510										+13,510		
(8) +1,000	+3,740									+4,740		
(9) −1,620											−1,620	
(10) +2,400	−2,400											
(11) −500												−500
40,590 +	1,340 +	2,850 +	10,800 +	32,400 =	2,850 +	3,000 +	36,000 +	30,000 +	18,250 −	1,620 −	500

$87,980 $87,980

Concept	Method	Assessment	TAKEAWAY 2.1
When should an event be recorded in a company's accounting records?	Review the event details. Does the event affect the company's assets, liabilities, or stockholders' equity?	If the event affects any of the elements of the accounting equation, it must be recorded in a company's accounting records.	

YOUR TURN! 2.1

The solution is on page 113.

Ford Aerobics Studio, Inc., operates as a corporation. The firm rents studio space (including a sound system) and specializes in offering aerobics classes to individuals and groups. On January 1, the assets, liabilities, and stockholders' equity of the business were as follows: Cash, $5,000; Accounts Receivable, $5,200; Accounts Payable, $1,000; Notes Payable, $2,500; Common Stock, $5,500; and Retained Earnings, $1,200. The January business activities for the studio were as follows:

1. Paid $600 cash on accounts payable.
2. Paid January rent of $3,600 cash.
3. Billed clients for January classes in the amount of $11,500.
4. Received a $500 invoice from a supplier for T-shirts given free to January's class members as an advertising promotion.
5. Collected $10,000 cash on account from clients for prior aerobics classes.
6. Paid employee wages of $2,400 cash.
7. Received a $680 invoice for January's utilities.
8. Paid $20 cash to the bank as January interest on an outstanding note payable.
9. Paid $900 cash in dividends to stockholders.
10. Paid $4,000 cash on January 31 to purchase a sound system to replace the rented system.

Required

a. Set up an expanded accounting equation in columnar form with the following individual assets, liabilities, and stockholders' equity accounts: Cash, Accounts Receivable, Equipment, Accounts Payable, Notes Payable, Common Stock, and Retained Earnings. Enter the January 1 balances below each account. (The beginning balance in the Equipment account is $0.)

b. Record the financial impact (increase or decrease) of each transaction (l) through (l0) on the beginning account balances. Then total the columns to demonstrate that total assets equal the sum of total liabilities plus stockholders' equity as of January 31.

THE "ACCOUNT" SYSTEM

The basic component of an accounting system is the **account**, which is an individual record of the increases and decreases in a specific asset, liability, or stockholders' equity item. An account is created for each individual asset, liability, and stockholders' equity item on a company's financial statements. Some common account titles are Cash, Accounts Receivable, Notes Payable, Fee Revenue, and Rent Expense.

LO3 Explain the nature, format, and purpose of an account.

T-account

A **T-account** is a simplified form of an account. T-accounts are so named because they resemble the letter "T." A T-account with the December changes in the Cash account for WebWork is presented in Exhibit 2-4.

Exhibit 2-4	Cash T-account	

To compute the T-account balance, sum the numbers in each column and subtract the smaller total from the larger total. In this example, subtract 45,320 from 85,910 to compute the 40,590 balance.

	Cash		
(1)	30,000	10,800	(2)
(4)	36,000	32,400	(5)
(6)	3,000	1,620	(9)
(7)	13,510	500	(11)
(8)	1,000		
(10)	2,400		
	85,910	45,320	
Bal.	40,590		

A T-account consists of: (1) the account title (such as Cash), (2) amounts reflecting increases and decreases, and (3) cross-references to other accounting records. It is customary to reference (or link) the data entries in a T-account with a number or a letter to identify the related accounting transaction that originated the data. This permits a systematic review of the data entries in the event of a recording error. It also enables a company, and its independent auditor, to review the company's set of accounts and match the account information with the related accounting transactions. The numerical references in the Cash T-account are the ones used to identify the December transactions for WebWork from Exhibit 2-3.

CORPORATE SOCIAL RESPONSIBILITY	What to Record?

An important element of the conceptual framework discussed in Appendix 1A in Chapter 1 is the monetary unit concept, which states that only those items that can be expressed in monetary terms are reported in financial statements. This causes many items of interest to be excluded from financial statements. Reporting of a company's social responsibility activities, for example, would be compromised if it were constrained to the activities that can be expressed in monetary terms. Reporting guidelines established by the Global Reporting Initiative, the organization that pioneered the world's most widely-used sustainability reporting framework, allow for a wider range of activities to be measured and reported. For example, **Bayer Group**, a global healthcare company, reports such items as greenhouse emissions, net water usage, and employee safety records in its annual sustainable development report. Bayer's sustainability report can be found at the Bayer Website.

System of Debits and Credits

LO4 **Describe** the system of debits and credits and its use in recording transactions.

One basic characteristic of all accounts is that data entries separately record the increases and decreases to an account. In some accounts, such as the Cash account in Exhibit 2-4, increases are recorded on the left side of the account and decreases are recorded on the right side. In other accounts, the reverse is true. The method of recording data entries in the accounts is a matter of convention; that is, a simple set of rules is followed, which involves debits and credits.

The terms **debit** and **credit** are used to refer to the left side and the right side, respectively, of an account as shown below:

increase (Any Type of Account)	decrease
Debit	**Credit**
Always the left side	Always the right side

Regardless of what amount is recorded in an account, a data entry made on the left side is a debit to the account; and, a data entry recorded on the right side is a credit to the account. The words *debit* and *credit* are abbreviated *dr.* (from the Latin *debere*) and *cr.* (from the Latin *credere*), respectively.

The system of debits and credits identifies which accounts are increased by debits (or by credits) and which accounts are decreased by debits (or by credits). Exhibit 2-5 summarizes these rules for each of the six primary categories of accounts: assets, liabilities, common stock, dividends, revenues, and expenses. Observe the following relations in Exhibit 2-5:

Hint: A "Retained Earnings" account would be included in Exhibit 2-5 for a continuing business that has not paid out its income with dividends. That account would have increases on the right and decreases on the left.

1. *Debit* always refers to the left side of an account; *credit* always refers to the right side.
2. Increases in asset, dividend, and expense accounts are debit entries. Increases in liability, common stock, and revenue accounts are credit entries.
3. Decreases in asset, dividend, and expense accounts are credit entries. Decreases in liability, common stock, and revenue accounts are debit entries.
4. The **normal balance** of an account is the side on which increases to the account are recorded. Thus, asset, dividend, and expense accounts normally have debit balances, whereas liabilities, common stock, and revenue accounts normally have credit balances. This is because increases in an account are usually greater than, or equal to, the decreases to an account.

The pattern of increases and decreases for asset accounts is opposite that for liability, common stock, and revenue accounts. The pattern of increases and decreases for revenue accounts is to be expected because revenue is a temporary subdivision of stockholders' equity. Following the same logic, the pattern of increases and decreases for dividends and expenses is opposite that because dividends and expenses reduce stockholders' equity.

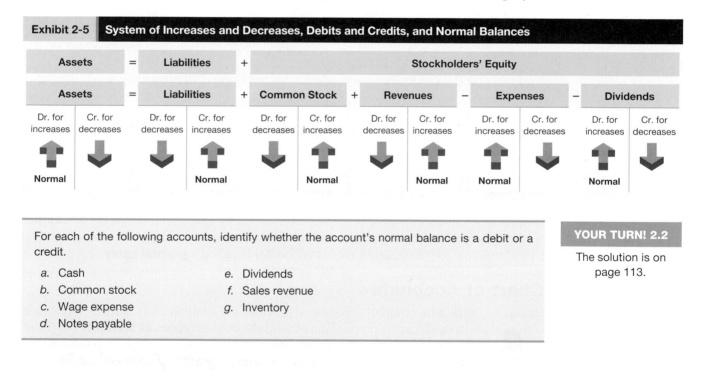

Exhibit 2-5   System of Increases and Decreases, Debits and Credits, and Normal Balances

For each of the following accounts, identify whether the account's normal balance is a debit or a credit.

a. Cash
b. Common stock
c. Wage expense
d. Notes payable
e. Dividends
f. Sales revenue
g. Inventory

YOUR TURN! 2.2

The solution is on page 113.

RECORDING TRANSACTIONS

Earlier in this chapter we analyzed the transactions of WebWork using the accounting equation. This approach enabled us to see how accounting transactions affect a company's financial position and operations. This approach is not feasible, however, for even a modest-sized business because of the large number of transactions. Consequently, we now explain the process of analyzing and recording accounting information in an actual accounting system.

An initial step in the analysis and recording process is to identify evidence of a business transaction. This usually comes in the form of a source document. **Source documents**

LO5 **Explain** the process of journalizing and posting transactions.

are printed forms or computer records that are generated when a firm engages in a business transaction. At a minimum, a source document usually specifies the dollar amount involved, the date of the transaction, and possibly the party dealing with the firm. Some examples of source documents include (1) a supplier's invoice showing evidence of a purchase of supplies on account, (2) a bank check indicating the payment of an obligation, (3) a deposit slip showing the amount of cash deposited in a bank, and (4) a cash receipt indicating the amount of cash received from a customer for services rendered. One example follows. Regardless of its form, the source document serves as the basis for the analysis of the underlying business event.

WebWork, Inc.   **INVOICE**

137 Technology Lane
Irvine, CA. 92614
Phone (949) 727-3555   INVOICE # [**100**]
                                                 DATE: DECEMBER 10, 2012

TO: FOR:
Pick Enterprises   Web design
1055 Kinrose Ave
Los Angeles, CA 90024
(310) 208-5570

DESCRIPTION	HOURS	RATE	AMOUNT
Design work for Website, including motion graphics	17.5	$125	$2,187.50
		TOTAL	$2,187.50

Make all checks payable to WebWork, Inc.
Total due in 15 days. Overdue accounts subject to a service charge of 1% per month.

Thank you for your business!

Once the source document has been analyzed to determine the accounts affected and the amounts involved, we then record the transaction. All accounting transactions are initially recorded in a journal. A **journal**, or *book of original entry,* is a tabular record in which a business's activities are reflected in terms of debits and credits and recorded in chronological order. A journal organizes information by date, and thus, serves as a chronological diary of a company's business activities. The word *journalize* means to record a transaction in a journal; and, an entry in a journal is called a **journal entry**.

A.K.A. A company's journals are also referred to as its "*books*."

A.K.A. Another term often used to describe the recording of a transaction is to "*book*" the transaction.

Chart of Accounts

Businesses maintain a chart of accounts to facilitate the analysis of a company's business activities and to assist in the preparation of journal entries. A **chart of accounts** is a list of the titles of all accounts in a business's accounting system. Account titles are grouped by, and in the order of, the five major components of the expanded accounting equation: assets, liabilities, stockholders' equity, revenues, and expenses. Exhibit 2-6 shows the chart of accounts for WebWork and indicates the account numbers that will be used throughout this illustration. (Each company maintains its own unique set of accounts and its own numbering system.)

General Journal

The **general journal** is a record with enough flexibility that any type of business transaction can be recorded in it. Like all journals in an accounting system, the general journal is a book of original entry in which accounting data are entered into a company's accounting system. Exhibit 2-7 shows the first transaction as it is recorded in WebWork's general journal. The procedure for recording entries in the general journal follows:

Exhibit 2-6	Chart of Accounts for WebWork

Assets	**Equity**
110 Cash	310 Common Stock
120 Accounts Receivable	320 Retained Earnings
130 Office Supplies	330 Dividends
150 Prepaid Rent	
170 Office Equipment	**Revenues**
175 Accumulated Depreciation—	410 Fee Revenue
Office Equipment	
	Expenses
Liabilities	510 Supplies Expense
210 Accounts Payable	520 Wage Expense
220 Interest Payable	530 Rent Expense
230 Wages Payable	540 Depreciation Expense—
250 Unearned Revenue	Office Equipment
260 Notes Payable	550 Interest Expense

❶ Indicate the year, month, and date of entry. (Usually the year and month are rewritten only at the top of each page of the journal or at the point in the journal where the year and month change.)

❷ Enter the titles of accounts affected (from the chart of accounts) in the Description column. Accounts to receive debits are entered close to the left margin and are recorded first. Accounts to receive credits are recorded next and indented slightly to the right.

❸ Enter dollar amounts in the left (Debit) and right (Credit) columns.

❹ Record an explanation of the transaction below the account titles; it should be brief, disclosing information necessary to understand the event recorded.

Exhibit 2-7	General Journal with First Entry of WebWork

GENERAL JOURNAL

Date	Description	Debit	Credit
2012			
❶ Dec. 1	Cash ❷	30,000 ❸	
	Common stock		30,000
	Issued stock in exchange for cash. ❹		

A journal entry that involves more than two accounts is called a **compound journal entry**. (The journal entry for Transaction 8 is an example of a compound journal entry involving three accounts. The credit of $4,740 to the Fee Revenue account is offset by debits of $1,000 to the Cash account and $3,740 to the Accounts Receivable account.) Any number of accounts can appear in a compound entry; but, regardless of how many accounts are used, the sum of the debit amounts always equals the sum of the credit amounts. Accordingly, each transaction entered in the general journal is recorded with equal dollar amounts of debits and credits. The account titles cited in the Description column should correspond to those from the chart of accounts. (To delineate between journal entries made in the general journal, we leave a blank line between each transaction entry.)

Posting Journal Entries to the General Ledger

After an accounting transaction is journalized in the general journal, the debits and credits in each journal entry are immediately transferred to another component of the accounting system called the general ledger. This transfer of data from the general journal to a company's general ledger is undertaken to facilitate the preparation of the company's financial statements. Although businesses can use various ledgers to accumulate detailed accounting information, all firms have a general ledger. A **general ledger** is a listing of each account of a company and the amounts making up each account.

The process of transferring the debit and credit information from the general journal to the general ledger is called **posting**. It is important to be able to trace each data entry appearing in a general ledger account to the general journal location from which it was posted; consequently, both the general journal and general ledger accounts have a **posting reference** code. The posting reference of the general journal indicates the account to which the related debit or credit has been posted. The posting references in the general journal and ledger accounts are entered when the journal entries are posted to the ledger accounts (automatically when computerized, or by hand for a manual system). We will use the transaction number as the posting reference in the examples that follow.

Illustration of the Recording Process

We now apply the recording process to the transactions of WebWork, that were summarized in Exhibit 2-3. For each transaction, we **(1) analyze** the transaction using the accounting equation, **(2) journalize** the transaction, and **(3) post** journal entries to the general ledger (for simplicity, we use the T-account structure for each ledger account).

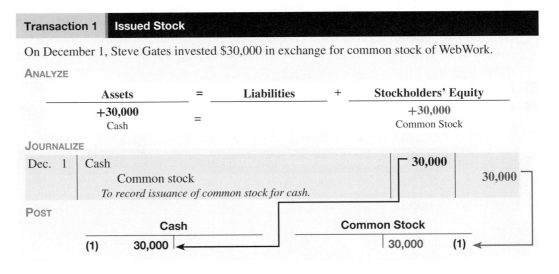

Transaction 1   Issued Stock

On December 1, Steve Gates invested $30,000 in exchange for common stock of WebWork.

ANALYZE

Assets	=	Liabilities	+	Stockholders' Equity
+30,000				+30,000
Cash	=			Common Stock

JOURNALIZE

Dec. 1	Cash		30,000	
	Common stock			30,000
	To record issuance of common stock for cash.			

POST

Cash		Common Stock	
(1) 30,000			30,000 (1)

Transaction 2   Paid Rent in Advance

On December 1, WebWork prepaid rent for the office covering the next six months, December 2012 through May 2013. Monthly rent is $1,800; the total amount prepaid was $10,800 cash.

ANALYZE

Assets		=	Liabilities	+	Stockholders' Equity
−10,800	+10,800	=			
Cash	Prepaid Rent				

JOURNALIZE

Dec. 1	Prepaid rent		10,800	
	Cash			10,800
	To record advance payment of six months' rent.			

POST

Prepaid Rent		Cash	
(2) 10,800		(1) 30,000	10,800 (2)

Transaction 3 | **Purchased Office Supplies on Account**

On December 1, WebWork purchased $2,850 of office supplies on account.

ANALYZE

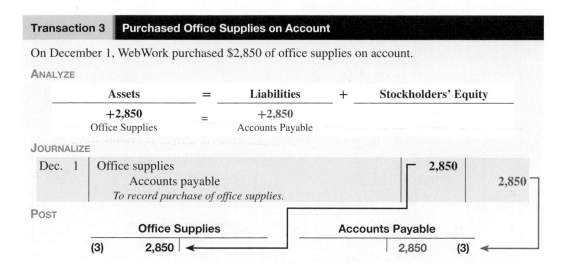

JOURNALIZE

Dec. 1	Office supplies	2,850	
	Accounts payable		2,850
	To record purchase of office supplies.		

POST

Office Supplies		Accounts Payable	
(3) 2,850			2,850 (3)

Transaction 4 | **Signed Bank Note in Exchange for Cash**

On December 1, WebWork obtained a two-year bank loan for $36,000, signing a note payable. Annual interest of 10 percent is due each November 30.

ANALYZE

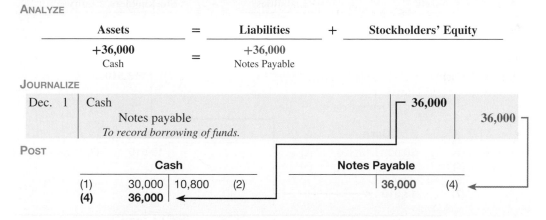

JOURNALIZE

Dec. 1	Cash	36,000	
	Notes payable		36,000
	To record borrowing of funds.		

POST

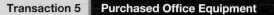

Cash		Notes Payable	
(1) 30,000	10,800 (2)		36,000 (4)
(4) 36,000			

Transaction 5 | **Purchased Office Equipment**

On December 2, WebWork used cash to purchase $32,400 of office equipment.

ANALYZE

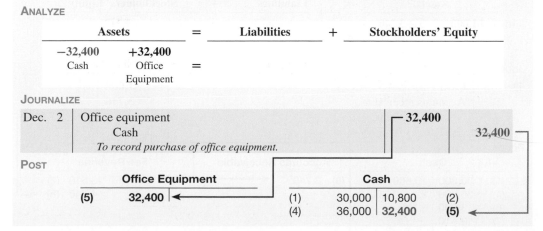

JOURNALIZE

Dec. 2	Office equipment	32,400	
	Cash		32,400
	To record purchase of office equipment.		

POST

Office Equipment		Cash	
(5) 32,400		(1) 30,000	10,800 (2)
		(4) 36,000	32,400 (5)

Transaction 6 | **Received Customer Prepayment**

On December 5, WebWork received $3,000 cash for services to be performed in the future.

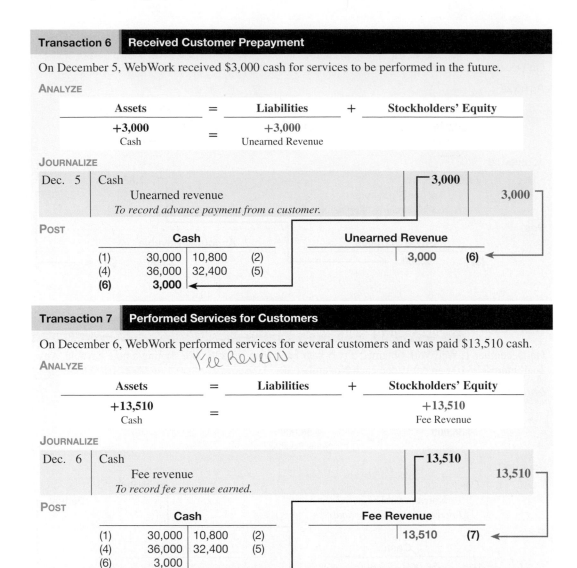

ANALYZE

Assets	=	Liabilities	+	Stockholders' Equity
+3,000	=	+3,000		
Cash		Unearned Revenue		

JOURNALIZE

Dec. 5	Cash	3,000	
	Unearned revenue		3,000
	To record advance payment from a customer.		

POST

	Cash				Unearned Revenue	
(1)	30,000	10,800	(2)		3,000	(6)
(4)	36,000	32,400	(5)			
(6)	3,000					

Transaction 7 | **Performed Services for Customers**

On December 6, WebWork performed services for several customers and was paid $13,510 cash.

Fee Revenue

ANALYZE

Assets	=	Liabilities	+	Stockholders' Equity
+13,510	=			+13,510
Cash				Fee Revenue

JOURNALIZE

Dec. 6	Cash	13,510	
	Fee revenue		13,510
	To record fee revenue earned.		

POST

	Cash				Fee Revenue	
(1)	30,000	10,800	(2)		13,510	(7)
(4)	36,000	32,400	(5)			
(6)	3,000					
(7)	13,510					

Transaction 8 | **Performed Services for Cash and on Account**

On December 8, WebWork performed $4,740 of services for which it received $1,000 cash with the remaining $3,740 to be paid in the future.

ANALYZE

Assets		=	Liabilities	+	Stockholders' Equity
+1,000	+3,740	=			+4,740
Cash	Accounts Receivable				Fee Revenue

JOURNALIZE

Dec. 8	Cash	1,000	
	Accounts receivable	3,740	
	Fee revenue		4,740
	To record fee revenue earned.		

POST

	Cash				Accounts Receivable			Fee Revenue	
(1)	30,000	10,800	(2)	(8)	3,740			13,510	(7)
(4)	36,000	32,400	(5)					4,740	(8)
(6)	3,000								
(7)	13,510								
(8)	1,000								

Transaction 9 **Paid Employee Wages**

On December 23, WebWork paid its employee $1,620 cash upon completion of her first two weeks on the job.

ANALYZE

Assets	=	Liabilities	+	Stockholders' Equity
−1,620	=			−1,620
Cash				Wage Expense

JOURNALIZE

Dec. 23	Wage expense		1,620	
	Cash			1,620
	To record payment of employee wages.			

POST

Wage Expense			Cash		
(9)	1,620	(1)	30,000	10,800	(2)
		(4)	36,000	32,400	(5)
		(6)	3,000	1,620	(9)
		(7)	13,510		
		(8)	1,000		

Transaction 10 **Received Payment on Account from Customer**

On December 27, WebWork received $2,400 cash from a customer for services previously performed on account.

ANALYZE

Assets		=	Liabilities	+	Stockholders' Equity
+2,400	−2,400	=			
Cash	Accounts Receivable				

JOURNALIZE

Dec. 27	Cash		2,400	
	Accounts receivable			2,400
	To record receipt of payment on account.			

POST

Cash			Accounts Receivable		
(1)	30,000	10,800 (2)	(8) 3,740	2,400	(10)
(4)	36,000	32,400 (5)			
(6)	3,000	1,620 (9)			
(7)	13,510				
(8)	1,000				
(10)	2,400				

Transaction 11 **Paid Cash Dividend**

On December 30, WebWork paid a $500 cash dividend.

ANALYZE

Assets	=	Liabilities	+	Stockholders' Equity
−500				−500
Cash				Dividends

JOURNALIZE

Dec. 30	Dividends		500	
	Cash			500
	To record payment of cash dividends.			

POST

Dividends			Cash		
(11)	500	(1)	30,000	10,800	(2)
		(4)	36,000	32,400	(5)
		(6)	3,000	1,620	(9)
		(7)	13,510	500	(11)
		(8)	1,000		
		(10)	2,400		

Summary Illustration of Journalizing and Posting Transactions

Exhibit 2-8 presents the general journal for WebWork for the month of December 2012. Also, Exhibit 2-9 presents the general ledger for WebWork as of December 31, 2012. All journal entries appearing in Exhibit 2-8 have been posted to the general ledger accounts in Exhibit 2-9. The accounts in WebWork's general ledger are grouped by category as follows: (1) assets, (2) liabilities, (3) stockholders' equity, (4) dividends, (5) revenues, and (6) expenses. Each general ledger account in Exhibit 2-9 has been totaled with the ending balance appearing in green.

Exhibit 2-8	General Journal for WebWork		
	General Journal		
Date	**Account Titles and Explanation**	**Debit**	**Credit**
2012			
(1) Dec. 1	Cash	30,000	
	Common stock		30,000
	To record issuance of common stock for cash.		
(2) 1	Prepaid rent	10,800	
	Cash		10,800
	To record advance payment of six months' rent.		
(3) 1	Office supplies	2,850	
	Accounts payable		2,850
	To record purchase of office supplies.		
(4) 1	Cash	36,000	
	Notes payable		36,000
	To record a bank loan, with a signed note payable.		
(5) 2	Office equipment	32,400	
	Cash		32,400
	To record purchase of office equipment.		
(6) 5	Cash	3,000	
	Unearned revenue		3,000
	To record a prepayment from a customer.		
(7) 6	Cash	13,510	
	Fee revenue		13,510
	To record fee revenue earned.		
(8) 8	Cash	1,000	
	Accounts receivable	3,740	
	Fee revenue		4,740
	To record fee revenue earned.		
(9) 23	Wage expense	1,620	
	Cash		1,620
	To record payment of employee wages.		
(10) 27	Cash	2,400	
	Accounts receivable		2,400
	To record receipt of payment on account.		
(11) 30	Dividends	500	
	Cash		500
	To record payment of cash dividends.		

Taccaunts

Exhibit 2-9	General Ledger for WebWork

General Ledger

| | Assets | | = | Liabilities | | + | Stockholders' Equity | |

add   subtract

Cash

(1)	30,000	10,800	(2)
(4)	36,000	32,400	(5)
(6)	3,000	1,620	(9)
(7)	13,510	500	(11)
(8)	1,000		
(10)	2,400		
Bal.	40,590		

Accounts Receivable

(8)	3,740	2,400	(10)
Bal.	1,340		

Office Supplies

(3)	2,850	
Bal.	2,850	

Prepaid Rent

(2)	10,800	
Bal.	10,800	

Office Equipment

(5)	32,400	
Bal.	32,400	

Accounts Payable

		2,850	(3)
		2,850	Bal.

Unearned Revenue

		3,000	(6)
		3,000	Bal.

Notes Payable

		36,000	(4)
		36,000	Bal.

Common Stock

		30,000	(1)
		30,000	Bal.

Dividends

(11)	500	
Bal.	500	

Fee Revenue

		13,510	(7)
		4,740	(8)
		18,250	Bal.

Wage Expense

(9)	1,620	
Bal.	1,620	

Assets = $87,980	=	Liabilities = $41,850	+	Stockholders' Equity = $46,130

For each of the transactions below, complete the following requirements.

1. Record the effect of each transaction using the accounting equation.
2. Prepare journal entries for each transaction.
3. Post the journal entries for each transaction to the appropriate T-accounts.

Transactions:

a. The company received $1,300 cash from clients for services rendered.
b. The company paid $2,400 cash for wages to employees.
c. The company collected $600 cash from clients on account.
d. The company paid a $400 cash dividend.
e. The company purchased $700 of office supplies on account.
f. The company billed clients $900 for services rendered, which were unpaid.
g. The company paid $500 cash to suppliers on account.

TRIAL BALANCE

A **trial balance** is a listing of all accounts from the general ledger with their respective debit or credit balance. A trial balance is prepared at the end of an accounting period after all transactions have been recorded. Exhibit 2-10

LO6   **Describe** the trial balance.

shows a trial balance for WebWork, Inc., as of December 31, 2012. The sequence of the accounts and the dollar amounts are taken directly from the general ledger T-accounts in Exhibit 2-9 (which follow the order of the account numbering system). The debit and credit columns from the trial balance are in balance; that is, the $90,100 sum of the debit account balances equals the $90,100 sum of the credit account balances.

Two principal reasons for preparing a trial balance are:

1. To serve as an interim check on whether the sum of the debit balances and the sum of the credit balances from the general ledger accounts are equal. If the totals are not equal, it would indicate the presence of some type of recording error.

2. To show all general ledger account balances in one location, which facilitates the preparation of financial statements. The trial balance, however, is *not* a financial statement.

A trial balance must be dated. In Exhibit 2.10, the trial balance of WebWork, Inc., was prepared as of December 31, 2012.

While it is required that a trial balance be in balance—that is, that the total of the debit column equal the total of the credit column—this equality does not guarantee that the accounting data is error-free. Potential data errors could still exist as a consequence of (1) transactions not being journalized, (2) journal entries not being posted, (3) journal entries being posted in the wrong amount, and (4) journal entries being posted to the wrong accounts.

Exhibit 2-10	Unadjusted Trial Balance for WebWork		

WEBWORK, INC.
Unadjusted Trial Balance
December 31, 2012

	Debit	Credit
Cash.	$40,590	
Accounts receivable.	1,340	
Office supplies	2,850	
Prepaid rent	10,800	
Office equipment	32,400	
Accounts payable.		$ 2,850
Unearned revenue		3,000
Notes payable		36,000
Common stock.		30,000
Dividends	500	
Fee revenue		18,250
Wage expense	1,620	
Totals	$90,100	$90,100

FORENSIC ACCOUNTING	**Fraudulent Reporting**

Verifying that the sum of the debit account balances from the general ledger is equal to the sum of the credit account balances is not sufficient to guarantee accuracy of financial records. The infamous accounting scandal at **WorldCom** provides a case in point. To inflate its net income, WorldCom improperly "capitalized expenses"—that is, they inappropriately debited property, plant, and equipment, an asset account, when they should have debited an expense account. While the sum of the debit account balances on WorldCom's books did equal the sum of the credit account balances, assets were overstated and expenses were understated by almost $7 billion. WorldCom's CEO Bernard Ebbers, the mastermind of its fraudulent accounting, was convicted of conspiracy to commit fraud, securities fraud, and making false filings with the SEC. Mr. Ebbers was sentenced to 25 years in prison.

YOUR TURN! 2.4

The solution is on page 114.

Each of the following accounts from the Devin Company has a normal balance. The unadjusted balances are as of December 31, 2013, the end of Devin's first year of operations:

Cash..............................	1,500	Common stock................	7,500
Accounts receivable.................	4,500	Sales revenue.................	12,000
Inventory.........................	3,750	Salary expense................	4,500
Property, plant, and equipment........	11,250	Administrative expenses	750
Accounts payable..................	2,250	Dividends....................	1,500
Notes payable	6,000		

Prepare an unadjusted trial balance for the Devin Company as of December 31, 2013.

Concept	Method	Assessment	TAKEAWAY 2.2
Is the trial balance in balance?	Ending balances for all of the general ledger accounts entered on the trial balance. Total the debit column and the credit column on the trial balance.	Verify the equality of the sum of the debit account balances and the sum of the credit account balances.	

REVIEW

COMPREHENSIVE PROBLEM

Juan Rios acted upon his entrepreneurial spirit and started a graphic design business called Juan's Designs. Based on an excellent business plan, Juan was able to raise sufficient capital to begin operations in October 2013. During the month of October, the following events occurred related to the business.

1. Stockholders invested $40,000 cash in the business in exchange for common stock.
2. Paid $2,500 cash for rent on an office suite for the month of October.
3. Purchased two desktop computers, software, and a printer for $10,000 cash.
4. Purchased miscellaneous supplies for $500 cash that will be used during the month, all on account.
5. Purchased an advertisement in a local newspaper for $300 cash, announcing the opening of his new business.
6. Performed $5,500 of design work on account.
7. Received $3,500 cash from customers for design work previously completed.
8. Paid $350 cash toward the company's accounts payable balance.
9. Paid $2,500 cash for wages of Juan Rios.

Required
a. Use the following accounts to create a general ledger using T-accounts.

Cash	Common Stock	Wage Expense
Accounts Receivable	Service Revenue	Advertising Expense
Equipment	Supplies Expense	Rent Expense
Accounts Payable		

Prepare journal entries and post the above accounting transactions to their general ledger T-accounts.
b. Prepare an unadjusted trial balance as of October 31, 2013.

Solution

Date	Description	Post Ref.	Debit	Credit
October	Cash	1	40,000	
	Common stock	1		40,000
	Owner purchased shares for cash.			

continued

continued from prior page

Date	Description	Post Ref.	Debit	Credit
October	Rent expense	2	2,500	
	Cash	2		2,500
	Paid rent for office suite.			
	Equipment	3	10,000	
	Cash	3		10,000
	Purchased office equipment.			
	Supplies expense	4	500	
	Accounts payable	4		500
	Purchased supplies on account to be used in current month.			
	Advertising expense	5	300	
	Cash	5		300
	Purchased advertising.			
	Accounts receivable	6	5,500	
	Service revenue	6		5,500
	Performed design work on account.			
	Cash	7	3,500	
	Accounts receivable	7		3,500
	Received cash from previously billed work.			
	Accounts payable	8	350	
	Cash	8		350
	Paid cash towards accounts payable.			
	Wage expense	9	2,500	
	Cash	9		2,500
	Paid wages.			

Cash

(1)	40,000	2,500	(2)
(7)	3,500	10,000	(3)
		300	(5)
		350	(8)
		2,500	(9)
Bal.	27,850		

Equipment

(3)	10,000

Common Stock

	40,000	(1)

Supplies Expense

(4)	500

Advertising Expense

(5)	300

Accounts Receivable

(6)	5,500	3,500	(7)
Bal.	2,000		

Accounts Payable

(8)	350	500	(4)
		150	**Bal.**

Service Revenue

	5,500	(6)

Wage Expense

(9)	2,500

Rent Expense

(2)	2,500

JUAN'S DESIGNS Unadjusted Trial Balance October 31, 2013	Debit	Credit
Cash.	$27,850	
Accounts receivable.	2,000	
Equipment	10,000	
Accounts payable.		$ 150
Common stock.		40,000
Service revenue		5,500
Supplies expense.	500	
Wage expense	2,500	
Advertising expense.	300	
Rent expense	2,500	
Totals	$45,650	$45,650

SUMMARY OF LEARNING OBJECTIVES

Identify the five major steps in the accounting cycle. (p. 58)   LO1

- Five major steps in the accounting cycle are:
  1. Analyze.
  2. Record.
  3. Adjust.
  4. Report.
  5. Close.

Analyze and record transactions using the accounting equation. (p. 59)   LO2

- The accounting equation provides a convenient way to summarize the recording of financial information.
- An initial step in the accounting process—analyze—is to determine just which transactions (if any) need to be recorded.
- An *accounting transaction* is an economic event that requires accounting recognition. An event that affects any of the elements of the basic accounting equation (assets, liabilities, or stockholders' equity) must be recorded.

Explain the nature, format, and purpose of an account. (p. 65)   LO3

- An account is an individual record of the increases and decreases in specific assets, liabilities, stockholders' equity, dividends, revenues, or expenses.
- Information provided by the account includes its title, amounts reflecting increases and decreases, cross-references to other accounting records, and dates and descriptive notations.

Describe the system of debits and credits and its use in recording transactions. (p. 66)   LO4

- The left side of an account is always the debit side; the right side of an account is always the credit side.
- Increases in assets, dividends, and expenses are debit entries; increases in liabilities, stockholders' equity, and revenues are credit entries. Decreases are the opposite.
- The normal balance of any account appears on the account side used for recording account increases.
- Each accounting transaction should be analyzed into equal amounts of debits and credits.
- All accounting transactions are analyzed using one or more of the basic account categories: (1) assets, (2) liabilities, (3) common stock, (4) dividends, (5) revenues, and (6) expenses. Retained earnings can also be included here.

Explain the process of journalizing and posting transactions. (p. 67)   LO5

- Source documents provide the basis for analyzing business transactions.
- Accounting entries are initially recorded in a journal in chronological order; the journal is a book of original entry and acts like a diary of a business's activities.
- A general ledger is a grouping of all of the accounts that are used to prepare the basic financial statements.

■ Posting is the transfer of information from a journal to the general ledger accounts.

■ Posting references are used to cross-reference the information in journals and the general ledger accounts.

LO6 **Describe the trial balance. (p. 75)**

■ A trial balance is a list of the accounts in the general ledger with their respective debit or credit balance.

■ A trial balance is prepared after all transactions have been recorded for an accounting period.

■ A trial balance serves as a mechanical check to evaluate the equality of the sum of the debit account balances and the sum of the credit account balances.

■ A trial balance facilitates the preparation of the financial statements by showing all account balances in one concise record.

SUMMARY	Concept	Method	Assessment
TAKEAWAY 2.1	When should an event be recorded in a company's accounting records?	Review the event details. Does the event affect the company's assets, liabilities, or stockholders' equity?	If the event affects any of the elements of the accounting equation, it must be recorded in a company's accounting records.
TAKEAWAY 2.2	Is the trial balance in balance?	Ending balances for all of the general ledger accounts entered on the trial balance. Total the debit column and the credit column on the trial balance.	Verify the equality of the sum of the debit account balances and the sum of the credit account balances.

KEY TERMS

Account (p. 65)	**Debit (entry)** (p. 66)	**Normal balance** (p. 67)
Accounting cycle (p. 58)	**Double-entry accounting** (p. 59)	**Posting** (p. 70)
Accounting transaction (p. 59)	**Fiscal year** (p. 59)	**Posting reference** (p. 70)
Calendar year (p. 59)	**General journal** (p. 68)	**Source documents** (p. 67)
Chart of accounts (p. 68)	**General ledger** (p. 70)	**T-account** (p. 65)
Compound journal entry (p. 69)	**Journal** (p. 68)	**Trial balance** (p. 75)
Credit (entry) (p. 66)	**Journal entry** (p. 68)	**Unearned revenue** (p. 62)

SELF-STUDY QUESTIONS

(Answers to Self-Study Questions are at the end of this chapter.)

LO2 **1. Which of the following transactions does not affect the balance sheet totals?**
   a. Purchased $500 supplies on account
   b. Paid off a $3,000 note payable
   c. Received $4,000 cash from a bank after signing a note payable
   d. Ordered a new machine that will be paid for upon its delivery in two months

LO2 **2. Tobias Company purchased inventory on account. This transaction will affect:**
   a. Only the balance sheet
   b. Only the income statement
   c. The income statement and the statement of retained earnings
   d. The income statement, balance sheet, and statement of retained earnings

LO2 **3. If assets increase by $100 and liabilities decrease by $30, stockholders' equity must:**
   a. Remain unchanged
   b. Increase by $130
   c. Decrease by $70
   d. Decrease by $130

4. **A T-account consists of how many parts?**   LO3
   a. One
   b. Two
   c. Three
   d. Four

5. **Which of the following is true?**   LO4
   a. The debit is on the right side of an asset account
   b. The debit is on the left side of an asset account
   c. The credit is on the left side of a liability account
   d. The debit is on the right side of an expense account

6. **Which of the following accounts has a normal debit balance?**   LO4
   a. Accounts Payable
   b. Notes Payable
   c. Common Stock
   d. Advertising Expense

7. **Which of the following accounts is increased by a credit?**   LO4
   a. Accounts Receivable
   b. Sales Revenue
   c. Dividends
   d. Advertising Expense

8. **Which of the following is true?**   LO4
   a. A debit will increase a liability account
   b. A credit will increase an asset account
   c. A credit will increase a revenue account
   d. A debit will decrease an expense account

9. **In applying the rules of debits and credits, which of the following statements is correct?**   LO4
   a. The word *debit* means to increase and the word *credit* means to decrease
   b. Asset, expense, and common stock accounts are debited for increases
   c. Liability, revenue, and common stock accounts are debited for increases
   d. Asset, expense, and dividends are debited for increases

10. **Which of these accounts has a normal debit balance?**   LO4
    a. Assets, expenses, dividends
    b. Assets, revenues, common stock
    c. Liabilities, revenues, common stock
    d. Assets, liabilities, dividends

11. **The general ledger includes accounts for all but which of the following?**   LO5
    a. Assets
    b. Expenses
    c. Dividends
    d. All of the above are in the general ledger

12. **Which of the following will cause a trial balance to be out of balance?**   LO6
    a. Mistakenly debiting an asset account instead of an expense account
    b. Posting $123 as $213 to both a debit and a credit account
    c. Posting the same transaction twice by mistake
    d. Posting only the debit part of a transaction

13. **A journal entry that contains more than just two accounts is called:**   LO5
    a. A posted journal entry
    b. An adjusting journal entry
    c. An erroneous journal entry
    d. A compound journal entry

14. **Posting refers to the process of transferring information from:**   LO5
    a. A journal to the general ledger accounts
    b. General ledger accounts to a journal
    c. Source documents to a journal
    d. A journal to source documents

LO1   **15.** **Which of the following is not one of the five steps in the accounting cycle?**
- *a.* Analyze
- *b.* Adjust
- *c.* Eliminate
- *d.* Report

LO2   **16.** **The purchase of $500 of supplies on account will:**
- *a.* Increase both assets and stockholders' equity by $500
- *b.* Increase assets and decrease liabilities by $500
- *c.* Increase assets and decrease stockholders' equity by $500
- *d.* Increase both assets and liabilities by $500

QUESTIONS

1. List the five major steps in the accounting cycle in their proper order.
2. Define the term *fiscal year*.
3. Provide three examples of source documents that underlie business transactions.
4. Provide an example of a transaction that would:
   - *a.* Increase one asset account but not change the amount of total assets.
   - *b.* Decrease an asset account and a liability account.
   - *c.* Decrease an asset account and increase an expense account.
   - *d.* Increase an asset account and a liability account.
5. Explain the financial effect (increase, decrease, or no effect) of each of the following transactions on stockholders' equity:
   - *a.* Purchased supplies for cash.
   - *b.* Paid an account payable.
   - *c.* Paid salaries.
   - *d.* Purchased equipment for cash.
   - *e.* Invested cash in business.
   - *f.* Rendered services to customers, on account.
   - *g.* Rendered services to customers, for cash.
6. The retained earnings on a balance sheet are $80,000. Without seeing the rest of the balance sheet, can you conclude that stockholders should be able to receive a dividend in the amount of $80,000 cash from the business? Justify your answer.
7. On December 31, 2013, the Miller Company had $700,000 in total assets and owed $220,000 to creditors. If the corporation's common stock amounted to $300,000, what amount of retained earnings should appear on the company's December 31, 2013, balance sheet?
8. Some accounting students believe that debits are good and credits are bad. Explain why this is not an accurate way to think about debits and credits.
9. What is an account?
10. What information is recorded in an account?
11. What does the term *debit* mean? What does the term *credit* mean?
12. What type of account—asset, liability, stockholders' equity, dividend, revenue, or expense—is each of the following accounts? Indicate whether a debit entry or a credit entry increases the balance of the account.

Professional Fees Earned	Common Stock
Accounts Receivable	Advertising Expense
Accounts Payable	Supplies
Cash	Dividends

13. How is the normal side of an account determined?
14. What is the normal balance (debit or credit) of each of the accounts in Discussion Question 12?
15. Describe the nature and purpose of a general journal.
16. What is the justification for the use of posting references?
17. Describe a compound journal entry.
18. What is a chart of accounts?

19. Explain the terms *general ledger* and *trial balance*. What are the primary reasons for preparing a trial balance?

20. Explain how it is possible for a trial balance to be in balance but still be in error.

21. What is a T-account and how is it used?

22. Is it possible for an accounting transaction to only affect the left side of the accounting equation and still leave the equation in balance? If so, provide an example.

23. Would a company record a transaction in its general ledger when an order is placed for the purchase of a machine that will be paid for at the time of its delivery in three months? Explain your answer.

SHORT EXERCISES

SE2-1. **Normal Balances** Indicate for each of the following accounts whether the normal balance is a debit or a credit: **LO4**

    a. Accounts Receivable
    b. Accounts Payable
    c. Dividends
    d. Wage Expense
    e. Inventory
    f. Interest Income
    g. Retained Earnings

SE2-2. **Debit and Credit Effects** Indicate the account that will be debited for each of the following transactions: **LO4**

    a. Issued common stock for cash
    b. Borrowed money from a bank
    c. Provided services on account
    d. Purchased inventory on account
    e. Collected cash from customers that owed a balance due

SE2-3. **Debit and Credit Effects** Indicate the account that will be credited for each of the following transactions: **LO4**

    a. Issued common stock for cash
    b. Borrowed money from a bank
    c. Provided services on account
    d. Purchased inventory on account
    e. Collected cash from customers that owed a balance due

SE2-4. **Determine a Transaction** The Pearce Company recorded a transaction by debiting Accounts Receivable and crediting Sales Revenue. What event was being recorded?   **LO4**

SE2-5. **Determine the Cash Balance** The beginning-of-the-period cash balance for the Travis Company was a $10,000 debit. Cash sales for the month were $5,000 and sales on account were $6,000. The company paid $3,500 cash for current-period purchases and also paid $2,000 cash for amounts due from last month. What is the ending debit or credit balance in the Cash account?   **LO4**

SE2-6. **Recording Transactions with the Accounting Equation** During the year, the Decker Company experienced the following accounting transactions: **LO2**

    1. Issued common stock in the amount of $100,000
    2. Paid a $30,000 cash dividend
    3. Borrowed $25,000 from a bank
    4. Made a principal payment of $2,500 on an outstanding bank loan
    5. Made an interest payment of $1,200 on an outstanding bank loan

Using the accounting equation, record each of the transactions in columnar format using the following template:

Assets	=	Liabilities	+	Stockholders' Equity		
Cash	=	Notes Payable	+	Common Stock	+	Retained Earnings

LO2 **SE2-7.** **Recording Transactions with the Accounting Equation** During the year, the Decker Company experienced the following accounting transactions:

1. Purchased equipment with cash in the amount of $100,000
2. Purchased supplies on account in the amount of $10,000
3. Collected $21,000 cash from customers
4. Paid a cash dividend of $15,000

Using the accounting equation, record each of the transactions in columnar format using the following template:

Assets				=	Liabilities	+	Stockholders' Equity
Cash +	Accounts Receivable	+ Supplies +	Equipment =		Accounts Payable	+	Retained Earnings

LO5 **SE2-8.** **Posting Transactions to T-accounts** Using the data from short exercise SE2-6, prepare journal entries and post your transaction analysis to the appropriate T-accounts.

LO5 **SE2-9.** **Posting Transactions to T-accounts** Using the data from short exercise SE2-7, prepare journal entries and post your transaction analysis to the appropriate T-accounts.

LO6 **SE2-10.** **Prepare a Trial Balance** The following balances were taken from the general ledger of Howser Corporation as of December 31. All balances are normal. Prepare a trial balance.

Cash............................	$ 6,000	Accounts receivable................	$10,800
Accounts payable..................	6,000	Common stock....................	36,000
Equipment	30,000	Dividends	2,400
Utilities expense..................	2,000	Administrative expense	8,000
Sales revenue....................	17,200		

LO6 **SE2-11.** **Prepare a Corrected Trial Balance** The following trial balance for Magill Company has errors that cause it to be out of balance. Prepare a corrected version of the trial balance for Magill Company.

MAGILL COMPANY Unadjusted Trial Balance December 31, 2013	Debit	Credit
Cash...	$ 20,000	
Inventory..		$ 85,000
Accounts receivable..	30,000	
Accounts payable..		12,000
Common stock...		40,000
Retained earnings		58,000
Sales revenue...	100,000	
Cost of goods sold...	60,000	
Selling expenses	15,000	
Totals	$225,000	$195,000

LO1 **SE2-12.** **The Accounting Cycle** The following is the correct order of the five steps in the accounting cycle:

a. Analyze; adjust; record; report; close
b. Analyze; record; adjust; report; close
c. Analyze; record; adjust; close; report
d. Analyze; report; adjust; record; close

LO3 **SE2-13.** **The Account** Which of the following is not part of the T-account?

a. Title
b. Amount
c. Cross-reference
d. Analysis

Assignments with the ✓ logo in the margin are available in my BusinessCourse.
See the Preface of the book for details.

EXERCISES—SET A

E2-1A. Accounting Equation Determine the missing amount in each of the following cases: **LO2** ✓

	Assets	Liabilities	Stockholders' Equity
a.	$200,000	$85,000	?
b.	?	$32,000	$28,000
c.	$93,000	?	$52,000

E2-2A. Transaction Analysis Following the example shown in (a) below, indicate the accounting effects   **LO2**
of the listed transactions on the assets, liabilities, and stockholders' equity of Martin & Company, a
corporation:

a.   Purchased, for cash, a desktop computer for use in the office.
     ANSWER: Increase assets (Office Equipment)
              Decrease assets (Cash)
b.   Rendered services and billed the client.
c.   Paid rent for the month.
d.   Rendered services to a client for cash.
e.   Received amount due from a client in Transaction (b).
f.   Purchased an office desk on account.
g.   Paid employees' salaries for the month.
h.   Paid for desk purchased in Transaction (f).
i.   The company paid a dividend.

E2-3A. Analysis of Accounts Calculate the unknown amount in each of the following five independent situ-   **LO2** ✓
ations. The answer to situation *(a)* is given as an example.

	Account	Beginning Balance	Ending Balance	Other Information
a.	Cash	$ 6,100	$ 5,250	Total cash disbursed, $5,400.
b.	Accounts receivable	8,500	9,300	Services on account, $16,500.
c.	Notes payable	15,000	20,000	Borrowed funds by issuing a note, $30,000.
d.	Accounts payable	3,280	1,720	Payments on account, $2,900.
e.	Stockholders' equity	32,000	46,000	Capital contribution, $5,000.

Unknown Amounts Required	
a. Total cash received	$4,550
b. Total cash collected from credit customers	_____
c. Notes payable repaid during the period	_____
d. Goods and services received from suppliers on account	_____
e. Net income, assuming that no dividends were paid	_____

E2-4A. Transaction Analysis The accounts below are from the general ledger of The Bast Company. For   **LO2, 5**
each letter given in the T-accounts, describe the type of business transaction(s) or event(s) that would
most likely be reflected by entries on that side of the account. For example, the answer to (a) is
amounts for services performed for clients on account.

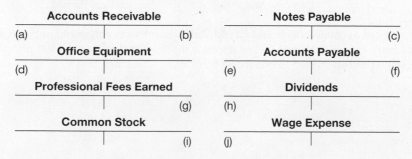

ASSIGNMENTS

LO4   E2-5A.   Transaction Analysis Match each of the following transactions of Lesch & Company with the appropriate letters, indicating the debits and credits to be made. The key for the letters follows the list of transactions. The correct answer for Transaction (1) is given as an illustration:

		Answer
1.	Purchased supplies on account.	*a, d*
2.	Paid interest on note payable.	_____
3.	Cash dividend was paid to stockholders.	_____
4.	Returned some defective supplies and received a reduction in the amount owed.	_____
5.	Made payment to settle note payable.	_____
6.	Received an invoice for utilities used.	_____
7.	Received payment in advance from client for work to be done next month.	_____
8.	The stockholders contributed additional capital to the business.	_____

Financial Effect of Transaction

a. Debit an asset		*g.* Debit dividends
b. Credit an asset		*h.* Credit dividends
c. Debit a liability		*i.* Debit a revenue
d. Credit a liability		*j.* Credit a revenue
e. Debit common stock		*k.* Debit an expense
f. Credit common stock		*l.* Credit an expense

LO5   E2-6A.   Transaction Entries Creative Designs, a firm providing art services for advertisers, began business on June 1. The following accounts in its general ledger are needed to record the transactions for June: Cash; Accounts Receivable; Supplies; Office Equipment; Accounts Payable; Common Stock; Dividends; Service Fees Earned; Rent Expense; Utilities Expense; and Salaries Expense. Use journal entries to record the following transactions for June in the general journal:

June   1   Lisa Ryan invested $12,000 cash to begin the business; she received common stock for her investment.
       2   Paid rent for June, $950.
       3   Purchased office equipment on account, $6,400.
       6   Purchased art materials and other supplies costing $3,800; paid $1,800 down with the remainder due within 30 days.
      11   Billed clients for services, $4,700.
      17   Collected $3,250 from clients on account.
      19   Paid $3,000 on account to office equipment company (see June 3 transaction).
      25   Lisa Ryan received a $2,000 dividend.
      30   Paid utility bill for June, $350.
      30   Paid salaries for June, $2,500.

LO5   E2-7A.   Source Documents For each transaction in E2-6A, indicate the related source document or documents that provide evidence supporting the transaction.

LO4, 5   E2-8A.   Nature of Accounts, Debit and Credit Rules For each of the accounts listed below, indicate whether the account is increased by a debit or a credit:

Accounts Payable	Dividends
Advertising Expense	Equipment
Cash	Land
Common Stock	Service Fees Earned

LO4, 5   E2-9A.   Nature of Accounts, Debit and Credit Rules In columns, enter *debit* or *credit* to describe the journal entry necessary to increase and decrease the account shown on the left, and which side of the account represents its normal balance.

	Increase	Decrease	Normal Balance
Asset............................	____	____	____
Liability........................	____	____	____
Common stock....................	____	____	____
Dividends.......................	____	____	____
Revenue........................	____	____	____
Expense........................	____	____	____

E2-10A. Nature of Accounts, Debit and Credit Rules For each of the accounts listed below, indicate whether the account is increased by a debit or a credit: **LO4, 5**

Accounts Receivable   Notes Payable
Advertising Revenue   Retained Earnings
Building   Supplies
Common Stock   Utilities Expense

E2-11A. Transaction Analysis Match each of the following transactions of L. Boyd & Company with the appropriate letters, indicating the debits and credits to be made. The key for the letters follows the list of transactions. The correct answer for Transaction 1 is given as an illustration: **LO2, 4**

		Answer
1.	Stockholders contributed cash to the business.	*a, f*
2.	Purchased equipment on account.	____
3.	Received and immediately paid advertising bill.	____
4.	Purchased supplies for cash.	____
5.	Borrowed money from a bank, giving a note payable.	____
6.	Billed customers for services rendered.	____
7.	Made a partial payment on account for equipment.	____
8.	Paid employee's salary.	____
9.	Collected amounts due from customers billed in Transaction 6.	____

Financial Effect of Transaction

a.	Debit an asset	*f.*	Credit common stock
b.	Credit an asset	*g.*	Debit a revenue
c.	Debit a liability	*h.*	Credit a revenue
d.	Credit a liability	*i.*	Debit an expense
e.	Debit common stock	*j.*	Credit an expense

E2-12A. Transaction Analysis and Trial Balance Make T-accounts for the following accounts that appear in the general ledger of Daniel Kelly, an attorney: Cash; Accounts Receivable; Office Equipment; Legal Database Subscription; Accounts Payable; Common Stock; Dividends; Legal Fees Earned; Salaries Expense; Rent Expense; and Utilities Expense. Prepare journal entries and record the following October transactions in the T-accounts and key all entries with the number identifying the transaction. Determine the balance in each account and prepare a trial balance sheet as of October 31. **LO5, 6**

Oct. 1 Kelly started his law practice by contributing $19,500 cash to the business on October 1, receiving shares of common stock in the company.
      2 Purchased office equipment on account, $10,400.
      3 Paid office rent for October, $700.
      4 Paid $9,600 to access online legal database for two years.
      5 Billed clients for services rendered, $11,300.
      6 Made $6,000 payment on account for the equipment purchased on October 2.
      7 Paid legal assistant's salary, $2,800.
      8 Collected $9,400 from clients previously billed for services.
      9 Received invoice for October utilities, $180; it will be paid in November.
     10 The company paid stockholders $1,500 as a cash dividend.

LO5, 6 ✓ **E2-13A. Transaction Analysis and Trial Balance** Make T-accounts for the following accounts that appear in the general ledger of Mead Pet Hospital, owned by R. Mead, a veterinarian: Cash; Accounts Receivable; Supplies; Office Equipment; Accounts Payable; Common Stock; Dividends; Professional Fees Earned; Salaries Expense; and Rent Expense. Prepare journal entries and record the following December transactions in the T-accounts and key all entries with the number identifying the transaction. Finally, determine the balance in each account and prepare a trial balance as of December 31.

Dec. 1 Mead opened a checking account on December 1 at United Bank in the name of Mead Pet Hospital and deposited $20,000 cash. Mead received common stock for his investment.
2 Paid rent for December, $1,100.
3 Purchased office equipment on account, $2,900.
4 Purchased supplies for cash, $1,700.
5 Billed clients for services rendered, $7,300.
6 Paid secretary's salary, $1,950.
7 Paid $1,500 on account for the equipment purchased on December 3.
8 Collected $5,800 from clients previously billed for services.
9 The company paid stockholders $2,200 as a cash dividend.

LO3 ✓ **E2-14A. The Account** The following transactions occurred during December, the first month of operations for Harris Company. Prepare journal entries and create a T-account for accounts payable that includes the following five transactions.

1. Purchased $500 of inventory on account.
2. Purchased $300 of inventory on account.
3. Paid suppliers $600.
4. Purchased $400 of inventory on account.
5. Paid suppliers $300.

EXERCISES—SET B

LO2 ✓ **E2-1B. Accounting Equation** Determine the missing amount in each of the following cases:

	Assets	Liabilities	Stockholders' Equity
a.	$400,000	$85,000	?
b.	?	$54,000	$28,000
c.	$193,000	?	$104,000

LO2 **E2-2B. Transaction Analysis** Following the example shown in (a) below, indicate the effects of the listed transactions on the assets, liabilities, and stockholders' equity of John Dallmus, certified public accountant, a corporation:

a. Purchased, for cash, a desktop computer for use in the office.
    ANSWER: Increase assets (Office Equipment)
            Decrease assets (Cash)
b. Rendered accounting services and billed client.
c. Paid utilities for month.
d. Rendered tax services to client for cash.
e. Received amount due from client in Transaction (b).
f. Purchased a copying machine on account.
g. Paid employees' salaries for month.
h. Paid for copying machine purchased in Transaction (f).
i. The company paid a dividend.

LO2 ✓ **E2-3B. Analysis of Accounts** Compute the unknown amount required in each of the following five independent situations. The answer to situation (a) is given as an illustration:

Account	Beginning Balance	Ending Balance	Other Information
a. Cash...............	$ 8,100	$ 5,250	Total cash disbursed, $5,400.
b. Accounts receivable.....	10,500	9,300	Services on account, $16,500.
c. Notes payable	17,000	20,000	Borrowed funds by issuing a note, $30,000.
d. Accounts payable.......	5,280	1,720	Payments on account, $3,900.
e. Stockholders' equity	34,000	46,000	Capital contribution, $5,000.

Unknown Amounts Required	
a. Total cash received	$2,550
b. Total cash collected from credit customers.................	_____
c. Notes payable repaid during the period....................	_____
d. Goods and services received from suppliers on account	_____
e. Net income, assuming that no dividends were paid	_____

E2-4B. Transaction Analysis The accounts below are from the general ledger of Andrew Miller & Company, an architectural firm. For each letter given in the T-accounts, describe the type of business transaction(s) or event(s) that would most likely be reflected by entries on that side of the account. For example, the answer to (a) is amounts for services performed for clients on account. **LO2, 5**

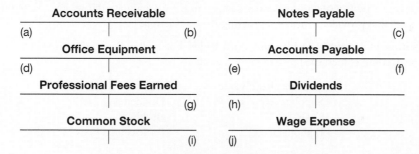

E2-5B. Transaction Analysis Match each of the following transactions of Ardon Peralta & Company, a landscape design firm, with the appropriate letters, indicating the debits and credits to be made. The key for the letters follows the list of transactions. The correct answer for Transaction 1 is given as an illustration: **LO4**

	Answer
1. Purchased supplies on account.	*a, d*
2. Paid interest on a bank loan.	_____
3. The business paid the stockholders a dividend.	_____
4. Returned some defective supplies and received a reduction in the amount owed.	_____
5. Made payment to repay bank loan.	_____
6. Received an invoice for supplies used.	_____
7. Received payment in advance from client for work to be done next month.	_____
8. Paid employee's salary.	_____
9. Peralta contributed additional capital to the business.	_____

Financial Effect of Transaction

a. Debit an asset	g. Debit dividends
b. Credit an asset	h. Credit dividends
c. Debit a liability	i. Debit a revenue
d. Credit a liability	j. Credit a revenue
e. Debit common stock	k. Debit an expense
f. Credit common stock	l. Credit an expense

LO5   **E2-6B.**   **Transaction Entries** Thoro Clean, a firm providing house-cleaning services, began business on April 1. The following accounts in its general ledger are needed to record the transactions for April: Cash; Accounts Receivable; Supplies; Prepaid Van Lease; Equipment; Accounts Payable; Notes Payable; Common Stock; Retained Earnings; Dividends; Cleaning Fees Earned; Wage Expense; Advertising Expense; and Fuel Expense. Prepare journal entries to record the following transactions for April in the general journal:

April   1   Randy Storm invested $9,000 cash to begin the business; he received common stock for his investment.
2   Paid six months' lease on a van, $2,850.
3   Borrowed $10,000 from a bank and signed a note payable agreeing to repay the $10,000 in one year plus 10 percent interest.
3   Purchased $5,500 of cleaning equipment; paid $2,500 down with the remainder due within 30 days.
4   Purchased cleaning supplies for $4,300 cash.
7   Paid $350 for newspaper advertisements to run during April.
21   Billed customers for services, $3,500.
23   Paid $3,000 on account to cleaning equipment firm (see April 3 transaction).
28   Collected $2,300 from customers on account.
29   Randy Storm received a $1,000 cash dividend.
30   Paid wages for April, $1,750.
30   Paid service station for gasoline used during April, $95.

LO5   **E2-7B.**   **Source Documents** For each transaction in E2-6B indicate the related source document or documents that provide evidence supporting the transaction.

LO4, 5   **E2-8B.**   **Nature of Accounts, Debit and Credit Rules** For each of the accounts listed below, indicate whether the account is increased by a debit or a credit:

Accounts Receivable	Common Stock
Supplies Expense	Dividends
Cash	Building
Equipment	Professional Fees Earned

LO4, 5   **E2-9B.**   **Nature of Accounts, Debit and Credit Rules** In the three columns, enter *debit* or *credit* to describe the journal entry necessary to increase and decrease the account shown to the left, and indicate which side of the account represents its normal balance.

	Increase	Decrease	Normal Balance
Cash.............................	_____	_____	_____
Accounts payable...................	_____	_____	_____
Common stock.....................	_____	_____	_____
Retained earnings	_____	_____	_____
Fee revenue	_____	_____	_____
Wage expense	_____	_____	_____

LO4, 5   **E2-10B.**   **Nature of Accounts, Debit and Credit Rules** For each of the accounts listed below, indicate whether the account is increased by a debit or a credit:

Accounts Receivable	Notes Payable
Sales Revenue	Retained Earnings
Equipment	Inventory
Common Stock	Rent Expense

LO2, 4   **E2-11B.**   **Transaction Analysis** Match each of the following transactions of R. Couche & Company, a printing company, with the appropriate letters, indicating the debits and credits to be made. The key for letters follows the list of transactions. The correct answer for Transaction (1) is given as an illustration:

	Answer
(1) Stockholders contributed cash to the business.	_a, f_
(2) Purchased inventory on account.	___
(3) Received and immediately paid a utility bill.	___
(4) Purchased supplies for cash.	___
(5) Borrowed money from a bank, giving a note payable.	___
(6) Billed customers for services rendered.	___
(7) Made a partial payment on account.	___
(8) Paid employee's salary.	___
(9) Collected amounts due from customers billed in Transaction 6.	___

Financial Effect of Transaction

a. Debit an asset	*f.* Credit common stock
b. Credit an asset	*g.* Debit a revenue
c. Debit a liability	*h.* Credit a revenue
d. Credit a liability	*i.* Debit an expense
e. Debit common stock	*j.* Credit an expense

E2-12B. Transaction Analysis and the Trial Balance Make T-accounts for the following accounts that **LO5, 6** appear in the general ledger of Matthew Thomas, an attorney: Cash; Accounts Receivable; Office Equipment; Legal Database Subscription; Accounts Payable; Common Stock; Dividends; Legal Fees Earned; Salaries Expense; Rent Expense; and Utilities Expense. Prepare journal entries and record the following October transactions in the T-accounts and key all entries with the number identifying the transaction. Determine the balance in each account and prepare a trial balance as of October 31.

Oct. 1 Thomas started his law practice by contributing $20,000 cash to the business on October 1; he received common stock for his investment.
   2 Purchased office equipment on account, $12,400.
   3 Paid office rent for October, $700.
   4 Paid $11,600 to access online legal database for two years.
   5 Billed clients for services rendered, $11,300.
   6 Made $6,000 payment on account for the equipment purchased on October 2.
   7 Paid legal assistant's salary, $2,800.
   8 Collected $9,400 from clients previously billed for services.
   9 Received invoice for October utilities, $180; it will be paid in November.
   10 The firm paid stockholders $2,000 cash as a dividend.

E2-13B. Transaction Analysis and Trial Balance Make T-accounts for the following accounts that appear in **LO5, 6** the general ledger of The Dog & Cat Hospital, owned by Kate Miller, a veterinarian: Cash; Accounts Receivable; Supplies; Office Equipment; Accounts Payable; Common Stock; Dividends; Professional Fees Earned; Salaries Expense; and Rent Expense. Prepare journal entries and record the following December transactions in the T-accounts and key all entries with the number identifying the transaction. Finally, determine the balance in each account and prepare a trial balance as of December 31.

Dec. 1 Miller opened a checking account on December 1 at Biltmore Bank in the name of The Dog & Cat Hospital and deposited $25,000 cash; Miller received common stock for her investment.
   2 Paid rent for December, $1,500.
   3 Purchased office equipment on account, $2,900.
   4 Purchased supplies for cash, $1,900.
   5 Billed clients for services rendered, $7,300.
   6 Paid secretary's salary, $1,950.
   7 Paid $1,500 on account for the equipment purchased on December 3.
   8 Collected $5,800 from clients previously billed for services.
   9 The firm paid stockholders $3,000 cash as a dividend.

E2-14B. The Account The following transactions occurred during January, the first month of operations for **LO3** Ruby Corporation. Prepare journal entries and create a T-account for inventory that includes the following five transactions. (*Hint:* When inventory is sold, it should be expensed to a Cost of Goods Sold expense account.)

1. Purchased $1,500 of inventory on account.
2. Purchased $1,300 of inventory on account.
3. Sold inventory with an original cost of $1,600.
4. Purchased $1,400 of inventory on account.
5. Sold inventory with an original cost of $1,300.

PROBLEMS—SET A

LO2 **P2-1A.** **Transaction Analysis** The accounting equation of L. Chen & Company as of the beginning of the accounting period is given below, followed by seven transactions whose effects on the accounting equation are shown. Describe each transaction that occurred. Of the transactions affecting Retained Earnings, transaction (e) had no effect on net income for the period.

	Cash	+	Accounts Receivable	+	Supplies	=	Accounts Payable	+	Notes Payable	+	Common Stock	+	Retained Earnings
Balance	$4,100	+	$9,000	+	$700	=	$800	+	$2,500	+	$2,000	+	$8,500
(a)	+6,500		−6,500										
(b)	−400				+400								
(c)			+7,000										+7,000
(d)	−800						−800						
(e)	−4,900												−4,900
(f)	−300				+300								
(g)	+1,200								+1,200				

LO2 **P2-2A.** **Transaction Analysis** An analysis of the transactions of Hewitt Detective Agency for the month of May appears below. Line 1 summarizes the company's accounting equation data as of May 1; lines 2–10 represent the transactions for May:

	Cash	+	Accounts Receivable	+	Supplies	+	Equipment	=	Accounts Payable	+	Notes Payable	+	Common Stock	+	Retained Earnings
(1)	$2,400	+	$7,600	+	$500	+	$8,000	=	$300	+	$5,000	+	$10,000	+	$3,200
(2)	+2,000										+2,000				
(3)	+6,100		−6,100												
(4)					+980						+980				
(5)			+6,800												+6,800
(6)	−300								−300						
(7)	+1,500														+1,500
(8)	−800														−800
(9)	−750						+750								
(10)	−2,500										−2,500				

Required

a. Show that assets equal liabilities plus stockholders' equity as of May 1.

b. Describe the apparent transaction indicated by each line. (For example, line 2: Borrowed $2,000, giving a note payable.) If any line could reasonably represent more than one type of transaction, describe each type.

c. Show that assets equal liabilities plus stockholders' equity as of May 31.

LO2 **P2-3A.** **Transaction Analysis** Grant Appraisal Service provides commercial and industrial appraisals and feasibility studies. On January 1, the assets and liabilities of the business were the following: Cash, $6,700; Accounts Receivable, $14,800; Accounts Payable, $600; and Notes Payable, $2,500. Common Stock had a balance of $18,400. Assume that Retained Earnings as of January 1, were zero. The following transactions occurred during the month of January:

Jan. 1 Paid rent for January, $950.
      2 Received $8,800 payment on customers' accounts.

Jan. 3 Paid $500 on accounts payable.
      4 Received $1,600 for services performed for cash customers.
      5 Borrowed $5,000 from a bank and signed a note payable for that amount.
      6 Billed the city $6,200 for a feasibility study performed; billed various other credit customers, $1,900.
      7 Paid the salary of an assistant, $4,000.
      8 Received invoice for January utilities, $410.
      9 Paid $6,000 cash for employee salaries.
     10 Purchased a van (on January 31) for business use, $9,800.
     11 Paid $50 to bank as January interest on the outstanding notes payable.

Required

a. Set up an accounting equation in columnar form with the following individual assets, liabilities, and stockholders' equity accounts: Cash, Accounts Receivable, Van, Accounts Payable, Notes Payable, Common Stock, and Retained Earnings. Enter the January 1 balances below each item. (*Note:* The beginning Van account balance is $0.)

b. Show the impact (increase or decrease) of transactions 1–11 on the beginning balances, and total the columns to show that assets equal liabilities plus stockholders' equity as of January 31.

P2-4A. Transaction Analysis On June 1, 2013, a group of bush pilots in Thunder Bay, Ontario, Canada, formed the Outpost Fly-In Service, Inc., by selling $50,000 of common stock for cash. The group then leased several amphibious aircraft and docking facilities, equipping them to transport campers and hunters to outpost camps owned by various resorts. The following transactions occurred during June 2013:   **LO2** ✔

June 1 Sold common stock for cash, $50,000.
      2 Paid June rent for aircraft, dockage, and dockside office, $4,800.
      3 Received invoice for the cost of a reception the firm gave to entertain resort owners, $1,600.
      4 Paid for June advertising in various sports magazines, $900.
      5 Paid insurance premium for June, $1,800.
      6 Rendered fly-in services for various groups for cash, $22,700.
      7 Billed the Canadian Ministry of Natural Resources for transporting mapping personnel, $2,900, and billed various firms for fly-in services, $13,000.
      8 Paid $1,500 on accounts payable.
      9 Received $13,200 on account from clients.
     10 Paid June wages, $16,000.
     11 Received invoice for the cost of fuel used during June, $3,500.
     12 Paid a cash dividend, $3,000.

Required

a. Set up an accounting equation in columnar form with the following column headings: Cash, Accounts Receivable, Accounts Payable, Common Stock, and Retained Earnings.

b. Show how the June transactions affect the items in the accounting equation, and total all columns to show that assets equal liabilities plus stockholders' equity as of June 30. (*Note:* Revenues, expenses, and dividends affect Retained Earnings.)

P2-5A. Accounting Equation Determine the following: **LO2** ✔

a. The stockholders' equity of a company that has assets of $450,000 and liabilities of $326,000.

b. The retained earnings of a company that has assets of $618,000, liabilities of $225,000, and common stock of $165,000.

c. The assets of a corporation that has liabilities of $400,000, common stock of $200,000, and retained earnings of $185,000.

P2-6A. Transaction Analysis Following the example shown in (a) below, indicate the effects of the listed transactions on the assets, liabilities, and stockholders' equity of Martin Andrews & Company.   **LO2**

a. Rendered legal services to clients for cash.
    ANSWER: Increase assets (Cash)
              Increase stockholders' equity (Revenue)

b. Purchased office supplies on account.

c. Andrews invested cash into the firm and received stock for his investment.
d. Paid amount due on account for office supplies purchased in (b).
e. Borrowed cash from a bank and signed a six-month note payable.
f. Rendered services and billed clients.
g. Purchased, for cash, a desk lamp for the office.
h. Paid interest on a note payable to the bank.
i. Received invoice for the current month's utilities.

LO2   P2-7A. Transaction Analysis On October 1, Alice Bloom started a consulting firm. The asset, liability, and stockholders' equity account balances after each of her first six transactions are shown below. Describe each of these six transactions:

	Cash	+	Accounts Receivable	+	Supplies	+	Equipment	=	Notes Payable	+	Common Stock	+	Retained Earnings
(a)	$6,000	+	$ 0	+	$ 0	+	$ 0	=	$ 0	+	$6,000	+	$ 0
(b)	4,000	+	0	+	2,000	+	0	=	0	+	6,000	+	0
(c)	7,500	+	0	+	2,000	+	0	=	3,500	+	6,000	+	0
(d)	2,500	+	0	+	2,000	+	5,000	=	3,500	+	6,000	+	0
(e)	2,500	+	1,000	+	2,000	+	5,000	=	3,500	+	6,000	+	1,000
(f)	3,000	+	500	+	2,000	+	5,000	=	3,500	+	6,000	+	1,000

LO2   P2-8A. Determination of Omitted Financial Statement Data For the four unrelated situations, A-D, calculate the unknown amounts indicated by the letters appearing in each column:

	A	B	C	D
Beginning				
Assets	$28,000	$12,000	$28,000	$ (d)
Liabilities	18,600	5,000	19,000	9,000
Ending				
Assets	30,000	26,000	34,000	40,000
Liabilities	17,300	(b)	15,000	19,000
During the Year				
Common stock	2,000	4,500	(c)	3,500
Sales revenues	(a)	28,000	18,000	24,000
Dividends	5,000	1,500	1,000	6,500
Expenses	8,500	21,000	11,000	17,000

LO2   P2-9A. Transaction Analysis Appearing below is an analysis of the June transactions for Rhode Consulting Services. Line 1 summarizes Rhode's accounting equation data as of June 1; lines 2-10 are the transactions for the month of June:

	Cash	+	Accounts Receivable	+	Supplies	+	Equipment	=	Accounts Payable	+	Notes Payable	+	Common Stock	+	Retained Earnings
(1)	$3,500	+	$5,200	+	$820	+	$9,000	=	$600	+	$3,000	+	$10,920	+	$4,000
(2)					+670				+670						
(3)							+5,000				+5,000				
(4)	+4,200		−4,200												
(5)			+7,800												+7,800
(6)	−600								−600						
(7)	−200				+200										
(8)	−4,600														−4,600
(9)	+2,000										+2,000				
(10)					+750								+750		

Required

a. Show that assets equal liabilities plus stockholders' equity as of June 1.

b. Describe the transaction indicated by each line. For example, line 2: Purchased supplies on account, $670. If any line could reasonably represent more than one type of transaction, describe each type.

c. Show that assets equal liabilities plus stockholders' equity as of June 30.

P2-10A. Transaction Analysis Grace Main began the Main Answering Service in December 2010. The firm provides services for professional people and is currently operating with leased equipment. On January 1, 2013, the assets and liabilities of the business were: Cash, $4,400; Accounts Receivable, $6,900; Accounts Payable, $600; and Notes Payable, $1,500. Assume that Retained Earnings as of January 1, 2013, were zero. The balance of Common Stock was $9,200. The following transactions occurred during the month of January: **LO2** ✓

Jan. 1 Paid rent on office and equipment for January, $800.
2 Collected $4,500 on account from clients.
3 Borrowed $2,000 from a bank and signed a note payable for that amount.
4 Billed clients for work performed on account, $9,500.
5 Paid $400 on accounts payable.
6 Received invoice for January advertising, $550.
7 Paid January salaries, $3,800.
8 Paid January utilities, $430.
9 Paid stockholders a dividend of $2,600 cash.
10 Purchased fax machine (on January 31) for business use, $1,400.
11 Paid $30 to the bank as January interest on the outstanding notes payable.

Required

a. Set up an accounting equation in columnar form with the following individual assets, liabilities, and stockholders' equity accounts: Cash, Accounts Receivable, Equipment, Accounts Payable, Notes Payable, Common Stock, and Retained Earnings. Enter the January 1 balances below each item. (*Note:* The beginning Equipment account balance is $0.)

b. Show the impact (increase or decrease) of the January transactions on the beginning balances, and total all columns to show that assets equal liabilities plus stockholders' equity as of January 31.

P2-11A. Transaction Analysis On December 1, Peter Allen started Career Services Inc., providing career and vocational counseling services. The following transactions took place during the month of December: **LO2** ✓

Dec. 1 Allen invested $7,000 in the business, receiving common shares.
2 Paid rent for December on furnished office space, $750.
3 Received invoice for December advertising, $500.
4 Borrowed $15,000 from a bank and signed a note payable for that amount.
5 Received $1,200 for counseling services rendered for cash.
6 Billed certain governmental agencies and other clients for counseling services, $6,800.
7 Paid secretary's salary, $2,200.
8 Paid December utilities, $370.
9 Paid stockholders a dividend of $900 cash.
10 Purchased land for cash to use as a site for a new facility, $13,000.
11 Paid $100 to the bank as December interest on a note payable.

Required

a. Set up an accounting equation in columnar form with the following column headings: Cash, Accounts Receivable, Land, Accounts Payable, Notes Payable, Common Stock, and Retained Earnings.

b. Show how the December transactions affect the items in the accounting equation, and total all columns to show that assets equal liabilities plus stockholders' equity as of December 31.

P2-12A. Transaction Analysis and the Effect of Errors on the Trial Balance The following T-accounts contain numbered entries for the May transactions of Carol Marsh, a market analyst, who opened her business on May 1, 2013:   **LO4, 5, 6**

Cash					Common Stock	
(1)	13,000	4,800	(2)		13,000	(1)
(9)	3,700	810	(4)			
		1,950	(6)			
		600	(8)			

Accounts Receivable					Dividends	
(5)	6,400	3,700	(9)	(8)	600	

Office Supplies			Professional Fees Earned	
(3)	2,800			6,400	(5)

Office Equipment			Rent Expense	
(2)	4,800		(4)	810

Accounts Payable					Utilities Expense	
(6)	1,950	2,800	(3)	(7)	270	
		270	(7)			

Required

a. Give a description of each of the nine numbered transactions entered in the above T-accounts. Example: (1) Carol Marsh invested $13,000 of her personal funds in her business.

b. The following trial balance, prepared from Marsh's data as of May 31, contains several errors. Itemize the errors and indicate the correct totals for the trial balance.

CAROL MARSH & COMPANY
Unadjusted Trial Balance
May 31, 2013

	Debit	Credit
Cash...	$ 8,450	
Accounts receivable.......................................	3,700	
Office supplies	2,800	
Office equipment	4,800	
Accounts payable..		$ 1,120
Common stock		13,000
Dividends		600
Professional fees earned		6,400
Rent expense..	810	
Totals	$20,560	$21,120

LO4, 5, 6 **P2-13A. Transaction Analysis and Trial Balance** Pam Brown owns Art Graphics, a firm providing designs for advertisers and market analysts. On July 1, the business's general ledger showed the following normal account balances:

Cash....................	$ 8,500	Accounts payable.......................	$ 2,100
Accounts receivable........	9,800	Notes payable.........................	5,000
		Common stock.........................	2,000
		Retained earnings	9,200
Total Assets	$18,300	Total Liabilities and Stockholders' Equity	$18,300

The following transactions occurred during the month of July:

July 1 Paid July rent, $670.
2 Collected $7,100 on account from customers.
3 Paid $2,500 installment due on the $5,000 noninterest-bearing note payable.
4 Billed customers for design services rendered on account, $16,550.
5 Rendered design services and collected from cash customers, $1,200.
6 Paid $1,400 to creditors on account.

July   7   Collected $12,750 on account from customers.
      8   Paid a delivery service for delivery of graphics to commercial firms, $400.
      9   Paid July salaries, $4,600.
     10   Received invoice for July advertising expense, to be paid in August, $600.
     11   Paid utilities for July, $350.
     12   Paid stockholders a dividend of $2,000 cash.
     13   Received invoice for supplies used in July, to be paid in August, $2,260.
     14   Purchased computer for $4,300 cash to be used in the business starting next month.

Required

a.   Set up accounts for the general ledger accounts with July 1 balances and enter the beginning balances. Also provide the following accounts: Equipment; Service Fees Earned; Rent Expense; Salaries Expense; Delivery Expense; Advertising Expense; Utilities Expense; Supplies Expense; and Dividends. Prepare journal entries and record the listed transactions in the appropriate T-accounts.
b.   Prepare a trial balance as of July 31.

P2-14A. Transaction Analysis and Trial Balance   Outpost Fly-In Service, Inc., operates leased amphibious aircraft and docking facilities, equipping the firm to transport campers and hunters from Vancouver, Canada, to outpost camps owned by various resorts. On August 1, 2013, the firm's trial balance was as follows: **LO4, 5, 6**

OUTPOST FLY-IN SERVICE, INC.
Unadjusted Trial Balance
August 1, 2013

	Debit	Credit
Cash	$52,600	
Accounts receivable	23,200	
Accounts payable		$ 1,700
Notes payable		3,000
Common stock		50,000
Retained earnings		21,100
Totals	$75,800	$75,800

During the month of August, the following transactions occurred:

Aug. 1   Paid August rental cost for aircraft, dockage, and dockside office, $5,000.
       2   Paid insurance premium for August, $1,800.
       3   Paid for August advertising in various sports magazines, $1,000.
       4   Rendered fly-in services for various groups for cash, $13,750.
       5   Billed the Canadian Ministry of Natural Resources for services in transporting mapping personnel, $3,200.
       6   Received $17,400 on account from clients.
       7   Paid $1,500 on accounts payable.
       8   Billed various clients for services, $16,400.
       9   Paid interest on a note payable for August, $25.
      10   Paid August wages, $12,800.
      11   Received invoice for the cost of fuel used during August, $3,200.
      12   Paid a cash dividend, $4,500 (debit Retained Earnings).

Required

a.   Set up accounts for each item in the August 1 trial balance and enter the beginning balances. Also provide accounts for the following items: Service Fees Earned, Wage Expense, Advertising Expense, Rent Expense, Fuel Expense, Insurance Expense, and Interest Expense. Prepare journal entries and record the transactions for August in the appropriate T-accounts, using the dates given.
b.   Prepare a trial balance as of August 31.

LO4, 5, 6   **P2-15A. Transaction Analysis and Trial Balance** Mary Aker opened a tax practice on June 1. The following accounts will be needed to record her transactions for June: Cash; Accounts Receivable; Office Supplies; Tax Library; Office Furniture and Fixtures; Accounts Payable; Notes Payable; Common Stock; Dividends; Professional Fees Earned; Rent Expense; Salaries Expense; Advertising Expense; Utilities Expense; and Interest Expense. The following transactions occurred during the month of June:

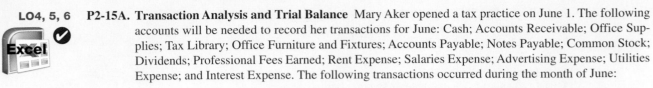

June 1   Aker opened a business checking account at a local bank, investing $16,000 in her practice in exchange for common stock.
2   Purchased office furniture and fixtures for $9,800, paid $2,800 cash, and gave a note payable for the balance.
3   Purchased books and software for a tax library on account, $3,700.
4   Purchased office supplies for cash, $560.
5   Paid rent for June, $750.
6   Returned $300 of books with defective bindings. The return reduced the amount owed to the supplier.
7   Billed clients for professional services rendered, $7,600.
8   Paid $1,700 on account for the library items purchased on June 3.
9   Collected $5,900 on account from clients billed on June 7.
10   Paid June salaries, $2,900.
11   Received invoice for June advertising, to be paid in July, $300.
12   Paid stockholders $800 cash as a dividend.
13   Paid utilities for June, $160.
14   Paid interest for June on note payable, $60.

Required
a.   Prepare journal entries and record the above transactions in T-accounts, and key entries with the number of the transactions.
b.   Prepare a trial balance as of June 30.

LO4, 5, 6   **P2-16A. Transaction Analysis and the Effect of Errors on the Trial Balance**
The following T-accounts contain numbered entries for the May transactions of Flores Corporation, an architectural firm, which opened its offices on May 1:

Cash					Accounts Payable			
(1)	20,000	1,400	(4)		(5)	310	1,530	(3)
(10)	5,200	5,950	(7)		(8)	1,000	290	(9)
		1,000	(8)					

Accounts Receivable					Common Stock			
(6)	8,750	5,200	(10)				20,000	(1)

Supplies					Professional Fees Earned			
(3)	1,530	310	(5)				8,750	(6)

Office Equipment					Rent Expense			
(2)	5,000				(4)	1,400		

Notes Payable					Utilities Expense			
		5,000	(2)		(9)	290		

Salaries Expense			
(7)	5,950		

Required
a.   Give a description of each of the 10 numbered transactions entered in the above accounts. Example: (1) Flores Corporation issued common stock for cash, $20,000.
b.   The following trial balance, prepared for Flores Corporation as of May 31, contains several errors. Itemize the errors, and indicate the correct totals for the trial balance.

FLORES CORPORATION
Unadjusted Trial Balance
May 31, 2013

	Debit	Credit
Cash.	$61,850	
Accounts receivable.	3,550	
Supplies	1,220	
Office equipment		$ 5,000
Accounts payable.		510
Notes payable		50,000
Common stock.		2,000
Professional fees earned		8,570
Rent expense	1,400	
Utilities expense.	290	
Salaries expense	5,950	
Totals	$74,260	$66,080

P2-17A. **Transaction Analysis and Trial Balance** James Behm, electrical contractor, began business on May 1. The following transactions occurred during the month of May: **LO5, 6** ✔

May 1   Behm invested $18,000 of his personal funds in the business in exchange for common stock.
 2   Purchased equipment on account, $4,200.
 3   Returned $200 of equipment that was not satisfactory. The return reduced the amount owed to the supplier.
 4   Purchased supplies on account, $860.
 5   Purchased a truck for $10,500. Behm paid $5,500 cash and gave a note payable for the balance.
 6   Paid rent for May, $875.
 7   Paid fuel cost for truck, $60.
 8   Billed customers for services rendered, $13,700.
 9   Paid $3,000 on account for equipment purchased on May 2.
 10   Paid utilities for May, $210.
 11   Received invoice for May advertising, to be paid in June, $280.
 12   Paid employees' wages, $3,350.
 13   Collected $8,600 on accounts receivable.
 14   Paid stockholders $1,500 cash as a dividend.
 15   Paid interest for May on an outstanding note payable, $40.

Required

a.   Prepare journal entries and record the above transactions in T-accounts, and key entries with the numbers of the transactions. The following accounts will be needed to record the transactions for May: Cash; Accounts Receivable; Supplies; Equipment; Truck; Accounts Payable; Notes Payable; Common Stock; Dividends; Service Revenue; Rent Expense; Wages Expense; Utilities Expense; Truck Expense; Advertising Expense; and Interest Expense.
b.   Prepare a trial balance as of May 31.

PROBLEMS—SET B

P2-1B.   **Transaction Analysis** The accounting equation of Matthew Thomas, attorney, at the beginning of an accounting period is given below, followed by seven transactions whose effects on the accounting equation are shown. Describe each transaction that occurred. Of the transactions affecting retained earnings, transaction (e) had no effect on net income for the period.   **LO2**

	Cash	+	Accounts Receivable	+	Supplies	=	Accounts Payable	+	Notes Payable	+	Common Stock	+	Retained Earnings
Balance	$4,100	+	$9,000	+	$900	=	$1,000	+	$2,500	+	$7,500	+	$3,000
(a)	+7,500		−7,500										
(b)					+400		+400						
(c)			+8,000										+8,000
(d)	−800						−800						
(e)	−4,900												−4,900
(f)	−300				+300								
(g)	+3,200								+3,200				

LO2   P2-2B.   Transaction Analysis An analysis of the transactions of Likert Shipping Services for the month of May appears below. Line 1 summarizes Likert's accounting equation data as of May 1; lines 2–10 represent the transactions for the month of May:

	Cash	+	Accounts Receivable	+	Supplies	+	Equipment	=	Accounts Payable	+	Notes Payable	+	Common Stock	+	Retained Earnings
(1)	$2,400	+	$7,600	+	$900	+	$9,000	=	$700	+	$6,000	+	$3,200	+	$10,000
(2)	+2,000										+2,000				
(3)	+6,100		−6,100												
(4)					+980				+980						
(5)			+6,800												+6,800
(6)	−300								−300						
(7)	+1,500														+1,500
(8)	−800														−800
(9)	−750						+750								
(10)	−2,500										−2,500				

Required

a. Show that assets equal liabilities plus stockholders' equity as of May 1.

b. Describe the apparent transaction indicated by each line. (For example, line 2: Borrowed $2,000, giving a note payable.) If any line could reasonably represent more than one type of transaction, describe each type.

c. Show that assets equal liabilities plus stockholders' equity as of May 31.

LO2   P2-3B.   Transaction Analysis Smith Appraisal Service provides commercial and industrial appraisals and feasibility studies. On January 1, the assets and liabilities of the business were the following: Cash, $8,700; Accounts Receivable, $16,800; Accounts Payable, $3,600; and Notes Payable, $6,500. Assume that Retained Earnings as of January 1, were zero. The balance of Common Stock was $15,400. The following transactions occurred during the month of January:

Jan. 1 Paid rent for January, $1,000.
      2 Received $9,800 on customers' accounts.
      3 Paid $900 on accounts payable.
      4 Received $1,600 for services performed for cash customers.
      5 Borrowed $8,000 from a bank and signed a note payable for that amount.
      6 Billed the city $8,200 for a feasibility study performed; billed various other credit customers, $2,900.
      7 Paid salary of assistant, $4,500.
      8 Received invoice for January utilities, $410.
      9 Paid $6,000 cash dividends.
     10 Purchased an automobile (on January 31) for business use, $9,800 cash.
     11 Paid $150 to the bank as January interest on an outstanding note payable.

Required

a. Set up an accounting equation in columnar form with the following individual assets, liabilities, and stockholders' equity accounts: Cash, Accounts Receivable, Automobile, Accounts Payable,

Notes Payable, Common Stock, and Retained Earnings. Enter January 1 balances below each item. (*Note:* The beginning Automobile amount is $0.)

b. Show the impact (increase or decrease) of transactions 1–11 on the beginning balances, and total the columns to show that assets equal liabilities plus stockholders' equity as of January 31.

P2-4B. Transaction Analysis On June 1, a group of bush pilots in British Columbia, Canada, formed the BC Back-Country Airlines, Inc., by selling $80,000 of common stock for cash. The group then leased several aircraft and docking facilities, equipping them to transport campers and hunters to outpost camps owned by various resorts. The following transactions occurred during June: **LO2**

June 1 Sold common stock for cash, $80,000.
  2 Paid June rent for aircraft, dockage, and dockside office, $5,500.
  3 Received invoice for the cost of a reception the firm gave to entertain resort owners, $2,600.
  4 Paid for June advertising in various sports magazines, $1,900.
  5 Paid insurance premium for June, $2,800.
  6 Rendered services for various groups for cash, $25,000.
  7 Billed the Canadian Ministry of Natural Resources for transporting mapping personnel, $3,900, and billed various firms for services, $15,000.
  8 Paid $1,500 on accounts payable.
  9 Received $13,200 on account from clients.
  10 Paid June wages, $16,000.
  11 Received an invoice for the cost of fuel used during June, $3,500.
  12 Paid a cash dividend, $5,000.

Required

a. Set up an accounting equation in columnar form with the following column headings: Cash, Accounts Receivable, Accounts Payable, Common Stock, and Retained Earnings.

b. Show how the June transactions affect the items in the accounting equation, and total all columns to show that assets equal liabilities plus stockholders' equity as of June 30.

P2-5B. Accounting Equation Determine the following: **LO2**

a. The stockholders' equity of a company that has assets of $480,000 and liabilities of $330,000.

b. The retained earnings of a company that has assets of $675,000, liabilities of $225,000, and common stock of $165,000.

c. The assets of a corporation that has liabilities of $500,000, common stock of $300,000, and retained earnings of $255,000.

P2-6B. Transaction Analysis Following the example shown in (a) below, indicate the effects of the listed transactions on the assets, liabilities, and stockholders' equity of McKay & Company: **LO2**

a. Rendered services to clients for cash.
    ANSWER: Increase assets (Cash)
         Increase stockholders' equity (Revenue)

b. Purchased office supplies on account.

c. Invested cash in the firm in exchange for common stock.

d. Paid amount due on account for supplies purchased in (b).

e. Borrowed cash from a bank and signed a six-month note.

f. Rendered services and billed clients.

g. Purchased, for cash, a desk lamp for the office.

h. Paid interest on note payable to bank.

i. Received an invoice for the current month's utilities.

P2-7B. Transaction Analysis On October 1, Deloitte & Coopers started a consulting firm. The asset, liability, and stockholders' equity account balances after each of the firm's first six transactions are shown below. Describe each of these six transactions.   **LO2**

	Cash	+	Accounts Receivable	+	Supplies	+	Equipment	=	Notes Payable	+	Common Stock	+	Retained Earnings
(a)	$6,000	+	$ 0	+	$ 0	+	$ 0	=	$ 0	+	$6,000	+	$ 0
(b)	4,000	+	0	+	2,000	+	0	=	0	+	6,000	+	0
(c)	7,500	+	0	+	2,000	+	0	=	3,500	+	6,000	+	0
(d)	2,500	+	0	+	2,000	+	5,000	=	3,500	+	6,000	+	0
(e)	2,500	+	2,000	+	2,000	+	5,000	=	3,500	+	6,000	+	2,000
(f)	3,000	+	1,500	+	2,000	+	5,000	=	3,500	+	6,000	+	2,000

LO2   P2-8B. Determination of Omitted Financial Statement Data For the four unrelated situations, A-D, below, calculate the unknown amounts indicated by the letters appearing in each column:

	A	B	C	D
Beginning				
Assets.	$38,000	$12,000	$28,000	$ (d)
Liabilities.	18,600	5,000	10,000	9,000
Ending				
Assets.	30,000	36,000	34,000	40,000
Liabilities.	17,300	(b)	15,000	15,000
During the Year				
Common stock	2,000	4,500	(c)	3,500
Revenues	(a)	28,000	18,000	24,000
Dividends	5,000	1,500	1,000	6,500
Expenses	8,500	21,000	11,000	17,000

LO2   P2-9B. Transaction Analysis Appearing below is an analysis of the June transactions for Carlton Communications Company. Line 1 summarizes Carlton's accounting equation data as of June 1; lines 2-10 are the transactions for June:

	Cash	+	Accounts Receivable	+	Supplies	+	Equipment	=	Accounts Payable	+	Notes Payable	+	Common Stock	+	Retained Earnings
(1)	$3,500	+	$5,200	+	$820	+	$12,000	=	$600	+	$3,000	+	$10,920	+	$7,000
(2)					+670				+670						
(3)							+6,000				+6,000				
(4)	+4,200		−4,200												
(5)			+7,800												+7,800
(6)	−600								−600						
(7)	−200				+200										
(8)	−4,600														−4,600
(9)	+3,000										+3,000				
(10)	−750						+750								

Required

a. Show that assets equal liabilities plus stockholders' equity as of June 1.

b. Describe the apparent transaction indicated by each line. For example, line 2: Purchased supplies on account, $670. If any line could reasonably represent more than one type of transaction, describe each type.

c. Show that assets equal liabilities plus stockholders' equity as of June 30.

LO2   P2-10B. Transaction Analysis Torrey Mann began the Mann Word Processing Service in December 2012. The firm provides word-processing services for businesses and is currently operating with leased equipment. On January 1, 2013, the assets and liabilities of the business were: Cash, $6,400; Accounts Receivable, $8,900; Accounts Payable, $900; and Notes Payable, $3,500. Assume that Retained Earnings as of January 1, 2010, were zero. Common Stock balance was $10,900. The following transactions occurred during the month of January:

Jan. 1 Paid rent on office and equipment for January, $900.
    2 Collected $6,500 on account from clients.
    3 Borrowed $5,000 from a bank and signed a note payable for that amount.
    4 Billed clients for work performed on account, $8,500.
    5 Paid $400 on accounts payable.
    6 Received invoice for January advertising, $750.
    7 Paid January salaries, $4,800.
    8 Paid January utilities, $230.
    9 Paid stockholders a dividend in the amount of $2,600.
  10 Purchased fax machine (on January 31) for business use, $1,400.
  11 Paid $130 to bank as January interest on the outstanding notes payable.

Required

a. Set up an accounting equation in columnar form with the following individual assets, liabilities, and stockholders' equity accounts: Cash, Accounts Receivable, Equipment, Accounts Payable, Notes Payable, Common Stock, Retained Earnings. Enter the January 1 balances below each item. (*Note:* The beginning Equipment amount is $0.)

b. Show the impact (increase or decrease) of the January transactions on the beginning balances, and total all columns to show that assets equal liabilities plus stockholders' equity as of January 31.

P2-11B. Transaction Analysis On December 1, Judy Johnson started Adult Career Services, which provided career and vocational counseling services to individuals. The following transactions took place during the month of December:

LO2

Dec. 1 Johnson invested $9,000 in the business in exchange for common stock.
    2 Paid rent for December on furnished office space, $950.
    3 Received invoice for December advertising, $800.
    4 Borrowed $25,000 from a bank and signed a note payable for that amount.
    5 Received $4,200 for counseling services rendered for cash.
    6 Billed certain governmental agencies and other clients for counseling services, $9,800.
    7 Paid secretary's salary, $3,200.
    8 Paid December utilities, $370.
    9 Paid stockholders a dividend in the amount of $900.
  10 Purchased land for cash to use as a site for the company's future offices, $23,000.
  11 Paid $100 to the bank as December interest on the outstanding note payable.

Required

a. Set up an accounting equation in columnar form with the following column headings: Cash, Accounts Receivable, Land, Accounts Payable, Notes Payable, Common Stock, and Retained Earnings.

b. Show how the December transactions affect the items in the accounting equation, and total all columns to show that assets equal liabilities plus stockholders' equity as of December 31.

P2-12B. Transaction Analysis and the Effect of Errors on the Trial Balance The following T-accounts contain numbered entries for the May transactions of Valerie Rankine who opened a consulting services business on May 1:

LO4, 5, 6

	Cash					Common Stock	
(1)	20,000	4,800	(2)			20,000	(1)
(9)	3,700	810	(4)				
		1,950	(6)				
		600	(8)				

	Accounts Receivable					Dividends	
(5)	6,400	3,700	(9)	(8)	600		

	Office Supplies				Professional Fees Earned		
(3)	2,800					6,400	(5)

Office Equipment			Rent Expense	
(2)	4,800		(4)	810
Accounts Payable			**Utilities Expense**	
(6)	1,950	2,800 (3)	(7)	270
		270 (7)		

Required

a. Give a description of each of the nine numbered transactions entered in the above accounts. Example: (1) Valerie Rankine invested $20,000 of her personal funds in the business in exchange for common stock.

b. The following trial balance, prepared for Rankine's firm as of May 31, contains several errors. Itemize the errors and indicate the correct totals for the trial balance.

RANKINE CONSULTING SERVICES Unadjusted Trial Balance May 31, 2013		
	Debit	Credit
Cash...	$15,450	
Accounts receivable................................	3,700	
Office supplies	2,800	
Office equipment	4,800	
Accounts payable...................................		$ 1,120
Common stock		20,000
Dividends		600
Professional fees earned		6,400
Rent expense......................................	810	
Totals	$27,560	$28,120

LO4, 5, 6

Excel ✓

P2-13B. **Transaction Analysis and Trial Balance** Ashley Somers owns San Diego Art Company, a firm providing designs for advertisers, market analysts, and others. On July 1, the business's general ledger showed the following normal account balances:

Cash.......................	$10,500	Accounts payable......................	$ 2,100
Accounts receivable............	9,800	Notes payable	5,000
		Common stock........................	11,200
		Retained earnings	2,000
Total assets	$20,300	Total Liabilities and Stockholders' Equity	$20,300

The following transactions occurred during the month of July:

July   1   Paid July rent, $670.
2   Collected $8,100 on account from customers.
3   Paid $2,500 installment due on the $5,000 noninterest-bearing note payable to a relative.
4   Billed customers for design services rendered on account, $19,550.
5   Rendered design services and collected from cash customers, $1,200.
6   Paid $1,700 to creditors on account.
7   Collected $14,750 on account from customers.
8   Paid a delivery service for delivery of graphics to commercial firms, $400.
9   Paid July salaries, $4,600.
10   Received invoice for July advertising expense, to be paid in August, $600.
11   Paid utilities for July, $350.
12   The business paid a $2,000 cash dividend.
13   Received invoice for supplies used in July, to be paid in August, $2,260.
14   Purchased a computer for $4,300 cash to be used in the business starting next month.

Required

a. Set up accounts for the general ledger accounts with July 1 balances and enter the beginning balances. Also provide the following accounts: Equipment; Dividends; Service Fees Earned;

Rent Expense; Salaries Expense; Delivery Expense; Advertising Expense; Utilities Expense; and Supplies Expense. Prepare journal entries and record the listed transactions in the appropriate T-accounts.

b. Prepare a trial balance as of July 31.

P2-14B. Transaction Analysis and Trial Balance BC Back-Country Airlines, Inc., operates leased amphibious aircraft and docking facilities, equipping the firm to transport campers and hunters from British Columbia, Canada, to outpost camps owned by various resorts. On August 1, the firm's trial balance was as follows:

LO4, 5, 6

✔

BC BACK-COUNTRY AIRLINES, INC.		
Unadjusted Trial Balance		
August 1, 2013		
	Debit	Credit
Cash	$ 82,600	
Accounts receivable	23,200	
Accounts payable		$ 1,700
Notes payable		3,000
Common stock		80,000
Retained earnings		21,100
Totals	$105,800	$105,800

During August the following transactions occurred:

Aug. 1 Paid August rental cost for aircraft, dockage, and dockside office, $6,000.
　　2 Paid the insurance premium for August, $2,800.
　　3 Paid for August advertising in various sports magazines, $1,500.
　　4 Rendered services for various groups for cash, $16,750.
　　5 Billed the Canadian Ministry of Natural Resources for services in transporting mapping personnel, $3,900.
　　6 Received $20,400 on account from clients.
　　7 Paid $1,700 on accounts payable.
　　8 Billed various clients for services, $19,400.
　　9 Paid interest on an outstanding note payable for August, $75.
　　10 Paid August wages, $14,800.
　　11 Received invoice for the cost of fuel used during August, $3,600.
　　12 Paid a cash dividend, $4,500 (debit Retained Earnings).

Required

a. Set up accounts for each item in the August 1 trial balance and enter the beginning balances. Also provide similar accounts for the following items: Service Fees Earned, Wages Expense, Advertising Expense, Rent Expense, Fuel Expense, Insurance Expense, and Interest Expense. Create journal entries and record the transactions for August in the appropriate T-accounts, using the dates given.

b. Prepare a trial balance as of August 31, 2013.

P2-15B. Transaction Analysis and Trial Balance William Groff opened a tax practice on June 1. The following accounts will be needed to record the business's transactions for June: Cash; Accounts Receivable; Office Supplies; Tax Library; Office Furniture and Fixtures; Accounts Payable; Notes Payable; Common Stock; Dividends; Professional Fees Earned; Rent Expense; Salaries Expense; Advertising Expense; Utilities Expense; and Interest Expense. The following transactions occurred in June:

LO4, 5, 6

✔

June 1 Groff opened a business checking account at a local bank, investing $20,000 in his practice in exchange for common stock.
　　2 Purchased office furniture and fixtures for $9,800, paid $2,800 cash, and gave a note payable for the balance.
　　3 Purchased books and software for a tax library on account, $5,700.
　　4 Purchased office supplies for cash, $560.
　　5 Paid rent for June, $950.

June 6 Returned $300 of books with defective bindings. The return reduced the amount owed to the supplier.

7 Billed clients for professional services rendered, $17,600.

8 Paid $1,700 on account for the library items purchased on June 3.

9 Collected $15,900 on account from clients billed on June 7.

10 Paid June salaries, $4,900.

11 Received an invoice for June advertising, to be paid in July, $300.

12 The business paid stockholders a cash dividend of $800.

13 Paid utilities for June, $160.

14 Paid interest for June on an outstanding note payable, $60.

Required

a. Prepare journal entries and record the above transactions in T-accounts, and key entries with the numbers of the transactions.

b. Prepare a trial balance from the general ledger as of June 30.

LO4, 5, 6 **P2-16B. Transaction Analysis and the Effect of Errors on the Trial Balance**

The following T-accounts contain numbered entries for the May transactions of the Claremont Corporation, an architectural firm, which opened its offices on May 1:

	Cash				Accounts Payable		
(1)	50,000	1,400	(4)	(5)	310	1,530	(3)
(10)	5,200	5,950	(7)	(8)	1,000	290	(9)
		1,000	(8)				

	Accounts Receivable				Common Stock	
(6)	8,750	5,200	(10)		50,000	(1)

	Supplies				Professional Fees Earned	
(3)	1,530	310	(5)		8,750	(6)

	Office Equipment			Rent Expense
(2)	5,000		(4)	1,400

	Notes Payable			Utilities Expense
	5,000	(2)	(9)	290

	Salaries Expense
(7)	5,950

Required

a. Give a description of each of the 10 numbered transactions entered in the above accounts. Example: (1) Claremont Corporation issued common stock for cash, $50,000.

b. The following trial balance, prepared for Claremont Corporation as of May 31, contains several errors. Itemize the errors, and indicate the correct totals for the trial balance.

CLAREMONT CORPORATION
Unadjusted Trial Balance
May 31, 2013

	Debit	Credit
Cash.	$ 91,850	
Accounts receivable.	3,550	
Supplies	1,220	
Office equipment		$ 5,000
Accounts payable.		510
Notes payable		50,000
Common stock.		50,000
Professional fees earned		8,570
Rent expense	1,400	
Utilities expense.	290	
Salaries expense	5,950	
Totals	$104,260	$114,080

P2-17B. Transaction Analysis and Trial Balance Walsh & Company, electrical contractors, began operations on May 1. The following transactions occurred during the month of May: **LO5, 6**

May   1   Stockholders invested $50,000 in the business in exchange for common stock.
2   Purchased equipment on account, $4,200.
3   Returned $200 of equipment that was not satisfactory. The return reduced the amount owed to the supplier.
4   Purchased supplies on account, $860.
5   Purchased a truck for $10,500. Walsh paid $5,500 cash and gave a note payable for the balance.
6   Paid rent for May, $875.
7   Paid fuel cost for truck, $60.
8   Billed customers for services rendered, $13,700.
9   Paid $3,000 on account for equipment purchased on May 2.
10   Paid utilities for May, $210.
11   Received invoice for May advertising, to be paid in June, $280.
12   Paid employees' wages, $3,350.
13   Collected $8,600 on accounts receivable.
14   Walsh paid stockholders a dividend of $1,500 cash.
15   Paid interest for May on an outstanding note payable, $80.

Required

a.   Create journal entries and record the above transactions in T-accounts, and key entries with the numbers of the transactions. The following accounts will be needed to record the transactions for May: Cash; Accounts Receivable; Supplies; Equipment; Truck; Accounts Payable; Notes Payable; Common Stock; Dividends; Service Revenue; Rent Expense; Wages Expense; Utilities Expense; Truck Expense; Advertising Expense; and Interest Expense.

b.   Prepare a trial balance as of May 31.

SERIAL PROBLEM: KATE'S CARDS

(Note: This is a continuation of the Serial Problem: Kate's Cards from Chapter 1.)

SP2.   In September 2013, Kate incorporated Kate's Cards after investigating different organizational forms, and began the process of getting her business up and running. The following events occurred during the month of September 2013:

1.   Kate deposited $10,000 that she had saved into a newly opened business checking account. She received common stock in exchange.
2.   Kate designed a brochure that she will use to promote her greeting cards at local stationery stores.
3.   Kate paid Fred Simmons $50 to critique her brochure before undertaking her final design and printing.
4.   Kate purchased a new iMac computer tablet, specialized graphic arts software, and commercial printer for the company, paying $4,800 in cash. She decided to record all of these items under the same equipment account.
5.   Kate purchased supplies such as paper and ink for $350 at the local stationery store. She opened a business account with the store and was granted 30 days credit on all purchases, including the one she just made.
6.   Kate designed her first 5 cards and prepared to show them to potential customers.
7.   The owner of the stationery store where Kate opened her account was impressed with Kate's work and ordered 1,000 of each of the five card designs at a cost of $1 per card, or $5,000 total. Kate tells the customer that she will have them printed and delivered within the week.
8.   Kate purchased additional supplies, on account, in the amount of $1,500.
9.   Kate delivered the 5,000 cards. Because the owner knows that Kate is just starting out, he paid her immediately in cash. He informed her that if the cards sell well that he will be ordering more, but would expect a 30-day credit period like the one he grants to his own business customers.
10.   The cost to Kate for the order was $1,750 of the supplies she had purchased. (*Hint:* This cost should be recorded as a debit to an expense called Cost of Goods Sold.)

11. Kate paid her balance due for the supplies in full.

12. Kate decided that she should have special renters' insurance to cover the business equipment she now owns. She purchased a one-year policy for $1,200, paying the entire amount in cash. (*Hint:* Two accounts will need to be debited here, one for the current month expense and one for the prepaid amount.)

13. Kate determined that all of her equipment will have a useful life of 4 years (48 months) at which time it will not have any resale or scrap value. (*Hint:* Kate will expense 1/48th of the cost of the equipment each month to Depreciation Expense. The credit will be to Accumulated Depreciation.)

14. Kate paid herself a salary of $1,000 for the month.

Required

a. Prepare a general ledger with the following accounts: Cash; Accounts Receivable; Supplies Inventory; Prepaid Insurance; Equipment; Accumulated Depreciation; Accounts Payable; Common Stock; Retained Earnings; Sales Revenue; Cost of Goods Sold; Consulting Expense; Insurance Expense; Depreciation Expense; Wages Expense. Prepare journal entries for the above transactions using these accounts.

b. Post the accounting transactions for the month of September 2013 to the general ledger T-accounts.

c. Prepare a trial balance for Kate's Cards as of September 30, 2013.

EXTENDING YOUR KNOWLEDGE

REPORTING AND ANALYSIS

COLUMBIA
SPORTSWEAR
COMPANY

EYK2-1.   **Financial Reporting Problem: Columbia Sportswear Company** The financial statements for the **Columbia Sportswear Company** can be found in Appendix A at the end of this book. The following selected accounts, in thousands, are from those statements:

Common stock.	$ 3,037
Accounts payable.	148,973
Accounts receivable.	351,538
Inventories	365,199
Prepaid expenses and other current assets.	36,392
Property, plant, and equipment	250,910
Net sales.	1,693,985

Required

a. For each of these accounts, indicate whether a debit or a credit is required to increase its balance.

b. What other account is likely involved when:
   1. Accounts receivable is increased?
   2. Accounts payable is decreased?
   3. Net sales are increased?

COLUMBIA
SPORTSWEAR
COMPANY

UNDER ARMOUR,
INC.

EYK2-2.   **Comparative Analysis Problem: Columbia Sportswear Company vs. Under Armour, Inc.** The financial statements for the **Columbia Sportswear Company** can be found in Appendix A and **Under Armour, Inc.**'s financial statements can be found in Appendix B at the end of this book.

Required

a. Each of the following accounts is listed in the company's financial statements:

	Columbia Sportswear		Under Armour, Inc.
1	Accounts receivable	1	Inventories
2	Property, plant, and equipment	2	Provision for income taxes
3	Accounts payable	3	Long term debt
4	Common stock	4	Retained earnings
5	Interest income	5	Cost of goods sold

Determine the normal balance (debit or credit) for each of the accounts listed above.

b. Identify the probable other account involved when:

1. Cost of goods sold is increased.
2. Interest income is increased.
3. Accounts receivable is decreased.
4. Income taxes payable is increased.

EYK2-3.   **Business Decision Problem**

Sarah Penney operates the Wildlife Picture Gallery, selling original art and signed prints received on consignment (rather than purchased) from recognized wildlife artists throughout the country. The firm receives a 30 percent commission on all art sold and remits 70 percent of the sales price to the artist. All art is sold on a cash basis.

Sarah began the business on March 1, 2013. She received a $10,000 loan from a relative to help her get started. Sarah signed a note agreeing to repay the loan in one year. No interest is being charged on the loan, but the relative does expect to receive a set of financial statements each month. On April 1, 2013, Sarah asks for your help in preparing the financial statements for the first month.

Sarah has carefully kept the firm's checking account up to date and provides you with the following complete listing of the cash receipts and disbursements for March 2013:

Cash Receipts

Original investment by Sarah Penney in exchange for common stock	$ 6,500
Loan from relative	10,000
Sales of art	95,000
Total cash receipts	$111,500

Cash Disbursements

Payments to artists for sales made	$ 54,000
Payment of March rent for gallery space	900
Payment of March staff wages	4,900
Payment of airfare for personal vacation of Sarah Penney (vacation will be taken in April)	500
Total cash disbursements	60,300
Cash balance, March 31, 2013	$ 51,200

Sarah also gives you the following documents she has received:

1. A $350 invoice for March utilities; payment is due by April 15, 2013.
2. A $1,700 invoice from Careful Express for the shipping of the artwork sold during March; payment is due by April 10, 2013.
3. The one-year lease she signed for the gallery space; as an incentive to sign the lease, the landlord reduced the first month's rent by 25 percent; the monthly rent starting in April is $1,200.

In your discussions with Sarah, she tells you that she has been so busy that she is behind in sending artists their share of the sales proceeds. She plans to catch up within the next week.

Required

From the above information, prepare the following financial statements for Wildlife Picture Gallery: (a) income statement for the month of March 2013; (b) statement of stockholders' equity for the month of March 2013; and (c) balance sheet as of March 31, 2013. To obtain the data needed, you may wish to use T-accounts to construct the company's accounts.

EYK2-4.   **Financial Analysis Problem**   Tim Johnson runs a local photography studio, Action Images, Inc. Action Images is organized as a corporation. Tim's primary sources of revenue are from the events he is contracted to photograph, mostly sporting events, and from photography lessons given at a local community college. Most of Tim's photographic event customers pay him soon after they receive an invoice from Tim, approximately one week after the event, although in some cases Tim receives payment on the day of the event. The community college pays Tim at the end of each month that he teaches a class. Tim maintains the following accounts to account for these revenue transactions: Cash, Accounts Receivable, Photographic Revenue, Teaching Revenue.

Tim leases the studio where he does most of his work. He owns all his equipment, which consists of cameras, lenses, lighting, a computer, printer, furniture, and miscellaneous office equipment. These assets are accounted for in the following accounts: Photographic Equipment, Office Equipment, and Furniture.

Tim does most of the work himself, but he does employ part-time help on days of his photo events, and he also employs a part-time bookkeeper. Most months Tim has expenses for the studio rent, utilities, advertising, supplies, and insurance. The following accounts are used to account for these expenses: Rent Expense, Utilities Expense, Salaries Expense, Advertising Expense, Supplies Expense, and Insurance Expense.

Tim pays himself a monthly salary. In addition, if his business does well, he will receive a dividend from Action Images. The following stockholders' equity accounts are maintained by Tim: Common Stock and Retained Earnings.

During the month of November, Tim hired a new bookkeeper while his regular bookkeeper was away on vacation. The new bookkeeper was inexperienced, and Tim is concerned that things may not have been recorded correctly. He has asked you to review the following transactions. For each transaction, Tim provides you with the account, the amount either debited or credited, and an explanation for the transaction. In each case, the explanation is correct.

	Account	Debit	Credit
1	Cash	5,000	
	Photographic revenue		5,000
	Issued common stock in exchange for cash.		
2	Cash	2,000	
	Teaching revenue		2,000
	Received $2,000 from the community college for course taught.		
3	Cash	4,500	
	Accounts receivable		5,400
	Received $4,500 from customers for work done last month.		
4	Photographic equipment	1,600	
	Cash		1,600
	Purchase of a new camera for $1,600.		
5	Utilities expense	3,000	
	Cash		3,000
	To pay the month's rent on the studio.		
6	Supplies expense	150	
	Accounts receivable		150
	Purchased printing supplies on account.		
7	Salaries expense	3,000	
	Cash		3,000
	Paid the salaries for the month.		

Required
a. For each entry, state if it is correct. If the entry is in error, make the necessary correction.
b. Will any of the errors cause the trial balance to be out of balance?
c. What effect did the errors have on Tim's net income for November?

CRITICAL THINKING

GENERAL MILLS, INC.

EYK2-5. **Accounting Research Problem** Go to this book's Website and locate the annual report of **General Mills, Inc.** for the year ending May 29, 2011 (fiscal year 2011).

Required
1. For each of the income statement accounts, indicate the normal balance.
2. For each of the balance sheet accounts, indicate the normal balance.

EYK2-6. **Accounting Communication Activity** Fred Jones is struggling with some accounting concepts and has come to you for help. In particular he does not understand what is meant by a debit and a credit. He was especially confused when he learned that sometimes debits result in account increases and sometimes debits result in account decreases.

Required

Write a short memorandum to Fred that explains what is meant by debits and credits as it applies to accounts used by a company.

EYK2-7. **Accounting Ethics Case** Andy Frame and his supervisor are sent on an out-of-town assignment by their employer. At the supervisor's suggestion, they stay at the Spartan Inn, across the street from the Luxury Inn. After three days of work, they settle their lodging bills and leave. On the return trip, the supervisor gives Andy what appears to be a copy of a receipt from the Luxury Inn for three nights of lodging. Actually, the supervisor indicates that he prepared the Luxury Inn receipt on his office computer and plans to complete his expense reimbursement request using the higher lodging costs from the Luxury Inn.

Required

What are the ethical considerations that Andy faces when he prepares his expense reimbursement request?

EYK2-8. **Corporate Social Responsibility Problem** The Global Reporting Initiative (GRI) is a network-based organization that has pioneered the development of the world's most widely used sustainability reporting framework. The GRI Website is located at http://www.globalreporting.org/. Sustainability reporting differs from financial reporting in several areas. One difference that is readily apparent is that sustainability reports contain performance metrics that are measured in units other than dollars. For example, greenhouse emissions may be measured in metric tons and employee in-kind volunteering may be measured in hours.

Required

Go to the GRI Website and near the bottom, left of the page, under Useful Pages, select Disclosure Database. Use the Search feature in the middle of the page to select a report of one of the listed firms. What are some of the areas that the company reports on, and what measures do they use?

EYK2-9. **Forensic Accounting Problem** Accrual accounting is based on the idea that revenue should be recognized when earned and that any resources consumed in the revenue-generating process (expenses) should be matched with those revenues in the same period. Another basic principle on which GAAP is based is that of the accounting period. This principle sets the time period for which the revenues and expenses are to be measured and matched. For many firms, this date is December 31. Revenues earned after December 31 are to be reported in the following period, and expenses in the following period are then matched to those revenues. One way that companies have been found to misrepresent their reported performance is to violate these principles by "holding the books open" beyond December 31. In other words, the firm will improperly record revenue earned after year-end as if it were earned in the current year, and at the same time, fail to properly match the expenses associated with those revenues. How might a forensic accountant who has been hired to investigate improper financial reporting catch this type of activity?

EYK2-10. **IFRS Financial Statements** Thomson Reuters is a global information company created by the 2008 merger of the Thomson Corporation, a Canadian company, with the Reuters Company, a United Kingdom-based company. The company operates in over 100 countries and has over 50,000 employees. The company provides financial, legal, scientific, and tax information services to the public on a fee basis. The shares of Thomson Reuters are listed on the New York Stock Exchange and the Toronto Stock Exchange. The company prepares its financial statements using Canadian GAAP but also reconciles them to IFRS. In 2011, the company reported net earnings of $2,579 billion U.S. dollars under Canadian GAAP but a loss of $1,392 billion U.S. dollars under IFRS, a difference of over $3,971 million. You can view the company's financial statements and the Canadian GAAP-IFRS reconciliation at www.thomsonreuters.com.

Required

1. What are the advantages of having a single, global set of accounting standards like IFRS?
2. A competitor of Thomson Reuters is U.S.-based Bloomberg L.P, a closely held financial software, news and data company founded by Michael Bloomberg, mayor of New York City. Bloomberg prepares its financial statements using U.S. GAAP. What constraints would you face in trying to compare the financial results of Thomson Reuters to Bloomberg?

EYK2-11. Working with the Takeaways

Part A

Each of the following accounts from the Furst Company has a normal balance as of December 31, 2013, the end of Furst's first year of operations.

Cash.............................	$100	Common stock.....................	$500
Accounts receivable.................	300	Dividends.........................	100
Inventory..........................	250	Sales revenue......................	800
Property, plant, and equipment........	750	Selling expenses	300
Accounts payable...................	150	Administrative expenses	50
Notes payable	400		

Required

Prepare a trial balance for Furst Company as of December 31, 2013.

Part B

Lampe Distributors was formed to serve as a distributor of fine furnishings imported from overseas manufacturers. Assume the following trial balance was prepared as of December 31, 2013, at the end of Lampe's first year of operations:

LAMPE DISTRIBUTORS Unadjusted Trial Balance December 31, 2013		
	Debit	**Credit**
Cash..	$ 23,000	
Accounts receivable.......................................	4,500	
Buildings...	72,000	
Equipment	20,500	
Inventory...	38,000	
Accounts payable..		$ 5,500
Notes payable		47,750
Common stock...		42,000
Dividends	6,000	
Sales revenue...		280,250
Wage expense	100,000	
Selling expenses	31,000	
Rent expense...	23,000	
Administrative expenses	15,750	
Tax expense..	23,000	
Totals	$356,750	$375,500

It is apparent that there is an error somewhere in the company's accounts since the sum of the debit account balances ($356,750) does not equal the sum of the credit account balances ($375,500). After further research, we learn the following:

1. A cash purchase of $20,000 in inventory, occurring near year-end, was not recorded.
2. By mistake, $5,000 that should have been recorded as Accounts Payable was recorded as Notes Payable.
3. A credit of $26,000 was accidentally recorded in the Wage Expense account rather than in Sales Revenue.
4. A sale on account of $18,750 was correctly recorded as Sales Revenue, but the other side of the entry was mistakenly never recorded.

Required

a. Which of the four errors, if any, is the reason that the trial balance is not in balance?
b. Which of the errors, if any, must be corrected?
c. Prepare a corrected trial balance.

ANSWERS TO SELF-STUDY QUESTIONS:

1. d, (pp. 102–106) 2. a, (pp. 102–106) 3. b, (pp. 102–106) 4. c, (pp. 107–108) 5. b, (p. 108)
6. d, (p. 108) 7. b, (p. 108) 8. c, (p. 109) 9. d, (p. 109) 10. a, (p. 109) 11. d, (p. 117)
12. d, (p. 118) 13. d, (p. 111) 14. a, (pp. 111–112) 15. c, (p. 100) 16. d, (p. 103)

YOUR TURN! SOLUTIONS

Solution 2.1

		Cash	+	Accounts Receivable	+	Equipment	=	Accounts Payable	+	Notes Payable	+	Common Stock	+	Retained Earnings
a.		$ 5,000	+	$ 5,200	+	$ 0	=	$1,000	+	$2,500	+	$5,500	+	$1,200
b.	(1)	−600						−600						
	(2)	−3,600												−3,600
	(3)			+11,500										+11,500
	(4)							+500						−500
	(5)	+10,000		−10,000										
	(6)	−2,400												−2,400
	(7)							+680						−680
	(8)	−20												−20
	(9)	−900												−900
	(10)	−4,000				+4,000								
		$ 3,480	+	$ 6,700	+	$4,000	=	$1,580	+	$2,500	+	$5,500	+	$4,600

$14,180 $14,180

Solution 2.2

a. Debit
b. Credit
c. Debit
d. Credit
e. Debit
f. Credit
g. Debit

Solution 2.3

1.

		Assets					Liabilities		Equity			
										Retained Earnings		
		Cash	+	Accounts Receivable	+	Office Supplies =	Accounts Payable	+	Revenues	− Expenses	− Dividends	
a.		$ 1,300	+	$ 0	+	$ 0 =	$ 0	+	$1,300	− $ 0	− $ 0	Service revenue
b.		−2,400								−2,400		Wages expense
c.		600		−600								
d.		−400									−400	Dividends
e.						700	700					
f.				900					900			Service revenue
g.		−500					−500					

2. a. | Cash | 1,300 |
  Service revenue | | 1,300
  Revenue payment for services rendered.

b. | Wages expense | 2,400 |
  Cash | | 2,400
  Paid employee wages.

c. | Cash | 600 |
  Accounts receivable | | 600
  Received payment from clients.

d. | Dividends | 400 |
  Cash | | 400
  Paid cash dividend.

e. | Office supplies | 700 |
  Accounts payable | | 700
  Purchased office supplies on account.

f. | Accounts receivable | 900 |
  Service revenue | | 900
  Billed clients for services rendered.

g. | Accounts payable | 500 |
  Cash | | 500
  Paid suppliers.

3.

	Cash					**Accounts Receivable**		
(a)	1,300	2,400	(b)		(f)	900	600	(c)
(c)	600	400	(d)					
		500	(g)					

	Office Supplies					**Accounts Payable**		
(e)	700				(g)	500	700	(e)

	Service Revenue					**Wages Expense**		
		1,300	(a)		(b)	2,400		
		900	(f)					

	Dividends		
(d)	400		

Solution 2.4

Devin Company
Unadjusted Trial Balance
December 31, 2013

	Debit	Credit
Cash..	$ 1,500	
Accounts receivable..	4,500	
Inventory..	3,750	
Property, plant, and equipment...............................	11,250	
Accounts payable...		$ 2,250
Notes payable		6,000
Common stock...		7,500
Dividends	1,500	
Sales revenue..		12,000
Salary expense...	4,500	
Administrative expenses	750	
Totals...	$27,750	$27,750

3

Accrual Basis of Accounting

PAST

Chapter 2 explained how we analyze and record transactions (the first two steps in the *accounting cycle*), including the system of debits and credits.

PRESENT

This chapter completes our examination of the final three steps in the five-step accounting cycle: adjust, report, and close.

FUTURE

Chapter 4 examines the balance sheet and income statement more closely and introduces techniques for analyzing and interpreting financial statements.

LEARNING OBJECTIVES

1. **Explain** the accrual basis of accounting and contrast it with the cash basis with reference to revenue and expense recognition. *(p. 118)*

2. **Describe** the adjusting process and **illustrate** the four major types of adjusting entries. *(p. 120)*

3. **Explain** the adjusted trial balance and use it to prepare financial statements. *(p. 129)*

4. **Describe** the closing process and **summarize** the accounting cycle. *(p. 131)*

5. Appendix 3A: **Describe** the process of closing to the Income Summary account and **summarize** the accounting cycle. *(p. 137)*

6. Appendix 3B: **Explain** how to use a worksheet in the adjusting and closing process. *(p. 140)*

MAKING DOUGH

Krispy Kreme is similar to other companies when it comes to the end-of-year accounting processes. As it closes its books for the year, its employees must get the accounting information organized to prepare the financial statements for its annual report. That process normally requires several accounting adjustments to properly determine how well a company performed and its financial condition.

Many estimates, assumptions, and judgments make up these accounting adjustments. Krispy Kreme's recent annual report had a fiscal year-end of January 29. However, because of those adjustments and other year-end procedures, it did not file its audited financial statements until March 30, two months later.

Accounting adjustments are important to investors and others that rely on financial statements for valuing company stock. Not long ago, Krispy Kreme was a high-flying company with a stock price of nearly $50 per share. Today, its stock is selling for just $6 per share.

What precipitated such a dramatic drop in its stock price? One reason suggested by Wall Street pundits is Krispy Kreme's accounting methods. It appears that some adjustments that Krispy Kreme made for its estimate of doubtful accounts, and its method of accounting for the purchase of franchise stores, propped up its earnings much like the yeast in its donuts. When investors began to question the "quality" of Krispy Kreme's earnings, a sharp sell-off of its stock followed as worried stockholders moved their money to alternative investments.

Why are accounting adjustments so important? This chapter focuses on that question. It explains the importance of those adjustments for financial statements. It also shows how companies account for adjustments and how financial statements are prepared from final adjusted numbers.

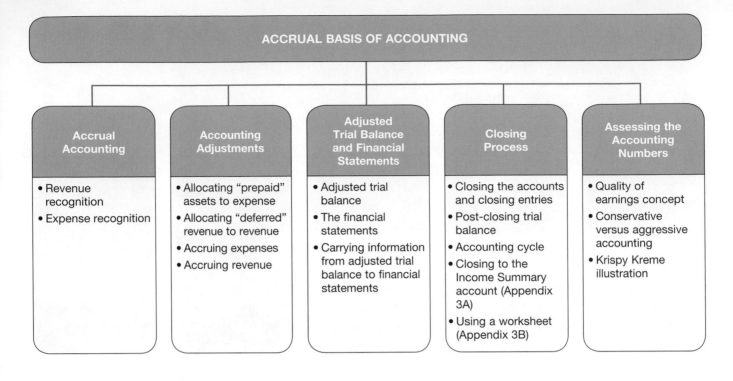

ACCRUAL BASIS OF ACCOUNTING

LO1 **Explain** the accrual basis of accounting and contrast it with the cash basis with reference to revenue and expense recognition.

Most individuals, and some small businesses, measure their financial performance by looking at their cash flow. For example, an individual who pays for all of her purchases from a checking account is likely to evaluate her financial well-being in terms of her available cash. If she ends the period with a higher cash balance than she started with, she is likely to conclude that she generated a profit.

The cash basis of accounting is not considered generally accepted for most businesses. Generally accepted accounting principles require that companies use the accrual basis of accounting. The accrual basis of accounting requires a business to measure and report its operating performance without the necessity of insuring that all revenues have been collected in cash and all expenses have been paid with cash.

Revenue Recognition Principle

Under the cash basis of accounting, the receipt and payment of cash is the determining factor for when sales revenue is recognized and when expenses are deducted. Under the accrual basis of accounting, sales revenue is recognized when it is earned, regardless of when the related cash is collected; and, expenses are recognized when incurred, regardless of whether cash has been paid. For most businesses, this means that its sales revenue is recognized at the time that goods and services are delivered to a customer. This may occur before, after, or at the same time that cash is received.

Cash Received *When* Revenue Is Earned

For most sales, **Krispy Kreme** will receive cash at the same time that the customer receives donuts. Under these circumstances, accrual accounting recognizes sales revenue at the same time that the company receives payment for its product. As a consequence, Krispy Kreme will debit Cash and credit Sales Revenue.

A = L + SE	April 30	Cash	100	
+100 + 100 Rev.		Sales revenue		100
		To record revenue at time of cash receipt.		

Cash Received *After* Revenue Is Earned

Safeway purchases large quantities of Krispy Kreme donuts for resale in their grocery stores. Assume that Safeway agrees to pay for the donuts in thirty days following each purchase. Even though Krispy Kreme has not received any payment for the delivered donuts, the company has earned the right to receive the cash, and consequently, Krispy Kreme must recognize the sales revenue prior to cash collection. In this case, it will debit Accounts Receivable and credit Sales Revenue.

April 30	Accounts receivable	100		A = L + SE	
	Sales revenue		100	+100 + 100 Rev.	
	To recognize revenue earned.				
May 30	Cash	100		A = L + SE	
	Accounts receivable		100	+100	
	To recognize cash received.			−100	

Cash Received *Before* Revenue Is Earned

Assume that Albertsons prepays for its donut purchases by giving Krispy Kreme a cash payment prior to receiving any donuts. Even though Krispy Kreme has received cash, it has not earned the revenue, and thus, will defer the recognition of any sales revenue until earned, which is at the time of product delivery. Krispy Kreme will record a liability account, Unearned Revenue, until such time as the donuts are delivered to Albertsons and it earns the revenue. As these examples demonstrate, it is the earning of sales revenue that determines when revenue is recognized by a company under the accrual basis of accounting, and not the timing of the cash collection.

April 30	Cash	100		A = L + SE	
	Unearned revenue		100	+100 +100	
	To recognize the receipt of cash prior to revenue being earned.				
May 30	Unearned revenue	100		A = L + SE	
	Sales revenue		100	−100 + 100 Rev.	
	To recognize earned revenue.				

Concept ➡	Method ➡	Assessment	TAKEAWAY 3.1
When should sales revenue be recognized?	Understand the nature of a company's earning process. Record revenue when it is earned.	Early recognition of revenue overstates current period revenue; recognizing revenue too late understates current period revenue.	

Expense Recognition (Matching) Principle

Accounting requires that the expenses incurred to generate revenues be recognized (matched) in the same period. In other words, business expenses are recognized (matched) with sales revenues so that they are reported on the same income statement. Like the recognition of revenue, the recognition of expenses can occur prior to, simultaneously with, or subsequent to the receipt of cash. It is the recognition of revenue, and not the payment of cash, that determines when expenses are recognized under the accrual basis of accounting.

Referring again to Krispy Kreme, assume the company pays $50 cash to acquire baking materials for its donuts. A cash purchase is not considered to be a business expense until Krispy Kreme sells the donuts it produces. The cash purchase of materials prior to sale would be accounted for as a reduction of cash and an increase in supplies, both assets.

May 15	Baking supplies	50		A = L + SE	
	Cash		50	+50	
	To record cash payment for supplies			−50	

The cash payment precedes the revenue recognition and the matching of expense. But what happens if the materials are purchased on account and used in donuts sold before the baking materials are paid for? In this case, the accrual basis of accounting dictates the recognition of expense prior to the cash payment for the materials so that the expense is properly matched with the earned revenue in the same accounting period.

A = L + SE	May 15	Baking supplies		50	
+50 +50		Accounts payable			50
		To record purchase of supplies on account			

In each of the above cases the expense is recognized when the donuts are sold with the following journal entry:

A = L + SE	May 15	Cost of goods sold		50	
−50 −50		Baking supplies			50
		To record cost of product sold			

The key point is that under accrual accounting the recognition of expense is matched to the recognition of revenue in the same period. This may occur after the cash expenditure, before the cash expenditure, or at the same time as the cash expenditure. In addition, it should be stressed that the purpose of accrual accounting is to adjust cash flows such that revenues and expenses are recognized in the period the revenue is earned and the corresponding resources to earn the revenue are used up. Ultimately both cash-based accounting and accrual accounting will yield the same results, however the results will likely differ period by period.

TAKEAWAY 3.2	**Concept** ➡	**Method** ➡	**Assessment**
	When should expenses be recognized?	Understand the nature of the company's earning process. Expenses should be recognized with the related revenue in the same accounting period.	Early recognition of expenses overstates current period expenses; recognizing expenses too late understates current period expenses.

ADJUSTING ACCOUNTS

LO2 Describe the adjusting process and **illustrate** the four major types of adjusting entries.

In Chapter 2, we analyzed a series of accounting transactions for WebWork, Inc., that occurred during the month of December. We prepared journal entries for those transactions and recorded them in the general journal. We then posted the company's journal entry data to the appropriate general ledger, which we set up in T-account form. Many of the general ledger account balances from Chapter 2, however, require an end-of-period adjustment to bring them to the correct balance for the preparation of WebWork's financial statements. For example, WebWork prepaid six months of rent for its office space on December 1. By December 31, one month's rent has expired, and thus, the prepaid rent account must be adjusted so that the account balance reflects the remaining amount of rent that is still prepaid. When it is time to prepare a company's financial statements, the company must review account balances and make any necessary end-of-period adjustments to bring those (unadjusted) accounts to their proper balance.

Unadjusted Trial Balance

The end-of-period adjustment process begins with the preparation of a trial balance of all general ledger accounts. Because this trial balance reports the account balances before any adjustments have been made, it is referred to as the **unadjusted trial balance**. An unadjusted trial balance is prepared to insure that the general ledger is in balance before the end-of-period adjusting process begins. Accumulating all general ledger account balances in one location makes it easier to review the accounts and determine which account balances must be adjusted. The unadjusted trial balance of WebWork, Inc., as of December 31 is in Exhibit 3-1.

Exhibit 3-1	Unadjusted Trial Balance for WebWork, Inc.	

WEBWORK, INC.
Unadjusted Trial Balance
December 31, 2012

	Debit	Credit
Cash..	$40,590	
Accounts receivable................................	1,340	
Office supplies.....................................	2,850	
Prepaid rent..	10,800	
Office equipment...................................	32,400	
Accounts payable...................................		$ 2,850
Unearned revenue...................................		3,000
Notes payable......................................		36,000
Common stock.......................................		30,000
Dividends...	500	
Fee revenue...		18,250
Wage expense..	1,620	
Totals..	$90,100	$90,100

Types of Adjustments

There are four types of accounting adjustments made at the end of an accounting period:

Prepaid Expenses	Unearned Revenues	Accrued Expenses	Accrued Revenues
Allocating previously recorded assets to expenses, to reflect the proper expenses incurred during that period.	Allocating previously recorded unearned revenue to earned revenue, to reflect revenues earned during the period.	Recording operating expenses that have not yet been paid or recorded, to reflect expenses incurred during the period.	Recording revenues that have not yet been received or recorded, to reflect revenue earned during the period.

Journal entries to record accounting adjustments are known as **adjusting entries**. Each adjusting entry affects one or more balance sheet accounts (an asset or liability account) and one or more income statement accounts (an expense or revenue account).

Adjustments in the first two categories—allocating "prepaid" assets to expense, and allocating "unearned" revenues to revenue—are referred to as **deferrals**. The distinguishing characteristic of a deferral is that the adjustment deals with an amount that has previously been recorded in a balance sheet account. The adjusting entry, in effect, decreases the balance sheet account and increases an income statement account. Adjustments in the last two categories—increasing expenses and increasing revenues—are referred to as **accruals**. The unique characteristic of an accrual is that the adjustment deals with an amount that has not previously been recorded in an account. Consequently, the adjusting entry increases both a balance sheet account and an income statement account.

Prepaid Expenses

Allocating Previously Recorded Assets to Expenses

Many expenditures benefit multiple accounting periods. These expenditures must be allocated over the periods benefited. Common examples include purchases of buildings, equipment, and supplies; prepayments of rent and advertising; and payments of insurance premiums covering more than one year. Outlays for these expenditures are normally debited to an asset account at the time of payment. Then, at the end of each accounting period, the estimated portion of the expenditure that has expired, or that has been used up, during the period is transferred from the asset account to an expense account to achieve a proper recognition of revenue and expenses.

These adjustments are commonly identified by inspecting the unadjusted trial balance for costs that benefit multiple accounting periods. For example, by looking at the December 31 trial balance of WebWork (Exhibit 3-1), we observe that adjustments are required to allocate costs of the purchased office supplies, the prepaid rent, and the office equipment to the current period (December) and subsequent accounting periods that benefit from these expenditures. The next three sections illustrate those adjustments.

Office Supplies

WebWork purchased office supplies on account and recorded the expenditure in an asset account, Office Supplies, as follows:

$$
\begin{array}{l}
A \;=\; L \;+\; SE \\
+2{,}850 \quad +2{,}850
\end{array}
$$

Dec. 1	Office supplies	2,850	
	Accounts payable		2,850
	To record the purchase of office supplies.		

During December, office supplies were used up as services were provided. The cost of office supplies used is an expense for December that reduces the amount of supplies available. It is unnecessary to record an expense as each individual supply item, such as a copier cartridge or LCD cleaner, is used up. Instead, at the end of December, the company physically counts the supplies still available and then subtracts that amount from the total amount purchased to determine the amount used up. For example, assume that a physical count of the office supplies reveals that $1,530 worth of WebWork's office supplies are available at the end of the month. This implies that $1,320 ($2,850 − $1,530) worth of supplies were used up during December. An adjusting entry is needed to transfer this amount to an expense account, Supplies Expense, as follows:

$$
\begin{array}{l}
A \;=\; L \;+\; SE \\
-1{,}320 \qquad\qquad -1{,}320 \\
\qquad\qquad\qquad\quad \text{Exp.}
\end{array}
$$

Dec. 31	Supplies expense	1,320	
	Office supplies		1,320
	To record expense of office supplies used in December.		

Office Supplies

Unadjusted	2,850		
		1,320	(a)
Adjusted	1,530		

Supplies Expense

Unadjusted	0	
(a)	1,320	
Adjusted	1,320	

When this adjusting entry is posted, it properly shows the $1,320 December expense for office supplies and reduces the asset account, Office Supplies, to $1,530, the actual amount of the asset remaining as of December 31.

Prepaid Rent

On December 1, WebWork paid six months' rent in advance and debited the $10,800 payment to Prepaid Rent, an asset account. As each day passes and the rented space is occupied, rent expense is being incurred, and the balance of the prepaid rent is decreasing. It is unnecessary to record rent expense on a daily basis because financial statements are not prepared daily; however, at the end of the accounting period, an adjusting entry is necessary to recognize the correct amount of rent expense for the period and to decrease the Prepaid Rent account. Specifically, on December 31, one month of WebWork's prepaid rent has been used up; consequently, WebWork will transfer $1,800 ($10,800/6 months) from the Prepaid Rent account to the Rent Expense account, as follows:

$$
\begin{array}{l}
A \;=\; L \;+\; SE \\
-1{,}800 \qquad\qquad -1{,}800 \\
\qquad\qquad\qquad\quad \text{Exp.}
\end{array}
$$

Dec. 31	Rent expense	1,800	
	Prepaid rent		1,800
	To record rent expense for December.		

The posting of this adjusting entry shows the correct rent expense ($1,800) for December in the Rent Expense account and reduces the Prepaid Rent account balance to the correct balance ($9,000) that remains prepaid as of December 31. (Examples of other prepaid expenses for which similar adjustments are made include prepaid insurance and prepaid advertising.)

Prepaid Rent			
Unadjusted	10,800		
		1,800	(b)
Adjusted	9,000		

Rent Expense		
Unadjusted	0	
(b)	1,800	
Adjusted	1,800	

Depreciation

The process of allocating the cost of buildings, equipment, and vehicles to the periods benefiting from their use is called **depreciation**. Because these long-lived assets help generate revenue for a company over many years, each accounting period in which the assets are used must reflect a portion of their cost as an expense. The allocation of a company's costs in these revenue-generating assets over the many periods that they help produce revenues is an application of the expense recognition principle; and, this periodic expense is known as *depreciation expense*.

There is no exact way to measure the amount by which these assets are used up each period, which means that the periodic depreciation expense is an estimate. The procedure used in this chapter estimates the annual amount of depreciation expense by dividing the acquisition cost of the asset by its estimated useful life in years. This method is called **straight-line depreciation**. (We will explore other depreciation methods in a later chapter.)

When recording depreciation expense, the asset account is not reduced directly. Instead, the reduction is recorded in a contra account called **Accumulated Depreciation**. The **contra accounts** are so named because they are used to record reductions in, or offsets against, a controlling account. The Accumulated Depreciation account has a normal credit balance and appears in the balance sheet as a deduction against its related asset account balance. Use of the contra account Accumulated Depreciation allows the original cost of the related asset to be reported in the company's balance sheet, followed by the accumulated amount of depreciation taken to date. Users of financial statements want to see both of these amounts so that they can estimate how much of an asset has been used up and how much remains to benefit the business in future periods.

Hint: A contra account is increased and decreased in the opposite way of its controlling account. Also, the normal balance of a contra account is opposite to the normal balance of its controlling account.

To illustrate, assume that the office equipment purchased by WebWork for $32,400 is expected to last six years. Straight-line depreciation is $5,400 per year ($32,400/6 years), or $450 per month ($5,400/12 months). At the end of December, WebWork would make the following adjusting entry:

Dec. 31	Depreciation expense	450	
	Accumulated depreciation—Office equipment		450
	To record December depreciation.		

A	= L	+	SE
−450			−450
			Exp

When the preceding adjusting entry is posted, it shows the estimated cost of using the asset during December, and shows the estimated expense ($450) in the company's December income statement. On the balance sheet, the accumulated depreciation is subtracted from the related asset account (Office Equipment). The resulting balance (acquisition cost less accumulated depreciation) is called the asset's **book value** and represents the unexpired asset cost to be applied as an expense against future periods. For example, the December 31, 2012, balance sheet shows WebWork's office equipment with a book value of $31,950, presented as follows:

Accumulated Depreciation—Office Equipment		
	0	Unadjusted
	450	(c)
	450	Adjusted

Depreciation Expense		
Unadjusted	0	
(c)	450	
Adjusted	450	

A.K.A. Book value is also called *carrying value.*

Office equipment	$32,400
Less: Accumulated depreciation	450
Office equipment, net.	$31,950

Unearned Revenues

Allocating Previously Recorded Unearned Revenue to Revenue

Sometimes a business receives fees for services or products before the services or products are rendered. Such transactions are initially recorded by debiting the Cash account and crediting a liability account called **Unearned Revenue**. The Unearned Revenue account is also called **Deferred Revenue** and represents an obligation to perform a service, or provide a product, in the future. Once the service or product is provided, the revenue is earned; and, this is recognized in the accounts by an adjusting entry with a debit to the Unearned Revenue account, which reduces the liability account, and a credit to the Revenue account for the amount of revenue earned in the current period.

Deferred Service Revenue

On December 5, WebWork signed a four-month contract to perform work for $750 per month, with the entire contract price of $3,000 received in advance. The journal entry made on December 5 was:

A   =   L   + SE
+3,000 +3,000

Dec. 5	Cash	3,000	
	Unearned revenue		3,000
	Received $3,000 advance payment on a four-month contract.		

On December 31, the following adjusting entry transfers $750, the revenue earned in December, to Fee Revenue and it reduces the liability Unearned Revenue by the same amount:

A = L   +   SE
     −750   +750 Rev..

Unearned Revenue

		3,000	Unadjusted
(d)	750		
		2,250	Adjusted

Fee Revenue

		18,250	Unadjusted
		750	(d)
		19,000	Adjusted

Dec. 31	Unearned revenue	750	
	Fee revenue		750
	To record portion of advance earned in December.		

After the journal entry is posted to the general ledger accounts, the liability account shows a balance of $2,250, the amount of future services still owed by WebWork and the Fee Revenue account reflects the $750 earned in December.

Other examples of revenues received in advance include rental prepayments by real estate management companies, insurance premiums received in advance by insurance companies, subscription revenues received in advance by magazine and newspaper publishers, and membership fees received in advance by health and fitness clubs. In each case, a liability account is established when the prepayment is initially received. Later, an adjusting entry is made to reflect the revenues earned from the services provided or products delivered during the current accounting period.

Accrued Expenses

Recording Previously Unrecorded Expenses

A company often incurs expenses before paying for them. Employee wages, utilities, and income taxes are all examples of expenses that are typically incurred by a business before payment is made. Usually the cash payments are made at regular time intervals, such as weekly, monthly, quarterly, or annually. If the accounting period ends on a date that does not coincide with a scheduled cash payment date, an adjusting entry must be recorded to reflect the expense incurred during the period. Such expenses are referred to as **accrued expenses**. WebWork has two such adjustments to make on December 31: for its employee wages and the interest on its bank loan.

Accrued Wages

WebWork's employee is paid every two weeks at the rate of $810 per week. The employee was paid $1,620 on Friday, December 23. At the close of business on Friday, December 30, the employee has worked one week during December for which wages are not paid until January. Because the employee's wages are $810 per week, an additional wage expense of $810 must be reflected in WebWork's income statement for December. The adjusting entry at the end of December to accrue one week of wage expense follows:

Dec. 31	Wage expense	810	
	Wages payable		810
	To record accrued wages for the final week of December.		

A = L + SE
    +810   −810
            Exp

Wages Payable

	0	Unadjusted
	810	(e)
	810	Adjusted

Wage Expense

Unadjusted	1,620	
(e)	810	
Adjusted	2,430	

This adjustment enables WebWork's December income statement to show the cost of all wages *incurred* during the month rather than just the wages *paid*. Also, its balance sheet will correctly show a liability for unpaid wages at the end of December.

When the employee is paid on the next regular payday in January, WebWork must insure that the one week of accrued wages for December are not again charged to expense. When the employee is paid $1,620 on Friday, January 6, the following entry is made:

Jan. 6	Wages payable	810	
	Wage expense	810	
	Cash		1,620
	To record two weeks wages paid.		

A = L + SE
−1,620   −810   −810
                Exp.

This entry eliminates the liability recorded in Wages Payable at the end of December and debits January Wage Expense for only those wages earned by the employee in January.

Accrued Interest

On December 1, 2012, WebWork obtained a bank loan in the amount of $36,000 and signed a two-year note payable. The annual interest rate on the note is 10 percent, with interest payable each November 30. The first year's interest of $3,600 ($36,000 × 10 percent) is due on November 30, 2013. Because interest accumulates as time passes, an adjusting entry is needed on December 31, 2012, to reflect the interest expense for December. December's interest is $300 ($3,600/12 months), and the adjusting entry at December 31 follows:

Dec. 31	Interest expense	300	
	Interest payable		300
	To record accrued interest expense for December.		

A = L + SE
    +300   −300
            Exp

Interest Payable

	0	Unadjusted
	300	(f)
	300	Adjusted

Interest Expense

Unadjusted	0	
(f)	300	
Adjusted	300	

When this adjusting entry is posted to the general ledger, the correct interest expense for December is shown as well as a liability for one month's interest that has accrued as of December 31.

When the first year's interest of $3,600 is paid on November 30, 2013, WebWork must remember that $300 of that amount relates to 2012. On November 30, 2013, the following entry records the interest payment:

Nov. 30	Interest payable	300	
	Interest expense	3,300	
	Cash		3,600
	To record payment of annual interest.		

A = L + SE
−3,600   −300   −3,300
                 Exp.

This entry eliminates the interest payable that was accrued on December 31, 2012, and debits the Interest Expense account for $3,300 ($300 times 11 months), the correct interest expense for the first 11 months of 2013.

Recording Previously Unrecorded Revenues

Accrued Revenues

Revenues from selling a product or providing a service must be recognized in the period in which the goods are sold or the services are performed. A company, however, may provide services during a period that are neither paid for by customers nor billed at the end of the period. The value of these services represents revenue that must be included in the current period income statement. To accomplish this, end-of-period adjusting entries are made to reflect any revenues for the period that have been earned, but have not yet been paid or billed. Such accumulated revenue is often called **accrued revenue**.

Accrued Fees

WebWork entered into a contract with a local company on December 2 that requires a December 31 adjusting entry to accrue revenue. Under the one-year contract, WebWork agreed to maintain that company's Website in exchange for a monthly fee of $150, payable at the end of every three months. By December 31, WebWork has earned one month of fee revenue, and the following adjusting entry is made:

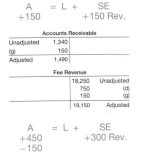

	A	= L +	SE	
	+150		+150 Rev.	

Dec. 31	Accounts receivable	150	
	Fee revenue		150
	To record accrued fee revenue earned in December.		

When WebWork receives the first $450 payment on February 28, 2013, the company must remember that $150 was previously earned and recorded in 2012. The following entry records the payment received on that date:

	A	= L +	SE	
	+450		+300 Rev.	
	−150			

Feb. 28	Cash	450	
	Accounts receivable		150
	Fee revenue		300
	To record receipt of quarterly payment.		

This entry eliminates the accounts receivable established on December 31, 2012, and records $300 of fee revenue earned for the first two months of 2013.

Accrued Interest

Another example of accrued revenue involves a company that has loaned money to another entity on which interest has been earned but that has not yet been collected at the end of the accounting period. The amount of the earned interest must be reflected in net income for the period. Interest revenue (or interest expense) is computed based on three factors: (1) the principal amount of the money loaned; (2) the rate of interest expressed as an annual rate; and (3) the amount of time in the calculation. Assume WebWork loaned $2,000 to James Corporation on November 1, 2012, with annual interest at the rate of 6 percent. The loan balance, along with interest, is to be repaid one year later. On December 31, 2012, WebWork would make the following entry:

	A	= L +	SE	
	+20		+20	

Dec. 31	Interest receivable	20	
	Interest income		20
	To record interest earned on note.		

The $20 interest is computed as follows:

Principal Amount of Note	×	Annual Interest Rate	×	Time as a fraction of a year	=	Interest
$2,000	×	6%	×	2/12	=	$20

Since WebWork did not actually have a loan to James Corporation, the adjustment calculated above will not be posted to the general ledger.

Summary of Accounting Adjustments

Exhibit 3-2 summarizes the adjusting entries for WebWork as recorded in its general journal. These adjustments are posted to the company's general ledger.

Exhibit 3-3 lists the four types of accounting adjustments along with showing (1) examples of how this type of adjustment arises, (2) the generic adjusting entry for each type of adjustment, and (3) what accounts are overstated or understated *prior to* any adjustment. As we explained, each adjustment affects one (or more) balance sheet (asset or liability) account and one (or more) income statement account (expense or revenue).

Exhibit 3-2	Adjusting Entries for WebWork, Inc.			

GENERAL JOURNAL

Date	Description	Debit	Credit	
2012				
Dec. 31	Supplies expense	1,320		(a)
	Office supplies		1,320	
	To record expense of office supplies used in December.			
Dec. 31	Rent expense	1,800		(b)
	Prepaid rent		1,800	
	To record rent expense for December.			
Dec. 31	Depreciation expense	450		(c)
	Accumulated depreciation—Office equipment		450	
	To record December depreciation.			
Dec. 31	Unearned revenue	750		(d)
	Fee revenue		750	
	To record portion of advance earned in December.			
Dec. 31	Wage expense	810		(e)
	Wages payable		810	
	To record accrued wages for the final week of December.			
Dec. 31	Interest expense	300		(f)
	Interest payable		300	
	To record accrued interest expense for December.			
Dec. 31	Accounts receivable	150		(g)
	Fee revenue		150	
	To record accrued fee revenue earned in December.			

Exhibit 3-3	Four Types of Accounting Adjustments			

Accounting Adjustment	Examples	Adjusting Entry	Financial Effects If Not Adjusted	
			Balance Sheet	Income Statement
Deferrals				
Prepaid expenses	Expiration of prepaid rent, insurance, and advertising; depreciation of buildings and equipment	Dr. Expense Cr. Asset (or contra asset)	Asset overstated Equity overstated	Expense understated
Unearned revenues	Use of prepayments on customer orders, gift cards, and subscriptions	Dr. Liability Cr. Revenue	Liability overstated Equity understated	Revenue understated
Accruals				
Accrued expenses	Incurred but not yet paid cash for wages, interest, and tax expenses	Dr. Expense Cr. Liability	Liabilty understated Equity overstated	Expense understated
Accrued revenues	Earned but not yet received cash for service, sales, and interest revenues	Dr. Asset Cr. Revenue	Asset understated Equity understated	Revenue understated

Concept →	Method →	Assessment	TAKEAWAY 3.3
When should an adjusting entry be made?	Individual account balances and transaction details such as contracts and agreements. Knowledge of the proper account balance is needed. Adjustments involve (1) allocating assets to expense, (2) allocating unearned revenue to revenue, (3) accruing expenses, or (4) accruing revenues.	Record an adjusting entry so that accounts are correctly reported; otherwise income and assets (and/or liabilities) are incorrectly reported.	

ADJUSTED TRIAL BALANCE AND FINANCIAL STATEMENTS

After the end-of-period adjustments are recorded in the general journal and posted to the general ledger, the company prepares an adjusted trial balance. The company then uses the adjusted trial balance to prepare financial statements.

Preparing the Adjusted Trial Balance

The **adjusted trial balance** lists all the general ledger account balances after the end-of-period adjustments have been posted. Exhibit 3-4 presents WebWork's adjusted trial balance as of December 31. Its adjusted trial balance is shown in the two right-hand columns of the exhibit. This exhibit begins with the unadjusted trial balance, shown in the two left-hand columns, and lists the seven adjustments in the middle columns. For example, the first adjusting entry adjusted office supplies for the $1,320 of supplies used in December. This adjustment is highlighted in Exhibit 3-4. First study Office Supplies which has a $2,850 debit balance in the unadjusted trial balance column. Next, the adjustment of a $1,320 credit appears in the credit column of the adjustments. This leads to a $1,530 debit balance in the adjusted trial balance. The adjusting entry also affects supplies expense, as shown in the exhibit. Supplies expense has a zero balance in the unadjusted trial balance. The adjustment appears as a $1,320 debit in the adjustments column, leading to a $1,320 debit balance in the adjusted trial balance for supplies expense. Using this presentation, managers can readily see the adjustments made and their impact on the financial accounting numbers. (Another common format for the adjusted trial balance is to only show the two right-hand columns as shown on the left side of Exhibit 3-5—either format is acceptable.)

Exhibit 3-4	Adjusted Trial Balance for WebWork, Inc.

WEBWORK, INC.
Adjusted Trial Balance
December 31, 2012

	Unadjusted Trial Balance		Adjustments				Adjusted Trial Balance	
	Debit	Credit	Debit		Credit		Debit	Credit
Cash..........................	$40,590						$40,590	
Accounts receivable.............	1,340		(g) $ 150				1,490	
Office supplies	2,850			(a)	$1,320		1,530	
Prepaid rent	10,800			(b)	1,800		9,000	
Office equipment	32,400						32,400	
Accumulated depreciation—								
Office equipment				(c)	450			$ 450
Accounts payable...............		$ 2,850						2,850
Interest payable				(f)	300			300
Wages payable..................				(e)	810			810
Unearned revenue		3,000	(d)	750				2,250
Notes payable		36,000						36,000
Common stock..................		30,000						30,000
Dividends	500						500	
Fee revenue		18,250		(d)	750			19,150
				(g)	150			
Supplies expense...............			(a)	1,320			1,320	
Wage expense	1,620		(e)	810			2,430	
Rent expense...................			(b)	1,800			1,800	
Depreciation expense...........			(c)	450			450	
Interest expense................			(f)	300			300	
Totals	$90,100	$90,100	$5,580		$5,580		$91,810	$91,810

YOUR TURN! 3.1

The solution is on page 175.

Prepare journal entries for each of the following end-of-year accounting adjustments.

1. Record depreciation expense adjustment of $700 on the company's buildings.
2. Record $1,500 for rent expense that was previously recorded as part of a $2,000 advance rent payment to the company's landlord.
3. Record $400 of revenue earned that was previously recorded as unearned revenue due to an advance payment from a customer.
4. Record $500 of accrued interest expense that applies to the company's bank loan. The $500 is part of the company's annual cash interest payment that is due next period.

Preparing Financial Statements

The adjusted trial balance is used to prepare the income statement, the statement of stockholders' equity, and the balance sheet. (It is also helpful in preparing the statement of cash flows; although other information is also necessary for it.) We illustrate the preparation of financial statements for Web-Work in Exhibit 3-5. Recall from Chapter 1 that financial statements are prepared in the following sequence: (1) the income statement, (2) the statement of stockholders' equity, (3) the balance sheet, and (4) the statement of cash flows.

LO3 **Explain** the adjusted trial balance and use it to prepare financial statements.

Income Statement

The income statement presents a company's revenues and expenses and discloses whether the company operated at a profit or a loss. WebWork's adjusted trial balance contains one revenue account and five expense accounts. The revenue and expense accounts are reported in WebWork's income statement located in the lower right side of Exhibit 3-5. As shown in this income statement, its net income for December is $12,850.

Statement of Stockholders' Equity

The statement of stockholders' equity reports the transactions and events causing a company's stockholders' equity to increase or decrease during an accounting period. The middle right side of Exhibit 3-5 presents WebWork's statement of stockholders' equity for December. The stockholders' equity accounts in the general ledger provides some of the information for this statement: the common stock and retained earnings balances at the beginning of the period, new common stock issuances, and dividends during the period. Since December was the first month of operations for WebWork, the beginning retained earnings balance is zero. The net income (or net loss) amount is obtained from the company's income statement.

Balance Sheet

The balance sheet reports a company's assets, liabilities, and stockholders' equity. The assets and liabilities for WebWork as of December 31, 2012, shown in the upper right side of Exhibit 3-5, come from the adjusted trial balance. The $12,350 amount reported as retained earnings is taken from the statement of stockholders' equity as of December 31.

Statement of Cash Flows

The statement of cash flows reports information regarding a company's cash inflows and outflows. The statement of cash flows classifies cash flows into three activity categories: operating, investing, and financing. The procedures for preparing a statement of cash flows are discussed in Chapter 12.

Exhibit 3-5	Financial Statements Prepared From the Adjusted Trial Balance

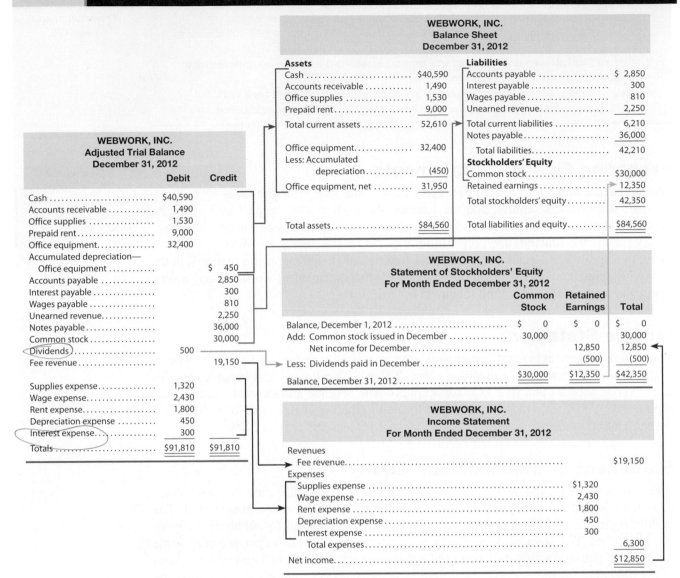

WEBWORK, INC.
Balance Sheet
December 31, 2012

Assets		Liabilities	
Cash	$40,590	Accounts payable	$ 2,850
Accounts receivable	1,490	Interest payable	300
Office supplies	1,530	Wages payable	810
Prepaid rent	9,000	Unearned revenue	2,250
Total current assets	52,610	Total current liabilities	6,210
		Notes payable	36,000
Office equipment	32,400	Total liabilities	42,210
Less: Accumulated		**Stockholders' Equity**	
depreciation	(450)	Common stock	$30,000
Office equipment, net	31,950	Retained earnings	12,350
		Total stockholders' equity	42,350
Total assets	$84,560	Total liabilities and equity	$84,560

WEBWORK, INC.
Adjusted Trial Balance
December 31, 2012

	Debit	Credit
Cash	$40,590	
Accounts receivable	1,490	
Office supplies	1,530	
Prepaid rent	9,000	
Office equipment	32,400	
Accumulated depreciation—		
Office equipment		$ 450
Accounts payable		2,850
Interest payable		300
Wages payable		810
Unearned revenue		2,250
Notes payable		36,000
Common stock		30,000
Dividends	500	
Fee revenue		19,150
Supplies expense	1,320	
Wage expense	2,430	
Rent expense	1,800	
Depreciation expense	450	
Interest expense	300	
Totals	$91,810	$91,810

WEBWORK, INC.
Statement of Stockholders' Equity
For Month Ended December 31, 2012

	Common Stock	Retained Earnings	Total
Balance, December 1, 2012	$ 0	$ 0	$ 0
Add: Common stock issued in December	30,000		30,000
Net income for December		12,850	12,850
Less: Dividends paid in December		(500)	(500)
Balance, December 31, 2012	$30,000	$12,350	$42,350

WEBWORK, INC.
Income Statement
For Month Ended December 31, 2012

Revenues		
Fee revenue		$19,150
Expenses		
Supplies expense	$1,320	
Wage expense	2,430	
Rent expense	1,800	
Depreciation expense	450	
Interest expense	300	
Total expenses		6,300
Net income		$12,850

PRINCIPLE ALERT	**Accounting Period Concept**

The income statement, the statement of stockholders' equity, and the statement of cash flows are financial statements covering periods of time. These statements illustrate the *accounting period concept*; the concept that useful financial statements can be prepared for arbitrary time periods within a company's total life span. Since a company does not complete all of its transactions by the end of an accounting period, accounting principles must provide a process to account for a company's continuing transactions. The end-of-period adjusting procedures provided by the accrual basis of accounting are that process. A major purpose of adjusting entries is to ensure that correct amounts of revenue and expense are reported for each accounting period.

YOUR TURN! 3.2	Cassi Company prepared the following adjusted trial balance to assist in the preparation of its December 31, 2013, financial statements.
The solution is on page 176.	

CASSI COMPANY Adjusted Trial Balance December 31, 2013	Debit	Credit
Cash...	$ 4,000	
Accounts receivable.............................	15,000	
Inventory......................................	18,000	
Prepaid rent...................................	5,000	
Equipment.....................................	50,000	
Accumulated depreciation.......................		$ 10,000
Accounts payable..............................		8,000
Salaries payable...............................		9,000
Dividends payable.............................		2,000
Unearned revenue.............................		5,000
Long-term debt................................		35,000
Common stock.................................		15,000
Retained earnings.............................		5,000
Sales revenue.................................		52,000
Cost of goods sold.............................	30,000	
Salaries expense..............................	5,000	
Rent expense..................................	6,000	
Depreciation expense..........................	6,000	
Dividends.....................................	2,000	
Totals..	$141,000	$141,000

Required

Prepare an income statement, a statement of stockholders' equity, and a balance sheet for Cassi Company using its December 31, 2013, adjusted trial balance. There were no changes in stockholders' equity during the year other than for net income and dividends.

The following section illustrates closing temporary accounts directly to Retained Earnings. Appendix 3A presents an alternative process that closes temporary accounts using the Income Summary account. Your instructor can choose to cover either one or both processes. If the process using Retained Earnings is skipped, then read Appendix 3A and return to the section (four pages ahead) titled, "Quality of Accounting Numbers."

CLOSING PROCESS

All accounts can be identified as either permanent accounts or temporary accounts. **Permanent accounts** are the accounts presented on the balance sheet. They consist of the asset, liability, and stockholders' equity accounts. The distinguishing feature of a permanent account is that any balance in the account at the end of an accounting period is carried forward to the following accounting period. **Temporary accounts** are used to gather information for a particular accounting period. Revenue, expense, and dividend accounts are temporary subdivisions of stockholders' equity. At the end of the accounting period, temporary account balances are transferred to Retained Earnings, which is a permanent stockholders' equity account. The process of transferring the balances in temporary accounts to Retained Earnings is referred to as the **closing process** or **closing procedures**.

A temporary account is *closed* when an entry is made that changes its account balance to zero—that is, the entry is equal in amount to the account's ending balance but is

LO4 **Describe** the closing process and **summarize** the accounting cycle.

A.K.A. Closing procedures are also known as *closing the books*.

opposite to the balance as a debit or credit. An account that is closed is said to be closed *to* the account that receives the offsetting debit or credit. Thus, a closing entry simply transfers the balance of one account to another account. Because closing entries bring temporary account balances to zero, the temporary accounts are then ready to start accumulating data for the next accounting period. In essence, closing the temporary accounts prevents information from the current accounting period from being carried forward to a subsequent period; and as a consequence, enables financial statement users to make meaningful comparisons of revenue and expenses from one period to the next. The following summarizes the classification of permanent and temporary accounts.

Permanent Accounts	Temporary Accounts
Assets	Revenues
Liabilities	Expenses
Common Stock	Dividends
Retained Earnings	

YOUR TURN! 3.3

The solution is on page 176.

For each of the following accounts, identify whether the account is either a permanent account or a temporary account:

a. Cash
b. Common Stock
c. Wage Expense
d. Notes Payable

e. Dividends
f. Sales Revenue
g. Inventory
h. Prepaid Expense

Journalizing and Posting the Closing Entries

The Retained Earnings account is used to close the temporary revenue, expense, and Dividends accounts. The closing entries occur only at the end of an accounting period and consist of three steps, which are graphically shown below.

1. **Close the revenue accounts.** Debit each revenue account for an amount equal to its current credit balance, and credit the Retained Earnings account for the total amount of earned revenue.
2. **Close the expense accounts.** Credit each expense account for an amount equal to its current debit balance, and debit the Retained Earnings account for the total amount of expenses.
3. **Close the Dividends account.** Debit the Retained Earnings account and credit the Dividends account for an amount equal to the balance in the Dividends account.

Closing Process for WebWork

Exhibit 3-6 illustrates the closing entries for WebWork as recorded in the company's general journal. The financial information in these entries is posted to the appropriate general ledger accounts, which is represented using T-accounts.

Exhibit 3-6	Closing Revenue, Expense, and Dividends Accounts—WebWork, Inc.		
	GENERAL JOURNAL		
Date	**Description**	**Debit**	**Credit**
2012			
1 Dec. 31	Fee revenue	19,150	
	Retained earnings		19,150
	To close the revenue account.		
2 Dec. 31	Retained earnings	6,300	
	Supplies expense		1,320
	Wage expense		2,430
	Rent expense		1,800
	Depreciation expense		450
	Interest expense		300
	To close the expense accounts.		
3 Dec. 31	Retained earnings	500	
	Dividends		500
	To close the dividends account.		

The financial effect of posting these entries on the general ledger is diagrammed below.

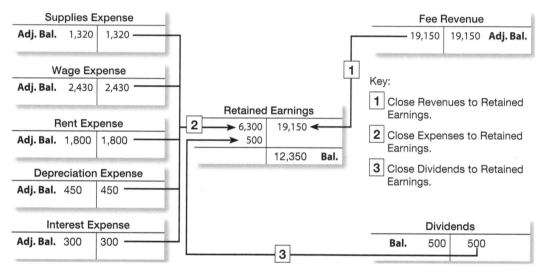

Preparing the Post-Closing Trial Balance

After closing entries are recorded in the general journal and posted to the general ledger, all of the temporary accounts have zero balances. At this point a **post-closing trial balance** is prepared. The post-closing trial balance provides evidence that an equality of debits and credits has been maintained in the general ledger throughout the adjusting and closing processes, and that the general ledger is in balance to start the next accounting period. Because the temporary accounts have been closed, only the balance sheet (or permanent) accounts appear in the post-closing trial balance. Exhibit 3-7 presents the post-closing trial balance for WebWork.

Exhibit 3-7	Post-Closing Trial Balance for WebWork, Inc.		

WEBWORK, INC.
Post-Closing Trial Balance
December 31, 2012

	Debit	Credit
Cash.	$40,590	
Accounts receivable.	1,490	
Office supplies	1,530	
Prepaid rent	9,000	
Office equipment	32,400	
Accumulated depreciation—Office equipment		$ 450
Accounts payable.		2,850
Interest payable		300
Wages payable.		810
Unearned revenue		2,250
Notes payable		36,000
Common stock.		30,000
Retained earnings		12,350
Totals	$85,010	$85,010

Summary of the Accounting Cycle

The sequence of accounting procedures known as the *accounting cycle* occurs each fiscal period and represents a systematic process for accumulating and reporting the financial data of a business. Exhibit 3-8 summarizes the five major steps in the accounting cycle as described in this and the preceding chapter.

Exhibit 3-8	The Accounting Cycle: A Summary

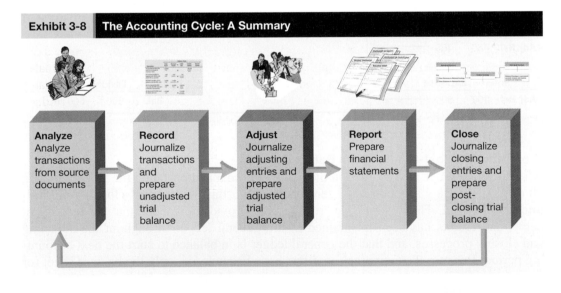

Analyze	**Record**	**Adjust**	**Report**	**Close**
Analyze transactions from source documents	Journalize transactions and prepare unadjusted trial balance	Journalize adjusting entries and prepare adjusted trial balance	Prepare financial statements	Journalize closing entries and prepare post-closing trial balance

YOUR TURN! 3.4

The solution is on page 177.

Prior to closing its books, the Morgan Company has the following balances in its temporary accounts as of December 31.

	Debit	Credit
Sales revenue		$79,000
Cost of goods sold	$41,000	
Wage expense	22,000	
Rent expense	3,000	
Depreciation expense	2,000	
Interest expense	4,000	
Dividends	5,000	

Required

Prepare closing entries as of December 31 for the Morgan Company.

For readers skipping the closing process using Retained Earnings, please resume reading here.

QUALITY OF ACCOUNTING NUMBERS

Earnings quality is a phrase used to characterize the degree to which a company's financial statements reflect its true financial condition and performance. The closer the statements represent the company's actual financial condition and performance, the higher a company's earnings quality is assumed to be.

While many end-of-period adjustments discussed in this chapter are based on direct calculations, such as the time remaining for a prepaid insurance policy or the interest rate on an outstanding loan, many other adjustments that we discuss in later chapters involve judgments on the part of the company's management. Examples of judgments leading to adjusting entries are the amount of future warranty work associated with a company's product, the amount of a company's accounts receivable that will not be collected, and the estimated depreciable lives of a company's plant and equipment. Each of these items involves estimates of future events that cannot be known with certainty. Consequently, each of these estimates can have a material effect on a company's reported financial results in any given period.

Wall Street analysts often evaluate a company's quality of earnings by the degree to which these estimates are considered conservative or aggressive. Conservative estimates are those that are more pessimistic, leading to lower reported net income and net asset values, while aggressive estimates are those that result in higher reported net income and net asset values. The more conservative a company's estimates are judged to be, the higher a company's earnings quality is assumed to be. Investors may punish a company that is judged to have a low quality of earnings, as we saw in this chapter's opening feature story regarding **Krispy Kreme**, because they worry that a company using aggressive accounting estimates can surprise them with poor future performance that will cause the company's stock price to fall.

Earnings Quality and Social Responsibility	CORPORATE SOCIAL RESPONSIBILITY

Does the stock market care about anything other than how much income a company earns? Apparently so, at least according to research performed by RateFinancials, Inc., an independent research firm. Using a proprietary methodology developed to rate the quality of earnings, along with certain corporate social responsibility (CSR) characteristics, RateFinancials found that companies with the poorest earnings quality and poorest CSR behavior underperformed the S&P 500 Index, a stock index based on the 500 largest U.S. companies, by a whopping 11 percent.

COMPREHENSIVE PROBLEM

Balke Laboratory began operations on July 1, 2011, and provides diagnostic services for physicians and medical clinics. The company's fiscal year ends on June 30, and the accounts are adjusted annually on this date. Balke's unadjusted trial balance as of June 30, 2013, is as follows:

BALKE LABORATORY Unadjusted Trial Balance June 30, 2013		
	Debit	Credit
Cash.	$ 1,000	
Accounts receivable.	9,200	
Prepaid insurance	6,000	
Supplies	31,300	
Laboratory equipment	270,000	
Accumulated depreciation—Laboratory equipment		$ 30,000
Accounts payable.		3,100
Diagnostic fees received in advance		4,000
Common stock.		90,000
Retained earnings		50,000
Diagnostic fees revenue.		220,400
Wage expense	58,000	
Rent expense	22,000	
Totals	$397,500	$397,500

The following information is also available:

1. The Prepaid Insurance account balance represents a premium paid on January 1, 2013, for two years of fire and casualty insurance coverage. Before 2013, Balke Laboratory had no insurance protection.
2. The supplies were physically counted at June 30, 2013. The count totaled $6,300.
3. All laboratory equipment was purchased on July 1, 2011. It is expected to last nine years.
4. Balke Laboratory received a $4,000 cash payment on April 1, 2013, from Boll Clinic for diagnostic services to be provided uniformly over the four months beginning April 1, 2013. Balke credited the payment to Diagnostic Fees Received in Advance. The services for April, May, and June have been provided to Boll Clinic.
5. Unpaid wages at June 30, 2013, were $600.
6. Balke Laboratory rents facilities for $2,000 per month. Because of cash flow problems, Balke was unable to pay the rent for June 2013. The landlord gave Balke permission to delay the payment until July.

Required
Make the necessary adjusting entries as of June 30, 2013.

Solution

June 30	Insurance expense	1,500	
	Prepaid insurance		1,500
	To record 6 months' insurance expense.		
	($6,000/4 = $1,500).		
30	Supplies expense	25,000	
	Supplies		25,000
	To record supplies expense for the year.		
	($31,300 – $6,300 = $25,000).		
30	Depreciation expense—Laboratory equipment	30,000	
	Accumulated depreciation—Laboratory equipment		30,000
	To record depreciation for the year.		
	($270,000/9 years = $30,000).		

June 30	Diagnostic fees received in advance	3,000	
	Diagnostic fees revenue		3,000
	To record portion of advance payment that has been earned.		
	($4,000 × 3/4 = $3,000).		
30	Wage expense	600	
	Wages payable		600
	To record unpaid wages at June 30.		
30	Rent expense	2,000	
	Rent payable		2,000
	To record rent expense for June.		

APPENDIX 3A: Closing Process—Using Income Summary Account

All accounts can be identified as either permanent accounts or temporary accounts. **Permanent accounts** are the accounts presented on the balance sheet. They consist of the asset, liability, and stockholders' equity accounts. The distinguishing feature of a permanent account is that any balance in the account at the end of an accounting period is carried forward to the following accounting period. **Temporary accounts** are used to gather information for a particular accounting period. Revenue, expense, and dividend accounts are temporary subdivisions of stockholders' equity. At the end of the accounting period, temporary account balances are transferred to retained earnings, which is a permanent stockholders' equity account. The process of transferring the balances in temporary accounts to retained earnings is referred to as the **closing process** or **closing procedures**.

> **LO5** Appendix 3A: **Describe** the process of closing to the Income Summary account and **summarize** the accounting cycle.

A temporary account is *closed* when an entry is made that changes its account balance to zero—that is, the entry is equal in amount to the account's ending balance but is opposite to the balance as a debit or credit. An account that is closed is said to be closed *to* the account that receives the offsetting debit or credit. Thus, a closing entry simply transfers the balance of one account to another account. Because closing entries bring temporary account balances to zero, the temporary accounts are then ready to start accumulating data for the next accounting period. In essence, closing the temporary accounts prevents information from the current accounting period from being carried forward to a subsequent period; and as a consequence, enables financial statement users to make meaningful comparisons of revenue and expenses from one period to the next. The following summarizes the classification of permanent and temporary accounts.

> **A.K.A.** Closing procedures are also known as *closing the books.*

Permanent Accounts	Temporary Accounts
Assets	Revenues
Liabilities	Expenses
Common Stock	Dividends
Retained Earnings	Income Summary

For each of the following accounts, identify whether the account is either a permanent account or a temporary account:

a.	Cash	*e.*	Dividends
b.	Common Stock	*f.*	Sales Revenue
c.	Wage Expense	*g.*	Inventory
d.	Notes Payable	*h.*	Prepaid Expense

> **YOUR TURN! 3A.1**
>
> The solution is on page 177.

Journalizing and Posting the Closing Entries

A summary account is traditionally used to close the temporary revenue and expense accounts. We use an account titled Income Summary (alternative titles for this account include Revenue and Expense Summary, Income and Expense Summary, and Profit and Loss Summary). The closing entries occur only at the end of an accounting period and consist of four steps, which are graphically shown as follows.

1. **Close the revenue accounts.** Debit each revenue account for an amount equal to its current credit balance, and credit the Income Summary account for the total amount of earned revenue.
2. **Close the expense accounts.** Credit each expense account for an amount equal to its current debit balance, and debit the Income Summary account for the total amount of expenses.

After steps 1 and 2, the balance of the Income Summary account equals the current period net income (if a credit balance) or net loss (if a debit balance).

3. **Close the Income Summary account.** In the case of net income, debit the Income Summary account and credit the Retained Earnings account for an amount equal to net income. In the case of a net loss, debit the Retained Earnings account and credit the Income Summary account for an amount equal to the net loss.
4. **Close the Dividends account.** Debit the Retained Earnings account and credit the Dividends account for an amount equal to the balance in the Dividends account.

Closing Process for WebWork

Exhibit 3A-1 illustrates the closing entries for the revenue and expense accounts for WebWork as recorded in the company's general journal. The financial information in these entries is posted to the appropriate general ledger accounts, which is represented using T-accounts.

Exhibit 3A-1	Closing Revenue and Expense Accounts—WebWork, Inc.		
	GENERAL JOURNAL		
Date	**Description**	**Debit**	**Credit**
2012			
Dec. 31	Fee revenue	19,150	
1	Income summary		19,150
	To close the revenue account.		
Dec. 31	Income summary	6,300	
	Supplies expense		1,320
	Wage expense		2,430
2	Rent expense		1,800
	Depreciation expense		450
	Interest expense		300
	To close the expense accounts.		

After steps 1 and 2, the Income Summary account has a credit balance equal to WebWork's net income of $12,850. Steps 3 and 4 close the Income Summary account and the Dividends account to the Retained Earnings account. These two entries are recorded in WebWork's general journal in Exhibit 3A-2. The financial effect of posting these entries on the general ledger is diagrammed below.

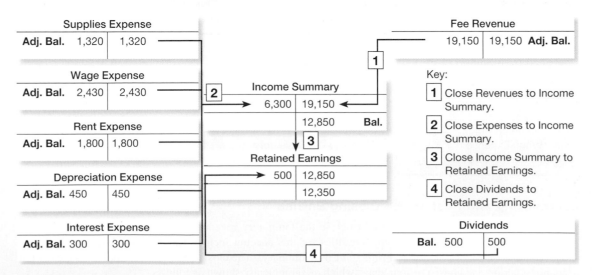

| Exhibit 3A-2 | Closing the Income Summary and Dividends Accounts—WebWork, Inc. |

GENERAL JOURNAL

Date	Description	Debit	Credit	
2012				
Dec. 31	Income summary	12,850		
	Retained earnings		12,850	3
	To close the Income Summary account.			
Dec. 31	Retained earnings	500		
	Dividends		500	4
	To close the Dividends account.			

Preparing the Post-Closing Trial Balance

After closing entries are recorded in the general journal and posted to the general ledger, all of the temporary accounts have zero balances. At this point a **post-closing trial balance** is prepared. The post-closing trial balance provides evidence that an equality of debits and credits has been maintained in the general ledger throughout the adjusting and closing processes, and that the general ledger is in balance to start the next accounting period. Because the temporary accounts have been closed, only the balance sheet (or permanent) accounts appear in the post-closing trial balance. Exhibit 3A-3 presents the post-closing trial balance for WebWork.

| Exhibit 3A-3 | Post-Closing Trial Balance for WebWork, Inc. |

WebWork, Inc.
Post-Closing Trial Balance
December 31, 2012

	Debit	Credit
Cash.	$40,590	
Accounts receivable.	1,490	
Office supplies	1,530	
Prepaid rent	9,000	
Office equipment	32,400	
Accumulated depreciation—Office equipment		$ 450
Accounts payable.		2,850
Interest payable		300
Wages payable.		810
Unearned revenue		2,250
Notes payable		36,000
Common stock.		30,000
Retained earnings		12,350
Totals	$85,010	$85,010

Summary of the Accounting Cycle

The sequence of accounting procedures known as the *accounting cycle* occurs each fiscal period and represents a systematic process for accumulating and reporting the financial data of a business. Exhibit 3A-4 summarizes the five major steps in the accounting cycle as described in this and the preceding chapter.

| Exhibit 3A-4 | The Accounting Cycle: A Summary |

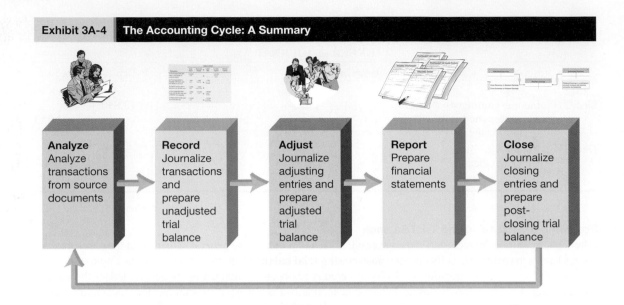

| | **Analyze**
Analyze transactions from source documents | **Record**
Journalize transactions and prepare unadjusted trial balance | **Adjust**
Journalize adjusting entries and prepare adjusted trial balance | **Report**
Prepare financial statements | **Close**
Journalize closing entries and prepare post-closing trial balance |

YOUR TURN! 3A-2

The solution is on page 177.

Prior to closing its books, the Morgan Company has the following balances in its temporary accounts as of December 31.

	Debit	Credit
Sales revenue.		$79,000
Cost of goods sold.	$41,000	
Wage expense	22,000	
Rent expense	3,000	
Depreciation expense.	2,000	
Interest expense.	4,000	
Dividends	5,000	

Required

Prepare closing entries as of December 31 for the Morgan Company.

APPENDIX 3B: Using a Worksheet

LO6 Appendix 3B:
Explain how to use a worksheet in the adjusting and closing process.

A worksheet can be used to facilitate the adjusting and closing processes, and ultimately, the preparation of a company's financial statements. A **worksheet** is an informal document that helps accumulate the accounting information needed to prepare the financial statements. A worksheet is a tool; it is not part of a company's formal accounting records. In this section, we explain how a worksheet can be used to help compile information for a set of financial statements. Computer programs such as Microsoft Excel can simplify the preparation of a worksheet.

Preparing a Worksheet

A worksheet is prepared at that stage in the accounting cycle when it is time to adjust the accounts and prepare the financial statements. The basic structure of a worksheet is illustrated in Exhibit 3B-1, which includes an explanation of the format used. The worksheet is prepared in the order indicated by the red colored numbers in the exhibit.

Exhibit 3B-1

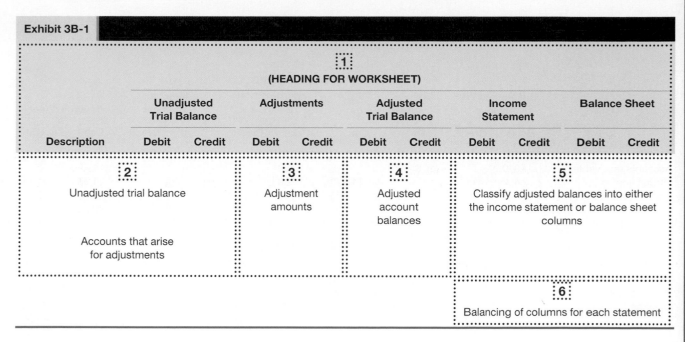

	Unadjusted Trial Balance		Adjustments		Adjusted Trial Balance		Income Statement		Balance Sheet	
Description	Debit	Credit	Debit	Credit	Debit	Credit	Debit	Credit	Debit	Credit

(HEADING FOR WORKSHEET) ①

② Unadjusted trial balance / Accounts that arise for adjustments

③ Adjustment amounts

④ Adjusted account balances

⑤ Classify adjusted balances into either the income statement or balance sheet columns

⑥ Balancing of columns for each statement

1. Heading The worksheet *heading* includes (1) the name of the entity, (2) the term *Worksheet* to indicate the type of analysis being performed, and (3) a date describing the period covered. The worksheet includes both income statement data (for the period described) and balance sheet data (for the end of the period described). Exhibit 3B-2 illustrates the heading for WebWork's worksheet. The worksheet has a description column and 10 amount (monetary) columns. A set of Debit and Credit columns is provided for each of the five headings: Unadjusted Trial Balance, Adjustments, Adjusted Trial Balance, Income Statement, and Balance Sheet.

2. Unadjusted Trial Balance The unadjusted trial balance is the starting point for the accounting analysis on the worksheet. It is entered in the worksheet's description column and the first pair of monetary columns. Once the trial balance is entered in the worksheet and double-ruled, it reflects the general ledger at the time the worksheet is prepared. Exhibit 3B-2 shows the worksheet placement of WebWork's unadjusted trial balance as of December 31, 2012.

3. Adjustments *When a worksheet is used, all adjustments are first entered on the worksheet.* This procedure permits the adjustments to be reviewed for completeness and accuracy. To adjust accounts already appearing in the unadjusted trial balance, we simply enter the amounts in the appropriate side (debit or credit) of the adjustments columns on the lines containing the accounts. When accounts not appearing in the unadjusted trial balance require adjustment, their titles are listed as needed in the Description column below the accounts already listed. Adjustments entered on the worksheet are not yet journalized; journalizing the adjustments occurs later. The adjustments recorded on WebWork's worksheet in Exhibit 3B-2 are identical to those illustrated in the chapter (see Exhibit 3-2). After recording all the adjusting entries on the worksheet, we total the adjustments columns to verify that the sum of the debit entries equals the sum of the credit entries.

4. Adjusted Trial Balance Once the adjustments have been entered on the worksheet, there is sufficient information available to complete an adjusted trial balance. The adjusted figures are determined by combining horizontally, line by line, the amounts in the first four money columns—that is, the unadjusted trial balance and the adjustments. We review the calculations for two lines of Exhibit 3B-2 to illustrate this process. The first line shows the Cash account with a debit amount of $40,590 in the unadjusted trial balance. Because Cash is not affected by any of the adjustments, the $40,590 appears in the debit column of the adjusted trial balance. On the third line, the Office Supplies account begins with a debit of $2,850 in the unadjusted trial balance and then shows a credit of $1,320 in the adjustments column. The $1,320 credit is subtracted from the $2,850 debit, and the remaining $1,530 is shown as a debit in the adjusted trial balance.

Exhibit 3B-2

WEBWORK, INC.
Worksheet
For Month Ended December 31, 2012

	Unadjusted Trial Balance Debit	Unadjusted Trial Balance Credit	Adjustments Debit	Adjustments Credit	Adjusted Trial Balance Debit	Adjusted Trial Balance Credit	Income Statement Debit	Income Statement Credit	Balance Sheet Debit	Balance Sheet Credit
Cash...............	$40,590				$40,590				$40,590	
Accounts receivable....	1,340		(g) $ 150		1,490				1,490	
Office supplies	2,850			(a) $1,320	1,530				1,530	
Prepaid rent	10,800			(b) 1,800	9,000				9,000	
Office equipment	32,400				32,400				32,400	
Accumulated depreciation—										
Office equipment				(c) 450		$ 450				$ 450
Accounts payable......		$ 2,850				2,850				2,850
Interest payable				(f) 300		300				300
Wages payable........				(e) 810		810				810
Unearned revenue		3,000	(d) 750			2,250				2,250
Notes payable		36,000				36,000				36,000
Common stock........		30,000				30,000				30,000
Dividends	500				500				500	
Fee revenue		18,250		(d) 750		19,150		$19,150		
				(g) 150						
Wage expense	1,620		(e) 810		2,430		2,430			
Supplies expense......			(a) 1,320		1,320		$ 1,320			
Rent expense			(b) 1,800		1,800		1,800			
Depreciation expense...			(c) 450		450		450			
Interest expense.......			(f) 300		300		300			
Totals	$90,100	$90,100	$5,580	$5,580	$91,810	$91,810	6,300	19,150	85,510	72,660
Net income...........							12,850			12,850
Totals							$19,150	$19,150	$85,510	$85,510

After calculating the adjusted trial balance amounts for all accounts on the worksheet, we total the two columns of the adjusted trial balance to verify that they are equal and that our worksheet is in balance.

⁙5⁙ Extension of the Adjusted Trial Balance　The amounts in the adjusted trial balance columns are extended into the two remaining pairs of columns as follows:

Expenses	→ Debit column of income statement
Revenues	→ Credit column of income statement
Assets and cash dividends	→ Debit column of balance sheet
Liabilities, Common Stock, Retained Earnings, and contra assets	→ Credit column of balance sheet

Expense and revenue account balances are extended to the income statement columns because these accounts will be used to prepare the income statement. Similarly, asset, contra asset, liability, and stockholders' equity accounts are balance sheet accounts, so their balances are extended to the balance sheet columns. In addition, the Dividends debit balance is extended to the balance sheet debit column, and the credit balances in the Common Stock and Retained Earnings accounts are extended to the balance sheet credit column. Exhibit 3B-2 shows the extension of WebWork's adjusted trial balance to the worksheet's income statement and balance sheet columns. Once the proper extensions are made, the worksheet is complete except for balancing the two pairs of statement columns containing the adjusted balances.

⁝6⁝ Balancing the Worksheet   The first step in balancing is to add each of the income statement and balance sheet columns and record their respective totals on the same line as the totals of the adjusted trial balance columns. The difference between the total debits and total credits in the income statement columns is the difference between total revenues and total expenses—that is, the net income or net loss for the period. The net income or net loss must be the amount by which the debit and credit columns for the balance sheet differ. This is true because the Retained Earnings account balance, as extended, does not yet reflect the net income or net loss for the current period.

When revenues exceed expenses, we balance the two pairs of statement columns by adding the net income figure to both the debit column of the income statement and the credit column of the balance sheet. Exhibit 3B-2 illustrates this balancing situation with WebWork's net income for December of $12,850. If expenses exceed revenues, we add the amount of net loss to the credit column of the income statement and to the debit column of the balance sheet. After we have added the net income (or loss) to the proper columns, we total and double-rule the four columns. The worksheet is now complete.

A completed worksheet aids in the last three steps of the accounting cycle—adjust, report, and close.

Adjust: The adjusting entries to be journalized and posted can be taken from the information in the adjustments columns. Because adjustments have first been entered on the worksheet, they can be reviewed for their financial effects before being journalized. Thus, the likelihood of incorrect adjustments appearing in the formal accounting records is reduced.

Report: The income statement can be prepared from the data in the income statement columns. Two pieces of information for the statement of stockholders' equity are available in the worksheet—the net income (or net loss) and dividends. The assets and liabilities needed for the balance sheet are available in the balance sheet columns (the ending Retained Earnings balance for the balance sheet is obtained from the statement of stockholders' equity).

Close: The closing entries to be journalized and posted can be prepared from data in the worksheet because it displays all of the temporary account balances. The revenue and expense account balances are shown in the income statement columns and the cash dividends account balance is shown in the balance sheet debit column.

SUMMARY OF LEARNING OBJECTIVES

Explain the accrual basis of accounting and contrast it with the cash basis with reference to revenue and expense recognition. (p. 118)   **LO1**

■   Revenue is recognized on an accrual basis at the time that it is earned. This may be prior to the receipt of cash, at the same time as the receipt of cash, or following the receipt of cash.

■   Expenses are matched against revenues in the same accounting period that the associated revenue is recognized. This may be prior to cash payment, at the same time as cash payment, or following cash payment.

■   Revenue recognition and the corresponding matching of expenses may differ in timing on an accrual basis versus on a cash basis.

Describe the adjusting process and illustrate the four major types of adjusting entries. (p. 120)   **LO2**

■   Adjusting entries are made to achieve the appropriate recognition of revenues and matching of expenses with revenues, and consist of four general types of adjustments:

1.   Allocating assets to operating expenses to reflect the total expenses incurred during the period.

2.   Allocating unearned revenue received in advance to revenue to reflect revenues earned during the period.

3.   Increasing operating expenses to reflect expenses incurred during the period that have not yet been paid or recorded.

4.   Increasing revenues to reflect revenue earned during the period that has not yet been received or recorded.

Explain the adjusted trial balance and use it to prepare financial statements. (p. 129)   **LO3**

■   An income statement, statement of stockholders' equity, balance sheet, and statement of cash flows may be prepared from an adjusted trial balance and other information.

■ The stockholders' equity account may need to be reviewed to obtain information regarding the beginning balances and additional capital contributions during the period for the statement of stockholders' equity.

LO4 **Describe the closing process and summarize the accounting cycle. (p. 131)**

■ *Closing the books* means closing the revenue, expense, and other temporary accounts. Revenue and expense account balances are transferred to the Retained Earnings account as is the balance in the Dividends account.

LO5 **Appendix 3A: Describe the process of closing to the Income Summary account and summarize the accounting cycle. (p. 137)**

■ *Closing the books* means closing the revenue, expense, and other temporary accounts. Revenue and expense account balances are transferred to the Income Summary account. The balances of the Income Summary account and the Dividends account are closed to the Retained Earnings account.

LO6 **Appendix 3B: Explain how to use a worksheet in the adjusting and closing process. (p. 140)**

A worksheet is an informal document that helps in compiling the information needed for the preparation of the financial statements. A worksheet is a tool of the accountant; it is not part of a company's formal accounting records. The worksheet consists of a heading, along with the following columns:

- *a.* Unadjusted trial balance
- *b.* Adjustments
- *c.* Adjusted trial balance
- *d.* Income statement
- *e.* Balance sheet

A completed worksheet aids in the last three steps of the accounting cycle: adjust, report, and close.

SUMMARY	Concept	Method	Assessment
TAKEAWAY 3.1	When should sales revenue be recognized?	Understand the nature of a company's earning process. Record revenue when it is earned.	Early recognition of revenue overstates current period revenue; recognizing revenue too late understates current period revenue.
TAKEAWAY 3.2	When should expenses be recognized?	Understand the nature of the company's earning process. Expenses should be recognized with the related revenue in the same accounting period.	Early recognition of expenses overstates current period expenses; recognizing expenses too late understates current period expenses.
TAKEAWAY 3.3	When should an adjusting entry be made?	Individual account balances and transaction details such as contracts and agreements. Knowledge of the proper account balance is needed. Adjustments involve (1) allocating assets to expense, (2) allocating unearned revenue to revenue, (3) accruing expenses, or (4) accruing revenues.	Record an adjusting entry so that accounts are correctly reported; otherwise income and assets (and/or liabilities) are incorrectly reported.

KEY TERMS

Accruals (p. 121)	**Adjusted trial balance** (p. 128)	**Contra accounts** (p. 123)
Accrued expenses (p. 124)	**Adjusting entries** (p. 121)	**Deferrals** (p. 121)
Accrued revenue (p. 125)	**Book value** (p. 123)	**Deferred revenue** (p. 124)
Accumulated depreciation (p. 123)	**Closing procedures** (p. 131, 137)	**Depreciation** (p. 123)
	Closing process (p. 131, 137)	**Earnings quality** (p. 135)

Permanent accounts	Straight-line	Unadjusted trial
(p. 131, 137)	depreciation (p. 123)	balance (p. 120)
Post-closing trial	Temporary accounts	Unearned revenue (p. 124)
balance (p. 133, 139)	(p. 131, 137)	Worksheet (p. 140)

SELF-STUDY QUESTIONS

(Answers to the Self-Study Questions are available at the end of the chapter.)

1. **Which of the following is an example of an adjusting entry?**　　　　　LO2
   a. Recording the purchase of supplies on account
   b. Recording depreciation expense on a truck
   c. Recording the billing of customers for services rendered
   d. Recording the payment of wages to employees

2. **An adjusting entry to record utilities used during a month for which no bill has yet been received is** 　LO2
   an example of
   a. Allocating assets to expense to reflect the actual operating expenses incurred during the accounting period
   b. Allocating revenues received in advance to revenue to reflect actual revenues earned during the accounting period
   c. Accruing expenses to reflect expenses incurred during the accounting period that are not yet paid or recorded
   d. Accruing revenues to reflect revenues earned during the accounting period that are not yet received or recorded

3. **Which of the following is not an example of a closing entry?**　　　　　LO4
   a. Close each revenue account to the Retained Earnings account
   b. Close each expense account to the Retained Earnings account
   c. Close the Dividends account to the Retained Earnings account
   d. Close Unearned Revenue to Retained Earnings

4. **Which of the following transactions does not affect the balance sheet totals?**　　　LO2
   a. Purchasing $500 supplies on account
   b. Paying a $3,000 note payable
   c. Collecting $4,000 from customers on account
   d. Payment of an $800 dividend

5. **The beginning and ending balances of retained earnings for the year were $30,000 and $35,000,** 　LO2
   respectively. If yearly dividends totaled $3,000, what was the net income or net loss for the year?
   a. $8,000 net loss
   b. $14,000 net income
   c. $2,000 net income
   d. $8,000 net income

6. **The ending balance of the Accounts Receivable account was $12,000. Services billed to customers** 　LO2
   for the period were $21,500, and collections on account from customers were $23,600. What was
   the beginning balance of Accounts Receivable?
   a. $33,500
   b. $14,100
   c. $9,900
   d. $33,100

7. **Kelly Corporation received an advanced payment of $20,000 in 2012 from Rufus Company for** 　LO2
   consulting services. Kelly performed half of the consulting in 2012 and the remainder in 2013.
   Kelly reports using the accrual basis of accounting. How much revenue from this consulting
   project will Kelly report in 2012?
   a. $20,000
   b. $10,000
   c. $0
   d. $15,000

QUESTIONS

1. Why is the adjusting step of the accounting cycle necessary?

2. What four different types of adjustments are frequently necessary at the close of an accounting period? Provide an example of each type.

3. On January 1, Prepaid Insurance was debited with the cost of a two-year premium in the amount of $1,872. What adjusting entry should be made on January 31 before the January financial statements are prepared?

4. What is a contra account? What contra account is used in reporting the book value of a depreciable asset?

5. At the beginning of January, the first month of the accounting year, the Supplies account had a debit balance of $825. During January, purchases of $260 of supplies were debited to the account. Although only $630 of supplies was on hand at the end of January, the necessary adjusting entry was omitted. How will the omission affect (a) the income statement for January and (b) the balance sheet prepared as of January 31?

6. The publisher of *International View*, a monthly magazine, received two-year subscriptions totaling $9,720 on January 1. (a) What entry should be made to record the receipt of the $9,720? (b) What entry should be made at the end of January before financial statements are prepared for the month?

7. Globe Travel Agency pays an employee $475 in wages each Friday for a five-day work week ending on that day. The last Friday of January falls on January 27. What adjusting entry should be made on January 31, the fiscal year-end?

8. The Bayou Company earns interest amounting to $360 per month on its investments. The company receives the interest every six months, on December 31 and June 30. Monthly financial statements are prepared. What adjusting entry should be made on January 31?

9. Define *permanent account*. Provide an example.

10. Define *temporary account*. Provide an example.

11. Which group of accounts is closed at the end of the accounting year? Why?

12. What is the purpose of a post-closing trial balance? Which of the following accounts should not appear in the post-closing trial balance: Cash, Unearned Revenue, Dividends, Depreciation Expense, Utilities Payable, Supplies Expense, Retained Earnings?

SHORT EXERCISES

LO4 **SE3-1.** **Steps in the Accounting Cycle** Listed below, out of order, are the steps in an accounting cycle.

1. Prepare the unadjusted trial balance.
2. Post journal entries to general ledger accounts.
3. Analyze transactions from source documents.
4. Journalize and post adjusting entries.
5. Prepare the financial statements.
6. Record transactions in a journal.
7. Prepare the post-closing trial balance.
8. Prepare the adjusted trial balance.
9. Journalize and post closing entries.

(a) Place the numbers from the above list in the order in which the steps in the accounting cycle are performed, and (b) identify the steps in the accounting cycle that occur daily.

LO1 **SE3-2.** **Accrual Accounting** Evan Corporation provided consulting services for Kensington Company in 2012. Evan incurred costs of $60,000 associated with the consulting and billed Kensington $90,000. Evan paid $40,000 of its costs in 2012 and the remaining $20,000 in 2013. Evan received $45,000 of its billing in 2012. Kensington paid the remaining $45,000 in 2013. Evan reports on the accrual basis of accounting. How much is Evan's 2012 and 2013 profit related to the Kensington consulting?

LO2 **SE3-3.** **Adjusting Accounts** MacKenzie Enterprises includes the following accounts in its general ledger. Explain why each of these accounts may need to be adjusted.

    a. Rent Payable
    b. Unearned Revenue
    c. Prepaid Subscriptions
    d. Depreciation Expense

SE3-4. **Adjusting Entry for Depreciation** Cowley Company just completed its first year of operations. The **LO2** December 31 equipment account has a balance of $20,000. There is no balance in the Accumulated Depreciation—Equipment account or in the Depreciation Expense account. The accountant estimates the yearly equipment depreciation to be $4,000. Prepare the required adjusting entry to record the yearly depreciation for equipment.

SE3-5. **Adjusting Entry for Prepaid Insurance** Cooper Inc. recorded the purchase of a three-year insur- **LO2** ance policy on July 1 in the amount of $3,600 by debiting Prepaid Insurance and crediting Cash. Prepare the necessary December 31 year-end adjusting entry.

SE3-6. **Accrual Adjusting Entries** Sparky Electronics requires adjusting entries for the following items: **LO2**

 a. Salaries for employees in the amount of $2,500 have not been paid.
 b. Interest expense of $1,200 for an outstanding note.
 c. Work performed but not yet billed for $3,500.

SE3-7. **Analyze an Adjusted Trial Balance** The trial balance of Fisher Supplies contains the following bal- **LO2** ance sheet accounts that require adjustment. Identify the likely income statement account that will be used to adjust these accounts.

 a. Prepaid Insurance
 b. Accumulated Depreciation
 c. Supplies
 d. Unearned Revenue
 e. Interest Payable

SE3-8. **Prepare an Income Statement from an Adjusted Trial Balance** The Century Company's ad- **LO3** justed trial balance contains the following balances as of December 31: Retained Earnings $8,500; Dividends $2,000; Sales $20,000; Cost of Goods Sold $8,000; Selling and Administrative Expenses $3,000; Interest Expense $1,500. Prepare an income statement for the year.

SE3-9. **Prepare Closing Entries Using the Income Summary Account** Use the data from SE3-8 to prepare **LO5** the closing entries for The Century Company. Close the temporary accounts to income summary. The balance of $8,500 in the retained earnings account is from the beginning of the year. What is the ending retained earnings balance after posting the closing entries?

SE3-10. **Prepare Closing Entries to Retained Earnings** Use the data from SE3-8 to prepare the closing **LO4** entries for The Century Company. Close the temporary accounts straight to retained earnings. The balance of $8,500 in the retained earnings account is from the beginning of the year. What is the ending retained earnings balance after posting the closing entries?

SE3-11. **Identify Financial Statements from Adjusted Trial Balance Accounts** Trownel Corp reports the **LO3** following balances in its adjusted trial balance. Identify which financial statement each account would appear on:

 a. Cash   d. Unearned Revenue
 b. Sales   e. Retained Earnings
 c. Accounts Payable   f. Interest Income

SE3-12. **The Accounting Worksheet** The adjusted trial balance section of Menlo Company's worksheet **LO6** shows a $1,500 debit balance in utility expense. At the end of the accounting period the accounting manager accrues an additional $300 of utility expense for the last week of the period. This will result in the following amounts appearing on Menlo's worksheet for utilities expense:

 a. $300 debit adjustment; $1,800 debit adjusted trial balance; $1,800 debit balance sheet
 b. $300 debit adjustment; $1,800 debit adjusted trial balance; $1,800 debit income statement
 c. $300 credit adjustment; $1,200 debit adjusted trial balance; $1,800 debit income statement
 d. $300 credit adjustment; $1,800 debit adjusted trial balance; $1,800 debit income statement

Assignments with the ✓ logo in the margin are available in BusinessCourse.
See the Preface of the book for details.

EXERCISES—SET A

E3-1A. **Transaction Entries and Adjusting Entries** Deluxe Building Services offers janitorial services on **LO2** both a contract basis and an hourly basis. On January 1, Deluxe collected $20,100 in advance on a ✓ six-month contract for work to be performed evenly during the next six months.

a. Provide the general journal entry on January 1 to record the receipt of $20,100 for contract work.

b. Provide the adjusting entry to be made on January 31, for the contract work done during January.

c. At January 31, a total of 30 hours of hourly rate janitor work was unbilled. The billing rate is $19 per hour. Provide the adjusting entry needed on January 31. (*Note:* The firm uses the account Fees Receivable to reflect amounts due but not yet billed.)

LO2 **E3-2A.** **Adjusting Entries** Selected accounts of Ideal Properties Inc., a real estate management firm, are shown below as of January 31, before any adjusting entries have been made:

	Debit	Credit
Prepaid insurance	$6,660	
Supplies	1,930	
Office equipment	5,952	
Unearned rent revenue		$ 5,250
Salaries expense	3,100	
Rent revenue		15,000

Monthly financial statements are prepared. Using the following information, record in a general journal the adjusting entries necessary on January 31:

a. Prepaid Insurance represents a three-year premium paid on January 1.

b. Supplies of $850 were on hand January 31.

c. Office equipment is expected to last eight years. Depreciation is recorded monthly.

d. On January 1, the firm collected six months' rent in advance from a tenant renting space for $875 per month.

e. Accrued salaries not recorded as of January 31 are $490.

LO2 **E3-3A.** **Adjusting Entries** For each of the following unrelated situations, prepare the necessary adjusting entry in general journal form:

a. Unrecorded depreciation on equipment is $610.

b. The Supplies account has a balance of $2,990. Supplies on hand at the end of the period totaled $1,100.

c. On the date for preparing financial statements, an estimated utilities expense of $390 has been incurred, but no utility bill has been received.

d. On the first day of the current month, rent for four months was paid and recorded as a $2,800 debit to Prepaid Rent and a $2,800 credit to Cash. Monthly statements are now being prepared.

e. Nine months ago, Solid Insurance Company sold a one-year policy to a customer and recorded the receipt of the premium by debiting Cash for $624 and crediting Unearned Premium Revenue for $624. No adjusting entries have been prepared during the nine-month period. Annual financial statements are now being prepared.

f. At the end of the accounting period, employee wages of $965 have been incurred but not paid.

g. At the end of the accounting period, $300 of interest has been earned but not yet received on notes receivable that are held.

LO3 **E3-4A.** **Statement of Stockholders' Equity** On January 1, the credit balance of the Retained Earnings account was $48,000. The company's Common Stock account had an opening balance of $70,000, and $6,000 in new capital contributions were made during the year. On December 31, at year-end, the Dividends account had a debit balance of $9,700 before closing. The income statement shows net income of $29,900. Prepare a statement of stockholders' equity for Strife & Company, architectural design firm.

LO4 **E3-5A.** **Closing Entries** The adjusted trial balance prepared as of December 31, for Phyllis Howell & Company, Consultant, contains the following revenue and expense accounts:

	Debit	Credit
Service fees earned		$80,300
Rent expense	$20,800	
Salaries expense	45,700	
Supplies expense	5,600	
Depreciation expense	10,200	
Retained earnings		67,000
Dividends	9,000	

Prepare journal entries to close the accounts directly to Retained Earnings. After these entries are posted, what is the balance in the Retained Earnings account?

E3-6A. Closing Entries Use the information provided in E3-5A to prepare journal entries to close the accounts using the Income Summary account. After these entries are posted, what is the balance in the Retained Earnings account?

LO5
(Appendix 3A)

E3-7A. Closing Entries In the midst of closing procedures, Echo Corporation's accountant became ill and was hospitalized. You have volunteered to complete the closing of the books, and you find that all revenue and expense accounts have zero balances and that the Income Summary account has a single debit entry for $308,800 and a single credit entry for $347,400. The Dividends account has a debit balance of $18,000, and the Retained Earnings account has a credit balance of $117,000. Prepare journal entries to complete the closing procedures as of year-end.

LO5
(Appendix 3A)
✔

E3-8A. Closing Entries In the midst of closing procedures, Echo Corporation's accountant became ill and was hospitalized. You have volunteered to complete the closing of the books. You find that all the revenue and expense accounts have zero balances. The Dividends account has a debit balance of $18,000. The Retained Earnings account has a beginning credit balance of $117,000. Expenses totaled $308,500, and revenues totaled $347,400. Prepare journal entries to complete the closing procedures as of year-end directly to Retained Earnings. After these entries are posted, what is the balance in the Retained Earnings account?

LO4
✔

E3-9A. Worksheet Identify each of the 10 amount columns of the worksheet and indicate to which column the adjusted balance of the following accounts would be extended:

LO6
(Appendix 3B)

a.	Accounts Receivable	*f.*	Rent Receivable
b.	Accumulated Depreciation	*g.*	Prepaid Insurance
c.	Dividends	*h.*	Service Fees Earned
d.	Wages Payable	*i.*	Common Stock
e.	Depreciation Expense	*j.*	Retained Earnings

E3-10A. Analysis of Adjusted Data Selected T-account balances for Coyle Company are shown below as of January 31; adjusting entries have already been posted. The firm uses a calendar-year accounting period and makes monthly adjustments.

LO2

Supplies		Supplies Expense	
Jan. 31 Bal. 800		Jan. 31 Bal. 960	

Prepaid Insurance		Insurance Expense	
Jan. 31 Bal. 574		Jan. 31 Bal. 82	

Wages Payable		Wages Expense	
	Bal. 500 Jan. 31	Jan. 31 Bal. 3,200	

Truck		Accumulated Depreciation—Truck	
Jan. 31 Bal. 8,700			Bal. 2,610 Jan. 31

a. If the amount in Supplies Expense represents the January 31 adjustment for the supplies used in January, and $620 worth of supplies were purchased during January, what was the January 1 balance of Supplies?

b. The amount in the Insurance Expense account represents the adjustment made at January 31 for January insurance expense. If the original insurance premium was for one year, what was the amount of the premium and on what date did the insurance policy start?

c. If we assume that no balance existed in Wages Payable or Wages Expense on January 1, how much cash was paid as wages during January?

d. If the truck has a useful life of five years, what is the monthly amount of depreciation expense and how many months has Coyle owned the truck?

E3-11A. Analysis of the Impact of Adjustments on Financial Statements At the end of the first month of operations, the Bradley Company's accountant prepared financial statements that showed the following amounts:

LO2
✔

Assets.	$60,000
Liabilities.	20,000
Stockholders' equity	40,000
Net income.	9,000

In preparing the statements, the accountant overlooked the following items:

a. Depreciation for the month, $1,000.
b. Service revenue earned but unbilled at month-end, $1,500.
c. Employee wages earned but unpaid at month-end, $250.

Determine the correct amounts of assets, liabilities, and stockholders' equity at month-end and net income for the month.

LO4 **E3-12A. Closing Entries** The adjusted trial balance of the Rose Corporation, prepared as of December 31, contains the following accounts:

	Debit	Credit
Service fees earned		$92,500
Interest income.		2,200
Salaries expense	$41,800	
Advertising expense.	4,300	
Depreciation expense.	8,700	
Income tax expense.	9,900	
Common stock.		75,000
Retained earnings		57,700
Cash dividends.	15,000	

Prepare journal entries to close the accounts directly to Retained Earnings. After these entries are posted, what is the ending balance in the Retained Earnings account?

LO5
(Appendix 3A) **E3-13A. Closing Entries** Use the information provided in E3-12A to prepare journal entries to close the accounts using the Income Summary account. After these entries are posted, what is the balance in the Retained Earnings account?

LO6
(Appendix 3B) **E3-14A. Worksheet** The adjusted trial balance columns of a worksheet for Bonn Corporation are shown below. The worksheet is prepared for the year ended December 31.

	Adjusted Trial Balance	
	Debit	Credit
Cash.	$ 4,000	
Accounts receivable.	6,500	
Equipment	78,000	
Accumulated depreciation		$ 14,000
Notes payable		10,000
Common stock.		43,000
Retained earnings		20,600
Cash dividends.	8,000	
Service fees earned		71,000
Rent expense.	18,000	
Salaries expense	37,100	
Depreciation expense.	7,000	
Totals	$158,600	$158,600

Complete the worksheet by (a) entering the adjusted trial balance, (b) putting in the worksheet income statement and balance sheet columns, (c) extending the adjusted trial balance to the income statement and balance sheet columns, and (d) balancing the worksheet.

LO1 **E3-15A. Revenue Recognition** Identify the proper point to recognize revenue for each of the following transactions.

a. Napoleon Industries sells a machine in January with terms of no payment due until six months later.
b. Emma Company collects an advance deposit of $700 in July toward the purchase of a $3,000 piece of equipment that is delivered to the customer the following September.
c. Ashley Corporation receives payment in October at the time of delivery of a rebuilt engine for a tractor.

EXERCISES—SET B

E3-1B. Transaction Entry and Adjusting Entries Beale Building Services offers janitorial services on both a contract basis and an hourly basis. On January 1, Beale collected $30,000 in advance on a six-month contract for work to be performed evenly during the next six months. **LO2** ✔

   a. Provide the general journal entry on January 1 to record the receipt of $30,000 for contract work.

   b. Provide the adjusting entry to be made on January 31, for the contract work done during January.

   c. At January 31, a total of 30 hours of hourly rate janitor work was unbilled. The billing rate is $25 per hour. Provide the adjusting entry needed on January 31. (*Note:* The firm uses the account Fees Receivable to reflect amounts due but not yet billed.)

E3-2B. Adjusting Entries Judy Brock began Brock Refinishing Service on July 1. Selected accounts are shown below as of July 31, before any adjusting entries have been made: **LO2** ✔

	Debit	Credit
Prepaid rent	$5,700	
Prepaid advertising.	630	
Supplies	3,000	
Unearned refinishing fees.		$ 600
Refinishing fees revenue		2,500

Using the following information, record in a general journal the necessary adjusting entries on July 31:

   a. On July 1, the firm paid one year's rent of $5,700.

   b. On July 1, $630 was paid to a local newspaper for an advertisement to run daily for the months of July, August, and September.

   c. Supplies on hand at July 31 total $1,100.

   d. At July 31, refinishing services of $800 have been performed but not yet billed to customers. The firm uses the account Fees Receivable to reflect amounts due but not yet billed.

   e. One customer paid $600 in advance for a refinishing project. At July 31, the project is one-half complete.

E3-3B. Adjusting Entries For each of the following unrelated situations, prepare the necessary adjusting entry in general journal form: **LO2** ✔

   a. Unrecorded depreciation on equipment is $900.

   b. The Supplies account has a balance of $3,000. Supplies on hand at the end of the period total $1,000.

   c. On the date for preparing financial statements, an estimated utilities expense of $400 has been incurred, but no utility bill has been received.

   d. On the first day of the current month, rent for four months was paid and recorded as a $2,800 debit to Prepaid Rent and a $2,800 credit to Cash. Monthly statements are now being prepared.

   e. Nine months ago, Macke Insurance Company sold a one-year policy to a customer and recorded the receipt of the premium by debiting Cash for $624 and crediting Unearned Premium Revenue for $624. No adjusting entries have been prepared during the nine-month period. Annual financial statements are now being prepared.

   f. At the end of the accounting period, employee wages of $600 have been incurred but not paid.

   g. At the end of the accounting period, $500 of interest has been earned but not yet received on notes receivable that are held.

E3-4B. Statement of Stockholders' Equity On January 1, the credit balance of the Retained Earnings account was $50,000. The company's common stock account had an opening balance of $60,000 and new contributions during the year totaled $7,000. On December 31, at year-end, the Dividends account had a debit balance of $5,700. The income statement shows net income of $30,000. Prepare a statement of stockholders' equity for A. Miller & Company, architectural design firm. **LO3** ✔

E3-5B. Closing Entries The adjusted trial balance prepared December 31, for Cheryl Fontaine & Company, shipping agent, contains the following accounts: **LO4**

	Debit	Credit
Commissions earned		$84,900
Wages expense	$36,000	
Insurance expense	1,900	
Utilities expense	8,200	
Depreciation expense	9,800	
Dividends	12,000	
Common stock		50,000
Retained earnings		22,100

Prepare journal entries to close the accounts directly to Retained Earnings. After these entries are posted, what is the ending balance in the Retained Earnings account?

LO5
(Appendix 3A)

E3-6B. **Closing Entries** Use the information provided in E3-5B to prepare journal entries to close the accounts using the Income Summary account. After these entries are posted, what is the balance in the Retained Earnings account?

LO5
(Appendix 3A)

E3-7B. **Closing Entries** In the midst of closing procedures, Claremont Corporation's accountant became ill. You have volunteered to complete the closing of the books, and you find that all revenue and expense accounts have zero balances and that the Income Summary account has a single debit entry for $318,800 and a single credit entry for $347,400. The Cash Dividends account has a debit balance of $29,000, and the Retained Earnings account has a credit balance of $117,000. Prepare journal entries to complete the closing procedures as of year-end.

LO4

E3-8B. **Closing Entries** In the midst of closing procedures, Claremont Corporation's accountant became ill and was hospitalized. You have volunteered to complete the closing of the books. You find that all the revenue and expense accounts have zero balances. The Dividends account has a debit balance of $29,000. The Retained Earnings account has a beginning credit balance of $117,000. Expenses totaled $318,800, and revenues totaled $347,400. Prepare journal entries to complete the closing procedures as of year-end directly to Retained Earnings. After these entries are posted, what is the balance in the Retained Earnings account?

LO6
(Appendix 3B)

E3-9B. **Worksheet** Identify each of the 10 amount columns of the worksheet and indicate to which column the adjusted balance of the following accounts would be extended:

a. Accounts Receivable
b. Accumulated Depreciation
c. Dividends
d. Salaries Payable
e. Wages Expense

f. Interest Receivable
g. Prepaid Rent
h. Service Fees Earned
i. Common Stock
j. Retained Earnings

LO2

E3-10B. **Analysis of Adjusted Data** Selected T-account balances for the Parris Company are shown below as of January 31; adjusting entries have already been posted. The firm uses a calendar-year accounting period and makes monthly adjustments.

Supplies		Supplies Expense	
Jan. 31 Bal. 800		Jan. 31 Bal. 1,960	
Prepaid Insurance		**Insurance Expense**	
Jan. 31 Bal. 910		Jan. 31 Bal. 182	
Wages Payable		**Wages Expense**	
	Bal. 500 Jan. 31	Jan. 31 Bal. 3,200	
Truck		**Accumulated Depreciation—Truck**	
Jan. 31 Bal. 8,700			Bal. 2,610 Jan. 31

a. If the amount in Supplies Expense represents the January 31 adjustment for the supplies used in January, and $620 worth of supplies were purchased during January, what was the January 1 balance of Supplies?

b. The amount in the Insurance Expense account represents the adjustment made at January 31 for January insurance expense. If the original insurance premium was for one year, what was the amount of the premium and on what date did the insurance policy start?

c. If we assume that no balance existed in Wages Payable or Wages Expense on January 1, how much cash was paid as wages during January?

    d.   If the truck has a useful life of five years, what is the monthly amount of depreciation expense and how many months has Parris owned the truck?

E3-11B. Analysis of the Impact of Adjustments on Financial Statements At the end of the first month of operations, the Omar Company's accountant prepared financial statements that showed the following amounts:

LO2 ✓

Assets.	$80,000
Liabilities.	30,000
Stockholders' equity	50,000
Net income.	11,000

In preparing the statements, the accountant overlooked the following items:

a.   Depreciation for the month, $3,000.

b.   Service revenue earned but unbilled at month-end, $1,500.

c.   Employee wages earned but unpaid at month-end, $250.

Determine the correct amounts of assets, liabilities, and stockholders' equity at month-end and net income for the month.

E3-12B. Closing Entries The adjusted trial balance of the Matthews Corporation, prepared December 31, contains the following accounts:

LO4 ✓

	Debit	Credit
Service fees earned		$97,500
Interest income.		5,200
Salaries expense	$49,800	
Advertising expense.	4,300	
Depreciation expense.	8,700	
Income tax expense.	9,900	
Common stock.		75,000
Retained earnings		57,700
Cash dividends.	15,000	

Prepare journal entries to close the accounts directly to Retained Earnings. After these entries are posted, what is the ending balance in the Retained Earnings account?

E3-13B. Closing Entries Use the information provided in E3-12B to prepare journal entries to close the accounts using the Income Summary account. After these entries are posted, what is the balance in the Retained Earnings account?

LO5
(Appendix 3A)
✓

E3-14B. Worksheet The adjusted trial balance columns of a worksheet for Frankfurt Corporation are shown below. The worksheet is prepared for the year ended December 31.

LO6
(Appendix 3B)
✓

	Adjusted Trial Balance	
	Debit	Credit
Cash.	$ 14,000	
Accounts receivable.	16,500	
Equipment	78,000	
Accumulated depreciation.		$ 24,000
Notes payable		10,000
Common stock.		43,000
Retained earnings		20,600
Cash dividends.	8,000	
Service fees earned		81,000
Rent expense.	18,000	
Salaries expense	37,100	
Depreciation expense.	7,000	
Totals	$178,600	$178,600

Complete the worksheet by (a) entering the adjusted trial balance, (b) putting in the worksheet income statement and balance sheet columns, (c) extending the adjusted trial balance to the income statement and balance sheet columns, and (d) balancing the worksheet.

LO1   **E3-15B. Expense Matching** Identify the proper point to recognize expenses for each of the following transactions.

     a.   Garner Inc. purchases for cash five custom dining tables for $1,000 each in March. Three tables are later sold for $1,750 each in April, and the remaining two tables are sold for $1,500 each in May.

     b.   Peyton Company purchases $300 of office supplies that are both paid for and used in August.

     c.   Kerra Company purchases $500 of inventory on account in July. The inventory is sold for $650 in August. Kerra pays its suppliers the $500 due in September.

PROBLEMS—SET A

LO2   **P3-1A. Transaction Entries, Posting, Trial Balance, and Adjusting Entries** Mark Ladd opened Ladd Roofing Service on April 1. Transactions for April are as follows:

April   1   Ladd contributed $11,500 of his personal funds in exchange for common stock to begin the business.

         2   Purchased a used truck for $6,100 cash.

         3   Purchased ladders and other equipment for a total of $3,100, paid $1,000 cash, with the balance due in 30 days.

         4   Paid two-year premium on liability insurance, $2,880.

         5   Purchased supplies on account, $1,200.

         6   Received an advance payment of $1,800 from a customer for roof repair work to be done during April and May.

         7   Billed customers for roofing services, $5,500.

         8   Collected $4,900 on account from customers.

         9   Paid bill for truck fuel used in April, $75.

      10   Paid April newspaper advertising, $100.

      11   Paid assistants' wages, $2,500.

      12   Billed customers for roofing services, $4,000.

Required

     a.   Set up a general ledger with the following accounts: Cash; Accounts Receivable; Supplies; Prepaid Insurance; Trucks; Accumulated Depreciation—Trucks; Equipment; Accumulated Depreciation—Equipment; Accounts Payable; Unearned Roofing Fees; Common Stock; Retained Earnings; Roofing Fees Earned; Fuel Expense; Advertising Expense; Wages Expense; Insurance Expense; Supplies Expense; Depreciation Expense—Trucks; and Depreciation Expense—Equipment.

     b.   Record these transactions in the general journal and post to the ledger accounts.

     c.   Prepare an unadjusted trial balance as of April 30.

     d.   Prepare the journal entries to adjust the books for insurance expense, supplies expense, depreciation expense on the truck, depreciation expense on the equipment, and roofing fees earned. Supplies on hand on April 30 amounted to $400. Depreciation for April was $125 on the truck and $35 on the equipment. One-fourth of the roofing fee received in advance was earned by April 30. Post the adjusting entries.

LO2   **P3-2A. Transaction Entries, Posting, Trial Balance, and Adjusting Entries** The Wellness Catering Service had the following transactions in July, its first month of operations:

July   1   Kelly Foster contributed $15,000 of personal funds to the business in exchange for common stock.

         2   Purchased the following items for cash from a catering firm that was going out of business (make a compound entry): delivery van, $3,780; equipment, $3,240; and supplies, $1,600.

         3   Paid premium on a one-year liability insurance policy, $1,080.

         4   Entered into a contract with a local service club to cater weekly luncheon meetings for one year at a fee of $750 per month. Received six months' fees in advance.

July 5   Paid rent for July, August, and September, $2,340.
     6   Paid employee's two weeks' wages (five-day week), $1,700.
     7   Billed customers for services rendered, $4,500.
     8   Purchased supplies on account, $3,400.
     9   Paid employee's two weeks' wages, $1,700.
    10   Paid July bill for gas, oil, and repairs on delivery van, $690.
    11   Collected $3,700 from customers on account.
    12   Billed customers for services rendered, $4,800.
    13   Foster received a $1,900 dividend.

Required

a.   Set up a general ledger that includes the following accounts: Cash; Accounts Receivable; Supplies; Prepaid Rent; Prepaid Insurance; Delivery Van; Accumulated Depreciation—Delivery Van; Equipment; Accumulated Depreciation—Equipment; Accounts Payable; Wages Payable; Unearned Catering Fees; Common Stock; Dividends; Retained Earnings; Catering Fees Revenue; Wages Expense; Rent Expense; Supplies Expense; Insurance Expense; Delivery Van Expense; Depreciation Expense—Delivery Van; and Depreciation Expense—Equipment.

b.   Record July transactions in the general journal and post to the ledger accounts.

c.   Prepare an unadjusted trial balance as of July 31.

d.   Record adjusting journal entries in the general journal and post to the ledger accounts. The following information is available on July 31:

    Supplies on hand, $1,500
    Accrued wages, $510
    Estimated life of delivery van, three years
    Estimated life of equipment, six years

Also, make any necessary adjusting entries for insurance, rent, and catering fees indicated by the July transactions.

P3-3A. **Trial Balance and Adjusting Entries** Photomake, Inc., a commercial photography studio, has just completed its first full year of operations on December 31. The general ledger account balances before year-end adjustments follow. No adjusting entries have been made to the accounts at any time during the year. Assume that all balances are normal.

LO2

Excel

Cash............................	$ 2,150	Accounts payable.................	$ 1,910
Accounts receivable...............	3,800	Unearned photography fees.........	2,600
Prepaid rent	12,600	Common stock....................	24,000
Prepaid insurance	2,970	Photography fees earned...........	34,480
Supplies	4,250	Wages expense	11,000
Equipment	22,800	Utilities expense..................	3,420

An analysis of the firm's records discloses the following items:

1.   Photography services of $925 have been rendered, but customers have not yet been billed. The firm uses the account Fees Receivable to reflect amounts due but not yet billed.

2.   The equipment, purchased January 1, has an estimated life of 10 years. *22800 ÷ 10*

3.   Utilities expense for December is estimated to be $400, but the bill will not arrive until January of next year.

4.   The balance in Prepaid Rent represents the amount paid on January 1, for a two-year lease on the studio. *12,600 ÷ 2*

5.   In November, customers paid $2,600 in advance for pictures to be taken for the holiday season. When received, these fees were credited to Unearned Photography Fees. By December 31, all fees are earned.

6.   A three-year insurance premium paid on January 1, was debited to Prepaid Insurance.

7.   Supplies on hand at December 31 are $1,520. *4,250 − 1,520*

8.   At December 31, wages expense of $375 has been incurred but not paid. *11,000*

Required

a.   Prove that the sum of the debits equals the sum of the credits for Photomake's unadjusted account balances by preparing an unadjusted trial balance as of December 31.

b.   Record adjusting entries in the general journal.

LO2   **P3-4A.**   **Adjusting Entries** Dole Carpet Cleaners ended its first month of operations on June 30. Monthly financial statements will be prepared. The unadjusted account balances are as follows:

DOLE CARPET CLEANERS Unadjusted Trial Balance June 30, 2012		
	Debit	Credit
Cash.	$ 1,180	
Accounts receivable.	450	
Prepaid rent	3,100	
Supplies	2,520	
Equipment	4,440	
Accounts payable.		$ 760
Common stock.		2,500
Retained earnings		5,000
Dividends	200	
Service fees earned		4,650
Wages expense	1,020	
	$12,910	$12,910

The following information is also available:

1. The balance in Prepaid Rent was the amount paid on June 1 for the first four months' rent.
2. Supplies on hand at June 30 were $820.
3. The equipment, purchased June 1, has an estimated life of five years.
4. Unpaid wages at June 30 were $210.
5. Utility services used during June were estimated at $300. A bill is expected early in July.
6. Fees earned for services performed but not yet billed on June 30 were $380. The firm uses the account Fees Receivable to reflect amounts due but not yet billed.

Required
Prepare the adjusting entries needed at June 30 for the general journal.

LO2   **P3-5A.**   **Adjusting Entries** The following information relates to December 31 adjustments for Finest Print, a printing company. The firm's fiscal year ends on December 31.

1. Weekly salaries for a five-day week total $1,800, payable on Fridays. December 31 of the current year is a Tuesday.
2. Finest Print has $20,000 of notes payable outstanding at December 31. Interest of $200 has accrued on these notes by December 31, but will not be paid until the notes mature next year.
3. During December, Finest Print provided $900 of printing services to clients who will be billed on January 2. The firm uses the account Fees Receivable to reflect amounts due but not yet billed.
4. Starting December 1, all maintenance work on Finest Print's equipment is handled by Prompt Repair Company under an agreement whereby Finest Print pays a fixed monthly charge of $90. Finest Print paid six months' service charge in advance on December 1, debiting Prepaid Maintenance for $540.
5. The firm paid $900 on December 15 for a series of radio commercials to run during December and January. One-third of the commercials have aired by December 31. The $900 payment was debited to Prepaid Advertising.
6. Starting December 16, Finest Print rented 400 square feet of storage space from a neighboring business. The monthly rent of $0.80 per square foot is due in advance on the first of each month. Nothing was paid in December, however, because the neighbor agreed to add the rent for one-half of December to the January 1 payment.
7. Finest Print invested $5,000 in securities on December 1 and earned interest of $38 on these securities by December 31. No interest will be received until January.
8. The annual depreciation on the firm's equipment is $2,175. No depreciation has been recorded during the year.

Required
Prepare the required December 31 adjusting entries in the general journal.

P3-6A. **Adjusting Entries** The following selected accounts appear in the Shaw Company's unadjusted trial balance as of December 31, the end of the fiscal year (all accounts have normal balances): **LO2**

Prepaid advertising.	$ 1,200	Unearned service fees	$ 5,400
Wages expense	43,800	Service fees earned	87,000
Prepaid insurance	3,420	Rental income	4,900

Required

Prepare the necessary adjusting entries in the general journal as of December 31, assuming the following:

1. Prepaid advertising at December 31 is $800.
2. Unpaid wages earned by employees in December are $1,300.
3. Prepaid insurance at December 31 is $2,280.
4. Unearned service fees at December 31 are $3,000.
5. Rent revenue of $1,000 owed by a tenant is not recorded at December 31.

P3-7A. **Adjusting Entries** The following selected accounts appear in the Birch Company's unadjusted trial balance as of December 31, the end of the fiscal year (all accounts have normal balances): **LO2**

Prepaid maintenance	$2,700	Commission fees earned	$84,000
Supplies	8,400	Rent expense	10,800
Unearned commission fees	8,500		

Required

Prepare the necessary adjusting entries in the general journal as of December 31, assuming the following:

1. On September 1, the company entered into a prepaid equipment maintenance contract. Birch Company paid $2,700 to cover maintenance service for six months, beginning September 1. The $2,700 payment was debited to Prepaid Maintenance.
2. Supplies on hand at December 31 are $3,200.
3. Unearned commission fees at December 31 are $4,000.
4. Commission fees earned but not yet billed at December 31 are $2,800. (*Note:* Debit Fees Receivable.)
5. Birch Company's lease calls for rent of $900 per month payable on the first of each month, plus an annual amount equal to 1 percent of annual commissions earned. This additional rent is payable on January 10 of the following year. (*Note:* Be sure to use the adjusted amount of commissions earned in computing the additional rent.)

P3-8A. **Financial Statements and Closing Entries** The adjusted trial balance shown below is for Fine Consulting Service as of December 31. Byran Fine made no capital contributions during the year. **LO3, 4**

	Adjusted Trial Balance	
	Debit	Credit
Cash.	$ 2,700	
Accounts receivable.	3,270	
Supplies	3,060	
Prepaid insurance	1,500	
Equipment	6,400	
Accumulated depreciation—Equipment		$ 1,080
Accounts payable.		845
Long-term notes payable.		7,000
Common stock.		2,000
Retained earnings		5,205
Dividends	2,900	
Service fees earned		58,400
Rent expense	12,000	
Salaries expense	33,400	
Supplies expense.	4,700	
Insurance expense.	3,250	
Depreciation expense—Equipment	720	
Interest expense.	630	
Totals	$74,530	$74,530

Required

a. Prepare an income statement and a statement of stockholders' equity for the year, and a balance sheet as of December 31.

b. Prepare closing entries directly to Retained Earnings in general journal form.

LO3, 5
(Appendix 3A)

Excel ✔

P3-9A. Financial Statements and Closing Entries   Use the information provided in P3-8A.

Required

a. Prepare an income statement, a statement of stockholders' equity, and a balance sheet as of December 31.

b. Prepare closing entries using the Income Summary account.

LO4 ✔

P3-10A. Closing Entries   The adjusted trial balance shown below is for Bayou, Inc., at December 31:

	Adjusted Trial Balance	
	Debit	Credit
Cash.	$ 3,500	
Accounts receivable.	8,000	
Prepaid insurance	3,600	
Equipment	72,000	
Accumulated depreciation		$ 12,000
Accounts payable.		600
Common stock.		30,000
Retained earnings		14,100
Cash dividends.	5,000	
Service fees earned		97,200
Miscellaneous income		4,200
Salaries expense	42,800	
Rent expense.	13,400	
Insurance expense.	1,800	
Depreciation expense.	8,000	
Income tax expense.	8,800	
Income tax payable		8,800
Totals	$166,900	$166,900

Required

a. Prepare closing entries directly to Retained Earnings in general journal form.

b. After the closing entries are posted, what is the ending balance in the Retained Earnings account?

c. Prepare a post-closing trial balance.

LO5
(Appendix 3A)
✔

P3-11A. Closing Entries   Use the information provided in P3-10A.

Required

a. Prepare closing entries in general journal form using the Income Summary account.

b. After the closing entries are posted, what is the ending balance in the Retained Earnings account?

c. Prepare a post-closing trial balance.

LO3 ✔

P3-12A. Balance Sheet and Net Income   At the beginning of 2012, Flynn's Parking Lots had the following balance sheet:

Assets		**Liabilities**	
Cash.	$ 4,800	Accounts payable.	$12,000
Accounts receivable.	14,700		
Land	60,000	**Stockholders' Equity**	
		Common stock.	20,000
		Retained earnings	47,500
		Total Liabilities and	
Total Assets	$79,500	Stockholders' Equity.	$79,500

a. At the end of 2012, Flynn had the following assets and liabilities: Cash, $8,800; Accounts Receivable, $17,400; Land, $60,000; and Accounts Payable, $7,500; and Common Stock, $20,000. Prepare a year-end balance sheet for Flynn's Parking Lots.

b. Assume that stockholders did not invest any money in the business during the year but received $12,000 as a dividend; what was Flynn's net income or net loss for 2012?

P3-13A. Determination of Retained Earnings and Net Income The following information appears in the records of Bock Corporation at the end of 2012:

LO3

Accounts receivable..............	$ 23,000	Retained earnings	$?
Accounts payable................	11,000	Supplies	9,000
Cash.........................	8,000	Equipment	138,000
Common stock..................	110,000		

a. Calculate the amount of retained earnings at the end of 2012.

b. Using your answer from part *a*, if the amount of the retained earnings at the beginning of 2012 was $30,000, and $12,000 in dividends were paid during 2012, what was the company's net income for 2012?

P3-14A. Transaction Analysis, Trial Balance, and Financial Statements Angela Mehl operates the Mehl Dance Studio. On June 1, the business's general ledger contained the following information:

LO2, 3

Cash.........................	$ 5,930	Accounts payable.................	$ 480
Accounts receivable..............	7,420	Notes payable	3,000
		Common stock..................	7,870
		Retained earnings	2,000
	$13,350		$13,350

The following transactions occurred during the month of June:

June 1 Paid June rent for practice studio, $975.
  2 Paid June piano rental, $90 (Rent Expense).
  3 Collected $5,320 from students on account.
  4 Borrowed $1,500 and signed a promissory note payable due in six months.
  5 Billed students for June instructional fees, $5,600.
  6 Paid interest for June on notes payable, $30.
  7 Paid $350 for advertising ballet performances.
  8 Paid costume rental, $400 (Rent Expense).
  9 Collected $2,100 admission fees from ballet performances given during the month.
  10 Paid $480 owed on account.
  11 Received invoice for June utilities, to be paid in July, $280.
  12 Paid stockholders $750 cash as a dividend.
  13 Purchased piano for $5,000 cash, to be used in business starting in July.

Required

a. Set up accounts for the general ledger with June 1 balances and enter the beginning balances. Also provide the following accounts: Piano; Dividends; Instructional Fees Earned; Performance Revenue; Rent Expense; Utilities Expense; Advertising Expense; and Interest Expense. Record the listed transactions in the accounts.

b. Prepare a trial balance as of June 30.

c. Prepare an income statement for the month of June.

d. Prepare a statement of stockholders' equity for the month of June.

e. Prepare a balance sheet as of June 30.

P3-15A. Transaction Analysis, Trial Balance, and Financial Statements On December 1, a group of individuals formed a corporation to establish the *Beeper,* a neighborhood weekly newspaper featuring want ads of individuals and advertising of local firms. The free paper will be mailed to about 8,000 local residents; revenue will be generated from advertising and want ads. The December transactions are summarized as follows:

LO2, 3

Dec. 1 Sold common stock of Beeper, Inc., for cash, $25,000.

2 Paid December rent on furnished office, $1,000.

3 Purchased for $750, on account, T-shirts displaying company logo. The T-shirts were distributed at a grand opening.

4 Paid to creditor on account, $750.

5 Collected "Help wanted" ad revenue in cash, $2,800.

6 Paid post office for cost of bulk mailing, $910.

7 Billed various firms for advertising in the first two issues of the newspaper, $5,300.

8 Paid Acme Courier Service for transporting newspapers to post office, $50.

9 Paid for printing newspaper, $2,900.

10 Collected "Help wanted" ad revenue in cash, $2,570.

11 Received invoice for December utilities, to be paid in January, $310.

12 Paid for printing newspaper, $2,900.

13 Paid December salaries, $4,100.

14 Billed various firms for advertising in two issues of the newspaper, $6,850.

15 Paid post office for cost of bulk mailing, $930.

16 Paid Acme Courier Service for transporting newspapers to post office, $50.

17 Collected $5,100 on accounts receivable.

18 Purchased fax machine for office in exchange for a six-month note payable, $1,100.

Required

a. Set up accounts for the following items: Cash, Accounts Receivable, Office Equipment, Accounts Payable, Notes Payable, Common Stock, Advertising Revenue, Want Ad Revenue, Printing Expense, Advertising Expense, Utilities Expense, Salaries Expense, Rent Expense, and Delivery Expense. Prepare journal entries in a general journal and record the foregoing transactions in the accounts.

b. Prepare a trial balance as of December 31.

c. Prepare an income statement for the month of December.

d. Prepare a balance sheet as of December 31. (*Note:* In this problem, the net income for December becomes the amount of retained earnings at December 31.)

LO3
P3-16A. Balance Sheets for a Corporation The following balance sheet data are given for Normandy Catering Service, a corporation, as of May 31:

Accounts receivable.	$18,300	Accounts payable.	$ 5,200
Notes payable	20,000	Cash	12,200
Equipment	55,000	Common stock.	42,500
Supplies	16,400	Retained earnings	?

Assume that on June 1, the following transactions occurred:

June 1 Purchased additional equipment costing $15,000, giving $2,000 cash and a $13,000 note payable.

1 Paid a cash dividend of $7,000.

Required

a. Prepare a balance sheet as of May 31.

b. Prepare a balance sheet as of June 2.

LO3
P3-17A. Determination of Net Income and Retained Earnings The following selected income statement and balance sheet information is available for Lloyd Appraisers at the end of the current month:

Supplies	$ 4,900	Accounts payable.	$ 4,000
Accounts receivable.	18,000	Salaries expense	15,000
Utilities expense	700	Appraisal fees earned.	31,000
Supplies expense.	1,300	Common stock	10,000
Rent expense	2,500	Retained earnings (beginning)	8,000
Cash.	3,600		

a. Calculate the net income or net loss for the month.

b. If Mr. Lloyd made no additional investment in the business during the month but received $7,000 as a dividend, what is the balance in Retained Earnings at the end of the month?

P3-18A. Trial Balance and Financial Statements The following account balances were taken (out of order) from the general ledger of R. Ladd & Company as of January 31. Ladd trains dogs for competitive championship field trials. The firm's accounting year began on January 1. All accounts have normal balances.

LO3 ✓

Land	$21,000	Office rent expense	$ 800
Maintenance expense	460	Supplies expense	760
Supplies	1,640	Utilities expense	200
Advertising expense	350	Fees earned	16,470
Common stock	20,000	Accounts receivable	8,200
Retained earnings	9,000		
Cash	7,300	Salaries expense	4,480
Accounts payable	820	Dividends	1,100

Required
a. Prepare a trial balance from the given data.
b. Prepare an income statement for the month of January.
c. Prepare a statement of stockholders' equity for the month of January.
d. Prepare a balance sheet as of January 31.

P3-19A. Trial Balance and Financial Statements The following account balances, in alphabetical order, are from the general ledger of Morgan's Waterproofing Service at January 31. The firm began business on January 1. All accounts have normal balances.

LO3 ✓

Accounts payable	$ 2,600	Notes payable	$ 6,000
Accounts receivable	21,000	Rent expense	1,700
Advertising expense	420	Salaries expense	8,000
Cash	10,400	Service fees earned	25,760
Common stock	29,740	Supplies	8,960
Dividends	3,000	Supplies expense	10,250
Interest expense	50	Utilities expense	320

Required
a. Prepare a trial balance from the given data.
b. Prepare an income statement for the month of January.
c. Prepare a statement of stockholders' equity for the month of January.
d. Prepare a balance sheet as of January 31.

P3-20A. Worksheet The following unadjusted trial balance was prepared as of March 31:

LO6
(Appendix 3B)
✓
Excel

FOCUS TRAVEL AGENCY Unadjusted Trial Balance March 31, 2012		
	Debit	**Credit**
Cash	$ 2,400	
Commissions receivable	5,000	
Supplies	1,750	
Prepaid insurance	1,800	
Equipment	13,000	
Accumulated depreciation		$ 2,600
Accounts payable		550
Unearned commissions		600
Common stock		4,000
Retained earnings		6,000
Dividends	900	
Commissions earned		18,990
Salaries expense	4,500	
Rent expense	1,770	
Advertising expense	1,000	
Utilities expense	620	
Totals	$32,740	$32,740

Focus Travel Agency's fiscal year ends on March 31. The following additional information is available:

1. Depreciation for the year is $1,300.
2. Supplies on hand at March 31 amount to $820.
3. By March 31, $400 of the unearned commissions was earned. The remainder will be earned in the next year.
4. Insurance expense for the year is $1,200.
5. Accrued salaries payable total $600 at March 31.

Required

Enter the trial balance on a worksheet and complete the worksheet using the adjustment data given above.

PROBLEMS—SET B

LO2 **P3-1B.** **Transaction Entries, Posting, Trial Balance, Adjusting Entries** Huang Karate School began business on June 1. Transactions for June were as follows:

June 1 Po Huang contributed $7,500 of his personal funds in exchange for common stock to begin the business.

2 Purchased equipment for $2,750, paying $750 cash, with the balance due in 30 days.

3 Paid six months' rent, $3,450.

4 Paid one-year premium on liability insurance, $876.

5 Paid June newspaper advertising, $225.

6 Billed participants for karate lessons to date, $2,200.

7 Received $555 from a local company to conduct a special three-session class on self-defense for its employees. The three sessions will be held on June 29, July 6, and July 13, at $185 per session.

8 Collected $1,800 on account from participants

9 Paid $275 to repair damage to wall caused by an errant kick.

10 Billed participants for karate lessons to date, $2,000.

11 Paid assistant's wages, $650.

Required

a. Set up a general ledger with the following accounts: Cash; Accounts Receivable; Prepaid Rent; Prepaid Insurance; Equipment; Accumulated Depreciation—Equipment; Accounts Payable; Utilities Payable; Unearned Karate Fees; Common Stock; Retained Earnings; Karate Fees Earned; Advertising Expense; Repairs Expense; Wages Expense; Rent Expense; Insurance Expense; Depreciation Expense—Equipment; and Utilities Expense.

b. Record these transactions in general journal form and post to the ledger accounts.

c. Prepare an unadjusted trial balance as of June 30.

d. Prepare the adjusting entries for rent expense, insurance expense, depreciation expense, utilities expense, and karate fees earned. Depreciation expense for June is $50, and estimated utilities expense for June is $120. Post the adjusting entries.

LO2 **P3-2B.** **Transaction Entries, Posting, Trial Balance, and Adjusting Entries** Market-Probe, a market research firm, had the following transactions in June, its first month of operations.

June 1 J. Witson invested $24,000 of personal funds in the firm in exchange for common stock.

2 The firm purchased the following from an office supply company: office equipment, $11,040; office supplies, $2,840. Terms called for a cash payment of $4,000, with the remainder due in 60 days. (Make a compound entry.)

3 Paid June rent, $875.

4 Contracted for three months' advertising in a local newspaper at $310 per month and paid for the advertising in advance.

5 Signed a six-month contract with an electronics firm to provide research consulting services at a rate of $3,200 per month. Received two months' fees in advance. Work on the contract started immediately.

6 Billed various customers for services rendered, $5,800.

June 7 Paid two weeks' salaries (five-day week) to employees, $3,600.
8 Paid J. Witson's travel expenses to business conference, $1,240.
9 Paid $520 cash for postage to mail questionnaire.
10 Paid two weeks' salaries to employees, $3,600.
11 Billed various customers for services rendered, $5,200.
12 Collected $7,800 from customers on account.
13 J. Witson received a $1,500 cash dividend.

Required

a. Set up a general ledger that includes the following accounts: Cash; Accounts Receivable; Office Supplies; Prepaid Advertising; Office Equipment; Accumulated Depreciation—Office Equipment; Accounts Payable; Salaries Payable; Unearned Service Fees; Common Stock; Dividends; Retained Earnings; Service Fees Earned; Salaries Expense; Advertising Expense; Supplies Expense; Rent Expense; Travel Expense; Depreciation Expense—Office Equipment; and Postage Expense.

b. Record June transactions in general journal form and post to the ledger accounts.

c. Prepare an unadjusted trial balance as of June 30.

d. Record adjusting journal entries in general journal form, and post to the ledger accounts. The following information is available on June 30:

Office supplies on hand, $1,530.
Accrued salaries, $725.
Estimated life of office equipment, eight years.

Also, make any necessary adjusting entries for advertising and for service fees indicated by the June transactions.

P3-3B. **Trial Balance and Adjusting Entries** Deliverall, a mailing service, has just completed its first full year of operations on December 31, 2012. The firm's general ledger account balances before year-end adjustments are given below. No adjusting entries have been made to the accounts at any time during the year. Assume that all balances are normal.

LO2

Excel

Cash	$ 2,300	Accounts payable	$ 2,700
Accounts receivable	5,120	Common stock	9,530
Prepaid advertising	1,680	Mailing fees earned	86,000
Supplies	6,270	Wages expense	38,800
Equipment	42,240	Rent expense	6,300
Notes payable	7,500	Utilities expense	3,020

An analysis of the firm's records reveals the following:

1. The balance in Prepaid Advertising represents the amount paid for newspaper advertising for one year. The agreement, which calls for the same amount of space each month, covers the period from February 1, 2012, to January 31, 2013. Deliverall did not advertise during its first month of operations.

2. The equipment, purchased January 1, has an estimated life of eight years.

3. Utilities expense does not include expense for December, estimated at $325. The bill will not arrive until January 2013.

4. At year-end, employees have earned $1,200 in wages that will not be paid until January.

5. Supplies on hand at year-end amounted to $1,520.

6. At year-end, unpaid interest of $450 has accrued on the notes payable.

7. The firm's lease calls for rent of $525 per month payable on the first of each month, plus an amount equal to ½ percent of annual mailing fees earned. The rental percentage is payable within 15 days after the end of the year.

Required

a. Demonstrate that the sum of the debits equals the sum of the credits for the unadjusted account balances shown above by preparing an unadjusted trial balance as of December 31, 2012.

b. Record adjusting entries in general journal form.

LO2 P3-4B. **Adjusting Entries** The Wheel Place, Inc., began operations on March 1 to provide automotive wheel alignment and balancing services. On March 31, 2012, the unadjusted balances of the firm's accounts are as follows:

THE WHEEL PLACE, INC. Unadjusted Trial Balance March 31, 2012		
	Debit	Credit
Cash	$ 1,900	
Accounts receivable	3,820	
Prepaid rent	4,770	
Supplies	3,700	
Equipment	36,180	
Accounts payable		$ 2,510
Unearned service revenue		1,000
Common stock		38,400
Service revenue		12,360
Wages expense	3,900	
Totals	$54,270	$54,270

The following information is also available.

1. The balance in Prepaid Rent was the amount paid on March 1 to cover the first six months' rent.
2. Supplies on hand on March 31 amounted to $1,720.
3. The equipment has an estimated life of nine years.
4. Unpaid wages at March 31 were $560.
5. Utility services used during March were estimated at $390. A bill is expected early in April.
6. The balance in Unearned Service Revenue was the amount received on March 1 from a new car dealer to cover alignment and balancing services on all new cars sold by the dealer in March and April. The Wheel Place agreed to provide the services at a fixed fee of $500 each month.

Required
Prepare the adjusting entries needed at March 31 in general journal form.

LO2 P3-5B. **Adjusting Entries** The following information relates to the December 31 adjustments for Water Barrier, a firm providing waterproofing services for commercial and residential customers. The firm's fiscal year ends December 31; no adjusting entries have been made during the year.

1. The firm paid a $2,340 premium for a three-year insurance policy, coverage to begin October 1. The premium payment was debited to Prepaid Insurance.
2. Weekly wages for a five-day work week total $1,225, payable on Fridays. December 31 is a Thursday.
3. Water Barrier received $3,600 in November for services to be performed during December through February of the following year. When received, this amount was credited to Unearned Service Fees. By December 31, one-third of this amount was earned.
4. Water Barrier receives a 5 percent commission from the manufacturer on sales of a waterproofing agent to Water Barrier's customers. By December 31, Water Barrier had sales of $9,000 (during November and December) for which no commissions had been received or recorded.
5. During December, fuel oil costs of $495 were incurred to heat the firm's buildings. Because the monthly bill from the oil company has not yet arrived, no entry has been made for this amount (fuel oil costs are charged to Utilities Expense).
6. The Supplies account has a balance of $16,900 on December 31. A count of supplies on December 31 indicates that $3,500 worth of supplies are still on hand.

7. On December 1, Water Barrier borrowed $9,000 from the bank, giving a note payable. Interest is not payable until the note is due near the end of the following January. However, the interest for December is $75.

8. Water Barrier rents parking spaces in its lot to firms in the office building next door. On December 1, Water Barrier received $10,000 as advance payments to cover parking privileges in the lot for December through March of the following year. When received, the $10,000 was credited to Unearned Parking Fees.

Required
Prepare the necessary December 31 adjusting entries in general journal form.

P3-6B. **Adjusting Entries** The following selected accounts appear in the Albany Company's unadjusted trial balance as of December 31, the end of the fiscal year (all accounts have normal balances): **LO2** ✓

Prepaid advertising.	$ 2,200	Unearned service fees	$ 5,400
Wages expense	43,800	Service fees earned	87,000
Prepaid insurance	5,420	Rental income	4,900

Required
Make the necessary adjusting entries in general journal form as of December 31 assuming the following:

a. Prepaid advertising at December 31 is $800.
b. Unpaid wages earned by employees in December are $1,700.
c. Prepaid insurance at December 31 is $2,280.
d. Unearned service fees at December 31 are $2,000.
e. Rent revenue of $3,500 owed by a tenant is not recorded at December 31.

P3-7B. **Adjusting Entries** The following selected accounts appear in the Burns Company's unadjusted trial balance as of December 31, the end of the fiscal year (all accounts have normal balances): **LO2** ✓

Prepaid maintenance	$ 3,000	Commission fees earned	$97,000
Supplies	10,400	Rent expense	10,800
Unearned commission fees	10,500		

Required
Make the necessary adjusting entries in general journal form at December 31, assuming the following:

1. On September 1, the company entered into a prepaid equipment maintenance contract. The Burns Company paid $3,000 to cover maintenance service for six months, beginning September 1. The $3,000 payment was debited to Prepaid Maintenance.

2. Supplies on hand at December 31 are $3,200.

3. Unearned commission fees at December 31 are $4,000.

4. Commission fees earned but not yet billed at December 31 are $3,500. (*Note:* Debit Fees Receivable.)

5. The Burns Company's lease calls for rent of $900 per month payable on the first of each month, plus an annual amount equal to 1 percent of annual commissions earned. This additional rent is payable on January 10 of the following year. (*Note:* Be sure to use the adjusted amount of commissions earned in calculating the additional rent.)

LO3, 4

P3-8B. **Financial Statements and Closing Entries** Outdoors, Inc., publishes magazines for skiers and hikers. The firm has the following adjusted trial balance at December 31:

OUTDOORS, INC. Adjusted Trial Balance December 31, 2012	Debit	Credit
Cash.	$ 5,400	
Accounts receivable.	18,600	
Supplies	4,200	
Prepaid insurance	930	
Office equipment	66,000	
Accumulated depreciation		$ 13,000
Accounts payable.		12,100
Unearned subscription revenue		10,000
Salaries payable.		3,500
Common stock.		25,000
Retained earnings		23,220
Subscription revenue		188,300
Advertising revenue		49,700
Salaries expense	120,230	
Printing and mailing expense.	85,600	
Rent expense.	8,800	
Supplies expense.	6,100	
Insurance expense.	1,860	
Depreciation expense.	5,500	
Income tax expense.	1,600	
Totals	$324,820	$324,820

Required
a. Prepare an income statement for 2012 and a balance sheet as of December 31.
b. Prepare closing entries directly to Retained Earnings in general journal form.

LO3, 5
(Appendix 3A)

P3-9B. **Financial Statements and Closing Entries** Use the information provided in P3-8B.

Required
a. Prepare an income statement for 2012 and a balance sheet as of December 31.
b. Prepare closing entries in general journal form using the Income Summary account.

P3-10B. Closing Entries The adjusted trial balance for Okay Moving Service as of December 31 is as follows: **LO4** ✔

	Adjusted Trial Balance	
	Debit	Credit
Cash.	$ 3,800	
Accounts receivable.	5,250	
Supplies	2,300	
Prepaid advertising.	3,000	
Trucks.	28,300	
Accumulated depreciation—Trucks.		$ 10,000
Equipment	7,600	
Accumulated depreciation—Equipment		2,100
Accounts payable.		1,200
Unearned service fees		2,700
Common stock.		10,000
Retained earnings		16,050
Dividends	5,500	
Service fees earned		72,500
Wages expense	29,800	
Rent expense.	10,200	
Insurance expense.	2,900	
Supplies expense.	5,100	
Advertising expense.	6,000	
Depreciation expense—Trucks	4,000	
Depreciation expense—Equipment	800	
Totals	$114,550	$114,550

Required
a. Prepare the closing entries at December 31 directly to Retained Earnings in general journal form.
b. After the closing entries are posted, calculate the ending balance in the Retained Earnings account.
c. Prepare a post-closing trial balance.

P3-11B. Closing Entries Use the information provided in P3-10B. **LO5 (Appendix 3A)** ✔

Required
a. Prepare closing entries at December 31 in general journal form using the Income Summary account.
b. After the closing entries are posted, calculate the ending balance in the Retained Earnings account.
c. Prepare a post-closing trial balance.

P3-12B. Balance Sheet and Net Income Determination At the beginning of 2012, Luxury Parking Services had the following balance sheet: **LO3** ✔

Assets		**Liabilities**	
Cash.	$ 5,800	Accounts payable.	$13,500
Accounts receivable.	14,700		
Land	60,500	**Stockholders' Equity**	
		Common stock.	60,000
		Retained earnings	7,500
		Total Liabilities and	
Total Assets	$81,000	Stockholders' Equity.	$81,000

a. At the end of 2012, Luxury Parking Services had the following assets and liabilities: Cash, $8,800; Accounts Receivable, $17,400; Land, $60,500; and Accounts Payable, $9,500. Prepare a year-end balance sheet for Luxury Parking Services assuming that no additional stock was issued.

b. Assuming that stockholders did not invest any money in the business during the year but received a $12,000 dividend, what was the company's net income or net loss for 2012?

LO3

P3-13B. Determination of Retained Earnings and Net Income The following information appears in the records of the Wellington Corporation at year-end 2012:

Accounts receivable...............	$ 33,000	Retained earnings	$?
Accounts payable.................	10,000	Supplies	7,000
Cash...........................	8,000	Equipment	140,000
Common stock..................	130,000		

a. Calculate the amount of retained earnings at the end of 2012.

b. Using your answer to part a, if the amount of the retained earnings at the beginning of 2012 was $30,000, and $9,000 in dividends were paid during 2012, what was the net income for 2012?

LO2, 3

P3-14B. Transaction Analysis, Trial Balance, and Financial Statements Kate Miller operates the Miller Dance Studio. On June 1, the studio's general ledger contained the following information:

Cash...........................	$ 8,930	Accounts payable..................	$ 480
Accounts receivable...............	17,420	Notes payable	3,000
		Common stock...................	9,870
		Retained earnings	13,000
	$26,350		$26,350

The following transactions occurred during the month of June:

June   1 Paid June rent for practice studio, $1,075.
       2 Paid June piano rental, $900 (Rent Expense).
       3 Collected $12,320 from students on account.
       4 Borrowed $5,500 and signed a promissory note payable due in six months.
       5 Billed students for June instructional fees, $7,600.
       6 Paid interest for June on the outstanding notes payable, $60.
       7 Paid $350 for advertising ballet performances.
       8 Paid costume rental, $600 (Rent Expense).
       9 Collected $4,100 admission fees from ballet performances given during June.
      10 Paid $480 owed on account.
      11 Received invoice for June utilities, to be paid in July, $280.
      12 The studio paid stockholders a cash dividend of $750.
      13 Purchased piano for $5,000 cash, to be used in business starting in July.

Required

a. Set up accounts for the general ledger with June 1 balances and enter the beginning balances. Also provide the following accounts: Piano; Dividends; Instructional Fees Earned; Performance Revenue; Rent Expense; Utilities Expense; Advertising Expense; and Interest Expense. Record the listed transactions in the accounts.

b. Prepare a trial balance as of June 30.

c. Prepare an income statement for the month of June.

d. Prepare a statement of stockholders' equity for the month of June.

e. Prepare a balance sheet as of June 30.

LO2, 3

P3-15B. Transaction Analysis, Trial Balance, and Financial Statements On December 1, a group of individuals formed a corporation to establish the *Arcadia News,* a neighborhood newspaper featuring "Help wanted" ads by individuals and advertising by local firms. The free paper will be mailed to about 20,000 local residents; revenue will be generated from advertising and the want ads. The December transactions are summarized below:

Dec. 1 Sold common stock for cash, $50,000.
  2 Paid December rent on furnished office, $3,000.
  3 Purchased for $750, on account, T-shirts displaying company logo. The T-shirts were distributed at a grand opening.
  4 Paid to creditor on account, $750.
  5 Collected want ad revenue in cash, $3,800.
  6 Paid post office for cost of bulk mailing, $910.
  7 Billed various firms for advertising in the first two issues of the newspaper, $7,300.
  8 Paid Tucson Courier Service for transporting newspapers to the post office, $50.
  9 Paid for printing newspaper, $2,900.
  10 Collected want ad revenue in cash, $2,570.
  11 Received invoice for December utilities, to be paid in January, $310.
  12 Paid for printing newspaper, $2,900.
  13 Paid December salaries, $4,100.
  14 Billed various firms for advertising in two issues of the newspaper, $6,950.
  15 Paid post office for cost of bulk mailing, $930.
  16 Paid Tucson Courier Service for transporting newspapers to the post office, $50.
  17 Collected $6,100 on accounts receivable.
  18 Purchased fax machine for the office in exchange for a six-month note payable, $2,100.

Required
a. Set up accounts for the following: Cash, Accounts Receivable, Office Equipment, Accounts Payable, Notes Payable, Common Stock, Advertising Revenue, Want Ad Revenue, Printing Expense, Advertising Expense, Utilities Expense, Salaries Expense, Rent Expense, and Delivery Expense. Prepare journal entries in a general journal and record the foregoing transactions in the accounts.
b. Prepare a trial balance as of December 31.
c. Prepare an income statement for the month of December.
d. Prepare a balance sheet as of December 31. (*Note:* In this problem, the net income for December becomes the amount of retained earnings at December 31.)

P3-16B. Balance Sheets The following balance sheet data are given for Cornell Catering Service, a corporation, at May 31:   **LO3** ✓

Accounts receivable	$28,300	Accounts payable	$ 5,200
Notes payable	20,000	Cash	12,200
Equipment	55,000	Common stock	62,500
Supplies	16,400	Retained earnings	?

Assume that on June 1, the following transactions occurred:

June 1 Purchased additional equipment costing $25,000, giving $5,000 cash and a $20,000 note payable.
  2 Paid a cash dividend of $7,000.

Required
a. Prepare a balance sheet as of May 31.
b. Prepare a balance sheet as of June 2.

P3-17B. Determination of Net Income and Stockholders' Equity The following selected income statement and balance sheet information is available for Zerbst Land Appraisers at the end of the current month: **LO3** ✓

Supplies	$ 4,900	Accounts payable	$ 4,000
Accounts receivable	18,000	Salaries expense	15,000
Utilities expense	700	Appraisal fees earned	31,000
Supplies expense	1,300	Common stock	15,000
Rent expense	2,500	Retained earnings (beginning)	3,000
Cash	3,600		

a. Calculate the net income or net loss for the month.

b. If stockholders made no additional investment during the month but received $5,000 as a dividend, what is the amount of stockholders' equity at the end of the month?

LO3 **P3-18B. Trial Balance and Financial Statements** The following account balances were prepared (out of order) from the general ledger of The Dog Whisperer, Inc. as of January 31. The company trains dogs having behavioral problems. The firm's business began on January 1. All accounts have normal balances.

Facilities	$31,000	Office rent expense	$ 800
Maintenance expense	460	Supplies expense.	760
Supplies	1,640	Utilities expense.	200
Advertising expense.	350	Fees earned	16,470
Common stock.	39,000	Accounts receivable.	8,200
Cash.	7,300	Salaries expense	4,480
Accounts payable.	820	Dividends	1,100

Required

a. Prepare a trial balance from the given data.

b. Prepare an income statement for the month of January.

c. Prepare a statement of stockholders' equity for the month of January.

d. Prepare a balance sheet as of January 31.

LO3 **P3-19B. Trial Balance and Financial Statements** The following account balances, in alphabetical order, are from the general ledger of The Columbus Service Company at January 31. The firm's business began on January 1. All accounts have normal balances.

Accounts payable.	$ 5,200	Notes payable	$12,000
Accounts receivable.	42,000	Rent expense	3,400
Advertising expense.	840	Salaries expense	16,000
Cash.	20,800	Service fees earned	51,520
Common stock	59,480	Supplies	17,920
Dividends	6,000	Supplies expense.	20,500
Interest expense.	100	Utilities expense.	640

Required

a. Prepare a trial balance from the given data.

b. Prepare an income statement for the month of January.

c. Prepare a statement of stockholders' equity for the month of January.

d. Prepare a balance sheet as of January 31.

P3-20B. Worksheet The July 31 unadjusted trial balance of Sharp Outfitters, a firm renting various types of equipment to canoeists and campers, follows.

LO6
(Appendix 3B)

Excel

SHARP OUTFITTERS Unadjusted Trial Balance July 31, 2013		
	Debit	**Credit**
Cash	$ 3,750	
Supplies	8,600	
Prepaid insurance	3,200	
Equipment	95,000	
Accumulated depreciation		$ 16,500
Accounts payable.		3,500
Unearned rental fees		8,850
Common stock.		30,000
Retained earnings		9,000
Dividends	1,200	
Rental fees earned		78,150
Wages expense	27,800	
Rent expense	3,300	
Advertising expense.	2,300	
Travel expense	850	
	$146,000	$146,000

Sharp Outfitters' fiscal year ends on July 31. The following additional information is available:

1. Supplies on hand at July 31 amount to $3,300.
2. Insurance expense for the year is $1,600.
3. Depreciation for the year is $8,250.
4. The unearned rental fees consist of deposits received from customers in advance when reservations are made. During the year, $4,850 of the unearned rental fees were earned. The remaining deposits apply to rentals for August and September 2013.
5. At July 31, revenue from rental services earned during July but not yet billed or received amounts to $2,500. (*Note:* Debit Fees Receivable.)
6. Accrued wages payable for equipment handlers and guides amounts to $900 at July 31.

Required
Enter the trial balance in a worksheet and complete the worksheet using the adjustment data given above.

SERIAL PROBLEM: KATE'S CARDS

(Note: This is a continuation of the Serial Problem: Kate's Cards from Chapters 1 and 2.)

SP3. Getting ready for the upcoming holiday season is traditionally a busy time for greeting card companies, and it was no exception for Kate. The following transactions occurred during the month of October:

1. Hired an assistant at an hourly rate of $10 per hour to help with some of the computer layouts and administrative chores.
2. Supplements her business by teaching a class to aspiring card designers. She charges and receives a total of $450.
3. Delivers greeting cards to several new customers. She bills them a total of $1,500.
4. Pays a utility bill in the amount of $250 that she determines is the business portion of her utility bill.

Kate's Cards

5. Receives an advance deposit of $500 for a new set of cards she is designing for a new customer.
6. Pays her assistant $200 for the work done this month.
7. Determines that the assistant has worked 10 additional hours this month that have not yet been paid.
8. Ordered and receives additional supplies in the amount of $1,000. These were paid for during the month.
9. Counts her remaining inventory of supplies at the end of the month and determines the balance to be $300. Don't forget to consider the supplies inventory balance at September 30, from Chapter 2. (*Hint:* This expense will be a debit to Cost of Goods Sold.)
10. Records the adjusting entries for depreciation and insurance expense for the month.
11. Pays herself a salary of $1,000.
12. Deciding she needs a little more cash, Kate pays herself a $500 dividend.
13. Receives her next utility bill during December and determines $85 applies to October's operations.

Required
Using the information that you gathered and the general ledger accounts that you prepared through Chapter 2, plus the new information above, complete the following:

a. Journalize the above transactions and adjusting entries.
b. Post the October transactions and adjusting entries. (Use the general ledger accounts prepared in Chapter 2 and add any new accounts that you may need.)
c. Prepare a trial balance as of October 31, 2012.
d. Prepare an income statement and a statement of stockholders' equity for the two-month period ending October 31, 2012, and a balance sheet as of October 31, 2012.
e. Prepare the closing entries as of October 31, 2012.
f. Prepare a post-closing trial balance.

EXTENDING YOUR KNOWLEDGE

REPORTING AND ANALYSIS

COLUMBIA
SPORTSWEAR
COMPANY

EYK3-1. **Financial Reporting Problem: Columbia Sportswear Company** The financial statements for the **Columbia Sportswear Company** can be found in Appendix A at the end of this book.

Required
Answer the following questions using Columbia's Consolidated Financial Statements and the Notes to the consolidated financial statements:

a. Identify an item that likely requires adjusting entries for prepayments.
b. Identify an item that likely requires an adjusting accrual.
c. Examine the statement of cash flows and identify the amount of depreciation and amortization expense for 2011. Where on the balance sheet was this accrual likely also shown?
d. Identify the items that will require closing entries. What account will they be ultimately closed to?

COLUMBIA
SPORTSWEAR
COMPANY

UNDER ARMOUR,
INC.

EYK3-2. **Comparative Analysis Problem: Columbia Sportswear Company vs. Under Armour, Inc.** The financial statements for the **Columbia Sportswear Company** can be found in Appendix A, and **Under Armour, Inc.**'s financial statements can be found in Appendix B at the end of this book.

Required
a. Examine the balance sheet of Columbia Sportswear and identify three items that indicate that the company uses the accrual method of accounting. In each case, identify the likely income statement account that is affected by these accruals.
b. Examine the balance sheet of Under Armour, Inc. and identify three items that indicate the company uses the accrual method of accounting. In each case, identify the likely income statement account that is affected by these accruals.

EYK3-3. **Business Decision Problem** Wyland Consulting Services, a firm started three years ago by Bruce Wyland, offers consulting services for material handling and plant layout. The balance sheet prepared by the firm's accountant at the close of 2012 is shown here.

WYLAND CONSULTING SERVICES						
Balance Sheet						
As of December 31, 2012						
Assets				**Liabilities**		
Cash.		$ 3,400		Notes payable		$30,000
Accounts receivable.		22,875		Accounts payable.		4,200
Supplies		13,200		Unearned consulting fees. . . .		11,300
Prepaid insurance		4,500		Wages payable.		400
Equipment	$68,500			Total Liabilities		45,900
Less: Accumulated depreciation . . .	(23,975)	44,525		**Stockholders' Equity**		
				Common stock.		20,000
				Retained earnings		22,600
				Total Stockholders' Equity . . .		42,600
				Total Liabilities and		
Total Assets		$88,500		Stockholders' Equity.		$88,500

Earlier in the year, Wyland obtained a bank loan of $30,000 for the firm. One of the provisions of the loan is that the year-end debt-to-equity ratio (ratio of total liabilities to total stockholders' equity) shall not exceed 1.0. Based on the above balance sheet, the ratio at the end of 2012 is 1.08 ($45,900/$42,600).

Wyland is concerned about being in violation of the loan agreement and asks your assistance in reviewing the situation. Wyland believes that his rather inexperienced accountant may have overlooked some items at year-end.

In discussions with Wyland and the accountant, you learn the following:

1. On January 1, 2012, the firm paid a $4,500 insurance premium for two years of coverage. The amount in Prepaid Insurance has not been adjusted.
2. Depreciation on the equipment should be 10 percent of cost per year. The accountant inadvertently recorded 15 percent for 2012.
3. Interest on the bank loan has been paid through the end of 2012.
4. The firm concluded a major consulting engagement in December, doing a plant layout analysis for a new factory. The $6,000 fee has not been billed or recorded in the accounts.
5. On December 1, 2012, the firm received an $11,300 advance payment from Croy Corporation for consulting services to be rendered over a two-month period. This payment was credited to the Unearned Consulting Fees account. One-half of this fee was earned by December 31, 2012.
6. Supplies costing $4,800 were on hand on December 31. The accountant filed the record of the count but made no entry in the accounts.

Required
a. What is the correct debt-to-equity ratio at December 31, 2012? Is the firm in violation of the loan agreement? Prepare a schedule to support your computation of the correct total liabilities and total stockholders' equity as of December 31, 2012.
b. Why might the loan agreement have contained the debt-to-equity provision?

EYK3-4. **Financial Analysis Problem** Purpose: To learn more about the Financial Accounting Standards Board (FASB)
Address: http://www.fasb.org

Required
Use the information on the FASB site to answer the following questiuons:
a. When was the FASB established?
b. What is the mission of the FASB?
c. Who has oversight responsibility for the FASB?
d. What are some of the current projects of the FASB?

CRITICAL THINKING

GENERAL MILLS,
INC.

EYK3-5. **Accounting Research Problem** Refer to the annual report of **General Mills, Inc.** for the year ending May 29, 2011 (fiscal year 2011), available on this book's Website. Review the consolidated balance sheets.

Required
a. Identify two assets listed in the consolidated balance sheets that indicate that General Mills uses the accrual basis of accounting. Which income statement accounts of General Mills are affected by adjustments to these assets accounts?
b. Identify two liabilities listed in the consolidated balance sheets that indicate that General Mills uses the accrual basis of accounting. Which income statement accounts of General Mills are affected by these adjustments?

EYK3-6. **Accounting Communications Activity** Many people do not understand the concept of accrual accounting and how it differs from accounting on a cash basis. In particular, they are confused as to why a company's results in any one accounting period can differ so much between the two methods of accounting. Because the cash basis is understood to a far larger degree, many people argue that the cash basis should be the primary basis of accounting.

Required
Write a short memorandum that explains the difference between accrual accounting and the cash basis of accounting. In your memo give a simple example of how the accrual basis can give a clearer picture of a company's performance in a given period.

EYK3-7. **Accounting Ethics Case** It is the end of an accounting year for Juliet Kravetz, controller of a medium-sized, publicly held corporation specializing in toxic waste cleanup. Within the corporation, only Kravetz and the president know that the firm has been negotiating for several months to land a very large contract for waste cleanup in Western Europe. The president has hired another firm with excellent contacts in Western Europe to help with the negotiations. The outside firm charges an hourly fee plus expenses, but has agreed not to submit a bill until the negotiations are in their final stages (expected to occur in another three to four months). Even if the contract falls through, the outside firm is entitled to receive payment for its services. Based upon her discussion with a member of the outside firm, Kravetz knows that its charge for services provided to date will be $150,000. This is a material amount for the company.

Kravetz knows that the president wants the negotiations to remain as secret as possible so that competitors will not learn of the European contract that the company is pursuing. Indeed, the president recently stated to her, "This is not the time to reveal our actions in Western Europe to other staff members, our auditors, or readers of our financial statements; securing this contract is crucial to our future growth." No entry has been made in the accounting records for the cost of the contract negotiations. Kravetz now faces an uncomfortable situation. The company's outside auditor has just asked her if she knows of any year-end adjustments that have not yet been recorded.

Required
What are the ethical considerations that Kravetz faces in answering the auditor's question? How should she respond to the question?

EYK3-8. **Corporate Social Responsibility Problem** Unlike financial reporting that requires all reported amounts to be expressed in monetary terms, Corporate Social Responsibility (CSR) reporting is often more qualitative than quantitative. This has caused some individuals to discount the CSR reports as too subjective.

Required
a. Can you identify any subjective areas within a financial statement prepared under GAAP?
b. Discuss the reasons both financial reporting, and to a larger extent CSR reporting, allow subjective estimates to be part of the report.

EYK3-9. **Forensic Accounting Problem** Most employees that choose to commit fraud against their employers feel justified in doing so. For example, a demotion with a corresponding pay cut can pro-

vide motivation to produce what is called "wages in kind," where the employee creates his or her own wages.

Required

What actions might an organization take to prevent "wages in kind"?

EYK3-10. IFRS Financial Statements Tesco PLC is the world's third largest retailer and is based in the United Kingdom. Tesco's IFRS financial statements are presented in Appendix C at the end of this textbook. Use these financial statements to answer the following questions:

Required

a. Identify two assets listed in the group balance sheets that indicate that Tesco uses the accrual basis of accounting. Which income statement accounts of Tesco are affected by adjustments to these assets accounts?

b. Identify two liabilities listed in the group balance sheets that indicate that Tesco uses the accrual basis of accounting. Which income statement accounts of Tesco are affected by these adjustments?

EYK3-11. Working with the Takeaways The Aspen Company has the following items that require adjustments as of December 31.

a. Service revenue of $600 had been received prior to work being performed. This amount was properly recorded as unearned revenue. At year-end, $400 of the services have now been performed.

b. Interest expense of $750 has not been recorded.

c. Services in the amount of $800 have been performed but not yet billed.

d. A physical count determined that supplies still available were $250. The Supplies asset account shows a balance of $700.

Required

Provide the adjusting entry needed to correct the balance in each of the affected accounts.

ANSWERS TO SELF-STUDY QUESTIONS:

1. b, (pp. 121–126) 2. c, (pp. 121–126) 3. d, (p. 138) 4. c, (p. 126) 5. d, (p. 129)
6. b, (p. 126) 7. b, (p. 124)

YOUR TURN! SOLUTIONS

Solution 3.1

1.	Dec. 31	Depreciation expense	700	
		Accumulated depreciation—Buildings		700
		To record depreciation on buildings.		
2.	Dec. 31	Rent expense	1,500	
		Prepaid rent		1,500
		To record rent expense.		
3.	Dec. 31	Unearned revenue	400	
		Revenue		400
		To recognize revenue earned on a previously recorded advance		
		payment from a customer.		
4.	Dec. 31	Interest expense	500	
		Interest payable		500
		To accrue interest expense.		

Solution 3.2

THE CASSI COMPANY Income Statement For the Year Ended December 31, 2013		
Sales revenues		$52,000
Expenses		
Cost of goods sold	$30,000	
Salaries expense	5,000	
Rent expense	6,000	
Depreciation expense	6,000	
Total expenses		47,000
Net income		$ 5,000

THE CASSI COMPANY Statement of Stockholders' Equity For the Year Ended December 31, 2013	Common Stock	Retained Earnings	Total
Balance, December 1, 2013	$15,000	$5,000	$20,000
Add: Net income for December		5,000	5,000
Less: Dividends in December		(2,000)	(2,000)
Balance, December 31, 2013	$15,000	$8,000	$23,000

THE CASSI COMPANY
Balance Sheet
As of December 31, 2013

Assets			Liabilities		
Current assets			Current liabilities		
Cash	$ 4,000		Accounts payable	$ 8,000	
Accounts receivable	15,000		Salaries payable	9,000	
Inventory	18,000		Dividends payable	2,000	
Prepaid rent	5,000		Unearned service	5,000	
Total current assets		$42,000	Total current liabilities		$24,000
			Long-term debt		35,000
Equipment	50,000		Total liabilities		59,000
Less: Accumulated depreciation	(10,000)	40,000	**Stockholders' Equity**		
			Common stock	15,000	
			Retained earnings	8,000	
			Total stockholders' equity		23,000
Total Assets		$82,000	Total Liabilities and Stockholders' Equity		$82,000

Solution 3.3

a. Permanent   e. Temporary
b. Permanent   f. Temporary
c. Temporary   g. Permanent
d. Permanent   h. Permanent

Solution 3.4

Dec. 31	Sales revenue	79,000	
	Retained earnings		79,000
	To close the revenue account.		

Dec. 31	Retained earnings	72,000	
	Cost of goods sold		41,000
	Wage expense		22,000
	Rent expense		3,000
	Depreciation expense		2,000
	Interest expense		4,000
	To close the expense accounts.		

Dec. 31	Retained earnings	5,000	
	Dividends		5,000
	To close the dividends account.		

Solution 3A.1

a. Permanent   e. Temporary
b. Permanent   f. Temporary
c. Temporary   g. Permanent
d. Permanent   h. Permanent

Solution 3A.2

Dec. 31	Sales revenue	79,000	
	Income summary		79,000
	To close the revenue account.		

Dec. 31	Income summary	72,000	
	Cost of goods sold		41,000
	Wage expense		22,000
	Rent expense		3,000
	Depreciation expense		2,000
	Interest expense		4,000
	To close the expense accounts.		

Dec. 31	Income summary	7,000	
	Retained earnings		7,000
	To close the Income Summary account.		

Dec. 31	Retained earnings	5,000	
	Dividends		5,000
	To close the Dividends account.		

4

Understanding Financial Statements

LEARNING OBJECTIVES

1. **Describe** a classified balance sheet. *(p. 180)*

2. **Describe** a classified (single-step and multi-step) income statement. *(p. 185)*

3. **Discuss** use of a balance sheet and ratios to assess liquidity and solvency. *(p. 188)*

4. **Discuss** use of the income statement and ratios to assess profitability. *(p. 191)*

5. **Explain** the components of the statement of stockholders' equity. *(p. 192)*

6. **Explain** use of the statement of cash flows to help assess solvency. *(p. 193)*

IDENTIFYING A WIN-WIN COMPANY

After a visit to one of **Apple**'s many retail stores, you will likely find it hard to believe that the company ever faced financial difficulties. The company has a cult-like following for its products including its Macintosh computer, the iPod, the iPhone, and the iPad. Things have not always been so good for the company that was established by Steve Jobs, Steve Wozniak, and Ronald Wayne. In fact, Apple suffered crippling financial losses and record low stock prices in the mid-1990s. Steve Jobs, who left the company in 1985 to start another business, was brought back to Apple in 1997 as chief executive officer (CEO). Over the next few years, Jobs was able to return the company to profitability.

Being a profitable company has allowed Apple to benefit from what some refer to as a virtuous cycle in which the company is able to both do good financially and do good socially. The company's solid financial resources provide the ability to do good, whereas doing good helps the company do well financially.

Apple realizes that a win-win situation can be obtained through its commitment to social responsibility. For example, Apple's Website explains how important it is to follow sound environmental policies to conserve natural resources. An example of this philosophy is its packaging for the iPhone, which is 42 percent smaller than the packing used for the original iPhone. The smaller packaging allows 80 percent more iPhone boxes to fit on each shipping pallet, which in turn enables more phones to fit on each boat and plane. Fitting more phones on each boat and plane results in fewer boats and planes used, which lowers the overall CO_2 emissions required by the shipping of the iPhone.

But what if we decide to consider investing in a company like Apple? How should we go about determining whether Apple is a good investment? We first want to do some research to determine if the company is profitable and financially sound. In this, and future chapters, we will begin to accumulate the financial skills needed to evaluate the financial health and operating performance of companies such as Apple.

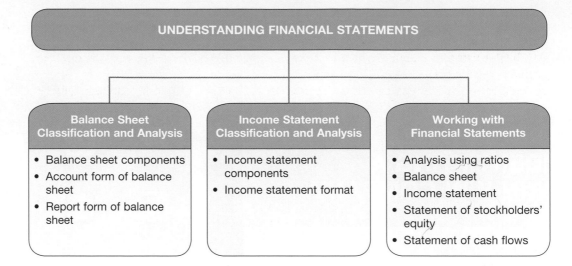

UNDERSTANDING FINANCIAL STATEMENTS

Balance Sheet Classification and Analysis	Income Statement Classification and Analysis	Working with Financial Statements
• Balance sheet components • Account form of balance sheet • Report form of balance sheet	• Income statement components • Income statement format	• Analysis using ratios • Balance sheet • Income statement • Statement of stockholders' equity • Statement of cash flows

BALANCE SHEET CLASSIFICATION AND ANALYSIS

LO1 — Describe a classified balance sheet.

A **classified balance sheet** presents the assets and liabilities of a business in separate subgroups. Such classification aids our financial analysis and business decision making. Exhibit 4-1 presents a list of the typical components of a classified balance sheet. A company need not use all of the components, and each company will use only those components necessary to report its financial position. Exhibit 4-1 shows that a company's assets are commonly classified into two subgroups: current assets and long-term assets. Similarly, liabilities are classified into two subgroups: current liabilities and long-term liabilities. Classified balance sheets are presented by most businesses.

Exhibit 4-1	Typical Components of a Classified Balance Sheet
Assets	**Liabilities and Stockholders' Equity**
Current Assets • Cash and cash equivalents • Accounts receivable • Inventory • Other current assets	**Current Liabilities** • Accounts payable • Accrued expenses payable • Short-term notes payable • Other current liabilities
Long-Term Assets • Property, plant, and equipment • Intangible assets • Other long-term assets	**Long-Term Liabilities** • Long-term notes payable • Other long-term liabilities **Stockholders' Equity**

Current Assets

Current assets consist of cash and other assets that will be converted into cash or used up within the normal operating cycle of a business or one year, whichever is longer. The **normal operating cycle** of a business is the average period of time between the use of cash to deliver a service or to buy goods for resale and the subsequent collection of cash from customers who purchase those services or products. For most businesses, the normal operating cycle is less than one year. For example, the normal operating cycle for a grocery store chain like **Safeway** might be as short as a week or two, on average, and even only a day or two for perishable products like bread and fresh sliced vegetables.

Current assets are listed on a classified balance sheet in the order of their expected liquidity. **Liquidity** is determined by the ability of an asset to be readily converted into cash. Exhibit 4-1 lists four examples of current assets in the order of their expected liquidity: cash, accounts receivable, inventory, and other current assets. Accounts receivable and inventory are converted into cash as part of the normal operations of a business; that is, inventory is sold for cash or on credit (accounts receivable) that is subsequently collected as cash from customers. Other current assets, such as supplies, are consumed during the normal operating cycle rather than converted into cash, and thus, represent the least liquid of the current assets. The following excerpt shows the current asset section of **Apple**.

APPLE INC. Balance Sheet (Partial) September 24, 2011 (in millions)	
Current assets	
Cash	$ 9,815
Accounts receivable	5,369
Inventory	776
Other current assets	29,028
Total current assets	$44,988

Long-Term Assets

Long-term assets are assets that the company does not expect to convert into cash within the next year or use up during the course of the normal operating cycle, whichever is longer. Long-term assets include property, plant, and equipment, intangible assets, and other long-term assets.

Property, Plant, and Equipment

Property, plant, and equipment consists of the land, buildings, equipment, vehicles, furniture, and fixtures that a company uses in its day-to-day operations. Investments into property, plant, and equipment, or PP&E, are often referred to as *capital expenditures* or capital investments. The following excerpt shows the PP&E section of **Apple**.

APPLE INC. Balance Sheet (Partial) September 24, 2011 (in millions)		
Property, plant, and equipment		
Land and buildings	$2,059	
Equipment.	7,110	
Leasehold improvements	2,599	$11,768
Less: accumulated depreciation and amortization.		3,991
Total property, plant, and equipment		$ 7,777

Intangible Assets

Intangible assets consist of brand names, copyrights, patents, and trademarks that a company acquires. These assets are referred to as "intangible" because, unlike buildings and equipment, they lack a physical presence. But, like buildings and equipment, intangible assets enable a company to generate revenue from its customers who recognize the quality associated with products bearing a brand name or trademark. The following excerpt shows the intangible asset section of **Apple**.

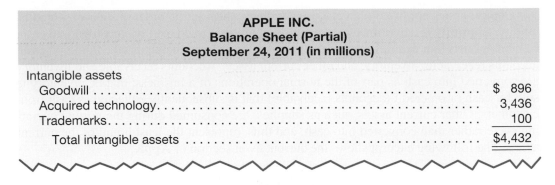

APPLE INC. Balance Sheet (Partial) September 24, 2011 (in millions)	
Intangible assets	
Goodwill	$ 896
Acquired technology.	3,436
Trademarks.	100
Total intangible assets	$4,432

Other Long-Term Assets

Other long-term assets consist of resources that a company consolidates into a single miscellaneous category. We discuss and illustrate the various types of assets that comprise this category of assets in later chapters. The following excerpt shows the other asset section of **Apple**.

APPLE INC. Balance Sheet (Partial) September 24, 2011 (in millions)	
Other long-term assets	
Long-term marketable securities	$55,618
Other assets	3,556
Total other long-term assets.	$59,174

Current Liabilities

Current liabilities consist of liabilities that must be settled within the normal operating cycle or one year, whichever is longer. Exhibit 4-1 lists four types of current liabilities: accounts payable, accrued expenses payable, short-term notes payable, and other current liabilities. Accounts payable reflects the amounts owed for inventory that was purchased from suppliers on credit. Accrued expenses payable include wages, utilities, interest, income tax, and property taxes that are legally owed by a company but which have not yet been paid. Short-term notes payable represent amounts owed that are specified in a formal contract called a note. Other current liabilities consist of current obligations that the company aggregates into a single miscellaneous category. One example is the advance payments received from customers (deferred revenue), such as for goods under a layaway plan that will be earned as revenue within the normal operating cycle or one year, whichever is longer. The following excerpt shows the current liabilities section of **Apple**.

APPLE INC. Balance Sheet (Partial) September 24, 2011 (in millions)	
Current liabilities	
Accounts payable.	$14,632
Accrued expenses	9,247
Deferred revenue	4,091
Total current liabilities.	$27,970

Long-Term Liabilities

Long-term liabilities consist of debt obligations not due to be settled within the normal operating cycle or one year. Long-term notes payable and bonds payable are two examples of long-term liabilities. Other long-term liabilities include unfunded employee retirement plans that will be funded by the company in the future. The following excerpt shows the long-term liabilities section of **Apple**.

A.K.A. *Long-term liabilities are also referred to as noncurrent liabilities.*

APPLE INC. Balance Sheet (Partial) September 24, 2011 (in millions)	
Long-term liabilities	
Deferred revenue	$ 1,686
Deferred tax liabilities	8,159
Other liabilities	1,941
Total long-term liabilities	$11,786

Stockholders' Equity

Stockholders' equity is the residual ownership interest in the assets of a business after its liabilities have been paid off. The stockholders' equity of a corporation is divided into two main categories: amounts invested by stockholders (common stock) and the cumulative net income of a business that has not yet been distributed to its stockholders as a dividend (retained earnings). The following excerpt shows the stockholders' equity section of **Apple**.

A.K.A. *Stockholders' equity is also referred to as shareholders' equity.*

APPLE INC. Balance Sheet (Partial) September 24, 2011 (in millions)	
Stockholders' equity	
Common stock	$13,331
Retained earnings	62,841
Other equity	443
Total stockholders' equity	$76,615

Presentation Format

There are two generally accepted formats for presenting a classified balance sheet—the account form and the report form. For the **account form**, assets are displayed on the left side and liabilities and stockholders' equity are displayed on the right side. For the **report form**, assets are displayed at the top, with liabilities displayed below the assets, and stockholders' equity displayed below liabilities. Apple's 2011 balance sheet in report form is presented in Exhibit 4-2. The report form is the more widely used format.

Hint: According to Accounting Trends and Techniques, a recent survey of 600 large U.S. companies shows that 88% use the report form for their balance sheet while 12% use the account form.

Exhibit 4-2	Report Form of a Classified Balance Sheet

APPLE INC.
Balance Sheet
September 24, 2011, and September 25, 2010

(in millions)	2011	2010
Assets		
Current assets		
Cash	$ 9,815	$11,261
Accounts receivable	5,369	5,510
Inventory	776	1,051
Other current assets	29,028	23,856
Total current assets	44,988	41,678
Long-term assets		
Property, plant and equipment	7,777	4,768
Intangible assets	4,432	1,083
Other long-term assets	59,174	27,654
Total long-term assets	71,383	33,505
Total assets	$116,371	$75,183
Liabilities		
Current liabilities		
Accounts payable	$ 14,632	$12,015
Other current liabilities	13,338	8,707
Total current liabilities	27,970	20,722
Long-term liabilities	11,786	6,670
Total liabilities	39,756	27,392
Stockholders' Equity		
Common stock	13,331	10,668
Retained earnings	62,841	37,169
Other equity	443	(46)
Total stockholders' equity	76,615	47,791
Total liabilities and stockholders' equity	$116,371	$75,183

IFRS ALERT!

Go to Appendix C at the end of this book and review the classified balance sheet of **Tesco PLC**. Tesco is the world's third largest retailer and is based in the United Kingdom. Tesco prepares its classified balance sheet using IFRS. After reviewing Tesco's balance sheet, prepare a list of differences between Tesco's IFRS balance sheet and Apple's U.S. GAAP balance sheet in Exhibit 4-2. Differences include: (a) Tesco presents noncurrent assets before its current assets—that is, it lists the company's assets in reverse order of liquidity; (b) Tesco calculates net assets by subtracting total liabilities from total assets; and (c) Tesco uses slightly different labeling for some of its balance sheet accounts, for instance common stock is referred to as "share capital."

YOUR TURN! 4.1

The solution is on page 217.

The President of Musicland Company requests that you prepare a classified balance sheet in report form for the company. The following financial data are available from the company's accounting records as of December 31, 2013.

Cash	$ 300	Accounts payable	$ 2,500
Accounts receivable	3,000	Other current liabilities	2,000
Inventory	12,200	Long-term notes payable	20,000
Other current assets	1,500	Stockholders' equity	17,500
Property, plant, & equipment, net	25,000		

INCOME STATEMENT CLASSIFICATION AND ANALYSIS

A **single-step income statement** is the simplest form of an income statement. The name originates from the way the statement is constructed. The sum of the expenses is subtracted from the sum of the revenues in a single step to arrive at net income. An example of a single-step income statement for Apple Inc. for the years ended September 24, 2011, and September 25, 2010, is in Exhibit 4-3.

LO2 Describe a classified (single-step and multi-step) income statement.

expenses subtracted from revenues

Exhibit 4-3	Single-Step Income Statement for Apple Inc.

APPLE INC.
Income Statement
For Years Ended September 24, 2011, and September 25, 2010

(in millions)	2011	2010
Revenues		
Net sales..	$108,249	$65,225
Interest and dividend income, net	415	155
Total revenues...............................	108,664	65,380
Expenses		
Cost of goods sold...........................	64,431	39,541
Research and development expenses..............	2,429	1,782
Selling, general and administrative.................	7,599	5,517
Income tax expense...........................	8,283	4,527
Total expenses...............................	82,742	51,367
Net income....................................	$ 25,922	$14,013

Specifically, Apple's 2011 revenues are totaled, yielding $108,664 million. Next, Apple's 2011 expenses of $82,742 million are totaled and subtracted from total revenues to yield Apple's 2011 net income of $25,922 million.

A **multi-step income statement** presents revenues and expenses in distinct categories to facilitate financial analysis and management decision making. A multi-step income statement provides financial statement users with more information, and thus, enables them to make better and more informed decisions about a business. The format of a multi-step income statement will differ depending on whether the company is a service firm or a merchandising firm. The difference in format between service firms and merchandising firms results because service firms do not sell a physical product and therefore do not have cost of goods sold. Examples of service companies include accounting firms, health care providers, and architects. In contrast, merchandising companies sell goods to customers. We discuss merchandisers in more detail in Chapter 5. For a service company, its total operating expenses are subtracted from its service revenues to determine its income from operations. Operating expenses are those expenses that relate to the primary operating activities of a business. Operating expenses are commonly classified as selling, general and administrative expenses. Revenue and expense items that do not relate to the primary operating activities of the company appear in a separate category called *Other Income and Expense*. The net amount of other income and expense is either added to or subtracted from income from operations to determine pretax income.

For a merchandising company, the cost of goods sold is subtracted from the firm's net sales to determine its gross profit on sales. **Gross profit**, or gross profit on sales, is defined as the difference between net sales and cost of goods sold and reveals the amount of sales revenue remaining after subtracting the cost of products sold. **Net sales**

A.K.A A multi-step income statement is also known as a classified income statement

A.K.A. *Gross profit* is often referred to as *gross margin*.

are total sales less an amount to record any **sales returns and allowances** and **sales discounts**. Sales returns and allowances represent the amount given to the customer for the return of merchandise or an amount given in lieu of a return. Sales discounts represent an amount allowed to the buyer for early payment. These items will be discussed further in Chapter 5. Gross profit also reveals how much sales revenue remains to cover a business's operating expenses. The remainder of the structure of a merchandising company's multi-step income statement (following gross profit) is the same as the structure of the service company's multi-step income statement.

Exhibit 4-4 presents a multi-step income statement for **Apple Inc.** for the year ended September 24, 2011. Apple's multi-step income statement provides more detail to the financial statement user with four measures of company performance: gross profit on sales, income from operations, income before income taxes, and net income. Gross profit on sales indicates just how well the company performed in terms of purchasing goods, warehousing those goods, and pricing the goods for sale. Income from operations reports Apple's performance after considering the cost of running its stores, paying its employees, advertising to its customers, and administering the business. The income before income taxes reports the company's performance after considering various nonoperating items like interest expense and interest income but before subtracting the expected cost of income taxes. Income tax is then subtracted from income before income taxes in order to compute net income. Income tax is computed as a percentage of income before income taxes.

A.K.A. Income before income tax is also known as pretax income.

Exhibit 4-4	Multi-Step Income Statement for a Merchandising Company		

APPLE INC.
Income Statement
For Years Ended September 24, 2011 and September 25, 2010

(in millions)	2011	2010
Net sales.	$108,249	$65,225
Less cost of goods sold.	64,431	39,541
Gross profit on sales	43,818	25,684
Operating expenses		
Research and development expenses	2,429	1,782
Selling, general and administrative expenses	7,599	5,517
Total operating expenses	10,028	7,299
Income from operations.	33,790	18,385
Other income and expenses		
Interest and dividend income, net	415	155
Income before income taxes	34,205	18,540
Income tax expense.	8,283	4,527
Net income	$ 25,922	$14,013

A multi-step income statement for a service firm will not have cost of goods sold nor will it have a subtotal for gross profit on sales

Net income reports Apple's bottom-line performance—that is, after all costs of running the business are subtracted. Net sales for Apple consists primarily of sales of hardware, software, digital content, and support contracts. Apple records reductions from these amounts for future product returns. Cost of goods sold represents the cost to Apple for the items sold. Cost of goods sold is typically the largest expense for a retail company such as Apple. Cost of goods sold is subtracted directly from net sales to highlight the gross profit on sales. The gross profit on sales is an important financial indicator for investment professionals who follow retail companies like Apple. Analysts compare the gross profit on sales between retailers as a way to assess the effectiveness of the retailer's pricing and purchasing policies.

The operating expenses section includes those expenses that relate to the primary operating activities of a business. Operating expenses consist primarily of selling expenses and administrative expenses. Examples of Apple's selling, general and administrative expenses include sales salaries expense, delivery expense, advertising expense, depreciation expense, rent expense, office salaries expense, and supplies expense.

The other income and expense section of the income statement is sometimes labeled nonoperating activities. Examples of revenues and expenses that do not relate to the primary operating activities of a merchandising firm include:

Other Expenses and Losses	Other Revenues and Gains
• Interest expense • Losses on asset sales	• Interest revenue • Gains on asset sales • Dividend revenue (income)

These items are reported in the other income and expense section that follows the financial information regarding a business's primary operating activities.

Exhibit 4.5 presents the components of a classified income statement for Webwork (a service company) and for Apple (a merchandising company). We see the absence of the cost of goods sold section, including the gross profit subtotal, in the service company's income statement. Otherwise, the income statements are identical.

Exhibit 4.5	Classified Income Statements for Service and Merchandising Companies

WEBWORK, INC. Income Statement For Year Ended December 31, 2012		APPLE INC. Income Statement For Year Ended September 24, 2011	
Revenues	$19,150	Net sales.	$108,249
		Less cost of goods sold.	64,431
		Gross profit on sales	43,818
Operating expenses		Operating expenses	
Wage, rent and supplies expenses. . . .	5,550	Research and development expenses	2,429
Depreciation and interest expenses . . .	750	Selling, general and administrative expenses . . .	7,599
Total operating expenses	6,300	Total operating expenses	10,028
Income from operations	12,850	Income from operations	33,790
Other income and expenses	—	Other income and expenses	
		Interest and dividend income, net	415
Income before income taxes	12,850	Income before income taxes	34,205
Income tax expense	3,855	Income tax expense	8,283
Net income	$ 8,995	Net income	$ 25,922

IFRS ALERT!

Appendix C at the end of this book presents the multi-step income statement for **Tesco PLC**. Tesco is a United Kingdom-based company and is the world's third largest retailer. Tesco is the parent company of Fresh and Easy Neighborhood Markets, a chain of small supermarkets located principally in the western United States. Tesco uses IFRS to prepare its multi-step income statement. Make a list of the similarities and any differences between Tesco's multi-step income statement and **Apple's** multi-step income statement in Exhibit 4.3. Like Apple, Tesco reports four measures of company performance: gross profit, operating profit, profit before tax, and profit for the year. Differences include: (1) Tesco uses the word "profit" instead of "income"; (2) Tesco lumps all of its noninventory operating expenses into one category called "administrative expenses"; and (3) Tesco refers to its interest income as "finance income" and its interest expense as "finance expense." Other than these labeling differences, Tesco's multi-step income statement under IFRS is strikingly similar to Apple's U.S. GAAP multi-step income statement.

YOUR TURN! 4.2

The solution is on page 217.

Musicland provides the following information and requests that we prepare a multi-step income statement for the year ended December 31, 2013. Musicland pays income tax at the rate of 30 percent of income.

Net sales.	$100,000	Research & development	
Cost of goods sold.	45,000	expense	$10,000
Selling, general and administrative expenses.	$ 25,000	Interest expense.	$ 5,000

WORKING WITH FINANCIAL STATEMENTS

Chapter 1 introduced the basic financial statements. We now extend that discussion by demonstrating how financial statements are used to address questions about a company's operating performance and financial health.

Analysis Based on Ratios

If Apple's net income in 2011 totaled $25,922 million, would we conclude that the company had a good year or a bad year? While $25,922 million is a large number, some frame of reference is needed before we can conclude that this amount represents a good, bad, or mediocre level of operating performance. For example, $25,922 million is a phenomenal performance if the company had only $1 million in assets to operate with during the year. But it is not as exceptional if the company had $100,000 million in assets to operate with during the year.

Investment professionals use a variety of methods to get a better understanding of how to interpret a net income number like $25,922 million. One such method involves ratio analysis. **Ratio analysis** expresses the relation of one relevant accounting number to another relevant accounting number through the process of division. The result of the division is expressed as a percentage, a rate, or as a proportion.

To illustrate how a ratio can provide additional meaning to Apple's net income of $25,922 million, we can divide Apple's net income by its total assets of $116,371 million, which is known as its **return on assets (ROA)**. The result is 22.3 percent and tells us that Apple earned a rate of return of 22.3 percent on each dollar of assets invested in the business in 2011. We can also compare this return with that of other technology companies to help us evaluate Apple's performance.

Although a single number like Apple's net income is difficult to interpret in isolation, a single ratio is also difficult to interpret without some point of reference or benchmark. Business professionals often use one of two techniques to further their understanding of ratios. **Trend analysis** is a process in which we compare a company's results, or the results of a ratio, over time. This technique helps the financial statement user identify any readily observable trends in a company's performance. **Benchmarking analysis** is where the analyst compares a company's performance, or a ratio, to that of its competitors, or to an industry average. Under benchmarking analysis, we are trying to compare, or benchmark, a company's performance against similar companies, or against an industry standard. Trend analysis and benchmarking analysis are powerful tools to place a company's results into a meaningful context.

Working with the Balance Sheet

LO3 **Discuss** use of a balance sheet and ratios to assess liquidity and solvency.

The balance sheet helps users evaluate how financially healthy a company is. The balance sheet also provides information on how the company finances the acquisition of its assets, with debt or with equity. Exhibit 4-2 presented a simplified version of Apple's balance sheet.

Terms such as liquidity and solvency refer to the financial well-being of a company. For a company to remain in business it must be able to pay its bills when they come due. Before a bank such as **Bank of America** will commit to extend a loan to a company like Apple, it needs to assess the likelihood that it will be repaid the amount borrowed and be paid the interest due on the amount borrowed, both in a timely manner. This assessment involves evaluating Apple's *liquidity*, the ability to pay obligations that come due in the current year, and *solvency*, the ability to pay obligations over the long term.

Liquidity

Liquidity refers to a company's ability to pay its short-term financial obligations. It depends on several factors, including the level of cash a company has and how quickly it can generate cash from operations or its assets.

Current Ratio   One widely-used measure of a company's liquidity is the **current ratio**. The current ratio is defined as current assets divided by current liabilities. Current assets provide a measure of the cash available and expected to be generated in the current period. Current liabilities provide a measure of the cash that will be needed in the current period to pay existing or expected obligations.

$$\text{Current ratio} = \frac{\text{Current assets}}{\text{Current liabilities}}$$

A current ratio greater than one implies that a company has more cash and current assets than needed to pay off its current obligations, and a ratio less than one implies the opposite. While this interpretation is overly simplistic, it does provide an easily understood assessment of a company's liquidity. In general, the greater the current ratio, the more liquid a company is, and the less concern a lender has in extending a loan to the company.

Exhibit 4-6	Current Ratio			
(in millions)		**2011**		**2010**
Apple	$\frac{\$44,988}{\$27,970}$ = 1.61:1		$\frac{\$41,678}{\$20,722}$ = 2.01:1	
Dell	$\frac{\$29,448}{\$22,001}$ = 1.34:1		$\frac{\$29,021}{\$19,483}$ = 1.49:1	

One of Apple's competitors is **Dell Inc.**, an online retailer of personal computers. The current ratio for both Apple and for Dell is in Exhibit 4-6. Both Apple and Dell report current ratios greater than one in 2011 and 2010; however, Apple reports a larger current ratio than does Dell in both years. Based on this ratio, we would conclude that Apple is more liquid than Dell, although each company appears to be sufficiently liquid to satisfy currently due obligations.

Concept ⟶	Method ⟶	Assessment	TAKEAWAY 4.1
Can a company meet its short-term obligations?	Current assets and current liabilities from the balance sheet. $\text{Current ratio} = \dfrac{\text{Current assets}}{\text{Current liabilities}}$	A larger current ratio implies greater liquidity and a greater ability to pay short-term obligations.	

Solvency

Lenders often provide loans that have repayment terms that extend over several years. In such cases the lender is interested in evaluating a company's solvency. **Solvency** refers to a company's ability to pay its long-term financial obligations. It depends on several factors, including the level of assets a company has. Solvency, therefore, is a measure of a company's ability to survive over the long term. (Both liquidity and solvency are important indicators of financial health; but, a company must first be liquid. If a company is unable to pay its bills in the short term, it is irrelevant whether it is solvent in the long term.)

Debt-to-Total-Assets Ratio   In general, the more debt a company uses to finance its assets and day-to-day operations, the riskier it is. This follows because the amount borrowed and the interest on that amount must be paid on a regular schedule. If a company is unable to meet the cash outflows required to satisfy its debt repayment schedule or meet its regular interest payments, a lender can legally demand immediate repayment of a loan, potentially forcing a company into bankruptcy if it is unable to repay that amount. The **debt-to-total-assets ratio**, calculated as total liabilities divided by total assets, provides a measure of this risk and is one ratio used to assess a company's solvency.

$$\text{Debt-to-total-assets ratio} = \frac{\text{Total liabilities}}{\text{Total assets}}$$

The greater the debt-to-total-assets ratio, the greater is a company's risk of not being able to pay its interest payments or principal repayments on a timely basis, and the lower is the company's solvency. Like the current ratio, the debt-to-total-assets ratio should not be used in isolation. There are many factors that must be considered when judging a company's solvency.

Exhibit 4-7 shows the debt-to-total-assets ratio for Apple and Dell. This exhibit reveals that in 2011, Dell used considerably more debt to finance its assets than did Apple (80.0 percent versus 34.2 percent). Consequently, Dell would be considered a riskier, less solvent company. A lender such as **Citibank** would likely be more concerned about the solvency of Dell than the solvency of Apple.

Exhibit 4-7	Debt-to-Total-Assets Ratio	
(in millions)	**2011**	**2010**
Apple	$\dfrac{\$39,756}{\$116,371} = 34.2\%$	$\dfrac{\$27,392}{\$75,183} = 36.4\%$
Dell	$\dfrac{\$35,616}{\$44,533} = 80.0\%$	$\dfrac{\$30,833}{\$38,599} = 79.9\%$

TAKEAWAY 4.2	Concept ⟶	Method ⟶	Assessment
	Can a company meet its long-term obligations?	Total assets and total liabilities from the balance sheet. $\text{Debt-to-total-assets ratio} = \dfrac{\text{Total liabilities}}{\text{Total assets}}$	A larger ratio implies reduced solvency and a reduced ability to repay outstanding obligations over the long term.

Working with the Income Statement

Apple generates income by selling computers, iPads, iPods, iPhones, peripherals, and downloads from its iTunes store. The company's income statement provides a report detailing how much net income Apple was able to generate from these activities. A review of a company's income and its components is called profitability analysis. Apple's net income of $25,922 million for the year ended September 24, 2011, indicates that Apple was able to sell these products at a price that exceeded the cost of manufacturing. Apple's income statement, presented in Exhibit 4-4, also shows that the company's profitability increased from 2010 to 2011.

LO4 Discuss use of the income statement and ratios to assess profitability.

Apple's net income increased by $11,909 million, from $14,013 million in 2010 to $25,922 million in 2011. During a similar period, Dell's net income rose by only $857 million, from $2,635 million to $3,492 million. This suggests that Apple outperformed one of its leading competitors during a difficult economic period. How was that possible? Perhaps Apple's success reflects its superior product line or possibly its greater diversity in products offered for sale. Alternatively, it might reflect the superior operating acumen of Apple's management team.

Measures for Profitability Analysis

There are many ways to measure a company's success. One such measure is profitability. Profitability indicates whether or not a company is able to bring its products or services to the market efficiently, and whether it produces products or services that are valued by the market. The more profitable a company is, the better are its long-term prospects. Consistently unprofitable companies are on a path to failure.

Return on Sales Ratio (Profit Margin)

It is somewhat unfair, and potentially misleading, to compare two companies of differing size on the basis of net income. A larger company is expected to generate a larger net income. But a large net income does not necessarily indicate that a company is performing more efficiently than a company with a smaller net income. One measure that facilitates a comparison of the profitability between companies of different size is the return on assets ratio, which we already explained. Another useful measure is the **return on sales (ROS) ratio**, calculated as net income divided by net sales.

A.K.A. Return on sales is often referred to as *profit margin*.

$$\text{Return on sales ratio} = \frac{\text{Net income}}{\text{Net sales}}$$

Exhibit 4-8 shows the calculation of return on sales for both Apple and Dell. Apple is a bit larger than Dell based on sales generated in 2011 ($108,249 million for Apple versus $62,071 million for Dell). Apple also generates much more income than Dell ($25,922 million for Apple versus $3,492 million for Dell in 2011). This translates into a much higher return on sales for Apple (23.9 percent for Apple versus 5.6 percent for Dell in 2011). An ROS of 23.9 indicates Apple has 23.9 cents left over for each dollar of sales revenue after subtracting all of its expenses. This is over four times as much as Dell, which generates just 5.6 cents for each dollar of sales revenue. This result suggests that Apple is a more profitable company than Dell, possibly because it is able to command a premium price for its products and/or because it runs a more efficient operation than does Dell.

Exhibit 4-8	Return on Sales		
(in millions)		2011*	2010
Apple		$\dfrac{\$25,922}{\$108,249} = 23.9\%$	$\dfrac{\$14,013}{\$65,225} = 21.5\%$
Dell		$\dfrac{\$3,492}{\$62,071} = 5.6\%$	$\dfrac{\$2,635}{\$61,494} = 4.3\%$

* One of the difficulties encountered in benchmarking is that companies often have different fiscal year-ends. Apple's year-end occurs in September, while Dell's year-end occurs in January.

TAKEAWAY 4.3	Concept ⟶	Method ⟶	Assessment
	How much net income does a company generate from each dollar of sales revenue?	Net sales and net income from the income statement. $\text{Return on sales ratio} = \dfrac{\text{Net income}}{\text{Net sales}}$	A larger ratio indicates that a company is more profitable on each sales dollar; this is because it commands a premium price for its products and/or is more operationally efficient.

Working with the Statement of Stockholders' Equity

LO5 Explain the components of the statement of stockholders' equity.

Chapter 1 introduced the statement of stockholder's equity, which summarizes the changes in a company's stockholders' equity during the period. The statement of stockholders' equity consists of two parts—contributed capital and earned capital. **Contributed capital** is a measure of the capital contributed by the stockholders of a company when they purchase ownership shares in the company. Ownership shares are called common shares or common stock. **Earned capital** is a measure of the capital that is earned by the company, reinvested in the business, and not distributed to its stockholders—that is, its retained earnings. Retained earnings at the end of a fiscal period is calculated as retained earnings at the start of the period, plus net income for the period, less any dividends paid during the period.

> **Retained earnings, beginning of period**
> **+ Net income**
> **− Dividends**
> _____
> **Retained earnings, end of period**

Exhibit 4-9 presents the statement of stockholders' equity for Apple. The column labeled Common Stock represents the change in Apple's contributed capital during the period covered by the statement. The change to common stock resulted from the issuance of additional shares. The newly issued shares may have been sold to Apple's existing stockholders, to new stockholders, or possibly to Apple's employees.

The column labeled Retained Earnings in Exhibit 4-9 represents Apple's earned capital. Because Apple does not pay a dividend, the primary adjustment to this column is the addition of net income for the period. Why has Apple's management decided not to distribute any of its net income as a dividend during this period? There are many factors that go into that decision, but one consideration is the investment opportunities that a company has for the money that it earns. As we saw earlier, Apple is able to generate a high return on each dollar of sales, so Apple might feel that it is better to retain its net income and invest it in the business than to make distributions to its stockholders who may have difficulty finding investments with equal or higher rates of return. Apple decided, however, to start paying a dividend in 2012.

| Exhibit 4-9 | Statement of Stockholders' Equity |

APPLE INC.
Statement of Stockholders' Equity

(in millions)	Common Stock	Retained Earnings	Other Equity	Total Equity
Balance at September 26, 2009........	$ 8,210	$23,353	$ 77	$31,640
Issuance of common stock	2,458			2,458
Net income........................		14,013		14,013
Other adjustments		(197)	(123)	(320)
Balance at September 25, 2010........	10,668	37,169	(46)	47,791
Issuance of common stock	2,663			2,663
Net income........................		25,922		25,922
Other adjustments		(250)	489	239
Balance at September 24, 2011........	$13,331	$62,841	$443	$76,615

| | Investing with a Social Conscience | CORPORATE SOCIAL RESPONSIBILITY |

Not all investors are singularly focused on the financial performance of businesses they invest in. For a segment of the investing community, corporate social responsibility goes hand in hand with financial performance in choosing an investment. **Socially responsible investing (SRI)**, also known as sustainable investing, considers a firm's environmental stewardship, consumer protection, human rights, and diversity, along with its financial performance. Investments in SRI funds are near $3 trillion and have grown in recent years at a pace almost six times greater than the growth of professionally managed investments.

Working with the Statement of Cash Flows

A common refrain heard from business people is that we do not pay bills with net income, we pay bills with cash! While net income is eventually converted into cash, it is the cash available that a company uses to run its business and pay its bills. Where can we find information about a company's cash resources? The answer is the statement of cash flows, which provides information on a company's sources and uses of cash.

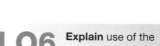
LO6 Explain use of the statement of cash flows to help assess solvency.

The statement of cash flows aids us in understanding the change in cash reported by a company over a period of time. The statement explains the change in the cash reported between two balance sheet dates. The statement of cash flows is segmented into three activity categories: (1) cash flow from operating activities, (2) cash flow from investing activities, and (3) cash flow from financing activities. The separation into these three activities increases the statement's usefulness. For example, knowing that cash increased is not as useful as knowing that cash increased because of increased operating cash flow or because of a bank loan.

Exhibit 4-10 shows a simplified version of Apple's statement of cash flows. Apple reported a decrease of $1,446 million in cash in 2011, decreasing from $11,261 million in 2010 to $9,815 million in 2011. These cash balances are on Apple's balance sheet in

Exhibit 4-2. Most of Apple's cash flow in 2011 was generated from operating activities ($37,529 million). Apple used much of its cash flow in its investing activities, with $32,464 million used for purchase of investments and $4,260 used to purchase additional property, plant, and equipment.

Free Cash Flow

Hint: When calculating a firm's free cash flow, "capital expenditures" amount is the cash spent for purchases of PP&E less the cash proceeds received from sale of PP&E. Both amounts are reported on a statement of cash flows.

The level of cash flow provided by operating activities is valuable information on a company's ability to generate cash from its day-to-day operations. One measure of cash flow health is **free cash flow**. Free cash flow is often calculated by subtracting a company's capital expenditures for PP&E from its cash flow provided by operating activities. A company's free cash flow is an indicator of its ability to expand operations, repay lenders, or pay stockholders a dividend after replacing the value of any property, plant and equipment used in operations. In general, the larger a company's free cash flow, the healthier a company is in terms of operating cash flow.

Free cash flow = Cash flow from operations − Capital expenditures

We calculate Apple's free cash flow in 2011 and 2010 with information reported in Apple's statement of cash flows in Exhibit 4-10.

(in millions)	2011	2010
Cash flow provided by operating activities	$37,529	$18,595
Less: Expenditures on property, plant, and equipment	(4,260)	(2,005)
Free cash flow	$33,269	$16,590

Apple's free cash flow of $33,269 in 2011 and $16,590 in 2010 indicates that it generates a healthy free cash flow. It also suggests that Apple should have no trouble financing future purchases of property, plant, and equipment, repaying its lenders, or paying dividends to its stockholders, using its operating cash flow.

TAKEAWAY 4.4	Concept ➡	Method ➡	Assessment
	How much free cash flow does a company generate?	Cash provided by operating activities less cash expended on purchases of property, plant, and equipment. Cash provided by operations − Capital expenditures = Free cash flow	Larger free cash flow indicates a greater ability to expand operations, repay debt, or pay dividends without external financing.

Exhibit 4-10	Statement of Cash Flows

APPLE INC.
Statement of Cash Flows
For Years Ended September 24, 2011, and September 25, 2010

(in millions)	2011	2010
Cash flow provided by operating activities		
Cash receipts less cash disbursements from operating activities	$37,529	$18,595
Net cash provided by operations	37,529	18,595
Cash flow provided by investing activities		
Net purchases of investments	(32,464)	(11,075)
Net payments for property, plant, and equipment	(4,260)	(2,005)
Other cash payments	(3,695)	(774)
Net cash used by investing.	(40,419)	(13,854)
Cash flow provided by financing activities		
Issuance of equity securities	1,964	1,663
Other payments	(520)	(406)
Net cash provided by financing	1,444	1,257
Net increase (decrease) in cash.	(1,446)	5,998
Cash at beginning of year	11,261	5,263
Cash at year-end	$ 9,815	$11,261

The following information is available from the financial statements of the Philips Company.

YOUR TURN! 4.3

The solution is on page 218.

	2013	2012
Net sales.	$120,000	$110,000
Net income.	20,000	15,000
Cash provided by operating activities	25,000	22,000
Expenditures on property, plant, and equipment.	7,000	6,000
Current assets	75,000	65,000
Current liabilities.	50,000	45,000
Total assets	220,000	190,000
Total liabilities.	150,000	145,000

Compute the following ratios and comment on any trends observed between 2012 and 2013: (1) return on sales ratio, (2) current ratio, (3) debt-to-total-assets ratio, and (4) free cash flow.

Accountant as Detective—Cash Fraud Schemes	FORENSIC ACCOUNTING

Frauds involving cash are the most common frauds, and are more common than corruption or fraudulent financial statements. The more common cash schemes include (1) skimming, where an employee accepts cash from a customer but does not record a sales transaction, (2) cash larceny, where an employee steals cash from the daily receipts before they are deposited in a bank, (3) check tampering, where an employee steals blank company checks and makes them out to themselves or an accomplice, and (4) cash register disbursement, where an employee fraudulently voids a sale on his or her cash register and steals the cash.

COMPREHENSIVE PROBLEM

Following are items reported on the financial statements of **Microsoft Corporation** as of June 30, 2011. (Some of the reported accounts have been combined for simplicity.) Amounts given are in millions of dollars.

Cash flow provided by operating activities	$26,994
Cash at June 30, 2010	5,505
Cash at June 30, 2011	9,610
Net revenue	69,943
Cash flow from investing activities	(14,616)
Inventory	1,372
Accounts receivable	14,987
Cost of goods sold	15,577
Cash flow from financing activities	(8,273)
Other current assets	48,949
Property, plant, and equipment	8,162
Operating expenses	27,205
Other income	910
Intangible assets	13,325
Other long-term assets	12,299
Income tax expense	4,921
Accounts payable	4,197
Other current liabilities	24,577
Long-term liabilities	22,847
Common stock	63,415
Retained earnings	(6,332)

Prepare a multi-step income statement, a classified balance sheet, and a statement of cash flows using the accounts listed above.

Solution

MICROSOFT CORPORATION
Income Statement
For Year Ended June 30, 2011 (in millions)

Net sales	$69,943
Less cost of goods sold	15,577
Gross profit on sales	54,366
Operating expenses	27,205
Income from operations	27,161
Other income	910
Income before income taxes	28,071
Income tax expenses	4,921
Net income	$23,150

MICROSOFT CORPORATION
Balance Sheet
June 30, 2011 (in millions)

Assets

Current assets

Cash	$ 9,610	
Account receivable	14,987	
Inventory	1,372	
Other current assets	48,949	
Total current assets		$ 74,918
Property, plant, and equipment		8,162
Intangible assets		13,325
Other long-term assets		12,299
Total assets		$108,704

continued

(continued)

Liabilities and Stockholders' Equity

Current liabilities

Accounts payable..	$ 4,197	
Other current liabilities...	24,577	
Total current liabilities..		$ 28,774
Long-term liabilities..		22,847
Total liabilities..		51,621
Stockholders' equity		
Common stock..	63,415	
Retained earnings..	(6,332)	
Total stockholders' equity..		57,083
Total liabilities and stockholders' equity		$108,704

MICROSOFT CORPORATION
Statement of Cash Flows
For Year Ended June 30, 2011 (in millions)

Cash flow provided by operating activities	$26,994
Cash flow used by investing activities	(14,616)
Cash flow used by financing activities...	(8,273)
Net decrease in cash	4,105
Cash at June 30, 2010	5,505
Cash at June 30, 2011	$ 9,610

SUMMARY OF LEARNING OBJECTIVES

Describe a classified balance sheet. (p. 180) **LO1**

- A classified balance sheet contains two subgroups of assets (current assets and long-term assets) and two subgroups of liabilities (current liabilities and long-term liabilities).
- A classified balance sheet can be presented in account form or report form.

Describe a classified (single-step and multi-step) income statement. (p. 185) **LO2**

- A multi-step income statement classifies items into subgroups in order to facilitate analysis and decision making.
- A multi-step income statement for a merchandising firm often includes one section for sales revenue; two sections for expenses: cost of goods sold and operating expenses; and a section for other income and expenses.
- A multi-step income statement for a service firm is similar, but does not have a section for cost of goods sold.

Discuss use of a balance sheet and ratios to assess liquidity and solvency. (p. 188) **LO3**

- Ratio analysis involves expressing the relation of one relevant accounting number with another relevant accounting number through the process of division. This process helps to provide a context to interpret a particular number.
- Two techniques that are often used in ratio analysis are (1) trend analysis where ratios are examined over time and (2) benchmarking analysis where a company's ratios are compared to those of another company or to an average of an industry as a whole.
- Liquidity refers to a company's ability to pay those obligations that are expected to come due in the next year.
- The current ratio, or current assets divided by current liabilities, provides a measure of a company's liquidity.
- Solvency refers to a company's ability to repay its debts over the long term.
- The debt-to-total-assets ratio, calculated as total debt divided by total assets, provides one measure of a company's solvency.

LO4　Discuss use of the income statement and ratios to assess profitability. (p. 191)

- Return on sales, or net income divided by net sales, provides a measure of a company's profitability by indicating how much net income a company earns on each dollar of sales revenue.

LO5　Explain the components of the statement of stockholders' equity. (p. 192)

- Stockholders' equity comprises two parts: (1) contributed capital and (2) earned capital.
- Contributed capital is the capital contributed to a firm by stockholders when they purchase ownership shares in the company.
- Earned capital represents the net income that has been earned by a company and not distributed to stockholders as a dividend.

LO6　Explain use of the statement of cash flows to help assess solvency. (p. 193)

- The statement of cash flows provides information regarding a company's sources and uses of cash.
- Free cash flow, calculated as cash provided from operating activities less cash expended on property, plant, and equipment, provides information regarding management's ability to expand operations, repay debt, or make distributions to stockholders, using a firm's operating cash flow.

SUMMARY	Concept	Method	Assessment
TAKEAWAY 4.1	Can a company meet its short-term obligations?	Current assets and current liabilities from the balance sheet. $$\text{Current ratio} = \frac{\text{Current assets}}{\text{Current liabilities}}$$	A larger current ratio implies greater liquidity and a greater ability to pay short-term obligations.
TAKEAWAY 4.2	Can a company meet its long-term obligations?	Total assets and total liabilities from the balance sheet. $$\text{Debt-to-total-assets ratio} = \frac{\text{Total liabilities}}{\text{Total assets}}$$	A larger ratio implies reduced solvency and a reduced ability to repay outstanding obligations over the long term.
TAKEAWAY 4.3	How much net income does a company generate from each dollar of sales revenue?	Net sales and net income from the income statement. $$\text{Return on sales ratio} = \frac{\text{Net income}}{\text{Net sales}}$$	A larger ratio indicates that a company is more profitable on each sales dollar; this is because it commands a premium price for its products and/or is more operationally efficient.
TAKEAWAY 4.4	How much free cash flow does a company generate?	Cash provided by operating activities less cash expended on purchases of property, plant, and equipment. $$\begin{array}{r}\text{Cash provided by operations}\\ -\text{ Capital expenditures}\\ \hline \text{Free cash flow}\end{array}$$	Larger free cash flow indicates a greater ability to expand operations, repay debt, or pay dividends without external financing.

GLOSSARY OF KEY TERMS

Account form (p. 183)

Benchmarking analysis (p. 188)

Classified balance sheet (p. 180)

Contributed capital (p. 192)

Current assets (p. 180)

Current liabilities (p. 182)

Current ratio (p. 189)

Debt-to-total-assets
　ratio (p. 190)

Earned capital (p. 192)

Free cash flow (p. 194)

Gross profit (p. 185)

Intangible assets (p. 181)

Liquidity (p. 181, 189)

Long-term liabilities (p. 183)

Multi-step income statement (p. 185)	**Report form** (p. 183)	**Single-step income statement** (p. 185)
Net sales (p. 185)	**Return on assets (ROA)** (p. 188)	**Socially responsible investing (SRI)** (p. 193)
Normal operating cycle (p. 180)	**Return on sales (ROS) ratio** (p. 191)	
Property, plant, and equipment (p. 181)	**Sales discounts** (p. 186)	**Solvency** (p. 190)
Ratio analysis (p. 188)	**Sales returns and allowances** (p. 186)	**Stockholders' equity** (p. 183)
		Trend analysis (p. 188)

SELF-STUDY QUESTIONS

(Answers to Self-Study Questions are at the end of this chapter.)

1. **Which of the following items will not be reported on a classified balance sheet?**   LO1
   a. Current assets
   b. Net income
   c. Total liabilities
   d. Common stock

2. **Which of the following would not be considered a current asset?**   LO1
   a. Inventory
   b. Accounts receivable
   c. Property, plant, and equipment
   d. Cash

3. **For the balance sheet to be in balance, the following must exist:**   LO1
   a. Total assets must be greater than total liabilities
   b. Total assets must be less than total liabilities
   c. Total assets must equal total liabilities plus stockholders' equity
   d. Total liabilities must equal total stockholders' equity

4. **Which of the following would be considered an intangible asset?**   LO1
   a. Cash
   b. Land
   c. Accounts payable
   d. Patents

5. **Which of the following would most likely be classified as a long-term liability?**   LO1
   a. Accounts payable
   b. Notes payable
   c. Accounts receivable
   d. Common stock

6. **Ratio analysis always involves which type of arithmetic operation?**   LO3
   a. Addition
   b. Subtraction
   c. Multiplication
   d. Division

7. **Which of the following is not a true statement?**   LO3
   a. Benchmarking analysis involves comparing a company to its industry's averages.
   b. Benchmarking analysis involves comparing a company to its competitors.
   c. Trend analysis involves comparing a company's ratios over time.
   d. Benchmarking analysis involves comparing a company's ratios over time.

8. **A company reported net income of $200 on net sales of $2,000. The company's return on sales is:**   LO4
   a. $1,800
   b. 10 percent
   c. 0.1 percent
   d. None of the above

LO4   **9.** The return on sales ratio does *not* provide insight on which of the following:
  a.   A company's net income per dollar of sales.
  b.   A measure of a company's financial performance.
  c.   A measure of a company's cash flow flexibility.
  d.   A measure of a company's operating efficiency.

LO5   **10.** Which of the following is not shown on the statement of stockholders' equity?
  a.   Contributed capital.
  b.   Retained earnings.
  c.   Common stock.
  d.   Total liabilities.

LO3   **11.** The following data appear in the financial statements of a company. Calculate its current ratio.

Current assets	$10,000
Current liabilities	$5,000

  a.   2:1
  b.   1:2
  c. $5,000
  d.   ($5,000)

LO5   **12.** The following data pertains to Smith Consulting, Inc. for 2013. Compute its ending retained earnings.

Beginning-of-year retained earnings	$120,000
Net income	37,500
Dividends paid	5,000

  a. $157,500
  b. $152,500
  c. $162,500
  d. $115,000

LO2   **13.** A merchandising company's multi-step income statement differs from that of a service company in what way?
  a.   There is no difference.
  b.   A service company does not include a line for cost of goods sold.
  c.   A service company has a line for selling expenses whereas a merchandising company does not.
  d.   A merchandising company will have a line for income from operations whereas a service company will not.

QUESTIONS

  1. List three subgroups of assets that may be found in the asset section of a classified balance sheet.

  2. Define *current asset* and *normal operating cycle*.

  3. Which of the following are current assets: land, cash, prepaid expense, building, accounts receivable, inventory, equipment?

  4. What is meant by corporate social responsibility?

  5. Define the following ratios: current ratio, debt-to-total-assets ratio, and return on sales ratio.

  6. What is meant by socially responsible investing?

  7. Which of the following measures are best computed using a classified balance sheet?
  a.   Liquidity
  b.   Solvency
  c.   Free cash flow
  d.   Both a. and b.

  8. Which of the following is a correct statement?
  a.   The current ratio is a measure of firm solvency.
  b.   The current ratio is a measure of firm liquidity.

    c. The debt-to-total-assets ratio is a measure of firm liquidity.

    d. None of the above is correct.

9. Free cash flow is measured using information from which financial statement?

    a. Balance sheet

    b. Income statement

    c. Statement of cash flows

    d. Statement of retained earnings

10. Socially responsible investing

    a. Means making as much money on your investments as you can as your only goal.

    b. Means investing in companies that adhere to environmental and social policies in their operations.

    c. Is too small of a concept to matter much.

SHORT EXERCISES

SE4-1. **Preparing a Classified Balance Sheet** Dino Company, a merchandising firm, reports the following data as of January 31, 2013:   **LO1**

Cash..	$ 400
Accounts receivable...........................	1,200
Inventory......................................	2,500
Property, plant, and equipment................	10,000
Accounts payable..............................	800
Other current liabilities.....................	600
Long-term notes payable.......................	8,000
Stockholders' equity..........................	4,700

Prepare a classified balance sheet for Dino Company as of January 31, 2013.

SE4-2. **Evaluating Firm Profitability** The following financial information is taken from the annual reports of the Smith Company and the Wesson Company: **LO4**

	Smith	Wesson
Net income....................................	$10,000	$100,000
Net sales.....................................	50,000	400,000

Calculate the return on sales ratio for each company and determine which firm is more profitable.

SE4-3. **Evaluating Firm Liquidity** The following financial information is taken from the balance sheets of the Drucker Company and the Ito Company: **LO3**

	Drucker	Ito
Current assets................................	$250,000	$50,000
Current liabilities...........................	100,000	15,000

Calculate the current ratio for each company and determine which firm has the higher level of liquidity.

SE4-4. **Evaluating Firm Solvency** The following financial information is taken from the balance sheets of the Lambeth Company and the Maritza Company: **LO3**

	Lambeth	Maritza
Total debt....................................	$350,000	$ 850,000
Total assets..................................	550,000	1,000,000

Calculate the debt-to-total-assets ratio and determine which firm has the higher level of solvency.

LO6 **SE4-5.** **Calculating Free Cash Flow** The following financial information is taken from the annual reports of the Jackson Company and the Pearce Company:

	Jackson	Pearce
Cash flow from operating activities	$250,000	$750,000
Cash investment in property & equipment.	75,000	240,000

Calculate the free cash flow for each company and determine which firm has better cash flow health.

LO6 **SE4-6.** **Statement of Cash Flows** Which of the following would not appear on a company's statement of cash flows?

    a.   Cash flow from operating activities
    b.   Net change in cash
    c.   Total assets
    d.   Cash flow for investing activities

LO3 **SE4-7.** **Debt-to-Total-Assets Ratio** Ruby Company's balance sheet reports the following totals: Assets = $40,000; Liabilities = $25,000; Stockholders' Equity = $15,000. Determine the company's debt-to-total-assets ratio.

    a.   37.5%
    b.   62.5%
    c. $15,000
    d.   166.7%

LO6 **SE4-8.** **Free Cash Flow** Lester Linens reports the following items on its statement of cash flows:

Cash flow provided by operating activities = $100,000
Cash flow used by investing activities = $50,000
Cash flow used by financing activities = $25,000
Capital expenditures = $40,000

Determine Lester's free cash flow:

    a. $40,000
    b. $5,000
    c.   40%
    d. $60,000

LO4 **SE4-9.** **Return on Sales** The following data are from the financial statements of Burkee Wines, Inc. Compute Burkee's return on sales ratio for 2011.

Total revenues for 2011: $3,500,000
Total expenses for 2011: $2,800,000

    a.   125%
    b.   80%
    c.   25%
    d.   20%

LO2 **SE4-10.** **The Multi-step Income Statement** Dino Company, a merchandising firm, reports the following data for the month ended January 31:

Net sales.	$10,000
Cost of goods sold.	4,000
Operating expenses.	3,000
Other income	500
Income tax expense.	1,200

Prepare a multi-step income statement for Dino Company for the month of January.

Assignments with the ✅ logo in the margin are available in BusinessCourse.
See the Preface of the book for details.

EXERCISES—SET A

E4-1A.   Preparing a Classified Balance Sheet From the following accounts, listed in alphabetical order, prepare a classified balance sheet for Berkly Wholesalers as of December 31, 2013. All accounts have normal balances.

LO1
✅

Accounts payable................	$ 43,000	Inventory.......................	$117,000
Accounts receivable..............	40,000	Land . non c.ueient asset.......	45,000
Building	67,000	Mortgage payable (long term)	78,000
Cash........................	26,000	Office supplies	2,000
Common stock..................	111,000	Retained earnings	? 58,000
		Salaries payable.................	7,000

E4-2A.   Multi-step Income Statement From the following accounts, listed in alphabetical order, prepare a multi-step income statement for Karlman Distributors for the year ended December 31. All accounts have normal balances.

LO2
✅

Selling, general and administrative expense	$186,000	Sales revenue............	$550,000
Cost of goods sold.......................	330,000	Income tax expense.......	10,000
Interest expense........................	3,000		

E4-3A.   Evaluating the Liquidity and Solvency of a Company Identify whether the following statements are true or false.

LO3, 4, 6

   a.   The current ratio is a measure of a firm's liquidity.
   b.   Free cash flow is a measure of a firm's solvency.
   c.   The return on sales ratio is a measure of a firm's liquidity.
   d.   The debt-to-total-assets ratio is a measure of a firm's liquidity.

E4-4A.   Classified Balance Sheet The Werthman Company collected the following information for the preparation of its December 31, 2013, classified balance sheet:

LO1
✅

Accounts receivable..............	$15,000	Property, plant, and equipment	$200,000
Cash..........................	17,000	Inventory.......................	65,000
Other current assets..............	25,000	Other long-term assets	40,000
Accounts payable.................	21,000	Common stock...................	95,000
Long-term liabilities	55,000	Retained earnings	?
Other current liabilities	18,000		

Prepare a classified balance sheet for Werthman Company.

E4-5A.   Profitability, Liquidity, and Solvency Ratios Shannon Corporation gathered the following information from its 2013 financial statements:

LO3, 4, 6
✅

Net sales..	$180,000
Net income..	25,200
Cash provided by operating activities	35,000
Expenditures on property, plant, and equipment.....................	14,000
Current assets	40,500
Current liabilities...	27,000
Total assets	130,000
Total liabilities...	97,500

Using the above data, calculate the following: (1) return on sales ratio, (2) current ratio, (3) debt-to-total-assets ratio, and (4) free cash flow.

LO3 ✔ **E4-6A. Return on Assets** The following information was taken from recent Apple Inc. financial statements. Numbers are in millions.

	2011	2010
Net income	$ 25,922	$14,013
Total assets	116,371	75,183

Required

a. What was Apple's return on assets for 2011 and 2010?
b. Based on your answer from part a., how did the company's performance change from 2010 to 2011?

LO5 ✔ **E4-7A. Statement of Stockholders' Equity** You have been asked to assist with the preparation of a statement of stockholders' equity for Maxx Company for the year ended December 31, 2013. You determine the following balances:

Common stock at December 31, 2012	$5,000
Retained earnings at December 31, 2012	7,500
Net income during 2013	2,500
Dividends during 2013	250
Issuance of common stock during 2013	400

Required

Prepare a statement of stockholders' equity for Maxx Company for 2013.

LO4 ✔ **E4-8A. Return on Sales** Kuyu Co.'s sales rose 10 percent over prior year sales of $100,000; however, net income increased by only 5 percent over the prior year's net income. If Kuyu's prior year return on sales ratio was 10 percent, what is the current year return on sales ratio?

LO6 ✔ **E4-9A. Free Cash Flow** Kat Co. reports the following financial data for the current year:

Cash flow from operating activities	$19,850
Cash flow from investing activities	(9,460)
Cash flow from financing activities	3,740
Cash disbursed for capital expenditures	(4,325)

Compute Kat's free cash flow.

LO5 ✔ **E4-10A. Statement of Stockholders' Equity** Prag Co. reported the following financial data for its most current year:

Beginning-of-year common stock	$ 80,000
Beginning-of-year retained earning	175,400
Net income	32,250
Dividends paid	8,500
Issuance of common stock	15,000

Compute Prag's end-of-year total stockholders' equity.

EXERCISES—SET B

LO1 ✔ **E4-1B. Preparing a Classified Balance Sheet** From the following accounts, listed in alphabetical order, prepare a classified balance sheet for Balford Wholesalers as of December 31, 2013. All accounts have normal balances.

Accounts payable.	$ 52,000	Inventory.	$142,000
Accounts receivable.	54,000	Land	58,000
Building and equipment	91,000	Mortgage payable (long-term)	100,000
Cash	40,000	Office supplies	2,000
Common stock.	136,000	Retained earnings	?
		Salaries payable.	8,000

E4-2B. **Multi-step Income Statement** From the following accounts, listed in alphabetical order, prepare a **LO2** ✔ multi-step income statement for Kokomo Wholesale for the year ended December 31. All accounts have normal balances.

Sellling, general, and administrative expenses . . .	$223,000	Sales revenue.	$658,000
Cost of goods sold.	400,000	Income tax expense.	8,000
Interest expense.	4,000		

E4-3B. **Statement of Cash Flows** Identify whether the following statements are true or false. **LO6**

a.   The statement of cash flows reveals whether a firm is "rich" or not.
b.   The statement of cash flows reveals a firm's financial health.
c.   The statement of cash flows reveals a firm's liquidity.
d.   The statement of cash flows reveals a firm's solvency.

E4-4B. **Classified Balance Sheet** The Cambridge Company collected the following information for the **LO1** ✔ preparation of its December 31, 2013, classified balance sheet:

Accounts receivable.	$15,000	Property, plant, and equipment	$200,000
Cash	20,000	Inventory.	65,000
Other current assets.	30,000	Other long-term assets	40,000
Accounts payable.	21,000	Common stock.	105,000
Long-term liabilities	55,000	Retained earnings	?
Other current liabilities	18,000		

Prepare a classified balance sheet for Cambridge Company.

E4-5B. **Profitability, Liquidity, and Solvency Ratios** O'Neill Corporation gathered the following informa- **LO3, 4, 6** ✔ tion from its 2013 financial statements:

Net sales.	$280,000	Current assets	$ 40,500
Net income.	75,000	Current liabilities.	27,000
Cash provided by operating activities	85,000	Total assets	130,000
Expenditures on property, plant, and equipment. . .	14,000	Total liabilities.	97,500

Using the above data, calculate the following: (1) return on sales ratio, (2) current ratio, (3) debt-to-total-assets ratio, and (4) free cash flow.

E4-6B. **Return on Assets** Daisy Company reports the following information in its financial statements. **LO3** ✔ Numbers are in thousands.

	2012	2013
Net sales.	$52,200	$48,750
Net income.	10,750	8,400
Total assets	63,900	61,450

There were 3,500 outstanding shares at December 31, 2013.

Required

a.   What was Daisy's return on assets ratio for 2013 and 2012?

b.   Based on your answer from part a., how did the company's performance change from 2012 to 2013?

LO5   **E4-7B.   Statement of Stockholders' Equity** You have been asked to assist with the preparation of a statement of stockholders' equity for Palatin Company for the year ended December 31, 2013. You determine the following balances:

Common stock at December 31, 2012	$45,000
Retained earnings at December 31, 2012	17,500
Net income during 2013	22,500
Dividends during 2013	9,250
Issuance of common stock during 2013	4,000

Required

Prepare a statement of stockholders' equity for Palatin Company for 2013.

LO4   **E4-8B.   Return on Sales** Bomont Co.'s sales rose 10 percent over prior year sales of $250,000, however net income increased by 15 percent over the prior year's net income. If Bomont's prior year return on sales ratio was 20 percent, what is the current year return on sales ratio?

LO6   **E4-9B.   Free Cash Flow** Bern Co. reports the following financial data for the current year:

Cash flow from operating activities	$39,600
Cash flow from investing activities	19,320
Cash flow from financing activities	13,150
Cash disbursed for capital expenditures	(11,425)

Compute Bern's free cash flow.

LO5   **E4-10B.   Statement of Stockholders' Equity** Stuart Co. reported the following financial data for its most current year:

Beginning-of-year common stock	$120,000
Beginning-of-year retained earning	325,500
Net loss	(23,750)
Dividends paid	8,000
Issuance of common stock	35,000

Compute Stuart's end-of-year total stockholders' equity.

PROBLEMS—SET A

LO1   **P4-1A.   Preparing a Classified Balance Sheet** The following financial data for Crane Distributors was collected as of December 31, 2013. All accounts have normal balances.

Cash	$ 15,200	Delivery equipment	$ 80,000
Accounts receivable	110,200	Accumulated depreciation	35,000
Inventory	114,000	Accounts payable	70,000
Prepaid insurance	2,400	Common stock	100,000
Supplies	6,400	Retained earnings	?

Required

Prepare a classified balance sheet as of December 31, 2013, for Crane Distributors.

P4-2A. **Preparing a Classified Balance Sheet** The following financial data for the Marshall Corporation was collected as of December 31, 2013. All accounts have normal balances.   LO1

Cash..................	$46,400	Furniture and equipment	$ 97,000
Accounts receivable...........	95,200	Accumulated depreciation—furniture and equipment....	38,800
Inventory....................	90,000	Accounts payable..............................	17,400
Prepaid insurance	300	Common stock..................................	200,000
		Retained earnings	?

Required
Prepare a classified balance sheet as of December 31, 2013.

P4-3A. **Multi-step Income Statements** The adjusted trial balance of Crane Distributors on December 31, 2013, is shown below.   LO2

CRANE DISTRIBUTORS Adjusted Trial Balance December 31, 2013		
	Debit	**Credit**
Cash.......................................	$ 15,200	
Accounts receivable........................	110,200	
Inventory..................................	84,000	
Prepaid insurance	2,400	
Supplies	6,400	
Delivery equipment........................	80,000	
Accumulated depreciation		$ 35,000
Accounts payable..........................		70,000
Common stock.............................		100,000
Retained earnings		42,000
Sales revenue.............................		785,800
Cost of goods sold........................	513,400	
Salaries expense	118,000	
Rent expense	40,000	
Supplies expense..........................	8,400	
Utilities expense...........................	4,000	
Depreciation expense......................	16,000	
Insurance expense.........................	4,800	
Income tax expense........................	30,000	
	$1,032,800	$1,032,800

Required
Prepare a multi-step income statement for the year ended December 31, 2013. Combine all the operating expenses into one line on the income statement for selling, general and administrative expenses.

P4-4A. **Preparing the Financial Statements** Listed below are items reported on the financial statements of the Huntington Company as of June 30, 2013:   LO1, 6

Cash flow provided by operating activities	$21,000	Other long-term assets	$17,500
Cash at June 30, 2012......................	9,000	Cash flow from financing activities......	1,300
Cash at June 30, 2013......................	16,000	Current liabilities....................	22,000
Inventory.................................	5,500	Long-term liabilities	18,250
Accounts receivable.......................	12,200	Intangible assets	9,500
Cash flow from investing activities.............	(15,300)	Common stock......................	51,000
Other current assets........................	1,500	Retained earnings	?
Property, plant and equipment...............	40,000		

Required

Prepare a classified balance sheet as of June 30, 2013, and statement of cash flows for 2013.

LO3, 4   **P4-5A.**   **Assessing a Firm's Profitability, Liquidity and Solvency**   Presented below is financial data for the Forrester Company as of year-end 2012 and 2013:

	2012	2013
Current assets	$ 35,000	$ 55,000
Total assets	120,000	170,000
Current liabilities	29,000	70,000
Total liabilities	72,000	112,000
Net sales	132,000	187,000
Net income	17,500	25,200

Required

Calculate Forrester's current ratio, debt-to-total-assets ratio, and return on sales ratio. Comment on the trend in the company's profitability, liquidity, and solvency from 2012 to 2013.

LO2, 4   **P4-6A.**   **Profitability and the Income Statement**   Presented below is income statement data for Longo & Company as of year-end 2013:

Income tax expense	$ 5,400	Net revenue	58,500
Cost of goods sold	12,300	Operating expenses	26,000
Other expenses	700		

Required

Prepare a multi-step income statement for 2013 and calculate the company's return on sales ratio. If Longo's return on sales was 20 percent in 2012, is the company's profitability improving or declining?

LO5   **P4-7A.**   **Preparing the Statement of Stockholders' Equity**   Presented below is financial data for Likert & Co. as of year-end 2013:

Cash	$ 6,000	Accumulated depreciation	$(14,000)
Retained earnings, Jan. 1, 2013	13,000	Net income	30,000
Intangible assets	22,000	Stockholders' equity, Jan. 1, 2013	63,000
Common stock	50,000	Retained earnings, Dec. 31, 2013	31,000
Accounts payable	4,000	Stockholders' equity, Dec. 31, 2013	81,000
Dividends paid	12,000		

Required

Prepare a statement of stockholders' equity for Likert & Co. as of December 31, 2013.

LO3, 4   **P4-8A.**   **Interpreting Liquidity, Solvency, and Profitability Ratios**   Presented below are financial data for two retail companies:

	Company A	Company B
Return on sales ratio	15.5%	13.9%
Current ratio	0.5	2.0
Debt-to-total-assets	65%	30%

Required

Consider the financial ratio data for the two companies. Which company represents the better investment opportunity in your view and why?

P4-9A. Ratio Analysis The following balances were reported in the financial statements for Nafooz Company.

LO3, 4

	2013	2012
Net sales.	$800,000	$700,000
Net income.	80,000	65,000
Current assets	200,000	175,000
Current liabilities.	80,000	100,000
Total liabilities.	250,000	225,000
Total assets	750,000	600,000

Required

1. Compute the following ratios for 2013 and 2012 for Nafooz Company.
   a. Return on sales ratio
   b. Current ratio
   c. Debt-to-total-assets ratio
2. Comment on changes to Nafooz Company's profitability, liquidity, and solvency.

P4-10A. Multi-step Income Statement and Adjusting Entries The Boston Trading Company, whose accounting year ends on December 31, had the following normal balances in its general ledger at December 31:

LO2

Cash	$13,000	Sales revenue	$630,000
Accounts receivable	56,600	Cost of goods sold	404,000
Inventory	73,000	Utilities expense	4,800
Prepaid insurance	6,000	Sales salaries expense	82,000
Office supplies	4,200	Delivery expense	10,800
Furniture and fixtures	21,000	Advertising expense	5,600
Accumulated depreciation—		Rent expense	14,400
furniture and fixtures	5,000	Office salaries expense	56,000
Delivery equipment	84,000	Income tax expense	9,000
Accumulated depreciation—			
delivery equipment	12,000		
Accounts payable	41,000		
Long-term notes payable	30,000		
Common stock	75,000		
Retained earnings	51,400		

During the year, the accounting department prepared monthly statements but no adjusting entries were made in the journals and ledgers. Data for the year-end procedures are as follows:

1. Prepaid insurance, December 31, was $1,200
2. Depreciation expense on furniture and fixtures for the year was $1,800
3. Depreciation expense on delivery equipment for the year was $13,000
4. Salaries payable, December 31, ($1,800 sales and $1,200 office) was $3,000
5. Unused office supplies on December 31 were $1,000

Required

a. Record the necessary adjusting entries at December 31.
b. Prepare a multi-step income statement for the year. Combine all the operating expenses into one line on the income statement for selling, general and administrative expenses.

PROBLEMS—SET B

LO1 ✓ **P4-1B.** **Preparing a Classified Balance Sheet** The following financial data for McKensie & Company was collected as of December 31, 2013. All accounts have normal balances.

Cash	$ 30,400	Delivery equipment	$160,000
Accounts receivable	221,000	Accumulated depreciation	70,000
Inventory	228,000	Accounts payable	140,000
Prepaid insurance	4,800	Common stock	200,000
Supplies	12,800	Retained earnings	?

Required
Prepare a classified balance sheet as of December 31, 2013, for McKensie & Company.

LO1 ✓ **P4-2B.** **Preparing a Classified Balance Sheet** The following financial data for the St. John Corporation was collected as of December 31, 2013. All accounts have normal balances.

Cash	$ 92.800	Furniture and equipment	$194,000
Accounts receivable	190,400	Accumulated Depreciation—	
Inventory	180,000	furniture and equipment	77,600
Prepaid insurance	600	Accounts payable	34,800
		Common stock	400,000
		Retained earnings	?

Required
Prepare a classified balance sheet as of December 31, 2013.

LO2 ✓ **P4-3B.** **Multi-step Income Statement** The adjusted trial balance of Marshall Corporation on December 31, 2013, is shown below.

Marshall Corporation Adjusted Trial Balance December 31, 2013	Debit	Credit
Cash	$ 46,400	
Accounts receivable	95,200	
Inventory	87,000	
Prepaid insurance	300	
Furniture and fixtures	32,000	
Accumulated depreciation—furniture and fixtures		$ 6,800
Delivery equipment	65,000	
Accumulated depreciation—delivery equipment		32,000
Accounts payable		17,400
Common stock		200,000
Retained earnings		59,600
Sales revenue		365,200
Cost of goods sold	214,800	
Salaries expense	92,000	
Rent expense	20,800	
Utilities expense	6,800	
Insurance expense	1,500	
Depreciation expense—furniture and fixtures	3,200	
Depreciation expense—delivery equipment	13,000	
Income tax expense	3,000	
	$681,000	$681,000

Required

Prepare a multi-step income statement for the year ended December 31, 2013. Combine all the operating expenses into one line on the income statement for selling, general and administrative expenses.

P4-4B.   Preparing the Financial Statements Listed below are items reported on the financial statements of the Manhattan Company as of June 30, 2013:

LO1, 6

Cash flow provided by operating activities	$ 42,000	Other long-term assets	$ 35,000
Cash at June 30, 2012	18,000	Cash flow from financing activities.	2,600
Cash at June 30, 2013	32,000	Current liabilities.	44,000
Inventory.	11,000	Long-term liabilities	36,500
Accounts receivable.	24,400	Intangible assets	19,000
Cash flow from investing activities.	(30,600)	Common stock.	102,000
Other current assets.	3,000	Retained earnings	?
Property, plant and equipment.	80,000		

Required

Prepare a classified balance sheet as of June 30, 2013, and statement of cash flows for 2013.

P4-5B.   Assessing a Firm's Profitability, Liquidity and Solvency Presented below is financial data for the Miller Company as of year-end 2012 and 2013:

LO3, 4

	2012	2013
Current assets	$ 70,000	$110,000
Total assets	240,000	340,000
Current liabilities.	58,000	140,000
Total liabilities.	144,000	224,000
Net sales	264,000	374,000
Net income.	35,000	50,400

Required

Calculate Miller's current ratio, debt-to-total-assets ratio, and return on sales ratio. Comment on the trend in the company's profitability, liquidity, and solvency from 2012 to 2013.

P4-6B.   Profitability and the Income Statement Presented below are income statement data for VanPool & Company for 2013:

LO2, 4

Operating expenses.	$ 52,000	Cost of goods sold.	25,200
Other expenses	1,000	Sales revenue.	116,500
Income taxes	10,500		

Required

Prepare a multi-step income statement for 2013 and calculate the company's return on sales ratio. If VanPool's return on sales was 26 percent in 2012, did the company's profitability increase or decrease in 2013?

P4-7B.   Preparing a Statement of Stockholders' Equity Presented below is financial data for Thomas & Co. as of December 31, 2013:

LO5

Cash.	$ 16,000	Inventory.	14,000
Retained earnings, Jan. 1, 2013.	26,000	Net income.	60,000
Building	44,000	Stockholders' equity, Jan. 1, 2013.	126,000
Common stock.	100,000	Retained earnings, Dec. 31, 2013	?
Accrued expenses payable	8,000	Stockholders' equity, Dec. 31, 2013 . . .	162,000
Dividends paid	24,000		

Required

Prepare a statement of stockholders' equity as of December 31, 2013.

LO3, 4   **P4-8B.   Interpreting Profitability, Liquidity, and Solvency Ratios** Presented below is financial data for two furniture manufacturing companies:

	Company B	Company D
Return on sales ratio	9.0%	10.9%
Current ratio	1.9	1.0
Debt-to-total-assets ratio	41%	59%

Required

Consider the financial data of the two companies. Which company represents the better investment opportunity in your opinion and why?

LO3, 4   **P4-9B.   Ratio Analysis** The following balances were reported in the financial statements for Ruby Company.

	2013	2012
Net sales	$1,600,000	$1,700,000
Net income	160,000	195,000
Current assets	400,000	525,000
Current liabilities	160,000	200,000
Total liabilities	500,000	675,000
Total assets	1,500,000	2,400,000

Required

1. Compute the following ratios for 2013 and 2012 for Ruby Company.
   a. Return on sales ratio
   b. Current ratio
   c. Debt-to-total-assets ratio
2. Comment on changes to Ruby Company's profitability, liquidity, and solvency.

LO2   **P4-10B.   Multi-step Income Statement and Adjusting Entries** Oregon Distributors, whose accounting year ends on December 31, had the following normal balances in its ledger accounts at December 31:

Cash	$ 32,800	Common stock	$ 100,000
Accounts receivable	92,000	Retained earnings	42,000
Inventory	82,000	Sales revenue	1,154,000
Prepaid insurance	7,200	Cost of goods sold	821,200
Office supplies	4,800	Utilities expense	8,600
Furniture and fixtures	28,000	Sales salaries expense	108,000
Accumulated depreciation—		Delivery expense	36,800
furniture and fixtures	10,800	Advertising expense	26,200
Delivery equipment	70,000	Rent expense	30,000
Accumulated depreciation—		Office salaries expense	72,000
delivery equipment	24,400		
Accounts payable	69,400		
Long-term notes payable	30,000		
Income tax expense	11,000		

During the year, the accounting department prepared monthly statements, but no adjusting entries were made in the journals and ledgers. Data for the year-end procedures are as follows:

1. Prepaid insurance, December 31, was $2,400
2. Depreciation expense on furniture and fixtures for the year was $2,000
3. Depreciation expense on delivery equipment for the year was $10,000
4. Salaries payable, December 31, was $1,600
5. Office supplies on hand, December 31, were $1,800

Required

a. Record the necessary adjusting entries in general journal form at December 31.

b. Prepare a multi-step income statement for the year. Combine all the operating expenses into one line on the income statement for selling, general and administrative expenses.

SERIAL PROBLEM: KATE'S CARDS

(Note: This is a continuation of the Serial Problem: Kate's Cards from Chapter 3.)

SP4. In order to learn more about the industry and to meet people who could give her advice, Kate attended several industry trade shows. At the most recent trade show, Kate was introduced to Fred Abbott, operations manager of "Sentiments," a national card distributor. After much discussion, Fred asked Kate to consider being one of Sentiments' card suppliers. He provided Kate with a copy of the company's recent financial statements. Fred indicated that he expects that Kate will need to supply Sentiments with approximately 50 card designs per month. Kate is to send Sentiments a monthly invoice, and she will be paid approximately 30 days from the date the invoice is received in Sentiments' corporate office. Naturally, Kate was thrilled with this offer, since this will certainly give her business a big boost.

Required

Kate has several questions. Answer the following questions for Kate.

a. What type of information does each of Sentiments' financial statements provide to Kate?

b. What financial statements would Kate need to evaluate whether Sentiments will have enough cash to meet its current liabilities? Explain what to look for.

c. What financial statement would Kate need to evaluate whether Sentiments will be able to survive over a long period of time? Explain what to look for.

d. What financial statement would Kate need to evaluate Sentiments' profitability? Explain what to look for.

e. Where can Kate find out whether Sentiments has outstanding debt? How can Kate determine whether Sentiments will be able to meet its interest and principal payments on any debts that it has?

f. How could Kate determine whether Sentiments pays a dividend?

g. In deciding whether to go ahead with this opportunity, are there other areas of concern that Kate should be aware of?

EXTENDING YOUR KNOWLEDGE

REPORTING AND ANALYSIS

EYK4-1. Financial Reporting Problem: Columbia Sportswear Company The financial statements for Columbia Sportswear can be found in Appendix A at the end of this textbook.

COLUMBIA
SPORTSWEAR
COMPANY

Required

Answer the following questions using the Consolidated Balance Sheet and the Notes to the consolidated financial statements:

a. What were the combined totals of Columbia's liabilities and stockholders' equity for 2011 and 2010?

b. How do these amounts compare with Columbia's total assets for each year?

c. What was the largest, in dollar value, of Columbia's assets each year? What does this asset represent?

d. What is the balance of accrued liabilities made up of?

COLUMBIA
SPORTSWEAR
COMPANY

UNDER ARMOUR,
INC.

EYK4-2.   **Comparative Analysis Problem: Columbia Sportswear Company vs. Under Armour, Inc.** The financial statements for **Columbia Sportswear** can be found in Appendix A and **Under Armour**'s financial statements can be found in Appendix B at the end of this textbook.

Required

a.   Calculate for each company the following ratios for 2011:
1.   Current ratio
2.   Debt-to-total-assets ratio
3.   Return on sales ratio
b.   Comment on the companies' relative profitability, liquidity, and solvency.

SANDISK

EYK4-3.   **Business Decision Problem** **SanDisk**, a maker of computer memory devices, reports the following information in its financial statements. Assume that you are a loan officer at a major bank and have been assigned the task of evaluating whether to extend a loan for a plant expansion to the company.

(in millions)	2011	2010	2009
Current assets	$ 4,356	$4,033	$2,915
Total assets	10,175	8,777	6,002
Current liabilities.	1,093	960	871
Total liabilities.	3,114	2,997	2,093
Retained earnings	1,797	813	(487)
Net sales.	5,662	4,827	3,567
Cost of goods sold.	3,223	2,565	2,282
Net income.	987	1,300	415
Cash flow from operating activities	1,054	1,452	488
Cash flow from investing activities.	(667)	(2,715)	(375)
Cash flow from financing activities.	(48)	991	25
Expenditures for property, plant, and equipment	(193)	(108)	(60)

Required

a.   Calculate the company's current ratio, debt-to-total-assets ratio, return on sales ratio, and free cash flow for each year.
b.   Comment on SanDisk's liquidity, solvency, and profitability.
c.   Based on what you have learned about SanDisk, would you recommend offering the company a loan?

EYK4-4.   **Financial Analysis Problem** As part of your internship at Walleys Inc. you have been assigned the job of developing a few important ratios from the company's financial statements. This information is intended to be used by the company to help Walleys obtain a large bank loan. In particular, the data will need to convince the bank that Walleys is a good loan risk based on its liquidity, solvency, and profitability. Below are the data you pulled together:

	2013	2012
Current ratio	2.2:1	1.5:1
Debt-to-total-assets ratio.	55 percent	63 percent
Return on sales ratio	9.3 percent	9.1 percent
Free cash flow	Up 17 percent	Up 19 percent
Net income.	Up 15 percent	Down 12 percent

Required

Prepare brief comments that discuss how each of these items can be used to support the argument that Walleys is showing improving financial health.

CRITICAL THINKING

EYK4-5.   **Accounting Research Problem** Go to this book's Website and locate the annual report of **General Mills, Inc.** for the year ending May 29, 2011 (fiscal year 2011).

GENERAL MILLS, INC.

Required
1. Calculate the company's return on sales for 2009, 2010, and 2011. What is the trend?
2. Calculate the company's current asset ratio for 2010 and 2011. What is the trend?
3. Calculate the company's debt-to-total-assets ratio for 2010 and 2011. What is the trend?
4. Calculate the company's free cash flow for 2009, 2010, and 2011. What is the trend?

EYK4-6.   **Accounting Communication Activity** V. J. Simmons is the President of Forward Engineering Associates. He is a very good engineer, but his accounting knowledge is quite limited.

Required
V. J. has heard that ratio analysis can help him determine the financial condition of his company. In particular, he would like you to explain to him in a memo how to calculate and interpret the following three ratios: (1) return on sales ratio, (2) current ratio, and (3) debt-to-total-assets ratio. Prepare a memo for V.J.

EYK4-7.   **Accounting Ethics Case** In the post-Enron environment, and with the enactment of the Sarbanes-Oxley legislation, many firms are proactively portraying themselves as being "ethical." Ethical behavior is, for example, part of the Corporate Social Responsibility movement. This behavior includes many dimensions, from the ethical treatment of employees and the environment, to ethical financial reporting. Academic research has found a positive correlation between a firm's reputation and its financial performance. Do you feel that strong ethics makes good business sense? Why do you think that there is a positive correlation between ethical behavior and successful corporate financial performance?

EYK4-8.   **Corporate Social Responsibility Problem** Many investors consider past performance, fees, and investment objectives as the sole criteria for selecting a mutual fund for investment purposes. A growing number of investors are also asking about the actions and philosophies of the companies that form a fund's underlying investment portfolio. Socially responsible mutual funds have been developed to fill this need. These funds are designed for investors who want to align their investments with their religious, political, or social convictions.

Because there is no universally accepted definition as to what makes a company responsible or an investment a socially responsible investment, socially responsible funds are quite diverse. Not surprisingly different funds may take opposite positions on certain controversial issues such as family planning, gay rights, or animal testing.

For the most part, socially responsible funds select their underlying investment firms through either a negative filter or a positive filter. A negative filter is used to screen out firms that are not considered acceptable to the positions advocated by the fund. Examples of firms that may be screened out include firms that are involved in gambling, alcohol, tobacco, or weapons. A positive filter is used to include firms that are seen to be leaders in areas advocated by the fund, such as environmental, diversity, or human rights records.

Required
a.   Go to the Websites of three socially responsible mutual funds
     1. Calvert Signature Funds: http://www.calvertgroup.com/sri-signature.html
     2. Domini Social Equity Fund: http://www.domini.com/domini-funds/Domini-Social-Equity-Fund/index.htm
     3. Green Century Balanced Fund: http://www.greencentury.com/funds/Green-Century-Balanced-Fund
b.   Compare the screening criteria used by each fund. How do they differ and how are they alike?

EYK4-9. **Forensic Accounting Problem** Debra Day, a business major at a local college, was recently hired for the summer at Sweet Delights, a popular ice cream parlor near the campus. Debra spent most of her time tending the cash register where she noticed that most of the customers paid in cash and never seemed to care about getting a receipt. Debra soon figured out that she could ring up a much lesser amount on the register, charge the customer the full amount, then toss the receipt. For example, on a $7 order she would charge and collect the full $7 from the customer, but only ring up $5. She would then deposit $5 in the register so that it would agree with the register tape and pocket the $2.

Required

a. What type of fraud is Debra committing?

b. The store manager recently hired you as a forensic accountant to critique the controls at Sweet Delights. He has noticed that while the store seems as busy as ever, and the cash in the register agrees with the tapes, the store is not as profitable as it previously was. What control would you recommend to help prevent the type of fraud being committed by Debra?

LOGITECH INTERNATIONAL

EYK4-10. **Working with the Takeaways** Throughout this chapter we have considered the financial statements of Apple Inc. and have undertaken select financial analysis using the Takeaways. Utilize these same tools to analyze the financial data of **Logitech International**, a manufacturer of computer peripherals. The following information was reported by Logitech in the company's financial statements as of year-end March 31, 2011 and 2010:

March 31 (in millions)	2011	2010
Current assets	$1,076	$ 794
Total assets	1,862	1,600
Current liabilities	471	440
Total liabilities	657	600
Net sales	2,363	1,967
Net income	128	65
Cash provided by operating activities	157	365
Expenditures on property, plant, and equipment	40	40

Required

1. Calculate the return on sales ratio for each year and comment on Logitech's profitability.
2. Calculate the current ratio for each year and comment on Logitech's liquidity.
3. Calculate the debt-to-total-assets ratio for each year and comment on Logitech's solvency.
4. Calculate the free cash flow for each year and comment on what this means for Logitech.
5. Apple's fiscal year-end occurs near the end of September, whereas Logitech uses a March year-end. How might this affect a comparison of the financial results of the two companies?

TESCO PLC

EYK4-11. **Evaluating Firm Liquidity, Solvency, Profitability and Free Cash Flow: IFRS Financial Statements** **Tesco PLC** is the world's third largest retailer and is headquartered in the United Kingdom. Tesco's IFRS financial statements are presented in Appendix C at the end of this textbook. Using this financial data, calculate the company's (a) return on sales ratio, (b) current ratio, (c) debt-to-total-assets ratio, and (d) free cash flow for 2010 and 2011. Comment on the trend in Tesco's liquidity, solvency, profitability, and free cash flow from 2010 to 2011.

ANSWERS TO SELF-STUDY QUESTIONS:

1. b, (p. 182) 2. c, (pp. 182–183) 3. c, (p. 185) 4. d, (p. 183) 5. b, (p. 185) 6. d, (p. 190) 7. d, (p. 190)
8. b, (p. 193) 9. c, (p. 193) 10. d, (p. 194) 11. a, (p. 191) 12. b, (p. 194) 13. b, (p. 187)

YOUR TURN! SOLUTIONS

Solution 4.1

MUSICLAND COMPANY BALANCE SHEET DECEMBER 31, 2013	
Assets	
Current assets	
Cash	$ 300
Accounts receivable	3,000
Inventory	12,200
Other current assets	1,500
Total current assets	17,000
Property, plant, & equipment	25,000
Total assets	$42,000
Liabilities and Stockholders' Equity	
Current liabilities	
Accounts payable	$ 2,500
Other current liabilities	2,000
Total current liabilities	4,500
Long-term notes payable	20,000
Total liabilities	24,500
Stockholders' equity	17,500
Total liabilities and stockholders' equity	$42,000

Solution 4.2

Musicland Company Income Statement For Year Ended December 31, 2013	
Net sales	$100,000
Less Cost of goods sold	45,000
Gross profit on sales	55,000
Operating expenses	
Selling, general and administrative	25,000
Research and development expenses	10,000
Total operating expenses	35,000
Income from operations	20,000
Other income and expense	
Interest expense	5,000
Income before income taxes	15,000
Income tax expense	4,500
Net income	$ 10,500

Solution 4.3

	2013	2012
Return on sales ratio	$\dfrac{\$20,000}{\$120,000} = 16.7\%$	$\dfrac{\$15,000}{\$110,000} = 13.6\%$
Current ratio	$\dfrac{\$75,000}{\$50,000} = 1.50{:}1$	$\dfrac{\$65,000}{\$45,000} = 1.44{:}1$
Debt-to-total-assets ratio.	$\dfrac{\$150,000}{\$220,000} = 68.2\%$	$\dfrac{\$145,000}{\$190,000} = 76.3\%$
Free cash flow	$\$25,000 - \$7,000 = \$18,000$	$\$22,000 - \$6,000 = \$16,000$

The Philips Company has improved its performance on every measure. The company is earning a higher amount of net income on every dollar of sales revenue as indicated by its return on sales ratio and has more cash for a possible plant expansion as seen in its increasing free cash flow. In addition, both its liquidity as reflected by the current ratio and its solvency as reflected by the debt-to-total-assets ratio are trending in a positive direction.

5

Accounting for Merchandising Operations

LEARNING OBJECTIVES

1. **Explain** the operations of a merchandise company and **contrast** that with the operations of a service company. *(p. 222)*

2. **Describe** the accounting for purchases of merchandise. *(p. 225)*

3. **Describe** the accounting for sales of merchandise. *(p. 229)*

4. **Define** the gross profit percentage and the return on sales ratio, and **explain** their use in profitability analysis. *(p. 232)*

5. Appendix 5A: **Describe** and **illustrate** a periodic inventory system. *(p. 236)*

RIGHT ON TARGET

Target Corporation is one of the largest merchandising companies in the world with more than 1,700 stores and with sales of nearly $70 billion. Target sells products, often referred to as *inventory*. However, Target does not manufacture or make its inventory. Instead, it buys this inventory from manufacturers such as **Sony** and **Panasonic**, and then resells that inventory to consumers. Some refer to companies such as Target as "middlemen."

Target's recent balance sheet reports that it carries nearly $8 billion in inventory, which is about 48 percent of its total current assets. Further, Target's income statement shows that its cost of goods (or inventory) sold of $47.9 billion makes up more than 74 percent of its total operating expenses. Target must track all of these purchases and sales of its inventory.

This chapter describes the most common inventory system that merchandisers apply in today's business world. This system *perpetually* tracks all purchases and sales of inventory. Such tracking is important for managers to effectively manage this key asset and to regularly compute measures that report on management's ability to generate profit from inventory.

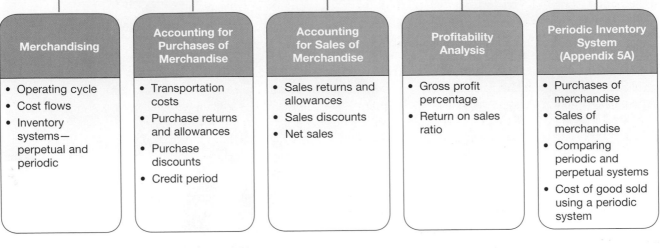

Merchandising	Accounting for Purchases of Merchandise	Accounting for Sales of Merchandise	Profitability Analysis	Periodic Inventory System (Appendix 5A)
• Operating cycle • Cost flows • Inventory systems—perpetual and periodic	• Transportation costs • Purchase returns and allowances • Purchase discounts • Credit period	• Sales returns and allowances • Sales discounts • Net sales	• Gross profit percentage • Return on sales ratio	• Purchases of merchandise • Sales of merchandise • Comparing periodic and perpetual systems • Cost of good sold using a periodic system

THE NATURE OF MERCHANDISING

LO1 **Explain** the operations of a merchandise company and **contrast** that with the operations of a service company.

Manufacturers, wholesalers, and retailers are companies that sell products rather than services. Wholesalers and retailers are both merchandising firms. **Merchandising firms** buy finished products, warehouse and display the products for varying periods of time, and then resell the products. Merchandising firms do not manufacture products nor do they consume the products that they purchase. Merchandising firms provide additional services to their customers, but their primary business is the resale of goods produced by other companies. Exhibit 5-1 illustrates the typical relationship among these three types of companies and the final consumer.

Exhibit 5-1	Distribution of Products to Individual Consumers

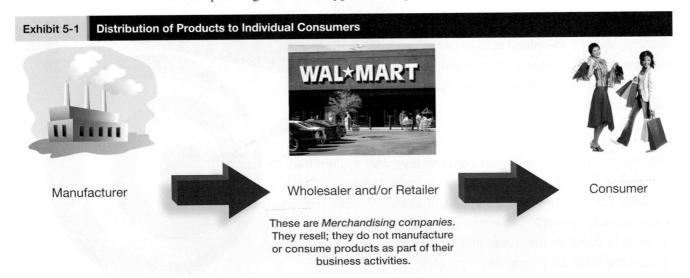

Manufacturer   Wholesaler and/or Retailer   Consumer

These are *Merchandising companies.*
They resell; they do not manufacture
or consume products as part of their
business activities.

A.K.A. Business-to-business transactions, such as Del Monte's sale of canned peaches to Safeway, are often referred to simply as B2B transactions.

Manufacturers convert raw materials and component parts into a finished product through the application of skilled labor and machine operations. **Ford Motor Company**, for example, converts raw materials such as sheets of steel and components such as tires into automobiles and trucks. Similarly, **Del Monte** converts such raw materials as fresh peaches and such components as metal cans into canned peaches. Manufacturers typically only sell their products to wholesale distributors. This process is referred to as a business-to-business (B2B) transaction.

Wholesalers buy finished products from manufacturing firms in large quantities. After warehousing the product for a period of time, the wholesale distributor sells and ships the product to various retailers in smaller quantities to satisfy the local demand for the product. Some wholesalers handle the products of only one manufacturer, while others handle the products of many manufacturers. **Retailers** typically buy products from wholesale distributors and resell the finished products to individual consumers in what is referred to as a business-to-consumer transaction (a B2C transaction). Retailers often have multiple store locations, including the Internet, where they display the products they are offering for sale, enabling customers to view and buy the products. Radio, television, newspaper, and online advertisements inform potential customers of product availability and price. Retailers may range in size from small, with only one store location, to large, with thousands of store locations along with an online Website, such as **Target.com**.

Operating Cycle of a Merchandising Firm

Exhibit 5-2 presents the **operating cycle** of a merchandising firm. There are three primary transactions involved in a merchandising firm's operating cycle: ❶ the purchase of merchandise and its placement in inventory; ❷ the removal of merchandise from inventory when sold and delivered to the customer; and ❸ the receipt of cash from the customer in payment for a cash-and-carry or prior credit purchase. These transactions involve three current asset accounts: cash, accounts receivable, and inventory. The purchased merchandise becomes part of the retailer's inventory until sold; an account receivable is created when the inventory is sold to a customer on credit; and, cash is received when the customer pays for the previously purchased goods. In cases where a customer pays immediately with cash for the purchased merchandise, no accounts receivable is created.

Exhibit 5-2	Comparison of Operating Cycle for a Merchandising Firm and a Service Firm

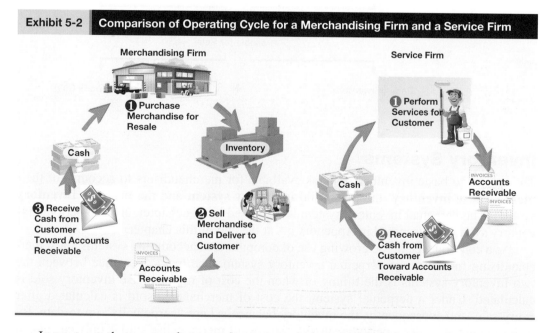

In contrast, there are only two primary transactions involved in the operating cycle of a service firm: ❶ performing a service, and ❷ receiving cash from the customer. Service firms have no inventory to warehouse or display, and consequently, the length of their operating cycle is typically much shorter than that of a merchandising firm.

The three primary transactions for a merchandising firm repeat frequently, creating the cycle depicted in Exhibit 5-2. The timing of the cash collection depends upon the credit terms associated with the sale. When a wholesaler sells to a retailer, a B2B transaction, the sale is usually concluded on a credit basis. That is, the retailer is allowed some period of time following the sale, frequently 30 days or more, to pay the wholesaler for the purchased goods. Some retailers call a credit sale a **sale on account** (also referred to as **sale on credit**). "On account" means on a credit basis.

When retailers such as **Nordstrom** sell to individual consumers, the consumer can (1) pay cash at the time of the sale; (2) use a credit card such as **Discover**, **MasterCard**, or **Visa**; or (3) use an "open account" with the retailer. An **open account** is a charge account provided by a retailer for its customers. Many retailers such as Nordstrom have their own branded credit card to facilitate open account sales. If a customer pays cash, the retailer receives cash immediately. If the customer uses a major credit card issued by a financial institution like **Citibank**, the retailer transmits the credit card information to the card-issuing financial institution and collects the cash either on the same day or within a few days following the credit-sale transaction. If the customer uses an open account, the retailer may not collect the cash from the customer for 30 to 60 days or longer, depending upon the length of the credit terms allowed by the retailer.

Cost Flows

The costs of inventory for merchandisers all flow through its accounting system as diagrammed below. Specifically, a company records its *costs of goods purchased* and adds this to any *beginning inventory* it might have. These two components make up the company's *cost of goods available for sale*. From that total, a company either sells part or all of this inventory, which is recorded in *cost of goods sold*, or carries some of its inventory into the next period, referred to as its *ending inventory*.

The mathematical representation of this cost flow relation is:

Beginning inventory
+ Cost of goods purchased
= Cost of goods available for sale
− Ending inventory
= Cost of goods sold

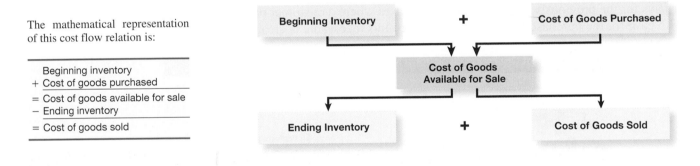

Inventory Systems

There are two basic inventory systems available for merchandisers to account for their **merchandise inventory**: the **perpetual inventory system** and the **periodic inventory system**. The perpetual inventory system is discussed in this chapter, and the periodic inventory system is discussed in Appendix 5A at the end of this chapter.

As a consequence of the growing use of computerized accounting systems, most merchandising firms use the perpetual inventory system. The main difference between the two inventory systems is the timing of when the cost of merchandise inventory sold is calculated. Under a perpetual system, the cost of merchandise sold is calculated after every sale, and consequently, the inventory balance is kept "perpetually" up-to-date. By way of contrast, under a periodic system, the cost of merchandise sold is only calculated "periodically," specifically when a physical count of the inventory is undertaken, which usually occurs only at the end of a fiscal period. As a consequence, the actual inventory balance remains unknown until the end of a fiscal period.

A major advantage of the perpetual system is the increased control it provides over the inventory. Since the inventory is being continuously updated, management is able to determine whether current inventory levels are adequate to satisfy pending or expected sales. In addition, having a record of exactly how much inventory is available allows management to compare these amounts to a physical count of the inventory. Management can then investigate any difference between the amounts to identify the presence of theft or spoilage (in the case of perishable goods).

ACCOUNTING FOR PURCHASES OF MERCHANDISE

When a company using the perpetual inventory system purchases merchandise, it debits the Inventory account for the acquisition cost of the merchandise purchased to reflect an increase in the amount of inventory and credits the Accounts Payable account to reflect an increase in the amount owed to the supplying company. For example, the Barton Wholesale Electronics' purchase invoice for inventory shown in Exhibit 5.3 requires Barton to record the company's purchase of merchandise from Malibu Manufacturing on November 10 with the following journal entry:

LO2 **Describe** the accounting for purchases of merchandise.

Nov 10	Inventory	21,000					
	Accounts payable		21,000	+21,000	+21,000		
	To record the purchase of 100 disk drives from Malibu Manufacturing with credit terms of 2/10, n/30.						

A = L + SE
+21,000 +21,000

Transportation Costs

Transportation Costs Incurred by Buyer

Transportation costs are sometimes incurred by a merchandising company when it acquires goods, and this cost is included as part of the acquisition cost of the inventory. When the buyer is responsible for shipping costs, it is referred to as **FOB shipping point**. (Shipping terms are explained further in Chapter 6.) Assume Barton (buyer) pays $126 to a freight company on November 11, for transportation costs on the 100 disk drives purchased from Malibu Manufacturing (seller). Barton makes the following journal entry to record the payment of $126:

Nov 11	Inventory	126				
	Cash		126	+126		
	To record the payment of $126 of transportation costs for the purchase of 100 disk drives.			−126		

A = L + SE
+126
−126

Exhibit 5-3	**Invoice for Inventory Purchase**

INVOICE

Date: November 10, 2013
Invoice # 1050

Malibu Manufacturing
100 Computer Way
Claremont, CA 91711
909-607-6064
Fax 909-610-1234
sales@malibu.com

SHIP TO: George Jones
Barton Wholesale Electronics
100 Main Street
Anytown, CA 91234
123-456-7890
Customer ID ABC12345

SALESPERSON	SHIPPING METHOD	SHIPPING TERMS	DELIVERY DATE	PAYMENT TERMS
Kate Kanzu	UPS	FOB Shipping Point	Nov 12, 2013	2/10, n/30

QUANTITY	ITEM #	DESCRIPTION	UNIT PRICE	DISCOUNT	LINE TOTAL
100	A30	1.5 TB Disk Drives	210		$21,000
				Total	$21,000

Make all checks payable to Malibu Manufacturing.
Thank you for your business.

PRINCIPLE ALERT	Cost Principle

The inclusion of transportation cost in the acquisition cost of inventory is consistent with the *cost principle*. The cost principle states that an asset is initially recorded at the amount paid to acquire the asset. There can be multiple expenditures associated with an asset acquisition, and all expenditures that are reasonable and necessary to acquire an asset are added to the asset's initial recorded cost.

Transportation Costs Incurred by Seller

When the seller is responsible for shipping costs, it is referred to as **FOB destination**. Instead of the shipping terms stated in the invoice, assume that the seller, Malibu Manufacturing, is responsible for and paid the $126 transportation costs. In this case the transportation cost would be considered an operating expense of the seller, and Malibu Manufacturing would debit an expense account titled Freight-out Expense as follows:

A = L + SE
−126   −126
                Exp

Nov 11	Freight-out expense	126	
	Cash		126
	To record payment for the transportation cost for goods sold.		

Malibu paid the freight charges on the Barton purchase of disk drives, and it will attempt to pass on this cost to the buyer in the form of a higher sales price for the items purchased.

Purchase Returns and Allowances

Occasionally, a purchaser is dissatisfied with some or all of the merchandise purchased because the merchandise was, for example, manufactured poorly, the wrong merchandise was shipped, or because the merchandise was damaged during shipping. When such circumstances are encountered, the purchaser and the seller can remedy the problem by agreeing to treat the value of the unwanted items either as a purchase return or as a purchase allowance.

With a **purchase return**, the purchaser ships the unsatisfactory merchandise back to the seller and receives a credit against the amount due equal to the **invoice price** of the returned merchandise. With a **purchase allowance**, the purchaser retains the merchandise, and the seller reduces the amount that the purchaser owes the seller for the shipment, in effect reducing the sales price.

A retailer can also return merchandise even though there is nothing wrong with the items. For example, textbook publishers often allow college bookstores to return any unsold textbooks to publishers at the conclusion of a term. When publishers allow bookstores to return unsold books, merchandise returns and merchandise allowances occur. In this case, the publisher increases its Inventory account balance by the invoice price of the returned textbooks.

As an example of a purchase return, assume that on November 15, Barton returns 10 of the 100 disk drives purchased on November 10. Barton has not yet paid Malibu Manufacturing for the goods purchased. Accordingly, Barton makes the following journal entry on November 15 to record the purchase return:

A = L + SE
−2,100 −2,100

Nov 15	Accounts payable	2,100	
	Inventory		2,100
	To record a purchase return of 10 disk drives at an invoice price of		
	$210 each to Malibu Manufacturing.		

This entry reduces the Inventory account balance and reduces the amount owed. When the purchaser and seller reach agreement on how to handle a purchase return, they also must agree on which party pays the freight charges on the returned merchandise. (Usually the seller pays freight charges when goods are returned, in an attempt to maintain a positive customer relationship and to increase the likelihood of future repeat business.)

Purchase Discounts

Credit Period

When merchandise is sold on credit, the **credit period** is the maximum amount of time, often stated in days, that a purchaser can take to pay a seller for the purchased items. A typical credit period for a wholesale distributor is 30 days. The credit period is frequently described as the *net credit period*, or net terms. Merchandisers use the notation "**n/**" followed by the number of days in the credit period to designate the time period that a customer can take before paying cash for purchased goods. For example, **n/30** indicates a credit period of 30 days, and n/45 indicates a credit period of 45 days.

To encourage the early payment of unpaid bills, many firms offer their customers a cash discount if payment is made within a designated discount period. A **cash discount**, or **sales discount**, is the amount that the seller deducts from the invoice price if payment is made within the allowed discount period. Some refer to the cash discount offered to credit customers as a "quick-pay incentive." Sellers usually state cash discounts as a percent of the invoice price. The **discount period** is the maximum amount of time, stated in days, that a purchaser has within which to pay the seller if the purchaser wants to claim the cash discount. The discount period is always shorter than the credit period. Most merchandisers use the format "cash discount percent/discount period" to designate the cash discount and the discount period. For example, 1/10 indicates a cash discount of one percent of the invoice price and a discount period of ten days following the invoice date. Finally, merchandisers usually combine the notation for the cash discount and the discount period with the notation for the credit period. For example, 1/10, n/30 represents a cash discount of one percent if paid within ten days of the sale with a total credit period of 30 days following the date of the sale.

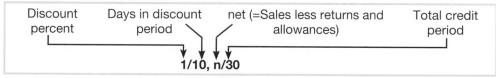

To illustrate, let's return to the Barton example in which Malibu Manufacturing and Barton agree on terms of 2/10, n/30, for the sale on November 10. Barton deducts two percent of the $21,000 invoice price ($420) if it pays Malibu by November 20. In that case, Barton pays $20,580 cash [computed as $21,000 \times (1 - 0.02)$]. If Barton pays Malibu after November 20 but no later than December 10, the amount that Barton must pay is $21,000. After December 10, the $21,000 amount would become overdue and often incurs additional interest cost depending on the invoice terms. Exhibit 5.4 illustrates this example.

Discounts are normally attractive to merchandisers. For instance, if Barton did not take the discount offered by Malibu, this is like Barton paying an interest rate of 2 percent on the $21,000 for 20 days (30-day credit period − 10-day discount period). This is similar to paying an annual interest rate of 36.5 percent, computed as 2 percent $\times$ 365/20. Barton can borrow money at lower rates.

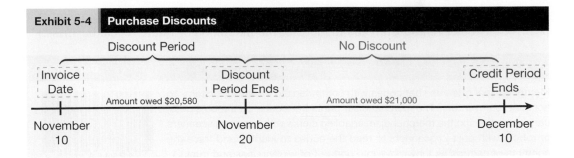

Exhibit 5-4	**Purchase Discounts**

Accounts Payable

		21,000	Nov. 10
Nov. 15	2,100		
		18,900	**Balance**

Accounting for Discounts

Let's extend the prior example where Barton owes $18,900 to Malibu Manufacturing; recall that Barton made a $21,000 purchase, then had a $2,100 purchase return, yielding an amount owed of $18,900. See T-account in the margin.

Pay Within Discount Period   Assume that Barton makes a cash payment to Malibu on November 20, the last day of the discount period. (November 11, the first day following the date of sale, is the first day of the discount period, and November 20 is the tenth or last day of the discount period.) Barton records the cash payment, less the cash discount, with the following journal entry:

A = L + SE
−378   −18,900
−18,522

Nov 20	Accounts payable	18,900	
	Inventory		378
	Cash		18,522
	To record the purchase discount and payment to Malibu		
	Manufacturing within the discount period.		

This entry reduces to zero the amount that Barton owes Malibu Manufacturing. It also records the purchase discount of two percent ($18,900 × 2 percent = $378) as a reduction of the cost in the Inventory account. The entry reveals that $18,522 in cash was paid by Barton to Malibu Manufacturing ($18,900 − $378 = $18,522). Two aspects of this transaction should be noted. First, the cash discount applies only to the cost of the merchandise and not to the transportation cost. Second, the invoice price of the returned merchandise is subtracted from the total invoice price before the cash discount is calculated.

The net total cost reflected in Barton's Inventory account for the disk drives follows:

Inventory

Purchase (+100 units)	Nov 10	21,000			
Freight-in	Nov 11	126			
			2,100	Nov 15	Purchase return (−10 units)
			378	Nov 20	Purchase discount
Balance		18,648			

A total cost of $18,648 is assigned to the 90 disk drives in Barton's inventory (100 purchased − 10 returned). This results in an average cost per disk drive of $207.20 ($18,648/90).

Pay After Discount Period   If Barton made a cash payment to Malibu sometime between November 21 and December 10, after the discount period expired, Barton is not eligible to receive the two percent purchase discount. Consequently, Barton would record a full cash payment on November 25 with the following journal entry:

A = L + SE
−18,900   −18,900

Nov 25	Accounts payable	18,900	
	Cash		18,900
	To record full payment to Malibu Manufacturing following expiration		
	of the discount period.		

When Barton makes the payment to Malibu outside of the allowed discount period, the net total cost in Barton's Inventory account for the 90 disk drives is:

		Inventory			
Purchase (+100 units)	Nov 10	21,000			
Freight-in	Nov 11	126			
			2,100	Nov 15	Purchase return (−10 units)
	Balance	19,026			

A total cost of $19,026 is assigned to the 90 disk drives in Barton's inventory, resulting in an average cost per disk drive of $211.40 ($19,026/90). The cost per disk drive is higher in this situation because Barton did not make the payment for the inventory in a timely fashion to make it eligible for the cash discount.

On June 1, Musicland Inc. purchases 125 CDs at $4.08 each on account from its distributor for a total of $510. The credit terms of the purchase were 2/10 n/30. Also on June 1, Musicland paid freight charges of $22.18 cash for delivery of the CDs. On June 4, Musicland returned 15 defective CDs for an account credit of $61.20. On June 8, Musicland paid $439.82 for the remaining 110 CDs.
Record these transactions in journal entry form for Musicland.

YOUR TURN! 5.1

The solution is on pages 256–257.

ACCOUNTING FOR SALES OF MERCHANDISE

Manufacturing firms and merchandising firms credit Sales Revenue when they sell products, regardless of whether the sales transaction is on credit or for cash. The Sales Revenue account has a normal credit balance.

LO3 Describe the accounting for sales of merchandise.

Let's return to our example and assume that Barton sells 15 disk drives purchased from Malibu Manufacturing (the assumed cost per unit = $18,648/90 disk drives = $207.20 per disk drive) to The Computer Outlet Store at a sales price of $280 per unit. Barton makes the credit sale on December 12, with terms of 1/10, n/15, and The Computer Outlet Store pays shipping cost. Barton makes the following *two* journal entries to record the sale:

Dec 12	Accounts receivable	4,200		A = L + SE		
	Sales revenue		4,200	+4,200		+4,200
	To record sale of 15 disk drives at a sales price of $280 each to The					Rev
	Computer Outlet Store with credit terms of 1/10, n/15.					
Dec 12	Cost of goods sold	3,108		A = L + SE		
	Inventory		3,108	−3,108		−3,108
	To record sale of 15 disk drives with a unit cost of $207.20 to The					Exp
	Computer Outlet Store.					

Revenue Side   The first journal entry records $4,200 of sales revenue ($280 × 15 disk drives) from the sale to Computer Outlet. The debit to Accounts Receivable increases the amount due from customers, and the credit to Sales Revenue increases the total revenue from sales of merchandise during the accounting period.

A.K.A. Sales revenue is also referred to as *revenue*.

Cost Side   The second journal entry transfers the $3,108 cost of merchandise sold ($207.20 × 15 disk drives) from the Inventory account, an asset account, to the Cost of Goods Sold account, an expense account. The debit to Cost of Goods Sold increases the total cost of merchandise sold during the accounting period, and the credit to Inventory removes the cost of the merchandise sold from the Inventory account. **Cost of goods sold** is the total cost of merchandise sold to customers during the accounting period.

A.K.A. Cost of goods sold is often referred to as *COGS*.
A.K.A Cost of goods sold is also referred to as *cost of sales*.

After recording this sale, the net cost in Barton's Inventory account related to the disk drives is $15,540, as follows:

	Inventory				
Purchase (+100 units)	Nov 10	21,000	2,100	Nov 15	Purchase return (−10 units)
Freight-in	Nov 11	126	378	Nov 20	Purchase discount
			3,108	Dec 12	Cost of goods sold (−15 units)
	Balance	15,540			

The $15,540 cost relates to the 75 disk drives (100 purchased − 10 returned − 15 sold) remaining in inventory. The average cost per disk drive remains $207.20 ($15,540/75 disk drives).

PRINCIPLE ALERT	**Revenue and Expense Recognition**

The entry to record sales revenue when 15 disk drives are sold to The Computer Outlet Store illustrates the *revenue recognition principle*. For a merchandising firm, the revenue recognition principle states that revenue is recorded when goods are sold. Normally, this is the earliest point in time that the revenue is both earned (the company has made the economic effort to sell goods) and realized (the company has received payment or has a claim to receive payment for the goods sold). The entry to record the cost of goods sold illustrates the *expense recognition (matching) principle*. Expense recognition states that expenses should be recorded in the same accounting period as the revenues they help generate.

Sales Returns and Allowances

When buyers have returns and allowances, there are sellers that must record those same returns and allowances. With a sales return, the customer ships the merchandise back to the seller and the customer receives a reduction in the amount due to the seller. With a sales allowance, the customer retains the merchandise, and the seller reduces the amount the customer owes, in effect reducing the sales price.

Accounting for **sales returns and allowances** requires two journal entries. The first entry offsets the sales revenue generated from the transaction and reduces the amount owed by the customer. The second entry transfers the cost of merchandise from Cost of Goods Sold back to the Inventory account. Extending the previous example, assume that on December 15, The Computer Outlet Store returned five of the disk drives that it had purchased on December 12. Computer Outlet returned the units because it ordered five units too many; there is nothing wrong with the disk drives. Barton records the sales return by making the following two journal entries:

A = L + SE
−1,400   −1,400
Contra-
Rev
	Dec 15	Sales returns and allowances
		    Accounts receivable
		    To record the return of 5 disk drives by The Computer Outlet Store,
		    with a sales price of $280 each.
			1,400	1,400

A = L + SE
+1,036   +1,036
Exp
	Dec 15	Inventory
		    Cost of goods sold
		    To record the return of 5 disk drives with a unit cost of $207.20 from
		    The Computer Outlet Store.
			1,036	1,036

The first entry offsets the revenue generated from the sale by debiting Sales Returns and Allowances and it reduces the amount the customer owes by crediting Accounts Receivable. The Sales Returns and Allowances account is a *contra-revenue account* and is subtracted from gross sales revenue on the income statement.

The second journal entry transfers the cost of the merchandise from Cost of Goods Sold back to the Inventory account by debiting Inventory (increasing it) and by crediting Cost of Goods Sold (decreasing it). After recording the transfer from Cost of Goods

Sold to Inventory, the net total cost in Barton's Inventory account related to the disk drives is:

Hint: Contra accounts, such as the contra-revenue account, are useful because they provide more information than if the related account were used by itself. For example, by using both the revenue and the contra-revenue accounts, it is possible to track how much of the original sales have had associated returns or allowances.

Inventory					
Purchase (+100 units)	Nov 10	21,000	2,100	Nov 15	Purchase return (−10 units)
Freight-in	Nov 11	126	378	Nov 20	Purchase discount
Sales return (+5 units)	Dec 15	1,036	3,108	Dec 12	Cost of goods sold (−15 units)
	Balance	16,576			

The $16,576 total cost relates to 80 units (100 purchased − 10 purchase return − 15 sold + 5 sales return); and, the average cost of the inventory remains $207.20 ($16,576/80).

Monitoring Sales Returns and Allowances	**ACCOUNTING IN PRACTICE**

Companies accumulate sales revenue in one account and sales returns and allowances in another account so that they can monitor the two. A high ratio of sales returns and allowances to sales revenue is undesirable, often indicating a problem in the quality of the merchandise or its packaging. A company can compare the ratio for the current year to prior-year ratios, or to a target ratio set for the current year, to determine how well the company is managing its product and packaging quality.

Sales Discounts

When making a cash payment for purchased goods, a customer is entitled to take a cash discount only if the payment is made during the allowed discount period. If a cash discount is taken, the seller records it in a separate account called Sales Discounts.

Pay Within Discount Period

Returning to the previous example, assume that The Computer Outlet Store agrees to terms of 1/10, n/15, and it then pays the amount due Barton after deducting the 1 percent cash discount on December 22, the last day of the cash discount period. (December 13 is the first day of the discount period, and December 22 is the tenth or last day of the discount period.) Barton makes the following journal entry to record the cash received from Computer Outlet:

Dec 22	Cash	2,772			A	= L +	SE
	Sales discounts	28			+2,772		−28
	Accounts receivable		2,800		−2,800		Contra-
	To record the sales discount and cash payment from The Computer						Rev
	Outlet Store within the allowed discount period.						

This entry reduces the amount the customer, Computer Outlet, owes the seller, Barton, to zero. The total undiscounted amount due from The Computer Outlet Store was $2,800 ($4,200 sale − $1,400 sales return). With terms of 1/10, n/15, the sales discount is $28 ($2,800 × 1 percent); and, the cash collected is $2,772 ($2,800 − $28).

Companies accumulate sales discounts in a separate account. This enables management to monitor the dollar amount of sales discounts being taken by customers. Sales Discounts is a *contra-revenue account* like Sales Returns and Allowances. Both accounts are contra to, or subtracted from, gross Sales Revenue on the income statement. There are two important aspects of the sales discount calculation. First, the cash discount applies only to the sales price of the merchandise sold and not to any transportation cost. Second, the sales price of any merchandise returned must be subtracted from the total amount before calculating the cash discount.

Pay After Discount Period

If The Computer Outlet Store makes a cash payment after December 22 (after the discount period has expired), the cash discount does not apply. For example, if cash is received in full payment from Computer Outlet on December 27, Barton would record the following journal entry:

A = L + SE	Dec 27	Cash	2,800
+2,800		Accounts receivable	2,800
−2,800		*To record cash received from The Computer Outlet Store outside the allowed discount period.*	

Net Sales

Net sales is the gross sales revenue generated through merchandise sales less any sales revenue given up through sales returns and allowances and any earned sales (cash) discounts. A company calculates its net sales for the period by subtracting the balances of the Sales Returns and Allowances account (normal debit balance) and the Sales Discounts account (normal debit balance) from the balance of the Sales Revenue account (normal credit balance).

> Gross sales revenue
> − Sales returns and allowances
> − Sales discounts
> = Net sales

YOUR TURN! 5.2

The solution is on page 257.

On June 15, a customer buys 75 CDs on account from Musicland for $10 each, for a total of $750. The **list price** of the CDs is $12 each, but Musicland gave the customer a $2 per CD discount because of the large order. On June 20, the customer returned, unopened, five of the CDs and was given a purchase credit of $50. The customer paid its full balance of $700 on June 25. Record these transactions in journal entry form for Musicland. The unit cost of the CDs in inventory is $4.20 each.*

*$4.20 is calculated from the prior Your Turn! as follows:
   Inventory cost = $510.00 + $22.18 − $61.20 − $8.98 = $462.00
   Inventory quantity = 125 − 15 = 110
   Cost per unit = $462.00/110 = $4.20

PROFITABILITY ANALYSIS

LO4 **Define** the gross profit percentage and the return on sales ratio, and **explain** their use in profitability analysis.

Gross Profit Percentage

Managers, investment professionals, and stockholders closely monitor a company's gross profit on sales. They know that if gross profit on sales declines from one year to the next, net income for the current and following year is also likely to decline. A declining gross profit can indicate problems in a company's purchasing activities or problems selling its goods at an acceptable price. For a merchandising company, the Cost of Goods Sold is subtracted from the firm's net sales to determine its gross profit on sales. **Gross profit**, or **gross profit on sales**, is defined as the difference between net sales and Cost of Goods Sold and reveals the amount of sales revenue remaining after subtracting the cost of products sold. (Recall that net sales equals gross sales revenue less any sales returns and allowances and sales discounts.)

A.K.A. Gross profit is often referred to as *gross margin*.

Financial statement users who monitor a company's gross profit on sales are also usually interested in its **gross profit percentage**—that is, the rate at which a company earns gross profit on its sales revenue. A merchandising company measures its gross profit percentage as follows:

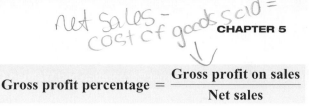

$$\text{Gross profit percentage} = \frac{\text{Gross profit on sales}}{\text{Net sales}}$$

Using the data in Exhibit 5-5, the 2011 gross profit percentage for **Target** is 31.5 percent, computed as $22,005/$69,865.

Financial analysis of the gross profit percentage frequently involves benchmarking the company against competitor companies. Gross profit percentages for a two-year period are presented in Exhibit 5.5 for both **Target Corporation** and one of its chief competitors, **Walmart Corporation**.

Exhibit 5-5	Gross Profit Percentage for Target Corporation and Walmart Corporation	
(in millions)	**2010**	**2011**
Target.....	$21,665/$67,390 = 32.1 percent	$22,005/$69,865 = 31.5 percent
Walmart ...	$106,903/$421,849 = 25.3 percent	$111,823/$446,950 = 25.0 percent

Target's gross profit percentage decreased 0.6 percent, from 32.1 percent in 2010 to 31.5 percent in 2011. Target has a higher gross profit percentage than Walmart. Walmart's gross profit percentage is only 25.3 percent in 2010 and 25.0 percent in 2011. Another explanation for the large difference between the gross profit percentages of the two companies is their different business strategies. Target attempts to sell higher-quality products at a reasonable price, whereas Walmart focuses more on low prices and less on product quality.

Concept ➡	Method ➡	Assessment	TAKEAWAY 5.1
Is a company able to maintain prices on its goods consistent with changes in the cost of its inventory?	Gross profit and net sales $\text{Gross profit percentage} = \dfrac{\text{Gross profit on sales}}{\text{Net sales}}$	A higher ratio suggests the company has market power to command higher retail prices. A lower ratio suggests competitive pressures on price setting.	

Return on Sales Ratio (Profit Margin)

First introduced in Chapter 4, the **return on sales ratio** reveals the net income earned on each dollar of net sales and is computed by dividing net income by net sales:

A.K.A. Return on sales is often referred to as *profit margin*.

$$\text{Return on sales ratio} = \frac{\text{Net income}}{\text{Net sales}}$$

Target's return on sales ratio for 2011 is 4.2%, computed as $2,929/$69,865. A company has a number of ways to improve its return on sales ratio, for example, by raising its retail prices or by purchase discounts by buying in larger quantities. It could also reduce operating expenses by reducing salaries, administrative costs, or selling and marketing costs. Analysts like to compare return on sales ratios for a company over time to detect any trends. They also like to compare the ratio with those of competitors. Return on sales ratios for **Target Corporation** and **Walmart Corporation** are presented in Exhibit 5-6.

Exhibit 5-6	Return on Sales Ratios for Target Corporation and Walmart Corporation	
(in millions)	2010	2011
Target.....	$2,920/$67,390 = 4.3 percent	$2,929/$69,865 = 4.2 percent
Walmart ...	$16,389/$421,849 = 3.9 percent	$15,699/$446,950 = 3.5 percent

Both Target and Walmart have similar return on sales ratios for 2011, with each company realizing net income of about 4 cents for each dollar of sales. This ratio allows us to compare a company's ability to earn profits on its sales regardless of company size. Walmart generates over six times the sales revenue as does Target ($69,865 million for Target versus $446,950 for Walmart), yet Target has a higher return on sales ratio. The return on sales for both companies decreased from 2010 to 2011, although Target's decrease was lesser.

TAKEAWAY 5.2	Concept ⟶	Method ⟶	Assessment ⟶
	Is a company able to maintain prices on its goods consistent with changes in its total expenses?	Net income and net sales $\text{Return on sales ratio} = \dfrac{\text{Net income}}{\text{Net sales}}$	A higher ratio suggests the company is providing a higher net income on each dollar of net sales.

YOUR TURN! 5.3

The solution is on page 257.

The President of Musicland has asked for help to evaluate the company's performance during the current year. In particular, we are requested to calculate Musicland's gross profit percentage and its return on sales ratio and then explain what these measures indicate. The following information is from Musicland's financial statements:

Net sales..	$100,000
Cost of goods sold..	45,000
Net income..	10,500

CORPORATE SOCIAL RESPONSIBILITY

Governance and Conflicts of Interest

An important component of good corporate responsibility is strong corporate governance. **Target** publishes a Business Conduct Guide for its employees as part of its governance program. Included in this handbook are guidelines concerning conflicts of interest. The list below provides examples of potential conflicts of interest:

- Owning a substantial amount of stock in any competing business or in any organization that does business with us.
- Serving as a director, manager, consultant, employee or independent contractor for any organization that does business with us, or is a competitor—except with our company's specific prior knowledge and consent.
- Accepting or receiving gifts of any value or favors, compensation, loans, excessive entertainment or similar activities from any individual or organization that does business or wants to do business with us, or is a competitor.
- Representing the company in any transaction in which you or a related person has a substantial interest.
- Disclosing or using for your benefit confidential or non-public information about Target or other organizations with which we do business.
- Taking personal advantage of a business opportunity that is within the scope of Target's business—such as by purchasing property that Target is interested in acquiring.

COMPREHENSIVE PROBLEM

Williams Distributing Company is a merchandising company. Williams uses the perpetual inventory system. Record each of the following transactions related to the company's purchasing and selling of merchandise:

March 1 Purchased merchandise on account for $6,000; terms were 2/10, n/30.
3 Paid $200 cash for freight on the March 1 purchase.
6 Returned merchandise costing $300 (part of the $6,000 purchase).
10 Paid for merchandise purchased on March 1.
12 Sold merchandise on account costing $8,000 for $10,000; terms were 2/10, n/30.
15 Accepted returned and undamaged merchandise from a customer costing $400 that had been sold on account for $500 (part of the $10,000 sale).
20 Received payment from customer for merchandise sold on March 12.

Solution

March	1	Inventory	6,000	
		Accounts payable		6,000
		Purchased merchandise with 2/10, n/30 terms.		
	3	Inventory	200	
		Cash		200
		Paid freight on March 1 purchase.		
	6	Accounts payable	300	
		Inventory		300
		Returned merchandise from March 1 purchase.		
	10	Accounts payable	5,700	
		Inventory		114
		Cash		5,586
		Paid for merchandise purchased on March 1 within the discount period		
		[($6,000 − $300) × 2% = $114].		
March	12	Accounts receivable	10,000	
		Sales revenue		10,000
		To record revenue from sale of merchandise.		
	12	Cost of goods sold	8,000	
		Inventory		8,000
		To record cost of merchandise sold and to reduce inventory.		
	15	Sales returns and allowances	500	
		Accounts receivable		500
		To record revenue lost from return by customer.		
	15	Inventory	400	
		Cost of goods sold		400
		To record cost of goods returned by customer.		
	20	Cash	9,310	
		Sales discounts	190	
		Accounts receivable		9,500
		To record receipt of cash from customer within the discount period.		

APPENDIX 5A: Periodic Inventory System

An alternative to the perpetual inventory system is the periodic inventory system. The **periodic inventory system** does not update the Inventory account or the Cost of Goods Sold account as merchandise transactions occur during the year. Instead, the Inventory account and the Cost of Goods Sold account are updated only at

LO5

Appendix 5A:
Describe and **illustrate** a periodic inventory system.

the end of the accounting period when a physical count of the inventory on hand is undertaken. The periodic inventory system is unacceptable for most companies because up-to-date inventory amounts are not available during the year for managerial decision making. The following section illustrates the journal entries that Barton Wholesale Electronics would make if it used the periodic inventory system. We utilize the same data used in the chapter to illustrate the perpetual inventory system to facilitate an easy comparison of the two systems.

Accounting for Purchases of Merchandise

When a company uses the periodic inventory system, it records the purchase of merchandise by debiting the cost of the merchandise to the Purchases account, rather than the Inventory account, and crediting the cost to Accounts Payable. (The Purchases account has a normal debit balance.) On November 10, Barton records the purchase of 100 disk drives with a list price of $210 each and terms of 2/10, n/30 by making the following journal entry:

A	=	L	+	SE				
		+21,000		−21,000	Nov 10	Purchases	21,000	
						Accounts payable		21,000
						To record the purchase of 100 disk drives from Malibu		
						with 2/10, n/30 terms.		

Transportation Costs

When a purchaser using the periodic inventory system bears the cost of transporting the merchandise from the seller, the purchaser records the transportation cost in the Freight In account, rather than in the Inventory account. (The Freight In account has a normal debit balance.) Barton makes the following journal entry on November 12 to record payment of $126 of transportation costs on the purchase of 100 disk drives:

A	=	L	+	SE				
−126				−126	Nov 12	Freight in	126	
						Cash		126
						To record the payment of $126 of transportation costs on the		
						purchase of 100 disk drives.		

Purchase Returns and Allowances

If a purchaser is dissatisfied with merchandise that was purchased and a purchase return or allowance is granted, the purchaser records the purchase return or allowance using the Purchase Returns and Allowances account, rather than the Inventory account. (Purchase Returns and Allowances is a contra-purchases account with a normal credit balance.) On November 15, Barton records the return of 10 disk drives to Malibu Manufacturing by making the following journal entry:

A	=	L	+	SE				
		−2,100		+2,100	Nov 15	Accounts payable	2,100	
						Purchase returns and allowances		2,100
						To record the return of 10 disk drives at a list price of $210.		

Purchase Discounts

If a purchaser makes a cash payment to the seller before the end of the allowed discount period, the purchaser deducts a cash discount. Otherwise, the purchaser pays the full invoice price. When a purchaser takes a cash discount, the purchaser credits the Purchase Discounts account, rather than the Inventory account. (Purchase Discounts is a contra-purchases account with a normal credit balance.) Barton makes the following journal entry on November 20 to record its cash payment to Malibu Manufacturing after deducting the cash discount:

A	=	L	+	SE				
−18,522		−18,900		+378	Nov 20	Accounts payable	18,900	
						Purchase discounts		378
						Cash		18,522
						To record the payment to Malibu Manufacturing within the allowed		
						discount period.		

If Barton makes payment between November 21 and December 10, after the discount period has expired, the cash discount does not apply. In this case, Barton records a cash payment on November 25 with the following journal entry:

Nov 25	Accounts payable	18,900		A = L + SE
	Cash		18,900	18,900 −18,900 −18,900
	To record the payment to Malibu Manufacturing outside the allowed discount period.			

YOUR TURN! 5.4

The solution is on page 257.

Assume that Musicland uses the *periodic system*. On June 1, Musicland purchased 125 CDs at $4.08 each on account from its distributor for $510. The terms of the purchase were 2/10, n/30. Also on June 1, Musicland paid in cash a freight charge of $22.18 for delivery of the CDs. On June 4, Musicland returned 15 defective CDs for a credit of $61.20. On June 8, Musicland paid $439.82 for the remaining 110 CDs. Record the transactions in journal entry form for Musicland.

Accounting for Sales of Merchandise

Under the periodic inventory system, a seller makes only one journal entry to record a sale of merchandise. The entry records an account receivable from the customer and the sales revenue from the sale by debiting Accounts Receivable and crediting Sales Revenue. Barton records the December 12 sale of 15 disk drives to The Computer Outlet Store at a sales price of $280 each with terms of 1/10, n/15 by making the following entry:

Dec 12	Accounts receivable	4,200		A = L + SE
	Sales revenue		4,200	+4,200 +4,200
	To record the sale of 15 disk drives at a sales price of $280 each to The Computer Outlet Store with credit terms of 1/10, n/15.			Rev

The same journal entry is made under the perpetual inventory system. Under the periodic inventory system, however, there is no concurrent entry to transfer the cost of merchandise sold from the Inventory account to the Cost of Goods Sold account.

Sales Returns and Allowances

Under the periodic inventory system, only one journal entry is used to record a sales return or allowance. The entry records the reduction of the revenue from the sale and the reduction of the account receivable from the customer by debiting Sales Returns and Allowances and crediting Accounts Receivable. Barton records the December 15 return by The Computer Outlet Store of five disk drives by making the following journal entry:

Dec 15	Sales returns and allowances	1,400		A = L + SE
	Accounts receivable		1,400	−1,400 −1,400
	To record the return of 5 disk drives by The Computer Outlet Store; sales price was $280 each.			Rev

This entry is the same as the first journal entry under the perpetual inventory system; however, Barton does not make the second journal entry that was made under the perpetual inventory system. Under the periodic inventory system, there is no immediate reinstatement of the returned merchandise to the Inventory account or corresponding reduction in the Cost of Goods Sold account.

Sales Discounts

The journal entry to record the receipt of a cash payment from a customer is exactly the same under either the perpetual inventory system or the periodic inventory system. If the payment is made within the allowed discount period, the entry includes a debit to Sales Discounts, a contra-sales account. Barton records the cash received from The Computer Outlet Store on December 22 (within the discount period) as follows:

Dec 22	Cash	2,772		A = L + SE
	Sales discounts	28		+2,772 −28
	Accounts receivable		2,800	−2,800 Rev
	To record the cash payment from The Computer Outlet Store within the discount period.			

If The Computer Outlet Store makes its cash payment any time between December 23 and December 27 (after the discount period), the cash discount does not apply. Barton records the cash received from Computer Outlet on December 27 with the following journal entry:

A = L + SE	Dec 27	Cash	2,800	
+2,800		Accounts receivable		2,800
−2,800		*To record the cash payment from The Computer Outlet Store outside*		
		the discount period.		

YOUR TURN! 5.5

The solution is on page 258.

Assume Musicland uses the *periodic system*. On June 15, a customer buys on account 75 CDs from Musicland for $10 each, for a total of $750. The list price of the CDs is $12 each, but Musicland provided the customer with a $2 per CD discount because of the large order. On June 20, the customer returned, unopened, five of the CDs and was given a credit of $50. The customer paid its full balance of $700 on June 25. Record these transactions on Musicland's books. The unit cost of the CDs in inventory is $4.20 each.*

*$4.20 is computed from Your Turn 5.1 as follows:
  Inventory cost = $510.00 + $22.18 − $61.20 − $8.98 = $462.00
  Inventory quantity = 125 − 15 = 110
  Cost per unit = $462.00/110 = $4.20

Comparison of Entries Under the Perpetual and Periodic Systems

Exhibit 5A-1 summarizes all key journal entries under both the perpetual and periodic inventory systems for purchases and sales of merchandise.

Exhibit 5A-1   **Comparison of Journal Entries under the Perpetual and Periodic Systems**

Date	Transaction	Perpetual Inventory System		Periodic Inventory System	

Nov 10	Purchase of merchandise on credit	Inventory
		    Accounts payable
			21,000
			21,000
				Purchases
				    Accounts payable
					21,000
					21,000

Nov 11	Freight cost	Inventory
		    Cash
			126
			126
				Freight In
				    Cash
					126
					126

Nov 15	Purchase returns	Accounts payable
		    Inventory
			2,100
			2,100
				Accounts payable
				    Purchase returns
					2,100
					2,100

Nov 20	Purchase discount and payment	Accounts payable
		    Inventory
		    Cash
			18,900
			378
			18,522
				Accounts payable
				    Purchase discounts
				    Cash
					18,900
					378
					18,522

Dec 12	Sale of merchandise on credit	Accounts receivable
		    Sales revenue
			4,200
			4,200
				Accounts receivable
				    Sales revenue
					4,200
					4,200

		Cost of goods sold Inventory	3,108 3,108	No entry	

Dec 15	Return of sales merchandise	Sales returns and allowances
		    Accounts receivable
			1,400
			1,400
				Sales returns and allowances
				    Accounts receivable
					1,400
					1,400

		Inventory Cost of goods sold	1,036 1,036	No entry	

Dec 22	Sales discount and payment	Cash
		Sales discounts
		    Accounts receivable
			2,772
			28
			2,800
				Cash
				Sales discounts
				    Accounts receivable
					2,772
					28
					2,800

Cost of Goods Sold Using a Periodic System

If a firm uses a periodic system rather than a perpetual system, it does not record cost of goods sold at the time sales revenue is recorded. Instead, cost of goods sold is calculated periodically at the end of the accounting period when the inventory is physically counted. Cost of goods sold is then backed into by subtracting the ending inventory from the **cost of goods available for sale**, which represents the total inventory that was available to be sold. The calculation of cost of goods sold using the periodic method is shown in Exhibit 5A-2.

Exhibit 5A-2	Cost of Goods Sold Computation Using the Periodic Method

	Beginning inventory
+	Cost of goods purchased during the period
=	Cost of goods available for sale
−	Ending inventory
=	Cost of goods sold

One additional difference between the periodic method and the perpetual method is how a company keeps track of items that affect the Inventory account. Under the perpetual system, items such as transportation charges, purchase returns, and purchase discounts, are debited and credited directly to the Inventory account. Under the periodic system, separate accounts are used for each of these items, which are then added to beginning inventory to arrive at the cost of goods available for sale. An illustration of this is shown in Exhibit 5A-3, assuming that there was no beginning inventory.

Exhibit 5A-3	Cost of Goods Sold Illustration Using the Periodic Method

BARTON WHOLESALE ELECTRONICS
Cost of Goods Sold
For Year Ended December 31, 2013

Inventory, January 1.			$ 0
Purchases.		$21,000	
Less: Purchase returns and allowances	$2,100		
Purchase discounts	378	2,478	
Net purchases		18,522	
Add: Freight-in		126	
Cost of goods purchased.			18,648
Cost of goods available for sale.			18,648
Less: Inventory, December 31			16,576
Cost of goods sold.			$ 2,072

YOUR TURN! 5.6

The solution is on page 258.

Assume that Musicland uses a periodic inventory system. Prepare a schedule of cost of goods sold as of December 31, 2012, using the following information:

Inventory, January 1, 2012.	$10,000
Purchases.	50,000
Purchase returns and allowances	2,000
Freight-in	200
Purchase discounts	1,000
Inventory, December 31, 2012.	12,200

SUMMARY OF LEARNING OBJECTIVES

LO1   **Explain the operations of a merchandise company and contrast that with the operations of a service company. (p. 222)**

■   Merchandise inventory is a stock of products that a company buys from another company and makes available for sale to its customers.

■   Merchandising firms sell merchandise. There are two types of merchandising firms: wholesale distributors and retailers.

■   Manufacturing companies convert raw materials and components into finished products through the application of skilled labor and machine operations; wholesale distributors buy finished product from manufacturing firms in large quantities and sell smaller quantities to retailers; retailers sell the products to individual consumers.

■   The operating cycle of a merchandising firm consists of three types of transactions: purchase merchandise for resale and warehouse the inventory, remove goods from inventory and ship to the customer at sale, and receive cash from the customer.

■   The primary revenue source for a service firm is from providing services to customers, rather than manufacturing or selling a physical product.

LO2   **Describe the accounting for purchases of merchandise. (p. 225)**

■   The perpetual inventory system records the cost of merchandise in the Inventory account at the time of purchase and updates the Inventory account for subsequent transactions as they occur.

■   When the perpetual inventory system is used, the Inventory account is affected by merchandise transactions as follows:
  - Debited for the invoice price of purchases.
  - Debited for transportation costs.
  - Credited for the cost of purchase returns and allowances.
  - Credited for cash discounts taken.
  - Credited for the cost of the merchandise sold.
  - Debited for the cost of any sales returns.

LO3   **Describe the accounting for sales of merchandise. (p. 229)**

■   When a perpetual inventory system is used, the following procedure is followed to account for the sale of merchandise:
  - Credit Sales Revenue at the time of the sale, and debit Cash or Accounts Receivable.
  - Debit Cost of Goods Sold and credit Inventory at the time of sale to match expenses with revenue and to update the inventory balance.

LO4   **Define the gross profit percentage and the return on sales ratio, and explain their use in profitability analysis. (p. 232)**

■   The gross profit percentage is the rate at which a company earns gross profit on net sales.

■   The gross profit percentage is calculated as net sales less the cost of goods sold, all divided by net sales.

■   The return on sales ratio reveals how much of each dollar of net sales is earned by the company after subtracting all expenses.

■   The return on sales ratio is calculated by dividing net income by net sales.

LO5   **Appendix 5A: Describe and illustrate a periodic inventory system. (p. 236)**

■   The periodic inventory system updates both the Inventory account and the Cost of Goods Sold account at the end of the accounting period when a physical count of the inventory is taken.

■   Under the periodic inventory system separate accounts are used to record merchandise purchases, transportation costs, purchase returns and allowances, and purchase discounts, rather than recording these items to the Inventory account.

Compute cost of goods sold (periodic system).

■   The periodic inventory system does not update the Inventory account or the Cost of Goods Sold account as merchandise transactions occur during the year. Instead, the Inventory account and the Cost of Goods

Sold account are updated only at the end of the accounting period when a physical count of the inventory is taken. Other accounts are used to record purchases, transportation costs, purchase returns and allowances, and purchase discounts.

■ Cost of goods sold is calculated by subtracting the remaining inventory on hand from the cost of goods available for sale, which represents the aggregate inventory that was available to be sold.

■ The basic formula for calculating the cost of goods sold under the periodic system is to calculate goods available for sale consisting of beginning inventory plus net purchases during the period, and then subtract ending inventory from this amount.

Concept	Method	Assessment	SUMMARY
Is a company able to maintain prices on its goods consistent with changes in the cost of its inventory?	Gross profit and net sales $\text{Gross profit percentage} = \dfrac{\text{Gross profit on sales}}{\text{Net sales}}$	A higher ratio suggests the company has market power to command higher retail prices. A lower ratio suggests competitive pressures on price setting.	TAKEAWAY 5.1
Is a company able to maintain prices on its goods consistent with changes in its total expenses?	Net income and net sales $\text{Return on sales ratio} = \dfrac{\text{Net income}}{\text{Net sales}}$	A higher ratio suggests the company is providing a higher net income on each dollar of net sales.	TAKEAWAY 5.2

KEY TERMS

Cash discount (p. 227)

Cost of goods available for sale (p. 239)

Cost of goods sold (p. 229)

Credit period (p. 227)

Discount period (p. 227)

FOB destination (p. 226)

FOB shipping point (p. 225)

Gross profit (gross margin) (p. 232)

Gross profit on sales (p. 232)

Gross profit percentage (p. 232)

Invoice price (p. 226)

List price (p. 232)

Manufacturers (p. 222)

Merchandise inventory (p. 224)

Merchandising firms (p. 222)

Net sales (p. 232)

Open account (p. 224)

Operating cycle (p. 223)

Periodic inventory system (p. 224)

Perpetual inventory system (p. 224)

Purchase allowance (p. 226)

Purchase return (p. 226)

Retailers (p. 223)

Return on sales ratio (profit margin) (p. 233)

Sale on account (p. 224)

Sale on credit (p. 224)

Sales discount (p. 227)

Sales returns and allowances (p. 230)

Wholesalers (p. 223)

SELF-STUDY QUESTIONS

(Answers to Self-Study Questions are at the end of this chapter.)

1. On March 1, Troy Company purchased merchandise with an invoice price of $2,700 and 2/10, n/30 **LO2**
terms. On March 3, Troy pays $100 transportation cost on the purchased goods. On March 10, Troy pays for the merchandise. What is Troy's total cost of the purchased merchandise?

   a. $2,700
   b. $2,744
   c. $2,746
   d. $2,800

LO2   2. Newman Company started business on January 1. During the year, the company purchased merchandise with an invoice price of $500,000. Newman also paid $20,000 freight on the merchandise. During the year, Newman also returned $80,000 of the merchandise to its suppliers. All purchases were paid for in a timely manner, and a $10,000 cash discount was taken. $418,000 of the merchandise was sold for $627,000. What is the December 31, balance in the Inventory account?

    a. $82,000   *c.* $12,000
    b. $32,000   *d.* $2,000

LO2   3. Saber Company uses the perpetual inventory system. Saber purchased merchandise with an invoice price of $800, terms 2/10, n/30. If Saber returns merchandise with an invoice price of $200 to the supplier, what should the journal entry to record the return include?

    a. Debit to Inventory of $200
    b. Debit to Inventory of $196
    c. Credit to Inventory of $200
    d. Credit to Inventory of $100

LO4   4. Ira Company reports net sales of $500, cost of sales of $300, and net income of $50. What is the gross profit percentage and return on sales ratio for Ira?

    a. Gross profit percentage is 10 percent and return on sales ratio is 40 percent.
    b. Gross profit percentage is 60 percent and return on sales ratio is 10 percent.
    c. Gross profit percentage is 40 percent and return on sales ratio is 10 percent.
    d. Gross profit percentage is 40 percent and return on sales ratio is 25 percent.

LO2   5. Smith & Sons purchased $5,000 of merchandise from the Claremont Company with terms of 3/10, n/30. How much discount is Smith & Sons entitled to take if it pays within the allowed discount period of 10 days?

    a. $50   *c.* $150
    b. $100   *d.* $300

LO2   6. Moonitz Inc. purchased merchandise with a list price of $6,000 from the Sprague Company. Sprague offers its customers credit terms of 2/10, n/30. What amount should Moonitz pay if the cash discount is taken?

    a. $5,940   *c.* $6,120
    b. $6,060   *d.* $5,880

LO5   7. Kali Company began the period with $20,000 in inventory. The company also purchased an additional $20,000 of inventory and returned $2,000 for a full credit. A physical count of the inventory at year-end revealed an inventory on hand of $16,000. What was Kali's cost of goods sold for the period?

    a. $16,000   *c.* $48,000
    b. $22,000   *d.* $50,000

LO4   8. The Arcadia Company is a merchandiser and reports the following data at year-end:

Net sales.	$100,000
Cost of goods sold.	60,000
Net income.	15,000

What is the company's gross profit percentage?

    a. 40 percent   *c.* 15 percent
    b. 60 percent   *d.* None of the above

LO4   9. Using the data in Question 8, what is The Arcadia Company's return on sales ratio?

    a. 40 percent   *c.* 15 percent
    b. 60 percent   *d.* None of the above

LO5   10. Denald Co. uses the periodic inventory system. When goods are purchased, Denald will:

    a. debit freight costs to Inventory.
    b. debit purchase returns and allowance for returned items.
    c. debit the Purchases account for purchases on account.
    d. debit the Inventory account for purchases on account.

11. **Which of the following statements regarding cost flows is true?**   **LO1**
    a. Cost of goods available for sale is equal to beginning inventory minus cost of goods purchased.
    b. Cost of goods available for sale is equal to beginning inventory plus cost of goods purchased.
    c. CGAS = beginning inventory minus ending inventory.
    d. CGAS = cost of goods sold minus cost of goods purchased.

QUESTIONS

1. Describe the differences between (a) a manufacturer, (b) a wholesale distributor, and (c) a retailer.

2. Describe the three primary transactions in the operating cycle of a merchandising firm.

3. What is the difference between a credit period and a discount period? What is a cash discount?

4. Sprague Company purchased merchandise with a list price of $2,000 from the Thompson Company. Thompson offers a two percent cash discount if payment is received within 10 days. What is the payment amount if the cash discount is taken?

5. Krane Company purchased $4,000 of merchandise and paid $250 in transportation costs to deliver the merchandise. Krane then returned $1,000 of the merchandise before paying the supplier within the discount period. Krane was entitled to a two percent cash discount. How much did Krane pay the supplier?

6. What is the primary difference between a merchandise return and a merchandise allowance?

7. Define the *return on sales ratio*. What does this ratio measure?

8. Define *gross profit on sales.*

9. Define *gross profit percentage.* How is this percentage used by analysts and investors?

10. When merchandisers and manufacturers prepare income statements for their annual reports to shareholders, they usually begin the statement with net sales. For internal reporting purposes, however, the income statements will show gross sales and the related contra-revenue accounts of sales returns and allowances and sales discounts. What might explain this difference in the financial information disclosed to external parties and management? Do you consider the more limited disclosure in the annual reports to be inconsistent with the full disclosure principle? Briefly explain your point of view.

SHORT EXERCISES

SE5-1. **Merchandising versus Service Firm** For each of the following accounts, indicate whether it would   **LO1**
be found in the records of a merchandising firm, a service firm, or both.

    a. Cost of goods sold.
    b. Service revenue.
    c. Purchase returns and allowances.
    d. Inventory.
    e. Accounts receivable.
    f. Accounts payable.
    g. Sales revenue.
    h. Freight-out.

SE5-2. **Accounting for Purchase Transactions** Debra Company began operations on June 1. The following   **LO2**
transactions took place in June:

    a. Purchases of merchandise on account were $600,000.
    b. The cost of freight to receive the inventory was $20,000. This was paid in cash.
    c. Debra returned $10,000 of the merchandise due to an ordering error. Debra received a full credit for the return.
    d. Debra paid the remaining balance for the merchandise.

Calculate the dollar amount that Debra will have in inventory at the end of the month. Assume Debra uses the perpetual inventory system and there were no sales.

LO2 **SE5-3.** **Accounting for Purchase Transactions** Use the data from SE5-2 and prepare the journal entries to record the June transactions.

LO2 **SE5-4.** **Accounting for Purchase Discounts** Ken Company purchased $5,000 of merchandise from Marilyn Company with terms of 3/10 n/45. What percent discount will Ken Company get if it pays within the allowed discount period? If Ken Company fails to pay within the discount period, how many days does Ken Company have from the date of purchase before the payment is considered to be late?

LO2 **SE5-5.** **Accounting for Purchase Discounts** Using the information in SE5-4, what amount will Ken Company pay to Marilyn Company if Ken Company takes advantage of the purchase discount?

LO3 **SE5-6.** **Accounting for Sales Transactions** Kate Company uses the perpetual inventory system. Record the journal entries for the following transactions:

    a. On July 16, Kate sold $600 of merchandise with terms of 2/10 n/30. The cost of the merchandise was $360.

    b. On July 19, the customer returned $100 of the merchandise from (*a*). The cost of the merchandise was $60.

    c. On July 22, the customer paid the entire balance due to Kate.

LO5
(Appendix 5A) **SE5-7.** **Cost of Goods Sold and the Periodic System** Kanzu Company uses the periodic inventory system. Kanzu started the period with $10,000 in inventory. The Company purchased an additional $25,000 of merchandise, and returned $1,000 for a full credit. A physical count of inventory at the end of the period revealed that there was an ending inventory balance of $8,000. What was Kanzu's cost of goods sold during the period?

LO5
(Appendix 5A) **SE5-8.** **Cost of Goods Sold and the Periodic System** Hermani Company uses the periodic inventory system. Hermani started the period with $20,000 in inventory. The Company purchased an additional $25,000 of merchandise and returned $3,000 for a full credit. If Hermani's cost of goods sold during the period was $35,000, what must have been the total of the physical inventory count?

LO4 **SE5-9.** **Gross Profit Percentage** Using the data below, compute Dino's gross profit percentage for the month of January.

Net sales.	$10,000
Cost of goods sold.	4,000
Operating expenses.	3,000
Other income.	500
Income tax expense.	1,200

LO4 **SE5-10.** **Return on Sales Ratio** Using the data in SE5-9, compute Dino's return on sales ratio for the month of January.

LO5
(Appendix 5A) **SE5-11.** **Journalize Periodic Inventory Entries** Prepare the journal entries to record the following transactions for the Walbright Company using a periodic inventory system.

    a. On June 2, Walbright purchased $350,000 of merchandise from the Ferway Company with terms, 3/15, n/30.

    b. On June 5, Walbright returned $50,000 of the merchandise purchased on June 2.

    c. On June 13, Walbright paid the balance due to Ferway.

Assignments with the ✔ logo in the margin are available in BusinessCourse.
See the Preface of the book for details.

EXERCISES—SET A

LO3 **E5-1A.** **Cash Discount Calculations** On June 1, Forest Company sold merchandise with a list price of $24,000. For each of the sales terms below, determine the proper amount of cash received:

	Credit Terms	Date Paid
1.	2/10, n/30	June 8
2.	1/10, n/30	June 15
3.	1/15, n/30	June 14
4.	n/30	June 28

E5-2A.   Journal Entries for Sale, Return, and Remittance—Perpetual System   On September 13, Brady Company sold merchandise with an invoice price of $900 ($600 cost), with terms of 2/10, n/30, to Dalton Company. On September 17, $150 of the merchandise ($100 cost) was returned because it was the wrong model. On September 23, Brady Company received a check for the amount due from Dalton Company.   **LO3** ✔

Required
Prepare the journal entries made by Brady Company for these transactions. Brady uses the perpetual inventory system.

E5-3A.   Journal Entries for Purchase, Return, and Remittance—Perpetual System   On April 13, the Kesselman Company purchased $22,000 of merchandise from the Krausman Company, with terms of 1/10, n/30. On April 15, Kesselman paid $300 to Ace Trucking Company for freight on the shipment. On April 18, Kesselman Company returned $1,000 of merchandise for credit. Final payment was made to Krausman on April 22. Kesselman Company records purchases using the perpetual inventory system.   **LO2** ✔

Required
Prepare the journal entries that Kesselman Company should make on April 13, 15, 18, and 22.

E5-4A.   Journal Entries for Merchandise Transactions on Seller's and Buyer's Books—Perpetual System   The following are selected transactions for Lamont, Inc., during the month of June: **LO2, 3** ✔

June 21	Sold and shipped on account to Lowery Company, $2,880 ($2,000 cost) of merchandise, with terms of 2/10, n/30.
28	Lowery Company returned defective merchandise billed at $280 on June 21 ($210 cost).
30	Received from Lowery Company a check for full settlement of the June 21 transaction.

Required
Prepare the necessary journal entries for (a) Lamont, Inc., and (b) Lowery Company. Both companies use the perpetual inventory system.

E5-5A.   Recording Purchases—Perpetual System   On July 1, Alvarez, Inc. purchased merchandise for $1,800, with terms of 2/10, n/30. On July 5, the firm returned $600 of the merchandise to the seller. Payment of the account occurred on July 8. Alvarez uses the perpetual inventory system.   **LO2** ✔

Required
a.   Prepare the journal entries for July 1, July 5, and July 8.
b.   Assuming that the account was paid on July 14, prepare the journal entry for payment on that date.

E5-6A.   Profitability Analysis   Shannon Enterprises reports the following information on its year-end income statement: **LO4** ✔

Net sales.	$150,000	Operating expenses	30,000
Cost of goods sold.	90,000	Other income	10,000

Required
Calculate Shannon's gross profit percentage and return on sales ratio.

LO5
(Appendix 5A)
✅

E5-7A.   Journal Entries for Sale, Return, and Remittance—Periodic System On June 8, Stevens Company sold merchandise listing for $1,600 to Dalton Company, terms 2/10, n/30. On June 12, $400 worth of the merchandise was returned because it was the wrong color. On June 18, Stevens Company received a check for the amount due.

Required
Record the journal entries made by Stevens Company for these transactions. Stevens uses the periodic inventory system.

LO5
(Appendix 5A)
✅

E5-8A.   Journal Entries for Purchase, Return, and Remittance—Periodic System On March 10, Horton Company purchased $18,000 worth of merchandise from James Company, terms 1/10, n/30. On March 12, Horton paid $160 freight on the shipment. On March 15, Horton returned $200 of merchandise for credit. Final payment was made to James on March 19. Horton Company uses the periodic inventory system.

Required
Prepare the journal entries that Horton should make on March 10, March 12, March 15, and March 19.

LO5
(Appendix 5A)
✅

E5-9A.   Journal Entries for Merchandise Transactions on Seller's and Buyer's Records—Periodic System The following are selected transactions for Franklin, Inc., during the month of April:

April   20   Sold and shipped on account to Lind Stores merchandise for $2,400, with terms of 2/10, n/30.
27   Lind Stores returned defective merchandise billed at $200 on April 20.
29   Received from Lind Stores a check for full settlement of the April 20 transaction.

Required
Prepare the necessary journal entries for (a) Franklin, Inc., and (b) Lind Stores. Both companies use the periodic inventory system.

EXERCISES—SET B

LO3
✅

E5-1B.   Cash Discount Calculations On April 1, the Fitzgerald Company sold merchandise with a list price of $40,000. For each of the sales terms below, determine the proper amount of cash received:

	Credit Terms	Date Paid
1.	1/15, n/30...	April 14
2.	n/30	April 28
3.	2/10, n/30...	April 8
4.	1/10, n/30...	April 15

LO3
✅

E5-2B.   Journal Entries for Sale, Return, and Remittance—Perpetual System On October 14, the Patrick Company sold merchandise with an invoice price of $1,000 ($750 cost), with terms of 2/10, n/30, to the Baxter Company. On October 18, $200 of merchandise ($150 cost) was returned because it was the wrong size. On October 24, the Patrick Company received a check for the amount due from the Baxter Company.

Required
Prepare the journal entries for the Patrick Company using the perpetual inventory system.

LO2
✅

E5-3B.   Journal Entries for Purchase, Return, and Remittance—Perpetual System On May 15, Monique Company purchased $25,000 of merchandise from the Terrell Company, with terms of 1/10, n/30. On May 17, Monique paid $260 to Swift Trucking Company for freight on the shipment. On May 20, Monique Company returned $500 of merchandise for credit. Final payment was made to Terrell on May 24. Monique Company records purchases using the perpetual inventory system.

Required
Prepare the journal entries that Monique Company should make on May 15, 17, 20, and 24.

E5-4B.   Journal Entries for Merchandise Transactions on Seller's and Buyer's Books—Perpetual System   **LO2, 3**
The following are selected transactions of Candello, Inc., during the month of June:

June   18   Sold and shipped on account to Dante Company $4,000 ($3,000 cost) of merchandise,
with terms of 2/10, n/30.
       25   Dante Company returned defective merchandise billed at $400 on June 18 ($300 cost).
       27   Received from Dante Company a check for full settlement of the June 18 transaction.

Required
Prepare the necessary journal entries for (a) Candello, Inc., and (b) Dante Company. Both companies use the perpetual inventory system.

E5-5B.   Recording Purchases—Perpetual System   On September 12, Evans, Inc., purchased merchandise   **LO2**
for $3,000, with terms of 2/10, n/30. On September 16, the firm returned $900 of the merchandise
to the seller. Payment of the account occurred on September 19. Evans uses the perpetual inventory
system.

Required
a.   Prepare the journal entries for September 12, September 16, and September 19.
b.   Assuming that the account was paid on September 25, prepare the journal entry for payment on
that date.

E5-6B.   Profitability Analysis   Alex Enterprises reports the following information on its year-end income   **LO4**
statement:

| Net sales. . . . . | $300,000 | Operating expenses . . . . | 60,000 |
| Cost of goods sold. . . . . | 180,000 | Other income . . . . | 20,000 |

Required
Calculate Alex's gross profit percentage and return on sales ratio.

E5-7B.   Journal Entries for Sale, Return, and Remittance—Periodic System   On March 10, the Sharon   **LO5**
Company sold merchandise listing for $2,000 to the Dillard Company with terms of 2/10, n/30. On   **(Appendix 5A)**
March 14, $500 of merchandise was returned because it was the wrong size. On March 20, Sharon
Company received a check for the amount due.

Required
Prepare the journal entries made by Sharon Company for these transactions. Sharon uses the periodic
inventory system.

E5-8B.   Journal Entries for Purchase, Return, and Remittance—Periodic System   On August 15, the Har-   **LO5**
ris Company purchased $20,000 of merchandise from Jason Company with terms of 2/10, n/30. On   **(Appendix 5A)**
August 17, Harris paid $200 freight on the shipment. On August 20, Harris returned $300 worth of
the merchandise for credit. Final payment was made to Jason on August 24. Harris Company records
purchases using the periodic inventory system.

Required
Prepare the journal entries that Harris should make on August 15, August 17, August 20, and August 24.

E5-9B.   Journal Entries for Merchandise Transactions on Seller's and Buyer's Books—Periodic System   **LO5**
The following are selected transactions of Fenton, Inc., during the month of January: **(Appendix 5A)**

Jan   18   Sold and shipped on account to Lawrence Stores merchandise listing for $1,500 with
terms of 2/10, n/30.
      25   Lawrence Stores was granted a $200 allowance on goods shipped January 18.
      27   Received from Lawrence Stores a check for full settlement of the January 18 transaction.

Required

Prepare journal entries for (a) Fenton, Inc., and (b) Lawrence Stores. Both companies use the periodic inventory system.

PROBLEMS—SET A

LO2, 3   **P5-1A.**   **Journal Entries for Merchandise Transactions on Seller's and Buyer's Books—Perpetual System**

Excel ✔

The following transactions occurred between the Decker Company and Mann Stores, Inc., during March:

Mar   8   Decker sold $13,200 worth of merchandise ($8,800 cost) to Mann Stores with terms of 2/10, n/30.
       10 Mann Stores paid freight charges on the shipment from Decker Company, $200.
       12 Mann Stores returned $1,200 of the merchandise ($800 cost) shipped on March 8.
       17 Decker received full payment for the net amount due from the March 8 sale.
       20 Mann Stores returned goods that had been billed originally at $600 ($400 cost). Decker issued a check for $588.

Required

Prepare the necessary journal entries for (a) the books of Decker Company and (b) the books of Mann Stores, Inc. Assume that both companies use the perpetual inventory system.

LO2, 3   **P5-2A.**   **Journal Entries for Merchandise Transactions—Perpetual System**   Rockford Corporation, which

✔

began business on August 1, sells on terms of 2/10, n/30. Credit terms for its purchases vary with the supplier. Selected transactions for August are given below. Unless noted, all transactions are on account and involve merchandise held for resale. The perpetual inventory system is used.

Aug   1   Purchased merchandise from Norris, Inc., $3,400, terms 2/10, n/30.
       5   Paid freight on shipment from Norris, Inc., $160.
       7   Sold merchandise to Denton Corporation, $4,800 ($3,400 cost).
       7   Paid $240 freight on August 7 shipment and billed Denton for the charges.
       9   Returned $600 worth of the merchandise purchased August 1 from Norris, Inc., because it was defective. Norris approved the return.
       9   Received $800 of returned merchandise ($600 cost) from Denton Corporation. Rockford approved the return.
       10 Paid Norris, Inc., the amount due.
       14 Purchased from Chambers, Inc., goods with a price of $8,000. Terms 1/10, n/30.
       15 Paid freight on shipment from Chambers, Inc., $280.
       17 Received the amount due from Denton Corporation.
       18 Sold merchandise to Weber, Inc., $9,600 ($6,600 cost).
       20 Paid $320 freight on August 18 shipment and billed Weber for the charges.
       24 Paid Chambers, Inc., the amount due.
       28 Received the amount due from Weber, Inc.

Required

Prepare journal entries for these transactions for Rockford Corporation.

LO2, 3   **P5-3A.**   **Effects of Transactions on the Inventory Account—Perpetual System**   Watt Wholesale Company

✔

purchases merchandise from a variety of manufacturers and sells the merchandise to a variety of retailers. All sales are subject to a cash discount (2/10, n/30). Watt uses a perpetual inventory system. The May 1 balance in Watt's Inventory account was a $60,000 debit. The following transactions occurred during May:

May   2   Purchased $4,500 of merchandise from Ajax Manufacturing; terms are 1/10, n/30.
       4   Paid $160 freight on the May 2 purchase.

May 12 Paid Ajax for the May 2 purchase.
   14 Purchased $3,000 of merchandise from Baker Manufacturing; terms are 2/10, n/45.
   16 Received a $200 allowance on the May 14 purchase since some of the merchandise was the wrong color. All of the merchandise is salable at regular prices.
   18 Purchased $2,500 of merchandise from Charles Industries; terms are 2/10, n/30.
   19 Sold merchandise with a list price of $2,000 ($1,200 cost) to Daytime Industries.
   22 Daytime Industries returned 30 percent of the merchandise from the May 19 sale.
   26 Paid Baker Manufacturing for the May 14 purchase.
   29 Paid Charles Industries for the May 18 purchase.

Required
Prepare a schedule that shows the impact of these transactions on Watt's Inventory account. Use the following headings:

Date	Transaction	Debit Amount	Credit Amount	Account Balance

P5-4A. **Journal Entries for Merchandise Transactions—Perpetual System** Cushing Distributing Company uses the perpetual inventory system. Cushing had the following transactions related to merchandise during the month of June: **LO2, 3** ✔

June 1 Purchased on account merchandise for resale for $8,000; terms were 2/10, n/30.
   3 Paid $350 cash for freight on the June 1 purchase.
   7 Returned merchandise costing $500 (part of the $8,000 purchase).
   10 Paid for merchandise purchased on June 1.
   13 Sold merchandise on account costing $7,000 for $10,000; terms were 2/10, n/30.
   16 Customer returned merchandise costing $650 that had been sold on account for $900 (part of the $10,000 sale).
   22 Received payment from customer for merchandise sold on June 13.

Required
Prepare journal entries for each of the transactions for the Cushing Distributing Company.

P5-5A. **Profitability Analysis** Kolby Enterprises reports the following information on its income statement: **LO4** ✔

Net sales.	$220,000	Administrative expenses	$10,000
Cost of goods sold.	140,000	Other income	15,000
Selling expenses	40,000	Other expense	5,000

Required
Calculate Kolby's gross profit percentage and return on sales ratio. Explain what each ratio tells us about Kolby's performance. Kolby is planning to add a new product and expects net sales to be $30,000 and cost of goods to be $25,000. No other income or expenses are expected to change. How will this affect Kolby's gross profit percentage and return on sales ratio? What do you advise regarding the new product offering?

P5-6A. **Journal Entries for Merchandise Transactions on Seller's and Buyer's Books—Periodic System** The following transactions occurred between Southwick Company and Mann Stores, Inc., during March: **LO5** **(Appendix 5A)** ✔

Mar 8 Southwick sold $6,600 worth of merchandise to Mann Stores, terms 2/10, n/30.
   10 Mann Stores paid freight charges on the shipment from Southwick Company, $100.
   12 Mann Stores returned $600 of the merchandise shipped on March 8.
   17 Southwick received full payment for the net amount due from the March 8 sale.
   20 Mann Stores returned goods that had been billed originally at $200. Southwick issued a check for $196.

Required

Prepare the necessary journal entries for (a) the books of Southwick Company and (b) the books of Mann Stores, Inc. Assume that both companies use the periodic inventory system.

LO5 **P5-7A.** **Journal Entries for Merchandise Transactions—Periodic System** The Malvado Corporation sells
(Appendix 5A) goods on terms of 2/10, n/30. Credit terms for its purchases vary with the supplier. Selected transactions for August are given below. Unless noted, all transactions are on account and involve merchandise held for resale. The periodic inventory system is used.

Aug   1   Purchased merchandise from Norris, Inc., $1,700; terms 2/10, n/30.
      5   Paid freight on shipment from Norris, Inc., $80.
      7   Sold merchandise to Denton Corporation, $2,400.
      7   Paid freight on shipment to Denton Corporation, $120, and billed Denton for the charges.
      9   Returned $300 worth of the merchandise purchased August 1 from Norris, Inc., because
          it was defective. Norris approved the return.
      9   Received $400 of returned merchandise from Denton Corporation.
     10   Paid Norris, Inc., the amount due.
     14   Purchased from Chambers, Inc., goods with a price of $3,000. Terms 1/10, n/30.
     15   Paid freight on shipment from Chambers, Inc., $140.
     17   Received the amount due from Denton Corporation.
     18   Sold merchandise to Weber, Inc., $4,800.
     20   Paid freight on August 18 shipment to Weber, Inc., $160 and billed Weber.
     24   Paid Chambers, Inc., the amount due.
     28   Received the amount due from Weber, Inc.

Required

Prepare the necessary journal entries for the Malvado Corporation.

PROBLEMS—SET B

LO2, 3 **P5-1B.** **Journal Entries for Merchandise Transactions on Seller's and Buyer's Books—Perpetual System**
Riggs Distributing Company had the following transactions with Arlington, Inc., during the month of November:

Nov 10   Riggs sold and shipped $6,000 worth of merchandise ($4,200 cost) to Arlington, terms
          2/10, n/30.
     12   Arlington, Inc., paid freight charges on the shipment from Riggs Company, $320.
     14   Riggs received $600 of merchandise returned by Arlington ($420 cost) from the
          November 10 sale.
     19   Riggs received payment in full for the net amount due on the November 10 sale.
     24   Arlington returned goods that had originally been billed at $300 ($210 cost). Riggs
          issued a check for $294.

Required

Prepare the necessary journal entries (a) on the books of Riggs Distributing Company and (b) on the books of Arlington, Inc. Assume that both companies use the perpetual inventory system.

LO2, 3 **P5-2B.** **Journal Entries for Merchandise Transactions—Perpetual System** Webster Company was established on July 1. Its sales terms are 2/10, n/30. Credit terms for its purchases vary with the supplier. Selected transactions for the first month of operations are given below. Unless noted, all transactions are on account and involve merchandise held for resale. Webster Company uses the perpetual inventory system.

July 1   Purchased goods from Dawson, Inc., $1,900; terms 1/10, n/30.
      2   Purchased goods from Penn Company, $4,200; terms 2/10, n/30.
      3   Paid freight on shipment from Dawson, $100.
      5   Sold merchandise to Ward, Inc., $1,300 ($975 cost).

July 5 Paid freight on shipment to Ward, Inc., $60. (*Hint:* debit Delivery Expense)

8 Returned $300 worth of the goods purchased July 1 from Dawson, Inc., because some goods were damaged. Dawson approved the return.

9 Received returned goods from Ward, Inc., worth $200 ($150 cost).

10 Paid Dawson, Inc., the amount due.

10 Purchased goods from Dorn Company with a list price of $2,400. Terms 2/10, n/30.

11 Paid freight on shipment from Dorn Company, $130.

15 Received the amount due from Ward, Inc.

15 Sold merchandise to Colby Corporation, $3,200 ($2,400 cost).

16 Mailed a check to Penn Company for the amount due on its July 2 invoice.

18 Received an allowance of $100 from Dorn Company for defective merchandise purchased on July 10.

19 Paid Dorn Company the amount due.

25 Received the amount due from Colby Corporation.

Required

Prepare the necessary journal entries for the Webster Company.

P5-3B. Effects of Transactions on the Inventory Account—Perpetual System Rand Wholesale Company **LO2, 3** purchases merchandise from a variety of manufacturers and sells the merchandise to a variety of retailers. All sales are subject to a cash discount (2/10, n/30). Rand has a perpetual inventory system. The February 1, balance in Rand's Inventory account was a $50,000 debit. The following transactions occurred during February:

Feb 2 Purchased $7,600 of merchandise from Sweet Manufacturing; terms are 1/10, n/30.

5 Paid $270 freight on the February 2 purchase.

11 Paid Sweet for the February 2 purchase.

13 Purchased $5,000 of merchandise from Tayler Manufacturing; terms are 2/10, n/45.

16 Received a $300 allowance on the February 13 purchase since some of the merchandise was the wrong size. All of the merchandise is salable at regular prices.

17 Purchased $4,200 of merchandise from Zorn Industries; terms are 2/10, n/30.

20 Sold merchandise with a list price of $4,000 ($2,200 cost) to Valley Mart.

22 Valley Mart returned 20 percent of the merchandise from the February 20 sale.

23 Paid Tayler Manufacturing for the February 13 purchase.

28 Paid Zorn Industries for the February 17 purchase.

Required

Prepare a schedule that shows the impact of these transactions on Rand's Inventory account. Use the following headings:

Date	Transaction	Debit Amount	Credit Amount	Account Balance

P5-4B. Journal Entries for Merchandise Transactions Janetto Distributing Company uses the perpetual **LO2, 3** inventory system. Janetto had the following transactions related to merchandise during the month of August:

Aug 10 Purchased on account merchandise for resale for $3,000; terms were 2/10, n/30.

12 Paid $120 cash for freight on the August 10 purchase.

16 Returned merchandise costing $200 (part of the $3,000 purchase).

19 Paid for merchandise purchased on August 10.

22 Sold merchandise on account costing $1,000 for $1,600; terms were 2/10, n/30.

25 Customer returned merchandise costing $65 that had been sold on account for $100 (part of the $1,600 sale).

31 Received payment from customer for merchandise sold on August 22.

Required

Record each of the transactions related to purchasing and selling merchandise for the Janetto Distributing Company.

LO4 **P5-5B.** **Profitability Analysis** Ashley Enterprises reports the following information on its income statement:

Net sales.	$440,000	Administrative expenses	$20,000
Cost of goods sold.	280,000	Other income	30,000
Selling expenses	80,000	Other expense	10,000

Required

Compute Ashley's gross profit percentage and return on sales ratio. Explain what each ratio tells us about Ashley's performance. Ashley is planning to add a new product and expects net sales to be $30,000 and cost of goods to be $25,000. No other income or expenses are expected to change. How will this affect Ashley's gross profit percentage and return on sales ratio? What do you advise regarding the new product offering?

LO5 **P5-6B.** **Journal Entries for Merchandise Transactions on Seller's and Buyer's Books—Periodic System**
(Appendix 5A) Fortune Distributing Company had the following transactions with Arlington, Inc., during November:

Nov 10 Fortune sold and shipped $6,000 worth of merchandise to Arlington, terms 2/10, n/30.
     12 Arlington, Inc., paid freight charges on the shipment from Fortune Company, $360.
     14 Fortune received $600 of merchandise returned by Arlington from the November 10 sale.
     19 Fortune received payment in full for the net amount due on the November 10 sale.
     24 Arlington returned goods that had originally been billed at $500. Fortune issued a check for $490.

Required

Prepare the necessary journal entries (a) on the books of Fortune Distributing Company and (b) on the books of Arlington, Inc. Assume that both companies use the periodic inventory system.

LO5 **P5-7B.** **Journal Entries for Merchandise Transactions—Periodic System** Polidor Company was estab-
(Appendix 5A) lished on July 1. Its sales terms are 2/10, n/30. Credit terms for its purchases vary with the supplier. Selected transactions for the first month of operations are given below. Unless noted, all transactions are on account and involve merchandise held for resale. All purchases are recorded using the periodic inventory system.

July 1 Purchased goods from Dawson, Inc., $1,900; terms 1/10, n/30.
     2 Purchased goods from Penn Company, $4,200; terms 2/10, n/30.
     3 Paid freight on shipment from Dawson, $80.
     5 Sold merchandise to Ward, Inc., $1,300.
     5 Paid freight on shipment to Ward, Inc., $60. (*Hint:* debit Delivery Expense)
     8 Returned $300 worth of the goods purchased July 1 from Dawson, Inc., because some goods were damaged. Dawson approved the return.
     9 Received returned merchandise from Ward, Inc., $200.
    10 Paid Dawson, Inc., the amount due.
    10 Purchased goods from Dorn Company with a price of $1,600. Terms 2/10, n/30.
    11 Paid freight on shipment from Dorn Company, $130.
    15 Received the amount due from Ward, Inc.
    15 Sold merchandise to Colby Corporation, $3,200.
    16 Mailed a check to Penn Company for the amount due on its July 2 invoice.
    18 Received an allowance of $100 from Dorn Company for defective merchandise purchased on July 10.
    19 Paid Dorn Company the amount due.
    25 Received the amount due from Colby Corporation.

Required

Prepare the necessary journal entries for Polidor Company.

SERIAL PROBLEM: KATE'S CARDS

(Note: This is a continuation of the Serial Problem: Kate's Cards from Chapters 1 through 4.)

SP5.   Kate was a little worried about some of the practices of Fred Abbott, the CEO of Sentiments, and decided that an association with Sentiments could damage the reputation of her own company. Kate is very concerned that her business be viewed as socially responsible and any damage to her reputation at this early stage could prove very difficult to overcome. She therefore decided to concentrate her efforts on producing a quality product that consumers would be proud to purchase and send to their loved ones.

As expected, November saw a boom in Kate's greeting card business. She invested in additional computer graphics equipment, which she partially funded with a bank loan of $15,000 and an additional investment of her own funds into the business. The loan carries an interest rate of six percent with interest payments required semiannually. The entire principal balance is due in one balloon payment in two years. Kate uses a perpetual inventory system. As of December 2, 2012, Kate's Cards had the following account balances:

Cash..........................	$11,900	Accumulated depreciation...........	$ 1,600
Accounts receivable...............	16,800	Accounts payable.................	13,800
Inventory.......................	16,000	Other current liabilities.............	900
Other current assets..............	3,600	Long-term note payable.............	15,000
Computer equipment..............	38,900	Common stock...................	25,000
		Retained earnings	30,900

The company had the following transactions during December 2012:

Dec   7   Paid $1,800 to employees. Of this amount, $900 was for an amount owed from November. Salaries due to employees at the end of each month are recorded as Other Current Liabilities.

      9   Received $5,400 from customers as payment on account.

    12   Sold, for cash, $9,000 of greeting cards. This merchandise had cost $6,000 to produce.

Dec   14   Purchased additional inventory totaling $7,000 on account with terms of 2/10, n/45.

    15   Paid cash for supplies (listed as Other Current Assets) in the amount of $600.

    19   Sold, on account with terms of 2/10, n/30, greeting cards totaling $6,000. The merchandise had cost $4,000 to produce.

    21   Paid additional salaries of $1,400.

    25   Paid the total owed for the merchandise that was purchased on December 14.

    28   Received payment in full from the customer that purchased the merchandise on December 19. Granted the discount of two percent since payment was within the allowed discount period.

    31   Depreciation for the month totaled $900.

    31   A physical count of inventory and supplies revealed that $13,000 and $2,000, respectively, were on hand at year-end. Assume that Other Current Assets consists only of the cost of supplies.

Required

a.   Prepare journal entries for the December transactions.

b.   Prepare a classified income statement for the month of December 2012.

c.   Calculate Kate's gross profit percentage and return on sales ratio for December 2012.

EXTENDING YOUR KNOWLEDGE

REPORTING AND ANALYSIS

EYK5-1.   **Financial Reporting Problem: The Columbia Sportswear Company** The financial statements for the **Columbia Sportswear Company** are in Appendix A at the end of this book.

COLUMBIA
SPORTSWEAR
COMPANY

Required

Using the company's Consolidated Statement of Operations (which is another name for Income Statement), answer the following questions.

a. What was the change in net sales and in net income from 2010 to 2011?

b. What was the gross profit percentage in each of the three years, 2009 through 2011? Comment on the trend in this ratio.

c. What was the return on sales ratio in each of the three years, 2009 through 2011? Comment on the trend in this ratio.

COLUMBIA
SPORTSWEAR
COMPANY

UNDER ARMOUR,
INC.

EYK5-2. **Comparative Analysis Problem: The Columbia Sportswear Company vs. Under Armour, Inc.** The financial statements for the **Columbia Sportswear Company** and **Under Armour, Inc.** are in Appendix A and B, respectively, at the end of this book.

Required

a. Based on the information you find in these financial statements, determine the following values for each company:

1. Gross profit for 2011
2. Gross profit percentage for 2011
3. Net income for 2011
4. Return on sales ratio for 2011

b. Based on this information, what can you say about the relative performance of these two companies?

EYK5-3. **Business Decision Problem** Northwestern Corporation started a retail clothing business on July 1, 2012. During 2012, Northwestern Corporation had the following summary transactions related to merchandise inventory:

	Purchases	Sales
July.	$240,000	$ 360,000
August	384,000	696,000
September	312,000	576,000
October	360,000	660,000
November.	900,000	1,020,000
December.	264,000	1,344,000

On average, Northwestern's cost of goods sold is 50 percent of sales. Assume that there were no sales returns and allowances or purchases returns and allowances during this six-month time period.

Required

a. Calculate the ending merchandise inventory for each of the six months.

b. Northwestern's purchases peaked during November; its sales peaked during December. Did Northwestern plan its purchases wisely? Should Northwestern expect a similar pattern in future years?

JOHNSON &
JOHNSON

EYK5-4. **Financial Analysis Problem** **Johnson & Johnson** is a worldwide manufacturer of health care products, including Band-Aid bandages and Mylanta antacid. It reported the following results for three recent years (Year 3 is the most recent):

(in millions)	Year 3	Year 2	Year 1
Net sales.	$63,747	$61,095	$53,324
Cost of goods sold.	18,511	17,751	15,057

Assume that similar-sized companies in the same basic industries have experienced an average gross profit percentage of 70 percent each year.

Required

a. Calculate the gross profit percentage for Johnson & Johnson for the three years.

b.   Compare the three-year trend in gross profit percentage for Johnson & Johnson to the assumed industry average. Analyze the trend and evaluate the performance of Johnson & Johnson compared to the assumed industry average.

CRITICAL THINKING

EYK5-5.   **Accounting Research Problem** Refer to the fiscal year 2011 annual report of **General Mills, Inc.**, available on this book's Website.

GENERAL MILLS, INC.

Required
a.   How much sales revenue did General Mills report in 2010 and 2011?
b.   What was the company's gross profit percentage in 2010 and 2011?
c.   How much net income did the company earn in 2010 and 2011?
d.   What was the company's return on sales for 2010 and 2011? What can we conclude about the company's performance over the two-year period?

EYK5-6.   **Accounting Communication Activity** Nobel Company produces custom machinery that has few competitors. As such, Nobel is able to charge a large markup that is reflected in its large gross profit percentage. Recently the marketing director proposed offering a new set of products that are more generic in nature, and therefore will not allow large markups. The accounting department has, however, determined the products will add to Nobel's overall net income. The following table provides estimates of Nobel's profitability both with and without the new product:

	Without New Product	With New Product
Net sales.	$250,000	$350,000
Cost of goods sold.	125,000	210,000
Net income.	25,000	31,500

Required
The President of Nobel, Jack Towne, has asked you to write a memo answering the following questions.

a.   How will the new product line affect the company's profitability as measured by its gross profit percentage and the return on sales ratio?
b.   How is it possible for net income to improve, while at the same time these profitability ratios may deteriorate?
c.   Should the company expand by offering this new product line?

EYK5-7.   **Accounting Ethics Case** During the last week of 2011, George Connors, controller of We 'R' Appliances, received a memorandum from the firm's president, Jane Anderson. The memorandum stated that Anderson had negotiated a very large sale with a new customer and directed Connors to see that the order was processed and the goods shipped before the end of the year. Anderson noted that she had to depart from the usual credit terms of n/30 and allow terms of n/60 to clinch the sale. Although the credit terms were unusual for the company, Connors was particularly pleased with the news because business had been somewhat slow. The goods were shipped on December 29 and the sale was incorporated into the 2011 financial data.

It is now mid-February 2012, and two events have occurred recently that, together, cause concern for Connors. First, he was inadvertently copied on a letter from the firm's bank to Anderson. The letter stated that the bank had reconsidered its decision to deny a loan to the company and is now granting the loan based on the new, and favorable, sales data supplied by the president. The bank was "particularly impressed with the sales improvement shown in December." Although Connors had been involved in the initial loan application that was denied, he had been unaware that the president had reapplied for the loan.

The second event was that all of the goods shipped on December 29, 2011, to the new customer had just been returned.

Required
What are the ethical considerations George Connors faces as a result of the recent events?

TARGET

EYK5-8. **Corporate Social Responsibility Problem** Target is one of a large growing number of companies that publish an annual corporate social responsibility report. Go to the Target Website and navigate to the section on corporate responsibility in order to download Target's latest corporate responsibility report. Discuss some of the ways that Target documents its good citizenship.

IFRS

EYK5-9. **Profitability Analysis: IFRS Financial Statements** Tesco PLC is the world's third largest retailer and is based in the United Kingdom. Tesco's IFRS financial statements are presented in Appendix C at the end of this textbook. Using the company's financial statements, calculate the company's (a) gross profit percentage and (b) return on sales ratio for 2010 and 2011. Comment on the trend in the company's profitability over the two-year period.

COSTCO

EYK5-10. **Working with the Takeaways** Costco Wholesale Corporation is the largest membership warehouse club chain in the world based on sales volume. It is the fifth largest general retailer in the United States. Costco is also one of the fastest growing retailers, having grown to over 600 locations since its start in 1983. A look at Costco's income statement reveals the following data:

COSTCO WHOLESALE CORPORATION		
(in millions)	**2010**	**2011**
Net sales.	$77,946	$88,915
Cost of goods sold.	67,995	77,739
Net income.	1,303	1,462

Required

Evaluate Costco's performance in terms of gross profit percentage and return on sales ratio. How does Costco compare to Target and Walmart? (See Exhibits 5-5 and 5-6 on pages 233 and 234.)

ANSWERS TO SELF-STUDY QUESTIONS:

1. c, (pp. 227–231) 2. c, (pp. 227–231) 3. c, (pp. 228–230) 4. c, (pp. 234–235) 5. c, (pp. 229–230)
6. d, (pp. 229–230) 7. b, (p. 241) 8. a, (pp. 234–235) 9. c, (p. 235) 10. c, (p. 238) 11. b, (p. 226)

YOUR TURN! SOLUTIONS

Solution 5.1

June 1	Inventory	510.00	
	Accounts payable		510.00
	To record merchandise purchased on account (125 CDs @ $4.08 each)		
June 1	Inventory	22.18	
	Cash		22.18
	To record payment of freight charges on merchandise purchased.		
June 4	Accounts payable	61.20	
	Inventory		61.20
	To record the return of defective merchandise		
	(15 units @ $4.08 per unit).		

June 8	Accounts payable	448.80	
	Cash		439.82
	Inventory		8.98
	To record full payment within discount period. Cash discount		
	earned = $8.98.		

Solution 5.2

June 15	Accounts receivable	750.00	
	Sales revenue		750.00
	To record the sale of 75 CDs on account.		

June 15	Cost of goods sold	315.00	
	Inventory		315.00
	To record cost of goods sold for 75 CDs.		

June 20	Sales revenue	50.00	
	Accounts receivable		50.00
	To record the return of 5 CDs for credit.		

June 20	Inventory	21.00	
	Cost of goods sold		21.00
	To record the return of 5 CDs for credit		

June 25	Cash	700.00	
	Accounts receivable		700.00
	To record cash payment from customer.		

The third journal entry for the return of merchandise has the effect of reversing a portion of the first two entries.

Solution 5.3

Gross profit percentage = ($100,000 − $45,000)/$100,000 = 55 percent
Return on sales ratio = $10,500/$100,000 = 10.5 percent

    A gross profit percentage of 55 percent indicates that Musicland was able to earn 55 cents for each dollar of net sales after considering just its cost of goods sold. In other words, Musicland still has 55 cents available from each dollar of net sales to cover its remaining expenses and to earn a net profit.

    A return on sales ratio of 10.5 percent indicates that Musicland was able to earn 10.5 cents in net income from each dollar of net sales after subtracting all of the business's expenses.

Solution 5.4

June 1	Purchases	510.00	
	Accounts payable		510.00
	To record merchandise purchased on account (125 @ $4.08 each).		

June 1	Freight in	22.18	
	Cash		22.18
	To record payment of freight charge on merchandise purchase.		

June 4	Accounts payable	61.20	
	Purchase returns		61.20
	To record the return of defective merchandise (15 units).		

June 8	Accounts payable	448.80	
	Cash		439.82
	Purchase discounts		8.98
	To record payment for merchandise purchased.		

Solution 5.5

June 15	Accounts receivable	750.00	
	Sales revenue		750.00
	To record the sale of 75 CDs on account.		
June 20	Sales returns	50.00	
	Accounts receivable		50.00
	To record the return of 5 CDs for credit.		
June 25	Cash	700.00	
	Accounts receivable		700.00
	To record cash payment from customer.		

The second entry for the return of merchandise has the effect of reversing a portion of the first entry.

Solution 5.6

MUSICLAND COMPANY
Cost of Goods Sold
For Year Ended December 31, 2012

Cost of goods sold			
Inventory, January 1			$10,000
Purchases		$50,000	
Less: Purchase returns and allowances	$2,000		
Purchase discounts	1,000	3,000	
Net purchases		47,000	
Add: Freight-in		200	
Cost of goods purchased			47,200
Cost of goods available for sale			57,200
Less: Inventory, December 31			12,200
Cost of goods sold			$45,000

6

Accounting for Inventory

LEARNING OBJECTIVES

1. **Explain** inventory concepts and modern inventory practices. *(p. 262)*
2. **Describe** inventory costing under specific identification, weighted-average cost, FIFO, and LIFO. *(p. 266)*
3. **Analyze** the financial effects of different inventory costing methods on company profit. *(p. 271)*
4. **Apply** the lower-of-cost-or-market method. *(p. 276)*
5. **Define** *inventory turnover* and *days' sales in inventory* and **explain** the use of these ratios. *(p. 278)*
6. Appendix 6A: **Describe** inventory costing under a perpetual inventory system using specific identification, weighted-average cost, FIFO, and LIFO. *(p. 281)*
7. Appendix 6B: **Define** the LIFO reserve and **explain** how it is used to compare the performance of companies using different inventory costing methods. *(p. 287)*

ACHIEVING THE BEST BUY

The recent years will likely be remembered as some of the most difficult years ever in the retail industry. Retail company bankruptcies during this time period include **Linens 'n Things**, **Mervyn's**, **Sharper Image**, **Steve and Barry's**, and **Wickes Furniture**. However, the bankruptcy of **Circuit City** was perhaps the biggest surprise. Circuit City had over 500 stores throughout the United States that were full of the latest flat screen TVs and electronics. What could explain the failure of Circuit City when the company's biggest rival, **Best Buy**, reported nearly $5 million in profits during the same time period? One key explanation, according to *Time* magazine, was ineffective inventory management.

Circuit City was unable to sell its existing inventory quickly enough, thereby failing to generate the necessary cash flow to enable the company to pay off its huge debt load and creating a backlog that prevented the company from ordering the newer models that consumers preferred. Best Buy, on the other hand, spent considerable time and effort revamping its supply chain and inventory management system to avoid such a fate. The Vice President of Logistics and Transportation with Best Buy observed that "Without better inventory management, Best Buy would have been a thing of the past."

With inventory comprising approximately one-third of Best Buy's assets, it is readily apparent why effective inventory management is so crucial to its financial health (and that of Circuit City). But how is Best Buy's inventory valued and recorded on its balance sheet? What measures exist for management and financial statement users to evaluate how effectively those inventories are being managed? We discuss answers to both of these important questions and others in this chapter.

Source: "Why Circuit City Busted, While Best Buy Boomed," by Anita Hamilton, Time.com, November 11, 2008; Best Buy 10-K report; Circuit City 10-K report.

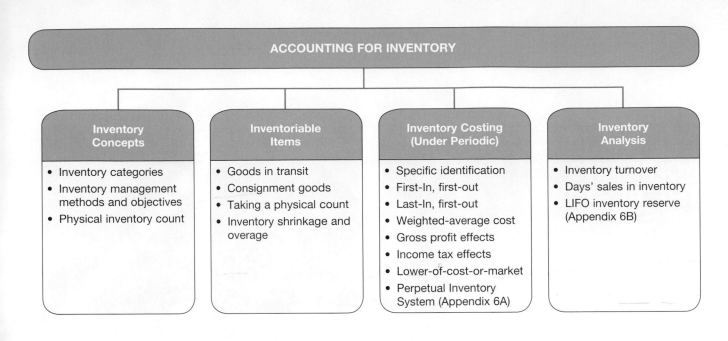

ACCOUNTING FOR INVENTORY

Inventory Concepts	Inventoriable Items	Inventory Costing (Under Periodic)	Inventory Analysis
• Inventory categories • Inventory management methods and objectives • Physical inventory count	• Goods in transit • Consignment goods • Taking a physical count • Inventory shrinkage and overage	• Specific identification • First-In, first-out • Last-In, first-out • Weighted-average cost • Gross profit effects • Income tax effects • Lower-of-cost-or-market • Perpetual Inventory System (Appendix 6A)	• Inventory turnover • Days' sales in inventory • LIFO inventory reserve (Appendix 6B)

INVENTORY CATEGORIES AND CONCEPTS

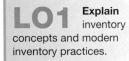

LO1 Explain inventory concepts and modern inventory practices.

This section explains the basic categories of inventory and introduces basic concepts of inventory management.

Categories of Inventory

We define *merchandise inventory* as the inventory of goods that a merchandising company buys from a manufacturing company and makes available for sale to its customers. All necessary costs incurred to acquire the merchandise inventory and deliver it to the buyer's place of business are included in the buyer's cost of inventory. This includes the purchase price of the merchandise, plus any transportation or freight-in costs, less any purchase returns and allowances and any purchase discounts. Wholesale distributors and retailing firms are two major types of merchandising firms.

Unlike merchandising firms, manufacturing firms do not purchase merchandise that is ready for sale. Instead, they purchase various raw materials and components and convert them into salable merchandise in their factories. At any point in time, manufacturing firms have units of merchandise at various stages of completion. Consequently, a manufacturing firm usually maintains three separate categories of inventory: raw materials inventory, work-in-process inventory, and finished goods inventory.

The **raw materials inventory** includes raw materials and components that have been purchased for use in the production of a product but that have not yet been placed into the production process. Sheets of steel are an example of raw material, and computer chips are an example of a component. A *component* is an item in the raw materials inventory account that was a finished product for the manufacturer that produced it. For example, **Intel Corporation** manufactures computer chips that other manufacturers incorporate into their final products. **Dell Inc.**, a computer manufacturer, is an example of a company that incorporates the finished goods of Intel into the computers that it manufactures.

The **work-in-process inventory** consists of units of product that have been placed into production in a factory but that are not fully assembled. All of the costs related to raw materials and components, human labor in the factory, factory utilities, and other factory-related resources are included in the work-in-process inventory. Items in this inventory category are not ready for sale since they are not yet a finished product.

The **finished goods inventory** includes all units that have been fully manufactured and are ready to be sold to customers. The cost of each item in the finished goods inventory is accumulated in the work-in-process inventory account and is then transferred to the finished goods inventory when the inventory is ready for sale.

Raw Materials   Work-in-Process   Finished Goods

Concepts of Inventory Management

Merchandising and manufacturing companies often find it desirable to maintain a large and varied inventory of merchandise to satisfy the diverse needs and preferences of their customers.

Just-in-Case Inventory

Manufacturing companies have traditionally maintained inventories as a buffer against unforeseen shipping delays and unforeseen demand by customers. This extra quantity is known as **just-in-case inventory**. Just-in-case inventories create **inventory carrying costs**, which include insurance, building usage costs, and the cost of the capital invested in the inventory.

Just-in-Time Manufacturing

Just-in-time (JIT) manufacturing seeks to eliminate or minimize inventory quantities and their related costs. The key to just-in-time manufacturing involves careful raw material purchase planning and careful management of the manufacturing and sales processes.

Quick Response Systems	**ACCOUNTING IN PRACTICE**

Many retailers have installed point-of-sale checkout systems to assist in inventory management. These systems either read Universal Product Code bar codes or specially-formed characters using either a plate scanner built into the checkout counter or a handheld scanner (or "wand") to identify the product being sold. Retailers also use a quick response system to optimize their inventory. A **quick response system** is designed to ensure that the retailer quickly reorders items that are being sold and quickly eliminates from inventory any items that are not selling. Special software on a business's computer identifies fast-selling and slow-selling items. The retailer reviews the list and orders more of the highly desirable items that are selling quickly. A retailer typically uses one (or both) of the following approaches to eliminate slow-moving items: (1) return the item to the supplier (if possible) and (2) reduce the unit selling price to (hopefully) induce a quick sale. Quick response systems tend to reduce both the size of inventory that a company must maintain and increase the dollar amount of its sales revenue.

INVENTORY OWNERSHIP AND PHYSICAL COUNT

To determine the quantity of inventory, it is necessary to take a physical count of the inventory at the end of a fiscal period. This involves not only physically counting the inventory, but also determining the ownership of the inventory.

Ownership of Inventory

Goods in Transit

Goods in transit can present some uncertainty when trying to determine the end-of-period inventory quantities. It is important to include all inventory items that are owned by a company and exclude any items that are no longer owned, regardless of whether a company has the merchandise in its physical possession or not. When merchandise is shipped by a common carrier—a railroad, trucking company, or an airline—the carrier prepares a *freight bill* in accordance with the instructions of the party making the transportation arrangements. The freight bill designates which party bears the shipping costs and which party has ownership of the merchandise that is being shipped, referred to as **goods in transit**.

Freight bills usually show shipping terms of **F.O.B. shipping point** or **F.O.B. destination**. *F.O.B.* is an abbreviation for "free on board." When the freight terms are F.O.B. shipping point, the buyer assumes ownership of the merchandise at the time the common carrier accepts the items from the seller. When the terms are F.O.B. destination, the seller maintains ownership of the merchandise until the buyer takes possession at delivery. In sum, ownership of goods in transit is directly linked to the freight terms when goods are shipped from a seller to a buyer as illustrated in Exhibit 6-1.

Consignment Goods

Another uncertainty when assessing inventory ownership involves consignment goods. **Consignment goods** are items held for sale by parties other than the item's owner. An example of a consignment good is used cars held for sale at a used car lot specializing in selling cars for private parties. The car lot owner does not assume ownership of the cars, but simply attempts to sell the cars, collecting a commission on any completed sales. Since consignment goods do not involve a transfer of title, they are included in the determination of the end-of-period inventory quantity by the seller until sold.

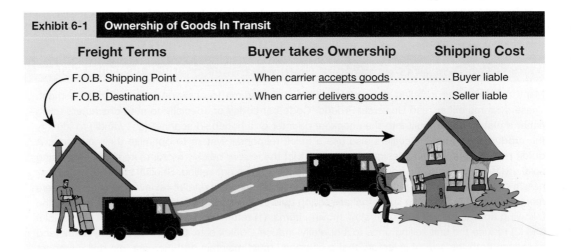

Exhibit 6-1	Ownership of Goods In Transit	
Freight Terms	**Buyer takes Ownership**	**Shipping Cost**
F.O.B. Shipping Point	When carrier <u>accepts goods</u>	Buyer liable
F.O.B. Destination	When carrier <u>delivers goods</u>	Seller liable

Physical Count of Inventory

A company takes a **physical count of inventory** to verify the balance of inventory. It is possible that changes in the quantity of particular items could have taken place without a transaction being recognized. For example, quantities of various items may have been stolen, damaged, or destroyed. Also, the seller might have shipped an incorrect quantity to a customer even though the seller reflected the correct quantity in a journal entry. The physical count of inventory is often taken at year-end and consists of the following steps:

1. Count the number of individual items of merchandise inventory available at the end of the period.

2. Determine the unit cost of each individual item and multiply the unit cost times the quantity to obtain the total cost for each individual inventory item.

3. Add the total cost of all the individual inventory items to obtain the total cost of the aggregate inventory available.

In a perpetual inventory system, if the physical count of inventory results in a total that does not agree with the balance in the Inventory account, the company makes a year-end adjusting entry. If the physical inventory total is less than the Inventory account balance, the company makes an adjusting entry debiting Cost of Goods Sold and crediting Inventory for the difference between the physical inventory total and the balance in the Inventory account. This entry decreases the balance in the Inventory account and adds the cost of the inventory shortage to Cost of Goods Sold. The cost associated with an inventory shortage is known as **inventory shrinkage**.

Employee Theft of Inventory	FORENSIC ACCOUNTING

Inventory shrinkage arises from employee and/or customer theft, physical damage or deterioration, and obsolescence. Shrinkage is typically discovered following a physical count of inventory. Shrinkage for U.S. retailers is estimated at over $40 billion, and the largest part, nearly $20 billion, is employee theft. Preventing inventory theft is difficult; however, there are ways to reduce it. Here are tips from AskDeb.com:

- Give different passwords to each cashier; using separate passwords and log-ins reveals which employee was manning the cash register at the times when theft occurs.
- Verify any transaction that is voided or canceled. This is a common way for inventory to be removed from a store.
- Review inventory reports daily to be sure sales match current inventory quantities.
- Install an alarm system on a store's back door that is activated each time the door is opened without authorization.
- Inspect the garbage nightly; use clear, plastic bags so that the contents are easily inspected to ensure that no inventory is hidden inside.
- Install security cameras in the store and in the back storage; this allows a store manager to keep an eye on items on the store racks as well as in stock.

If the physical inventory total is greater than the Inventory account balance, the company makes an adjusting entry debiting Inventory and crediting Cost of Goods Sold for the difference between the physical inventory and the Inventory account balance. This entry increases the balance in the Inventory account and subtracts the cost of this **inventory overage** from Cost of Goods Sold.

To illustrate shrinkage (the usual situation), assume that the December 31 balance of the Inventory account (including all items) is $120,600. Also assume that a physical count of the inventory produced a total cost at December 31 of $120,000. The following period-end adjusting entry is required at December 31 to adjust the balance in the Inventory account from $120,600 to $120,000:

A	=	L	+	SE	Dec 31	Cost of Goods Sold		600	
−600				−600		Inventory			600
				Exp		*To adjust the inventory account balance to the total cost determined by*			
						a physical inventory count in a perpetual inventory system.			

YOUR TURN! 6.1

The solution is on page 311.

The Counter Company just completed the year-end physical count of its inventory. The total value of inventory was determined to be $300,000. The following additional information came to light following the conclusion of the physical count:

1. The company included $20,000 of inventory that was shipped F.O.B. destination.
2. The company included $15,000 of inventory that was shipped F.O.B. shipping point.
3. The company did not include $25,000 of inventory that was being sold on consignment by Johnson Sales, a consignment dealer.

Discuss how this additional information affects the $300,000 value that The Counter Company initially determined to be the value of its ending inventory.

INVENTORY COSTING METHODS

LO2 **Describe** inventory costing under specific identification, weighted-average cost, FIFO, and LIFO.

In general, the value of a company's inventory is entered into the accounting records at its acquisition cost. Inventory costing is simple when the acquisition cost remains constant. For example, assume that the Fletcher Motor Company purchased electric motors four times during the year:

Exhibit 6-2	Illustration of Cost Flows When Prices Do Not Change
February 10 purchase	100 motors at $180 each
April 25 purchase	150 motors at $180 each
July 16 purchase	150 motors at $180 each
October 8 purchase	200 motors at $180 each
December 31 ending inventory	40 motors at $? each

The December 31 ending inventory for Fletcher Motor Company includes 40 electric motors, some from the July 16 purchase and some from the October 8 purchase. In this case, it is easy to determine the cost to be assigned to the 40 motors ($40 \times \$180 = \$7{,}200$) since all of the inventory purchases were made at the exact same purchase price of $180. In real business situations, however, the purchase price of an item of inventory often changes. The trend is usually toward increasing prices, but some purchase prices may actually decline. When purchase prices change during the year, a company must either keep track of the acquisition cost of each specific unit or make an assumption about which units have been sold and which units remain in inventory. Most companies choose the latter option and make an assumption about which units have been sold and which are still available because the cost of keeping track of exactly which units are sold can be prohibitively expensive.

Goods Flow vs. Cost Flow

Two concepts that are helpful in understanding the problem of assigning a cost to inventory when purchase prices are changing are goods flow and cost flow. **Goods flow** describes the actual physical movement of inventory through a business. **Cost flow** is the assumed assignment of costs to goods sold and to ending inventory. The cost flow need not, and often does not, reflect the actual goods flow through a business.

Generally accepted accounting principles permit businesses to use a cost flow that does not reflect the company's actual goods flow. For example, the goods flow in a grocery store chain like **Safeway** will almost always be such that the goods brought in first will be the first goods to be sold. This physical goods flow results in the least amount of loss due to spoilage. However, just because Safeway operates with this physical goods flow through its stores does not mean that the company is required to adopt a similar cost flow to calculate the value of its inventory. The *cost flow assumption* adopted could be one in which the most recent goods added to inventory are assumed to be the first goods sold.

The following sections on inventory costing use the periodic system. Appendix 6A uses the perpetual system. Your instructor can choose to cover either one or both systems. If the following periodic system is skipped, then read Appendix 6A and return to the section (five pages ahead) titled "Income Tax Effects."

Data for Illustration of Cost Flow Assumptions

In this section, we introduce and illustrate four generally accepted methods of costing inventories: (1) specific identification, (2) first-in, first-out (FIFO), (3) last-in, first-out (LIFO), and (4) weighted-average cost. Following an illustration of the four methods, a comparative analysis of the financial results of the methods is presented. To facilitate a comparison of their results, we use a common set of data. Assume that the Claremont Company had the following purchases and sales of inventory during the year.

Exhibit 6-3	Purchases and Sales for Application of Inventory Methods				
Date	**Event**	**No. of Units**	**Unit Cost**		**Total Cost**
Jan. 1	Beginning inventory	60	@ $10	=	$ 600
Mar. 27	Purchase inventory.	90	@ $11	=	$ 990
May 2	**Sell inventory**	(130)			
Aug. 15	Purchase inventory.	100	@ $13	=	$1,300
Nov. 6	Purchase inventory.	50	@ $16	=	$ 800
Dec. 10	**Sell inventory**	(90)			
Dec. 31	Ending inventory.	80			

The four inventory costing methods differ in the way they assign costs to the 80 units in ending inventory and the 220 units in cost of goods sold. Under the periodic inventory system, the Inventory account and the Cost of Goods Sold account are updated only at the end of the period, following a physical count of the ending inventory. Once the total cost of ending inventory is determined, the ending inventory amount is subtracted from cost of goods available for sale to derive the period's cost of goods sold.

Specific Identification Method

The **specific identification method** involves (1) keeping track of the purchase cost of each specific unit available for sale and (2) costing the ending inventory at the actual costs of the specific units not sold. Assume that the 80 unsold units consist of 10 units from beginning inventory, 20 units from the August 15 purchase, and all 50 of the units purchased on November 6. The cost assigned to the ending inventory and cost of goods sold is shown in Exhibit 6-4. Observe that the entire $3,690 of cost of the goods available for sale is assigned as either ending inventory or as cost of goods sold.

This information is used to compute ending inventory

Exhibit 6-4	Specific Identification Method							
		Goods Available			**Ending Inventory**			
Date	Event	Units	Cost	Total	Units	Cost		Total
Jan. 1 Beginning inventory		60 @	$10	= $ 600	10 @	$10	=	$ 100
Mar. 27 Purchase		90 @	11	= 990				
Aug. 15 Purchase		100 @	13	= 1,300	20 @	13	=	260
Nov. 6 Purchase		50 @	16	= 800	50 @	16	=	800
		300		$3,690	80			$1,160

Cost of goods available for sale. . . $3,690
Less: Ending inventory   1,160
Cost of goods sold $2,530

Ending Inventory $1,160

$100 $500

$990

$260 $1,040

$800

Cost of Goods Sold $2,530

First-In, First-Out (FIFO) Method

The **first-in, first-out (FIFO) method** assumes that the oldest goods (or earliest purchased) are sold first. This implies that ending inventory is *always* made up of the most recent purchases. FIFO results in the cost allocations as shown in Exhibit 6-5. This method assumes the first 220 units acquired are sold first and that the last 80 units purchased are those remaining.

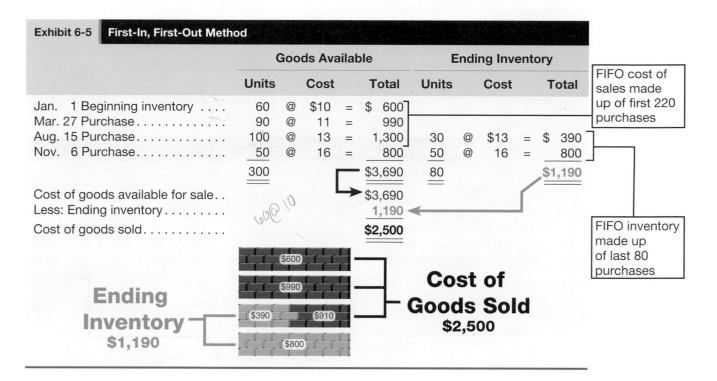

Exhibit 6-5   First-In, First-Out Method

	Goods Available			Ending Inventory		
	Units	Cost	Total	Units	Cost	Total
Jan. 1 Beginning inventory	60 @	$10 =	$ 600			
Mar. 27 Purchase............	90 @	11 =	990			
Aug. 15 Purchase............	100 @	13 =	1,300	30 @	$13 =	$ 390
Nov. 6 Purchase............	50 @	16 =	800	50 @	16 =	800
	300		$3,690	80		$1,190
Cost of goods available for sale..			$3,690			
Less: Ending inventory.........			1,190			
Cost of goods sold...........			$2,500			

FIFO cost of sales made up of first 220 purchases

FIFO inventory made up of last 80 purchases

Ending Inventory $1,190

$600
$990
$390 $910
$800

Cost of Goods Sold $2,500

Last-In, First-Out (LIFO) Method

The **last-in, first-out (LIFO) method** assumes that the most recent purchases are sold first. Exhibit 6-6 illustrates the calculation of LIFO cost of goods sold. LIFO assumes that the 220 units last (most recently) purchased are sold first, and that the 80 oldest units available for sale remain at the end of the period.

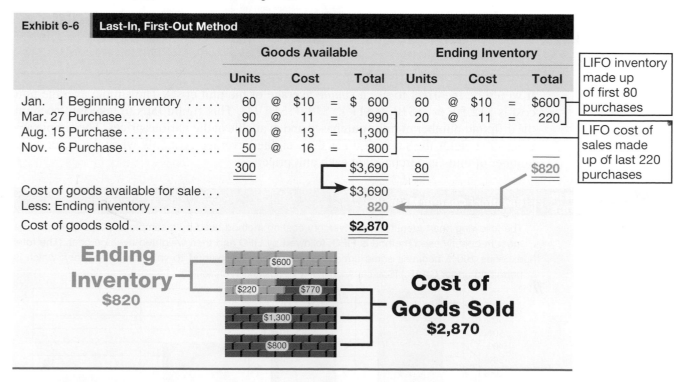

Exhibit 6-6   Last-In, First-Out Method

	Goods Available			Ending Inventory		
	Units	Cost	Total	Units	Cost	Total
Jan. 1 Beginning inventory	60 @	$10 =	$ 600	60 @	$10 =	$600
Mar. 27 Purchase.............	90 @	11 =	990	20 @	11 =	220
Aug. 15 Purchase.............	100 @	13 =	1,300			
Nov. 6 Purchase.............	50 @	16 =	800			
	300		$3,690	80		$820
Cost of goods available for sale...			$3,690			
Less: Ending inventory..........			820			
Cost of goods sold...........			$2,870			

LIFO inventory made up of first 80 purchases

LIFO cost of sales made up of last 220 purchases

Ending Inventory $820

$600
$220 $770
$1,300
$800

Cost of Goods Sold $2,870

Weighted-Average Cost Method

The **weighted-average cost method** spreads the total dollar cost of the goods available for sale equally among all units. In our illustration, the weighted-average cost per unit is $12.30, computed as $3,690/300. Exhibit 6-7 diagrams the assignment of costs under this method. The entire cost of goods available for sale is allocated between ending inventory and cost of goods sold.

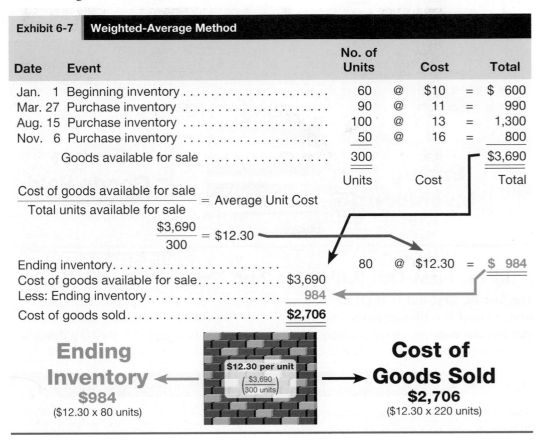

Exhibit 6-7	Weighted-Average Method				
Date	**Event**	**No. of Units**		**Cost**	**Total**
Jan. 1	Beginning inventory	60	@	$10 =	$ 600
Mar. 27	Purchase inventory	90	@	11 =	990
Aug. 15	Purchase inventory	100	@	13 =	1,300
Nov. 6	Purchase inventory	50	@	16 =	800
	Goods available for sale	300			$3,690
		Units		Cost	Total

$$\frac{\text{Cost of goods available for sale}}{\text{Total units available for sale}} = \text{Average Unit Cost}$$

$$\frac{\$3,690}{300} = \$12.30$$

Ending inventory . . . . 80 @ $12.30 = $ 984

Cost of goods available for sale $3,690
Less: Ending inventory 984
Cost of goods sold **$2,706**

Ending Inventory
$984
($12.30 x 80 units)

$12.30 per unit
($3,690 / 300 units)

Cost of Goods Sold
$2,706
($12.30 x 220 units)

It would be incorrect to use a *simple* average of the unit costs. The simple average unit cost is $12.50, or $[(\$10 + \$11 + \$13 + \$16)/4]$. This figure fails to take into account the different number of units purchased and available at the various prices. The simple average cost yields the same result as the weighted-average cost only when the exact same number of units is purchased at each unit price.

ACCOUNTING IN PRACTICE	Inventory Costing Methods

The following chart identifies the inventory costing method used by a sample of 600 U.S. firms. The most frequently used method is FIFO, followed by LIFO and then weighted-average cost. (The total exceeds 100% because some firms use more than one method to value their inventory, which is permitted under GAAP.) [Source: Accounting Trends and Techniques]

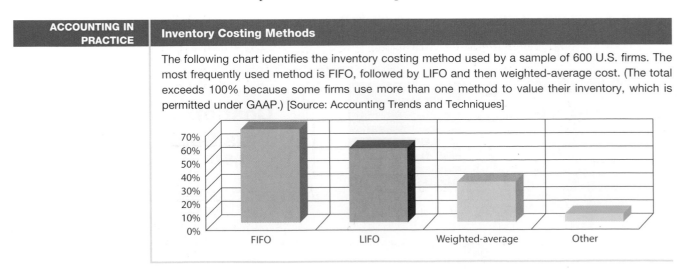

Comparative Analysis of Inventory Costing Methods

The purchase price data used in the Claremont Company illustration has an important characteristic: the purchase price of the inventory increased each time that a purchase was made, from $11 per unit to $13 per unit to $16 per unit. Increasing inventory prices are frequently encountered in the real world where price inflation is common and price deflation is uncommon. Exhibit 6-8 summarizes the results of applying the four inventory costing methods to the Claremont Company data and reveals that the FIFO method produces the lowest cost of goods sold ($2,500), while the LIFO method produces the highest cost of goods sold ($2,870). The exhibit also reveals that FIFO produces the highest year-end value of ending inventory ($1,190), while LIFO produces the lowest year-end value of ending inventory ($820). Specific identification and weighted-average cost produce ending inventory values and cost of goods sold values that fall in between the results obtained using FIFO and LIFO.

> **LO3** **Analyze** the financial effects of different inventory costing methods on company profit.

These results, however, are highly dependent on the purchase prices for the inventory. If the inventory's purchase price had been decreasing rather than increasing, the financial effects would have been just the opposite, with LIFO producing the lowest cost of goods sold and FIFO the highest. If, on the other hand, the purchase prices had been perfectly stable, there would be no difference between the cost of goods sold or the ending inventory for any of the four methods.

Exhibit 6-8	Results of Different Inventory Costing Methods			
	Specific Identification	FIFO	LIFO	Weighted-Average
Cost of goods sold...................	$2,530	$2,500	$2,870	$2,706
Ending inventory.....................	1,160	1,190	820	984

Impacts of Cost Flow Assumptions

Under generally accepted accounting principles, a company is permitted to select one or more of the four methods for purposes of assigning cost to its ending inventory and its cost of goods sold. Which method (or methods, since a company may elect to value some of its inventory using FIFO, some using LIFO, and some using weighted-average cost) is selected by a company depends upon a number of factors—the type of product produced, the cost of producing the product, whether the product is perishable, whether the company desires to report a high or a low net income, and income tax considerations.

Specific Identification Method

Specific identification is typically used by companies that manufacture a small volume of products with relatively high unit values. Airplanes, jewelry, and construction equipment are examples of products that would justify the cost of tracking the specific unit cost of each inventory item. Specific identification is usually not cost-justified for companies that manufacture products that have a low unit cost or involve high volumes of production. It can be very expensive to trace the exact costs of producing a product, especially a product manufactured in high volumes.

FIFO Method

Many companies, especially those with perishable, time-dated, or style-affected merchandise, attempt to sell their oldest merchandise first. This is especially true for companies that sell food products, chemicals, and drugs. For these types of companies, the cost flow produced by the FIFO method most closely matches the actual goods flow. However, a company is not required to use the cost flow assumption that most closely matches its actual goods flow. When costs are rising, FIFO will result in the lowest cost of goods sold, and therefore, the highest net income. The desire to show a higher net income by some companies partly explains the popularity of the FIFO method.

LIFO Method

Although LIFO does not reflect the actual goods flow for most businesses, its popularity is likely linked to the potential income tax savings associated with its use. For some industries, however, LIFO does depict the actual goods flow. For example, in industries that extract natural resources, such as mining, the product is frequently dumped onto a storage pile from an overhead trestle, and sold inventory is taken from the top of the pile. One disadvantage of using LIFO when beginning inventories have been maintained or increased is that a firm's ending inventory can be substantially undervalued since old purchase prices tend to be retained on a company's books under the LIFO method. This, in turn, will cause a firm's current assets and total assets to likewise be undervalued.

Weighted-Average Cost Method

Weighted-average cost is best suited for businesses that warehouse a large volume of undifferentiated goods in a common area. Liquid fuels, grains, and other commodities are examples. Weighted-average cost typically generates a cost of goods sold amount that is neither high nor low as compared to the other methods, as is revealed in Exhibit 6-8.

Summary of Impacts

We can broadly summarize the impacts of the cost flow assumptions as follows:

1. Specific identification most closely identifies the actual cost of goods sold and ending inventory.
2. FIFO approximates the actual physical goods flow for most firms.
3. LIFO is popular because of the income tax savings associated with its use.
4. Weighted-average cost is most often associated with businesses in which undifferentiated goods are commingled in a common area like a warehouse.

Analysis of Costing Methods and Gross Profit

To illustrate the financial effects of the different inventory costing methods, assume that the 220 units sold by the Claremont Company were sold for $20 each, producing sales of $4,400 ($20 × 220). Exhibit 6-9 shows the difference in gross profit under each of the four inventory costing methods. Remember that the difference in reported gross profit results from the assumptions made about cost flow, not from any difference in actual goods flow. In each case, 220 units were sold and 80 units remained. Each of the inventory costing methods is in accord with generally accepted accounting principles, yet one method's financial impact on gross profit and net income is different from the financial impact of another method.

Exhibit 6-9	Gross Profit Using Alternative Inventory Costing Methods			
	Specific Identification	FIFO	LIFO	Weighted-Average
Sales (220 units @ $20)	$4,400	$4,400	$4,400	$4,400
Cost of goods sold.	2,530	2,500	2,870	2,706
Gross profit.	$1,870	$1,900	$1,530	$1,694
Increased gross profit compared with LIFO. .	$ 340	$ 370		$ 164

Income Statement and Balance Sheet Effects

As Exhibit 6-9 reveals, LIFO results in the smallest gross profit ($1,530), with FIFO producing the highest ($1,900) gross profit. This result occurs because the purchase price of inventory was increasing throughout the year, from $11 per unit to $13 per unit to $16 per unit. Most agree that when costs are rising, FIFO tends to overstate gross profit (and income) because older, lower unit costs are included in the cost of goods sold and matched with current sales prices. In other words, in the illustration, all of the units sold are charged to costs of goods sold under FIFO at unit costs of $10, $11, and $13. If the latest purchase price reflects the inventory's current acquisition cost, the units sold must be replaced by units costing $16 (or more if costs continue to rise).

It is frequently argued that LIFO provides a better matching of current costs with current revenues since the cost of the most recent purchases constitutes the LIFO cost of goods sold. While LIFO associates the current, higher unit costs with cost of goods sold, it assigns costs to ending inventory using the older, lower unit costs. As a consequence, the value of the LIFO ending inventory on the balance sheet is often undervalued in terms of the inventory's current value. When inventory quantities are maintained or increased, the LIFO method prevents older costs from appearing in the cost of goods sold. No doubt, some firms still carry LIFO inventories at unit costs that existed more than 10 years ago. Under FIFO, the ending inventory is measured at relatively recent costs, which means the ending inventory reflects relatively current costs.

For readers skipping the periodic system, please resume reading here.

Consistency and Full Disclosure	**PRINCIPLE ALERT**

Inventory costing requires the application of *consistency* and *full disclosure*. Because of the possible variation in gross profit and ending inventory values that result from the use of different inventory costing methods, it is important that a firm use the same inventory costing method from one fiscal period to the next. This application of consistency enhances the comparability of a firm's cost of goods sold, gross profit, net income, inventory, current assets, and total assets over time. In addition, a firm should disclose which inventory costing method it is using, either in its financial statements or in the notes to the statements. This information is required by the full disclosure principle and is important to users who compare financial data across firms.

Income Tax Effects

During periods of rising purchase prices, LIFO results in a lower gross profit than any of the alternative inventory costing methods. A lower gross profit, and net income, means that lower amounts of income taxes need to be paid. Hence, the desire to reduce current income tax payments is a major reason for widespread use of LIFO.

To illustrate LIFO's income tax advantage, assume that the Huntington Corporation has beginning inventory of 10 units costing $500 each, and that only two transactions occur. In the first transaction, it purchases 10 more units costing $630 each, for a total cash purchase price of $6,300. In the second transaction, it sells 10 units for $700 each, for a total cash sale of $7,000. Both transactions are for cash and, for simplicity, we assume that the company's operating expenses are zero and the applicable income tax rate is 35 percent. Exhibit 6-10 presents the income statements and cash flows for Huntington under both FIFO and LIFO.

Under FIFO, it reports $1,300 of net income, but cash from sales ($7,000) is only enough to replace the inventory sold ($6,300) and pay the income tax ($700) on the $2,000 in FIFO pretax net income. The net income of $1,300 is not realized in cash, and consequently, is unavailable to pay dividends, or be reinvested in the business, or replace the sold inventory. As a consequence, FIFO net income is sometimes referred to as *phantom profit*.

Exhibit 6-10	FIFO vs. LIFO Comparison: Phantom Profit Effect and Tax Benefit				
		FIFO		LIFO	
		Income Statement	Cash In (Out)	Income Statement	Cash In (Out)
Sales (10 @ $700).		$ 7,000	$7,000	$ 7,000	$7,000
Cost of goods sold					
Beginning inventory (10 @ $500)		5,000		5,000	
Purchases (10 @ $630).		6,300	(6,300)	6,300	(6,300)
Goods available (20 units).		11,300		11,300	
Ending inventory					
10 @ FIFO		6,300			
10 @ LIFO				5,000	
Cost of goods sold.		5,000		6,300	
Pretax income		2,000		700	
Income tax (at 35%).		700	(700)	245	(245)
Net income.		$ 1,300		$ 455	
Net cash proceeds			$ 0		$ 455

Under LIFO, it reports net income of $455 as a consequence of its larger cost of goods sold ($6,300). With a lower net income, it incurs a smaller cash outflow ($245) for income taxes. The attractiveness of LIFO during periods of rising inventory purchase prices is evidenced by LIFO's more favorable net cash flow ($455) as compared with FIFO ($0). Use of LIFO during times of falling inventory purchase prices, however, has the opposite income tax effect.

Management is usually free to select different accounting treatments for financial reporting to shareholders and for income tax reporting to the Internal Revenue Service (IRS). For example, it is acceptable for a business to use different methods of computing inventory when reporting under GAAP on the income statement and for reporting under income tax regulations on a company's income tax return. This situation has led some individuals to correctly infer that U.S. corporations effectively maintain two sets of financial records—one for reporting to shareholders and one for reporting to the IRS. An exception to this flexibility occurs when a company chooses to use LIFO for income tax reporting to benefit from the lower income taxes that result from the use of LIFO when purchase prices are rising. A U.S. federal tax regulation known as the **LIFO conformity rule** requires any company that selects LIFO for income tax reporting to also use LIFO for financial reporting to shareholders. It is currently not possible to report lower taxable income to the IRS using LIFO while also reporting higher net income to shareholders using FIFO. (The elimination of LIFO for income tax purposes has been discussed during the budget debate in an effort to generate additional tax revenues to help close the U.S. budget deficit.)

YOUR TURN! 6.2

The solution is on page 311.

The following inventory information is gathered from the accounting records of a company:

Beginning inventory	4,000 units at $5 each
Purchases.	6,000 units at $7 each
Sales.	9,000 units at $10 each

Calculate (a) ending inventory, (b) cost of goods sold, and (c) the gross profit using each of the following methods (i) FIFO, (ii) LIFO, and (iii) weighted-average cost.

Errors in the Inventory Count

A physical count of a business's inventory is necessary to determine the value of a company's ending inventory regardless of what inventory method is used. Unfortunately, errors in the inventory count, for example failing to count some items or counting some items twice, can occur. These errors affect not only the value of ending inventory reported on the balance sheet in the period of the error, but also cost of goods sold and current net income. Further, the error is not limited to only the current period—net income in the following period is also affected. To illustrate, assume that the Arrow Company began operations in 2012. Exhibit 6.11 summarizes Arrow's 2012 and 2013 transactions. For simplicity, assume that the only expense that it incurs is its cost of goods sold.

Exhibit 6-11	Inventory Transactions for Arrow Company			
		Inventory Units	Inventory Balance	Sales
2012	Beginning inventory	0	0	
	Purchased 1,000 units of merchandise inventory for $3 per unit	1000	$3,000	
	Sold 400 units of merchandise inventory for $7 per unit	(400)	(1,200)	$ 2,800
	Ending inventory.	600	$1,800	
2013	Beginning inventory	600	$1,800	
	Purchased 2,000 units of merchandise inventory for $3 per unit	2,000	6,000	
	Sold 1,500 units of merchandise inventory for $7 per unit	(1,500)	(4,500)	$10,500
	Ending inventory.	1,100	$3,300	

Assume that Arrow Company made an error in its physical count of inventory at the end of 2012, mistakenly double-counting 40 units of inventory, and consequently, overstating ending inventory by $120 (40 units × $3). As illustrated in Exhibit 6-12, both the value of ending inventory and cost of goods sold in 2012 are affected. Further, because ending inventory in 2012 becomes beginning inventory in 2013, cost of goods sold in 2013 is also misstated. Exhibit 6-12 illustrates these effects on both the 2012 and 2013 Arrow Company income statements.

Exhibit 6-12	Inventory Error Effects			
Cost of goods sold	=	Beginning Inventory	+ Purchases −	Ending Inventory
2012: $1,080 (instead of $1,200). . . =		$ 0	+ $ 3,000 −	$1,920
2013: $4,620 (instead of $4,500). . . =		$ 1,920	+ $ 6,000 −	$3,300

Key figures	No Error	With Error
2012		
Sales.	$ 2,800	$ 2,800
Cost of goods sold	1,200	1,080 ↓
Net income	$ 1,600	$ 1,720
2013		
Sales.	$10,500	$10,500
Cost of goods sold	4,500	4,620 ↑
Net income	$ 6,000	$ 5,880

In sum, an error in the ending inventory account in the current year affects the value of ending inventory in the current year, as well as current year net income through cost of goods sold. The error also affects, in an opposite direction, net income in the following year (through its effect on cost of goods sold). To show this, and using the company in Exhibit 6-12, notice that the combined net income for both years is $7,600, without the error ($1,600 + $6,000) or with the error ($1,720 + $5,880). Further, we see that ending inventory was overstated in 2012 by $120, which resulted in: 2012 ending inventory being overstated by $120, 2012 cost of goods sold being understated by $120, and 2012 net income being overstated by $120. The same $120 error is carried through to 2013 where it causes cost of goods sold to be overstated by $120 (because of the overstatement of beginning inventory), and net income to be understated by $120.

FORENSIC ACCOUNTING	**Fraudulent Reporting**

Most errors in inventory result from honest mistakes; however, there are inventory counts that have been intentionally overstated. One such case involved a retail company called **Crazy Eddie**, which was a discount electronics store. Court records indicate that Eddie, the founder, hired his nephew, Sammy, who had earned a degree in accounting, to inflate sales by $15 to $20 million per year, and falsified inventories to justify the inflated figures. The U.S. Securities and Exchange Commission ultimately charged Eddie with securities fraud and he was sentenced to 8 years in prison and ordered to pay more than $150 million in fines.

LOWER-OF-COST-OR-MARKET METHOD

LO4 Apply the lower-of-cost-or-market method.

In general, inventory is valued at its acquisition cost using the common inventory costing methods explained in this chapter. However, it can be necessary to report inventory at a lower value if there is evidence that the inventory's utility to a business—that is, the inventory's revenue-generating ability—has fallen below its acquisition cost. Such *inventory write-downs* can occur when (1) merchandise must be sold at reduced prices because it is damaged or otherwise not in normal salable condition or when (2) the cost of replacing the ending inventory has declined below the inventory's recorded acquisition cost.

Net Realizable Value

Damaged, physically deteriorated, or obsolete merchandise should be measured and reported at its net realizable value on the balance sheet when this value is less than the inventory's acquisition cost. **Net realizable value** is an item's estimated selling price less the expected cost of disposal. For example, assume that an inventory item cost $300 but can be sold for only $200 because it is damaged. If the related selling costs are estimated to be $20, the inventory should be written down to $180 ($200 estimated selling price less $20 estimated disposal cost) and a $120 inventory write-down loss ($300 − $180) should be reported on the income statement for the current period.

Lower-of-Cost-or-Market Method

The **lower-of-cost-or-market (LCM)** method provides for the recognition of an inventory write-down loss when the inventory's replacement cost declines below its recorded acquisition cost. Under LCM, a loss is reported in the period when the inventory's replacement cost declines, rather than during a subsequent period when the actual sale of the inventory takes place. *Market, for purposes of applying the LCM method,* is defined as the current replacement cost of the inventory. This procedure assumes that decreases in the replacement cost of inventory will be accompanied by proportionate decreases in the selling price of the inventory. The LCM method values the ending inventory at its lower (replacement) market value. Consequently, income decreases by the amount that the ending inventory is written down. When the ending inventory becomes part of the cost of goods sold in a future period, its reduced carrying value helps maintain normal profit margins in the period when sold.

To illustrate, assume that an inventory item that cost $80 has been selling at a retail price of $100, yielding a gross profit percentage of 20 percent. Assume also that by year-end, the item's replacement cost has declined to $60—a 25 percent decline—and a proportionate reduction in its selling price from $100 to $75 is expected in the following period. In this case, the inventory is written down to its $60 replacement cost, reducing the current period's net income by a $20 write-down loss ($80 − $60 = $20). When the inventory is sold in a subsequent period for $75, the normal gross profit percentage of 20 percent on sales is reported ($75 − $60 = $15 gross profit). The LCM method is applied to each individual item in inventory. It can also be applied to different categories of inventory.

In Exhibit 6-13, LCM is applied on an *individual item-by-item* basis, and the value of ending inventory is $6,820. Inventory replacement costs are in such sources as current catalogs, purchase contracts with suppliers, and other forms of price quotations.

Exhibit 6-13	Application of the Lower-of-Cost-or-Market					
		Per Unit		**Total**		**LCM**
Inventory Item	**Quantity**	**Cost**	**Market**	**Cost**	**Market**	**Individual Item**
Cameras						
Model V70.	40	$80	$75	$3,200	$3,000	$3,000
Model V85.	30	60	64	1,800	1,920	1,800
Subtotal.				$5,000	$4,920	—
Calculators						
Model C20	90	13	15	$1,170	$1,350	1,170
Model C40	50	20	17	1,000	850	850
Subtotal.				$2,170	$2,200	—
Total				$7,170	$7,120	$6,820

Conservatism | **PRINCIPLE ALERT**

The lower-of-cost-or-market method for inventory is a good illustration of *conservatism*. When the current replacement cost for an inventory item falls below its acquisition cost, there is increased uncertainty about the future profitability of the item. Conservatism is the reaction to significant uncertainties in the measurement of net assets and net income. In choosing between alternative financial measures, conservatism causes the least optimistic measure to be selected. When an item's market value (current replacement cost of inventory) falls below its historical acquisition cost, the least optimistic measure is its lower market value.

IFRS ALERT!

Under IFRS, LIFO is *not* generally accepted. Further, under U.S. GAAP inventory may not be revalued above its acquisition cost. IFRS permits inventory to be revalued upwards if the inventory's fair value appreciates above acquisition cost. When inventory is revalued upward under IFRS a parallel increase is made to an equity account called Asset Revaluation Reserve. To illustrate, assume that **Tesco**'s ending inventory at year-end is valued on its books at 2,669 million British pounds. Also assume that a review by management concluded that the fair value of its inventory had appreciated to 3,000 million British pounds. Under IFRS, we make the following journal entry to revalue inventory:

A = L + SE		
+331 +331		

Inventories	331	
Asset revaluation reserve		331
To write up inventory to its fair market value.		

Appendix C at the end of this book presents the IFRS financial statements of Tesco. Tesco's asset revaluation reserve is in the equity section of its balance sheet.

YOUR TURN! 6.3

The solution is on page 311.

The Images Company sells three types of video equipment—DSLR cameras, Point and Shoot cameras, and Camcorders. The cost and market value of its inventory of video equipment follow:

	Cost	Market
DSLR	$110,000	$125,000
Point and Shoot	73,000	92,000
Camcorders	57,000	48,000

Compute the value of the Images Company's ending inventory under the lower-of-cost-or-market method applied on an item-by-item basis.

INVENTORY ANALYSIS

LO5 Define *inventory turnover* and *days' sales in inventory* and **explain** the use of these ratios.

Inventory Turnover and Days' Sales in Inventory

The **inventory turnover ratio** indicates how many times a year, on average, a firm sells its inventory, and it is calculated as:

$$\text{Inventory turnover} = \frac{\text{Cost of goods sold}}{\text{Average inventory}}$$

This ratio relates data from two financial statements: the income statement and the balance sheet. Cost of goods sold is taken from the income statement, while the average inventory is calculated from balance sheet data—that is, the beginning and ending inventories are summed and the total is divided by two.

In general, the faster a company can turn over its inventory, the more profitable the company will be. Further, the higher the inventory turnover ratio, the less time a firm has its funds tied up in its inventory and the less risk the firm faces from trying to sell out-of-date merchandise. What is considered to be a satisfactory inventory turnover varies from industry to industry. A grocery store chain like **Safeway**, for example, should have a much higher inventory turnover than a jewelry store like **Zales**.

To illustrate the inventory turnover ratio, **Best Buy** reported the following financial data:

($ millions)	2011	2010	2009
Cost of goods sold.	$38,113	$37,197	$37,201
Beginning inventory	5,897	5,486	4,753
Ending inventory.	5,731	5,897	5,486

Best Buy's inventory turnover in 2011 is 6.56, computed as $38,113/[($5,897 + $5,731)/2]. Similar calculations reveal that Best Buy's inventory turnover in 2010 was 6.54 and it was 7.27 in 2009, indicating that its inventory turnover was relatively stable over the last two years, but has decreased since 2009.

The inventory turnover ratio can be influenced by a firm's choice of inventory costing method. Inventory amounts calculated using LIFO, for example, will typically be smaller than the same inventory calculated using FIFO. An investor comparing inventory turnover ratios between different firms will need to verify that the firms are using the same inventory costing method; otherwise, any ratio comparisons will be apples-to-oranges rather than apples-to-apples.

An extension of the inventory turnover ratio is the **days' sales in inventory**, calculated as:

$$\text{Days' sales in inventory} = \frac{365}{\text{Inventory turnover}}$$

This ratio indicates how many days it takes, on average, for a firm to sell its inventory. During 2011, for example, Best Buy's days' sales in inventory was 55.6 days, or 365/6.56; that is, Best Buy took over 55 days to sell its inventory. Similar calculations reveal it took an average of 55.8 days for Best Buy to sell its inventory in 2010 and 50.2 days in 2009. Do these ratio results indicate that Best Buy is doing a good job of managing its investment in inventory? Without comparable ratio data from a competitor like Target Corporation, it is difficult to conclude whether a days' sales in inventory ratio of 55.6 days indicates that Best Buy is doing a good or bad job of managing its inventory.

A.K.A. The days' sales in inventory ratio is also referred to as the *days' inventory-on-hand ratio* and the *inventory-on-hand period*.

Concept ➡	Method ➡	Assessment	**TAKEAWAY 6.1**
How long, on average, does it take to sell the inventory?	Cost of goods sold, beginning inventory, and ending inventory $\text{Inventory turnover} = \dfrac{\text{Cost of goods sold}}{\text{Average inventory}}$ $\text{Days' sales in inventory} = \dfrac{365}{\text{Inventory turnover}}$	A higher inventory turnover or a lower days' sales in inventory indicates that the company is able to sell its inventory more quickly.	

YOUR TURN! 6.4

The solution is on page 311.

Flip Company installed a new inventory management system at the beginning of 2013. Shown below are financial data from the company's accounting records:

	2012	2013
Sales revenue.	$4,000,000	$4,400,000
Cost of goods sold.	2,000,000	2,300,000
Beginning inventory	450,000	430,000
Ending inventory.	430,000	320,000

Calculate the inventory turnover and days' sales in inventory for 2012 and 2013. Discuss your findings.

CORPORATE SOCIAL RESPONSIBILITY	**Best Buy and an Ethical Supply Chain**

Many businesses strive to not only do well financially, but also to do good environmentally and socially. **Best Buy** serves as the ultimate seller of many products manufactured by other companies, such as TVs by **Sony**, cameras by **Nikon**, and computers by **Dell**. Best Buy also sells its exclusive brands. As the manufacturer of these products, Best Buy faces decisions on how and where these products are produced. Best Buy's Corporate Responsibility Report states, "While manufacturing expertise, lower labor costs and an efficient global supply chain make production in southeastern Asia a viable proposition, our operations there have not been without challenges." Best Buy meets these challenges through their ethical manufacturing program that includes supplier compliance standards that embody standards of the Fair Labor Association Workplace Code of Conduct and the core labor standards of the International Labor Organization. Best Buy also has a factory audit program to identify environmental and social problems at its suppliers.

COMPREHENSIVE PROBLEM

The Montclair Corporation had the following inventory transactions for its only product during 2012:

Purchases	
February 15............	2,000 units @ $27.00 each
April 20	3,000 units @ $28.40 each
October 25	1,200 units @ $31.25 each
Sales	
March 1...............	1,200 units @ $50.00 each
June 12...............	2,000 units @ $52.00 each
August 10	1,000 units @ $53.00 each
December 14	1,600 units @ $55.00 each

The Montclair Corporation had 1,000 units in its January 1, 2012, beginning inventory with a unit cost of $24 each. Montclair uses the periodic inventory system.

Required

a. Determine the cost assigned to Montclair's December 31, 2012, ending inventory and Montclair's cost of goods sold for 2012 under each of the following inventory costing methods:
   1. Weighted-average cost
   2. FIFO
   3. LIFO
b. Determine Montclair's gross profit for 2012 under each of the following inventory costing methods:
   1. Weighted-average cost
   2. FIFO
   3. LIFO
c. Determine Montclair's inventory turnover and days' sales in inventory for 2012 under each of the following inventory costing methods:
   1. Weighted-average cost
   2. FIFO
   3. LIFO

Solution

a. Units available:

1,000 units @ $24.00 =	$ 24,000
2,000 units @ $27.00 =	54,000
3,000 units @ $28.40 =	85,200
1,200 units @ $31.25 =	37,500
7,200	$200,700

1. **Weighted-average cost:**

   Weighted-average unit cost: $200,700/7,200 units = $ 27.875

   Ending inventory: 1,400 units × $27.875 = $ 39,025

   Cost of goods sold: $200,700 − $39,025 = $161,675

2. **FIFO:**

   Ending inventory: 1,200 units @ $31.25 = $ 37,500
   200 units @ $28.40 = 5,680
   1,400 $ 43,180

   Cost of goods sold: $200,700 − $43,180 = $157,520

3. **LIFO:**

   Ending inventory: 1,000 units @ $24.00 = $ 24,000
   400 units @ $27.00 = 10,800
   1,400 $ 34,800

   Cost of goods sold: $200,700 − $34,800 = $165,900

b. Sales revenue:
   1,200 units @ $50.00 = $ 60,000
   2,000 units @ $52.00 = 104,000
   1,000 units @ $53.00 = 53,000
   1,600 units @ $55.00 = 88,000
   5,800 $305,000

   1. Weighted-average gross profit = $305,000 − $161,675 = $143,325
   2. FIFO gross profit = $305,000 − $157,520 = $147,480
   3. LIFO gross profit = $305,000 − $165,900 = $139,100

c.

	Inventory Turnover	Days' Sales in Inventory
Weighted-average cost	5.13	71.15 days
FIFO	4.69	77.83 days
LIFO	5.64	64.72 days

APPENDIX 6A: Inventory Costing Methods and the Perpetual Inventory System

This appendix illustrates the accounting for inventories using the perpetual inventory system under the four costing methods of: (1) specific identification; (2) first-in, first-out; (3) last-in, first-out; and (4) weighted-average cost. All four methods are illustrated using the following data for Claremont Company.

LO6 Describe inventory costing under a perpetual inventory system using specific identification, weighted-average cost, FIFO, and LIFO.

Date	Event	No. of Units	Unit Cost		Total Cost
Jan. 1	Beginning inventory	60	@ $10 =		$ 600
Mar. 27	Purchase inventory.	90	@ 11 =		990
Aug. 15	Purchase inventory.	100	@ 13 =		1,300
Nov. 6	Purchase inventory.	50	@ 16 =		800
	Goods available for sale.	300			$3,690
May 2	Sell inventory	(130)			
Dec. 10	Sell inventory	(90)			
Dec. 31	Ending inventory.	80			

Under all four inventory costing methods, the Inventory account is increased each time a purchase occurs for the amount of the purchase and is decreased each time a sale occurs by an amount equal to the cost of goods sold. The methods differ only in the computation of cost of goods sold, consisting of 220 units (130 + 90 = 220), and the year-end Inventory account balance, consisting of 80 units remaining.

Specific Identification Method

Under the **specific identification method**, the actual cost of the specific units sold is identified and used to compute the cost of goods sold. To illustrate, assume that (1) 50 of the 130 units sold on May 2 came from the beginning inventory of 60 units and the remaining 80 units sold (50 + 80 = 130) came from the purchase of 90 units on March 27, and that (2) 10 of the 90 units sold on December 10 came from the purchase of 90 units on March 27 and the remaining 80 units sold (10 + 80 = 90) came from the purchase of 100 units on August 15. Exhibit 6A-1 illustrates the calculation of cost of goods sold and ending inventory using specific identification. The cost of goods sold is $2,530 (sum of the Sold Total column), and the ending inventory of 80 units is valued at $1,160 (final amount in the Inventory Balance Total column).

Exhibit 6A-1	**Specific Identification Method (Perpetual Inventory System)**								
	Purchased			**Sold**			**Inventory Balance**		
Date	Units	Unit Cost	Total	Units	Unit Cost	Total	Units	Unit Cost	Total
Jan. 1							60	$10	$ 600
Mar. 27	90	$11	$ 990				60	10	⎫
							90	11	⎬ 1,590
May 2				50	$10	$ 500	10	10	⎫
				80	11	880	10	11	⎬ 210
Aug. 15	100	13	1,300				10	10	⎫
							10	11	⎬ 1,510
							100	13	⎭
Nov. 6	50	16	800				10	10	⎫
							10	11	⎬ 2,310
							100	13	
							50	16	⎭
Dec. 10				10	11	110	10	10	⎫
				80	13	1,040	20	13	⎬ 1,160
							50	16	⎭
Total						$2,530			

First-In, First-Out (FIFO) Method

Under the **first-in, first-out (FIFO) method**, each time that a sale is made the cost of the oldest goods are charged to cost of goods sold. Visually, the FIFO method appears like a conveyor belt. Items of inventory are placed on the belt and then move along to the end. As items reach the end of the conveyor belt, they are assumed to be sold. Those items still on the belt (which are the last items placed on the belt) are assumed to remain in inventory until they reach the end of the conveyor belt. This visualization is illustrated in Exhibit 6A-2.

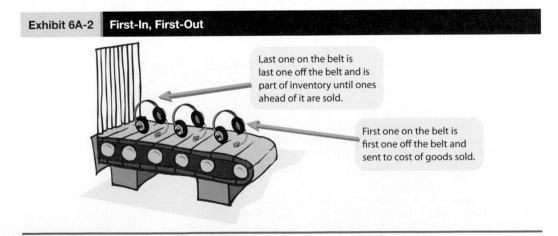

Exhibit 6A-2   **First-In, First-Out**

Last one on the belt is last one off the belt and is part of inventory until ones ahead of it are sold.

First one on the belt is first one off the belt and sent to cost of goods sold.

Results of the FIFO method are in Exhibit 6A-3. FIFO handles the May 2 sale of 130 units as follows: The oldest units are the units in the January 1 beginning inventory. These are the first 60 units assumed to be sold. The next oldest units are the units purchased on March 27 and 70 units are needed from this purchase (130 sold − 60 from January 1) to provide all of the units sold on May 2. After the May 2 sale, only 20 units remain, all from the March 27 purchase.

The December 10 sale of 90 units is handled in a similar manner. The oldest units at December 10 are the 20 units remaining from the March 27 purchase. These are the first units assumed to be sold. The next oldest units are the 100 units purchased on August 15 and 70 additional units are needed for the sale (90 sold − 20 from the March 27 purchase). Therefore, 70 of the 100 units purchased on August 15 are assumed to be included in the units sold on December 10. After the December 10 sale, 30 units remain from the August 15 purchase and 50 units remain from the November 6 purchase.

Cost of goods sold using the FIFO method is $2,500 (sum of the Sold Total column), and the ending inventory is $1,190 (final amount in the Inventory Balance Total column).

Exhibit 6A-3	**First-In, First-Out Method (Perpetual Inventory System)**								
	Purchased			**Sold**			**Inventory Balance**		
Date	**Units**	**Unit Cost**	**Total**	**Units**	**Unit Cost**	**Total**	**Units**	**Unit Cost**	**Total**
Jan. 1							60	$10	$ 600
Mar. 27	90	$11	$ 990				60	10	⎱ 1,590
							90	11	⎰
May 2				60	$10	$ 600			
				70	11	770	20	11	220
Aug. 15	100	13	1,300				20	11	⎱ 1,520
							100	13	⎰
Nov. 6	50	16	800				20	11	⎱
							100	13	2,320
							50	16	⎰
Dec. 10.				20	11	220	30	13	⎱ 1,190
				70	13	910	50	16	⎰
Total						$2,500			

Last-In, First-Out (LIFO) Method

When the **last-in, first-out (LIFO) method** is used, the cost of the most recent inventory purchased is charged to cost of goods sold when a sale occurs. Visually, the LIFO method appears like a stack of bricks. Each new brick entered into inventory is placed on top of the existing stack of bricks. When a brick is sold, the last brick placed on the stack is pulled from the top of the stack and given to the customer. The bricks at the bottom of the stack are assumed to remain in inventory until the newer bricks from the top of the stack are first sold. This visualization is illustrated in Exhibit 6A-4.

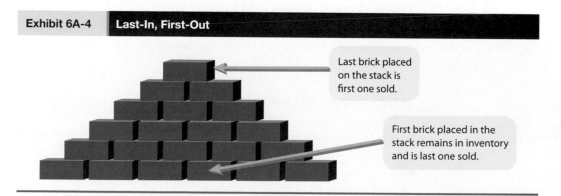

Exhibit 6A-4	**Last-In, First-Out**

Last brick placed on the stack is first one sold.

First brick placed in the stack remains in inventory and is last one sold.

Exhibit 6A-5 illustrates the results using LIFO. The LIFO method handles the May 2 sale of 130 units as follows: The most recently purchased units (newest units) are the units from the March 27 purchase. These are the first 90 units assumed to be sold. The next newest units are the units in the January 1 beginning inventory and 40 units from the January 1 units are needed (130 sold − 90 from the March 27 purchase) to provide all of the units sold on May 2. After the May 2 sale, only 20 units remain, all from the January 1 beginning inventory.

The December 10 sale of 90 units is handled in a similar manner. The newest units at December 10 are the 50 units purchased on November 6. These are the first units assumed to be sold. The next newest units are the 100 units purchased on August 15 and 40 additional units are needed for the sale (90 sold − 50 from the November 6 purchase). Therefore, 40 of the 100 units purchased on August 15 are assumed to be included in the units sold on December 10. After the sale, 20 units remain from the January 1 inventory and 60 units remain from the August 15 purchase.

Cost of goods sold using LIFO is $2,710 (sum of the Sold Total column), and the ending inventory is $980 (final amount in the Inventory Balance Total column).

Exhibit 6A-5	Last-In, First-Out Method (Perpetual Inventory System)								
	Purchased			**Sold**			**Inventory Balance**		
Date	**Units**	**Unit Cost**	**Total**	**Units**	**Unit Cost**	**Total**	**Units**	**Unit Cost**	**Total**
Jan. 1							60	$10	$ 600
Mar. 27	90	$11	$ 990				60	10	} 1,590
							90	11	
May 2				90	$11	$ 990			
				40	10	400	20	10	200
Aug. 15	100	13	1,300				20	10	} 1,500
							100	13	
Nov. 6	50	16	800				20	10	
							100	13	} 2,300
							50	16	
Dec. 10				50	16	800	20	10	} 980
				40	13	520	60	13	
Total						$2,710			

Weighted-Average Cost Method

When the **weighted-average cost method** is used, a new weighted-average unit cost is calculated for the goods (**total cost divided by total units**) each time that goods are purchased and added to inventory. The cost of goods sold for each sale is calculated by multiplying the weighted-average unit cost at the time of sale by the number of units sold. Exhibit 6A-6 illustrates the calculation of cost of goods sold and ending inventory under the weighted-average cost method. The weighted-average unit cost is calculated three times in Exhibit 6A-6. On March 27, 90 units were purchased at a unit cost of $11, and the updated weighted-average unit cost on this date is:

$$[\$600 + \$990]/[60 \text{ Units} + 90 \text{ Units}] = \$10.60$$

On August 15, 100 units were purchased at a unit cost of $13. The updated weighted-average unit cost on this date is:

$$[\$212 + \$1,300]/[20 \text{ Units} + 100 \text{ Units}] = \$12.60$$

On November 6, 50 units were purchased at a unit cost of $16. The updated weighted-average unit cost on this date is:

$$[\$1,512 + \$800]/[120 \text{ Units} + 50 \text{ Units}] = \$13.60$$

The cost of goods sold is $2,602 (sum of the Sold Total column), and the ending inventory is $1,088 (final amount in the Inventory Balance Total column).

| Exhibit 6A-6 | Weighted-Average Cost Method (Perpetual Inventory System) |

	Purchased			Sold			Inventory Balance		
Date	Units	Unit Cost	Total	Units	Unit Cost	Total	Units	Unit Cost	Total
Jan. 1							60	$10.00	$ 600
Mar. 27	90	$11	$ 990				150	10.60	1,590
May 2				**130**	**$10.60**	**$1,378**	20	10.60	212
Aug. 15	100	13	1,300				120	12.60	1,512
Nov. 6	50	16	800				170	13.60	2,312
Dec. 10				**90**	**13.60**	1,224	80	13.60	1,088
Total						$2,602			

Comparative Analysis of Inventory Costing Methods

The purchase price data used in the Claremont Company illustration has an important characteristic: the purchase price of the inventory increased each time that a purchase was made, from $11 per unit to $13 per unit to $16 per unit. Increasing inventory prices are frequently encountered in the real world where price inflation is common and price deflation is uncommon. Exhibit 6A-7 summarizes the results of applying the four inventory costing methods to the Claremont Company data and reveals that the FIFO method produces the lowest cost of goods sold ($2,500), while the LIFO method produces the highest cost of goods sold ($2,710). The exhibit also reveals that FIFO produces the highest year-end value of ending inventory ($1,190), while LIFO produces the lowest year-end value of ending inventory ($980). Specific identification and weighted-average cost produce ending inventory values and cost of goods sold values that fall in between the results obtained using FIFO and LIFO.

These results, however, are highly dependent on the purchase prices for the inventory. If the inventory's purchase price had been decreasing rather than increasing, the financial effects would have been just the opposite, with LIFO producing the lowest cost of goods sold and FIFO the highest. If, on the other hand, the purchase prices had been perfectly stable, there would be no difference between the cost of goods sold or the ending inventory for any of the four methods.

| Exhibit 6A-7 | Results of Different Inventory Costing Methods |

	Specific Identification	FIFO	LIFO	Weighted-Average
Cost of goods sold.	$2,530	$2,500	$2,710	$2,602
Ending inventory.	1,160	1,190	980	1,088

Impacts of Cost Flow Assumptions

Under generally accepted accounting principles, a company is permitted to select one or more of the four methods for purposes of assigning cost to its ending inventory and its cost of goods sold. Which method (or methods, since a company may elect to value some of its inventory using FIFO, some using LIFO, and some using weighted-average cost) is selected by a company depends upon a number of factors—the type of product produced, the cost of producing the product, whether the product is perishable, whether the company desires to report a high or a low net income, and income tax considerations.

Specific Identification Method

Specific identification is typically used by companies that manufacture a small volume of products with relatively high unit values. Airplanes, jewelry, and construction equipment are examples of products that would justify the cost of tracking the specific unit cost of each inventory item. Specific identification is usually not cost-justified for companies that manufacture products that have a low unit cost or involve high volumes of production. It can be very expensive to trace the exact costs of producing a product, especially a product manufactured in high volumes.

FIFO Method

Many companies, especially those with perishable, time-dated, or style-affected merchandise, attempt to sell their oldest merchandise first. This is especially true for companies that sell food products, chemicals, and drugs. For these types of companies, the cost flow produced by the FIFO method most closely matches the actual goods flow. However, a company is not required to use the cost flow assumption that most closely matches its actual goods flow. When costs are rising, FIFO will result in the lowest cost of goods sold, and therefore, the highest net income. The desire to show a higher net income by some companies partly explains the popularity of the FIFO method.

LIFO Method

Although LIFO does not reflect the actual goods flow for most businesses, its popularity is likely linked to the potential income tax savings associated with its use. For some industries, however, LIFO does depict the actual goods flow. For example, in industries that extract natural resources, such as mining, the product is frequently dumped onto a storage pile from an overhead trestle, and sold inventory is taken from the top of the pile. One disadvantage of using LIFO when beginning inventories have been maintained or increased is that a firm's ending inventory can be substantially undervalued since old purchase prices tend to be retained on a company's books under the LIFO method. This, in turn, will cause a firm's current assets and total assets to likewise be undervalued.

Weighted-Average Cost Method

Weighted-average cost is best suited for businesses that warehouse a large volume of undifferentiated goods in a common area. Liquid fuels, grains, and other commodities are examples. Weighted-average cost typically generates a cost of goods sold amount that is neither high nor low as compared to the other methods, as is revealed in Exhibit 6A-7.

Summary of Impacts

We can broadly summarize the impacts of the cost flow assumptions as follows:

1. Specific identification most closely identifies the actual cost of goods sold and ending inventory.
2. FIFO approximates the actual physical goods flow for most firms.
3. LIFO is popular because of the income tax savings associated with its use.
4. Weighted-average cost is most often associated with businesses in which undifferentiated goods are commingled in a common area like a warehouse.

Analysis of Costing Methods and Gross Profit

To illustrate the financial effects of the different inventory costing methods, assume that the 220 units sold by the Claremont Company were sold for $20 each, producing sales of $4,400 ($20 × 220). Exhibit 6A-8 shows the difference in gross profit under each of the four inventory costing methods. Remember that the difference in reported gross profit results from the assumptions made about cost flow, not from any difference in actual goods flow. In each case, 220 units were sold and 80 units remained. Each of the inventory costing methods is in accord with generally accepted accounting principles, yet one method's financial impact on gross profit and net income is different from the financial impact of another method.

Exhibit 6A-8	Gross Profit Using Alternative Inventory Costing Methods			
	Specific Identification	FIFO	LIFO	Weighted-Average
Sales (220 units @ $20)	$4,400	$4,400	$4,400	$4,400
Cost of goods sold	2,530	2,500	2,710	2,602
Gross profit	$1,870	$1,900	$1,690	$1,798
Increased gross profit compared with LIFO	$ 180	$ 210		$ 108

Income Statement and Balance Sheet Effects

As Exhibit 6A-8 reveals, LIFO results in the smallest gross profit ($1,690) with FIFO producing the highest ($1,900) gross profit. This result occurs because the purchase price of inventory was increasing throughout the year, from $11 per unit to $13 per unit to $16 per unit. Most agree that when costs are rising, FIFO tends to overstate gross profit (and income) because older, lower unit costs are included in the cost of goods sold and matched with current sales prices. In other words, in the illustration, all of the units sold are charged to costs of goods sold under FIFO at unit costs of $10, $11, and $13. If the latest purchase price reflects the inventory's current acquisition cost, the units sold must be replaced by units costing $16 (or more if costs continue to rise).

It is frequently argued that LIFO provides a better matching of current costs with current revenues since the cost of the most recent purchases constitutes the LIFO cost of goods sold. While LIFO associates the current, higher unit costs with cost of goods sold, it assigns costs to ending inventory using the older, lower unit costs. As a consequence, the value of the LIFO ending inventory on the balance sheet is often undervalued in terms of the inventory's current value. When inventory quantities are maintained or increased, the LIFO method prevents older costs from appearing in the cost of goods sold. No doubt, some firms still carry LIFO inventories at unit costs that existed more than 10 years ago. Under FIFO, the ending inventory is measured at relatively recent costs.

Comparison of Inventory Costing Methods

Exhibit 6A-9 summarizes the results of applying the periodic and perpetual costing methods to the same Claremont data. The specific identification method and the FIFO method yield the exact same results for ending inventory and cost of goods sold regardless of whether the periodic or the perpetual method is being used. For specific identification, ending inventory and cost of goods sold are identical under both the periodic and perpetual inventory systems. The same is true for FIFO. Only LIFO and weighted-average methods produce different results under the periodic and perpetual systems.

Exhibit 6A-9	**Summary Results of Different Inventory Costing Methods**	
Costing Method	**Ending Inventory**	**Cost of Goods Sold**
Specific identification		
Periodic..............................	$1,160	$2,530
Perpetual.............................	1,160	2,530
FIFO		
Periodic..............................	1,190	2,500
Perpetual.............................	1,190	2,500
LIFO		
Periodic..............................	820	2,870
Perpetual.............................	980	2,710
Average		
Periodic..............................	984	2,706
Perpetual.............................	1,088	2,602

Choice of a periodic vs perpetual system does *not* impact specific identification or FIFO

Choice of a periodic vs perpetual system does impact LIFO and weighted-average results

APPENDIX 6B: LIFO Reserve

As shown in this chapter, the LIFO inventory costing method can produce significantly different results relative to other inventory costing methods for both cost of goods sold, and therefore gross profit and net income, and ending inventory. The difference is greatest when compared to results obtained using FIFO. When costs are rising, FIFO will result in higher reported ending inventory, lower cost of goods sold, and higher net income.

LO7 Define the LIFO reserve and explain how it is used to compare the performance of companies using different inventory costing methods.

To make comparisons between companies using LIFO and companies using FIFO, we need to use the **LIFO inventory reserve**, or simply *LIFO reserve*. Companies that use LIFO are required under generally accepted accounting principles to report the difference between ending inventory using LIFO and the inventory that would have been reported under FIFO. This difference is called the LIFO inventory reserve and is disclosed in notes to financial statements.

Referring again to Exhibit 6-8, FIFO ending inventory is valued at $1,190 and LIFO ending inventory at $820. The LIFO reserve is $370 ($1,190 − $820). Use of LIFO can have a material impact on many ratios, and one way to compensate for these effects is to use the LIFO reserve to restate the reported inventory. To illustrate, assume that Claremont Company, whose inventory costing method results are contrasted in Exhibit 6-8, has current assets of $2,100 and current liabilities of $1,400 under the LIFO method. Exhibit 6B-1 calculates the current ratio (current assets divided by current liabilities) under both LIFO and FIFO. (The current ratio is discussed in Chapter 2.)

Hint: *The LIFO reserve is also used to restate the LIFO cost of goods sold to that under FIFO. The LIFO cost of good sold minus the change in the LIFO reserve from the beginning to the end of the period equals FIFO cost of goods sold.*

Exhibit 6B-1	Impact of the LIFO Inventory Reserve on the Current Ratio	
	LIFO	**FIFO**
Current ratio	$\dfrac{\$2,100}{\$1,400} = 1.50$	$\dfrac{(\$2,100 + \$370)}{\$1,400} = 1.76$

As shown in Exhibit 6B-1, the current ratio is much higher under FIFO (1.76) than under LIFO (1.50). Differences occur between LIFO and FIFO companies for many ratios, with FIFO resulting in more favorable ratios in most cases since FIFO generally results in higher inventory values and higher net earnings. For some ratios, however, LIFO produces more favorable results. Two examples are the inventory turnover ratio and the days' sales in inventory ratio. Because LIFO results in lower inventory values, the inventory turnover (and consequently, the days' sales in inventory) under LIFO appears higher (lower) than it does under FIFO. (The LIFO reserve also affects cost of goods sold and therefore the numerator of the inventory turnover ratio; in most cases the adjustment to cost of goods sold is much smaller than the adjustment to average inventory, leading to a higher inventory turnover under LIFO than under FIFO.)

TAKEAWAY 6.2	Concept ➝	Method ➝	Assessment
	What effect does the use of LIFO have on ending inventory relative to the use of FIFO?	Ending inventory and the LIFO inventory reserve The value of LIFO ending inventory + the LIFO inventory reserve = The value of FIFO ending inventory	If the LIFO reserve is material it can have a significant impact on many ratios when compared to FIFO. The calculation of these ratios can be adjusted using the LIFO inventory reserve to provide a more comparable set of results.

SUMMARY OF LEARNING OBJECTIVES

LO1 **Explain inventory concepts and modern inventory practices. (p. 262)**

- Merchandise inventory is a stock of inventory that a merchandising company buys from a manufacturer and makes available for sale to its customers.
- A manufacturing firm maintains three different inventory categories: raw materials inventory, work-in-process inventory, and finished goods inventory.
- Traditionally, manufacturers have maintained just-in-case inventories of raw materials and components to provide for unplanned production or delayed raw material shipments, resulting in high levels of inventory carrying costs.
- Today, many manufacturers have adopted the just-in-time (JIT) manufacturing philosophy which is designed to eliminate or minimize raw materials, work-in-process, and finished goods inventories. The key to JIT manufacturing is careful inventory order planning and sophisticated production management.
- Ownership of goods in transit depends on the shipping terms. The buyer assumes ownership of goods in transit shipped F.O.B. shipping point, whereas the seller maintains ownership of goods shipped F.O.B. destination until the buyer assumes possession at delivery.
- Consignment goods are goods held for sale by parties other than the seller. The seller maintains legal ownership of these inventory items while they are held for sale by the consignment seller.
- The year-end physical count of inventory is taken to verify the inventory balance. It consists of three steps:
  - Count the number of individual items of merchandise on hand at the end of the year.
  - Determine the unit cost of each individual item and multiply the unit cost times the quantity on hand to obtain the total cost for each individual item of merchandise.
  - Add together the total cost of all the individual items to obtain the total cost of the inventory on hand.

LO2 **Describe inventory costing under specific identification, weighted-average cost, FIFO, and LIFO. (p. 266)**

- To assign cost to units sold (cost of goods sold) and units available (inventory), a company must either keep track of the cost of each specific unit (specific identification method) or make an assumption about which units have been sold (weighted-average cost, FIFO, and LIFO methods).

■ The weighted-average cost method assumes that a mix of the goods available is sold; the FIFO method assumes that the oldest goods are sold first; and, the LIFO method assumes that the newest goods are sold first.

Analyze the financial effects of different inventory costing methods on company profit. (p. 271)   **LO3**

■ Each of the alternative inventory costing methods produces a different cost of goods sold and gross profit.

■ When costs are rising, the LIFO method does the best job of matching current costs with revenues; LIFO also produces a lower gross profit and lower income taxes than either weighted-average cost or FIFO.

Apply the lower-of-cost-or-market method. (p. 276)   **LO4**

■ Damaged, physically deteriorated, or obsolete merchandise should be valued and reported at its net realizable value—that is, its estimated selling price less the expected cost of disposal.

■ The lower-of-cost-or-market method provides for inventory write-downs to be recorded in the period that the replacement cost of inventory declines below the inventory's acquisition cost.

Define *inventory turnover* and *day's sales in inventory* and explain the use of these ratios. (p. 278)   **LO5**

■ Inventory turnover and days' sales in inventory indicate, respectively, how many times on average during the year a firm sells its inventory and how many days on average it takes a firm to sell its inventory.

■ Inventory turnover and days' sales in inventory provide evidence regarding a firm's ability to sell its inventory and its ability to effectively manage its investment in inventory.

Appendix 6A: Describe inventory costing under a perpetual inventory system using specific identification, weighted-average cost, FIFO, and LIFO. (p. 281)   **LO6**

■ To assign cost to units sold (cost of goods sold) and units available (inventory), a company must either keep track of the cost of each specific unit (specific identification method) or make an assumption about which units have been sold (weighted-average cost, FIFO, and LIFO methods).

■ The weighted-average cost method assumes that a mix of the goods available is sold; the FIFO method assumes that the oldest goods are sold; and, the LIFO method assumes that the newest goods are sold.

■ The specific identification method and the FIFO method yield the exact same results for ending inventory and for cost of goods sold regardless of whether the periodic or the perpetual method is being used. Only LIFO and weighted-average methods produce different results.

Appendix 6B: Define the LIFO reserve and explain how it is used to compare the performance of companies using different inventory costing methods. (p. 287)   **LO7**

■ The LIFO inventory reserve represents the difference between the value of LIFO ending inventory and what the ending inventory would have been valued at under FIFO.

■ The LIFO inventory reserve can cause a material effect on many ratios. These ratios should be adjusted for the LIFO inventory reserve when comparing a company using LIFO with a FIFO company.

Concept ➡	Method ➡	Assessment	SUMMARY
How long, on average, does it take to sell the inventory?	Cost of goods sold, beginning inventory, and ending inventory $$\text{Inventory turnover} = \frac{\text{Cost of goods sold}}{\text{Average inventory}}$$ $$\text{Days' sales in inventory} = \frac{365}{\text{Inventory turnover}}$$	A higher inventory turnover or a lower days' sales in inventory indicates that the company is able to sell its inventory more quickly.	TAKEAWAY 6.1
What effect does the use of LIFO have on ending inventory relative to the use of FIFO?	Ending inventory and the LIFO inventory reserve The value of LIFO ending inventory + the LIFO inventory reserve = The value of FIFO ending inventory	If the LIFO reserve is material it can have a significant impact on many ratios when compared to FIFO. The calculation of these ratios can be adjusted using the LIFO inventory reserve to provide a more comparable set of results.	TAKEAWAY 6.2

KEY TERMS

Consignment goods (p. 264)

Cost flow (p. 267)

Days' sales in inventory (p. 279)

Finished goods
   inventory (p. 263)

First-in, first-out (FIFO)
   method (p. 268, 282)

F.O.B. destination (p. 264)

F.O.B. shipping point (p. 264)

Goods flow (p. 267)

Goods in transit (p. 264)

Inventory carrying
   costs (p. 263)

Inventory overage (p. 265)

Inventory shrinkage (p. 265)

Inventory turnover
   ratio (p. 278)

Just-in-case inventory (p. 263)

Just-in-time (JIT)
   manufacturing (p. 263)

Last-in, first-out (LIFO)
   method (p. 269, 283)

LIFO conformity rule (p. 274)

LIFO inventory reserve (p. 287)

Lower-of-cost-or-market
   (LCM) (p. 276)

Net realizable value (p. 276)

Physical count of
   inventory (p. 265)

Quick response system (p. 263)

Raw materials
   inventory (p. 262)

Specific identification
   method (p. 268, 282)

Weighted-average cost
   method (p. 270, 284)

Work-in-process
   inventory (p. 262)

SELF-STUDY QUESTIONS

(Answers to Self-Study Questions are at the end of this chapter.)

LO1 1. **Which of the following concepts relates to the elimination or minimization of inventories by a manufacturing firm?**
   a. Quick response
   b. Just-in-time
   c. Just-in-case
   d. Specific identification

LO2 2. **Which inventory costing method assumes that the most recently purchased merchandise is sold first?**
   a. Specific identification
   b. Weighted-average cost
   c. FIFO
   d. LIFO

LO3 3. **Which inventory costing method results in the highest-valued ending inventory during a period of rising unit costs?**
   a. Specific identification
   b. Weighted-average cost
   c. FIFO
   d. LIFO

LO1 4. **Under which of the following freight terms does the seller retain ownership of the shipped goods?**
   a. F.O.B. shipping point
   b. F.O.B. destination

LO4 5. **When should ending inventory be written down below its acquisition cost on the balance sheet?**
   a. When units are damaged, physically deteriorated, or obsolete.
   b. When the inventory's replacement cost exceeds its acquisition cost.
   c. When the inventory's replacement cost is below its acquisition cost.
   d. Both a and c.

LO3 6. **Which inventory costing method results in the highest net income during a period of rising unit prices?**
   a. Specific identification
   b. Weighted-average cost
   c. FIFO
   d. LIFO

7. **Which inventory costing method is expensive to implement?**   LO2
   a.   Specific identification
   b.   Weighted-average cost
   c.   FIFO
   d.   LIFO

8. **Which inventory costing method is frequently used when undifferentiated units are stored in a**   LO2
   common area?
   a.   Specific identification
   b.   Weighted-average cost
   c.   FIFO
   d.   LIFO

9. **Which inventory costing method results in the lowest net income during a period of rising unit**   LO3
   prices?
   a.   Specific identification
   b.   Weighted-average cost
   c.   FIFO
   d.   LIFO

10. **Which inventory costing method does not require the use of the lower-of-cost-or-market method?**   LO4
    a.   Specific identification
    b.   Weighted-average cost
    c.   FIFO
    d.   All methods require the use of LCM.

11. **Tracker Corp. reported annual cost of goods sold of $30,000 and average inventory on hand during**   LO5
    the year of $3,750. What was Tracker's inventory turnover?
    a.   0.125 times
    b.   8.0 times
    c. $26,250
    d.   8.0%

12. **The Avner Company reports ending inventory under the LIFO method of $15,000. Had Avner used**   LO7
    FIFO, the ending inventory would have been reported as $16,500. Avner's LIFO inventory reserve is: **(Appendix 6B)**
    a. $31,500
    b. $15,000
    c. $1,500
    d.   91%

13. **The periodic inventory system differs from the perpetual inventory system:**   LO6
    a.   because the periodic system is not compatible with modern technology.   **(Appendix 6A)**
    b.   because the perpetual system continually updates inventory, while the periodic inventory system
         only updates inventory at the end of the period.
    c.   because the periodic system continually updates inventory, while the perpetual inventory system
         only updates inventory at the end of the period.
    d.   because the periodic system is more complex and costly.

QUESTIONS

1. What are the three inventory accounts maintained by a manufacturing firm? Define each.

2. ShopMart Stores uses point-of-sale equipment at its checkout counters to read universal bar codes. It also
   uses a quick response system. What is a quick response system?

3. What are *just-in-case inventory* and *inventory carrying costs?*

4. What is the *just-in-time manufacturing philosophy?* Describe it.

5. What is meant by *goods flow* and *cost flow?*

6. Describe how each of the following inventory costing methods is used with the perpetual inventory system: (a) Specific identification; (b) Weighted-average cost; (c) First-in, first-out; and (d) Last-in, first-out.

7. What is an appropriate operating situation (that is, goods flow corresponds with cost flow) for each of the following approaches to inventory costing: Specific identification, Weighted-average cost, FIFO, and LIFO?

8. Why do relatively stable purchase prices reduce the significance of the choice of an inventory costing method?

9. What is the nature of FIFO *phantom profits* during periods of rising inventory purchase prices?

10. If costs have been rising, which inventory costing method—weighted-average cost; first-in, first-out; or last-in, first-out—yields (a) the lowest ending inventory value? (b) the lowest net income? (c) the largest ending inventory value? (d) the largest net income?

11. Even though it does not represent their goods flow, why might firms adopt last-in, first-out inventory costing during periods when inventory costs are rising?

12. Describe two situations in which merchandise may be valued on the balance sheet at an amount less than its acquisition cost.

13. Which of the following is not an inventory costing method?
    a. Specific identification
    b. Weighted-average cost
    c. Just-in-time manufacturing
    d. FIFO

14. What is the effect on reported net income of applying the lower-of-cost-or-market method to ending inventory?

15. How do the accounting principles of consistency and full disclosure apply to inventory costing?

16. Which party, the seller or the buyer, bears the freight cost when the terms are F.O.B. shipping point? When the terms are F.O.B. destination?

17. What is a LIFO inventory reserve and how can it be useful to an analyst?

18. Moyer Company has an inventory turnover of 4.51. What is Moyer's days' sales in inventory?

19. In a recent annual report, Craftmade International, Inc., describes its inventory accounting policies as follows:

> Inventories are stated at the lower-of-cost-or-market, with inventory cost determined using the first-in, first-out (FIFO) method. The cost of inventory includes freight-in and duties on imported goods.

Also in a recent annual report, Kaiser Aluminum Corporation made the following statement in discussing its inventories:

> The Company recorded pretax charges of approximately $19.4 million because of a reduction in the carrying values of its inventories caused principally by prevailing lower prices for alumina, primary aluminum, and fabricated products.

What accounting principle did Craftmade International follow when it included the costs of freight-in and duties on imported goods in its Inventory account? Briefly describe how a firm determines which costs to include in its inventory account. What accounting principle did Kaiser Aluminum follow when it recorded the $19.4 million pretax charge? Briefly describe the rationale for this principle.

20. What are the three steps that make up the year-end physical count of inventory?

SHORT EXERCISES

LO4   **SE6-1.**   **Departures from Acquisition Cost**   At year-end, The Appliance Shop has a refrigerator that has been used as a demonstration model. The refrigerator cost $350 and sells for $500 when new. In its present condition, the refrigerator will be sold for $325. Related selling costs are an estimated $15. At what amount should the refrigerator be carried in inventory?

a. $350
b. $335

c. $325
d. $310

SE6-2. **Inventory Costing Methods** Which inventory costing method requires that a company keep track of the cost of each specific unit of inventory? **LO2**

    a. Specific identification

    b. Lower-of-cost-or-market method

    c. LIFO

    d. All of the above

SE6-3. **LIFO Inventory Reserve** Lamil Company reports ending inventory of $150,000 on a LIFO basis and also reports a LIFO inventory reserve of $27,000. If Lamil had used FIFO rather than FIFO, ending inventory would have been: **LO7** **(Appendix 6B)**

    a. $123,000.

    b. $150,000.

    c. $177,000.

    d. $182,500.

SE6-4. **Lower-of-Cost-or-Market Method** The Claremont Company's ending inventory is composed of 50 units that had cost $20 each and 100 units that had cost $15 each. If the company can replace all 150 units at a price of $16 each, what value should be assigned to the company's ending inventory assuming that it applies LCM? **LO4**

SE6-5. **Lower-of-Cost-or-Market Method** The McQuenny Company's ending inventory is composed of 100 units that had an acquisition cost of $25 per unit and 50 units that had an acquisition cost of $30 per unit. If the company can replace all 150 units at a replacement cost of $27 per unit, what value should be assigned to the company's ending inventory assuming that it applies the LCM method? **LO4**

SE6-6. **Inventory Turnover and Days' Sales in Inventory** W. Glass & Company reported the following information in its recent annual report: **LO5**

	2012	2013
Cost of goods sold.	$4,000,000	$4,600,000
Beginning inventory	900,000	860,000
Ending inventory.	860,000	640,000

Calculate the company's inventory turnover and days' sales in inventory for both years.

SE6-7. **Inventory Turnover and Days' Sales in Inventory** Herberger & Company disclosed the following information in its recent annual report: **LO5**

	2012	2013
Cost of goods sold.	$16,000,000	$20,000,000
Beginning inventory	2,000,000	4,000,000
Ending inventory.	4,000,000	5,000,000

Calculate the company's inventory turnover and days' sales in inventory for both years.

SE6-8. **Inventory Costing Methods and the Periodic Method** Lambeth Company experienced the following events in January: **LO2**

Date	Event	Units		Unit Cost	Total Cost
Jan. 10	Purchased inventory.	100	@	$12	$1,200
Jan. 20	Purchased inventory.	200	@	14	2,800
Jan. 30	Sold inventory	150			

If the Lambeth Company uses the FIFO inventory costing method, calculate the company's cost of goods sold and its ending inventory as of January 31 assuming the periodic method.

LO2   **SE6-9.** **Inventory Costing Methods and the Periodic Method** Lambeth Company experienced the following events in February:

Date	Event	Units		Unit Cost	Total Cost
Feb. 1	Purchased inventory............................	100	@	$20	$2,000
Feb. 4	Sold inventory	50			
Feb. 9	Purchased inventory............................	100	@	$22	$2,200
Feb. 27	Sold inventory	100			

If the Lambeth Company uses the LIFO inventory costing method, calculate the company's cost of goods sold and ending inventory as of February 28 assuming the periodic method.

LO6   **SE6-10.** **Inventory Costing Methods and the Perpetual Method** Refer to the information in SE6-9 and as-
(Appendix 6A)   sume the perpetual inventory system is used. Use the LIFO inventory costing method to calculate the company's cost of goods sold and ending inventory as of February 28.

LO2   **SE6-11.** **Inventory Costing Methods and the Periodic Method** McKay & Company experienced the following events in March:

Date	Event	Units		Unit Cost	Total Cost
Mar. 1	Purchased inventory............................	100	@	$15	$1,500
Mar. 3	Sold inventory	60			
Mar. 15	Purchased inventory............................	100	@	$18	$1,800
Mar. 20	Sold inventory	40			

If McKay & Company uses the weighted-average cost method, calculate the company's cost of goods sold and ending inventory as of March 31 assuming the periodic method.

LO6   **SE6-12.** **Inventory Costing Methods and the Perpetual Method** Refer to the information in SE6-11 and
(Appendix 6A)   assume the perpetual inventory system is used. Use the weighted-average inventory costing method to calculate the company's cost of goods sold and ending inventory as of March 31. Round your final answers to the nearest dollar.

LO1   **SE6-13.** **Identify Goods to Be Included in Inventory** Patterson Company has the following items at year-end. Identify which items should be included in Patterson's year-end inventory count.

1. Goods held on consignment by Sell For You Company.
2. Goods held by Patterson on consignment that will be sold for another company.
3. Goods in transit sent to a client F.O.B. shipping point.
4. Goods in transit sent to a client F.O.B. destination.

LO3   **SE6-14.** **Errors in Inventory Count** Bow Corp. accidentally overstated its 2012 ending inventory by $750. Assume that ending 2013 inventory is accurately counted. The error in 2012 will have what effect on Bow Corp.?

a. 2012 net income is understated by $750.
b. 2012 net income is overstated by $750.
c. 2013 net income is understated by $750.
d. Both b and c are correct.

Assignments with the ✔ logo in the margin are available in ᵐʸBusinessCourse.
See the Preface of the book for details.

EXERCISES—SET A

LO1   **E6-1A.** **Just-in-Time Inventories** Raymond Manufacturing Company uses the perpetual inventory system and plans to use raw materials costing $600,000 in manufacturing its products during 2012. Raymond will operate its factory 300 days during 2012. Currently, Raymond follows the just-in-case philosophy with its raw materials inventory, keeping raw materials costing $15,000 in its raw materials inventory. Raymond plans to switch to the just-in-time manufacturing philosophy by keeping only the raw materials needed for the next two days of production. Calculate the new raw materials inventory level after Raymond implements the just-in-time manufacturing philosophy in its factory.

E6-2A. **Inventory Costing Methods—Periodic Method** The Lippert Company uses the periodic inventory system. The following July data are for an item in Lippert's inventory:

LO2

July 1 Beginning inventory, 30 units @ $8 per unit.
10 Purchased 50 units @ $9 per unit.
15 Sold 60 units.
26 Purchased 25 units @ $10 per unit.

Calculate the cost of goods sold for July and ending inventory at July 31 using (a) first-in, first-out, (b) last-in, first-out, and (c) the weighted-average cost methods. Round your final answers to the nearest dollar.

E6-3A. **Inventory Costing Methods—Perpetual Method** Refer to the information in E6-2A and assume the perpetual inventory system is used. Calculate the cost of goods sold for the July 15 sale using (a) first-in, first-out, (b) last-in, first-out, and (c) the weighted-average cost methods. Round your final answers to the nearest dollar.

LO6
(Appendix 6A)

E6-4A. **Inventory Costing Methods—Periodic Method** Archer Company is a retailer that uses the periodic inventory system. On August 1, it had 80 units of product A at a total cost of $1,600. On August 5, Archer purchased 100 units of A for $2,116. On August 8, it purchased 200 units of A for $4,416. On August 11, it sold 150 units of A for $4,800. Calculate the August cost of goods sold and the ending inventory at August 31 using (a) first-in, first-out, (b) last-in, first-out, and (c) the weighted-average cost methods. Round your final answers to the nearest dollar.

LO2

E6-5A. **Inventory Costing Methods—Perpetual Method** Refer to the information in E6-4A and assume the perpetual inventory system is used. Calculate the inventory cost of item A on August 11 (after the sale) using (a) first-in, first-out, (b) last-in, first-out, and (c) the weighted-average cost methods. Round your final answers to the nearest dollar.

LO6
(Appendix 6A)

E6-6A. **Departures from Acquisition Cost** Determine the proper total inventory value for each of the following items in Viking Company's ending inventory:

LO4

a. Viking has 600 video games in stock. The games cost $36 each, but their year-end replacement cost is $30. Viking has been selling the games for $60, but competitors are now selling them for $50. Viking plans to drop its price to $50. Viking's normal gross profit on video games is 40 percent.

b. Viking has 300 rolls of camera film that are past the expiration date marked on the film's box. The films cost $1.65 each and are normally sold for $3.30. New replacement films still cost $1.65. To clear out these old films, Viking will drop their selling price to $1.40. There are no related selling costs.

c. Viking has five cameras in stock that have been used as demonstration models. The cameras cost $180 and normally sell for $280. Because these cameras are in used condition, Viking has set the selling price at $160 each. Expected selling costs are $10 per camera. New models of the camera (on order) will cost Viking $200 and will be priced to sell at $320.

E6-7A. **Inventory Costing Methods—Periodic Method** The following information is for the Bloom Company for 2012; the company sells just one product:

LO2

	Units	Unit Cost
Beginning inventory	200	$10
Purchases: Feb. 11	500	14
May 18	400	16
October 23	100	20

At December 31, 2012, there was an ending inventory of 360 units. Assume the use of the periodic inventory method. Calculate the value of ending inventory and the cost of goods sold for the year using (a) first-in, first-out, (b) last-in, first-out, and (c) the weighted-average cost method.

LO2 **E6-8A.** **Inventory Costing Methods—Periodic Method** The following data are for the Bloom Company, which sells just one product:

		Units	Unit Cost
Beginning inventory, January 1		200	$10
Purchases:	February 11	500	14
	May 18	400	16
	October 23	100	20
Sales	March 1	400	
	July 1	400	

Calculate the value of ending inventory and cost of goods sold using the periodic method and (a) first-in, first-out, (b) last-in, first-out, and (c) weighted-average cost method.

LO6 **E6-9A.** **Inventory Costing Methods—Perpetual Method** Refer to the information in E6-8A and assume the
(Appendix 6A) perpetual inventory system is used. Calculate the value of ending inventory and cost of goods sold using the perpetual method and (a) first-in, first-out, (b) last-in, first-out, and (c) weighted-average cost method.

LO4 **E6-10A.** **Lower-of-Cost-or-Market (LCM) Method** The following data are taken from the Browning Corporation's inventory accounts:

Item Code	Quantity	Unit Cost	Replacement Cost
ACE	100	$25	$24
BDF	300	30	31
GHJ	400	20	18
MBS	200	23	27

Calculate the value of the company's ending inventory using the lower-of-cost-or-market method applied to each item of inventory.

LO5 **E6-11A.** **Inventory Turnover and Days' Sales in Inventory** The Southern Company installed a new inventory management system at the beginning of 2012. Shown below are data from the company's accounting records as reported out by the new system:

	2012	2013
Sales revenue	$8,000,000	$10,000,000
Cost of goods sold	4,000,000	4,900,000
Beginning inventory	500,000	530,000
Ending inventory	530,000	600,000

Calculate the company's (a) inventory turnover and (b) days' sales in inventory for 2012 and 2013. Comment on your results.

LO7 **E6-12A.** **The LIFO Inventory Reserve** Midwestern Steel Company uses the LIFO inventory costing method
(Appendix 6B) to value its ending inventory. The following data were obtained from the company's accounting records:

Current assets (under FIFO)	$8,000,000
Current liabilities	5,500,000
Inventory under LIFO	2,000,000
Inventory under FIFO	2,700,000

Calculate the company's (a) LIFO inventory reserve and (b) the current ratio assuming (i) FIFO and (ii) LIFO.

E6-13A. Applying IFRS LVMH is a Paris-based manufacturer of luxury goods that prepares its financial statements using IFRS. During the year, the management of the company undertook a review of the fair value of its inventory and found that the inventory had appreciated above its book value of 10 million euros. According to the company's management, the inventory was undervalued by 1 million euros. Prepare the journal entry to revalue the company's inventory. How would the revaluation immediately affect the company's (a) current ratio, (b) inventory turnover, and (c) days' sales in inventory?   **LO4**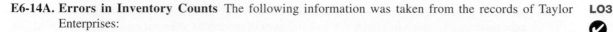

E6-14A. Errors in Inventory Counts The following information was taken from the records of Taylor Enterprises: **LO3**

	2013	2012
Beginning inventory	$ 60,000	$ 50,000
Cost of goods purchased	420,000	400,000
Cost of goods available for sale	480,000	450,000
Ending inventory	55,000	60,000
Cost of goods sold	$425,000	$390,000

The following two errors were made in the physical inventory counts:

1. 2012 ending inventory was understated by $10,000.
2. 2013 ending inventory was overstated by $5,000.

Compute the correct cost of goods sold for both 2012 and 2013.

E6-15A. Year-End Physical Inventory The December 31 inventory for the Hayes Company included five products. The year-end physical count revealed the following: **LO1**

Product	Quantity Available
A	26
B	50
C	34
D	75
E	40

The related unit costs were: A, $10; B, $6; C, $5; D, $8; and E, $7.

Required
Calculate the total cost of the December 31 physical inventory.

EXERCISES—SET B

E6-1B. Just-in-Time Inventories Carson Manufacturing Company uses the perpetual inventory system and plans to use raw material costing $1,650,000 in making its products during 2012. Carson will operate its factory 275 days during 2012. Currently, Carson follows the just-in-case philosophy with its raw materials inventory, keeping raw materials costing $35,000 in its raw materials inventory. Carson plans to switch to the just-in-time manufacturing philosophy by keeping only the raw materials needed for the next two days of production. Calculate the new raw materials inventory level after Carson implements the just-in-time manufacturing philosophy.   **LO1**

E6-2B. Inventory Costing Methods—Periodic Method Merritt Company uses the periodic inventory system. The following May data are for an item in Merritt's inventory: **LO2**

May   1   Beginning inventory, 150 units @ $30 per unit.
     12   Purchased 100 units @ $35 per unit.
     16   Sold 180 units.
     24   Purchased 160 units @ $36 per unit.

Calculate the cost of goods sold for May and ending inventory at May 31 using (a) first-in, first-out, (b) last-in, first-out, and (c) the weighted-average cost method. Round your final answers to the nearest dollar.

LO6
(Appendix 6A)
✓

E6-3B. **Inventory Costing Methods—Perpetual Method** Refer to the information in E6-2B and assume the perpetual inventory system is used. Calculate the cost of goods sold for the May 16 sale using (a) first-in, first-out, (b) last-in, first-out, and (c) the weighted-average cost method. Round your final answers to the nearest dollar.

LO2
✓

E6-4B. **Inventory Costing Methods—Periodic Method** Spangler Company is a retailer that uses the periodic inventory system. On March 1, it had 100 units of product M at a total cost of $1,590. On March 6, Spangler purchased 200 units of M for $3,600. On March 10, it purchased 150 units of M for $3,000. On March 15, it sold 180 units of M for $5,400. Calculate the March cost of goods sold and the ending inventory at March 31 using (a) first-in, first-out, (b) last-in, first-out, and (c) the weighted-average cost method. Round your final answers to the nearest dollar.

LO6
(Appendix 6A)
✓

E6-5B. **Inventory Costing Methods—Perpetual Method** Refer to the information in E6-4B and assume the perpetual inventory system is used. Calculate the ending inventory cost of item M on March 15 (after the sale) using (a) first-in, first-out, (b) last-in, first-out, and (c) the weighted-average cost method. Round your final answers to the nearest dollar.

LO4
✓

E6-6B. **Lower-of-Cost-or-Market (LCM) Method** The following data refer to the Froning Company's ending inventory:

Item Code	Quantity	Unit Cost	Unit Market
LXC.	60	$45	$48
KWT	210	38	34
MOR.	300	22	20
NES	100	27	32

Calculate the value of the company's ending inventory by using the lower-of-cost-or-market method applied to each item of inventory.

LO2
✓

E6-7B. **Inventory Costing Methods—Periodic Method** The Toon Company, which uses the periodic inventory system, has the following records for 2012:

		Units	Unit Cost
Beginning inventory		100	$49
Purchases:	Jan. 6	650	42
	July 15	550	38
	Dec. 28	200	36

Ending inventory at December 31, 2012, was 350 units. Compute the ending inventory and the cost of goods sold for the year using (a) first-in, first out, (b) weighted-average cost, and (c) last-in, first-out.

LO2
✓

E6-8B. **Inventory Costing Methods—Periodic Method** The following data are for the Miller Corporation, which sells just one product:

		Units	Unit Cost
Beginning inventory, January 1		200	$12
Purchases	February 11	500	13
	May 18	400	15
	October 23	100	18
Sales	March 1	400	
	July 1	400	

Calculate the value of ending inventory and cost of goods sold using the periodic method and (a) first-in, first-out, (b) last-in, first-out, and (c) weighted-average cost method. Round your final answers to the nearest dollar.

E6-9B.   Inventory Costing Methods—Perpetual Method Refer to the information in E6-8B and assume the perpetual inventory system is used. Calculate the value of ending inventory and cost of goods sold using the perpetual method and (a) first-in, first-out, (b) last-in, first-out, and (c) weighted-average cost method. Round your final answers to the nearest dollar.

LO6
(Appendix 6A)

E6-10B.   Lower-of-Cost-or-Market (LCM) Method The following data are taken from the Smith & Wesson Corporation's inventory accounts:

LO4

Item Code	Quantity	Unit Cost	Replacement Cost
ZKE.....................................	100	$22	$20
XYF.....................................	300	33	34
MNJ	400	22	20
UBS	200	33	37

Calculate the value of the company's ending inventory using the lower-of-cost-or-market method applied to each item of inventory.

E6-11B.   Inventory Turnover and Days' Sales in Inventory The Northern Company installed a new inventory management system at the beginning of 2012. Shown below are data from the company's accounting records as reported by the new system:

LO5

	2012	2013
Sales revenue...	$9,000,000	$11,000,000
Cost of goods sold.......................................	5,000,000	5,900,000
Beginning inventory	600,000	630,000
Ending inventory..	630,000	700,000

Calculate the company's (a) inventory turnover and (b) days' sales in inventory for 2012 and 2013. Comment on your results.

E6-12B.   The LIFO Inventory Reserve Midwestern Steel Company uses the LIFO inventory costing method to value its ending inventory. The following data were obtained from the company's accounting records for 2012:

LO7
(Appendix 6B)

Current assets (under LIFO)...	$9,000,000
Current liabilities...	7,500,000
Inventory under LIFO	4,000,000
Inventory under FIFO	4,700,000

Calculate the company's (a) LIFO inventory reserve and (b) current ratio assuming (i) FIFO and (ii) LIFO.

E6-13B.   Applying IFRS The French Petroleum Company is a Paris-based oil and gas company that prepares its financial statements using IFRS. During the year, the management of the company undertook a review of the fair value of its oil and gas inventory and found that the inventory had appreciated above its book value of 50 million euros. According to the company's management, the oil and gas inventory was undervalued by 5 million euros. Prepare the journal entry to revalue the company's inventory. How would the revaluation immediately affect the company's (a) current ratio, (b) inventory turnover, and (c) days' sales in inventory?

LO4

E6-14B.   Errors in Inventory Counts The following information was taken from the records of Spencer Enterprises:

LO3

	2013	2012
Beginning inventory	$ 55,000	$ 75,000
Cost of goods purchased...	540,000	500,000
Cost of goods available for sale.......................................	595,000	575,000
Ending inventory..	85,000	55,000
Cost of goods sold..	$510,000	$520,000

The following two errors were made in the physical inventory counts:

1. 2012 ending inventory was overstated by $25,000.
2. 2013 ending inventory was understated by $20,000.

Compute the correct cost of goods sold for both 2012 and 2013.

LO1 **E6-15B. Year-End Physical Inventory** The December 31, inventory for the Simmons Company included five products. The year-end physical count revealed the following quantities on hand:

Product	Quantity Available
K	40
L	36
M	60
N	52
P	55

The related unit costs K, $7; L, $10; M, $8; N, $5; and P, $4.

Required
Calculate the total cost of the December 31, physical inventory.

PROBLEMS—SET A

LO1 **P6-1A. Just-in-Time Inventory** The Dixon Manufacturing Company uses the perpetual inventory system with its raw material inventory. During 2012, Dixon plans to include raw material costing $1,960,000 in the products that it manufactures. John Dixon, president of the company, wants to adopt the just-in-time manufacturing philosophy for the raw materials inventory during 2012. He wants to have only the raw material needed for the next day's production at the end of each day. The factory operates 280 days each year. Historically, the raw materials inventory balance at the end of the day has averaged $50,000 cost. Dixon has an annual inventory carrying cost equal to 20 percent of total inventory cost.

Required
a. What is the anticipated inventory carrying cost (in dollars) if Dixon does not adopt the just-in-time manufacturing philosophy?
b. Calculate the average level (in dollars) for the raw materials inventory if Dixon adopts the just-in-time manufacturing philosophy.
c. Calculate the reductions in the raw materials inventory level and the raw materials inventory annual carrying cost if Dixon adopts the just-in-time manufacturing philosophy.
d. What other factors or situations should Dixon consider before deciding to have only one day's supply of raw material? (*Hint:* Consider factors and situations related to environment, supplier problems, labor problems, etc.)

LO2 **P6-2A. Inventory Costing Methods—Periodic Method** Fortune Stores uses the periodic inventory system for its merchandise inventory. The April 1 inventory for one of the items in the merchandise inventory consisted of 120 units with a unit cost of $325. Transactions for this item during April were as follows:

April 9 Purchased 40 units @ $345 per unit.
14 Sold 80 units @ $550 per unit.
23 Purchased 20 units @ $350 per unit.
29 Sold 40 units @ $550 per unit.

Required
a. Calculate the cost of goods sold and the ending inventory cost for the month of April using the weighted-average cost method. Round your final answers to the nearest dollar.
b. Calculate the cost of goods sold and the ending inventory cost for the month of April using the first-in, first-out method.
c. Calculate the cost of goods sold and the ending inventory cost for the month of April using the last-in, first-out method.

P6-3A. **Inventory Costing Methods—Perpetual Method** Refer to the information in P6-2A and assume the perpetual inventory system is used.

LO6
(Appendix 6A)

Required
a.   Calculate the cost of goods sold and the ending inventory cost for the month of April using the weighted-average cost method.
b.   Calculate the cost of goods sold and the ending inventory cost for the month of April using the first-in, first-out method.
c.   Calculate the cost of goods sold and the ending inventory cost for the month of April using the last-in, first-out method.

P6-4A. **Inventory Costing Methods—Periodic Method** Chen Sales Corporation uses the periodic inventory system. On January 1, 2012, Chen had 1,000 units of product A with a unit cost of $20 per unit. A summary of purchases and sales during 2012 follows:

LO2, 3

	Unit Cost	Units Purchased	Units Sold
Feb. 2			400
Apr. 6	$22	1,800	
July 10			1,600
Aug. 9	26	800	
Oct. 23			800
Dec. 30	29	1,200	

Required
a.   Assume that Chen uses the first-in, first-out method. Compute the cost of goods sold for 2012 and the ending inventory balance at December 31, 2012, for product A.
b.   Assume that Chen uses the last-in, first-out method. Compute the cost of goods sold for 2012 and the ending inventory balance at December 31, 2012, for product A.
c.   Assume that Chen uses the weighted-average cost method. Compute the cost of goods sold for 2012 and the ending inventory balance at December 31, 2012, for product A.
d.   Assuming that Chen's products are perishable items, which of the three inventory costing methods would you choose to:
   1.   Reflect the likely goods flow through the business?
   2.   Minimize income taxes for the period?
   3.   Report the largest amount of net income for the period?
   Explain your answers.

P6-5A. **Inventory Costing Methods—Perpetual Method** Refer to the information in P6-4A and assume the perpetual inventory system is used.

LO6
(Appendix 6A)

Required
a.   Assume that Chen uses the first-in, first-out method. Compute the cost of goods sold for 2012 and the ending inventory balance at December 31, 2012, for product A.
b.   Assume that Chen uses the last-in, first-out method. Compute the cost of goods sold for 2012 and the ending inventory balance at December 31, 2012, for product A.
c.   Assume that Chen uses the weighted-average cost method. Compute the cost of goods sold for 2012 and the ending inventory balance at December 31, 2012, for product A.
d.   Assuming that Chen's products are perishable items, which of the three inventory costing methods would you choose to:
   1.   Reflect the likely goods flow through the business?
   2.   Minimize income taxes for the period?
   3.   Report the largest amount of net income for the period?
   Explain your answers.

P6-6A. **Goods in Transit** The Cardinal Wholesale Company sells merchandise to a variety of retailers. Cardinal uses different freight terms with its various customers and suppliers. All sales are made on account.

LO1

Required

For each of the following transactions, indicate which company has ownership of the goods in transit:

a. Cardinal sold merchandise to X-Mart Stores, with shipping terms of F.O.B. shipping point.

b. Cardinal purchased merchandise from Zendo Manufacturing Company, with shipping terms of F.O.B. destination.

c. Cardinal sold merchandise to Mary's Boutique, with shipping terms of F.O.B. destination.

d. Sunshine Manufacturing Company sold merchandise to Cardinal, with shipping terms of F.O.B. shipping point.

e. Cardinal purchased merchandise from Warfield Manufacturing Company, with freight terms of F.O.B. shipping point.

f. Stevenson Stores purchased merchandise from Cardinal, with shipping terms of F.O.B. shipping point.

LO4 **P6-7A.** **Lower-of-Cost-or-Market (LCM) Method** The Venner Company had the following inventory at year-end:

	Quantity	Unit Price Cost	Unit Price Market
Fans			
Model X1	300	$18	$19
Model X2	250	22	24
Model X3	400	29	26
Heaters			
Model B7	500	24	28
Model B8	290	35	32
Model B9	100	41	38

Required

a. Determine the value of ending inventory after applying the lower-of-cost-or-market method to each item of inventory.

b. Would the net income be lower under the cost method or the lower-of-cost-or-market method?

LO2 **P6-8A.** **Inventory Costing Methods—Periodic Method** The following data are for the Portet Corporation, which sells just one product:

		Units	Unit Cost
Beginning inventory, January 1		1,200	$ 8
Purchases	February 11	1,500	9
	May 18	1,400	10
	October 23	1,100	12
Sales	March 1	1,400	
	July 1	1,400	
	October 29	1,000	

Calculate the value of ending inventory and cost of goods sold at year-end using the periodic method and (a) first-in, first-out, (b) last-in, first-out, and (c) weighted-average cost method. Round the cost per unit to 3 decimal places and round your final answers to the nearest dollar. If the replacement cost of the inventory at year-end is $13, how will the cost of goods sold under each method be affected?

LO6 **P6-9A.** **Inventory Costing Methods—Perpetual Method** Using the data in P6-8A, assume that Portet Cor-
(Appendix 6A) poration uses the perpetual inventory system. Calculate the value of ending inventory and cost of goods sold at year-end using the perpetual method and (a) first-in, first-out, (b) last-in, first-out, and (c) weighted-average cost method. Round the cost per unit to 3 decimal places and round your final answers to the nearest dollar. If the replacement cost of the inventory at year-end is $13, how will the cost of goods sold under each method be affected?

P6-10A. Lower-of-Cost-or-Market (LCM) Method The following data are taken from the Simpson Corporation's inventory accounts:

LO4

Item Code	Quantity	Unit Cost	Replacement Cost
Product 1			
ZKE...	100	$22	$20
ZKF...	300	33	34
Product 2			
MNJ	400	22	19
MNS	200	33	37

Calculate the value of the company's ending inventory using the lower-of-cost-or-market method applied to each item of inventory.

P6-11A. Inventory Turnover and Days' Sales in Inventory The Eastern Corporation installed a new inventory management system at the beginning of 2012. Shown below are data from the company's accounting records as reported by the new system:

LO5

	2012	2013
Sales revenue..	$18,000,000	$20,000,000
Cost of goods sold...	8,000,000	8,900,000
Beginning inventory.......................................	2,500,000	2,530,000
Ending inventory..	2,530,000	2,600,000

Calculate the company's (a) inventory turnover and (b) days' sales in inventory for 2012 and 2013. Comment on your results.

P6-12A. The LIFO Inventory Reserve Waterloo Manufacturing Company uses the LIFO inventory costing method to value its ending inventory. The following data were obtained from the company's accounting records for 2012:

LO7
(Appendix 6B)

Current assets (under FIFO)...............................	$18,000,000
Current liabilities..	15,500,000
Inventory under LIFO	7,000,000
Inventory under FIFO	7,700,000

Calculate the company's (a) LIFO inventory reserve and (b) current ratio assuming (i) FIFO and (ii) LIFO. If the company's LIFO gross profit was $10,000,000 and the change in the LIFO inventory reserve from 2011 to 2012 was $1,200,000, calculate the company's gross profit under FIFO.

P6-13A. Physical Inventory Count and Adjusting Entry Apache Stores conducted a physical inventory at December 31. The items counted during the physical inventory are listed below. Apache's accountant provided the unit costs.

LO1

Item Description	December 31 Count	Unit Cost
Colorado wool sweaters....................................	48	$32
Magnum wool sweaters.....................................	27	34
Johnson jackets..	50	28
Magnum caps..	45	12
Evans caps..	26	10
Colorado shirts..	72	18
Johnson shirts	68	15
Magnum boots...	40	60

Required
Prepare a schedule to determine the total cost of each item in the inventory and the total cost of the complete inventory at December 31.

PROBLEMS—SET B

LO1

P6-1B. **Just-in-Time Inventory** The Field Manufacturing Company uses the perpetual inventory system for its raw materials inventory. During 2012, Field plans to include raw material costing $2,400,000 in the products that it manufactures. Henry Field, president of the company, wants to adopt the just-in-time manufacturing philosophy for the raw materials inventory during 2012. He wants to have only the raw material needed for the next day's production at the end of each day. The factory operates 300 days each year. Historically, the raw materials inventory balance at the end of the day has averaged $60,000 cost. Field has an annual inventory carrying cost equal to 22 percent of total inventory cost.

Required
a. What is the anticipated annual inventory carrying cost (in dollars) if Field does not adopt the just-in-time manufacturing philosophy?
b. Calculate the average level (in dollars) for the raw materials inventory if Field adopts the just-in-time manufacturing philosophy.
c. Calculate the reduction in the raw materials inventory level and the raw materials inventory annual carrying cost if Field adopts the just-in-time manufacturing philosophy.
d. What other factors or situations should Field consider before deciding to have only one day's supply of material? (*Hint:* Consider factors and situations related to environment, supplier problems, labor problems, etc.)

LO2

P6-2B. **Inventory Costing Methods—Periodic Method** The Shiloh Company uses the periodic inventory system for its merchandise inventory. The June 1 inventory for one of the items in the merchandise inventory consisted of 60 units with a unit cost of $40. Transactions for this item during June were as follows:

June   5 Purchased 40 units @ $50 per unit.
    13 Sold 50 units @ $90 per unit.
    25 Purchased 30 units @ $52 per unit.
    29 Sold 20 units @ $100 per unit.

Required
a. Compute the cost of goods sold and the ending inventory cost for the month of June using the weighted-average cost method. Round the cost per unit to 3 decimal places and round your final answers to the nearest dollar.
b. Compute the cost of goods sold and the ending inventory cost for the month of June using the first-in, first-out method.
c. Compute the cost of goods sold and the ending inventory cost for the month of June using the last-in, first-out method.

LO6
(Appendix 6A)

P6-3B. **Inventory Costing Methods—Perpetual Method** Refer to the information in P6-2B and assume the perpetual inventory system is used.

Required
a. Compute the cost of goods sold and the ending inventory cost for the month of June using the weighted-average cost method.
b. Compute the cost of goods sold and the ending inventory cost for the month of June using the first-in, first-out method.
c. Compute the cost of goods sold and the ending inventory cost for the month of June using the last-in, first-out method.

P6-4B. **Inventory Costing Methods—Periodic Method** The Gleem Sales Corporation uses the periodic in-   **LO2, 3**
ventory system. On January 1, 2012, Gleem had 2,600 units of product B with a unit cost of $40 per unit.
A summary of purchases and sales during 2012 follows:

	Unit Cost	Units Purchased	Units Sold
Jan. 3			1,600
Mar. 8	$44	3,000	
June 13.			2,000
Sept. 19	50	800	
Nov. 23.	55	1,200	
Dec. 28.			1,800

Required
a. Assume that Gleem uses the first-in, first-out method. Compute the cost of goods sold for 2012
    and the ending inventory balance at December 31, 2012, for product B.
b. Assume that Gleem uses the last-in, first-out method. Compute the cost of goods sold for 2012
    and the ending inventory balance at December 31, 2012, for product B.
c. Assume that Gleem uses the weighted-average cost method. Compute the cost of goods sold for
    2012 and the ending inventory balance at December 31, 2012, for product B.
d. Assuming that Gleem sells items that quickly become obsolete, which of these three inventory
    costing methods would you choose to:
    1. Reflect the likely goods flow through the business?
    2. Minimize income tax for the period?
    3. To report the largest amount of net income for the period?
    Explain your answers.

P6-5B. **Inventory Costing Methods—Perpetual Method** Refer to the information in P6-4B and assume the   **LO6**
perpetual inventory system is used.   **(Appendix 6A)**

Required
a. Assume that Gleem uses the first-in, first-out method. Compute the cost of goods sold for 2012
    and the ending inventory balance at December 31, 2012, for product B.
b. Assume that Gleem uses the last-in, first-out method. Compute the cost of goods sold for 2012
    and the ending inventory balance at December 31, 2012, for product B.
c. Assume that Gleem uses the weighted-average cost method. Compute the cost of goods sold for
    2012 and the ending inventory balance at December 31, 2012, for product B.
d. Assuming that Gleem sells items that quickly become obsolete, which of these three inventory
    costing methods would you choose to:
    1. Reflect the likely goods flow through the business?
    2. Minimize income tax for the period?
    3. To report the largest amount of net income for the period?
    Explain your answers.

P6-6B. **Goods in Transit** Marshall Distributors sells merchandise to a variety of retailers. Marshall uses dif-   **LO1**
ferent freight terms with its various customers and suppliers. All sales are made on account.

Required
For each of the following transactions, indicate which company has ownership of the goods in transit:
a. Marshall sold merchandise to Clay Boutique, with shipping terms of F.O.B. destination.
b. Marshall purchased merchandise from Campbell Manufacturing Company, with freight terms of
    F.O.B. shipping point.
c. Marshall sold merchandise to Save-A-Lot Stores, with shipping terms of F.O.B. shipping point.
d. Marshall purchased merchandise from Central Manufacturing Company, with shipping terms of
    F.O.B. destination.

e. Levinson Stores purchased merchandise from Marshall, with shipping terms of F.O.B. shipping point.

f. Connor Manufacturing Company sold merchandise to Marshall, with shipping terms of F.O.B. shipping point.

LO4 **P6-7B.** **Lower-of-Cost-or-Market (LCM) Method** The Crane Company had the following inventory at year-end:

		Unit Price	
	Quantity	Cost	Market
Desks			
Model 9001	70	$190	$210
Model 9002	45	280	268
Model 9003	20	350	360
Cabinets			
Model 7001	120	60	64
Model 7002	80	95	88
Model 7003	50	130	126

Required

a. Determine the value of the ending inventory after applying the lower-of-cost-or-market method to each item of inventory.

b. Would the net income be lower under the cost method or the lower-of-cost-or-market method?

LO2 **P6-8B.** **Inventory Costing Methods—Periodic Method** The following data are for the Graham Corporation, which sells just one product:

		Units	Unit Cost
Beginning inventory, January 1		1,200	$18
Purchases	February 11	1,500	19
	May 18	1,400	20
	October 23	1,100	22
Sales	March 1	1,400	
	July 1	1,400	
	October 29	1,000	

Calculate the value of ending inventory and cost of goods sold for the year using the periodic method and (a) first-in, first-out, (b) last-in, first-out, and (c) weighted-average cost method. Round the cost per unit to 3 decimal places and round your final answers to the nearest dollar. If the replacement cost of the inventory at year-end is $23, how will the cost of goods sold under each method be affected?

LO6 **P6-9B.** **Inventory Costing Methods—Perpetual Method** Using the data in P6-8B, assume that Graham
(Appendix 6A) Corporation uses the perpetual inventory system. Calculate the value of ending inventory and cost of goods sold for the year using the perpetual method and (a) first-in, first-out, (b) last-in, first-out, and (c) weighted-average cost method. Round the cost per unit to 3 decimal places and round your final answers to the nearest dollar. If the replacement cost of the inventory at year-end is $23, how will the cost of goods sold under each method be affected?

LO4 **P6-10B.** **Lower-of-Cost-or-Market (LCM) Method** The following data are taken from the Smithfield Corporation's inventory accounts:

Item Code	Quantity	Unit Cost	Replacement Cost
Product 1			
XKE	100	$32	$30
XKF	300	43	44
Product 2			
ZNJ	400	32	29
ZNS	200	43	47

Calculate the value of the company's ending inventory using the lower-of-cost-or-market method applied to each item of inventory.

P6-11B. Inventory Turnover and Days' Sales in Inventory The Western States Corporation installed a new **LO5** inventory management system at the beginning of 2012. Shown below are data from the company's accounting records as reported by the new system:

	2012	2013
Sales revenue	$48,000,000	$40,000,000
Cost of goods sold	28,000,000	28,900,000
Beginning inventory	16,500,000	16,530,000
Ending inventory	16,530,000	20,600,000

Calculate the company's (a) inventory turnover and (b) days' sales in inventory for 2012 and 2013. Comment on your results.

P6-12B. The LIFO Inventory Reserve The Peoria Manufacturing Company uses the LIFO inventory costing **LO7** method to value its ending inventory. The following data were obtained from the company's account- **(Appendix 6B)** ing records for 2012:

Current assets (under LIFO)	$48,000,000
Current liabilities	35,500,000
Inventory under LIFO	15,000,000
Inventory under FIFO	18,700,000

Calculate the company's (a) LIFO inventory reserve and (b) current ratio assuming (i) FIFO and (ii) LIFO. If the company's LIFO gross profit was $18,000,000 and the change in the LIFO inventory reserve from 2011 to 2012 was $2,200,000, calculate the company's gross profit under FIFO.

P6-13B. Physical Inventory Calculations—Periodic System Furniture City conducted a physical inventory **LO1** at December 31. The items counted during the physical inventory are listed below. Furniture City's accountant provided the unit costs.

Item Description	December 31 Count	Unit Cost
Taylor sofas	10	$250
Georgia sofas	8	300
Taylor chairs	22	175
Taylor recliners	12	200
Georgia recliners	4	210
Carolina lamps	16	30
Chicago lamps	18	28
Georgia tables	8	150

Required
Prepare a schedule to determine the total cost of each item in the inventory and the total cost of the complete inventory at December 31.

SERIAL PROBLEM: KATE'S CARDS

(Note: This is a continuation of the Serial Problem: Kate's Cards from Chapters 1 through 5.)

SP6. As expected, the holiday season was very busy for Kate and her greeting card company. In fact, most of her supplies were fully depleted by year-end, necessitating a restocking of inventory. Assume that

Kate uses the periodic method of accounting for inventory and that her January beginning inventory was $0. The following transactions occurred for Kate's Cards during January of the New Year:

Purchases	Units		Unit Cost	Total Cost
Jan. 10	400	@	$3.00 per unit	$1,200
Jan. 17	500	@	$3.50 per unit	1,750
Jan. 23	300	@	$4.00 per unit	1,200
Total	1,200			$4,150

Sales	Units
Jan. 15	360
Jan. 21	420
Jan. 27	380
Total	1,160

Required

a. Calculate the company's cost of goods sold and value of ending inventory for the month of January using (1) FIFO, (2) LIFO, and (3) the weighted-average cost method. Round the cost per unit to 3 decimal places and round your final answers to the nearest dollar.

b. If the replacement cost of Kate's inventory is $4.00 per unit on January 31, what value should be reported for her ending inventory on the January 31 balance sheet under each of the three inventory costing methods?

EXTENDING YOUR KNOWLEDGE

REPORTING AND ANALYSIS

COLUMBIA
SPORTSWEAR
COMPANY

EYK6-1. **Financial Reporting Problem: The Columbia Sportswear Company** The financial statements for the **Columbia Sportswear Company** can be found in Appendix A at the end of this textbook.

Required
Answer the following questions using Columbia's Consolidated Financial Statements:
a. How much inventory does Columbia carry on its balance sheet? What percentage of Columbia's total assets does inventory represent in 2011 and 2010?
b. Compute the inventory turnover and days' sales in inventory for 2011 and 2010. Inventory at December 31, 2009, was $222.2 million.
c. Is Columbia's inventory management improving?

COLUMBIA
SPORTSWEAR
COMPANY

UNDER ARMOUR,
INC.

EYK6-2. **Comparative Analysis Problem: Columbia Sportswear Company vs Under Armour, Inc.** The financial statements for **Columbia Sportswear Company** can be found in Appendix A at the end of this textbook, and the financial statements of **Under Armour, Inc.** can be found in Appendix B.

Required
a. Compare the dollar value of inventory carried on the balance sheet by each company in 2011 and 2010. Which company carries the greatest dollar amount of inventory? Compare the ratio of inventory divided by total assets for each company for 2011 and 2010. Which company carries the largest relative investment in inventory?
b. Calculate the inventory turnover and days' sales in inventory for 2011 and 2010 for each company. Inventory at December 31, 2009, for Columbia and Under Armour, Inc. was $222.2 million and $148.5 million, respectively.
c. Which company appears to be doing the better job of managing its investment in inventory?

EYK6-3. **Business Decision Problem** Mackenzie Company is a wholesaler that uses the perpetual inventory system. On January 1, 2012, Mackenzie had 3,000 units of its product at a cost of $5 per unit. Transactions related to inventory during 2012 were as follows:

Purchases				Sales			
Feb. 5	9,000 units	@	$6	March 8	8,000 units	@	$ 9
May 19	20,000 units	@	7	June 21	19,000 units	@	10
Dec. 15	3,000 units	@	9	Dec. 28	4,000 units	@	12

Mackenzie is trying to decide whether to use the first-in, first-out (FIFO) inventory costing method or the last-in, first-out (LIFO) inventory costing method.

Required
a. Assume that Mackenzie decides to use the FIFO inventory costing method.
   1. What would gross profit be for 2012?
   2. How would Mackenzie's gross profit and ending inventory for 2012 change if the December 15, 2012, purchase had been made on January 3, 2013, instead?
   3. How would Mackenzie's gross profit and ending inventory for 2012 change if the December 15, 2012, purchase had been for 6,000 units instead of 3,000 units?
b. Assume that Mackenzie decides to use the LIFO inventory costing method.
   1. What would gross profit be for 2012?
   2. How would Mackenzie's gross profit and ending inventory for 2012 change if the December 15, 2012, purchase had been made on January 3, 2013, instead?
   3. How would Mackenzie's gross profit and ending inventory for 2012 change if the December 15, 2012, purchase had been for 6,000 units instead of 3,000 units?
c. Which inventory costing method should Mackenzie choose and why?

EYK6-4. **Financial Analysis Problem** Purpose: To use annual financial report filings to learn about how a company accounts for its inventory.

Select any publicly traded company not discussed in this chapter and go to its Website. Find the section on investor information and download its latest annual report (you may download its 10K report rather than the annual report).

Required
Using this report, answer the following questions.
a. What is the name of the company you chose and what is the primary industry that it operates in?
b. Does the company list inventory on its balance sheet? If so, where on the balance sheet does it appear?
c. Does the company have a separate note in the notes to the financial statements that provides a more detailed breakdown of the amount of inventory listed? If so, what is that breakdown?
d. What inventory method does the company use?
e. Calculate the inventory turnover ratio and days' sales in inventory for the most current year shown.

CRITICAL THINKING

EYK6-5. **Accounting Research Problem** The fiscal year 2011 annual report of General Mills, Inc. is available on this book's Website.

GENERAL MILLS, INC.

Required
a. What percentage of total assets are represented by General Mills' investment in inventory in 2011 and 2010?
b. Compute the inventory turnover and days' sales in inventory for General Mills for 2011 and 2010. In 2009, the ending inventory was $1.347 billion.
c. Is the company doing a better job of managing its investment in inventory in 2011?
d. What inventory costing method does General Mills use?
e. What is the value of the company's LIFO reserve at year-end 2011? (Appendix 6B)

PACTIV
CORPORATION

EYK6-6. **Accounting Communications Activity** **Pactiv Corporation** is a leader in the consumer and foodservice packaging market. In December 2009 the company announced a change in the accounting for inventories. www.businesswire.com/news/home/20091221005622/en/Pactiv-Announces-Inventory-Accounting-Change-LIFO-FIFO

Required

Sarah Jenkins, CEO of a competing firm, read this announcement, but was confused about what exactly Pactiv was doing. She asked that you write a memo explaining the following items.

a. What about its accounting for inventory was Pactiv changing?

b. Why does Pactiv believe the new method is preferable?

c. What benefit does Pactiv believe will be realized from the change?

EYK6-7. **Accounting Ethics Case** Reed Kohler is in his final year of employment as controller for Quality Sales Corporation; he hopes to retire next year. As a member of top management, Kohler participates in an attractive company bonus plan. The overall size of the bonus is a function of the firm's net income before bonus and income taxes—the larger the net income, the larger the bonus.

Due to a slowdown in the economy, Quality Sales Corporation has encountered difficulties in managing its cash flow. To improve its cash flow by reducing cash payments for income taxes, the firm's auditors have recommended that the company change its inventory costing method from FIFO to LIFO. This change would cause a significant increase in the cost of goods sold for the year. Kohler believes the firm should not switch to LIFO this year because its inventory quantities are too large. He believes that the firm should work to reduce its inventory quantities and then switch to LIFO (the switch could be made in a year or two). After expressing this opinion to the firm's treasurer, Kohler is stunned when the treasurer replies: "Reed, I can't believe that after all these years with the firm, you put your personal interests ahead of the firm's interests."

Explain why Kohler may be viewed as holding a position that favors his personal interests. What can Kohler do to increase his credibility when the possible change to LIFO is discussed at a meeting of the firm's top management next week?

BEST BUY

EYK6-8. **Corporate Social Responsibility Problem** The Corporate Social Responsibility highlight in this chapter discussed how **Best Buy** is working to make sure its supply chain complies with the company's high ethical standards. One of the ways this is done is for Best Buy's Global Sourcing team to work with their Social and Environmental Responsibility team.

Go to the Best Buy Website and navigate to the section on sustainability, and then locate the section on product stewardship within Best Buy's Sustainability Report. Click on Supply Chain Integrity and explain how their current Factory Audit Program works.

CRAZY EDDIE

COMPTRONIX
CORPORATION

LESLIE FAY
COMPANY

LARIBEE
MANUFACTURING
COMPANY

PHAR-MOR

EYK6-9. **Forensic Accounting Problem** The chapter highlights an inventory fraud case at **Crazy Eddie**. Unfortunately there have been many other serious inventory frauds where the auditors were fooled by illegal acts. A few of these cases include (1) **Comptronix Corporation**, (2) **Leslie Fay Company**, (3) **Laribee Manufacturing Company**, and (4) **Phar-Mor** drug stores.

Do a computer search of one of these cases and explain how inventory was used to commit the fraud. List some ways the auditors can lessen the chance such frauds could go undetected.

LO5

IFRS

EYK6-10. **Inventory Turnover and Days' Sales in Inventory: IFRS Financial Statements** Tesco PLC is the world's third largest retailer and is based in the United Kingdom. Tesco's IFRS financial statements are presented in Appendix C at the end of this textbook. Using these financial statements, calculate the company's (a) inventory turnover and (b) days' sales in inventory for 2010 and 2011. Tesco's 2009 ending inventory was 2,669 million British pounds. Comment on the company's trend in inventory management effectiveness.

LO7
(Appendix 6B)

EYK6-11. **Working with the Takeaways** Felix Company uses the LIFO inventory costing method to value inventory. The following financial data was obtained from its accounting records for the current year:

Current assets (including inventory)	$4,000
Current liabilities	2,000
Inventory under LIFO	575
Inventory under FIFO	775

Compute (a) the current ratio assuming (i) LIFO and (ii) FIFO and (b) the LIFO inventory reserve.

ANSWERS TO SELF-STUDY QUESTIONS:

1. b, (p. 265)   2. d, (p. 271)   3. c, (pp. 273–274)   4. b, (p. 266)   5. d, (pp. 278–279)   6. c, (pp. 273–274)
7. a, (p. 273)   8. b, (p. 274)   9. d, (p. 275)   10. d, (pp. 278–279)   11. b, (p. 280)   12. c, (p. 289)
13. b, (p. 289)

YOUR TURN! SOLUTIONS

Solution 6.1

The $15,000 of goods shipped F.O.B. shipping point should be deducted from the inventory valuation, and the $25,000 of consignment goods should be included in the inventory valuation. The corrected ending inventory total should be $310,000 ($300,000 − $15,000 + $25,000).

Solution 6.2

a. Ending inventory using:
   i. FIFO: 1,000 × $7 = $7,000
   ii. LIFO: 1,000 × $5 = $5,000
   iii. Weighted-average cost: 1,000 × [(4,000 × $5) + (6,000 × $7)]/10,000 = 1,000 × $6.20 = $6,200

b. Cost of goods sold using:
   i. FIFO: (4,000 × $5) + (5,000 × $7) = $55,000
   ii. LIFO: (6,000 × $7) + (3,000 × $5) = $57,000
   iii. Weighted-average cost: 9,000 × [(4,000 × $5) + (6,000 × $7)]/10,000 = 9,000 × $6.20 = $55,800

c. Gross profit using:
   i. FIFO: $90,000 − $55,000 = $35,000
   ii. LIFO: $90,000 − $57,000 = $33,000
   iii. Weighted-average cost: $90,000 − $55,800 = $34,200

Solution 6.3

The lowest value for each inventory item is: DSLR $110,000, Point and Shoot $73,000, and Camcorders $48,000. The total of the inventory is therefore valued under LCM at $231,000 ($110,000 + $73,000 + $48,000).

Solution 6.4

	2012	2013
Inventory turnover	$\dfrac{\$2,000,000}{(\$450,000 + \$430,000)/2} = 4.55$	$\dfrac{\$2,300,000}{(\$430,000 + \$320,000)/2} = 6.13$
Days' sales in inventory	365/4.55 = 80.22 days	365/6.13 = 59.54 days

The company increased its sales by $400,000 from 2012 to 2013, and at the same time, decreased its average inventory by $65,000 ($440,000 − $375,000) as a consequence of improved inventory management. This resulted in a significantly improved inventory turnover (6.13 versus 4.55) and 20.68 (80.22 − 59.54) less days' sales in inventory. It appears that the new inventory management system is a financial success.

7

Internal Control and Cash

PAST

Chapter 6 explained the accounting for inventory. We described and applied the costing methods of specific identification, FIFO, LIFO, and weighted-average.

PRESENT

In this chapter, we focus our attention on another current asset, cash. In addition, we study how internal control can be used to prevent errors and fraud associated with assets such as cash and inventory.

FUTURE

Chapter 8 explains the accounting for accounts and notes receivable. We will explain the reporting of uncollectible accounts and how managers monitor such accounts.

LEARNING OBJECTIVES

1. **Define** the three elements of fraud and **discuss** the role of internal control in a business to prevent fraud. *(p. 314)*

2. **Define** cash and **discuss** the accounting for cash. *(p. 321)*

3. **Describe** the internal controls for cash. *(p. 323)*

4. **Describe** the four primary activities of effective cash management. *(p. 334)*

5. Appendix 7A **Describe** financial statement audits and operational audits. *(p. 336)*

BERNARD L. MADOFF INVESTMENT SECURITIES LLC

The collapse and subsequent bankruptcy of **Enron Corporation** in 2001 was the largest bankruptcy in American history at the time. The losses were staggering, with stockholders losing over $70 billion. The demise of Enron, mostly attributed to a massive accounting scandal, contributed to the downfall of Arthur Anderson; one of the five largest accounting firms in the world and the independent auditor for Enron.

Enron's collapse was followed by the passage of the landmark **Sarbanes-Oxley Act** in 2002; legislation aimed at preventing another Enron-type accounting scandal. A major provision of the Act requires that senior management certify the adequacy of a company's internal controls and that the external auditors provide an opinion as to the adequacy of those internal controls. The factors required to be reported include the controls to prevent or detect fraud and the controls over the financial reporting process.

It wasn't supposed to happen again. At least that is what most of us thought after the regulations put in place after Enron and the other large accounting scandals in the early years of the decade. Then, in March of 2009, **Bernard Madoff** pleaded guilty to 11 federal felonies for defrauding thousands of investors in his wealth management company. Madoff was convicted of fraud and was sentenced to 150 years in prison. Madoff ran what turned out to be a giant Ponzi scheme in which funds from new investors were used to pay high returns to prior investors. In retrospect, Madoff never should have been able to get away with this fraud for so long. In fact several red flags led financial analyst Harry Markopolos to report Madoff to the SEC; claiming the returns provided by Madoff were not possible. Madoff's company was audited by a one-person accounting firm whose sole accountant was a close family friend of Madoff and an investor in Madoff's fund. Despite the regulations put in place to prevent accounting fraud, Madoff's fraud left investors with billions of dollars in losses and the dubious honor of being named one of the top ten accounting scandals of all time.

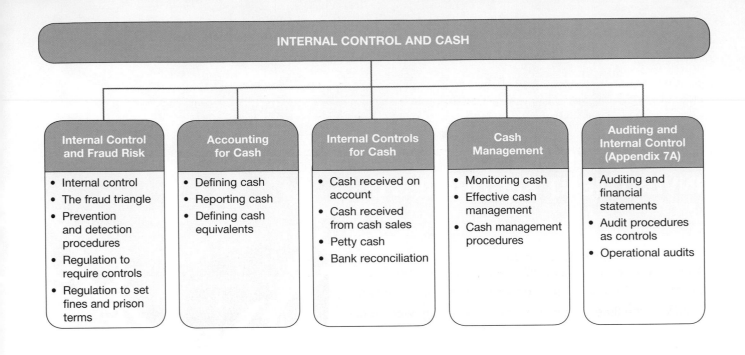

INTERNAL CONTROL AND CASH				
Internal Control and Fraud Risk	**Accounting for Cash**	**Internal Controls for Cash**	**Cash Management**	**Auditing and Internal Control (Appendix 7A)**
• Internal control • The fraud triangle • Prevention and detection procedures • Regulation to require controls • Regulation to set fines and prison terms	• Defining cash • Reporting cash • Defining cash equivalents	• Cash received on account • Cash received from cash sales • Petty cash • Bank reconciliation	• Monitoring cash • Effective cash management • Cash management procedures	• Auditing and financial statements • Audit procedures as controls • Operational audits

INTERNAL CONTROL

LO1 **Define** the three elements of fraud and **discuss** the role of internal control in a business to prevent fraud.

The feature story involving **Enron Corporation** and **Madoff Investment Securities LLC** illustrate the potential cost that fraud can have on so many people. Unfortunately, it is nearly impossible to completely prevent fraud; however, we do know much about why fraud is committed and what can be done to lower the risk of it occurring. Research has shown that any individual, under the right circumstances, can commit fraud. This does not mean, however, that everyone will commit fraud. What it does mean is that it is very difficult to determine prior to the commission of a fraud exactly which employee will be the one to commit fraud.

Fraud refers to any act by the management or employees of a business involving an intentional deception for personal gain. Fraud may include, among other acts, embezzlement of a business's cash, theft of assets, filing false insurance claims, filing false health claims, and financial statement fraud. Fraud is a punishable crime and is also a violation of civil law. Research has shown that three elements are almost always present when a fraud occurs. These elements are often referred to as the **fraud triangle** and include (1) a perceived pressure, (2) some way to rationalize the fraudulent act, and (3) a perceived opportunity. Reducing or suppressing any of the three elements of the fraud triangle reduces the likelihood of fraud occurring in a business.

Unfortunately, the fraud triangle is not well understood. Because of this, nearly all fraud prevention efforts by businesses are devoted to the third element—reducing the opportunity to commit fraud. As we will discuss in this chapter, this often involves implementing a system of internal control, including such measures as physical control over cash and proper authorization over cash disbursements. Too often, little effort is expended on the other elements of fraud even though it has been shown that efforts in any one area can reduce the effort needed in the other two areas.

Pressure

Pressure can be divided into several categories, but research has shown that nearly all frauds are committed by individuals who feel perceived pressure from some sort of financial need. Financial pressure could come from living beyond one's means and being unable to pay one's bills, experiencing large medical bills, or the financial pressure from vices like gambling, drugs or alcohol. The latter pressure is sometimes referred to as vice pressure.

Financial statement fraud, such as the overstatement of revenues or the understatement of expenses, usually occurs because of pressure on management to "make the numbers," either to satisfy Wall Street analyst expectations or to attain a company-sponsored monetary bonus.

While it is not possible to completely eliminate this element of fraud, numerous methods have proven successful at lowering the risk of financial statement fraud. An obvious action is to perform careful personnel screening before hiring any employee to reduce the likelihood of employing individuals with known histories of fraud.

Rationalization

Very few individuals want to commit fraud since they recognize that it is wrong. In order to overcome this tremendous feeling of guilt, most employees need to come up with some form of rationalization so that they can live with the knowledge of what they did. Common rationalizations include such attitudes as (1) I am underpaid and the company owes it to me; (2) Everyone else is doing it; or (3) I am only borrowing the money and I will pay it back later.

The best way to reduce this element of fraud is to create an environment in which it is difficult to rationalize unethical behavior. A company that promotes a culture of honesty and integrity, within which unethical behavior is considered unacceptable, is much less likely to encounter fraudulent behavior by management or its employees. The key to building organization-wide attitudes regarding ethical behavior starts with the "tone at the top"—that is, the behaviors and attitudes displayed by a company's CEO or president.

Opportunity

The third element of the fraud triangle is perceived opportunity. An individual will only attempt to commit a fraud if he or she perceives that there is an opportunity to succeed. Of course this element is related to the other two elements. For example, if an employee is under tremendous pressure either at work or outside the workplace, he may attempt to commit a fraud even if he perceives only a small chance of success, while an individual under much less pressure will likely only attempt the fraud if it is perceived to be easy to commit.

Governance and Conflicts of Interest	CORPORATE SOCIAL RESPONSIBILITY

Much of what was done at **Enron** was perfectly legal. Enron's management became very skilled at staying within the letter of the law, even if it meant violating the spirit of the law. Examples include the use of specialized accounting rules that allowed Enron to mask the true level of its debt so that financial statement users would be unable to obtain a transparent view of the company's financial position. Top executives at Enron created a culture of deceit within the company that provided employees with an easy rationalization for their own misdeeds. Corporate Social Responsibility, by way of contrast, espouses the notion that not only is it important to make money, but it is important to do so in a responsible way. Cutting corners and playing fast and loose with the rules may work in the short term, but it is not sustainable as the Enron saga reveals. Creating a culture of ethical behavior within a business is perhaps the most important internal control that exists to not only prevent fraud, but to provide a foundation for a sustainable enterprise.

The accounting system represents a cornerstone of the control environment that is necessary to reduce the opportunity for, and success of, fraudulent behavior. A critical aspect of the accounting system is a strong system of internal control. **Internal controls** are the measures undertaken by a business to ensure the reliability of its accounting data, protect its assets from theft or unauthorized use, ensure that employees are following the company's policies and procedures, and evaluate the performance of employees, departments, divisions, and the company as a whole. A company implements internal controls to improve the chances that employees will function according to the plans and standard operating procedures developed by the management team. Internal controls are meant to reduce the likelihood that errors will occur, and if they do occur, that any errors will be caught.

Management is responsible for designing, installing, and monitoring internal controls throughout a business. In designing the controls, management tries to attain "reasonable assurance," rather than "absolute assurance," that the controls will meet their objectives.

Internal control exists in many forms, including policies, standard operating procedures, records, equipment, supervision, and insurance. An internal control can be either a prevention control or a detection control. A **prevention control** is intended to deter a problem or fraud before it can arise. A **detection control**, on the other hand, is designed to discover any problems or fraud shortly after it arises. Prevention controls are generally more desirable and preferred than detection controls, reflecting the old saying that "an ounce of prevention is worth a pound of detection."

A company should incorporate the following elements when it designs its prevention and detection controls:

1. Establish clear lines of authority and responsibility.
2. Implement segregation of duties.
3. Hire competent personnel.
4. Use control numbers on all business documents.
5. Develop plans and budgets.
6. Maintain adequate accounting records.
7. Provide physical and electronic controls.
8. Conduct internal audits.

We consider each of these elements in the following paragraphs and provide examples of their use.

1. Establish Clear Lines of Authority and Responsibility

The organizational structure of a company defines the lines of authority and responsibility within the company. When a company assigns authority to an employee to perform certain functions, it also makes that employee responsible for accomplishing certain objectives. This structure provides the overall framework for planning, directing, and controlling the company's operations. It informs employees about who is in charge of which functions and to whom each person reports.

Supervision is an important internal control. The existence of an identified supervisor is a preventive control. Employees know that the supervisor is evaluating their performance; consequently, they are more likely to perform according to a company's established policies and rules. Supervision is also a detection control. A supervisor is likely to discover errors or irregularities when he or she reviews the work performance of employees.

Management must also make sure that all employees understand a company's philosophy and operating style as well as the authority and responsibility relationships. To guide employees in performing their duties, top management should develop written policy statements, procedure manuals, and job descriptions.

| Proper Authorization as an Internal Control | ACCOUNTING IN PRACTICE |

It is important that proper authorization be maintained, and this means that only those employees with proper authorization should be given access to items that they have the authority to possess. In one documented case, over $900,000 was stolen from a business because of a breach of this internal control. In this particular case, the defrauded company went to considerable lengths to maintain proper authorization to access its automated payment system. This involved, among other things, authorized users obtaining a special code that could be used only once from the internal control register clerk. Unfortunately, the control was circumvented when a charismatic employee gained the trust of fellow employees, including the internal control register clerk. The employee explained to the clerk that one of the authorized users had asked him to pick up access codes for him. The employee then went on to use the codes to access the system, submitting false documents for building maintenance services and eventually stealing over $900,000 from the company.

Source: Davia, *Fraud 101* (2000), pp. 45-46.

2. Implement Segregation of Duties

Segregation of duties requires that when allocating various duties within the accounting system, management should make sure that no employee is assigned too many different responsibilities. As a general rule, no individual employee should be able to perpetrate and conceal irregularities in the transaction processing system. To accomplish this, management must separate three functions: the authorization function, the recording function, and the custody function. Ideally, for any particular transaction, an individual employee should have the authority to perform only one of the three functions.

For example, if an employee "authorizes" a sales transaction by approving a customer's credit, that employee should not "record" the transaction in the accounting records or have physical "custody" of the merchandise sold or the cash received from the customer. This separation of duties is an important preventive control. When an employee prepares a purchase order to buy merchandise, that employee is effectively "authorizing" the transaction. When the merchandise is received, a second employee should prepare the receiving report when he or she gains "custody" of the merchandise. And, neither of these two employees should be allowed to "record" either the purchase order, the receipt of the merchandise, or the payment of cash for the goods in the accounting records. The separation of work functions in this manner will reduce the likelihood of fraud occurring because committing a fraud when work duties are separated requires collusion among multiple employees.

| Segregation of Duties Functions as an Internal Control | ACCOUNTING IN PRACTICE |

In a case of a company giving a salesman too much responsibility, an advertising salesman not only sold the ads, but also had the authority to bill the customer and collect on the accounts receivable. In addition, the salesman was authorized to offer discounts to customers. This authority proved too much of a temptation, and resulted in free travel, lodging, and other gifts in return for greatly reduced, and sometimes even free, ads. In total, it was determined that the salesman gave away over $20,000 in advertising revenues in return for the bribes that he was given.

Source: Wells, *Principles of Fraud Examination* (2005), p. 264.

3. Hire Competent Personnel

Because people are the most important element of an accounting system, it is vital that a company hire competent personnel. Management must screen each job applicant to determine that he or she has sufficient education, training, and experience to qualify for the job. After hiring an employee, the company should provide specific formal training so that the employee is able to complete all of the tasks that the job requires. The training should refer to written policy statements, procedure manuals, and job descriptions so that the employee can become familiar with all aspects and expectations of his or her job.

Some companies routinely rotate personnel among various jobs. For example, a company might switch jobs between an employee working exclusively with the accounts receivable and an employee working exclusively with accounts payable. This rotation may disclose errors or irregularities resulting from over-familiarity with a job or just carelessness. Requiring employees to take vacations of at least one week in duration may also disclose errors or irregularities when another employee performs the vacationing employee's duties.

ACCOUNTING IN PRACTICE	**Job Rotation and Mandatory Vacations as Internal Controls**

Job rotation and mandatory vacations is one of the best internal controls for uncovering fraud. For many frauds, it is necessary for the perpetrator to actively cover up their misdeeds through the falsification of accounting records. Requiring job rotation and vacations allows another employee to perform these job responsibilities, often leading to the discovery of fraud. And you thought your employer was only giving you that vacation to be nice!

Source: Association of Certified Fraud Examiners 2008 Report.

4. Use Control Numbers on All Business Documents

All business documents such as purchase orders, sales invoices, credit memos, and checks should have **control numbers** preprinted on them. Each control number should be unique for that type of document. For example, the bank checks that you use to pay your personal expenses have control numbers on them, usually in the upper right-hand corner of the check, referred to as a *check number*. These numbers are an internal control enabling you to track each check written, and to insure that no one has written an improper check against your account.

To provide proper control to the accounting process, a company should use the following three rules related to control numbers on business documents. First, have a commercial printer place the control numbers on the documents when they are printed. Second, use the documents in strict numerical sequence. That is, use check number 101 first, then check 102, then 103, and so on. Third, for each type of business document, periodically account for all the numbers in the sequence to make sure that all were processed. Use of control numbers with this type of reconciliation helps to ensure that a company records all transactions and does not record a transaction multiple times.

5. Develop Plans and Budgets

Top management should initiate the planning and budgeting process to establish forward thinking about the business and to provide a basis for evaluating department and employee performance. Every company should prepare an annual operating plan and budget. These items provide guidance for all levels of management regarding how to respond to various situations. The **budget** also provides a basis for comparing actual operating results to planned results when management evaluates operating unit performance. An example of evaluating performance involves comparing the actual advertising expense to the budgeted advertising expense. When variances between actual and budgeted amounts are observed, those variances should be investigated by management. This type of internal control is both a prevention control and a detection control.

6. Maintain Adequate Accounting Records

Previously we discussed a number of internal controls that help ensure that a business has adequate accounting records. These controls include using the double-entry approach to record transactions (debits must equal credits), preparing trial balances (total debits must equal total credits), and taking a physical count of the inventory on hand (physical inventory total should equal perpetual inventory total).

Many internal controls related to maintaining accurate accounting records involve comparisons of various amounts. For instance, each business should periodically make a physical inspection of its plant assets to compare the data in the plant assets' ledger account to the plant assets actually in use. This inspection identifies any missing assets and any assets not recorded in the asset account. Similarly, a business should periodically confirm the amounts owed to suppliers (Accounts Payable) and the amounts due from customers (Accounts Receivable) by contacting the suppliers and customers to verify any amounts owing and to be received. This internal control process is known as accounts receivable confirmation and accounts payable confirmation.

7. Provide Physical and Electronic Controls

Physical and electronic controls take many forms. Locked doors are an important physical control. Locked doors help prevent the theft of assets and protect the integrity of the accounting system. Many companies install safes and vaults to store cash prior to depositing it in a bank and to hold important business documents such as mortgages and securities. Any installed safes and vaults should be of sufficient quality that they can withstand fire and such natural disasters as flooding and tornados. Fencing off company property and assigning security guards at the gates are other commonly used physical controls.

Physical Control of Assets as an Internal Control	**ACCOUNTING IN PRACTICE**

Failure to adequately maintain physical control of assets is especially risky when it comes to items like cash. In one documented case, checks were left overnight on the desks of employees because processing was not complete. This proved too tempting of a target for a member of the overnight janitorial cleaning crew. The janitor found the checks, forged the endorsements of the payees, and then cashed the checks at a local liquor store.

Source: Wells, *Principles of Fraud Examination* (2005), p. 139.

Electronic controls are also widely used by businesses. Merchandising firms use electronic cash registers to ensure that each salesperson records each transaction as it occurs and that the salesperson stores cash in a locked drawer. Retailers, convenience stores, and banks use observation cameras to monitor their operations. Retailers also attach special plastic tags to merchandise, which activate electronic sensors and set off alarms if an individual attempts to leave a store without having the plastic tag removed by a salesperson.

8. Conduct Internal Audits

In a small company, internal auditing is a function typically assigned to an employee who has other duties as well. In a large company, internal auditing is an activity assigned to an independent department that reports to top management or the board of directors of the corporation. **Internal auditing** is a company function that provides independent appraisals of the company's financial statements, its internal control, and its operations.

The evaluation of a company's internal control involves two phases. First, the internal auditor determines whether sufficient internal controls are in place. Second, the internal auditor determines whether the internal controls in place are actually functioning as planned. After completing the appraisal, the internal auditor makes recommendations to management regarding additional controls that are needed or improvements that are required for existing controls.

ACCOUNTING IN PRACTICE	**Internal Audit as an Internal Control**

Sometimes it takes a little luck to uncover a fraud; however, having a strong internal audit department helps that luck to happen. That was exactly the case at **Deerfield College's School of Dentistry**, when a married supervisor in the business office took his girlfriend on a business trip using school funds. In order to cover up the identity of his actual traveling partner, the supervisor unwisely named a senior internal control auditor as the person he was traveling with. As luck would have it, the named auditor was the individual who reviewed the bogus travel report as part of a routine audit of employee expense reports. Because of the unexpected discovery, a larger audit was performed on the business office. During the audit, a much larger unrelated fraud was discovered involving an administrative assistant who had been issuing checks to a bogus vendor and taking the money for herself. The administrative assistant had a drug addiction and was under tremendous pressure to pay for her habit.

Source: McNeal, One fraud leads to another, *Internal Auditor Magazine,* December 2008.

Control Failures

Occasionally, internal controls fail. For example, an employee may forget to lock an exterior door and a thief will steal some merchandise. Or, an employee with custody responsibilities steals cash received from customers. A company cannot completely prevent these types of incidents from occurring. Consequently, many businesses purchase insurance to compensate the company if any of these types of incidents do occur. Casualty insurance provides financial compensation to a business for losses from fire, natural disasters, and theft. A **fidelity bond** is an insurance policy that provides financial compensation for theft by employees specifically covered by the insurance.

Another reason that internal controls fail is **employee collusion**. When two or more employees work together to circumvent or avoid prescribed internal controls, this act is known as *employee collusion.* For example, an employee with custody of an asset (like cash) can work with an employee with recording responsibilities to steal the asset and cover up the theft in the accounting records. Employee collusion is difficult to prevent or detect. Hiring high-quality employees and paying them market wages is the best approach to avoid collusion. Close employee supervision is also important.

THINKING GLOBALLY	

While it might appear that financial fraud occurs only in the United States, that is far from the truth. In 2003, the Italian agricultural conglomerate **Parmalat SpA** filed for bankruptcy after revealing that it had massively underreported its outstanding net debt—that is, its debt minus its liquid current assets—by approximately $16 billion. The financial fraud had been perpetuated for over a decade and had gone undetected by the company's independent auditor, **Grant Thorton**. The underreporting of Parmalat's net debt had been achieved by overreporting the amount of cash on hand and by retaining worthless accounts receivable on the company's balance sheet. In a similar situation, in 2008, India's leading software services firm, **Satyam Computer Services**, was found to have defrauded stockholders for over a decade by overstating the company's revenues and its cash by over $1 billion. The company's independent auditors, **PricewaterhouseCoopers**, were arrested shortly thereafter on charges of being an accomplice to the financial fraud.

As with employee collusion, senior management can often circumvent internal controls. Additionally, in small companies where proper segregation of duties is not possible, the owner must serve as the mitigating control. This requires the owner to be present most of the time and also provides opportunity for the owner to circumvent internal controls. The opening vignette about Bernard Madoff's Ponzi scheme provides an illustration of what can happen when upper management proves to be dishonest.

The Sarbanes-Oxley Act

For public companies, strong internal control like that described above is no longer simply a matter of good business practice, it is required by law. Following the **Enron** and **WorldCom** accounting scandals, the U.S. Congress passed landmark legislation called the Sarbanes-Oxley Act (SOX). This Act mandates that all publicly traded U.S. corporations maintain an adequate system of internal control. Further, top management must ensure the reliability of these controls and outside independent auditors must attest to the adequacy of the controls. Failing to do so can result in prison sentences of up to 20 years and/or monetary fines of up to $5 million.

Identify which internal control concept is being violated and explain how this may cause an opportunity for fraud to occur within a business:

1. The supervisor for the purchasing department has not taken a vacation in three years.
2. Inventory is left in a receiving area at the back of the store by an open door.
3. The purchasing supervisor has the authority to order a purchase and also to receive the merchandise, record its receipt, and authorize the accounting department to issue a check.
4. Order slips are used to order meals at a restaurant; however, the slips are not prenumbered.

YOUR TURN! 7.1

The solution is on pages 357–358.

Concept	Method	Assessment	TAKEAWAY 7.1
Are the internal controls adequate?	Independent auditors' attestation report. The principles of good internal control include: (1) Establish clear lines of authority and responsibility; (2) Segregation of duties; (3) Hire competent personnel; (4) Use control numbers on all business documents; (5) Develop plans and budgets; (6) Maintain adequate accounting records; (7) Provide physical and electronic controls; (8) Conduct internal audits.	Be sure that the report does not indicate any weaknesses in the company's internal control. If weaknesses are reported, be cautious in relying on the reported financial statements.	

ACCOUNTING FOR CASH

Cash includes coins, currency (paper money), checks, money orders, traveler's checks, and funds on deposit at a financial institution in a company's checking accounts and savings accounts. An item is considered to be an element of cash if (1) it is accepted by a bank or other financial institution (brokerage firm or credit union) for deposit, and (2) it is free from restrictions that would prevent its use for paying debts.

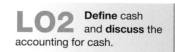

LO2 Define cash and **discuss** the accounting for cash.

Many near-cash items such as certificates of deposit, postdated checks, not-sufficient-funds checks, and IOUs are not considered to be cash. **Certificates of deposit** (CDs) are securities issued by a bank when cash is invested for a short period of time, typically three months to one year. CDs pay a fixed rate of interest on any deposited funds. A **postdated check** is a check from another person or company with a date that is later than the current date. A postdated check does not become equivalent to cash until the actual calendar date on the check. A **not-sufficient-funds check** (NSF check) is a check from an individual or company that had an insufficient cash balance in the bank when the holder of the check presented it to the bank for payment. IOU is a slang term for a note receivable—that is, a written document that states that one party promises to pay another party a certain amount of cash on a certain date. CDs are accounted for as investments, whereas post-dated checks, NSF checks, and IOUs are accounted for as Other Receivables.

Reporting Cash

A company may have only one Cash account in the general ledger or it may have multiple cash accounts, such as Cash in Bank, Cash on Hand, and Petty Cash. Cash in Bank includes any cash held in a company's checking accounts and savings accounts, while Cash on Hand includes cash items not yet deposited in the bank. Petty Cash is an example of cash on hand that is used for small disbursements and is maintained at the company's business location.

When a company has several bank accounts, it may maintain a separate general ledger account for each account or use a single Cash in Bank account. Although a company may prepare for internal use only a balance sheet that shows each individual bank account separately, the balance sheet that the company prepares for external users typically shows the combined balances of all bank accounts and other cash accounts under a single heading of Cash. Management is likely to want to see the detail involving the multiple cash accounts that the company maintains so that it can monitor and control the various accounts and on hand amounts. Most external users, however, are only interested in the total amount of cash and its relationship to other items on the balance sheet.

ACCOUNTING IN PRACTICE	Balance Sheet Title for Cash

Cash is cash, or is it? Companies often include many other items, such as certificates of deposit, that are very similar to cash in their Cash account. Companies also vary in the title they use for their Cash account on their balance sheet. In fact, Cash is not the most common term used. Cash and Cash Equivalents is by far the most commonly used label. The following table identifies the label used by a sample of 600 large U.S. firms for their Cash account on the balance sheet:

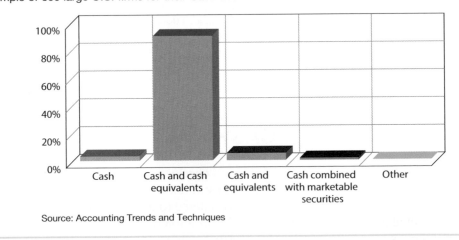

Source: Accounting Trends and Techniques

Cash is a current asset and is shown first in the balance sheet listing of assets. Some of a company's cash may be **restricted cash**, in which case it is restricted for a special purpose. For example, a company may have a restriction on its cash to cover a litigation settlement. Restricted cash should be reported separately on the balance sheet as either a current or noncurrent asset depending on the length of the restriction. Sometimes a company's total cash includes one or more compensating balances. A **compensating balance** is a minimum cash balance that a bank requires a firm to maintain in its bank account as part of a borrowing arrangement. Compensating balances related to short-term borrowings are current assets, which, if significant, are reported separately from the cash amount among the current assets. Compensating balances related to long-term borrowings are reported as long-term assets.

Cash and Cash Equivalents

A company may combine certain short-term, highly liquid investments with cash and present a single amount called **cash and cash equivalents** on the balance sheet. Cash equivalents are highly liquid, short-term investments of 90 days maturity or less in such risk-free securities as U.S. Treasury bills and money market funds. A company presents this combined amount on the balance sheet so that it reconciles with the change in cash and cash equivalents appearing on the company's statement of cash flows. The statement of cash flows explains the changes in a firm's total cash and cash equivalents during an accounting period.

Concept	Method	Assessment	TAKEAWAY 7.2
Are there any restrictions on a company's use of its cash and cash equivalents?	Balance sheet and the notes to the financial statements. Are there any restrictions to cash or compensating cash balances reported?	Any assessments of liquidity should consider any existing cash restrictions.	

INTERNAL CONTROL OF CASH RECEIPTS TRANSACTIONS

Most companies develop elaborate internal controls to protect their cash because it is their most liquid asset, and in all likelihood, their most important asset. Cash is highly desirable, easily taken and concealed, and quickly converted into other assets. In addition, a high percentage of a company's transactions involve cash. Cash is received from customers following a sale and cash is paid to suppliers and employees for goods and services. A company receives cash from customers, for example, as payment on account and as payment for cash sales. The following sections describe cash handling procedures and the related internal controls for these two types of cash receipts.

LO3 Describe the internal controls for cash.

Cash Received on Account

A company receives cash through the mail from customers who are making payments on their accounts receivable balance. Four departments play major roles in processing cash receipts that arrive via the mail: the mailroom, the treasurer's department, the controller's department, and the internal audit department. Exhibit 7-1 and the following paragraphs describe the role that each department plays in processing mailed cash receipts.

Mailroom

A company often sets up a separate post office box and requests that its customers mail any cash payments on account to that post office box. All other mail and company correspondence are directed to another company address or a different post office box. This approach automatically sorts a company's mail into two groups: (1) cash receipts from customers and (2) all other mail.

Mailroom employees open the envelopes containing cash receipts from customers. Each envelope should contain two items: a check and a remittance advice. A **remittance advice** is a form that accompanies a check to inform the company receiving the check about the purpose of the check. The remittance advice includes the customer's name, the amount paid, and such reference numbers as the invoice number and the customer account number.

Mailroom employees ensure that the dollar amount on each check and the related remittance advice are the same and then place the two documents in separate piles. An employee then endorses each check "For Deposit Only" so that no one can cash the check. The mailroom employees also prepare a remittance list. A **remittance list** is a list of all of the checks received on a given day. For each check, the remittance list includes the customer name and/or account number, the check number, and the amount received.

Exhibit 7-1	Processing Cash Received on Account Through the Mail

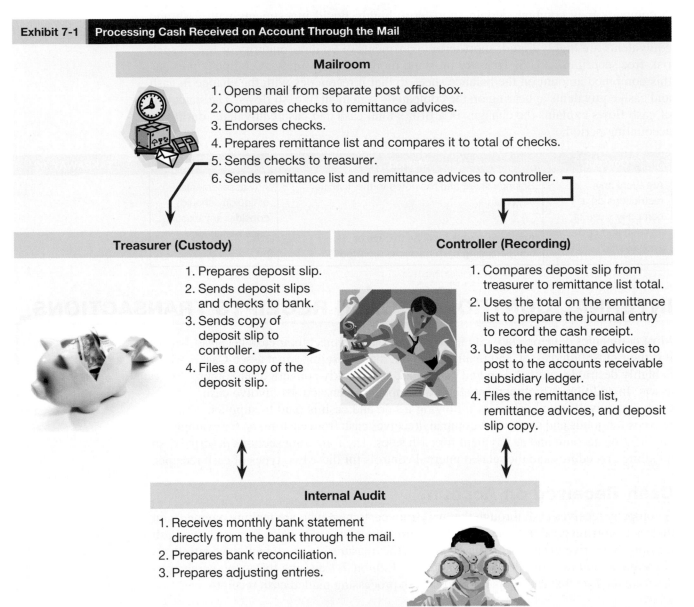

Mailroom
1. Opens mail from separate post office box.
2. Compares checks to remittance advices.
3. Endorses checks.
4. Prepares remittance list and compares it to total of checks.
5. Sends checks to treasurer.
6. Sends remittance list and remittance advices to controller.

Treasurer (Custody)
1. Prepares deposit slip.
2. Sends deposit slips and checks to bank.
3. Sends copy of deposit slip to controller.
4. Files a copy of the deposit slip.

Controller (Recording)
1. Compares deposit slip from treasurer to remittance list total.
2. Uses the total on the remittance list to prepare the journal entry to record the cash receipt.
3. Uses the remittance advices to post to the accounts receivable subsidiary ledger.
4. Files the remittance list, remittance advices, and deposit slip copy.

Internal Audit
1. Receives monthly bank statement directly from the bank through the mail.
2. Prepares bank reconciliation.
3. Prepares adjusting entries.

A separate mailroom employee compares the remittance list total to a list totaling the checks and another list totaling the remittance advices to ensure that the check amounts are listed correctly and that they agree with the remittance advices. The mailroom then sends the checks to the treasurer's department and the remittance list and the remittance advices to the controller's department.

Treasurer
The treasurer's department is a *custodial* department. It maintains custody of the received customer checks. *It has no responsibilities for any recording or posting activities.* The

duties of this department include preparing a bank deposit slip (original plus two copies) for each batch of checks received and sending the original deposit slip and the customer checks to the bank. One copy of the deposit slip is forwarded to the controller's department; and, the treasurer's department files the second copy for future reference.

Controller

The controller's department is a *recording* department. It records the cash receipts in a journal and posts the cash receipts to the company's general ledger and the Accounts Receivable account. *The controller's department never has access to, or custody of, the received customer checks.*

Before recording and posting the cash receipts, the controller's department compares the total on the deposit slip copy from the treasurer's department to the remittance list obtained from the mailroom to ensure that the treasurer's department deposited all of the checks sent from the mailroom. The controller's department then prepares a journal entry (debit Cash and credit Accounts Receivable) to record the cash receipts. The dollar amount of the debit and credit is the total from the deposit slip.

The controller's department uses the individual remittance advices to post the cash payments to the Accounts Receivable account of each individual customer. After processing, the remittance list, the remittance advices, and the deposit slip copy are filed in the controller's department for future reference.

Internal Audit

Internal audit is an independent department; it has no recurring custody, recording, or authorization duties related to accounting transactions. Once each month, the internal audit department performs its independent review and reconciliation duties related to the cash received. The internal auditor receives the monthly bank statement directly from the bank through the mail. This ensures that no one can alter the information returned with the bank statement. The internal audit department uses the bank statement to prepare the monthly bank reconciliation and create any needed journal entries. The preparation of the bank reconciliation and related journal entries are discussed later in this chapter.

Cash Received from Retail Cash Sales

A retailer receives cash from customers when the retailer sells merchandise. The retailer must design internal controls to protect any cash received. Five groups play major roles in collecting, protecting, processing, and recording cash received from retail customers: the retail sales area, the retail sales supervisor, the treasurer's department, the controller's department, and the internal audit department. Exhibit 7-2 and the following paragraphs describe the role that each group plays.

Retail Sales Area

Sales associates use cash registers to record cash sales and to control and protect the cash collected from customers. Some retailers such as **Safeway Food Stores** place all of the company's cash registers near the store exit. Other retailers such as **Macy's Department Stores** place the cash registers throughout the store in the various departments such as men's clothing, cosmetics, and women's shoes.

Each sales associate uses a unique **password** or key to identify him or herself to the cash register. Each associate should have a separate cash drawer for collecting cash from customers and making change. Each sales associate begins each business day with a fixed amount of change in his or her cash drawer. The sales associates enter details of each sale into the cash register and place any cash received from customers into the assigned cash drawer. The cash register prints a paper tape listing the description and price of the items sold and the total amount due. The cash register also records this information either in the memory of the cash register or in a computer memory that the cash register accesses.

EXHIBIT 7-2	Processing Cash Received from Retail Cash Sales

Retail Sales Area

1. Begin each day with a fixed amount of change in drawer of each cash register.
2. Sales associate enters details of each sale into a cash register and places cash received from the customer into the cash register drawer assigned to that sales associate.

Retail Sales Supervisor

1. Observes the sales operation during the day.
2. Approves any unusual transactions during the day.
3. At the end of the day, counts the contents of each drawer with the sales associate responsible for the drawer.
4. Compares the amount in the drawer in excess of the beginning amount to the sales total accumulated by the cash register for that sales associate.
5. Prepares written report of sales and cash received.
6. Sends cash and a copy of the written report to the treasurer.
7. Sends cash register tape and a copy of the report to the controller.

Treasurer (Custody)

1. Prepares deposit slip.
2. Sends deposit slip and cash to bank.
3. Sends copy of deposit slip to controller.
4. Files a copy of the deposit slip.

Controller (Recording)

1. Compares deposit slip from treasurer to written report and cash register tape.
2. Uses the written report to prepare the journal entry to record cash sales.
3. Files written report and deposit slip.

Internal Auditor

1. Receives monthly bank statement directly from the bank through the mail.
2. Prepares bank reconciliation.
3. Prepares adjusting entries.

Retail Sales Supervisor

The retail sales supervisor oversees the retail sales operations of a business. Throughout the day, the supervisor approves any unusual transactions such as merchandise returns. At the end of the day, the supervisor counts the contents of each cash drawer. He or she compares the amount of cash in each drawer in excess of the beginning amount of change to the sales total accumulated by the cash register for each sales associate. The supervisor then prepares a written report (three copies) to document the total sales and the total cash received.

The supervisor delivers the cash in excess of the initial change amount and a copy of the written report to the treasurer's department. The cash register tape and another copy of the written report are taken to the controller's department. The supervisor files the third copy of the written report for future use if needed.

Treasurer

The treasurer's department takes custody of any cash from the retail sales supervisor after signing a receipt that the supervisor retains as proof of the cash delivery. Employees of the treasurer's department count the cash and prepare a deposit slip (original plus two copies). The employees then send the original deposit slip and cash to the bank for deposit. One copy of the deposit slip is sent to the controller's department; and, the treasurer's department files the final copy for future reference.

Controller

The controller's department is responsible for recording cash sales. The controller's department never has access to or custody of the cash or any checks. Before recording and posting the cash receipts, the controller's department compares the total on the deposit slip copy from the treasurer's department to the written report from the retail sales supervisor to ensure that the treasurer's department deposited all of the cash received. The controller's department then prepares a journal entry to record the cash sales. This entry also reflects any shortage or overage of cash, should this occur.

Internal Audit

The duties of the internal audit department with respect to cash received from retail sales are identical to its duties with respect to cash received on account. Note again that the bank sends the monthly bank statement directly to a company's internal auditor. If a company does not have an internal auditor, the bank sends the monthly bank statement to an appropriate person designated by the company, usually someone who does not have custody or recording responsibilities for cash. The internal audit department prepares a bank reconciliation statement and makes any needed journal entries.

Checks

When a company opens a checking account at a bank, the bank requires each company employee who will sign checks to sign a signature card. Occasionally, a bank employee compares the signatures on the checks presented for payment by various parties to the authorized signatures on the signature cards. This comparison provides an internal control for the bank that it is not cashing a check written by an unauthorized employee. The bank is responsible for any amounts erroneously paid out of a company's checking account.

A **check** is a written order signed by a checking account owner (also known as the *maker*) directing the bank (called the *payer*) to pay a specified amount of money to the person or company named on the check (called the *payee*). A check is a negotiable instrument; it can be transferred to another person or company by writing "pay to the order of" and the name of the other person or company on the back of the check and then signing the back of the check.

Magnetic Characters on Checks

The routing number on a check tells the various banks handling the check how to route it through the U.S. Federal Reserve System to properly transfer the cash between bank accounts. The routing number has two formats: the fraction format (item 3 in Exhibit 7-3) and the MICR format (item 4 in Exhibit 7-3). Both formats are printed on each check. In the fraction format in Exhibit 7-3, the number 79 represents the state in which the bank is located, the number 123 represents the number of the bank where the checking account is located, and the number 759 represents the Federal Reserve District and bank through which the check must clear. In the MICR format, the number 0759 identifies the Federal Reserve District and bank, the number 0123 identifies the specific bank, and the number 8 is the check digit.

Exhibit 7-3 presents a sample check. As noted previously, proper internal control requires that business documents such as checks be prenumbered in numerical sequence. The printed check number appears in two locations in Exhibit 7-3: in standard type in the upper right corner ❶ and in MICR (magnetic ink character recognition) form on the bottom of the check ❷. Also printed twice on the check are alternative formats of the routing number for the check, a fraction format ❸ and an MICR format ❹. (See Accounting in Practice.) The check printer also places the customer's account number on the check in MICR form ❺. When the check is processed by the banking system, the MICR check amount ❻ is added at the bottom right of the check. Banks use special equipment that reads MICR codes directly into computer files.

EXHIBIT 7-3	Sample Check

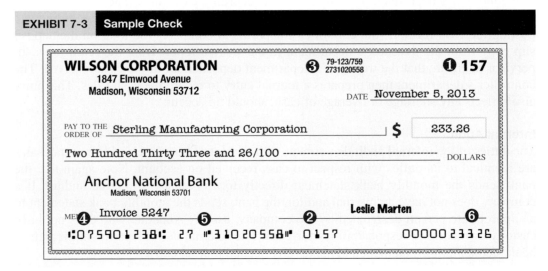

Using Electronic Funds Transfer

Many companies use electronic funds transfer to pay suppliers rather than writing and mailing checks. **Electronic funds transfer**, commonly known as EFT, involves sending an electronic message from one computer to another to cause a transfer of money from one financial institution to another, or directly to a company. Actually, two electronic messages are sent. To illustrate, assume that a company wants to use EFT to transfer money to a second company to pay an invoice. The paying company has its computer send a message to its bank's computer to request the funds transfer. This is known as *retail EFT*. Then, the paying company's bank uses EFT to transfer funds to the receiving company's bank. This is known as *wholesale EFT* or *bank-to-bank EFT*. Wholesale EFT usually involves a central bank (such as a Federal Reserve Bank) that acts as an automated clearinghouse by increasing the balance of one bank and decreasing the balance of the other bank.

The Petty Cash Fund

Most businesses find it inconvenient and expensive to write checks for small expenditures. Instead, these businesses establish a petty cash fund. A **petty cash fund** is a small amount of cash, for example $300, that is placed in a secure location on a business's premises to be used to pay for small expenditures such as postage, delivery service charges, and minor purchases of supplies. The size of the petty cash fund depends on how often it is used and the amount of the disbursements. Firms often select an amount that will last for three or four weeks.

Although the use of a petty cash fund violates the rule that all cash payments should be made by check, control can be maintained by handling the fund on an imprest basis with documented procedures. An imprest fund contains a fixed amount of cash. A business establishes a petty cash fund by writing a check against the firm's checking account and cashing the check at the bank. All replenishments of the petty cash fund are also made by check. As a result, all expenditures are ultimately controlled by check, providing a paper trail of all cash transfers to the petty cash fund.

YOUR TURN! 7.2

The solution is on page 358.

Match the internal control function from the left-hand column with the area of responsibility in the right-hand column:

1. Prepares deposit receipt.
2. Approves unusual transactions.
3. Prepares remittance list.
4. Prepares bank reconciliation.
5. Compares deposit receipt to remittance list.

a. Retail sales supervisor
b. Mailroom
c. Treasurer's department
d. Controller's department
e. Internal audit department

The Bank Statement

At the end of each month, a business's bank prepares a bank statement for each checking account that the company maintains and then sends the statement to the internal audit department of the company that owns the checking account. Exhibit 7-4 is the bank statement from Anchor National Bank for the Wilson Corporation's checking account as of November 30, 2013.

In the body of the bank statement, the bank lists Wilson's deposits and other credits on the left, Wilson's checks (in numerical order) and other debits in the center, and Wilson's daily account balance on the right. The daily account balance is the balance in the account as of the end of each day listed. The bank presents a summary calculation of Wilson's ending account balance near the bottom of the statement.

The bank defines a series of code letters at the bottom of the statement. These code letters identify debits and credits not related to paying checks or making deposits. These code letters are not standard from bank to bank. In Exhibit 7-4, EC identifies corrections of errors made by the bank; DM (debit memo) identifies automatic loan payments and bank charges for items such as collecting notes; CM (credit memo) identifies amounts collected by the bank for the depositor; SC (service charge) identifies fees charged by the bank for the checking account; OD (overdraft) indicates a negative balance in the account; RT (returned item) identifies items such as posted checks and NSF checks for which the bank could not collect cash; and IN (interest earned) identifies interest added to the account. The bank statement for the Wilson Corporation does not show any interest because federal regulations do not allow corporate checking accounts to earn interest.

The Bank Reconciliation

The internal audit department prepares a bank reconciliation as of the end of each month. A **bank reconciliation** is a schedule that (1) accounts for all differences between the end-

EXHIBIT 7-4   Bank Statement of Wilson Corporation

ANCHOR NATIONAL BANK
123 Center Street
Madison, Wisconsin 53701

Wilson Corporation
1847 Elmwood Avenue
Madison, Wisconsin 53712

Account Number   27-31020558
Statement Date   November 30, 2013

Deposits and Credits		Checks and Debits			Daily Balance	
Date	Amount	Number	Date	Amount	Date	Amount
Nov. 01	420.00	149	Nov. 02	125.00	Nov. 01	6,060.30
Nov. 02	630.00	154	Nov. 03	56.25	Nov. 02	6,565.30
Nov. 07	560.80	155	Nov. 10	135.00	Nov. 03	6,509.05
Nov. 10	480.25	156	Nov. 08	315.10	Nov. 07	6,801.19
Nov. 14	525.00	157	Nov. 07	233.26	Nov. 08	6,486.09
Nov. 17	270.25	158	Nov. 11	27.14	Nov. 10	6,831.34
Nov. 21	640.20	159	Nov. 18	275.00	Nov. 11	6,804.20
Nov. 26	300.00CM	160	Nov. 15	315.37	Nov. 14	7,329.20
Nov. 26	475.00	161	Nov. 17	76.40	Nov. 15	7,013.83
Nov. 30	471.40	162	Nov. 21	325.60	Nov. 17	7,207.68
		163	Nov. 21	450.00	Nov. 18	6,932.68
		164	Nov. 23	239.00	Nov. 21	6,731.58
		165	Nov. 21	65.70	Nov. 23	6,492.58
		166	Nov. 28	482.43	Nov. 26	7,262.58
		169	Nov. 28	260.00	Nov. 28	6,520.15
		170	Nov. 30	122.50	Nov. 30	6,488.95
		171	Nov. 30	370.10		
			Nov. 07	35.40RT		
			Nov. 26	5.00DM		
			Nov. 30	10.00SC		

Beginning Balance	+	Deposits and Credits	−	Checks and Debits	=	Ending Balance
$5,640.30	+	$4,772.90	−	$3,924.25	=	$6,488.95

Item Codes:

EC: Error Correction	DM: Debit Memo	CM: Credit Memo
SC: Service Charge	OD: Overdraft	RT: Returned Item
IN: Interest Earned		

ing cash balance on the bank statement and the ending cash balance in the Cash account in the company's general ledger and (2) determines the reconciled cash balance as of the end of the month. The internal audit department employee preparing the bank reconciliation needs access to the bank statement, the general ledger, cash receipts records, and cash disbursements records to prepare the reconciliation.

ACCOUNTING IN PRACTICE

Debits or Credits?

Debit and credit terminology may seem backward on a bank statement. Debits decrease a bank account balance and credits increase a bank account balance. When a company deposits cash in its checking account, the bank debits Cash and credits a liability account called a Customer Deposit. The bank statement sent to a company each month is a statement of its Customer Deposit account held by the bank. As with any liability, debits decrease its balance and credits increase its balance.

Bank Reconciliation Structure

Exhibit 7-5 outlines the structure of a company's bank reconciliation. The bank reconciliation is really two schedules prepared side by side. The schedule on the left includes bank items, and the schedule on the right includes items related to the company's general ledger.

EXHIBIT 7-5	**Structure of a Company's Bank Reconciliation**

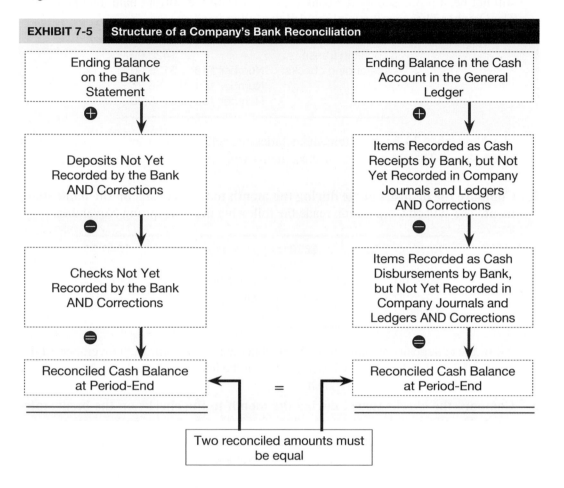

The schedule on the left begins with the ending cash balance from the bank statement (the month-end balance according to the bank's records). The internal audit department employee preparing the reconciliation adds (1) deposits not yet recorded by the bank, called **deposits in transit**, and (2) any corrections not yet made by the bank that will increase the bank balance. The preparer then subtracts (1) checks not yet recorded by the bank, called **outstanding checks**, and (2) any corrections not yet made by the bank that will decrease the bank balance. The resulting total is the *reconciled cash balance at the end of the month.*

The schedule on the right begins with the ending balance in the Cash account in the company's general ledger. The internal audit department employee adds (1) items recorded as cash receipts by the bank but not yet recorded in the company's journals and (2) any corrections not yet made by the company that will increase the general ledger cash balance. The preparer subtracts (1) items recorded as cash disbursements by the bank but not yet recorded in the company's journals and (2) any corrections not yet made by the company that will decrease the general ledger cash balance. The resulting total is the *reconciled cash balance at the end of the month.* The totals of the two schedules should be the same.

Bank Reconciliation Illustrated   Assume that the internal auditor of the Wilson Corporation is preparing the November 30, 2013, bank reconciliation. She uses the following procedures to reconcile the November 30 bank statement balance of $6,488.95 to the November 30 general ledger Cash account balance of $5,322.69:

1. **Trace outstanding items on the bank reconciliation for the previous month to the current bank statement.** Any items on the previous bank reconciliation that have still not been processed by the bank must appear on the current bank reconciliation. The October 31 reconciliation included the following:

Deposit in transit		$420.00
Outstanding checks:	Number 149	$125.00
	Number 154	56.25
	Number 155	135.00

    The November 30 bank statement includes the $420 deposit and all three checks listed above. Therefore, none of these items will appear on the November 30 bank reconciliation.

2. **Compare the deposits made during the month to the deposits on the bank statement.** The Wilson Corporation made the following deposits during November:

November 2	$630.00	November 21	$640.20
November 7	560.80	November 26	475.00
November 10	480.25	November 29	471.40
November 14	525.00	November 30	225.00
November 17	270.25		

    All of these deposits appear on the bank statement except for the November 30 deposit of $225. The $225 deposit will appear on the left side of the November 30 bank reconciliation as a deposit in transit.

3. **Compare the checks issued during the month to the checks on the bank statement.** The Wilson Corporation issued the following checks during November:

Number 156	$315.10	Number 165	$ 65.70
Number 157	233.26	Number 166	482.43
Number 158	27.14	Number 167	301.66
Number 159	275.00	Number 168	149.50
Number 160	315.37	Number 169	260.00
Number 161	76.40	Number 170	122.50
Number 162	325.60	Number 171	370.10
Number 163	450.00	Number 172	450.00
Number 164	239.00	Number 173	240.50

    Four of the checks—numbers 167, 168, 172, and 173—do not appear on the bank statement. These four checks will appear on the left side of the November 30 bank reconciliation as outstanding checks.

4. **Scan the bank statement for charges and credits not yet reflected in the general ledger.** The Wilson Corporation's bank statement contains a charge of $35.40 for a returned item, a debit memo of $5.00, and a service charge of $10.00 in the checks and other debits column. The deposits and other credits column contains a credit memo for $300.00. Supplemental information sent by the bank with the bank statement reveals that the bank charged a $35.40 NSF check against Wilson's account, collected a $300.00 note for Wilson and charged a $5.00 collection fee, and that the service charge for the month of November was $10.00. These four items have not yet

been recorded by Wilson Corporation. Therefore, they must be listed on the right side of the bank reconciliation.

After the four preceding procedures have been completed, the November 30 bank reconciliation for the Wilson Corporation appears as shown in Exhibit 7-6. Note that both the left side and the right side of the reconciliation end with a reconciled cash balance and that the two amounts are the same. This reconciled cash balance is the amount that will appear on the November 30 balance sheet for the company.

EXHIBIT 7-6	**November 30, 2013, Bank Reconciliation for Wilson Corporation**

WILSON CORPORATION
Bank Reconciliation
November 30, 2013

Ending balance from bank statement . . .	$6,488.95	Balance from general ledger			$5,322.69
Add: Deposits in transit	225.00	Add: Collection of note.	$300.00		
		Less: Collection fee	5.00		295.00
	6,713.95				5,617.69
Less: Outstanding checks:		Less: NSF check		35.40	
No. 167 . . . . $301.66		Service charge		10.00	45.40
No. 168 . . . . 149.50					
No. 172 . . . . 450.00					
No. 173 . . . . 240.50	1,141.66				
Reconciled cash balance	$5,572.29	Reconciled cash balance . . .			$5,572.29

Before the Wilson Corporation prepares its financial statements for November, Wilson must make journal entries to bring the balance in the Cash account into agreement with the reconciled cash balance on the bank reconciliation. These entries incorporate the items on the company's side of the bank reconciliation as follows:

Nov. 30	Cash	295.00		A = L + SE
	Miscellaneous expense	5.00		+295.00
	Notes receivable		300.00	−5.00 Exp
	To record a note collected by the bank, less a collection fee.			−300.00
Nov. 30	Accounts receivable	35.40		A = L + SE
	Cash		35.40	+35.40
	To reclassify an NSF check as an account receivable.			−35.40
Nov. 30	Miscellaneous expense	10.00		A = L + SE
	Cash		10.00	−10.00 Exp
	To record bank service charge for November.			−10.00

YOUR TURN! 7.3

The solution is on page 358.

Match the reconciling items from the left-hand column with the proper reconciling action from the right-hand column:

1. Deposits in transit
2. Outstanding checks
3. Bank service charge
4. Cash collected by bank on note

a. Add to bank statement balance
b. Subtract from bank statement balance
c. Add to cash general ledger account
d. Subtract from cash general ledger account

EFFECTIVE CASH MANAGEMENT

LO4 **Describe** the four primary activities of effective cash management.

Cash is a company's most important asset. Without cash, a company would be unable to pay its employees or its suppliers. In short, a company would be unable to continue operating. As a consequence, managers spend considerable time and effort managing and monitoring this key asset. Similarly, investors and lenders spend considerable time understanding where a company's cash came from and how the company spent it.

Monitoring Cash

The most effective tool for external parties to monitor a company's cash is the statement of cash flows.[1] As discussed in Chapter 1, the statement of cash flows identifies a company's cash inflows and cash outflows, segmenting them into the three business activities of operating, investing, and financing. Exhibit 7-7 presents the statement of cash flows for WebWork Inc. for the month ended December 31, 2013.

EXHIBIT 7-7	Statement of Cash Flows for WebWork, Inc.

WEBWORK, INC.
Statement of Cash Flows
For Month Ended December 31, 2013

Cash flow from operating activities		
Cash received from clients.	$19,910	
Cash paid to employees and suppliers	(1,620)	
Cash paid for rent.	(10,800)	
Cash provided by operating activities		$ 7,490
Cash flow from investing activities		
Purchase of office equipment.	(32,400)	
Cash used by investing activities		(32,400)
Cash flow from financing activities		
Stock issued.	30,000	
Borrowing from bank	36,000	
Cash dividends.	(500)	
Cash provided by financing activities.		65,500
Net increase in cash.		40,590
Cash at December 1, 2013		0
Cash at December 31, 2013		$40,590

The positive numbers on the statement of cash flows represent a company's cash inflows and the negative numbers represent a company's cash outflows. The larger positive numbers represent the major cash inflows and the larger negative numbers represent the major cash outflows. WebWork's primary cash inflows involved the sale of stock ($30,000) and its bank borrowings ($36,000). The company's primary uses of cash involved the purchase of office equipment ($32,400) and the payment of rent ($10,800). Not only does the statement of cash flows identify the sources and uses of cash, but it also identifies whether a company's cash balance increased or decreased for the period. Exhibit 7-7 reveals that WebWork's cash account increased by $40,590 for the month of December.

---

[1] The statement of cash flows provides an after-the-fact monitoring of cash sources and uses. Many companies use a cash budget in order to plan anticipated cash inflows and outflows so that they are able to manage the amount of cash on hand at an appropriate level. Cash budgets are covered in most managerial accounting textbooks.

While having some cash on hand is important to enable a company to pay its employees and its suppliers on a timely basis, having too much cash on hand may indicate that a company is not maximizing the return on its assets. Thus, it is important for managers to not only monitor a company's cash but also to manage it effectively to insure that the company is earning an adequate return on this key asset.

Primary Activities of Effective Cash Management

Effective cash management generally involves four primary activities:

1. Manage accounts receivable. Since accounts receivable rarely include interest charges for late payment, the sooner that cash from sales can be collected, the sooner the cash can be used to pay suppliers, pay debt, or be invested in operations. Thus, managers should try to increase the rate at which accounts receivable are collected.

2. Manage inventory levels. Inventory should be maintained at levels that allow a company to satisfy customer needs while, at the same time, avoid having too much of the company's resources tied up in inventory for extended periods of time. Thus, managers should try to keep inventory levels as low as possible without losing any sales.

3. Manage accounts payable. Since accounts payable rarely include an interest charge for late payment, the longer a manager takes to pay off these accounts, the longer a company can use its cash to fund operations. Thus, managers should delay the payment of accounts payable; however, they should not be delayed beyond the point that their credit rating may be harmed. Where accounts payable have credit terms that provide a discount for prompt payment, managers must evaluate the trade-off involved by delaying the payment of accounts payable versus the reduced purchase price that results from timely payment.

4. Invest excess cash. Since cash on hand or in a bank account yields a very low rate of return, it is important to invest any excess cash. Thus, an important management activity is forecasting a company's cash needs by constructing a cash budget each period. Only a sufficient amount of cash necessary to cover a company's day-to-day needs should be kept on hand; any excess amounts should be invested in an effort to earn an adequate rate of return on this asset.

COMPREHENSIVE PROBLEM

At December 31, 2013, the Cash account in the Tyler Company's general ledger had a debit balance of $18,434.27. The December 31, 2013, bank statement showed a balance of $19,726.40. In reconciling the two amounts, you discover the following:

1. Bank deposits made by Tyler on December 31 amounting to $2,145.40 do not appear on the bank statement.
2. A non-interest-bearing note receivable from the Smith Company for $2,000, left with the bank for collection, was collected by the bank at the end of December. The bank credited the proceeds, less a $5 collection charge, on the bank statement. Tyler Company has not recorded the collection.
3. Accompanying the bank statement is a debit memorandum indicating that John Miller's check for $450 was charged against Tyler's bank account on December 30 because of insufficient funds.
4. Check No. 586, written for advertising expense of $869.10, was recorded as $896.10 by Tyler Company.
5. A comparison of the paid checks returned by the bank with the recorded disbursements revealed that the following checks are still outstanding as of December 31:

No. 561	$306.63	No. 591	$190.00
No. 585	440.00	No. 592	282.50
No. 588	476.40	No. 593	243.00

6. The bank mistakenly charged Tyler Company's account for check printing costs of $30.50, which should have been charged to Taylor Company.

7. The bank charged Tyler Company's account $42.50 for the rental of a safe deposit box. No entry has been made in Tyler's records for this expense.

Required

a. Prepare a bank reconciliation as of December 31, 2013.

b. Prepare any necessary journal entries at December 31, 2013.

Solution

a.

TYLER COMPANY
Bank Reconciliation
December 31, 2013

Ending balance from bank statement		$19,726.40	Balance from general ledger			$18,434.27
Add: Deposits not credited by bank.		2,145.40	Add: Collection of note.	$2,000.00		
Error by bank (Check printing			Less: Collection charge	5.00		1,995.00
charge of Taylor Co.)		30.50	Error in recording check No. 586			27.00
		21,902.30				20,456.27
Less: Outstanding checks:			Less:			
No. 561.	$306.63		NSF check	450.00		
No. 585	440.00		Charge for safe deposit box	42.50		492.50
No. 588	476.40					
No. 591	190.00					
No. 592	282.50					
No. 593	243.00	1,938.53				
Reconciled cash balance		$19,963.77	Reconciled cash balance			$19,963.77

A = L + SE
+1,995.00
        −5.00
−2,000.00
	b. Dec. 31	Cash
		Miscellaneous expense
		        Notes receivable—Smith Company
		        To record collection of Smith Company's note by bank,
		        less collection charge.
			1,995.00
			5.00
				
				2,000.00

A = L + SE
+27.00
        +27.00
	31	Cash
		        Advertising expense
		        To correct error in recording advertising expense.
			27.00	
				27.00

A = L + SE
+450.00
−450.00
	31	Accounts receivable—John Miller
		        Cash
		        To reclassify NSF check as an account receivable.
			450.00	
				450.00

A = L + SE
        −42.50
−42.50
	31	Miscellaneous expense
		        Cash
		        To record rental expense of safety deposit box.
			42.50	
				42.50

APPENDIX 7A: Auditing and Internal Control

LO5 **Describe** financial statement audits and operational audits.

One of the internal control concepts previously discussed was conducting internal company audits. Internal audits provide appraisals of a company's financial statements, its internal control, and its operations. Internal auditors, who are employees of the company that they audit, conduct internal audits under the direction of top management or a company's board of directors. Parties outside the company, such as bankers and stockholders, prefer independent appraisals of a company's performance. These parties are usually unwilling to accept an audit report prepared by company-employed internal auditors because of possible bias and conflicts of interest.

Consequently, creditors and stockholders usually require that an independent, professional auditing firm conduct an audit of the annual financial statements. Moreover, U.S. securities law requires that all corporations whose common stock is publicly traded have an independent firm of certified public accountants (CPAs) audit the company's annual financial statements.

Not Your Ordinary Audit	**FORENSIC ACCOUNTING**

The financial statement audit is performed to enable the independent auditor to express an opinion regarding whether the financial statements present fairly, in all material respects, the financial position and results of operations of a company. In so doing, the independent auditor is looking for material errors, whether the errors are a result of unintentional misstatement or fraud. To perform the audit, the auditor will perform statistical sampling of the reported transactions to make judgments regarding the fairness of the reported statements. The auditor is not specifically looking for fraud, and likely will not find it even if present, because the financial statement audit is not designed to uncover fraud. The forensic accountant, by way of contrast, is specifically looking for fraud. Forensic accountants concentrate their efforts where fraud is likely to occur or is suspected, rather than on the financial statements as a whole. The forensic accountant will also utilize additional investigative techniques and follow leads suggested by what appear to be immaterial items. The forensic accountant will often have additional skills not common to financial statement auditors, such as surveillance tactics and interviewing and interrogation skills.

Financial Statement Audits

A **financial statement audit** is an examination of a company's annual financial statements by a firm of independent certified public accountants. (The quarterly financial reports of U.S. publicly traded companies are "reviewed" by an independent audit firm but they are not subject to a full audit like the annual financial statements.) The independent audit firm conducts this examination so it can prepare a report that expresses an opinion regarding whether (or not) the financial statements fairly present the results of operations, cash flows, and financial position of a company.

Going Concern Concept	**PRINCIPLE ALERT**

The *going concern concept* assumes that a business entity will continue to operate indefinitely. As part of the annual audit, a company's independent auditors must assess the likelihood that the company that they are auditing will continue as a going concern for a reasonable period. Events such as recurring losses, pending litigation, and the loss of a major customer or supplier may raise concern about a firm's ability to maintain its going-concern status. In such cases, the independent auditors should assess management's response to the problem and the type of financial statement disclosure being made about the problem. When substantial doubt exists about a company's going-concern status, the independent auditors may include a paragraph in the audit report expressing their concern regarding this issue.

Audit Procedures

The independent audit firm conducts the annual financial statement audit according to standards established by the **Public Company Accounting Oversight Board (PCAOB)**, a quasi-governmental agency established by the Sarbanes-Oxley Act. The PCAOB is responsible for establishing auditing standards, inspecting the auditing practices of independent audit firms, and disciplining those firms that fail to maintain acceptable audit standards and practices.

The annual financial statement audit includes many different stages of work. During the early stage of an audit, the independent auditor reviews and evaluates the internal controls imbedded in a company's accounting system and other systems. This review and evaluation helps the auditor determine what additional investigative steps, if any, should be included in the audit. The auditor then collects and analyzes data that substantiates the amounts in the financial statements. The auditor obtains most of these data from accounting records (such as journals and ledgers), business documents (such as purchase orders, sales invoices, and payment approval forms), and outside sources (such as banks, insurance companies, and suppliers).

The Audit Report

The **audit report** that the independent auditor issues following the annual audit specifies the financial statements that were audited, summarizes the audit process, and states the auditor's opinion regarding the financial statement data. The opinion usually states that the financial statements "fairly present" the results of operations, cash flow, and financial position of the company. The independent auditor does not conduct the audit to determine whether the financial statements are absolutely correct. Instead, the audit is conducted to determine whether the financial statements are a fair representation of operating results, cash flow, and financial position.

The primary purpose of the annual financial statement audit is *not* the discovery of fraudulent acts by management or employees of the company. Many audit procedures use statistical samples of transactions and data rather than examining the complete population of transactions. The auditors use samples to minimize the time required to conduct the audit, and consequently, to minimize its cost. As a result, there is the possibility that some errors or irregularities will exist in the transactions and data that the auditor does not review or evaluate. However, the independent auditor carefully designs the sampling procedures to detect errors and irregularities that are material in relation to the financial statements.

> **Report of Independent Registered Public Accounting Firm**
>
> In our opinion, such consolidated financial statements present fairly, in all material respects, the financial position of the Company as of December 31, 2011 and 2010, and the results of its operations and its cash flows for each of the three years in the period ended December 31, 2011, in conformity with accounting principles generally accepted in the United States of America. Also, in our opinion, such a financial statement schedule, when considered in relation to the basic consolidated financial statements taken as a whole, presents fairly, in all material respects, the information set forth therein.
>
> *DELOITTE & TOUCHE LLP*

Operational Audits

Both internal audit departments and independent audit firms perform operational audits. An **operational audit** is an evaluation of activities, systems, and internal controls within a company to determine their efficiency, effectiveness, and economy. Operational auditing goes beyond accounting records and financial statements to obtain a full understanding of the operations of a company. Companies dedicated to continuous quality improvement often use operational audits to identify specific areas where they need to improve the quality of their operations or products.

Auditors design operational audits to assess the quality and efficiency of operational performance, identify opportunities for improvement, and develop specific recommendations for improvement. The scope of an operational audit can be very narrow, such as a review and evaluation of the procedures for processing cash receipts, or quite broad, such as a review and evaluation of all of the internal controls in a computerized accounting system.

YOUR TURN! 7.4

The solution is on page 358.

Match the description in the left-hand column with the type of audit in the right-hand column:

1. Conducted by company employees
2. Conducted by independent auditors
3. Conducted by both independent auditors and internal auditors
4. Primary purpose is to report on the fairness of a company's financial statements
5. Evaluation of the efficiency and effectiveness of company activities

a. Internal audit
b. Financial statement audit
c. Operational audit

SUMMARY OF LEARNING OBJECTIVES

Define the three elements of fraud and discuss the role of internal control in a business to prevent fraud. (p. 314)

LO1

■ The fraud triangle consists of three parts: (1) pressure, (2) rationalization, and (3) opportunity.

■ Internal controls are the measures undertaken by a company to ensure the reliability of its accounting data, protect its assets from theft or unauthorized use, insure that employees follow the company's policies and procedures, and evaluate the performance of employees, departments, divisions, and the company as a whole.

■ A prevention control is designed to deter problems before they arise. A detection control is designed to discover problems soon after they arise. Prevention controls are generally more desirable than detection controls.

■ A company should incorporate the following concepts when it designs its internal control:
  • Establish clear lines of authority and responsibility.
  • Implement segregation of duties.
  • Hire competent personnel.
  • Use control numbers on all business documents.
  • Develop plans and budgets.
  • Maintain adequate accounting records.
  • Provide physical and electronic controls.
  • Conduct internal audits.

Define cash and discuss the accounting for cash. (p. 321)

LO2

■ Cash includes coins, currency (paper money), checks, money orders, traveler's checks, and funds on deposit at a financial institution in a company's checking accounts and savings accounts.

■ A company can have one or more cash accounts in its general ledger. Cash is a current asset.

■ A company may combine certain short-term, highly liquid investments with cash and present a single amount called *cash and cash equivalents*.

■ Not all of the company's cash may be available for general use. Restricted cash represents cash that has been restricted for specific uses. A compensating balance is an amount that a company must maintain in a bank account as part of a loan agreement.

Describe the internal controls for cash. (p. 323)

LO3

■ Companies develop elaborate internal controls to protect cash, their most liquid asset.

■ Four departments play major roles in processing cash received on account: the mailroom (open mail, endorse checks, list checks), the treasurer's department (deposit checks), the controller's department (update general ledger accounts), and the internal audit department (reconcile bank statement).

■ Five departments play major roles in processing cash received from retail sales: the retail sales area (enter sales in cash register and place cash in drawer), the retail sales supervisor (count cash and prepare reports), the treasurer's department (deposit cash), the controller's department (update general ledger), and the internal audit department (reconcile bank statement).

■ A petty cash fund is a small amount of cash placed in a secure location on a company's premises to be used to pay for small expenditures such as postage and delivery service.

■ A bank reconciliation is a schedule that (1) accounts for all differences between the ending cash balance of the bank statement and the ending cash balance of the Cash account in a company's general ledger and (2) determines the reconciled cash balance as of the end of the month.

■ The procedure used to prepare the bank reconciliation involves four steps:
  • Trace outstanding items on the bank reconciliation from the previous month to the current bank statement.
  • Compare the deposits made during the month to the deposits on the bank statement.
  • Compare the checks issued during the month to the checks on the bank statement.
  • Scan the bank statement for charges and credits not yet reflected in the general ledger.

Describe the four primary activities of effective cash management. (p. 334)

LO4

■ Cash should be monitored using the statement of cash flows.

■ Effective cash management includes monitoring and managing accounts receivable, inventory, and accounts payable, and investing any excess cash.

LO5   **Appendix 7A: Describe financial statement audits and operational audits. (p. 336)**

■   A financial statement audit is an examination of a company's financial statements by a firm of independent certified public accountants. The firm issues an audit report upon completion of the audit.

■   An operational audit is an evaluation of activities, systems, and internal controls within a company to determine their efficiency, effectiveness, and economy.

SUMMARY	Concept ➜	Method ➜	Assessment
TAKEAWAY 7.1	Are the internal controls adequate?	Independent auditors' attestation report. The principles of good internal control include: (1) Establish clear lines of authority and responsibility, (2) Segregation of duties, (3) Hire competent personnel, (4) Use control numbers on all business documents, (5) Develop plans and budgets, (6) Maintain adequate accounting records, (7) Provide physical and electronic controls, (8) Conduct internal audits.	Be sure that the report does not indicate any weaknesses in the company's internal control. If weaknesses are reported, be cautious in relying on the reported financial statements.
TAKEAWAY 7.2	Are there any restrictions on a company's use of its cash and cash equivalents?	Balance sheet and the notes to the financial statements. Are there any restrictions to cash or compensating cash balances reported?	Any assessments of liquidity should consider any existing cash restrictions.

KEY TERMS

Audit report (p. 338)
Bank reconciliation (p. 329)
Budget (p. 318)
Cash (p. 321)
Cash and cash equivalents (p. 323)
Certificates of deposit (p. 321)
Check (p. 327)
Compensating balance (p. 322)
Control numbers (p. 318)
Deposits in transit (p. 331)
Detection control (p. 316)

Electronic funds transfer (p. 328)
Employee collusion (p. 320)
Fidelity bond (p. 320)
Financial statement audit (p. 337)
Fraud (p. 314)
Fraud triangle (p. 314)
Internal auditing (p. 319)
Internal controls (p. 315)
Not-sufficient-funds check (p. 322)
Operational audit (p. 338)

Outstanding checks (p. 331)
Password (p. 325)
Petty cash fund (p. 329)
Postdated check (p. 321)
Prevention control (p. 316)
Public Company Accounting Oversight Board (PCAOB) (p. 337)
Remittance advice (p. 323)
Remittance list (p. 324)
Restricted cash (p. 322)
Segregation of duties (p. 317)

SELF-STUDY QUESTIONS

(Answers to the Self-Study Questions are at the end of the chapter.)

1. **Which of the following is not one of the three elements of the fraud triangle?**
    a.   Pressure
    b.   Rationalization
    c.   Embezzlement
    d.   Opportunity

2. **Which of the following is not a common internal control concept?**
    a.   Establish clear lines of responsibility
    b.   Provide physical and electronic controls
    c.   Collusion among employees
    d.   Separate work functions

3. **Which of the following are considered good internal control practice?**
   - *a.* Job rotation
   - *b.* Required vacations
   - *c.* Only promoting from within
   - *d.* Both *a* and *b*

4. **Burton Company should utilize all except one of the following concepts related to placing control numbers on business documents. Which concept should Burton not use?**
   - *a.* Write the control number on the document when it is used.
   - *b.* Place control numbers on all business documents.
   - *c.* Use the documents in strict numerical sequence.
   - *d.* Periodically account for all numbers used.

5. **An operational audit is:**
   - *a.* Just another word for a financial statement audit
   - *b.* Only performed by independent auditors
   - *c.* Used to assess the quality and efficiency of operational performance
   - *d.* Usually reported to the public along with the financial statements

6. **Which of the following statements is correct regarding the reporting of cash?**
   - *a.* Restricted cash is always shown as a noncurrent asset
   - *b.* Cash is shown as the first asset on the balance sheet
   - *c.* Restricted cash is usually combined with unrestricted cash on the balance sheet
   - *d.* If a company maintains more than one bank account, each must be shown separately on the balance sheet

7. **The treasurer is responsible for each of the following except:**
   - *a.* Prepare the deposit slip
   - *b.* Send deposit slips and checks to the bank
   - *c.* Prepare the bank reconciliation
   - *d.* File a copy of the deposit receipt

8. **What is a bank reconciliation?**
   - *a.* A formal financial statement that lists all of a firm's bank account balances
   - *b.* A merger of two banks that previously were competitors
   - *c.* A statement sent monthly by a bank to a depositor that lists all deposits, checks paid, and other credits and charges to the depositor's account for the month
   - *d.* A schedule that accounts for differences between a firm's cash balance as shown on its bank statement and the balance shown in its general ledger Cash account

9. **In a bank reconciliation, outstanding checks are:**
   - *a.* Deducted from the bank balance
   - *b.* Added to the bank balance
   - *c.* Deducted from the general ledger balance
   - *d.* Added to the general ledger balance

10. **Which of the following statements about a petty cash fund is not true?**
    - *a.* The fund is managed on an imprest basis.
    - *b.* The fund is used to pay for minor items such as postage and delivery charges.
    - *c.* The fund should have a balance large enough to support one replenishment per year.
    - *d.* All replenishments are made by check.

QUESTIONS

1. Describe the three elements of the fraud triangle and how they relate to each other.
2. Explain why supervision is an important internal control.
3. Define and contrast prevention controls and detection controls. Which are more desirable?
4. Yates Company is reviewing its internal procedures to try to improve the company's internal control. It specifically wants to separate work functions. What three types of work functions must be separated to improve internal control?

5. Janet Jones is considered one of the rising stars at Finch Company. Janet is very hard working and has not taken a vacation in three years. Explain why this is a violation of good internal control.

6. Kwong Industries is redesigning its business documents. What three rules should Kwong follow relative to the use of control numbers on business documents?

7. In what way did the Sarbanes-Oxley Act impact the need for internal control?

8. How are a financial statement audit and an operational audit similar and different?

9. What types of items are included in cash? What are the two important characteristics of an item of cash?

10. Which of the following are considered to be cash: paper money, certificates of deposit, postdated checks, traveler's checks, funds in a checking account, and money orders?

11. What is a remittance advice? What types of data are included on a remittance advice?

12. What is electronic funds transfer (EFT)? What are retail EFT and wholesale EFT?

13. What is the purpose of a bank reconciliation?

14. In preparing a bank reconciliation, how should you determine (a) deposits not recorded in the bank statement and (b) outstanding checks?

15. Indicate whether the following bank reconciliation items should be (1) added to the bank statement balance, (2) deducted from the bank statement balance, (3) added to the ledger account balance, or (4) deducted from the ledger account balance:
    a. Bank service charge.
    b. NSF check.
    c. Deposit in transit.
    d. Outstanding check.
    e. Bank error charging company's account with another company's check.
    f. Difference of $270 in amount of check written for $410 but recorded by the company as $140.

16. Which of the items listed in Discussion Question 15 require a journal entry on the company's books?

17. What is an imprest petty cash fund? How is such a fund established and replenished?

18. Carter Manufacturing Company makes a variety of consumer products. For the year just ended (and the two prior years), sales of private-label product to Mega-Mart (1,200 stores nationwide) have made up 60 to 65 percent of total sales. On December 31 of the year just ended, Mega-Mart informed Carter that it would be buying all private-label products from another manufacturer under a five-year contract. Losing this business will result in a 50 to 55 percent reduction in total gross profit for Carter.
    a. What is the going concern concept and how does it apply to this situation?
    b. How should the full disclosure principle be applied when preparing the annual report for the year just ended?
    c. What is the independent auditor's responsibility in this situation?

SHORT EXERCISES

LO1 **SE7-1.** **The Fraud Triangle** Each of the following is part of the fraud triangle except:
    a. pressure.
    b. opportunity.
    c. concealment.
    d. rationalization.

LO1 **SE7-2.** **Segregation of Duties** Having one person responsible for the related activities of ordering merchandise, receiving the merchandise, and paying for the merchandise:
    a. provides increased security over the firm's assets.
    b. is an example of good internal control.
    c. is a good example of segregation of duties.
    d. increases the potential of fraud.

LO1 **SE7-3.** **Internal Control** Internal controls do each of the following except:
    a. protect assets from theft.
    b. evaluate the performance of employees.
    c. guarantee the accuracy of the accounting records.
    d. increase the likelihood that any errors will be caught.

SE7-4. **Auditors** Which of the following is true? LO5
    a. Internal auditors are independent of the company they audit.
    b. Internal audits provide appraisals of a company's internal control.
    c. The company being audited cannot pay the external auditing firm since this would violate their independence.
    d. Outside parties prefer appraisals by internal auditors over those of external auditors since they know more about the company being audited.

SE7-5. **Financial Statement Audit** The financial statement audit is: LO5
    a. conducted by the internal auditors. **(Appendix 7A)**
    b. conducted by auditors overseen by the American Institute of Certified Public Accountants.
    c. conducted by auditors overseen by the Public Company Accounting Oversight Board.
    d. only necessary if fraud is suspected.

SE7-6. **Cash** Cash includes each of the following except: LO2
    a. a postdated check.
    b. currency.
    c. money orders.
    d. funds in a checking account.

SE7-7. **Restricted Cash** Restricted cash: LO2
    a. must be shown as a current asset.
    b. must be shown as a noncurrent asset.
    c. is shown as a liability.
    d. is reported separate from unrestricted cash.

SE7-8. **Electronic Funds Transfer** Electronic funds transfer (EFT) involves transferring cash from one lo- LO3
cation to another using:
    a. armored trucks.
    b. computers.
    c. bicycle messengers.
    d. the mail service.

SE7-9. **Cash Internal Control** Good internal control over cash received on account involves the mailroom LO3
doing each of the following activities except:
    a. Open the mail.
    b. Prepare the deposit receipt.
    c. Prepare the remittance list.
    d. Send checks to the treasurer.

SE7-10. **Cash Management** Effective cash management involves all the following except: LO4
    a. Manage accounts receivable.
    b. Manage inventory.
    c. Invest excess cash.
    d. Conduct internal audits.

Assignments with the ✅ logo in the margin are available in *my*BusinessCourse.
See the Preface of the book for details.

EXERCISES—SET A

E7-1A. **Internal Control** Explain how each of the following procedures strengthens a company's internal LO1
control:
    a. After preparing a check for a cash disbursement, the accountant for Travis Lumber Company cancels the supporting business documents (purchase order, receiving report, and invoice) by stamping them PAID.
    b. The salespeople for Davis Department Store give each customer a cash register receipt along with the proper change. A sign on each cash register states that no refunds or exchanges are allowed without the related cash register receipt.
    c. The ticket-taker at the Esquire Theater tears each admission ticket in half and gives one half back to the ticket purchaser. The seat number is printed on each half of the ticket.

  d. John Renaldo's restaurant provides servers with prenumbered customers' checks. The servers are to void checks with mistakes on them and issue new ones rather than make corrections on them. Voided checks must be given to the manager every day.

LO3 **E7-2A.** **Internal Controls for Cash Received on Account** Hudson Company sells supplies to restaurants. Most sales are made on open account (credit sales). Hudson has requested your help in designing procedures for processing checks received from its customers. Briefly describe the procedures that should be used in each of the following departments:

  a. Mailroom
  b. Treasurer's department
  c. Controller's department

LO3 **E7-3A.** **Bank Reconciliation** Use the following information to prepare a bank reconciliation for Young Company at June 30:

  1. Balance per Cash account, June 30, $7,055.80.
  2. Balance per bank statement, June 30, $7,300.25.
  3. Deposits not reflected on bank statement, $725.
  4. Outstanding checks, June 30, $1,260.45.
  5. Service charge on bank statement not recorded in books, $11.
  6. Error by bank—Yertel Company check charged on Young Company's bank statement, $550.
  7. Check for advertising expense, $250, incorrectly recorded in books as $520.

LO3 **E7-4A.** **Bank Reconciliation Components** Identify the requested amount in each of the following situations:

  a. Munsing Company's May 31 bank reconciliation shows deposits in transit of $1,400. The general ledger Cash in Bank account shows total cash receipts during June of $57,300. The June bank statement shows total cash deposits of $55,900 (and no credit memos). What amount of deposits in transit should appear in the June 30 bank reconciliation?
  b. Sandusky Company's August 31 bank reconciliation shows outstanding checks of $2,100. The general ledger Cash in Bank account shows total cash disbursements (all by check) during September of $50,300. The September bank statement shows $49,200 of checks clearing the bank. What amount of outstanding checks should appear in the September 30 bank reconciliation?
  c. Fremont Corporation's March 31 bank reconciliation shows deposits in transit of $800. The general ledger Cash in Bank account shows total cash receipts during April of $38,000. The April bank statement shows total cash deposits of $37,100 (including $1,300 from the collection of a note; the note collection has not yet been recorded by Fremont). What amount of deposits in transit should appear in the April 30 bank reconciliation?

LO5
(Appendix 7A) **E7-5A.** **External versus Internal Audit** Explain why parties outside the company, such as bankers and stockholders, prefer an independent appraisal of the company's financial results rather than relying on the work of internal auditors.

LO5
(Appendix 7A) **E7-6A.** **Operational Audits** Explain the nature of an operational audit.

LO2 **E7-7A.** **Cash and Cash Equivalents** Identify each of the following items as either cash (C), cash equivalents (CE), or neither (N):

  a. Coin
  b. U.S. treasury bills
  c. Checks
  d. Six-month certificate of deposit
  e. Currency

LO1 **E7-8A.** **Internal Control** Explain how each of the following actions strengthens a company's system of internal control:

  a. Separate work functions.
  b. Hire competent personnel.
  c. Develop plans and budgets.
  d. Use control numbers on all business documents.

E7-9A. **Effective Cash Management** Explain how each of the following activities can improve a company's   **LO4**
cash management:

    a. Manage accounts receivable.
    b. Manage inventory.
    c. Manage accounts payable.
    d. Invest excess cash.

EXERCISES—SET B

E7-1B. **Internal Control** Explain how each of the following procedures strengthens a company's internal   **LO1**
control:

    a. Western Corporation's photocopy machines are activated by keying a code number. Each employee is assigned a different, confidential code number. Each copy machine keeps track of the number of copies run under each employee number.
    b. Picket Company's bank requires a signature card on file for each Picket Company employee who is authorized to sign checks.
    c. Fast Stop Convenience Stores have programmed their cash registers to imprint a blue star on every 300th receipt printed. A sign by each cash register states that the customer will receive $2 if his or her receipt has a blue star on it.
    d. Wilson Corporation has a policy that every employee must take two weeks of vacation each year.

E7-2B. **Internal Controls for Cash Received from Retail Sales** Edwards Company operates a retail depart-   **LO3**
ment store. Most customers pay cash for their purchases. Edwards has asked you to help it design procedures for processing cash received from customers for cash sales. Briefly describe the procedures that should be used in each of the following departments:

    a. Retail sales departments
    b. Retail sales supervisor
    c. Treasurer's department
    d. Controller's department

E7-3B. **Bank Reconciliation** Use the following information to prepare a bank reconciliation for Dillon Com-   **LO3**
pany at April 30:

    1. Balance per Cash account, April 30, $6,042.10.
    2. Balance per bank statement, April 30, $6,300.28.
    3. Deposits not reflected on bank statement, $650.
    4. Outstanding checks, April 30, $1,140.18.
    5. Service charge on bank statement not recorded in books, $12.
    6. Error by bank—Dillard Company check charged on Dillon Company's bank statement, $400.
    7. Check for advertising expense, $130, incorrectly recorded in books as $310.

E7-4B. **Bank Reconciliation Components** Identify the requested amount in each of the following situations: **LO3**

    a. Howell Company's August 31 bank reconciliation shows deposits in transit of $2,400. The general ledger Cash in Bank account shows total cash receipts during September of $91,200. The September bank statement shows total cash deposits of $88,000 (and no credit memos). What amount of deposits in transit should appear in the September 30 bank reconciliation?
    b. Wright Corporation's March 31 bank reconciliation shows deposits in transit of $1,600. The general ledger Cash in Bank account shows total cash receipts during April of $63,100. The April bank statement shows total cash deposits of $66,200 (including $2,000 from the collection of a note; the note collection has not yet been recorded by Wright). What amount of deposits in transit should appear in the April 30 bank reconciliation?
    c. Braddock Company's October 31 bank reconciliation shows outstanding checks of $2,600. The general ledger Cash in Bank account shows total cash disbursements (all by check) during November of $68,700. The November bank statement shows $67,200 of checks clearing the bank. What amount of outstanding checks should appear in the November 30 bank reconciliation?

E7-5B. **External versus Internal Audit** Compare the purpose of an external audit to that of an internal audit.   **LO5**
(Appendix 7A)

LO5
(Appendix 7A)

E7-6B. **The External Audit and Fraud** Explain why the external audit is not considered a fraud audit.

LO2

E7-7B. **Cash and Cash Equivalents** Identify each of the following items as either cash (C), cash equivalents (CE), or neither (N):

a. Money market funds
b. Euros
c. A postdated check
d. A savings account
e. Traveler's checks

LO1

E7-8B. **Internal Control** Explain how each of the following items strengthens a company's system of internal control:

a. Conduct internal audits.
b. Establish clear lines of authority and responsibility.
c. Maintain adequate accounting records.
d. Provide physical and electronic controls.

LO4

E7-9B. **Effective Cash Management** Presented below is the statement of cash flows for Smith & Sons for the month ended December 31. Identify (a) the major sources of cash, (b) the major uses of cash, and (c) the change in the cash balance during the month.

SMITH & SONS Statement of Cash Flows For the Month Ended December 31	
Cash flows from operating activities	
Cash receipts from customers	$13,275
Cash payments for operating activities	(11,131)
Cash provided by operating activities	2,144
Cash flows from investing activities	
Net purchases of investments	(140)
Net capital expenditures	(30,000)
Cash used by investing activities	(30,140)
Cash flows for financing activities	
Repurchase of common stock	(7,300)
Cash dividends paid	(6,000)
Cash used in financing activities	(13,300)
Net decrease in cash	(41,296)
Cash at beginning of month	95,000
Cash at end of month	$53,704

PROBLEMS—SET A

LO1, 3

P7-1A. **Internal Control** Regent Company encountered the following situations:

a. The person who opens the mail for Regent, Bill Stevens, stole a check from a customer and cashed it. To cover up the theft, he debited Sales Returns and Allowances and credited Accounts Receivable in the general ledger. He also posted the amount to the customer's account in the accounts receivable subsidiary ledger.
b. The purchasing agent, Susan Martin, used a company purchase order to order building materials from Builders Mart. Later, she telephoned Builders Mart and changed the delivery address to her home address. She told Builders Mart to charge the material to the company. At month-end, she approved the invoice from Builders Mart for payment.
c. Nashville Supply Company sent two invoices for the same order: the first on June 10 and the second on July 20. The accountant authorized payment of both invoices and both were paid.

d. On January 1, Jack Monty, a junior accountant for Regent, was given the responsibility of recording all general journal entries. At the end of the year, the auditors discovered that Monty had made 150 serious errors in recording transactions. The chief accountant was unaware that Monty had been making mistakes.

Required

For each situation, describe any violations of good internal control procedures and identify the steps that you would take to prevent each situation.

P7-2A. Internal Control Each of the following lettered paragraphs briefly describes an independent situation involving some aspect of internal control.   **LO1, 3**

Required

Answer the questions at the end of each paragraph or numbered section.

a. Robert Flynn is the office manager of Oswald Company, a small wholesaling company. Flynn opens all incoming mail, makes bank deposits, and maintains both the general ledger and the accounts receivable subsidiary ledger. An assistant records transactions in the credit sales journal and the cash receipts journal. The assistant also prepares a monthly statement for each customer and mails the statements to the customers. These statements list the beginning balance, credit sales, cash receipts, adjustments, and ending balance for the month.

1. If Flynn stole Customer A's $200 check (payment in full) and made no effort to conceal his embezzlement in the ledgers, how would the misappropriation be discovered?
2. What routine accounting procedure would disclose Flynn's $200 embezzlement in part (1), even if Flynn destroyed Customer A's subsidiary ledger account?
3. What circumstances might disclose Flynn's theft if he posted a payment to Customer A's account in the accounts receivable subsidiary ledger and set up a $200 account for a fictitious customer?
4. In part (3), why might Flynn be anxious to open the mail himself each morning?
5. In part (3), why might Flynn want to have the authority to write off accounts considered uncollectible?

b. A doughnut shop uses a cash register that produces a printed receipt for each sale. The register also prints each transaction on a paper tape that is locked inside the cash register. Only the supervisor has access to the cash-register tape. A prominently displayed sign promises a free doughnut to any customer who is not given a cash-register receipt with his or her purchase. How is this procedure an internal control device for the doughnut shop?

c. Jason Miller, a swindler, sent several businesses invoices requesting payment for office supplies that had never been ordered or delivered to the businesses. A five percent discount was offered for prompt payment. What internal control procedures should prevent this swindle from being successful?

d. The cashier for Uptown Cafeteria is located at the end of the food line. After customers have selected their food items, the cashier rings up the prices of the food and the customer pays the bill. The customer line frequently stalls while the person paying searches for the correct amount of cash. To speed things up, the cashier often collects money from the next customer or two who have the correct change without ringing up their food on the register. After the first customer finally pays, the cashier rings up the amounts for the customers who have already paid. What is the internal control weakness in this procedure? How might the internal control over the collection of cash from the cafeteria customers be strengthened?

P7-3A. Internal Controls for Cash Received on Account Schoff Company sells plumbing supplies to plumbing contractors on account. The procedures that Schoff uses to handle checks received from customers via the mail are described below: **LO3**

a. Schoff instructs its customers to send payment checks to its street address, 619 Main Street, Scottsdale, Arizona.
b. Schoff does not provide a remittance advice to its customers for return with payment checks.
c. Checks are endorsed by the treasurer's office just prior to sending the checks to the bank for deposit.
d. The mailroom prepares a remittance list of all the checks received and files the only copy of the remittance list in a mailroom file cabinet.

e. The checks are sent to the controller's office. The controller's office uses the checks to post the accounts receivable subsidiary ledger and prepare the journal entry to record cash receipts. The checks are then sent to the treasurer's office.

f. The treasurer's office prepares the deposit slip (two copies) and sends one copy and the checks to the bank. The other copy of the deposit slip is filed in the treasurer's file cabinet.

g. The bank statement is sent to the controller, who prepares the bank reconciliation.

Required

For each of these procedures, indicate how Schoff could improve it. (Refer to Exhibit 7-1 in the chapter to help you generate ideas.)

LO3 **P7-4A.** **Bank Reconciliation** On July 31, Sullivan Company's Cash in Bank account had a balance of $7,216.60. On that date, the bank statement indicated a balance of $9,098.55. A comparison of returned checks and bank advices revealed the following:

1. Deposits in transit July 31 amounted to $3,576.95.
2. Outstanding checks July 31 totaled $1,467.90.
3. The bank erroneously charged a $325 check of Solomon Company against the Sullivan bank account.
4. A $25 bank service charge has not yet been recorded by Sullivan Company.
5. Sullivan neglected to record $4,000 borrowed from the bank on a ten percent six-month note. The bank statement shows the $4,000 as a deposit.
6. Included with the returned checks is a memo indicating that J. Martin's check for $640 had been returned NSF. Martin, a customer, had sent the check to pay an account of $660 less a $20 discount.
7. Sullivan Company recorded a $109 payment for repairs as $1,090.

Required

a. Prepare a bank reconciliation for Sullivan Company at July 31.
b. Prepare the journal entry (or entries) necessary to bring the Cash in Bank account into agreement with the reconciled cash balance on the bank reconciliation.

LO3 **P7-5A.** **Bank Reconciliation** The bank reconciliation made by Winton, Inc., on August 31 showed a deposit in transit of $1,280 and two outstanding checks, No. 597 for $830 and No. 603 for $640. The reconciled cash balance on August 31 was $14,110.

The following bank statement is available for September:

Bank Statement						
TO Winton, Inc. St. Louis, MO					September 30 STATE BANK	
Date	**Deposits**	**No.**	**Date**	**Charges**	**Date**	**Balance**
					Aug. 31	$14,300
Sept. 1	$1,280	597	Sept. 1	$ 830	Sept. 1	14,750
2	1,120	607	5	1,850	2	15,870
5	850	608	5	1,100	5	13,770
9	744	609	9	552	8	13,130
15	1,360	610	8	640	9	13,322
17	1,540	611	17	488	15	14,008
25	1,028	612	15	674	17	15,060
30	680	614	25	920	25	15,168
		NSF	29	1,028	29	14,140
		SC	30	36	30	14,784
Item Codes:	EC: Error Correction SC: Service Charge IN: Interest Earned		DM: Debit Memo OD: Overdraft NSF: Non-sufficient Funds		CM: Credit Memo RT: Returned Item	

A list of deposits made and checks written during September is shown below:

Deposits Made		Checks Written	
Sept. 1	$1,120	No. 607	$1,850
4	850	608	1,100
8	744	609	552
12	1,360	610	640
16	1,540	611	488
24	1,028	612	746
29	680	613	310
30	1,266	614	920
	$8,588	615	386
		616	420
			$7,412

The Cash in Bank account balance on September 30 was $15,286. In reviewing checks returned by the bank, the accountant discovered that check No. 612, written for $674 for advertising expense, was recorded in the cash disbursements journal as $746. The NSF check for $1,028, which Winton deposited on September 24, was a payment on account from customer D. Walker.

Required

a. Prepare a bank reconciliation for Winton, Inc., at September 30.

b. Prepare the necessary journal entries to bring the Cash in Bank account into agreement with the reconciled cash balance on the bank reconciliation.

P7-6A. **Reporting Cash** Jenkins Company has the following items at year-end.   **LO2** ✔

Currency and coin in safe.	$ 3,500
Funds in savings account (requires $2,000 compensating balance)	25,250
Funds in checking account	6,750
Traveler's checks	500
Postdated check	1,250
Not-sufficient-funds check.	850
Money market fund	32,400

Required

Identify the amount of the above items that should be reported as cash and cash equivalents on Jenkins Company's balance sheet.

P7-7A. **Internal Control** Bart Simons has worked for Dr. Homer Spring for many years. Bart has been   **LO1** a model employee. He has not taken a vacation in over four years, always stating that work was too important. One of Bart's primary jobs at the clinic is to open mail and list the checks received. He also collects cash from patients at the cashier's window as patients leave. There are times that things are so hectic that Bart does not bother to give the patient a receipt; however, he assures them that he will make sure their account is properly credited. When things slow down at the clinic Bart often offers to help Lisa post payments to the patients' accounts receivable ledger. Lisa is always happy to receive help since she is also quite busy and because Bart is such a careful worker.

Required

Identify any internal control principles that may be violated in Dr. Spring's clinic.

P7-8A. **Internal Control** Listed below are (a) four potential errors or problems that could occur in the process-   **LO1, 3** ing of cash transactions and (b) internal control principles. Review each error or problem and identify an internal control principle that could reduce the chance of the error or problem occurring. You may also cite more than one principle if more than one applies, or write none if none of the principles will correct the error or problem.

1. An employee steals cash collected from a customer's accounts receivable and hides the theft by issuing a credit memorandum indicating the customer returned the merchandise.

2. An official with authority to sign checks is able to steal blank checks and issue them without detection.

3. Due to a labor shortage many employees are hired without sufficient skills with the thought they can "learn on the job."

4. A salesperson often rings up a sale for less than the actual amount and then pockets the additional cash collected from the customer.

Internal control principles:

a. Establish clear lines of authority and responsibility.
b. Segregation of duties.
c. Hire competent personnel.
d. Use control numbers on all business documents.
e. Develop plans and budgets.
f. Maintain adequate accounting records.
g. Provide physical and electronic controls.
h. Conduct internal audits.

LO3 **P7-9A. Bank Reconciliation** The Seattle Boat Company's bank statement for the month of September indicated a balance of $14,000. The company's cash account in the general ledger showed a balance of $11,318 on September 30. Other relevant information includes the following:

1. Deposits in transit on September 30 total $10,400.

2. The bank statement shows a debit memorandum for an $80 check printing charge.

3. Check number 238 payable to Simon Company was recorded in the accounting records for $496 and cleared the bank for this same amount. A review of the records indicated that the Simon account now has a $72 credit balance and the check to them should have been $568.

4. Outstanding checks as of September 30 totaled $11,600.

5. Check No. 276 was correctly written and paid by the bank for $818. The check was recorded in the accounting records as a debit to accounts payable and a credit to cash for $980.

6. The bank returned a NSF check in the amount of $1,120.

7. The bank included a credit memorandum for $2,520 representing a collection of a customer's note. The principle portion was $2,400 and the interest portion was $120. The interest had not been accrued.

Required
a. Prepare the September bank reconciliation for Seattle Boat Company.
b. Prepare any necessary adjusting entries.

LO4 **P7-10A. Effective Cash Management** Longo LLP is a new law firm struggling to manage its cash flow. Like all new businesses, the firm has not yet developed a sufficient client base to cover its operating costs. Additionally, the firm faced a number of large initial, but nonrecurring, start-up costs at the beginning of the year. Ongoing monthly costs include office rent and salary for a paralegal staff member. Another problem that the firm faces is that several of its major clients have failed to pay their current, but overdue, bills. Mick Longo, one of the two founding partners, has not taken any salary since the firm began operations over eight months ago, and has decided to maintain a part-time job bartending on weekends at a local resort to insure that he has some cash to cover day-to-day expenses like travel.

Required
What suggestions would you make to Mick Longo to improve his firm's cash management practices?

PROBLEMS—SET B

LO1, 3 **P7-1B. Internal Control** Wheeler Company encountered the following situations:

a. Jenny Farrell, head of the receiving department, created a fictitious company named Quick Forms and used it to send invoices to Wheeler Company for business documents that Wheeler never ordered or received. Farrell prepared receiving reports that stated that the business documents had been received. Wheeler's controller compared the receiving reports to the invoices and paid each one.

b. Wheeler Company lost one day's cash receipts. An employee took the receipts to the bank after the bank's closing hours to deposit them in the night depository slot. A creative thief had placed a sign on the slot saying it was out of order and all deposits should be placed in a metal canister placed next to the building. Wheeler's employee placed the deposit in the canister and left. Employees from two other companies did the same thing. Later that night, the thief returned and stole the deposits from the canister. (This is an actual case.)

c. Wheeler Company does not prenumber the sales invoices used for over-the-counter sales. A cashier pocketed cash receipts and destroyed all copies of the related sales invoices.

Required

For each situation, describe any violations of good internal control procedures and identify the steps that you would take to prevent each situation.

P7-2B. **Internal Control** The Mountain Twister amusement ride has the following system of internal control over cash receipts. All persons pay the same price for a ride. A person taking the ride pays cash to the cashier and receives a prenumbered ticket. The tickets are issued in strict number sequence. The individual then walks to the ride site, hands the ticket to a ticket-taker (who controls the number of people getting on each ride), and passes through a turnstile. At the end of each day, the beginning ticket number is subtracted from the ending ticket number to determine the number of tickets sold. The cash is counted and compared with the number of tickets sold. The turnstile records how many people pass through it. At the end of each day, the beginning turnstile count is subtracted from the ending count to determine the number of riders that day. The number of riders is compared with the number of tickets sold.   **LO1, 3**

Required

Which internal control feature would reveal each of the following irregularities?

a. The ticket-taker lets her friends on the ride without tickets.
b. The cashier gives his friends tickets without receiving cash from them.
c. The cashier gives too much change.
d. The ticket-taker returns the tickets she has collected to the cashier. The cashier then resells these tickets and splits the proceeds with the ticket-taker.
e. A person sneaks into the ride line without paying the cashier.

P7-3B. **Internal Controls for Cash Received from Retail Sales** Midland Stores is a retailer of men's clothing. Most customers pay cash for their purchases. The procedures that Midland uses for handling cash are described below: **LO3**

a. Each department begins the day with whatever amount of cash remains in the cash register from the prior day. This is not a predetermined amount.
b. All sales associates share one cash drawer.
c. Each sales associate can handle all transactions, including returns and unusual transactions, without approval from a supervisor.
d. At the end of each day, one of the sales associates takes the cash drawer and the cash register totals to a private area where no one can observe what is being done, counts the cash in the drawer, and prepares a written report of sales and cash received. The cash, the register tape, and a copy of the report are sent to the controller's department.
e. The controller prepares the deposit slip and sends the deposit to the bank. The controller then prepares the journal entry to record the cash sales.
f. The controller does not keep any copies of the written report or the deposit slip.
g. The bank statement is sent to the controller, who prepares the bank reconciliation.

Required

For each of these procedures, indicate how Midland could improve it. (Refer to Exhibit 7-2 in the chapter to help you generate ideas.)

P7-4B. **Bank Reconciliation** On May 31, the Cash in Bank account of Wallace Company, a sole proprietorship, had a balance of $6,122.50. On that date, the bank statement indicated a balance of $7,933.50. A comparison of returned checks and bank advices revealed the following: **LO3** ✅

1. Deposits in transit May 31 totaled $2,709.05.
2. Outstanding checks May 31 totaled $3,088.25.

3. The bank added to the account $27.80 of interest income earned by Wallace during May.

4. The bank collected a $2,400 note receivable for Wallace and charged a $20 collection fee. Both items appear on the bank statement.

5. Bank service charges in addition to the collection fee, not yet recorded, were $20.

6. Included with the returned checks is a memo indicating that L. Ryder's check for $686 had been returned NSF. Ryder, a customer, had sent the check to pay an account of $700 less a 2% discount.

7. Wallace Company incorrectly recorded the payment of an account payable as $690; the check was for $960.

Required

a. Prepare a bank reconciliation for Wallace Company at May 31.

b. Prepare the journal entry (or entries) necessary to bring the Cash in Bank account into agreement with the reconciled cash balance on the bank reconciliation.

LO3 **P7-5B.** **Bank Reconciliation** The bank reconciliation made by Sandler Company, a sole proprietorship, on March 31 showed a deposit in transit of $1,100 and two outstanding checks, No. 797 for $450 and No. 804 for $890. The reconciled cash balance on March 31 was $11,720.

The following bank statement is available for April 2012:

			Bank Statement			
TO	Sandler Company Fairbanks, AK				April 30 FAIRBANKS NATIONAL BANK	
Date	Deposits	No.	Date	Charges	Date	Balance
					Mar. 31	$11,960
Apr. 1	$1,100	804	Apr. 2	$ 890	Apr. 1	13,060
3	1,680	807	3	730	2	12,170
7	1,250	808	7	1,140	3	13,120
13	1,020	809	7	838	7	12,392
18	840	810	16	1,040	13	13,086
23	790	811	13	326	16	12,046
27	1,340	813	27	540	18	12,386
30	1,160	814	23	600	23	12,576
30	60IN	NSF	18	500	27	13,376
		SC	30	40	30	14,556

Item Codes:	EC: Error Correction	DM: Debit Memo	CM: Credit Memo
	SC: Service Charge	OD: Overdraft	RT: Returned Item
	IN: Interest Earned	NSF: Non-sufficient Funds	

A list of deposits made and checks written during April is shown below:

Deposits Made		Checks Written	
Apr. 2	$1,680	No. 807	$ 730
6	1,250	808	1,140
10	1,020	809	838
17	840	810	1,040
22	790	811	272
24	1,340	812	948
29	1,160	813	540
30	1,425	814	600
		815	372
	$9,505	816	875
			$7,355

The Cash in Bank account balance on April 30 was $13,870. In reviewing checks returned by the bank, the accountant discovered that check No. 811, written for $326 for delivery expense, was recorded in the cash disbursements journal as $272. The NSF check for $500 was that of customer R. Koppa, deposited in April. Interest for April added to the account by the bank was $60.

Required

a. Prepare a bank reconciliation for Sandler Company at April 30.

b. Prepare the necessary journal entries to bring the Cash in Bank account into agreement with the reconciled cash balance on the bank reconciliation.

P7-6B. Reporting Cash Jenkins Company has the following items at year-end:

LO2

Currency and coin in safe.	$ 5,500
Funds in savings account (requires $3,000 compensating balance)	15,250
Funds in checking account	1,750
Traveler's checks	1,500
Postdated check	2,250
Not-sufficient-funds check.	450
Money market fund	12,600

Required

Identify the amount of the above items that should be reported as cash and cash equivalents on Jenkins Company's balance sheet.

P7-7B. Internal Control Jerry Finch has worked for Jones Hardware for many years. Jerry has been a model employee. He has not taken a vacation in over three years, always stating that work was too important. One of Jerry's primary jobs at the store is to open mail and list the checks received. He also collects cash from customers at the store's outdoor nursery area. There are times that things are so hectic that Jerry does not bother to use the register, simply making change from cash he carries with him. When things slow down at the store Jerry often offers to help Cindy post payments to the customer's accounts receivable ledger. Cindy is always happy to receive help since she is also quite busy and because Jerry is such a careful worker.

LO1

Required

Identify any internal control principles that may be violated in Jones Hardware store.

P7-8B. Internal Control Listed below are (a) four potential errors or problems that could occur in the processing of cash transactions and (b) internal control principles. For each error or problem, identify an internal control principle that could reduce the chance of the error or problem occurring. You may also cite more than one principle if more than one applies, or write none if none of the principles will correct the error or problem.

LO1, 3

1. Three cashiers use one cash register and the cash in the drawer is often short of the recorded balance.

2. The same employee is responsible for opening the mail, listing any checks received, preparing the deposit receipt, and recording to the accounts receivable journal. Several customers have complained that their balances are incorrect.

3. In an effort to save printing costs, generic receipts without numbers are used for customer sales.

4. Because things have been hectic, no budgets were prepared this year. One department seems to be doing less volume in revenue, but cost of goods sold appear to be high relative to sales.

Internal control principles:

a. Establish clear lines of authority and responsibility.
b. Segregation of duties.
c. Hire competent personnel.
d. Use control numbers on all business documents.
e. Develop plans and budgets.
f. Maintain adequate accounting records.
g. Provide physical and electronic controls.
h. Conduct internal audits.

P7-9B. Bank Reconciliation The Chicago Scooter Company's bank statement for the month of June indicated a balance of $3,500. The company's cash account in the general ledger showed a balance of $2,890 on June 30. Other relevant information includes the following:

LO3

1. Deposits in transit on June 30 total $2,600.

2. The bank statement shows a debit memorandum for a $20 check printing charge.
3. Check No. 160 payable to Simon Company was recorded in the accounting records for $124 and cleared the bank for this same amount. A review of the records indicated that the Simon account now has an $18 credit balance and the check to them should have been $142.
4. Outstanding checks as of June 30 totaled $2,900.
5. Check No. 176 was correctly written and paid by the bank for $203. The check was recorded in the accounting records as a debit to accounts payable and a credit to cash for $245.
6. The bank returned a NSF check in the amount of $342.
7. The bank included a credit memorandum for $630 representing a collection of a customer's note. The principal portion was $600 and the interest portion was $30. The interest had not been accrued.

Required
a. Prepare the June bank reconciliation for the Chicago Scooter Company.
b. Prepare any necessary adjusting entries.

SERIAL PROBLEM: KATE'S CARDS

(Note: This is a continuation of the Serial Problem: Kate's Cards from Chapters 1 through 6.)

SP7. On February 15, 2013, Kate Collins, owner of Kate's Cards, asks you to investigate the cash handling activities in her business. She believes that a new employee might be stealing funds. "I have no proof," she says, "but I'm fairly certain that the January 31, 2013, undeposited receipts amounted to more than $12,000, although the January 31 bank reconciliation prepared by the cashier (who works in the treasurer's department) shows only $7,238.40. Also, the January bank reconciliation doesn't show several checks that have been outstanding for a long time. The cashier told me that these checks needn't appear on the reconciliation because he had notified the bank to stop payment on them and he had made the necessary adjustment on the books. Does that sound reasonable to you?"

At your request, Kate shows you the following January 31, 2013, bank reconciliation prepared by the cashier:

KATE'S CARDS
Bank Reconciliation
January 31, 2013

Ending balance from bank statement		$ 4,843.69	Balance from general ledger			$10,893.89
Add: Deposits in transit		7,238.40				
		$12,082.09				
Less:			Less:			
Outstanding checks:			Bank service charge	$ 60.00		
No. 2351	$1,100.20		Unrecorded credit	1,200.00	(1,260.00)	
No. 2353	578.32					
No. 2354	969.68	(2,448.20)				
Reconciled cash balance		$ 9,633.89	Reconciled cash balance			$ 9,633.89

You discover that the $1,200 unrecorded bank credit represents a note collected by the bank on Kate's behalf; it appears in the deposits column of the January bank statement. Your investigation also reveals that the December 31, 2012, bank reconciliation showed three checks that had been outstanding longer than 10 months: No. 1432 for $600, No. 1458 for $466.90, and No. 1512 for $253.10. You also discover that these items were never added back into the Cash account in Kate's books. In confirming that the checks shown on the cashier's January 31 bank reconciliation were outstanding on that date, you discover that check No. 2353 was actually a payment of $1,658.32 and had been recorded on the books for that amount.

To confirm the amount of undeposited receipts at January 31, you request a bank statement for February 1–12 (called a cutoff bank statement). This indeed shows a January 1 deposit of $7,238.40.

Required

a. Calculate the amount of funds stolen by the employee.

b. Describe how the employee concealed the theft.

c. What suggestions would you make to Kate about cash control procedures?

EXTENDING YOUR KNOWLEDGE

REPORTING AND ANALYSIS

EYK7-1. **Financial Reporting Problem: Columbia Sportswear Company** The financial statements for the Columbia Sportswear Company can be found in Appendix A at the end of this book.

COLUMBIA
SPORTSWEAR
COMPANY

Required

Use the financial statements and the accompanying notes to the financial statements to answer the following questions about Columbia Sportswear:

a. What title is used on Columbia's consolidated balance sheet for cash?

b. According to the information given in Note 2, what is the makeup of the cash and cash equivalents account?

c. According to information in Item 9A. Controls and Procedures, who is responsible for establishing and maintaining adequate internal control over financial reporting?

d. Deloitte and Touche, the independent auditor of Columbia Sportswear, issued a report on their audit of Columbia's internal control. What did they conclude?

EYK7-2. **Comparative Analysis Problem: Columbia Sportswear Company vs. Under Armour, Inc.** The financial statements for Columbia Sportswear Company can be found in Appendix A and Under Armour, Inc.'s financial statements can be found in Appendix B at the end of this book.

COLUMBIA
SPORTSWEAR
COMPANY

UNDER ARMOUR,
INC.

Required

Use the information in the companies' financial statements to answer the following questions:

a. What is the balance in cash and cash equivalents as of December 31, 2011?

b. What percentage of each company's total assets is made up of cash and cash equivalents as of December 31, 2011?

c. How much did cash and cash equivalents change during 2011 for each firm?

d. For each company, how did the change in cash for 2011 compare to its cash provided by operating activities?

EYK7-3. **Business Decision Problem** Qualitec Electronics Company is a distributor of microcomputers and related electronic equipment. The company has grown very rapidly. It is located in a large building near Chicago, Illinois. Jack Flanigan, the president of Qualitec, has hired you to perform an internal control review of the company. You conduct interviews of key employees, tour the operations, and observe various company functions. You discover the following:

1. Qualitec has not changed its ordering procedures since it was formed eight years ago. Anyone in the company can prepare a purchase order and send it to the vendor without getting any managerial approval. When the invoice arrives from the vendor, it is compared only to the purchase order before authorizing payment.

2. Qualitec does not have an organization chart. In fact, employees are encouraged to work on their own, without supervision. Flanigan believes that this approach increases creativity.

3. Business documents have been carefully designed by the controller. When the printer prints the documents, no control numbers are printed on them. Instead, employees using a form write the next sequential number on the form. The controller believes that this approach ensures that a proper sequencing of numbers will be maintained.

4. No budgets are prepared for the company.

5. All doors to the building remain unlocked from 7:00 a.m. to 11:00 p.m. Employees normally work from 7:30 a.m. to 5:00 p.m. A private security firm drives to the building to unlock it

each morning and lock it each night. The security firm's employee leaves immediately after unlocking or locking. The company does not use time clocks or employee badges.

6. Flanigan believes that audits (either external or internal) are a waste of time. He has resisted the bank president's urging to hire a CPA firm to conduct an audit.

Required

Analyze the findings listed above. Then list all the internal control weaknesses that you can identify. For each weakness, describe one or more internal controls that Qualitec should install to overcome the weakness.

EYK7-4.   **Financial Analysis Problem** The **Public Company Accounting Oversight Board (PCAOB)** was created as part of the Sarbanes-Oxley legislation to provide oversight to U.S. accounting firms. The PCAOB's address is http://www.pcaobus.org

Required

Answer the following questions:

a.   What is the mission of the PCAOB?
b.   What is the title of the first auditing standard issued by the PCAOB?
c.   According to the rules section of the site, what is required for a PCAOB rule to take effect?

CRITICAL THINKING

GENERAL MILLS,
INC.

EYK7-5.   **Accounting Research Problem** Refer to the consolidated balance sheets in the fiscal year 2011 annual report of **General Mills, Inc.** available on this book's Website.

Required

a.   What was the amount of cash and cash equivalents as of May 29, 2011?
b.   By what amount did cash and cash equivalents increase or decrease during the year?
c.   What statement elsewhere in the annual report contains an explanation of the increase or decrease in the cash and cash equivalents amount? In that statement, what amount of cash was provided or used by (1) operating activities, (2) investment activities, and (3) financing activities?
d.   What members of the company signed off as to the assessment of the company's internal control (see Reports of management and Independent Registered Public Accounting Firm)?
e.   What firm conducted the audit of General Mills?
f.   What opinion did the accounting firm express about General Mills' financial statements?
g.   In addition to their audit of the financial statements, what else did the auditing firm audit?

EYK7-6.   **Accounting Communication Activity** You were recently hired as the head of a company's ethics division. As one of your first acts, you decide to prepare a letter to the company's Chairman of the Board explaining the importance of ethics within the company. What are some of the items that should be included in your letter?

EYK7-7.   **Accounting Ethics Case** Gina Pullen is the petty cash cashier for a large family-owned restaurant. She has been presented on numerous occasions with properly approved receipts for reimbursement from petty cash that she believes are personal expenses of one of the five owners of the restaurant. She reports to the controller of the company. The controller is also a family member and is the person who approves the receipts for payment out of petty cash.

Required

What are the accounting implications if Pullen is correct? What alternatives should she consider?

EYK7-8.   **Corporate Social Responsibility Problem** Corporate Social Responsibility and fraud prevention are often related. One way that the two are connected is in the creation of a culture of honesty and the ethical treatment of employees. This is often the result of the tone from the top, where the company leaders not only talk about these concepts, but also practice them.

Required

Discuss how a culture of honesty and the ethical treatment of employees can reduce the risk of fraud.

EYK7-9. **Forensic Accounting Problem** Internal control follows the concept of reasonable assurance. Pete Simmons, the chief compliance officer of Salem Company, stated that he does not want simply reasonable assurance. He wants absolute assurance in all aspects that apply to the financial statements of the company. Specifically, Pete stated, "As long as I am working here, we will run a perfectly tight system that ensures absolutely no fraud in our financial statements." Betty Flint, the controller, disagreed with Pete and argued that anything more than reasonable assurance is both financially and practically impossible.

Required
Do you agree with Pete or Betty, and why?

EYK7-10. **Analyzing IFRS Financial Statements** Tesco PLC is the world's third largest retailer and is headquartered in the United Kingdom. The complete annual report for **Tesco PLC** for year-ended February 26, 2011 is available on this book's Website.

Required
a. What was the amount of cash and cash equivalents as of 26 February, 2009?
b. By what amount did cash and cash equivalents increase or decrease during the year?
c. What statement elsewhere in the annual report contains an explanation of the increase or decrease in the cash and cash equivalents amount? In that statement, what amount of cash was provided or used by (1) operating activities, (2) investment activities, and (3) financing activities?
d. What firm conducted the audit of Tesco's financial statements?
e. What opinion did the accounting firm express about Tesco's financial statements?

EYK7-11. **Working with the Takeaways** The following conditions of material weaknesses were reported in a prior year independent auditors' report on internal control of the U.S. Department of Transportation Highway Trust Fund (HTF):
1. Weaknesses with respect to journal entry preparation:
   a. Lack of indication of preparer
   b. Lack of supporting documentation
   c. Lack of proper review and approval
2. Weaknesses with respect to the consolidated financial statement preparation and analysis process:
   a. Inadequate analysis of abnormal balances
   b. Inadequate analysis of account relationships
   c. Inadequate controls over journal entry processing
   d. Lack of oversight related to allocation transfers

Required
a. What is the possible negative effect of these material weaknesses?
b. If you were the reporting auditor, what would you recommend be done?

ANSWERS TO SELF-STUDY QUESTIONS:

1. c, (p. 314) 2. c, (p. 316) 3. d, (p. 318) 4. a, (p. 318) 5. c, (p. 338) 6. b, (p. 322) 7. c, (p. 324)
8. d, (p. 329) 9. a, (p. 331) 10. c, (p. 329)

YOUR TURN! SOLUTIONS

Solution 7.1

1. This is a human resources control violation. The supervisor may be committing a fraud and covering up his acts. If the supervisor were forced to take a vacation, the employee filling in might observe some suspicious activity and uncover the fraud.
2. This is a physical control violation. The unattended inventory could be stolen through the open door.

3. This is a segregation of duties violation. The supervisor is in a position to order an improper purchase, receive the goods for his own purposes, record the goods as received by the company, and then have the company pay for the purchase.

4. This is a violation of the use of control numbers. An employee could defraud the company by writing up a meal purchase, receiving the cash from the customer, then destroying the order slip and keeping the cash.

Solution 7.2

1. Treasurer's department
2. Retail sales supervisor
3. Mailroom
4. Internal audit department
5. Controller's department

Solution 7.3

1. Add to bank statement balance
2. Subtract from bank statement balance
3. Subtract from cash general ledger account
4. Add to cash general ledger account

Solution 7.4

1. Internal audit
2. Financial statement audit
3. Operational audit
4. Financial statement audit
5. Operational audit

8

Accounting for Receivables

PAST

In Chapter 7 we studied how companies can prevent errors and fraud with the use of internal controls.

PRESENT

In this chapter we turn our attention to the accounting for two important assets—accounts and notes receivable.

FUTURE

In Chapter 9 we will continue our study of a company's assets by looking at long-lived assets.

LEARNING OBJECTIVES

1. **Define** accounts receivable, explain losses from uncollectible accounts, and **describe** the allowance method of accounting for doubtful accounts. *(p. 362)*

2. **Describe** and **illustrate** the percentage of net sales method and the accounts receivable aging method for estimating a business's bad debts expense. *(p. 367)*

3. **Discuss** the accounting treatment of credit card sales. *(p. 371)*

4. **Illustrate** a promissory note receivable, **discuss** the calculation of interest on notes receivable, and **present** journal entries to record notes receivable and interest. *(p. 372)*

5. **Define** accounts receivable turnover and average collection period and **explain** their use in the analysis and management of accounts and notes receivable. *(p. 376)*

6. Appendix 8A: **Illustrate** the direct write-off method and **contrast** it with the allowance method for accounting for doubtful accounts. *(p. 379)*

MGM RESORTS INTERNATIONAL— MANAGING CREDIT FOR BIGGER PROFITS

MGM Resorts International is among the largest gaming companies in the world. The company owns 15 casino resorts, including Bellagio, MGM Grand Las Vegas, Mandalay Bay, Luxor, Excalibur, Monte Carlo, New York-New York, Circus Circus, and The Mirage. These establishments provide gaming, hotel accommodations, dining, and other entertainment for their clientele. Gaming, however, is the primary revenue-producing activity for these businesses.

Casino credit is an important marketing tool for gaming companies like MGM Resorts International. When used intelligently, it can result in significant increases in revenue since high-end casinos like Bellagio and The Mirage rely heavily on clientele that gamble on credit. Granting credit to gamblers also increases player loyalty because gamblers are inclined to play at casinos where they have a line of credit. Once credit is established, the gambler is allowed to write a marker and withdraw money to use to gamble. The credit, however, is only granted to clientele who utilize it. While there is no requirement that a gambler lose in order to maintain a line of credit, the credit is lost if it is not used. In other words, a casino grants credit to its clientele with the expectation that the more a gambler uses the line of credit, the more likely the casino is to win.

While credit lines clearly provide a boost to a casino's revenue, it is critical that the casino carefully manage these receivables. MGM Resorts International, for example, maintains strict controls over the issuance of markers and "aggressively pursues collection from those customers who fail to repay their markers on a timely basis." GAAP requires MGM Resorts International to recognize the likelihood that a casino may be unable to collect all of its outstanding markers on its financial statements. At year-end 2011, despite aggressive collection efforts, MGM Resorts International reported over $100 million dollars in doubtful collections.

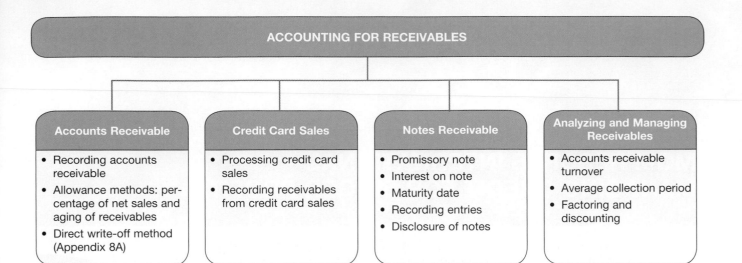

ACCOUNTING FOR RECEIVABLES

Accounts Receivable	Credit Card Sales	Notes Receivable	Analyzing and Managing Receivables
• Recording accounts receivable • Allowance methods: percentage of net sales and aging of receivables • Direct write-off method (Appendix 8A)	• Processing credit card sales • Recording receivables from credit card sales	• Promissory note • Interest on note • Maturity date • Recording entries • Disclosure of notes	• Accounts receivable turnover • Average collection period • Factoring and discounting

RECEIVABLES

Receivables are assets representing a company's right to receive cash or other assets at some point in the future. Receivables may be classified as either a current asset or a non-current asset, depending upon the date of the expected receipt of cash or other assets. The most common types of receivables are accounts and notes receivable, which arise when a company sells its products or services to its customers on credit. Other types of receivables include loans to employees, loans to other companies, and any interest receivable on such outstanding loans.

ACCOUNTING IN PRACTICE	Accounts Receivable

Accounts receivable can amount to a large percentage of total assets for a company. Below are representative accounts receivable as a percentage of total assets appearing on the recent balance sheets of four well known companies in different industries.

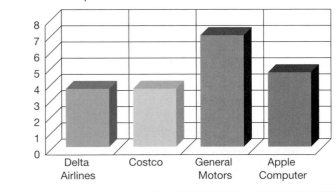

ACCOUNTS RECEIVABLE

LO1 **Define** accounts receivable, explain losses from uncollectible accounts, and **describe** the allowance method of accounting for doubtful accounts.

Many businesses sell goods and services to their customers on a credit basis, allowing customers to pay for their purchases over a period of time called the credit period. **Accounts receivable** is the current asset that is created when a sale or service transaction is executed on a credit basis.

When a company executes a credit sale, it debits the Accounts Receivable account and credits the Sales Revenue account. This transaction is posted to the general ledger, increasing both the Accounts Receivable and Sales Revenue balances. To illustrate, assume that on December 1, 2013, the Claremont Company sells $20,000 of merchandise on account. The company will make the following journal entry on its books for the credit sale transaction:

2013			
Dec. 1	Accounts receivable	20,000	
	Sales revenue		20,000
	To record credit sales to customers.		

A = L + SE
+20,000   +20,000
                       Rev

When the credit sale is collected on December 20, the following entry is made:

Dec. 20	Cash	20,000	
	Accounts receivable		20,000
	To record cash collection.		

A = L + SE
+20,000
−20,000

Accounts receivable includes only those amounts relating to credit sales of goods or services. Other amounts due, such as from advances to employees or loans to affiliated companies, should be included with the Other Receivables account on the balance sheet. Other Receivables may be either a current asset or a noncurrent asset.

A.K.A. Accounts receivable are also sometimes referred to as *trade receivables*.

Balance Sheet Title for Accounts Receivable	**ACCOUNTING IN PRACTICE**

Regardless of what it is called, accounts receivable are not cash until they are collected. So, what should we call these receivables? Uncollected cash may seem like an appropriate account title, but this title is not commonly used by businesses. Instead, companies use several other titles, as can be seen from a survey of 600 large U.S. companies:

Source: Accounting Trends and Techniques

LOSSES FROM VALUING ACCOUNTS RECEIVABLE

Businesses that extend credit to their customers anticipate some amount of credit losses—that is, losses from customers who fail to pay for their credit purchases. The magnitude of these losses is usually closely related to a firm's credit-granting policy. A **credit-granting policy** is a policy that a company follows to decide which customers should be allowed to buy goods and services on credit and how much credit those customers should be granted. Companies often base their credit-granting policy on a computerized credit score. (See Accounting in Practice: Credit Scoring Systems.) A company may deliberately relax its credit-granting policy to increase its sales, fully anticipating a parallel increase in its credit losses.

Businesses must also establish a **credit-collection policy**; that is, a policy establishing the amount of time that its customers may take before they are required to pay their outstanding accounts receivable. In Chapter 5, we discussed the credit period, or the allowed time period that a customer may take to pay for their credit purchases, and sales discounts, or the dollar amount that a customer may deduct from the purchase price of goods if they pay within an allowed discount period. Together, any sales discount, the discount period, and the credit period constitute a company's credit-collection policy. Maintaining an effective credit-collection policy is important for those businesses that allow their customers to buy goods and services on credit, since companies can have millions of dollars of their cash tied up in unpaid accounts receivable.

Most large companies have credit departments that administer the company's credit-granting and credit-collection policies. Credit personnel conduct credit investigations, establish credit limits, and follow up on any unpaid accounts. They also decide, following written collection procedures, when an account receivable is uncollectible, and consequently, when an account receivable should be written off a company's balance sheet as uncollectible.

A.K.A. The Bad Debts Expense is also sometimes referred to as the *Loss from Doubtful Accounts*, the *Loss from Uncollectible Accounts*, or the *Uncollectible Accounts Expense*.

Credit losses are considered to be an operating expense of a business, and consequently, they are debited to an account called **Bad Debts Expense**. Normally, the Bad Debts Expense account is classified as a selling expense on the income statement, although some companies include it as part of their administrative expenses.

ACCOUNTING IN PRACTICE	**Credit Scoring Systems**

Most companies use a computerized credit scoring system to decide whether to extend credit to their customers. The credit scoring system is based on a set of formulas with multiple variables. Data from a customer's credit application and from credit reporting agencies are used by the system to calculate a credit score. The system then compares the score to predetermined limits and recommends whether or not credit be extended.

If credit is extended, the scoring system often recommends an upper limit on the amount of credit to be extended. Scoring systems focus on a customer's ability to generate net income and cash flow, the customer's current level of debt and required repayment schedule, and current assets. Many of the financial statement ratios discussed throughout this text are incorporated into credit scoring systems.

Allowance Method

Credit losses are an unfortunate but predictable consequence of extending credit to a business's customers. At the time that a credit sale is made, the seller does not know whether the account receivable will be collected in full, in part, or not at all. Further, any loss from an uncollectible account may not be known for several months, or even a year or more, following the credit sale. To achieve a proper matching of sales revenues and expenses, however, a company's accountants must estimate the amount of the bad debts expense to report on the income statement. This estimate is reported in an end-of-period adjusting entry. The process of estimating and recording the bad debts expense for a business is most often executed using the **allowance method**.

PRINCIPLE ALERT	**Matching Concept**

The *matching concept* states that expenses should be linked with, or matched with, the revenues that they help to generate. A company sells its goods and services on credit because this business practice attracts more customers and, therefore, more sales revenue than if the company only permitted cash transactions. One of the costs associated with extending credit to customers is the bad debts expense. The matching concept requires that this expense be reported in the same accounting period as the related sales revenue. To accomplish the appropriate matching of sales revenue and expenses, accountants must estimate the bad debts expense because the specific accounts that will be uncollectible may not be known until a later time period.

Recording Estimated Bad Debt Expense Under the Allowance Method

The allowance method receives its name because the end-of-period adjusting entry credits a contra-asset account called the *Allowance for Doubtful Accounts*. The allowance method not only matches credit losses with the related credit sales in the same time period in which the sale occurs, but it also reports accounts receivable at their estimated realizable value in the end-of-period balance sheet. To illustrate, assume that the Claremont Corporation estimates its bad debts expense for 2013 to be $4,000 and makes the following adjusting entry in its general journal:

2013			
Dec. 31	Bad debts expense	4,000	
	Allowance for doubtful accounts		4,000
	To record the bad debts expense for the year.		

A = L + SE
−4,000   −4,000
Exp

Notice that the credit entry is made to the **Allowance for Doubtful Accounts** rather than directly against the Accounts Receivable account. The reason for this is because when a firm records its estimate of the amount of its uncollectible accounts, it does not know precisely which of its customer accounts will be uncollectible.

A.K.A. The Allowance for Doubtful Accounts is also often referred to as the *Allowance for Uncollectible Accounts.*

The Allowance for Doubtful Accounts is a contra-asset account with a normal credit balance. To report the expected collectible amount of accounts receivable on the balance sheet, the Allowance for Doubtful Accounts is subtracted from the Accounts Receivable account. Assuming that the Claremont Corporation had $100,000 of accounts receivable (and a zero balance in the Allowance for Doubtful Accounts prior to the December 31, 2013, adjusting entry), the year-end balance sheet presentation would appear as follows:

Current Assets		
Cash		$ 52,000
Accounts receivable	$100,000	
Less: Allowance for doubtful accounts	4,000	96,000
Inventory		125,000
Other current assets		31,000
Total Current Assets		$304,000

Going Concern Concept	**PRINCIPLE ALERT**

Accounts receivable are reported on the balance sheet at the amount that a company expects to collect in the future from its credit customers. This presentation assumes that the company will be in existence long enough to collect its accounts receivable, and therefore, it is an example of the *going concern concept*. As a principle of accounting, the going concern concept assumes that a business entity will continue to operate indefinitely in the future.

Writing Off Specific Accounts Receivable under the Allowance Method A company's credit department manager is usually the employee with the authority to determine when an account receivable is uncollectible, and hence, when a specific account receivable should be written off and removed from a company's balance sheet. Assume, for example, that the credit manager of the Claremont Corporation authorizes a $300 write off of the Monroe Company's account receivable. When the accounting department is notified of the credit department manager's decision, it will make the following journal entry:

2014			
Jan. 5	Allowance for doubtful accounts	300	
	Accounts receivable—Monroe Company		300
	To write off the Monroe Company's account receivable.		

A = L + SE
+300
−300

The journal entry to write off an account receivable does not affect a company's net income or total assets. By means of the year-end adjusting entry, the bad debts expense is reported in the period when the related sales revenue is recorded. Because the Allowance for Doubtful Accounts is deducted from the Accounts Receivable account on the balance sheet, the *net* realizable value of accounts receivable is unchanged by the account write off. After the Monroe Company's account receivable has been written off, the Accounts Receivable and the Allowance for Doubtful Accounts T-accounts appear as follows:

Accounts Receivable				Allowance for Doubtful Accounts			
Beg.	100,000	300	Jan. 5	Jan. 5	300	4,000	Beg.
Bal.	99,700					3,700	Bal.

As can be seen in the above T-accounts, the net realizable value of Claremont's accounts receivable as of January 1, 2014, is $96,000 ($100,000 less $4,000 allowance for doubtful accounts). Following the January 5, 2014, account write off, the net realizable value of the Claremont Corporation's accounts receivable remains $96,000 ($99,700 less $3,700 allowance for doubtful accounts) since both the Accounts Receivable account and the Allowance for Doubtful Accounts are reduced by the same amount ($300). The following table summarizes the allowance method.

Action	Journal Entry	Balance Sheet Effect (Increase/Decrease)	Income Statement Effect (Increase/Decrease)
Recording Estimated Bad Debt Expense (In period when sale occurred)	**DEBIT** Bad debt expense **CREDIT** Allowance for doubtful accounts	▲ Allowance for doubtful accounts ▼ Accounts receivable, net	▲ Bad debt expense ▼ Net income
Writing-Off Bad Debt (When receivable is determined uncollectible)	**DEBIT** Allowance for doubtful accounts **CREDIT** Accounts receivable	▼ Accounts receivable ▼ Allowance for doubtful accounts **No Change** Accounts receivable, net	**No Change**

Balance Sheet Title for Uncollectible Accounts

No doubt about it, not all receivables will be collected! So how should a company title the amount that they likely will be unable to collect? Allowance for Doubtful Accounts is the most common account title, although several other titles are also used, as can be seen from a survey of 600 large U.S. companies:

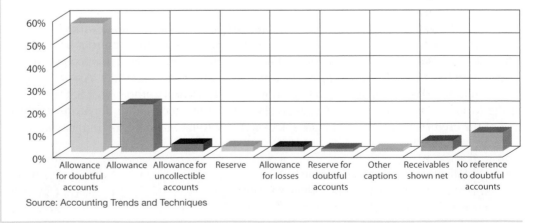

Source: Accounting Trends and Techniques

ESTIMATING CREDIT LOSSES

When the allowance method is used, estimates of a company's expected credit losses are generally based on past business experience, with additional consideration given to forecasts of future sales activity, economic conditions, and any planned changes to a company's credit-granting policy. The most commonly used estimates of expected credit losses are related either to a company's credit sales for the period, or to the amount of accounts receivable outstanding at the end of a fiscal period.

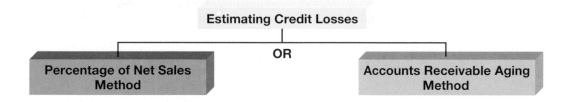

Percentage of Net Sales Method

Through years of business experience, some companies have learned to estimate their expected credit losses as a percentage of their credit sales for a given period. Under this approach, the amount of the end-of-period adjusting entry for a business's expected bad debts expense is determined by multiplying the company's total credit sales for the period by a historical percentage that reflects past credit losses. For example, suppose that credit sales for 2013 for the Claremont Corporation are $500,000 and that past experience indicates that the company is likely to sustain a two percent loss on its credit sales. The adjusting entry for Claremont's expected credit losses for 2013 (2 percent × $500,000) would be recorded as follows in the general journal:

LO2 **Describe** and **illustrate** the percentage of net sales method and the accounts receivable aging method for estimating a business's bad debts expense.

2013			
Dec. 31	Bad debts expense	10,000	
	Allowance for doubtful accounts		10,000
	To record the bad debts expense for the year.		

A = L + SE
−10,000   −10,000
                Exp

Because the periodic estimate for doubtful accounts under this procedure is related to credit sales, a firm should review its allowance account regularly to ensure that the account maintains a reasonable balance. If the allowance account balance is too large or too small, the percentage used to estimate the periodic credit losses should be revised accordingly.

A company that uses the **percentage of net sales method** usually applies the estimated uncollectible percentage only to its credit sales, excluding cash sales, since only credit sales are subject to credit losses. Further, any sales discounts and sales returns and allowances should be deducted from total credit sales before applying the historical uncollectible percentage.

> Taylor Company estimates three percent of its $600,000 credit sales will prove uncollectible. What journal entry will Taylor Company use to record this estimate?

YOUR TURN! 8.1

The solution is on page 402.

Accounts Receivable Aging Method

A second approach to estimating a company's bad debts expense is to determine the appropriate balance for the Allowance for Doubtful Accounts account at year-end, and then determine the appropriate estimate of the bad debts expense. The year-end balance in the Allowance for Doubtful Accounts represents a firm's estimate of the year-end accounts receivable that will prove uncollectible. By adding any existing debit balance or subtracting any existing credit balance in the allowance account to the year-end projected Allowance for Doubtful Accounts balance, it is possible to indirectly determine the appropriate current period estimate of the company's bad debts expense. This approach is called the **accounts receivable aging method**.

When using the accounts receivable aging method, a company determines the amount needed in the allowance account by analyzing the age structure of its outstanding accounts receivable balances. An aging schedule similar to the one in Exhibit 8-1 would be used. An **aging schedule** is simply an analysis that reveals how much time has elapsed since a credit sale originally occurred, and consequently, how long a customer's account receivable has remained unpaid. Assume, for example, that the firm whose aging schedule appears in Exhibit 8-1 sells its goods on credit with a credit period of 30 days. The exhibit reveals that the Alton account is current, which means that the $320 billing was made within the last 30 days; however, the Bailey account is 0–30 days *past due,* which means that the account receivable is from 31 to 60 days old. The aging schedule also reveals that the Wall balance consists of a $50 billing made from 91 to 150 days ago and a $100 billing made from 151 days to seven months ago, and so on.

Exhibit 8-1	Aging Schedule of Customer Balances, December 31, 2013							
					Past Due			
Customer	Account Balance	Current	0–30 Days	31–60 Days	61–120 Days	121 Days to 6 Mos.	Over 6 Mos.	
Alton, J.	320	$ 320						
Bailey, C.	400		$ 400					
many more accts . . .	...	...	...	...	...	...	...	
Wall, M..	150					50	100	
Zorn, W.	210			210				
	$50,000	$42,000	$4,000	$2,000	$1,000	$800	$200	

Companies that analyze their uncollectible accounts experience using aged account balances develop probability-of-collection percentages to correspond with each age category. The probability of collection is subtracted from 100 percent to arrive at the probability of noncollection. At the end of each period, the probability-of-noncollection percentages are applied to the totals of each age category to determine the appropriate allowance account balance for a given category. For our example, these percentages are shown in the table below. Applying the percentages to the totals in our aging schedule, we can calculate the required balance for the Allowance for Doubtful Accounts—that is, $1,560:

	Amount	Probability of Noncollection	Allowance Required
Current	$42,000	2%	$ 840
0–30 days past due	4,000	3%	120
31–60 days past due	2,000	5%	100
61–120 days past due	1,000	20%	200
121-180 days past due	800	25%	200
Over 180 days past due	200	50%	100
Total allowance required.			$1,560

Since the aging method is just an estimation process, estimation errors are likely to occur, causing the allowance account to sometimes be over or underestimated. If, for example, the Allowance for Doubtful Accounts has an existing $400 credit balance (implying an overestimation error in the prior period), the year-end adjusting entry is:

2013				
Dec. 31	Bad debts expense	1,160		
	Allowance for doubtful accounts		1,160	
	To record the bad debts expense for the period.			

A = L + SE
−1,160   −1,160 Exp

This entry brings the credit balance in the Allowance for Doubtful Accounts account to the required amount—$1,560, as shown below:

Allowance for Doubtful Accounts

400	Beg.
1,160	Dec. 31
1,560	Bal.

Hint: In contrast to the percentage of net sales method, the accounts receivable aging method takes into account the beginning balance for doubtful accounts.

It is also possible to have a debit balance in the allowance account before the year-end adjustment, implying an underestimation error in the prior period. This would occur whenever the write-off of specific accounts receivable during the year exceeded the credit balance in the account as of the beginning of the year. Assume, for example, that the Allowance for Doubtful Accounts had a $350 debit balance prior to the recording of the December 31, 2013, adjusting entry, and that the aging schedule showed that the allowance account should have a $1,560 credit balance. The year-end adjusting entry would then be as follows:

2013				
Dec. 31	Bad debts expense	1,910		
	Allowance for doubtful accounts		1,910	
	To record the bad debts expense for the period.			

A = L + SE
−1,910   −1,910 Exp

The following Allowance for Doubtful Accounts T-account shows that this entry creates the desired year-end credit balance in the allowance account of $1,560:

Allowance for Doubtful Accounts

Beg.	350	1,910	Dec. 31
		1,560	Bal.

THINKING GLOBALLY

Just when an account receivable is judged to be uncollectible is very much a cultural issue. In some Central and South American countries, buying goods and services on credit is almost unheard of! In these countries, it is considered in bad taste to owe someone money, and consequently, to preserve a company's good reputation and standing in the business community, companies pay cash for their purchases and avoid buying goods and services on credit. Therefore, in these countries it is extremely rare to see accounts receivable on the financial statements of businesses. In the United States, on the other hand, buying goods and services on credit is considered to be a normal business activity. In fact, a business manager would be chastised for failing to take advantage of any offered trade credit by paying cash for purchased goods or services. In the United States, most large businesses consider an account receivable to be uncollectible when it becomes 120 days old. Buying goods and services on credit in China is, likewise, quite common; however, buyers often take several years to pay for purchased goods, and consequently, accounts receivable are not considered to be uncollectible until 2 to 3 years have elapsed since the original credit sales transaction.

TAKEAWAY 8.1	Concept ⟶	Method ⟶	Assessment
	Are the accounts receivable being collected in a timely manner?	List of accounts receivable along with how long they have been outstanding. Prepare an aging schedule.	Accounts in the older categories require additional collection attention.

Recoveries of Accounts Written Off under the Allowance Method   Occasionally, an account written off against the allowance for doubtful accounts as uncollectible will later prove to be wholly or partially collectible. In such situations, a firm should first reinstate the customer's account receivable for the amount recovered before recording the collection of cash. Then the cash payment can be recorded in the customer's account. The journal entry made for the original account write-off is reversed to the extent of the recovery amount and the receipt of cash is recorded in the usual manner. For example, assume that the Claremont Corporation is using the allowance method and wrote off the Monroe Company's $300 account on January 5, 2014, but subsequently received a $200 payment on April 20, 2014. The following journal entries (including write-off) illustrate the recovery procedure:

To write off the account

A = L + SE +300 −300	**2014** Jan. 5	Allowance for doubtful accounts Accounts receivable—Monroe Company *To write off the Monroe Company's account.*	300 300

To reinstate the account

A = L + SE +200 −200	Apr. 20	Accounts receivable—Monroe Company Allowance for doubtful accounts *To reinstate the Monroe Company's account to the extent of the recovery.*	200 200

To record receipt of cash

A = L + SE +200 −200	Apr. 20	Cash Accounts receivable—Monroe Company *To record collection of cash on account.*	200 200

These last two journal entries are prepared the same way even if the recovery occurs more than a year following the period in which the account was originally written off.

FORENSIC ACCOUNTING	**Lapping**

One type of fraud that forensic accountants are trained to detect is "lapping." Lapping is not actually a fraud, but rather is a technique that a fraudster uses to cover up a fraud, typically involving the theft of funds. Under lapping, an employee who has access to incoming payments from the collection of accounts receivables will steal some of the cash received from credit customers. The employee then applies another customer's payment to the outstanding balance from the individual's account whose payment was stolen, in order to cover up the theft. The process is repeated in an effort to cover up the original misappropriation. In other words, after the initial theft, the fraudster must continually "rob Peter to pay Paul." One audit procedure that may detect a lapping scheme involves the confirmation of accounts receivable. As part of the year-end independent audit, or as part of a regular internal audit, a company's accountant will send out confirmation letters to a sample of customers from the list of outstanding accounts receivable and pay particular attention to replies from customers disputing the timing of their payments.

Phisher, Inc., analyzed its accounts receivable at the end of its first year of operations, and arrived at the aged balances listed below, along with the percentage that is estimated to be uncollectible:

Age Group	Balance	Estimated Loss Percentage
0–30 days past due	$100,000	1
31–60 days past due	15,000	3
61–120 days past due	10,000	5
Over 120 days past due................................	20,000	10
	$145,000	

The company handles credit losses with the allowance method.

a. Prepare the adjusting entry for estimated credit losses on December 31, 2012.

b. Prepare the journal entry to write off Phorest Company's account on May 12, 2013, in the amount of $480.

YOUR TURN! 8.2

The solution is on page 402.

CREDIT CARD SALES

Many businesses, especially retailers, allow their customers to use credit cards for their purchase transactions. Popular credit cards include VISA, MasterCard, Discover, and American Express. When a customer uses a credit card to make a purchase, the seller collects cash from the credit card company, and the customer pays cash to the credit card company when billed at a later date. To facilitate this process, the seller prepares a sales slip using the credit card. The seller either imprints the card number on a slip using the card or uses an electronic device such as a cash register with a card reader to read the card number from the magnetic strip on the back of the credit card, and then prints a sales slip with the card number on it. The second approach also allows for the electronic accumulation and transmission of credit card sales data. In either case, the customer is usually asked to sign the sales slip to authenticate the transaction.

LO3 Discuss the accounting treatment of credit card sales.

The issuer of a credit card, frequently a financial institution like **Chase Bank** or **Citibank**, will charge the seller a fee each time a card is used. The **credit card fee** usually ranges from one percent to five percent of the amount of the credit card purchase. Businesses are willing to incur this fee because credit cards provide considerable benefits to a seller. For example, the seller does not have to evaluate the creditworthiness of the customer using a credit card, and the business avoids any risk of noncollection of the account since this risk remains with the credit card issuer. Finally, the seller typically receives the cash from the credit card issuer faster than if the customer were granted trade credit by the seller.

Depending upon the type of credit card, there are two ways that a seller may collect from the credit card issuer: (1) immediately upon deposit of the credit card sales slip or (2) on a delayed basis after the credit card slips have been processed by the credit card issuer. For cards issued by a financial institution, cash is received immediately upon deposit of the sales slip at the financial institution. The journal entry to record a $1,000 credit card sale of this type on March 15, with a three percent credit card fee, is as follows:

Mar. 15	Cash	970	
	Credit card fee expense	30	
	Sales revenue		1,000
	To record credit card sales and collection, less a three percent fee.		

A = L + SE
+970 −30 Exp
+1,000 Rev

If, instead, sales slips are sent to a credit card company for subsequent cash settlement, the journal entries to record the $1,000 credit card sale with subsequent collection on March 23 are as follows:

A = L + SE					
+970	−30 Exp	Mar. 15	Accounts receivable—Credit Card Company	970	
	+1,000 Rev		Credit card fee expense	30	
			Sales revenue		1,000
			To record credit card sales.		

A = L + SE					
+970		Mar. 23	Cash	970	
−970			Accounts receivable—Credit Card Company		970
			To record collection from credit card company.		

YOUR TURN! 8.3

The solution is on page 402.

Nafooz Company pays a two percent credit card fee on all credit sales, and receives a cash deposit immediately following each credit card transaction. If credit sales for the company total $50,000, what journal entry should be recorded to recognize the receipt of cash and the credit card fee expense?

NOTES RECEIVABLE

LO4 **Illustrate** a promissory note receivable, **discuss** the calculation of interest on notes receivable, and **present** journal entries to record notes receivable and interest.

Promissory notes receivable are often used in sale transactions when the credit period is longer than the 30 to 60 day credit period that is typical for accounts receivable. Promissory notes are also used frequently in sales involving equipment and property because the dollar amount of these transactions can be quite large. Occasionally, a note will be substituted for an account receivable when an extension of the usual credit period is granted. Also, promissory notes are normally prepared when financial institutions make a loan to a business or an individual.

A **promissory note** is a written promise to pay a certain sum of money on demand or at a fixed (or determinable) future date. The note is signed by the **maker** and made payable to the order of either a specific **payee** or to the **bearer**. The interest rate specified on the note is typically an annual rate. Exhibit 8.2 illustrates a promissory note.

Exhibit 8-2	A Promissory Note

$2,000.00	Los Angeles, CA	May 3, 2013

Sixty days _____ after date I promise to pay to

the order of _____ Susan Robinson _____

Two thousand and no/100 · dollars

for value received with interest at _____ 9% _____

payable at _____ First Bank of Los Angeles, CA _____

James Stone ·

A note from a debtor is called a **note receivable** by the noteholder. A note is usually regarded as a stronger claim against a debtor than an account receivable because the terms of payment are specified in writing.

Interest on Notes Receivable

Interest is a charge for the use of money over time. Interest incurred on a promissory note receivable is interest income to the noteholder or payee of the note and interest expense to the maker of the note. Businesses are required to distinguish between operating and non-operating items in their income statements; consequently, they place any interest expense or interest income on outstanding notes under the other income and expense heading in the income statement so that financial statement users will readily identify interest income or expense as being nonoperating in nature. Interest expense is a financing expense, not an operating expense, and interest income is financing income, not operating income.

Interest on a short-term promissory note is paid at the maturity date of the note. The formula for determining the amount of interest expense to the maker and interest income to the noteholder is as follows:

$$\textbf{Interest} = \textbf{Principal} \times \textbf{Interest rate} \times \textbf{Interest time}$$

The principal is the face amount of a note; and, the interest rate is the annual rate of interest specified in the note agreement. Interest time is the fraction of a year that a note receivable is outstanding.

When a note is written for a certain number of months, interest time is expressed in twelfths of a year. For example, interest on a six-month note for $2,000 with a nine percent annual interest rate is calculated as:

$$\textbf{Interest} = \textbf{\$2,000} \times \textbf{0.09} \times \textbf{6/12} = \textbf{\$90}$$

When a note's duration, or time to maturity, is given in days, interest time is expressed as a fraction of a year; the numerator is the number of days that the note receivable will be outstanding and the denominator is 360 days. (Some lenders use 360 days, while others use 365 days; we use 360 days in our examples, exercises, and problems.) For example, interest on a 60 day note for $2,000 with a nine percent annual interest rate is:

$$\textbf{Interest} = \textbf{\$2,000} \times \textbf{0.09} \times \textbf{60/360} = \textbf{\$30}$$

Determining Maturity Date

When a note's duration is expressed in days, it is customary to count the exact number of days in each calendar month to determine the note's **maturity date**. For example, a 90 day note dated July 21 has an October 19 maturity date, which is determined as follows:

10	days in July (remainder of month—31 days minus 21 days)
31	days in August
30	days in September
19	days in October (number of days required to total 90)
90	

If the duration of a note is expressed in months, the maturity date is calculated simply by counting the number of months from the date of issue. For example, a two-month note dated January 31 would mature on March 31, a three-month note of the same date would mature on April 30 (the last day of the month), and a four-month note would mature on May 31.

Recording Notes Receivable and Interest

When a note is exchanged to settle an account receivable, a journal entry is made to reflect the note receivable and to reduce the balance of the related account receivable. For example, suppose that Jordon Company sold $12,000 of merchandise on account to Bowman Company. On October 1, after the regular credit period had elapsed, the Bowman Company gave the Jordon Company a 60 day, nine percent note receivable for $12,000. Jordon Company makes the following journal entry to record receiving the note:

A = L + SE
+12,000
−12,000
	Oct. 1	Notes receivable—Bowman Company
		        Accounts receivable—Bowman Company
		        Received 60 day, nine percent note in payment of account.
			12,000
			
				12,000

If the Bowman Company pays its note receivable on the November 30 maturity date, the Jordon Company makes the following journal entry:

A = L + SE
+12,180   +180
            Rev
−12,000
	Nov. 30	Cash
		        Interest income
		        Notes receivable—Bowman Company
		        Collected Bowman Company note.
		        ($12,000 × 0.09 × 60/360 = $180).
			12,180
			
				180
				12,000

Recording Dishonored Notes

In the prior example, interest for 60 days at nine percent is recorded on the maturity date of the note even if the maker of the note (Bowman Company) defaults on or dishonors the note. When a note is dishonored at maturity, the amount of the combined principal plus interest is converted to an account receivable. This procedure leaves only the current, unmatured notes in the noteholder's Notes Receivable account. If the Bowman Company, for example, failed to pay its note on November 30 as expected, the Jordon Company would make the following journal entry:

A = L + SE
+12,180   +180
            Rev
−12,000
	Nov. 30	Accounts receivable—Bowman Company
		        Interest income
		        Notes receivable—Bowman Company
		        To record the dishonoring of a note by Bowman Company.
			12,180
			
				180
				12,000

Adjusting Entry for Interest

When the term of a promissory note extends beyond the end of an accounting period, a year-end adjusting entry is necessary to reflect the interest earned. To illustrate, assume that Jordon Company has a note receivable outstanding at December 31, 2013. The note receivable from the Garcia Company is dated December 21, 2013, has a principal amount of $6,000, an interest rate of 12 percent, and a maturity date of February 19, 2014. The adjusting entry that Jordon Company makes at December 31, 2013, to record the earned, but uncollected, interest income is as follows:

A = L + SE
+20   +20 Rev
	Dec. 31
	Ⓐ
		Interest receivable
		        Interest income
		        To accrue interest income on the note from Garcia Company
		        ($6,000 × 0.12 × 10/360 = $20).
			20
			
				20

When the note is subsequently paid on February 19, 2014, Jordon Company makes the following journal entry:

A = L + SE
+6,120   +100
            Rev
−20
−6,000
	Feb. 19
	Ⓑ
		Cash
		        Interest income
		        Interest receivable
		        Notes receivable—Garcia Company
		        Received payment of principal and interest from Garcia Company
		        ($6,000 × 0.12 × 50/360 = $100).
			6,120
			
				100
				20
				6,000

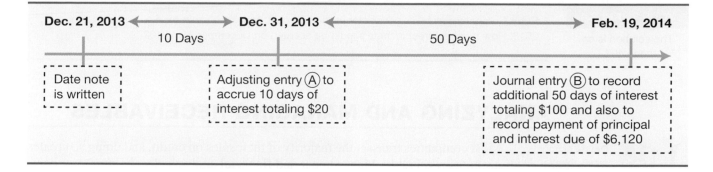

| Revenue Recognition Principle | PRINCIPLE ALERT |

The adjusting entry to accrue interest income on an outstanding promissory note receivable at year-end illustrates the *revenue recognition principle*. This principle states that revenue should be recognized when services are performed or goods are sold. The holder of a promissory note provides the maker of the note with a service: the use of money for a specified time period. This service is provided each day that a note is outstanding; and, interest is the payment for this service. Interest income is not recorded each day. Normally, interest income for a note's full term is recorded when it is collected at the note's maturity. If the accounting period ends before a note's maturity date, an adjusting entry is made to record the accrued interest income for the services provided in the current period.

Reporting Notes Receivable on the Balance Sheet

Short-Term Notes Receivable are a current asset on the balance sheet. Since these notes can normally be readily converted into cash, they are often placed below Accounts Receivable in the current asset section. As with accounts receivable, notes receivable are reported separately from other notes receivable from officers and employees and notes representing advances to affiliated companies. If the notes are not short term, they should be classified as noncurrent assets. Interest Receivable on a note receivable is also a current asset.

Sometimes companies with a large volume of notes receivable must provide for possible losses on the outstanding notes. Frequently, the Allowance for Doubtful Accounts also covers potential credit losses on notes as well. In such cases, the Allowance for Doubtful Accounts account is deducted from the aggregate total of Accounts Receivable and Notes Receivable on the balance sheet. Estimating the potential credit losses on outstanding notes receivable follows the same procedures as for accounts receivable.

| Responsible Gaming | CORPORATE SOCIAL RESPONSIBILITY |

Perhaps it may seem odd to equate good corporate citizenship with the gaming industry, but that does not mean that gaming companies should not do all that they can to be good citizens. MGM Resorts International's mission statement aims to portray the company as a responsible corporate citizen:

> "MGM Resorts International is the leader in entertainment & hospitality—a diverse collection of extraordinary people, distinctive brands and best in class destinations. Working together, we create partnerships and experiences that engage, entertain and inspire."

MGM Resorts International's Website further discusses their commitment to sustainability:

> "MGM Resorts International is committed to be a global leader in sustainability and stewardship of the environment, bringing value to communities and shareholders alike. Our company operates smarter and more efficiently as we extend sustainable business practices to existing properties and new projects. The results we achieve include using resources more efficiently; reducing construction impact; minimizing waste; managing supply chains; and increasing awareness. This commitment helps our business grow responsibly."

YOUR TURN! 8.4

The solution is on page 402.

Ruby Company received a four month, five percent note receivable for $40,000 on October 1, 2013. How much interest income should be accrued on December 31, 2013?

ANALYZING AND MANAGING RECEIVABLES

LO5 **Define** accounts receivable turnover and average collection *period* and **explain** their use in the analysis and management of accounts and notes receivable.

Most companies transact the majority of their sales on credit, and doing so creates accounts receivable. Management and financial analysts closely monitor a company's accounts receivable using a variety of financial measures, including the accounts receivable turnover ratio and the average collection period. **Accounts receivable turnover** indicates how many times a year a firm collects its average accounts receivable, and thus, measures how fast accounts receivable are being converted into cash. Accounts receivable turnover is calculated as follows:

$$\text{Accounts receivable turnover} = \frac{\text{Net sales}}{\text{Average accounts receivable (net)}}$$

The numerator in this ratio is net sales. Ideally, the numerator should be net credit sales, but financial information available to financial statement users does not usually divide net sales into credit sales and cash sales. For many businesses like the **Johnson & Johnson Company**, the maker of Band-Aids and baby shampoo, over 99 percent of the company's sales are credit sales; and thus, it is common to assume that a company's net sales is a good proxy for its credit sales. Average accounts receivable (net of the allowance for doubtful accounts) is calculated by summing the beginning and ending accounts receivable (net) balances and dividing the sum by two.

To illustrate these financial indicators, consider the financial results for the Claremont Corporation.

	2013	2012
Net sales.	$40,831	$33,548
Beginning accounts receivable (net)	1,848	1,948
Ending accounts receivable (net).	1,799	1,848

Claremont's accounts receivable turnover for 2013 is 22.39, or $40,831/[$1,848 + $1,799)/2], and for 2012 is 17.68, or $33,548/[($1,948 + $1,848)/2]. In general, the higher the accounts receivable turnover ratio, the faster a company is converting its receivables into cash. The increase in accounts receivable turnover from 2012 to 2013 is a positive sign regarding how well the Claremont Corporation is managing its accounts receivable.

An extension of the accounts receivable turnover ratio is the **average collection period**, calculated as follows:

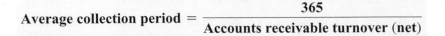

$$\text{Average collection period} = \frac{365}{\text{Accounts receivable turnover (net)}}$$

This ratio indicates how many days it takes on average to collect an account receivable. During 2013, Claremont's average collection period was 16.3 days, or 365/22.39. During 2012, Claremont's average collection period was 20.6 days, or 365/17.68. The ratio reveals that Claremont is taking four fewer days to collect its accounts receivable in 2013 than in 2012, another sign of improved accounts receivable management.

The average collection period may also be used to evaluate the effectiveness of a company's credit policies. One rule of thumb states that the average collection period should not exceed a business's allowed credit period by more than 15 days. Thus, if a firm grants credit terms of 30 days to its customers, its average collection period should not exceed 45 days.

The Forrester Corporation disclosed the following financial information (in millions) in its recent annual report:

	2013
Net sales.	$30,000
Beginning accounts receivable (net)	2,800
Ending accounts receivable (net)	3,200

a. Calculate the accounts receivable turnover ratio for 2013.
b. Calculate the average collection period for 2013.

YOUR TURN! 8.5

The solution is on page 403.

Factoring and Discounting

A company can accelerate the collection of cash on an account receivable or a note receivable by selling the receivable to a finance company or a financial institution. Selling an account receivable is called **factoring** and selling a note receivable is called **discounting**. Finance companies and financial institutions that buy receivables are called **factors**.

When receivables are sold, the factor pays the selling company the amount of the account receivable or note receivable less a fee, often ranging from two percent to five percent of the value of the sold receivable. The factor then collects the cash payments directly from the customer who originally purchased the goods or services on credit. This approach speeds the collection of cash to the selling company and releases it from the work of billing and collecting the account.

Accounts and notes receivable may be sold under two conditions—with recourse and without recourse. "With recourse" indicates that in the event that a factor is unable to collect a specific customer's account or note receivable, the factor has the right to request that the selling company return the amount of the uncollected receivable. "Without recourse" indicates that a factor is unable to request reimbursement from the selling company if the factor is unable to collect a specific account or note receivable. Selling receivables without recourse is more expensive than selling receivables with recourse because the factor is forced to assume additional collection risk.

Concept	Method	Assessment	TAKEAWAY 8.2
Are any of the existing accounts receivable in need of further attention?	Net sales and average accounts receivable $\text{Accounts receivable turnover} = \dfrac{\text{Net sales}}{\text{Average accounts receivable}}$ $\text{Average collection period} = \dfrac{365}{\text{Accounts receivable turnover}}$	Compare the average collection period to the company credit policy. Longer collection periods suggest the need for management attention.	

COMPREHENSIVE PROBLEM

At December 31, 2012, the following selected accounts appeared in Delta Company's unadjusted trial balance:

Accounts receivable.	$81,000
Allowance for doubtful accounts	1,200 (credit)
Notes receivable (Jason, Inc.)	12,000

Net credit sales for 2012 were $250,000. The $12,000 note receivable was a 90 day, eight percent note dated December 13, 2012. The following adjusting entries and transactions occurred at the end of 2012 and during 2013:

2012

Dec. 31 Recorded the adjusting entry for the bad debts expense, at $1\frac{1}{2}$ percent of net credit sales.
      31 Recorded the adjusting entry for interest on the $12,000 note receivable.

2013

Mar. 12 Received payment on the $12,000 note receivable from Jason, Inc., plus interest.
Apr.   5 Wrote off the account of Abilene Company, $2,850.
July   9 Wrote off the account of Acme Suppliers, $1,450.
Sept. 5 Received payment from Acme Suppliers, which is in bankruptcy proceedings, for $450 in final settlement of the account written off on July 9.
Dec.   6 Wrote off the account of Walton, Inc., $1,300.
      31 Changed from the percentage-of-net-sales method of providing for uncollectible accounts to an estimate based on the accounts receivable aging method. The account analysis indicated a desired credit balance of $4,500 in the Allowance for Doubtful Accounts.

Required
Prepare the journal entries for these adjustments and transactions.

Solution

2012			
Dec. 31	Bad debts expense	3,750	
	Allowance for doubtful accounts		3,750
	To provide for bad debts expense at $1\frac{1}{2}$ percent of		
	net credit sales, $250,000.		
31	Interest receivable	48	
	Interest income		48
	To accrue interest on Jason, Inc., note receivable		
	($12,000 × 0.08 × 18/360 = $48).		
2013			
Mar. 12	Cash	12,240	
	Interest income		192
	Interest receivable		48
	Notes receivable—Jason, Inc.		12,000
	To record receipt of payment of Jason, Inc., note receivable		
	($12,000 × 0.08 × 72/360 = $192).		
Apr. 5	Allowance for doubtful accounts	2,850	
	Accounts receivable—Abilene Company		2,850
	To write off the account of Abilene Company as uncollectible.		
July 9	Allowance for doubtful accounts	1,450	
	Accounts receivable—Acme Suppliers		1,450
	To write off the account of Acme Suppliers as uncollectible.		

Sept. 5	Accounts receivable—Acme Suppliers	450	
	Allowance for doubtful accounts		450
	To reinstate $450 of the account of Acme Suppliers that proved collectible.		
5	Cash	450	
	Accounts receivable—Acme Suppliers		450
	To record payment of Acme Suppliers' account.		
Dec. 6	Allowance for doubtful accounts	1,300	
	Accounts receivable—Walton, Inc.		1,300
	To write off the account of Walton, Inc., as uncollectible.		
Dec. 31	Bad debts expense	4,700	
	Allowance for doubtful accounts		4,700
	To provide for bad debts expense		
	($4,500 desired balance + $200 existing debit balance = $4,700).		

APPENDIX 8A: Direct Write-Off Method

The direct write-off method of accounting for credit losses is an alternative to the allowance method. Under the **direct write-off method**, doubtful accounts are charged to the bad debts expense on the income statement in the period in which the accounts are determined to be uncollectible. Under this approach, there is no attempt to estimate the bad debts expense, nor is there any attempt to match this expense with sales revenues in the period in which the credit sales transaction originally occurred. As a consequence, U.S. GAAP does not permit the use of the direct write-off method unless the amount of the credit losses is immaterial. The reason for this is because the direct write-off method does not properly match credit losses with credit sales in the appropriate time period, violating the matching concept.

LO6 Illustrate the direct write-off method and **contrast** it with the allowance method for accounting for doubtful accounts.

For example, an account receivable may not be determined to be uncollectible, and therefore written off, until several periods after the actual credit sales revenue is recorded. By way of contrast, the allowance method, through the use of an estimate of the bad debt expense, properly matches this expense with the associated sales revenue in the same period. The use of the direct write-off method also causes a consistent overstatement of accounts receivable on the balance sheet. Although not generally accepted for accounting purposes for most businesses, the direct write-off method is used by all companies for U.S. federal income tax purposes.

The journal entries made when the direct write-off method is used are illustrated below using data from the Claremont Corporation illustration:

To write off the account

2014

Jan. 5	Bad debts expense	300		A	= L +	SE	
	Accounts receivable—Monroe Company		300	−300		−300 Exp	
	To write off the Monroe Company's account.						

To reinstate the account

Apr. 20	Accounts receivable—Monroe Company	200		A	= L +	SE	
	Bad debts expense		200	+200		+200 Exp	
	To reinstate the Monroe Company's account to the extent of the recovery.						

To record receipt of cash

Apr. 20	Cash	200		A	= L +	SE	
	Accounts receivable—Monroe Company		200	+200 −200			
	To record collection of cash on account.						

If an account receivable written off in a prior year is reinstated during the current year and the Bad Debts Expense account has no existing balance from other write-offs (and no more write-offs are expected), then the account credited in the reinstatement entry is the Doubtful Accounts Recovery, a revenue account.

YOUR TURN! 8.6

The solution is on page 403.

Harley Company has determined an account receivable in the amount of $750 from Rhea Inc. will be uncollectible and has decided to write the account off. Harley Company uses the direct write-off method because write-offs are considered immaterial. Provide the journal entry to write off the Rhea account.

SUMMARY OF LEARNING OBJECTIVES

LO1 **Define accounts receivable, explain losses from uncollectible accounts, and describe the allowance method of accounting for doubtful accounts. (p. 362)**

- Accounts receivable is a current asset created when a sales transaction is executed on a credit basis.
- Accounts receivable does not include such receivables as loans to affiliate companies or advances to employees.
- The credit department of a company is responsible for conducting credit investigations of customers, establishing credit limits, and following up on overdue accounts.
- The allowance method is designed to record the bad debts expense in the same accounting period as the related credit sale.
- When the allowance method is used, specific accounts are written off by debiting the Allowance for Doubtful Accounts and crediting the Accounts Receivable account.

LO2 **Describe and illustrate the percentage of net sales method and the accounts receivable aging method for estimating a business's bad debts expense. (p. 367)**

- The percentage of net sales method is used to determine estimated credit losses directly. Estimated credit losses are determined by multiplying credit sales (net of any sales discounts and sales returns and allowances) times the estimated percentage of uncollectible credit sales.
- The accounts receivable aging method determines the estimated credit loss indirectly. The balance in the Accounts Receivable account is segmented into age categories. Then the balance of each category is multiplied by the estimated uncollectible percentage for that age category. The results are added to obtain the desired balance in the Allowance for Doubtful Accounts. The desired balance is then compared to the existing balance in the Allowance for Doubtful Accounts to determine the estimated credit losses and bad debts expense for the period.
- Occasionally, accounts written off against the Allowance for Doubtful Accounts later prove to be wholly or partially collectible. When this happens, the Accounts Receivable account is first reinstated to the extent of the recovery, and then the cash collection is recorded.

LO3 **Discuss the accounting treatment of credit card sales. (p. 371)**

- The credit card issuer can reimburse the merchant accepting the credit card immediately upon deposit of any sales slips or subsequently after processing the sales slips.
- In both situations, the credit card fee expense is recognized when the credit card sales slips are remitted to the credit card issuer.

LO4 **Illustrate a promissory note receivable, discuss the calculation of interest on notes receivable, and present journal entries to record notes receivable and interest. (p. 372)**

- Interest on a short-term promissory note is determined using the following formula:

$$\text{Interest} = \text{Principal} \times \text{Interest rate} \times \text{Interest time}$$

- When a note is received in payment of an account receivable balance, the Notes Receivable account is debited and the Accounts Receivable account is credited.
- The noteholder recognizes interest income at the maturity date or in an end-of-period adjusting entry if the financial statements are prepared before the note matures.

LO5 **Define *accounts receivable turnover* and *average collection period* and explain their use in the analysis and management of accounts and notes receivable. (p. 376)**

- Accounts receivable turnover = Net sales/Average accounts receivable

- Average collection period = 365/Accounts receivable turnover
- *Accounts receivable turnover* indicates how many times a year, on average, that a firm collects its accounts receivable. *Average collection period* indicates how many days it takes, on average, to collect an account receivable.

Appendix 8A: Illustrate the direct write-off method and contrast it with the allowance method for accounting for doubtful accounts. (p. 379) **LO6**

- Under the direct write-off method, uncollectible accounts are charged to the bad debts expense in the period in which they are determined to be uncollectible.
- For most companies, the direct write-off method is not a generally accepted method of accounting for credit losses; however, most companies use the direct write-off method for income tax purposes.

Concept	Method	Assessment	SUMMARY
Are the accounts receivable being collected in a timely manner?	List of accounts receivable along with how long they have been outstanding. Prepare an aging schedule.	Accounts in the older categories require additional collection attention.	TAKEAWAY 8.1
Are any of the existing accounts receivable in need of further attention?	Net sales and average accounts receivable Accounts receivable turnover = $\dfrac{\text{Net sales}}{\text{Average accounts receivable}}$ Average collection period = $\dfrac{365}{\text{Accounts receivable turnover}}$	Compare the average collection period to the company credit policy. Longer collection periods suggest the need for management attention.	TAKEAWAY 8.2

KEY TERMS

Accounts receivable (p. 362)
Accounts receivable aging method (p. 368)
Accounts receivable turnover (p. 376)
Aging schedule (p. 368)
Allowance for Doubtful Accounts (p. 365)
Allowance method (p. 364)

Average collection period (p. 376)
Bad Debts Expense (p. 364)
Bearer (p. 372)
Credit card fee (p. 371)
Credit-collection policy (p. 363)
Credit-granting policy (p. 363)
Direct write-off method (p. 379)
Discounting (p. 377)

Factoring (p. 377)
Factors (p. 377)
Maker (p. 372)
Maturity date (p. 373)
Note receivable (p. 372)
Payee (p. 372)
Percentage of net sales method (p. 367)
Promissory note (p. 372)

SELF-STUDY QUESTIONS

(Answers to the Self-Study Questions are available at the end of this chapter.)

1. **A firm, using the allowance method of recording credit losses, wrote off a customer's account in the amount of $500. Later, the customer paid the account. The firm reinstated the account by means of a journal entry and then recorded the collection. What is the result of these procedures?** **LO1**
    a. Increases total assets by $500
    b. Decreases total assets by $500
    c. Decreases total assets by $1,000
    d. Has no effect on total assets

LO2 2. A firm has accounts receivable of $90,000 and a debit balance of $900 in the Allowance for Doubtful Accounts. Two-thirds of the accounts receivable are current and one-third is past due. The firm estimates that two percent of the current accounts and five percent of the past due accounts will prove to be uncollectible. The adjusting entry to provide for the bad debts expense under the aging method should be for what amount?
   a. $2,700
   b. $3,600
   c. $1,800
   d. $4,500

LO4 3. A firm receives a six-month note from a customer. The note has a face amount of $4,000 and an interest rate of nine percent. What is the total amount of interest to be received?
   a. $1,080
   b. $30
   c. $360
   d. $180

LO5 4. A business has net sales of $60,000, a beginning balance in Accounts Receivable of $5,000, and an ending balance in Accounts Receivable of $7,000. What is the company's accounts receivable turnover?
   a. 10.0
   b. 12.0
   c. 8.6
   d. 9.2

LO5 5. A business has an accounts receivable turnover of ten. What is the company's average collection period?
   a. 36.0
   b. 30.8
   c. 34.6
   d. 36.5

LO4 6. Miller Company received a 90 day, six percent note receivable for $10,000 on December 1. How much interest should be accrued on December 31?
   a. $150
   b. $90
   c. $50
   d. $25

LO1, 2 7. Smith Company uses the allowance method to record its expected credit losses. It estimates its losses at one percent of credit sales, which were $750,000 during the year. The Accounts Receivable balance was $220,000 and the Allowance for Doubtful Accounts had a credit balance of $1,000 at year-end. What amount is the debit to the Bad Debt Expense?
   a. $7,500
   b. $8,500
   c. $6,500
   d. $3,200

LO3 8. Rankine & Company pays a three percent credit card fee on all credit sales, and receives a cash deposit immediately following each credit card transaction. If credit sales for the company total $15,000 on December 13, what journal entry should be recorded to recognize the receipt of cash and the credit card fee expense?
   a. Debit Cash $14,550; debit Credit Card Fee Expense $450.
   b. Debit Cash $15,000; credit Credit Card Fee Expense $450.
   c. Debit Cash $15,450; debit Credit Card Fee Expense $450.
   d. Debit Cash $15,450; credit Credit Card Fee Expense $450.

LO1, 2, 6 9. Which of the following statements is true?
   a. The direct write-off method is generally accepted.
   b. The percentage of net sales method estimates the bad debts expense indirectly.
   c. The accounts receivable aging method estimates the bad debts expense indirectly.
   d. None of the above is true.

10. **On September 1, the Pavoreal Company accepted a $24,000, 60 day, nine percent, promissory**   **LO4**
    note in exchange for overdue accounts receivable balance for the same amount from the Wagner
    Company. On November 30, the Wagner Company dishonored the note. What journal entry should
    be recorded on November 30?
    a.   Debit Dishonored Note Receivable Expense; credit Notes Receivable.
    b.   Debit Allowance for Doubtful Accounts; credit Notes Receivable.
    c.   Debit Accounts Receivable; credit Interest Income; credit Notes Receivable.
    d.   None of the above entries is correct.

QUESTIONS

1. In dealing with receivables, what do the terms *factoring* and *discounting* mean?

2. How does a credit scoring system work?

3. How do the allowance method and the direct write-off method of handling credit losses differ with respect to the timing of bad debt expense recognition?

4. When a firm provides for credit losses under the allowance method, why is the Allowance for Doubtful Accounts credited rather than Accounts Receivable?

5. What are the two most commonly used methods of estimating the bad debts expense when the allowance method is employed? Describe them.

6. Murphy Company estimates its bad debts expense by aging its accounts receivable and applying percentages to various age groups of the accounts. Murphy calculated a total of $2,100 in possible credit losses as of December 31. Accounts Receivable has a balance of $98,000, and the Allowance for Doubtful Accounts has a credit balance of $500 before adjustment at December 31. What is the December 31 adjusting entry to provide for credit losses? What is the net amount of accounts receivable that should be included in current assets?

7. On June 15, 2012, Rollins, Inc. sold $750 worth of merchandise to Dell Company. On November 20, 2012, Rollins, Inc., wrote off Dell's account. On March 10, 2013, Dell Company paid the account in full. What are the journal entries that Rollins, Inc. should make for the write-off and the recovery assuming that Rollins, Inc., uses (a) the allowance method of handling credit losses and (b) the direct write-off method?

8. Wood Company sold a $675 refrigerator to a customer who charged the sale using a VISA credit card. Wood Company deposits credit card sales slips daily; cash is deposited in Wood Company's checking account at the same time. Wood Company's bank charges a credit card fee of four percent of sales revenue. What journal entry should Wood Company make to record the sale?

9. Volter Inc. received a 60 day, nine percent note for $15,000 on March 5 from a customer. What is the maturity date of the note?

10. Stanley Company received a 150 day, eight percent note for $15,000 on December 1. What adjusting entry is needed to accrue the interest due on December 31?

11. Define *accounts receivable turnover* and explain its use. How is the *average collection period* determined?

12. At a recent board of directors meeting of Ascot, Inc., one of the directors expressed concern over the Allowance for Doubtful Accounts appearing on the company's balance sheet. "I don't understand this account," he said. "Why don't we just show accounts receivable at the amount we would receive if we sold them to a financial institution and get rid of that allowance account?"

    Prepare a written response to the director. Include in your response (1) an explanation of why the company has an allowance account, (2) what the balance sheet presentation of accounts receivable is supposed to show, and (3) how the basic principles of accounting relate to the analysis and presentation of accounts receivable.

13. What generally accepted accounting principle is being implemented when a company estimates its potential credit losses from its outstanding accounts receivable?

14. Why is the direct write-off method of accounting for credit losses not generally accepted?

15. When a previously written-off account receivable is collected, it must first be reinstated by debiting the Accounts Receivable account and crediting the Allowance for Doubtful Accounts. Explain the credit portion of the reinstatement journal entry.

SHORT EXERCISES

LO1, 2 **SE8-1.** **Accounting for Doubtful Accounts** Rankine Company estimates its bad debts expense by aging its accounts receivable and applying percentages to various age groups of the accounts. Rankine calculated a total of $4,000 in possible credit losses as of December 31. Accounts Receivable has a balance of $128,000, and the Allowance for Doubtful Accounts has a credit balance of $500 before adjustment at December 31. What is the December 31 adjusting entry to provide for credit losses? What is the net amount of accounts receivable that should be included in current assets?

LO2 **SE8-2.** **Reinstating Written-Off Accounts** The Watergate Company uses the allowance method of recording credit losses and wrote off a customer's account in the amount of $800. Later, the customer paid the account. The company reinstated the account by means of a journal entry and then recorded the collection. What is the result of these procedures?

    a. Increases total assets by $800
    b. Decreases total assets by $800
    c. Decreases total assets by $1,600
    d. Has no effect on total assets

LO2 **SE8-3.** **Estimating the Bad Debts Expense** Winstead & Company has accounts receivable of $120,000 and a debit balance of $1,000 in the Allowance for Doubtful Accounts. Two thirds of the accounts receivable are current and one third is past due. The firm estimates that two percent of the current accounts and five percent of the past due accounts will prove to be uncollectible. The adjusting entry to provide for the bad debts expense under the aging method should be for what amount?

    a. $3,600
    b. $4,600
    c. $2,600
    d. $1,600

LO6
(Appendix 8A) **SE8-4.** **Direct Write-Off Method** The direct write-off method is not generally accepted because:

    a. The method overstates the bad debt expense.
    b. It is too complex.
    c. The method fails to match sales revenue with expenses in the appropriate time period.
    d. The method causes liabilities to be overstated.

LO4 **SE8-5.** **Recording Dishonored Promissory Notes Receivable** On September 30, the Camelback Company accepted a $50,000, 60 day, nine percent, promissory note in exchange for an overdue accounts receivable balance for the same amount from the Schwartz Company. On November 30, the Schwartz Company dishonored the note. What journal entry should be recorded on November 30?

    a. Debit Dishonored Note Receivable Expense; credit Notes Receivable.
    b. Debit Allowance for Doubtful Accounts; credit Notes Receivable.
    c. Debit Accounts Receivable; credit Interest Income; credit Notes Receivable.
    d. None of the above entries is correct.

LO3 **SE8-6.** **Accounting for Credit Card Sales** Chassoul & Company pays a three percent credit card fee on all credit sales, and receives a cash deposit immediately following each credit card transaction. If credit sales for the company total $30,000 on January 15, what journal entry should be recorded to recognize the receipt of cash and the credit card fee expense?

    a. Debit Cash $29,100; debit Credit Card Fee Expense $900.
    b. Debit Cash $29,100; credit Credit Card Fee Expense $900.
    c. Debit Cash $30,900; debit Credit Card Fee Expense $900.
    d. Debit Cash $30,900; credit Credit Card Fee Expense $900.

LO4 **SE8-7.** **Calculating Accrued Interest Income on Promissory Notes Receivable** Likert Company received a 90 day, six percent note receivable for $20,000 on November 1. How much interest income should be accrued on December 31?

    a. $100
    b. $200
    c. $300
    d. $400

SE8-8. **Calculating Interest on Promissory Notes Receivable** Dallas Company receives a six-month note **LO4** from a customer. The note has a face amount of $8,000 and an interest rate of nine percent. What is the total amount of interest income to be received?

a. $720
b. $540
c. $360
d. $180

SE8-9. **Accounts Receivable Turnover** Tarrant Company has net sales of $120,000, a beginning balance in **LO5** Accounts Receivable of $10,000, and an ending balance in Accounts Receivable of $14,000. What is the company's accounts receivable turnover?

a.   10.0
b.   12.0
c.   8.6
d.   9.2

SE8-10. **Average Collection Period** Smith & Sons has an accounts receivable turnover of 20. What is the **LO5** company's average collection period?

a.   18.25 days
b.   20.0 days
c.   22.25 days
d.   24.25 days

Assignments with the ✔ logo in the margin are available in ᵐʸBusinessCourse.
See the Preface of the book for details.

EXERCISES—SET A

E8-1A. **Credit Losses Based on Credit Sales** Lewis Company uses the allowance method for recording its **LO2** expected credit losses. It estimates credit losses at 1 percent of credit sales, which were $900,000 dur- ✔ ing the year. On December 31, the Accounts Receivable balance was $150,000, and the Allowance for Doubtful Accounts had a credit balance of $10,200 before adjustment.

a.   Prepare the adjusting entry to record the credit losses for the year.
b.   Show how Accounts Receivable and the Allowance for Doubtful Accounts would appear in the December 31 balance sheet.

E8-2A. **Credit Losses Based on Accounts Receivable** Hunter, Inc., analyzed its accounts receivable bal- **LO1, 2** ances at December 31, and arrived at the aged balances listed below, along with the percentage that is ✔ estimated to be uncollectible:

Age Group	Balance	Probability of Noncollection
0–30 days past due	$ 90,000	1
31–60 days past due	20,000	2
61–120 days past due	11,000	5
121–180 days past due	6,000	10
Over 180 days past due...............................	4,000	25
	$131,000	

The company handles credit losses using the allowance method. The credit balance of the Allowance for Doubtful Accounts is $520 on December 31, before any adjustments.

a.   Prepare the adjusting entry for estimated credit losses on December 31.
b.   Prepare the journal entry to write off the Rose Company's account on April 10 of the following year in the amount of $425.

E8-3A. **Allowance Method versus Direct Write-Off Method** On March 10, Gardner, Inc., declared a $900 **LO6** account receivable from the Gates Company as uncollectible and wrote off the account. On November **(Appendix 8A)** 18, Gardner received a $400 payment on the account from Gates. ✔

a.   Assume that Gardner uses the allowance method of handling credit losses. Prepare the journal entries to record the write-off and the subsequent recovery of Gates's account.

b.   Assume that Gardner uses the direct write-off method of handling credit losses. Prepare the journal entries to record the write-off and the subsequent recovery of Gates's account.

c.   Assume that the payment from Gates arrives on February 5 of the following year rather than on November 18 of the current year. (1) Prepare the journal entries to record the write-off and subsequent recovery of Gates's account under the allowance method. (2) Prepare the journal entries to record the write-off and subsequent recovery of Gates's account under the direct write-off method.

LO3   **E8-4A.   Credit Card Sales** Ruth Anne's Fabrics accepts cash, personal checks, and two credit cards when customers buy merchandise. With the Great American Bank Card, Ruth Anne's Fabrics receives an immediate deposit in its checking account when credit card sales slips are deposited at the bank. The bank charges a four percent fee. With the United Merchants Card, Ruth Anne's Fabrics mails the credit card sales slips to United Merchants' regional processing center each day. United Merchants accumulates these slips for three days and then mails a check to Ruth Anne's Fabrics, after deducting a three percent fee. Prepare journal entries to record the following:

a.   Sales for March 15 were as follows:

Cash and checks	$ 850
Great American Bank Card (Deposited at the end of the day).	1,100
United Merchants Card (Mailed at the end of the day)	700
	$2,650

b.   Received a check for $3,978 from United Merchants on March 20.

LO4   **E8-5A.   Maturity Dates of Notes Receivable** Determine the maturity date and compute the interest for each of the following notes:

	Date of Note	Principal	Interest Rate (%)	Term
a.	August 5	$ 6,000	8	120 days
b.	May 10	16,800	7	90 days
c.	October 20	24,000	9	45 days
d.	July 6	4,500	10	60 days
e.	September 15.	9,000	8	75 days

LO4   **E8-6A.   Computing Accrued Interest** Compute the interest accrued on each of the following notes receivable held by Northland, Inc., on December 31:

Maker	Date of Note	Principal	Interest Rate (%)	Term
Maple	11/21	$18,000	10	120 days
Wyman	12/13	14,000	9	90 days
Nahn.	12/19	21,000	8	60 days

LO5   **E8-7A.   Accounts Receivable Turnover and Average Collection Period** The Forrester Corporation disclosed the following financial information (in millions) in its recent annual report:

	2012	2013
Net sales.	$67,096	$81,662
Beginning accounts receivable (net)	3,896	3,696
Ending accounts receivable (net).	3,696	3,598

a.   Calculate the accounts receivable turnover ratio for both years.

b.   Calculate the average collection period for both years.

c.   Is the company's accounts receivable management improving or deteriorating?

E8-8A. Credit Losses Based on Credit Sales Smith & Sons uses the allowance method of handling its credit losses. It estimates credit losses at one percent of credit sales, which were $1,800,000 during the year. On December 31, the Accounts Receivable balance was $300,000, and the Allowance for Doubtful Accounts had a credit balance of $20,400 before adjustment.   **LO2**

a. Prepare the adjusting entry to record the credit losses for the year.

b. Show how Accounts Receivable and the Allowance for Doubtful Accounts would appear in the December 31 balance sheet.

E8-9A. Credit Losses Based on Accounts Receivable Miller, Inc., analyzed its accounts receivable balances at December 31 and arrived at the aged balances listed below, along with the percentage that is estimated to be uncollectible: **LO1, 2**

Age Group	Balance	Probability of Noncollection
0–30 days past due	$180,000	1
31–60 days past due	40,000	2
61–120 days past due	22,000	5
121–180 days past due	12,000	10
Over 180 days past due	8,000	25
	$262,000	

The company handles credit losses using the allowance method. The credit balance of the Allowance for Doubtful Accounts is $1,040 on December 31, before any adjustments.

a. Prepare the adjusting entry for estimated credit losses on December 31.

b. Prepare the journal entry to write off the Lyons Company's account on April 10 of the following year in the amount of $425.

E8-10A. Allowance Method versus Direct Write-Off Method On March 10, Mize, Inc., declared an $1,800 account receivable from Anders Company as uncollectible and wrote off the account. On November 18, Mize received an $800 payment on the account from Anders.   **LO6 (Appendix 8A)**

a. Assume that Mize uses the allowance method of handling credit losses. Prepare the journal entries to record the write-off and the subsequent recovery of Anders's account.

b. Assume that Mize uses the direct write-off method of handling credit losses. Prepare the journal entries to record the write-off and the subsequent recovery of Anders's account.

c. Assume that the payment from Anders arrives on the following February 5, rather than on November 18 of the current year. (1) Prepare the journal entries to record the write-off and subsequent recovery of Anders's account under the allowance method. (2) Prepare the journal entries to record the write-off and subsequent recovery of Anders's account under the direct write-off method.

E8-11A. Credit Card Sales The Tin Roof accepts cash, personal checks, and two credit cards when customers buy merchandise. With the Great American Bank Card, The Tin Roof receives an immediate deposit in its checking account when credit card sales slips are deposited at the bank. The bank charges a four percent fee. With the United Merchants Card, The Tin Roof mails the credit card sales slips to United Merchants' regional processing center each day. United Merchants accumulates these slips for three days and then mails a check to The Tin Roof, after deducting a three percent fee. Prepare journal entries to record the following: **LO3**

a. Sales for March 15 were as follows:

Cash and checks	$1,700
Great American Bank Card (Deposited at the end of the day)	2,200
United Merchants Card (Mailed at the end of the day)	1,400
	$5,300

b. Received a check for $7,956 from United Merchants on March 20.

LO4

E8-12A. Maturity Dates of Notes Receivable Determine the maturity date and compute the interest for each of the following notes:

	Date of Note	Principal	Interest Rate (%)	Term
a.	August 5	$12,000	8	120 days
b.	May 10	33,600	7	90 days
c.	October 20	48,000	9	45 days
d.	July 6	9,000	10	60 days
e.	September 15	18,000	8	75 days

LO4

E8-13A. Computing Accrued Interest Compute the interest accrued on each of the following notes receivable held by Kierland, Inc., on December 31:

Maker	Date of Note	Principal	Interest Rate (%)	Term
Abel	11/21	$36,000	10	120 days
Baker	12/13	28,000	9	90 days
Charlie	12/19	42,000	8	60 days

LO5

E8-14A. Accounts Receivable Turnover and Average Collection Period VanPoole Corporation disclosed the following financial information (in millions) in its recent annual report:

	2012	2013
Net sales	$167,096	$181,662
Beginning accounts receivable (net)	13,896	13,696
Ending accounts receivable (net)	13,696	13,598

    a. Calculate the accounts receivable turnover ratio for both years.
    b. Calculate the average collection period for both years.
    c. Is the company's accounts receivable management improving or deteriorating?

LO1

E8-15A. Recognizing Accounts Receivable On June 7, Bixby Co. sells $750 of merchandise to Jasmine Co. on account. Jasmine Co. pays for this merchandise on June 21.

    a. Prepare the entry on Bixby's books to record the sale.
    b. Prepare the entry on Bixby's books to record the receipt of payment.

EXERCISES—SET B

LO2

E8-1B. Credit Losses Based on Credit Sales Highland Company uses the allowance method of handling credit losses. It estimates losses at one percent of credit sales, which were $1,200,000 during the year. On December 31, the Accounts Receivable balance was $280,000, and the Allowance for Doubtful Accounts had a credit balance of $1,700 before adjustment.

    a. Prepare the adjusting entry to record credit losses for the year.
    b. Show how the Accounts Receivable account and the Allowance for Doubtful Accounts would appear on the December 31 balance sheet.

LO1, 2

E8-2B. Credit Losses Based on Accounts Receivable Maxwell, Inc. analyzed its accounts receivable balances at December 31 and arrived at the aged balances listed below, along with the percentage that is estimated to be uncollectible:

Age Group	Balance	Probability of Noncollection
0–30 days past due	$100,000	1
31–60 days past due	18,000	3
61–120 days past due	20,000	6
121–180 days past due	7,000	10
Over 180 days past due	2,000	20
	$147,000	

The company handles credit losses with the allowance method. The credit balance of the Allowance for Doubtful Accounts is $840 on December 31, before any adjustments.

a. Prepare the adjusting entry for estimated credit losses on December 31.

b. Prepare the journal entry to write off Porter Company's account on the following May 12, in the amount of $480.

E8-3B. **Allowance Method versus Direct Write-Off Method** On April 12, Maddox Company declared a $1,000 account receivable from the Ward Company as uncollectible and wrote off the account. On December 5, Maddox received a $700 payment on the account from Ward.

LO6
(Appendix 8A)

a. Assume that Maddox uses the allowance method of handling credit losses. Prepare the journal entries to record the write-off and the subsequent recovery of Ward's account.

b. Assume that Maddox uses the direct write-off method of handling credit losses. Prepare the journal entries to record the write-off and the subsequent recovery of Ward's account.

c. Assume that the payment from Ward arrives on the following January 18, rather than on December 5 of the current year. (1) Prepare the journal entries to record the write-off and subsequent recovery of Ward's account under the allowance method. (2) Prepare the journal entries to record the write-off and subsequent recovery of Ward's account under the direct write-off method.

E8-4B. **Credit Card Sales** Historically, 60 percent of the customer bills at the Andrews' Supper Club have been paid with cash or check, and 40 percent have been paid using either the Great American Bank Card or the United Merchants Card. Andrews pays a four percent fee with both cards. Great American Bank deposits cash in Andrews' checking account when the credit card sales slips are deposited. United Merchants makes an electronic funds transfer three days after the sales slips are mailed. Prepare journal entries to record the following:

LO3

a. Sales for September 10 were as follows:

Cash and checks	$1,340
Great American Bank Card (Deposited at the end of the day).	500
United Merchants Card (Mailed at the end of the day)	300
	$2,140

b. On September 13, Andrews received an electronic funds transfer from United Merchants for the September 10 sales.

E8-5B. **Maturity Dates of Notes Receivable** Determine the maturity date and compute the interest for each of the following notes:

LO4

	Date of Note	Principal	Interest Rate (%)	Term
a.	July 10	$ 7,200	9	90 days
b.	April 14	12,000	8	120 days
c.	May 19	11,200	$7\frac{1}{2}$	120 days
d.	June 10	5,400	8	45 days
e.	October 29	30,000	8	75 days

E8-6B. **Computing Accrued Interest** Compute the interest accrued on each of the following notes receivable held by Galloway, Inc., on December 31:

LO4

Maker	Date of Note	Principal	Interest Rate (%)	Term
Barton.	12/4	$10,000	8	120 days
Lawson.	12/13	24,000	9	90 days
Riley	12/19	9,000	10	60 days

E8-7B. **Accounts Receivable Turnover and Average Collection Period** The Andrew Miller Corporation disclosed the following financial information (in millions) in its recent annual report:

LO5

	2012	2013
Net sales..	$97,096	$111,662
Beginning accounts receivable (net)	6,896	6,696
Ending accounts receivable (net).....................................	6,696	6,598

a. Calculate the accounts receivable turnover ratio for both years.
b. Calculate the average collection period for both years.
c. Is the company's accounts receivable management improving or deteriorating?

LO2

E8-8B. Credit Losses Based on Credit Sales Harris Company uses the allowance method of handling its credit losses. It estimates credit losses at one percent of credit sales, which were $2,700,000 during the year. On December 31, the Accounts Receivable balance was $450,000, and the Allowance for Doubtful Accounts had a credit balance of $30,600 before adjustment.

a. Prepare the adjusting entry to record the credit losses for the year.
b. Show how Accounts Receivable and the Allowance for Doubtful Accounts would appear in the December 31 balance sheet.

LO1, 2

E8-9B. Credit Losses Based on Accounts Receivable Graham, Inc., analyzed its accounts receivable balances at December 31 and arrived at the aged balances listed below, along with the percentage that is estimated to be uncollectible:

Age Group	Balance	Probability of Noncollection
0–30 days past due	$270,000	1
31–60 days past due	60,000	2
61–120 days past due	33,000	5
121–180 days past due	18,000	10
Over 180 days past due....................................	12,000	25
	$393,000	

The company handles credit losses using the allowance method. The credit balance of the Allowance for Doubtful Accounts is $1,560 on December 31, before any adjustments.

a. Prepare the adjusting entry for estimated credit losses on December 31.
b. Prepare the journal entry to write off the Matthews Company's account on the following April 10, in the amount of $425.

LO6
(Appendix 8A)

E8-10B. Allowance Method versus Direct Write-Off Method On March 10, Barrett, Inc., declared a $2,700 account receivable from Lamas Company as uncollectible and wrote off the account. On November 18, Barrett received a $1,200 payment on the account from Lamas.

a. Assume that Barrett uses the allowance method of handling credit losses. Prepare the journal entries to record the write-off and the subsequent recovery of Lamas's account.
b. Assume that Barrett uses the direct write-off method of handling credit losses. Prepare the journal entries to record the write-off and the subsequent recovery of Lamas's account.
c. Assume that the payment from Lamas arrives on the following February 5, rather than on November 18 of the current year. (1) Prepare the journal entries to record the write-off and subsequent recovery of Lamas's account under the allowance method. (2) Prepare the journal entries to record the write-off and subsequent recovery of Lamas's account under the direct write-off method.

LO3

E8-11B. Credit Card Sales The Bedroom Store accepts cash, personal checks, and two credit cards when customers buy merchandise. With the Great American Bank Card, The Bedroom Store receives an immediate deposit in its checking account when credit card sales slips are deposited at the bank. The bank charges a four percent fee. With the United Merchants Card, The Bedroom Store mails the credit card sales slips to United Merchants' regional processing center each day. United Merchants accumulates these slips for three days and then mails a check to The Bedroom Store, after deducting a three percent fee. Prepare journal entries to record the following:

a. Sales for March 15 were as follows:

Cash and checks	$2,550
Great American Bank Card (Deposited at the end of the day).	3,300
United Merchants Card (Mailed at the end of the day)	2,100
	$7,950

b. Received a check for $11,934 from United Merchants on March 20.

E8-12B. Maturity Dates of Notes Receivable Determine the maturity date and compute the interest for each of the following notes: **LO4** ✔

	Date of Note	Principal	Interest Rate (%)	Term
a.	August 5.	$18,000	8	120 days
b.	May 10	50,400	7	90 days
c.	October 20	72,000	9	45 days
d.	July 6	13,500	10	60 days
e.	September 15.	27,000	8	75 days

E8-13B. Computing Accrued Interest Compute the interest accrued on each of the following notes receivable held by Northland, Inc., on December 31: **LO4** ✔

	Maker	Date of Note	Principal	Interest Rate (%)	Term
a.	Delta.	11/21	$54,000	10	120 days
b.	Echo	12/13	42,000	9	90 days
c.	Foxtrot	12/19	63,000	8	60 days

E8-14B. Accounts Receivable Turnover and Average Collection Period The Longo Corporation disclosed the following financial information (in millions) in its recent annual report: **LO5** ✔

	2012	2013
Net sales.	$127,096	$111,662
Beginning accounts receivable (net)	8,896	7,696
Ending accounts receivable (net)	7,696	6,598

a. Calculate the accounts receivable turnover ratio for both years.
b. Calculate the average collection period for both years.
c. Is the company's accounts receivable management improving or deteriorating?

E8-15B. Recognizing Accounts Receivable On August 9, Gunner Co. sells $300 of merchandise to Taylor Co. on account. Taylor Co. pays for this merchandise on September 1. **LO1** ✔

a. Prepare the entry on Gunner's books to record the sale.
b. Prepare the entry on Gunner's books to record the receipt of payment.

PROBLEMS—SET A

P8-1A. Allowance Method Fullerton Company, which has been in business for three years, makes all of its sales on account and does not offer cash discounts. The firm's credit sales, collections from customers, and write-offs of uncollectible accounts for the three-year period are summarized below: **LO2** ✔

Year	Sales	Collections	Accounts Written Off
2012	$300,000	$287,000	$2,100
2013	385,000	380,000	3,350
2014	420,000	407,000	3,650

Required

a. If Fullerton Company had used the allowance method of recognizing credit losses and had provided for such losses at the rate of 1.2 percent of credit sales, what amounts in accounts receivable and the allowance for doubtful accounts would appear on the firm's balance sheet at the end of 2014? What total amount of bad debts expense would have appeared on the firm's income statement during the three year period?

b. Comment on the use of the 1.2 percent rate to provide for credit losses in part *a*.

LO1, 2   **P8-2A.**   **Journal Entries for Credit Losses**   At the beginning of the year, Whitney Company had the following accounts on its books:

Accounts receivable.	$122,000 (debit)
Allowance for doubtful accounts	7,900 (credit)

During the year, credit sales were $1,173,000 and collections on account were $1,150,000. The following transactions, among others, occurred during the year:

Feb.   17   Wrote off R. Lowell's account, $3,600.

May   28   Wrote off G. Boyd's account, $2,400.

Oct.   13   Received $600 from G. Boyd, who is in bankruptcy proceedings, in final settlement of the account written off on May 28. This amount is not included in the $1,150,000 collections.

Dec.   15   Wrote off K. Marshall's account, $1,500.

        31   In an adjusting entry, recorded the allowance for doubtful accounts at 0.8 percent of credit sales for the year.

Required

a. Prepare journal entries to record the credit sales, the collections on account, and the preceding transactions and adjustment.

b. Show how Accounts Receivable and the Allowance for Doubtful Accounts would appear on the December 31 balance sheet.

LO2   **P8-3A.**   **Credit Losses Based on Accounts Receivable**   At December 31, Schuler Company had a balance

of $370,000 in its Accounts Receivable account and a credit balance of $4,200 in the Allowance for Doubtful Accounts account. The accounts receivable T-account consisted of $375,000 in debit balances and $5,000 in credit balances. The company aged its accounts as follows:

Current	$304,000
0–60 days past due	44,000
61–180 days past due	18,000
Over 180 days past due	9,000
	$375,000

In the past, the company has experienced credit losses as follows: one percent of current balances, five percent of balances 0–60 days past due, 15 percent of balances 61–180 days past due, and 40 percent of balances over six months past due. The company bases its allowance for doubtful accounts on an aging analysis of accounts receivable.

Required

a. Prepare the adjusting entry to record the allowance for doubtful accounts for the year.

b. Show how Accounts Receivable (including the credit balances) and the Allowance for Doubtful Accounts would appear on the December 31 balance sheet.

LO3   **P8-4A.**   **Credit Card Sales**   Valderi's Gallery sells quality art work, with prices for individual pieces ranging from $500 to $25,000. Sales are infrequent, typically only three to five pieces per week. The following transactions occurred during the first week of June 2012. Perpetual inventory is used.

On June 1, sold an $800 framed print ($500 cost) to Kerwin Antiques on account, with 2/10, n/30 credit terms.

On June 2, sold three framed etchings totaling $2,400 ($1,500 cost) to Maria Alvado, who used the United Merchants Card to charge the cost of the etchings. Valderi mailed the credit card sales slip to United Merchants the same day. United Merchants will send a check within seven days after deducting a one percent fee.

On June 4, sold an $1,800 oil painting ($1,000 cost) to Shaun Chandler, who paid with a personal check.

On June 5, sold a $2,000 watercolor ($1,300 cost) to Julie and John Malbie, who used their Great American Bank Card to charge the purchase of the painting. Valderi deposited the credit card sales slip the same day and received immediate credit in the company's checking account. The bank charged a two percent fee.

On June 6, received payment from Kerwin Antiques for its June 1 purchase.

On June 7, received a check from United Merchants for the June 2 sale.

Required
Prepare journal entries to record the Valderi Gallery transactions.

P8-5A. **Journal Entries for Accounts and Notes Receivable** Lancaster Inc. began business on January 1. Certain transactions for the year follow:

LO2, 4

June	8	Received a $15,000, 60 day, eight percent note on account from R. Elliot.
Aug.	7	Received payment from R. Elliot on her note (principal plus interest).
Sept.	1	Received an $18,000, 120 day, nine percent note from B. Shore Company on account.
Dec.	16	Received a $14,400, 45 day, ten percent note from C. Judd on account.
	30	B. Shore Company failed to pay its note.
	31	Wrote off B. Shore's account as uncollectible. Lancaster, Inc. uses the allowance method of providing for credit losses.
	31	Recorded expected credit losses for the year by an adjusting entry. Accounts written off during this first year have created a debit balance in the Allowance for Doubtful Accounts of $22,600. An analysis of aged receivables indicates that the desired balance of the allowance account should be $19,500.
	31	Made the appropriate adjusting entries for interest.

Required
Record the foregoing transactions and adjustments in general journal form.

P8-6A. **Allowance Method** The Huntington Company, which has been in business for three years, makes all of its sales on account and does not offer cash discounts. The firm's credit sales, collections from customers, and write-offs of uncollectible accounts for the three-year period are summarized below:

LO2

Year	Sales	Collections	Accounts Written Off
2012	$600,000	$574,000	$4,200
2013	770,000	760,000	6,700
2014	840,000	814,000	7,300

Required
a. If the Huntington Company had used the allowance method of recognizing credit losses and had provided for such losses at the rate of 1.2 percent of credit sales, what amounts in Accounts Receivable and the Allowance for Doubtful Accounts would appear on the firm's balance sheet at the end of 2014? What total amount of bad debts expense would have appeared on the firm's income statement during the three year period?
b. Comment on the use of the 1.2 percent rate to provide for credit losses in part *a*.

P8-7A. **Journal Entries for Credit Losses** At the beginning of the year, the Houston Company had the following accounts on its books:

LO1, 2

Accounts receivable..	$244,000 (debit)
Allowance for doubtful accounts	15,800 (credit)

During the year, credit sales were $2,346,000 and collections on account were $2,300,000. The following transactions, among others, occurred during the year:

Feb.   17 Wrote off R. St. John's account, $7,200.
May   28 Wrote off G. Herberger's account, $4,800.
Oct.   13 Received $1,200 from G. Herberger, who is in bankruptcy proceedings, in final settlement of the account written off on May 28. This amount is not included in the $2,300,000 collections.
Dec.   15 Wrote off R. Clancy's account, $3,000.
       31 In an adjusting entry, recorded the allowance for doubtful accounts at 0.8 percent of credit sales for the year.

Required
a. Prepare journal entries to record the credit sales, the collections on account, and the preceding transactions and adjustment.
b. Show how Accounts Receivable and the Allowance for Doubtful Accounts would appear on the December 31 balance sheet.

LO2 **P8-8A.** **Credit Losses Based on Accounts Receivable** At December 31, the Selling Company had a balance of $740,000 in its Accounts Receivable account and a credit balance of $8,400 in the Allowance for Doubtful Accounts account. The accounts receivable T-account consisted of $750,000 in debit balances and $10,000 in credit balances. The company aged its accounts as follows:

Current	$608,000
0–60 days past due	88,000
61–180 days past due	36,000
Over 180 days past due	18,000
	$750,000

In the past, the company has experienced credit losses as follows: one percent of current balances, five percent of balances 0–60 days past due, 15 percent of balances 61–180 days past due, and 40 percent of balances over six months past due. The company bases its allowance for doubtful accounts on an aging analysis of accounts receivable.

Required
a. Prepare the adjusting entry to record the allowance for doubtful accounts for the year.
b. Show how Accounts Receivable (including the credit balances) and the Allowance for Doubtful Accounts would appear on the December 31 balance sheet.

LO3 **P8-9A.** **Credit Card Sales** Le Kai Gallery sells quality art work, with prices for individual pieces ranging from $1,000 to $50,000. Sales are infrequent, typically only six to ten pieces per week. The following transactions occurred during the first week of June. Perpetual inventory is used.

On June 1, sold an $1,600 framed print ($1,000 cost) to Likert Antiques on account, with 2/10, n/30 credit terms.

On June 2, sold three framed etchings totaling $4,800 ($3,000 cost) to Annabelle Herrera, who used the United Merchants Card to charge the cost of the etchings. Le Kai mailed the credit card sales slip to United Merchants the same day. United Merchants will send a check within seven days after deducting a one percent fee.

On June 4, sold a $3,600 oil painting ($2,000 cost) to Ryan LaLander, who paid with a personal check.

On June 5, sold a $4,000 watercolor ($2,600 cost) to Julie and Bobby Herman, who used their Great American Bank Card to charge the purchase of the painting. Le Kai deposited the credit card sales slip the same day and received immediate credit in the company's checking account. The bank charged a two percent fee.

On June 6, received payment from Likert Antiques for its June 1 purchase.

On June 7, received a check from United Merchants for the June 2 sale.

Required
Prepare journal entries to record the Le Kai Gallery transactions.

P8-10A. Journal Entries for Accounts and Notes Receivable Pittsburgh, Inc., began business on January 1.   **LO2, 4**
Certain transactions for the year follow:

June   8   Received a $30,000, 60 day, eight percent note on account from J. Albert.
Aug.   7   Received payment from J. Albert on his note (principal plus interest).
Sept.   1   Received a $36,000, 120 day, nine percent note from R.T. Matthews Company on account.
Dec.   16   Received a $28,800, 45 day, ten percent note from D. LeRoy on account.
        30   R.T. Matthews Company failed to pay its note.
        31   Wrote off R.T. Matthews' account as uncollectible. Pittsburgh, Inc., uses the allowance
             method of providing for credit losses.
        31   Recorded expected credit losses for the year by an adjusting entry. Accounts written off
             during this first year have created a debit balance in the allowance for doubtful accounts
             of $45,200. An analysis of aged receivables indicates that the desired balance of the
             allowance account should be $39,000.
        31   Made the appropriate adjusting entries for interest.

Required
Record the foregoing transactions and adjustments in general journal form.

PROBLEMS—SET B

P8-1B. Allowance Method Steinbrook Company, which has been in business for three years, makes all of its   **LO2**
sales on account and does not offer cash discounts. The firm's credit sales, collections from customers, and write-offs of uncollectible accounts for the three-year period are summarized as follows:

Year	Sales	Collections	Accounts Written Off
2012	$751,000	$733,000	$5,300
2013	876,000	864,000	5,800
2014	972,000	938,000	6,500

Required
a.   If Steinbrook Company used an allowance method of recognizing credit losses and provided for
     such losses at the rate of one percent of credit sales, what amounts of accounts receivable and the
     allowance for doubtful accounts should appear on the firm's balance sheet at the end of 2014?
     What total amount of bad debts expense should appear on the firm's income statement during the
     three-year period?
b.   Comment on the use of the one percent rate to provide for credit losses in part *a*.

P8-2B. Journal Entries for Credit Losses At January 1, the Griffin Company had the following accounts   **LO1, 2**
on its books:

Accounts receivable.	$126,000 (debit)
Allowance for doubtful accounts	6,800 (credit)

During the year, credit sales were $811,000 and collections on account were $794,000. The following
transactions, among others, occurred during the year:

Jan.   11   Wrote off J. Wolf's account, $2,800.
Apr.   29   Wrote off B. Avery's account, $1,000.
Nov.   15   Received $1,000 from B. Avery to pay a debt that had been written off April 29. This
             amount is not included in the $794,000 collections.
Dec.   5   Wrote off D. Wright's account, $2,150.
        31   In an adjusting entry, recorded the allowance for doubtful accounts at one percent of
             credit sales for the year.

Required

a. Prepare journal entries to record the credit sales, the collections on account, the transactions, and the adjustment.

b. Show how Accounts Receivable and the Allowance for Doubtful Accounts appear on the December 31 balance sheet.

LO2 **P8-3B.** **Credit Losses Based on Accounts Receivable** At December 31, Rinehart Company had a balance of $304,000 in its Accounts Receivable account and a credit balance of $2,800 in the Allowance for Doubtful Accounts account. The accounts receivable T-account consisted of $309,600 in debit balances and $5,600 in credit balances. The company has aged its accounts as follows:

Current	$262,000
0–60 days past due	28,000
61–180 days past due	11,200
Over 180 days past due	8,400
	$309,600

In the past, the company has experienced credit losses as follows: two percent of current balances, six percent of balances 0–60 days past due, 15 percent of balances 61–180 days past due, and 30 percent of balances more than six months past due. The company bases its allowance for doubtful accounts on an aging analysis of accounts receivable.

Required

a. Prepare the adjusting journal entry to record the provision for credit losses for the year.

b. Show how Accounts Receivable (including the credit balances) and the Allowance for Doubtful Accounts appear on the December 31 balance sheet.

LO3 **P8-4B.** **Credit Card Sales** Captain Paul's Marina sells boats and other water recreational vehicles (approximately three vehicles are sold each week). The following transactions occurred during the third week of May:

On May 15, sold a $600 boat trailer ($400 cost) to Sam and Myrna Marston, who paid using a personal check.

On May 16, sold a $10,000 boat ($6,500 cost) to the Calumet Lake Patrol on account, with 2/10, n/30 terms.

On May 18, sold a $1,200 water scooter ($700 cost) to Kyle Bronson, who used the United Merchants Card to charge the cost of the water scooter. Captain Paul's mailed the credit card sales slip to United Merchants the same day. United Merchants will send a check within seven days, net of a two percent fee.

On May 19, sold a $5,000 fishing boat ($3,000 cost) to Michael Ferguson, who used the Great American Bank Card to pay for the boat. Captain Paul's deposited the credit card sales slip the same day and received an immediate credit in the company's checking account, net of a two percent fee.

On May 20, received payment from Calumet Lake Patrol for the boat purchased on May 16.

On May 21, received payment from United Merchants for the May 18 transaction.

Required

Prepare journal entries to record these transactions. Captain Paul's Marina uses the perpetual inventory system.

LO2, 4 **P8-5B.** **Journal Entries for Accounts and Notes Receivable** Armstrong, Inc., began business on January 1. Several transactions for the year follow:

May	2	Received a $14,400, 60 day, ten percent note on account from the Holt Company.
July	1	Received payment from Holt for its note plus interest.
	1	Received a $27,000, 120 day, ten percent note from B. Rich Company on account.
Oct.	30	B. Rich failed to pay its note.

Dec. 9 Wrote off B. Rich's account as uncollectible. Armstrong, Inc., uses the allowance method of providing for credit losses.

11 Received a $21,000, 90 day, nine percent note from W. Maling on account.

31 Recorded expected credit losses for the year by an adjusting entry. The allowance for doubtful accounts has a debit balance of $28,300 as a result of accounts written off during this first year. An analysis of aged accounts receivables indicates that the desired balance of the allowance account is $5,800.

31 Made the appropriate adjusting entries for interest.

Required

Record the foregoing transactions and adjustments in general journal form.

P8-6B. Allowance Method The Wallbrook Company, which has been in business for three years, makes all of its sales on account and does not offer cash discounts. The firm's credit sales, collections from customers, and write-offs of uncollectible accounts for the three-year period are summarized below:

LO2

Year	Sales	Collections	Accounts Written Off
2012	$1,502,000	$1,466,000	$10,600
2013	1,752,000	1,728,000	11,600
2014	1,944,000	1,876,000	13,000

Required

a. If the Wallbrook Company used an allowance method of recognizing credit losses and provided for such losses at the rate of one percent of credit sales, what amounts of accounts receivable and the allowance for doubtful accounts should appear on the firm's balance sheet at the end of 2014? What total amount of bad debts expense should appear on the firm's income statement during the three year period?

b. Comment on the use of the one percent rate to provide for credit losses in part *a*.

P8-7B. Journal Entries for Credit Losses At January 1, the Chesley Company had the following accounts on its books:

LO1, 2

Accounts receivable.	$252,000 (debit)
Allowance for doubtful accounts	13,600 (credit)

During the year, credit sales were $1,622,000 and collections on account were $1,588,000. The following transactions, among others, occurred during the year:

Jan. 11 Wrote off J. Smith's account, $5,600.

Apr. 29 Wrote off B. Bird's account, $2,000.

Nov. 15 Received $1,000 from B. Bird to pay a debt that had been written off April 29. This amount is not included in the $1,588,000 collections.

Dec. 5 Wrote off D. Finger's account, $4,300.

31 In an adjusting entry, recorded the allowance for doubtful accounts at one percent of credit sales for the year.

Required

a. Prepare journal entries to record the credit sales, the collections on account, the transactions, and the adjustment.

b. Show how Accounts Receivable and the Allowance for Doubtful Accounts appear on the December 31 balance sheet.

P8-8B. Credit Losses Based on Accounts Receivable At December 31, the Hope Company had a balance of $608,000 in its accounts receivable account and a credit balance of $5,600 in the allowance for doubtful accounts account. The accounts receivable T-account consisted of $619,200 in debit balances and $11,200 in credit balances. The company has aged its accounts as follows:

LO2

Current	$524,000
0–60 days past due	56,000
61–180 days past due	22,400
Over 180 days past due	16,800
	$619,200

In the past, the company has experienced credit losses as follows: two percent of current balances, six percent of balances 0–60 days past due, 15 percent of balances 61–180 days past due, and 30 percent of balances more than six months past due. The company bases its allowance for doubtful accounts on an aging analysis of accounts receivable.

Required

a.   Prepare the adjusting journal entry to record the provision for credit losses for the year.

b.   Show how Accounts Receivable (including the credit balances) and the Allowance for Doubtful Accounts appear on the December 31 balance sheet.

LO3 **P8-9B.** **Credit Card Sales** Lake Pleasant Marina sells boats and other water recreational vehicles (approximately three vehicles are sold each week). The following transactions occurred during the third week of May:

On May 15, sold a $1,200 boat trailer ($800 cost) to Ed and Jane Peeler, who paid using a personal check.

On May 16, sold a $20,000 boat ($13,000 cost) to the Lake Pleasant Lake Patrol on account, with 2/10, n/30 terms.

On May 18, sold a $2,400 water scooter ($1,400 cost) to Bryan Wagner, who used the United Merchants Card to charge the cost of the water scooter. Lake Pleasant Marina mailed the credit card sales slip to United Merchants the same day. United Merchants will send a check within seven days, net of a two percent fee.

On May 19, sold a $10,000 fishing boat ($6,000 cost) to Michael Moffett, who used the Great American Bank Card to pay for the boat. Lake Pleasant Marina deposited the credit card sales slip the same day and received an immediate credit in the company's checking account, net of a two percent fee.

On May 20, received payment from the Lake Pleasant Lake Patrol for the boat purchased on May 16.

On May 21, received payment from United Merchants for the May 18 transaction.

Required

Prepare journal entries to record these transactions. The Lake Pleasant Marina uses a perpetual inventory system.

LO2, 4 **P8-10B.** **Journal Entries for Accounts and Notes Receivable** Dallmus, Inc., began business on January 1. Several transactions for the year follow:

May   2   Received a $28,800, 60 day, ten percent note on account from the Haskins Company.
July   1   Received payment from Haskins for its note plus interest.
        1   Received a $54,000, 120 day, ten percent note from R. Longo Company on account.
Oct. 30   R. Longo failed to pay its note.
Dec.   9   Wrote off R. Longo's account as uncollectible. Dallmus, Inc., uses the allowance method of providing for credit losses.
        11   Received a $42,000, 90 day, nine percent note from R. Canal on account.
        31   Recorded expected credit losses for the year by an adjusting entry. The Allowance for Doubtful Accounts has a debit balance of $56,600 as a result of accounts written off during this first year. An analysis of aged accounts receivables indicates that the desired balance of the allowance account is $11,600.
        31   Made the appropriate adjusting entries for interest.

Required

Record the foregoing transactions and adjustments in general journal form.

SERIAL PROBLEM: KATE'S CARDS

(Note: This is a continuation of the Serial Problem: Kate's Cards from Chapters 1 through 7.)

SP8. Kate has put a lot of time and effort into streamlining the process to design and produce a greeting card. She has documented the entire process in a QuickTime video she produced on her iMac. The video takes the viewer through the step-by-step process of selecting hardware and software, and shows how to design and produce the card. Kate has met many people who would like to get into the production of greeting cards, but are overwhelmed by the process. Kate has decided to sell the entire package (hardware, software, and video tutorial) to aspiring card producers. The cost of the entire package to Kate is $4,500 and she plans to mark it up by $500 and sell it for $5,000.

John Stevens, an individual Kate met recently at a greeting card conference, would like to buy the package from Kate. Unfortunately, John does not have this much cash and would like for Kate to extend credit.

Kate believes that many of her customers will not be able to pay cash and, therefore, she will need to find some way to provide financing. One option she is exploring is to accept credit cards. She learned that the credit card provider charges a 2.5 percent fee and provides immediate cash upon receiving the sales receipts.

Kate would like you to answer the following questions:

1. What are the advantages and disadvantages of offering credit?
2. What precautions should she take before offering credit to people like John?
3. If Kate grants credit to John, the terms will be 2/10, n/30. Assuming the payment is made during the 10-day discount period, what would be the journal entry to record the sale and then the subsequent payment?
4. If instead of paying early, John pays in 25 days, what would be the journal entry to record the payment?
5. Rather than providing the financing directly, assume that Kate decides to allow the use of credit cards. Further, assume that during the month there is $15,000 worth of credit card sales. Provide the journal entry to record the sales, along with the associated credit card fee. The cost of the goods sold total $13,500.

EXTENDING YOUR KNOWLEDGE

REPORTING AND ANALYSIS

EYK8-1. **Financial Reporting Problem: Columbia Sportswear Company** The annual report of the **Columbia Sportswear Company** is presented in Appendix A at the end of this book.

COLUMBIA
SPORTSWEAR
COMPANY

    a. What was the amount of the Accounts Receivables and the Allowance for Doubtful Accounts at the end of 2010 and 2011?

    b. What percent of total accounts receivables was the allowance for doubtful accounts at the end of 2010 and 2011?

EYK8-2. **Comparative Analysis Problem: Columbia Sportswear Company vs. Under Armour, Inc.** The annual report of the **Columbia Sportswear Company** is presented in Appendix A at the end of this book and the complete annual report of **Under Armour, Inc.** is on this book's Website.

COLUMBIA
SPORTSWEAR
COMPANY

UNDER ARMOUR,
INC.

Required

    a. Calculate the accounts receivable turnover and the average collection period for Columbia Sportswear and Under Armour, Inc. for 2011 and 2010. (To calculate the accounts receivable turnover, use the ending net accounts receivable balance as the denominator rather than average net accounts receivable.)

    b. Compare the average collection periods for the two companies and comment on possible reasons for the difference in the average collection periods for the two companies.

EYK8-3. **Business Decision Problem** Sally Smith owned a dance studio in San Francisco, California. Students could buy access to the dance classes by paying a monthly fee. Unfortunately, many of Sally's students were struggling actors and actresses who lacked the ability to pay their bills in a timely manner. And, although the students were expected to pay for classes in advance, Sally had begun offering credit to many of her students in order to grow her business. This, however, created a serious liquidity problem for Sally.

Age Classification	Trade Receivables Outstanding Balance	Historical Estimate of Noncollection
0–30 days	$44,000	4%
31–60 days	31,000	8%
61–90 days	22,000	12%
91–120 days	13,000	14%
121–150 days	9,000	20%
> 150 days	5,000	50%

Sally's accountant, Matt Thomas, had tried to help her get a handle on the receivable problem, but to little avail. One trick he had successfully used in the past to make Sally realize the seriousness of the problem was to overestimate the extent of Sally's bad debt problem; consequently, there currently existed a balance in the Allowance for Uncollectible Accounts totaling $2,700.

Required

1. The first step to help get Sally's business back on track is to write off all receivables having a very low probability of collection (i.e., those accounts over 150 days). Which accounts are affected and by what amount, to execute this action?

2. Prepare an aging of Sally's remaining accounts receivable. What should be the balance in the Allowance for Uncollectible Accounts?

3. Sally is in need of an immediate cash infusion and Matt has advised her to sell some of her receivables. A local bank has offered her two alternatives:
   a. Factor $40,000 of "current" receivables (i.e., 0–30 days old) on a nonrecourse basis at a flat fee of eleven percent of the receivables sold.
   b. Factor $40,000 of "current" receivables on a recourse basis at a flat fee of six percent of the receivables sold.
   Which option should Sally choose? Why?

ABBOTT
LABORATORIES

PFIZER INC.

EYK8-4. **Financial Analysis Problem** **Abbott Laboratories** is a diversified health care company devoted to the discovery, development, manufacture, and marketing of innovative products that improve diagnostic, therapeutic, and nutritional practices. Abbott markets products in more than 130 countries and employs 50,000 people. **Pfizer Inc.** is a research-based, global health care company. Its mission is to discover and develop innovative, value-added products that improve the quality of life of people around the world. Pfizer manufactures products in 31 countries and markets these products worldwide. These two companies reported the following information in their financial reports:

(in millions)	2008	2009
Abbott Laboratories		
Net sales..	$29,528	$30,765
Beginning accounts receivable (net).................	4,947	5,466
Ending accounts receivable (net)....................	5,466	6,542
Pfizer Inc.		
Net sales..	$48,296	$50,009
Beginning accounts receivable (net).................	9,843	8,958
Ending accounts receivable (net)....................	8,958	14,645

Required

a. Calculate the accounts receivable turnover and the average collection period for Abbott Laboratories and Pfizer Inc. for 2008 and 2009.

b. Compare the average collection periods for the two companies and comment on possible reasons for the difference in average collection periods for the two companies.

CRITICAL THINKING

EYK8-5. Accounting Research Problem Access the fiscal year 2011 annual report of **General Mills, Inc.,** available on this book's Website.

GENERAL MILLS,
INC.

Required

a. What was the amount of total Accounts Receivables and the Allowance for Doubtful Accounts at the end of fiscal-year 2011 and 2010? (Note: This information can be found in note 17.)

b. What percent of total accounts receivables was the allowance for doubtful accounts at the end of 2011 and 2010?

c. Calculate the accounts receivable turnover and the average collection period for General Mills for 2011 and 2010. (For purposes of calculating the accounts receivable turnover, use the ending total accounts receivable balance as the denominator rather than the average total accounts receivable.)

d. Comment on whether General Mills' management of accounts receivable improved (or not) over the two year period.

EYK8-6. Accounting Communications Activity You have been hired as the accounting manager of Taylor, Inc., a provider of custom furniture. The company recently switched its method of paying its salespeople from a straight salary to a commission basis in order to encourage them to increase sales. The salespeople receive ten percent of the sales price at the time of the sale. You have noticed that the company's accounts receivable balance is growing because the salespeople are granting more credit to their customers.

Required

Draft a memorandum explaining why it is important to closely monitor the company's accounts receivable balance and why a large balance could lead to cash flow problems.

EYK8-7. Accounting Ethics Case Tractor Motors' best salesperson is Marie Glazer. Glazer's largest sales have been to Farmers Cooperative, a customer she brought to the company. Another salesperson, Bryan Blanchard, has been told in confidence by his cousin (an employee of Farmers Cooperative) that Farmers Cooperative is experiencing financial difficulties and may not be able to pay Tractor Motors what is owed.

Both Glazer and Blanchard are being considered for promotion to a new sales manager position.

Required

What are the ethical considerations that face Bryan Blanchard? What alternatives does he have?

EYK8-8. Corporate Social Responsibility Problem **MGM Resorts International** is committed to responsible gaming and strictly adheres to the Code of Conduct established by the American Gaming Association. The company's efforts include employee training, public awareness, and support for research initiatives through the National Center for Responsible Gaming.

MGM RESORTS
INTERNATIONAL

Since MGM Resorts International makes money when people gamble, and the more people gamble, the more money the company makes, why would MGM Resorts International work to curtail gambling by some of the people they could make a lot of money from? Does this form of good citizenship run counter to the company's responsibilities to its stockholders?

EYK8-9. Forensic Accounting Problem The chapter highlight on forensic accounting discussed the technique of covering up receivables theft by lapping (see Forensic Accounting: Lapping on page 370), where one account is credited with the receipt from another account. The highlight stated that lapping may be detected by an auditor through the confirmation of accounts receivables. While detection is important, it is far better to prevent lapping from occurring in the first place. Can you think of any controls that can be put in place to help prevent lapping?

EYK8-10. Analyzing IFRS Financial Statements **Tesco PLC** is the world's third largest retailer and is headquartered in the United Kingdom. Tesco's IFRS financial statements are presented in Appendix C at the end of this book, and the complete annual report is available on this book's Website. Using this financial data, respond to the following questions. At year-end 2011 (2010), Tesco's allowance for doubtful accounts was 44 (47) million British pounds.

TESCO PLC

Required

a. What was the gross amount of Trade and Other Receivables at fiscal year-end 2010 and 2011?

b. What percent of total trade and other receivables was the allowance for doubtful accounts as of the end of 2010 and 2011?

c. Calculate the accounts receivable turnover and the average collection period for the company for 2010 and 2011. (For purposes of calculating the accounts receivable turnover, the 2009 ending Trade and Other Receivables was 1,820 million pounds.)

d. Comment on whether Tesco's management of its trade receivables improved (or not) over the two year period.

MGM RESORTS INTERNATIONAL

EYK8-11. **Working with the Takeaways** Below are selected data from a recent **MGM Resorts International** financial statement. Amounts are in thousands.

Net sales:	$7,208,767
Beginning of year accounts receivable:	412,933
End of year accounts receivable:	303,416

Required

Calculate the MGM Resorts International (a) accounts receivable turnover, and (b) average collection period.

ANSWERS TO SELF-STUDY QUESTIONS:

1. d, (p. 370) 2. b, (p. 368) 3. d, (p. 373) 4. a, (p. 376) 5. d, (p. 376) 6. c, (p. 374)
7. a, (p. 367) 8. a, (p. 381) 9. c, (p. 368) 10. c, (p. 374)

YOUR TURN! SOLUTIONS

Solution 8.1

Bad debt expense	18,000	
Allowance for doubtful accounts		18,000
To record the bad debt expense for the period.		

Solution 8.2

a.	Bad debt expense	3,950	
	Allowance for doubtful accounts		3,950
	To record the bad debt expense for the period.		
b.	Allowance for doubtful accounts	480	
	Accounts receivable		480
	To write off the Phorest Company uncollectible account.		

Solution 8.3

Cash	49,000	
Credit card fee expense	1,000	
Sales revenue		50,000
To record credit sales and collection, less a two percent fee.		

Solution 8.4

$40,000 \times .05 \times 3/12 = \$500$

Solution 8.5

a. Accounts receivable turnover = $30,000/[($2,800 + $3,200)/2] = 10

b. Average collection period = 365/10 = 36.5 days

Solution 8.6

Bad debt expense	750	
Accounts receivable		750
To write off the Rhea Inc. uncollectible account.		

9

Accounting for Long-Lived and Intangible Assets

PAST

In Chapter 8 we studied how to account for accounts and notes receivable.

PRESENT

This chapter focuses on another important set of assets—long-lived plant assets and intangible assets.

FUTURE

Chapter 10 begins our study of the accounting for liabilities.

LEARNING OBJECTIVES

1. **Discuss** the nature of long-lived assets and **identify** the accounting guidelines relating to their initial measurement. *(p. 407)*

2. **Discuss** the nature of depreciation, **illustrate** three depreciation methods, and **explain** impairment losses. *(p. 410)*

3. **Discuss** the distinction between revenue expenditures and capital expenditures. *(p. 418)*

4. **Explain** and **illustrate** the accounting for disposals of plant assets. *(p. 420)*

5. **Discuss** the nature of, and the accounting for, intangible assets. *(p. 421)*

6. **Illustrate** the balance sheet presentation of plant assets and intangible assets. *(p. 425)*

7. **Define** the return on assets ratio and the asset turnover ratio and **explain** their use. *(p. 426)*

CUMMINS INC.

Cummins Inc. is a multinational, Fortune 500 company based in Columbus, Indiana. The company is best known for its production of large diesel engines that power tractor-trailer trucks and buses. Cummins is no longer just an engine manufacturer. Today, the company is a global power manufacturer with over $18 billion in sales. Cummins, however, was not always so big. The company was founded in 1919 as Cummins Engine Company to develop the commercial potential of the unproven diesel engine. The company saw little success over the next decade. In fact, it was not until several decades later when the United States embarked on a national interstate highway construction program that Cummins cemented its place as the principal provider of the engines to power much of the equipment used to build those roads and power the trucks that drove on the roads.

Manufacturers like Cummins require large investments in plant assets such as land, buildings, and equipment in order to produce the products they sell. Companies like Cummins also typically maintain large investments in such intangible assets as trademarks and patents. Plant assets and intangible assets comprised 19.6 percent and 4.9 percent, respectively, of the company's total assets. Because of its large investment in these long-lived, revenue-producing assets, Cummins is referred to as a capital-intensive company. Wall Street analysts evaluate the capital intensity of companies by calculating a capital-intensity ratio, calculated as the value of plant assets plus the value of intangible assets divided by the value of a company's total assets. Cummins' capital-intensity ratio is consistently about 25 percent.

Plant Assets	Intangible Assets	Analyzing Long-Lived Assets
• Measuring acquisition cost of plant assets • Recording plant assets • Computing depreciation • Revenue expenditures • Disposing of plant assets	• Measuring intangible asset costs • Recording intangible assets • Computing amortization • Examples of intangible assets • Balance sheet presentation of intangible assets	• Return on assets • Asset turnover

OVERVIEW OF LONG-LIVED ASSETS

A.K.A. Plant assets are often referred to as *fixed assets*.

A.K.A. Property, plant and equipment is often referred to simply as *PP&E*.

Consider for a moment the asset structure of Cummins Inc. Approximately 25 percent of the assets used to fulfill the company's mission of manufacturing and distributing power products are in two long-term asset categories: *plant assets* and *goodwill and other intangible assets*. **Plant assets** refer to a firm's *long-lived property, plant and equipment*. Cummins reports plant assets of over $2 billion. Intangible assets, on the other hand, refer to those economic resources that benefit a company's operations but which lack the physical substance that characterizes plant assets. Examples of intangible assets include copyrights, franchises, and patents. The benefits provided to a firm by its plant assets and its intangible assets extend over many accounting periods. In this chapter, we discuss the accounting for these long-lived assets.

The carrying value of long-lived assets is initially based on the asset's historical cost—that is, the cost incurred to acquire and place the asset into a revenue-producing state. The costs related to the use of long-lived assets must be matched with the revenues that they help to generate to insure that a business's net income is correctly determined. The portion of an asset's cost that is consumed or used up in any given period is called *depreciation expense, when referring to plant assets,* and *amortization expense, when referring to intangible assets.* Both of these terms have an equivalent meaning in accounting: that is, amortization and depreciation refer to the process of allocating a portion of an asset's acquisition cost to expense on the income statement to reflect the consumption of the asset as it produces revenue for a business.

Exhibit 9-1 provides several examples of both categories of assets. The exhibit also identifies the appropriate term for the periodic consumption of the asset and its write-off to expense. Note that site land—that is, the land on which a business is operated—has an indefinite useful life, and therefore, does not require any periodic write-off to expense.

Exhibit 9-1	Long-Lived Assets That Require Periodic Write-Off	
Asset Category	**Examples**	**Term for the Periodic Write-Off to Expense**
Plant Assets	Buildings, equipment, tools, furniture, fixtures, vehicles	Depreciation
 **Coca-Cola** Intangible Assets	Patents, copyrights, leaseholds, franchises, trademarks, brand names	Amortization

ACCOUNTING FOR LONG-LIVED ASSETS (COST DETERMINATION)

Exhibit 9-2 is a graphic presentation of the accounting issues associated with long-lived assets during an asset's useful life. The accounting issues include: ❶ Identifying the type, and amount, of expenditures that make up the acquisition cost of the asset. ❷ Determining the appropriate amount of an asset's cost to periodically charge against revenue to reflect the asset's consumption. This involves estimating the asset's useful life and its probable salvage value at disposal. ❸ Differentiating those expenditures related to the maintenance of an asset from those expenditures that increase an asset's productive capacity or extend its useful life. ❹ Determining any gain or loss to be recognized when a long-lived asset is disposed of.

LO1 **Discuss** the nature of long-lived assets and **identify** the accounting guidelines relating to their initial measurement.

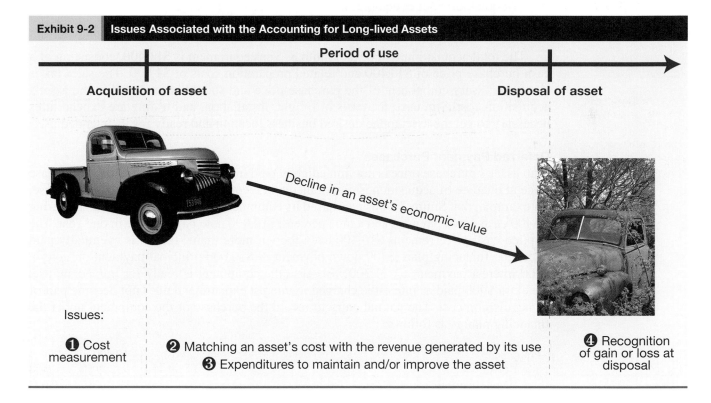

| Exhibit 9-2 | Issues Associated with the Accounting for Long-lived Assets |

Acquisition Cost of Long-Lived Assets

Long-lived assets are initially recorded on the balance sheet at their acquisition cost. This measure is also called the asset's *historical cost* because it represents the amount expended when the asset was originally acquired. In general, the acquisition cost of a long-lived asset equals the cash and/or cash equivalent given up to acquire the asset *and* to prepare it for its intended use.

| | Cost Principle | PRINCIPLE ALERT |

The initial valuation of long-lived assets follows directly from the *cost principle* discussed in Chapter 2. To measure an asset's acquisition cost, accountants must not only identify the asset's cash-equivalent purchase price, but also identify whether any additional costs were incurred to get the asset to a company's place of business and in a condition for use by the business. Both costs are added to the asset's balance sheet value and are considered part of the asset's acquisition cost.

Cash Purchases

An asset's acquisition cost is often simply the amount of cash paid when the asset is acquired and readied for use by a business. Consider, for example, the following expenditures for a piece of equipment by Smith & Sons:

Purchase price components:		
Gross invoice price...	$10,000	
Less: Cash discount (1/10, n/30)	100	
Sales tax...	500	$10,400
Related expenditures:		
Freight charges..	200	
Installation costs.......................................	500	
Testing of installed machine..............................	300	1,000
Acquisition cost of equipment.........................		**$11,400**

The total acquisition cost of the Smith & Sons equipment is $11,400, consisting of a cash purchase price of $10,400 and related preparation costs of $1,000. The sales tax is also a necessary component of the purchase price and should be included in the asset's acquisition cost. Similarly, the costs of freight, installation, and testing are expenditures necessary to get the asset to the desired business location and ready for its intended use.

Deferred Payment Purchases

If an asset's purchase price is not immediately paid in cash, the cash-equivalent purchase price at the date of acquisition is determined and recorded in the asset account. Suppose, for example, that Smith & Sons purchased its equipment under a financing plan requiring a $400 cash down payment and a nine percent, $10,000 note payable due in one year. The implied cash price remains $10,400 even though more than $10,400 is eventually paid under the financing plan ($400 down payment + $10,000 principal payment on note + $900 interest payment = $11,300). Because the equipment is ready for immediate use, the extra $900 paid as interest is charged to interest expense and does not become part of its acquisition cost. The journal entry to record the purchase of the equipment under the financing plan is as follows:

Equipment	10,400	
Cash		400
Notes payable		10,000
To record purchase of equipment.		

A = L + SE
+10,400
−400   +10,000

As in the case of a cash purchase, the expenditures for freight, installation, and testing are debited to the Equipment account when incurred.

Package Purchases

Sometimes several long-lived assets are purchased as a package. For example, assume that Smith & Sons purchased a freight terminal that included land, a building, and some loading equipment for an aggregate price of $190,000. For accounting purposes, the total purchase price should be divided among the three assets because (1) they should be reported in different asset accounts on the balance sheet to properly reflect the company's asset structure, (2) only the building and equipment are subject to depreciation, and (3) the equipment is likely to have an estimated useful life different from that of the building.

The total package price is allocated among the acquired assets on the basis of their relative market or appraisal values. For example, if the estimated market value of the land, building, and equipment is $60,000, $120,000, and $20,000, respectively, the allocation of the $190,000 acquisition price would be as follows:

Asset	Estimated Market Value	Percent of Total	Allocation of Purchase Price	Estimated Useful Life
Land	$ 60,000	30	$ 57,000 (30% × $190,000)	Indefinite
Building	120,000	60	114,000 (60% × $190,000)	30 years
Equipment	20,000	10	19,000 (10% × $190,000)	8 years
Totals	$200,000	100	$190,000	

Expenditures Related to Land

The purchase of land often raises a number of accounting issues. Suppose, for example, that Smith & Sons retains a local real estate broker at a fee of $2,000 to locate an appropriate site for the company's new office building. Assume, also, that the property selected for purchase has an existing building on it which will need to be razed. The terms of the sale include a down payment of $40,000 to the seller, with the buyer paying off an existing mortgage of $10,000 and $300 of accrued interest. In addition, Smith & Sons agrees to pay accrued real estate taxes of $800 owed by the seller. Other related expenditures include legal fees of $400 and a title insurance premium of $500. A local salvage company will be hired to raze the old building, paying Smith & Sons $200 for reclaimed materials. Applying the cost principle, the acquisition cost of the land is calculated as follows:

Payment to the seller	$40,000
Commission to real estate agent	2,000
Payment of mortgage and accrued interest due at time of sale	10,300
Payment of property taxes owed by seller.	800
Legal fees.	400
Title insurance premium.	500
	$54,000
Less: Net recovery from material reclamation	**200**
Cost of land	$53,800

Again, any expenditure for the property taxes, insurance, and legal fees should be capitalized, or added to, the acquisition cost of the land because they are necessary to complete the purchase transaction. Similarly, removing the old building also prepares the land for its intended use. The $200 net recovery from razing the existing structure, therefore, *reduces* the land's cost. A net payment to remove the old building would have *increased* the land's cost.

When a land site is acquired in an undeveloped area, a firm may pay a special assessment to the local government for such property improvements as streets, sidewalks, and sewers. These improvements are considered to be permanent improvements; and consequently, the special assessment is capitalized to (added to) the acquisition cost of the land.

A firm may also make property improvements that have limited lives. Classified as **land improvements**, they include such improvements as paved parking lots, driveways, private sidewalks, and fences. Expenditures for these assets are charged to a separate Land Improvement account on the balance sheet and depreciated over the estimated useful life of the improvements.

Leasehold Improvements

Expenditures made by a business to alter or improve leased property are called **leasehold improvements**. For example, a merchandising firm may make improvements, with the permission of the owner, to a leased building. **The Home Depot, Inc.,** a home improvement retail chain, leases a significant portion of its more than 2,000 U.S. stores and reports nearly $1.4 billion of leasehold improvements on its balance sheet. The improvements, or alterations, become part of the leased property and revert to the owner of the property at the end of the lease. The cost of the leasehold improvements is capitalized to the Leasehold Improvements account on the balance sheet and is depreciated over the life of the lease or the life of the improvements, whichever is shorter.

YOUR TURN! 9.1

The solution is on page 445.

Kelly Company purchased manufacturing equipment for $20,000 cash. In addition to the $20,000 purchase price, Kelly paid sales tax of $1,600, freight costs of $400, installation costs of $600, testing costs of $100, and $300 for unrelated supplies from the same company. Explain the accounting treatment for each of the expenditures.

CORPORATE SOCIAL RESPONSIBILITY

It is unlikely that the first company that you think of when asked to name the top companies in an annual ranking of socially-responsible businesses is a manufacturer of diesel engines. Perhaps you may need to revise your thinking. **Cummins Inc.** is a perennial top 10 finisher among Business Ethics 100 Best Corporate Citizens, a prestigious annual ranking by *Business Ethics* magazine. In fact, Cummins placed number one in the ranking in 2005!

Cummins is one of the best manufacturing companies in the world when it comes to air-emissions reduction research. The company's research efforts have paid off with a 90 percent reduction in diesel-engine emissions. Cummins' ten-year goal is to achieve zero, or close to zero, engine emissions.

NATURE OF DEPRECIATION

LO2   **Discuss** the nature of depreciation, **illustrate** three depreciation methods, and **explain** impairment losses.

With the exception of site land, the use of plant assets to generate revenue consumes the economic benefit provided by the assets. At some point—usually before they are totally worthless—these assets are disposed of, and often replaced. A diagram of a typical pattern of plant asset utilization is illustrated below:

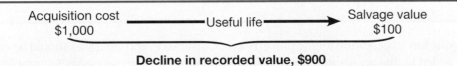

Acquisition cost $1,000 ————————Useful life————————► Salvage value $100

Decline in recorded value, $900

In this example, a plant asset is acquired for $1,000, used for several accounting periods, and then sold for $100. The $900 decline in recorded value is called **depreciation** and is an expense of generating the revenues recognized during the periods that the asset was in use. Thus, if a company's net income is to be a meaningful representation of the business's operating performance, $900 of expense must be allocated to the periods of asset use and matched with sales revenue. Failure to do so would overstate the company's net income for these periods.

As part of this allocation process, it is first necessary to estimate the asset's useful life and its expected future salvage value. **Useful life** is the expected period of economic usefulness to a business—that is, the period from the date of acquisition to the expected date of disposal. **Salvage value** (or *residual value*) is the expected net recovery (sales proceeds – disposal costs) when the asset is sold or removed from service. When the salvage value is insignificant, it may be ignored in the depreciation process under the materiality concept.

A.K.A. The salvage value of a plant asset is also often referred to as its *scrap value*.

Allocation versus Valuation: Depreciation Accounting

Although the idea is theoretically appealing, accountants do not base an asset's periodic depreciation expense on changes in the asset's market value or on the measured wear of the asset, primarily because a reliable, objective, and practical source for such data rarely exists. Rather, **depreciation accounting** is simply an attempt to allocate, in a *systematic* and *rational* manner, the difference between an asset's acquisition cost and its estimated salvage value over the *estimated* useful life of the asset. Consequently, depreciation accounting techniques are just convenient expedients for estimating asset utilization and should not be considered precise. Although imprecise, depreciation estimates facilitate a better assessment of a business's net income than would result from expensing the asset at either its date of acquisition or its date of disposal.

Expense Recognition (Matching) Concept	**PRINCIPLE ALERT**

Depreciation accounting represents an application of the expense recognition (*matching*) concept. Depreciable plant assets are used in a business's operating activities to help generate revenues. Each period that benefits from the use of a plant asset is assigned part of the asset's cost as depreciation expense. In so doing, the depreciation expense is matched with the sales revenue that the asset helps to generate. The matching that occurs through this allocation process extends throughout the asset's useful life.

Several factors are related to the periodic allocation of depreciation. Depreciation can be caused by wear from use, from natural deterioration, and from technical obsolescence. Each factor reduces the economic value of an asset. To some extent, maintenance (lubrication, adjustments, parts replacements, and cleaning) may partially arrest or offset wear and deterioration. Thus, when an asset's useful life and salvage value are estimated, a given level of maintenance is assumed.

Calculating Depreciation Expense

Estimating the periodic depreciation of a long-lived asset can be achieved in many ways. In this section, three widely used methods for calculating depreciation are illustrated.

1. Straight-line
2. Declining-balance
3. Units-of-production

For each method, we assume that equipment is purchased for $1,000. The equipment is assumed to have an estimated useful life of five years and has an estimated salvage value of $100.

Straight-Line Method

The **straight-line method** is the easiest depreciation method to understand and calculate. Consequently, this method is the most widely used depreciation method by U.S. businesses. Under the straight-line method, an equal amount of depreciation expense is allocated to each period of an asset's useful life. Straight-line depreciation is calculated as follows:

$$\text{Annual depreciation} = \frac{(\text{Acquisition cost} - \text{Salvage value})}{\text{Estimated useful life (in months or years)}}$$

For the purchased equipment, the annual straight-line depreciation expense is:

$$\frac{(\$1,000 - \$100)}{5 \text{ years}} = \$180 \text{ per year}$$

And, the journal entry to record the annual depreciation expense is:

Depreciation expense—Equipment	180		A	=	L +	SE
Accumulated depreciation—Equipment		180	−180			−180
To record depreciation expense for the year.						Exp

Like other expense accounts, Depreciation Expense is deducted from sales revenue on the income statement and is closed at year-end to the Income Summary account. The offsetting credit entry is posted to a contra-asset account, Accumulated Depreciation, which is deducted from the Equipment account on the balance sheet to calculate the asset's book value. In this manner, the original acquisition cost of the asset is maintained in the asset account, and the cumulative balance of depreciation taken to date is carried in the contra-asset account, as long as the asset is in service. When an asset is disposed of, the asset's acquisition cost and accumulated depreciation are both removed from the accounts.

The following table shows the various account balances during the equipment's five-year life under the straight-line method:

Year of Useful Life	Balance of Equipment Account	Annual Depreciation Expense	End-of-Period Balance Accumulated Depreciation Account	End-of-Period Balance Asset's Book Value
1	$1,000	$180	$180	$820
2	1,000	180	360	640
3	1,000	180	540	460
4	1,000	180	720	280
5	1,000	180	900	100
Total		$900		

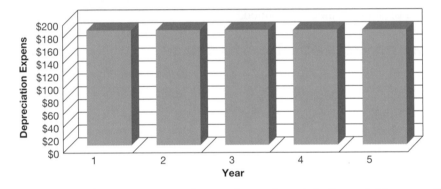

Notice that (1) the Equipment account always shows the original acquisition cost ($1,000) of the asset; (2) each period reflects $180 of depreciation expense; (3) the Accumulated Depreciation account balance is cumulative and shows the portion of the acquisition cost taken as depreciation to date; (4) the asset's book value is the original acquisition cost of the asset less the accumulated depreciation taken to date; and (5) the asset's book value at the end of the five-year period is equal to the asset's estimated salvage value. Thus, an asset's book value declines to its estimated salvage value as the asset is depreciated over its useful life.

For periods of less than one year, straight-line depreciation amounts are simply proportions of the annual depreciation charge. For example, if an asset is acquired on April 1, depreciation for the period ended December 31 would be $135, or 9/12 × $180. Assets acquired or disposed of during the first half of any month are usually treated as if the acquisition or disposal occurred on the first day of the month. When either event occurs during the last half of any month, it is assumed that the event occurred on the first day of the following month.

PRINCIPLE ALERT	Going Concern Concept

Note the role of the *going concern concept* in depreciation accounting. Absent evidence to the contrary, the going concern concept assumes that a business has an indefinite life. Depreciation accounting allocates an asset's acquisition cost to expense over the asset's useful life. Any depreciation method that allocates an asset's acquisition cost over many years—whether the useful life is five years or 25 years (or more)—implicitly assumes that a business will be in existence for at least that number of years.

Declining-Balance Method

The **declining-balance method** is an **accelerated depreciation method**. It calculates a company's depreciation expense as a constant percentage of an asset's book value as of the beginning of each period. The method takes its name from the fact that, over time, an asset's book value (acquisition cost − accumulated depreciation) declines as the asset is used up, yielding a decreasing depreciation expense. An asset's salvage value is not considered in the calculation of declining-balance depreciation, except that the depreciation of an asset stops when the asset's book value equals its estimated salvage value.

The declining-balance method is considered to be an "accelerated" method because the constant depreciation percentage it uses is a multiple of the straight-line depreciation rate (the straight-line depreciation rate = 100 percent/expected useful life in years). There are many versions of the declining-balance method because different multiples of the straight-line rate may be used. *Double-declining balance depreciation* uses a depreciation rate that is twice the straight-line rate; similarly, *150 percent-declining balance depreciation* uses a depreciation rate that is one and one-half times the straight-line rate.

For example, the straight-line depreciation rate for an asset with a five-year useful life is 20 percent per year (100 percent/5 years). Thus, to depreciate a five-year asset on an accelerated basis, the double-declining balance method uses a 40 percent depreciation rate (2 × 20 percent); and, the 150 percent declining-balance method uses a 30 percent depreciation rate (1.5 × 20 percent).

Under the double-declining balance method, the annual depreciation expense is calculated as follows:

Annual depreciation = Book value at beginning of year × Double-declining balance rate

Referring to our example of the equipment purchased for $1,000, with a useful life of five years and an expected salvage value of $100, the periodic double-declining balance depreciation would be calculated as follows (amounts rounded to the nearest dollar):

Year of Useful Life	Acquisition Cost	Beginning Accumulated Depreciation	Beginning Book Value	Twice Straight-line Percentage		Annual Depreciation Expense
1	$1,000	$ 0	$1,000	× 40 percent	=	$400
2	1,000	400	600	× 40 percent	=	240
3	1,000	640	360	× 40 percent	=	144
4	1,000	784	216	× 40 percent	=	86
5	1,000	870	130	[exceeds limit]		30
Total						$900

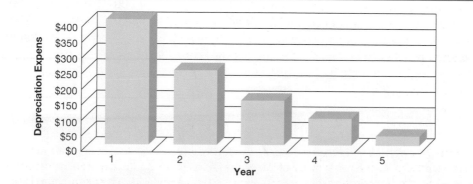

Hint: An asset's salvage value must be considered when calculating the depreciation expense for an asset using the straight-line method or the units-of-production method; but, an asset's salvage value is not considered when calculating double-declining balance depreciation, until the final year.

Notice in the fifth year that the depreciation expense is only $30, the amount needed to reduce the asset's book value to its estimated salvage value of $100. Assets are not depreciated below their estimated salvage value.

If an asset is purchased during a fiscal period, a pro-rata allocation of the first year's depreciation is calculated. If, for example, an asset is acquired on April 1, depreciation for the period ended December 31 would be $300, or [9/12 × (40 percent × $1,000)]. In subsequent periods, the usual procedure is followed; that is, the asset's book value at the beginning of the period is multiplied by the constant depreciation rate. For example, in the second year, depreciation on the asset would be $280, or [40 percent × ($1,000 − $300)].

Units-of-Production Method

The **units-of-production method** allocates depreciation in proportion to an asset's use in operations. Under this method, the depreciation per unit of production is first calculated by dividing the total depreciable cost of the asset (in our example, $1000 − $100 = $900) by the asset's projected units-of-production capacity:

$$\text{Depreciation per unit} = \frac{(\text{Acquisition cost} - \text{Salvage value})}{\text{Total estimated units of production}}$$

The total estimated units of production may represent the total expected miles that an asset will be driven, the total tons expected to be hauled, the total hours expected to be used, or the total number of expected cuttings, drillings, or stampings of parts by a piece of equipment. To illustrate, assume that a drilling tool will drill an estimated 45,000 parts during its expected useful life. The tool is purchased for $1,000 and has an expected salvage value of $100. Consequently, the depreciation per unit of production is:

$$\frac{(\$1,000 - \$100)}{45,000 \text{ parts}} = \$0.02 \text{ per part}$$

To find the asset's annual depreciation expense, the depreciation per unit of production is multiplied by the number of units actually produced during a given year:

Annual depreciation = Depreciation per unit × Units of production for the period

Assuming that the number of parts drilled over the five years were 8,000, 14,000, 10,000, 4,000, and 9,000, respectively, in Year 1 through Year 5, the units-of-production depreciation expense is calculated as follows:

Year of Useful Life	Depreciation per Unit		Annual Units of Production		Annual Depreciation Expense
1	$0.02	×	8,000	=	$160
2	0.02	×	14,000	=	280
3	0.02	×	10,000	=	200
4	0.02	×	4,000	=	80
5	0.02	×	9,000	=	180
Total					$900

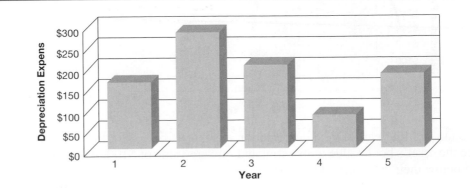

A Comparison of Alternative Depreciation Methods

The following charts compare the periodic depreciation expense from our equipment illustration for the straight-line and the double-declining balance methods. The charts visually display the accelerated nature of the double-declining balance method relative to the straight-line method. Notice, for example, that the depreciation expense in Year 1 under the double-declining balance method is $400 but is only $180 under the straight-line method. In Year 2, the double-declining balance depreciation is $240 but again is only $180 for the straight-line method. It is not until Year 3 that the straight-line method produces a depreciation charge that exceeds the double-declining balance charge. The units-of-production method chart, as shown, reflects the assumptions presented previously in the chapter. There is no general pattern for the annual depreciation expense under this method. The annual depreciation for the units-of-production method depends on the yearly productive activity of an asset, and this activity will vary from asset to asset.

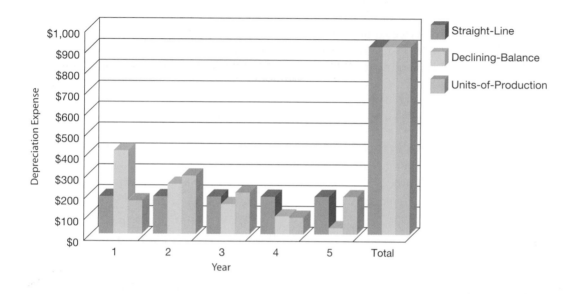

| **Depreciation Methods** | ACCOUNTING IN PRACTICE |

So many assets, so little time. Some accountants may feel that way when it comes to calculating the periodic depreciation expense for a business. They may also feel that variety is the spice of life. At least it appears that way given the various methods that companies choose to calculate the depreciation expense that appears on their income statements. Below are the depreciation methods used by 600 large U.S. companies. As can be seen, the straight-line method is by far the most popular depreciation method used:

- Group/composite 1.8%
- Units-of-production 3.3%
- Accelerated method—not specified 4%
- Sum-of-the-years'-digits <1%
- Declining-balance 2.2%
- Straight-line 99%

*The totals exceed 100 percent because some firms use more than one method.
Source: Accounting Trends and Techniques

Depreciation Method Estimate Changes

It is important to remember that a business's periodic depreciation expense is based on estimates of both an asset's useful life and its salvage value. Circumstances change, however, and original estimates of both an asset's useful life and its salvage value may subsequently be found to be too high or too low. Once it is determined that the original estimates of either an asset's useful life or salvage value were incorrect, the calculation of the periodic depreciation expense for an asset's remaining useful life may be revised. When a depreciation estimate revision is found to be warranted, the revision is executed by allocating the undepreciated balance of the asset's book value over the revised remaining useful life. To illustrate this process, refer again to our example of equipment costing $1,000, with a five year life, and an estimated salvage value of $100.

If, based on original estimates, straight-line depreciation of $180 has been recorded for each of the first three years of the asset's useful life, the accumulated depreciation to date would total $540, or 3 × $180. Now, suppose that just before recording the depreciation expense for the fourth year, circumstances indicate that the equipment's useful life will total six years instead of five, and that its salvage value at the end of the sixth year will be $40 instead of $100. The revised depreciation expense to be taken during the revised remaining useful life (Year Four through Year Six) of the equipment is calculated as follows:

Original acquisition cost.	$1,000
Depreciation previously recorded (3 years @ $180)	(540)
Book value at start of fourth year.	$ 460
Revised salvage value	(40)
Revised remaining depreciable cost.	$ 420
Revised remaining useful life	3 years
Revised depreciation for fourth, fifth, and sixth years	$420/3 = $140 per year

Impairment Losses

Sometimes a change in the circumstances relating to a depreciable asset is so severe that the future cash flows from the asset's use and disposal are estimated to be *less* than its current book value. If an asset's remaining book value cannot be recovered through the future cash flows expected to be generated from the asset's use, the asset's value is said to be *impaired*. Under these circumstances, an impairment loss is recorded on the income statement, and the asset's book value on the balance sheet is reduced. The **impairment loss** is calculated as the difference between the asset's current book value and its current fair value.

To illustrate, assume that two years ago Cummins purchased equipment costing $500,000, with an estimated useful life of six years and a salvage value of $20,000. The equipment's book value is currently $340,000 ($500,000 cost less $160,000 accumulated depreciation). Unanticipated technological advances in equipment used by competitors, however, now severely limits the use of Cummins' equipment. An analysis by the company's CFO indicates that Cummins now expects that the net future cash flows to be generated from the use and disposal of the equipment over the next four years is $300,000. The limited uses for the equipment cause its current fair value to be only $200,000.

Cummins' equipment is impaired because its book value is not recoverable through its expected future cash flows—the $300,000 of expected future cash flows is less than the equipment's $340,000 current book value. Thus, an impairment loss is computed by comparing the equipment's book value with its current fair value, as follows:

Equipment book value	$340,000
Equipment current fair value	**(200,000)**
Impairment loss	$140,000

The journal entry to record the impairment loss is as follows:

Impairment loss on equipment	140,000	
Accumulated depreciation—Equipment		140,000
To record impairment loss on equipment.		

A = L + SE
−140,000   −140,000
Loss

PRINCIPLE ALERT

Conservatism Concept

The accounting for impaired plant assets illustrates the *conservatism concept*. In selecting between alternative accounting measures, the conservatism concept states that the least optimistic measure should be used. When a plant asset is impaired, it is reported on the balance sheet at its current fair value, an amount lower than its book value before any impairment loss is recorded. Unimpaired plant assets remain on the balance sheet at their book value, however, even though current fair values may be higher. U.S. GAAP mandates that asset values be written down when impaired, but prohibits the write-up of assets when their value appreciates.

IFRS ALERT!

While U.S. GAAP requires that long-lived assets be written down in value when they are judged to be impaired, they may not be written up in value if there is a subsequent recovery in their fair market value. Under International Financial Reporting Standards (IFRS), however, the accounting treatment of long-lived asset value recoveries is substantially different. Under IFRS, if an asset's value increases above its current book value, the asset's balance sheet value may be written up to the higher value by debiting the asset account for the amount of the increase. The balancing credit entry is to a stockholders' equity account called the asset revaluation reserve.

To illustrate, assume that Peabody International PLC, based in the United Kingdom, owns land in London that was originally purchased for 20 million British pounds. Current real estate appraisals, however, indicate that the fair market value of the land is now worth 50 million pounds. To recognize the increase in the land's fair market value, Peabody International would record the following journal entry:

Land	30 million pounds	
Asset revaluation reserve—Land		30 million pounds
To record the revaluation of land.		

Depreciation for Income Tax Purposes

Depreciation expense may be deducted by a business on its federal income tax return as a normal business expense. As a consequence, some refer to the tax deductibility of depreciation as a "tax shield" since depreciation expense lowers a business's pre-tax net income, and hence, lowers the actual income taxes that must be paid. The depreciation expense deducted on a business's income tax return, however, may differ substantially from the depreciation expense reported on a company's income statement because the calculation of tax depreciation follows income tax regulations referred to as the **modified accelerated cost recovery system (MACRS)**.

MACRS establishes eight asset classes with prescribed useful lives ranging from three years to 31.5 years. Most machinery and equipment, for example, are in the seven-year asset class. When acquired, an asset is placed in the appropriate asset class (per MACRS guidelines) and depreciated over the prescribed useful life specified for that class.[1]

MACRS was introduced into U.S. tax law to encourage companies to invest in plant assets. Because the useful life specified under MACRS is usually shorter than an asset's accounting useful life, this method provides larger depreciation deductions during an asset's early years than was previously possible, much like the declining-balance method used for financial statement reporting. In a sense, the accelerated deductions under MACRS provide an interest-free loan to a business because they allow the firm to pay less income tax in the early years of an asset's life and more in the later years. During the intervening time period, the firm can use the postponed income tax payments to support the business's operations, without incurring any interest charges.

Change and modification characterize U.S. tax law. Tax depreciation guidelines will likely be modified again in the future. Keep in mind, however, that depreciation changes in the tax law do not affect the depreciation method and estimates that a firm may use in preparing its financial statements using U.S. GAAP for its shareholders and lenders.

YOUR TURN! 9.2

The solution is on page 445.

The Salsbury Company purchased equipment costing $10,000 at the start of the year. The equipment has an estimated useful life of five years and a salvage value of $2,000. The CEO is unsure if the company should use the straight-line method or the double-declining balance method to depreciate the new equipment.

Required:
Prepare the journal entry for depreciation for the second year under each of the alternative depreciation accounting methods.

REVENUE EXPENDITURES

LO3 Discuss the distinction between revenue expenditures and capital expenditures.

Revenue expenditures are expenditures relating to plant assets that are expensed when incurred. The following list identifies two common types of revenue expenditures:

1. Expenditures for ordinary maintenance and repairs of existing plant assets.
2. Expenditures to acquire low-cost items that benefit the firm for several periods.

Maintenance and Repairs

Some level of maintenance and repairs must be assumed when estimating the useful lives and salvage values of property, plant, and equipment. For example, a plant asset that is not maintained or repaired will have a shorter useful life than a similar asset that is properly maintained. Periodic upkeep—such as lubrication, cleaning, and replacement of minor parts—is necessary to maintain an asset's expected level and length of usefulness. These periodic upkeep costs—referred to as maintenance costs—are charged to expense as they are incurred.

Low-Cost Items

Most businesses purchase items that provide years of service at a relatively small cost, such as paperweights, staplers, and wastebaskets. Because of the small dollar amounts involved, establishing these items as assets on the balance sheet and depreciating them over

---

[1] Depreciation in most asset classes must follow a half-year convention whereby one-half of the first year's depreciation expense is taken in the first year, regardless of when the asset was acquired, and one-half of the asset's last year's depreciation is taken in the year of disposal. The half-year convention means that assets in the three-year asset class are effectively depreciated over four different accounting periods, assets in the five-year property class are depreciated over six different accounting periods, and so on.

their expected useful lives serves no useful purpose. The effect on the financial statements is insignificant; and consequently, expensing these expenditures at the time of purchase is more efficient. The accounting for such low-cost items is thus completed in the period in which they are acquired.

Materiality Concept	**PRINCIPLE ALERT**

The practice of accounting for small dollar transactions in the most expedient fashion follows the *materiality concept*. Under this accounting concept, generally accepted accounting principles apply only to items of significance to the users of financial statements. Because the judgment of users will be unaffected by the accounting for immaterial dollar amounts, their immediate expensing does not diminish the usefulness of financial statements.

Capital Expenditures

Capital expenditures increase the book value of long-lived assets. To *capitalize* an amount means to increase an asset's book value by that amount. The following list identifies two typical capital expenditures related to property, plant, and equipment:

1. Initial acquisitions and additions.
2. Betterments.

Initial Acquisitions and Additions

At the beginning of this chapter, the accounting guidelines governing the initial measurement of long-lived assets were discussed. At that time, it was noted that expenditures equal to an asset's implied cash purchase price, plus any costs necessary to prepare the asset for use, were debited to the asset account. These amounts are commonly referred to as capital expenditures.

These same accounting guidelines apply for additions to existing plant assets. Adding a new wing to a building or expanding the size of an asphalt parking lot are examples of additions. These capital expenditures should also be debited to an asset account. A separate account (and depreciation schedule) should be used for an addition when its estimated useful life differs from the remaining useful life of the existing plant asset.

Betterments

Betterments are expenditures that (1) extend the useful life of an asset, (2) improve the quality and/or quantity of the asset's output, or (3) reduce the asset's operating expenses. Examples include overhauling the engine or adding a power winch to a highway service truck, improving the precision of a machining device to reduce defects, or converting a building to solar power. Expenditures for betterments are generally debited to the appropriate asset account, and the subsequent periodic depreciation expense is increased to allocate the additional cost over the asset's remaining useful life.

Hastings Company recorded the following expenditures during the year with regard to its delivery van:

1. Changed the engine oil
2. Repainted the van
3. Overhauled the engine that is expected to increase the useful life of the van
4. Repaired a dent in a fender
5. Converted the van to run on a biofuel with an estimated annual fuel cost savings of 30 percent.

Required:
Determine whether each of the above expenditures is a revenue expenditure or a capital expenditure.

YOUR TURN! 9.3

The solution is on page 446.

FORENSIC ACCOUNTING	WorldCom's Bad Accounting

 On the surface, the decision to capitalize or expense an expenditure related to a long-lived asset does not seem like the subject matter for one of the most infamous accounting scandals of all time. Unfortunately, to the many investors in **WorldCom** who saw the value of their investment disappear, this accounting decision had profound consequences.

Beginning in 2001, and continuing through mid-2002, WorldCom, under the direction of its CEO, CFO, Controller, and Director of General Accounting, used fraudulent accounting methods to portray a false picture of the company's financial health. The principal accounting gimmickry used by the company was to misclassify "line costs," a cost that should have been expensed each year, as a capital expenditure, thus, adding to WorldCom's assets rather than adding to its expenses.

A small team of internal auditors working in secret, mostly at night, to investigate and uncover this fraud, brought the fraud to the attention of WorldCom's Board of Directors. The Securities and Exchange Commission followed with its own investigation. The final conclusion—WorldCom's assets and pre-tax net income had been inflated by nearly $11 billion! Following a conviction for filing false financial reports with the SEC, WorldCom's CEO Bernard Ebbers was sentenced to 25 years in prison.

DISPOSALS OF PLANT ASSETS

LO4 **Explain** and **illustrate** the accounting for disposals of plant assets.

A business may dispose of its plant assets in a variety of ways. An asset may be sold, retired, or exchanged as partial payment for a new asset. The asset's usefulness to a firm may also be ended by an unfavorable or unanticipated event—the asset may be stolen or destroyed by a natural disaster.

Depreciation must extend through an asset's total useful life to a business. Consequently, depreciation must be recorded up to the disposal date, regardless of the manner of the asset's disposal. Should the disposal date not coincide with the end of an accounting period, a journal entry must record depreciation for the partial period—that is, the period from the date that depreciation was last recorded to the asset's disposal date.

The following data is used to illustrate the disposal of plant assets:

Equipment's acquisition cost.	$1,000
Estimated salvage value after five years	100
Annual straight-line depreciation	180
(Assume that depreciation to the date of disposal has been recorded.)	

Sale of Plant Assets

Most sales of plant assets involve the following factors:

1. The sale transaction involves an exchange of a used plant asset for cash. Because the plant asset sold is no longer on hand, a journal entry must remove the asset account and the accumulated depreciation account from the books. These amounts together reflect the asset's book value.

2. Because plant assets are often sold for an amount higher or lower than their book value, a gain or loss will result. Sale proceeds in excess of book value create a gain, whereas book values in excess of sales proceeds create a loss.

Asset Sales for More Than Book Value

Assume that the equipment is sold for $230 midway through its fifth year of use. Depreciation was last recorded at the end of the fourth year. The journal entries to record the sale are:

Depreciation expense—Equipment	90				
Accumulated depreciation—Equipment		90	A = L + SE		
To record depreciation expense for six months ($180/2).			−90		−90 Exp

Cash	230				
Accumulated depreciation—Equipment	810		A = L + SE		
Equipment		1,000	+230		+40 Gain
Gain on sale of plant assets		40	+810		
To record the sale of equipment for $230.			−1,000		

Note that recording depreciation to the date of sale adds $90 to the Accumulated Depreciation account, which totals $810, calculated as [(4 × $180) + $90]. To reflect the sale properly, it is necessary to remove the entire amount of accumulated depreciation ($810) from the books. The gain of $40 is calculated as the sale proceeds of $230 minus the asset's book value of $190 ($1,000 − $810).

Asset Sales for Less Than Book Value

Assume that the equipment is sold for $30 at the end of the fifth year. The journal entry to record this sale is:

Cash	30				
Loss on sale of plant assets	70		A = L + SE		−70
Accumulated depreciation—Equipment	900		+30		Loss
Equipment		1,000	+900		
To record the sale of equipment for $30.			−1,000		

The loss on the asset sale equals the book value of $100 minus the sales proceeds of $30. The cash received is recorded, and the balances from both the Equipment account and the Accumulated Depreciation account are removed from the books.

If the equipment is sold for an amount exactly equal to its book value, no gain or loss results. Should the equipment be abandoned, stolen, or destroyed (with no insurance coverage) before the end of its expected useful life, a loss equal to its book value is recorded. Similarly, if the equipment is retired at the end of its useful life and has no salvage value, a loss equal to its book value is recorded.

Exchange of Plant Assets

A plant asset may be exchanged for another plant asset. The accounting for long-lived asset exchanges can be complex depending upon the relationship between the new asset and the asset being traded in. Consequently, the accounting for asset exchanges is covered in intermediate accounting textbooks.

YOUR TURN! 9.4

The solution is on page 446.

The Jones Company is self-insured; and consequently, the company does not receive any insurance payments if it is involved in an accident. One of the Jones Company trucks was involved in a major accident and the company decided to sell the truck for scrap. At the time of the accident, the truck had a cost basis of $22,500 and accumulated depreciation of $15,000. The proceeds from the sale totaled $750.

Required:
Record the journal entry for the disposal of the truck.

INTANGIBLE ASSETS

Intangible assets are the various resources that benefit a business's operations, but which lack physical characteristics or substance. Intangible assets include, for example, the exclusive rights or privileges obtained from a governmental unit or by legal contract, such as patents, copyrights, franchises, trademarks, and leaseholds. Another intangible asset is goodwill, which reflects the beneficial

LO5 Discuss the nature of, and the accounting for, intangible assets.

attributes acquired in the acquisition of another company that cannot be attributed to any other recorded asset.

The term *intangible asset* is not used with precision in accounting. By convention, only certain assets are included in the intangible asset category. Some resources that lack physical substance, such as prepaid insurance, accounts receivable, and investments, are not classified as intangible assets. Because intangible assets lack physical characteristics, the related accounting procedures are more subjective than for such tangible assets as property, plant, and equipment.

Measurement of Intangible Assets (Cost Determination)

A firm should record intangible assets acquired from outside entities at their acquisition cost. Similarly, some intangible assets created internally by a firm are measured at their cost. For example, the costs to secure a trademark—such as attorney's fees, registration fees, and design costs—are charged to a Trademarks account.

The accounting for other expenditures related to intangible assets varies depending upon the type of expenditure and the nature of the intangible asset. **Research and development costs** are not capitalized to the balance sheet as an intangible asset because GAAP guidelines require that these expenditures be expensed when incurred. As a consequence, many significant costs incurred by a firm associated with developing a patentable product or process are not capitalized to the balance sheet. Legal costs associated with patent work may be capitalized, however. The costs of developing, maintaining, or restoring an intangible asset are also expensed when incurred, provided that the asset is not specifically identifiable or has an indeterminate life. As a result of these accounting procedures, some companies may have important intangible assets that are carried at a nominal amount, or may even fail to appear at all on the firm's balance sheet.

It is noteworthy that one U.S. industry is exempted from the conservative accounting treatment of research and development costs. Under U.S. GAAP, software development companies may capitalize the development of second generation software, although the cost of first generation software must be expensed as incurred.

IFRS Alert!

The accounting for some intangible assets under IFRS differs significantly from the accounting under U.S. GAAP. For instance, under U.S. GAAP, all research and development costs must be expensed when incurred; however, under IFRS, development costs may be capitalized if a commercially viable product results from the original research effort. A significant consequence of this alternative accounting treatment is that IFRS-accounted companies enjoy a more fairly presented balance sheet, since most intangible assets are fully disclosed. On the balance sheets of many U.S. GAAP-accounted companies, there are many unreported intangible assets.

To illustrate, assume that British Laboratories PLC, a biotechnology company, spends five million British pounds on research for a cure for diabetes. The research leads to a promising compound that is shown in tests to effectively control the disease. Further testing is needed, however; and consequently, the company spends an additional three million British pounds to develop and test the drug compound before receiving a patent from the British Patent Office. Under these circumstances, the company would record an expense for its initial research effort, and an asset for the subsequent expenditure to develop the drug, as follows:

Research expense	5 million pounds	
Cash		5 million pounds
To record research expense.		
Development costs	3 million pounds	
Cash		3 million pounds
To capitalize development costs.		

In short, under IFRS, all research costs must be expensed when incurred; however, development costs may be capitalized to the balance sheet when a commercially viable product is evident.

Amortization of Intangibles

The **amortization** of an intangible asset carried on the balance sheet involves the periodic expensing of the asset's cost over the term of its expected useful life. Because salvage values are ordinarily not involved, the amortization of intangible assets typically entails (1) determining the asset's cost, (2) estimating the period over which it will benefit a company, and (3) allocating the cost in equal amounts to each accounting period involved. Straight-line amortization is typically used for intangible assets unless another method is shown to be more appropriate.

The amortization entry debits the Amortization Expense account, while the credit entry goes directly to the Intangible Asset account. An Accumulated Amortization account could be used for the credit entry, but generally there is no particular benefit to financial statement users from accumulating amortization in a separate contra-asset account. In the following examples, we will reduce the intangible asset account directly for its periodic amortization.

EXAMPLES OF INTANGIBLE ASSETS

Patents

A **patent** is an exclusive privilege granted to an inventor by the U.S. Patent Office for a period of 20 years from the date the patent application is filed. A patent gives the patent holder the right to exclude others from making, using, or selling the invention. Patent laws were originated to encourage inventors by protecting them from imitators who might usurp the invention for commercial gain. Just what qualifies as a patentable idea, however, has become quite complex in the modern realm of technical knowledge. Consequently, long periods of patent "searching," and frequently, successful defense of infringement suits may precede the validation of a patent. Even though patents have a legal life of 20 years from application date, changes in technology or consumer tastes may shorten their economic life. Because of their uncertain value, patents are accounted for conservatively by most businesses. For example, most businesses amortize patents over a shorter period than 20 years. When patents are purchased, the buyer enjoys patent protection for the patent's remaining legal life.

To illustrate the accounting for patents, assume that a company incurs $30,000 in legal costs to obtain a patent on a new product. The journal entry to recognize the awarding of the patent is:

Patents	30,000		A = L + SE
Cash		30,000	+30,000
To record legal costs of acquiring patent.			−30,000

If the company expects the patent to provide benefits for 15 years, the following journal entry is made to record the first year's amortization using the straight-line method:

Amortization expense—Patents	2,000		A = L + SE
Patents		2,000	−2,000 −2,000
To record patent amortization ($30,000/15 years = $2,000).			Exp

Because an accumulated amortization account is not normally used, the intangible asset account balance reflects the asset's book value. The balance sheet presentation of the patent at year-end would appear as follows:

Patents (cost less amortization to date).	$28,000

Copyright

A **copyright** protects its owner against the unauthorized reproduction of a specific written work, recorded work, or artwork. A copyright lasts for the life of the author plus 70 years. The purchase price of valuable copyrights can be substantial, and proper measurement and amortization are necessary for valid business income determination.

Franchises

Franchises most often involve exclusive rights to operate or sell a specific brand of products in a given geographic area. Franchises may be for definite or indefinite periods. Although many franchises are agreements between two private firms, various governmental units award franchises for public utility operations within their legal jurisdictions. The right to operate a **Kentucky Fried Chicken (KFC)** restaurant or to sell **Midas Mufflers** in a specific area illustrates franchise agreements in the private sector.

ACCOUNTING IN PRACTICE	**Types of Intangible Assets**

Intangible assets are perhaps the most difficult asset category to fully comprehend. Intangible assets appearing on a company's balance sheet represent a varied collection of assets as can be seen from a sample of 600 large U.S. firms:

Type of Intangible Asset	Number	%
Goodwill	542	90%
Trademarks, brand names, copyrights	330	55%
Customer lists/relationships	320	53%
Technology	162	27%
Patents	161	27%
Licenses, franchises, memberships	114	19%
Non-compete covenants	112	18.7%
Contracts, agreements	104	17.3%
Other—described	65	10.8%

Source: Accounting Trends and Techniques.

Trademarks

Trademarks and **trade names** represent the exclusive and continuing right to use certain terms, names, or symbols, usually to identify a brand or family of products. An original trademark or trade name can be registered with the U.S. federal government for a nominal cost. A company may spend considerable time and money to determine an appropriate name or symbol for a product. Also, the purchase of well-known, and thus valuable, trademarks or trade names may involve substantial amounts of money. When the cost of a trademark or trade name is material, the amount is debited to an appropriate intangible asset account—Trademarks—and amortized over the period of expected benefit to a business.

Goodwill

Goodwill is an often misunderstood concept. In common usage, goodwill may represent the favorable reputation a firm has earned based on its prior operations, quality of service, or positive product characteristics. The term goodwill, however, has a much different meaning when used in accounting and finance. Goodwill represents the amount paid by one company in the acquisition of another company, above the amount that can be attributed to the identifiable net assets of the acquired company. The measurement of goodwill is complex because it can stem from many factors. Examples of such factors include exceptional customer relations, advantageous business location, operating efficiency, superior personnel, favorable financial sources, or perceived synergies between the acquiring company and the acquired company. Unlike most intangible assets, goodwill is not subject to periodic amortization. Instead, goodwill is evaluated annually for any impairment in value. If a company's goodwill is found to be impaired, the Goodwill account is written down to its fair value and an Impairment Loss is recorded on the income statement.

Although accountants only record goodwill when another business entity is purchased (to the extent that the purchase price exceeds the fair value of the identifiable net assets acquired), the balance sheets of many major corporations contain significant amounts of goodwill. Recent balance sheets, for example, show the following amounts of goodwill: **Bank of America Corporation**, $86.3 billion; **General Electric Company**, $65.6 billion; **AT&T Inc.**, $73.3 billion; and **Procter & Gamble Company**, $54.0 billion. These amounts are evidence of the active acquisition efforts of these major corporations, and also of the large amounts that may be paid for goodwill in acquisition transactions.

Match the descriptive explanation below with the correct term:

Amortization	Patent	Copyright
Franchise	Trademark	

1. An exclusive right that protects an owner against the unauthorized reproduction of a specific written work.
2. The periodic write-off of an intangible asset to expense on the income statement.
3. An exclusive and continuing right to use a certain symbol to identify a brand or family of products.
4. An exclusive right to operate or sell a specific brand of products in a given geographic area.
5. An exclusive privilege granted to an inventor that gives the asset holder the right to exclude others from making, using, or selling the invention.

YOUR TURN! 9.5

The solution is on page 446.

BALANCE SHEET PRESENTATION

Plant assets and intangible assets are presented on the balance sheet below the Long-term Investments category. (Recall that the assets are listed on a classified balance sheet in descending order of liquidity.) For example, Exhibit 9-3 reveals how these assets appear on the balance sheet of **Cummins Inc.** Notice that Cummins lists its intangible assets and goodwill separately. This convention is followed because while Cummins amortizes its intangible assets, it does not amortize its goodwill. Goodwill is subject to an annual impairment test of its current value, but it is not subject to periodic amortization.

LO6 **Illustrate** the balance sheet presentation of plant assets and intangible assets.

Exhibit 9-3 Cummins Inc.

CUMMINS INC
Balance Sheet (asset section only)
December 31, 2011 and 2010

(in $ millions)	2011	2010
Current Assets		
Cash and cash equivalent	$ 1,484	$ 1,023
Short-term investments	277	339
Net receivables	2,520	2,249
Other current assets	2,810	2,678
Total Current Assets	7,091	6,289
Long-term investments	838	734
Property, plant, and equipment (net)	2,288	2,041
Goodwill	339	367
Intangible assets	227	222
Other assets	885	749
Total assets	$11,668	$10,402

RETURN ON ASSETS AND ASSET TURNOVER

LO7 Define the return on assets ratio and the asset turnover ratio, and **explain** their use.

The ability of a firm to use its assets effectively and efficiently is a sign of a healthy, well-managed company. The rate of return generated on a company's assets, referred to as the *return on assets ratio,* is a widely used indicator that focuses on this dimension of a firm's financial health. In practice, there is some variation in the calculation of this ratio; however, one commonly used definition of the **return on assets** is:

$$\text{Return on assets} = \frac{\text{Net income}}{\text{Average total assets}}$$

This ratio relates data from two financial statements—the income statement and the balance sheet. The numerator consists of the net income for the year from the income statement.[2] The denominator in the ratio is the average balance of total assets for the year (sum the total assets at the beginning of the year with the total assets at the end of the year and divide the sum by two) obtained from the balance sheet.

To illustrate the calculation of the return on assets ratio, we use data from Cummins Inc. The company reported 2011 net income of $1,848 million, total assets at the beginning of the year of $10,402 million, and year-end total assets of $11,668 million. Cummins' return on assets for the year is 16.7 percent, calculated as $1,848/[($10,402 + $11,668)/2].

To evaluate a firm's return on assets, it is useful to consider the trend in the ratio, the return for other firms in the same industry, the industry average return on assets, and the economic environment that the company faced. For example, in the same year that Cummins generated a 16.7 percent return on its assets, Caterpillar, Inc., a competitor of Cummins, generated only a 6.8 percent return on assets. These results suggest that, for 2011, Cummins utilized its assets more efficiently and profitably than did Caterpillar.

TAKEAWAY 9.1	Concept	Method	Assessment
	How effective is a company in using its assets to produce net income?	Net income and average total assets $\text{Return on assets ratio} = \dfrac{\text{Net income}}{\text{Average total assets}}$	A higher ratio value implies a higher, more effective level of asset utilization.

The **asset turnover** ratio is another ratio that evaluates a company's effective use of its assets. This ratio measures how effectively a firm uses its assets to generate sales revenue. The asset turnover ratio is calculated as follows:

$$\text{Asset turnover} = \frac{\text{Net sales}}{\text{Average total assets}}$$

Referring again to the Cummins' data for 2011, the company reported net operating revenues (which is equivalent to net sales), of $18,048 million. Consequently, Cummins' asset turnover for the year is 1.64, or $18,048/[($10,402 + $11,668)/2], indicating that the company was able to generate $1.64 of sales revenue for every dollar invested in assets. A high asset turnover ratio indicates that a company is very effective in using its assets to generate sales revenue. For the preceding year, Cummins' asset turnover was 1.38. Thus, Cummins generated $1.38 in net sales in 2010 for each dollar invested in total assets. The increase in Cummins' asset turnover from 1.38 to 1.64 indicates that the firm used its assets more effectively in 2011 than in 2010 to generate sales revenue.

---

[2] An alternative calculation of the return on assets ratio adds interest expense to net income in the ratio's numerator. This calculation keeps the method of financing a company's assets from influencing the calculation of the ratio.

Concept	→	Method	→	Assessment	TAKEAWAY 9.2
How effective is a company in generating sales revenue using its assets?		Average total assets and net sales $\text{Asset turnover ratio} = \dfrac{\text{Net sales}}{\text{Average total assets}}$		A higher ratio value implies a higher level of sales revenue generated for each dollar invested in assets.	

COMPREHENSIVE PROBLEM

Segman Company purchased a machine on January 2 for $24,300. The machine has an expected useful life of three years and an expected salvage value of $900. The company expects to use the machine for 1,400 hours in the first year, 2,000 hours in the second year, and 1,600 hours in the third year.

Required

a. Calculate the depreciation expense for each year using each of the following depreciation methods: (1) straight-line, (2) units-of-production (assume that actual usage equals expected usage), (3) double-declining balance.

b. Assume that the machine was purchased June 1. Calculate the depreciation expense for each year using the following depreciation methods: (1) straight-line, (2) double-declining balance.

Solution

a. 1. Straight-line:
    Year 1: ($24,300 − $900)/3 = $7,800
    Year 2: ($24,300 − $900)/3 = $7,800
    Year 3: ($24,300 − $900)/3 = $7,800

    2. Units-of-production:
    Depreciation per hour = ($24,300 − $900)/5,000 hours = $4.68 per hour
    Year 1: 1,400 hours × $4.68 = $6,552
    Year 2: 2,000 hours × $4.68 = $9,360
    Year 3: 1,600 hours × $4.68 = $7,488

    3. Double-declining balance:
    Depreciation rate = (100/3) × 2 = 66 2/3 percent
    Year 1: $24,300 × 66 2/3 percent = $16,200
    Year 2: ($24,300 − $16,200) × 66 2/3 percent = $5,400
    Year 3: ($24,300 − $21,600) × 66 2/3 percent = $1,800

b. 1. Straight-line: Refer to calculations in (a)1.
    Year 1: $7,800 × 7/12 = $4,550
    Year 2: $7,800 (full year's depreciation)
    Year 3: $7,800 (full year's depreciation)
    Year 4: $7,800 × 5/12 = $3,250

    2. Double-declining balance Refer to calculations in (a)3.
    Year 1: $16,200 × 7/12 = $9,450
    Year 2: ($24,300 − $9,450) × 66 2/3 percent = $9,900
    Year 3: ($24,300 − $19,350) × 66 2/3 percent= $3,300
    Year 4: $750 [This amount reduces the machine's book value to its salvage value of $900 and is the maximum depreciation expense for the year. ($24,300 − $22,650) × 66 2/3 percent = $1,100 gives an amount in excess of the maximum $750 depreciation.]

REVIEW

SUMMARY OF LEARNING OBJECTIVES

LO1   Discuss the nature of long-lived assets and identify the accounting guidelines relating to their initial measurement. (p. 407)

- The accounting for long-lived assets involves the determination of an asset's acquisition cost, periodic depreciation expense, subsequent capital expenditures, and disposal.
- The initial cost of a plant asset is its implied cash price plus any expenditure necessary to prepare the asset for its intended use.

LO2   Discuss the nature of depreciation, illustrate three depreciation methods, and explain impairment losses. (p. 410)

- Depreciation is a cost allocation process; it allocates a long-lived asset's depreciable cost (acquisition cost less salvage value) in a systematic manner over the asset's estimated useful life.
- The most commonly used depreciation methods are straight-line, units-of-production, and declining-balance.
- Revisions of depreciation estimates are accomplished by recalculating depreciation charges for current and subsequent periods.
- When a plant asset is impaired, a loss is recognized equal to the difference between the asset's book value and its current fair value.

LO3   Discuss the distinction between revenue expenditures and capital expenditures. (p. 418)

- Revenue expenditures are expensed as incurred and include the cost of ordinary repairs and maintenance and the purchase of low-cost items.
- Capital expenditures, which increase a plant asset's book value, include initial acquisitions, additions, and betterments.

LO4   Explain and illustrate the accounting for disposals of plant assets. (p. 420)

- When a firm disposes of a plant asset, depreciation must be recorded on the asset up to the disposal date.
- Gains and losses on plant asset dispositions are determined by comparing an asset's book value to the proceeds received.

LO5   Discuss the nature of, and the accounting for, intangible assets. (p. 421)

- Intangible assets acquired from other entities are initially valued at their acquisition cost. Some internally created intangible assets are also measured at their cost, but most expenditures related to internally developed intangible assets are expensed rather than capitalized.
- Research and development costs related to a firm's products and its production processes are expensed as incurred.
- Amortization is the periodic write-off to expense of an intangible asset's cost over the asset's useful life.
- Goodwill may be shown in the accounts only when it has been purchased as part of the acquisition of another business.

LO6   Illustrate the balance sheet presentation of plant assets and intangible assets. (p. 425)

- Plant assets and intangible assets are shown on the balance sheet after long-term investments. Although technically an intangible asset, goodwill is reported separately on the balance sheet since it is not subject to amortization.

LO7   Define the return on assets ratio and the asset turnover ratio, and explain their use. (p. 426)

- The return on assets ratio is calculated by dividing net income by average total assets; it represents an overall measure of a firm's profitability and how efficiently a company is using its assets to generate net income.
- The asset turnover ratio is calculated by dividing net sales by average total assets; it provides an indication of the effective utilization of business assets to generate sales revenues.

Concept	→	Method	→	Assessment	SUMMARY
How effective is a company in using its assets to produce net income?		Net income and average total assets $\text{Return on assets ratio} = \dfrac{\text{Net income}}{\text{Average total assets}}$		A higher ratio value implies a higher, more effective level of asset utilization.	TAKEAWAY 9.1
How effective is a company at generating sales using its assets?		Average total assets and net sales $\text{Asset turnover ratio} = \dfrac{\text{Net sales}}{\text{Average total assets}}$		A higher ratio value implies a higher level of sales revenue generated for each dollar invested in assets.	TAKEAWAY 9.2

KEY TERMS

Accelerated depreciation method (p. 413)

Amortization (p. 423)

Asset turnover (p. 426)

Betterments (p. 419)

Capital expenditures (p. 419)

Copyright (p. 423)

Declining-balance method (p. 413)

Depreciation (p. 410)

Depreciation accounting (p. 410)

Franchises (p. 424)

Goodwill (p. 424)

Impairment loss (p. 416)

Intangible assets (p. 421)

Land improvements (p. 409)

Leasehold improvements (p. 409)

Modified accelerated cost recovery system (MACRS) (p. 417)

Patent (p. 423)

Plant assets (p. 406)

Research and development costs (p. 422)

Return on assets (p. 426)

Revenue expenditures (p. 418)

Salvage value (p. 410)

Straight-line method (p. 411)

Trademarks (p. 424)

Trade names (p. 424)

Units-of-production method (p. 414)

Useful life (p. 410)

SELF-STUDY QUESTIONS

(Answers for the Self-Study Questions are available at the end of this chapter.)

1. **The acquisition cost of a plant asset is equal to the asset's implied cash price and:**   **LO1**
   a. The interest paid on any debt incurred to finance the asset's purchase.
   b. The market value of any noncash assets given up to acquire the plant asset.
   c. The reasonable and necessary costs incurred to prepare the asset for its intended use.
   d. The asset's estimated salvage value.

2. **On January 1, Rio Company purchased a delivery truck for $10,000. The company estimates the truck will be driven 80,000 miles over its eight-year useful life. The estimated salvage value is $2,000. The truck was driven 12,000 miles in its first year. Which method results in the largest depreciation expense for the first year?**   **LO2**
   a. Units-of-production
   b. Straight-line
   c. Double-declining balance

3. **On the first day of the current year, Blakely Company sold equipment for less than its book value. Which of the following is part of the journal entry to record the sale?**   **LO4**
   a. A debit to Equipment
   b. A credit to Accumulated Depreciation—Equipment
   c. A credit to Gain on Sale of Plant Assets
   d. A debit to Loss on Sale of Plant Assets

4. **Accounting for the periodic amortization of intangible assets is similar to which depreciation method?**   **LO5**
   a. Straight-line
   b. Units-of-production
   c. Double-declining balance

LO5 5. **An exclusive right to operate or sell a specific brand of products in a given geographic area is called:**
    a. A franchise.
    b. Goodwill.
    c. A patent.
    d. A copyright.

LO5 6. **Which of the following statements is true?**
    a. Goodwill is subject to amortization.
    b. Research and development costs may be capitalized to the balance sheet.
    c. Intangible assets are amortized to expense on the income statement.
    d. Goodwill arises because of a company's positive corporate image among its customers.

LO3 7. **Which of the following statements is false?**
    a. Expenditures for ordinary repairs are a capital expenditure.
    b. Betterment expenditures are a capital expenditure.
    c. Expenditures to acquire low-cost assets are revenue expenditures.
    d. Material additions to a plant asset are capital expenditures.

LO6 8. **Which of the following statements is true?**
    a. Intangible assets are shown on the balance sheet net of the Accumulated Amortization account.
    b. Goodwill is shown on the balance sheet net of the Accumulated Amortization account.
    c. The Accumulated Depreciation account need not be used for plant assets.
    d. Plant assets are shown on the balance sheet net of the Accumulated Depreciation account.

LO7 9. **A company reports net income of $6,000, net sales of $15,000, and total assets of $24,000. What is the company's return on assets?**
    a. 62.5 percent
    b. 25.0 percent
    c. 40.0 percent
    d. None of the above

LO7 10. **A company reports net income of $6,000, net sales of $15,000, and average total assets of $24,000. What is the company's asset turnover?**
    a. 0.625
    b. 0.25
    c. 0.40
    d. None of the above

LO4 11. **Harley Company sold one of its worn out delivery trucks on December 31, 2013. The truck was purchased on January 1, 2010, for $50,000 and was depreciated on a straight-line basis over a 5-year life. There was no salvage value associated with the truck. If the truck was sold for $14,000, what was the amount of gain or loss recorded at the time of the sale?**
    a. $4,000 loss
    b. $14,000 gain
    c. $4,000 gain
    d. $6,000 loss

QUESTIONS

1. What are the two major types of long-term assets that require a periodic write-off? Present examples of each, and indicate for each type of asset the term that denotes the periodic write-off to expense.

2. In what way is land different from other plant assets?

3. In general, what amounts constitute the acquisition cost of plant assets?

4. Foss Company bought land with a vacant building for $400,000. Foss will use the building in its operations. Must Foss allocate the purchase price between the land and building? Why or why not? Would your answer be different if Foss intends to raze the building and build a new one? Why or why not?

5. Why is the recognition of depreciation expense necessary to match revenue and expense properly?

6. What is the pattern of plant asset utilization (or benefit) that is appropriate for each of the following depreciation methods: (a) straight-line, (b) units-of-production, (c) double-declining balance?

7. How should a revision of depreciation charges due to a change in an asset's estimated useful life or salvage value be handled? Which periods—past, present, or future—are affected by the revision?

8. When is a plant asset considered to be impaired? How is an impairment loss calculated?

9. What is the benefit of accelerating depreciation for income tax purposes when the total depreciation taken is no more than if straight-line depreciation were used?

10. Identify two types of revenue expenditures. What is the proper accounting for revenue expenditures?

11. Identify two types of capital expenditures. What is the proper accounting for capital expenditures?

12. What factors determine the gain or loss on the sale of a plant asset?

13. Folger Company installed a conveyor system that cost $192,000. The system can be used only in the excavation of gravel at a particular site. Folger expects to excavate gravel at the site for 10 years. Over how many years should the conveyor be depreciated if its physical life is estimated at (a) 8 years and (b) 12 years?

14. What are five different types of intangible assets? Briefly explain the nature of each type.

15. How should a firm account for research and development costs?

16. Under what circumstances is goodwill recorded?

17. How is the *return on assets* ratio calculated? What does this ratio reveal about a business?

18. How is the *asset turnover ratio* calculated? What does this ratio reveal about a business?

SHORT EXERCISES

SE9-1. Calculate Amount to Capitalize The Miller Company paid $10,000 to acquire a 100 ton press. Freight charges to deliver the equipment amounted to $1,500 and were paid by Miller. Installation costs amounted to $570, and machine testing charges amounted to $250. Calculate the amount that should be capitalized to the Equipment account. **LO1**

SE9-2. Depreciation Expense Using the Straight-Line Method The Pack Company purchased an office building for $4,500,000. The building had an estimated useful life of 40 years and an expected salvage value of $500,000. Calculate the depreciation expense for the second year using the straight-line method. **LO2**

SE9-3. Depreciation Expense Using the Double-Declining Balance Method The Pack Company purchased an office building for $4,500,000. The building had an estimated useful life of 40 years and an expected salvage value of $500,000. Calculate the depreciation expense for the second year using the double-declining balance method. **LO2**

SE9-4. Depreciation Expense Using the Units-of-Production Method The Likert Company is a coal company based in West Virginia. The company recently purchased a new coal truck for $60,000. The truck had an expected useful life of 200,000 miles and an expected salvage value of $2,000. Calculate the depreciation expense using the units-of-production method assuming the truck travelled 40,000 miles on company business during the year. **LO2**

SE9-5. Sale of a Building The Miller Company sold a building for $400,000 that had a book value of $450,000. The building had originally cost the company $12,000,000 and had accumulated depreciation to date of $11,550,000. Prepare a journal entry to record the sale of the building. **LO4**

SE9-6. Goodwill Impairment Bruceton Farms Equipment Company had goodwill valued at $80 million on its balance sheet at year-end. A review of the goodwill by the company's CFO indicated that the goodwill was impaired and was now only worth $50 million. Prepare a journal entry to record the goodwill impairment on the books of the company. **LO5**

SE9-7. Amortization Expense Smith & Sons obtained a patent for a new optical scanning device. The fees incurred to file for the patent and to defend the patent in court against several companies which challenged the patent amounted to $45,000. Smith & Sons concluded that the expected economic life of the patent was 12 years. Calculate the amortization expense that should be recorded in the second year, and record the journal entry for the amortization expense on the books of Smith & Sons. **LO5**

SE9-8. Return on Assets The Kingwood Company reported net income of $50,000 and average total assets of $450,000. Calculate the company's return on assets. **LO7**

SE9-9. Asset Turnover The Kingwood Company reported sales revenue of $520,000 and average total assets of $450,000. Calculate the company's asset turnover. **LO7**

LO7   SE9-10. Return on Assets and Asset Turnover Last year, the Miller Company reported a return on assets of 15 percent and an asset turnover of 1.6. In the current year, the company reported a return on assets of 19 percent but an asset turnover of only 1.2. If sales revenue remained unchanged from last year to the current year, what would explain the two ratio results?

LO4   SE9-11. Sale of Equipment Prepare the journal entry for the following transactions: (1) Geysler Company sold some old equipment that initially cost $30,000 and had $25,000 of accumulated depreciation and received cash in the amount of $3,000. (2) Assume the same facts except Geysler received $9,000.

LO6   SE9-12. Financial Statement Placement Name the financial statement where each of the following will appear: (IS) Income Statement; (BS) Balance Sheet; (SCF) Statement of Cash Flows; (N) None.

    a.   Book value of equipment purchased five years ago
    b.   Market value of equipment purchased five years ago
    c.   Cash proceeds from the sale of land
    d.   Gain on the sale of buildings
    e.   Accumulated depreciation on equipment
    f.   Impairment loss on land

Assignments with the ✓ logo in the margin are available in BusinessCourse.
See the Preface of the book for details.

EXERCISES—SET A

LO1   E9-1A. Acquisition Cost of Long-Lived Asset The following data relate to a firm's purchase of a machine used in the manufacture of its product:

Invoice price.	$20,000
Applicable sales tax	1,200
Cash discount taken for prompt payment	400
Freight paid	260
Cost of insurance coverage on machine while in transit	125
Installation costs	1,000
Testing and adjusting costs	475
Repair of damages to machine caused by the firm's employees	550
Prepaid maintenance contract for first year of machine's use.	300

Determine the acquisition cost of the machine.

LO1   E9-2A. Allocation of Package Purchase Price Tamock Company purchased a plant from one of its suppliers. The $975,000 purchase price included the land, a building, and factory machinery. Tamock also paid $5,000 in legal fees to negotiate the purchase of the plant. An appraisal showed the following values for the items purchased:

Property	Assessed Value
Land	$126,000
Building	486,000
Machinery.	288,000
Total	$900,000

Using the assessed value as a guide, allocate the total purchase price of the plant to the land, building, and machinery accounts in Tamock Company's records.

LO2   E9-3A. Depreciation Methods A delivery truck costing $18,000 is expected to have a $1,500 salvage value at the end of its useful life of four years or 125,000 miles. Assume that the truck was purchased on January 2. Calculate the depreciation expense for the second year using each of the following depreciation methods: (a) straight-line, (b) double-declining balance, and (c) units-of-production. (Assume that the truck was driven 28,000 miles in the second year.)

LO2   E9-4A. Revision of Depreciation On January 2, 2009, Mosler, Inc., purchased equipment for $66,000. The equipment was expected to have a $6,000 salvage value at the end of its estimated six-year useful life. Straight-line depreciation has been recorded. Before adjusting the accounts for 2013, Mosler decided that the useful life of the equipment should be extended by two years and the salvage value decreased to $4,000.

a.   Prepare a journal entry to record depreciation expense on the equipment for 2013.

b.   What is the book value of the equipment at the end of 2013 (after recording the depreciation expense for 2013)?

E9-5A.   Impairment Loss   On July 1, 2009, Okin Company purchased equipment for $225,000; the esti- mated useful life was 10 years and the expected salvage value was $25,000. Straight-line depreciation is used. On July 1, 2013, economic factors cause the market value of the equipment to decrease to $90,000. On this date, Okin evaluates if the equipment is impaired and estimates future cash flows relating to the use and disposal of the equipment to be $125,000.

LO2

a.   Is the equipment impaired at July 1, 2013? Explain.

b.   If the equipment is impaired at July 1, 2013, calculate the amount of the impairment loss.

c.   If the equipment is impaired at July 1, 2013, prepare the journal entry to record the impairment loss.

E9-6A.   Revenue and Capital Expenditures   Shively Company built an addition to its chemical plant. Indi- cate whether each of the following expenditures related to the addition is a revenue expenditure or a capital expenditure:

LO3

a.   Shively's initial application for a building permit was denied by the city as not conforming to environmental standards. Shively disagreed with the decision and spent $6,000 in attorney's fees to convince the city to reverse its position and issue the permit.

b.   Due to unanticipated sandy soil conditions, and on the advice of construction engineers, Shively spent $58,000 to extend the footings for the addition to a greater depth than originally planned.

c.   Shively spent $3,000 to send each of the addition's subcontractors a side of beef as a thank-you gift for completing the project on schedule.

d.   Shively invited the mayor to a ribbon-cutting ceremony to open the plant addition. It spent $25 to purchase the ribbon and scissors.

e.   Shively spent $4,100 to have the company logo sandblasted into the concrete above the entrance to the addition.

E9-7A.   Sale of Plant Asset   Raine Company has a machine that originally cost $68,000. Depreciation has been recorded for five years using the straight-line method, with a $5,000 estimated salvage value at the end of an expected nine-year life. After recording depreciation at the end of the fifth year, Raine sells the machine. Prepare the journal entry to record the machine's sale for:

LO4

a. $37,000 cash.

b. $33,000 cash.

c. $28,000 cash.

E9-8A.   Amortization Expense   For each of the following unrelated situations, calculate the annual amortiza- tion expense and prepare a journal entry to record the expense:

LO5

a.   A patent with a 15-year remaining legal life was purchased for $270,000. The patent will be com- mercially exploitable for another nine years.

b.   A patent was acquired on a device designed by a production worker. Although the cost of the patent to date consisted of $42,300 in legal fees for handling the patent application, the patent should be commercially valuable during its entire remaining legal life of 18 years and is currently worth $378,000.

c.   A franchise granting exclusive distribution rights for a new solar water heater within a three-state area for four years was obtained at a cost of $63,000. Satisfactory sales performance over the four years permits renewal of the franchise for another four years (at an additional cost determined at renewal).

E9-9A.   Return on Assets Ratio and Asset Turnover Ratio   Campo Systems reported the following financial data (in millions) in its annual report:

LO7

	2012	2013
Net income.	$ 8,052	$ 6,134
Net sales.	39,540	36,117
Total assets	58,734	68,128

If the company's total assets are $55,676 in 2011, calculate the company's (a) return on assets and (b) asset turnover for 2012 and 2013.

LO7   **E9-10A.** **Return on Assets Ratio and Asset Turnover Ratio: Using IFRS Financial Statements** Tesco PLC is the world's third largest retailer and is headquartered in the United Kingdom. Tesco's IFRS financial statements are presented in Appendix C at the end of this book. Using this financial data, calculate the company's (a) return on assets and (b) asset turnover for 2011 and 2010. Tesco's 2009 total assets were 46,053 million British pounds. Comment on the trend in Tesco's ratios.

LO6 ✔   **E9-11A. Financial Statement Presentation** Vera Corp. reported the following amounts for the year just ended:

Land	$120,000
Patents	25,000
Equipment	40,000
Buildings.	150,000
Goodwill	35,000
Accumulated amortization	10,000
Accumulated depreciation	80,000

Prepare a partial balance sheet for these amounts.

EXERCISES—SET B

LO1 ✔   **E9-1B.** **Acquisition Cost of Long-Lived Asset** Fischer Construction purchased a used front-end loader for $28,000, terms 1/10, n/30, F.O.B. shipping point, freight collect. Fischer paid the freight charges of $270 and sent the seller a check for $27,720 one week after the machine was delivered. The loader required a new battery, which cost Fischer $150. Fischer also spent $240 to have the company name printed on the loader and $375 for one year's insurance coverage on it. Fischer hired a new employee to operate it at a wage of $19 per hour; the employee spent one morning (four hours) practicing with the machine and went to work at a construction site that afternoon. Calculate the amount at which the front-end loader should be reported on the company's balance sheet.

LO1 ✔   **E9-2B.** **Allocation of Package Purchase Price** Andrew Lupino went into business by purchasing a car lubrication station, consisting of land, a building, and equipment. The seller's original asking price was $210,000. Lupino hired an appraiser for $2,000 to appraise the assets. The appraised valuations were land, $38,000; building, $95,000; and equipment, $57,000. After receiving the appraisal, Lupino offered $175,000 for the business. The seller refused this offer. Lupino then offered $185,000 for the business, which the seller accepted. Using the appraisal values as a guide, allocate the total purchase price of the car lubrication station to the Land, Building, and Equipment accounts.

LO2 ✔   **E9-3B.** **Depreciation Methods** A machine costing $145,800 was purchased May 1. The machine should be obsolete after three years and, therefore, no longer useful to the company. The estimated salvage value is $5,400. Calculate the depreciation expense for each year of its expected useful life using each of the following depreciation methods: (a) straight-line, (b) double-declining balance.

LO2 ✔   **E9-4B.** **Revision of Depreciation** Associated Clinic purchased a special machine for use in its laboratory on January 2, 2010. The machine cost $84,000 and was expected to last 10 years. Its salvage value was estimated to be $6,000. By early 2012, it was evident that the machine will be useful for a total of only seven years. The salvage value after seven years was estimated to be $7,500. Associated Clinic uses straight-line depreciation. Compute the proper depreciation expense on the machine for 2012.

LO2 ✔   **E9-5B.** **Impairment Loss** On May 1, 2010, Silky, Inc., purchased machinery for $315,000; the estimated useful life was eight years and the expected salvage value was $15,000. Straight-line depreciation is used. On May 1, 2012, economic factors cause the market value of the machinery to decrease to $190,000. On this date, Silky evaluates whether the machinery is impaired.

   a.   Assume that on May 1, 2012, Silky estimates future cash flows relating to the use and disposal of the machinery to be $260,000. Is the machinery impaired at May 1, 2012? Explain. If it is impaired, what is the amount of the impairment loss?

   b.   Assume that on May 1, 2012, Silky estimates future cash flows relating to the use and disposal of the machinery to be $230,000. Is the machinery impaired at May 1, 2012? Explain. If it is impaired, what is the amount of the impairment loss?

E9-6B. **Revenue and Capital Expenditures** Indicate whether each of the following expenditures is a rev-   **LO3**
enue expenditure or a capital expenditure for Blare Company:

   a. Paid $280 to replace a truck windshield that was cracked by a stone thrown up by another vehicle while the truck was being used to make a delivery.
   b. Paid $10 for a "No Smoking" sign for the conference room.
   c. Paid $900 to add a hard disk to an employee's computer.
   d. Paid $15 for a dust cover for a computer printer.
   e. Paid $280 to replace a cracked windshield on a used truck that was just purchased for company use. The company bought the truck knowing the windshield was cracked.
   f. Paid $500 for a building permit from the city for a storage shed the company is going to have built.

E9-7B. **Sale of Plant Asset** Noble Company has equipment that originally cost $63,000. Depreciation has   **LO4**
been recorded for six years using the straight-line method, with a $7,000 estimated salvage value at
the end of an expected eight-year life. After recording depreciation at the end of the sixth year, Noble
sells the equipment. Prepare the journal entry to record the equipment's sale for:

   a. $27,000 cash.
   b. $21,000 cash.
   c. $18,000 cash.

E9-8B. **Amortization Expense** For each of the following unrelated situations, calculate the annual amortiza-   **LO5**
tion expense and prepare a journal entry to record the expense:

   a. A patent with a 15-year remaining legal life was purchased for $595,000. The patent will be commercially exploitable for another seven years.
   b. A patent was acquired on a device designed by a production worker. Although the cost of the patent to date consisted of $84,600 in legal fees for handling the patent application, the patent should be commercially valuable during its entire remaining legal life of 18 years and is currently worth $720,000.
   c. A franchise granting exclusive distribution rights for a new wind turbine within a three-state area for four years was obtained at a cost of $66,400. Satisfactory sales performance over the four years permits renewal of the franchise for another four years (at an additional cost determined at renewal).

E9-9B. **Return on Assets Ratio and Asset Turnover Ratio** Allied Systems reported the following financial   **LO7**
data (in millions) in its annual report:

	2012	2013
Net income.	$18,052	$16,134
Net sales.	49,540	46,117
Total assets	68,734	78,128

If the company's total assets are $65,676 in 2011, calculate the company's (a) return on assets and
(b) asset turnover for 2012 and 2013.

E9-10B. **Financial Statement Presentation** Evae Corp. reported the following amounts for the year just   **LO6**
ended:

Land.	$ 60
Trademarks	15
Equipment	80
Buildings.	110
Goodwill.	25
Accumulated amortization	5
Accumulated depreciation	55

Prepare a partial balance sheet for these amounts.

PROBLEMS—SET A

LO1 **P9-1A.** **Acquisition Cost of Long-Lived Assets** The following items represent expenditures (or receipts) related to the construction of a new home office for Lowrey Company.

Cost of land site, which included an old apartment building appraised at $75,000	$ 165,000
Legal fees, including fee for title search.	2,100
Payment of apartment building mortgage and related interest due at time of sale.	9,300
Payment for delinquent property taxes assumed by the purchaser	4,000
Cost of razing the apartment building	17,000
Proceeds from sale of salvaged materials.	(3,800)
Grading to establish proper drainage flow on land site	1,900
Architect's fees on new building	300,000
Proceeds from sales of excess dirt (from basement excavation) to owner of adjoining property (dirt was used to fill in a low area on property)	(2,000)
Payment to building contractor	5,000,000
Payment of medical bills of employee accidentally injured while inspecting building construction	1,400
Special assessment for paving city sidewalks (paid to city)	18,000
Cost of paving driveway and parking lot	25,000
Cost of installing lights in parking lot.	9,200
Premium for insurance on building during construction	7,500
Cost of open house party to celebrate opening of new building.	8,000

Required
From the given data, calculate the proper balances for the Land, Building, and Land Improvements accounts of Lowrey Company.

LO1, 2 **P9-2A.** **Allocation of Package Purchase Price and Depreciation Methods** To expand its business, Small Company paid $754,000 for most of the property, plant, and equipment of a small trucking company that was going out of business. Before agreeing to the price, Small hired a consultant for $6,000 to appraise the assets. The appraised values were as follows:

Land.	$120,000
Building	440,000
Trucks.	144,000
Equipment	96,000
Total	$800,000

Small issued two checks totaling $760,000 to acquire the assets and pay the consultant on July 1. Small depreciated the assets using the straight-line method on the building and on the equipment, and the double-declining balance method on the trucks. Estimated useful lives and salvage values were as follows:

	Useful Life	Salvage Value
Building	20 years	$42,000
Trucks.	4 years	15,000
Equipment	7 years	10,000

Required
a. Calculate the amounts allocated to the various types of plant assets acquired on July 1.
b. Prepare the July 1 journal entries to record the purchase of the assets and the payment to the consultant.
c. Prepare the December 31 journal entries to record depreciation expense for the year on the building, trucks, and equipment.

LO2 **P9-3A.** **Depreciation Methods** On January 2, Roth, Inc. purchased a laser cutting machine to be used in the fabrication of a part for one of its key products. The machine cost $80,000, and its estimated useful life was four years or 1,000,000 cuttings, after which it could be sold for $5,000.

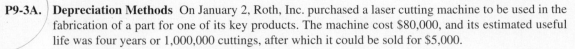

Required

Calculate the depreciation expense for each year of the machine's useful life under each of the following depreciation methods:

a.   Straight-line.

b.   Double-declining balance.

c.   Units-of-production. Assume annual production in cuttings of 200,000; 350,000; 260,000; and 190,000.

P9-4A.   **Accounting for Plant Assets**   Basin Corporation had the following transactions related to its delivery truck: **LO1, 2, 3**

Year 1

Jan.   5   Purchased for $14,300 cash a new truck with an estimated useful life of four years and a salvage value of $2,300.

Feb.   20   Installed a new set of side-view mirrors at a cost of $68 cash.

June   9   Paid $285 for an engine tune-up, wheel balancing, and a periodic chassis lubrication.

Aug.   2   Paid a $250 repair bill for the uninsured portion of damages to the truck caused by Basin's own driver.

Dec.   31   Recorded depreciation on the truck for the year.

Year 2

May   1   Installed a set of parts bins in the truck at a cost of $800 cash. This expenditure was not expected to increase the salvage value of the truck.

Dec.   31   Recorded depreciation on the truck for the year.

Year 3

Dec.   31   Recorded depreciation on the truck for the year.

Basin's depreciation policies include (1) using straight-line depreciation, (2) recording depreciation to the nearest whole month, and (3) expensing all truck expenditures of $75 or less.

Required

Prepare journal entries to record these transactions and adjustments.

P9-5A.   **Disposal of Plant Asset**   Citano Company has a used executive charter plane that originally cost $800,000. Straight-line depreciation on the plane has been recorded for six years, with an $80,000 expected salvage value at the end of its estimated eight-year useful life. The last depreciation entry was made at the end of the sixth year. Eight months into the seventh year, Citano disposes of the plane.   **LO4**

Required

Prepare journal entries to record:

a.   Depreciation expense to the date of disposal.

b.   Sale of the plane for cash at its book value.

c.   Sale of the plane for $215,000 cash.

d.   Sale of the plane for $195,000 cash.

e.   Destruction of the plane in a fire. Citano expects a $190,000 insurance settlement.

P9-6A.   **Accounting for Intangible Assets and Leasehold Improvements**   Berdahl Company owns several retail outlets. During the year, it expanded operations and entered into the following transactions: **LO1, 2, 5**

Jan.   2   Signed an eight-year lease for additional retail space for an annual rent of $23,400. Paid the first year's rent on this date. (*Hint:* Debit the first year's rent to Prepaid Rent.)

           3   Paid $22,800 to a contractor for installation of a new oak floor in the leased facility. The oak floor's life is an estimated 50 years with no salvage value.

Mar.   1   Paid $45,000 to obtain an exclusive area franchise for five years to distribute a new line of perfume.

July   1   Paid $38,000 to LogoLab, Inc., for designing a trademark for a new line of gourmet chocolates that Berdahl will distribute nationally. Berdahl will use the trademark for as long as the firm remains in business. Berdahl expects to be in business for at least another 50 years.

           1   Paid $25,000 for advertisement in a national magazine (June issue) introducing the new line of chocolates and the trademark.

Required

a.   Prepare journal entries to record these transactions.

b.   Prepare the necessary adjusting entries on December 31 for these transactions. Berdahl makes adjusting entries once a year. Berdahl uses straight-line depreciation and amortization.

LO6   **P9-7A.   Preparation of Balance Sheet** Dooley Company's December 31 post-closing trial balance contains the following normal balances:

Cash.	$ 9,000
Accounts payable.	18,000
Building	439,500
Long-term notes payable.	785,000
Common stock.	900,000
Retained earnings	70,000
Accumulated depreciation—Equipment	180,000
Land	829,500
Accounts receivable.	22,500
Accumulated depreciation—Building.	135,000
Wages payable.	6,000
Patent (net of amortization)	120,000
Notes payable (short term).	131,000
Inventory.	206,000
Equipment	600,000
Allowance for doubtful accounts	1,500

Required

Prepare a December 31 classified balance sheet for Dooley Company.

LO1, 2, 3   **P9-8A.   Journal Entries for Plant Assets** During the first few days of the year, Coast Company entered into the following transactions:

1.   Purchased a parcel of land with a building on it for $900,000 cash. The building, which will be used in operations, has an estimated useful life of 25 years and a salvage value of $60,000. The assessed valuations for property tax purposes show the land at $80,000 and the building at $720,000.

2.   Paid $30,000 for the construction of an asphalt parking lot for customers. The parking lot is expected to last 12 years and has no salvage value.

3.   Paid $25,000 for the construction of a new entrance to the building.

4.   Purchased store equipment, paying the invoice price (including seven percent sales tax) of $74,900 in cash. The estimated useful life of the equipment is eight years, and the salvage value is $6,000.

5.   Paid $220 freight on the new equipment.

6.   Paid $1,500 to repair damages to floor caused when the store equipment was accidentally dropped as it was moved into place.

7.   Paid $40 for an umbrella holder to place inside front door (customers may place wet umbrellas in the holder). The holder is expected to last 20 years.

Required

a.   Prepare journal entries to record these transactions.

b.   Prepare the December 31 journal entries to record depreciation expense for the year. Double-declining balance depreciation is used for the equipment, and straight-line depreciation is used for the building and parking lot.

LO1, 2, 5   **P9-9A.   IFRS** Sovereign Biotechnology PLC is a U.K.-based biotechnology company. During the year, the company's London office property was appraised at 100 million British pounds, or 20 million pounds more than its current book value on the company's balance sheet. The company also spent 12 million British pounds on original research seeking a cure for cancer. Finally, the company spent 6 million British pounds on development costs associated with a promising new molecule combination that had, in early human tests, shown that it could substantially reduce the likelihood that patients with immune deficiency syndrome would develop pneumonia.

Required

Prepare journal entries to record the above information.

PROBLEMS—SET B

P9-1B. **Acquisition Cost of Long-Lived Assets** The following items represent expenditures (or receipts) related to the construction of a new home office for Secrest Investment Company.

LO1
✓

Cost of land site, which included an abandoned railroad spur	$ 175,000
Legal fees, including title search, relating to land purchase	4,300
Cost of surveying land to confirm boundaries	1,100
Cost of removing railroad tracks	6,500
Payment of delinquent property taxes assumed by the purchaser	6,000
Proceeds from sale of timber from walnut trees cut down to prepare site for construction	(18,000)
Proceeds from sale of salvaged railroad track.	(3,500)
Grading to prepare land site for construction	4,000
Cost of basement excavation (contracted separately).	3,700
Architect's fees on new building	128,000
Payment to building contractor—original contract price	3,200,000
Cost of changes during construction to make building more energy efficient	91,000
Cost of replacing windows broken by vandals	2,400
Cost of paving driveway and parking lot	17,000
Out-of-court settlement for mud slide onto adjacent property	10,000
Special assessment for paving city sidewalks (paid to city)	22,000
Cost of brick and wrought iron fence installed across front of property	16,500

Required

From the given data, compute the proper balances for the Land, Building, and Land Improvements accounts of Secrest Investment Company.

P9-2B. **Allocation of Package Purchase Price and Depreciation Methods** In an expansion move, Beam Company paid $2,180,000 for most of the property, plant, and equipment of a small manufacturing firm that was going out of business. Before agreeing to the price, Beam hired a consultant for $20,000 to appraise the assets. The appraised values were as follows:

LO1, 2
✓

Land	$ 384,000
Building	912,000
Equipment	960,000
Trucks.	144,000
Total	$2,400,000

Beam issued two checks totaling $2,200,000 to acquire the assets and pay the consultant on April 1. Beam depreciated the assets using the straight-line method for the building and equipment, and the double-declining balance method for the trucks. Estimated useful lives and salvage values were as follows:

	Useful Life	Salvage Value
Building	15 years	$86,000
Equipment	9 years	70,000
Trucks.	5 years	13,000

Required

a. Calculate the amounts allocated to the various types of plant assets acquired on April 1.
b. Prepare the April 1 journal entries to record the purchase of the assets and the payment of the consultant.
c. Prepare the December 31 journal entries to record the depreciation expense on the building, equipment, and trucks for the year.

P9-3B. **Depreciation Methods** On January 2, 2012, Alvarez Company purchased an electroplating machine to help manufacture a part for one of its key products. The machine cost $218,700 and was estimated to have a useful life of six years or 700,000 platings, after which it could be sold for $23,400.

LO2
✓

Required

a. Calculate each year's depreciation expense for the period 2012–2017 under each of the following depreciation methods:
  1. Straight-line.
  2. Double-declining balance.
  3. Units-of-production. (Assume annual production in platings of 140,000; 180,000; 100,000; 110,000; 80,000; and 90,000.)

b. Assume that the machine was purchased on September 1, 2012. Calculate each year's depreciation expense for the period 2012–2018 under each of the following depreciation methods:
  1. Straight-line.
  2. Double-declining balance.

LO1, 2, 3

P9-4B. **Journal Entries for Plant Assets** Stellar Delivery Service had the following transactions related to its delivery truck:

Year 1

Mar.	1	Purchased for $28,500 cash a new delivery truck with an estimated useful life of five years and a $2,800 salvage value.
	2	Paid $580 for painting the company name and logo on the truck.
Dec.	31	Recorded depreciation on the truck for the year.

Year 2

July	1	Installed air conditioning in the truck at a cost of $1,808 cash. Although the truck's estimated useful life was unaffected, its estimated salvage value was increased by $400.
Sept.	7	Paid $430 for truck tune-up and safety inspection.
Dec.	31	Recorded depreciation on the truck for the year.

Year 3

| Sept. | 3 | Installed a set of front and rear bumper guards at a cost of $130 cash. |
| Dec. | 31 | Recorded depreciation on the truck for the year. |

Year 4

| Dec. | 31 | Recorded depreciation on the truck for the year. |

Stellar's depreciation policies include (1) using straight-line depreciation, (2) recording depreciation to the nearest whole month, and (3) expensing all truck expenditures of $150 or less.

Required

Prepare journal entries to record these transactions and adjustments.

LO2, 3

P9-5B. **Revision of Depreciation and Capital Expenditure** Richter Company uses straight-line depreciation in accounting for its machines. On January 2, 2007, Richter purchased a new machine for $122,000 cash. The machine's estimated useful life was seven years with a $10,000 salvage value. In 2012, the company decided its original useful life estimate should be increased by three years. Beginning in 2012, depreciation was based on a 10-year total useful life, and no change was made in the salvage value estimate. On January 3, 2013, Richter added an automatic cut-off switch and a self-sharpening blade mechanism to the machine at a cost of $8,800 cash. These improvements did not change the machine's useful life but did increase the estimated salvage value to $11,200.

Required

a. Prepare journal entries to record (1) the purchase of the machine, (2) 2007 depreciation expense, (3) 2012 depreciation expense, (4) the 2013 improvements, and (5) 2013 depreciation expense.
b. Calculate the book value of the machine at the end of 2013 (that is, after recording the depreciation expense for 2013).

LO4

P9-6B. **Disposal of Plant Asset** Canyon Company has a used delivery truck that originally cost $27,200. Straight-line depreciation on the truck has been recorded for three years, with a $2,000 expected salvage value at the end of its estimated six-year useful life. The last depreciation entry was made at the end of the third year. Four months into the fourth year, Canyon disposes of the truck.

Required

Prepare journal entries to record:

a. Depreciation expense to the date of disposal.

b. Sale of the truck for cash at its book value.
c. Sale of the truck for $15,000 cash.
d. Sale of the truck for $12,000 cash.
e. Theft of the truck. Canyon carries no insurance for theft.

P9-7B. Accounting for Plant and Intangible Assets Selected transactions of Continental Publishers, Inc., for 2013 are given below: **LO1, 2, 5** ✓

Jan.   2 Paid $90,000 to purchase copyrights to a series of romantic novels. The copyrights expire in 40 years, although sales of the novels are expected to stop after 10 years.

Mar.   1 Discovered a satellite dish antenna has been destroyed by lightning. The loss is covered by insurance and a claim is filed today. The antenna cost $9,180 when installed on July 1, 2012, and was being depreciated over 12 years with a $900 salvage value. Straight-line depreciation was last recorded on December 31, 2012. Continental expects to receive an insurance settlement of $8,100.

April 1 Paid $120,000 to remodel space to create an employee exercise area on the lower level in a leased building. The building's remaining useful life is 40 years; the lease on the building expires in 12 years.

July   1 Paid $270,000 to acquire a patent on a new publishing process. The patent has a remaining legal life of 15 years. Continental estimates the new process will be utilized for 6 years before it becomes obsolete.

Nov.   1 Paid $63,000 to obtain a four-year franchise to sell a new series of computerized do-it-yourself manuals.

Required
a. Prepare journal entries to record these transactions.
b. Prepare the December 31 journal entries to record depreciation and amortization expense for assets acquired during the year. Continental uses straight-line depreciation and amortization.

P9-8B. Preparation of Balance Sheet Conlon Corporation's December 31 post-closing trial balance contains the following normal account balances: **LO6** ✓

Interest payable	$ 24,000
Allowance for doubtful accounts	1,000
Accumulated depreciation—Equipment	130,000
Inventory	137,000
Organization costs (net of amortization)	19,000
Notes payable (short term)	80,000
Cash	2,000
Building	280,000
Accounts receivable	21,000
Patent (net of amortization)	50,000
Equipment	266,000
Common stock	400,000
Retained earnings	353,000
Accumulated depreciation—Building	70,000
Accounts payable	13,000
Leasehold improvements	140,000
Land	1,128,000
Long-term notes payable	950,000
Accumulated depreciation—Leasehold improvements	22,000

Required
Prepare a December 31 classified balance sheet for Conlon Corporation.

ASSIGNMENTS

SERIAL PROBLEM: KATE'S CARDS

(Note: This is a continuation of the Serial Problem: Kate's Cards from Chapters 1 through 8.)

SP9. Kate's business is growing faster than she had predicted. In order to keep up, she will need to purchase improved computer hardware. Kate has learned that the software that she uses runs much faster if her computer has a lot of memory. In addition, her files are very large and she is running out of free space on her existing hard drive. Finally, Kate has heard horror stories about hard disk drive crashes and the possibility that all of her work will be destroyed. In order to protect against this possibility, she has decided to invest in a large commercial grade backup system.

The cost of the memory and hard disk drive upgrade to Kate's computer will total $420. The cost of the backup system is $3,000. The memory and hard disk upgrade will increase the productivity of Kate's current computer; however, it will not extend its useful life. The backup system is expected to have a 5-year useful life.

Kate would like to know the following items:

1. How should the expenditure for the memory and hard disk drive upgrade be recorded? Provide the journal entry.
2. Kate's current computer has 42 months remaining for depreciation purpose (under the straight-line method). The original cost of the computer was $4,800 and had a four-year useful life. The current monthly depreciation is $100. How will this current expenditure affect the monthly depreciation?
3. Kate would like to know how depreciation on the backup system under both the straight-line method and the double-declining method differ. She is assigning a $500 salvage value to the equipment. Construct a table showing yearly depreciation under both methods.

EXTENDING YOUR KNOWLEDGE

REPORTING AND ANALYSIS

COLUMBIA
SPORTSWEAR
COMPANY

EYK9-1. Financial Reporting Problem: Columbia Sportswear Company The financial statements for the **Columbia Sportswear Company** can be found in Appendix A at the end of this book.

Required
Answer the following questions.

a. What was the total cost of Columbia's property, plant, and equipment at December 31, 2011?
b. What was the total accumulated depreciation at December 31, 2011?
c. What percentage of the total cost of property, plant, and equipment at December 31, 2011, was from building and improvements?
d. How much depreciation and amortization expense was taken in 2011?
e. What amount of property, plant, and equipment purchases (capital expenditures) occurred in 2011?

COLUMBIA
SPORTSWEAR
COMPANY

UNDER ARMOUR,
INC.

EYK9-2. Comparative Analysis Problem: Columbia Sportswear Company vs. Under Armour, Inc. The financial statements for the **Columbia Sportswear Company** can be found in Appendix A at the end of this book, and the financial statements of **Under Armour, Inc.** can be found in Appendix B (the complete annual report is available on this book's Website).

Required
a. Calculate the following ratios for Columbia Sportswear and for Under Armour, Inc. for 2011:
   1. Return on assets
   2. Asset turnover
b. Comment on your findings.

EYK9-3. Business Decision Problem Lyle Fleming, president of Fleming, Inc., wants you to resolve his dispute with Mia Gooden over the amount of a finder's fee due Gooden. Fleming hired Gooden to locate a new plant site to expand the business. By agreement, Gooden's fee was to be 15 percent of the "cost of the property (excluding the finder's fee), measured according to generally accepted accounting principles."

Gooden located Site 1 and Site 2 for Fleming to consider. Each site had a selling price of $150,000, and the geographic locations of both sites were equally acceptable to Fleming. Fleming employed an engineering firm to conduct the geological tests necessary to determine the relative quality of the two sites for construction. The tests, which cost $10,000 for each site, showed that Site 1 was superior to Site 2.

The owner of Site 1 initially gave Fleming 30 days—a reasonable period—to decide whether or not to buy the property. However, Fleming procrastinated in contracting the geological tests, and the results were not available by the end of the 30-day period. Fleming requested a two-week extension. The Site 1 owner granted Fleming the additional two weeks but charged him $6,000 for the extension (which Fleming paid). Fleming eventually bought Site 1.

Fleming sent Gooden a fee of $24,000, which was 15 percent of a cost computed as follows:

Sales price, Site 1.	$150,000
Geological tests, Site 1	10,000
Total	$160,000

Gooden believes that she is entitled to $26,400, based on a cost computed as follows:

Sales price, Site 1.	$150,000
Geological tests, Site 1	10,000
Geological tests, Site 2	10,000
Fee for time extension	6,000
Total	$176,000

Required
What fee is Gooden entitled to under the agreement? Explain.

EYK9-4.   **Financial Analysis Problem** **Best Buy Co., Inc.**, is headquartered in Minneapolis, Minnesota. The company sells brand name consumer electronics, personal computers, home office products, major appliances, entertainment software, and photographic equipment. Selected financial data for Best Buy Co. follow (amounts in millions):

BEST BUY CO., INC.

	2010	2009	2008
Total assets, beginning of year	$18,302	$15,826	$12,758
Total assets, end of year	$17,849	$18,302	$15,826
Revenues for the year	$49,747	$49,243	$45,015
Net income for the year	$ 1,277	$ 1,317	$ 1,003

Required
a.   Calculate the return on assets for 2008–2010.
b.   In 2010 and 2009 Best Buy's revenues grew by 15.6 and 24.0 percent, respectively. How did this revenue growth correspond to Best Buy's ROA for 2010 and 2009?

CRITICAL THINKING

EYK9-5.   **Accounting Research Problem** The 2011 annual report of **General Mills, Inc.**, for fiscal year 2011 is available on this book's Website. Review the consolidated statements of earnings, the consolidated balance sheets, and Notes 2 and 17.

GENERAL MILLS, INC.

Required
a.   What is General Mills' gross cost of land, buildings, and equipment at May 29, 2011?
b.   What depreciation method is used in the financial statements?
c.   How much depreciation and amortization were expensed in fiscal 2011?
d.   How much depreciation has accumulated by May 29, 2011?

    e. How much research and development cost was expensed in fiscal 2011?

    f. What is General Mills' return on assets for fiscal 2011?

EYK9-6. **Accounting Communication Activity** Peggy Zimmer, a friend of yours taking her first accounting class, is confused as to why there is a separate accumulated depreciation account. She argues that it would be much simpler to just credit the asset that is being depreciated directly instead of crediting accumulated depreciation.

Required

Explain to your friend in an informal memo a possible advantage that keeping the cost and accumulated depreciation separate can have for an analyst.

EYK9-7. **Accounting Ethics Case** Linda Tristan, assistant controller for Ag-Growth, Inc., a biotechnology firm, has concerns about the accounting analysis for the firm's purchase of a land site and building from Hylite Corporation. The price for this package purchase was $1,800,000 cash. A memorandum from the controller, Greg Fister, stated that the journal entry for this purchase should debit Land for $1,350,000, debit Building for $450,000, and credit Cash for $1,800,000. The building, a used laboratory facility, is to be depreciated over 10 years with a zero salvage value.

    The source documents supporting the transaction include two appraisals of the property, one done for Ag-Growth and one done for Hylite Corporation. The appraisal for Ag-Growth valued the land at $1,000,000 and the building at $500,000. The appraisal for Hylite Corporation (done by a different appraiser) valued the land at $1,500,000 and the building at $750,000. Negotiations between the two firms finally settled on an overall price of $1,800,000 for the land and the building.

    Tristan asked Fister how he arrived at the amounts to be recorded for the land and building since each appraisal valued the land at only twice the building's value. "Well," replied Fister, "I used the $1,500,000 land value from Hylite's appraiser and the $500,000 building value from our appraiser. That relationship shows the land to be worth three times the building's value. Using that relationship, I assigned 75 percent of our actual purchase price of $1,800,000 to the land and 25 percent of the purchase price to the building."

    "But why do it that way?" asked Tristan.

    "Because it will improve our profits, before income taxes, by $150,000 over the next decade," replied Fister.

    "But it just doesn't seem right," commented Tristan.

Required

    a. How does the accounting analysis by Fister improve profits before income taxes by $150,000 over the next decade?

    b. Is the goal of improving profits a sufficient rationale to defend the accounting analysis by Fister?

    c. Do you agree with Fister's analysis? Briefly explain.

    d. What actions are available to Tristan to resolve her concerns with Fister's analysis?

CUMMINS INC.

EYK9-8. **Corporate Social Responsibility Problem** Go to the **Cummins'** Website at http://cummins.com and navigate to the section on sustainability.

Required

    1. Articulate Cummins' approach to corporate responsibility.

    2. Cummins states that "corporate responsibility contributes directly to the long-term health, growth and profitability of our company." Explain how being a good corporate citizen may lead to increased growth and profitability.

WASTE
MANAGEMENT,
INC.

EYK9-9. **Forensic Accounting Problem** **Waste Management** is a leading provider of comprehensive trash and waste removal, recycling, and waste management services. In 2002, the Securities and Exchange Commission sued several members and former members of Waste Management's management team for fraud. Go to the S.E.C. press release at: http://www.sec.gov/news/headlines/wastemgmt6.htm to answer the following questions:

    1. What does the complaint claim about Dean L. Buntrock, the company's founder, chairman of the board, and chief executive officer?

    2. What accounting methods does the complaint claim were used by Waste Management in order to perpetuate the fraud?

EYK9-10. **Analyzing IFRS Financial Statements** Tesco PLC is the world's third largest retailer and is headquartered in the United Kingdom. The complete annual report for **Tesco PLC** for year-ended February 26, 2011, is available on this book's Website.

TESCO PLC

IFRS

Required

a.   What is Tesco's net cost of property, plant, and equipment at 2/26/2011?
b.   What depreciation method is used in the company?
c.   What is Tesco's net cost of goodwill and other intangible assets at 2/26/2011?
d.   What amortization method is used by the company?
e.   How does Tesco account for its research costs? development costs?
f.   What is Tesco's return on assets for the year ended 2/26/2011?

EYK9-11. **Working with the Takeaways** The following data (in millions) is taken from **Google**'s 2011 financial statements:

GOOGLE INC.

	2011	2010
Net sales.	$37,905	$29,321
Net income.	$ 9,737	$ 8,505
Total assets	$72,574	$57,851

Calculate Google's 2011 asset turnover and return on assets.

ANSWERS TO SELF-STUDY QUESTIONS:

1. c, (p. 407)   2. c, (pp. 411–414)   3. d, (p. 421)   4. a, (p. 423)   5. a, (p. 424)   6. c, (p. 423)
7. a, (p. 418)   8. d, (p. 425)   9. b, (p. 426)   10. a, (p. 426)   11. c, (p. 421)

YOUR TURN! SOLUTIONS

Solution 9.1

All of the costs, with the exception of the unrelated supplies, are considered to be part of the equipment's acquisition cost, and therefore, should be capitalized to the equipment account. This includes the $20,000 purchase price, along with the $1,600 sales tax, $400 freight cost, $600 installation cost, and $100 testing cost, for a total acquisition cost of $22,700. The cost of the $300 of supplies should be accounted for as a supplies inventory (an asset) and allocated to expense on the income statement as it is used.

Solution 9.2

(a) Under the straight-line method, the annual depreciation expense is calculated as ($10,000 − $2,000)/5 years = $1,600 for each year. Thus, depreciation for the second year will require the following journal entry:

Depreciation expense	1,600	
Accumulated depreciation		1,600
To record depreciation expense.		

(b) The depreciation rate for a five-year asset under the double-declining balance method is 40 percent, or [(100 percent/5 years) × 2]. And, the depreciation expense is calculated as 40 percent times the book value of the asset as of the beginning of the year. Thus, the first year depreciation is $4,000 (40 percent × $10,000) and the second year depreciation is $2,400 [40 percent × ($10,000 − $4,000)]. Thus, the required journal entry is:

Depreciation expense	2,400	
Accumulated depreciation		2,400
To record depreciation expense.		

Solution 9.3

Items (1), (2), and (4) are revenue expenditures. Item (3) increases the van's useful life and item (5) reduces the van's operating costs; consequently, items (3) and (5) are capital expenditures.

Solution 9.4

Cash	750	
Accumulated depreciation	15,000	
Loss on sale of truck	6,750	
Truck		22,500
To record the sale of truck.		

Solution 9.5

1. Copyright
2. Amortization
3. Trademark
4. Franchise
5. Patent

10

Accounting for Liabilities

PAST

Chapter 9 concluded our investigation of the accounting for assets.

PRESENT

In this chapter we turn our attention to the accounting for liabilities.

FUTURE

Chapter 11 examines the accounting for stockholders' equity.

LEARNING OBJECTIVES

1. **Describe** the nature of liabilities and **define** *current liabilities*. *(p. 450)*

2. **Illustrate** the accounting for long-term liabilities. *(p. 457)*

3. **Define** *contingent liabilities* and **explain** their disclosure in the financial statements. *(p. 466)*

4. **Define** the *current ratio, quick ratio,* and *times-interest-earned ratio* and **explain** their use. *(p. 469)*

5. Appendix 10A: **Explain** bond pricing and **illustrate** the effective interest method of amortizing bond discounts/premiums. *(p. 472)*

6. Appendix 10B: **Define** *capital leases* and *operating leases* and **distinguish** between them. *(p. 478)*

MICROSOFT CORPORATION

Microsoft Corporation is one of the world's most well-recognized companies. Founded in 1975 by Bill Gates and Paul Allen in Albuquerque, New Mexico, the company moved its headquarters in 1979 to Bellevue, Washington. That same year, Steve Ballmer joined the company and years later succeeded Gates as Microsoft's CEO. By 2012, Microsoft had global annual revenue of over $70 billion, employing over 90,000 employees in over 100 countries.

Until 2009, Microsoft remained largely debt free. The company's business model was so successful that it was unnecessary for the company to utilize debt financing. The high profit margins on the company's products enabled Microsoft to generate a significant free cash flow year in and year out and to finance its growth using internally generated operating cash flow. In 2009, however, the company issued its first bonds to the capital market. Wall Street analysts speculated that Microsoft really didn't need the cash provided by the debt issuance but rather sold the bonds to take advantage of the extremely low interest rates available at that time. Investment professionals speculated that CEO, Steve Ballmer, may have decided to "bulk up" the company's cash position in anticipation of a major corporate acquisition.

In this chapter, we examine how companies, like Microsoft, value and disclose liabilities on their balance sheets. We consider such current liabilities as accounts payable and accrued expenses payable, such noncurrent liabilities as bonds payable and term loans payable, and such contingent liabilities as pending lawsuits and environmental cleanup obligations.

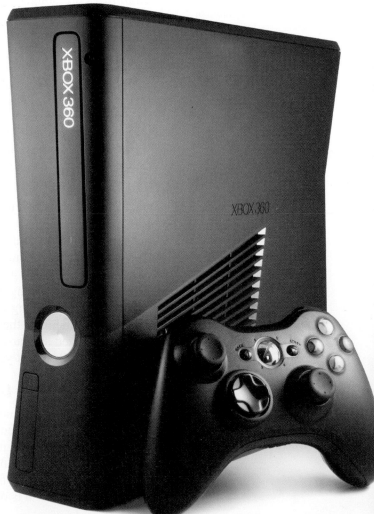

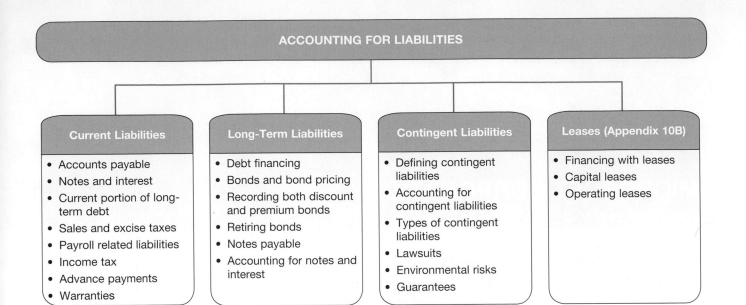

ACCOUNTING FOR LIABILITIES

Current Liabilities	Long-Term Liabilities	Contingent Liabilities	Leases (Appendix 10B)
• Accounts payable • Notes and interest • Current portion of long-term debt • Sales and excise taxes • Payroll related liabilities • Income tax • Advance payments • Warranties	• Debt financing • Bonds and bond pricing • Recording both discount and premium bonds • Retiring bonds • Notes payable • Accounting for notes and interest	• Defining contingent liabilities • Accounting for contingent liabilities • Types of contingent liabilities • Lawsuits • Environmental risks • Guarantees	• Financing with leases • Capital leases • Operating leases

CURRENT LIABILITIES

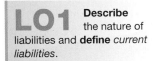

LO1 Describe the nature of liabilities and **define** *current liabilities*.

Liabilities are obligations resulting from past transactions or events that require a business to pay money, provide goods, or perform services in the future. **Current liabilities** are obligations that will require, within the coming year or the normal operating cycle, whichever is longer, (1) the use of existing current assets or (2) the creation of other current liabilities. Most current liabilities are settled by using current assets, but sometimes a current liability is settled by the issuance of another current liability. A past due account payable, for example, may be settled by issuing a short-term note payable. Liabilities are classified as current using the same time frame used to classify current assets—the longer of one year or a firm's normal operating cycle. In the following section, we consider some typical current liabilities.

Accounts Payable

In a balance sheet listing of current liabilities, amounts due to short-term creditors on notes payable and accounts payable are commonly shown first. Short-term creditors send invoices specifying the amount owed for goods or services that they have provided. As a result, the amount of any account or note payable is easily determined because it is based on the invoices received from a creditor.

At the end of an accounting period, accountants need to know whether any goods are in transit and what the shipping terms are for such goods. If the goods are shipped F.O.B. shipping point, ownership of the goods has transferred to the buyer and an account payable should be recorded at year-end (as well as an increase in inventory) even though the goods and an invoice have not yet arrived.

Notes Payable and Interest

Promissory notes are often issued in transactions when the credit period is longer than the 30 or 60 days typical for accounts payable. Although promissory notes are commonly used in credit sales transactions involving equipment and real property, a note may sometimes be exchanged for merchandise. A note payable may also be substituted for an account payable when an extension of the usual credit period is granted. And, a promissory note is prepared when a loan is obtained from a bank.

Interest is a charge for the use of money. Consequently, interest incurred on a promissory note is an expense to the maker of a note. Since businesses are required under GAAP to distinguish between operating and nonoperating expenses in their income statements, interest expense is reported under the Other Income and Expense category to highlight the fact that this expense is not considered to be an operating expense, and instead, is a financing expense of the business.

Interest on promissory notes can be structured in either of two ways: (1) it is an amount paid in addition to the face amount of the note, called the *add-on interest method*, or (2) it is an amount included in the face amount of the note, called the *discount method*. The add-on interest method is most commonly used, and consequently, we focus on that approach.

Add-On Interest Method   *Most common*

Interest on a short-term note payable using the *add-on interest method* is paid at the maturity date of the note. The formula for determining the amount of interest to be paid is as follows:

$$\textbf{Interest} = \textbf{Principal} \times \textbf{Interest rate} \times \textbf{Interest time}$$

The principal, or face amount, of a note is the amount borrowed. The interest rate is the annual rate of interest. Interest time is the fraction of a year that a note is outstanding.

When a note is written for a certain number of months, time is expressed in twelfths of a year. For example, interest on a three-month note for $4,000, with a nine percent annual interest rate is:

$$\textbf{Interest} = \textbf{\$4,000} \times \textbf{0.09} \times \textbf{3/12} = \textbf{\$90}$$

When a note's duration—that is, the length of the borrowing period—is given in days, time is expressed as a fraction of a year; the numerator is the number of days that the note will be outstanding and the denominator is 360 days. (Some lenders use 360 days, while others use 365 days; we will use 360 days in our examples.) For example, interest on a 60-day note for $3,000, with a nine percent annual interest rate is:

$$\textbf{Interest} = \textbf{\$3,000} \times \textbf{0.09} \times \textbf{60/360} = \textbf{\$45}$$

Determining the Maturity Date of a Note

When a note's duration is expressed in days, the exact number of days in each calendar month is counted to determine the note's **maturity date**. For example, a 90-day note dated July 21 has an October 19 maturity date, determined as follows:

10 days in July (**remainder of month, 31 days minus 21 days**)
31 days in August
30 days in September
19 days in October (**number of days required to total 90**)
90

If the duration of a note is expressed in months, the maturity date is determined by counting the number of months from the date of issue. For example, a two-month note dated January 31 matures on March 31, a three-month note of the same date matures on April 30 (the last day of the month), and a four-month note matures on May 31.

Recording Notes Payable and Interest Expense

When a note payable is exchanged to settle an account payable, a journal entry is made to reflect the note payable and to reduce the balance of the related account payable. For example, suppose that the Jordon Company sold $12,000 of merchandise on account to Bowman Company. On October 1, after the regular credit period had expired, Bowman Company gave the Jordon Company a 60-day, nine percent note for $12,000. As a consequence, the Bowman Company makes the following journal entry on October 1:

A	=	L	+	SE
−12,000				
+12,000				

Oct. 1	Accounts payable—Jordon Company	12,000	
	Notes payable—Jordon Company		12,000
	Gave 60-day, 9 percent note in payment of account.		

If the Bowman Company pays the note on the November 30 maturity date, the company makes the following journal entry:

A	=	L	+	SE
−12,180		−12,000		−180 Exp

Nov. 30	Notes payable—Jordon Company	12,000	
	Interest expense	180	
	Cash		12,180
	Paid note to Jordon Company ($12,000 × 0.09 × 60/360 = $180).		

Interest Payable

At the end of the fiscal year, adjusting entries must be made to reflect any accrued, but unpaid, interest expense. For example, assume that the Bowman Company has one note payable outstanding at December 31, 2012, to Garcia Company, which is dated December 21, 2012, has a principal amount of $6,000, an interest rate of 12 percent, and a maturity date of February 19, 2013. The adjusting entry that Bowman Company makes at December 31, 2012, is as follows:

A	=	L	+	SE
		+20		−20 Exp

2012			
Dec. 31	Interest expense	20	
	Interest payable		20
	To accrue interest expense on the note to Garcia Company		
	($6,000 × 0.12 × 10/360 = $20).		

When the note payable to Garcia Company is subsequently paid on February 19, 2013, the Bowman Company makes the following entry:

A	=	L	+	SE
−6,120		−6,000		−100
		−20		Exp

2013			
Feb. 19	Notes payable—Garcia Company	6,000	
	Interest payable	20	
	Interest expense	100	
	Cash		6,120
	Paid principal and interest to Garcia Company		
	($6,000 × 0.12 × 50/360 = $100).		

Current Portion of Long-Term Debt

The repayment of many long-term obligations involves a series of principal payment installments over several years. To report liabilities involving installments properly, any principal due within one year (or the operating cycle, if longer) is reported as a current liability on the balance sheet. Failure to reclassify the currently maturing portion of any long-term debt due within the next year as a current liability can mislead readers regarding the total current obligations of a business.

Sales and Excise Taxes Payable

Many products and services are subject to sales and excise taxes. The laws governing these taxes usually require the selling firm to collect the tax at the time of sale and to send the collections periodically to the appropriate tax collection agency. For example, assume that a particular product selling for $1,000 is subject to a six percent state sales tax and a ten percent federal excise tax. Each tax should be figured on the basic sale price only. The sale is recorded as follows:

			A = L + SE
Accounts receivable (*or* Cash)	1,160		+1,160 +60 +1,000
Sales revenue		1,000	Rev
Sales tax payable		60	+100
Excise tax payable		100	
To record sales and related taxes.			

The selling firm will periodically complete a tax reporting form and send the period's tax collections to the appropriate collection agency. The tax liability accounts are then debited and the Cash account is credited.

Payroll-Related Liabilities

Salaries and wages represent a major outlay in the cost structure of many businesses. For service firms, the largest expense category is usually the compensation paid to employees and the related payroll taxes and fringe benefits paid by the employer. Three types of current liabilities arise from a company's payroll: (1) accrued salaries and wages payable (discussed in Chapter 4), (2) amounts withheld from employees' paychecks by the employer, and (3) payroll taxes and fringe benefits paid by the employer.

Amounts Withheld from Employee Paychecks

When a business hires an employee, the firm establishes the employee's rate of pay. At the end of each pay period, the employer uses the employee's salary to determine the employee's **gross pay**, the amount earned before any withholdings. The employer then subtracts any withheld amounts to determine the employee's **net pay**, the amount of the paycheck. Exhibit 10-1 demonstrates these relations.

Amounts Withheld by Legal Mandate Some amounts withheld from an employee's gross pay are mandated by law. These amounts include federal income tax, state income tax, Social Security taxes, and Medicare taxes.

The amount of federal income tax withheld from an employee's paycheck is determined by referencing a table that uses the amount of the employee's gross pay, the employee's marital status, and the number of withholding allowances to which the employee is entitled to calculate the amount to be withheld. Most states require employers to use similar information in calculating state income tax withholding.

The **Federal Insurance Contributions Act (FICA)** dictates the percentages to be used in calculating the withholding amounts for Social Security and Medicare. The rates for employee withholding for 2012 were 4.2 percent of the first $110,100 of gross pay for Social Security and 1.45 percent of all gross pay for Medicare.[1]

Amounts Withheld by Employee Request Other amounts are withheld from an employee's gross pay by employee request. These amounts include premiums for life or health insurance, union dues, and payments into a self funded retirement plan.

Recording Gross Pay and Net Pay

To illustrate the recording of employee gross and net pay, assume that the payroll for the week ended August 15 for Centerline Company totaled $6,000. Amounts withheld were $1,200 for federal income tax, $405 for state income tax, $252 for Social Security, and $87 for Medicare. In addition, Centerline withheld $100 for union dues and $320 for health insurance premiums. Centerline makes the following entry to record the payroll:

---

[1] For the years 2011 and 2012, Congress legislated a temporary payroll tax holiday that reduced the employee rate from 6.2 percent to 4.2 percent. This legislation was designed to put more money into the hands of American workers.

A	=	L	+	SE			
		+1,200		−6,000			
				Exp			
		+405					
		+339					
		+100					
		+320					
		+3,636					

Aug. 15	Salaries and wage expense	6,000	
	Federal income tax withholding payable		1,200
	State income tax withholding payable		405
	FICA taxes payable		339
	Union dues payable		100
	Health insurance premiums payable		320
	Payroll payable		3,636
	To record the payroll for the week ended August 15.		

At the appropriate time, the employer will remit the amounts withheld from employees to the proper recipients. To the extent that any of the payable amounts are not paid at the end of an accounting period, they are reported as current liabilities.

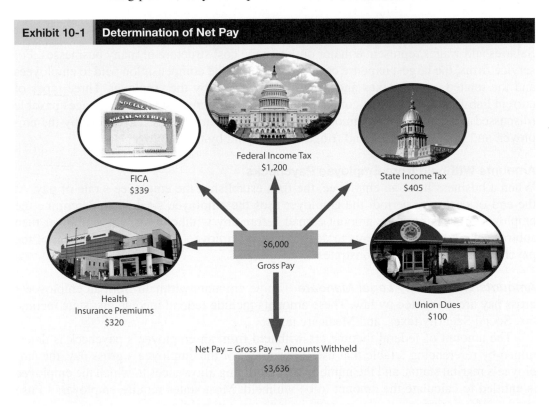

Exhibit 10-1   Determination of Net Pay

FICA $339

Federal Income Tax $1,200

State Income Tax $405

$6,000 Gross Pay

Health Insurance Premiums $320

Union Dues $100

Net Pay = Gross Pay − Amounts Withheld

$3,636

Payroll Taxes Paid by the Employer

An employer pays three types of taxes on the gross payroll amount: FICA taxes (Social Security and Medicare), federal unemployment tax, and state unemployment tax.

Each employer is required to pay an amount equal to the FICA taxes withheld from the employees' gross pay (2012 rates were 6.2 percent of the first $110,100 of gross pay for Social Security and 1.45 percent of gross pay for Medicare). As a result, the total Social Security collected in 2012 for each employee was 10.4 percent of the first $110,100 of gross pay, and the total Medicare collected was 2.9 percent of all gross pay.

Federal and state unemployment taxes are levied only on employers as a percentage of the gross payroll, subject to various limits. The current federal unemployment tax rate is 6.0 percent of the first $7,000 of an employee's gross pay. However, an employer is entitled to a credit against this tax for unemployment taxes paid to the state. The maximum credit allowed is 5.4 percent of the first $7,000 of gross pay. Many states set their basic unemployment tax rate at this maximum credit. In these states, the effective federal unemployment tax rate is 0.6 percent (6.0 percent − 5.4 percent), and the effective state unemployment tax rate is 5.4 percent.

Recording Payroll Taxes Paid by the Employer   Assume that the payroll for the week ended August 15 for Centerline Company totaled $6,000. Amounts withheld included $372 for Social Security and $87 for Medicare. Federal unemployment tax payable for the week was $36 (0.6 percent) and state unemployment tax payable was $324 (5.4 percent). Centerline makes the following entry to record its payroll taxes:

Aug. 15	Payroll tax expense	819	
	FICA taxes payable		459
	Federal unemployment tax payable		36
	State unemployment tax payable		324
	To record the payroll taxes for the week ended August 15.		

A = L + SE
+459   −831 Exp
+36
+324

    If payroll taxes have not been remitted to the proper government agency by the end of the accounting period, they are classified as current liabilities in the balance sheet.

Archer Corporation had the following payroll data for April:

Office salaries.	$ 40,000
Sales salaries	86,000
Federal income taxes withheld.	25,600
Health insurance premiums withheld. . . . . . ∙.	1,850
Union dues withheld.	950
Salaries (included above):	
Subject to both FICA taxes.	126,000
Subject to federal unemployment taxes.	76,000
Subject to state unemployment taxes	88,000

    The combined FICA tax rate (for both employee withholding and employer) is 7.65 percent (6.2 percent plus 1.45 percent), the federal unemployment compensation tax rate is 0.6 percent, and the state unemployment compensation tax rate is 5.4 percent. The amounts subject to these taxes are given above.

Required
Prepare journal entries to record the following on April 30:
a. Accrual of the payroll.
b. Payment of the net payroll.
c. Accrual of the employer's payroll taxes.
d. Payment of all liabilities related to the payroll. (Assume that all liabilities are paid at the same time.)

YOUR TURN! 10.1

The solution is on page 501.

Income Taxes Payable

The U.S. Federal Government, most states, and some municipalities levy income taxes against corporations, individuals, estates, and trusts. Sole proprietorships and partnerships are not taxable entities—their owners include any business income on the owner's personal income tax return.

    The tax due is determined in accordance with tax law, rulings by taxing agencies, and court decisions. Because the administration of tax law is quite complex and many honest differences exist in their interpretation, the tax obligation reported on a tax return is only an estimate until the government reviews and accepts a firm's (or individual's) calculations.

    Because corporations are separate taxable entities, they incur a legal obligation for income taxes whenever income is earned. Therefore, corporate financial statements routinely include income tax liabilities. For example, business income taxes of $8,000 are recorded as follows:

Income tax expense	8,000	
Income tax payable		8,000
To record estimated income tax.		

A = L + SE
+8,000   −8,000 Exp

Corporations usually pay their estimated income taxes quarterly, with an annual tax return and final payment due within a few months following the end of a calendar year. Thus, any liability for income taxes in the financial statements is classified as a current liability since payment is expected in the short-term.

Advance Payments—Unearned Revenue

Airline tickets, gift cards, cruise-line tickets, season football tickets, and cellular phone connection charges are examples of advance payments for services. A customer pays cash in advance for these services and the service provider agrees to provide future services. As an example, assume that **Southwest Airlines Co.** sells a ticket for $400 on March 20 for travel on May 25. American makes the following entry when the ticket is sold:

A = L + SE
+400   +400

Mar. 20	Cash	400	
	Unearned ticket revenue		400
	To record the sale of an airline ticket.		

When the passenger takes the scheduled flight, the airline makes the following entry:

A = L + SE
     −400   +400
           Rev

May 25	Unearned ticket revenue	400	
	Ticket revenue		400
	To record ticket revenue earned.		

Liabilities for Product Warranties

Many firms guarantee their products for a period of time following their sale. A proper matching of sales revenue and expenses requires that the estimated cost of honoring and servicing these **product warranties** be recognized as an expense in the period of sale rather than in a later period when the warranty costs may actually be incurred and paid.

     To illustrate, assume that a firm sells a product for $300 per unit, which includes a 30-day warranty against defects. Past experience indicates that three percent of the units will prove defective and that the average repair cost will be $40 per defective unit. Furthermore, during a particular month, product sales were $240,000, and 13 of the units sold during the month were defective and were repaired. Using this information, the accrued liability for product warranties at the end of the month can be calculated as follows:

Number of units sold ($240,000/$300)	800
Rate of projected defective units	× 0.03
Total units expected to fail	24
Less: Units that failed in the month of sale	**13**
Units expected to fail in the remainder of the warranty period	11
Average repair cost per unit	× $40
Estimated liability for product warranty at end of month	$440

This accrued liability is recorded at the end of the month of sale as follows:

A = L + SE
     +440   −440
           Exp

	Product warranty expense	440	
	Estimated liability for product warranty		440
	To record estimated warranty expense.		

     When a unit fails in a future period, the repair costs will be recorded by debiting the Estimated Liability for Product Warranty account and crediting Cash, Supplies, and so forth.

Matching Concept	**PRINCIPLE ALERT**

The accounting for product warranties follows the *expense recognition (matching) concept*. This accounting concept states that expenses must be recorded in the same accounting period as the revenues they help generate. Product warranties make a company's products more attractive to buyers; consequently, product warranties help generate incremental sales revenues. Hence, one of the expenses that must be matched with sales revenues is the cost of honoring and servicing a product warranty. Because most warranty costs are incurred in periods following the period of sale, it is necessary to estimate these costs and record them in the same period when the sale of the product occurs, to achieve a proper matching of revenues and expenses.

Aligning Business and Citizenship	**CORPORATE SOCIAL RESPONSIBILITY**

Being socially responsible does not mean simply trying to solve the world's problems single-handedly. To do things that one has no particular competence in is wasteful, and it makes far more sense and is far more responsible to do things to help others using one's strengths. Few would contest that one of **Microsoft Corporation**'s strengths is technology. Although technology has led to phenomenal advances in productivity and economic growth in developed countries, much of the world still has little access to this technology. Microsoft, through its Unlimited Potential effort, brings the benefits of "relevant, accessible and affordable technology to people at the middle and bottom of the economic pyramid." Unlimited Potential combines Microsoft's technology, business strategies, and citizenship efforts with global partners to take aim at the needs of local communities. The Unlimited Potential program addresses three interrelated areas of education, innovation, and job creation. The impact of these partnerships spans the world, with 110 Microsoft Innovation Centers in 60 countries and 29,000 Microsoft-supported Community Technology Centers in 102 countries.

LONG-TERM LIABILITIES

At various times during a business's operating life, the business will need to secure long-term funds to finance its operations or the acquisition of various operating assets. When a business elects to finance its growth with long-term borrowing, it may do so by issuing bonds or borrowing money with long-term notes. A **bond** is a long-term debt instrument that promises to pay interest periodically as well as a principal amount at maturity, to the bond investor. In the United States, bond interest is usually paid semiannually. The principal amount is referred to as the bond's face value (because it is printed on the face of the bond certificate), par value, or maturity value. Whereas bonds are usually issued to the general public with a large number of buyers, long-term notes are usually arranged with a single lender. The borrower typically signs a note payable and the debt is referred to as a **term loan**.

LO2 Illustrate the accounting for long-term liabilities.

Types of Bonds

Bond agreements may be formulated to capitalize on certain lending situations, appeal to special investor groups, or provide special repayment patterns.

Secured bonds, for example, pledge specific property as security for meeting the terms of the bond agreement. The specific title of the bonds may indicate the type of property pledged—for example, real estate mortgage bonds (land or buildings), chattel mortgage bonds (machinery or equipment), and collateral trust bonds (negotiable securities).

Bonds that have no specific property pledged as security for their repayment are called **debenture bonds**. Buyers of debenture bonds rely on a borrower's general credit reputation. Because a lender's risk is usually greater than with secured bonds, the sale of unsecured bonds may require offering a higher rate of interest to attract bond buyers.

The maturity dates of **serial bonds** are staggered over a series of years. For example, a serial bond issue of $15 million may provide for $1 million of the bonds to mature each year for 15 years. An advantage of serial bonds is that bond investors can choose bonds with maturity dates that correspond with their desired length of investment.

Convertible bonds grant the bondholder the right to convert the bonds into a company's common stock at some specific exchange (or conversion) ratio. This provision gives an investor the security of being a creditor during a certain stage of a firm's life, with the option of becoming a stockholder if the firm becomes sufficiently profitable. Because the conversion feature is attractive to potential investors, a company may issue convertible bonds at a lower interest rate than it would pay without the conversion feature.

Zero-coupon bonds are bonds that pay no periodic interest payments but are issued at a substantial discount from their face value. The face value is paid to the bondholder at maturity. The total interest implicit in the bond contract is the difference between the bond's original issue price and its face value at maturity. For example, a five-year, $1,000 zero-coupon bond issued for $713 will pay the lender $1,000 at the end of the five years. The total interest associated with this bond is $287 ($1,000 – $713). Zero-coupon bonds are particularly helpful to a borrower when the project being financed with the bond proceeds provides no cash inflows until the bond maturity date.

Exhibit 10-2	Bond Certificate

Bond Issuer ⟶

General Electric Company

Face value ⟶ **$5,000,000,000**

Interest rate ⟶ **5% Notes due 2013**

Issue price: 99.626%

We will pay interest on the notes semiannually on February 1 and August 1 of each year, beginning August 1, 2003. The notes will mature on February 1, 2013. We may not redeem the notes prior to maturity.

Maturity date ⟶

The notes will be unsecured obligations and rank equally with our other unsecured debt securities that are not subordinated obligations. The notes will be issued in registered form in denominations of $1,000.

Neither the Securities and Exchange Commission nor any state securities commission has approved or disapproved of the notes or determined if this prospectus supplement or the accompanying prospectus is truthful or complete. Any representation to the contrary is a criminal offense.

	Per Note	Total
Public Offering Price(1)	99.626%	$4,981,300,000
Underwriting Discounts	.425%	$ 21,250,000
Proceeds to General Electric Company (before expenses)	99.201%	$4,960,050,000

(1) Plus accrued interest from January 28, 2003, if settlement occurs after that date.

The underwriters expect to deliver the notes in book-entry form only through the facilities of The Depository Trust Company, Clearstream, Luxembourg or the Euroclear System, as the case may be, on or about January 28, 2003.

Joint Bookrunners

Morgan Stanley   **Salomon Smith Barney**

Senior Co-Managers

| Banc of America Securities LLC
Goldman. Sachs & Co. | Credit Suisse First Boston
JPMorgan
UBS Warburg | Deutsche Bank Securities
Merrill Lynch & Co. |

Co-Managers

| Banc One Capital Markets, Inc.
BNP PARIBAN
HSBC
Utendahl Capital Partners, L.P. | Barclays Capital
Dresdner Kleinwort Wasserstein
Loop Capital Markets
The Williams Capital Group, L.P. | Blaylock & Partners, L.P.
Guzman & Company
Ormes Capital Markets, Inc. |

Bond Risk Ratings	**ACCOUNTING IN PRACTICE**

The relative riskiness of different bonds may vary considerably. Bond investors who want to know the relative quality of a particular bond issue can consult a bond-rating service. Two major firms that rate the riskiness of bonds are **Standard & Poor's Corporation** (S&P) and **Moody's Investors Service** (Moody's). The rating categories used by these firms are similar. The schedule below shows the relationship between the ratings and the degree of risk using Standard & Poor's rating system:

Low Risk							High Risk
AAA	AA	A	BBB	BB	B	CCC	D

I- - - - - - - - - Investment Grade Bonds - - - - - - - - -I- - - - - - - - Junk Bonds - - - - - - - -I

Investment grade bonds are highly-rated bonds with little risk that the issuing company will fail to pay interest as scheduled or fail to repay the principal at a bond's maturity. Junk bonds, on the other hand, are low-quality, high-yield bonds. In the S&P rating system, junk bonds are any bond rated BB and lower. Generally, bonds with poor credit ratings must offer higher interest rates than highly-rated bonds to attract potential buyers.

A.K.A. Junk bonds are often referred to as *high-yield bonds* because of the higher yield rates that typically accompany this type of debt investment.

Bond Features

Bonds with a **call provision** allow the bond issuer to call in the bonds for redemption. Usually, an extra amount or premium must be paid to the holders of a called bond. A call provision offers borrowers additional financing flexibility that may be significant if funds become available at interest rates substantially lower than those currently being paid on the bonds. Borrowers can, in effect, also "call" any of their bonds by buying them in the open market.

A **sinking fund provision** requires that a borrower retire a portion of its outstanding bonds each year or, in some bond issues, make payments each year to a trustee who is responsible for managing the funds needed to retire the bonds at maturity. The orderly retirement of bonds, or the accumulation of funds needed at maturity, as required by a sinking fund provision is generally viewed as making any bond safer (less risky) for the bondholders.

Microsoft Bond Issuance and Company Value	**ACCOUNTING IN PRACTICE**

As noted in the opening feature story, **Microsoft** was essentially debt free until 2009. Following the $3.75 billion in bonds that Microsoft issued in late 2009, part of a larger $6 billion debt issue that the board of directors approved, analysts weighed in on why they thought this occurred. Noting that Microsoft also authorized a plan to buy back $40 billion of its own stock over the following five years, Sid Parakh, an analyst at McAdams Wright Ragen stated, "They said a few months ago they would like to leverage the balance sheets; that's what they're doing. Lowering the cost of capital will probably benefit shareholder value in the long term."

Bond Prices

Bonds are typically sold in units of $1,000 face (maturity) value, and the market price is expressed as a percentage of face value. Thus, a $1,000 face value bond that is quoted at 98 will sell for $980. Generally, bond prices fluctuate in response to changes in market interest rates, which are determined by government monetary policies (managing the demand and supply of money) and economic expectations. Bond prices are also affected by the financial outlook for the issuing firm.

A bond specifies a pattern of future cash flows, usually a series of interest payments and a single payment at maturity equal to the bond's face value. The amount of the

A.K.A. A bond's face value is also referred to as its *maturity value, stated value,* or *settlement value.*

A.K.A. A bond's coupon rate of interest is also referred to as its *nominal rate* or *stated rate* of interest.

periodic interest payment is determined by the **coupon rate** stated on the bond certificate. Interest rates are usually quoted as annual rates, so the coupon rate will need to be converted to a per period interest rate when interest is paid more than once a year. For example, in the U.S., bond interest is usually paid semiannually, with the payments six months apart. Thus, the amount of interest paid semiannually is calculated by multiplying one-half the coupon rate of interest times the bond's face value.

A bond's market price is determined by discounting the bond's future cash flows (both its principal and interest payments) to the present using the current **market rate of interest** for the bond as the discount rate, a process known as *computing the bond's present value.* The market rate is the rate of return investors expect on their investment.

A.K.A. A bond's market rate of interest is also referred to as its *real rate of interest* or its *effective yield rate.*

IFRS ALERT!

U.S. GAAP and IFRS are substantially aligned when it comes to the reporting of liabilities. Under both accounting systems, for example, current liabilities (Accounts Payable) are reported at their settlement or future value, or the amount of money required to satisfy the obligation when it becomes due. Similarly, both systems require that long-term liabilities, like Bonds Payable, be reported at their present value, or the amount of money necessary to currently satisfy the obligation. Where the two systems diverge is in regards to the reporting of some contingent liabilities (to be discussed shortly).

When issued, a bond's price may be equal to, less than, or greater than its face value. Bonds sell at *face value* when the market rate of interest equals the bond's coupon rate. Bonds sell at a *discount* (less than face value) when the market interest rate exceeds the bond's coupon rate; and, bonds sell at a *premium* (more than face value) when the market interest rate is less than the bond's coupon rate.

Since bonds are usually printed and sold at different times, the market rate and coupon rate will often differ. Market rates and coupon rates are frequently stated in percentage terms, although increasingly, these rates are stated as "basis points." One percentage point is equal to one hundred basis points. Thus, a bond with a coupon rate of three percent is said to have a coupon rate of 300 basis points.

Exhibit 10-3 shows the calculation of a bond's selling price using different market rates of interest. (See Appendix 10A for a discussion of the calculation of a bond's present value.) The bond is a $1,000, eight percent annual coupon rate, four-year bond with interest payable semiannually; the periodic interest payment is $40 ($1,000 × 0.08 × 1/2). As shown in the exhibit, the bond will:

1. Sell at a *discount* ($936 bond price) when the market rate (ten percent) exceeds the coupon rate (eight percent).

2. Sell at *face value* ($1,000 bond price) when the market rate (eight percent) equals the coupon rate (eight percent).

3. Sell at a *premium* ($1,070 bond price) when the market rate (six percent) is less than the coupon rate (eight percent).

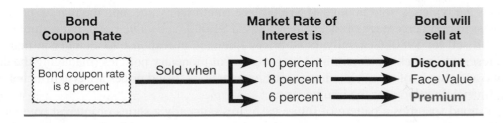

Exhibit 10-3	Calculation of Bond Selling Price at Different Market Rates		

Four-year $1,000 bond, eight percent annual coupon rate, interest payable semiannually. Eight semiannual interest payments of $40 ($1,000 × 0.08 × 1/2)

	Yield Rate, Compounded Semiannually		
	10%	**8%**	**6%**
Present value of $1,000 at maturity			
$1,000 × 0.677 present value factor*....... =	**$677**		
$1,000 × 0.731 present value factor .... =		$ 731	
$1,000 × 0.789 present value factor .... =			$ 789
Present value of eight $40 interest payments (rounded to nearest dollar)			
$40 × 6.463 present value factor* .... =	**259**		
$40 × 6.733 present value factor .... =		269	
$40 × 7.020 present value factor.......... =			281
Bond selling price........................	**$936**	$1,000	$1,070
Bond priced at	**Discount**	Face value	Premium

*See Appendix 10A for a discussion of present value factors.

Recording Bonds

Bonds Issued at Face Value

To provide a simple illustration, we use a bond with a short period to maturity. Assume that on December 31, 2012, Reid, Inc., issues at face value $100,000 of eight percent bonds that mature in four years with interest paid on June 30 and December 31. The following entry records the bond, which is sold at its face value:

2012			
Dec. 31	Cash	100,000	
	Bonds payable		100,000
	To record the issuance of bonds.		

A   =   L   + SE
+100,000 +100,000

Interest of $4,000 ($100,000 × 0.08 × 6/12) will be paid on each of the eight payment dates (four years, semiannual payments). For example, the entry on June 30, 2013, the first interest payment date, is:

2013			
June 30	Bond interest expense	4,000	
	Cash		4,000
	To record the payment of semiannual interest on bonds.		

A   = L +   SE
−4,000   −4,000
              Exp

When the bonds mature, Reid, Inc., records their retirement as follows (this assumes the December 31 interest payment is separately recorded):

2016			
Dec. 31	Bonds payable	100,000	
	Cash		100,000
	To record the retirement of bonds.		

A   =   L   + SE
−100,000 −100,000

Issuance Between Interest Dates

Not all bonds are sold on the exact day on which their interest payment period begins. Investors who buy bonds after the interest period begins are expected to "buy" any interest that has accrued on the bonds. Such bonds are said to be sold at a given price "plus accrued interest." The accrued interest is returned to the investor at the next interest payment date. This procedure simplifies the bond issuer's administrative work. Regardless of when bonds are issued, a full six months' interest is paid to all bondholders on each interest payment date.

To illustrate, let us assume that Reid, Inc. sold its $100,000, eight percent, four-year bonds at 100 plus accrued interest on February 28, 2013, instead of on December 31, 2012. The following journal entry is made:

A	=	L	+ SE
+101,333		+100,000	
		+1,333	

2013			
Feb. 28	Cash	101,333	
	Bonds payable		100,000
	Bond interest payable		1,333
	To record bond issuance at 100 plus two months' accrued interest.		

The interest accrued on the bonds on February 28 is $1,333 ($100,000 × 0.08 × 2/12, rounded). On the first interest payment date, June 30, 2013, Reid, Inc., makes the following entry:

A	=	L	+ SE
−4,000		−1,333	−2,667 Exp

2013			
June 30	Bond interest payable	1,333	
	Bond interest expense	2,667	
	Cash		4,000
	To record the payment of semiannual interest on bonds payable.		

Bond interest expense recorded by Reid relates only to the four months since the bonds were issued.

Bonds Issued at a Discount

If the coupon rate of interest on the bonds issued is less than the current market rate, the bonds will be sold at a price less than their face value. In such cases, investors "discount" the price of the bonds to enable the buyer to earn the current market rate of interest. For example, assume that Reid, Inc.'s $100,000 issue of eight percent, four-year bonds is sold on December 31, 2012, for $93,552. This price permits investors to earn an interest rate of ten percent. (For calculations, please see Appendix 10A.) The following entry records the issuance of the bonds at a discount:

A	=	L	+ SE
+93,552		−6,448	
		+100,000	

2012			
Dec. 31	Cash	93,552	
	Discount on bonds payable	**6,448**	
	Bonds payable		100,000
	To record the issuance of bonds.		

The $6,448 discount is not an immediate loss or expense to Reid, Inc. It represents an adjustment of interest expense over the life of the bonds. This can be illustrated by comparing the funds that Reid, Inc., receives with the funds it must pay to the bondholders. Regardless of their selling price, the bonds represent an agreement to pay $132,000 to the bondholders ($100,000 principal plus eight semiannual interest payments of $4,000 each).

Total funds paid to bondholders	$132,000
Total funds received from bond sale	(93,552)
Difference equals total interest expense	38,448
Total semiannual interest payments ([$100,000 × 8% = $8,000] × 4 years) . .	(32,000)
Increase in interest expense beyond semiannual interest payments	
(aka *bond discount*)	**$ 6,448**

The total interest expense for this four-year bond issue is $38,448, the difference between the total cash paid to the bondholders and the proceeds from the sale of the bonds. The semiannual interest payments to bondholders total $32,000, so an additional $6,448 must be recognized as interest expense over the life of the bonds. The $6,448 is the amount of the bond discount. To reflect the larger periodic interest expense, the bond discount is *amortized over the eight interest payment periods*. Amortization of a bond discount means that, periodically, an amount is transferred from the Discount on Bonds Payable account to the Bond Interest Expense account.

There are two methods of bond amortization: the straight-line method and the effective interest method. Under the *straight-line method*, equal amounts are transferred from bond discount to interest expense for each interest payment period. The *effective interest method*, on the other hand, reflects a constant rate of interest over the life of the bonds. We use the effective interest method in Appendix 10A since that is the method more commonly used in the bond market.

Bonds Issued at a Premium

If the market rate of interest had been below the eight percent offered by Reid, Inc., investors would have been willing to pay a premium to buy the bonds. Suppose that the **effective interest rate** was six percent. Reid Inc.'s $100,000, eight percent, four-year bonds would sell for $106,980 (for calculations, please see Appendix 10A). The issuance of the bonds on December 31, 2012, is recorded as follows:

2012			
Dec. 31	Cash	106,980	
	Bonds payable		100,000
	Premium on bonds payable		**6,980**
	To record issuance of bonds.		

A = L + SE
+106,980 +100,000
+6,980

When bonds are issued at a premium, the book value of the bond liability is determined by adding the Premium on Bonds Payable account balance to the Bonds Payable account balance.

Like a bond discount, a bond premium is considered an adjustment of interest expense over the life of the bonds. We saw that a bond discount represents the excess of total interest expense over the total semiannual interest payments. A similar analysis shows that a bond premium represents the amount by which the total semiannual interest payments exceed the total interest expense. The analysis begins by comparing the total funds that will be paid to the bondholders over the four years (again, it is $132,000) with the proceeds received when the bonds are issued:

Total funds paid to bondholders	$132,000
Total funds received from bond sale	(106,980)
Difference equals total interest expense	25,020
Total semiannual interest payments ([$100,000 × 8% = $8,000] × 4 years) . . .	(32,000)
Decrease in interest expense below semiannual interest payments (aka *bond premium*)	$ 6,980

The total interest expense for this four-year bond issue is $25,020, an amount that is $6,980 less than the total semiannual interest payments to be made to bondholders. The $6,980 is the amount of the bond premium. The bond premium is amortized to cause the periodic interest expense to be less than the semiannual interest payment.

Year-End Adjustments

When a periodic interest payment does not correspond with the fiscal year-end, an adjusting entry should be recorded reflecting the amount of interest expense incurred but not yet recorded. The adjusting entry includes a pro rata amortization of bond discount or bond premium for the portion of the year involved.

PRINCIPLE ALERT	**Matching Concept**
	The adjusting entry to record interest expense incurred but not yet recorded is an application of the *expense recognition (matching) concept*. This accounting concept states that all expenses incurred to generate sales revenue must be recorded, regardless of when the expense is paid in cash. Interest is a charge for the use of money, and this charge is incurred every day that a borrower has use of, and benefits from, borrowed funds.

Bonds Payable Disclosed on the Balance Sheet

Bonds payable that mature more than one year in the future are classified as long-term liabilities on the balance sheet. Bonds payable maturing within the next year, on the other hand, are classified as current liabilities. The Discount on Bonds Payable is classified as a deduction from and Premium on Bonds Payable as an addition to the face value of the bonds reported in the balance sheet. Many companies do not separately disclose the Discount on Bonds Payable account or the Premium on Bonds Payable account on their publicly disseminated balance sheet, but rather net these amounts against the Bonds Payable account.

At December 31, 2013, the Reid, Inc., bonds issued at a discount (see Exhibit 10A-2) appear on Reid's balance sheet as follows:

Bonds payable	$100,000	
Less: Discount on bonds payable	5,058	$94,942

On the same date, the Reid Inc. bonds issued at a premium (see Exhibit 10A-3) appear as follows:

Bonds payable	$100,000	
Add: Premium on bonds payable.	5,375	$105,375

Retirement of Bonds Before Maturity

Bonds are usually retired at their maturity dates with a journal entry debiting the Bonds Payable account and crediting the Cash account for the face value of the bonds. However, bonds can be retired before maturity—for example, to take advantage of more attractive financing terms. In accounting for the retirement of bonds before maturity, the following steps are used:

1. Remove the book value of the bonds being retired from the accounts (that is, remove the Bonds Payable amount and any related bond premium or discount).

2. Record the cash paid to retire the bonds.

3. Recognize any difference between the bonds' book value and the cash paid as a gain or loss on bond retirement.

To illustrate, assume that the Reid, Inc., bonds issued for $106,980 in our previous example were called for retirement at 105 at the end of 2015, after paying the semiannual interest on December 31, 2015. According to Exhibit 10A-3, the bonds' book value at the end of 2015 is $101,865. The following entry records the bond retirement:

A = L + SE	2015			
−105,000 −100,000 −3,135	Dec. 31	Bonds payable	100,000	
−1,865 Loss		Premium on bonds payable	1,865	
		Loss on bond retirement	3,135	
		Cash		105,000
		To retire bonds at 105 and record loss on retirement.		

Long-Term Notes (Term Loans)

An obligation in the form of a written note due after the current period is referred to as a **term loan** or long-term note payable. Term loans are often repaid in equal periodic installments. The agreement may require installment payments to be made monthly, quarterly, or semiannually. Each payment contains an interest amount and a partial repayment of principal. Because the installment payments are equal, each installment payment contains different amounts of interest and principal repayment. These component amounts change with each installment because the interest is computed on the unpaid principal, and the unpaid principal is reduced with each payment.

To illustrate, assume that on December 31, 2012, Reid, Inc., borrows $100,000 from a bank on a 12 percent, ten-year mortgage note payable. The note is to be repaid with equal quarterly installments of $4,326 (please see Appendix E for explanation on how to do this calculation). Thus, there will be 40 quarterly payments; and, the quarterly interest rate is three percent (12 percent/4 quarters). Exhibit 10-4 presents the first eight quarterly payments (of the complete 40 quarterly payment schedule) and their division between interest expense and principal repayment. The entry to record the first quarterly payment follows:

2013

Mar. 31	Interest expense	3,000	
	Mortgage note payable	1,326	
	Cash		4,326
	To record quarterly mortgage loan payment.		

A = L + SE
−4,326 −1,326 −3,000
Exp

| **Exhibit 10-4** | **Partial Mortgage Note Payment Schedule** |

$100,000 mortgage note payable with quarterly payments of $4,326 and quarterly interest rate of three percent

Payment Date	A Cash Payment	B Interest Expense (3% × D)*	C Principal Repaid (A − B)	D Book Value of Note (Unpaid Principal)
2012				
December 31 (issue date)....				$100,000
2013				
March 31.................	$4,326	$3,000	$1,326	98,674
June 30..................	4,326	2,960	1,366	97,308
September 30.............	4,326	2,919	1,407	95,901
December 31	4,326	2,877	1,449	94,452
2014				
March 31.................	4,326	2,834	1,492	92,960
June 30..................	4,326	2,789	1,537	91,423
September 30.............	4,326	2,743	1,583	89,840
December 31	4,326	2,695	1,631	88,209

* 3 percent × Unpaid principal after previous payment (rounded to nearest dollar).

FORENSIC ACCOUNTING	Accounting Software

 One definition of forensic accounting is "the use of accounting records and documents to determine the legality of past activities." Possible uses of forensic accounting include financial statements, government investigations, contract disputes, or even culling through a shoebox of receipts in preparation for an IRS audit. As a business owner, would you rather defend yourself in an investigation with a shoebox full of documents or with a detailed set of accounting records? While some small business owners feel that entry-level accounting systems such as **Intuit**'s Quickbooks are fine for their needs, they may want to consider the benefits of a more robust accounting package, such as **Microsoft** Dynamics GP accounting system. In today's technology driven society, a security breach is only a few keystrokes away. A hacker will have a much easier time penetrating the single layer of security in most entry-level packages than the eight levels of security in Microsoft Dynamics GP. In addition, the more robust accounting systems provide a richer data repository from which a forensic accountant can mine data in an effort to identify inconsistencies, a major weapon in the detection of fraud.

CONTINGENT LIABILITIES

LO3 Define *contingent liabilities* and **explain** their disclosure in the financial statements.

Previously, a *liability* was defined as an obligation resulting from past transactions or events that require a firm to pay money, provide goods, or perform services in the future. Even though a past transaction or event has taken place, the existence of some liabilities still depends on the occurrence of a future event. These types of liability are called **contingent liabilities**. Whether or not a contingent liability is recorded in the accounts depends on the likelihood of the future event occurring and the measurability of the obligation.

If the future event will *probably occur* and the amount of the liability can be *reasonably estimated,* an estimated liability should be recorded in the accounts. The estimated liability for product warranty, discussed earlier in the chapter, is a good example of this situation. The analysis assumed that customers were likely to make claims under a warranty for goods that they had purchased, and that a reasonable estimate of the amount of the warranty obligation could be made.

Some contingent liabilities are not recorded in the accounts but must be disclosed in a note to the financial statements. Contingent liabilities disclosed in this manner are (1) those for which the likelihood of the future event occurring is probable but no reasonable estimate of the future obligation is determinable or (2) those for which the likelihood of the future event occurring is *reasonably possible* (but not probable), regardless of the ability to measure the future amount. When the future amount is not determinable, the note should state that the amount cannot be estimated.

PRINCIPLE ALERT	Measuring Unit Concept and Full Disclosure Principle

The accounting guidelines for contingent liabilities illustrate the application of two principles of accounting: the *measuring unit concept* and the *full disclosure principle*. The measuring unit concept requires that information reported in the body of the financial statements be expressed in money terms. If a reasonable estimate of a contingent liability's dollar amount cannot be made, the measuring unit concept prevents the item from appearing in the balance sheet, even if its future occurrence is probable. However, the full disclosure principle requires that firms disclose all significant financial facts and circumstances to financial statement users. This principle leads to the reporting of likely, but unmeasurable contingent liabilities in the notes to the financial statements.

If the likelihood of the future event occurring is *remote,* the contingent liability is not recorded in the accounts nor disclosed in the notes to the financial statements, regardless of the ability to measure the future amount. One exception to this guideline, however, is when a company guarantees the credit of others (discussed in the following section). Even remote contingent liabilities associated with credit guarantees must be disclosed in the notes to the financial statements.

Estimated Liabilities Resulting from Lawsuits	ACCOUNTING IN PRACTICE

Walmart Stores, Inc., is the world's largest retailer with over 10,000 stores around the globe. Each week, 200 million customers visit a Walmart store to take advantage of the company's notorious low prices. But while Walmart may be cheered by consumers for its low prices, others are more critical of the company. Walmart, for example, has been criticized and sued by community groups, trade unions, and environmental groups for, among other things, its extensive foreign product sourcing, treatment of employees and product suppliers, environmental policies, and store impact on local communities. One such lawsuit alleges that female employees were discriminated against in pay and promotions. The following description of the lawsuit appeared in the company's 2009 annual report:

> . . . The Company is a defendant in Dukes v. Walmart Stores, Inc., a class-action lawsuit . . . The complaint alleges that the Company engaged in a pattern and practice of discriminating against women in promotions, pay, training, and job assignments . . . If the company is not successful in its appeal . . . the resulting liability could be material to the company . . . However, because of the uncertainty of the outcome of the appeal . . . the Company cannot reasonably estimate the possible loss or range of loss which may arise from the litigation.

Walmart's description of its pending litigation illustrates a common problem with measuring and reporting lawsuit liabilities—it is impossible in most cases to arrive at a reasonable estimate of a company's possible losses. For this reason, lawsuit liabilities are most commonly disclosed in the notes to the financial statements and not on the face of the income statement or the balance sheet.

Examples of Contingent Liabilities

Situations that may create contingent liabilities are discussed in the following sections. In each of these situations, accountants must assess the likelihood of the future event occurring and the measurability of the future amount because these factors determine the proper accounting treatment of the contingent liability.

Lawsuits

In the course of its operations, a firm may pursue a claim in a court of law by filing a **lawsuit**. At any point, a firm may also be a defendant in one or more lawsuits involving potentially material financial settlements. Examples of litigation issues include product liability, patent infringement, unfair labor practices (see the Walmart Accounting in Practice on previous page), and environmental matters. The resolution of a lawsuit may take many years. During the time a lawsuit is pending, the defendant has a contingent liability for any future financial settlement.

Environmental Cleanup Costs

Past actions by many companies in disposing of various types of industrial waste have caused subsequent environmental damage. Some estimates of the total cleanup costs for the United States run as high as $100 billion. Firms owning sites that require environmental remediation or that may require clean-up face a contingent liability for the remediation costs. Cleanup costs for a particular site may be very difficult to estimate. The party responsible for bearing the cost—the company or its insurance company—may also be at issue.

Credit Guarantees

To accommodate important, but less financially secure suppliers or customers, a firm may create a **credit guarantee** by cosigning a note payable. Until the original debtor satisfies the obligation, the cosigning firm is contingently liable for the debt. Even when the likelihood of default by a debtor is considered remote, the contingent liability associated with credit guarantees must be disclosed in the notes to the financial statements.

Exhibit 10-5 summarizes the accounting for different types of liabilities according to their unique characteristics.

Exhibit 10-5	Liabilities: Criteria and Financial Statement Treatment					
Different Characteristics that Determine the Type of Liability and How it is Recorded	**Recorded in Accounts and Reported on Balance Sheet**		**Disclosed in Footnote to Financial Statements**			**No Disclosure Required**
	Noncontingent	Contingent	Contingent	Contingent		Contingent
Dependent on future event. . .	No	No	Yes	Yes	Yes	Yes
Likelihood of future event.	Already Occurred	Already Occurred	**Probable**	**Probable**	**Reasonably possible**	**Remote**
Amount of future obligation	Known	Reasonably estimable	Reasonably estimable	Not reasonably estimable	Known, or Reasonably estimable, or Not reasonably estimable	Known, or Reasonably estimable, or Not reasonably estimable
Common examples	Notes payable, Accounts payable, Dividends payable	Income tax payable, Estimated liability for frequent use awards	Estimated liability for product warranty	Lawsuits, Environmental cleanup, Guarantee of others' credit	Lawsuits, Environmental cleanup, Guarantee of others' credit	Lawsuits, Environmental cleanup

TAKEAWAY 10.1	Concept ➞	Method ➞	Assessment
	Does the company have any contingent or off-balance sheet liabilities?	Notes to the financial statements Read the notes to the financial statements to identify contingent liabilities and operating leases	Consider the likely outcome and size of contingent liabilities and the amount of operating leases. If significant, consider these items in the analysis of the firm's liabilities.

Advantages and Disadvantages of Long-Term Bonds and Notes

Issuing bonds and notes versus issuing common stock is an alternative way for a corporation to obtain needed long-term funds. The advantages of obtaining long-term funds by issuing bonds and notes instead of common stock include:

1. **No dilution of ownership interest.** Bondholders and noteholders are creditors, not shareholders, of a corporation. Issuing bonds and notes rather than common stock maintains the number of outstanding shares of stock at their current level.

2. **Tax deductibility of interest expense.** Interest expense is deductible as an expense on a corporation's income tax return. Dividend payments to shareholders are not tax deductible.

3. **Income to common shareholders can increase. Leverage** refers to the use of borrowed funds, particularly long-term debt, to finance a business's growth. When a firm is able to earn a return on its borrowed funds that exceeds the cost of borrowing the funds, then leverage is said to build shareholder value.

For example, assume that a firm can earn 15 percent on $5,000,000 obtained by issuing bonds and notes that have a ten percent interest rate. If the firm pays income taxes at a 40 percent rate, its net income will increase $150,000 each year, as follows:

Earnings on funds borrowed: 15 percent × $5,000,000	$750,000
Interest cost on funds borrowed: 10 percent × $5,000,000	**(500,000)**
Increase in income before income tax expense.	$250,000
Income tax expense on increase: 40 percent × $250,000	**(100,000)**
Increase in net income.	$150,000

The $150,000 increase in net income accrues exclusively to the company's common stockholders.

Not all aspects of issuing bonds and notes, however, are necessarily desirable for the borrowing company. Among the disadvantages of issuing bonds and notes are the following:

1. **Interest expense is a contractual obligation.** In contrast with dividends on common stock, interest represents a fixed periodic expenditure that the firm is contractually obligated to pay.

2. **Funds borrowed have a specific repayment date.** Because bonds and notes normally have a defined maturity date, the borrower has a specific obligation to repay the borrowings at maturity.

3. **Borrowing agreement can restrict company actions.** The legal document setting forth the terms of a debt issue is called an *indenture*. Some of the provisions in an indenture may involve restrictions on dividend payments, restrictions on additional financing, and specification of minimum financial ratios that must be maintained. These provisions, called debt covenants, are intended to provide protection for debtholders by limiting a company's flexibility to act.

IFRS Alert!

The accounting for some contingent liabilities under U.S. GAAP and IFRS differs significantly. For example, under U.S. GAAP, purchase commitments—that is, an agreement by one company to buy merchandise from another company at a future date—are not reported on the balance sheet but, if material in amount, are disclosed in the notes to the financial statements. Under IFRS, however, purchase commitments are reported on the balance sheet when a company has a clear and demonstrable commitment to a second company to buy its goods. In essence, IFRS adopts a broader definition of what constitutes an accounting liability than does U.S. GAAP. Under U.S. GAAP, while purchase commitments are acknowledged to be economic liabilities of a business, they do not constitute an accounting liability until an exchange of assets occurs between the two companies.

ANALYZING LIABILITIES

Current Ratio and Quick Ratio

The **working capital** of a firm is the difference between the value of its current assets and the value of its current liabilities. In general, having a higher working capital position is preferred to having a lower working capital position. In analyzing the adequacy of a firm's working capital, the current ratio is a widely used financial metric. The **current ratio** is calculated as follows:

LO4 Define the current ratio, quick ratio, and times-interest-earned ratio and **explain** their use.

$$\text{Current ratio} = \frac{\text{Current assets}}{\text{Current liabilities}}$$

Historically, a current ratio of 2.00 has been considered an acceptable current ratio; however, this is a general guide only. Many businesses operate successfully with a current ratio below 2.00, particularly service firms, because they do not need to maintain large amounts of inventory among their current assets. Similarly, many fast-food franchises operate successfully with a negative working capital position. These businesses produce large amounts of operating cash flow, have no accounts receivable, and extensively utilize the trade credit (accounts payable) provided by their suppliers.

The **quick ratio** is another ratio used to evaluate a company's working capital position. The quick ratio is calculated as follows:

$$\text{Quick ratio} = \frac{[\textbf{Cash and cash equivalents} + \textbf{Short-term investments} + \textbf{Accounts receivable}]}{\textbf{Current liabilities}}$$

Cash and cash equivalents, short-term investments, and accounts receivable are also known as quick assets. Quick assets are converted to cash more quickly than inventory or prepaid assets.

Comparing the quick ratio to the current ratio, the main current assets omitted from the numerator when calculating the quick ratio are inventory and prepaid assets. Consequently, the quick ratio is often preferred by investment professionals because it gives a more accurate picture of a company's ability to pay current liabilities.

The following are examples of the current and quick ratios for companies in different industries:

	Current Ratio	Quick Ratio
Verizon Communications (telecommunications)	1.01	0.84
Johnson & Johnson (health care products)	2.38	1.88
Duke Energy (utility)	1.24	0.56
Google (technology)	5.92	5.62

As can be seen from the above data, the current and quick ratios vary dramatically between industries.

THINKING GLOBALLY   **Forensic Accounting**

One of the key measures indicating the amount of liabilities, or leverage, used by a company is its net debt. Net debt is calculated as a firm's total liabilities minus its liquid (or quick) assets. The higher a firm's net debt, the higher the firm's leverage, or use of debt financing. Because of the widespread use of net debt as an indicator of a firm's use of leverage by investment professionals, some firms have attempted to manage the level of their reported net debt. To illustrate, consider the case of **Parmalat SpA**, an Italian dairy company. In late 2003, the company filed for bankruptcy after revealing that it had massively underreported its outstanding net debt. According to the company's forensic investigative auditor, **PricewaterhouseCoopers LLP**, Parmalat underreported its net debt position by overstating the amount of cash on hand and retaining worthless accounts receivable on the company's balance sheet.

TAKEAWAY 10.2	Concept	➡ Method ➡	Assessment
	Can a firm pay its current liabilities?	Current assets, Quick assets, Current liabilities $\text{Current ratio} = \dfrac{\text{Current assets}}{\text{Current liabilities}}$ $\text{Quick ratio} = \dfrac{\text{Quick assets}}{\text{Current liabilities}}$	A higher current ratio and quick ratio indicates that a firm can readily pay its current liabilities.

Times-Interest-Earned Ratio

A financial ratio of particular interest to current and potential long-term creditors is the times-interest-earned ratio. The **times-interest-earned ratio** is computed as follows:

$$\text{Times-interest-earned ratio} = \frac{\text{Income before interest expense and income taxes}}{\text{Interest expense}}$$

The principal on long-term debt, such as bonds payable, is not due until maturity, which may be many years into the future. Interest payments, however, are due every six months, and possibly monthly on term loans. Thus, creditors examine the times-interest-earned ratio to help assess the ability of a company to meet its periodic interest commitments. The ratio indicates the number of times that the fixed interest charges were earned during the year. Many investment professionals believe that the times-interest-earned ratio should be at least in the range of 3.0–4.0 for the extension of long-term credit to be considered a safe investment. The trend of the ratio in recent years and the nature of the industry (volatile or stable, for example) also influence the interpretation of this ratio.

A.K.A. The times-interest-earned ratio is also referred to as the *interest coverage ratio*.

Both the numerator and denominator in the times-interest-earned ratio are obtained from the income statement. The numerator uses income before interest expense and income taxes because that is the amount available to cover a business's current interest charges. The denominator is the business's total interest expense for the period. To illustrate, Reid, Inc., issued $100,000 of eight percent bonds at face value. The annual interest expense was $8,000. If this was Reid's only interest expense and Reid's income before interest expense and income taxes the first year were $28,000, Reid's times-interest-earned ratio for the year would be 3.5, or $28,000/$8,000.

The times-interest-earned ratio may differ substantially among industries and firms, depending upon a company's decision to use leverage to finance its assets and operations. The following are examples of times-interest-earned ratios for several companies in different industries:

Kellogg Company (grocery products)	8.4
MeadWestvaco Corporation (paper and paper products)	3.3
Amazon.com Inc. (online retailing)	15.4
Cisco Systems, Inc. (computer communications equip.)	18.0

Concept	Method	Assessment	TAKEAWAY 10.3
Can a firm pay its current periodic interest payments?	Income before income taxes and interest expense, Interest expense Times-interest-earned ratio $= \dfrac{\text{Income before income taxes and interest expense}}{\text{Interest expense}}$	A higher times-interest-earned ratio indicates that a firm will have less difficulty paying its current interest expense.	

COMPREHENSIVE PROBLEM

The following are selected transactions for Tyler, Inc., for 2011 and 2012. The firm closes its books on December 31.

2011

Dec. 31   Issued $500,000 of 12 percent, ten-year bonds for $562,360, yielding an effective rate of ten percent. Interest is payable June 30 and December 31.

REVIEW

2012

June 30   Paid semiannual interest and recorded semiannual premium amortization on bonds.

Dec. 31   Paid semiannual interest and recorded semiannual premium amortization on bonds.

    31   Called one-half of the bonds in for retirement at 104.

Required

Record the transactions using effective interest amortization. Round amounts to nearest dollar. It will be helpful to read Appendix 10A prior to attempting this comprehensive problem.

Solution:

	a.	**2011**	Cash	562,360	
A = L + SE		Dec. 31	Bonds payable		500,000
+562,360 +500,000			Premium on bonds payable		62,360
+62,360			*Issued $500,000 of 12 percent, ten-year bonds for $562,360.*		

	b.	**2012**	Bond interest expense	28,118	
A = L + SE		June 30	Premium on bonds payable	1,882	
−30,000 −1,882 −28,118			Cash		30,000
Exp			*To record semiannual interest payment and premium amortization [$562,360 × 0.05 = $28,118].*		

A = L + SE		Dec. 31	Bond interest expense	28,024	
−30,000 −1,976 −28,024			Premium on bonds payable	1,976	
Exp			Cash		30,000
			To record semiannual interest payment and premium amortization [($562,360 − $1,882) × 0.05 = $28,024, rounded].		

A = L + SE		31	Bonds payable	250,000	
−260,000 −250,000 +19,251			Premium on bonds payable	29,251	
−29,251 Gain			Cash		260,000
			Gain on bond retirement		19,251
			To record retirement of $250,000 of bonds; book value of bonds retired:		

Face amount. $250,000

Add: Premium (50 percent × $58,502)   29,251

Book value. $279,251

Retirement payment: $250,000 × 1.04 = $260,000.

APPENDIX 10A: Bond Pricing

L05   **Explain** bond pricing and **illustrate** the effective interest method of amortizing bond discounts/premiums.

We explained that (1) a bond agreement specifies a pattern of future cash flows—usually a series of interest payments and a single payment at maturity equal to the face value—and that (2) bonds are often sold at premiums or discounts to adjust their effective interest rates to the prevailing market rate of interest when they are issued.

Because of the role played by interest, the selling price of a bond that is necessary to yield a specific rate can be determined as follows:

❶ Use Appendix E's Table III to calculate the present value of the future principal repayment at the bond's effective rate of interest.

❷ Use Appendix E's Table IV to calculate the present value of the future series of interest payments at the bond's effective rate of interest.

❸ Add the two present value calculations obtained in steps one and two.

Exhibit 10-6 illustrates the pricing of a $100,000 issue of eight percent, four-year bonds paying interest semiannually and sold on the date of issue to yield (1) eight percent, (2) ten percent, and (3) six percent. The price of the eight-percent bonds sold to yield eight percent equals the face (or par) value of the bonds. However, the bonds must sell for $93,552 to provide a yield of ten percent, whereas the bonds must sell for $106,980 to provide a yield of six percent.

Exhibit 10A-1	Calculating Bond Issue Price Using Present Value Tables

❶ $100,000 of eight percent, four-year bonds with interest payable semiannually sold to yield eight percent:

Future Cash Flows	Multiplier (Table III)	Multiplier (Table IV)	Present Values at 4% Semiannually
Principal repayment, $100,000 (a single amount received eight semiannual periods hence)..............	0.731		$ 73,100
Interest payments, $4,000 at end of each of eight semiannual interest periods.....................		6.733	26,900 (rounded)
Total present value (or issue price) of bonds.................			$100,000

❷ $100,000 of eight percent, four-year bonds with interest payable semiannually sold to yield ten percent:

Future Cash Flows	Multiplier (Table III)	Multiplier (Table IV)	Present Values at 5% Semiannually
Principal repayment, $100,000 (a single amount received eight semiannual periods hence)..............	0.677		$ 67,700
Interest payments, $4,000 at end of each of eight semiannual interest periods.....................		6.463	25,852
Total present value (or issue price) of bonds.................			$ 93,552

❸ $100,000 of eight percent, four-year bonds with interest payable semiannually sold to yield six percent:

Future Cash Flows	Multiplier (Table III)	Multiplier (Table IV)	Present Values at 3% Semiannually
Principal repayment, $100,000 (a single amount received eight semiannual periods hence)..............	0.789		$ 78,900
Interest payments, $4,000 at end of each of eight semiannual interest periods.......................		7.020	28,080
Total present value (or issue price) of bonds.................			$106,980

Effective Interest Method of Discount Amortization

A bond premium or discount can be amortized to interest expense using the straight-line method or the effective interest method. GAAP requires the effective interest method, except in cases where the differences between the two methods is not material. The **effective interest method** of amortization recognizes a constant percentage of the book value of a bond as interest expense for each interest payment period. For bonds issued at a discount, the book value of a bond is the balance in the Bonds Payable account less the balance in the Discount on Bonds Payable account. To obtain a period's interest expense under the effective interest method, we multiply the bond's book value at the beginning of each period by the effective interest rate. The **effective interest rate** is the market rate of interest used to price the bonds when they are originally issued. The difference between this amount and the amount of interest paid (coupon interest rate × face value of bonds) is the amount of discount amortized. When using the effective interest method of amortization, accountants often prepare an amortization schedule similar to the one in Exhibit 10A-1. This schedule covers the four-year life of the Reid, Inc., bonds issued at a discount.

Exhibit 10A-1 presents the various components for the Reid, Inc., bonds for the six-month interest payment periods. The interest rates shown in columns A and B are one-half the annual rates. Column A lists the constant amounts of interest paid each six months—that is, the coupon interest rate times the face value (4 percent × $100,000). The amounts in Column B are obtained by multiplying the book value as of the beginning of each period (column E) by the 5 percent effective interest rate. For example, the $4,678 interest expense for the first period is 5 percent times $93,552; for the second period, it is 5 percent times $94,230, or $4,712, and so on. The reported value of the bonds changes each period. For discounted bonds, the value increases each period because the book value increases over the life of the bonds until it reaches the face value on the maturity date. The amount of discount amortization for each period, given in column C, is the difference between the corresponding amounts in columns A and B. Column D lists the amount of unamortized discount at the end of each period.

Exhibit 10A-2	**Bonds Sold at a Discount: Effective Interest Method**					
	$100,000 of 8%, four-year bonds with interest payable semiannually issued on December 31, 2012, at $93,552 to yield 10%					
		A	**B**	**C**	**D**	**E**
Year	Interest Period	Interest Paid (4% of face value)	Interest Expense (5% of bond book value)	Periodic Amortization (B − A)	Balance of Unamortized Discount (D − C)	Book Value of Bonds, End of Period ($100,000 − D)
At issue....					$6,448	$ 93,552
2013......	1	$4,000	$4,678	$678	5,770	94,230
	2	4,000	4,712	712	5,058	94,942
2014......	3	4,000	4,747	747	4,311	95,689
	4	4,000	4,784	784	3,527	96,473
2015......	5	4,000	4,824	824	2,703	97,297
	6	4,000	4,865	865	1,838	98,162
2016......	7	4,000	4,908	908	930	99,070
	8	4,000	4,930*	930	0	100,000

*Adjusted for cumulative rounding error of $24

The amounts recorded for each interest payment can be read directly from the amortization schedule. The following journal entries record the interest expense and discount amortization at the time of the first two interest payments:

A = L + SE	**2013**			
−4,000 +678 −4,678	June 30	Bond interest expense	4,678	
Exp		Discount on bonds payable		678
		Cash		4,000
		To record semiannual interest payment and amortization.		

A = L + SE	Dec. 31	Bond interest expense	4,712	
−4,000 +712 −4,712		Discount on bonds payable		712
Exp		Cash		4,000
		To record semiannual interest payment and amortization.		

Amortizing the bond discount over the four-year life of the bonds leaves a zero balance in the Discount on Bonds Payable account on the maturity date of the bonds. The retirement of the bonds at maturity is then recorded by debiting Bonds Payable and crediting Cash for $100,000, the amount of their face value.

PRINCIPLE ALERT	**Materiality Concept**

Under U.S. GAAP, the effective interest method is the preferred method of bond amortization. It is generally accepted because it uses the actual market rate of interest when the bonds were originally issued to determine the amount of the periodic amortization. The effective interest method, however, is somewhat more complex than the straight-line method. Accounting standards permit the straight-line method of amortization to be used when the results are not materially different from those achieved under the effective interest method. This exception represents an application of the *materiality concept*. As previously discussed, the materiality concept permits insignificant accounting transactions to be recorded most expediently. Here, the materiality concept permits a simpler (and, thus, more expedient) straight-line method to be used when it results in insignificant differences from the theoretically superior effective interest method.

Effective Interest Method of Premium Amortization

The effective interest method of amortizing a bond premium is handled the same way as a bond discount amortization. Each interest period, a constant percentage of the bonds' book value as of the beginning of the period is recognized as interest expense; the difference between the interest expense and the semiannual interest payment is the amount of the premium amortization.

Exhibit 10A-3 shows the amortization schedule for the four-year life of the Reid, Inc., bonds that were issued at a premium. The coupon rate of 4 percent in column A and the effective interest rate of 3 percent in column B are one-half the annual rates because the calculations are for six-month periods.

Exhibit 10A-3	Bonds Sold at a Premium: Effective Interest Method				
	$100,000 of 8%, four-year bonds with interest payable semiannually issued on December 31, 2012, at $106,980 to yield 6%				
		A	**B**	**C**	**D**	**E**
Year	**Interest Period**	**Interest Paid (4% of face value)**	**Interest Expense (3% of bond book value)**	**Periodic Amortization (A − B)**	**Balance of Unamortized Premium (D − C)**	**Book Value of Bonds, End of Period ($100,000 + D)**
At issue....					$6,980	$106,980
2013......	1	$4,000	$3,209	$791	6,189	106,189
	2	4,000	3,186	814	5,375	105,375
2014......	3	4,000	3,161	839	4,536	104,536
	4	4,000	3,136	864	3,672	103,672
2015......	5	4,000	3,110	890	2,782	102,782
	6	4,000	3,083	917	1,865	101,865
2016......	7	4,000	3,056	944	921	100,921
	8	4,000	3,079*	921	0	100,000

*Adjusted for cumulative rounding error of $51

The journal entries for each interest payment are taken directly from the amortization schedule. The entries for the first two interest payments (June 30 and December 31) follow. Note that the periodic interest expense is less than the semiannual interest payment.

2013				
June 30	Bond interest expense	3,209	
	Premium on bonds payable		791
	Cash		4,000
	To record semiannual interest payment and amortization.		

A   =   L   +   SE
−4,000   −791   −3,209
Exp

Dec. 31	Bond interest expense	3,186	
	Premium on bonds payable		814
	Cash		4,000
	To record semiannual interest payment and amortization.		

A   =   L   +   SE
−4,000   −814   −3,186
Exp

After amortizing the bond premium over the four-year life of the bonds, the balance in the Premium on Bonds Payable account is zero. When the bonds are retired at the end of four years, the journal entry to record the retirement debits Bonds Payable and credits Cash for the $100,000 face value of the bonds.

Using a Financial Calculator

While present value tables can provide a handy method to solve some time value of money problems, they are not suitable for many real-world situations. For example, many real-world interest rates are not "even integers" like those appearing in Table I through Table IV of Appendix E, nor are many problems limited to the number of time periods appearing in the tables. While it is still possible to solve these problems with the provided formulas, a financial calculator provides a quicker solution. Financial calculators can be distinguished from other calculators by the presence of dedicated keys for present and future values, along with keys for the number of periods, interest rates, and annuity payments. There exists many brands of financial calculators; however, all of them work in much the same way. We will illustrate the calculation of bond issuance prices from Exhibit 10A-1 using a Hewlett-Packard 10BII financial calculator, as illustrated in Exhibit 10A-4. (It is usually necessary to do some preliminary setup on a financial calculator before performing time value of money calculations. For example, the HP 10BII calculator has a default setting of monthly compounding; this may need to be changed if the problem calls for a different number of compounding periods, such as annual. In addition, the calculator assumes annuity payments occur at the end of each period; this will need to be changed if the problem requires beginning of period payments. See your calculator manual to determine how to make these setting changes.)

Exhibit 10A-4	Hewlett-Packard 10BII Financial Calculator

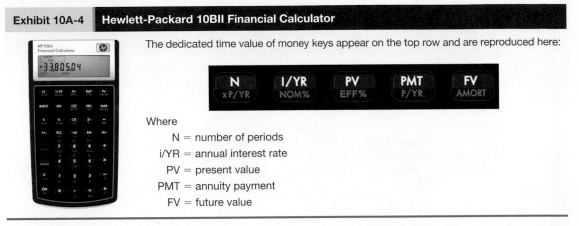

The dedicated time value of money keys appear on the top row and are reproduced here:

N xP/YR	I/YR NOM%	PV EFF%	PMT P/YR	FV AMORT

Where

N = number of periods
i/YR = annual interest rate
PV = present value
PMT = annuity payment
FV = future value

To solve a time value of money problem using a financial calculator, input the known values and then press the key of the unknown value. Exhibit 10A-5 illustrates the bond value calculations from Exhibit 10A-1. Calculator solutions can be slightly different from the solutions using either the tables or the formulas due to rounding of the future value and present value multipliers.

Exhibit 10A-5	Calculating Bond Issue Prices Using a Financial Calculator

(1) $100,000 of eight percent, four-year bonds with interest payable semiannually sold to yield eight percent:

Enter		Display		
8	N	N	=	8
8	I/YR	I/YR	=	8
4,000	PMT	PMT	=	4,000
100,000	FV	FV	=	100,000
Press	PV	PV	=	−100,000

(2) $100,000 of eight percent, four-year bonds with interest payable semiannually sold to yield ten percent:

Enter		Display		
8	N	N	=	8
10	I/YR	I/YR	=	10
4,000	PMT	PMT	=	4,000
100,000	FV	FV	=	100,000
Press	PV	PV	=	−93,537

(3) $100,000 of eight percent, four-year bonds with interest payable semiannually sold to yield six percent:

Enter		Display		
8	N	N	=	8
6	I/YR	I/YR	=	6
4,000	PMT	PMT	=	4,000
100,000	FV	FV	=	100,000
Press	PV	PV	=	−107,020

(The calculator must be preset to semiannual compounding.)

Using an Electronic Spreadsheet

In addition to formulas, tables, and financial calculators, a fourth way to solve time value of money problems is with an electronic spreadsheet such as Excel. Excel has several built-in functions that allow calculation of time value of money problems. Depending upon the version of Excel, these functions are accessed differently. Within Excel 2010, go to the Insert function f_x in the Formulas ribbon. The required functions are located under the FINANCIAL option. Below are examples of how to use Excel to solve the same problems we previously solved using a financial calculator.

Example 1

Find the selling price (present value) of $100,000 of eight percent, four-year bonds with interest payable semi-annually sold to yield eight percent. Use the PV function and enter the values as follows:

Function Arguments		? X
PV		
Rate	.04	= 0.04
Nper	8	= 8
Pmt	4000	= 4000
Fv	100000	= 100000
Type		= number
		= -100000

Returns the present value of an investment: the total amount that a series of future payments is worth now.

Rate is the interest rate per period. For example, use 6%/4 for quarterly payments at 6% APR.

Formula result = -100000

Example 2

Find the selling price (present value) of $100,000 of eight percent, four-year bonds with interest payable semi-annually sold to yield ten percent. Use the PV function and enter the values as follows:

Function Arguments		? X
PV		
Rate	.05	= 0.05
Nper	8	= 8
Pmt	4000	= 4000
Fv	100000	= 100000
Type		= number
		= -93536.78724

Returns the present value of an investment: the total amount that a series of future payments is worth now.

Rate is the interest rate per period. For example, use 6%/4 for quarterly payments at 6% APR.

Formula result = -93536.78724

Example 3

Find the selling price (present value) of $100,000 of eight percent, four-year bonds with interest payable semi-annually sold to yield six percent. Use the PV function and enter the values as follows:

Function Arguments		? X
PV		
Rate	.03	= 0.03
Nper	8	= 8
Pmt	4000	= 4000
Fv	100000	= 100000
Type		= number
		= -107019.6922

Returns the present value of an investment: the total amount that a series of future payments is worth now.

Rate is the interest rate per period. For example, use 6%/4 for quarterly payments at 6% APR.

Formula result = -107019.6922

APPENDIX 10B: Leases

LO6 Define *captial leases* and *operating leases* and **distinguish** between them.

A firm may rent property for a specified period of time under a contract called a **lease**. The company acquiring the right to use the property is the **lessee**, while the owner of the property is the **lessor**. The rights transferred to the lessee are called a **leasehold**. Examples of leased assets include land, buildings, factory machinery, and office equipment. A lessee's accounting treatment of a leased asset and lease liability depends upon whether a lease is a capital lease or an operating lease.

Capital Leases

A **capital lease** transfers to the lessee substantially all of the benefits and risks related to ownership of a leased asset. A lease meeting at least one of the following criteria is considered to be a capital lease:

1. The lease transfers ownership of the property to the lessee by the end of the lease term.
2. The lease contains a bargain purchase option, enabling the lessee to acquire the leased asset at a price below its fair market value.
3. The lease term is at least 75 percent of the remaining estimated economic life of the leased asset.
4. The present value of the lease payments is at least 90 percent of the fair value of the leased asset.

The economic effect of a capital lease is similar to that of an installment purchase. The lessee accounts for a capital lease by recording the leased property as an asset and establishing a liability for the lease obligation. The present value of the future lease payments determines the dollar amount of the capitalized lease asset and capitalized lease liability. For example, assume that Reid, Inc., leases equipment under a capital lease for ten years at $40,000 per year, and that the present value of the ten lease payments is $226,000.[2] Consequently, Reid records the capital lease as follows:

A	=	L	+ SE			
+226,000		+226,000		Leased equipment	226,000	
				Lease obligation		226,000
				To record 10-year capital lease.		

The leased equipment is depreciated over the life of the lease and appears among the firm's plant assets in the balance sheet. The total lease obligation is divided between current liabilities and long-term liabilities in the balance sheet based on the settlement dates for the obligation. The accounting for each lease payment is similar to the accounting for an installment note payment illustrated in the previous section. Part of each lease payment made by the lessee is charged to interest expense, and the remainder reduces the lease obligation.

Operating Leases

The typical rental agreement illustrates an **operating lease**: the lessee pays for the use of an asset for a limited period of time, and the lessor retains the usual risks and rewards of owning the asset. The lessee usually charges each lease payment to rent expense on the income statement. No leased asset or lease obligation is recorded on the lessee's balance sheet.

Lessees usually prefer to have any leases classified as operating leases rather than capital leases because this classification avoids reporting a lease obligation among the lessee's balance sheet liabilities. Having fewer balance sheet liabilities may make it easier for a lessee to borrow money from other lenders. Structuring a lease so that no liability is recorded (that is, having it qualify as an operating lease) is an example of a practice known as **off-balance-sheet financing**.

IFRS Alert!

The accounting for leases varies dramatically around the world. In some countries, all leases are accounted for as operating leases—that is, as off-balance-sheet debt. Many countries, like the United States, attempt to differentiate between capital and operating leases. The issue of lease accounting is on the agenda of the joint FASB/IASB convergence project committee. The prevailing view of the convergence project committee is that all noncancellable leases should be accounted for as a capital lease and placed on the balance sheet as a liability.

---

[2] Annual lease payments of $40,000 times present value of an ordinary annuity with a factor of 5.650 (12%) equals $226,000 (See Appendix E).

| | Leasing in the Airline Industry | ACCOUNTING IN PRACTICE |

Companies in the airline industry use leases to finance most of their flight equipment. The following are the (undiscounted) dollar amounts of capital and operating leases reported by several airlines:

Airline	Capital Lease Obligation	Operating Lease Obligation	Total Lease Obligation
American (AMR Corp.)	$1,118,000	$10,613,000	$11,731,000
Continental	1,852,000	9,421,000	11,273,000
Delta	1,127,000	14,268,000	15,395,000

These data reveal several important points. First, observe that the dominant form of airline equipment leasing, by a wide margin, is operating leasing. For example, over 90 percent ($14,268/$15,395) of Delta Airlines' total lease obligation is in the form of operating leases. Second, since operating leases are carried off-balance sheet, the data suggest that most of the airline industry's total debt is not reported on the balance sheets of the respective airline carriers.

SUMMARY OF LEARNING OBJECTIVES

Describe the nature of liabilities and define *current liabilities*. (p. 450)   **LO1**

■ Liabilities are obligations resulting from past transactions or events that require a business to pay money, provide goods, or perform services in the future.

■ Current liabilities are obligations that will require, within the coming year or the normal operating cycle, whichever is longer, (1) the use of existing current assets or (2) the creation of other current liabilities.

Illustrate the accounting for bonds. (p. 457)   **LO2**

■ A bond is a long-term debt instrument used by many businesses to provide financing for operations or asset purchases.

■ Discounts and premiums are recorded when the bonds are issued.

■ Bonds payable are shown in the long-term liabilities section of the balance sheet, with any unamortized premium added or unamortized discount deducted.

■ The entry for the retirement of bonds removes both the bonds payable and any related bond premium or bond discount from the accounts at the date of retirement and recognizes any gain or loss on retirement.

Define *contingent liabilities* and explain their disclosure in the financial statements. (p. 466)   **LO3**

■ Even though a past transaction or event has taken place, the existence of some liabilities, called contingent liabilities, depends on the occurrence of a future event. Whether or not a contingent liability is recorded in the accounts depends on the likelihood of the future event occurring and the measurability of the obligation:

1. If the future event will probably occur and the amount of the liability can be reasonably estimated, the contingent liability should be recorded in the accounts.

2. If the likelihood of the future event occurring is probable, but no reasonable estimate of the future obligation is determinable, or the likelihood of the future event occurring is reasonably possible (but not probable), regardless of the ability to measure the future amount, the contingent liability should be disclosed in a note to the financial statements, but not recorded in the accounts.

3. If the likelihood of the future event occurring is remote, the contingent liability is not recorded in the accounts or disclosed in a note to the financial statements. The only exception is a credit guarantee, which must be disclosed in a note to the financial statements.

Define the *current ratio*, *quick ratio*, and *times-interest-earned ratio* and explain their use. (p. 469)   **LO4**

■ The current ratio is calculated as follows:

$$\text{Current ratio} = \frac{\text{Current assets}}{\text{Current liabilities}}$$

■ The quick ratio is calculated as follows:

$$\text{Quick ratio} = \frac{[\text{Cash and cash equivalents} + \text{Short-term investments} + \text{Accounts receivable}]}{\text{Current liabilities}}$$

- Both ratios measure a firm's ability to pay its current liabilities, as well as the strength of its working capital position.
- The times-interest-earned ratio measures the ability of a firm to meet its periodic interest commitments, and is calculated as:

$$\text{Times-interest-earned ratio} = \frac{\text{Income before interest expense and income taxes}}{\text{Interest expense}}$$

LO5 **Explain bond pricing and illustrate the effective interest method of amortizing bond discounts/ premiums. (p. 472)**

- Because of the role played by interest, the selling price of the bond often differs from the face amount of the bond.
- We account for this difference by utilizing bond premium (when the market rate of interest is less than the coupon rate) and bond discount (when the market rate of interest is more than the coupon rate) accounts, which affect the book value of the liability.
- The preferred method according to GAAP for amortizing bond premiums and discounts is the effective interest method.

LO6 **Appendix 10B: Define *capital leases* and *operating leases* and distinguish between them. (p. 478)**

- A capital lease transfers most of the usual risks and rewards of property ownership to the lessee. At the inception of the lease, the lessee records an asset (a leased asset) and a liability (a lease obligation). The asset is depreciated over its expected useful life, and the liability is reduced as the periodic lease payments are made.
- Under an operating lease, the lessor retains the usual risks and rewards of owning the property. The lessee records no lease asset or lease liability at the start of the lease. Each lease payment made by the lessee is charged to rent expense.

SUMMARY	Concept ——►	Method ——————►	Assessment
TAKEAWAY 10.1	Does the company have any contingent or off-balance sheet liabilities?	Notes to the financial statements Read the notes to the financial statements to identify contingent liabilities and operating leases	Consider the likely outcome and size of contingent liabilities and the amount of operating leases. If significant, consider these items in the analysis of the firm's liabilities.
TAKEAWAY 10.2	Can a firm pay its current liabilities?	Current assets, Quick assets, Current liabilities $\text{Current ratio} = \dfrac{\text{Current assets}}{\text{Current liabilities}}$ $\text{Quick ratio} = \dfrac{\text{Quick assets}}{\text{Current liabilities}}$	A higher current ratio and quick ratio indicates that a firm can readily pay its current liabilities.
TAKEAWAY 10.3	Can a firm pay its current periodic interest payments?	Income before income taxes and interest expense, Interest expense Times-interest-earned ratio $= \dfrac{\text{Income before income taxes and interest expense}}{\text{Interest expense}}$	A higher times-interest-earned ratio indicates that a firm will have less difficulty paying its current interest expense.

KEY TERMS

Bond (p. 457)

Call provision (p. 459)

Capital lease (p. 478)

Contingent liabilities (p. 466)

Convertible bonds (p. 458)

Coupon rate (p. 460)

Credit guarantee (p. 467)

Current liabilities (p. 450)

Current ratio (p. 469)

Debenture bonds (p. 457)

Effective interest method (p. 473)

Effective interest rate (p. 463, 473)

Federal Insurance Contributions Act (FICA) (p. 453)

Gross pay (p. 453)

Lawsuit (p. 467)

Lease (p. 478)

Leasehold (p. 478)

Lessee (p. 478)

Lessor (p. 478)

Leverage (p. 468)

Liabilities (p. 450)

Market rate of interest (p. 460)

Maturity date (p. 451)

Net pay (p. 453)

Off-balance-sheet financing (p. 478)

Operating lease (p. 478)

Product warranties (p. 456)

Quick ratio (p. 470)

Secured bonds (p. 457)

Serial bonds (p. 458)

Sinking fund provision (p. 459)

Term loan (p. 457, 465)

Times-interest-earned ratio (p. 471)

Working capital (p. 469)

Zero-coupon bonds (p. 458)

SELF-STUDY QUESTIONS

(Answers to the Self-Study Questions are available at the end of this chapter.)

1. **Goldsteen Corporation obtained a $5,000 loan from a bank on April 1. If the bank charges eight percent interest annually, how much interest will be accrued at December 31?** **LO1**
   a. $400
   b. $300
   c. $275
   d. $250

2. **Wong, Inc., sold merchandise on account for $1,840, which is subject to a ten percent excise tax and a five percent sales tax. What would the entry to record this sale include?** **LO1**
   a. A debit of $1,600 to Accounts Receivable
   b. A debit of $2,116 to Accounts Receivable
   c. A credit of $1,600 to Sales
   d. A dedit of $1,840 to Sales

3. **Jansen Company sells a product for $400 per unit, which includes a 30-day warranty against product defects. Experience indicates that four percent of the units sold will prove defective, requiring an average repair cost of $50 per unit. During the first month of business, product sales were $320,000, and 20 of the units sold were found to be defective and repaired during the month. What is the accrued liability for product warranties at month-end?** **LO1**
   a. $1,000
   b. $600
   c. $1,600
   d. $2,000

4. **Which of the following payroll related taxes are not withheld from an employee's earnings?** **LO1**
   a. Medicare taxes
   b. Income taxes
   c. Federal unemployment taxes
   d. Social Security taxes

5. **Which of the following is *not* considered to be a contingent liability?** **LO3**
   a. Environmental cleanup costs
   b. Notes payable
   c. Credit guarantees
   d. Lawsuit

6. **On May 1, 2013, a firm issued $400,000 of 12-year, nine percent bonds payable at 96 1/2 plus accrued interest. The bonds are dated January 1, and interest is payable on January 1 and July 1 of each year. The amount the firm receives on May 1 from the sale of the bonds (see Appendix 10A) is:** **LO2**
   a. $386,000.
   b. $422,000.
   c. $392,000.
   d. $398,000.

LO5 7. A firm issued $250,000 of ten-year, 12 percent bonds payable on January 1, for $281,180, yielding an effective rate of ten percent. Interest is payable on January 1 and July 1 each year. The firm records amortization on each interest date. Bond interest expense for the first six months using effective interest amortization (see Appendix 10A) is:

    a. $15,000.
    b. $16,870.80.
    c. $14,059.
    d. $14,331.

LO2 8. In financial statement presentations, the Discount on Bonds Payable account is:

    a. Added to Bond Interest Expense.
    b. Deducted from Bonds Payable.
    c. Added to Bonds Payable.
    d. Deducted from Bond Interest Expense.

LO6 9. An example of off-balance-sheet financing is a(n):

    a. Term loan.
    b. Operating lease.
    c. Zero-coupon bond.
    d. Capital lease.

LO4 10. Apolo Company reported year-end current assets of $75,000 and current liabilities of $25,000. The company's current ratio is:

    a. 1/3
    b. 3
    c. 4
    d. $50,000

LO4 11. Cristo Company reported net income of $50,000 after subtracting $10,000 for interest expense and $20,000 for taxes. Compute the company's times-interest-earned ratio:

    a. 2.5
    b. 5
    c. 8
    d. 3

QUESTIONS

1. For accounting purposes, how are liabilities defined?

2. At what amount are current liabilities presented on the balance sheet?

3. What does the term *current liabilities* mean?

4. What formula should Hardy Company use to calculate the total amount of interest on a note payable that uses add-on interest?

5. Gordon Company signed a note payable on November 20. Gordon has a December 31 year-end. It paid the note, including interest, on the maturity date, February 20. What accounts did Gordon debit and what account did it credit on February 20?

6. Jack Swanson gave a creditor a 90-day, eight percent note payable for $7,200 on December 16. What adjusting entry should Swanson make on December 31?

7. What are two examples of voluntary deductions from an employee's gross pay?

8. On whom is the FICA tax levied? What does the FICA tax finance?

9. What is the difference between accounting for product warranties on (a) failed units repaired in the month of sale and (b) failed units repaired in a subsequent month but that are still covered by warranty?

AMERICAN PAGING, INC.
10. **American Paging, Inc.**, is the seventh largest paging company in the United States. In a recent balance sheet, it reported a current liability of $8,452,379 that was labeled Unearned Revenues and Deposits. A note to the financial statements explained:

Unearned revenues and deposits primarily represent monthly charges to customers for radio paging rental and dispatch billed in advance. Such revenues and deposits are recognized in the following month when service is provided or are applied against the customer's final bill or last month's rent.

What basic principle of accounting guides American Paging's handling of its unearned revenues and deposits?

11. What do the following terms mean? (a) term loan, (b) bonds payable, (c) trustee, (d) secured bonds, (e) serial bonds, (f) call provision, (g) convertible bonds, (h) face value, (i) coupon rate, (j) bond discount, (k) bond premium, and (l) amortization of bond premium or discount.

12. What are the advantages and disadvantages of issuing bonds rather than common stock?

13. A $3,000,000 issue of ten-year, nine percent bonds was sold at 98 plus accrued interest three months after the bonds were dated. What net amount of cash is received when the bonds are sold?

14. If the effective interest amortization method is used for bonds payable, how does the periodic interest expense change over the life of the bonds when they are issued (a) at a discount and (b) at a premium?

15. On April 30, one year before maturity, Eastern Company retired $200,000 of nine percent bonds payable at 101. The book value of the bonds on April 30 was $197,600. Bond interest was last paid on April 30. What is the gain or loss on the retirement of the bonds?

16. What are *contingent liabilities*? List three examples of contingent liabilities. When should contingent liabilities be recorded in the accounts?

17. What is the difference between an operating lease and a capital lease?

18. Define the terms *current ratio* and *quick ratio*. What does each ratio tell us?

19. Define the times-interest-earned ratio and explain how it is used.

SHORT EXERCISES

SE10-1.   **Contingent Liabilities** The CEO of Smith & Sons, Inc., negotiated with its principal supplier of raw materials to purchase 10,000 units for a total price of $100,000. The units are to be delivered in 90 days. The CEO is uncertain whether she should record the purchase commitment on the company's balance sheet as a liability or not. She asks for your advice. What would you advise her?   **LO1**

SE10-2.   **Determining Bond Premium or Discount** Smith & Sons, Inc., decides to sell $1,000,000 in bonds to finance the construction of a new warehouse. The bonds will carry an annual coupon rate of interest of four percent, to be paid semiannually, and will mature in five years. (a) If the market rate of interest at the time of issuance is five percent, will the bonds sell at their face value, a discount, or a premium? (b) If the market rate of interest at the time of issuance is four percent, will the bonds sell at their face value, a discount, or a premium? (c) If the market rate of interest at the time of issuance is three percent, will the bonds sell at their face value, a discount, or a premium?   **LO2**

SE10-3.   **Contingent Liabilities** Smith & Sons, Inc., received notification from a local attorney that the company was being sued for $5,000,000 for patent infringement. A review of the situation by the company's CEO led to the conclusion that Smith & Sons had indeed infringed upon the other company's patented product. Nonetheless, the CEO thought the amount of $5,000,000 was excessive and intended to litigate the issue. How should the lawsuit be reported in Smith & Sons' annual report?   **LO3**

SE10-4.   **Operating and Capital Leases** The CEO of Smith & Sons, Inc., was considering a lease for a new administrative headquarters building. The building was old, but was very well located near the company's principal customers. The leasing agent estimated that the building's remaining useful life was ten years, and at the end of its useful life, the building would probably be worth $100,000. The proposed lease term was eight years, and as an inducement to Smith & Sons' CEO to sign the lease, the leasing agent indicated a willingness to include a statement in the lease agreement that would allow Smith & Sons to buy the building at the end of the lease for only $75,000. As the CEO   **LO6**

considered whether or not to sign the lease, she wondered whether the lease could be accounted for as an off-balance-sheet operating lease. What would you advise her?

The following information relates to SE10-5 through SE10-7:

SMITH & SONS, INC.
Income Statement
For Years Ended December 31, 2013 and 2012

(in millions)	2013	2012
Net sales.	$10,000	$ 9,500
Cost of goods sold.	5,500	5,200
Gross profit.	4,500	4,300
Selling and administrative expenses	2,800	2,700
Income from operations	1,700	1,600
Interest expense.	300	250
Income before income taxes	1,400	1,350
Income tax expense.	420	400
Net income.	$ 980	$ 950

SMITH & SONS, INC.
Balance Sheet
December 31, 2013 and 2012

(in millions)	2013	2012
Assets		
Current assets		
Cash and cash equivalents	$ 200	$ 400
Accounts receivable.	900	800
Inventory.	500	650
Other current assets.	400	250
Total current assets	2,000	2,100
Property, plant, & equipment (net)	2,600	2,500
Other assets.	5,700	5,900
Total Assets	$10,300	$10,500
Liabilities and Stockholders' Equity		
Current liabilities.	$ 3,000	$ 2,900
Long-term liabilities	5,000	5,400
Total liabilities.	8,000	8,300
Stockholders' equity – common.	2,300	2,200
Total Liabilities and Stockholders' Equity	$10,300	$10,500

LO4   SE10-5.   Current Ratio Calculate the current ratio for Smith & Sons, Inc., for 2012 and 2013, and comment on the company's working capital position. Did the company's ability to pay its current liabilities improve over the two years?

LO4   SE10-6.   Quick Ratio Calculate the quick ratio for Smith & Sons, Inc., for 2012 and 2013, and comment on the company's working capital position. Did the company's ability to pay its current liabilities improve over the two years?

LO4   SE10-7.   Times-Interest-Earned Ratio Calculate the times-interest-earned ratio for Smith & Sons, Inc., for 2012 and 2013, and comment on the company's ability to pay its current interest payments. Did the company's ability to pay its current interest charges improve?

LO2   SE10-8.   Premium and Discount of a Bond or Debenture The Johnson & Johnson Company reported the following borrowings in a prior annual report:

Borrowing ($ in millions)		Amount	Effective Interest Rate (%)
a.	3.00 percent, zero-coupon bond, due 2020	$202	3.00
b.	4.95 percent debentures, due 2033	500	5.00
c.	3.80 percent debentures, due 2017	500	3.82
d.	6.95 percent bonds, due 2025	293	6.90

For each borrowing, indicate whether the bond or debenture was originally sold at its face value, a discount, or a premium.

SE10-9. **Bond Interest Expense** Smith & Sons, Inc., sold $100,000 face value, six percent coupon rate, four-year bonds, for an aggregate issue price of $96,000. Calculate the total interest expense to be recorded by the company over the four-year life of the bonds. **LO2**

SE10-10. **Bond Interest Expense** During 2010, Smith & Sons, Inc., issued $400 million of zero-coupon bonds, due in 2020. The proceeds from the bond issuance were $186.6 million. Calculate the total interest expense that the company will incur over the life of the bonds. **LO2**

Assignments with the ✓ logo in the margin are available in ᵐʸBusinessCourse.
See the Preface of the book for details.

EXERCISES—SET A

E10-1A. **Liabilities on the Balance Sheet** For each of the following situations, indicate the amount shown as a liability on the balance sheet of Kane, Inc., at December 31: **LO1**

    a. Kane has accounts payable of $110,000 for merchandise included in the year-end inventory.

    b. Kane agreed to purchase a $28,000 drill press in the following January.

    c. During November and December of the current year, Kane sold products to a firm and guaranteed them against product failure for 90 days. Estimated costs of honoring this provision next year are $2,200.

    d. On December 15, Kane declared a $70,000 cash dividend payable on January 15 of the following year to shareholders of record on December 31.

    e. Kane provides a profit-sharing bonus for its executives equal to five percent of the reported before-tax income for the current year. The estimated before-tax income for the current year is $600,000.

E10-2A. **Maturity Dates of Notes Payable** Determine the maturity date and compute the interest for each of the following notes payable with add-on interest: **LO1** ✓

	Date of Note	Principal	Interest Rate (%)	Term
a.	August 5	$15,000	8	120 days
b.	May 10	8,400	7	90 days
c.	October 20	12,000	9	45 days
d.	July 6	4,500	10	60 days
e.	September 15	13,500	8	75 days

E10-3A. **Accrued Interest Payable** Compute the interest accrued on each of the following notes payable owed by Northland, Inc., on December 31: **LO1** ✓

Lender	Date of Note	Principal	Interest Rate (%)	Term
Maple	11/21	$18,000	10	120 days
Wyman	12/13	14,000	9	90 days
Nahn	12/19	16,000	12	60 days

LO1 ✔ **E10-4A.** **Adjusting Entries for Interest** The following note transactions occurred during the year for Towell Company:

Nov. 25 Towell issued a 90-day, nine percent note payable for $8,000 to Hyatt Company for merchandise.

Dec. 7 Towell signed a 120-day, $12,000 note at the bank at ten percent.

22 Towell gave Barr, Inc., a $12,000, ten percent, 60-day note in payment of account.

Prepare the general journal entries necessary to adjust the interest accounts at December 31.

LO1 ✔ **E10-5A.** **Excise and Sales Tax Calculations** Barnes Company has just billed a customer for $1,044, an amount that includes a ten percent excise tax and a six percent state sales tax.

a. What amount of revenue is recorded?

b. Prepare a general journal entry to record the transaction on the books of Barnes Company.

LO1 ✔ **E10-6A.** **Advance Payments for Goods** The Chicago Daily Times Corporation (CDT) publishes a daily newspaper. A 52-week subscription sells for $208. Assume that CDT sells 100 subscriptions on January 1. None of the subscriptions are cancelled as of March 31.

a. Prepare a journal entry to record the receipt of the subscriptions on January 1.

b. Prepare a journal entry to record one week of earned revenue on March 25.

LO1 ✔ **E10-7A.** **Warranty Costs** Milford Company sells a motor that carries a 60-day unconditional warranty against product failure. Based on a reliable statistical analysis, Milford knows that between the sale and the end of the product warranty period, two percent of the units sold will require repair at an average cost of $50 per unit. The following data reflect Milford's recent experience:

	October	November	December	Dec. 31 Total
Units sold	23,000	22,000	25,000	70,000
Known product failures from sales in:				
October.	120	180	160	460
November		130	220	350
December			210	210

Calculate, and prepare a journal entry to record, the estimated liability for product warranties at December 31. Assume that warranty costs of known failures have already been reflected in the records.

LO2 ✔ **E10-8A.** **Bonds Payable Journal Entries; Effective Interest Amortization** On December 31, 2011, Daggett Company issued $800,000 of ten-year, nine percent bonds payable for $750,232, yielding an effective interest rate of ten percent. Interest is payable semiannually on June 30 and December 31. Prepare journal entries to reflect (a) the issuance of the bonds, (b) the semiannual interest payment and discount amortization (effective interest method) on June 30, 2012, and (c) the semiannual interest payment and discount amortization on December 31, 2012. Round amounts to the nearest dollar.

LO2 ✔ **E10-9A.** **Bonds Payable Journal Entries; Effective Interest Amortization** On December 31, 2011, Coffey Company issued $300,000 of 15-year, ten percent bonds payable for $351,780, yielding an effective interest rate of eight percent. Interest is payable semiannually on June 30 and December 31. Prepare journal entries to reflect (a) the issuance of the bonds, (b) the semiannual interest payment and premium amortization (effective interest method) on June 30, 2012, and (c) the semiannual interest payment and premium amortization on December 31, 2012. Round amounts to the nearest dollar.

LO2 **E10-10A.** **Financial Statement Presentation of Bond Accounts** Indicate the proper financial statement classification for each of the following accounts:

Gain on Bond Retirement (material amount)

Discount on Long-term Bonds Payable

Mortgage Notes Payable

Long-term Bonds Payable

Bond Interest Expense

Bond Interest Payable

Premium on Long-term Bonds Payable

E10-11A. Early Retirement of Bonds Elston Company issued $400,000 of 11 percent, 20-year bonds at 108 on January 1, 2010. Interest is payable semiannually on July 1 and January 1. Through January 1, 2016, Elston amortized $5,000 of the bond premium. On January 1, 2016, Elston retired the bonds at 103 (after making the interest payment on that date). Prepare the journal entry to record the bond retirement on January 1, 2016.

LO2

E10-12A. Installment Term Loan On December 31, 2009, Thomas, Inc. borrowed $700,000 on a 12 percent, 15-year mortgage note payable. The note is to be repaid in equal semiannual installments of $50,854 (payable on June 30 and December 31). Prepare journal entries to reflect (a) the issuance of the mortgage note payable, (b) the payment of the first installment on June 30, 2010, and (c) the payment of the second installment on December 31, 2010. Round amounts to the nearest dollar.

LO2

E10-13A. Leases On January 1, Spider, Inc., entered into two lease contracts. The first lease contract was a six-year lease for a computer with $15,000 annual lease payments due at the end of each year. Spider took possession of the computer on January 1. The second lease contract was a six-month lease, beginning January 1 for warehouse storage space with $1,000 monthly lease payments due the first of each month. Spider made the first month's payment on January 1. The present value of the lease payments under the first contract is $74,520. The present value of the lease payments under the second contract is $5,853.

LO6

a. The first lease contract is a capital lease. Prepare the journal entry for this lease on January 1.
b. The second lease contract is an operating lease. Prepare the journal entry for this lease on January 1.

E10-14A. Contingent Liabilities Determine which of the following transactions represent contingent liabilities for Hermani Rental and indicate the proper accounting treatment at the company's fiscal year-end, by placing the letter of the correct accounting treatment in the space provided.

LO3

A. Accrue a liability and disclose in the financial statement notes
B. Disclose in the financial statement footnotes only
C. No disclosure

1. Hermani Rental cosigned a loan for $75,000 due in one year for Wyler Company. Wyler is a very profitable company and is very liquid, making it a remote chance Hermani will have to pay the loan.	
2. One of Hermani's rental tents collapsed at a wedding and injured the bride and groom. Hermani's legal counsel believes it is probable that Hermani will have to pay damages of $400,000.	
3. Hermani Rental is being audited by the Internal Revenue Service. Its tax returns for the past two years are being examined. At the company's year-end, the audit is still in process. Hermani's CPA believes that payment of significant taxes is possible.	

E10-15A. Ratio Analysis Presented below are summary financial data from Pompeo's annual report:

LO4

Amounts in millions	
Balance sheet	
Cash and cash equivalents	$ 1,808
Marketable securities	18,085
Accounts receivable (net)	9,367
Total current assets	39,088
Total assets	123,078
Current liabilities	37,724
Long-term debt	7,279
Shareholders' equity	68,278
Income Statement	
Interest expense	359
Net income before taxes	14,007

Calculate the following ratios:
a. Times-interest-earned ratio
b. Quick ratio
c. Current ratio

LO2, 5 **E10-16A.** **Issue Price of a Bond** Conner Enterprises issued $100,000 of 10%, five-year bonds with interest payable semiannually. Determine the issue price if the bonds are priced to yield (a) 10%, (b) 8%, and (c) 12%.

LO2, 5 **E10-17A.** **Issue Price of a Bond** Lunar, Inc., plans to issue $900,000 of 10% bonds that will pay interest semiannually and mature in five years. Assume that the effective interest rate is 12 percent per year compounded semiannually. Calculate the selling price of the bonds.

EXERCISES—SET B

LO1 **E10-1B.** **Liabilities on the Balance Sheet** For each of the following situations, indicate the amount shown as a liability on the balance sheet of Anchor, Inc., at December 31:

a. Anchor's general ledger shows a credit balance of $125,000 in Long-Term Notes Payable. Of this amount, a $25,000 installment becomes due on June 30 of the following year.

b. Anchor estimates its unpaid income tax liability for the current year is $34,000; it plans to pay this amount in March of the following year.

c. On December 31, Anchor received a $15,000 invoice for merchandise shipped on December 28. The merchandise has not yet been received. The merchandise was shipped F.O.B. shipping point.

d. During the year, Anchor collected $10,500 of state sales tax. At year-end, it has not yet remitted $1,400 of these taxes to the state department of revenue.

e. On December 31, Anchor's bank approved a $5,000, 90-day loan. Anchor plans to sign the note and receive the money on January 2 of the following year.

LO1 **E10-2B.** **Maturity Dates of Notes Payable** Determine the maturity date and compute the interest for each of the following notes payable:

	Date of Note	Principal	Interest Rate (%)	Term
a.	July 10	$7,200	9	90 days
b.	April 14	6,000	8	120 days
c.	May 19	5,600	7 ½	120 days
d.	June 10	5,400	8	45 days
e.	October 29	7,500	8	75 days

LO1 **E10-3B.** **Accrued Interest Payable** Compute the interest accrued on each of the following notes payable owed by Galloway, Inc., on December 31:

Lender	Date of Note	Principal	Interest Rate (%)	Term
Barton	12/4	$10,000	12	120 days
Lawson	12/13	12,000	9	90 days
Riley	12/19	15,000	10	60 days

LO1 **E10-4B.** **Adjusting Entries for Interest** The following note transactions occurred during the year for Zuber Company:

Nov. 25 Zuber issued a 90-day, 12 percent note payable for $6,000 to Porter Company for merchandise.

Dec. 10 Zuber signed a 120-day, $7,200 note at the bank at ten percent.

23 Zuber gave Dale, Inc., a $9,000, ten percent, 60-day note in payment of account.

Prepare the journal entries necessary to adjust the interest accounts at December 31.

E10-5B. **Excise and Sales Tax Calculations** Allied Company has just billed a customer for $1,102, an amount that includes a ten percent excise tax and a six percent state sales tax.

    a. What amount of revenue is recorded?

    b. Prepare a journal entry to record the transaction on the books of Allied Company.

E10-6B. **Advance Payment for Services** The Columbus Bluebirds football team sells a 12-game season ticket for $180. Assume that the team sells 1,000 season tickets on August 10. The tickets are all used for admission.

    a. Prepare a journal entry to record the sale of the season tickets on August 10.

    b. Prepare a journal entry to record one game of earned revenue on September 12.

E10-7B. **Warranty Costs** Brigham Company sells an electric timer that carries a 60-day unconditional warranty against product failure. Based on a reliable statistical analysis, Brigham knows that between the sale and the end of the product warranty period, three percent of the units sold will require repair at an average cost of $35 per unit. The following data reflect Brigham's recent experience:

	October	November	December	Dec. 31 Total
Units sold	36,000	34,000	45,000	115,000
Known product failures from sales in:				
October.	320	550	210	1,080
November.		230	360	590
December.			410	410

Calculate, and prepare a journal entry to record, the estimated liability for product warranties at December 31. Assume that warranty costs of known failures have already been reflected in the records.

E10-8B. **Bonds Payable Journal Entries; Effective Interest Amortization** On December 31, 2009, Blair Company issued $600,000 of 20-year, 11 percent bonds payable for $554,718, yielding an effective interest rate of 12 percent. Interest is payable semiannually on June 30 and December 31. Prepare journal entries to reflect (a) the issuance of the bonds, (b) the semiannual interest payment and discount amortization (effective interest method) on June 30, 2010, and (c) the semiannual interest payment and discount amortization on December 31, 2010. Round amounts to the nearest dollar.

E10-9B. **Bonds Payable Journal Entries; Effective Interest Amortization** On December 31, 2009, Kay Company issued $400,000 of five-year, 13 percent bonds payable for $446,372, yielding an effective interest rate of ten percent. Interest is payable semiannually on June 30 and December 31. Prepare journal entries to reflect (a) the issuance of the bonds, (b) the semiannual interest payment and premium amortization (effective interest method) on June 30, 2010, and (c) the semiannual interest payment and premium amortization on December 31, 2010. Round amounts to the nearest dollar.

E10-10B. **Bonds Payable on the Balance Sheet** The adjusted trial balance for the Lancer Corporation at the end of 2011 contains the following accounts:

Bond interest payable	$ 25,000
9% Bonds payable due 2013.	600,000
10% Bonds payable due 2015.	500,000
Discount on 9% bonds payable.	19,000
Premium on 10% bonds payable.	15,000
Zero coupon bonds payable due 2017	170,500
8% Bonds payable due 2019.	100,000

Prepare the long-term liabilities section of the balance sheet. Indicate the balance sheet classification for any accounts listed above that do not belong in the long-term liabilities section.

E10-11B. **Early Retirement of Bonds** Norwich, Inc., issued $250,000 of 8 percent, 15-year bonds at 96 on June 30, 2009. Interest is payable semiannually on December 31 and June 30. Through June 30, 2015, Norwich amortized $3,000 of the bond discount. On June 30, 2015, Norwich retired the bonds at 101 (after making the interest payment on that date). Prepare the journal entry to record the bond retirement on June 30, 2015.

LO1

LO1

LO1

LO2

LO2

LO2

LO2

LO2   **E10-12B. Installment Term Loan** On December 31, 2009, Beam, Inc., borrowed $500,000 on an eight per-cent, ten-year mortgage note payable. The note is to be repaid in equal quarterly installments of $18,278 (beginning March 31, 2010). Prepare journal entries to reflect (a) the issuance of the mort-gage note payable, (b) the payment of the first installment on March 31, 2010, and (c) the payment of the second installment on June 30, 2010. Round amounts to the nearest dollar.

LO6 **E10-13B. Leases** On January 1, Cooper, Inc., entered into two lease contracts. The first lease contract was a seven-year lease for a sound system with $25,000 annual lease payments due at the end of each year. Spider took possession of the sound system on January 1. The second lease contract was a nine-month lease, beginning January 1 for warehouse storage space with $1,500 monthly lease payments due the first of each month. Cooper made the first month's payment on January 1. The present value of the lease payments under the first contract is $140,000. The present value of the lease payments under the second contract is $13,000.

a. The first lease contract is a capital lease. Prepare the journal entry for this lease on January 1.
b. The second lease contract is an operating lease. Prepare the journal entry for this lease on January 1.

LO3 **E10-14B. Contingent Liabilities** Determine which of the following transactions represent contingent liabili-ties for Koby Leasing and indicate the proper accounting treatment at the company's fiscal year-end, by placing the letter of the correct accounting treatment in the space provided.

A. Accrue a liability and disclose in the financial statement notes
B. Disclose in the financial statement footnotes only
C. No disclosure

1. Koby Leasing was sued by a customer who claimed the equipment they leased was not up to the standards described by Koby. Koby stands by its claims and can support all the item's specifications. Koby plans to vigorously defend itself and believes the chances of losing the lawsuit are remote.	
2. A government audit of Koby found that the company is in violation of several work safety regulations. Koby has been notified that it will be assessed a fine of $25,000. Koby has agreed to make the safety changes so that it will be in compliance with the regulations.	
3. Koby Leasing has been served a lawsuit by a customer that claims he was injured from one of the products leased from Koby. Koby plans to defend itself in court, but its lawyers believe there is a 50/50 chance that they will lose and be forced to pay $50,000.	

LO4   **E10-15B. Ratio Analysis** Presented below are summary financial data from the Jackson Co. annual report:

Amounts in millions	
Balance sheet	
Cash and cash equivalents	$ 2,200
Marketable securities	15,300
Accounts receivable (net)	10,000
Total current assets	42,000
Total assets	155,000
Current liabilities	28,000
Long-term debt	47,500
Shareholders' equity	79,500
Income Statement	
Interest expense	3,200
Net income before taxes	36,800

Calculate the following ratios:

a. Times-interest-earned ratio
b. Quick ratio
c. Current ratio

E10-16B. Issue Price of a Bond Maggie Enterprises issued $100,000 of 6%, five-year bonds with interest payable semiannually. Determine the issue price if the bonds are priced to yield (a) 6%, (b) 8%, and (c) 4%.

LO2, 5

E10-17B. Issue Price of a Bond Tide, Inc., plans to issue $500,000 of 9% bonds that will pay interest semiannually and mature in ten years. Assume that the effective interest is 8 percent per year compounded semiannually. Calculate the selling price of the bonds.

LO2, 5

PROBLEMS—SET A

P10-1A. Journal Entries for Accounts and Notes Payable Logan Company had the following transactions:

LO1

Apr.	8	Issued a $4,800, 75-day, eight percent note payable in payment of an account with Bennett Company.
May	15	Borrowed $36,000 from Lincoln Bank, signing a 60-day note at nine percent.
June	22	Paid Bennett Company the principal and interest due on the April 8 note payable.
July	6	Purchased $12,000 of merchandise from Bolton Company; signed a 90-day note with ten percent interest.
July	14	Paid the May 15 note due Lincoln Bank.
Oct.	2	Borrowed $24,000 from Lincoln Bank, signing a 120-day note at 12 percent.
	4	Defaulted on the note payable to Bolton Company.

Required
a. Record these transactions in general journal form.
b. Record any adjusting entries for interest in general journal form. Logan Company has a December 31 year-end.

P10-2A. Adjusting Entries for Interest At December 31, 2011, Hoffman Corporation had two notes payable outstanding (notes 1 and 2). At December 31, 2012, Hoffman also had two notes payable outstanding (notes 3 and 4). These notes are described below:

LO1

	Date of Note	Principal Amount	Interest Rate	Number of Days
December 31, 2011				
Note 1.................	11/16/2011	$12,000	8%	120
Note 2.................	12/4/2011	16,000	9	60
December 31, 2012				
Note 3.................	12/7/2012	9,000	9	60
Note 4.................	12/21/2012	18,000	10	30

Required
a. Prepare the adjusting entries for interest at December 31, 2011.
b. Assume that the adjusting entries were made at December 31, 2011. Prepare the 2012 journal entries to record payment of the notes that were outstanding at December 31, 2011.
c. Prepare the adjusting entries for interest at December 31, 2012.

P10-3A. Recording Payroll and Payroll Taxes Beamon Corporation had the following payroll for April:

LO1

Officers' salaries...	$32,000
Sales salaries..	67,000
Federal income taxes withheld...	19,000
FICA taxes withheld...	7,500
Health insurance premiums withheld...	1,600
Union dues withheld...	1,200
Salaries (included above) subject to federal unemployment taxes	55,000
Salaries (included above) subject to state unemployment taxes................	60,000

Required
Prepare journal entries on April 30 to record:

a. Accrual of the monthly payroll.

b. Payment of the net payroll.

c. Accrual of employer's payroll taxes. (Assume that the FICA tax matches the amount withheld, the federal unemployment tax is 0.6 percent, and the state unemployment tax is 5.4 percent.)

d. Payment of all liabilities related to this payroll. (Assume that all are settled at the same time.)

LO1 P10-4A. Recording Payroll and Payroll Taxes The following data are taken from Fremont Wholesale Company's May payroll:

Administrative salaries	$34,000
Sales salaries	47,000
Custodial salaries	7,000
Total payroll	$88,000
Salaries subject to 1.45 percent Medicare tax	$88,000
Salaries subject to 6.2 percent Social Security tax	74,000
Salaries subject to federal unemployment taxes	14,000
Salaries subject to state unemployment taxes	20,000
Federal income taxes withheld from all salaries	17,800

Assume that the company is subject to a two percent state unemployment tax (due to a favorable experience rating) and a 0.6 percent federal unemployment tax.

Required

Record the following in general journal form on May 31:

a. Accrual of the monthly payroll.

b. Payment of the net payroll.

c. Accrual of the employer's payroll taxes.

d. Payment of these payroll-related liabilities. (Assume that all are settled at the same time.)

LO1 P10-5A. Excise and Sales Tax Calculations Fulton Corporation initially records its sales at amounts that exclude any related excise and sales taxes. During June, Fulton recorded total sales of $400,000. An analysis of June sales indicated the following:

1. Thirty percent of sales were subject to both a ten percent excise tax and a six percent sales tax.

2. Fifty percent of sales were subject only to the sales tax.

3. The balance of sales was for labor charges not subject to either excise or sales tax.

Required

a. Calculate the related liabilities for excise and sales taxes for June.

b. Prepare the necessary journal entry at June 30 to record the monthly payment of excise tax and sales tax to the government.

LO1, 3 P10-6A. Noncontingent and Contingent Liabilities The following independent situations represent various types of liabilities:

1. One of the employees of Martin Company was severely injured when hit by one of Martin's trucks in the parking lot. The 35-year-old employee will never be able to work again. Insurance coverage is minimal. The employee has sued Martin Company and a jury trial is scheduled.

2. A shareholder has filed a lawsuit against Sweitzer Corporation. Sweitzer's attorneys have reviewed the facts of the case. Their review revealed that similar lawsuits have never resulted in a cash award and it is highly unlikely that this lawsuit will either.

3. Armstrong Company signed a 60-day, ten percent note when it purchased merchandise from Fischer Company.

4. Richmond Company has been notified by the Department of Environment Protection (DEP) that a state where it has a plant is filing a lawsuit for groundwater pollution against Richmond and another company that has a plant adjacent to Richmond's plant. Test results have not identified the exact source of the pollution. Richmond's manufacturing process can produce by-products that pollute ground water.

5. Fredonia Company has cosigned a note payable to a bank for one of its customers. The customer received all of the proceeds of the note. Fredonia will have to repay the loan if the customer fails to do so. Fredonia Company believes that it is unlikely that it will have to pay the note.

6. Holt Company manufactured and sold products to Z-Mart, a retailer that sold the products to consumers. The manufacturer's warranty offers replacement of the product if it is found to be defective within 90 days of the sale to the consumer. Historically, 1.2 percent of the products are returned for replacement.

Required
Prepare a multicolumn analysis that presents the following information for each of these situations:

a. Number of the situation.
b. Type of liability: (1) noncontingent or (2) contingent.
c. Accounting treatment: (1) record in accounts, (2) disclose in a note to the financial statements, or (3) neither record nor disclose.

P10-7A. **Bonds Payable Journal Entries; Issued at Par Plus Accrued Interest** Askew, Inc., which closes its books on December 31, is authorized to issue $500,000 of nine percent, 15-year bonds dated May 1, with interest payments on November 1 and May 1.   LO2

Required
Prepare journal entries to record the following events, assuming that the bonds were sold at 100 plus accrued interest on October 1:

a. The bond issuance.
b. Payment of the first semiannual period's interest on November 1.
c. Accrual of bond interest expense at December 31.
d. Payment of the semiannual interest on May 1 of the following year.
e. Retirement of $300,000 of the bonds at 101 on May 1, Year 2 (immediately after the interest payment on that date).

P10-8A. **Effective Interest Amortization** On December 31, Caper, Inc., issued $250,000 of eight percent, nine-year bonds for $220,900, yielding an effective interest rate of ten percent. Semiannual interest is payable on June 30 and December 31 each year. The firm uses the effective interest method to amortize the discount.   LO2

Required
a. Prepare an amortization schedule showing the necessary information for the first two interest periods. Round amounts to the nearest dollar.
b. Prepare the journal entry for the bond issuance on December 31.
c. Prepare the journal entry to record the bond interest payment and discount amortization at June 30 of the following year.
d. Prepare the journal entry to record the bond interest payment and discount amortization at December 31 of the following year.

P10-9A. **Effective Interest Amortization** On January 1, Eagle, Inc., issued $800,000 of nine percent, 20-year bonds for $878,948, yielding an effective interest rate of eight percent. Semiannual interest is payable on June 30 and December 31 each year. The firm uses the effective interest method to amortize the premium.   LO2

Required
a. Prepare an amortization schedule showing the necessary information for the first two interest periods. Round amounts to the nearest dollar.
b. Prepare the journal entry for the bond issuance on January 1.
c. Prepare the journal entry to record the bond interest payment and premium amortization at June 30.
d. Prepare the journal entry to record the bond interest payment and premium amortization at December 31.

LO4 **P10-10A. Current Ratio, Quick Ratio, and Times-Interest-Earned Ratio** The following data is from the current accounting records of Florence Company:

Cash...	$120
Accounts receivable (net of allowance of 40)..	200
Inventory..	150
Other current assets...	80
Accounts payable...	110
Other current liabilities..	170

The president of the company is concerned that the company is in violation of a debt covenant that requires the company to maintain a minimum current ratio of 2.0. He believes the best way to rectify this is to reverse a bad debt write-off in the amount of $10 that the company just recorded. He argues that the write-off was done too early, and that the collections department should be given more time to collect the outstanding receivables. The CFO argues that this will have no effect on the current ratio, so a better idea is to use $10 of cash to pay accounts payable early.

Required
a. Which idea, the president's or the CFO's, is better for attaining a minimum 2.0 current ratio?
b. Will either the quick ratio or the times-interest-earned ratios be affected by either of these ideas?

PROBLEMS—SET B

LO1 **P10-1B. Journal Entries for Accounts Payable and Notes Payable** Simon Company had the following transactions:

Apr.	15	Issued a $6,000, 75-day, eight percent note payable in payment of an account with Marion Company.
May	22	Borrowed $30,000 from Sinclair Bank, signing a 60-day note at nine percent.
June	29	Paid Marion Company the principal and interest due on the April 15 note payable.
July	13	Purchased $12,000 of merchandise from Sharp Company; signed a 90-day note with ten percent interest.
	21	Paid the May 22 note due Sinclair Bank.
Oct.	2	Borrowed $36,000 from Sinclair Bank, signing a 120-day note at 12 percent.
	11	Defaulted on the note payable to Sharp Company.

Required
a. Record these transactions in general journal form.
b. Record any adjusting entries for interest in general journal form. Simon Company has a December 31 year-end.

LO1 **P10-2B. Adjusting Entries for Interest** At December 31, 2011, Portland Corporation had two notes payable outstanding (notes 1 and 2). At December 31, 2012, Portland also had two notes payable outstanding (notes 3 and 4). These notes are described below.

	Date of Note	Principal Amount	Interest Rate	Number of Days
December 31, 2011				
Note 1................	11/25/2011	$27,000	8%	90
Note 2................	12/16/2011	16,800	9	60
December 31, 2012				
Note 3................	12/11/2012	15,400	9	120
Note 4................	12/7/2012	18,000	10	90

Required
a. Prepare the adjusting entries for interest at December 31, 2011.

b. Assume that the adjusting entries were made at December 31, 2011, and that no adjusting entries were made during 2012. Prepare the 2012 journal entries to record payment of the notes that were outstanding at December 31, 2011.

c. Prepare the adjusting entries for interest at December 31, 2012.

P10-3B. **Recording Payroll and Payroll Taxes** Manchester, Inc., had the following payroll for March: **LO1**

Officers' salaries..	$39,000
Sales salaries	65,000
Federal income taxes withheld...	21,000
FICA taxes withheld	7,900
Health insurance premiums withheld...................................	2,200
Salaries (included above) subject to federal unemployment taxes	65,000
Salaries (included above) subject to state unemployment taxes........	70,000

Required

Prepare journal entries on March 31 to record:

a. Accrual of the monthly payroll.

b. Payment of the net payroll.

c. Accrual of employer's payroll taxes. (Assume that the FICA tax matches the amount withheld, the federal unemployment tax is 0.6 percent, and the state unemployment tax is 5.4 percent.)

d. Payment of all liabilities related to this payroll. (Assume that all are settled at the same time.)

P10-4B. **Recording Payroll and Payroll Taxes** The following data are taken from Jefferson Distribution Company's March payroll: **LO1**

Administrative salaries	$29,000
Sales salaries	55,000
Custodial salaries...	8,000
Total payroll	$92,000
Salaries subject to FICA tax (6.2 percent + 1.45 percent).............	$92,000
Salaries subject to federal unemployment taxes	68,000
Salaries subject to state unemployment taxes	76,000
Federal income taxes withheld from all salaries	18,600

Assume that the company is subject to a 5.4 percent state unemployment tax and an 0.6 percent federal unemployment tax.

Required

Record the following in general journal form on March 31:

a. Accrual of the monthly payroll.

b. Payment of the net payroll.

c. Accrual of the employer's payroll taxes.

d. Payment of these payroll-related liabilities. (Assume that all are settled at the same time.)

P10-5B. **Excise and Sales Tax Calculations** Madison Corporation initially records its sales at amounts that exclude any related excise and sales taxes. During May, Madison recorded total sales of $600,000. An analysis of May sales indicated the following: **LO1**

1. Twenty percent of sales were subject to both a ten percent excise tax and a five percent sales tax.

2. Sixty percent of sales were subject only to the sales tax.

3. The balance of sales was for labor charges not subject to either excise or sales tax.

Required

a. Calculate the related liabilities for excise and sales taxes for May.

b. Prepare the necessary journal entry at May 31, to record the monthly payment of excise tax and sales tax to the government.

LO1, 3 **P10-6B.** **Noncontingent and Contingent Liabilities** The following independent situations represent various types of liabilities:

1. Marshall Company has a manufacturing plant located in a small, rural community. The only other major employer in the area is Baker Company, which is experiencing financial problems. Marshall agrees to guarantee a loan for Baker, so Baker will remain in the community. Baker will receive all the proceeds of the loan. However, Marshall will have to repay the loan if Baker fails to do so. Marshall believes that Baker will repay the loan.

2. The village of High Creek and the town of Middlebury have been jointly using a rural dump site for 25 years. The state Department of Natural Resources has notified the two municipalities that wells on the nearby farms are polluted and that the dump site will be closed while further testing is done. Cleanup could cost as much as $25 million.

3. Two people walking on the sidewalk in front of the building owned by First United Bank were injured when part of the building collapsed on them. They are 25 years old and both are totally disabled. The building had been in poor condition for a long time. Insurance coverage is minimal. Both are suing First United Bank, and a jury trial is scheduled.

4. Winters Company sells garden tractors through 120 dealers located throughout the United States. Winters provides a two-year warranty for all parts and labor on these tractors. Each year, the average warranty cost per tractor sold is approximately $40.

5. Cronnin Company signed a 90-day note when it bought a new delivery truck for $25,000.

6. The CPA firm of Boyd and Lampe is being sued by one of the owners of an audit client that went bankrupt three years after Boyd and Lampe conducted an audit. The CPA firm has no insurance for this type of lawsuit. The attorneys for the CPA firm have stated that similar cases have never been successful, and they expect the same result here.

Required

Prepare a multicolumn analysis that presents the following information for each of these situations:

a. Number of the situation.

b. Type of liability: (1) noncontingent or (2) contingent.

c. Accounting treatment: (1) record in accounts, (2) disclose in a note to the financial statements, or (3) neither record nor disclose.

LO2 **P10-7B.** **Bonds Payable Journal Entries; Issued at Par Plus Accrued Interest** Cheney, Inc., which closes its books on December 31, is authorized to issue $800,000 of nine percent, 20-year bonds dated March 1, with interest payments on September 1 and March 1.

Required

Prepare journal entries to record the following events, assuming that the bonds were sold at 100 plus accrued interest on July 1.

a. The bond issuance.

b. Payment of the semiannual interest on September 1.

c. Accrual of bond interest expense at December 31.

d. Payment of the semiannual interest on March 1 of the following year.

e. Retirement of $200,000 of the bonds at 101 on March 1, Year 3 (immediately after the interest payment on that date).

LO2 **P10-8B.** **Effective Interest Amortization** On December 31, 2011, Echo, Inc., issued $720,000 of 11 percent, ten-year bonds for $678,852, yielding an effective interest rate of 12 percent. Semiannual interest is payable on June 30 and December 31 each year. The firm uses the effective interest method to amortize the discount.

Required

a. Prepare an amortization schedule showing the necessary information for the first two interest periods. Round amounts to the nearest dollar.

b. Prepare the journal entry for the bond issuance on December 31, 2011.

c. Prepare the journal entry to record bond interest expense and discount amortization at June 30, 2012.

d. Prepare the journal entry to record bond interest expense and discount amortization at December 31, 2012.

P10-9B. **Effective Interest Amortization** On January 1, 2012, Raines, Inc., issued $250,000 of six percent, 15-year bonds for $206,690, yielding an effective interest rate of eight percent. Semiannual interest is payable on June 30 and December 31 each year. The firm uses the effective interest method to amortize the discount.

LO2

Required

   a. Prepare an amortization schedule showing the necessary information for the first two interest periods. Round amounts to the nearest dollar.

   b. Prepare the journal entry for the bond issuance on January 1, 2012.

   c. Prepare the journal entry to record the bond interest payment and discount amortization at June 30.

   d. Prepare the journal entry to record the bond interest payment and discount amortization at December 31.

P10-10B. **Current Ratio, Quick Ratio, and Times-Interest-Earned Ratio** The following data is from the current accounting records of Sierra Company:

LO4

Cash.	$240
Accounts receivable (net of allowance of 80).	400
Inventory.	300
Other current assets.	160
Accounts payable.	220
Other current liabilities	340

The president of the company is concerned that the company may be in violation of a debt covenant that requires the company to maintain a minimum current ratio of 2.0. He believes the best way to rectify the problem is to reverse a bad debt write-off in the amount of $20 that the company just recorded. He argues that the write-off was done too early and that the collections department should be given more time to collect the outstanding amounts. The CFO argues that this will have no effect on the current ratio, so a better idea is to use $20 of cash to pay accounts payable early.

Required

   a. Which idea, the president's or the CFO's, is better for attaining a minimum 2.0 current ratio?

   b. Will either the quick ratio or the times-interest-earned ratios be affected by either of these ideas?

SERIAL PROBLEM: KATE'S CARDS

(Note: This is a continuation of the Serial Problem: Kate's Cards from Chapters 1 through 9.)

SP10. Recall that Kate previously obtained a $15,000 bank loan, signing a note payable, on November 30. The note required semiannual interest payments at the rate of six percent. The entire principal balance was due two years from the origination date of the note. Kate has been accruing interest on a monthly basis in the amount of $75. Kate would like to know how she should record the interest in May, the month she makes the first interest payment. She is unsure how much expense will need to be recorded in May.

      The upcoming interest payment is really not Kate's main concern right now. She was just notified by a lawyer that she is being sued for copyright infringement. Mega Cards Incorporated, one of the largest greeting card companies, believes that one of Kate's designs is too similar to one of Mega's designs for it to be coincidence, and has, therefore, decided to sue Kate's Cards. Mega has a prior reputation for suing small companies and settling out of court for lesser damages. Kate, however, knows that her design is original and that she had never previously seen the Mega design that is the subject of the lawsuit. She has determined to fight the lawsuit, regardless of the cost. She doesn't know, however, how this will affect her financial statements.

   1. Record the May journal entry for Kate's first interest payment. How much interest expense is reported in May?

   2. How should Kate report the copyright infringement lawsuit in her financial statements?

EXTENDING YOUR KNOWLEDGE

REPORTING AND ANALYSIS

COLUMBIA
SPORTSWEAR
COMPANY

EYK10-1. Financial Reporting Problem: Columbia Sportswear Company The financial statements for the **Columbia Sportswear Company** can be found in Appendix A at the end of this book.

Required
Answer the following questions:

a. How much were Columbia's current liabilities as of December 31, 2011?
b. What two items made up the largest percentage of Columbia's December 31, 2011, current liabilities?
c. What was the largest component of Columbia's December 31, 2011, accrued liabilities?
d. What was the largest component of Columbia's December 31, 2011, other long-term liabilities?

COLUMBIA
SPORTSWEAR
COMPANY

UNDER ARMOUR,
INC.

EYK10-2. Comparative Analysis Problem: Columbia Sportswear Company vs Under Armour Inc. The financial statements for the **Columbia Sportswear Company** can be found in Appendix A at the end of this book, and the financial statements of **Under Armour, Inc.** can be found in Appendix B (the complete annual report is available on this book's Website).

Required
Answer the following questions:

a. Compute the current ratio for Columbia Sportswear and Under Armour, Inc. as of December 31, 2011, and comment on what this ratio implies about each company's liquidity and working capital position.
b. Compute the debt-to-total assets ratio for Columbia Sportswear and Under Armour, Inc. as of December 31, 2011, and comment on what this ratio implies about each company's solvency.

EYK10-3. Business Decision Problem Kingston Corporation has total assets of $5,200,000 and has been earning an average of $800,000 before income taxes the past several years. The firm is planning to expand plant facilities to manufacture a new product and needs an additional $2,000,000 in funds, on which it expects to earn 18 percent before income tax. The income tax rate is expected to be 40 percent for the next several years. The firm has no long-term debt outstanding and presently has 75,000 shares of common stock outstanding. The firm is considering three alternatives:

1. Obtain the $2,000,000 by issuing 25,000 shares of common stock at $80 per share.
2. Obtain the $2,000,000 by issuing $1,000,000 of ten percent, 20-year bonds at face value and 12,500 shares of common stock at $80 per share.
3. Obtain the $2,000,000 by issuing $2,000,000 of ten percent, 20-year bonds at face value.

Required
As a shareholder of Kingston Corporation, which of the three alternatives would you prefer if your main concern is enhancing the firm's earnings per share? (Hint: Divide net income by the number of outstanding common shares to determine the company's earnings per share.)

ABBOTT
LABORATORIES

EYK10-4. Financial Analysis Problem **Abbott Laboratories** is a diversified health care company devoted to the discovery, development, manufacture, and marketing of innovative products that improve diagnostic, therapeutic, and nutritional practices. The company's balance sheet for three recent years contains the following data:

	2011	2010	2009
Cash and cash equivalents	$ 6,812,820	$ 3,648,371	$ 8,809,339
Investment securities	1,284,539	1,803,079	1,122,709
Trade receivables (net of allowance)	7,683,920	7,184,034	6,541,941
Inventories	3,284,249	3,188,734	3,264,877
Other current assets	4,703,246	6,493,311	3,575,025
Total current assets	$23,768,774	$22,317,529	$23,313,891
Total current liabilities	$15,480,228	$17,262,434	$13,049,489

Required

a. Compute the current ratio for 2009–2011.
b. Compute the quick ratio for 2009–2011.
c. Comment on the three-year trend in these ratios.

CRITICAL THINKING

EYK10-5. Financial Analysis on the Web: General Mills, Inc. The fiscal year 2011 annual report of **General Mills, Inc.** is available on this book's Website. Refer to the consolidated statement of earnings, the consolidated balance sheets, and Notes 8 and 15.

GENERAL MILLS, INC.

Required

a. What was the total dollar amount of current liabilities as of May 29, 2011?
b. What percent of long-term debt was considered current as of May 29, 2011?
c. What were the current ratio and quick ratio as of May 29, 2011?
d. What is the total amount of long-term liabilities reported by General Mills as of May 29, 2011?
e. How much principal payments on the long-term debt is General Mills anticipating paying in fiscal year 2012?
f. Are General Mills' leases capital leases or operating leases? Explain.

EYK10-6. Accounting Communication Activity Cedric Salos is considering different ways to raise money for the expansion of his company's operations. Cedric is not sure about the advantages of issuing bonds versus issuing common stock. In addition, he is not sure which features he should consider including with the bonds if he selects that form of financing. He asks you to explain, in simple terms, the answers to his questions.

Required

Write a short memorandum to Cedric explaining the advantages of issuing bonds over issuing common stock and the features that should be considered for inclusion with the bonds.

EYK10-7. Accounting Ethics Case Sunrise Pools, Inc., is being sued by the Crescent Club for negligence when installing a new pool on Crescent Club's property. Crescent Club alleges that the employees of Sunrise Pools damaged the foundation of the clubhouse and part of the golf course while operating heavy machinery to install the pool.

The lawsuit is for $1.5 million. At the time of the alleged incident, Sunrise Pools carried only $600,000 of liability insurance.

While reviewing the draft of Sunrise Pools' annual report, its president deletes all references to this lawsuit. She is concerned that disclosure of this lawsuit in the annual report will be viewed by Crescent Club as admission of Sunrise's wrongdoing, even though she privately admits that Sunrise employees were careless and believes that Sunrise Pools will be found liable for an amount in excess of $1 million. The president sends the amended draft of the annual report to the vice president of finance with a note stating that the lawsuit will not be disclosed in the annual report and that the lawsuit will not be disclosed to the board of directors.

Required

Is the president's concern valid? What ethical problems will the vice president of finance face if he follows the president's instructions?

EYK10-8. Corporate Social Responsibility Problem The chapter highlight on Microsoft's corporate social responsibility efforts (see Page 457) discussed the company's Unlimited Potential partnerships. Go to Microsoft's Website and navigate to the section "About Microsoft;" then navigate to the section on corporate citizenship. Download the Corporate Citizenship Report. In addition to Unlimited Potential, what are some other ways that Microsoft demonstrates its commitment to being a good corporate citizen?

EYK10-9. Forensic Accounting Problem Billing schemes are frauds in which an employee causes the victim organization to issue fraudulent payments by submitting invoices for nonexistent goods or services, inflated invoices, or invoices for personal items. One type of billing scheme uses a shell company that is set up for the purpose of committing the fraud. The shell company is often nothing more than a fake corporate name and a post-office mailbox.

What are some of the ways that shell company invoices can be detected?

EYK10-10. Working with the Takeaways Below are selected data from Microsoft's 2012 financial statements:

	2012	2011
Net income.	$16,978	$23,150
Tax expense.	5,289	4,921
Interest expense.	0	0
Cash and cash equivalents	6,938	9,610
Short-term investments	56,102	43,162
Accounts receivable.	17,815	17,454
Other current assets.	4,229	4,692
Current liabilities.	32,688	28,774

Required

Calculate the following ratios for 2012 and 2011 and comment on the trend:

a. Current ratio
b. Quick ratio

EYK10-11. IFRS Financial Statements Tesco PLC is the world's third largest retailer and is based in the United Kingdom. Tesco also operates a chain of grocery stores in the Western U.S. called Fresh-n-Easy. Tesco prepares its financial statements using IFRS. Selected data from Tesco's 2011 annual report is presented in Appendix C at the end of this book. Using Tesco's financial data for 2010 and 2011, calculate the company's (a) current ratio, (b) quick ratio, and (c) times-interest-earned ratio. Is Tesco's working capital position improving or declining over the two-year period? Can Tesco readily service its interest payments from its income before interest expense and income taxes? (Hint: Tesco's interest expense is labeled "Finance costs" on its group income statement.)

ANSWERS TO SELF-STUDY QUESTIONS:

1. b, (p. 453)   2. b, (p. 455)   3. b, (p. 458)   4. c, (p. 456)   5. b, (p. 468)   6. d, (p. 464)
7. c, (p. 477)   8. b, (p. 466)   9. b, (p. 481)   10. b, (p. 472)   11. c, (p. 473)

YOUR TURN! SOLUTIONS

Solution 10.1

a.

Apr. 30	Office salaries expense		40,000	
	Sales salaries expense		86,000	
	Federal income tax withholding payable			25,600
	FICA tax payable			9,639
	Health insurance premiums payable			1,850
	Union dues payable			950
	Payroll payable			87,961
	To accrue payroll for April			
	(FICA taxes = 0.0765 × $126,000 = $9,639).			

b.

30	Payroll payable		87,961	
	Cash			87,961
	To pay April payroll.			

c.

30	Payroll tax expense		14,847	
	FICA tax payable			9,639
	Federal unemployment tax payable			456
	State unemployment tax payable			4,752
	To record employer's payroll taxes (FICA Tax = 0.0765 ×			
	$126,000 = $9,639; Federal Unemployment Tax = 0.006 ×			
	$76,000 = $456; State Unemployment Tax = 0.054 × $88,000			
	= $4,752).			

d.

30	Federal income tax withholding payable		25,600	
	FICA tax payable		19,278	
	Health insurance premiums payable		1,850	
	Union dues payable		950	
	Federal unemployment tax payable		456	
	State unemployment tax payable		4,752	
	Cash			52,886
	To record the payment of payroll-related liabilities.			

Solution 10.2

(a)

Cash			325,000	
Bonds payable				300,000
Premium on bonds payable				25,000
To record the issuance of bonds payable				

(b)

Long-term liabilities
Bonds payable $300,000
Add: Premium on bonds payable. 25,000 $325,000

11

Stockholders' Equity

PAST

Chapter 10 examined the accounting for liabilities.

PRESENT

In this chapter, we turn our attention to the accounting for stockholders' equity.

FUTURE

In Chapter 12, we shift our focus to the statement of cash flows.

LEARNING OBJECTIVES

1. **Define** the corporate form of organization and **discuss** its principal characteristics. *(p. 504)*

2. **Explain** the difference between par value stock and no-par value stock. *(p. 507)*

3. **Identify** and **discuss** the two types of capital stock and their respective stockholder rights. *(p. 508)*

4. **Describe** the accounting for issuances of capital stock. *(p. 512)*

5. **Define** and **discuss** the accounting for stock splits. *(p. 514)*

6. **Explain** the accounting for treasury stock. *(p. 515)*

7. **Identify** and **distinguish** between cash dividends and stock dividends. *(p. 516)*

8. **Illustrate** the statement of retained earnings and the statement of stockholders' equity. *(p. 520)*

9. **Define** the *return on common stockholders' equity, dividend yield,* and *dividend payout ratio* and **explain** their use. *(p. 522)*

STARBUCKS

Starbucks is the largest coffeehouse company in the world, with approximately 20,000 stores in 49 countries. The first Starbucks coffeehouse was opened in Seattle, Washington, in 1971 to sell high quality coffee beans and equipment.

An important event in Starbucks' history occurred in 1982 when Howard Schultz joined the company. Schultz had a different strategic vision for Starbucks. He believed that the company should not only sell coffee beans, but coffee and espresso drinks as well. Starbucks' owners, however, rejected the idea. Schultz was so committed to his vision that he decided to leave the company and start the Il Giornale coffee bar chain in 1985.

In 1987, the Starbucks chain was sold to Schultz's Il Giornale, which was re-branded as Starbucks. Soon after, the company began to rapidly expand at an explosive rate. During the 1990s, Starbucks opened a new store almost every workday!

Where do firms get the necessary capital for expansion? While not every large firm is a corporation, many are; and, one of the most important characteristics of the corporate form of organization is the ability to raise new capital by selling ownership shares in the company. Starbucks had its initial public offering of its common shares in 1992.

Without a doubt, the modern corporation dominates the national and international economic landscape. In the United States, corporations generate well over three-fourths of the combined sales revenue of all forms of business organization, even though less than one of every five businesses is organized as a corporation. The corporate form of organization is used in a variety of business settings—from large multinational corporations with more than a million stockholders operating in countries all over the world, to small, family-owned businesses operating only in their local community.

Why do fast growing firms like Starbucks choose the corporate form of organization? There are several reasons, but certainly one of the primary reasons is the relative ease of attracting large amounts of capital as compared to other organizational forms of business.

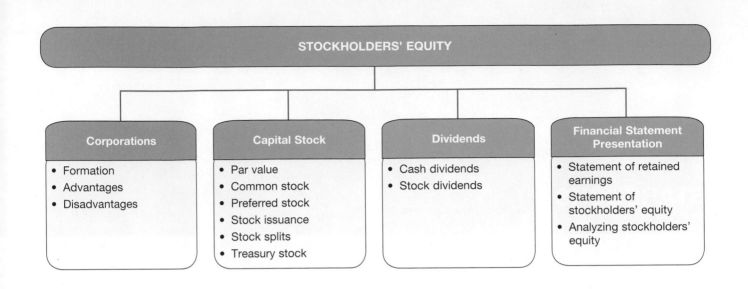

Corporations	Capital Stock	Dividends	Financial Statement Presentation
• Formation • Advantages • Disadvantages	• Par value • Common stock • Preferred stock • Stock issuance • Stock splits • Treasury stock	• Cash dividends • Stock dividends	• Statement of retained earnings • Statement of stockholders' equity • Analyzing stockholders' equity

NATURE AND FORMATION OF A CORPORATION

LO1 **Define** the corporate form of organization and **discuss** its principal characteristics.

A **corporation** is a legal entity created with the approval of a governmental authority. The right to conduct business as a corporation is a privilege granted by the state in which a corporation is formed (or chartered). All states have laws specifying the requirements for creating a corporation.

To form a corporation, the incorporators (founders) must apply for a charter. The incorporators prepare and file the **articles of incorporation**, which define the basic structure of the corporation, including the purpose for which it is formed and the amount of capital stock to be authorized. If the incorporators meet the requirements of the law, the government issues a charter or certificate of incorporation. After a charter has been granted, the founders hold an organizational meeting to elect the first board of directors and adopt the corporation's bylaws.

Because assets are essential to starting any business, a corporation issues (or sells) *certificates of capital stock* to obtain the necessary funds to acquire its operating assets. As owners of a corporation, capital stock *stockholders* are entitled to a voice in the control and management of the company. Stockholders with voting stock may vote on specific issues at the annual meeting and participate in the election of the board of directors. The board of directors establishes the overall policies of a corporation and declares dividends. Normally, the board also hires a group of corporate officers, including a president, a chief financial officer, one or more vice presidents, a controller, a treasurer, and a secretary, to execute the day-to-day operations of the company. The officers implement the policies of the board of directors and actively manage the affairs of the corporation. Exhibit 11-1 depicts the responsibilities of these stakeholders in a corporation.

Advantages of the Corporate Form of Organization

A corporation has several advantages when compared with a sole proprietorship or partnership.

Separate Legal Entity
The corporation, as a separate legal entity, may acquire assets, incur debt, enter into contracts, sue, and be sued—all in its own name. The stockholders of a corporation, however, are separate and distinct from the corporation. This characteristic contrasts with proprietorships and partnerships, which are accounting entities but not legal entities apart from their owners.

| EXHIBIT 11-1 | Responsibilities of Selected Corporate Stakeholders |

STOCKHOLDERS
Owners of the corporation; those with voting shares elect the board of directors.

↓

BOARD OF DIRECTORS
Establish overall policies, declare dividends, and select corporate officers.

↓

OFFICERS
Implement operating policies and manage day to day operations.

↓

EMPLOYEES
Execute management's operating plans and procedures.

Limited Liability

The liability of stockholders with respect to a company's business affairs is usually limited to the value of their investment in the corporation. By way of contrast, the owners of proprietorships and partnerships can be held financially responsible, separately and collectively, for any unsatisfied obligations of the business. To protect a corporation's creditors, state laws limit the distribution of contributed capital. Distributions of retained earnings (undistributed profits) are not legal unless the board of directors formally votes to declare a dividend. Because of the legal constraints regarding the amount of stockholder capital available for distribution, corporations must maintain clear distinctions in the accounts to identify the various elements of stockholders' equity.

Transferability of Ownership

Shares in a corporation may be routinely transferred without affecting a company's operations. The corporation merely notes such transfers of ownership in the stockholder records. Although a corporation must have stockholder records to notify stockholders of meetings and to pay dividends, the price at which shares transfer between investors is not recognized in the corporation's accounts.

Continuity of Existence

Because routine transfers of ownership do not affect a corporation's affairs, the corporation is said to have continuity of existence. In a partnership, any change in ownership technically results in a discontinuation of the old partnership and the formation of a new one.

| Entity Concept and Going Concern Concept | PRINCIPLE ALERT |

Two characteristics of the corporate form of organization mesh well with the basic principles of accounting. The separate legal status conferred upon a corporation conforms, for example, with the *entity concept*. When the corporation is the unit of focus for accounting purposes, the entity concept requires that the economic activity of the corporation be accounted for separately from the activities of its owners. Legally, the corporate entity is also distinct from its owners. Consequently, the corporation's continuity of existence also aligns well with the *going concern concept*, which assumes that the accounting entity will continue indefinitely into the future.

Capital Raising Capability

The limited liability of stockholders and the ease with which shares of stock may be transferred from one investor to another are attractive features to potential stockholders. These characteristics enhance the ability of the corporation to raise large amounts of capital by issuing shares of stock. Since both large and small investors may acquire ownership interests in a corporation, there exists a wide spectrum of potential investors. Corporations with thousands of stockholders are not uncommon.

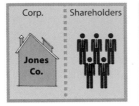

Separate Legal Entity

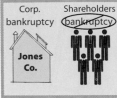

Limited Liability

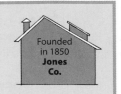

Transferability of Ownership

Continuous Existence

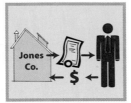

Capital Raising Capability

Disadvantages of the Corporate Form of Organization

There are some disadvantages to organizing as a corporation as compared with a proprietorship or partnership.

Organization Costs

Creating a corporation is more costly than organizing a proprietorship or partnership. The expenditures incurred to organize a corporation are charged to Organization Costs and expensed on the income statement when incurred. These costs include attorney's fees, fees paid to the state, and the costs of promoting the enterprise.

Taxation

As separate legal entities, corporations are subject to federal income taxes on any earned income. Stockholders are likewise subject to income taxation on any income received from a corporation as dividends, leading to a situation of double taxation of a corporation's distributed earnings.

Usually, corporations are subject to state income taxes in the states in which they are incorporated or are doing business. They may also be subject to real estate, personal property, and franchise taxes.

THINKING GLOBALLY

The equity ownership structure of most U.S. and United Kingdom companies is characterized by small diffuse investors, each of whom owns only a small fraction of the firm. But the ownership structure of public companies in most of the rest of the world is strikingly different, and is more commonly characterized by the presence of a large investor who holds a controlling interest in the company's shares. These large owners usually consist of families and are typically directly involved in managing the company's operations. To illustrate, consider the following seven East Asian countries and the percentage of their public companies that are controlled by families. South Korea has the highest percentage of family-controlled public companies at 78 percent:

Country	Percentage of Family-Controlled Companies
Hong Kong	65%
Indonesia	75
Malaysia	71
Singapore	50
South Korea	78
Taiwan	55
Thailand	68

Regulation and Supervision

Corporations are subject to greater degrees of regulation and supervision than are proprietorships and partnerships. Each state maintains the right to regulate the corporations it charters. State laws also limit the powers a corporation may exercise, identify reports that must be filed by a corporation, and define the rights and liabilities of stockholders. If shares of stock are issued to the public, the corporation must comply with any securities laws governing the sale of corporate securities. Furthermore, corporations whose shares are listed and traded on organized security exchanges, such as the New York Stock Exchange, are subject to the various reporting and disclosure requirements of these exchanges.

Accounting for Stockholders' Equity in Alternative Organizational Forms

Differences exist between the accounting for the stockholders' equity of a corporation and for that of a sole proprietorship or partnership. In a sole proprietorship, only a single owner's capital account is needed to reflect increases from capital contributions and net income as well as decreases from owner withdrawals and net losses. A similar situation exists in most partnerships, which customarily maintain capital and drawing accounts for each partner.

A corporation, on the other hand, is subject to certain legal restrictions imposed by the government approving its creation. These restrictions focus on the distinction between contributed capital and retained earnings and make accounting for stockholders' equity somewhat more complex for corporations than for other types of business organizations.

The following attributes are associated with the corporate form of organization. Identify each one as either an advantage or a disadvantage of the corporate form over other forms of organization:

1. Taxation
2. Limited liability
3. Capital raising capability
4. Regulation
5. Cost to organize
6. Transferability of ownership

YOUR TURN! 11.1

The solution is on page 546.

PAR VALUE STOCK AND NO-PAR VALUE STOCK

A corporate charter may specify a face value, or **par value**, for each share of capital stock. In the early days of corporate stock issuances, par value represented the market value of the stock when it was issued. In more recent times, however, par values have typically been set at amounts well below a stock's fair market value on the date of issue. As a consequence, a stock's par value has no economic significance today.

LO2 Explain the difference between par value stock and no-par value stock.

Par value, however, may have legal implications. In some states, par value may represent the minimum amount that must be paid in per share of stock. If stock is issued at a *discount* (that is, at less than its par value), the stockholder may have a liability for the amount of the discount should any creditor claims remain unsatisfied following a company's liquidation. Issuing stock at a discount rarely occurs, however, because boards of directors have generally established par values below fair market values at the time of issue. For example, **PepsiCo, Inc.** set the par value of its common stock at $0.0167 and **The Charles Schwab Corporation** set the par value of its common stock at $0.01.

Par value may also be used in some states to define a corporation's legal capital. *Legal capital* is the minimum amount of contributed capital that must remain in a corporation as a margin of protection for creditors. However, given the low par values typically assigned to common stock today, this protection has limited usefulness for creditors. Still, given the role that par value may play in defining legal capital, accountants carefully segregate and record the par value of stock transactions in an appropriate capital stock account.

Most states permit the issuance of capital stock without a par value, called **no-par value stock**. The company's board of directors, however, usually sets a **stated value** for the no-par stock. In such cases, the stated value will determine the corporation's legal capital. For accounting purposes, stated value amounts are treated similarly to par value amounts. In the absence of a stated value, the entire proceeds from the issuance of no-par value stock will likely establish a corporation's legal capital.

CORPORATE SOCIAL RESPONSIBILITY	Starbucks
	To some, corporate social responsibility (CSR) means doing things for non-stockholder stakeholders, even if it means a lower rate of return for stockholders. This sort of thinking pits CSR against stockholder gains, as if the two were competitors for the corporate dollar. Companies that truly understand CSR have come to see CSR in a more strategic light, where doing good can lead to doing well. Further, these companies realize that they would not have the resources to do good if they were not making money. Starbucks is known to be not only a highly profitable company with 2010 profits of nearly $1 billion U.S. dollars, but also a company on the leading edge of social responsibility. Starbucks believes businesses should have a positive impact on the communities they serve. The company has set goals in such areas as ethical sourcing, recycling, diversity, and philanthropy.

TYPES OF CAPITAL STOCK

LO3 **Identify** and **discuss** the two types of capital stock and their respective stockholder rights.

The amounts and kinds of capital stock that a corporation may issue are specified in a company's charter of incorporation. Providing for the sale of several classes of capital stock permits a company to raise capital from different types of investors with diverse risk preferences. The charter also specifies a corporation's **authorized shares**—the maximum number of shares of each class of capital stock that may be issued. Shares that have been sold and issued to stockholders constitute the **issued shares** of a corporation. Some of these shares may be repurchased by the corporation. When shares are repurchased, they may be retired and cancelled or held for reissuance. Shares actually held by stockholders are called **outstanding shares**, whereas those reacquired by a corporation (and not cancelled) are called *treasury stock*. We will discuss treasury stock later in the chapter.

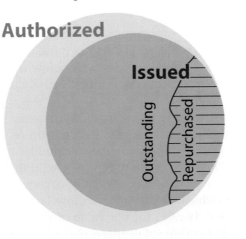

Common Stock

When only one class of stock is issued, it is called **common stock**. Common stockholders have the right to vote on corporate matters, to share in the corporation's net income, to participate in additional issuances of stock, and in the case of a corporate liquidation, to share in any asset distributions after any prior claims against the corporation by its creditors have been settled.

As the owners of a corporation, the common stockholders elect the board of directors and vote on all matters requiring the approval of the owners. Common stockholders are entitled to one vote for each share of stock they own. Stockholders who do not attend the annual stockholders' meetings may vote by proxy.

A common stockholder has the right to a proportionate share of the corporation's earnings that are distributed as dividends. All earnings belong to the corporation, however, until the board of directors formally votes to declare a dividend.

Each stockholder of a corporation has a **preemptive right** to maintain his or her proportionate ownership interest in the corporation. If a company issues additional shares of stock, the current owners of that type of capital stock receive the first opportunity to acquire, on a pro rata basis, the new shares. In certain situations, management may request stockholders to waive their preemptive right. For example, a corporation may wish to issue additional shares of capital stock for use to acquire another company.

Preemptive Right Prevents Wealth Transfer	ACCOUNTING IN PRACTICE

A major reason for the preemptive right is to protect stockholders against a transfer of their wealth to new stockholders. To illustrate, assume that a firm has 10,000 shares of common stock outstanding with a market price of $20 per share. Thus, the firm's total market value is $200,000 (10,000 shares × $20). If the firm sells another 10,000 common shares at $10 per share (a price below its current market value), the additional $100,000 cash received would raise the firm's total market value to $300,000. With a new market value of $15 per share ($300,000/20,000 shares), the new share issuance causes the old stockholders to lose $5 per share and the new stockholders to gain $5 per share—that is, the sale of the new shares at a lower price caused a wealth transfer from the old stockholders to the new stockholders. The preemptive right protects the existing stockholders from such wealth transfers by enabling them to purchase any newly issued shares.

When a corporation liquidates, it converts its assets to a form suitable for distribution, usually cash, which it then distributes to all parties having claims on the corporate assets. Any assets remaining after all claims have been satisfied belong to the residual owners of the corporation—that is, the common stockholders. Common stockholders are entitled to the final distribution of the balance of any remaining assets in a corporate liquidation.

A company may occasionally issue *classified* common stock; that is, it may issue more than one class of common stock. For example, when two classes of common stock are issued, they are often identified as Class A and Class B. The two classes usually differ in either their respective dividend rights or their respective voting powers. Usually, classified common stock is issued when the founders of a corporation wish to acquire funds from the public while retaining voting control of the corporation.

Preferred Stock

Preferred stock is a class of stock with characteristics that differentiate it from common stock. Preferred stock, for example, has one or more preferences over common stock, usually with reference to (1) the payment of dividends and (2) the distribution of assets when a corporation liquidates. To determine the features of a particular preferred stock issue, it is necessary to examine the preferred stock contract. The majority of preferred shares issues, however, have certain typical features, which are discussed below.

Dividend Preference

When the board of directors declares a distribution of the company's net income, preferred stockholders are entitled to an annual dividend before common stockholders may receive any dividend distribution. The amount is usually specified in the preferred stock contract as a percentage of the par value of the stock or in dollars per share if the stock lacks a par value. Thus, if the preferred stock has a $100 par value and a six percent dividend rate, the preferred stockholders receive $6 per share in dividends. However, the dividend is owed to the stockholders only if, and when, declared by the board of directors.

From both a legal and an accounting standpoint, preferred stock is disclosed as part of stockholders' equity on the balance sheet. Dividends are distributions of earnings and, unlike interest on bonds, are not shown as expenses on the income statement. Also, because of the legal classification of preferred stock as stockholders' equity, the company cannot deduct dividends as expenses for income tax purposes, whereas interest on debt can be deducted as an expense.

Preferred dividends are usually **cumulative**—that is, regular dividends to preferred stockholders omitted in the past must be paid in addition to the current year's dividend before any dividend distribution can be made to the common stockholders. If a preferred stock is **noncumulative**, omitted dividends do not carry forward.

To illustrate the difference between cumulative and noncumulative preferred stock, assume that a company ending its second year of operations has 1,000 shares of $100 par value, six percent preferred stock and 100,000 shares of $1 par value common stock outstanding. The company declared no dividends last year. This year a dividend of $27,000 is declared. The distribution of the $27,000 between the two stockholder classes depends upon whether the preferred stock is cumulative or noncumulative. If the preferred stock is cumulative, preferred stockholders receive $12 per share before common stockholders receive anything, as illustrated below:

	Preferred	Common	Total
Total par value of outstanding shares	$100,000	$100,000	$200,000
Preferred stock is cumulative			
Preferred dividends in arrears (6 percent)	$ 6,000		$ 6,000
Regular preferred dividend (6 percent).	6,000		6,000
Remainder to common.		$ 15,000	15,000
Total distribution	$ 12,000	$ 15,000	$ 27,000
Preferred stock is noncumulative			
Regular preferred dividend (6 percent).	$ 6,000		$ 6,000
Remainder to common.		$ 21,000	21,000
Total distribution	$ 6,000	$ 21,000	$ 27,000

Dividends in arrears (that is, dividends omitted in past years) on cumulative preferred stock are not an accounting liability and do not appear in the liability section of the balance sheet. They do not become an obligation of the corporation until the board of directors formally declares such dividends. Any dividends in arrears are disclosed to investors in the notes to the financial statements.

Asset Distribution Preference

Preferred stockholders normally have a preference over common stockholders with respect to the receipt of assets in the event of a corporate liquidation. When a corporation liquidates, any creditor claims are settled first. Preferred stockholders then have the right to receive assets equal to the par value of their shares, or a larger stated liquidation value per share, before any assets are distributed to common stockholders. The preferred stockholders' preference to assets in liquidation also includes any dividends in arrears.

Other Preferred Stock Features

Although preferred stockholders do not ordinarily have the right to vote in the election of the board of directors, this right can be accorded by contract. Some state laws require that all capital stock issued by a corporation be given voting rights. Further, preferred stock may contain features that cause the shares to resemble common stock. Preferred stock may, for example, be **convertible** into common stock at a specified conversion rate. When this feature is present, the market price of the preferred shares often moves in a fashion consistent with the related common shares; that is, when the price of the common stock rises, the value of the conversion feature is enhanced, and consequently, the value of the preferred shares should also rise. When preferred stock is converted into a company's common stock, the newly issued common stock assumes the book value of the preferred stock; that is, the Preferred Stock—Par Value and the Paid-in Capital in Excess of Par Value—Preferred Stock are debited while the Common Stock—Par Value and Paid-in Capital in Excess of Par Value—Common Stock are credited.

Preferred stock may be **participating**. A *participating preferred stock* shares any special dividend distributions with common stock beyond the regular preferred stock dividend rate. After receiving its regular dividend preference, preferred stock normally does not participate in any special dividend distribution until the common stock is allowed a dividend amount corresponding to the regular preferred stock dividend rate (Special dividends are discussed on p. 517). At this point, the two classes of stock begin to share the special dividend distribution at the same rate. The preferred stock participation feature may be partial (which limits the participation to a certain amount) or full (which places no limit on the rate of participation).

Preferred stock may be **callable**, which means that a corporation can redeem the shares after a length of time and at a price specified in the stock contract. The call feature makes the preferred stock similar to a bond, since many bonds are callable or have a limited life. Most preferred stocks are callable, with the call or redemption price set slightly above the original preferred stock issuance price.

Benford's Law Aids Accounting Sleuths	FORENSIC ACCOUNTING

How often should the number 9 appear as the first digit of an amount reported on a financial statement? If you say one out of ten times you, like most people, would be wrong. It turns out the number 9 should appear less than five percent of the time, whereas the number 1 will appear as the first digit of a reported amount over thirty percent of the time! This numerical phenomenon, known as Benford's Law, was discovered by Frank Benford while working as a physicist at the GE Research Laboratories.

An intuitive explanation of Benford's Law appeared in the *Journal of Accountancy* in the article "I've Got Your Number" written by Mark Nigrini. Nigrini offered an explanation that considered "the total assets of a mutual fund that is growing at 10 percent per year. When the total assets are $100 million, the first digit of total assets is 1. The first digit will continue to be 1 until total assets reach $200 million. This will require a 100 percent increase (from 100 to 200), which, at a growth rate of 10 percent per year, will take about 7.3 years (with compounding). At $500 million the first digit will be 5. Growing at 10 percent per year, the total assets will rise from $500 million to $600 million in about 1.9 years, significantly less time than assets took to grow from $100 million to $200 million. At $900 million, the first digit will be 9 until total assets reach $1 billion, or about 1.1 years at 10 percent. Once total assets are $1 billion the first digit will again be 1, until total assets again grow by another 100 percent. The persistence of a 1 as a first digit will occur with any phenomenon that has a constant (or even an erratic) growth rate."

Benford's Law has been applied to the detection of fraudulent financial statements by forensic accountants with some success. The reasoning is simply that when somebody chooses to make up numbers to produce a fraudulent financial statement they are more likely to choose numbers more randomly than what Benford has shown will occur.

ACCOUNTING IN PRACTICE	**Preferred Shares and the Capital Market**

Although legally, and from an accounting standpoint, preferred shares are considered to be part of a company's stockholders' equity, the capital market takes a different point of view. Most investment professionals consider a company's preferred stock to be part of the company's debt structure. Thus, from a capital market perspective, the only true stockholders of a business are its common stockholders. This point of view is apparent in the calculation of such ratios as the return on common stockholders' equity, discussed shortly, which excludes a company's preferred stockholders' equity.

YOUR TURN! 11.2

The solution is on page 546.

Match the description in the right column with the appropriate term in the left column:

1. Authorized	a. The right to receive dividends omitted in prior years.
2. Outstanding	b. The most basic class of stock ownership.
3. Common stock	c. Stock with one or more preferences over common stock.
4. Preemptive right	d. The maximum number of shares of each class of stock that may be issued.
5. Preferred stock	e. Shares actually held by stockholders.
6. Cumulative preference	f. The right to maintain a proportionate ownership interest in a corporation.

STOCK ISSUANCES FOR CASH

LO4 Describe the accounting for issuances of capital stock.

When issuing capital stock to investors, a corporation may use the services of an investment bank, a specialist in marketing securities to the capital market. The investment bank may *underwrite* a stock issue by agreeing to sell the shares on a firm commitment basis— that is, buying the shares from the corporation and then reselling them to investors. Under a firm commitment agreement, a corporation does not risk being unable to sell its stock. The underwriter bears this risk in return for the fees and profits generated by selling the shares to investors at a price higher than it paid to the corporation. An investment bank that is unwilling to underwrite a stock issue may handle the issuance of the shares on a *best efforts* basis. In this case, the investment bank agrees to sell as many shares as possible at a set price, but the corporation bears the risk of any unsold shares.

When capital stock is issued to investors, the appropriate capital stock account is credited for the par value of the stock issued, or if the stock is no-par value stock, with its stated value, if any. The asset received in exchange for the stock (usually cash) is debited, and any difference is credited to the Paid-in Capital in Excess of Par Value account.

To illustrate the journal entries to record various stock issuances in exchange for cash, assume that Smith & Sons issued two different types of capital stock during its first year of operations:

Issuing Stock At A Premium

1. Issued 1,000 shares of $100 par value, 9% preferred stock at $107 cash per share:

A = L + SE
+107,000   +100,000
                        PS
                +7,000 PS

Cash	107,000	
Preferred stock		100,000
Paid-in capital in excess of par value—Preferred stock		7,000

In this transaction, the preferred stock is issued at a price greater than its par value—that is, the shares were sold at a premium. The par value of the preferred stock issued is credited to the Preferred Stock account and the $7,000 premium is credited to the Paid-in Capital in Excess of Par Value account. If there is more than one class of par value stock, the account title may indicate the class of stock to which the premium relates, in this case Paid-in Capital in Excess of Par Value—Preferred Stock.

Issuing No-Par Stock

2. Issued 30,000 shares of no-par value common stock, stated value $5, at $8 cash per share:

Cash	240,000	
Common stock		150,000
Paid-in capital in excess of stated value—Common stock		90,000

A = L + SE
+240,000   +150,000
             CS
             +90,000
             CS

When no-par value stock has a stated value, as in Entry 2, the stated value of the total shares issued is credited to the proper capital stock account, and any additional amount received is credited to the account Paid-in Capital in Excess of Stated Value. If there is no stated value for the no-par value stock, the entire proceeds are credited to the appropriate capital stock account. In the second journal entry, if the common stock had no stated value, the entire $240,000 amount would have been credited to the Common Stock account.

These two stock issuances are reflected in Exhibit 11-2, which presents the stockholders' equity section from Smith & Sons' year-end balance sheet. (Retained earnings are assumed to be $25,000.) The stockholders' equity section is divided into two major categories: ❶ Paid-in Capital and ❷ Retained Earnings. **Paid-in capital** is the amount of capital contributed to the corporation from various capital stock transactions such as the issuance of preferred stock and common stock. The capital contributed by stockholders through the issuance of stock is divided between the legal capital (the par value or stated value of the stock) and the amounts received in excess of the legal capital. Later in this chapter we discuss treasury stock transactions that may affect a corporation's paid-in capital. **Retained earnings** represent the cumulative net income and losses of the company that have not been distributed to stockholders as a dividend.

EXHIBIT 11-2	Stockholders' Equity Section of the Balance Sheet

❶	Paid-in Capital		
	9% Preferred stock, $100 par value, 1,000 shares authorized, issued, and outstanding.	$100,000	
	No-par common stock, stated value $5, 40,000 shares authorized; 30,000 shares issued and outstanding	150,000	$250,000
	Additional paid-in capital		
	In excess of par value—Preferred stock.	7,000	
	In excess of stated value—Common stock	90,000	97,000
	Total Paid-in Capital		347,000
❷	Retained earnings		25,000
	Total Shareholders' Equity		$372,000

Noncash Stock Issuances

Sometimes a corporation will exchange its common stock for services, operating assets, or for its own convertible debt. For example, some start-up companies lacking cash will exchange their common stock for professional services provided by attorneys and accountants. When this occurs, a journal entry is made to debit the Professional Services Expense account and a credit is made to Common Stock—Par Value and to the Paid-in Capital in Excess of Par Value—Common Stock account for the fair value of the services received.

When common stock is exchanged for operating assets, a similar journal entry is made, although the debit in this case is to the Land or Equipment account. When common stock is exchanged for convertible bonds (discussed in Chapter 10), the value of the newly issued stock is assumed to be equal to the book value of the bonds. An exchange of convertible bonds for common stock is executed by debiting the Bonds Payable account and the Premium on Bonds Payable account (or crediting the Discount on Bonds Payable account) and crediting the Common Stock account and the Paid-in Capital in Excess of Par Value—Common Stock for any excess of the bonds' book value over the stock's par value.

YOUR TURN! 11.3

The solution is on page 546.

Wyatt Industries began operations on June 1 by issuing 10,000 shares of $1 par value common stock for cash at $9 per share. How much Additional Paid-in Capital will be reported by Wyatt Industries?

STOCK SPLITS

LO5 **Define** and **discuss** the accounting for stock splits.

Occasionally, a corporation may issue additional shares of common stock to its stockholders through a **forward stock split**. The principal reason that companies execute a forward stock split is to reduce the market price of their shares. A forward stock split increases the number of shares outstanding and is accounted for by reducing the par value or stated value of the stock affected. A forward stock split does not change the balances of any of the stockholders' equity accounts; however, a memorandum entry is made in the general journal to show the altered par value or stated value of the stock and to note the increase in the number of shares issued and outstanding. For example, if Smith & Sons has 10,000 shares of $10 par value common stock outstanding and announces a 2-for-1 forward stock split, it would simply reduce the par value of its common stock to $5 per share and issue to its stockholders 10,000 new common shares. Thus, after the forward stock split, each stockholder would have twice the number of shares held prior to the split, and the value of the Common Stock account would remain unchanged at $100,000 (10,000 shares × $10 = 20,000 shares × $5 = $100,000). If you owned one share of Smith & Sons $10 par value stock before the 2-for-1 forward stock split you would own two shares of Smith & Sons $5 par value stock after the stock split.

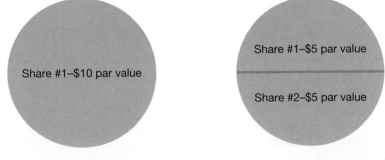

Before 2-for-1 forward stock split   After 2-for-1 forward stock split

Occasionally, a company may execute a *reverse stock split* by increasing the par value of the stock and reducing the number of shares outstanding. Reverse stock splits are designed to increase a company's stock price. Most major stock exchanges have a minimum trading price that a company must meet or exceed in order to be traded on the exchange. When a company's stock price falls below the minimum trading price, the shares may be delisted, making it difficult for stockholders to find buyers for their shares. Meeting and exceeding an exchange's minimum listing price is one of the principal reasons for reverse stock splits.

TREASURY STOCK

When a corporation acquires its own outstanding shares for a purpose other than retiring (cancelling) them, the acquired shares are called **treasury stock**. Treasury stock may be purchased for a variety of reasons, to include reissuing them to officers and employees in profit sharing programs or employee stock option plans. Whatever the purpose, treasury stock purchases reduce a company's stockholders' equity. The repurchased shares do not carry voting privileges or preemptive rights, are not paid dividends, and do not receive assets in the event of a corporation's liquidation.

LO6 Explain the accounting for treasury stock.

	ACCOUNTING IN PRACTICE
Greenmail	

Corporations usually purchase their own shares by buying them through a brokerage firm on the open market or by making a tender offer to stockholders. Under a tender offer, the company offers to buy back its shares of stock at a specified price per share. Another way to acquire treasury stock is to negotiate a purchase of shares from a single large stockholder. In some cases, this latter technique may involve greenmail. *Greenmail* is a ploy in which an investor purchases a large number of a company's shares, threatens to take control of the company, and then sells the shares back to the company at a premium. Management pays the premium to entice the investor to "be quiet and go away." Although it is not illegal, payment of an unjustified greenmail premium is likely to upset other stockholders and may lead to legal action against a company.

Accounting for Treasury Stock

Accountants commonly record treasury stock at its acquisition cost, debiting the Treasury Stock account and crediting the Cash account. The Treasury Stock account is a contra-stockholders' equity account, and its balance is deducted when deriving total stockholders' equity on the balance sheet. To illustrate the accounting for the purchase of treasury stock, assume that Smith & Sons had 20,000 shares of $10 par value common stock outstanding and then purchased 1,000 shares at $12 per share. The journal entry to record the purchase is:

Treasury stock	12,000	
Cash		12,000
To record purchase of 1,000 shares of treasury stock at $12 per share.		

$$A = L + SE$$
$$-12,000 \qquad -12,000 \text{ TS}$$

If a balance sheet is prepared following this transaction, the stockholders' equity section would appear as follows (the values for Paid-in Capital in Excess of Par Value and Retained Earnings are assumed):

SMITH & SONS, INC. Stockholders' Equity	
Paid-in Capital	
Common stock, $10 par value, authorized and issued 20,000 shares; 1,000 shares in treasury, 19,000 shares outstanding	$200,000
Paid-in capital in excess of par value	20,000
Total Paid-in Capital	220,000
Retained earnings	40,000
	260,000
Less: Treasury stock (1,000 shares) at cost	**12,000**
Total Stockholders' Equity	$248,000

Note that the $200,000 par value of all *issued* stock is disclosed, although the 1,000 treasury shares are no longer outstanding. The total cost of the 1,000 shares, however, is later deducted as the last component in the presentation of total stockholders' equity.

If Smith & Sons subsequently resells 500 shares of its treasury stock at $14 per share, the following journal entry is made:

A = L + SE			
+7,000 +6,000 TS	Cash	7,000	
+1,000 TS	Treasury stock		6,000
	Paid-in capital—Treasury stock		1,000

Note that the $1,000 "gain" on the resale of the treasury stock is accounted for as an increase in shareholders' equity and not as net income.

IFRS Alert!

Under IFRS and U.S. GAAP, treasury stock is reported on the balance sheet as a contra stockholders' equity account; that is, the repurchase cost of any treasury stock is subtracted from total stockholders' equity. In addition, both IFRS and U.S. GAAP preclude the recognition of any gain or loss by a company from stock transactions involving its own shares—that is, any "gain" or "loss" from trading in a company's own shares is recorded as part of Paid-in Capital in Excess of Par Value. By way of contrast, some countries permit treasury stock to be reported on the asset side of the balance sheet as an investment in marketable securities. Under IFRS and U.S. GAAP, treasury stock does not satisfy the definition of an asset, and therefore, cannot be reported on the balance sheet as marketable securities. It is also noteworthy that in some countries, treasury stock purchases are illegal because they are viewed as a form of stock price manipulation.

YOUR TURN! 11.4

The solution is on page 546.

The Fullerton Corporation purchased 5,000 shares of its outstanding $2 par value common stock for $75,000 cash on November 1. Management anticipates holding the stock in the treasury until it resells the stock. By how much would the Fullerton Corporation debit Treasury Stock for this purchase?

CASH DIVIDENDS AND STOCK DIVIDENDS

LO7 Identify and distinguish between cash dividends and stock dividends.

Dividends are a distribution of assets or shares of stock from a corporation to its stockholders. A corporation can distribute dividends to stockholders only after its board of directors has formally voted to declare a distribution. Dividends are usually paid in cash but may also be paid as property or additional shares of stock in the firm. Legally, declared dividends are an obligation of the firm, and an entry to record the dividend obligation is made on the *dividend declaration date*. Cash and property dividends payable are carried as liabilities, and stock dividends to be issued are shown in the stockholders' equity section of the balance sheet. At the date of declaration, a *record date* and *payment date* are also established. For example, assume that on April 25 (the declaration date), the board of directors of Smith & Sons declares a cash dividend payable on June 1 (the payment date) to those investors who own shares of stock on May 15 (the record date). Stockholders owning stock on the record date receive the dividend even if they dispose of their shares before the payment date. Therefore, shares sold between the record date and the payment date are sold *ex dividend*—that is, they are sold without the right to receive the dividend.

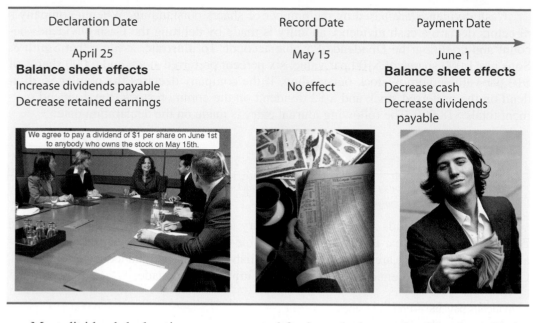

Most dividend declarations are accounted for by reducing retained earnings. Under certain conditions, however, state laws may permit distributions from additional paid-in capital. Stockholders should be informed of the source of such dividends, because, in a sense, any dividend paid from a company's paid-in capital is a nontaxable return of capital rather than a taxable distribution of earnings.

THINKING GLOBALLY

While U.S. corporations principally distribute cash and/or stock dividends, property dividend distributions are common among Japanese corporations. For example, **McDonald's Holding Company of Japan** annually distributes to its stockholders coupons for a free Big Mac as a property dividend. And, **DyDo Drinco, Inc.**, distributes to its stockholders samples of its beverage products as a property dividend. Companies that distribute their products or coupons for their products to stockholders as a property dividend believe that by making stockholders more familiar with the company's products, they will retain the investment commitment of their stockholders on a longer term basis than would otherwise be the case.

Cash Dividends

The majority of dividends distributed by corporations are paid in cash. Although companies may pay such dividends annually, many firms pay quarterly dividends. Dividends that are paid routinely are called regular dividends. The **Johnson & Johnson Company** and **PepsiCo, Inc.**, for example, pay regular quarterly dividends. Some companies occasionally pay a special dividend. Special dividends occur infrequently and represent the distribution of excess cash that has been accumulated by a business and for which the business has no immediate operational need.

When a company declares a cash dividend, the company must have both an appropriate amount of retained earnings and the necessary amount of cash on hand. Uninformed investors often believe that a large retained earnings balance automatically permits generous dividend distributions. A company, however, may successfully accumulate earnings and at the same time not be sufficiently liquid to pay large cash dividends. Many companies, especially new firms in growth industries, finance their expansion from assets generated through earnings and pay out small cash dividends or none at all.

Cash dividends are based on the number of shares outstanding. When a company's directors declare a cash dividend, an entry is made by debiting the Cash Dividends account and crediting the Dividends Payable account. To illustrate, assume that Smith & Sons has 1,000 shares of $100 par value, six percent preferred stock and 6,000 shares of $10 par value common stock outstanding. If the company declares the regular $6 dividend on the preferred stock and a $2 dividend on the common stock, the dividend payment totals $18,000. The following journal entry is made on the declaration date:

A = L + SE	Cash dividends	18,000	
+6,000 −18,000	Dividends payable—Preferred stock		6,000
Div	Dividends payable—Common stock		12,000
+12,000	*To record the declaration of $6 dividend on preferred stock and*		
	$2 dividend on common stock.		

The Cash Dividends account is a temporary account that is closed to the Retained Earnings account at year-end.[1] Dividends Payable—Preferred Stock and Dividends Payable—Common Stock are reported as current liabilities on the balance sheet until paid. On the dividend payment date, the following journal entry is made:

A = L + SE	Dividends payable—Preferred stock	6,000	
−18,000 −6,000	Dividends payable—Common stock	12,000	
−12,000	Cash		18,000
	To record the payment of dividends on preferred and common shares.		

Stock Dividends

Companies frequently distribute shares of their own stock as dividends to stockholders in lieu of, or in addition to, cash dividends. A company may issue **stock dividends** when it does not wish to deplete its working capital by paying a cash dividend. Young and growing companies often issue stock dividends because cash is usually needed to acquire new facilities and to expand.

The accounting for a stock dividend results in a transfer of a portion of retained earnings to the paid-in capital accounts. Thus, the distribution of a stock dividend signals investors of management's desire to "plow back" earnings into the company. Although stock dividends may take a number of forms, usually common shares are distributed to common stockholders. We limit our discussion to this type of stock dividend distribution.

Small Stock Dividends

Small stock dividends are share distributions that involve less than 25 percent of the total number of shares previously outstanding. Small stock dividends are *recorded at the market value* of the shares issued, causing retained earnings to decrease and paid-in capital to increase by this amount. To illustrate the journal entries for a declaration of a small stock dividend, assume that the stockholders' equity of Smith & Sons is as follows prior to the declaration of a ten percent stock dividend:

Common stock, $5 par value, 20,000 shares issued and outstanding	$100,000
Paid-in capital in excess of par value.	**20,000**
Total Paid-in Capital	120,000
Retained earnings	**65,000**
Total Stockholders' Equity	$185,000

---

[1] Some companies, especially those paying regular dividends, debit the Retained Earnings account directly on the dividend declaration date.

With 20,000 shares outstanding, the declaration of a ten percent stock dividend requires the issuance of an additional 2,000 shares (10 percent × 20,000 shares). If the current market price per share is $11, the total market value of the shares to be distributed is $22,000 (2,000 shares × $11), resulting in the following journal entry:

Stock dividends	22,000		A = L + SE
Stock dividend distributable		10,000	−22,000
Paid-in capital in excess of par value		12,000	Div
To record declaration of 10 percent stock dividend on common shares.			+10,000
			CS
			+12,000
			CS

The amount of the credit to the Stock Dividend Distributable account is the par value of the shares to be distributed (2,000 shares × $5). If a balance sheet is prepared between the declaration date and the distribution date of a stock dividend, the Stock Dividend Distributable account is shown in stockholders' equity immediately after the Common Stock account. When the shares are distributed, the following journal entry is made:

Stock dividend distributable	10,000		A = L + SE
Common stock		10,000	−10,000
To record issuance of stock dividend on common shares.			CS
			+10,000
			CS

The Stock Dividends account is a temporary account that is closed to the Retained Earnings account at year-end, as shown by the following journal entry:

Retained earnings	22,000		A = L + SE
Stock dividends		22,000	−22,000
To close the Stock Dividends account.			RE
			+22,000
			Div

After the shares are distributed and the Stock Dividends account is closed, a comparison of the stockholders' equity and outstanding shares before and after the stock dividend appears below. Note that retained earnings decreased by $22,000 and paid-in capital increased by $22,000, but total stockholders' equity remains unchanged:

	Before Stock Dividend	After Stock Dividend
Common stock, $5 par value.	$100,000	$110,000
Paid-in capital in excess of par value.	20,000	32,000
Total Paid-in Capital.	120,000	142,000
Retained earnings	65,000	43,000
Total Stockholders' Equity	$185,000	$185,000
Common shares issued and outstanding	20,000	22,000

The relative ownership interest of a common stockholder is unaltered by the receipt of a common stock dividend. If a ten percent stock dividend is distributed, all stockholders increase their proportionate holdings by ten percent, and the total shares outstanding are increased in the same proportion. Small stock dividends rarely affect the market value of the underlying stock.

Large Stock Dividends

When the number of shares issued as a stock dividend is large enough to impact the stock's market value per share, the stockholders may not perceive the same benefits as they do for a small stock dividend. Accordingly, the accounting for large stock dividends (those over 25 percent) differs from the accounting for small stock dividends. The journal entry to record the declaration of a large stock dividend debits the Stock Dividends account and credits the

Stock Dividend Distributable account for the par or stated value of the shares issued. Once the stock is issued, the increase in paid-in capital is reflected in the Common Stock account.[2]

Fango Company's president would like to know the financial impact that a cash dividend and a stock dividend will have on the company's retained earnings account. The current balance in retained earnings is $500,000. The company has 10,000 shares of $1 par value common stock outstanding with a current market value of $20 per share. The potential cash dividend will be $3 per share and the potential stock dividend will be ten percent.

Required
Compute the Fango Company retained earnings balance after

a. A $3 per share cash dividend
b. A ten percent stock dividend

RETAINED EARNINGS AND THE STATEMENT OF STOCKHOLDERS' EQUITY

LO8 Illustrate the statement of retained earnings and the statement of stockholders' equity.

A **statement of retained earnings** presents an analysis of the Retained Earnings account for a given accounting period. An example of a statement of retained earnings is presented in Exhibit 11-3. The statement begins with the retained earnings balance as of the beginning of the period ❶, then reports the items that caused retained earnings to change during the period ❷, and ends with the end-of-period balance in retained earnings ❸.

EXHIBIT 11-3	Statement of Retained Earnings

GEYSER CORPORATION Statement of Retained Earnings For Year Ended December 31, 2013	
❶ { Retained earnings, January 1, 2013	$48,000
❷ { Add: Net income	32,000
	80,000
Less: Cash dividends declared	19,000
❸ { Retained earnings, December 31, 2013	$61,000

Statement of Stockholders' Equity

Rather than reporting a statement of retained earnings, most corporations integrate the information regarding retained earnings into a more comprehensive statement called a **statement of stockholders' equity**. This statement shows an analysis of all of the stockholders' equity accounts for the period. Exhibit 11-4 presents an example of a statement of stockholders' equity. The statement begins with the beginning balances of the various stockholders' equity accounts ❶, reports the items causing changes in these accounts ❷, and ends with the end-of-period balances ❸.

---

[2] A large stock dividend is similar in many respects to a stock split (discussed earlier in the chapter). A stock's par value or stated value per share is not changed by a stock dividend; however, a stock split reduces the par value or stated value in proportion to the increase in the number of shares issued. This difference leads to a difference in accounting treatment—only a memorandum entry is made for a stock split, whereas a large stock dividend requires a journal entry to transfer the legal capital of the shares to be issued from retained earnings to common stock.

The statement of stockholders' equity in Exhibit 11-4 reveals all of the events affecting the Geyser Corporation's stockholders' equity during 2013. These events are the issuance of common stock, the issuance of treasury stock, the earning of net income, the declaration of a cash dividend, and the acquisition of treasury stock. Note that the information in the retained earnings column (highlighted using a dotted red box) contains the same information as a statement of retained earnings.

EXHIBIT 11-4	Statement of Stockholders' Equity

GEYSER CORPORATION
Statement of Stockholders' Equity
For Year Ended December 31, 2013

	Common Stock	Paid-in Capital in Excess of Par Value	Paid-in Capital from Treasury Stock	Retained Earnings	Treasury Stock	Total
❶ Balance, January 1, 2013.......	$200,000	$120,000	$18,000	$48,000	$(14,000)	$372,000
6,000 Common shares issued ...	30,000	24,000				54,000
500 Treasury shares issued			2,000		3,500	5,500
❷ Net income.................				32,000		32,000
Cash dividends declared				(19,000)		(19,000)
200 Treasury shares acquired ...					(2,000)	(2,000)
❸ Balance, December 31, 2013....	$230,000	$144,000	$20,000	$61,000	$(12,500)	$442,500

IFRS Alert!

IFRS

There exist a number of significant terminology differences between U.S. GAAP and IFRS with respect to the reporting of stockholders' equity.

U.S. GAAP	IFRS
Common stock	Share capital
Paid-in capital in excess of par value	Share premium
Retained earnings	Retained profits
Accumulated other comprehensive income	Other reserve accounts

---

YOUR TURN! 11.6

The solution is on page 546.

Dior Company had beginning balances at January 1, 2012, of $100,000 Common Stock, $900,000 Paid-in Capital in Excess of Par Value, and $50,000 Retained Earnings, $(10,000) Treasury Stock. Net income for the year was $30,000. Dior paid a cash dividend of $8,000. Dior also issued 1,000 new $1 par value common shares for $15 each.

Required
Prepare a statement of stockholders' equity for the Dior Company for 2012.

ANALYZING STOCKHOLDERS' EQUITY

Return on Common Stockholders' Equity

A financial ratio of particular interest to common stockholders is the return on common stockholders' equity. This ratio measures the profitability of the common stockholders'

LO9 **Define** the *return on common stockholders' equity*, *dividend yield*, and *dividend payout ratio* and **explain** their use.

investment in a company. The **return on common stockholders' equity** is calculated as follows:

$$\text{Return on common stockholders' equity} = \frac{(\text{Net income} - \text{Preferred stock dividends})}{\text{Average common stockholders' equity}}$$

By subtracting the preferred stock dividends from net income, the numerator represents the net income available exclusively to the common stockholders. The denominator averages the common stockholders' equity for the year (sum the beginning and ending common stockholders' equity and then divide by 2). If a company has preferred stock outstanding, the common stockholders' equity is calculated by subtracting the preferred stockholders' equity (the sum of the preferred stock par value and the preferred stock paid-in capital in excess of par value) from total stockholders' equity.

To illustrate the calculation of the return on common stockholders' equity, financial data from **Johnson Controls, Inc.**, is used. Johnson Controls manufactures automotive seating systems, environmental control systems, automotive batteries, and plastic packaging. The company's 2012 financial data are as follows (in millions of dollars):

Net income.	$ 1,353
Preferred stock dividends	0
Preferred stockholders' equity, beginning of year	0
Preferred stockholders' equity, end of year.	0
Common stockholders' equity, beginning of year	11,042
Common stockholders' equity, end of year.	11,555

Johnson Controls' return on common stockholders' equity for the year is 12.0 percent, calculated as $1,353 − $0/[($11,042 + $11,555)/2].

TAKEAWAY 11.1	**Concept**	**Method**	**Assessment**
	How profitable is the stockholders' investment in a company?	Statement of stockholders' equity and the income statement. Calculate the return on common stockholders' equity.	The higher the return on common stockholders' equity, the higher the profitability of the stockholders' investment in a business.

Dividend Yield and Dividend Payout Ratio

Investors differ in their expectations regarding their investments—some investors are primarily interested in appreciation in the market value of their shares, while other investors focus on receiving current income in the form of dividends. Dividend yield and dividend payout ratio are ratios that are helpful to this latter group of investors.

Dividend Yield

Dividend yield measures the current rate of return in cash dividends from an investment in a company's shares. The ratio may be calculated for either common or preferred shares, and is calculated by dividing the latest annual dividend per share by the current market price of the stock:

$$\text{Dividend yield} = \frac{\text{Annual dividend per share}}{\text{Market price per share}}$$

To illustrate, **Worthington Industries**, a manufacturer of steel and plastic products, declared cash dividends per common share of $0.61. At its fiscal year-end, Worthington's common stock had a market price of $13.99 per share. Consequently, at year-end, the company's dividend yield was 4.4 percent, or $0.61/$13.99.

Dividend yields are included in the stock tables published in *The Wall Street Journal* and *Barrons,* as well as online resources such as Yahoo! Finance, so it is easy for investors to compare current dividend yields for different stocks. The following are dividend yields for several well-known companies:

The Coca-Cola Company	2.5 percent
AT&T	4.7 percent
IBM Corporation	1.6 percent
J.C. Penney Company	2.5 percent
Chevron Corp.	3.0 percent
Wal-Mart Stores, Inc.	2.2 percent

Concept	Method	Assessment	TAKEAWAY 11.2
What is a company's current rate of return to stockholders in the form of dividends?	Statement of stockholders' equity and a company's current market price per share. Calculate the company's dividend yield by dividing the annual dividend per share by the company's market price per share.	The higher a company's dividend yield, the greater the rate of return to stockholders in the form of dividends.	

Dividend Payout Ratio

The **dividend payout ratio** measures the percentage of net income available to common stockholders that is paid out as dividends. The ratio is calculated as follows:

$$\text{Dividend payout ratio} = \frac{\text{Annual dividend per share}}{\text{Earnings per share}}$$

Dividend payout ratios vary considerably among corporations. Companies that are considered "growth" companies often have low payout ratios because they use the net income generated by operations to help finance their growth. By way of contrast, "mature" companies that lack significant growth opportunities often distribute a high percentage of their net income as dividends. A good example of a mature company is the local utility company whose growth is limited by the net increase of new homes and businesses in the community and the approved rate increases by the local public utility commission.

Some corporations try to maintain a reasonably stable dividend payout ratio, so their payout ratios do not vary much from one year to the next. Other corporations try to keep their dividend per share either constant or increasing each year at a constant rate. If net income fluctuates quite a bit from year to year, these latter corporations will show dividend payout ratios that are quite variable over time.

The following are the dividend payout ratios for some well-known corporations:

Best Buy Co. Inc. (retail)	18 percent
Microsoft Corporation (technology)	25 percent
Procter & Gamble Co. (consumer goods)	44 percent

TAKEAWAY 11.3	Concept	Method	Assessment
	What percentage of a company's net income is paid out to stockholders as a dividend?	Statement of stockholders' equity and the income statement. Calculate the dividend payout ratio by dividing the annual dividend per share by a company's earnings per share.	The higher the dividend payout ratio, the higher the percentage of net income paid to stockholders as a dividend.

COMPREHENSIVE PROBLEM

Following is the stockholders' equity section of Bayside Corporation's December 31 balance sheet:

Paid-in Capital		
7 Percent preferred stock, $50 par value, 5,000 shares authorized, issued, and outstanding	$ 250,000	
Common stock, $6 par value, 700,000 shares authorized; 200,000 issued, of which 10,000 shares are in the treasury	1,200,000	$1,450,000
Additional Paid-in Capital		
In excess of par value—Preferred stock	80,000	
In excess of par value—Common stock	1,000,000	
From treasury stock	22,000	1,102,000
Total Paid-in Capital		2,552,000
Retained earnings		2,223,000
		4,775,000
Less: Treasury stock (10,000 common shares) at cost		140,000
Total Stockholders' Equity		$4,635,000

Required

a. What is Bayside's legal capital at December 31?
b. What is the number of common shares outstanding at December 31?
c. What is the average amount per share received from the original issuance of common stock?
d. Assuming that the preferred stock is cumulative with no dividends in arrears, what total dollar amount of preferred dividends needs to be declared at December 31, before the common stockholders may receive a dividend?
e. Has Bayside ever sold treasury stock for more than the treasury stock cost when it was acquired? Briefly explain.
f. Assume that Bayside splits its common stock 3-for-1 on the following January 1. What is the total amount of paid-in capital immediately after the split?

Solution

a. $1,450,000 (the par value of the issued preferred stock and common stock).
b. 190,000 shares (200,000 issued common shares less 10,000 shares in the treasury).
c. $11 [($1,200,000 par value of issued shares + $1,000,000 paid-in capital in excess of par value)/200,000 issued shares].
d. $17,500 (7 percent × $250,000).
e. Yes, the stockholders' equity section shows additional paid-in capital of $22,000 from treasury stock. This type of paid-in capital represents the excess of proceeds from the sale of treasury stock over that treasury stock's cost.
f. $2,552,000 (splitting the common stock does not change any of the account balances composing paid-in capital; the common stock's par value will decrease to $2 per share, and the common shares issued will increase to 600,000).

SUMMARY OF LEARNING OBJECTIVES

Define the corporate form of organization and discuss its principal characteristics. (p. 504)   **LO1**

- A corporation is a separate legal entity chartered by the state in which it is formed.
- The liability of corporate stockholders for the debts of a business is limited to the value of their ownership interest in a corporation, whereas claims against partners and sole proprietors may extend to their personal resources.
- Unlike proprietorships and partnerships, corporations must report paid-in capital separately from the accumulated balance of retained earnings. Distributions to stockholders are limited by the amount of retained earnings and other capital as specified by state law.

Explain the difference between par value stock and no-par value stock. (p. 507)   **LO2**

- Par value is the face value printed on a stock certificate. It has no economic significance but may have legal significance.
- No-par value stock has no face value printed on the stock certificate, although generally the board of directors sets a stated value for a corporation's capital stock.

Identify and discuss the two types of capital stock and their respective stockholder rights. (p. 508)   **LO3**

- Common stock represents a corporation's basic ownership class of stock; common shares carry the right to vote and may or may not pay a dividend.
- Preferred stocks may differ from common stock in several ways. Typically, preferred stocks have, at a minimum, some type of dividend preference and a prior claim to assets in the event of a corporate liquidation, relative to common stock.

Describe the accounting for issuances of capital stock. (p. 512)   **LO4**

- When capital stock is issued, the appropriate capital stock account is credited with the par value or stated value of the shares issued. The asset exchanged for the stock (usually cash) is debited for its fair value. Any difference is placed in the Paid-in Capital in Excess of Par Value account.

Define and discuss the accounting for stock splits. (p. 514)   **LO5**

- Stock splits change the par or stated value of capital stock and affect the number of shares outstanding. Only a memorandum notation records stock splits in the general journal. Forward stock splits increase the number of shares outstanding and lower its par or stated value, while reverse stock splits do the opposite.

Explain the accounting for treasury stock. (p. 515)   **LO6**

- Treasury stock represents reacquired shares of a firm's capital stock. It is commonly recorded at its acquisition cost and is deducted from total stockholders' equity on the balance sheet.

Identify and distinguish between cash dividends and stock dividends. (p. 516)   **LO7**

- Cash dividends reduce retained earnings and are a current liability when declared.
- Stock dividends are accounted for by a transfer of retained earnings to the appropriate capital stock and paid-in capital accounts at the fair market value of the shares distributed for small stock dividends and at par value for large stock dividends.

Illustrate the statement of retained earnings and the statement of stockholders' equity. (p. 520)   **LO8**

- A statement of retained earnings presents the financial effect of events causing retained earnings to change during an accounting period.
- A statement of stockholders' equity presents the financial effect of events causing each component of stockholders' equity (including retained earnings) to change during an accounting period.

Define the *return on common stockholders' equity, dividend yield,* and *dividend payout ratio* and explain their use. (p. 522)   **LO9**

- The return on common stockholders' equity is computed as (net income − preferred stock dividends)/ average common stockholders' equity. It indicates the profitability of the common stockholders' investment in a company.
- Dividend yield is computed by dividing a stock's annual dividend per share by its current market price per share. For investors, this ratio identifies the annual rate of return in dividends from an investment in a company's shares.
- The dividend payout ratio is computed by dividing the annual dividend per share by a company's earnings per share.

SUMMARY	Concept ➡	Method ➡	Assessment
TAKEAWAY 11.1	How profitable is the stockholders' investment in a company?	Statement of stockholders' equity and the income statement. Calculate the return on common stockholders' equity.	The higher the return on common stockholders' equity, the higher the profitability of the stockholders' investment in a business.
TAKEAWAY 11.2	What is a company's current rate of return to stockholders in the form of dividends?	Statement of stockholders' equity and a company's current market price per share. Calculate the company's dividend yield by dividing the annual dividend per share by the company's market price per share.	The higher a company's dividend yield, the greater the rate of return to stockholders in the form of dividends.
TAKEAWAY 11.3	What percentage of a company's net income is paid out to stockholders as a dividend?	Statement of stockholders' equity and the income statement. Calculate the dividend payout ratio by dividing the annual dividend per share by a company's earnings per share.	The higher the dividend payout ratio, the higher the percentage of net income paid to stockholders as a dividend.

KEY TERMS

Articles of
incorporation (p. 504)
Authorized shares (p. 508)
Callable (p. 511)
Common stock (p. 508)
Convertible (p. 511)
Corporation (p. 504)
Cumulative (p. 510)
Dividend payout ratio (p. 523)
Dividends (p. 516)

Dividend yield (p. 522)
Forward stock split (p. 514)
Issued shares (p. 508)
Noncumulative (p. 510)
No-par value stock (p. 508)
Outstanding shares (p. 508)
Paid-in capital (p. 513)
Participating (p. 511)
Par value (p. 507)
Preemptive right (p. 509)

Preferred stock (p. 509)
Retained earnings (p. 513)
Return on common
stockholders' equity (p. 522)
Stated value (p. 508)
Statement of retained
earnings (p. 520)
Statement of stockholders'
equity (p. 520)
Stock dividends (p. 518)
Treasury stock (p. 515)

SELF-STUDY QUESTIONS

(Answers to the Self-Study Questions are available at the end of this chapter.)

LO1 1. **What is the usual liability of stockholders for corporation actions?**
   a. Unlimited
   b. Limited to the par value or stated value of the shares of stock they hold
   c. Limited to the amount of their investment in the corporation
   d. Limited to the amount of a corporation's retained earnings

LO3 2. **Which type of stock may have dividends in arrears?**
   a. Cumulative preferred stock
   b. Common stock
   c. Noncumulative preferred stock
   d. Treasury stock

LO4 3. **Wyler Company issued 20,000 shares of $10 par value common stock in exchange for a building with a current fair value of $1,000,000. In recording this transaction, what amount should be credited to the Paid-in Capital in Excess of Par Value account?**
   a. $1,000,000   *c.* $800,000
   b. $200,000   *d.* $980,000

4. **Which of the following accounts has a normal debit balance?**   LO6
   a.   Common Stock
   b.   Paid-in Capital in Excess of Stated Value
   c.   Preferred Stock
   d.   Treasury Stock

5. **Which of the following events decreases a corporation's stockholders' equity?**   LO7
   a.   A payment of a previously declared cash dividend
   b.   A declaration of a six percent stock dividend
   c.   A 2-for-1 forward stock split
   d.   A declaration of a $1 cash dividend per share on preferred stock

6. **When a company wants to reduce the market price per share of its stock, what action should it take?**   LO5
   a.   Issue a cash dividend
   b.   Issue a stock dividend
   c.   Do a reverse stock split
   d.   Do a forward stock split

7. **What type of company is typically characterized by a high dividend payout ratio?**   LO9
   a.   Technology company
   b.   High-growth company
   c.   Mature, low-growth company
   d.   All of the above

8. **Preferred stock that may be converted into common stock has which of the following characteristics?**   LO3
   a.   Call feature
   b.   Cumulative feature
   c.   Participation feature
   d.   Convertible feature

9. **A dividend that is paid every quarter or every year is called?**   LO7
   a.   Regular dividend
   b.   Special dividend
   c.   Property dividend
   d.   Stock dividend

10. **The statement of stockholders' equity includes each of the following except:**   LO8
    a.   Retained Earning
    b.   Treasury Stock
    c.   Paid-in Capital in Excess of Par Value
    d.   Accounts Receivable

QUESTIONS

1. What is the meaning of each of the following terms and, when appropriate, how do they interrelate: *corporation, articles of incorporation, corporate charter, board of directors, corporate officers,* and *organization costs*?

2. What is meant by the limited liability of a stockholder? Does this characteristic enhance or reduce a corporation's ability to raise capital?

3. Contrast the federal income taxation of a corporation with that of a sole proprietorship and a partnership. Which of the three types of organizations must file a federal income tax return?

4. Define *par value stock*. What is the significance of a stock's par value?

5. What is the preemptive right of a stockholder?

6. What are the basic differences between preferred stock and common stock? What are the typical features of preferred stock?

7. What features make preferred stock similar to debt? Similar to common stock?

8. What is meant by dividend in arrears? If dividends are two years in arrears on $500,000 of six percent preferred stock and dividends are declared this year, what amount of total dividends must preferred stockholders receive before any distributions can be made to common stockholders?

9. Distinguish between authorized shares and issued shares. Why might the number of shares issued be more than the number of shares outstanding?

10. What are two different sources of paid-in capital?

11. Define a *forward stock split*. What is the major reason for a forward stock split?

12. Define *treasury stock*. Why might a corporation acquire treasury stock? How is treasury stock shown on the balance sheet?

13. If a corporation purchases 600 shares of its own common stock at $10 per share and resells the shares at $14 per share, where would the $2,400 [($14 − $10) × 600 shares] increase in capital appear in the financial statements? Why is no gain reported?

14. Assume that a corporation has preferred shares outstanding. How is the return on common stockholders' equity computed?

15. What is a stock dividend? How does a common stock dividend paid to common stockholders affect their respective ownership interests?

16. What is the difference between the accounting for a small stock dividend versus the accounting for a large stock dividend?

17. What information is presented in a statement of retained earnings? a statement of stockholders' equity?

18. Where do the following accounts (and their balances) appear in the balance sheet?
    a. Dividends Payable—Common Stock
    b. Stock Dividend Distributable

19. How is a corporation's dividend yield calculated?

20. Bleaker Company declares and pays its annual dividend near the end of its fiscal year. For the current year, Bleaker's dividend payout ratio was 40 percent, its earnings per common share were $5.80, and it had 50,000 shares of common stock outstanding all year. What total amount of dividends did Bleaker declare and pay in the current year?

SHORT EXERCISES

LO1   **SE11-1.**   **Issuance of Common Stock** Smith & Sons, Inc., is authorized to issue one million shares of $1 par value common stock. In the company's initial public offering, 500,000 shares are sold to the investing public at a price of $5 per share. One month following Smith & Sons' initial public offering, 1,000 of its common shares were sold by one investor to another at a price of $10 per share. How should this transaction be recorded in the accounts of Smith & Sons? Why?

LO2   **SE11-2.**   **Issuance of No-Par Common Stock** Jackson & Company issued 100,000 shares of $1 par value common stock at a price of $5 per share and issued 10,000 shares of no-par value common stock at a price of $10 per share. Prepare the journal entry to record the issuance of the no-par value common stock. How does this entry differ from the entry to record the $1 par value common stock?

LO3   **SE11-3.**   **Allocating Liquidation Between Common Stockholders and Preferred Stockholders** The Arcadia Company is liquidating. After paying off all of its creditors, the company has $1 million to distribute between its preferred stockholders and its common stockholders. The aggregate par value of the preferred stock is $900,000 and the aggregate par value of its common stock is $2 million. How much of the remaining $1 million in assets should be distributed to the preferred stockholders and how much should be distributed to the common stockholders?

LO4   **SE11-4.**   **Issuance of Common Stock** Smith & Sons, Inc., is authorized to issue one million shares of $1 par value common stock. The company actually sells 500,000 shares at $10 per share. Prepare the journal entry to record the issuance of the 500,000 shares.

LO5   **SE11-5.**   **Outstanding Shares** Pearce & Company has 10 million shares of $2 par value common stock outstanding. The company believes that its current market price of $100 per share is too high and decides to execute a 4-for-1 forward stock split to lower the price. How many shares will be outstanding following the stock split, and what will be the new par value per share?

SE11-6. **Treasury Stock Purchase** Jackson & Company has no-par value common stock outstanding that is selling at $20 per share. The company's CEO believes that the stock price is undervalued and decides to buy back 10,000 shares. Prepare the journal entry to record the purchase of the treasury stock.   **LO6**

SE11-7. **Dividends Paid and Dividends in Arrears** The Arcadia Company has 100,000 shares of cumulative, six percent, $100 par value preferred stock outstanding. Last year the company failed to pay its regular dividend, but the board of directors would like to resume paying its regular dividend this year. Calculate the dividends in arrears and the total dividend that must be paid this year.   **LO7**

The following information relates to SE11-8 through SE11-10:

Smith & Sons, Inc., disclosed the following information in a recent annual report:

	2012	2013
Net income.	$ 35,000	$ 55,000
Preferred stock dividends	3,000	3,000
Average common stockholders' equity	1,200,000	1,500,000
Dividend per common share	1.20	1.20
Earnings per share	1.90	2.05
Market price per common share, year-end	19.50	21.00

SE11-8. **Return on Common Stockholders' Equity** Calculate the return on common stockholders' equity for Smith & Sons for 2012 and 2013. Did the return improve from 2012 to 2013?   **LO9**

SE11-9. **Dividend Yield** Calculate the dividend yield for Smith & Sons for 2012 and 2013. Did the dividend yield improve from 2012 to 2013?   **LO9**

SE11-10. **Dividend Payout Ratio** Calculate the dividend payout for Smith & Sons for 2012 and 2013. Did the dividend payout increase from 2012 to 2013?   **LO9**

SE11-11. **Change in Stockholders' Equity** Nikron Corporation issued 10,000 shares of $0.50 par value common stock during the year for $20 each. Nikron also repurchased treasury stock for $15,000. Net income for the year was $120,000. The company also paid cash dividends of $25,000. What was the total change in Nikron's stockholders' equity for the year?   **LO9**

Assignments with the ✓ logo in the margin are available in BusinessCourse.
See the Preface of the book for details.

EXERCISES—SET A

E11-1A. **Dividend Distribution** Lakeside Company has the following shares outstanding: 20,000 shares of $50 par value, six percent cumulative preferred stock and 80,000 shares of $10 par value common stock. The company declared cash dividends amounting to $160,000.   **LO7**

 a. If no dividends in arrears on the preferred stock exist, how much in total dividends, and in dividends per share, is paid to each class of stock?

 b. If one year of dividends in arrears exist on the preferred stock, how much in total dividends, and in dividends per share, is paid to each class of stock?

E11-2A. **Share Issuances for Cash** Finlay, Inc., issued 8,000 shares of $50 par value preferred stock at $68 per share and 12,000 shares of no-par value common stock at $10 per share. The common stock has no stated value. All issuances were for cash.   **LO4** ✓

 a. Prepare the journal entries to record the share issuances.

 b. Prepare the journal entry for the issuance of the common stock assuming that it had a stated value of $5 per share.

 c. Prepare the journal entry for the issuance of the common stock assuming that it had a par value of $1 per share.

E11-3A. **Forward Stock Split** On March 1 of the current year, Sentry Corporation has 400,000 shares of $20 par value common stock that are issued and outstanding. The general ledger shows the following account balances relating to the common stock: **LO5** ✓

Common stock.	$8,000,000
Paid-in capital in excess of par value.	3,400,000

On March 2, Sentry Corporation splits its stock 2-for-1 and reduces the par value to $10 per share.

a. How many shares of common stock are issued and outstanding immediately following the stock split?

b. What is the balance in the Common Stock account immediately following the stock split?

c. What is the balance in the Paid-in Capital in Excess of Par Value account immediately following the stock split?

d. Is a journal entry required to record the forward stock split? If yes, prepare the entry.

LO4, 6   **E11-4A.** **Treasury Stock** Coastal Corporation issued 25,000 shares of $5 par value common stock at $17 per share and 6,000 shares of $50 par value, eight percent preferred stock at $78 per share. Later, the company purchased 3,000 shares of its own common stock at $20 per share.

a. Prepare the journal entries to record the share issuances and the purchase of the common shares.

b. Assume that Coastal sold 2,000 shares of the treasury stock at $26 per share. Prepare the general journal entry to record the sale of this treasury stock.

c. Assume that Coastal sold the remaining 1,000 shares of treasury stock at $19 per share. Prepare the journal entry to record the sale of this treasury stock.

LO7   **E11-5A.** **Cash Dividends** Sanders Corporation has the following shares outstanding: 6,000 shares of $50 par value, six percent preferred stock and 40,000 shares of $1 par value common stock. The company has $328,000 of retained earnings. At year-end, the company declares its regular $3 per share cash dividend on the preferred stock and a $2.20 per share cash dividend on the common stock. Three weeks later, the company pays the dividends.

a. Prepare the journal entry for the declaration of the cash dividends.

b. Prepare the journal entry for the payment of the cash dividends.

LO7   **E11-6A.** **Stock Dividends** Witt Corporation has 70,000 shares of $5 par value common stock outstanding. At year-end, the company declares a four percent stock dividend. The market price of the stock on the declaration date is $21 per share. Four weeks later, the company issues the shares of stock to stockholders.

a. Prepare the journal entry for the declaration of the stock dividend.

b. Prepare the journal entry for the issuance of the stock dividend.

c. Assume that the company declared a 40 percent stock dividend rather than a four percent stock dividend. Prepare the journal entries for (1) the declaration of the stock dividend and (2) the issuance of the stock dividend.

LO8   **E11-7A.** **Statement of Retained Earnings** Use the following data to prepare a statement of retained earnings for Shepler Corporation.

Total retained earnings originally reported at January 1	$324,000
Cash dividends declared during the year.	75,000
Net income for the year	193,000
Stock dividend declared during the year	30,000

LO3   **E11-8A.** **Conversion of Preferred Stock into Common Stock** Smith & Sons, Inc., has 12,000 shares of $100 par value, six percent preferred stock and 80,000 shares of $0.50 par value common stock outstanding. The preferred stock is convertible into the company's common stock at a conversion rate of 1-to-20; that is, each share of preferred stock is convertible into 20 shares of common stock. The preferred stock had been sold for its par value when issued. Prepare the journal entry to record the conversion of all of the company's preferred stock into common stock.

LO5   **E11-9A.** **Reverse Stock Split** Titanium Metals Company had 20,000,000 shares of $0.01 par value common stock outstanding which had been sold for an aggregate amount of $300,000,000. The company's shares are traded on the New York Stock Exchange, which has a minimum listing price of $1 per share. Recently, the company's common stock has been trading on the exchange below $1 per share, and the exchange has notified the company that its common stock would be delisted in 30 days if the stock price did not rebound above its minimum listing price. In response to this notification, Titanium Metals authorized a 1-for-10 reverse stock split. Following the reverse stock split:

a. How many common shares will be outstanding?
b. What will be the new par value per share?
c. How will the reverse stock split be recorded in the company's accounts?

E11-10A. Return on Common Stockholders' Equity, Dividend Yield, and Dividend Payout The following information relates to Waterloo Components, Inc.: **LO9**

	2012	2013
Net income.	$ 55,000	$ 75,000
Preferred stock dividends	5,000	5,000
Average common stockholders' equity	2,000,000	2,100,000
Dividend per common share	1.50	1.60
Earnings per share	2.90	2.95
Market price per common share, year-end	29.50	30.00

a. Calculate the company's return on common stockholders' equity for 2012 and 2013.
b. Calculate the company's dividend yield for 2012 and 2013.
c. Calculate the company's dividend payout for 2012 and 2013.

E11-11A. Characteristics of a Corporation Label each of the following characteristics of a corporation as either an (A) advantage, or a (D) disadvantage: **LO1**

a. Limited liability
b. Taxation
c. Regulations
d. Transferability of ownership

EXERCISES—SET B

E11-1B. Dividend Distribution Bower Corporation has the following shares outstanding: 15,000 shares of $50 par value, eight percent preferred stock and 50,000 shares of $5 par value common stock. During its first three years in business, the firm declared no dividends in the first year, $280,000 of dividends in the second year, and $60,000 of dividends in the third year. **LO7**

a. If the preferred stock is cumulative, determine the total amount of dividends paid to each class of stock in each of the three years.
b. If the preferred stock is noncumulative, determine the total amount of dividends paid to each class of stock in each of the three years.

E11-2B. Cash and Noncash Share Issuances Chavoy Corporation was organized on July 1. The company's charter authorizes 100,000 shares of $10 par value common stock. On August 1, the attorney who helped organize the corporation accepted 800 shares of Chavoy common stock in settlement for the services provided (the services were valued at $9,600). On August 15, Chavoy issued 5,000 common shares for $75,000 cash. On October 15, Chavoy issued 3,000 common shares to acquire a vacant land site appraised at $48,000. Prepare the journal entries to record the stock issuances on August 1, August 15, and October 15. **LO4**

E11-3B. Forward Stock Split On September 1, Oxford Company has 250,000 shares of $15 par value common stock that are issued and outstanding. The general ledger shows the following account balances relating to the common stock: **LO5**

Common stock.	$3,750,000
Paid-in capital in excess of par value.	$2,250,000

On September 2, Oxford splits its stock 3-for-2 and reduces the par value to $10 per share.

a. How many shares of common stock are issued and outstanding immediately following the stock split?

    b. What is the balance in the Common Stock account immediately following the stock split?

    c. What is the likely reason that Oxford Company split its stock?

LO4, 6 **E11-4B.** **Stock Issuance and Treasury Stock** Diva, Inc., recorded certain capital stock transactions shown in the following journal entries: (1) issued common stock for $19 cash per share, (2) purchased treasury shares at $22 per share, and (3) sold some of the treasury shares:

1. Cash	437,000	
Common stock		46,000
Paid-in capital in excess of par value		391,000
2. Treasury stock	77,000	
Cash		77,000
3. Cash	62,400	
Treasury stock		52,800
Paid-in capital from treasury stock		9,600

    a. How many shares were originally issued?

    b. What was the par value of the shares issued?

    c. How many shares of treasury stock were acquired?

    d. How many shares of treasury stock were sold?

    e. At what price per share was the treasury stock sold?

LO7 **E11-5B.** **Cash and Stock Dividends** Mandrich Corporation has 25,000 shares of $10 par value common stock outstanding. The company has $405,000 of retained earnings. At year-end, the company declares a cash dividend of $1.90 per share and a four percent stock dividend. The market price of the stock at the declaration date is $35 per share. Four weeks later, the company pays the dividends.

    a. Prepare the journal entry for the declaration of the cash dividend.

    b. Prepare the journal entry for the declaration of the stock dividend.

    c. Prepare the journal entry for the payment of the cash dividend.

    d. Prepare the journal entry for the payment of the stock dividend.

LO5, 7 **E11-6B.** **Large Stock Dividend and Forward Stock Split** Key Corporation has 40,000 shares of $10 par value common stock outstanding and retained earnings of $820,000. The company declares a 100 percent stock dividend. The market price at the declaration date is $17 per share.

    a. Prepare the journal entries for (1) the declaration of the dividend and (2) the issuance of the dividend.

    b. Assume that the company splits its stock 2-for-1 and reduces the par value from $10 to $5 rather than declaring a 100 percent stock dividend. How does the accounting for the forward stock split differ from the accounting for the 100 percent stock dividend?

LO8 **E11-7B.** **Statement of Retained Earnings** Use the following data to prepare a statement of retained earnings for Schauer Corporation.

Total retained earnings originally reported as of January 1	$347,000
Stock dividends declared during the year	28,000
Cash dividends declared during the year	35,000
Net income for the year	94,000

LO3 **E11-8B.** **Conversion of Preferred Stock into Common Stock** Groff & Sons, Inc., has 20,000 shares of $50 par value, nine percent preferred stock and 100,000 shares of $1.00 par value common stock outstanding. The preferred stock is convertible into the company's common stock at a conversion rate of 1-to-40; that is, each share of preferred stock is convertible into 40 shares of common stock. The preferred stock had been sold for its par value when issued. Prepare the journal entry to record the conversion of all of the company's preferred stock into common stock.

LO5 **E11-9B.** **Reverse Stock Split** The Waterford Company had 50,000,000 shares of $0.10 par value common stock outstanding which had been sold for an aggregate amount of $500,000,000. The company's shares are traded on the New York Stock Exchange, which has a minimum listing price of $1 per share. Recently, the company's common stock has been trading on the exchange below $1 per share, and the exchange has notified the company that its common stock would be delisted in 30 days if the stock price did not rebound above its minimum listing price. In response to this notification, Waterford authorized a 1-for-20 reverse stock split. Following the reverse stock split:

a. How many common shares will be outstanding?
b. What will be the new par value per share?
c. How will the reverse stock split be recorded in the company's accounts?

E11-10B. Return on Common Stockholders' Equity, Dividend Yield, and Dividend Payout The following information relates to Litchfield, Inc.:

LO9

	2012	2013
Net income.	$ 110,000	$ 150,000
Preferred stock dividends	15,000	15,000
Average common stockholders' equity	4,000,000	4,200,000
Dividend per common share	3.00	3.20
Earnings per share	5.80	5.90
Market price per common share, year-end	58.00	59.50

a. Calculate the company's return on common stockholders' equity for 2012 and 2013.
b. Calculate the company's dividend yield for 2012 and 2013.
c. Calculate the company's dividend payout for 2012 and 2013.

E11-11B. Characteristics of a Corporation Label each of the following characteristics of a corporation as either an (A) advantage, or a (D) disadvantage:

LO1

a. Organizational costs
b. Continuity of existence
c. Capital raising capability
d. Separate legal entity

PROBLEMS—SET A

P11-1A. Dividend Distribution Rydon Corporation began business on March 1, 2010. At that time, it issued 20,000 shares of $60 par value, seven percent cumulative preferred stock and 100,000 shares of $5 par value common stock. Through the end of 2012, there had been no change in the number of preferred and common shares outstanding.

LO7

Required
a. Assume that Rydon declared dividends of $0 in 2010, $183,000 in 2011, and $200,000 in 2012. Calculate the total dividends and the dividends per share paid to each class of stock in 2010, 2011, and 2012.
b. Assume that Rydon declared dividends of $0 in 2010, $84,000 in 2011, and $150,000 in 2012. Calculate the total dividends and the dividends per share paid to each class of stock in 2010, 2011, and 2012.

P11-2A. Stockholders' Equity: Transactions and Balance Sheet Presentation Tunic Corporation was organized on April 1, with an authorization of 25,000 shares of six percent, $50 par value preferred stock and 200,000 shares of $5 par value common stock. During April, the following transactions affecting stockholders' equity occurred:

LO4

Apr. 1 Issued 80,000 shares of common stock at $15 cash per share.
     3 Issued 2,000 shares of common stock to attorneys and promoters in exchange for their services in organizing the corporation. The services were valued at $31,000.
     8 Issued 3,000 shares of common stock in exchange for equipment with a fair market value of $48,000.
     20 Issued 6,000 shares of preferred stock for cash at $55 per share.

Required

a. Prepare journal entries to record the above transactions.

b. Prepare the stockholders' equity section of the balance sheet at April 30. Assume that the net income for April is $49,000.

LO4, 6 P11-3A. Stockholders' Equity: Transactions and Balance Sheet Presentation The stockholders' equity accounts of Windham Corporation at January 1 appear below:

8 Percent preferred stock, $25 par value, 50,000 shares authorized; 6,800 shares issued and outstanding.	$170,000
Common stock, $10 par value, 200,000 shares authorized; 50,000 shares issued and outstanding.	500,000
Paid-in capital in excess of par value—Preferred stock	68,000
Paid-in capital in excess of par value—Common stock	200,000
Retained earnings	270,000

During the year, the following transactions occurred:

Jan. 10 Issued 28,000 shares of common stock for $17 cash per share.

23 Purchased 8,000 shares of common stock as treasury stock at $19 per share.

Mar. 14 Sold one-half of the treasury shares acquired January 23 for $21 per share.

July 15 Issued 3,200 shares of preferred stock in exchange for equipment with a fair market value of $128,000.

Nov. 15 Sold 1,000 of the treasury shares acquired January 23 for $24 per share.

Dec. 31 Closed the net income of $59,000 to the Retained Earnings account.

Required

a. Set up T-accounts for the stockholders' equity accounts as of the beginning of the year and enter the January 1 balances.

b. Prepare journal entries to record the foregoing transactions and post to T-accounts (set up any additional T-accounts needed). Do not prepare the journal entry for the Dec. 31 transaction, but post the appropriate amount to the Retained Earnings T-account. Determine the ending balances for the stockholders' equity accounts.

c. Prepare the December 31 stockholders' equity section of the balance sheet.

LO4, 5, 6 P11-4A. Stockholders' Equity: Transactions and Balance Sheet Presentation The stockholders' equity of Summit Corporation at January 1 follows:

7 Percent preferred stock, $100 par value, 20,000 shares authorized; 5,000 shares issued and outstanding.	$ 500,000
Common stock, $15 par value, 100,000 shares authorized; 40,000 shares issued and outstanding.	600,000
Paid-in capital in excess of par value—Preferred stock	24,000
Paid-in capital in excess of par value—Common stock	360,000
Retained earnings	325,000
Total Stockholders' Equity	$1,809,000

The following transactions, among others, occurred during the year:

Jan. 12 Announced a 3-for-1 common stock split, reducing the par value of the common stock to $5 per share. The authorization was increased to 300,000 shares.

Mar. 31 Converted $40,000 face value of convertible bonds payable (the book value of the bonds was $43,000) to common stock. Each $1,000 bond converted to 125 shares of common stock.

June 1 Acquired equipment with a fair market value of $60,000 in exchange for 500 shares of preferred stock.

Sept. 1 Acquired 10,000 shares of common stock for cash at $10 per share.

Oct. 12 Sold 1,500 treasury shares at $12 per share.

Nov. 21 Issued 5,000 shares of common stock at $11 cash per share.

Dec.   28   Sold 1,200 treasury shares at $9 per share.

31   Closed net income of $83,000 to the Retained Earnings account.

Required

a.   Set up T-accounts for the stockholders' equity accounts as of the beginning of the year and enter the January 1 balances.

b.   Prepare journal entries for the given transactions and post them to the T-accounts (set up any additional T-accounts needed). Do not prepare the journal entry for the Dec. 31 transaction, but post the appropriate amount to the Retained Earnings T-account. Determine the ending balances for the stockholders' equity accounts.

c.   Prepare the stockholders' equity section of the balance sheet at December 31.

P11-5A.   **Stockholders' Equity: Information and Entries from Comparative Data** Comparative stockholders' equity sections from two successive years of balance sheets from Smiley, Inc., are as follows:

LO4, 6

✔

	Dec. 31, 2012	Dec. 31, 2011
Paid-in Capital		
8 Percent preferred stock, $50 par value, authorized 20,000 shares; issued and outstanding, 2011: 8,000 shares; 2012: 12,000 shares . . .	$ 600,000	$ 400,000
Common stock, no-par value, $20 stated value, authorized 80,000 shares; issued, 2011: 32,000 shares; 2012: 40,000 shares	800,000	640,000
Additional Paid-in Capital		
In excess of par value—Preferred stock.	224,000	144,000
In excess of stated value—Common stock	232,000	160,000
From treasury stock	21,000	
Retained earnings	300,000	229,000
		$1,573,000
Less: Treasury stock (7,000 shares common) at cost	0	196,000
Total Stockholders' Equity	$2,177,000	$1,377,000

No dividends were declared or paid during 2012.

Required

Prepare the journal entries for the transactions affecting stockholders' equity that occurred during 2012. Do not prepare the journal entry for closing net income to retained earnings. Assume that any share transactions were for cash.

P11-6A.   **Retained Earnings: Transactions and Statement** The stockholders' equity accounts of Rayburn Corporation as of January 1 appear below:

LO7, 8

✔

Common stock, $5 par value, 400,000 shares authorized; 160,000 shares issued and outstanding.	$800,000
Paid-in capital in excess of par value.	920,000
Retained earnings	513,000

During the year, the following transactions occurred:

June   7   Declared a ten percent stock dividend; market value of the common stock was $11 per share.

28   Issued the stock dividend declared on June 7.

Dec.   5   Declared a cash dividend of $1.25 per share.

26   Paid the cash dividend declared on December 5.

Required

a.   Prepare journal entries to record the foregoing transactions.

b.   Prepare a statement of retained earnings. The net income for the year is $412,000.

LO7, 8   **P11-7A.**   **Retained Earnings: Transactions and Statement** The stockholders' equity of Cyclone Corporation at January 1 follows:

6 Percent preferred stock, $25 par value, 40,000 shares authorized; 20,000 shares issued and outstanding..	$ 500,000
Common stock, $5 par value, 300,000 shares authorized; 80,000 shares issued and outstanding	400,000
Paid-in capital in excess of par value—Common stock	560,000
Retained earnings	830,000
Total Stockholders' Equity	$2,290,000

The following transactions, among others, occurred during the year:

June   18   Declared a 50 percent stock dividend on all outstanding shares of common stock. The market value of the stock was $14 per share.

July   1   Issued the stock dividend declared on June 18.

Dec.   20   Declared the annual cash dividend on the preferred stock and a cash dividend of $1.30 per share on the common stock, payable on January 20 to stockholders of record on December 28.

Required

a.   Prepare journal entries to record the foregoing transactions.

b.   Prepare a statement of retained earnings. The net income for the year is $379,000.

LO4, 5, 6   **P11-8A.**   **Stockholders' Equity Transactions, Journal Entries, and T-Accounts** The stockholders' equity of Fremantle Corporation at January 1 follows:

8 Percent preferred stock, $100 par value, 20,000 shares authorized; 4,000 shares issued and outstanding	$ 400,000
Common stock, $1 par value, 100,000 shares authorized; 40,000 shares issued and outstanding	40,000
Paid-in capital in excess of par value—Preferred stock	200,000
Paid-in capital in excess of par value—Common stock	800,000
Retained earnings	550,000
Total Stockholders' Equity	$1,990,000

The following transactions, among others, occurred during the year:

Jan.   1   Announced a 2-for-1 common stock split, reducing the par value of the common stock to $0.50 per share.

Mar.   31   Converted $80,000 face value of convertible bonds payable (the book value of the bonds was $83,000) to common stock. Each $1,000 bond converted to 125 shares of common stock.

June   1   Acquired equipment with a fair market value of $45,000 in exchange for 300 shares of preferred stock.

Sept.   1   Acquired 10,000 shares of common stock for cash at $20 per share.

Nov.   21   Issued 5,000 shares of common stock at $22 cash per share.

Dec.   28   Sold 1,000 treasury shares at $23 per share.

    31   Closed net income of $103,000, to the Retained Earnings account.

Required

a.   Set up T-accounts for the stockholders' equity accounts as of the beginning of the year and enter the January 1 balances.

b.   Prepare journal entries for the given transactions and post them to the T-accounts (set up any additional T-accounts needed). Do not prepare the journal entry for the Dec. 31 transaction, but post the appropriate amount to the Retained Earnings T-account. Determine the ending balances for the stockholders' equity accounts.

P11-9A. **Stockholders' Equity Section of the Balance Sheet** Using your analysis from P11-8A, prepare the stockholders' equity section of the Fremantle Corporation's balance sheet.

LO4, 5, 6

PROBLEMS—SET B

P11-1B. **Dividend Distribution** Gardner Corporation began business on June 30, 2010. At that time, it issued 18,000 shares of $50 par value, six percent, cumulative preferred stock and 90,000 shares of $10 par value common stock. Through the end of 2012, there had been no change in the number of preferred and common shares outstanding.

LO7

Required

a.   Assume that Gardner declared dividends of $63,000 in 2010, $0 in 2011, and $378,000 in 2012. Calculate the total dividends and the dividends per share paid to each class of stock in 2010, 2011, and 2012.

b.   Assume that Gardner declared dividends of $0 in 2010, $108,000 in 2011, and $189,000 in 2012. Calculate the total dividends and the dividends per share paid to each class of stock in 2010, 2011, and 2012.

P11-2B. **Stockholders' Equity: Transactions and Balance Sheet Presentation** Beaker Corporation was organized on July 1, with an authorization of 50,000 shares of $4 no-par value preferred stock ($4 is the annual dividend) and 100,000 shares of $10 par value common stock. During July, the following transactions affecting stockholders' equity occurred:

LO4

July   1   Issued 31,000 shares of common stock at $17 cash per share.
       12 Issued 3,500 shares of common stock in exchange for equipment with a fair market value of $63,000.
       15 Issued 5,000 shares of preferred stock for cash at $44 per share.

Required

a.   Prepare journal entries to record the foregoing transactions.

b.   Prepare the stockholders' equity section of the balance sheet at July 31. The net income for July is $38,000.

P11-3B. **Stockholders' Equity: Transactions and Balance Sheet Presentation** The stockholders' equity accounts of Scott Corporation at January 1 follow:

LO4, 6

Common stock, $5 par value, 350,000 shares authorized;	
150,000 shares issued and outstanding.	$750,000
Paid-in capital in excess of par value.	600,000
Retained earnings	346,000

During the year, the following transactions occurred:

Jan.   5   Issued 10,000 shares of common stock for $12 cash per share.
       18 Purchased 4,000 shares of common stock as treasury stock at $14 cash per share.
Mar.   12 Sold one-fourth of the treasury shares acquired January 18 for $17 per share.
July   17 Sold 500 shares of the remaining treasury stock for $13 per share.
Oct.   1   Issued 5,000 shares of eight percent, $25 par value preferred stock for $35 cash per share. These are the first preferred shares issued out of 50,000 authorized shares.
Dec.   31 Closed the net income of $72,500 to the Retained Earnings account.

Required

a.   Set up T-accounts for the stockholders' equity accounts as of the beginning of the year and enter the January 1 balances.

b.   Prepare journal entries to record the foregoing transactions and post to T-accounts (set up any additional T-accounts needed). Do not prepare the journal entry for the Dec. 31 transaction, but post the appropriate amount to the Retained Earnings T-account. Determine the ending balances for the stockholders' equity accounts.

c.   Prepare the December 31 stockholders' equity section of the balance sheet.

LO4, 5, 6 **P11-4B.** **Stockholders' Equity: Transactions and Balance Sheet Presentation** The following is the stockholders' equity of Clipper Corporation at January 1:

8 Percent preferred stock, $50 par value, 10,000 shares authorized; 7,000 shares issued and outstanding.	$ 350,000
Common stock, $20 par value, 50,000 shares authorized; 25,000 shares issued and outstanding.	500,000
Paid-in capital in excess of par value—Preferred stock	70,000
Paid-in capital in excess of par value—Common stock	385,000
Retained earnings	238,000
Total Stockholders' Equity	$1,543,000

The following transactions, among others, occurred during the year:

Jan. 15 Issued 1,000 shares of preferred stock for $62 cash per share.
  20 Issued 4,000 shares of common stock at $36 cash per share.
  31 Converted $20,000 face value of convertible bonds payable (the book value of the bonds is $18,500) to common stock. Each $1,000 bond converted to 25 shares of common stock.
May 18 Announced a 2-for-1 common stock split, reducing the par value of the common stock to $10 per share. The authorization was increased to 100,000 shares.
June 1 Acquired equipment with a fair market value of $40,000 in exchange for 2,000 shares of common stock.
Sept. 1 Purchased 2,500 shares of common stock as treasury stock at $18 cash per share.
Oct. 12 Sold 900 treasury shares at $21 per share.
Dec. 22 Issued 500 shares of preferred stock for $59 cash per share.
  28 Sold 1,100 of the remaining treasury shares at $16 per share.
  31 Closed net income of $85,000 to the Retained Earnings account.

Required

a. Set up T-accounts for the stockholders' equity accounts as of the beginning of the year and enter the January 1 balances.
b. Prepare journal entries for the given transactions and post them to the T-accounts (set up any additional T-accounts needed). Do not prepare the journal entry for the Dec. 31 transaction, but post the appropriate amount to the Retained Earnings T-account. Determine the ending balances for the stockholders' equity accounts.
c. Prepare the stockholders' equity section of the balance sheet at December 31.

LO4, 6 **P11-5B.** **Stockholders' Equity: Transaction Descriptions from Account Data** The following T-accounts contain keyed entries representing five transactions involving the stockholders' equity of Riverview, Inc.:

Cash			
(1)	80,600	12,800	(4)
(2)	35,000		
(5)	6,080		

Land	
(3)	93,000

Preferred Stock, $50 Par		
	65,000	(1)

Paid-in Capital in Excess of Par Value—Preferred Stock		
	15,600	(1)

Common Stock, $10 Par		
	35,000	(2)
	60,000	(3)

Paid-in Capital in Excess of Par Value—Common Stock		
	33,000	(3)

Paid-in Capital from Treasury Stock		
	960	(5)

Treasury Stock			
(4)	(800 shares of common)	5,120	(5)
		12,800	

Required

Using this information, give detailed descriptions, including number of shares and price per share when applicable, for each of the five transactions.

P11-6B. **Retained Earnings: Transactions and Statement** The stockholders' equity of Striker Corporation at January 1 appears below: LO7, 8

Common stock, $10 par value, 200,000 shares authorized;	
80,000 shares issued and outstanding....................................	$800,000
Paid-in capital in excess of par value..	480,000
Retained earnings	305,000

During the year, the following transactions occurred:

May 12 Declared a seven percent stock dividend; market value of the common stock was $18 per share.

June 6 Issued the stock dividend declared on May 12.

Dec. 5 Declared a cash dividend of 75 cents per share.

30 Paid the cash dividend declared on December 5.

Required

a. Prepare journal entries to record the foregoing transactions.

b. Prepare a statement of retained earnings. Net income for the year is $283,000.

P11-7B. **Retained Earnings: Transactions and Statement** The stockholders' equity of Elson Corporation at January 1 is shown below: LO7, 8

5 Percent preferred stock, $100 par value, 10,000 shares authorized;	
4,000 shares issued and outstanding......................................	$ 400,000
Common stock, $5 par value, 200,000 shares	
authorized; 50,000 shares issued and outstanding	250,000
Paid-in capital in excess of par value—Preferred stock	40,000
Paid-in capital in excess of par value—Common stock	300,000
Retained earnings	656,000
Total Stockholders' Equity	$1,646,000

The following transactions, among others, occurred during the year:

Apr. 1 Declared a 100 percent stock dividend on all outstanding shares of common stock. The market value of the stock was $11 per share.

15 Issued the stock dividend declared on April 1.

Dec. 7 Declared a three percent stock dividend on all outstanding shares of common stock. The market value of the stock was $14 per share.

17 Issued the stock dividend declared on December 7.

20 Declared the annual cash dividend on the preferred stock and a cash dividend of 80 cents per common share, payable on January 15 to common stockholders of record on December 31.

Required

a. Prepare journal entries to record the foregoing transactions.

b. Prepare a statement of retained earnings. Net income for the year is $253,000.

P11-8B. **Stockholders' Equity: Transactions and Statement** The stockholders' equity section of Day Corporation's balance sheet at January 1 follows: LO4, 6, 7, 8

Common stock, $10 par value, 200,000 shares authorized, 35,000 shares issued, 4,000 shares are in the treasury..........................		$350,000
Additional paid-in capital		
In excess of par value..	$315,000	
From treasury stock	18,000	333,000
Retained earnings (see note)		298,000
		981,000
Less: Treasury stock (4,000 shares) at cost.........................		84,000
Total Stockholders' Equity.......................................		$897,000

The following transactions affecting stockholders' equity occurred during the year:

Jan.   8   Issued 10,000 shares of previously unissued common stock for $23 cash per share.

Mar.   12   Sold all of the treasury shares for $26 cash per share.

June   30   Declared a six percent stock dividend on all outstanding shares of common stock. The market value of the stock was $30 per share.

July   10   Issued the stock dividend declared on June 30.

Oct.   7   Acquired 1,500 shares of common stock as treasury stock at $27 cash per share.

Dec.   18   Declared a cash dividend of 90 cents per outstanding common share, payable on January 9 to stockholders of record on December 31.

Required

a.   Prepare journal entries to record the foregoing transactions.

b.   Prepare a statement of stockholders' equity. Net income for the year is $186,000.

LO4, 5, 6   **P11-9B.**   **Stockholders' Equity Transactions, Journal Entries, and T-Accounts** The stockholders' equity of Xeltron Corporation at January 1 follows:

9 % Preferred stock, $100 par value, 20,000 shares authorized; 6,000 shares issued and outstanding	$ 600,000
Common stock, $2 par value, 100,000 shares authorized; 40,000 shares issued and outstanding..	80,000
Paid-in capital in excess of par value—Preferred stock	400,000
Paid-in capital in excess of par value—Common stock	800,000
Retained earnings	750,000
Total Stockholders' Equity	$2,630,000

The following transactions, among others, occurred during the year:

Jan.   1   Announced a 2-for-1 common stock split, reducing the par value of the common stock to $1.00 per share.

Mar.   31   Converted $100,000 face value of convertible bonds payable (the book value of the bonds was $103,000) to common stock. Each $1,000 bond converted to 125 shares of common stock.

June   1   Acquired equipment with a fair market value of $30,000 in exchange for 200 shares of preferred stock.

Sept.   1   Acquired 10,000 shares of common stock for cash at $20 per share.

Nov.   21   Issued 5,000 shares of common stock at $22 cash per share.

Dec.   28   Sold 1,000 treasury shares at $23 per share.

      31   Closed net income of $200,000 to the Retained Earnings account.

Required

a.   Set up T-accounts for the stockholders' equity accounts as of the beginning of the year and enter the January 1 balances.

b.   Prepare journal entries for the given transactions and post them to the T-accounts (set up any additional T-accounts needed). Do not prepare the journal entry for the Dec. 31 transaction, but post the appropriate amount to the Retained Earnings T-account. Determine the ending balances for the stockholders' equity accounts.

P11-10B. The Stockholders' Equity Section of the Balance Sheet Using your analysis from P11-9B, prepare the Stockholders' Equity section of the Xeltron Corporation's balance sheet.

LO4, 5, 6

SERIAL PROBLEM: KATE'S CARDS

(Note: This is a continuation of the Serial Problem: Kate's Cards from Chapters 1 through 10.)

SP11.   Kate's business continues to flourish. It hardly seems that just eleven months ago, in September of 2012, that Kate started the business. She is especially pleased that she was able to successfully defend herself against what turned out to be a mistaken attempt to sue her for copyright infringement. She was able to clearly demonstrate that her card designs were unique and significantly different from the designs sold by Mega Cards.

Kate has decided to take on an investor. Taylor Kasey believes that Kate's Cards represents a good investment and wishes to invest money to help Kate expand the business. Kate, however, is somewhat unsure how to structure Taylor's investment. Taylor wishes to be an equity investor rather than simply providing a loan to Kate. Kate wants to know whether she should issue Taylor common stock or preferred stock for her investment.

1. Discuss the difference between the two classes of stock and suggest which type is more appropriate for Kate to issue.

    Kate has decided that she does not want to give up voting control of Kate's Cards. Since Taylor prefers to be a passive investor, but does wish to have a steady income from dividends, the decision is made to issue 50 shares of $100 par value, 6 percent cumulative preferred stock.

2. Provide the journal entry to record the issuance of the preferred stock for cash.

    Kate also wishes to pay dividends on both her common shares and the preferred stock. She is a little confused between cash and stock dividends.

3. Explain the difference between a cash dividend and a stock dividend. Since Kate is the only stockholder of the common stock, what would be the effect of issuing a 10 percent stock dividend?

    Kate decides to issue cash dividends on both the common stock and the preferred stock. Currently there are 50 outstanding preferred shares and 500 common shares outstanding. The dividends that Kate paid were $6 per share on the preferred shares and $2 per share on the common shares.

4. Provide the journal entry for the payment of the cash dividends.

    Kate's Cards has a net income of $1,500 for the current month of August 2013. Kate had decided that the business will have a fiscal year-end of August 31, so this is the completion of the company's first year. Kate will be preparing her annual financial statements; however, she would also like to see a monthly statement of retained earnings for August 2013. In addition, she would like to see how the stockholders' equity section of the balance sheet will look after the addition of the preferred stock. The stockholders' equity section from July 2013 is shown below:

Stockholders' Equity	
Common stock (5,000 shares authorized, 500 shares issued and outstanding)	$ 500
Paid-in capital in excess of par value—common stock	9,500
Retained earnings	15,000
Total stockholders' equity	$25,000

5. Prepare a statement of retained earnings for the month of August 2013 and the stockholders' equity section of the balance sheet as of August 31, 2013.

EXTENDING YOUR KNOWLEDGE

REPORTING AND ANALYSIS

COLUMBIA
SPORTSWEAR
COMPANY

EYK11-1. Financial Reporting Problem: Columbia Sportswear Company The financial statements for the **Columbia Sportswear Company** can be found in Appendix A at the end of this book.

Required
Answer the following questions:

a. How many shares of common stock are authorized at the end of 2011?
b. What percentage of the common shares authorized are outstanding at the end of 2011?
c. Does Columbia Sportswear have any preferred shares outstanding at the end of 2011?
d. How many shares of common stock did Columbia Sportswear repurchase in 2011? What was the dollar amount of this repurchase?
e. What amount of dividends per share did Columbia Sportswear report for 2011? 2010? 2009?

COLUMBIA
SPORTSWEAR
COMPANY

UNDER ARMOUR,
INC.

EYK11-2. Comparative Analysis Problem: Columbia Sportswear Company vs Under Armour, Inc. The financial statements for the **Columbia Sportswear Company** can be found in Appendix A at the end of this book, and the financial statements of **Under Armour, Inc.** can be found in Appendix B (the complete annual report is available on this book's Website).

Required
Answer the following questions:

a. Calculate the return on common stockholders' equity for each company for 2011.
b. Calculate the dividend payout ratio for each company for 2011.
c. Based on these ratios, which company performed better for its shareholders during 2011?

EYK11-3. Business Decision Problem Egghead, Inc., was a software chain that had over 100 stores across the U.S. Initially its founders and employees owned the company privately. The company eventually went public with an initial public offering (IPO) of 3.6 million shares (the company had 12 million shares prior to the IPO). The new shares were priced at $15 each. The company did not hold any treasury shares.

Required

a. Assume that the common shares had a $1 par value. Provide the journal entry to record the issuance of new shares.
b. Discuss whether you think Egghead's board of directors and existing shareholders had to approve the public issuance before it occurred.
c. Provide some reasons why Egghead wished to raise $54 million with equity rather than debt.

GILLETTE
COMPANY

PROCTER &
GAMBLE

COLGATE-
PALMOLIVE
COMPANY

EYK11-4. Financial Analysis Problem The following data was obtained prior to the acquisition of **Gillette Company** by **Procter & Gamble**. Gillette Company, the Procter & Gamble Company, and **Colgate-Palmolive Company** are three firms in the personal care consumer products industry. During the prior year, the average return on common stockholders' equity for the personal care consumer products industry was 28.1 percent. In the same year, the relevant financial data for Gillette, Procter & Gamble, and Colgate-Palmolive were as follows (in millions):

	Gillette	Procter & Gamble	Colgate-Palmolive
Preferred stockholders' equity, beginning	$ 99.2	$1,969.0	$ 418.3
Preferred stockholders' equity, ending	99.0	1,942.0	414.3
Preferred dividends	4.7	102.0	21.6
Common stockholders' equity, beginning	1,397.2	5,472.0	2,201.5
Common stockholders' equity, ending	1,380.0	6,890.0	1,460.7
Net income	426.9	2,211.0	548.1

Required

a. Calculate Gillette Company's return on common stockholders' equity.

b. Evaluate Gillette Company's return on common stockholders' equity by comparing it with the following:
1. The average for the personal care consumer products industry.
2. The return earned by the Procter & Gamble Company.
3. The return earned by Colgate-Palmolive Company.
4. The return earned by Gillette Company in the previous year (in the previous year, Gillette's net income was $513.4 million, preferred stock dividends were $4.8 million, and average common stockholders' equity was $1,227.3 million).

CRITICAL THINKING

EYK11-5. **Financial Analysis on the Web: General Mills, Inc.** The fiscal year 2011 annual report of **General Mills, Inc.** is available on this book's Website.

GENERAL MILLS, INC.

Required
a. How many shares of common stock is General Mills authorized to issue? How many common shares are issued as of May 29, 2011?
b. What is the par value of General Mills' common stock?
c. Does General Mills have any preferred shares? If so, how many shares of preferred stock are outstanding on May 29, 2011?
d. How many treasury shares did General Mills purchase on the open market during the 2011 fiscal year? What did General Mills pay to purchase these shares? How many common shares are in the treasury as of May 29, 2011?
e. What is General Mills' return on common stockholders' equity for the 2011 fiscal year?
f. What is the cash dividend per share declared by General Mills in fiscal year 2011? 2010? 2009?
g. What are General Mills' basic earnings per share in fiscal year 2011? 2010? 2009?
h. What is General Mills' dividend payout ratio for fiscal year 2011? 2010? 2009?

EYK11-6. **Accounting Communication Activity** Your neighbor, Norman Vetter, has always been tinkering in his garage with his inventions. He believes he has finally come up with one that could really sell well. He is a little concerned about some potential safety issues, but he believes those issues will be worked out. He wants to form a business to manufacture and sell his invention and has come to you for advice. In particular, he would like to know the advantages and disadvantages of forming a corporation, rather than simply organizing as a sole proprietor.

Required
Write a brief memorandum to your neighbor explaining the advantages and disadvantages of the corporate form of organization.

EYK11-7. **Accounting Ethics Case** Colin Agee, chairperson of the board of directors and chief executive officer of Image, Inc., is pondering a recommendation to make to the firm's board of directors in response to actions taken by Sam Mecon. Mecon recently informed Agee and other board members that he (Mecon) had purchased 15 percent of the voting stock of Image at $12 per share and is considering an attempt to take control of the company. His effort to take control would include offering $16 per share to stockholders to induce them to sell shares to him. Mecon also indicated that he would abandon his takeover plans if the company would buy back his stock at a price 50 percent over its current market price of $13 per share.

Agee views the proposed takeover by Mecon as a hostile maneuver. Mecon has a reputation of identifying companies that are undervalued (that is, their underlying net assets are worth more than the price of the outstanding shares), buying enough shares to take control of the company, replacing top management, and, on occasion, breaking up the company (that is, selling off the various divisions to the highest bidder). The process has proven profitable to Mecon and his financial backers. Stockholders of the companies taken over have also benefited because Mecon paid them attractive prices to buy their shares.

Agee recognizes that Image is currently undervalued by the stock market but believes that eventually the company will significantly improve its financial performance to the long-run benefit of its stockholders.

Required

What are the ethical issues that Agee should consider in arriving at a recommendation to make to the board of directors regarding Mecon's offer to be "bought out" of his takeover plans?

EYK11-8. **Corporate Social Responsibility Problem** In the corporate social responsibility highlight regarding Starbucks on page 508 in this chapter, it was stated that Starbucks believes in measuring and monitoring the company's CSR progress. One of Starbucks' commitments is to ethical coffee sourcing. Two of the metrics that the company uses in this regard are the pounds of coffee purchased from C.A.F.E. and the pounds of green coffee purchased from Fair Trade Certified cooperatives. Go to the Starbucks Website and navigate to the section on global responsibility to download the report on Ethical Coffee Sourcing. Identify how the company is doing with respect to these two metrics.

EYK11-9. **Forensic Accounting Problem** Wayne James Nelson, a manager in the office of the Arizona State Treasurer, was found guilty of trying to defraud the state of nearly $2 million. Nelson's scheme involved issuing checks to bogus vendors. The amounts of the 23 checks issued are shown below:

The table lists the checks that a manager in the office of the Arizona State Treasurer wrote to divert funds for his own use. The vendors to whom the checks were issued were fictitious.

Date of Check	Amount
October 9, 1992	$ 1,927.48
	27,902.31
October 14, 1992	86,241.90
	72,117.46
	81,321.75
	97,473.96
October 19, 1992	93,249.11
	89,658.17
	87,776.89
	92,105.83
	79,949.16
	87,602.93
	96,879.27
	91,806.47
	84,991.67
	90,831.83
	93,766.67
	88,338.72
	94,639.49
	83,709.28
	96,412.21
	88,432.86
	71,552.16
TOTAL	**$1,878,687.58**

Required

Refer to the chart shown below that reports the occurrences of various digits in a number. Compare the first digit of the fraudulent checks to the table of Benford's Law. How do the two compare? Are there any other unusual patterns you detect in the check amounts?

Position of digit in number				
Digit	**First**	**Second**	**Third**	**Fourth**
0	.	.11968	.10178	.10018
1	.30103	.11389	.10138	.10014
2	.17609	.10882	.10097	.10010
3	.12494	.10433	.10057	.10006
4	.09691	.10031	.10018	.10002
5	.07918	.09668	.09979	.09998
6	.06695	.09337	.09940	.09994
7	.05799	.09035	.09902	.09990
8	.05115	.08757	.09864	.09986
9	.04576	.08500	.09827	.09982

Example: The number 147 has three digits, with 1 as the first digit, 4 as the second digit and 7 as the third digit. The table shows that under Benford's Law the expected proportion of numbers with a first digit 1 is 30.103% and the expected proportion of numbers with a third digit 7 is 9.902%.

Source: "A Taxpayer Compliance Application of Benford's Law," by M. J. Nigrini. *The Journal of American Taxation Association* 18, 1996.

EYK11-10. Working With The Takeaways The following data is from a recent **General Electric Company** annual report. All amounts, except per share data, are in $ millions).

GENERAL ELECTRIC COMPANY

Net income.	$ 17,410
Preferred stock dividends	75
Average common stockholders' equity	110,112
Dividends per share.	1.24
Earnings per share.	1.72
Per share market price of common stock at year-end.	16.20

Required
Compute the following ratios for the General Electric Company:

a. Return on common stockholders' equity
b. Dividend yield
c. Dividend payout

EYK11-11. IFRS Financial Statements Tesco PLC is the world's third largest retailer and is based in the United Kingdom. Tesco prepares its financial statements using IFRS. The complete annual report for Tesco PLC for year-ended February 26, 2011, is available on this book's Website. Calculate Tesco's (a) return on common stockholders' equity, (b) dividend yield, and (c) dividend payout for 2010 and 2011. Additional information that you will need are the following:

LO9
TESCO PLC

	2009	2010	2011
Total equity (millions of British pounds)	12,906		
Dividend per share (in British pence)		13.05	14.46
Market price per share (in British pence)		419.70	404.20

ANSWERS TO SELF-STUDY QUESTIONS:

1. c, (p. 505)   2. a, (p. 510)   3. c, (p. 514)   4. d, (p. 515)   5. d, (p. 517)   6. d, (p. 514)
7. c, (p. 523)   8. d, (p. 511)   9. a, (p. 517)   10. d, (p. 521)

YOUR TURN! SOLUTIONS

Solution 11.1

1. Disadvantage
2. Advantage
3. Advantage
4. Disadvantage
5. Disadvantage
6. Advantage

Solution 11.2

1. d   **2.** e   **3.** b   **4.** f   **5.** c   **6.** a

Solution 11.3

Paid-in capital in excess of par value = ($9 − $1) × 10,000 shares = $80,000

Solution 11.4

$75,000

Solution 11.5

a. A cash dividend will lower retained earnings by $30,000 ($3 × 10,000 shares) to $470,000.
b. A ten percent stock dividend will lower retained earnings by $20,000 (.10 × 10,000 × $20) to $480,000.

Solution 11.6

	Common Stock	Paid-in Capital in Excess of Par Value	Retained Earnings	Treasury Stock	Total
DIOR COMPANY **Statement of Stockholders' Equity** **For Year Ended December 31, 2012**					
Balance, January 1, 2012.	$100,000	$900,000	$50,000	$(10,000)	$1,040,000
1,000 common shares issued	1,000	14,000			15,000
Net income.			30,000		30,000
Cash dividend			(8,000)		(8,000)
Balance, December 31, 2012.	$101,000	$914,000	$72,000	$(10,000)	$1,077,000

12

Statement of Cash Flows

PAST

Chapter 11 examined the accounting for stockholders' equity.

PRESENT

In this chapter we turn our attention to the statement of cash flows.

FUTURE

Chapter 13 completes our study of financial accounting by looking at the analysis and interpretation of financial statements.

LEARNING OBJECTIVES

1. **Discuss** the content and format of the statement of cash flows. *(p. 550)*

2. **Explain** the preparation of a statement of cash flows using the indirect method. *(p. 556)*

3. **Define** several ratios used to analyze the statement of cash flows and **explain** their use. *(p. 564)*

4. Appendix 12A: **Explain** the preparation of a statement of cash flows using the direct method. *(p. 568).*

HOME DEPOT: A Company with a Vision

Home Depot is the largest home improvement retailer in the United States. Home Depot was founded in 1978 in Atlanta, Georgia, with only a few stores. Today, the company operates over 2,200 stores in the United States and Canada. The company's founders had a vision that led to the company's tremendous growth:

> "We founded [The Home Depot] with a special vision—to create a company that would keep alive the values that were important to us. Values like respect among all people, excellent customer service and giving back to communities and society."
>
> —Arthur Blank, co-founder, Home Depot

It takes a lot of cash to build and operate over 2,200 stores, especially when the average Home Depot store is over 105,000 square feet. In fiscal year 2011 Home Depot spent over $1.2 billion on capital expenditures. This represents the second year in a row that the company expended over $1 billion dollars in capital expenditures.

How can a financial statement user determine where a company obtained the cash to fund such growth? In this chapter we examine the statement of cash flows and learn how a company discloses both the sources and uses of its cash. Understanding the content, format, and construction of the statement of cash flows will enable a financial statement user to assess just how a company like Home Depot was able to finance its capital expenditures for new store growth.

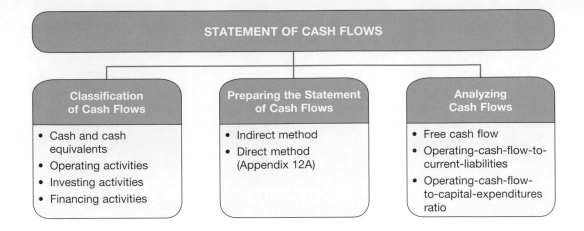

CASH AND CASH EQUIVALENTS

LO1 **Discuss** the content and format of the statement of cash flows.

Do you maintain a checkbook in which you record the checks you write and the bank deposits you make? If so, you are keeping a record of your cash flows—the checks you write are your cash outflows and the bank deposits you make are your cash inflows. Businesses also experience cash inflows and outflows; but, they do more than just record their cash flows because GAAP requires that businesses prepare an entirely separate financial statement explaining where their cash flow came from and how it was used.

The statement of cash flows complements the balance sheet and the income statement. While a balance sheet reports a company's financial position as of a point in time, usually the end of a fiscal period, the statement of cash flows explains the change in one component of a company's financial position—its cash—from one balance sheet date to the next. The income statement, on the other hand, reveals the results of a company's operating activities for the period, and these operating activities are a major source and use of the cash reported in a company's statement of cash flows.

In the eyes of most creditors, investors, and managers, cash is a business's most important asset. Without cash, a business would be unable to pay its employees, its lenders, its suppliers, its service providers, or its shareholders. In short, cash is the only asset that a business can't operate without.

The dilemma for most managers, however, is knowing exactly how much cash to keep on hand. Although managers know that they need to keep some cash on hand in a checking account and/or petty cash fund to pay their immediate bills, they also know that cash is the lowest return generating asset that a business has. Keeping too much cash on hand means that a business is not maximizing the value of its assets. For this reason, most managers spend considerable time assessing their cash needs—an activity called **cash management**. Because the science of cash management is inexact, managers have derived ways to help them minimize the amount of cash that they need to keep on hand while also maximizing the return on a business's assets. One such method is to invest any excess cash in alternative investments that are readily convertible back into cash and earn a higher rate of return than cash, but which do not place the invested cash at risk of loss. These alternative investments are known as cash equivalents.

Cash equivalents are short-term, highly liquid investments that are (1) easily convertible into cash and (2) close enough to maturity so that their market value is relatively insensitive to interest rate changes (generally, investments with maturities of three months or less). U.S. Treasury bills, certificates of deposit (CDs), commercial paper (short-term notes issued by corporations), and money market funds are examples of cash equivalents. Because firms may differ as to exactly which investments they consider to be cash equivalents, GAAP requires that each firm disclose in the notes to the financial statements the company's policy regarding which investments are treated as cash equivalents.

When preparing a statement of cash flows, the cash and cash equivalents are added together and treated as a single amount. This is done because the purchase and sale of investments in cash equivalents are considered to be part of a firm's overall cash management strategy rather than a source or use of cash. As financial statement users evaluate a firm's cash flows, it should not matter whether the cash is on hand, deposited in a bank account, or invested in cash equivalents. Transfers back and forth between a firm's Cash account and its investments in cash equivalents, consequently, are not treated as cash inflows or outflows in the statement of cash flows.

When discussing the statement of cash flows, accountants often just use the word *cash* rather than the term *cash and cash equivalents*. We follow that practice in this chapter.

Definition of Cash Equivalents	**ACCOUNTING IN PRACTICE**

There exist some differences between firms as to just which investments of cash are considered to be cash equivalents. For example, **PepsiCo, Inc.**, the beverage and snack food company, states in the notes to its financial statements that "Cash equivalents are investments with original maturities of three months or less." **International Game Technology**, a manufacturer of gaming machines and proprietary gaming software systems, on the other hand, notes that "In addition to cash deposits at major banks, cash and equivalents include other marketable securities with original matures of 90 days or less, primarily in U.S. Treasury-backed money market funds." The commonality among all firms, however, is that cash equivalents represent a temporary investment of excess cash in risk-free investments until such time as the cash is needed to support a business's operations.

ACTIVITY CLASSIFICATIONS IN THE STATEMENT OF CASH FLOWS

A statement of cash flows classifies a company's cash receipts and cash payments into three major business activity categories: operating activities, investing activities, and financing activities. Grouping cash flows into these categories identifies the effect on cash of each of the major business activities of a firm (see Chapter 1). The combined effects on cash from all three categories explain the net change in cash for the period. The net change in cash is then reconciled with the beginning and ending balances of cash from the balance sheet. Exhibit 12-1 illustrates the basic format for a statement of cash flows.

Exhibit 12-1	Format for the Statement of Cash Flows

SAMPLE COMPANY
Statement of Cash Flows
For Year Ended December 31, 2013

Cash Flow from Operating Activities		
(Details of cash flow from operating activities).....................	$###	
Cash provided (used) by operating activities.......................		$###
Cash Flow from Investing Activities		
(Details of investing cash inflows and outflows).....................	###	
Cash provided (used) by investing activities		###
Cash Flow from Financing Activities		
(Details of financing cash inflows and outflows)	###	
Cash provided (used) by financing activities		###
Net increase (decrease) in cash...................................		###
Cash at beginning of year		###
Cash at end of year		$###

Operating Activities

A company's income statement reflects the transactions and events that constitute its operating activities. The focus of a firm's operating activities involves selling goods or rendering services. The cash flow from **operating activities** is defined broadly enough, however, to include any cash receipts or payments that are not classified as investing activities or financing activities. For example, cash received from a lawsuit settlement and cash payments to charity are treated as cash flow from operating activities. The following are examples of cash inflows and outflows relating to a firm's operating activities:

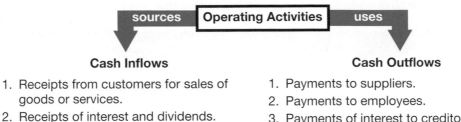

Cash Inflows

1. Receipts from customers for sales of goods or services.
2. Receipts of interest and dividends.
3. Other receipts that are not related to investing or financing activities, such as lawsuit settlements and refunds received from suppliers.

Cash Outflows

1. Payments to suppliers.
2. Payments to employees.
3. Payments of interest to creditors.
4. Payments of taxes to governmental agencies.
5. Other payments that are not related to investing or financing activities, such as contributions to charity.

Investing Activities

A firm's **investing activities** include those transactions involving (1) the acquisition or disposal of plant assets and intangible assets, (2) the purchase or sale of stocks, bonds, and other securities (that are not cash equivalents), and (3) the lending and subsequent collection of money.[1] The related cash receipts and cash payments appear in the investing activities section of the statement of cash flows. Examples of these cash flows include:

Cash Inflows

1. Receipts from the sale of plant assets and intangible assets.
2. Receipts from sales of investments in stocks, bonds, and other securities (other than cash equivalents).
3. Receipts from repayments of loans by borrowers.

Cash Outflows

1. Payments to purchase plant assets and intangible assets.
2. Payments to purchase stocks, bonds, and other securities (other than cash equivalents).
3. Payments made to lend money to borrowers.

Financing Activities

A firm engages in **financing activities** when it obtains cash from shareholders, returns cash to shareholders, borrows from creditors, and repays amounts borrowed from creditors. Cash flows related to these events are reported in the financing activities section of the statement of cash flows. Examples of these cash flows include:

---

[1] There are exceptions to the classification of these events as investing activities. For example, the purchase or sale of mortgage loans by a mortgage banker, like Bank of America, and the purchase or sale of securities in the trading account of a broker/dealer in financial securities, like Merrill Lynch, represent operating activities for these businesses.

| sources | **Financing Activities** | uses |

Cash Inflows

1. Receipts from the issuance of common stock and preferred stock and from sales of treasury stock.
2. Receipts from the issuance of bonds payable, mortgage notes payable, and other notes payable.

Cash Outflows

1. Payments to acquire treasury stock.
2. Payments of dividends.
3. Payments to settle outstanding bonds payable, mortgage notes payable, and other notes payable.

Observe that paying cash to settle such obligations as accounts payable, wages payable, interest payable, and income tax payable is an operating activity, not a financing activity. Also observe that cash received as interest and dividends and cash paid as interest are classified as cash flows from operating activities, although cash paid as dividends to a company's stockholders is classified as a financing activity.

IFRS ALERT!

Although the statement of cash flows under U.S. GAAP has three activity categories—operations, investing, and financing—this is not the case under International Financial Reporting Standards (IFRS). Under IFRS, the statement of cash flows may have either four or five activity categories: Operations, Investing, Debt Financing, Equity Financing, and sometimes a category called the Effect of Foreign Currency Translation. In essence, IFRS segments the financing activities category into two separate categories relating to financing with debt and financing with equity. The sum of these two categories is exactly equivalent to the single category of financing activities under U.S. GAAP.

An Illustration of Activity Classification Usefulness

The classification of cash flows into the three business activity categories helps financial statement users analyze and interpret a company's cash flow data. To illustrate, assume that companies D, E, and F operate in the same industry, and that each company reported a $100,000 increase in cash during the period. Information from each company's statement of cash flows is summarized below:

	Company		
	D	**E**	**F**
Cash flow from operating activities	$100,000	$ 0	$ 0
Cash flow from investing activities:			
Sale of plant assets	0	100,000	0
Cash flow from financing activities:			
Issuance of notes payable	0	0	100,000
Net increase in cash.	$100,000	$100,000	$100,000

Although each company's increase in cash was exactly $100,000, the source of the cash increase varied by company. This variation affects the analysis of the cash flow data, particularly for potential creditors who must evaluate the likelihood of the repayment of funds loaned to a company. Based only on this cash flow data, a potential creditor would feel more comfortable lending money to Company D than to either Company E or F. D's cash increase came from its operating activities, whereas E's cash increase came from the sale of plant assets, a source that is unlikely to recur, and F's cash increase came from borrowed funds. Company F faces additional future uncertainty when the interest and principal payments on the existing notes become due, and for this reason, a potential creditor would be less inclined to extend additional loans to Company F.

NONCASH INVESTING AND FINANCING ACTIVITIES

A secondary objective of the statement of cash flows is to present summary information about a firm's investing and financing activities. Although many of these activities affect cash and therefore are already included in the investing and financing sections of the statement of cash flows, some significant investing and financing events do not affect current cash flow. Examples of **noncash investing and financing activities** are the issuance of stock or bonds in exchange for plant assets or intangible assets, the exchange of long-term assets for other long-term assets, and the conversion of long-term debt into common stock. A common feature among each of these transactions is that no cash is exchanged between the parties involved in the transaction.

Noncash investing and financing transactions generally do, however, affect future cash flows. Issuing bonds in exchange for equipment, for example, requires future cash payments for interest and principal on the bonds. On the other hand, converting bonds into common stock eliminates the future cash payments related to the bonds' interest and principal. Knowledge of these types of events, therefore, should be helpful to financial statement users who wish to evaluate a firm's future cash flows.

Information regarding noncash investing and financing transactions is disclosed in a separate accounting schedule. The separate schedule may be placed immediately below the statement of cash flows or it may be placed among the notes to the financial statements.

PRINCIPLE ALERT	**Objectivity Principle**
	The *objectivity principle* asserts that the usefulness of financial statements is enhanced when the underlying data are objective and verifiable. Measuring cash and the changes in cash are among the most objective measurements that accountants make. The statement of cash flows, therefore, is the most objective financial statement required under generally accepted accounting principles. This characteristic of the statement of cash flows is welcomed by investors and creditors interested in evaluating the quality of a firm's net income and assets. Financial statement users often feel more confident about the quality of a company's net income and assets when there is a high correlation between, or relationship with, a company's cash flow from operating activities and its net income.

USING THE STATEMENT OF CASH FLOWS

The Financial Accounting Standards Board believes that one of the principal objectives of financial reporting is to help financial statement users assess the amount, timing, and uncertainty of a business's future cash flows. These assessments, in turn, help users evaluate prospective future cash receipts from their investments in, or loans to, a business. Although the statement of cash flows describes a company's past cash flows, the statement is also useful for assessing future cash flows since the recent past is often a very good predictor of the future.

A statement of cash flows shows the cash effects of a firm's operating, investing, and financing activities. Distinguishing among these different categories of cash flow helps financial statement users compare, evaluate, and predict a business's future cash flows. With cash flow information, creditors and investors are better able to assess a company's ability to repay its liabilities and pay dividends. A firm's need for outside financing can also be evaluated using the statement of cash flows. Further, the statement enables users to observe and analyze management's investing and financing policies, plans, and strategies.

A statement of cash flows also provides information useful in evaluating a firm's financial flexibility. **Financial flexibility** is a company's ability to generate sufficient amounts of cash to respond to unanticipated needs and opportunities. Information about past cash flows, particularly the cash flow from operations, helps in assessing financial flexibility. An evaluation of a firm's ability to survive an unexpected drop in demand for its goods and services, for example, may include a review of its past cash flow from operations. The larger these past cash flows, the greater will be a firm's ability to withstand adverse changes in future economic conditions.

Some investors and creditors find the statement of cash flows useful in evaluating the "quality" of a firm's net income. As we saw in Chapter 4, determining net income under the accrual basis of accounting requires many accruals, deferrals, allocations, and valuations. These adjustment and measurement procedures introduce greater subjectivity into a company's income determination than some financial statement users are comfortable with. Consequently, these users can relate a more objective performance measure—a firm's cash flow from operations—to net income. To these users, the higher the relationship between a company's net income and the cash flow from operations, the higher is the quality of the firm's net income.

CASH FLOW FROM OPERATING ACTIVITIES

The first section of the statement of cash flows presents a firm's cash flow from operating activities. *Two alternative formats are available to present the cash flow from operating activities: the indirect method and the direct method. Both methods report the same amount of cash flow from operating activities and differ only in how the cash flow from operating activities is presented.*

The **indirect method** starts with net income using the accrual basis of accounting and applies a series of adjustments to convert it to net income under the cash basis of accounting, which is equivalent to the cash flow from operating activities. The adjustments to net income do not represent specific cash flows; consequently, the indirect method does not report any detail concerning individual operating cash inflows and outflows.

The **direct method** shows individual amounts of cash inflows and cash outflows for the major operating activities. The net difference between these inflows and outflows is the cash flow from operating activities.

The Financial Accounting Standards Board encourages companies to use the direct method but permits the use of the indirect method. Despite the FASB's preference for the direct method, *more than 95 percent of companies preparing the statement of cash flows use the indirect method.* The indirect method is popular because (1) it is easier and less expensive to prepare than the direct method and (2) the direct method requires a supplemental disclosure showing the indirect method.

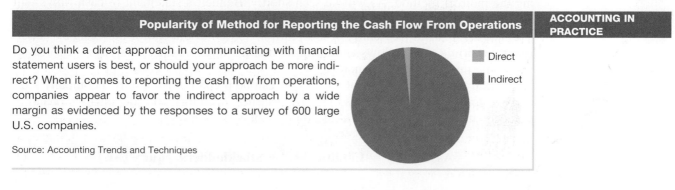

| **Popularity of Method for Reporting the Cash Flow From Operations** | **ACCOUNTING IN PRACTICE** |

Do you think a direct approach in communicating with financial statement users is best, or should your approach be more indirect? When it comes to reporting the cash flow from operations, companies appear to favor the indirect approach by a wide margin as evidenced by the responses to a survey of 600 large U.S. companies.

Source: Accounting Trends and Techniques

YOUR TURN! 12.1

The solution is on page 596.

Classify each of the cash flow events listed below as either an (1) operating activity, (2) investing activity, or (3) financing activity:

1. Cash received from customers
2. Cash sale of land
3. Cash paid to suppliers
4. Cash purchase of equipment
5. Payment on note payable
6. Cash dividend payment
7. Cash wages paid
8. Purchase of treasury stock
9. Cash sale of investments

The following section on preparing the statement of cash flows uses the indirect method. Appendix 12A uses the direct method. Your instructor can choose to cover either one or both methods. If the indirect method is skipped, then read Appendix 12A and return to the section (8 pages ahead) titled "Analyzing Cash Flows."

PREPARING THE STATEMENT OF CASH FLOWS USING THE INDIRECT METHOD

LO2 **Explain** the preparation of a statement of cash flows using the indirect method.

To prepare a statement of cash flows using the indirect method, the following information is needed: a company's income statement, comparative balance sheets, and possibly additional data taken from the company's financial statements. Exhibit 12-2 presents this information for the Bennett Company. We will use this data to prepare Bennett's 2013 statement of cash flows using the indirect method. As will be seen shortly, Bennett's statement of cash flows will explain the $25,000 increase in the company's cash account that occurred during 2013 (from $10,000 at the beginning of the year to $35,000 at the end of the year) by classifying the firm's cash inflows and outflows into the three business activity categories of operating, investing, and financing.

To see that the statement of cash flows can be prepared using only a company's income statement and the changes in its balance sheet accounts, consider again the balance sheet equation that was first introduced in Chapter 1:

$$\text{Assets (A)} = \text{Liabilities (L)} + \text{Stockholders' equity (SE)} \qquad (1)$$

Separating a firm's assets into its cash (CA) and noncash assets (NCA) gives:

$$CA + NCA = L + SE \qquad (2)$$

And, rewriting the balance sheet equation in changes form yields:

$$\Delta CA + \Delta NCA = \Delta L + \Delta SE \qquad (3)$$

Finally, rearranging the components of the equation shows that the change in cash (which is the end result of the statement of cash flows) can be computed from the change in all of the other balance sheet accounts:

$$\Delta CA = \Delta L - \Delta NCA + \Delta SE \qquad (4)$$

Exhibit 12-2	Financial Data of Bennett Company

BENNETT COMPANY
Income Statement
For Year Ended December 31, 2013

Sales revenue.		$250,000
Cost of goods sold.	$148,000	
Wages expense	52,000	
Insurance expense	5,000	
Depreciation expense.	10,000	
Income tax expense	11,000	
Gain on sale of plant assets	(8,000)	218,000
Net income.		$ 32,000

Additional Data for 2013
1. Sold plant assets costing $20,000 for $28,000 cash.
2. Declared and paid cash dividends of $13,000.

BENNETT COMPANY
Balance Sheets

As of December 31	2013	2012
Assets		
Cash.	$ 35,000	$ 10,000
Accounts receivable.	39,000	34,000
Inventory.	54,000	60,000
Prepaid insurance	17,000	4,000
Long-term investments	15,000	—
Plant assets	180,000	200,000
Accumulated depreciation	(50,000)	(40,000)
Patent.	60,000	—
Total assets	$350,000	$268,000
Liabilities and Equity		
Accounts payable.	$ 10,000	$ 19,000
Income tax payable	5,000	3,000
Common stock.	260,000	190,000
Retained earnings	75,000	56,000
Total liabilities and equity.	$350,000	$268,000

IFRS ALERT!

Currently, both U.S. GAAP and IFRS permit a company to present its statement of cash flows using either the direct method or the indirect method. A topic being considered by the FASB/IASB convergence project would limit the preparation of the statement of cash flows to just the direct method. The direct method is currently preferred by both the FASB and the IASB, although most U.S. firms present their statement of cash flows using the indirect method.

Five Steps to Preparing a Statement of Cash Flows

The process to prepare a statement of cash flows using the indirect method involves five steps. The approach begins by focusing initially only on the balance sheet and then proceeds to integrate a business's income statement through a series of systematic adjustments to a preliminary statement of cash flows derived solely from balance sheet data.

Step One Using just the beginning and ending balance sheets (see Columns 1 and 2 in Exhibit 12-3), calculate the change in each balance sheet account by subtracting the beginning balance sheet amount from the ending amount. The results of this step for the Bennett Company are presented in Column 3 of Exhibit 12-3. To simplify this step, the change in the Plant Assets account is combined with the Accumulated Depreciation account—that is, the change in the Plant Assets account is calculated on a net of accumulated depreciation basis.

To verify the accuracy of the Step One calculations, simply compare the sum of the changes in the asset accounts ($82,000) with the sum of the changes in the liability and stockholders' equity accounts ($82,000). These totals must be equal. If the totals are not equal, it indicates the presence of a subtraction error that must be identified and corrected before progressing to Step Two.

Exhibit 12-3	Preparing a Statement of Cash Flows: The Indirect Method			

BENNETT COMPANY
Balance Sheet
December 31, 2013

	(1) Beginning of Year	(2) End of Year	(3) Change for Year	(4) Cash Flow Classification
Assets				
Cash.	$ 10,000	$ 35,000	**$25,000**	**Cash flow increase**
Accounts receivable.	34,000	39,000	5,000	Operating
Inventory.	60,000	54,000	(6,000)	Operating
Prepaid insurance	4,000	17,000	13,000	Operating
Long-term investments	0	15,000	15,000	Investing
Plant assets (net)	160,000	130,000	(30,000)	Investing/Operating
Patent.	0	60,000	60,000	Investing/Operating
Total assets	$268,000	$350,000	$82,000	
Liabilities and Equity				
Accounts payable.	$ 19,000	$ 10,000	$ (9,000)	Operating
Income tax payable	3,000	5,000	2,000	Operating
Common stock.	190,000	260,000	70,000	Financing
Retained earnings	56,000	75,000	19,000	Operating/Financing
Total liabilities and equity. . . .	$268,000	$350,000	$82,000	

An important figure identified during Step One is the "bottom line" of the statement of cash flows, namely the change in the cash account. The highlighted area in Exhibit 12-3 reveals that the cash account of the Bennett Company increased by $25,000 from the beginning of the year to the end of the year. Hence, all of the various cash inflows and outflows for the company must aggregate to this figure.

Step Two Identify the appropriate business activity category—operating, investing, or financing—for each balance sheet account. The cash flow activity classifications are presented in Column 4 of Exhibit 12-3.

Although measuring the change in the balance sheet accounts in Step 1 is a straightforward arithmetic activity, there can be some confusion over the correct activity classification for some of the balance sheet accounts in Step 2. The change in accounts receivable, inventory, prepaid insurance, accounts payable, and income tax payable are all easily identified as operating activities because they are associated with the day-to-day operations of a business. The change in common stock, on the other hand, is clearly a financing activity because it is associated with raising capital to finance a business. The change in net plant assets, however, can be both an investing activity and an operating activity. Purchases and sales of plant assets are associated with the capital investment needed to run a business, and thus are an investing activity; but, the depreciation expense associated with plant assets is an operating activity since the depreciation of plant assets is deducted as an expense in the calculation of a company's net income. Similarly, the change in intangible assets such as patents can be both an investing activity and an operating activity because the acquisition or sale of intangibles is an investing activity, whereas the amortization of intangibles is an expense deducted in the calculation of net income, and hence, an operating activity. Finally, the change in retained earnings can be both an operating activity and a financing activity because retained earnings is increased by net income, an operating activity, but decreased by the payment of dividends, a financing activity.

As a general rule, the following cash flow activity classifications apply, although exceptions exist:

Balance Sheet Account	Cash Flow Activity Category
Current assets	Operating
Noncurrent assets	Investing/Operating
Current liabilities.	Operating
Noncurrent liabilities.	Financing
Capital stock	Financing
Retained earnings	Operating/Financing

Examples of exceptions to the above cash flow activity classifications include the following:

- Marketable securities, a current asset, are an investing activity item.
- Current maturities of long-term debt, a current liability, are a financing activity item.
- Employee pension obligations, a noncurrent liability, are an operating activity item.

Step Three   Having completed Steps One and Two, you are now ready to build a preliminary statement of cash flows using the calculated increases or decreases in the various balance sheet accounts from Step One and the identified activity classifications from Step Two. The preliminary statement of cash flows for the Bennett Company using the change values from Column 3 of Exhibit 12-3 and the cash flow activity classifications from Column 4 is presented in Exhibit 12-4.

Because a statement of cash flows measures the inflows and outflows of cash for a business, it is important to note that the sign of the asset account changes calculated in Step One must be reversed for purposes of preparing the preliminary statement of cash flows in Exhibit 12-4. This can be seen in equation (4) above in which the change in noncash assets has a negative sign. For instance, Exhibit 12-4 shows that the change in accounts receivable was an increase of $5,000, whereas the change in inventory was a decrease of $6,000. When preparing the indirect method statement of cash flows, a $5,000 increase in accounts receivable represents a subtraction from net income (a cash outflow), and a decline in inventory of $6,000 represents an addition to net income (a cash inflow), to arrive at the cash flow from operations. To illustrate why an increase in accounts receivable must be subtracted from net income to arrive at operating cash flow, consider how sales revenue is initially recorded. Assume that a $2,000 sale of goods is paid for with $1,200 in cash and the remaining amount recorded as an increase in accounts receivable. In this example, net income increases by $2,000, but cash is increased by only $1,200. Therefore, net income must be reduced by the $800 increase in accounts receivable in order to yield the correct cash flow from operations. Hence, when preparing the preliminary statement of cash flows in Step Three, it is important to remember to reverse the sign of the change values for the asset accounts. This is unnecessary for the liability and stockholders' equity accounts as can also be seen from equation (4) above.

Exhibit 12-4	An Illustration of a Preliminary Statement of Cash Flows: The Indirect Method

BENNETT COMPANY
Preliminary Statement of Cash Flows
For Year Ended December 31, 2013

Operating Activities

Retained earnings	$19,000
Accounts receivable	(5,000)
Inventory	6,000
Prepaid insurance	(13,000)
Accounts payable	(9,000)
Income tax payable	2,000
Cash flow from operating activities	0
Investing Activities	
Long-term investments	(15,000)
Plant assets (net)	30,000
Patent	(60,000)
Cash flow for investing activities	(45,000)
Financing Activities	
Common stock	70,000
Cash flow from financing activities	70,000
Change in cash (from the balance sheet)	$25,000

Exhibit 12-4 presents the preliminary statement of cash flows for the Bennett Company. This preliminary statement suggests that the firm's cash flow from operating activities was $0, the cash flow from investing activities was negative $45,000, and the cash flow from financing activities was $70,000. As required, the cash inflows and outflows aggregate to the change in cash from the balance sheet, an increase of $25,000.

Step Four To this point we have used the balance sheet exclusively to provide the needed inputs to our statement of cash flows. For most businesses, however, cash flow will also be generated by a firm's ongoing operations. Hence, it is now appropriate to introduce the operations related data found on the company's income statement (see Exhibit 12-2).

In this step, we accomplish two important actions involving the preliminary statement of cash flows in Exhibit 12-4. First, the change in retained earnings from the balance sheet will be replaced by net income from the income statement. For the Bennett Company, the change in retained earnings of $19,000 does not equal net income of $32,000. The difference of $13,000 ($32,000 − $19,000) represents a cash dividend paid to Bennett's shareholders. Thus, when we replace retained earnings of $19,000 with net income of $32,000, it is also necessary to report the $13,000 cash dividend payment as a cash outflow under the financing activities section in Exhibit 12-5. Increasing the cash flow from operations and decreasing the cash flow from financing activities by an equivalent amount ($13,000) allows the statement of cash flows to remain in balance with the net change in cash of $25,000.

Second, we adjust the Bennett Company's net income for any **noncash expenses** such as the depreciation of plant assets and the amortization of intangibles that were deducted in the process of calculating the firm's accrual basis net income.[2] These noncash expenses must be added back to net income in the operating activities section to correctly measure the firm's operating cash flow. However, to keep the preliminary statement of cash flows in balance with an increase in cash of $25,000, it is also necessary to subtract equivalent amounts in the investing activities section.

---

[2] Depreciation expense and amortization expense are called noncash expenses because these expenses do not involve any current period cash outflow. Depreciation expense, for example, represents the allocation of the purchase price of plant assets over the many periods that these assets produce sales revenue for a business. The matching principle requires that the cost of plant assets be matched with the sales revenue produced by these assets, and this is accomplished on the income statement by the deduction of the periodic depreciation charge.

To summarize, the adjustments to the Bennett Company's preliminary statement of cash flows in Exhibit 12-4 are:

1. Net income of $32,000 replaces the change in retained earnings of $19,000 in the operating activities section. This action adds $13,000 to the cash flow from operating activities. To keep the statement of cash flows in balance with the change in cash of $25,000, it is necessary to subtract $13,000 elsewhere on the statement. Since retained earnings is calculated as follows:

| Retained earnings (beginning) |
| + Net income for the period |
| − Dividends declared |
| = Retained earnings (ending) |

the outflow of $13,000 is also reflected as a cash dividend to shareholders under the financing activities section.

2. Depreciation expense of $10,000, a noncash deduction from net income, is added back to net income to avoid understating the cash flow from operations. However, to keep the statement of cash flows in balance with the change in cash of $25,000, a similar amount is subtracted from plant assets under the investing activities section.

The results of these adjustments are displayed in Exhibit 12-5, which presents the final statement of cash flows for Bennett. Note that the company's statement of cash flows remains in balance with the change in cash of $25,000 after the two adjustments. This result is possible because whatever amount was added to (or subtracted from) net income under the cash flow from operating activities, an equivalent amount was subtracted from (or added to) the investing activities or the financing activities.

Exhibit 12-5	**Statement of Cash Flows—The Indirect Method**

BENNETT COMPANY
Statement of Cash Flows
For Year Ended December 31, 2013

Cash Flow from Operating Activities		
Net income	$32,000	
Add (deduct) items to convert net income to cash basis		
Depreciation	10,000	
Gain on sale of plant assets	(8,000)	
Accounts receivable increase	(5,000)	
Inventory decrease	6,000	
Prepaid insurance increase	(13,000)	
Accounts payable decrease . . . . . . ·	(9,000)	
Income tax payable increase	2,000	
Cash provided by operating activities		$15,000
Cash Flow from Investing Activities		
Purchase of long-term investments	(15,000)	
Sale of plant assets	28,000	
Purchase of patent	(60,000)	
Cash used by investing activities		(47,000)
Cash Flow from Financing Activities		
Issuance of common stock	70,000	
Payment of dividends	(13,000)	
Cash provided by financing activities		57,000
Net increase in cash		25,000
Cash at beginning of year		10,000
Cash at end of year		$35,000

Step Five   To provide the most useful cash flow data, a final step is required: Make any appropriate adjustments to the operating activities section to calculate a company's operating cash flow. As noted above, a firm's operating cash flow should include only the cash flows from operating activities. Consequently, to calculate the cash flow from operating activities of a business, it is necessary to review a company's income statement to identify and remove the financial effects of any nonoperating transactions included in net income.[3]

To illustrate this point, note that the Bennett Company sold plant assets during the year at a gain of $8,000 ($28,000 sales price less $20,000 cost). This event is an investing activity and therefore properly belongs under the investing activities. To correctly assess Bennett's operating cash flow, it is necessary to remove this gain from the operating activity section and to add it to plant assets under the investing activities section. These actions allow us to correctly measure Bennett's cash flow from operating activities, as well as its cash flow from plant assets.

Exhibit 12-5 presents the final statement of cash flows for Bennett Company and includes not only the adjustments from Step Four, but also the adjustment to remove any nonoperating gains and losses from the cash flow from operating activities (Step 5). Bennett's statement of cash flows in Exhibit 12-5, using the indirect method, reveals that the cash flow from operating activities is $15,000, the cash flow used for investing activities is negative $47,000, and the cash flow provided by financing activities is $57,000. The resulting cash flow of $25,000 exactly equals the increase in cash on the balance sheet of $25,000, as required.

The following illustration summarizes the five-step process to prepare an indirect method statement of cash flows:

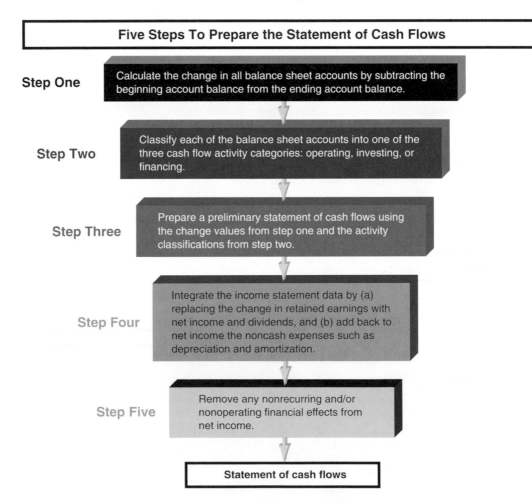

Five Steps To Prepare the Statement of Cash Flows

Step One   Calculate the change in all balance sheet accounts by subtracting the beginning account balance from the ending account balance.

Step Two   Classify each of the balance sheet accounts into one of the three cash flow activity categories: operating, investing, or financing.

Step Three   Prepare a preliminary statement of cash flows using the change values from step one and the activity classifications from step two.

Step Four   Integrate the income statement data by (a) replacing the change in retained earnings with net income and dividends, and (b) add back to net income the noncash expenses such as depreciation and amortization.

Step Five   Remove any nonrecurring and/or nonoperating financial effects from net income.

Statement of cash flows

---

[3] An exception is interest expense, which most investment professionals view as a financing activity. Regardless, interest payments are required to be included in the cash flow from operating activities.

According to **Home Depot**, "Our values are our beliefs, principles and standards that do not change over time. Values are the resources we draw on when asked to make decisions. They form the groundwork for our ethical behavior. All that we do at The Home Depot must be consistent with the values of the Company. We believe in *Doing the Right Thing*, having *Respect for all People*, building *Strong Relationships*, *Taking Care of Our People*, *Giving Back*, providing *Excellent Customer Service*, *Encouraging Entrepreneurial Spirit* and providing strong *Shareholder Returns*."

Home Depot believes that "Doing the Right Thing" leads to doing well for all its stakeholders, including its shareholders. As Home Depot states, "We will conduct our business and ourselves in a way that enhances and preserves the reputation of the Company while providing our shareholders with a fair return on their investment." There seems to be a lot of truth in this as Home Depot has managed to stay profitable even as the poor U.S. economy has battered the construction industry. In fiscal years 2008 and 2007, during the height of the construction downturn, the company managed to produce cash flows from operating activities each year in excess of $5 billion.

Husky Company's 2013 income statement and comparative balance sheets as of December 31 of 2013 and 2012 are shown below:

YOUR TURN! 12.2

The solution is on page 596.

HUSKY COMPANY
Income Statement
For Year Ended December 31, 2013

Sales revenue. . . . . . . :		$1,270,000
Cost of goods sold.	$860,000	
Wages expense	172,000	
Insurance expense.	16,000	
Depreciation expense.	34,000	
Interest expense.	18,000	
Income tax expense.	58,000	1,158,000
Net income.		$ 112,000

HUSKY COMPANY
Balance Sheets

	Dec. 31, 2013	Dec. 31, 2012
Assets		
Cash.	$ 22,000	$ 10,000
Accounts receivable.	82,000	64,000
Inventory.	180,000	120,000
Prepaid insurance	10,000	14,000
Plant assets	500,000	390,000
Accumulated depreciation	(136,000)	(102,000)
Total assets	$658,000	$496,000
Liabilities and Stockholders' Equity		
Accounts payable.	$ 14,000	$ 20,000
Wages payable.	18,000	12,000
Income tax payable	14,000	16,000
Bonds payable	260,000	150,000
Common stock.	180,000	180,000
Retained earnings	172,000	118,000
Total liabilities and stockholders' equity	$658,000	$496,000

Cash dividends of $58,000 were declared and paid during 2013. Plant assets were purchased for cash, and bonds payable were issued for cash. Accounts payable relate to merchandise purchases.

Required

Prepare a 2013 statement of cash flows for the Husky Company using the indirect method.

> *For readers skipping the indirect method, please resume reading here.*

ANALYZING CASH FLOWS

LO3 **Define** several ratios used to analyze the statement of cash flows and **explain** their use.

Data from the statement of cash flows are often used to calculate financial measures to evaluate a company's cash flow health. Three such measures include a company's free cash flow, the operating cash flow to current liabilities ratio, and the operating cash flow to capital expenditures ratio.

Free Cash Flow

Free cash flow (FCF) is often used by investment professionals and investors to evaluate a company's cash-flow strength. FCF is an important performance reference point for investment professionals because it is less subject to the accounting trickery that often characterizes accrual basis net income. Free cash flow is calculated as follows:

FCF = Cash flow from operating activities − Capital expenditures

As discussed in Chapter 9, capital expenditures refer to the required reinvestment in a business's plant and intangible assets necessary to enable a firm to remain a going concern. A firm with strong free cash flow will carry a higher stock value than one with weak (or no) free cash flow.

TAKEAWAY 12.1	**Concept** ⟶	**Method** ⟶	**Assessment**
	Does a company generate cash flows in excess of its capital expenditure needs?	Statement of cash flows. FCF = Cash flow from operating activities − Capital expenditures	The higher the free cash flow, the greater is a company's ability to generate cash for needs other than capital expenditures.

Operating-Cash-Flow-to-Current-Liabilities Ratio

Two measures previously introduced—the current ratio and the quick ratio—emphasize the relationship of a company's current or quick assets to its current liabilities in an attempt to measure the ability of a firm to pay its current liabilities. The **operating-cash-flow-to-current-liabilities ratio** is another measure of a company's ability to pay its current liabilities. While the current and quick ratios focus on a firm's ability to pay liabilities using existing current or quick assets, the operating cash flow to current liabilities highlights a firm's ability to pay its current liabilities using its operating cash flow. The ratio is calculated as follows:

$$\text{Operating-cash-flow-to-current-liabilities ratio} = \frac{\text{Cash flow from operating activities}}{\text{Average current liabilities}}$$

The cash flow from operating activities is obtained from the statement of cash flows. The denominator is the average of the beginning and ending current liabilities for the year.

The following amounts (in thousands of dollars) were taken from the financial statements of the **Gannett Co., Inc.**, a diversified news and information company that publishes *USA Today:*

Cash flow from operating activities	$1,017,186,000
Current liabilities at beginning of the year	962,163,000
Current liabilities at end of the year	1,153,141,000

The operating cash flow to current liabilities ratio for the Gannett Co. is calculated as follows:

$$\frac{\$1,017,186,000}{\left[\dfrac{(\$962,163,000 + \$1,153,141,000)}{2}\right]} = 0.96$$

The higher this ratio, the greater is a firm's ability to pay current liabilities using its operating cash flow. A ratio of 0.5 is considered a strong ratio; consequently, Gannett's ratio of 0.96 would be interpreted as very strong. A ratio of 0.96 indicates that Gannett generates $0.96 of operating cash flow for every dollar of current liabilities.

Concept ⟶	Method ⟶	Assessment	TAKEAWAY 12.2
Will a company have sufficient cash to pay its current liabilities as they become due?	Statement of cash flows and balance sheet. $\text{Operating-cash-flow-to-current-liabilities ratio} = \dfrac{\text{Cash flow from operating activities}}{\text{Average current liabilities}}$	The higher the ratio, the higher the probability that a company will have sufficient operating cash flow to pay its current liabilities as they become due.	

Operating-Cash-Flow-to-Capital-Expenditures Ratio

To remain competitive, a business must be able to replace, and expand when appropriate, its property, plant, and equipment. A ratio that evaluates a firm's ability to finance its capital investments from operating cash flow is the **operating-cash-flow-to-capital-expenditures ratio**. This ratio is calculated as follows:

$$\text{Operating-cash-flow-to-capital expenditures ratio} = \frac{\textbf{Cash flow from operating activities}}{\textbf{Annual net capital expenditures}}$$

The numerator in this ratio comes from the statement of cash flows. Information for the denominator may be found in one or more places in the financial statements. Data on capital expenditures are part of the required industry segment disclosures in the notes to the financial statements. Data regarding a company's capital expenditures are also presented in the investing activities section of the statement of cash flows. (When capital expenditures are reported in the statement of cash flows, the amount is often broken into two figures—(1) Proceeds from the sale of property, plant and equipment and (2) Purchases of property, plant and equipment. The appropriate "capital expenditures" figure for purpose of calculating this ratio is the net of the two amounts.) Finally, management's discussion and analysis of the financial statements may identify a company's annual capital expenditures.

A ratio in excess of 1.0 indicates that a firm's current operating activities are providing cash in excess of the amount needed to fund its desired investment in plant and intangible assets and would normally be considered a sign of financial strength. The interpretation of this ratio is influenced by the trend in recent years, the ratio being achieved by other firms in the same industry, and the stage of a firm's life cycle. A firm in the early stages of its life cycle—when periods of rapid expansion may occur—may be expected to experience a lower ratio than a firm in the later stage of its life cycle—when maintenance of plant capacity may be more likely than an expansion of plant capacity.

To illustrate the ratio's calculation, **Abbott Laboratories**, a manufacturer of pharmaceutical and health care products, reported capital expenditures of $1,287,724,000. Abbott's cash flow from operating activities was $6,994,620,000. Thus, Abbott's operating-cash-flow-to-capital-expenditures ratio for the year was 5.43, or

($6,994,620,000/$1,287,724,000). The following are operating-cash-flow-to-capital-expenditures ratios for other well-known companies:

PepsiCo Inc. (Consumer foods and beverages)	2.98
Lockheed Martin Corporation (Aerospace).	4.77
Norfolk Southern Corporation (Freight transportation services).	1.87
Federal Mogul Corporation (Precision parts)	2.04

TAKEAWAY 12.3	Concept	→ Method →	Assessment
	Does a company generate sufficient operating cash flows to finance its capital expenditure needs?	Statement of cash flows. Operating-cash-flow-to-capital-expenditures ratio $= \dfrac{\text{Cash flow from operating activities}}{\text{Annual net capital expenditures}}$	The higher the ratio, the higher the probability that a company will generate sufficient operating cash flow to finance its capital expenditure needs.

YOUR TURN! 12.3

The solution is on page 597.

The following selected data were obtained from the financial statements of Blake Enterprises:

Cash flow from operating activities	$40,000
Annual net capital expenditures.	12,500
Average current liabilities	30,000

Calculate the following financial measures for Blake Enterprises:

1. Free cash flow
2. Operating-cash-flow-to-current-liabilities ratio
3. Operating-cash-flow-to-capital-expenditures ratio

COMPREHENSIVE PROBLEM

Terry Company's income statement and comparative balance sheets at December 31, 2013 and 2012, are as follows:

TERRY COMPANY Income Statement For Year Ended December 31, 2013		
Sales revenue.		$385,000
Dividend income.		5,000
		390,000
Cost of goods sold.	$233,000	
Wages expense	82,000	
Advertising expense.	10,000	
Depreciation expense.	11,000	
Income tax expense.	17,000	
Loss on sale of investments.	2,000	355,000
Net income.		$ 35,000

REVIEW

TERRY COMPANY Balance Sheets	Dec. 31, 2013	Dec. 31, 2012
Assets		
Cash.	$ 8,000	$ 12,000
Accounts receivable.	22,000	28,000
Inventory.	94,000	66,000
Prepaid advertising.	12,000	9,000
Long-term investments—available for sale	30,000	41,000
Fair value adjustment to investments.	—	(1,000)
Plant assets	178,000	130,000
Accumulated depreciation	(72,000)	(61,000)
Total assets	$272,000	$224,000
Liabilities and Stockholders' Equity		
Accounts payable.	$ 27,000	$ 14,000
Wages payable.	6,000	2,500
Income tax payable	3,000	4,500
Common stock.	139,000	125,000
Retained earnings	97,000	79,000
Unrealized loss on investments	—	(1,000)
Total liabilities and stockholders' equity	$272,000	$224,000

Cash dividends of $17,000 were declared and paid during 2013. Plant assets were purchased for cash, and, later in the year, additional common stock was issued for cash. Investments costing $11,000 were sold for cash at a $2,000 loss; an unrealized loss of $1,000 on these investments had been recorded in 2012 (at December 31, 2013, the cost and fair value of the unsold investments are equal).

Required

a. Calculate the change in cash that occurred during 2013.

b. Prepare a 2013 statement of cash flows using the indirect method.

Solution

a. $8,000 ending balance − $12,000 beginning balance = $4,000 decrease in cash

b. 1. Use the indirect method to determine the cash flow from operating activities.

   • The adjustments to convert Terry Company's net income of $35,000 to the cash provided by operating activities of $38,000 are shown in the following statement of cash flows.

2. Analyze changes in remaining noncash asset (and contra asset) accounts to determine cash flows from investing activities.

   • Long-term investments: $11,000 decrease resulted from sale of investments for cash at a $2,000 loss. Cash received from sale of investments = $9,000 ($11,000 cost − $2,000 loss).

   • Fair value adjustment to investments: $1,000 decrease resulted from the elimination of this account balance (and the unrealized loss of investments) at the end of 2013. No cash flow effect.

   • Plant assets: $48,000 increase resulted from purchase of plant assets for cash. Cash paid to purchase plant assets = $48,000.

   • Accumulated depreciation: $11,000 increase resulted from the recording of 2013 depreciation. No cash flow effect.

3. Analyze changes in remaining liability and stockholders' equity accounts to determine cash flows from financing activities.

   • Common stock: $14,000 increase resulted from the issuance of stock for cash. Cash received from issuance of common stock = $14,000.

   • Retained earnings: $18,000 increase resulted from net income of $35,000 and dividend declaration of $17,000. Cash paid as dividends = $17,000.

   • Unrealized loss on investments: $1,000 decrease resulted from the elimination of this account balance (and the fair value adjustment to investments) at the end of 2013. No cash flow effect.

The statement of cash flows (indirect method) is as follows:

TERRY COMPANY Statement of Cash Flows For the Year Ended December 31, 2013		
Cash Flow from Operating Activities		
Net income	$35,000	
Add (deduct) items to convert net income to cash basis		
Depreciation	11,000	
Loss on sale of investments	2,000	
Accounts receivable decrease	6,000	
Inventory increase	(28,000)	
Prepaid advertising increase	(3,000)	
Accounts payable increase	13,000	
Wages payable increase	3,500	
Income tax payable decrease	(1,500)	
Cash provided by operating activities		$38,000
Cash Flow from Investing Activities		
Sale of investments	9,000	
Purchase of plant assets	(48,000)	
Cash used by investing activities		(39,000)
Cash Flow from Financing Activities		
Issuance of common stock	14,000	
Payment of dividends	(17,000)	
Cash used by financing activities		(3,000)
Net decrease in cash		(4,000)
Cash at beginning of year		12,000
Cash at end of year		$ 8,000

APPENDIX 12A: Preparing the Statement of Cash Flows Under the Direct Method

LO4 Explain the preparation of a statement of cash flows using the direct method.

Although it is quite straightforward to create a direct method statement of cash flows given access to a company's internal accounting records, such access is rarely available to anyone except a company's management team. All that is necessary is to pull the numbers directly off the Cash general ledger account and place them in the appropriate section of the statement of cash flows. This is why, in fact, the direct method is referred to as "direct." The cash flow from operations is taken directly from the company's general ledger, rather than being indirectly computed from net income. Unfortunately, investment professionals, lenders, and stockholders rarely have access to such proprietary internal data. Thus, it is necessary to be able to create direct method cash flow information using only such publicly available data as the indirect method statement of cash flows.

The process to convert an indirect method statement of cash flows to the direct method requires two steps. First, replace net income (the first line item under the operating activities section of the indirect method statement format) with the line items appearing on a firm's income statement. For instance, Bennett Company's income statement in Exhibit 12-2 contains the following line items:

Sales revenue	$250,000
Cost of goods sold	(148,000)
Wages expense	(52,000)
Insurance expense	(5,000)
Depreciation expense	(10,000)
Income tax expense	(11,000)
Gain on sale of plant assets	8,000
Net income	$ 32,000

Thus, for the Bennett Company, we begin by replacing the net income of $32,000 under the operating activities section in Exhibit 12-5 with the seven income statement line items shown above, which aggregate to $32,000.

The second step involves adjusting the income statement line items identified in Step One with the remaining line items from the operating activities section of the indirect method statement of cash flows. Exhibit 12A-1 summarizes the procedures for converting individual income statement items to the corresponding cash flows from operating activities.

Exhibit 12A-1	**Direct Method Conversion Schedule: Adjustments to Convert Income Statement Items to Operating Activity Cash Flows**

Income Statement Item	Adjustment to Cash Flow	Operating Activity Cash Flow
Sales revenue	+ Decrease in accounts receivable *or* − Increase in accounts receivable	= Receipts from customers
Cost of goods sold	− Increase in inventory *or* + Decrease in inventory **and** − Decrease in accounts payable *or* + Increase in accounts payable	= Payments for merchandise
Operating expenses Interest expense Income tax expense (excluding items listed below)	− Increase in related prepaid expense *or* + Decrease in related prepaid expense **and** − Decrease in related accrued liability *or* + Increase in related accrued liability	= Payments for expenses
Depreciation expense Depletion expense Amortization expense	+ Depreciation expense + Depletion expense + Amortization expense	= 0
Gains (investing/financing) Losses (investing/financing)	Omit: Not related to operating activities	= 0

Using Bennett Company's data in Exhibit 12-5, those adjustments would appear as follows:

Income Statement Line Items		Operating Activities Line Items		Direct Method Cash Flow	
Sales revenue............	$250,000	**Less**	**$5,000 accounts receivable**	Cash received from customers	$245,000
Cost of goods sold........	(148,000)	Add **Less**	$6,000 inventory **$9,000 accounts payable**	Cash paid for merchandise	(151,000)
Wage expense	(52,000)			Cash paid to employees..........	(52,000)
Insurance expense........	(5,000)	**Less**	**$13,000 prepaid insurance**	Cash paid for insurance	(18,000)
Depreciation expense......	(10,000)	Add	$10,000 depreciation		
Income tax expense.......	(11,000)	Add	$2,000 income tax payable	Cash paid for income taxes	(9,000)
Gain on sale of plant assets	8,000	**Less**	**$8,000 gain on sale of plant assets**		
Net income..............	$ 32,000			Cash flow from operations........	$ 15,000

Exhibit 12A-2 presents the Bennett Company's direct method statement of cash flows after undertaking the above two steps. As expected, the direct method cash flow from operating activities of $15,000 is exactly equivalent to the indirect method result of $15,000 as reported in Exhibit 12-5. Note that the cash flow from investing activities and the cash flow from financing activities are exactly the same in both Exhibit 12-5 and Exhibit 12A-2. The only difference between the two exhibits is the manner in which the cash flow from operating activities is calculated. In Exhibit 12-5, the cash flow from operating activities is calculated by beginning with net income and then adjusting for various noncash expenses (depreciation expense) and nonoperating transactions (gain on sale of plant assets), as well as adjusting for the changes in the various working capital accounts (accounts receivable, inventory, prepaid insurance, accounts payable, and taxes payable). In Exhibit 12A-2, net income is replaced with the income statement line items and the noncash expenses and working capital adjustments are disaggregated to the individual line items. But in each case, the operating cash flow of $15,000 remains the same.

Exhibit 12A-2	Statement of Cash Flows Under the Direct Method

BENNETT COMPANY
Statement of Cash Flows
For Year Ended December 31, 2013

Cash Flow from Operating Activities

Cash received from customers		$245,000
Cash paid for merchandise purchased	$(151,000)	
Cash paid to employees	(52,000)	
Cash paid for insurance	(18,000)	
Cash paid for income taxes	(9,000)	(230,000)
Cash provided by operating activities		15,000
Cash Flow from Investing Activities		
Purchase of long-term investments	(15,000)	
Sale of plant assets	28,000	
Purchase of patent	(60,000)	
Cash used by investing activities		(47,000)
Cash Flow from Financing Activities		
Issuance of common stock	70,000	
Payment of dividends	(13,000)	
Cash provided by financing activities		57,000
Net increase in cash		25,000
Cash at beginning of year		10,000
Cash at end of year		$ 35,000

YOUR TURN! 12.4

The solution is on page 597.

Husky Company's 2013 income statement and comparative balance sheets as of December 31 of 2013 and 2012 are shown below:

HUSKY COMPANY
Income Statement
For the Year Ended December 31, 2013

Sales revenue		$1,270,000
Cost of goods sold	$860,000	
Wages expense	172,000	
Insurance expense	16,000	
Depreciation expense	34,000	
Interest expense	18,000	
Income tax expense	58,000	1,158,000
Net income		$ 112,000

HUSKY COMPANY
Balance Sheets

	Dec. 31, 2013	Dec. 31, 2012
Assets		
Cash	$ 22,000	$ 10,000
Accounts receivable	82,000	64,000
Inventory	180,000	120,000
Prepaid insurance	10,000	14,000
Plant assets	500,000	390,000
Accumulated depreciation	(136,000)	(102,000)
Total assets	$658,000	$496,000

HUSKY COMPANY
Balance Sheets

	Dec. 31, 2013	Dec. 31, 2012
Liabilities and Stockholders' Equity		
Accounts payable.	$ 14,000	$ 20,000
Wages payable.	18,000	12,000
Income tax payable	14,000	16,000
Bonds payable.	260,000	150,000
Common stock.	180,000	180,000
Retained earnings	172,000	118,000
Total liabilities and stockholders' equity	$658,000	$496,000

Cash dividends of $58,000 were declared and paid during 2013. Plant assets were purchased for cash, and bonds payable were issued for cash. Bond interest is paid semiannually on June 30 and December 31. Accounts payable relate to merchandise purchases.

Required
Prepare a 2013 statement of cash flows using the direct method.

SUMMARY OF LEARNING OBJECTIVES

Discuss the content and format of the statement of cash flows. (p. 550)   LO1
- A statement of cash flows explains the net increase or decrease in cash and cash equivalents during the period.
- A statement of cash flows separates cash flows into operating, investing, and financing activity categories.
- A secondary objective of cash flow reporting is to provide information regarding a firm's investing and financing activities. A required supplemental disclosure reports noncash investing and financing activities.
- A statement of cash flows should help users compare, evaluate, and predict a firm's cash flows and also help evaluate its financial flexibility.

Explain the preparation of a statement of cash flows using the indirect method. (p. 556)   LO2
- The indirect method reconciles net income to cash flow from operating activities.

Define several ratios used to analyze the statement of cash flows and explain their use. (p. 564)   LO3
- Free cash flow is defined as a company's cash flow from operations less its capital expenditures; the metric provides a measure of a firm's cash flow that can be used to fund business activities beyond the replacement of property, plant, and equipment.
- The operating-cash-flow-to-current-liabilities ratio is calculated by dividing a company's cash flow from operating activities by its average current liabilities for the year; the ratio reveals a firm's ability to repay current liabilities from operating cash flow.
- The operating-cash-flow-to-capital-expenditures ratio is calculated by dividing a firm's cash flow from operating activities by its annual net capital expenditures; the ratio evaluates a firm's ability to fund its capital investment using operating cash flow.

Appendix 12A: Explain the preparation of a statement of cash flows using the direct method. (p. 568)   LO4
- The direct method shows the major categories of operating cash receipts and payments.
- The FASB encourages use of the direct method but permits use of either the direct or the indirect method.
- A firm using the direct method must separately disclose the reconciliation of net income to cash flow from operating activities.

SUMMARY	Concept	Method	Assessment
TAKEAWAY 12.1	Does a company generate cash flows in excess of its capital expenditure needs?	Statement of cash flows. FCF = Cash flow from operating activities − Capital expenditures	The higher the free cash flow, the greater is a company's ability to generate cash for needs other than capital expenditures.
TAKEAWAY 12.2	Will a company have sufficient cash to pay its current liabilities as they become due?	Statement of cash flows and balance sheet. $\text{Operating-cash-flow-to-current-liabilities ratio} = \dfrac{\text{Cash flow from operating activities}}{\text{Average current liabilities}}$	The higher the ratio, the higher the probability that a company will have sufficient operating cash flow to pay its current liabilities as they become due.
TAKEAWAY 12.3	Does a company generate sufficient operating cash flows to finance its capital expenditure needs?	Statement of cash flows. $\text{Operating-cash-flow-to-capital-expenditures ratio} = \dfrac{\text{Cash flow from operating activities}}{\text{Annual net capital expenditures}}$	The higher the ratio, the higher the probability that a company will generate sufficient operating cash flow to finance its capital expenditure needs.

KEY TERMS

Cash equivalents (p. 550)
Cash management (p. 550)
Direct method (p. 555)
Financial flexibility (p. 555)
Financing activities (p. 552)

Free cash flow (FCF) (p. 564)
Indirect method (p. 555)
Investing activities (p. 552)
Noncash expenses (p. 560)
Noncash investing and financing activities (p. 554)

Operating activities (p. 552)
Operating-cash-flow-to-capital-expenditures ratio (p. 565)
Operating-cash-flow-to-current-liabilities ratio (p. 564)

SELF-STUDY QUESTIONS

(Answers to the Self-Study Questions are at the end of the chapter.)

LO1   1. **Which of the following is not disclosed in a statement of cash flows?**
   a. A transfer of cash to a cash equivalent investment
   b. The amount of cash at year-end
   c. Cash outflows from investing activities during the period
   d. Cash inflows from financing activities during the period

LO1   2. **Which of the following events will appear in the cash flows from investing activities section of the statement of cash flows?**
   a. Cash received as interest
   b. Cash received from issuance of common stock
   c. Cash purchase of truck
   d. Cash payment of dividends

LO1   3. **Which of the following events will appear in the cash flows from financing activities section of the statement of cash flows?**
   a. Cash purchase of equipment
   b. Cash purchase of bonds issued by another company
   c. Cash received as repayment for funds loaned
   d. Cash purchase of treasury stock

4. Tyler Company has net income of $49,000 and the following related items: **LO2**

Depreciation expense.	$ 5,000
Accounts receivable increase	2,000
Inventory decrease.	10,000
Accounts payable decrease.	4,000

Using the indirect method, what is Tyler's cash flow from operations?
   a. $42,000
   b. $46,000
   c. $58,000
   d. $38,000

5. Which of the following methods will disclose the cash received from customers in the statement of   **LO4**
cash flows?   **(Appendix 12A)**
   a. Indirect method
   b. Reconciliation method
   c. Direct method
   d. Both direct and indirect methods

6. Which of the following events will not appear in the cash flows from financing activities section of   **LO1**
the statement of cash flow?
   a. Borrowing cash from a bank
   b. Issuance of stock in exchange for plant assets
   c. Sales of common stock
   d. Payment of dividends on preferred stock

7. Smith & Sons reports sales revenue of $1,000,000 on its income statement. Its balance sheet reveals   **LO4**
beginning and ending accounts receivable of $60,000 and $92,000, respectively. What is the amount   **(Appendix 12A)**
of cash collected from customers of the company?
   a. $1,032,000
   b. $968,000
   c. $1,060,000
   d. $1,092,000

8. Which of the following is not a cash equivalent?   **LO1**
   a. Short-term U.S. Treasury bill
   b. Short-term certificate of deposit
   c. Money-market account
   d. IBM common stock

9. Which of the following expenses are not added back to net income when using the indirect method   **LO2**
to prepare a statement of cash flows?
   a. Amortization expense
   b. Depletion expense
   c. Interest expense
   d. Depreciation expense

10. Smith & Sons reports interest expense of $90,000 on its income statement. The beginning and   **LO4**
ending balances for interest payable reported on its balance sheet are $10,000 and $15,000,   **(Appendix 12A)**
respectively. How much cash did Smith & Sons pay for interest expense this period?
   a. $85,000
   b. $95,000
   c. $100,000
   d. $105,000

11. Free cash flow is a measure of a firm's   **LO3**
   a. interest free debt.
   b. ability to generate net income.
   c. ability to generate cash and invest in new capital expenditures.
   d. ability to collect accounts receivable in a timely manner.

LO3 12. Taylor Company reports free cash flow of $15,000, total cash of $18,000, net income of $50,000, current assets of $90,000, average current liabilities of $60,000, and cash flow from operating activities of $48,000. Compute the operating-cash-flow-to-current-liabilities ratio for Taylor Company.

    a. 0.83

    b. 0.80

    c. 0.30

    d. 1.25

QUESTIONS

1. What is the definition of *cash equivalents?* Give three examples of cash equivalents.

2. Why are cash equivalents included with cash in a statement of cash flows?

3. What are the three major types of activities classified on a statement of cash flows? Give an example of a cash inflow and a cash outflow in each classification.

4. In which of the three activity categories of a statement of cash flows would each of the following items appear? Indicate for each item whether it represents a cash inflow or a cash outflow:

    a. Cash purchase of equipment

    b. Cash collection on loans

    c. Cash dividends paid

    d. Cash dividends received

    e. Cash proceeds from issuing stock

    f. Cash receipts from customers

    g. Cash interest paid

    h. Cash interest received

5. Why is a statement of cash flows a useful financial statement?

6. What is the difference between the direct method and the indirect method of presenting the cash flow from operating activities?

7. In determining the cash flow from operating activities using the indirect method, why is it necessary to add depreciation back to net income? Give an example of another item that is added back to net income under the indirect method.

8. Vista Company sold land for $98,000 cash that had originally cost $70,000. The company recorded a gain on the sale of $28,000. How is this event reported in a statement of cash flows using the indirect method?

9. A firm uses the indirect method. Using the following information, what is its cash flow from operating activities?

Net income	$88,000
Accounts receivable decrease	13,000
Inventory increase	9,000
Accounts payable decrease	3,500
Income tax payable increase	1,500
Depreciation expense	6,000

10. If a business had a net loss for the year, under what circumstances would the statement of cash flows show a positive cash flow from operating activities?

11. A firm is converting its accrual revenues to corresponding cash amounts using the direct method. Sales revenue on the income statement are $925,000. Beginning and ending accounts receivable on the balance sheet are $58,000 and $44,000, respectively. What is the amount of cash received from customers?

12. A firm reports $86,000 wages expense in its income statement. If beginning and ending wages payable are $3,900 and $2,800, respectively, what is the amount of cash paid to employees?

13. A firm reports $43,000 advertising expense in its income statement. If beginning and ending prepaid advertising are $6,000 and $7,600, respectively, what is the amount of cash paid for advertising?

14. Rusk Company sold equipment for $5,100 cash that had cost $35,000 and had $29,000 of accumulated depreciation. How is this event reported in a statement of cash flows using the direct method?

15. What separate disclosures are required for a company that reports a statement of cash flows using the direct method?

16. How is the *operating-cash-flow-to-current-liabilities ratio* calculated? Explain its use.

17. How is the *operating-cash-flow-to-capital-expenditures ratio* calculated? Explain its use.

18. The statement of cash flows provides information that may be useful in predicting future cash flows, evaluating financial flexibility, assessing liquidity, and identifying a company's financing needs. It is not, however, the best financial statement for learning about a firm's financial performance during a period. Information about a company's financial performance is provided by the income statement. Two basic principles—the revenue recognition principle and the matching concept—work to distinguish the income statement from the statement of cash flows. (a) Define the revenue recognition principle and the matching concept. (b) Briefly explain how these two principles work to make the income statement a better report regarding a firm's periodic financial performance than the statement of cash flows.

SHORT EXERCISES

Use the following information regarding the Seville Corporation to answer Short Exercises 12-1 through 12-3:

Accounts payable increase	$ 9,000
Accounts receivable increase	4,000
Accrued liabilities decrease	3,000
Amortization expense	6,000
Cash balance, January 1	22,000
Cash balance, December 31	15,000
Cash paid as dividends	29,000
Cash paid to purchase land	90,000
Cash paid to retire bonds payable at par	60,000
Cash received from issuance of common stock	35,000
Cash received from sale of equipment	17,000
Depreciation expense	29,000
Gain on sale of equipment	4,000
Inventory decrease	13,000
Net income	76,000
Prepaid expenses increase	2,000

SE12-1. **Cash Flow from Operating Activities** Using the information for the Seville Corporation above, calculate the cash flow from operating activities. **LO1, 2**

SE12-2. **Cash Flow from Investing Activities** Using the information for the Seville Corporation above, calculate the cash flow from investing activities. **LO1, 2**

SE12-3. **Cash Flow from Financing Activities** Using the information for the Seville Corporation above, calculate the cash flow for financing activities. **LO1, 2**

SE12-4. **Direct Method** Using the following data for Smith & Sons, calculate the cash paid for rent: **LO4** (Appendix 12A)

Rent expense	$80,000
Prepaid rent, January 1	10,000
Prepaid rent, December 31	8,000

SE12-5. **Direct Method** Using the following data for Smith & Sons, calculate the cash received as interest: **LO4** (Appendix 12A)

Interest income	$26,000
Interest receivable, January 1	3,000
Interest receivable, December 31	3,700

LO4
(Appendix 12A)

SE12-6. **Direct Method** Using the following data for Smith & Sons, calculate the cash paid for merchandise purchased:

Cost of goods sold.	$108,000
Inventory, January 1.	19,000
Inventory, December 31.	22,000
Accounts payable, January 1.	11,000
Accounts payable, December 31.	7,000

LO4
(Appendix 12A)

SE12-7. **Converting Sales Revenue to Cash** Smith & Sons is converting its sales revenues to corresponding cash amounts using the direct method. Sales revenue on the income statement are $1,025,000. Beginning and ending accounts receivable on the balance sheet are $58,000 and $34,000, respectively. Calculate the amount of cash received from customers.

The following information for Smith & Sons relates to Short Exercises 12-8 through 12-10:

Cash flow from operating activities	$1,500,000
Capital expenditures	850,000
Current liabilities, beginning of year.	300,000
Current liabilities, end of year.	360,000

LO3   **SE12-8.**   **Free Cash Flow** Using the above data, calculate the free cash flow for Smith & Sons.

LO3   **SE12-9.**   **Operating-Cash-Flow-to-Current-Liabilities Ratio** Using the above data, calculate the operating-cash-flow-to-current-liabilities ratio for Smith & Sons.

LO3   **SE12-10.**   **Operating-Cash-Flow-to-Capital-Expenditures Ratio** Using the above data, calculate the operating-cash-flow-to-capital-expenditures ratio for Smith & Sons.

Assignments with the ✓ logo in the margin are available in BusinessCourse.
See the Preface of the book for details.

EXERCISES—SET A

LO1   **E12-1A.**   **Classification of Cash Flows** For each of the items below, indicate whether the cash flow item relates to an operating activity, an investing activity, or a financing activity:

a.   Cash receipts from customers for services rendered
b.   Sale of long-term investments for cash
c.   Acquisition of plant assets for cash
d.   Payment of income taxes
e.   Bonds payable issued for cash
f.   Payment of cash dividends declared in previous year
g.   Purchase of short-term investments (not cash equivalents) for cash

LO1   **E12-2A.**   **Classification of Cash Flows** For each of the items below, indicate whether it is (1) a cash flow from an operating activity, (2) a cash flow from an investing activity, (3) a cash flow from a financing activity, (4) a noncash investing and financing activity, or (5) none of the above:

a.   Paid cash to retire bonds payable at a loss
b.   Received cash as settlement of a lawsuit
c.   Acquired a patent in exchange for common stock
d.   Received advance payments from customers on orders for custom-made goods
e.   Gave large cash contribution to local university
f.   Invested cash in 60-day commercial paper (a cash equivalent)

LO2   **E12-3A.**   **Cash Flow from Operating Activities (Indirect Method)** The Lincoln Company owns no plant assets and had the following income statement for the year:

Sales revenue		$750,000
Cost of goods sold	$470,000	
Wages expense	110,000	
Rent expense	42,000	
Insurance expense	15,000	637,000
Net income		$113,000

Additional information about the company includes:

	End of Year	Beginning of Year
Accounts receivable	$54,000	$49,000
Inventory	60,000	66,000
Prepaid insurance	8,000	7,000
Accounts payable	22,000	18,000
Wages payable	9,000	11,000

Use the preceding information to calculate the cash flow from operating activities using the indirect method.

E12-4A. **Statement of Cash Flows (Indirect Method)** Use the following information regarding the Lund Corporation to (a) prepare a statement of cash flows using the indirect method and (b) compute Lund's operating-cash-flow-to-current-liabilities ratio.   **LO2, 3** ✔

Accounts payable increase	$ 9,000
Accounts receivable increase	4,000
Accrued liabilities decrease	3,000
Amortization expense	6,000
Cash balance, January 1	22,000
Cash balance, December 31	15,000
Cash paid as dividends	29,000
Cash paid to purchase land	90,000
Cash paid to retire bonds payable at par	60,000
Cash received from issuance of common stock	35,000
Cash received from sale of equipment	17,000
Depreciation expense	29,000
Gain on sale of equipment	4,000
Inventory decrease	13,000
Net income	76,000
Prepaid expenses increase	2,000
Average current liabilities	100,000

E12-5A. **Operating Cash Flows (Direct Method)** Calculate the cash flow in each of the following cases: **LO4 (Appendix 12A)** ✔

a. Cash paid for advertising:

Advertising expense	$62,000
Prepaid advertising, January 1	11,000
Prepaid advertising, December 31	15,000

b. Cash paid for income taxes:

Income tax expense	$29,000
Income tax payable, January 1	7,100
Income tax payable, December 31	4,900

c. Cash paid for merchandise purchased:

Cost of goods sold	$180,000
Inventory, January 1	30,000
Inventory, December 31	25,000
Accounts payable, January 1	10,000
Accounts payable, December 31	12,000

LO4
(Appendix 12A)
✓

E12-6A. **Statement of Cash Flows (Direct Method)** Use the following information regarding the cash flows of Mason Corporation to prepare a statement of cash flows using the direct method:

Cash balance, December 31	$ 12,000
Cash paid to employees and suppliers	148,000
Cash received from sale of land	40,000
Cash paid to acquire treasury stock	10,000
Cash balance, January 1	16,000
Cash received as interest	6,000
Cash paid as income taxes	11,000
Cash paid to purchase equipment	89,000
Cash received from customers	194,000
Cash received from issuing bonds payable	30,000
Cash paid as dividends	16,000

LO4
(Appendix 12A)
✓

E12-7A. **Operating Cash Flows (Direct Method)** Refer to the information in Exercise E12-3A. Calculate the cash flow from operating activities using the direct method. Show a related cash flow for each revenue and expense.

LO2, 4
(Appendix 12A)
✓

E12-8A. **Investing and Financing Cash Flows** During the year, Paxon Corporation's Long-Term Investments account (at cost) increased $15,000, the net result of purchasing stocks costing $80,000 and selling stocks costing $65,000 at a $6,000 loss. Also, the Bonds Payable account decreased by $40,000, the net result of issuing $100,000 of bonds at 103 and retiring bonds with a face value (and book value) of $140,000 at a $9,000 gain. What items and amounts will appear in the (a) cash flows from investing activities and the (b) cash flows from financing activities sections of Paxon's statement of cash flows?

LO2
✓

E12-9A. **Cash Flow from Operating Activities (Indirect Method)** The Arcadia Company owns no plant assets and had the following income statement for the year:

Sales revenue		$950,000
Cost of goods sold	$670,000	
Wages expense	210,000	
Rent expense	42,000	
Utilities expense	15,000	937,000
Net income		$ 13,000

Additional information about the company includes:

	End of Year	Beginning of Year
Accounts receivable	$64,000	$59,000
Inventory	60,000	86,000
Prepaid rent	8,000	7,000
Accounts payable	22,000	28,000
Wages payable	9,000	6,000

Use the preceding information to calculate the cash flow from operating activities using the indirect method.

E12-10A. Statement of Cash Flows (Indirect Method) Use the following information regarding the New-   **LO2**
castle Corporation to prepare a statement of cash flows using the indirect method:

Accounts payable decrease.	$ 5,000
Accounts receivable increase	7,000
Wages payable decrease.	3,000
Amortization expense.	16,000
Cash balance, January 1	30,000
Cash balance, December 31	7,000
Cash paid as dividends	6,000
Cash paid to purchase land.	100,000
Cash paid to retire bonds payable at par.	75,000
Cash received from issuance of common stock	45,000
Cash received from sale of equipment	12,000
Depreciation expense.	39,000
Gain on sale of equipment.	14,000
Inventory increase	13,000
Net income.	96,000
Prepaid expenses increase	8,000

E12-11A. Cash Flow Ratios Spencer Company reports the following amounts in its annual financial   **LO3**
statements:

Cash flow from operating activities	$50,000	Capital expenditures	$ 35,000*
Cash flow from investing activities.	(40,000)	Average current assets.	80,000
Cash flow from financing activities.	(5,000)	Average current liabilities.	60,000
Net income.	25,000	Total assets	150,000

* This amount is a cash outflow

a.   Compute Spencer's free cash flow.
b.   Compute Spencer's operating-cash-flow-to-current-liabilities ratio.
c.   Compute Spencer's operating-cash-flow-to-capital-expenditures ratio.

EXERCISES—SET B

E12-1B. Classification of Cash Flows For each of the items below, indicate whether the cash flow item   **LO1**
relates to an operating activity, an investing activity, or a financing activity:

a.   Cash loaned to borrowers
b.   Cash paid as interest on bonds payable
c.   Cash received from issuance of preferred stock
d.   Cash paid as state income taxes
e.   Cash received as dividends on stock investments
f.   Cash paid to acquire treasury stock
g.   Cash paid to acquire a franchise to distribute a product line

E12-2B. Classification of Cash Flows For each of the items below, indicate whether it is (1) a cash flow   **LO1**
from an operating activity, (2) a cash flow from an investing activity, (3) a cash flow from a financing activity, (4) a noncash investing and financing activity, or (5) none of the above:

a.   Received cash as interest earned on bond investment
b.   Received cash as refund from supplier
c.   Borrowed cash from bank on six-month note payable
d.   Exchanged, at a gain, stock held as an investment for a parcel of land   noncash
e.   Invested cash in a money market fund (cash may be easily withdrawn from the fund)
f.   Loaned cash to help finance the start of a new biotechnology firm

LO2, 3   E12-3B.   Cash Flow from Operating Activities (Indirect Method) The following information was obtained from Galena Company's comparative balance sheets:

	End of Year	Beginning of Year
Cash	$ 19,000	$ 9,000
Accounts receivable	44,000	35,000
Inventory	55,000	49,000
Prepaid rent	6,000	8,000
Long-term investments	21,000	34,000
Plant assets	150,000	106,000
Accumulated depreciation	(40,000)	(32,000)
Accounts payable	24,000	20,000
Income tax payable	4,000	6,000
Common stock	121,000	92,000
Retained earnings	106,000	91,000
Capital expenditures	13,200	

Assume that Galena Company's income statement showed depreciation expense of $8,000, a gain on sale of investments of $9,000, and a net income of $45,000. (a) Calculate the cash flow from operating activities using the indirect method and (b) compute Galena's operating-cash-flow-to-capital-expenditures ratio.

LO2   E12-4B.   Cash Flow from Operating Activities (Indirect Method) Cairo Company had a $21,000 net loss from operations. Depreciation expense for the year was $8,600, and a dividend of $6,000 was declared and paid. The balances of the current asset and current liability accounts at the beginning and end of the year are as follows:

	End	Beginning
Cash	$ 3,500	$ 7,000
Accounts receivable	16,000	25,000
Inventory	50,000	53,000
Prepaid expenses	6,000	9,000
Accounts payable	12,000	8,000
Accrued liabilities	5,000	7,600

Did Cairo Company's operating activities provide or use cash? Use the indirect method to determine your answer.

LO4
(Appendix 12A)

E12-5B.   Operating Cash Flows (Direct Method) Calculate the cash flow in each of the following cases:

a.   Cash paid for rent:

Rent expense	$60,000
Prepaid rent, January 1	10,000
Prepaid rent, December 31	8,000

b.   Cash received as interest:

Interest income	$16,000
Interest receivable, January 1	3,000
Interest receivable, December 31	3,700

c.   Cash paid for merchandise purchased:

Cost of goods sold	$98,000
Inventory, January 1	19,000
Inventory, December 31	22,000
Accounts payable, January 1	11,000
Accounts payable, December 31	7,000

E12-6B. **Operating Cash Flows (Direct Method)** The Howell Company's current year income statement contains the following data:

LO4
(Appendix 12A)

Sales revenue..	$825,000
Cost of goods sold..	550,000
Gross profit...	$275,000

Howell's comparative balance sheets show the following data (accounts payable relate to merchandise purchases):

	End of Year	Beginning of Year
Accounts receivable...	$ 71,000	$60,000
Inventory..	109,000	96,000
Prepaid expenses..	3,000	8,000
Accounts payable..	31,000	37,000

Compute Howell's current-year cash received from customers and cash paid for merchandise purchased.

E12-7B. **Statement of Cash Flows (Direct Method)** Use the following information regarding the cash flows of Gilbert Corporation to prepare a statement of cash flows using the direct method:

LO4
(Appendix 12A)

Cash balance, December 31	$ 30,000
Cash paid to employees and suppliers	151,000
Cash received from sale of equipment	98,000
Cash paid to retire bonds payable.................................	70,000
Cash balance, January 1	20,000
Cash paid as interest	7,000
Cash paid as income taxes	24,000
Cash paid to purchase patent	66,000
Cash received from customers	216,000
Cash received from issuing common stock..........................	35,000
Cash paid as dividends	21,000

E12-8B. **Investing and Financing Cash Flows** Refer to the information in Exercise 12-3B. During the year, Galena Company purchased plant assets for cash, sold investments for cash (the entire $9,000 gain developed during the year), and issued common stock for cash. The firm also declared and paid cash dividends. What items and amounts will appear in (a) the cash flow from investing activities and (b) the cash flow from financing activities sections of a statement of cash flows?

LO2, 4
(Appendix 12A)

E12-9B. **Cash Flow From Operating Activities (Indirect Method)** The Smithfield Company owns no plant assets and had the following income statement for the year:

LO2

Sales revenue...		$1,150,000
Cost of goods sold...................................	$770,000	
Wages expense	210,000	
Rent expense	62,000	
Insurance expense...................................	45,000	1,087,000
Net income..		$ 63,000

Additional information about the company includes:

	End of Year	Beginning of Year
Accounts receivable.	$74,000	$49,000
Inventory.	70,000	86,000
Prepaid insurance	5,000	7,000
Accounts payable.	26,000	28,000
Wages payable.	12,000	13,000

Use the preceding information to calculate the cash flow from operating activities using the indirect method

LO2 **E12-10B. Statement of Cash Flows (Indirect Method)** Use the following information regarding the Fremantle Corporation to prepare a statement of cash flows using the indirect method:

Accounts payable increase	$ 11,000
Accounts receivable increase	4,000
Accrued liabilities decrease	3,000
Amortization expense.	26,000
Cash balance, January 1	22,000
Cash balance, December 31	117,000
Cash paid as dividends	49,000
Cash paid to purchase land.	100,000
Cash paid to retire bonds payable at par.	70,000
Cash received from issuance of common stock	75,000
Cash received from sale of equipment	17,000
Depreciation expense.	69,000
Gain on sale of equipment	14,000
Inventory decrease.	13,000
Net income.	126,000
Prepaid expenses increase	2,000

LO3 **E12-11B. Cash Flow Ratios** Morgan Company reports the following amounts in its annual financial statements:

Cash flow from operating activities	$60,000	Capital expenditures	$ 52,500*
Cash flow from investing activities.	(60,000)	Average current assets.	120,000
Cash flow from financing activities.	(7,500)	Average current liabilities	90,000
Net income.	37,500	Total assets	225,000

* This amount is a cash outflow

a. Compute Morgan's free cash flow.
b. Compute Morgan's operating-cash-flow-to-current-liabilities ratio.
c. Compute Morgan's operating-cash-flow-to-capital-expenditures ratio.

PROBLEMS—SET A

LO2, 3 **P12-1A. Statement of Cash Flows (Indirect Method)** The Wolff Company's income statement and comparative balance sheets at December 31 of 2013 and 2012 are shown below:

WOLFF COMPANY
Income Statement
For the Year Ended December 31, 2013

Sales revenue.		$635,000
Cost of goods sold.	$430,000	
Wages expense	86,000	
Insurance expense.	8,000	
Depreciation expense.	17,000	
Interest expense.	9,000	
Income tax expense.	29,000	579,000
Net income.		$ 56,000

WOLFF COMPANY
Balance Sheets

	Dec. 31, 2013	Dec. 31, 2012
Assets		
Cash.	$ 11,000	$ 5,000
Accounts receivable.	41,000	32,000
Inventory.	90,000	60,000
Prepaid insurance	5,000	7,000
Plant assets	250,000	195,000
Accumulated depreciation	(68,000)	(51,000)
Total assets	$329,000	$248,000
Liabilities and Stockholders' Equity		
Accounts payable.	$ 7,000	$ 10,000
Wages payable.	9,000	6,000
Income tax payable	7,000	8,000
Bonds payable	130,000	75,000
Common stock.	90,000	90,000
Retained earnings	86,000	59,000
Total liabilities and stockholders' equity	$329,000	$248,000

Cash dividends of $29,000 were declared and paid during 2013. Plant assets were purchased for cash and bonds payable were issued for cash. Bond interest is paid semi-annually on June 30 and December 31. Accounts payable relate to merchandise purchases.

Required
a.   Calculate the change in cash that occurred during 2013.
b.   Prepare a statement of cash flows using the indirect method.
c.   Compute free cash flow.
d.   Compute the operating-cash-flow-to-current-liabilities ratio.
e.   Compute the operating-cash-flow-to-capital-expenditures ratio.

P12-2A.   Statement of Cash Flows (Indirect Method) Arctic Company's income statement and comparative balance sheets as of December 31 of 2013 and 2012 follow:

LO2

ARCTIC COMPANY
Income Statement
For the Year Ended December 31, 2013

Sales revenue		$728,000
Cost of goods sold	$534,000	
Wages expense	190,000	
Advertising expense	31,000	
Depreciation expense	22,000	
Interest expense	18,000	
Gain on sale of land	(25,000)	770,000
Net loss		$ 42,000

ARCTIC COMPANY
Balance Sheets

	Dec. 31, 2013	Dec. 31, 2012
Assets		
Cash	$ 49,000	$ 28,000
Accounts receivable	42,000	50,000
Inventory	107,000	113,000
Prepaid advertising	10,000	13,000
Plant assets	360,000	222,000
Accumulated depreciation	(78,000)	(56,000)
Total assets	$490,000	$370,000
Liabilities and Stockholders' Equity		
Accounts payable	$ 17,000	$ 31,000
Interest payable	6,000	—
Bonds payable	200,000	—
Common stock	245,000	245,000
Retained earnings	52,000	94,000
Treasury stock	(30,000)	—
Total liabilities and stockholders' equity	$490,000	$370,000

During 2013, Arctic sold land for $70,000 cash that had originally cost $45,000. Arctic also purchased equipment for cash, acquired treasury stock for cash, and issued bonds payable for cash. Accounts payable relate to merchandise purchases.

Required
a. Calculate the change in cash that occurred during 2013.
b. Prepare a statement of cash flows using the indirect method.

LO2 **P12-3A.** **Statement of Cash Flows (Indirect Method)** The Dairy Company's income statement and comparative balance sheets as of December 31 of 2013 and 2012 follow:

DAIRY COMPANY
Income Statement
For the Year Ended December 31, 2013

Sales revenue		$700,000
Cost of goods sold	$440,000	
Wages and other operating expenses	95,000	
Depreciation expense	22,000	
Goodwill amortization expense	7,000	
Interest expense	10,000	
Income tax expense	36,000	
Loss on bond retirement	5,000	615,000
Net income		$ 85,000

DAIRY COMPANY Balance Sheets	Dec. 31, 2013	Dec. 31, 2012
Assets		
Cash.	$ 27,000	$ 18,000
Accounts receivable.	53,000	48,000
Inventory.	103,000	109,000
Prepaid expenses.	12,000	10,000
Plant assets	360,000	336,000
Accumulated depreciation	(87,000)	(84,000)
Goodwill	43,000	50,000
Total assets	$511,000	$487,000
Liabilities and Stockholders' Equity		
Accounts payable.	$ 32,000	$ 26,000
Interest payable	4,000	7,000
Income tax payable	6,000	8,000
Bonds payable	60,000	120,000
Common stock.	252,000	228,000
Retained earnings	157,000	98,000
Total liabilities and stockholders' equity	$511,000	$487,000

During the year, the company sold for $17,000 cash old equipment that had cost $36,000 and had
$19,000 accumulated depreciation. New equipment worth $60,000 was acquired in exchange for
$60,000 of bonds payable. Bonds payable of $120,000 were retired for cash at a loss. A $26,000 cash
dividend was declared and paid. All stock issuances were for cash.

Required

a.   Compute the change in cash that occurred in 2013.

b.   Prepare a statement of cash flows using the indirect method.

P12-4A.   Statement of Cash Flows (Indirect Method) The Rainbow Company's income statement and
comparative balance sheets as of December 31 of 2013 and 2012 follow:

LO2

RAINBOW COMPANY Income Statement For Year Ended December 31, 2013		
Sales revenue.		$750,000
Dividend income.		15,000
		765,000
Cost of goods sold.	$440,000	
Wages and other operating expenses	130,000	
Depreciation expense.	39,000	
Patent amortization expense	7,000	
Interest expense.	13,000	
Income tax expense.	44,000	
Loss on sale of equipment.	5,000	
Gain on sale of investments.	(10,000)	668,000
Net income.		$ 97,000

RAINBOW COMPANY Balance Sheets	Dec. 31, 2013	Dec. 31, 2012
Assets		
Cash and cash equivalents	$ 19,000	$ 25,000
Accounts receivable......................................	40,000	30,000
Inventory..	103,000	77,000
Prepaid expenses..	10,000	6,000
Long-term investments—available for sale	—	50,000
Fair value adjustment to investments.....................	—	7,000
Land	190,000	100,000
Buildings..	445,000	350,000
Accumulated depreciation—Buildings......................	(91,000)	(75,000)
Equipment	179,000	225,000
Accumulated depreciation—Equipment	(42,000)	(46,000)
Patents...	50,000	32,000
Total assets	$903,000	$781,000
Liabilities and Stockholders' Equity		
Accounts payable..	$ 20,000	$ 16,000
Interest payable	6,000	5,000
Income tax payable	8,000	10,000
Bonds payable	155,000	125,000
Preferred stock ($100 par value)	100,000	75,000
Common stock ($5 par value)	379,000	364,000
Paid-in-capital in excess of par value—Common	133,000	124,000
Retained earnings	102,000	55,000
Unrealized gain on investments..........................	—	7,000
Total liabilities and stockholders' equity	$903,000	$781,000

During the year, the following transactions occurred:

1. Sold long-term investments costing $50,000 for $60,000 cash. Unrealized gains totaling $7,000 related to these investments had been recorded in earlier years. At year-end, the fair value adjustment and unrealized gain account balances were eliminated.
2. Purchased land for cash.
3. Capitalized an expenditure made to improve the building.
4. Sold equipment for $14,000 cash that originally cost $46,000 and had $27,000 accumulated depreciation.
5. Issued bonds payable at face value for cash.
6. Acquired a patent with a fair value of $25,000 by issuing 250 shares of preferred stock at par value.
7. Declared and paid a $50,000 cash dividend.
8. Issued 3,000 shares of common stock for cash at $8 per share.
9. Recorded depreciation of $16,000 on buildings and $23,000 on equipment.

Required
a. Calculate the change in cash and cash equivalents that occurred during 2013.
b. Prepare a statement of cash flows using the indirect method.

LO3, 4 **P12-5A.** **Statement of Cash Flows (Direct Method)** Refer to the data given for the Wolff Company in Prob-
(Appendix 12A) lem P12-1A.

Required
a. Calculate the change in cash that occurred during 2013.
b. Prepare a statement of cash flows using the direct method.
c. Compute free cash flow.
d. Compute the operating-cash-flow-to-current-liabilities ratio.
e. Compute the operating-cash-flow-to-capital-expenditures ratio.

P12-6A. **Statement of Cash Flows (Direct Method)** Refer to the data given for the Arctic Company in
Problem P12-2A.

LO4
(Appendix 12A)

Required
a. Calculate the change in cash that occurred during 2013.
b. Prepare a statement of cash flows using the direct method.

P12-7A. **Statement of Cash Flows (Direct Method)** Refer to the data given for the Dairy Company in Problem P12-3A.

LO4
(Appendix 12A)

Required
a. Compute the change in cash that occurred in 2013.
b. Prepare a statement of cash flows using the direct method. Use one cash outflow for "cash paid
for wages and other operating expenses." Accounts payable relate to inventory purchases only.

P12-8A. **Statement of Cash Flows (Direct Method)** Refer to the data given for the Rainbow Company in
Problem P12-4A.

LO4
(Appendix 12A)

Required
a. Calculate the change in cash that occurred in 2013.
b. Prepare a statement of cash flows using the direct method. Use one cash outflow for "cash paid
for wages and other operating expenses." Accounts payable relate to inventory purchases only.

P12-9A. **Analyzing Cash Flow Ratios** Molly Enterprises reported the following information for the past
year of operations:

LO3

Transaction	Free Cash Flow $250,000	Operating-Cash-Flow-to-Current-Liabilities Ratio 1.0 times	Operating-Cash-Flow-to-Capital-Expenditures Ratio 3.0 times
a. Recorded credit sales of $5,000			
b. Collected $3,000 owed from customers			
c. Purchased $20,000 of equipment on long-term credit			
d. Purchased $15,000 of equipment for cash			
e. Paid $4,000 of wages with cash			
f. Recorded utility bill of $1,500 that has not been paid			

For each transaction, indicate whether the ratio will (I) increase, (D) decrease, or (N) have no effect.

PROBLEMS—SET B

P12-1B. **Statement of Cash Flows (Indirect Method)** The Rural Company's income statement and comparative balance sheets as of December 31 of 2013 and 2012 are shown below:

LO2, 3

RURAL COMPANY Income Statement For the Year Ended December 31, 2013		
Sales revenue		$630,000
Cost of goods sold	$376,000	
Wages expense	107,000	
Depreciation expense	20,000	
Rent expense	28,000	
Income tax expense	31,000	562,000
Net income		$ 68,000

RURAL COMPANY Balance Sheets	Dec. 31, 2013	Dec. 31, 2012
Assets		
Cash.	$ 20,000	$ 37,000
Accounts receivable.	52,000	60,000
Inventory.	137,000	110,000
Prepaid rent	14,000	12,000
Plant assets	420,000	300,000
Accumulated depreciation	(125,000)	(105,000)
Total assets	$518,000	$414,000
Liabilities and Stockholders' Equity		
Accounts payable.	$ 29,000	$ 17,000
Wages payable.	12,000	7,000
Income tax payable	5,000	8,000
Common stock.	294,000	252,000
Paid-in-capital in excess of par value	72,000	58,000
Retained earnings	106,000	72,000
Total liabilities and stockholders' equity	$518,000	$414,000

Cash dividends of $34,000 were declared and paid during 2013. Plant assets were purchased for cash and additional common stock was issued for cash. Accounts payable relate to merchandise purchases.

Required
a. Calculate the change in cash that occurred during 2013.
b. Prepare a statement of cash flows using the indirect method.
c. Compute free cash flow.
d. Compute the operating-cash-flow-to-current-liabilities ratio.
e. Compute the operating-cash-flows-to-capital-expenditures ratio.

LO2 **P12-2B.** **Statement of Cash Flows (Indirect Method)** The Sweet Company's income statement and comparative balance sheets as of December 31 of 2013 and 2012 are presented below:

SWEET COMPANY Income Statement For the Year Ended December 31, 2013		
Sales revenue.		$946,000
Cost of goods sold.	$507,000	
Wages expense	203,000	
Depreciation expense.	60,000	
Insurance expense.	13,000	
Interest expense.	12,000	
Income tax expense.	57,000	
Gain on sale of equipment	(16,000)	836,000
Net income.		$110,000

SWEET COMPANY Balance Sheets		
	Dec. 31, 2013	Dec. 31, 2012
Assets		
Cash.	$ 23,000	$ 31,000
Accounts receivable.	68,000	43,000
Inventory.	177,000	126,000
Prepaid insurance	9,000	11,000
Plant assets	887,000	770,000
Accumulated depreciation	(189,000)	(175,000)
Total assets	$975,000	$806,000
Liabilities and Stockholders' Equity		
Accounts payable.	$ 37,000	$ 27,000
Interest payable	5,000	—
Income tax payable	12,000	16,000
Bonds payable	135,000	80,000
Common stock.	660,000	585,000
Retained earnings	178,000	98,000
Treasury stock	(52,000)	—
Total liabilities and stockholders' equity	$975,000	$806,000

During the year, Sweet Company sold equipment for $27,000 cash that originally cost $57,000 and had $46,000 accumulated depreciation. New equipment was purchased for cash. Bonds payable and common stock were issued for cash. Cash dividends of $30,000 were declared and paid. At the end of the year, shares of treasury stock were purchased for cash. Accounts payable relate to merchandise purchases.

Required
a. Compute the change in cash that occurred during 2013.
b. Prepare a statement of cash flows using the indirect method.

P12-3B. **Statement of Cash Flows (Indirect Method)** The Huber Company's income statement and comparative balance sheets as of December 31 of 2013 and 2012 follow:

LO2

HUBER COMPANY Income Statement For the Year Ended December 31, 2013		
Sales revenue.		$800,000
Cost of goods sold.	$530,000	
Wages and other operating expenses	172,000	
Depreciation expense.	27,000	
Patent amortization expense	6,000	
Interest expense.	18,000	
Income tax expense.	25,000	
Gain on exchange of land for patent	(36,000)	742,000
Net income.		$ 58,000

HUBER COMPANY Balance Sheets		
	Dec. 31, 2013	Dec. 31, 2012
Assets		
Cash.	$ 34,000	$ 16,000
Accounts receivable.	64,000	49,000
Inventory.	85,000	64,000
Land.	117,000	160,000
Building and equipment	441,000	361,000
Accumulated depreciation	(120,000)	(100,000)
Patent.	73,000	—
Total assets	$694,000	$550,000
Liabilities and Stockholders' Equity		
Accounts payable.	$ 36,000	$ 26,000
Interest payable	13,000	5,000
Income tax payable	7,000	12,000
Bonds payable	175,000	75,000
Common stock.	350,000	350,000
Retained earnings	113,000	82,000
Total liabilities and stockholders' equity	$694,000	$550,000

During 2013, $27,000 of cash dividends were declared and paid. A patent valued at $79,000 was obtained in exchange for land. Equipment that originally cost $20,000 and had $7,000 accumulated depreciation was sold for $13,000 cash. Bonds payable were sold for cash and cash was used to pay for structural improvements to the building.

Required

a. Compute the change in cash that occurred during 2013.

b. Prepare a statement of cash flows using the indirect method.

LO2 **P12-4B.** **Statement of Cash Flows (Indirect Method)** The Towne Company's income statement and comparative balance sheets as of December 31 of 2013 and 2012 follow:

TOWNE COMPANY Income Statement For the Year Ended December 31, 2013		
Service fees earned		$317,000
Dividend and interest income.		14,000
		$331,000
Wages and other operating expenses	$285,000	
Depreciation expense.	52,000	
Franchise amortization expense	10,000	
Loss on sale of equipment	7,000	
Gain on sale of investments.	(17,000)	337,000
Net loss		$ 6,000

TOWNE COMPANY Balance Sheets	Dec. 31, 2013	Dec. 31, 2012
Assets		
Cash.	$ 43,000	$ 36,000
Accounts receivable.	13,000	18,000
Interest receivable	—	4,000
Prepaid expenses.	16,000	8,000
Long-term investments—available for sale	—	70,000
Fair value adjustment to investments.	—	10,000
Plant assets	696,000	655,000
Accumulated depreciation	(234,000)	(185,000)
Franchise	91,000	29,000
Total assets	$625,000	$645,000
Liabilities and Stockholders' Equity		
Accrued liabilities	$ 12,000	$ 14,000
Notes payable	—	27,000
Common stock ($10 par value)	595,000	535,000
Retained earnings	38,000	59,000
Unrealized gain on investments.	—	10,000
Treasury stock	(20,000)	—
Total liabilities and stockholders' equity	$625,000	$645,000

During the year, the following transactions occurred:

1. Sold equipment for $9,000 cash that originally cost $19,000 and had $3,000 accumulated depreciation.
2. Sold long-term investments that had cost $70,000 for $87,000 cash. Unrealized gains totaling $10,000 related to these investments had been recorded in earlier years. At year-end, the fair value adjustment and unrealized gain account balances were eliminated.
3. Paid cash to extend the company's exclusive franchise for another three years.
4. Paid off a note payable at the bank on January 1.
5. Declared and paid a $15,000 dividend.
6. Purchased treasury stock for cash.
7. Acquired land valued at $60,000 by issuing 6,000 shares of common stock.

Required
a. Compute the change in cash that occurred in 2013.
b. Prepare a statement of cash flows using the indirect method.

P12-5B.   Statement of Cash Flows (Direct Method) Refer to the data given for the Rural Company in Problem P12-1B.

LO3, 4
(Appendix 12A)
✓

Required
a. Compute the change in cash that occurred during 2013.
b. Prepare a statement of cash flows using the direct method.
c. Compute free cash flow.
d. Compute the operating-cash-flow-to-current-liabilities ratio.
e. Compute the operating-cash-flow-to-capital-expenditures ratio.

P12-6B.   Statement of Cash Flows (Direct Method) Refer to the data given for the Sweet Company in Problem P12-2B.

LO4
(Appendix 12A)
✓

Required
a. Compute the change in cash that occurred during 2013.
b. Prepare a statement of cash flows using the direct method.

ASSIGNMENTS

LO4
(Appendix 12A) ✓

P12-7B. **Statement of Cash Flows (Direct Method)** Refer to the data given for the Huber Company in Problem P12-3B.

Required
a. Compute the change in cash that occurred during 2013.
b. Prepare a statement of cash flows using the direct method. Use one cash outflow for "cash paid for wages and other operating expenses." Accounts payable relate to inventory purchases only.

LO4
(Appendix 12A) ✓

Excel

P12-8B. **Statement of Cash Flows (Direct Method)** Refer to the data given for the Towne Company in Problem P12-4B.

Required
a. Compute the change in cash that occurred during 2013.
b. Prepare a statement of cash flows using the direct method. Use one cash outflow for "cash paid for wages and other operating expenses."

LO3 ✓

Excel

P12-9B. **Analyzing Cash Flow Ratios** Molly Enterprises reported the following information for the past year of operations:

Transaction	Free Cash Flow $300,000	Operating-Cash-Flow-to-Current-Liabilities Ratio 1.2 times	Operating-Cash-Flow-to-Capital-Expenditures Ratio 4.0 times
a. Recorded credit sales of $10,000			
b. Collected $9,000 owed from customers			
c. Purchased $50,000 of equipment on long-term credit			
d. Purchased $65,000 of equipment for cash			
e. Paid $14,000 of wages with cash			
f. Recorded utility bill of $11,500 that has not been paid			

For each transaction, indicate whether the ratio will (I) increase, (D) decrease, or (N) have no effect.

SERIAL PROBLEM: KATE'S CARDS

(Note: This is a continuation of the Serial Problem: Kate's Cards from Chapter 1 through Chapter 11.)

Kate's Cards

SP12. Kate has just completed her first year running Kate's Cards. She has been preparing monthly income statements and balance sheets, so she knows that her company has been profitable and that there is cash in the bank. She has not, however, prepared a statement of cash flows. Kate provides you with the year-end income statement and balance sheet and asks that you prepare a statement of cash flows for Kate's Cards.

Additional information:

1. There was no disposals of equipment during the year.
2. Dividends in the amount of $1,300 were paid in cash during the year.
3. Prepaid expenses relate to operating expenses.

Required
a. Prepare a statement of cash flows for Kate's Cards for the year ended August 31, 2013, using the indirect method. Hint: Since this was Kate's first year of operations, the beginning balance sheet account balances were zero.
b. Prepare a statement of cash flows for Kate's Cards for the year ended August 31, 2013, using the direct method. (Appendix 12A)

KATE'S CARDS
Income Statement
Year Ended August 31, 2013

Sales revenue	$135,000
Cost of goods sold	72,000
Gross profit	63,000
Operating expenses	
Wages	18,000
Consulting	11,850
Insurance	1,200
Utilities	2,400
Depreciation	3,250
Total operating expenses	36,700
Income from operations	26,300
Interest expense	900
Income before income tax	25,400
Income tax expense	8,900
Net income	$ 16,500

KATE'S CARDS
Balance Sheet
As of August 31, 2013

Assets	
Current assets	
Cash	$12,300
Accounts receivable	11,000
Inventory	16,000
Prepaid insurance	1,000
Total current assets	40,300
Equipment	17,500
Accumulated depreciation	3,250
Total assets	$54,550
Liabilities	
Current liabilities	
Accounts payable	$6,200
Unearned revenue	1,250
Other current liabilities	1,900
Total current liabilities	9,350
Note payable	15,000
Total liabilities	24,350
Stockholders' equity	
Common stock	500
Additional paid-in-capital	9,500
Preferred stock	5,000
Retained earnings	15,200
Total stockholders' equity	30,200
Total liabilities and stockholders' equity	$54,550

EXTENDING YOUR KNOWLEDGE

REPORTING AND ANALYSIS

EYK12-1.   Financial Reporting Problem: Columbia Sportswear Company The financial statements for the **Columbia Sportswear Company** can be found in Appendix A at the end of this book.

COLUMBIA
SPORTSWEAR
COMPANY

Required

Answer the following questions:

a. How much did Columbia Sportswear's cash and cash equivalents increase in 2011?
b. What was the largest source of cash and cash equivalents in 2011?
c. What was the single largest use of cash and cash equivalents in 2011?
d. How much dividends were paid in 2011?
e. Why do depreciation and amortization, both noncash items, appear on Columbia's statement of cash flows?

COLUMBIA
SPORTSWEAR
COMPANY

UNDER ARMOUR,
INC.

EYK12-2. **Comparative Analysis Problem: Columbia Sportswear Company vs Under Armour, Inc.** The financial statements for the Columbia Sportswear Company can be found in Appendix A at the end of this book, and the financial statements of Under Armour, Inc. can be found in Appendix B (the complete annual report is available on this book's Website).

Required

Answer the following questions:

a. Compute the free cash flow in 2011 for both Columbia Sportswear and Under Armour, Inc.
b. Compute the operating cash flows to capital expenditures for both Columbia Sportswear and Under Armour, Inc.
c. Comment on the ability of each company to finance its capital expenditures.

EYK12-3. **Business Decision Problem** Recently hired as assistant controller for Finite, Inc., you are sitting next to the controller as she responds to questions at the annual stockholders' meeting. The firm's financial statements contain a statement of cash flows prepared using the indirect method. A stockholder raises his hand.

Stockholder: "I notice that depreciation expense is shown as an addition in the calculation of the cash flow from operating activities."

Controller: "That's correct."

Stockholder: "What depreciation method do you use?"

Controller: "We use the straight-line method for all plant assets."

Stockholder: "Well, why don't you switch to an accelerated depreciation method, such as double-declining balance, increase the annual depreciation amount, and thus increase the cash flow from operating activities?"

The controller pauses, turns to you, and replies, "My assistant will answer your question."

Required

Prepare an answer to the stockholder's question.

PARKER HANNIFIN
CORPORATION

EYK12-4. **Financial Analysis Problem** **Parker Hannifin Corporation**, headquartered in Cleveland, Ohio, manufactures motion control and fluid system components for a variety of industrial users. The firm's financial statements contain the following data (Year 3 is the most recent year; dollar amounts are in thousands):

	Year 3	Year 2	Year 1
Current assets at year-end.........................	$1,018,354	$1,056,443	$1,055,776
Current liabilities at year-end	504,444	468,254	358,729
Current liabilities at beginning of year	468,254	358,729	345,594
Cash provided by operating activities	259,204	229,382	235,186
Capital expenditures	99,914	91,484	84,955

a. Calculate Parker Hannifin's current ratio (current assets/current liabilities) for Years 1, 2, and 3.
b. Calculate Parker Hannifin's operating-cash-flow-to-current-liabilities ratio for Years 1, 2, and 3.
c. Comment on the three-year trend in Parker Hannifin's current ratio and operating-cash-flow-to-current-liabilities ratio. Do the trends in these two ratios reinforce each other or contradict each other as indicators of Parker Hannifin's ability to pay its current liabilities?
d. Calculate Parker Hannifin's operating-cash-flow-to-capital-expenditures ratio for Years 1, 2, and 3. Comment on the strength of this ratio over the three-year period.

CRITICAL THINKING

EYK12-5. **Accounting Research Problem: General Mills, Inc.** The fiscal year 2011 annual report of General Mills, Inc. is available on this book's Website.

GENERAL MILLS, INC.

Required

a.   Refer to Note 2. How does General Mills define its cash equivalents?

b.   What method does General Mills use to report its cash provided by operating activities?

c.   What is the change in cash and cash equivalents experienced by General Mills during fiscal 2011? What is the amount of cash and cash equivalents as of May 29, 2011?

d.   What is General Mills' operating-cash-flow-to-capital-expenditures ratio for fiscal year 2011?

e.   Calculate General Mills' 2011 operating-cash-flow-to-current-liabilities ratio.

EYK12-6. **Accounting Communication Activity** Susan Henderson, the vice president of marketing, was told by the CEO that she needs to understand the numbers because the company's existence depends on making money. It has been a long time since Susan took a class in accounting. She recalls that companies report net income and cash flows in two separate statements. She feels pretty comfortable with the income statement, but is somewhat lost looking at the statement of cash flows. She asks you to help explain this statement.

Required

Write a brief memo to Susan explaining the form and content of the statement of cash flows, along with a short discussion of how to analyze the statement.

EYK12-7. **Accounting Ethics Case** Due to an economic recession, Anton Corporation faces severe cash flow problems. Management forecasts that payments to some suppliers will have to be delayed for several months. Jay Newton, controller, has asked his staff for suggestions on selecting the suppliers for which payments will be delayed.

"That's a fairly easy decision," observes Tim Haslem. "Some suppliers charge interest if our payment is late, but others do not. We should pay those suppliers that charge interest and delay payments to the ones that do not charge interest. If we do this, the savings in interest charges will be quite substantial."

"I disagree," states Tara Wirth. "That position is too 'bottom line' oriented. It's not fair to delay payments only to suppliers who don't charge interest for late payments. Most suppliers in that category are ones we have dealt with for years; selecting these suppliers would be taking advantage of the excellent relationships we have developed over the years. The fair thing to do is to make pro-rata payments to each supplier."

"Well, making pro-rata payments to each supplier means that *all* our suppliers will be upset because no one receives full payment," comments Sue Myling. "I believe it is most important to maintain good relations with our long-term suppliers; we should pay them currently and delay payments to our newer suppliers. The interest costs we end up paying these newer suppliers is the price we must pay to keep our long-term relationships solid."

Required

Which suppliers should Jay Newton select for delayed payments? Discuss.

EYK12-8. **Corporate Social Responsibility Problem** The corporate social responsibility highlighted in this chapter (see page 563) mentions that **Home Depot** believes in giving back. One of the ways the company has done this is through its Team Depot program of employee volunteerism. Under this program, Home Depot employees volunteer their own time to work together on projects that benefit communities in which the company does business. Each year the program provides millions of hours of employee volunteerism.

THE HOME DEPOT, INC.

One of the many programs that benefits from Team Depot is Habitat for Humanity. Do a computer search and report how Team Depot has helped Habitat for Humanity.

EYK12-9. **Forensic Accounting Problem** Cash larceny involves the fraudulent stealing of an employer's cash. These schemes often target the company's bank deposits. The fraudster steals the money after the deposit has been prepared, but before the deposit is taken to the bank. Most often these schemes involve a deficiency in the internal control system where segregation of duties is not present. The perpetrator is often in charge of recording receipts, preparing the deposit, delivering the deposit to the bank, and verifying the receipted deposit slip. Without proper segregation of duties, the fraudster is able cover up the theft.

In addition to segregation of duties, what internal control procedures might help deter and detect cash larceny?

EYK12-10. Working with the Takeaways Home Depot reports (in millions) cash provided by operating activities of $6,651. For the same period, average current liabilities were reported to be $9,376 and annual capital expenditures were $1,221. Calculate the free cash flow, operating-cash-flow-to-current-liabities ratio, and the operating-cash-flow-to-capital-expenditures ratio for Home Depot and comment on the results.

TESCO PLC

IFRS

EYK12-11. IFRS Financial Statements **Tesco PLC** is the world's third largest retailer and is based in the United Kingdom. Tesco prepares its financial statements (see Appendix C at the end of this textbook) using IFRS. Calculate Tesco's (a) free cash flow, (b) operating-cash-flow-to-current-liabilities ratio (use the year-end current liabilities instead of the average current liabilities), and (c) operating-cash-flow-to-capital-expenditures ratio for 2010 and 2011. What do the ratio results reveal about Tesco?

ANSWERS TO SELF-STUDY QUESTIONS:

1. a, (p. 553) 2. c, (p. 554) 3. d, (p. 555) 4. c, (p. 559) 5. c, (p. 571) 6. b, (p. 555)
7. b, (p. 571) 8. d, (p. 552) 9. c, (p. 562) 10. a, (p. 571) 11. c, (p. 566) 12. b, (p. 566)

YOUR TURN! SOLUTIONS

Solution 12.1

1. Operating
2. Investing
3. Operating
4. Investing
5. Financing
6. Financing
7. Operating
8. Financing
9. Investing

Solution 12.2

HUSKY COMPANY Statement of Cash Flows For the Year Ended December 31, 2013		
Cash Flow from Operating Activities		
Net income	$112,000	
Add (deduct) items to convert net income to cash basis		
Depreciation	34,000	
Accounts receivable increase	(18,000)	
Inventory increase	(60,000)	
Prepaid insurance decrease	4,000	
Accounts payable decrease	(6,000)	
Wages payable increase	6,000	
Income tax payable decrease	(2,000)	
Cash provided by operating activities		$ 70,000
Cash Flow from Investing Activities		
Purchase of plant assets		(110,000)
Cash Flow from Financing Activities		
Issuance of bonds payable	110,000	
Payment of dividends	(58,000)	
Cash provided by financing activities		52,000
Net increase in cash		12,000
Cash at beginning of year		10,000
Cash at end of year		$ 22,000

Solution 12.3

Free cash flow: $40,000 − $12,500 = $27,500

Operating-cash-flow-to-current-liabilities-ratio: $40,000/$30,000 = 1.33

Operating-cash-flow-to-capital-expenditures-ratio: $40,000/$12,500 = 3.20

Solution 12.4

Supporting Calculations:

Cash received from customers:

$1,270,000 Sales revenue − $18,000 Accounts receivable increase = $1,252,000

Cash paid for merchandise purchased:

$860,000 Cost of goods sold + $60,000 Inventory increase + $6,000 Accounts payable decrease = $926,000

Cash paid to employees:

$172,000 Wages expense − $6,000 Wages payable increase = $166,000

Cash paid for insurance:

$16,000 Insurance expense − $4,000 Prepaid insurance decrease = $12,000

Cash paid for interest:

Equal to the $18,000 balance in interest expense

Cash paid for income taxes:

$58,000 Income tax expense + $2,000 Income tax payable decrease = $60,000

Purchase of plant assets:

$500,000 Ending plant assets − $390,000 Beginning plant assets = $110,000

Issuance of bonds payable:

$260,000 Ending bonds payable − $150,000 Beginning bonds payable = $110,000

Payment of dividends

$58,000 given in problem data

Other Analysis

Accumulated depreciation increased by $34,000, which is the amount of depreciation expense.

Common stock account balance did not change.

Retained earnings increased by $54,000, which is the difference between the net income of $112,000 and the dividends declared of $58,000.

HUSKY COMPANY
Statement of Cash Flows (Direct Method)
For the Year Ended December 31, 2013

Cash Flow from Operating Activities		
Cash received from customers		$1,252,000
Cash paid for merchandise purchased	$(926,000)	
Cash paid to employees	(166,000)	
Cash paid for insurance	(12,000)	
Cash paid for interest	(18,000)	
Cash paid for income taxes	(60,000)	(1,182,000)
Cash provided by operating activities		70,000
Cash Flow from Investing Activities		
Purchase of plant assets		(110,000)
Cash Flow from Financing Activities		
Issuance of bonds payable	110,000	
Payment of dividends	(58,000)	
Cash provided by financing activities		52,000
Net increase in cash		12,000
Cash at beginning of year		10,000
Cash at end of year		$ 22,000

13

Analysis and Interpretation of Financial Statements

PAST

In Chapter 12, we examined the statement of cash flows.

PRESENT

In this chapter we complete our study of financial accounting by looking at the analysis and interpretation of financial statements.

LEARNING OBJECTIVES

1. **Identify** persistent earnings and **discuss** the content and format of the income statement. *(p. 600)*

2. **Identify** the sources of financial information used by investment professionals and **explain** horizontal financial statement analysis. *(p. 604)*

3. **Explain** vertical financial statement analysis. *(p. 611)*

4. **Define** and **discuss** financial ratios for analyzing a firm. *(p. 612)*

5. **Discuss** the limitations of financial statement analysis. *(p. 627)*

6. Appendix 13A: **Describe** financial statement disclosures. *(p. 629)*

PROCTER & GAMBLE

The **Procter & Gamble Company (P&G)** is one of America's oldest companies, dating back to 1837 when candle maker William Procter and soap maker James Gamble combined their small businesses. Over the next few decades the company introduced such well-known products as Ivory soap and Crisco shortening that are still sold today.

P&G has continued to grow, with annual sales of over $80 billion. Not all of the company's growth, however, is the result of internally developed products like Crest toothpaste, Head & Shoulders shampoo, and Pampers diapers. A significant part of P&G's growth has come from mergers and acquisitions. P&G's largest acquisition occurred in 2005 when it acquired Gillette for $57 billion.

Acquisitions, such as the one involving Gillette, are complex transactions. Perhaps the hardest part of any merger or acquisition is to determine the appropriate price to pay—in this case $57 billion. How did P&G determine how much to pay for Gillette? Many factors go into such an analysis, but it often comes down to how much a company like Gillette will be able to add to P&G's future persistent earnings.

In this chapter we explore some of the ways that investment professionals determine how much a company is worth. The process involves analyzing a company's persistent earnings potential as well as the various risks associated with a company's day-to-day operations.

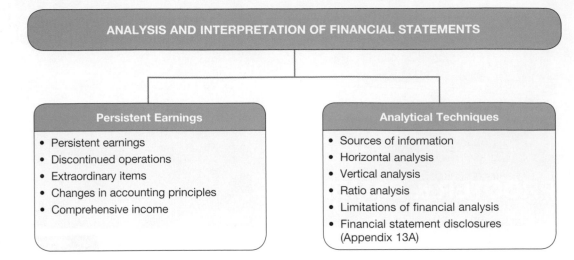

ANALYSIS AND INTERPRETATION OF FINANCIAL STATEMENTS

Persistent Earnings
- Persistent earnings
- Discontinued operations
- Extraordinary items
- Changes in accounting principles
- Comprehensive income

Analytical Techniques
- Sources of information
- Horizontal analysis
- Vertical analysis
- Ratio analysis
- Limitations of financial analysis
- Financial statement disclosures (Appendix 13A)

PERSISTENT EARNINGS AND THE INCOME STATEMENT

LO1 **Identify** persistent earnings and **discuss** the content and format of the income statement.

Net income is the "bottom line" measure of firm performance. It is a measure that depends on such accrual accounting procedures as the revenue recognition and expense matching policies selected by a firm's management. Generally accepted accounting practice has historically emphasized the importance of accounting earnings because past accounting earnings have been found to be a good predictor of a firm's future operating cash flow. Modern valuation theory tells us that the economic value of a company is the present value of the company's future operating cash flows. Thus, an important role for accounting numbers is their use by investment professionals when assessing the economic value of a company (like Gillette in the feature story).

One of the determinants of the ability of historical accounting earnings to predict future cash flow is the extent to which earnings recur over time, or what is known as *earnings persistence*. Since the value of a share of common stock today is a function of a firm's ability to consistently generate earnings year in and year out, the persistence (or sustainability) of a company's operating earnings is closely linked to its economic value. **Persistent earnings** are also sometimes referred to as *sustainable earnings* or *permanent earnings*, whereas non-persistent earnings are often referred to as transitory earnings. In general, **transitory earnings** include such single-period events as extraordinary gains/ losses, special items, restructuring charges, changes in accounting principle, and discontinued operations.

A.K.A. Persistent earnings are also referred to as *sustainable earnings* or *permanent earnings*.

To assist investors in their assessment of a company's persistent earnings, and hence in assessing a firm's economic value, companies are required under GAAP to classify income statement accounts in a manner that aids a financial statement user in assessing persistent earnings. In Chapter 5, we discussed the classified income statement. In this chapter, we discuss a refinement of the classified income statement called the multi-step income statement.

Exhibit 13-1 illustrates the basic format of the multi-step income statement. While a **single-step income statement** derives the net income of a business in one step by subtracting total expenses from total revenues, a **multiple-step income statement** derives one or more intermediate performance measures before net income is reported. Examples of such intermediate performance measures are gross profit, net operating income, and net income from continuing operations before taxes.

The income statement is organized in such a way that items with greater persistence are reported higher up in the income statement, whereas items considered more transi-

Exhibit 13-1	The Multi-Step Income Statement

KALI COMPANY
Income Statement
For Year Ended December 31, 2013

Sales revenue.		$ 500	Usual and frequent
Cost of goods sold.		200	Usual and frequent
Gross profit.		300	
Operating expenses.		250	Usual and frequent
Net operating income.		50	
Other income and expense			
Interest income.	25		**Unusual**
Interest expense.	(35)		**Unusual**
Gain on sale of equipment.	15	5	**Unusual**
Net income from continuing operations before tax		55	
Income tax		20	Usual and frequent
Net income from continuing operations		35	
Gain from operations of discontinued division, net of tax	15		Infrequent
Loss on disposal of discontinued division (net of tax)	(5)	10	
Net income before extraordinary item		45	
Extraordinary gain (loss), net of tax		(15)	**Unusual** and **infrequent**
Net income		$ 30	
Earning per share (100 shares outstanding).		$0.30	

tory are reported further down in the statement. Thus, accounts representing financial events that are both usual and frequent are reported first. Usual refers to whether an item is central to a firm's core operations, whereas **unusual items** display a high degree of abnormality and/or are unrelated, or only incidentally related to the normal activities of a business. Frequent refers to how often an item is expected to occur, with infrequent items not reasonably expected to recur in the foreseeable future. Usual and frequent items typically consist of such income statement accounts as sales revenue, cost of goods sold, and other operating expenses. Just below these usual and frequent items are items that are either unusual or infrequent, but not both. Examples of these include such financial events as asset write-downs and restructuring charges. While these items are not expected to occur regularly, they are not considered unusual in nature. Income statement accounts such as interest expense, interest income, and gains on sales of equipment are often frequently recurring items; however, they are not considered part of a firm's central operations and therefore are considered unusual.

Each of the above items is reported as part of a company's continuing operations and is shown before any income tax expense. GAAP, however, requires certain single-period items, or one-time events, to be reported on an after-tax basis. For example, discontinued operations, or the part of a business which is being shuttered or sold, are shown net of the financial effect of any applicable income taxes. Reporting discontinued operations on a net-of-tax basis allows the income tax expense reported on the income statement to reflect only the income taxes associated with a firm's continuing operations.

Most believe that the income statement is more useful when certain types of transactions and events are reported in separate sections. For this reason, information about discontinued operations is disclosed separately in the income statement. Segregating these categories of information from the results of continuing operations makes it easier for financial statement users to identify a company's persistent earnings.

The creation of sections within the income statement, however, complicates the reporting of a company's income tax expense. Items affecting the overall amount of income tax expense may appear in more than one section. If this is the case, accountants allocate a company's total income tax expense among those sections of the income statement in which the items affecting the tax expense appear.

The income statement's usefulness is also enhanced if it contains information on a firm's earnings per share. Since stock prices are quoted on the New York Stock Exchange and the NASDAQ exchange on a per share basis, it is customary for businesses to also report their net income on a per common share basis, called earnings per share. Accordingly, earnings per share are also reported on the income statement, immediately following net income.

> ### IFRS ALERT!
>
> Like U.S. GAAP, IFRS encourages companies to use a multi-step income statement when presenting a company's periodic performance. Tesco, the world's third largest retailer, presents its IFRS accounted income statement in Appendix C at the end of this book. Examining Tesco's income statement reveals that the retailer presents four measures of firm performance: gross profit, operating profit, profit before tax, and profit for the year. These indicators correspond to the four performance measures reported by the Kali Company in Exhibit 13.1: gross profit, net operating income, net income from continuing operations before tax, and net income. Although the income statements under U.S. GAAP and IFRS are very similar, with only minor labeling differences—like using "profit" instead of "income"—one significant difference relates to extraordinary items, which are separately disclosed on U.S. GAAP income statements but which are not separately disclosed on IFRS accounted income statements.

Discontinued Operations

Discontinued Operations

When a company sells, abandons, or otherwise disposes of a segment of its operations, a **discontinued operations** section of the income statement reports information about the discontinued business segment. The discontinued operations section presents two categories of information:

1. The income or loss from the segment's operations for the portion of the year before its discontinuance.

2. Any gain or loss from the disposal of the segment.

This section is reported on the income statement immediately after information regarding a firm's continuing operations.

To illustrate the reporting of discontinued operations, assume that on July 1, 2013, Kali Company, a diversified manufacturing company, sold its pet food division. Exhibit 13-1 illustrates the income statement for Kali Company, including information regarding its pet food division in the discontinued operations section. From January 1 through June 30, Kali's pet food division operated at a profit, net of income taxes, of $15. The loss, net of income taxes, from the sale of the division's assets and liabilities was $5. Note that when there is a discontinued operations section, the difference between a firm's continuing sales revenues and expenses is labeled net income from continuing operations.

Extraordinary Items

Extraordinary Item

Extraordinary items are transactions and events that are both *unusual in nature* and *occur infrequently*. An item that is unusual in nature is highly abnormal and significantly different from a firm's typical activities. To determine a firm's typical activities, it is necessary to consider such factors as the type of operations, lines of business, operating policies, and the environment in which the firm operates. The operating environment includes the characteristics of the industry, the geographic location of a firm's facilities, and the type of government regulations imposed on the industry and firm. A transaction or event is considered to occur infrequently if the firm does not expect it to recur in the foreseeable future.

The fact that the two criteria—unusual nature and infrequent occurrence—must *both* be present substantially restricts the events and transactions that qualify as extraordinary. For example, suppose a farmer suffers crop loss from a flood that normally happens every few years. The history of floods creates a reasonable expectation that another flood will occur in the foreseeable future. The crop loss, therefore, does not meet the criteria for classification as an extraordinary item. Now consider a second farmer in a location rarely exposed to flooding and who suffers flood damage to his crop for the first time from a broken dam. The dam is repaired and is not expected to fail again in the foreseeable future. The flood loss in this circumstance would be considered an extraordinary item.

In addition to natural disasters, other events that may generate extraordinary losses include expropriations of property by foreign governments (such as Venezuela's 2007 nationalization of ExxonMobil's assets located in that country), and prohibitions under newly enacted laws (such as a government ban on a currently marketed product).

Earthquake and Tsunami Loss for Sony Corporation | **ACCOUNTING IN PRACTICE**

In March of 2011, Japan experienced a massive earthquake and tsunami that caused significant damage to Sony Corporation's buildings, machinery, and equipment. In addition, Sony incurred other losses for idle facility costs at manufacturing sites. Sony reported nearly 20,000 million yen of uninsured costs in its financial statements ending March 31, 2011. Sony reported these costs primarily as an unusual item in other operating expenses. Given the frequency of earthquakes in this part of Japan, this natural disaster would not qualify as extraordinary since it was not both unusual and infrequent.

Changes in Accounting Principles

Occasionally a company may implement a **change in accounting principle**—that is, a switch from one generally accepted method to another. Examples include a change in inventory costing method, such as from FIFO to weighted-average cost. Such changes are permitted when a business can demonstrate that the reported financial results under the new accounting method are superior to the results reported under the replaced method.

Changing accounting principles can present a problem for financial statement users analyzing a company's performance over time because different accounting principles are likely to produce different financial statement results. This concern led to the adoption of the GAAP practice that financial statements of prior years, issued in comparative form with current year financial statements, should be restated using any new accounting principles. This means that a change in accounting principle is accounted for by restating prior financial statements as if the new method had been used all along.

Consistency Principle | **PRINCIPLE ALERT**

The *consistency principle* states that, unless otherwise disclosed, financial statements use the same accounting methods from one period to the next. A consistent use of accounting methods enhances the comparability of financial data across time. The consistency principle impacts the accounting for a change in accounting principles in several ways. First, to change an accounting principle, a company must be able to justify that the reported results under the new principle are preferable. Second, a company must restate its prior year financial statements as though the new principle had been in use all along. In actual practice, only the prior year financial statements presented with the current year financial statements must be restated to reflect the financial effect of the new accounting method. For all financial statements prior to those presented with the current statements, a lump sum financial restatement is made to retained earnings on the statement of retained earnings and the statement of stockholders' equity.

Comprehensive Income

Most items that generate wealth changes in a business are required to be shown on the income statement. There are, however, a few items that do not appear as part of the regular content of the income statement and instead are classified under a category labeled **comprehensive income**. A business's comprehensive income includes its net income, any changes in the market value of certain marketable securities (see Appendix D at the end of this book), and any unrealized gains and losses from translating foreign currency denominated financial statements into U.S. dollars. This latter topic is covered in more advanced accounting textbooks.

Companies are given some flexibility as to how they report their comprehensive income. They are allowed to utilize three alternative formats under GAAP: (1) appending comprehensive income to the bottom of the income statement; (2) creating a separate statement of comprehensive income; or, (3) including comprehensive income in the statement of stockholders' equity. In addition to comprehensive income for the current period, GAAP requires a company to report accumulated other comprehensive income as part of stockholders' equity on the balance sheet. Accumulated other comprehensive income serves the same role for comprehensive income as retained earnings serves for regular net income—it reports the cumulative amount of comprehensive income as of the balance sheet date.

CORPORATE SOCIAL RESPONSIBILITY	**Pampers and UNICEF**

Maternal and neonatal tetanus is a disease that kills 59,000 people annually. **P&G**, through its Pampers product, has teamed up with UNICEF to fight this completely preventable disease. For every purchase of a pack of Pampers, P&G donates one dose of the tetanus vaccine. Pampers' funding has helped protect 100 million women and their babies against maternal and neonatal tetanus (MNT) and has helped eliminate this disease in Myanmar and Uganda. P&G and UNICEF are committed to the elimination of MNT from the face of the earth.

P&G and UNICEF have gone even further in their teamwork. P&G offers its employees in Europe, the Middle East, and Africa, a three-month paid sabbatical to work with UNICEF. The program is aimed at employees who have always wanted to perform humanitarian work but have lacked the financial resources to do so.

YOUR TURN! 13.1	Conner Company, a retail company, entered into the following transactions during the year:

The solution is on page 663.

1. Sold merchandise to customers
2. Settled a major lawsuit
3. Wrote down the book value of a closed warehouse
4. Paid employee wages
5. Disposed of a line of discount stores
6. Paid income taxes

Required
Classify each of the above items as either persistent earnings or transitory earnings.

SOURCES OF INFORMATION

LO2 **Identify** the sources of financial information used by investment professionals and **explain** horizontal financial statement analysis

Except for closely held companies, businesses publish their financial statements at least annually. Most large companies also issue quarterly financial data. Normally, annual financial statements are attested to by a certified public accountant, and investment professionals carefully review the independent accountant's opinion to assess the reliability of the published financial data. Companies listed on stock exchanges must also submit annual financial statements, called a 10-K for the annual report and 10-Q for the quarterly report, to the U.S. Securities and Exchange Commission (SEC). These statements are available to any interested party and are generally more useful than annual reports because they contain greater detail.

Investment professionals may also want to compare the performance of a particular firm with that of the other firms in the same industry. Data on industry norms, median ratios by industry, and other relationships are available from such data collection services as Dun & Bradstreet, Moody's, and Standard and Poor's. In addition, some brokerage firms compile industry norms and ratios from their own computer databases.

SEC EDGAR Database	ACCOUNTING IN PRACTICE

An example of a financial database is **EDGAR**, the Electronic Data Gathering, Analysis, and Retrieval system, maintained by the U.S. SEC. This computer database aids financial statement analysis by performing automated data collection, validation, indexing, acceptance, and forwarding of submissions by companies and others who are required by law to file forms with the U.S. Securities and Exchange Commission. The primary intent of the SEC in creating EDGAR was to increase the efficiency of the securities market for the benefit of investors, corporations, and the economy, by accelerating the receipt, acceptance, dissemination, and analysis of corporate information filed with the agency. An "efficient" securities market means that investors are able to make the best possible decisions regarding where and when to invest their funds.

Analytical Techniques

The absolute dollar amounts of net income, sales revenue, total assets, and other key data are usually not meaningful when analyzed in isolation. For example, knowing that a company's annual net income is $1 million is of little informational value unless the amount of the income can be related to other factors. A $1 million profit might represent excellent performance for a company with less than $10 million in invested capital. On the other hand, $1 million in net income would be considered meager for a firm that had several hundred million dollars in invested capital. Thus, significant information can be derived by examining the relationship between two or more accounting variables, such as net income and total assets, net income and sales revenue, and net income and stockholders' equity. To describe these relationships clearly and to make comparisons easy, the relationships are often expressed in terms of ratios or percentages.

For example, we might express the relationship of $15,000 in net income to $150,000 in sales revenue as a ten percent ($15,000/$150,000) rate of return on sales. To describe the relationship between sales revenue of $150,000 and inventory of $20,000, we might use a ratio or a percentage; ($150,000/$20,000) may be expressed as 7.5, 7.5:1, or 750 percent.

Changes in selected financial statement items compared in successive financial statements are often expressed as percentages. For example, if a firm's net income increased from $40,000 last year to $48,000 this year, the $8,000 increase related to last year (the base year) is expressed as a 20 percent increase ($8,000/$40,000) in net income. To express a dollar increase or decrease as a percentage, however, the analyst must make the base year amount a positive figure. If, for example, a firm had a net loss of $4,000 in one year and net income of $20,000 in the next, the $24,000 increase cannot be meaningfully expressed as a percentage. Similarly, if a firm reported no marketable securities in last year's balance sheet but showed $15,000 of such securities in this year's statement, the $15,000 increase cannot be expressed as a meaningful percentage.

When evaluating a firm's financial statements for two or more years, analysts often use **horizontal analysis**. Horizontal analysis is a technique that can be useful for detecting an improvement or deterioration in a firm's performance and for spotting trends regarding a firm's financial well-being. The term **vertical analysis** is used to describe the analysis of a single year of financial data.

HORIZONTAL ANALYSIS

Comparative Financial Statements

The type of horizontal analysis most often used by investment professionals is **comparative financial statement analysis** for two or more years, showing dollar and/or percentage changes for important financial statement items and totals. Dollar increases and decreases are divided by the earliest year's data to obtain percentage changes. To illustrate, the 2011 and 2010 financial statements of Procter & Gamble (P&G) are presented in Exhibits 13-2, 13-3, and 13-4. We will use the data in these statements throughout this chapter to illustrate various analytical techniques.

Exhibit 13-2	Procter & Gamble Income Statement

THE PROCTER & GAMBLE COMPANY
Consolidated Income Statements

(in millions)	Year Ended 2011	Common-Size	Year Ended 2010	Common-Size	$ Change	% Change
Net sales.	$82,559	100.0%	$78,938	100.0%	$3,621	4.6%
Cost of goods sold.	40,768	49.4%	37,919	48.0%	2,849	7.5%
Gross margin	41,791	50.6%	41,019	52.0%	772	1.9%
Selling, general, and administrative expense.	25,973	31.5%	24,998	31.7%	975	3.9%
Operating income.	15,818	19.2%	16,021	20.3%	(203)	(1.3)%
Interest expense.	831	1.0%	946	1.2%	(115)	(12.2)%
Other non-operating income . .	202	0.2%	(28)	0.0%	230	(821.4)%
Earnings from continuing operations before taxes	15,189	18.4%	15,047	19.1%	142	0.9%
Income taxes on continuing operations.	3,392	4.1%	4,101	5.2%	(709)	(17.3)%
Net earnings from continuing operations.	11,797	14.3%	10,946	13.9%	851	7.8%
Net earnings from discontinued operations, net of taxes			1,790	2.3%	(1,790)	(100.0)%
Net earnings	$11,797	14.3%	$12,736	16.1%	$ (939)	(7.4)%
Earnings per share	4.12		4.32		(0.20)	(4.6)%
Dividends per share	1.97		1.80		0.17	9.4%

When analyzing financial statements, the investment professional is likely to focus his or her immediate attention on those financial statement items or percentages that are significant in amount. Although percentage changes are helpful in identifying significant items, they can sometimes be misleading. An unusually large percentage change may occur simply because the dollar amount of the base year is small. For example, assume that P&G had an increase in interest expense of $25, from $10 in 2010 to $35 in 2011. This increase amounts to a percentage change of 250 percent, yet the dollar amount is quite small and insignificant relative to the other reported dollar amounts on P&G's income

Exhibit 13-3	Procter & Gamble Balance Sheet

THE PROCTER & GAMBLE COMPANY
Consolidated Balance Sheets

(in millions)	2011		2010		$ Change	% Change
Assets						
Current assets						
Cash and cash equivalents.......	$ 2,768	2.0%	$ 2,879	2.2%	$ (111)	(3.9)%
Accounts receivable............	6,275	4.5%	5,335	4.2%	940	17.6%
Inventories	7,379	5.3%	6,384	5.0%	995	15.6%
Other current assets............	5,548	4.0%	4,184	3.3%	1,364	32.6%
Total current assets..........	21,970	15.9%	18,782	14.7%	3,188	17.0%
Property, plant, and equipment, net .	21,293	15.4%	19,244	15.0%	2,049	10.6%
Intangible assets, net............	90,182	65.2%	85,648	66.8%	4,534	5.3%
Other noncurrent assets..........	4,909	3.5%	4,498	3.5%	411	9.1%
Total assets................	$138,354	100.0%	$128,172	100.0%	$10,182	7.9%
Liabilities and Stockholders' Equity						
Current liabilities						
Accounts payable..............	$ 8,022	5.8%	$ 7,251	5.7%	$ 771	10.6%
Other current liabilities	19,271	13.9%	17,031	13.3%	2,240	13.2%
Total current liabilities........	27,293	19.7%	24,282	18.9%	3,011	12.4%
Long-term debt	22,033	15.9%	21,360	16.7%	673	3.2%
Other noncurrent liabilities	21,027	15.2%	21,091	16.5%	(64)	(0.3)%
Total liabilities	70,353	50.8%	66,733	52.1%	3,620	5.4%
Preferred stock..................	1,234	0.9%	1,277	1.0%	(43)	(3.4)%
Common stock..................	4,008	2.9%	4,008	3.1%	–	0.0%
Additional paid-in capital	62,405	45.1%	61,697	48.1%	708	1.1%
Accumulated other comprehensive income (loss).................	(3,050)	(2.2)%	(8,848)	(6.9)%	(5,798)	(65.5)%
Treasury stock	(67,278)	(48.6)%	(61,309)	(47.8)%	5,969	9.7%
Retained earnings	70,682	51.1%	64,614	50.4%	6,068	9.4%
Total stockholders' equity......	68,001	49.2%	61,439	47.9%	6,562	10.7%
Total liabilities and stockholders' equity	$138,354	100.0%	$128,172	100.0%	$10,182	7.9%

statement. The financial statement user's attention should be directed first to changes in key financial statement totals: sales revenue, operating income, net income, total assets, total liabilities, and so on. Next, the changes in significant individual items, such as accounts receivable, inventory, and property, plant and equipment should be examined.

For example, P&G's total assets increased 7.9 percent from 2010 to 2011 (see Exhibit 13-3), and net sales increased 4.6 percent over the same time period (see Exhibit 13-2). (Note: Some companies, like P&G, use the label "net sales" to refer to their sales revenue, the top line of the income statement.) A small percentage increase in net sales coincided with a larger increase in total assets, reflecting a recovery of the world economy in 2011, and indicating that P&G undertook certain business strategies to increase capacity to meet increasing demand. Note that P&G's 15.6 percent increase in inventory levels is consistent with this strategy. One potential note of concern is the relationship between cost of products sold and net sales. While net sales increased by 4.6 percent, cost of products sold increased by 7.5 percent, leading to a deterioration in P&G's gross profit margin percentage and ultimately to net earnings which decreased 7.4 percent in 2011. (Note: Some companies, like P&G, use the label "net earnings" to refer to their net income.) It should

Exhibit 13-4	Procter & Gamble Statement of Cash Flows

THE PROCTER & GAMBLE COMPANY
Consolidated Statements of Cash Flows

(in millions)	Year Ended 2011	Year Ended 2010	$ Change	% Change
Operating activities				
Net earnings.	11,797	12,736		
Depreciation and amortization.	2,838	3,108		
Gain on sale of business	(203)	(2,670)		
Other noncash items	542	489		
Change in accounts receivable	(426)	(14)		
Change in inventories.	(501)	86		
Change in accounts payable, accrued and other liabilities	358	2,446		
Change in other operating assets and liabilities	(1,190)	(305)		
Other.	16	196		
Net cash flow provided by operating activities.	13,231	16,072	(2,841)	(17.7)%
Investing activities				
Capital expenditures	(3,306)	(3,067)		
Proceeds from asset sales.	225	3,068		
Acquisitions, net.	(474)	(425)		
Change in investments.	73	(173)		
Net cash flow used by investing activities	(3,482)	(597)	(2,885)	(483.2)%
Financing activities				
Dividends	(5,767)	(5,458)		
Change in short-term debt.	151	(1,798)		
Additions to long-term debt.	1,536	3,830		
Reductions of long-term debt	(206)	(8,546)		
Treasury stock purchases	(7,039)	(6,004)		
Other.	1,302	721		
Net cash used by financing activities.	(10,023)	(17,255)	7,232	41.9%
Effect of exchange rate changes	163	(122)		
Change in cash and cash equivalents	(111)	(1,902)		
Beginning cash and cash equivalents	2,879	4,781		
Ending cash and cash equivalents.	$ 2,768	$ 2,879		

be noted that an additional factor contributing to the decrease in net earnings in 2011 was the absence of earnings from discontinued operations that was present in 2010.

We can also see from P&G's statement of cash flow (Exhibit 13-4) that the company's cash flow from operations declined from 2010 to 2011; and, that P&G increased its capital spending from 2010 to 2011, consistent with what we noticed above in the balance sheet. Finally, Exhibit 13-4 reveals that P&G chose to repurchase its common stock (treasury stock) in both 2010 and 2011, perhaps to take advantage of the depressed share prices that characterized the U.S. stock market during this time period.

From this limited analysis of comparative financial statements, an investment professional might conclude that P&G's operating performance for 2011 was slightly better when compared with that of 2010, mostly the result of factoring in the impact of discontinued operations in 2010. Further analysis using some of the techniques summarized later in the chapter, however, may cause that opinion to be modified. The foregoing analysis did reveal one "red flag"—a deteriorating gross profit margin.

Trend Analysis

To observe percentage changes over time in selected financial data, investment professionals often calculate **trend percentages**. Most companies provide summaries of their key financial data for the past five or ten years in their annual reports. With such information, the financial statement user can examine changes over periods longer than just the past two years. For example, suppose an analyst is interested in the trend in sales and net income for P&G for the past five years. The following are P&G's sales revenue and net income figures for 2007 through 2011:

	PROCTER & GAMBLE COMPANY Annual Performance									
	2007		**2008**		**2009**		**2010**		**2011**	
	Millions of Dollars	Percentage of Base Year	Millions of Dollars	Percentage of Base Year	Millions of Dollars	Percentage of Base Year	Millions of Dollars	Percentage of Base Year	Millions of Dollars	Percentage of Base Year
Net sales..............	$74,832	100	$81,748	109	$76,694	102	$78,938	105	$82,559	110
Net income............	10,340	100	12,075	117	13,436	130	12,736	123	11,797	114

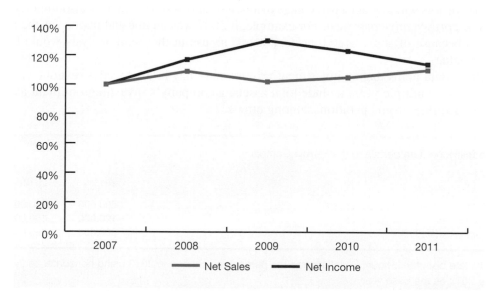

These data suggest an inconsistent growth pattern for the company, but the pattern of change from year to year can be determined more precisely by calculating trend percentages. To do this, we select a *base year* and then divide the data for each of the remaining years by the base-year data. The resultant figures are actually indexes of the changes occurring throughout the period. If, for example, 2007 is selected as the base year, all data for 2008 through 2011 will be related to 2007, which is represented as 100 percent.

To create the table of data displayed above, we divide each year's net sales—from 2008 through 2011—by $74,832, P&G's 2007 net sales (in millions of dollars). Similarly, P&G's net income for 2008 through 2011 is divided by $10,340, the company's 2007 net income (in millions of dollars).

PRINCIPLE ALERT	**Consistency Principle**

Horizontal analysis is a process of analyzing a firm's financial data across two or more years by examining dollar changes, percentage changes, and/or trend percentages. The utility of horizontal analysis, however, is dependent upon the effective implementation of the *consistency principle*. This accounting principle requires that a firm use the same accounting methods from one period to the next or, if a firm finds it necessary (or required) to change an accounting method, that the financial effects of any change be fully disclosed in the financial statements. The consistency principle assures financial analysts that, unless otherwise noted, changes in the accounts over time represent underlying economic changes in a business, and not the result of an accounting method change.

P&G's trend percentages above reveal that the company's growth in net income outstripped its growth in net sales for the entire five-year period. The horizontal analysis of P&G's financial data also reveals that, while net sales declined in 2009 and 2010, P&G appeared to take steps to counter the adverse impact on its profitability. The trend data indicate that P&G's performance actually showed a large (13 percent) increase in its net income growth in 2009. This increase was largely attributable to a gain from discontinued operations, and therefore not the result of persistent earnings as we see from later years where P&G is not able to maintain this percentage gain in net income.

It is important to exercise care when interpreting trend percentages. Since all index percentages are related to a base year, it must be remembered that the change between the 2010 net sales index (105 percent) and the 2011 net sales index (110 percent) represents a 5 percent increase in terms of *base year* dollars. To express the increase as a percentage of 2010 dollars, we divide the $3,621 increase in net sales from 2010 to 2011 ($82,559 − $78,938) by 2010 net sales of $78,938 to yield a percentage increase of only 4.6 percent. It is also important to select a *representative* base year. For example, if 2007 was an unusual period for the firm, perhaps because of some large transitory items, its use in the trend analysis would be of limited value.

Other data items that an investment professional may relate to sales revenue and net income over multiple years include total assets, a company's investment in plant assets, and its cash flow from operations, among others.

YOUR TURN! 13.2	The following data pertain to the Farrow Company:

The solution is on page 663.

	2013	2012
Sales revenue.	$800,000	$750,000
Net income.	120,000	100,000
Total assets	300,000	290,000

Calculate both the amount in dollars and the percentage change in 2013 using horizontal analysis and 2012 as the base year.

TAKEAWAY 13.1	Concept	→	Method	→	Assessment
	How does a company's current performance compare with the prior year?		Income statement and balance sheet for current and prior year. The income statement and balance sheet should be compared using the prior year as the base. Percentage changes in net income and total assets can be computed as the change between years divided by the base year amount.		Significant changes should be analyzed to determine the reason for any change.

VERTICAL ANALYSIS

The relative importance of various accounts in a company's financial statements for a single year can be highlighted by showing them as a percentage of a key financial statement figure. A financial statement that presents the various account balances as a percentage of a key figure is called a **common-size financial statement**. Sales revenue (or net sales) is the key figure used to construct a common-size income statement, whereas total assets is the key figure used to construct a common-size balance sheet.

LO3 Explain vertical financial statement analysis.

A financial statement may present both the dollar amounts and common-size percentages. For example, Exhibit 13-2 presents P&G's 2011 income statement in dollars and common-size percentages. The common-size percentages show each item in the income statement as a percentage of the company's net sales.

The common-size income statement allows financial statement users to readily compare P&G's ability to manage and control its various expenses while the level of its sales revenue changes over time. For example, P&G's net earnings decreased from 16.1 percent of net sales in 2010 to 14.3 percent of net sales in 2011. We can also observe that there are only small changes in almost all of the line items as a percentage of net sales and that almost all of the percentage decrease in P&G's net income comes from its net earnings from discontinued operations. Common-size income statements are also useful when comparing different firms to one another, especially when the firms are significantly different in size. While we should expect different size firms in similar industries to report dissimilar sales revenues and expenses on a dollar basis, we would expect far more similarities when the comparison is done on a common-size basis.

Common-size percentages can also be used to analyze balance sheet data. For example, by examining a firm's current assets and long-term assets as a percentage of total assets, we can determine whether a company is becoming more or less liquid over time. Another use of common-size percentages with balance sheet data is to evaluate the changing sources of financing used by a business. For example, the proportion of total assets supplied by short-term creditors, long-term creditors, preferred stockholders, and common stockholders of P&G are shown in Exhibit 13-3.

P&G's common-size balance sheets reveal that P&G is relying less on debt financing than equity financing in 2011 as compared to 2010. The primary means that P&G used to make this shift in financing appears to be through the use of treasury stock purchases, growing from 47.8 percent of total assets in 2010 to 48.6 percent of total assets in 2011. We also see that although P&G experienced a rather large increase in total assets, the relative composition of those assets remained quite stable between 2010 and 2011.

The Sanford Company reported the following income statement in 2012:

YOUR TURN! 13.3

The solution is on page 664.

SANFORD COMPANY Income Statement For the Year Ended December 31, 2012	
Sales revenue	$13,500
Cost of goods sold	5,400
Gross profit	8,100
Selling and administrative expenses	1,350
Income from operations	6,750
Interest expense	675
Other expense	135
Income before income taxes	5,940
Income tax expense	2,295
Net income	$ 3,645

Hint: When preparing common-size income statements, expenses are expressed as a positive percentage of net sales even though they are subtractions on the income statement.

Required
Prepare a 2012 common-size income statement for Sanford Company.

TAKEAWAY 13.2	Concept ⟶	Method ⟶	Assessment
	How do the relationships within a company's income statement and balance sheet compare to those of prior years?	Income statement and balance sheet for current and prior year. Each income statement item should be presented as a percentage of sales revenue and each balance sheet item should be presented as a percentage of total assets. Financial statements in this form are called common-size statements.	The percentages should be analyzed for differences between years and significant changes should be analyzed to determine the reason for any change.

THINKING GLOBALLY

Financial statement analysis is executed, worldwide, in exactly the same way. Common-size financial statements and the financial ratios discussed below are currency neutral and can be effectively used anywhere in the world. Not all ratios are relevant, however, in all countries. For example, in emerging countries that lack the financial infrastructure to support a credit system, ratios involving accounts receivable and accounts payable are likely to be irrelevant since sales transactions in those countries are only executed on a cash basis. Similarly, solvency ratios like the times-interest-earned ratio (discussed shortly) are irrelevant since bank financing in lesser-developed countries is rare (although it is becoming more prevalent with the advent of micro-finance in these countries).

RATIO ANALYSIS

LO4 **Define** and **discuss** financial ratios for analyzing a firm.

In prior chapters, a number of financial ratios were introduced. At this juncture, we classify those ratios by their analytical objective and review their analysis and interpretation by calculating them for a single company. P&G's financial statements in Exhibit 13-2 , Exhibit 13-3 and Exhibit 13-4. provide the data for these calculations (all amounts are in millions). Also, representative industry averages are presented for comparison purposes where available. Some of the financial ratios that are commonly calculated by investment professionals, lenders, and managers are presented and explained in Exhibit 13-5.

Analyzing Firm Profitability

Several ratios assist in evaluating how efficiently a firm has performed in its quest for profits, or what is referred to as firm profitability. These ratios include (1) the gross profit percentage, (2) the return on sales, (3) asset turnover, (4) the return on assets, and (5) the return on common stockholders' equity.

Gross Profit Percentage

The **gross profit percentage** is a closely watched ratio for both retailers and manufacturers. The ratio is calculated as:

A.K.A Gross profit is often referred to as *gross margin*.

$$\text{Gross profit percentage} = \frac{\text{Gross profit on sales}}{\text{Net sales}}$$

Exhibit 13-5	Key Financial Ratios	
Ratio	**Definition**	**Expla**

Analyzing Firm Profitability

- Gross profit percentage

$$\frac{\text{Gross profit on sales}}{\text{Net sales}}$$

Percentage of incom ...erated from sales after deducting the cost of goods sold.

- Return on sales

$$\frac{\text{Net income}}{\text{Net sales}}$$

Percentage of net income remaining from a dollar of sales after subtracting all expenses.

- Asset turnover

$$\frac{\text{Net sales}}{\text{Average total assets}}$$

Amount of sales generated from each dollar invested in assets.

- Return on assets

$$\frac{\text{Net income}}{\text{Average total assets}}$$

Rate of return generated on a company's investment in assets from all sources.

- Return on common stockholders' equity

$$\frac{(\text{Net income} - \text{Preferred stock dividends})}{\text{Average common stockholders' equity}}$$

Rate of return generated by a business for its common shareholders.

Analyzing Short-Term Firm Liquidity

- Working capital

Current assets − Current liabilities

The difference between a firm's current assets and its current liabilities.

- Current ratio

$$\frac{\text{Current assets}}{\text{Current liabilities}}$$

Amount of current assets available to service current liabilities

- Quick ratio

$$\frac{(\text{Cash and cash equivalents} + \text{Short-term investments} + \text{Accounts receivable})}{\text{Current liabilities}}$$

Amount of liquid assets available to service current liabilities

- Operating-cash-flow-to-current-liabilities ratio

$$\frac{\text{Cash flow from operating activities}}{\text{Average current liabilities}}$$

Amount of cash flow from operating activities available to service current liabilities.

- Accounts receivable turnover

$$\frac{\text{Net sales}}{\text{Average accounts receivable (net)}}$$

Number of sales/collection cycles experienced by a firm.

- Average collection period

$$\frac{365}{\text{Accounts receivable turnover (net)}}$$

Number of days required, on average, to collect an outstanding accounts receivable.

- Inventory turnover

$$\frac{\text{Cost of goods sold}}{\text{Average inventory}}$$

Number of production/sales cycles experienced by a firm.

- Days' sales in inventory

$$\frac{365}{\text{Inventory turnover}}$$

Number of days, on average, required to sell the inventory currently on hand.

Analyzing Long-Term Firm Solvency

- Debt-to-equity ratio

$$\frac{\text{Total liabilities}}{\text{Total stockholders' equity}}$$

Percentage of total assets provided by creditors.

- Times-interest-earned ratio

$$\frac{\text{Income before interest expense and income taxes}}{\text{Interest expense}}$$

Extent to which current operating income covers current debt service charges.

- Operating-cash-flow-to-capital-expenditures ratio

$$\frac{\text{Cash flow from operating activities}}{\text{Annual net capital expenditures}}$$

The ability of a firm's operations to provide sufficient cash to replace and expand its property, plant, and equipment.

Financial Ratios for Common Stockholders

- Earnings per share

$$\frac{(\text{Net income} - \text{Preferred stock dividends})}{\text{Weighted-average number of common shares outstanding}}$$

The net income available to common shareholders calculated on a per share basis.

- Price-earnings ratio

$$\frac{\text{Market price per share}}{\text{Earnings per share}}$$

A measure of the price of a share of common stock relative to the share's annual earnings.

- Dividend yield

$$\frac{\text{Annual dividend per share}}{\text{Market price per share}}$$

The earnings on an investment in stock coming from dividends.

- Dividend payout ratio

$$\frac{\text{Annual dividend per share}}{\text{Earnings per share}}$$

The percentage of net income paid out to shareholders as dividends.

This ratio reflects the impact on firm profitability associated with changes in a firm's product pricing structure, sales mix, and merchandise costs. The cost of goods sold is subtracted from the firm's net sales to determine its gross profit on sales. **Gross profit**, or **gross profit on sales**, is defined as the difference between net sales and cost of goods sold and reveals the amount of sales revenue remaining after subtracting the cost of products sold. (Recall that net sales equals gross sales revenue less any sales returns and allowances and sales discounts.)

P&G's common-size income statements (see Exhibit 13-2) reveal that its gross profit percentage decreased from 52.0 percent in 2010 to 50.6 percent in 2011. These percentages are derived using the following figures:

	2011	2010
Gross profit.	$41,791	$41,019
Net sales.	82,559	78,938
Gross profit percentage.	**50.6%**	**52.0%**
Industry average.	23.5%	

While P&G's gross profit percentage decreased slightly from 2010 to 2011, its ratio is well above the industry average. This suggests that P&G is still able to command premium prices for its well-known consumer products.

Return on Sales (Profit Margin)

A.K.A Return on sales is often referred to as *profit margin*.

Another important measure of firm profitability is the **return on sales**. This ratio reveals the percentage of each dollar of net sales that remains as profit after subtracting all operating and nonoperating expenses. The return on sales is calculated as follows:

$$\text{Return on sales} = \frac{\text{Net income}}{\text{Net sales}}$$

When common-size income statements are available, the return on sales equals the net income percentage. P&G's common-size income statements in Exhibit 13-2 reveal that its return on sales decreased from 16.1 percent in 2010 to 14.3 percent in 2011. These percentages are calculated using the following figures:

	2011	2010
Net income.	$11,797	$12,736
Net sales.	82,559	78,938
Return on sales.	**14.3%**	**16.1%**
Industry average.	3.8%	

The decrease in the return on sales for P&G is disappointing, however as noted above, P&G's increase in its return on sales is mostly attributable to the company's net earnings from discontinued operations in 2010 that did not occur in 2011. Additionally, P&G's 2011 return on sales exceeds the industry average.

The return on sales and gross profit percentages should be used only when analyzing companies from the same industry or when comparing a firm's performance across multiple time periods (as we did above) since the ratio may vary widely across industries. Retail jewelers, for example, have much larger gross profit percentages (an industry average of 45.0 percent) than do retail grocers (an industry average of 23.0 percent). Industry averages for the asset turnover ratio, discussed next, would also be expected to vary significantly from one industry to another.

Asset Turnover

The **asset turnover ratio** measures how efficiently a firm uses its assets to generate sales revenue by calculating the amount of sales dollars generated annually for each dollar of assets invested in the company. This ratio is calculated as follows:

$$\text{Asset turnover} = \frac{\textbf{Net sales}}{\textbf{Average total assets}}$$

P&G's asset turnover is (total assets were $134,833 at year-end 2009):

		2011	2010
Net sales.		$ 82,559	$ 78,938
Total assets			
Beginning of year	(a)	128,172	134,833
End of year	(b)	138,354	128,172
Average [(a + b)/2]		133,263	131,503
Asset turnover		**0.62**	**0.60**
Industry average.		2.1	

P&G's asset turnover increased from 2010 to 2011, indicating an improvement in how effectively the company used its assets to generate its sales revenue. Specifically, the company generated $0.62 in net sales for every dollar invested in total assets during 2011. This ratio result, however, is well below the industry average of 2.1 for the same time period, indicating that other firms in the consumer products industry significantly outperformed P&G on this financial metric.

Some industries that are characterized by low gross profit percentages manage to generate relatively high asset turnover ratios. Retail grocery chains, for example, typically turnover their assets five to six times per year. By way of contrast, retail jewelers average only one to two asset turnovers per year. These industry differences largely reflect the high cost of products sold by jewelers versus the low cost of products sold by retail grocers.

Return on Assets

The rate of return on total assets, called the **return on assets**, is an overall measure of a firm's profitability. It reveals the rate of profit earned per dollar of assets under a firm's control. The return on assets is calculated as follows:[1]

$$\text{Return on assets} = \frac{\textbf{Net income}}{\textbf{Average total assets}}$$

P&G's return on assets is:

	2011	2010
Net income.	$ 11,797	$ 12,736
Average total assets (*see asset turnover calculation above*) . . .	133,263	131,503
Return on assets	**8.9%**	**9.7%**
Industry average.	8.9%	

---

[1] An alternative calculation adds interest expense to a company's net income in the ratio's numerator. This action prevents the method of financing a company's assets from influencing the ratio result.

P&G's return on assets declined from 9.7 percent in 2010 to 8.9 percent in 2011; however the return is consistent with the industry average. As noted above, this decrease in return on assets is primarily the result of net income decreasing as a result of the discontinued operations reported in 2010 not occuring again in 2011.

The return on asset ratio summarizes the financial impact of two component ratios: the return on sales and asset turnover; that is, the return on assets is the multiplicative product of these latter two ratios, as follows:

Ratio:	Return on sales × Asset turnover = Return on assets
Ratio calculation:	$\dfrac{\text{Net income}}{\text{Net sales}} \times \dfrac{\text{Net sales}}{\text{Average total asset}} = \dfrac{\text{Net income}}{\text{Average total assets}}$
P&G:	**14.3 percent × 0.62 = 8.9 percent**

Return on Common Stockholders' Equity

The **return on common stockholders' equity** measures the profitability of the ownership interest held by a company's common stockholders. The ratio shows the percentage of profit earned on each dollar of common stockholder equity invested in a business. The return is earned on the equity invested throughout the year, and consequently, the ratio uses the average common stockholders' equity as its denominator, as follows:

$$\text{Return on common stockholders' equity} = \frac{(\textbf{Net income} - \textbf{Preferred stock dividends})}{\textbf{Average common stockholders' equity}}$$

The return on common stockholders' equity for P&G is (common stockholders' equity was $61,775 at year-end 2009):

		2011	2010
Net income..............................		$11,797	$12,736
Less: Preferred stock dividends..................		233	219
Common stock earnings		$11,564	$12,517
Common stockholders' equity:			
Beginning of year	(a)	$59,838	$61,775
End of year	(b)	66,406	59,838
Average [(a + b)/2]........................		63,122	60,807
Return on common stockholders' equity.........		**18.3%**	**20.6%**
Industry average...............................		23.5%	

P&G's return on common stockholders' equity declined by 2.3 percent, from 20.6 percent in 2010 to 18.3 percent in 2011. Unlike the return on assets, P&G's return on common stockholders' equity is below the industry average.

YOUR TURN! 13.4

The solution is on page 664.

The following data was obtained from the current financial statements for Kelly Corporation:

Net sales..	$30,000
Cost of goods sold...	10,500
Net income..	4,500
Average total assets..	50,000
Average common stockholders' equity	35,000
Preferred dividends	500

Required

Calculate the following ratios for Kelly Corporation:

a. Gross profit percentage
b. Return on sales
c. Asset turnover
d. Return on assets
e. Return on common stockholders' equity

Concept	Method	Assessment	TAKEAWAY 13.3
How much profit is a company generating relative to the amount of assets invested in the company?	Income statement and balance sheet. Calculate the return on assets by dividing net income by the average total assets for the year.	The higher the return on assets, the better a company is doing in terms of generating profits utilizing the assets under its control.	

Analyzing Short-Term Firm Liquidity

A firm's **working capital** is the difference between its current assets and current liabilities. Maintaining an adequate working capital enables a firm to repay its current obligations on a timely basis and to take advantage of any available purchase discounts associated with the timely payment of accounts payable. Shortages of working capital, on the other hand, can force a company into borrowing at inopportune times and unfavorable interest rates. As a consequence, many long-term debt contracts contain provisions that require the borrowing firm to maintain an adequate working capital position. A firm's working capital is calculated as follows:

$$\text{Working capital} = \text{Current assets} - \text{Current liabilities}$$

Analysis of a firm's short-term liquidity utilizes several financial ratios that relate to various aspects of a company's working capital. These ratios are (1) the current ratio, (2) the quick ratio, (3) operating-cash-flow-to-current-liabilities ratio, (4) accounts receivable turnover and average collection period, and (5) inventory turnover and days' sales in inventory.

Current Ratio

The **current ratio** is calculated as a firm's current assets divided by its current liabilities:

$$\text{Current ratio} = \frac{\text{Current assets}}{\text{Current liabilities}}$$

This ratio is a widely used measure of a firm's ability to meet its current obligations and to have funds available for use in daily operations. The following calculations reveal that P&G's current ratio improved from 0.77 in 2010 to 0.80 (or 0.80:1) in 2011:

	2011	2010
Current assets	$21,970	$18,782
Current liabilities.	27,293	24,282
Current ratio	**0.80**	**0.77**
Industry average.	1.4	

In essence, P&G had $0.80 in current assets for every $1 in current liabilities at the end of 2011.

In the past, a generally accepted rule of thumb was that a firm's current ratio should be approximately 2:1, indicating that a company should maintain twice the dollar amount of current assets as was needed to satisfy its current liabilities. Improved cash flow management techniques and alternate forms of short-term financing (such as bank lines of credit) have reduced the need for businesses to maintain such a high current ratio. Still, many creditors prefer to see a higher current ratio and consider a low ratio as a potential warning sign of short-term liquidity problems.

Evaluating the adequacy of a firm's current ratio may involve comparing it with the recent past (P&G's current ratio improved slightly from 2010 to 2011) or with an industry average (P&G's ratio is below the industry average of 1.4). What is considered an appropriate current ratio varies by industry. A service firm with little or no inventory, such as a car wash service, would be expected to have a smaller current ratio than would a firm carrying a large inventory, such as a hardware retailer. The composition (or mix) of a firm's current assets significantly influences any evaluation of a firm's short-term liquidity. The quick ratio, discussed next, explicitly considers the composition of a firm's current assets when evaluating short-term liquidity.

Quick Ratio

The **quick ratio** (or *acid-test ratio*) reveals the relationship between a firm's liquid, or *quick,* assets and its current liabilities. Quick assets include cash and cash equivalents, short-term investments, and accounts receivable. The quick ratio omits a company's inventory and prepaid assets, which may not be particularly liquid. Consequently, the quick ratio may give a more accurate picture of a company's ability to meet its current obligations since the ratio ignores a firm's potentially illiquid inventory and prepaid expenses.

The quick ratio and the current ratio together also indicate the financial impact of a company's inventory on its working capital. For example, a company might have an acceptable current ratio, but if its quick ratio falls to an unacceptable level, a financial analyst is likely to be concerned about the amount of inventory on hand, and consequently, analyze the company's inventory position more thoroughly.

The quick ratio is calculated as follows:

$$\textbf{Quick ratio} = \frac{\left(\textbf{Cash and cash equivalents + Short-term investments + Accounts receivable}\right)}{\textbf{Current liabilities}}$$

The quick ratio for P&G is:

	2011	2010
Cash and cash equivalents, short-term investments, and accounts receivable.	$ 9,043	$ 8,214
Current liabilities.	27,293	24,282
Quick ratio.	**0.33**	**0.34**
Industry average.	0.6	

P&G's quick ratio declined slightly from 0.34 in 2010 to 0.33 in 2011; and, its 2011 quick ratio is well below the industry average of 0.6. P&G may feel that it is unnecessary to maintain a higher quick ratio if the company has other sources of liquidity, such as a bank line of credit.

Operating-Cash-Flow-to-Current-Liabilities Ratio

Ultimately, cash will be needed to settle a business's current liabilities. Another ratio indicating a firm's ability to pay its current liabilities as they come due focuses on a company's operating cash flow. The **operating-cash-flow-to-current-liabilities ratio** is calculated as follows:

$$\text{Operating-cash-flow-to-current-liabilities ratio} = \frac{\textbf{Cash flow from operating activities}}{\textbf{Average current liabilities}}$$

The operating-cash-flow-to-current-liabilities ratio relates the net cash available as a result of operating activities to the average current liabilities outstanding during the period. A higher ratio indicates that a firm has a greater ability to settle its current liabilities using its operating cash flow.

P&G's operating-cash-flow-to-current-liabilities ratio is (current liabilities at the end of 2009 was $30,901; no industry average is available):

		2011	2010
Cash flow from operating activities		$13,231	$16,072
Current liabilities			
Beginning of year	(a)	24,282	30,901
End of year	(b)	27,293	24,282
Average [(a+b)/2]		25,788	27,592
Operating-cash-flow-to-current-liabilities ratio		**0.51**	**0.58**

P&G's operating-cash-flow-to-current-liabilities ratio declined from 2010 to 2011, a result of a decline in cash provided by operating activities and a smaller percentage decline in average current liabilities.

Accounts Receivable Turnover

The speed with which accounts receivable are collected is of considerable interest to investment professionals when evaluating a firm's short-term liquidity. **Accounts receivable turnover** indicates how many times a year a firm collects its average outstanding accounts receivable, and thus, measures how fast a firm converts its accounts receivable into cash. The quicker a firm is able to convert its accounts receivables into cash, the less cash the company needs to keep on hand to satisfy its current liabilities. Accounts receivable turnover is calculated as follows:

$$\textbf{Accounts receivable turnover} = \frac{\textbf{Net sales}}{\textbf{Average accounts receivable (net)}}$$

The accounts receivable turnover for P&G is (accounts receivable at the end of 2009 were $5,836):

		2011	2010
Net sales.		$82,559	$78,938
Average accounts receivable (net)			
Beginning of year	(a)	5,335	5,836
End of year	(b)	6,275	5,335
Average [(a + b)/2]		5,805	5,586
Accounts receivable turnover		**14.22**	**14.13**
Industry average.		9.0	

The higher the accounts receivable turnover, the faster a company is able to convert its accounts receivable into cash. P&G's accounts receivable turnover increased slightly from 14.13 in 2010 to 14.22 in 2011. Moreover, P&G's 2011 accounts receivable turnover is well above the industry average of 9.0 for the year.

Average Collection Period

An extension of the accounts receivable turnover is the **average collection period**. The average collection period reveals how many days it takes, on average, for a company to collect an account receivable. The ratio is calculated as follows:

$$\text{Average collection period} = \frac{365}{\text{Accounts receivable turnover (net)}}$$

P&G's average collection period is calculated as follows:

	2011	2010
Average collection period 2011: 365/14.22; 2010: 365/14.13.	**25.7 days**	**25.8 days**
Industry average.	40.6 days	

P&G reduced its average collection period slightly in 2011. This may have resulted from such actions as a tightening of the credit standards offered by the company to its customers or by shortening the allowed credit period. Alternatively, it may reflect that P&G's customers have improved their cash flows, and thus, are able to pay their accounts payable more promptly. Knowledge of P&G's credit terms would permit a more complete analysis of these results. If, for example, P&G's credit terms are n/20, then an average collection period of 25.7 days indicates that the company has a problem with slow-paying customers. If, on the other hand, P&G's credit terms are n/30, then the 2011 average collection period shows no particular problem with the company's speed of receivable collection.

Inventory Turnover

An analyst concerned about a company's inventory position is likely to evaluate the company's **inventory turnover**. This ratio indicates whether the inventory on hand is disproportionate to the amount of sales revenue. Excessive inventories not only tie up company funds and increase storage costs but may also lead to subsequent losses if the goods become outdated or unsalable. The calculation of inventory turnover is as follows:

$$\text{Inventory turnover} = \frac{\text{Cost of goods sold}}{\text{Average inventory}}$$

P&G's inventory turnover is (inventory at the end of 2009 was $6,880):

		2011	2010
Cost of goods sold.		$40,768	$37,919
Inventory			
Beginning of year	(a)	6,384	6,880
End of year	(b)	7,379	6,384
Average [(a + b)/2].		6,882	6,632
Inventory turnover		**5.92**	**5.72**
Industry average.		7.4	

P&G's inventory turnover increased from 5.72 in 2010 to 5.92 in 2011. (Recall that, in general, a higher turnover is preferred to a lower turnover.) However the company's 2011 inventory turnover of 5.92 is below the industry average of 7.4 and indicates a problem area that the company's management will want to address.

The cost of goods sold is used in the calculation of inventory turnover because the inventory measure in the denominator is a *cost* figure; consequently, it is appropriate to also use a cost figure in the numerator. By way of contrast, accounts receivable turnover uses net sales in the calculation because accounts receivable is based on sales revenue, which includes a markup for the company's expected profit.

A low inventory turnover can result from an overextended inventory position or from inadequate sales volume. For this reason, an appraisal of a firm's inventory turnover should be accompanied by a review of the quick ratio and an analysis of trends in both inventory and sales revenue.

Days' Sales in Inventory

The **days' sales in inventory** ratio is derived from a firm's inventory turnover ratio and reveals how many days it takes, on average, for a firm to sell its inventory on hand. The ratio is calculated as follows:

$$\text{Days' sales in inventory} = \frac{365}{\text{Inventory turnover}}$$

P&G's days' sales in inventory is:

	2011	2010
Days' sales in inventory		
2011: 365/5.92; 2010: 365/5.72	**61.7 days**	**63.8 days**
Industry average	49.3 days	

P&G's days' sales in inventory reveals that the average amount of time required to sell its inventory decreased by over two days from 63.8 days in 2010 to 61.7 days in 2011. However, P&G's average length of time to sell its inventory is higher than the industry average by over twelve days. The improvement in P&G's day's sales in inventory will positively impact the company's profitability due to the related decrease in inventory storage costs and a decrease in its inventory financing costs.

By combining the days' sales in inventory with the average collection period, it is possible to estimate the average time period from the acquisition of inventory, to the sale of inventory, to the eventual collection of cash. In 2011, for example, it took P&G 87.4 days (61.7 days' sales in inventory + 25.7 days average collection period) to sell its average inventory and collect the related cash from its customers. This time period is better than the industry average of 89.9 days by about three days and better than P&G's 2010 period of 89.6 days (63.8 days + 25.8 days).

YOUR TURN! 13.5

The solution is on page 664.

The following selected data was obtained from the financial statements of Justin Corporation:

Current assets	$ 60,000
Current liabilities for both current and prior year	40,000
Cash flow from operating activities	55,000
Net sales.	100,000
Average accounts receivable	15,000
Cost of goods sold.	70,000
Average inventory.	9,000

Required

Calculate the following financial measures and ratios for Justin Corporation:

a. Working capital

b. Current ratio

c. Operating-cash-flow-to-current-liabilities ratio

d. Accounts receivable turnover

e. Days' sales in inventory

TAKEAWAY 13.4	Concept ⟶	Method ⟶	Assessment
	How financially capable is a company to pay its current liabilities as they come due?	Income statement, balance sheet, and statement of cash flows. Calculate the current ratio, the quick ratio, and the operating-cash-flow-to-current-liabilities ratio.	The higher the ratios, the higher the probability that a company will have the ability to pay its current liabilities as they become due.

Analyzing Long-Term Firm Solvency

The preceding set of ratios examined a firm's short-term liquidity. A separate set of ratios analyzes a firm's long-term solvency, or its long-term debt repayment capability. Ratios in this latter group include (1) the debt-to-equity ratio, (2) the times-interest-earned ratio, and (3) the operating-cash-flow-to-capital-expenditures ratio.

Debt-to-Equity Ratio

The **debt-to-equity ratio** evaluates the financial structure of a firm by relating a company's total liabilities to its total stockholders' equity. This ratio considers the extent to which a company relies on creditors versus stockholders to provide financing for a business. The debt-to-equity ratio is calculated as follows:

$$\text{Debt-to-equity ratio} = \frac{\textbf{Total liabilities}}{\textbf{Total stockholders' equity}}$$

This ratio uses year-end balances for the ratio's components, rather than averages, since we are interested in the firm's capital structure as of a particular point in time. The total stockholders' equity for a business is its total assets minus its total liabilities.

The debt-to-equity ratio gives potential creditors an indication of the margin of protection available to them (creditors' claims to assets have priority over stockholders' claims). The lower the ratio, the greater the protection being provided to creditors. A firm with a low ratio also has greater flexibility when seeking additional borrowed funds at a low rate of interest than does a firm with a high ratio.

P&G's debt-to-equity ratio is:

	2011	2010
Total liabilities (year-end)	$70,353	$66,733
Total stockholders' equity (year-end).	68,001	61,439
Debt-to-equity ratio	**1.03**	**1.09**
Industry average.	1.1	

P&G's debt-to-equity ratio decreased from 1.09 in 2010 to 1.03 in 2011, indicating a decreasing reliance on creditors for financing; in addition, the company's 2011 ratio is below the industry average, suggesting a positive aspect of the firm's long-term financial strength.

Times-Interest-Earned Ratio

A.K.A. The times-interest-earned ratio is also referred to as the *interest coverage ratio*.

To evaluate the ability of a company to pay its current interest charges from its operating income, an analyst may investigate the relationship between the company's current interest charges and its net income. For example, an extremely high debt-to-equity ratio for a company may indicate extensive borrowing by the company; however, if its operating earnings are sufficient to meet the interest charges on the debt several times over, an analyst may regard the situation quite favorably.

Analysts, particularly long-term credit analysts, almost always consider the **times-interest-earned ratio** of a company with interest-bearing debt. This ratio is calculated by dividing the income before interest expense and income taxes by the annual interest expense:

$$\text{Times-interest-earned ratio} = \frac{\text{Income before interest expense and income taxes}}{\text{Interest expense}}$$

P&G's times-interest-earned ratio is:

	2011	2010
Income before interest expense and income taxes	$16,020	$15,993
Interest expense.	831	946
Times-interest-earned ratio	**19.3**	**16.9**
Industry average.	5.1	

P&G's operating income available to meet its interest charges increased from 16.9 times in 2010 to 19.3 times in 2011. This ratio is well above the industry average of 5.1, and indicates that P&G exhibits an exceptionally good margin of safety for creditors. Generally speaking, a company that earns its interest charges several times before taxes is generally regarded as a satisfactory risk by long-term creditors.

Operating-Cash-Flow-to-Capital-Expenditures Ratio

The ability of a firm's operations to provide sufficient cash to replace and expand its property, plant, and equipment is revealed by the **operating-cash-flow-to-capital-expenditures ratio**. To the extent that acquisitions of plant assets can be financed using cash provided by operating activities, a firm does not have to use other financing sources, such as long-term debt. This ratio is calculated as follows:

$$\text{Operating-cash-flow-to-capital-expenditures ratio} = \frac{\text{Cash flow from operating activities}}{\text{Annual net capital expenditures}}$$

A ratio of 1.0 indicates that a firm's current operating activities provide sufficient cash to fully fund any investment in plant capacity. A ratio in excess of 1.0 indicates that a company has more than sufficient operating cash flow to fund any needed expansion in plant capacity.

The operating-cash-flow-to-capital-expenditures ratio for P&G is (no industry average is available):

	2011	2010
Cash flow from operating activities	$13,231	$16,072
Annual net capital expenditures (see Exhibit 13-4)	3,081	(1)
Operating-cash-flow-to-capital-expenditures ratio	**4.3**	**n/a**

In 2011, P&G's operating-cash-flow-to capital-expenditures ratio was 4.3. In 2010, P&G sold as many assets as they bought, so we don't calculate a ratio for that year. It appears that P&G is generating plenty of operating cash flow to cover its net capital expenditures for both years.

YOUR TURN! 13.6

The solution is on
page 664.

The following selected data was obtained from the financial statements for the Hartford Corporation:

Total liabilities.	$180,000
Total stockholders' equity	600,000
Cash flow from operating activities	100,000
Annual capital expenditures.	30,000
Net income.	55,000
Interest expense.	5,000
Income tax expense.	25,000

Required
Calculate the following ratios for Hartford Corporation:
a. Debt-to-equity ratio
b. Times-interest-earned ratio
c. Operating-cash-flow-to-capital-expenditures ratio

TAKEAWAY 13.5	Concept	⟶	Method	⟶	Assessment
	How solvent is a company?		Income statement, balance sheet, and statement of cash flows. Calculate the debt-to-equity ratio, the times-interest-earned ratio, and the operating-cash-flow-to-capital-expenditures ratio.		The higher the times-interest-earned ratio and the operating-cash-flow-to-capital-expenditures ratios, and the lower the debt-to-equity ratio, the greater is a company's solvency.

Financial Ratios for Common Stockholders

Present and potential common stockholders share an interest with a business's creditors in analyzing the profitability, short-term liquidity, and long-term solvency of a company. There are also other financial ratios that are primarily of interest to common stockholders. These ratios include (1) earnings per share, (2) the price-earnings ratio, (3) dividend yield, and (4) the dividend payout ratio.

Earnings per Share

Because stock market prices are quoted on a per-share basis, the reporting of earnings per share of common stock is useful to investors. Accounting guidelines require the disclosure of earnings per share data as part of the company's income statement.

Earnings per share (EPS) are calculated by dividing the net income available to common stockholders by the weighted average number of common shares outstanding during a year. The net income available to common stockholders is a company's net income less any preferred stock dividends. Preferred stock dividends are subtracted from net income to arrive at the net income available exclusively to a company's common stock stockholders. Thus, earnings per share is calculated as follows:

$$\frac{\textbf{Earnings}}{\textbf{per share}} = \frac{(\textbf{Net income} - \textbf{Preferred stock dividends})}{\textbf{Weighted-average number of common shares outstanding}}$$

Since earnings per share are a required disclosure on a company's income statement, investment professionals do not have to calculate this financial metric. P&G's income statements reveal the following earnings per share (see Exhibit 13-2):

	2011	2010
Earnings per share	$4.12	$4.32

Even though P&G's net income decreased about 7.4 percent in 2011, the company's earnings per share only decreased 4.6 percent due to a large increase in treasury share purchases during the year.

Price-Earnings Ratio

The **price-earnings ratio** is calculated by dividing the market price per share of common stock by a company's earnings per share:

A.K.A. The price-earnings ratio is also referred to as the *P/E multiple*.

$$\text{Price-earnings ratio} = \frac{\textbf{Market price per share}}{\textbf{Earnings per share}}$$

For many analysts and investors, this ratio is an important tool for assessing a stock's fair value. For example, after evaluating the financial strengths of several comparable companies, an analyst may decide which company to invest in by comparing the price-earnings ratio of each company. Assuming that the companies have equivalent persistent earnings and financial risk profiles, the company with the lowest price-earnings ratio may represent the best investment opportunity.

When calculating the price-earnings ratio, it is customary to use the latest market price per share and the earnings per share for the last four quarters of a company's operations. P&G's price-earnings ratios as of the end of fiscal years 2010 and 2011 are:

	2011	2010
Market price per share (at year-end)	$63.57	$59.98
Earnings per share	4.12	4.32
Price-earnings ratio	**15.4**	**13.9**
Industry average.	16.1	

The market price of a share of P&G's common stock at year-end 2011 was 15.4 times the company's 2011 earnings per share. Since P&G's price-earnings ratio at the end of 2011 is below industry average, this may indicate that the company's shares are under valued, and thus, that its stock may represent a fair investment.

Dividend Yield

Investor expectations vary greatly with personal economic circumstances and with the overall economic outlook. Some investors are more interested in the potential share price appreciation of a stock than in any dividends that a company may pay on its outstanding shares. When shares are disposed of in the future, the capital gains provision of U.S. income tax law may tax capital gains at a rate that is lower than the tax rate applied to dividend income. Some investors, on the other hand, are more concerned with dividends than with stock price appreciation. These investors desire a high **dividend yield** on their investments. Dividend yield is calculated by dividing a company's current annual dividend per share by the current market price per share:

$$\text{Dividend yield} = \frac{\textbf{Annual dividend per share}}{\textbf{Market price per share}}$$

P&G's dividend yield per common share is (the dividend per share is disclosed in Exhibit 13-2):

	2011	2010
Annual dividend per share	$ 1.97	$ 1.80
Market price per share (at year-end)	63.57	59.98
Dividend yield	**3.1%**	**3.0%**
Industry average.	3.25%	

P&G's dividend yield increased from 3.0 percent in 2010 to 3.1 percent in 2011, and is slightly below the industry average of 3.25 percent.

Dividend Payout Ratio

Investors who emphasize the yield on their investments may also be interested in a firm's **dividend payout ratio**—that is, the percentage of net income paid out as dividends to stockholders. The payout ratio indicates whether a firm has a conservative or a liberal dividend policy, and may also indicate whether a firm is conserving funds for internal financing of its growth. The dividend payout ratio is calculated as follows:

$$\text{Dividend payout ratio} = \frac{\textbf{Annual dividend per share}}{\textbf{Earnings per share}}$$

P&G's dividend payout ratio is:

	2011	2010
Annual dividends per share	$1.97	$1.80
Earnings per share	4.12	4.32
Dividend payout ratio.	**47.8%**	**41.7%**

P&G's dividend payout ratio increased from 41.7 percent in 2010 to 47.8 percent in 2011. This payout ratio is consistent with the payout ratio for most comparable mature U.S. industrial corporations.

Payout ratios for mature industrial corporations vary between 40 percent and 60 percent of net income. Many corporations, however, need funds for internal financing of growth and pay out little (if any) of their net income as dividends. At the other extreme, some companies—principally utility companies—may pay out as much as 70 percent of their net income as dividends.

YOUR TURN! 13.7

The solution is on page 664.

The following selected data was obtained from financial statements for Baylor Corporation:

Earnings per share	$ 4.50
Market price per share of common stock	54.00
Dividends per share of common stock	1.50

Required

Calculate the following ratios for Baylor Corporation:

a. Dividend yield

b. Dividend payout ratio

Concept	Method	Assessment	TAKEAWAY 13.6
How much dividends are common stockholders likely to receive?	Earnings per share, dividends per share, and market price of common stock. Calculate the dividend yield and dividend payout ratio.	The higher the dividend yield and the dividend payout ratio, the greater the company's dividend distribution policy.	

LIMITATIONS OF FINANCIAL STATEMENT ANALYSIS

The ratios, percentages, and other relationships described in this chapter reflect the analytical techniques used by investment professionals and experienced investors. Nonetheless, they must be interpreted with due consideration of the general economic conditions, the conditions of the industry in which a company operates, and the relative position of individual companies within an industry.

LO5 **Discuss** the limitations of financial statement analysis.

Financial statement users must also be aware of the inherent limitations of financial statement data. Problems of comparability are frequently encountered. Companies within the same industry may use different accounting methods that can cause problems in comparing certain key relationships. For instance, inventory turnover is likely to be quite different for a company using LIFO than for one using FIFO. Inflation may also distort certain financial data and ratios, especially those resulting from horizontal analysis. For example, trend percentages calculated from data unadjusted for inflation may be deceptive.

Financial statement users must also be careful when comparing companies within a particular industry. Factors such as firm size, diversity of product line, and mode of operations can make firms within the same industry completely dissimilar in their reported results. Moreover, some firms, particularly conglomerates, are difficult to classify by industry. If segment information is available, the financial statement user may compare the statistics for several industries. Often, trade associations prepare industry statistics that are stratified by size of firm or type of product, facilitating financial statement analysis.

FORENSIC ACCOUNTING

It is generally considered more difficult to deter financial statement fraud than it is to deter other types of fraud such as embezzlement. The best approach to fraud deterrence is to put into place a strong set of internal controls. Unfortunately, senior management, such as a firm's CEO and CFO, are the most likely employees to commit financial statement fraud. These individuals are able to use their position of authority to override most internal controls. Thus, it is important to consider alternative approaches to fraud deterrence. Potential alternative approaches are based on the fraud triangle concept, in which fraud is related to the interaction of three factors: (1) pressure, (2) opportunity, and (3) rationalization.

The fraud element of pressure can be reduced by avoiding the practice of setting unachievable financial goals and utilizing compensation systems that are considered fair but which do not create excessive incentives to commit fraud. Although internal controls may be circumvented by senior management, it is still important to maintain a strong system of internal controls and to establish clear and uniform accounting procedures with no exception clauses. In addition, a strong internal control department reporting to the board of directors provides further deterrence. Finally, the creation and promotion of a culture of honesty and integrity throughout an organization makes the rationalization of financial statement fraud much more difficult.

COMPREHENSIVE PROBLEM

Knox Instruments, Inc., is a manufacturer of various medical and dental instruments. Financial statement data for the firm follow:

(thousands of dollars, except per-share amount)	2013
Sales revenue.	$200,000
Cost of goods sold.	98,000
Net income.	10,750
Dividends	4,200
Cash provided by operating activities	7,800
Earnings per share	3.07

KNOX INSTRUMENTS, INC.
Balance Sheets

(thousands of dollars)	Dec. 31, 2013	Dec. 31, 2012
Assets		
Cash.	$ 3,000	$ 2,900
Accounts receivable (net).	28,000	28,800
Inventory.	64,000	44,000
Total current assets	95,000	75,700
Plant assets (net)	76,000	67,300
Total Assets	$171,000	$143,000
Liabilities and Stockholders' Equity		
Current liabilities.	$ 45,200	$ 39,750
10% Bonds payable.	20,000	14,000
Total Liabilities	65,200	53,750
Common stock, $10 par value.	40,000	30,000
Retained earnings	65,800	59,250
Total Stockholders' Equity.	105,800	89,250
Total Liabilities and Stockholders' Equity	$171,000	$143,000

Required

a. Using the given data, calculate financial ratios one through nine for 2013. Compare the ratio results for Knox Instruments, Inc., with the following industry averages and comment on its operations.

Median Ratios for the Industry

1.	Current ratio	2.7
2.	Quick ratio	1.6
3.	Average collection period	73 days
4.	Inventory turnover	2.3
5.	Operating-cash-flow-to-current-liabilities ratio	NA
6.	Debt-to-equity ratio	0.50
7.	Return on assets	4.9 percent
8.	Return on common stockholders' equity	10.2 percent
9.	Return on sales	4.1 percent

b. Calculate the dividends paid per share of common stock. (Use the average number of shares outstanding during the year.) What was the dividend payout ratio?

c. If the 2013 year-end market price per share of Knox's common stock is $25, what is the company's (1) price-earnings ratio and (2) dividend yield?

Solution

a.

1. Current ratio = $95,000/$45,200 = 2.10
2. Quick ratio = $31,000/$45,200 = 0.69
3. Average collection period:
   Accounts receivable turnover = $200,000/($28,800 + $28,000)/2 = 7.04
   Average collection period = 365/7.04 = 51.8 days
4. Inventory turnover = $98,000/($44,000 + $64,000)/2 = 1.81
5. Operating-cash-flow-to-current-liabilities ratio = $7,800/($39,750 + $45,200)/2 = 0.18
6. Debt-to-equity ratio = $65,200/$105,800 = 0.62
7. Return on assets = $10,750/($143,000 + $171,000)/2 = 6.8 percent
8. Return on common stockholders' equity = $10,750/($89,250 + $105,800)/2 = 11.0 percent
9. Return on sales = $10,750/$200,000 = 5.4 percent

Although the firm's current ratio of 2.10 is below the industry median, it is still acceptable; however, the quick ratio of 0.69 is well below the industry median. This indicates that Knox's inventory (which is omitted from this calculation) is excessive. This is borne out by the firm's inventory turnover of 1.81 times, which compares with the industry median of 2.3 times. The firm's average collection period of 51.8 days is significantly better than the industry median of 73 days. No industry median is available for the operating-cash-flow-to-current-liabilities ratio. Knox's debt-to-equity ratio of 0.62 indicates that the firm has proportionately more debt in its capital structure than the median industry firm, which has a debt-to-equity ratio of 0.50. Knox's operations appear efficient as its return on assets, return on common stockholders' equity, and return on sales all exceed the industry medians.

b. Average number of shares outstanding = (4,000,000 + 3,000,000)/2 = 3,500,000 shares.
   $4,200,000 dividends/3,500,000 shares = $1.20 dividend per share.
   Dividend payout ratio = $1.20/$3.07 = 39.1 percent.

c. Price-earnings ratio = $25/$3.07 = 8.1.
   Dividend yield = $1.20/$25 = 4.8 percent.

APPENDIX 13A: Financial Statement Disclosures

Disclosures related to a company's financial statements fall into one of three categories: (1) parenthetical disclosures on the face of the financial statements, (2) notes to the financial statements, and (3) supplementary information. Most disclosures amplify or explain aggregated information contained in the financial statements. Some disclosures, however, add new information.

LO6 **Describe** financial statement disclosures.

Parenthetical Disclosures

Parenthetical disclosures are placed next to an account title or other descriptive label in the financial statements. Their purpose is to provide additional detail regarding the item or account.

An example of parenthetical disclosures follows:

	2011	2010
Accounts receivable, less allowances for doubtful accounts (2011—$7,545; 2010—$7,098).	$351,538	$300,181

Notes to the Financial Statements

Although much information is gathered, summarized, and reported in a company's financial statements, the financial statements alone are limited in their ability to convey a complete picture of a company's financial status. *Notes* are added to the financial statements to help fill in these gaps. In fact, over time, accountants have given so much attention to the financial statement notes that the notes now consume more page space in the annual report than the financial statements themselves. Notes may cover a wide variety of topics. Typically, they deal with significant accounting policies, explanations of complex or special transactions, details of reported amounts, commitments, contingencies, business segments, quarterly data, and subsequent material events.

Significant Accounting Policies

GAAP contains a number of instances for which alternative accounting procedures are equally acceptable. For example, there are several generally accepted depreciation and inventory valuation methods, and there are different ways to recognize sales revenue. The particular accounting policies selected by a company affect the financial data presented. Knowledge of a firm's specific accounting principles and methods of applying these principles helps users more fully understand a company's financial statements. Accordingly, these principles and methods are disclosed in a **summary of significant accounting policies**.

For example, the annual report of the **Columbia Sportswear Company**, included in Appendix A of this book, contains the following description of its inventory policy:

> Inventories are carried at the lower of cost or market. Cost is determined using the first-in, first-out method. The Company periodically reviews its inventories for excess, close-out or slow moving items and makes provisions as necessary to properly reflect inventory value.

Explanations of Complex or Special Transactions

The complexity of certain transactions means that not all important aspects are likely to be reflected in the accounts. Financial statement notes, therefore, report additional relevant details about such transactions. Typical examples include notes discussing the financial aspects of pension plans, profit-sharing plans, acquisitions of other companies, borrowing agreements, stock option and other incentive plans, and income taxes.

Transactions with related parties are special transactions requiring disclosure in the financial statement notes. *Related party transactions* include transactions between a firm and its (1) principal owners, (2) members of management, (3) subsidiary companies, or (4) affiliate companies.

Details of Reported Amounts

Financial statements often summarize several groups of accounts into a single aggregate dollar amount. For example, a balance sheet may show one asset account labeled *Property, Plant, and Equipment,* or it may list *Long-Term Debt* as a single amount among the liabilities. Notes report more detail, presenting schedules that list the types and amounts of property, plant, and equipment and long-term debt. Other items that may be summarized in the financial statements and detailed in the notes include inventories, other current assets, notes payable, accrued liabilities, stockholders' equity, and a company's income tax expense.

The notes to Columbia Sportswear Company's annual report (see Appendix A at the end of this book) contain several examples of financial statement items that are detailed, including inventories (**Note 5**), property, plant, and equipment (**Note 6**), short-term borrowing and credit lines (**Note 8**), accrued liabilities (**Note 9**), other long-term liabilities (**Note 11**), and income taxes (**Note 10**).

Commitments

A firm may have contractual arrangements existing as of a balance sheet date in which both parties to the contract still have acts yet to be completed. If performance under these **commitments** will have a significant financial impact on a firm, the existence and nature of the commitments should be disclosed in the notes to the financial statements. Examples of commitments reported in the notes include commitments under operating leases, contracts to purchase materials or equipment, contracts to construct facilities, salary commitments to executives, commitments to retire or redeem stock, and commitments to deliver goods.

Columbia Sportswear Company reports the following commitments in its annual report:

> During its normal course of business, the Company has made certain indemnities, commitments and guarantees under which it may be required to make payments in relation to certain transactions. These include (i) intellectual property indemnities to the Company's customers and licensees in connection with the use, sale and/or license of Company products, (ii) indemnities to various lessors in connection with facility leases for certain claims arising from such facility or lease, (iii) indemnities to customers, vendors and service providers pertaining to claims based on the negligence or willful misconduct of the Company, (iv) executive severance arrangements and (v) indemnities involving the accuracy of representations and warranties in certain contracts. The duration of these indemnities, commitments and guarantees varies, and in certain cases, may be indefinite. The majority of these indemnities, commitments and guarantees do not provide for any limitation of the maximum potential for future payments the Company could be obligated to make. The Company has not recorded any liability for these indemnities, commitments and guarantees in the accompanying Consolidated Balance Sheets.

Contingencies

Contingent liabilities were discussed in Chapter 10. As noted there, if the future event that would turn a contingency into an obligation is not likely to occur, or if the liability cannot be reasonably estimated, the **contingency** is disclosed in a note to the financial statements. Typical contingencies disclosed in the notes include pending lawsuits, environmental cleanup costs, possible income tax assessments, credit guarantees, and discounted notes receivable.

Under Armour, Inc. reports the following regarding contingencies in its annual report:

The company is, from time to time, involved in routine legal matters incidental to its business. The company believes that the ultimate resolution of any such current proceedings and claims will not have a material adverse effect on its consolidated financial position, results of operations or cash flows.

Segments

Many firms diversify their business activities and operate in several different industries. A firm's financial statements often combine information from all of a company's operations into aggregate amounts. This complicates the financial statement user's ability to analyze the statements because the interpretation of financial data is influenced by the industry in which a firm operates. Different industries face different types of risk and have different rates of profitability. In making investment and lending decisions, financial statement users evaluate risk and required rates of return. Having financial data available by industry segment is helpful to such evaluations.

The FASB recognizes the usefulness of industry data to investors and lenders. Public companies with significant operations in more than one industry must report certain financial information by industry **segment**. Typically, these disclosures are in the financial statement notes. The major disclosures by industry segment are sales revenue, operating profit or loss, identifiable assets (the assets used by the segment), capital expenditures, and depreciation.

Other types of segment data may also be disclosed. Business operations in different parts of the world are subject to different risks and opportunities for growth. Thus, public companies with significant operations in foreign countries must report selected financial data by foreign geographic area. The required data disclosures include sales revenue, operating profit or loss (or other profitability measure), and identifiable assets. Also, if a firm has export sales or sales revenue to a single customer that are ten percent or more of total sales revenue, the amount of such sales revenue must be separately disclosed.

Note 18 to **Columbia Sportswear's** financial statements in its annual report (see Appendix A at the end of this book) illustrates segment disclosures by foreign versus domestic segments.

Quarterly Data

Interim financial reports cover periods shorter than one year. Companies that issue interim reports generally do so quarterly. These reports provide financial statement users with timely information on a firm's progress and are useful in predicting a company's annual financial results. The SEC requires that certain companies disclose selected quarterly financial data in their annual reports to stockholders. Included among the notes, the data reported for each quarter include sales revenue, gross profit, net income, and earnings per share. **Quarterly data** permit financial statement users to analyze such things as the seasonal nature of operations, the impact of diversification on quarterly activity, and whether the firm's activities lead or lag general economic trends.

The Columbia Sportswear Company provides quarterly financial information as supplemental data in its annual report (see the Columbia Annual Report in Appendix A).

Subsequent Events

If a company issues a large amount of securities or suffers a casualty loss after the balance sheet date, this information should be reported in a note, even though the situation arose subsequent to the balance sheet date. Firms are responsible for disclosing any significant events that occur between the balance sheet date and the date the financial statements are issued. This guideline recognizes that it takes several weeks for financial statements to be prepared and audited before they are issued. Events occurring during this period may have a material effect on a firm's operations and should be disclosed. Other examples of **subsequent events** requiring disclosure are sales of assets, significant changes in long-term debt, and acquisitions of other companies.

For example, **Under Armour, Inc.** reported the following subsequent event in its annual report:

In February 2012, 150.0 thousand shares of Class B Convertible Common Stock were converted into shares of Class A Common Stock on a one-for-one basis in connection with a stock sale.

Supplementary Information

Supplementing the financial statements are several additional disclosures—management's discussion and analysis of the financial statements and selected financial data covering a five- to ten-year period along with possible other *supplementary* disclosures that are either required of certain companies by the SEC or recommended (but not required) by the FASB.

Management Discussion and Analysis

A.K.A. The management discussion and analysis is also referred to simply as the *MD&A*.

Management may increase the usefulness of financial statements by sharing some of their knowledge about a company's financial condition and operations. This is the purpose of the disclosure devoted to the management discussion and analysis. In this supplement to the financial statements, management identifies and comments on events and trends influencing a company's liquidity, operating results, and financial resources. Management's position within a company not only provides it with insights unavailable to outsiders, but also may introduce certain biases into the analysis. Nonetheless, management's comments, interpretations, and explanations should contribute to a better understanding of a company's financial statements.

Comparative Selected Financial Data

The analysis of a company's financial performance is enhanced when financial data for several years are available. By analyzing trends over time, it is possible for a financial statement user to learn much more about a company than would be possible by analyzing only a single year of data. Year-to-year changes may give clues as to a firm's future growth or may highlight areas for concern. Corporate annual reports to stockholders present complete financial statements in comparative form, showing the current year and one or more preceding years. Beyond this, however, the financial statements are supplemented by a summary of selected key financial statistics for a five- or ten-year period. The financial data presented in this historical summary usually include sales revenue, net income, dividends, earnings per share, working capital, and total assets.

SUMMARY OF LEARNING OBJECTIVES

LO1   **Identify persistent earnings and discuss the content and format of the income statement. (p. 600)**

- Persistent earnings are earnings that are likely to recur, while transitory earnings are unlikely to recur.
- The continuing income of a business may be reported in a single-step format or in a multiple-step format.
- Gains and losses from discontinued operations are reported in a special income statement section following income from continuing operations.
- Extraordinary items are both unusual *and* infrequent; they are reported in a separate section of the income statement.
- The effect of most changes in accounting principle requires restatement of prior financial statements as if the new method had been applied all along.
- Companies are required to report other comprehensive income in addition to regular income in their financial statements.

LO2   **Identify the sources of financial information used by investment professionals and explain horizontal financial statements analysis. (p. 604)**

- Data sources for investment professionals include published financial statements, filings with the U.S. Securities and Exchange Commission, and statistics available from financial data services.
- A common form of horizontal analysis involves analyzing dollar and percentage changes in comparative financial statements for two or more years.
- Analyzing trend percentages of key figures, such as sales revenue, net income, and total assets for a number of years, related to a base year, is often useful.

LO3   **Explain vertical financial statement analysis. (p. 611)**

- Vertical analysis deals with the relationship of financial statement data for a single year.
- Common-size statements express financial statement items as a percentage of another key item, such as expressing income statement items as a percentage of sales revenue and balance sheet items as a percentage of total assets.

LO4   **Define and discuss financial ratios for analyzing a firm. (p. 612)**

- Ratios for analyzing firm profitability include the gross profit percentage, the return on sales, asset turnover, the return on assets, and the return on common stockholders' equity.

- Ratios for analyzing short-term firm liquidity include the current ratio, quick ratio, operating-cash-flow-to-current-liabilities ratio, accounts receivable turnover, average collection period, inventory turnover, and days' sales in inventory.
- Ratios for analyzing long-term firm solvency include the debt-to-equity ratio, the times-interest-earned ratio, and the operating-cash-flow-to-capital-expenditures ratio.
- Ratios of particular interest to common stockholders include a company's earnings per share, the price-earnings ratio, dividend yield, and the dividend payout ratio.

Discuss the limitations of financial statement analysis. (p. 627) **LO5**

- When analyzing financial statements, financial statement users must be aware of a firm's accounting methods, the effects of inflation, and the difficulty of currently identifying a firm's industry classification.

Appendix 13A: Describe financial statement disclosures. (p. 629) **LO6**

- Parenthetical disclosures on the face of the financial statements provide additional detail regarding the item or account.
- Notes to the financial statements provide information on significant accounting policies, explanations of complex or special transactions, details of reported amounts, commitments, contingencies, segments, quarterly data, and subsequent events.
- Supplemental information includes the management discussion and analysis, and comparable selected financial information.

SUMMARY OF FINANCIAL STATEMENT RATIOS

Analyzing Firm Profitability

$$\text{Gross profit percentage} = \frac{\text{Gross profit on sales}}{\text{Net sales}}$$

$$\text{Return on sales} = \frac{\text{Net income}}{\text{Net sales}}$$

$$\text{Asset turnover} = \frac{\text{Net sales}}{\text{Average total assets}}$$

$$\text{Return on assets} = \frac{\text{Net income}}{\text{Average total assets}}$$

$$\text{Return on common stockholders' equity} = \frac{(\text{Net income} - \text{Preferred stock dividends})}{\text{Average common stockholders' equity}}$$

Analyzing Short-Term Firm Liquidity

$$\text{Current ratio} = \frac{\text{Current assets}}{\text{Current liabilities}}$$

$$\text{Quick ratio} = \frac{(\text{Cash and cash equivalents} + \text{Short-term investments} + \text{Accounts receivable})}{\text{Current liabilities}}$$

$$\text{Operating-cash-flow-to-current-liabilities ratio} = \frac{\text{Cash flow from operating activities}}{\text{Average current liabilities}}$$

$$\text{Accounts receivable turnover} = \frac{\text{Net sales}}{\text{Average accounts receivable (net)}}$$

$$\text{Average collection period} = \frac{365}{\text{Accounts receivable turnover (net)}}$$

$$\text{Inventory turnover} = \frac{\text{Cost of goods sold}}{\text{Average inventory}}$$

$$\text{Days' sales in inventory} = \frac{365}{\text{Inventory turnover}}$$

Analyzing Long-Term Firm Solvency

$$\text{Debt-to-equity ratio} = \frac{\text{Total liabilities}}{\text{Total stockholders' equity}}$$

$$\text{Times-interest-earned ratio} = \frac{\text{Income before interest expense and income taxes}}{\text{Interest expense}}$$

$$\text{Operating-cash-flow-to-capital-expenditures ratio} = \frac{\text{Cash flow from operating activities}}{\text{Annual net capital expenditures}}$$

Financial Ratios for Common Stockholders

$$\text{Earnings per share} = \frac{(\text{Net income} - \text{Preferred stock dividends})}{\text{Weighted average common shares outstanding}}$$

$$\text{Price-earnings ratio} = \frac{\text{Market price per share}}{\text{Earnings per share}}$$

$$\text{Dividend yield} = \frac{\text{Annual dividend per share}}{\text{Market price per share}}$$

$$\text{Dividend payout ratio} = \frac{\text{Annual dividend per share}}{\text{Earnings per share}}$$

SUMMARY	Concept ⟶	Method ⟶	Assessment
TAKEAWAY 13.1	How does a company's current performance compare with the prior year?	Income statement and balance sheet for current and prior year. The income statement and balance sheet should be compared using the prior year as the base. Percentage changes in net income and total assets can be computed as the change between years divided by the base year amount.	Significant changes should be analyzed to determine the reason for any change.
TAKEAWAY 13.2	How do the relationships within a company's income statement and balance sheet compare to those of prior years?	Income statement and balance sheet for current and prior year. Each income statement item should be presented as a percentage of sales revenue and each balance sheet item should be presented as a percentage of total assets. Financial statements in this form are called common-size statements.	The percentages should be analyzed for differences between years and significant changes should be analyzed to determine the reason for any change.
TAKEAWAY 13.3	How much profit is a company generating relative to the amount of assets invested in the company?	Income statement and balance sheet. Calculate the return on assets by dividing net income by the average total assets for the year.	The higher the return on assets, the better a company is doing with respect to generating profits utilizing the assets under its control.
TAKEAWAY 13.4	How financially capable is a company to pay its current liabilities as they come due?	Income statement, balance sheet, and statement of cash flows. Calculate the current ratio, the quick ratio, and the operating-cash-flow-to-current-liabilities ratio.	The higher the ratios, the higher the probability that a company will have the ability to pay its current liabilities as they come due.

Concept	⟶ Method ⟶	Assessment	SUMMARY
How solvent is a company?	Income statement, balance sheet, and statement of cash flows. Calculate the debt-to-equity ratio, the times-interest-earned ratio, and the operating-cash-flow-to-capital-expenditures ratio.	The higher the times-interest-earned and the operating-cash-flow-to-capital-expenditures ratios, and the lower the debt-to-equity ratio, the greater is a company's solvency.	TAKEAWAY 13.5
How much dividends are common stockholders likely to receive?	Earnings per share, dividends per share, and market price of common stock. Calculate the dividend yield and dividend payout ratio.	The higher the dividend yield and the dividend payout ratio, the greater the company's dividend distribution policy.	TAKEAWAY 13.6

KEY TERMS

Accounts receivable turnover (p. 619)

Asset turnover ratio (p. 615)

Average collection period (p. 620)

Change in accounting principle (p. 603)

Commitments (p. 630)

Common-size financial statement (p. 611)

Comparative financial statement analysis (p. 606)

Comprehensive income (p. 604)

Contingency (p. 631)

Current ratio (p. 617)

Days' sales in inventory (p. 621)

Debt-to-equity ratio (p. 622)

Discontinued operations (p. 602)

Dividend payout ratio (p. 626)

Dividend yield (p. 625)

Earnings per share (EPS) (p. 624)

Extraordinary items (p. 602)

Gross profit (p. 614)

Gross profit on sales (p. 614)

Gross profit percentage (p. 612)

Horizontal analysis (p. 605)

Inventory turnover (p. 620)

Multiple-step income statement (p. 600)

Operating-cash-flow-to-capital-expenditures ratio (p. 623)

Operating-cash-flow-to-current-liabilities ratio (p. 619)

Persistent earnings (p. 600)

Price-earnings ratio (p. 625)

Quarterly data (p. 631)

Quick ratio (p. 618)

Return on assets (p. 615)

Return on common stockholders' equity (p. 616)

Return on sales (p. 614)

Segment (p. 631)

Single-step income statement (p. 600)

Subsequent events (p. 631)

Summary of significant accounting policies (p. 630)

Times-interest-earned ratio (p. 623)

Transitory earnings (p. 600)

Trend percentages (p. 609)

Unusual items (p. 601)

Vertical analysis (p. 606)

Working capital (p. 617)

SELF-STUDY QUESTIONS

(Answers to the Self-Study Questions are at the end of this chapter.)

1. **Assume that an income statement contains each of the four sections listed below. Which will be the last section presented in the income statement?**   LO1
   a. Extraordinary items
   b. Gross profit
   c. Income from continuing operations
   d. Discontinued operations

2. **When constructing a common-sized income statement, all amounts are expressed as a percentage of:**   LO3
   a. net income.
   b. gross profit.
   c. net sales.
   d. income from operations.

Questions 3–10 of the Self-Study Questions are based on the following data:

HYDRO COMPANY			
Balance Sheet			
December 31, 2012			
Cash............................	$ 40,000	Current liabilities..........................	$ 80,000
Accounts receivable (net)............	80,000	10% Bonds payable......................	120,000
Inventory........................	130,000	Common stock.......................	200,000
Plant and equipment (net)	250,000	Retained earnings	100,000
Total Assets	$500,000	Total Liabilities and Stockholders' Equity	$500,000

Sales revenues for 2012 were $800,000, gross profit was $320,000, and net income was $36,000. The income tax rate was 40 percent. One year ago, accounts receivable (net) were $76,000, inventory was $110,000, total assets were $460,000, and stockholders' equity was $260,000. The bonds payable were outstanding all year and the 2012 interest expense was $12,000.

LO4 3. **The current ratio of Hydro Company at 12/31/2012, calculated using the above data, was 3.13 and the company's working capital was $170,000. Which of the following would happen if the firm paid off $20,000 of its current liabilities on January 1, 2013?**
   a. Both the current ratio and working capital would decrease.
   b. Both the current ratio and working capital would increase.
   c. The current ratio would increase, but working capital would remain the same.
   d. The current ratio would increase, but working capital would decrease.

LO4 4. **What was the firm's inventory turnover for 2012?**
   a. 6.67
   b. 4
   c. 6
   d. 3.69

LO4 5. **What was the firm's return on common stockholders' equity for 2012?**
   a. 25.7 percent
   b. 12.9 percent
   c. 17.1 percent
   d. 21.4 percent

LO4 6. **What was the firm's average collection period for 2012?**
   a. 36.5 days
   b. 37.4 days
   c. 35.6 days
   d. 18.3 days

LO4 7. **What was the firm's times-interest-earned ratio for 2012?**
   a. 4
   b. 3
   c. 5
   d. 6

LO4 8. **What was the firm's return on sales for 2012?**
   a. 4.0 percent
   b. 4.5 percent
   c. 5.0 percent
   d. 5.5 percent

LO4 9. **What was the firm's return on assets for 2012?**
   a. 6.0 percent
   b. 7.0 percent
   c. 7.5 percent
   d. 8.0 percent

LO2 10. **When performing trend analysis, each line item is expressed as a percentage of:**
   a. net income.
   b. the base year amount.
   c. the prior year amount.
   d. total assets.

LO5 11. **Recognized limitations of financial statement analysis include each of the following except:**
   a. companies in the same industry using different accounting methods.
   b. inflation.
   c. different levels of profitability between companies.
   d. difficulty of classifying by industry conglomerates.

LO6 12. **Financial statement disclosures include each of the following except:**
   a. notes to the financial statements.
   b. parenthetical disclosures.
   c. supplementary information.
   d. promotional giveaways.

QUESTIONS

1. What is the difference between a single-step income statement and a multiple-step income statement?

2. Which of the following amounts would appear only in a multiple-step income statement?
   a. Income from continuing operations.
   b. Income before extraordinary item.
   c. Gross profit on sales.
   d. Net income.

3. What is a business *segment*? Why are gains and losses from a discontinued segment reported in a separate section of the income statement?

4. Define *extraordinary items*. How are extraordinary items disclosed in the income statement?

5. A manufacturing plant of Park Corporation was destroyed by an earthquake, which is rare in the region where the plant was located. Where should this loss be classified on the income statement?

6. A Florida citrus grower incurs substantial frost damage to crops. Frost damage typically is experienced every few years. How should the loss on the crop damage be shown in the income statement?

7. How do horizontal analysis and vertical analysis of financial statements differ?

8. "Financial statement users should focus attention on each item showing a large percentage change from one year to the next." Is this statement correct? Why?

9. What are trend percentages and how are they calculated? What pitfalls must financial statement users avoid when preparing trend percentages?

10. What are common-size financial statements and how are they used?

11. What item is the key figure (that is, 100 percent) in a common-size income statement? a common-size balance sheet?

12. During the past year, Lite Company had net income of $5 million, and Scanlon Company had net income of $8 million. Both companies manufacture electrical components for the construction industry. What additional information would you need to compare the profitability of the two companies?

13. Under what circumstances can the return on sales be used to assess the profitability of a company? Can this ratio be used to compare the profitability of companies from different industries? Explain.

14. What is the relationship between asset turnover, return on assets, and return on sales?

15. Blare Company had a return on sales of 6.5 percent and an asset turnover of 2.40. What is Blare's return on assets?

16. What does the return on common stockholders' equity measure?

17. How does the quick ratio differ from the current ratio?

18. For each of the following ratios, is a high ratio or low ratio considered, in general, a positive sign?
   a. Current ratio
   b. Quick ratio
   c. Operating-cash-flow-to-current-liabilities ratio
   d. Accounts receivable turnover
   e. Average collection period
   f. Inventory turnover
   g. Days' sales in inventory

19. What is the significance of the debt-to-equity ratio and how is it computed?

20. What does the times-interest-earned ratio indicate and how is it calculated?

21. What does the operating-cash-flow-to-capital-expenditures ratio measure?

22. Clair, Inc., earned $4.50 per share of common stock in the current year and paid dividends of $2.34 per share. The most recent market price per share of the common stock is $46.80. What is the company's (a) price-earnings ratio, (b) dividend yield, and (c) dividend payout ratio?

23. What are two inherent limitations of financial statement data?

SHORT EXERCISES

Use the following financial data for Hi-Tech Instruments to answer Short Exercises 13-1 through 13-10:

2011 (Thousands of Dollars, except Earnings per Share)	
Sales revenue.	$210,000
Cost of goods sold.	125,000
Net income.	8,300
Dividends.	2,600
Earnings per share.	4.15

HI-TECH INSTRUMENTS, INC.
Balance Sheets

(Thousands of Dollars)	Dec. 31, 2013	Dec. 31, 2012
Assets		
Cash.	$ 18,300	$ 18,000
Accounts receivable (net).	46,000	41,000
Inventory.	39,500	43,700
Total Current Assets.	103,800	102,700
Plant assets (net)	52,600	50,500
Other assets.	15,600	13,800
Total Assets	$172,000	$167,000
Liabilities and Stockholders' Equity		
Notes payable—banks.	$ 6,000	$ 6,000
Accounts payable.	22,500	18,700
Accrued liabilities.	16,500	21,000
Total Current Liabilities.	45,000	45,700
9% Bonds payable.	40,000	40,000
Total Liabilities	85,000	85,700
Common stock, $25 par value (2,000,000 shares).	50,000	50,000
Retained earnings	37,000	31,300
Total Stockholders' Equity	87,000	81,300
Total Liabilities and Stockholders' Equity	$172,000	$167,000

Industry Average Ratios for Competitors	
Quick ratio	1.3
Current ratio	2.4
Accounts receivable turnover.	5.9 times
Inventory turnover	3.5 times
Debt-to-equity ratio	0.73
Gross profit percentage	42.8 percent
Return on sales	4.5 percent
Return on assets	7.6 percent

LO4 **SE13-1.** **Quick Ratio** Calculate the company's quick ratio for 2013 and compare the result to the industry average.

LO4 **SE13-2.** **Current Ratio** Calculate the company's current ratio for 2013 and compare the result to the industry average.

LO4 **SE13-3.** **Accounts Receivable Turnover** Calculate the company's accounts receivable turnover for 2013 and compare the result to the industry average.

LO4 **SE13-4.** **Inventory Turnover** Calculate the company's inventory turnover for 2013 and compare the result to the industry average.

SE13-5. **Debit-to-Equity Ratio** Calculate the company's 2013 debt-to-equity ratio and compare the result to the industry average.   **LO4**

SE13-6. **Gross Profit Percentage** Calculate the company's 2013 gross profit percentage and compare the result to the industry average.   **LO4**

SE13-7. **Return on Sales** Calculate the company's return on sales for 2013 and compare the result to the industry average.   **LO4**

SE13-8. **Return on Assets** Calculate the company's return on assets for 2013 and compare the result to the industry average.   **LO4**

SE13-9. **Dividends per Share** Calculate the company's dividend paid per share of common stock. What was the dividend payout ratio?   **LO4**

SE13-10. **Earnings per Share** If the company's most recent price per share of common stock is $62.25, what is the company's price-earnings ratio and dividend yield?   **LO4**

SE13-11. **Persistent Earnings** Identify each of the following items as either (P) persistent, or (T) transitory.   **LO1**

    a. Sale of merchandise.
    b. Settlement of a lawsuit.
    c. Interest income.
    d. Payment to vendors.
    e. Loss from expropriations of property by a foreign government.

SE13-12. **Horizontal Analysis** Total assets were $1,000,000 in 2012, $900,000 in 2011, and $950,000 in 2010. What was the percentage change from 2010 to 2011 and from 2011 to 2012? Was the change an increase or a decrease?   **LO2**

SE13-13. **Common-Size Income Statement** A partial common-size income statement for Prag Company for three years is shown below.   **LO3**

Item	2013	2012	2011
Net sales.	100.0	100.0	100.0
Cost of goods sold.	60.5	63.0	62.5
Other expenses	21.0	19.0	20.5

Did Prag's net income as a percentage of net sales increase, remain the same, or decrease over the three-year period?

SE13-14. **Financial Statement Disclosures** Which of the following is not a common form of financial statement disclosure?   **LO6**

    a. Notes to financial statements.
    b. Supplemental information.
    c. Parenthetical disclosure.
    d. Bullet points.

SE13-15. **Financial Statement Analysis Limitations** Which of the following is not considered a limitation of financial statement analysis?   **LO5**

    a. Firms may use different accounting methods.
    b. Firms may be audited by different auditing firms.
    c. Inflation may distort trend analysis.
    d. It may be difficult to classify large conglomorate firms by industry.

Assignments with the ✓ logo in the margin are available in BusinessCourse.
See the Preface of the book for details.

EXERCISES—SET A

E13-1A. **Income Statement Sections** During the current year, Dale Corporation incurred an extraordinary tornado loss of $300,000 and sold a segment of its business at a gain of $196,000. Until it was sold, the segment had a current period operating loss of $75,000. Also, the company discovered that an error caused last year's ending inventory to be understated by $31,000 (a material amount). The company had $800,000 income from continuing operations for the current year. Prepare the lower part of   **LO1**

the income statement, beginning with the $800,000 income from continuing operations. Follow tax allocation procedures, assuming that all changes in income are subject to a 40 percent income tax rate. Disregard earnings per share disclosures.

LO4 **E13-2A.** **Earnings per Share** Lucky Corporation began the year with a simple capital structure consisting of 200,000 shares of outstanding common stock. On April 1, 10,000 additional common shares were issued, and another 30,000 common shares were issued on August 1. The company had net income for the year of $572,000. Calculate the earnings per share of common stock.

LO2 **E13-3A.** **Comparative Income Statements** Consider the following income statement data from the Ross Company:

	2013	2012
Sales revenue.	$525,000	$450,000
Cost of goods sold.	336,000	279,000
Selling expenses	105,000	99,000
Administrative expenses	60,000	54,000
Income tax expense.	7,800	5,400

a. Prepare a comparative income statement, showing increases and decreases in dollars and in percentages.
b. Comment briefly on the changes between the two years.

LO3 **E13-4A.** **Common-Size Income Statements** Refer to the income statement data given in Exercise E13-3A.

a. Prepare common-size income statements for each year.
b. Compare the common-size income statements and comment briefly.

LO4 **E13-5A.** **Ratios Analyzing Firm Profitability** The following information is available for Buhler Company:

Annual Data	2013	2012
Net sales.	$8,600,000	$8,000,000
Gross profit on sales	3,053,000	2,736,000
Net income.	567,600	488,000

Year-End Data	Dec. 31, 2013	Dec. 31, 2012
Total assets	$6,500,000	$6,100,000
Stockholders' equity	3,800,000	3,200,000

Calculate the following ratios for 2013:

a. Gross profit percentage
b. Return on sales
c. Asset turnover
d. Return on assets
e. Return on common stockholders' equity (Buhler Company has no preferred stock.)

LO4 **E13-6A.** **Working Capital and Short-Term Liquidity Ratios** Bell Company has a current ratio of 2.85 (2.85:1) on December 31. On that date the company's current assets are as follows:

Cash.	$ 26,400
Short-term investments	49,000
Accounts receivable (net).	169,000
Inventory.	200,000
Prepaid expenses.	11,600
Current assets	$456,000

Bell Company's current liabilities at the beginning of the year were $135,000 and during the year its operating activities provided a cash flow of $50,000.

a. What are the firm's current liabilities on December 31?
b. What is the firm's working capital on December 31?
c. What is the quick ratio on December 31?
d. What is Bell's operating-cash-flow-to-current-liabilities ratio?

E13-7A. Accounts Receivable and Inventory Ratios Bell Company, whose current assets at December 31 are shown in Exercise E13-6A, had net sales for the year of $950,000 and cost of goods sold of $552,900. At the beginning of the year, Bell's accounts receivable (net) were $155,000 and its inventory was $194,000. **LO4**

a. What is the company's accounts receivable turnover for the year?
b. What is the company's average collection period for the year?
c. What is the company's inventory turnover for the year?
d. What is the company's days' sales in inventory for the year?

E13-8A. Ratios Analyzing Long-Term Firm Solvency The following information is available for Antler Company: **LO4**

Annual Data	2013	2012
Interest expense.	$ 88,000	$ 82,000
Income tax expense.	203,500	185,000
Net income.	496,500	395,000
Capital expenditures	320,000	400,000
Cash provided by operating activities	425,000	390,000

Year-End Data	Dec. 31, 2013	Dec. 31, 2012
Total liabilities.	$2,200,000	$1,900,000
Total stockholders' equity	4,000,000	3,600,000

Calculate the following:

a. 2013 debt-to-equity ratio.
b. 2013 times-interest-earned ratio.
c. 2013 operating-cash-flow-to-capital-expenditures ratio.

E13-9A. Financial Ratios for Common Stockholders Kluster Corporation has only common stock outstanding. The firm reported earnings per share of $5.10 for the year. During the year, Kluster paid dividends of $2.04 per share. At year end the current market price of the stock was $63 per share. Calculate the following: **LO4**

a. Year-end price-earnings ratio
b. Dividend yield
c. Dividend payout ratio

E13-10A. Financial Statement Notes The notes to financial statements present information on significant accounting policies, complex or special transactions, details of reported amounts, commitments, contingencies, segments, quarterly data, and subsequent events. Indicate which type of note disclosure is illustrated by each of the following notes: **LO6**

a. The company has agreed to purchase seven EMB-120 aircraft and related spare parts. The aggregate cost of these aircraft is approximately $35,500,000, subject to a cost escalation provision. The aircraft are scheduled to be delivered over the next two fiscal years.
b. The company has deferred certain costs related to major accounting and information systems enhancements that are anticipated to benefit future years. Upon completion, the related cost is amortized over a period not exceeding five years.
c. The company has guaranteed loans and leases of independent distributors approximating $26,800,000 as of December 31 of the current year.

d.   An officer of the company is also a director of a major raw material supplier of the company. The amount of raw material purchases from this supplier approximated $365,000 in the current year.

LO5   **E13-11A. Financial Statement Limitations**   You have been asked to perform financial statement analysis on the Patton Company. The Patton Company is a large chain of retail outlets that sells a wide range of household items. Last year the company introduced its own credit card and is pleased that profit from this financing activity now accounts for over twenty percent of the company's total profit. As part of your analysis you have chosen to compare the Patton Company to Johnson Stores, a much larger chain of stores. Johnson Stores sells household items and groceries, but it does not have its own credit card. Your analysis includes both horizontal trend analysis and vertical analysis. Identify some of the limitations from the description above.

EXERCISES—SET B

LO1   **E13-1B. Income Statement Sections**   During the current year, Newtech Corporation sold a segment of its business at a loss of $230,000. Until it was sold, the segment had a current period operating loss of $200,000. Also, the company had an extraordinary gain of $90,000 during the year as the result of an expropriation settlement received from a foreign government. The company has $800,000 income from continuing operations for the current year. Prepare the lower part of the income statement, beginning with the $800,000 income from continuing operations. Follow tax allocation procedures, assuming that all changes in income are subject to a 40 percent income tax rate. Disregard earnings per share disclosures.

LO4   **E13-2B. Earnings per Share**   Ewing Corporation began the year with a simple capital structure consisting of 38,000 shares of common stock outstanding. On May 1, 10,000 additional common shares were issued, and another 1,000 common shares were issued on September 1. The company had a net income for the year of $234,000. Calculate the earnings per share of common stock.

LO2   **E13-3B. Comparative Balance Sheets**   Consider the following balance sheet data for Great Buy Co., Inc., an electronics and major appliance retailer, at February 26, 2013 and February 27, 2012 (amounts in thousands):

	Feb. 26, 2013	Feb. 27, 2012
Cash and cash equivalents	$ 59,872	$ 7,138
Accounts receivables	52,944	37,968
Merchandise inventories	637,950	249,991
Other current assets	13,844	9,829
Current Assets	764,610	304,926
Property and equipment (net)	172,724	126,442
Other assets	15,160	7,774
Total Assets	$952,494	$439,142
Current Liabilities	$402,028	$186,005
Long-term liabilities	239,022	70,854
Total Liabilities	641,050	256,859
Common stock	2,087	1,149
Additional paid-in-capital	224,089	137,151
Retained earnings	85,268	43,983
Total Stockholders' Equity	311,444	182,283
Total Liabilities and Stockholders' Equity	$952,494	$439,142

a.   Prepare a comparative balance sheet, showing increases in dollars and percentages.
b.   Comment briefly on the changes between the two years.

E13-4B.   Common-Size Balance Sheets Refer to the balance sheet data given in Exercise E13-3B.   **LO3**

    a.   Prepare common-size balance sheets for each year (use total assets as the base amount for computing percentages).

    b.   Compare the common-size balance sheets and comment briefly.

E13-5B.   Ratios Analyzing Firm Profitability The following information is available for Crest Company: **LO4**

Annual Data	2013	2012
Sales revenue.	$6,400,000	$6,000,000
Cost of goods sold.	4,006,400	3,720,000
Net income.	307,200	264,000

Year-End Data	Dec. 31, 2013	Dec. 31, 2012
Total assets	$2,850,000	$2,360,000
Common stockholders' equity.	1,900,000	1,800,000

Calculate the following ratios for 2013:

    a.   Gross profit percentage

    b.   Return on sales

    c.   Asset turnover

    d.   Return on assets

    e.   Return on common stockholders' equity (Crest Company declared and paid preferred stock dividends of $25,000 in 2013.)

E13-6B.   Working Capital and Short-Term Firm Liquidity Ratios Favor Company has a current ratio of   **LO4**
2.08 (2.08:1) on December 31. On that date its current assets are as follows:

Cash and cash equivalents	$ 28,000
Short-term investments	87,000
Accounts receivable (net).	125,000
Inventory.	178,500
Prepaid expenses.	9,980
Current assets	$428,480

Favor Company's current liabilities at the beginning of the year were $192,000 and during the year its operating activities provided a cash flow of $33,830.

    a.   What are the firm's current liabilities at December 31?

    b.   What is the firm's working capital on December 31?

    c.   What is the quick ratio on December 31?

    d.   What is the firm's operating-cash-flow-to-current-liabilities ratio?

E13-7B.   Accounts Receivable and Inventory Ratios Favor Company, whose current assets at December   **LO4**
31 are shown in Exercise E13-6B, had net sales for the year of $522,750 and cost of goods sold of
$345,900. At the beginning of the year, accounts receivable (net) were $121,000 and inventory was
$165,700.

    a.   What is the company's accounts receivable turnover?

    b.   What is the company's average collection period?

    c.   What is the company's inventory turnover?

    d.   What is the company's days' sales in inventory?

LO4 **E13-8B.** **Ratios Analyzing Long-Term Firm Solvency** The following information is available for Percy Company:

Annual Data	2013	2012
Interest expense.	$175,000	$166,000
Income tax expense.	126,000	117,000
Net income.	294,000	273,000
Capital expenditures	440,000	350,000
Cash provided by operating activities	247,000	223,000

Year-End Data	Dec. 31, 2013	Dec. 31, 2012
Total liabilities.	$3,300,000	$2,900,000
Total stockholders' equity	2,200,000	1,900,000

Calculate the following:

a. 2013 debt-to-equity ratio
b. 2013 times-interest-earned ratio
c. 2013 operating-cash-flow-to-capital-expenditures ratio

LO4 **E13-9B.** **Financial Ratios for Common Stockholders** Henshue Corporation has only common stock outstanding. The firm reported earnings per share of $1.80 for the year. During the year, Henshue paid dividends of $0.81 per share. At year end, the current market price of the stock was $35.15 per share.
Calculate the following:

a. Year-end price-earnings ratio
b. Dividend yield
c. Dividend payout ratio

LO6 **E13-10B.** **Financial Statement Notes** Notes to the financial statements present information on significant accounting policies, complex or special transactions, details of reported amounts, commitments, contingencies, segments, quarterly data, and subsequent events. Indicate the type of note disclosure that is illustrated by each of the following notes:

a. Sales by the Farm and Equipment segment to independent dealers are recorded at the time of shipment to those dealers. Sales through company-owned retail stores are recorded at the time of sale to retail customers.
b. Members of the board of directors, the advisory board, and employees are not charged the vendor's commission on property sold at auction for their benefit. (From the notes of an auctioneer company.)
c. Sales to an airline company accounted for approximately 43 percent of the company's net sales in the current year.
d. The company's product liability insurance coverage with respect to insured events occurring after January 1 of the current year is substantially less than the amount of that insurance available in the recent past. The company is now predominantly self-insured in this area. The reduction in insurance coverage reflects trends in the liability insurance field generally and is not unique to the company.

LO5 **E13-11B.** **Financial Statement Limitations** You have been asked to perform financial statement analysis on the Anderson Company. The Anderson Company is a large manufacturer of construction machinery and vehicles. Last year the company closed down a segment of the business that produced mining equipment because it was not providing an adequate return on assets. This segment represented fifteen percent of the company's total assets. As part of your analysis you have chosen to compare the Anderson Company to Bertran, Inc., a much smaller manufacturer of equipment, although Bertran, Inc. also performs contract repairs for many other brands of equipment. Your analysis includes both horizontal trend analysis and vertical analysis. Identify some of the limitations from the description above.

PROBLEMS—SET A

P13-1A. Income Statement Format The following information from Belvidere Company's current operations is available: **LO1** ✓

Administrative expenses	$ 69,000
Cost of goods sold.	464,000
Sales revenue.	772,000
Flood loss (considered unusual and infrequent)	25,000
Selling expenses	87,000
Interest expense.	7,000
Loss from operations of discontinued segment.	60,000
Gain on disposal of discontinued segment	40,000
Income taxes:	
Amount applicable to ordinary operations	58,000
Reduction applicable to loss from operations of discontinued segment	24,000
Amount applicable to gain on disposal of discontinued segment	16,000
Reduction applicable to flood loss	10,000

Required
a.   Prepare a multiple-step income statement. (Disregard earnings per share.)
b.   Prepare a single-step income statement. (Disregard earnings per share.)

P13-2A. Earnings per Share Leland Corporation began the year with 120,000 shares of common stock outstanding. On March 1 an additional 10,000 shares of common stock were issued. On August 1, another 16,000 shares of common stock were issued. On November 1, 6,000 shares of common stock were acquired as Treasury Stock. Leland Corporation's net income for the calendar year is $501,000.   **LO4** ✓

Required
Calculate the company's earnings per share.

P13-3A. Earnings per Share and Multiple-Step Income Statement The following summarized data relate to Bowden Corporation's current operations: **LO1, 4** ✓

Sales revenue.	$745,000
Cost of goods sold.	450,000
Selling expenses	58,000
Administrative expenses	72,000
Loss from earthquake damages (considered unusual and infrequent)	40,000
Loss on sale of equipment.	5,000
Income tax expense (not allocated)	48,000
Shares of common stock	
Outstanding at January 1.	15,000 shares
Additional issued at May 1	7,000 shares
Additional issued at November 1	2,000 shares

Required
Prepare a multiple-step income statement for Bowden Corporation for the year. Assume a 40 percent income tax rate. Allocate income tax expense within the income statement. Include earnings per share disclosure at the bottom of the income statement.

LO2 **P13-4A.** **Trend Percentages** Net sales, net income, and total asset figures for Vibrant Controls, Inc., for five consecutive years are given below (Vibrant manufactures pollution controls):

	Annual Amounts (Thousands of Dollars)				
	Year 1	Year 2	Year 3	Year 4	Year 5
Net sales..............................	$71,500	$79,800	$84,250	$88,400	$94,700
Net income...........................	3,200	3,650	3,900	4,160	4,790
Total assets	42,500	45,400	48,700	51,000	54,900

Required
a. Calculate trend percentages, using Year 1 as the base year.
b. Calculate the return on sales for each year. (Rates above 2.8 percent are considered good for manufacturers of pollution controls; rates above 6.4 percent are considered very good.)
c. Comment on the results of your analysis.

LO4 **P13-5A.** **Changes in Various Ratios** Presented below is selected information for Brimmer Company:

	2013	2012
Sales revenue...	$910,000	$840,000
Cost of goods sold......................................	575,000	542,000
Interest expense..	20,000	20,000
Income tax expense.....................................	27,000	24,000
Net income...	61,000	52,000
Cash flow from operating activities	65,000	55,000
Capital expenditures	42,000	45,000
Accounts receivable (net), December 31	126,000	120,000
Inventory, December 31.................................	196,000	160,000
Stockholders' equity, December 31......................	450,000	400,000
Total assets, December 31.............................	730,000	660,000

Required
a. Calculate the following ratios for 2013. The 2012 results are given for comparative purposes.

		2012
1.	Gross profit percentage	35.5 percent
2.	Return on assets	8.3 percent
3.	Return on sales	6.2 percent
4.	Return on common stockholders' equity (no preferred stock was outstanding)...............................	13.9 percent
5.	Accounts receivable turnover....................................	8.00
6.	Average collection period.......................................	45.6 days
7.	Inventory turnover	3.61
8.	Times-interest-earned ratio	4.80
9.	Operating-cash-flow-to-capital-expenditures ratio	1.22

b. Comment on the changes between the two years.

LO2, 3, 4 **P13-6A.** **Ratios from Comparative and Common-Size Data** Consider the following financial statements for Waverly Company.

During 2013, management obtained additional bond financing to enlarge its production facilities. The company faced higher production costs during the year for such things as fuel, materials, and freight. Because of temporary government price controls, a planned price increase on products was delayed several months.

As a holder of both common and preferred stock, you decide to analyze the financial statements:

WAVERLY COMPANY Balance Sheets (Thousands of Dollars)	Dec. 31, 2013	Dec. 31, 2012
Assets		
Cash and cash equivalents	$ 18,000	$ 12,000
Accounts receivable (net)	55,000	43,000
Inventory	120,000	105,000
Prepaid expenses	20,000	14,000
Plant and other assets (net)	471,000	411,000
Total Assets	$684,000	$585,000
Liabilities and Stockholders' Equity		
Current liabilities	$ 90,000	$ 82,000
10% Bonds payable	225,000	160,000
9% Preferred stock, $50 Par Value	75,000	75,000
Common stock, $10 Par Value	200,000	200,000
Retained earnings	94,000	68,000
Total Liabilities and Stockholders' Equity	$684,000	$585,000

WAVERLY COMPANY Income Statements (Thousands of Dollars)	2013	2012
Sales revenue	$820,000	$678,000
Cost of goods sold	541,200	433,920
Gross profit on sales	278,800	244,080
Selling and administrative expenses	171,400	149,200
Income before interest expense and income taxes	107,400	94,880
Interest expense	22,500	16,000
Income before income taxes	84,900	78,880
Income tax expense	22,900	21,300
Net income	$ 62,000	$ 57,580
Other financial data (thousands of dollars)		
Cash provided by operating activities	$ 65,200	$ 60,500
Preferred stock dividends	6,750	6,750

Required

a. Calculate the following for each year: current ratio, quick ratio, operating-cash-flow-to-current-liabilities ratio (current liabilities were $78,000,000 at January 1, 2012), inventory turnover (inventory was $87,000,000 at January 1, 2012), debt-to-equity ratio, times-interest-earned ratio, return on assets (total assets were $493,000,000 at January 1, 2012), and return on common stockholders' equity (common stockholders' equity was $236,000,000 at January 1, 2012).

b. Calculate common-size percentages for each year's income statement.

c. Comment on the results of your analysis.

P13-7A.   Constructing Statements from Ratio Data The following are the 2012 financial statements for Omicron Company, with almost all dollar amounts missing: **LO4**

✓

OMICRON COMPANY
Balance Sheet
December 31, 2012

Cash..........................	$	?	Current liabilities..............	$	?
Accounts receivable (net).........		?	8% Bonds payable............		?
Inventory......................		?	Common stock...............		?
Equipment (net)		?	Retained earnings		900,000
			Total Liabilities and		
Total Assets..................	$5,900,000		Stockholders' Equity.........	$5,900,000	

OMICRON COMPANY
Income Statement
For the Year Ended December 31, 2012

Sales revenue...	$	?
Cost of goods sold.......................................		?
Gross profit...		?
Selling and administrative expenses		?
Income before interest expense and income taxes................		?
Interest expense..		80,000
Income before income taxes		?
Income tax expense (30%).................................		?
Net income...		$560,000

The following information is available about Omicron Company's financial statements:

1. Quick ratio, 0.90.
2. Inventory turnover (inventory at January 1 was $924,000), 5 times.
3. Return on sales, 8.0 percent.
4. Accounts receivable turnover (accounts receivable (net) at January 1 were $860,000), 8 times.
5. Gross profit percentage, 32 percent.
6. Return on common stockholders' equity (common stockholders' equity at January 1 was $3,300,000), 16 percent.
7. The interest expense relates to the bonds payable that were outstanding all year.

Required
Compute the missing amounts, and complete the financial statements of Omicron Company. *Hint:* Complete the income statement first.

LO4   P13-8A.   Ratios Compared with Industry Averages Because you own the common stock of Phantom Corporation, a paper manufacturer, you decide to analyze the firm's performance for the most recent year. The following data are taken from the firm's latest annual report:

	Dec. 31, 2013	Dec. 31, 2012
Quick assets..	$ 600,000	$ 552,000
Inventory and prepaid expenses	372,000	312,000
Other assets.......................................	4,788,000	4,176,000
Total Assets	$5,760,000	$5,040,000
Current liabilities..	$ 624,000	$ 540,000
10% Bonds payable......................................	1,440,000	1,440,000
8% Preferred stock, $100 par value.........................	480,000	480,000
Common stock, $10 par value.............................	2,700,000	2,160,000
Retained earnings	516,000	420,000
Total Liabilities and Stockholders' Equity	$5,760,000	$5,040,000

For 2013, net sales amount to $11,280,000, net income is $573,600, and preferred stock dividends paid are $38,400.

Required

a. Calculate the following ratios for 2013:
   1. Return on sales
   2. Return on assets
   3. Return on common stockholders' equity
   4. Quick ratio
   5. Current ratio
   6. Debt-to-equity ratio

b. Trade association statistics and information provided by credit agencies reveal the following data on industry norms:

	Median	Upper Quartile
Return on sales	4.9 percent	8.6 percent
Return on assets	6.5 percent	11.2 percent
Return on common stockholders' equity	10.6 percent	17.3 percent
Quick ratio	1.0	1.8
Current ratio	1.8	3.0
Debt-to-equity-ratio	1.08	0.66

   Compare Phantom Corporation's performance with industry performance.

P13-9A. **Ratios Compared with Industry Averages** Packard Plastics, Inc., manufactures various plastic and synthetic products. Financial statement data for the firm follow:

LO4

	2013 (Thousands of Dollars, except Earnings per Share)
Sales revenue	$815,000
Cost of goods sold	540,000
Net income	50,500
Dividends	14,000
Earnings per share	4.04

Packard Plastics, Inc. Balance Sheets (Thousands of Dollars)	Dec. 31, 2013	Dec. 31, 2012
Assets		
Cash	$ 4,100	$ 2,700
Accounts receivable (net)	66,900	60,900
Inventory	148,000	140,000
Total Current Assets	219,000	203,600
Plant assets (net)	215,000	194,000
Other assets	5,300	3,900
Total Assets	$439,300	$401,500
Liabilities and Stockholders' Equity		
Notes payable—banks	$ 31,000	$ 25,000
Accounts payable	27,600	23,000
Accrued liabilities	25,100	24,800
Total Current Liabilities	83,700	72,800
10% Bonds payable	150,000	150,000
Total Liabilities	233,700	222,800
Common stock, $10 par value (12,500,000 shares)	125,000	125,000
Retained earnings	80,600	53,700
Total Stockholders' Equity	205,600	178,700
Total Liabilities and Stockholders' Equity	$439,300	$401,500

Required

a. Using the given data, calculate items 1 through 8 below for 2013. Compare the performance of Packard Plastics, Inc., with the following industry averages and comment on its operations.

		Median Ratios for Manufacturers of Plastic and Synthetic Products
1.	Quick ratio	1.2
2.	Current ratio	1.9
3.	Accounts receivable turnover.	7.9
4.	Inventory turnover	7.8
5.	Debt-to-equity ratio	0.95
6.	Gross profit percentage	32.7 percent
7.	Return on sales	3.5 percent
8.	Return on assets	6.3 percent

b. Calculate the dividends paid per share of common stock. What was the dividend payout ratio?

c. If the most recent price per share of common stock is $47.75, what is the price-earnings ratio? The dividend yield?

LO2, 4   **P13-10A.** **Financial Statement Notes: Quarterly Data** Quarterly data are presented below for Company A and Company B. One of these companies is Gibson Greetings, Inc., which manufactures and sells greeting cards. The other company is Hon Industries, Inc., which manufactures and sells office furniture. Both companies are on a calendar year basis.

	(Amounts in Thousands)				
	First Quarter	Second Quarter	Third Quarter	Fourth Quarter	Year
Company A					
Net sales.	$186,111	$177,537	$203,070	$213,608	$780,326
Gross profit.	55,457	53,643	64,024	69,374	242,498
Company B					
Net sales.	$ 84,896	$ 83,796	$142,137	$235,336	$546,165
Gross profit.	53,900	52,983	66,018	104,961	277,862

Required

a. Compute the percent of annual net sales generated each quarter by Company A. Round to the nearest percent.

b. Compute the percent of annual net sales generated each quarter by Company B. Round to the nearest percent.

c. Which company has the most seasonal business? Briefly explain.

d. Which company is Gibson Greetings, Inc.? Hon Industries, Inc.? Briefly explain.

e. Which company's interim quarterly data are probably most useful for predicting annual results? Briefly explain.

PROBLEMS—SET B

LO1   **P13-1B.** **Income Statement Format** The following information from Tricon Company's operations is available:

Administrative expenses	$ 138,000
Cost of goods sold	928,000
Sales revenue	1,544,000
Selling expenses	174,000
Interest expense	14,000
Loss from operations of discontinued segment	120,000
Flood loss (considered unusual and infrequent)	50,000
Gain on disposal of discontinued segment	80,000
Income taxes	
Amount applicable to ordinary operations	116,000
Reduction applicable to loss from operations of discontinued segment	68,000
Amount applicable to gain on disposal of discontinued segment	32,000
Reduction applicable to flood loss	20,000

Required

a.   Prepare a multiple-step income statement. (Disregard earnings per share amounts.)

b.   Prepare a single-step income statement. (Disregard earnings per share amounts.)

P13-2B.   **Earnings per Share**   Island Corporation began the year with 25,000 shares of common stock outstanding. On May 1, an additional 9,000 shares of common stock were issued. On July 1, 6,000
shares of common stock were acquired as treasury stock. On September 1, the 6,000 treasury shares
of common stock were reissued. Island Corporation's net income for the calendar year is $230,000.

LO4

Required
Compute earnings per share.

P13-3B.   **Earnings per Share and Multiple-Step Income Statement**   The following summarized data are
related to Garner Corporation's operations:

LO1, 4

Sales revenue	$2,220,000
Cost of goods sold	1,290,000
Selling expenses	180,000
Administrative expenses	143,000
Gain from expropriation of property by foreign government	190,000
Loss from plant strike	97,000
Shares of common stock	
Outstanding at January 1	61,000 shares
Additional issued at April 1	17,000 shares
Additional issued at August 1	3,000 shares

Required
Prepare a multiple-step income statement for Garner Corporation. Assume a 40 percent income tax
rate. Include earnings per share disclosure at the bottom of the income statement. Garner Corporation
has no preferred stock.

P13-4B.   **Trend Percentages**   Sales of automotive products for Ford Motor Company and General Motors
Corporation for a five-year period are:

LO2

	Net Sales of Automotive Products (Millions of Dollars)				
	Year 1	Year 2	Year 3	Year 4	Year 5
Ford Motor Company	$82,879	$81,844	$72,051	$ 84,407	$ 91,568
General Motors Corporation	99,106	97,312	94,828	103,005	108,027

Net sales for Pfizer Inc. and Abbott Laboratories for the same five years follow:

	Net Sales (Millions of Dollars)				
	Year 1	Year 2	Year 3	Year 4	Year 5
Pfizer Inc.	$5,672	$6,406	$6,950	$7,230	$7,478
Abbott Laboratories	5,380	6,159	6,877	7,852	8,408

Required

a. Calculate trend percentages for all four companies, using Year 1 as the base year.
b. Comment on the trend percentage of Ford Motor Company and General Motors Corporation.
c. Comment on the trend percentages of Pfizer Inc. and Abbott Laboratories.

LO2, 4   P13-5B.   Changes in Various Ratios Selected information follow for Cycle Company:

	2013	2012
Sales revenue.	$675,000	$520,000
Cost of goods sold.	407,700	310,000
Interest expense.	18,000	14,000
Income tax expense.	6,200	5,100
Net income.	24,600	20,300
Cash flow from operating activities	29,500	26,500
Capital expenditures	40,000	25,000
Accounts receivable (net), December 31	182,000	128,000
Inventory, December 31.	225,000	180,000
Stockholders' equity, December 31.	205,000	165,000
Total assets, December 31.	460,000	350,000

Required

a. Calculate the following ratios for 2013. The 2012 results are given for comparative purposes.

		2012
1.	Gross profit percentage	40.4 percent
2.	Return on assets	6.3 percent
3.	Return on sales	3.9 percent
4.	Return on common stockholders' equity (no preferred stock was outstanding).	14.0 percent
5.	Accounts receivable turnover.	4.77
6.	Average collection period.	76.5 days
7.	Inventory turnover	2.07
8.	Times-interest-earned ratio	2.81
9.	Operating-cash-flow-to-capital-expenditures ratio	1.06

b. Comment on the changes between the two years.

LO2, 3, 4   P13-6B.   Ratios from Comparative and Common-Size Data Consider the following financial statements for Vega Company.

  During the year, management obtained additional bond financing to enlarge its production facilities. The plant addition produced a new high-margin product, which is supposed to improve the average rate of gross profit and return on sales.

  As a potential investor, you decide to analyze the financial statements:

VEGA COMPANY Balance Sheets (Thousands of Dollars)	Dec. 31, 2013	Dec. 31, 2012
Assets		
Cash..	$ 21,000	$ 16,100
Accounts receivable (net).................................	39,000	21,400
Inventory...	105,000	72,000
Prepaid expenses.......................................	1,500	3,000
Plant and other assets (net)	463,500	427,500
Total Assets	$630,000	$540,000
Liabilities and Stockholders' Equity		
Current liabilities.......................................	$ 76,000	$ 45,000
9% Bonds payable......................................	187,500	150,000
8% Preferred stock, $50 par value.......................	60,000	60,000
Common stock, $10 par value............................	225,000	225,000
Retained earnings	81,500	60,000
Total Liabilities and Stockholders' Equity	$630,000	$540,000

VEGA COMPANY Income Statements (Thousands of Dollars)	2013	2012
Sales revenue..	$840,000	$697,500
Cost of goods sold......................................	552,000	474,000
Gross profit on sales....................................	288,000	223,500
Selling and administrative expenses	231,000	174,000
Income before interest expense and income taxes...........	57,000	49,500
Interest expense.......................................	16,800	13,500
Income before income taxes	40,200	36,000
Income tax expense.....................................	14,100	12,600
Net income..	$ 26,100	$ 23,400
Other financial data (thousands of dollars):		
Cash provided by operating activities	$ 30,000	$ 25,000
Preferred stock dividends............................	4,800	4,800

Required

a. Calculate the following for each year: current ratio, quick ratio, operating-cash-flow-to-current-liabilities ratio (current liabilities were $42 million at January 1, 2012), inventory turnover (inventory was $68 million at January 1, 2012), debt-to-equity ratio, times-interest-earned ratio, return on assets (total assets were $472 million at January 1, 2012), and return on common stockholders' equity (common stockholders' equity was $266 million at January 1, 2012).

b. Calculate common-size percentage for each year's income statement.

c. Comment on the results of your analysis.

P13-7B. Constructing Statements from Ratio Data The following are the financial statements for Timber Company, with almost all dollar amounts missing:

LO4

✓

TIMBER COMPANY			
Balance Sheet			
December 31			
Cash..........................	$?	Current liabilities.................	$?
Accounts receivable (net)..........	?	10% Bonds payable..............	144,000
Inventory.......................	?	Common stock..................	?
Equipment (net)	?	Retained earnings	48,000
		Total Liabilities and	
Total Assets	$576,000	Stockholders' Equity...........	$576,000

TIMBER COMPANY	
Income Statement	
For the Year Ended December 31	
Sales revenue...	$?
Cost of goods sold..	?
Gross profit on sales	?
Selling and administrative expenses	?
Income before interest expense and income taxes.....................	?
Interest expense...	?
Income before income taxes	?
Income tax expense (35%)..	?
Net income..	$70,200

The following information is available about Timber Company's financial statements:

1. Quick ratio, 1.65.
2. Current ratio, 3.15.
3. Return on sales, 7.5 percent.
4. Return on common stockholders' equity (common stockholders' equity at January 1 was $342,000), 20 percent.
5. Gross profit percentage, 30 percent.
6. Accounts receivable turnover (accounts receivable (net) at January 1 were $97,200), 10 times.
7. The interest expense relates to the bonds payable that were outstanding all year.

Required
Compute the missing amounts, and complete the financial statements of Timber Company. (*Hint:* Complete the income statement first.)

LO4 **P13-8B.** **Ratios Compared with Industry Averages** You are analyzing the performance of Lumite Corporation, a manufacturer of personal care products, for the most recent year. The following data are taken from the firm's latest annual report:

	Dec. 31, 2013	Dec. 31, 2012
Quick assets.......................................	$ 290,000	$ 250,000
Inventory and prepaid expenses	945,000	820,000
Other assets.......................................	4,165,000	3,700,000
Total Assets	$5,400,000	$4,770,000
Current liabilities....................................	$ 500,000	$ 400,000
10% Bonds payable...................................	1,300,000	1,300,000
7% Preferred stock	900,000	900,000
Common stock, $5 par value...........................	1,900,000	1,800,000
Retained earnings	800,000	370,000
Total Liabilities and Stockholders' Equity	$5,400,000	$4,770,000

In 2013, net sales amount to $8,600,000, net income is $675,000, and preferred stock dividends paid are $63,000.

Required

a. Calculate the following for 2013:
   1. Return on sales
   2. Return on assets
   3. Return on common stockholders' equity
   4. Quick ratio
   5. Current ratio
   6. Debt-to-equity ratio

b. Trade association statistics and information provided by credit agencies reveal the following data on industry norms:

	Median	Upper Quartile
Return on sales	3.7 percent	10.6 percent
Return on assets	5.8 percent	14.2 percent
Return on common stockholders' equity	18.5 percent	34.2 percent
Quick ratio	1.0	1.8
Current ratio	2.2	3.7
Debt-to-equity ratio	1.07	0.37

Compare Lumite Corporation's performance with industry performance.

P13-9B. **Ratios Compared with Industry Averages** Avery Instrument, Inc., is a manufacturer of various measuring and controlling instruments. Financial statement data for the firm are as follows:

LO4

	2013 (Thousands of Dollars, except Earnings per Share)
Sales revenue	$210,000
Cost of goods sold	125,000
Net income	8,300
Dividends	2,600
Earnings per share	4.15

AVERY INSTRUMENTS, INC. Balance Sheets (Thousands of Dollars)	Dec. 31, 2013	Dec. 31, 2012
Assets		
Cash	$ 18,300	$ 18,000
Accounts receivable (net)	46,000	41,000
Inventory	39,500	43,700
Total Current Assets	103,800	102,700
Plant assets (net)	52,600	50,500
Other assets	15,600	13,800
Total Assets	$172,000	$167,000
Liabilities and Stockholders' Equity		
Notes payable—banks	$ 6,000	$ 6,000
Accounts payable	22,500	18,700
Accrued liabilities	16,500	21,000
Total Current Liabilities	45,000	45,700
9% Bonds payable	40,000	40,000
Total Liabilities	85,000	85,700
Common stock, $25 par value (2,000,000 shares)	50,000	50,000
Retained earnings	37,000	31,300
Total Stockholders' Equity	87,000	81,300
Total Liabilities and Stockholders' Equity	$172,000	$167,000

Required

a.   Using the given data, calculate ratios 1 through 8 for 2013. Compare the performance of Avery Instruments, Inc., with the following industry averages and comment on its operations.

		Median Ratios for Manufacturers of Measuring and Controlling Instruments
1.	Quick ratio	1.3
2.	Current ratio.............................	2.4
3.	Accounts receivable turnover................	5.9 times
4.	Inventory turnover	3.5 times
5.	Debt-to-equity ratio	0.73
6.	Gross profit percentage....................	42.8 percent
7.	Return on sales	4.5 percent
8.	Return on assets	7.6 percent

b.   Calculate the dividends paid per share of common stock. What was the dividend payout ratio?

c.   If the most recent price per share of common stock is $62.25, what is the price-earnings ratio? The dividend yield?

LO2, 4   **P13-10B.** **Financial Statement Notes: Quarterly Data** Quarterly data are presented below for Company C and Company D. One of these companies is Toys "R" Us, a children's specialty retail chain. The company's fiscal year ends on the Saturday nearest to January 31. The other company is the Gillette Company prior to its acquisition by Procter & Gamble. Gillette manufactures and sells blades, razors, and toiletries. Gillette was on a calendar year basis.

	(Amounts in Thousands)				
	First Quarter	Second Quarter	Third Quarter	Fourth Quarter	Year
Company C					
Net Sales	$1,216.6	$1,237.3	$1,339.7	$1,617.2	$5,410.8
Gross profit..................	753.1	773.6	839.0	1,000.8	3,366.5
Company D					
Net Sales	$1,172.5	$1,249.1	$1,345.8	$3,401.8	$7,169.2
Gross profit..................	362.5	384.6	423.2	1,030.3	2,200.6

Required

a.   Compute the percentage of annual net sales generated each quarter by Company C. Round to the nearest percent.

b.   Compute the percentage of annual net sales generated each quarter by Company D. Round to the nearest percent.

c.   Which company has the most seasonal business? Briefly explain.

d.   Which company is Toys "R" Us? The Gillette Company? Briefly explain.

SERIAL PROBLEM: KATE'S CARDS

(Note: This is a continuation of the Serial Problem: Kate's Cards from Chapter 1 through Chapter 12.)

SP13.   Kate is very pleased with the results of the first year of operations for Kate's Cards. She ended the year on a high note, with the company's reputation for producing quality cards leading to more business than she can currently manage. Kate is considering expanding and bringing in several employees. In order to do this, she will need to find a larger location and also purchase more equipment. All this means additional financing. Kate has asked you to look at her year-end financial statements as if you were a banker considering giving Kate a loan. Comment on your findings and provide calculations to support your comments.

KATE'S CARDS
Income Statement
Year Ended August 31, 2013

Sales revenue	$135,000
Cost of goods sold	72,000
Gross profit	63,000
Operating expenses	
Wages	18,000
Consulting	11,850
Insurance	1,200
Utilities	2,400
Depreciation	3,250
Total operating expenses	36,700
Income from operations	26,300
Interest expense	900
Income before income tax	25,400
Income tax expense	8,900
Net income	$ 16,500

KATE'S CARDS
Balance Sheet
August 31, 2013

Assets	
Current assets	
Cash	$12,300
Accounts receivable	11,000
Inventory	16,000
Prepaid insurance	1,000
Total current assets	40,300
Equipment	17,500
Accumulated depreciation	3,250
Total assets	$54,550
Liabilities	
Current liabilities	
Accounts payable	$ 6,200
Unearned revenue	1,250
Other current liabilities	1,900
Total current liabilities	9,350
Note payable	15,000
Total liabilities	24,350
Stockholders' equity	
Common stock	500
Additional paid-in-capital	9,500
Preferred stock	5,000
Retained earnings	15,200
Total stockholders' equity	30,200
Total liabilities and stockholders' equity	$54,550

KATE'S CARDS Statement of Cash Flows Year Ended August 31, 2013	
Cash flow from operating activities	
Net income	$16,500
Add depreciation	3,250
Increase in accounts receivable	(11,000)
Increase in inventory	(16,000)
Increase in prepaid expenses	(1,000)
Increase in accounts payable	6,200
Increase in unearned revenue	1,250
Increase in other current liabilities	1,900
Cash provided by operating activities	1,100
Cash flow from investing activities	
Purchase of equipment	(17,500)
Cash used by investing activities	(17,500)
Cash flow from financing activities	
Proceeds from bank note	15,000
Issuance of common stock	10,000
Issuance of preferred stock	5,000
Cash dividends	(1,300)
Cash provided by financing activities	28,700
Net increase in cash	12,300
Cash at beginning of year	0
Cash at end of year	$12,300

EXTENDING YOUR KNOWLEDGE

REPORTING AND ANALYSIS

COLUMBIA
SPORTSWEAR
COMPANY

EYK13-1. Financial Reporting Problem: Columbia Sportswear Company The financial statements for the Columbia Sportswear Company can be found in Appendix A at the end of this book.

You are considering an investment in Columbia Sportswear after a recent outdoor trip in which you really liked some of the clothes you purchased from the company. You decide to do an analysis of the company's financial statements in order to help you make an informed decision.

Required

a. Using the five year selected financial data reported in the annual report, produce a 5-year trend analysis, using 2007 as a base year, of (1) net sales, (2) net income, and (3) total assets. Comment on your findings.

b. Calculate the (1) gross profit percentage, (2) return on sales, and (3) return on assets for 2010 and 2011. Comment on Columbia Sportswear's profitability. (2009 total assets = $1,212,883,000)

c. Calculate the (1) current ratio, (2) quick ratio, and (3) operating-cash-flow-to-current-liabilities ratio for 2010 and 2011. (2009 current liabilities = $179,287,000) Comment on Columbia Sportswear's liquidity.

d. Calculate the debt-to-equity ratio for 2010 and 2011. Comment on Columbia Sportswear's solvency.

COLUMBIA
SPORTSWEAR
COMPANY

UNDER ARMOUR,
INC.

EYK13-2. Comparative Analysis Problem: Columbia Sportswear Company vs Under Armour, Inc. The financial statements for the Columbia Sportswear Company can be found in Appendix A at the end of this book, and the financial statements of Under Armour, Inc. can be found in Appendix B (the complete annual report is available on this book's Website).

Required

Based on the information from the financial statements of each company, do the following.

a.   Calculate the percentage change in (1) net sales, (2) net income, (3) cash flow from operating activities, and (4) total assets from 2010 to 2011.

b.   What conclusions can you draw from this analysis?

EYK13-3.   Business Decision Problem   Crescent Paints, Inc., a paint manufacturer, has been in business for five years. The company has had modest profits and has experienced few operating difficulties until this year, 2013, when president Alice Becknell discussed her company's working capital problems with you, a loan officer at Granite Bank. Becknell explained that expanding her firm has created difficulties in meeting obligations when they come due and in taking advantage of cash discounts offered by manufacturers for the timely payment of the company's accounts payable. She would like to borrow $50,000 from Granite Bank. At your request, Becknell submits the following financial data for the past two years:

	2013	2012
Sales revenue.	$2,000,000	$1,750,000
Cost of goods sold.	1,320,000	1,170,000
Net income.	42,000	33,600
Dividends	22,000	18,000
December 31, 2011, data.		
Total assets	1,100,000	
Accounts receivable (net).	205,000	
Inventory.	350,000	

CRESCENT PAINTS, INC.		
Balance Sheets	Dec. 31, 2013	Dec. 31, 2012
Assets		
Cash.	$ 31,000	$ 50,000
Accounts receivable (net).	345,000	250,000
Inventory.	525,000	425,000
Prepaid expenses.	11,000	6,000
Total Current Assets.	912,000	731,000
Plant assets (net)	483,000	444,000
Total Assets	$1,395,000	$ 1,175,000
Liabilities and Stockholders' Equity		
Notes payable—banks.	$ 100,000	$ 35,000
Accounts payable.	244,000	190,000
Accrued liabilities	96,000	85,000
Total Current Liabilities.	440,000	310,000
10% Mortgage payable	190,000	250,000
Total Liabilities	630,000	560,000
Common stock.	665,000	535,000
Retained earnings	100,000	80,000
Total Stockholders' Equity	765,000	615,000
Total Liabilities and Stockholders' Equity	$1,395,000	$1,175,000

Calculate the following items for both years from the given data and then compare them with the median ratios for paint manufacturers provided by a commercial credit firm:

	Median Ratios for Paint Manufacturers
1. Current ratio	2.5
2. Quick ratio	1.3
3. Accounts receivable turnover.	8.1
4. Average collection period.	44.9 days
5. Inventory turnover	4.9
6. Debt-to-equity ratio	0.78
7. Return on assets	4.8%
8. Return on sales	2.4%

Required

Based on your analysis, decide whether and under what circumstances you would grant Becknell's request for a loan. Explain the reasons for your decision.

HONEYWELL INTERNATIONAL, INC.

THE DOW CHEMICAL COMPANY

ABBOTT LABORATORIES

EYK13-4. **Financial Analysis Problem** Listed below are selected financial data for three corporations: **Honeywell International, Inc.** (environmental controls), **The Dow Chemical Company** (chemicals and plastic products), and **Abbott Laboratories** (health care products). These data cover five years (Year 5 is the most recent year; net income in thousands):

	Year 5	Year 4	Year 3	Year 2	Year 1
Honeywell International, Inc.					
Net income.	$278,900	$322,200	$246,800	$331,100	$381,900
Earnings per common share	$2.15	$2.40	$1.78	$2.35	$2.52
Dividend per common share	$1.00	$0.91	$0.84	$0.77	$0.70
The Dow Chemical Company					
Net income.	$938,000	$644,000	$276,000	$942,000	$1,384,000
Earnings per common share	$3.88	$2.33	$0.99	$3.46	$5.10
Dividend per common share	$2.60	$2.60	$2.60	$2.60	$2.60
Abbott Laboratories					
Net income*	$1,399,100	$1,239,100	$1,088,700	$965,800	$859,800
Earnings per common share*.	$1.69	$1.47	$1.27	$1.11	$0.96
Dividend per common share	$0.68	$0.60	$0.50	$0.42	$0.35

*Before extraordinary gain and accounting change

Required

a. Calculate the dividend payout ratio for each company for each of the five years.
b. Companies may differ in their dividend policy; that is, they may differ in whether they emphasize a constant dividend amount per share, a steady growth in dividend amount per share, a target or constant dividend payout ratio, or some other criterion. Based on the data available, identify what appears to be each of the above firm's dividend policy over the five-year period.

CRITICAL THINKING

GENERAL MILLS, INC.

EYK13-5. **Accounting Research Problem: General Mills, Inc.** The fiscal year 2011 annual report of General Mills, Inc. is available on this book's Website.

Required

a. Calculate (or identify) the following financial ratios for 2010 and 2011:
   1. Gross profit percentage
   2. Return on sales
   3. Asset turnover (2009, total assets = $17,874.8 million)
   4. Return on assets (2009, total assets = $17,874.8 million)
   5. Return on common stockholders' equity (2009, total stockholders' equity = $5,172.3 million)
   6. Current ratio
   7. Quick ratio

8. Operating-cash-flow-to-current-liabilities ratio (2009, current liabilities = $3,606 million)
9. Accounts receivable turnover (2009, accounts receivable = $953.4 million)
10. Average collection period
11. Inventory turnover (2009, inventory = $1,346.8 million)
12. Days' sales in inventory
13. Debt-to-equity ratio
14. Times-interest-earned ratio
15. Operating-cash-flow-to-capital-expenditures ratio
16. Earnings per share
17. Price-earnings ratio (Use year-end adjusted closing stock price of $37.44 for 2011 and $32.91 for 2010.)
18. Dividend yield
19. Dividend payout ratio

    b.   Comment briefly on the changes from fiscal 2010 to fiscal 2011 in the ratios computed above.

EYK13-6. **Accounting Communication Activity** Pete Hollingsworth is currently taking an accounting course and is confused about what his professor told the class about analyzing financial statements. Pete would like you to lead a study session on the topic. In order to help everyone out, you decide to write a short memo describing some of the key points.

Required
Include the following items in your memo:
a.   What is meant by trend analysis and how is it helpful?
b.   How are common-size statements constructed and what are their uses?
c.   What are a few common profitability, liquidity, and solvency ratios and how are they interpreted?
d.   What are some limitations of financial statement analysis?

EYK13-7. **Accounting Ethics Case** Chris Nelson, the new assistant controller for Grand Company, is preparing for the firm's year-end closing procedures. On December 30, 2012, a memorandum from the controller directed Nelson to make a journal entry debiting Cash and crediting Long-Term Advances to Officers for $1,000,000. Not finding the $1,000,000 in the cash deposit prepared for the bank that day, Nelson went to the controller for a further explanation. In response, the controller took from her desk drawer a check for $1,000,000 payable to Grand Company from Jason Grand, chief executive officer of the firm. Attached to the check was a note from Jason Grand saying that if this check were not needed to return it to him next week.

"This check is paying off a $1,000,000 advance the firm made to Jason Grand six years ago," stated the controller. "Mr. Grand has done this every year since the advance; each time we have returned the check to him in January of the following year. We plan to do so again this time. In fact, when Mr. Grand retires in four years, I expect the board of directors will forgive this advance. However, if the firm really needed the cash, we would deposit the check."

"Then why go through this charade each year?" inquired Nelson.

"It dresses up our year-end balance sheet," replied the controller. "Certain financial statement ratios are improved significantly. Further, the notes to the financial statements don't have to reveal a related-party loan. Lots of firms engage in year-end transactions designed to dress up their financial statements."

Required
a.   What financial statement ratios are improved by making the journal entry contained in the controller's memorandum?
b.   Is the year-end handling of Jason Grand's advance an ethical practice? Discuss.

EYK13-8. **Corporate Social Responsibility Problem** The chapter highlighted one way in which the **Procter & Gamble Company** demonstrates its commitment to being a good corporate citizen (see Page 604). Go to Procter & Gamble's Website and navigate to the section on sustainability. From there you can download their annual sustainability report. The report contains a section on social responsibility. In addition to the joint effort with UNICEF, what are some other ways that P&G demonstrates its commitment to being a good corporate citizen?

PROCTER
& GAMBLE
COMPANY

EYK13-9.   **Forensic Accounting Problem**   Accrual accounting is based on the principle that revenue should be reported when earned and that expenses associated with that revenue should be matched against the revenue in the same period. Some financial statement frauds violate this fundamental concept in order to overstate net income in the current year. Provide an example of how this may be accomplished.

EYK13-10. **Working with the Takeaways**   Below are income statements and balance sheets for the Fango Company for 2013 and 2012:

FANGO COMPANY Income Statement For the Years Ended December 31, 2013 and 2012		
(in millions)	**2013**	**2012**
Sales revenue.	$10,000	$9,500
Cost of goods sold.	5,500	5,200
Gross profit.	4,500	4,300
Selling and administrative expenses	2,800	2,700
Income from operations.	1,700	1,600
Interest expense.	300	250
Income before income taxes	1,400	1,350
Income tax expense.	420	400
Net income.	$ 980	$ 950

FANGO COMPANY Balance Sheet December 31, 2013 and 2012		
(in millions)	**2013**	**2012**
Assets		
Current assets		
Cash and cash equivalents	$ 200	$ 400
Accounts receivable.	900	800
Inventory.	700	650
Other current assets.	400	250
Total current assets	2,200	2,100
Property, plant, & equipment (net)	2,600	2,500
Other assets.	5,700	5,900
Total assets	$10,500	$10,500
Liabilities and Stockholders' Equity		
Current liabilities.	$ 3,000	$ 2,900
Long-term liabilities	5,000	5,400
Total liabilities.	8,000	8,300
Stockholders' equity—common.	2,500	2,200
Total liabilities and stockholders' equity	$10,500	$10,500

Required

Calculate the following ratios for the Fango Company for 2013 and 2012 and discuss your findings:

1. Profitability
   a.   Return on sales
   b.   Return on common stockholders' equity (common stockholders' equity was $2,000 on December 31, 2011)

2. Liquidity
  a. Current ratio
  b. Accounts receivable turnover (accounts receivable was $780 on December 31, 2011)
  c. Inventory turnover (inventory was $620 on December 31, 2011)
3. Solvency
  a. Debt-to-equity ratio
  b. Times-interest-earned ratio

EYK13-11. Ratios Using IFRS Financial Statements Tesco PLC is the world's third largest retailer. The
company is based out of the United Kingdom and prepares its financial statements using IFRS.
The complete annual report for Tesco PLC is in Appendix C at the end of this book. Calculate the
following ratios for the company for 2010 and 2011 and comment on your results:

 LO4
TESCO PLC

 a. Current ratio
 b. Quick ratio
 c. Accounts receivable turnover
 d. Inventory turnover
 e. Debt-to-equity ratio
 f. Times-interest-earned ratio
 g. Return on sales
 h. Return on assets
 i. Return on common stockholders' equity
 Hint: Additional 2009 year-end data (in millions of pounds):

Accounts receivable.	1,820
Inventories	2,669
Total assets	45,564
Total stockholders' equity	12,906

ANSWERS TO SELF-STUDY QUESTIONS:

1. a, (p. 601) 2. c, (p. 612) 3. c, (p. 617) 4. b, (p. 620) 5. b, (p. 616) 6. c, (p. 620)
7. d, (p. 623) 8. b, (p. 614) 9. c, (p. 615) 10. b, (p. 609) 11. c, (p. 627) 12. d, (p. 629)

YOUR TURN! SOLUTIONS

Solution 13.1

1. Persistent
2. Transitory
3. Transitory
4. Persistent
5. Transitory
6. Persistent

Solution 13.2

	Increase in 2013	
	Amount	**Percent**
Sales revenue.	$50,000	6.7 percent [($800,000 − $750,000)/$750,000]
Net income.	20,000	20.0 percent [($120,000 − $100,000)/$100,000]
Total assets	10,000	3.4 percent [($300,000 − $290,000)/$290,000]

Solution 13.3

SANFORD COMPANY Income Statement For the Year Ended December 31, 2012		
	Amount	**Percent**
Sales revenue.	$13,500	100.0
Cost of goods sold.	5,400	40.0
Gross profit.	8,100	60.0
Selling and administrative expenses	1,350	10.0
Income from operations.	6,750	50.0
Interest expense.	675	5.0
Other expense	135	1.0
Income before income taxes	5,940	44.0
Income tax expense.	2,295	17.0
Net income.	$ 3,645	27.0

Solution 13.4

a. Gross profit percentage = ($30,000 − $10,500)/$30,000 = 65.0 percent

b. Return on sales = $4,500/$30,000 = 15.0 percent

c. Asset turnover = $30,000/$50,000 = 0.60

d. Return on assets = $4,500/$50,000 = 9.0 percent

e. Return on common stockholders' equity = ($4,500 − $500)/$35,000 = 11.4 percent

Solution 13.5

a. Working capital = $60,000 − $40,000 = $20,000

b. Current ratio = $60,000/$40,000 = 1.5

c. Operating-cash-flow-to-current-liabilities ratio = $55,000/$40,000 = 1.375

d. Accounts receivable turnover = $100,000/$15,000 = 6.67 times

e. Days' sales in inventory = 365/($70,000/$9,000) = 46.9 days

Solution 13.6

a. Debt-to-equity ratio = $180,000/$600,000 = 0.30

b. Times-interest-earned ratio = ($55,000 + $5,000 + $25,000)/$5,000 = 17.0 times

c. Operating-cash-flow-to-capital-expenditures ratio = $100,000/$30,000 = 3.33 times

Solution 13.7

a. Dividend yield = $1.50/$54.00 = 2.8 percent

b. Dividend payout ratio = $1.50/$4.50 = 33.3 percent

Appendix A

Columbia Sportswear Company: Annual Report and Social Responsibility Report

The law requires publicly traded companies to submit an audited annual report to the Securities and Exchange Commission (SEC) within two months of the close of their fiscal year. This annual report is called Form 10-K. Companies also provide their stockholders with an annual report that contains many of the items included in Form 10-K, along with a letter to the shareholders and public relations and marketing material. Although each annual report is different, all annual reports typically include the following elements:

- Letter to the Shareholders
- Management Discussion and Analysis
- Independent Auditor's Report
- Financial Statements
- Notes to Financial Statements
- Report on Internal Control
- Management's Certification of Financial Statements
- Supplemental Information

In addition, most publicly traded companies also provide a voluntary report on their corporate social responsibility commitments. Because this report is voluntary, its content varies to a greater degree from company to company. Most reports, however, discuss the company's commitment in the areas of both social and environmental impact.

The following pages include data from Columbia Sportswear's 2011 Annual Report, along with highlights from its social responsibility reporting. Appendix A is organized as follows:

Occasionally, companies restate financial data for previous years, which may cause specific amounts to change in their financial statements. The data in this appendix reflect the most current financial data available at the time this book was printed.

LETTER TO SHAREHOLDERS

Dear Fellow Shareholders:

INNOVATION.
ENHANCED DESIGN.
COMPELLING MARKETING.

Those three simple ideas explain how Columbia Sportswear Company has succeeded for 74 years, and how we will continue to succeed in the future.

In 2011, we achieved many of the financial and operational goals we set for the company at the beginning of the year. Record sales of $1.69 billion, up 14 percent from 2010, were driven by double-digit growth from the Columbia, Sorel and Mountain Hardwear brands, as well as from each of our international regions.

More importantly, we improved the company's profitability, increasing operating margins to 8.1 percent, compared to 7.0 percent in 2010, and expanding net income by 34 percent, to $103.5 million, or $3.03 per share, compared to $77.0 million, or $2.26 per diluted share in 2010. We continue to maintain a very strong balance sheet, with more than $240 million in cash and short-term investments, and no long-term debt as of December 31, 2011.

Each of our brands grew stronger in 2011, as we introduced new technologies and designs to clearly differentiate our products from competitors'. With clear strategies for each of our brands, a pipeline of innovations and design concepts that extend several seasons into the future, and a disciplined approach to cost management, we are well-positioned to drive further growth and improve profitability.

ELEVATING THE BRAND THROUGH INNOVATION

Sales of our Columbia brand reached a record $1.39 billion in 2011, up 10 percent from 2010 and 30 percent higher than 2009. Since we sharpened Columbia's emphasis on innovation four years ago, we have focused on 14 major technologies to help keep people warm, dry, cool and protected in the outdoors year-round. One of our long-term goals is to increase consumer adoption of Columbia products for use in all climates and all seasons, diversifying our business to generate greater sales and profitability in the first half of the year and become less dependent on the fall and winter seasons to achieve our profitability targets.

During 2011, expansion of our award-winning Omni-Heat® technology into Omni-Heat® Reflective baselayer and Omni-Heat® Electric heated apparel, gloves and footwear completed a full-body warmth portfolio. We also launched footwear and gloves with OutDry® technology to deliver superior waterproof breathability. For 2012, we're extending our lightweight,

waterproof, breathable + wicking platform, introducing Omni-Dry® with Omni-Wick® EVAP in apparel to keep consumers dry inside and out. In addition Omni-Freeze® Ice will introduce outdoor consumers to an active ingredient that helps keep them cool. These innovations, combined with enhanced design and compelling marketing, are succeeding in elevating the Columbia brand. As evidence, brand-enhancing outdoor specialty and sporting goods retailers have been the brand's fastest growing channels of distribution in the U.S. for the past two years, and influential outdoor industry and consumer media have recognized numerous Columbia products with awards for innovation, performance and design.

We have made great progress with the Columbia brand and are working closely with our wholesale partners around the world, as well as through our direct-to-consumer channels in each region, to ensure that more consumers are exposed to Columbia's newest and best designs.

YOUNG, FASHION-FORWARD FEMALE CONSUMERS.

We launched a strategic repositioning of Sorel two years ago, targeting young, fashion-forward female consumers with new assortments featuring premium materials and provocative designs, while staying true to Sorel's authentic heritage. The results have been resounding. Sorel was our fastest growing brand in 2011, posting a 68 percent increase in global sales to $150 million.

We've invested in the creation of a separate sales and marketing organization focused exclusively on Sorel's global growth opportunities as more consumers discover and adopt the brand. Sorel has succeeded in garnering great exposure on the feet of influential icons of film, music and fashion, virally increasing awareness and adoption among our target consumers.

Columbia

SOREL

As pleased as we are with the growth of Sorel, it remains today primarily a winter brand with a 90-day presence on retail shelves. Our product creation team is focused on expanding Sorel's offering into Fall, Spring and Summer products, creating an opportunity for our growing base of high-quality footwear retail partners to showcase the brand year-round. In addition, we have yet to attack the potential market for Sorel in Russia, Korea, Japan or China, and we believe each of those countries represents a fertile market that can play a significant role in Sorel's future growth.

MOUNTAIN HARD WEAR

SERVING HIGH-PERFORMANCE NEEDS OF ALPINISTS

Mountain Hardwear sales grew 17 percent in 2011, totaling $142 million. With its successful launch of Dry.Q™ waterproof, breathable fabric systems, the Mountain Hardwear brand reinforced its commitment to serving the high-performance needs of alpinists and mountaineers who test the edges of human potential.

Working directly with several of today's leading alpinists, including Swiss speed-climber Ueli Steck, Mountain Hardwear pioneered an assortment of high-performance apparel and equipment that reduced the weight of the typical ascent kit by more than 50 percent. These innovations, and the amazing athletes who depend upon them, are redefining the sport and elevating the brand to the pinnacle of the market.

With just five countries – the U.S., Korea, United Kingdom, Canada and Japan – accounting for more than 90 percent of Mountain Hardwear's annual sales, we are confident the brand has potential for global expansion in the years ahead.

Our best is yet to come.

While 2011 was our second consecutive year of strong sales and earnings growth, we are mindful that our business is not insulated from the lingering effects of unseasonable weather and macro-economic storms in large markets. We expect those external forces to slow our sales growth in 2012.

In response, our management team has formulated a 2012 spending plan that correlates with this lower anticipated sales growth, while maintaining funding for our most important strategic initiatives.

We are very clear about two things:

- We remain firmly committed to investing in innovation, enhanced design, an expanded direct-to-consumer platform and compelling marketing to elevate our brands and gain market share.

- We are firmly committed to investing in information technology and process improvements to increase operational and resource efficiencies and, ultimately, our profitability.

We remain confident about the long-term market opportunities of our brands and are aligned behind the most impactful opportunities to drive long-term top-line growth and improve profitability.

Our best is yet to come.

Sincerely,

Timothy P. Boyle
President and Chief Executive Office

MANAGEMENT DISCUSSION AND ANALYSIS

Item 7.   *MAN AGEMENT'S DISCUSSION AND ANALYSIS OF FINANCIAL CONDITION AND RESULTS OF OPERATIONS*

This annual report, including Item 1 of Part I and Item 7 of Part II, contains forward-looking statements. Forward-looking statements include any statements related to our expectations regarding future performance or market position, including any statements regarding anticipated sales across markets, distribution channels and product categories, access to raw materials and factory capacity, financing and working capital requirements and resources and our exposure to market risk associated with interest rates and foreign currency exchange rates.

These forward-looking statements, and others we make from time to time, are subject to a number of risks and uncertainties. Many factors may cause actual results to differ materially from those projected in forward-looking statements, including the risks described above in Item 1A, Risk Factors. We do not undertake any duty either to update forward-looking statements after the date they are made or to conform them to actual results or to changes in circumstances or expectations.

Our Business

As one of the largest outdoor apparel and footwear companies in the world, we design, source, market and distribute active outdoor apparel, footwear, accessories and equipment under the Columbia, Mountain Hardwear, Sorel and Montrail brands. Our products are sold through a mix of wholesale distribution channels, independent distributors, our own direct-to-consumer channels and licensees.

The popularity of outdoor activities, changing design trends and consumer adoption of innovative performance technologies affect consumer desire for our products. Therefore, we seek to drive, anticipate and respond to trends and shifts in consumer preferences by adjusting the mix of available product offerings, developing new products with innovative performance features and designs, and creating persuasive and memorable marketing communications to generate consumer awareness and demand. Failure to anticipate or respond to consumer needs and preferences in a timely and adequate manner could have a material adverse effect on our sales and profitability.

Seasonality and Variability of Business

Our business is affected by the general seasonal trends common to the outdoor industry and is heavily dependent upon weather and discretionary consumer spending patterns. Our products are marketed on a seasonal basis and our product mix is weighted substantially toward the fall season, while our operating costs are more equally distributed throughout the year. Since 2008, the expansion of our direct-to-consumer operations has increased the proportion of sales and profits that we generate in the fourth calendar quarter. As a result, our sales and profits tend to be highest in the third and fourth calendar quarters. In 2011, approximately 65 percent of our net sales and all of our profitability were realized in the second half of the year, illustrating our dependence upon sales results in the second half of the year, as well as the less seasonal nature of our operating costs.

We generally solicit orders from wholesale customers and independent distributors for the fall and spring seasons based on seasonal ordering deadlines that we establish to aid our efforts in planning manufacturing volumes to meet demand for each of our selling seasons.

We typically ship the majority of our advance fall season orders to wholesale customers and independent distributors beginning in June and continuing through November. Similarly, the majority of our advance spring season orders ship to wholesale customers and independent distributors beginning in December and continuing through May. Generally, orders are subject to cancellation prior to the date of shipment.

Results of operations in any period should not be considered indicative of the results to be expected for any future period, particularly in light of persistent volatility in economic conditions. Sales of our products are subject to substantial cyclical fluctuation, the effects of unseasonable weather conditions, and the continued popularity of outdoor activities as part of an active lifestyle in key markets. Volatile economic environments in key markets, coupled with inflationary cost pressures and input cost volatility, reduces the predictability of our business.

Business Outlook

The global business climate continues to present us with a great deal of uncertainty, making it more difficult to predict future results. Factors that could significantly affect our full year 2012 outlook include:

- Unseasonable weather conditions or other unforeseen factors affecting consumer demand and the resulting effect on order cancellations, reorders, direct-to-consumer sales and suppressed demand in subsequent seasons;

- Changes in mix and volume of full price sales in contrast with closeout product sales;

- Volatile input costs across our supply chain;

- Increased fixed costs to support growth and our multi-year business process, supply chain and information technology infrastructure investments and projects;

- Our ability to implement adequate cost containment measures in order to limit the growth of selling, general and administrative ("SG&A") expenses to a rate comparable to sales growth;

- Costs of expedited transportation;

- Lower incremental sales through our expanding direct-to-consumer operations;

- Changes in consumer spending activity; and

- Fluctuating currency exchange rates.

Like other branded consumer product companies, our business is heavily dependent upon discretionary consumer spending patterns. Continuing high levels of unemployment and concerns about potential increases in consumer prices in our key markets continue to pose significant challenges and risks.

Over the past several years we have made significant investments in our go-to-market process to position us for growth. Among other things we have:

- Sharpened our focus on product innovation;

- Built a multi-channel and multi-country direct-to-consumer platform, including expanded retail store and e-commerce operations;

- Refocused our marketing efforts behind new brand campaigns and media strategies for each of our major brands; and

- Restructured our sales organizations to build relationships with new partners and strengthen those with existing accounts.

We have made improvements to our operational processes, involving significant investments in initiatives to improve our information technology infrastructure and our enterprise data and information management, which are designed to improve operational flexibility and performance. These investments are the foundation for a multi-year implementation of a new global enterprise resource planning, or ERP, system that began in late 2010.

As a result of these continuing initiatives, we expect our SG&A expenses in 2012 to increase compared to 2011.

As our business model and strategies have evolved, management expects certain trends to continue to affect our business and operating results, including:

- A higher amount of fixed operating expenses to support, among other things, direct-to-consumer activities and our multi-year ERP implementation;

- A greater reliance on sales growth through the company's global direct-to-consumer platform; and

- Higher product input costs.

We expect the unseasonably warm weather in the northern hemisphere during the 2011 and 2012 winter season to subdue retailer confidence as they plan their orders for the Fall 2012 season. However, we remain firmly committed to investing in innovation, enhanced design, our direct-to-consumer platform and compelling marketing to elevate our brands and gain market share, and to investing in information technologies and process improvements to increase operational and supply chain efficiencies and profitability. We are currently implementing cost containment measures with the goal of limiting 2012 SG&A growth at a rate comparable to anticipated 2012 sales growth.

These factors and others may have a material effect on our financial condition, results of operations, or cash flows, particularly with respect to quarterly comparisons.

OVERVIEW OF FINANCIAL PERFORMANCE

Results of Operations

The following discussion of our results of operations and liquidity and capital resources should be read in conjunction with the Consolidated Financial Statements and accompanying Notes that appear elsewhere in this annual report. All references to years relate to the calendar year ended December 31.

In 2011, we consolidated our categorical net sales reporting from four categories to two categories to better reflect product category management oversight and structure. Net sales within the new apparel, accessories and equipment product category consist of the combination of previously reported net sales of the outerwear, sportswear and accessories and equipment product categories. The footwear product categorical reporting remained unchanged. Previously reported product category net sales information for fiscal years 2010 and 2009 has been recast to reflect this change.

Highlights of the Year Ended December 31, 2011

- Net sales increased $210.5 million, or 14%, to $1,694.0 million in 2011 from $1,483.5 million in 2010. Changes in foreign currency exchange rates compared with 2010 contributed approximately three percentage points of benefit to the consolidated net sales comparison.

- Net income increased 34% to $103.5 million in 2011 from $77.0 million in 2010, and diluted earnings per share increased to $3.03 in 2011 compared to $2.26 in 2010.

- We paid cash dividends totaling $0.86 per share, or $29.1 million, in 2011, which included a 10% increase in the quarterly dividend to $0.22 per share from $0.20 per share in March 2011.

The following table sets forth, for the periods indicated, the percentage relationship to net sales of specified items in our Consolidated Statements of Operations:

	2011	2010	2009
Net sales	100.0%	100.0%	100.0%
Cost of sales	56.6	57.6	57.9
Gross profit	43.4	42.4	42.1
Selling, general and administrative expense	36.3	36.0	35.7
Net licensing income	1.0	0.6	0.7
Income from operations	8.1	7.0	7.1
Interest income, net	0.0	0.1	0.1
Income before income tax	8.1	7.1	7.2
Income tax expense	(2.0)	(1.9)	(1.8)
Net income	6.1%	5.2%	5.4%

Year Ended December 31, 2011 Compared to Year Ended December 31, 2010

   Net Sales: Consolidated net sales increased $210.5 million, or 14%, to $1,694.0 million in 2011 from $1,483.5 million in 2010. Net sales increased across all geographic regions, in each product category and across all major brands. Changes in foreign currency exchange rates compared with 2010 contributed approximately three percentage points of benefit to the consolidated net sales comparison.

Sales by Geographic Region

   Net sales by geographic region are summarized in the following table:

	Year Ended December 31,		
	2011	2010	% Change
	(In millions, except for percentage changes)		
United States	$ 948.0	$ 881.0	8%
LAAP	341.0	263.4	29%
EMEA	275.4	222.4	24%
Canada	129.6	116.7	11%
	$1,694.0	$1,483.5	14%

   Net sales in the United States increased $67.0 million, or 8%, to $948.0 million in 2011 from $881.0 million in 2010. The increase in net sales in the United States by product category was led by apparel, accessories and equipment, followed by a net sales increase in footwear. The net sales increase by brand was led by the Columbia brand, followed by the Sorel brand and the Mountain Hardwear brand. The net sales increase by channel was primarily driven by our direct-to-consumer business, followed by our wholesale business. The increase in net sales in our direct-to-consumer business was driven by strong comparable store sales growth, increased e-commerce sales and the net addition of two outlet stores.

   Net sales in the LAAP region increased $77.6 million, or 29%, to $341.0 million in 2011 from $263.4 million in 2010. Changes in foreign currency exchange rates contributed six percentage points of benefit to the LAAP net sales comparison. The net sales increase in the LAAP region by product category was primarily driven by a net sales increase in apparel, accessories and equipment, followed by a net sales increase in footwear. The LAAP net sales increase was concentrated in the Columbia brand and was led by Korea, followed by Japan and our LAAP distributor business. The increase in Korea net sales was primarily due to increased sales from existing stores, a greater number of retail stores operating during 2011 and the favorable effect of foreign currency exchange rates. The increase in Japan net sales was primarily the result of the favorable effect of foreign currency exchange rates and increased wholesale net sales. Net sales to our LAAP distributors increased due to increased demand in key distributor markets coupled with a higher percentage of spring 2012 advance orders shipping in the fourth quarter compared to the spring 2011 season.

   Net sales in the EMEA region increased $53.0 million, or 24%, to $275.4 million in 2011 from $222.4 million in 2010. Changes in foreign currency exchange rates contributed four percentage points of benefit to the EMEA net sales comparison. The increase in net sales in the EMEA region by product category was led by footwear, followed by a net sales increase in apparel, accessories and equipment. The net sales increase by channel was led by our EMEA direct business, followed by our EMEA distributors. The increase in EMEA direct net sales was primarily driven by the Sorel brand, followed by the Columbia brand.

   Net sales in Canada increased $12.9 million, or 11%, to $129.6 million in 2011 from $116.7 million in 2010. Changes in foreign currency exchange rates compared to 2010 contributed six percentage points of benefit to the Canada net sales comparison. By product category, the increase in net sales was led by apparel, accessories and equipment, followed by a net sales increase in footwear. By brand, the increase in net sales was led by the Columbia brand, followed by the Sorel and Mountain Hardwear brands. The increase in net sales was concentrated in our wholesale business.

Sales by Product Category

Net sales by product category are summarized in the following table:

	Year Ended December 31,		
	2011	2010	% Change
	(In millions, except for percentage changes)		
Apparel, Accessories and Equipment	$ 1,334.9	$ 1,213.3	10%
Footwear	359.1	270.2	33%
	$ 1,694.0	$ 1,483.5	14%

Net sales of apparel, accessories and equipments increased $121.6 million, or 10%, to $1,334.9 million in 2011 from $1,213.3 million in 2010. The increase in apparel, accessories and equipment net sales was primarily concentrated in the Columbia brand and was led by the LAAP region, followed by the United States, the EMEA region and Canada. The apparel, accessories and equipment net sales increase in the LAAP region was led by Korea, followed by our LAAP distributor business and Japan. The net sales increase in apparel, accessories and equipment in the United States was led by our direct-to-consumer business, partially offset by a net sales decrease in our wholesale business.

Net sales of footwear increased $88.9 million, or 33%, to $359.1 million in 2011 from $270.2 million in 2010. The increase in footwear net sales by brand was led by the Sorel brand, followed by the Columbia brand. The footwear net sales increase by region was led by the United States, followed by the EMEA region, the LAAP region and Canada. The net sales increase in footwear in the United States was primarily driven by our wholesale business, followed by our direct-to-consumer business. The footwear net sales increase in the EMEA region was primarily driven by our EMEA direct business, followed by our EMEA distributor business. The LAAP footwear net sales increase was led by Japan, followed by Korea and our LAAP distributor business.

Sales by Brand

Net sales by brand are summarized in the following table:

	Year Ended December 31,		
	2011	2010	% Change
	(In millions, except for percentage changes)		
Columbia	$1,391.5	$1,262.4	10%
Mountain Hardwear	142.3	121.9	17%
Sorel	150.3	89.7	68%
Other	9.9	9.5	4%
	$1,694.0	$1,483.5	14%

The net sales increase in 2011 compared to 2010 was led by the Columbia brand, followed by the Sorel and Mountain Hardwear brands. Columbia brand net sales increased in both product categories and across all regions, led by the LAAP region, followed by the United States, the EMEA region and Canada. Sorel brand net sales increased across all regions led by the EMEA region, followed by the United States, Canada, and the LAAP region. Mountain Hardwear net sales increased in three regions, led by the United States, the LAAP region and Canada, partially offset by a slight decline in the EMEA region.

Gross Profit: Gross profit as a percentage of net sales increased to 43.4% in 2011 from 42.4% in 2010, driven primarily by lower airfreight costs compared to 2010. Other factors favorably affecting gross margin included:

- Favorable foreign currency hedge rates; and
- A higher proportion of direct-to-consumer sales at higher gross margins;

partially offset by:

- Increased product costs;
- A higher proportion of close-out product sales; and
- An increased proportion of shipments to EMEA and LAAP distributors.

Our gross profit may not be comparable to those of other companies in our industry because some of these companies include all of the costs related to their distribution network in cost of sales while we, like many others, include these expenses as a component of SG&A expense.

Selling, General and Administrative Expense: SG&A expense includes all costs associated with our design, merchandising, marketing, distribution and corporate functions, including related depreciation and amortization.

SG&A expense increased $80.6 million, or 15%, to $614.7 million in 2011, from $534.1 million in 2010. The SG&A expense increase was primarily due to:

- The expansion of direct-to-consumer operations globally, including a net increase of $3.2 million in store impairment charges;
- Increased advertising expenses;
- Additions to staff and other expenses to support business initiatives and growth;
- Information technology initiatives, including our ERP implementation; and
- The unfavorable effect of foreign currency translation.

As a percentage of net sales, SG&A expense increased to 36.3% of net sales in 2011 from 36.0% of net sales in 2010. Depreciation and amortization included in SG&A expense totaled $42.9 million in 2011, compared to $37.8 million in 2010.

Net Licensing Income: Net licensing income increased $7.8 million, or 98%, to $15.8 million in 2011 from $8.0 million in 2010. The increase in net licensing income was primarily due to increased apparel and footwear licensing in the LAAP region, where a third party distributor is licensed to locally manufacture Columbia brand apparel and footwear for sale in local markets.

Interest Income, Net: Net interest income was $1.3 million in 2011, compared to $1.6 million in 2010. The decrease in interest income was primarily driven by lower average cash and investment balances and lower interest rates in 2011 compared to 2010. Interest expense was nominal in both 2011 and 2010.

Income Tax Expense: Income tax expense increased to $34.2 million in 2011 from $27.9 million in 2010. Our effective income tax rate decreased to 24.8% from 26.6% in 2010, primarily because we earned a higher proportion of our income from foreign jurisdictions with tax rates that are generally lower than the U.S. tax rate.

Net Income: Net income increased $26.4 million, or 34%, to $103.5 million in 2011 from $77.0 million in 2010. Diluted earnings per share was $3.03 in 2011 compared to $2.26 in 2010.

Year Ended December 31, 2010 Compared to Year Ended December 31, 2009

   Net Sales: Consolidated net sales increased $239.5 million, or 19%, to $1,483.5 million in 2010 from $1,244.0 million in 2009. Net sales increased across all geographic regions, in each product category and across all major brands. Changes in foreign currency exchange rates compared with 2009 contributed approximately one percentage point of benefit to the consolidated net sales comparison.

Sales by Geographic Region

   Net sales by geographic region are summarized in the following table:

	Year Ended December 31,		
	2010	2009	% Change
	(In millions, except for percentage changes)		
United States	$ 881.0	$ 736.9	20%
LAAP	263.4	203.2	30%
EMEA	222.4	197.4	13%
Canada	116.7	106.5	10%
	$1,483.5	$1,244.0	19%

   Net sales in the United States increased $144.1 million, or 20%, to $881.0 million in 2010 from $736.9 million in 2009. The increase in net sales in the United States by product category was led by outerwear, followed by sportswear, footwear and accessories and equipment. The net sales increase by channel was led by our wholesale business, followed by our direct-to-consumer business. The increase in net sales in our wholesale business was primarily concentrated in the Columbia brand resulting from improved economic conditions compared to the same period in 2009 and stronger advance orders. The net sales increase in our direct-to-consumer business was primarily concentrated in the Columbia brand and was driven by increased sales within existing stores, increased sales through our Columbia and Sorel brand e-commerce sites, which were launched in the third and fourth quarter of 2009, respectively, incremental sales from our Mountain Hardwear brand e-commerce site which was launched in the third quarter of 2010, and an increase in the number of retail stores, with 4 more retail stores operating at December 31, 2010 than at December 31, 2009.

   Net sales in the LAAP region increased $60.2 million, or 30%, to $263.4 million in 2010 from $203.2 million in 2009. Changes in foreign currency exchange rates contributed seven percentage points of benefit to the LAAP net sales comparison. The net sales increase in the LAAP region by product category was led by sportswear, followed by outerwear, footwear and accessories and equipment. The LAAP net sales increase was primarily concentrated in the Columbia brand and was led by Korea, followed by Japan and our LAAP distributor business. The increase in Korea net sales was primarily due to increased sales from existing stores, the favorable effect of foreign currency exchange rates and a greater number of retail stores operating during 2010. The increase in Japan net sales was primarily the result of the favorable effect of foreign currency exchange rates, increased wholesale net sales to the sporting goods channel and continued growth in our direct-to-consumer business. Net sales to our LAAP distributors increased due to improved macro-economic conditions in certain distributor markets, increased advance orders for both the Spring and Fall seasons, as well as a shift in the timing of shipments as a higher percentage of spring 2011 shipments occurred in the fourth quarter of 2010, while a higher percentage of spring 2010 shipments occurred in the first quarter of 2010.

   Net sales in the EMEA region increased $25.0 million, or 13%, to $222.4 million in 2010 from $197.4 million in 2009. Changes in foreign currency exchange rates compared to 2009 negatively affected the net sales comparison by four percentage points. The increase in net sales in the EMEA region by product category was led by footwear, followed by sportswear, outerwear and accessories and equipment. The net sales increase by channel was led by EMEA distributors, followed by our EMEA direct business. The increase in net sales to EMEA distributors was partially the result of improved macro-economic conditions in Russia, coupled with a shift in the timing of shipments as a higher percentage of spring 2011 shipments occurred in the fourth quarter of 2010, while a higher percentage of spring 2010 shipments occurred in the first quarter of 2010. The increase in EMEA direct net sales was primarily the result of increased net sales of Sorel-branded footwear.

Net sales in Canada increased $10.2 million, or 10%, to $116.7 million in 2010 from $106.5 million in 2009. Changes in foreign currency exchange rates compared to 2009 contributed eight percentage points of benefit to the Canada net sales comparison.

Sales by Product Category

Net sales by product category are summarized in the following table:

	Year Ended December 31,		
	2010	2009	% Change
	(In millions, except for percentage changes)		
Apparel, accessories and equipment	$1,213.3	$1,029.4	18%
Footwear	270.2	214.6	26%
	$1,483.5	$1,244.0	19%

Net sales of apparel, accessories and equipment increased $183.9 million, or 18%, to $1,213.3 million in 2010 from $1,029.4 million in 2009. The increase in apparel, accessories and equipment net sales was primarily concentrated in the Columbia brand and was led by the United States, followed by the LAAP region, Canada and the EMEA region. The net sales increase in apparel, accessories and equipment in the United States was led by our wholesale business, followed by our direct-to-consumer business. The apparel, accessories and equipment net sales increase in the LAAP region was led by Korea, followed by Japan and our LAAP distributor business.

Net sales of footwear increased $55.6 million, or 26%, to $270.2 million in 2010 from $214.6 million in 2009. The increase in footwear net sales by brand was led by the Sorel brand, followed by the Columbia brand. The footwear net sales increase by region was led by the United States, followed by the EMEA region, the LAAP region and Canada. The net sales increase in footwear in the United States was led by our wholesale business, followed by our direct-to-consumer business. The footwear net sales increase in the EMEA region was led by our EMEA direct business, followed by our EMEA distributor business. The LAAP footwear net sales increase was led by our LAAP distributor business, followed by Korea and Japan.

Sales by Brand

Net sales by brand are summarized in the following table:

	Year Ended December 31,		
	2010	2009	% Change
	(In millions, except for percentage changes)		
Columbia	$ 1,262.4	$ 1,072.5	18%
Mountain Hardwear	121.9	100.5	21%
Sorel	89.7	60.6	48%
Other	9.5	10.4	(9)%
	$ 1,483.5	$ 1,244.0	19%

The net sales increase by brand in 2010 compared to 2009 was primarily concentrated in the Columbia brand, followed by the Sorel and Mountain Hardwear brands. The Columbia brand net sales increased across all product categories, led by sportswear, followed by outerwear, footwear and accessories and equipment. The Columbia brand net sales increased across all regions led by the United States, followed by the LAAP region, the EMEA region and Canada.

Gross Profit: Gross profit as a percentage of net sales increased to 42.4% in 2010 from 42.1% in 2009. Gross profit margins expanded primarily due to a higher volume of direct-to-consumer sales at higher gross margins, improved gross margins on close-out product sales and favorable foreign currency hedge rates, largely offset by increased costs to expedite production and delivery of fall 2010 orders to wholesale customers.

Selling, General and Administrative Expense: SG&A expense increased $89.4 million, or 20%, to $534.1 million in 2010 from $444.7 million in 2009. The SG&A expense increase was primarily due to:

- Increased global personnel costs resulting from the continued internalization of our sales organization in the United States, the EMEA region and Canada, additional personnel to support our growth initiatives, reinstatement of personnel and benefit programs that were curtailed or postponed in 2009, and higher incentive compensation;

- Incremental expenses to support our expanded direct-to-consumer businesses in the United States, the EMEA region and Canada;

- Expenses associated with various initiatives to improve our information technology infrastructure, including increased costs associated with our multi-year global ERP implementation; and

- Increased advertising expense.

As a percentage of net sales, SG&A expense increased to 36.0% of net sales in 2010 from 35.7% of net sales in 2009. Depreciation and amortization included in SG&A expense totaled $37.8 million in 2010, compared to $35.5 million in 2009.

Net Licensing Income: Net licensing income decreased $0.4 million, or 5%, to $8.0 million in 2010 from $8.4 million in 2009. The decrease in net licensing income was primarily due to decreased net licensing income in our socks category in the United States, as we began directly producing this formerly licensed category. The decrease in our U.S. licensing business was partially offset by increased apparel and footwear net licensing income in the LAAP region.

Interest Income, Net: Net interest income was $1.6 million in 2010, compared to $2.1 million in 2009. The decrease in interest income was primarily driven by lower interest rates in 2010 compared to 2009. Interest expense was nominal in both 2010 and 2009.

Income Tax Expense: Income tax expense increased to $27.9 million in 2010 from $22.8 million in 2009. This increase resulted from higher income before tax as well as an increase in our effective income tax rate to 26.6% in 2010, compared to 25.4% in 2009. Our effective tax rates in 2010 and 2009 were reduced by the recognition of tax benefits associated with the favorable resolution of uncertain tax positions, foreign tax credits and non-U.S. income generally taxed at lower tax rates.

Net Income: Net income increased $10.0 million, or 15%, to $77.0 million in 2010 from $67.0 million in 2009. Diluted earnings per share was $2.26 in 2010, compared to $1.97 in 2009.

Liquidity and Capital Resources

Our primary ongoing funding requirements are for working capital, investing activities associated with the expansion of our global operations and general corporate needs. At December 31, 2011, we had total cash and cash equivalents of $241.0 million compared to $234.3 million at December 31, 2010. In addition, we had short-term investments of $2.9 million at December 31, 2011 compared to $68.8 million at December 31, 2010. At December 31, 2011, approximately 29% of our cash and short-term investments were held by our foreign subsidiaries where a repatriation of those funds to the United States would likely result in a significant tax expense to the Company. However, based on the capital and liquidity needs of our foreign operations, as well as the status of current tax law, it is our intent to indefinitely reinvest these funds outside the United States. In addition, our United States operations do not require the repatriation of these funds to meet our currently projected liquidity needs.

2011 compared to 2010

Net cash provided by operating activities was $63.8 million in 2011 compared to $23.5 million in 2010. The increase in cash provided by operating activities was primarily due to increased income from operations, combined with a reduction in the rate of growth of accounts receivable and inventory; partially offset by a reduction in the rate of growth of accounts payable and accrued liabilities, an increase in prepaid expenses and an increase in income taxes paid compared to 2010.

Net cash used in investing activities was $12.5 million in 2011 compared to $91.2 million in 2010. For 2011, net cash used in investing activities primarily consisted of $78.4 million for capital expenditures, partially offset by $65.7 million for net sales of short-term investments. For 2010, net cash used in investing activities primarily consisted of $46.1 million for net purchases of short-term investments, $28.8 million for capital expenditures and $16.3 million for acquisitions.

Net cash used in financing activities was $39.2 million in 2011 compared to $82.3 million in 2010. For 2011, net cash used in financing activities primarily consisted of dividend payments of $29.1 million and the repurchase of common stock at an aggregate price of $20.0 million, partially offset by net proceeds of $8.0 million from the issuance of common stock. For 2010, net cash used in financing activities primarily consisted of dividend payments of $75.4 million, including a $50.5 million special dividend paid in December 2010, and the repurchase of common stock at an aggregate price of $13.8 million, partially offset by net proceeds of $6.5 million from the issuance of common stock.

2010 compared to 2009

Net cash provided by operating activities was $23.5 million in 2010 compared to $214.4 million in 2009. The decrease in cash provided by operating activities was primarily the result of increases in inventory and accounts receivable in 2010 compared to decreases in accounts receivable and inventory in 2009, partially offset by increases in accounts payable and accrued liabilities in 2010 compared to a net decrease in accounts payable and accrued liabilities in 2009. The increase in inventory was due to a larger volume of excess fall 2010 inventory designated for sale primarily through our own outlet retail stores compared to fall 2009 inventory, earlier receipt of spring 2011 inventory compared to spring 2010 inventory, increased 2010 replenishment inventory compared to 2009 and incremental inventory to support increased direct-to-consumer sales. The increase in accounts receivable was in line with the 19% increase in net sales and was also due to an increase in close-out product sales and shipment of spring 2011 advance orders close to the end of the 2010 period.

Net cash used in investing activities was $91.2 million in 2010 compared to net cash used in investing activities of $33.2 million in 2009. For the 2010 period, net cash used in investing activities primarily consisted of $46.1 million for the net purchases of short-term investments, $28.8 million for capital expenditures and $16.3 million for acquisitions. For the 2009 period, net cash used in investing activities primarily consisted of capital expenditures of $33.1 million.

Net cash used in financing activities was $82.3 million in 2010 compared to $29.6 million in 2009. For the 2010 period, net cash used in financing activities primarily consisted of dividend payments of $75.4 million, including a $50.5 million special dividend paid in December 2010, and the repurchase of common stock at an aggregate price of $13.8 million, partially offset by proceeds from issuance of common stock of $6.5 million. For the 2009 period, net cash used in financing activities included dividend payments of $22.3 million and the repurchase of common stock at an aggregate price of $7.4 million.

We have an unsecured, committed $125.0 million revolving line of credit available to fund our domestic working capital requirements. At December 31, 2011, no balance was outstanding under this line of credit and we were in compliance with all associated covenants. Internationally, our subsidiaries have local currency operating lines of credit in place guaranteed by the parent company with a combined limit of approximately $89.7 million at December 31, 2011, of which $3.2 million is designated as a European customs guarantee. At December 31, 2011, no balance was outstanding under these lines of credit.

We expect to fund our future capital expenditures with existing cash, operating cash flows and credit facilities. If the need arises, we may need to seek additional funding. Our ability to obtain additional financing will depend on many factors, including prevailing market conditions, our financial condition, and our ability to negotiate favorable terms and conditions. Financing may not be available on terms that are acceptable or favorable to us, if at all.

Our operations are affected by seasonal trends typical in the outdoor apparel industry, and have historically resulted in higher sales and profits in the third and fourth calendar quarters. This pattern has resulted primarily from the timing of shipments of fall season products to wholesale customers and proportionally higher sales from our direct-to-consumer operations in the fourth quarter. We believe that our liquidity requirements for at least the next 12 months will be adequately covered by existing cash, cash provided by operations and existing short-term borrowing arrangements.

The following table presents our estimated contractual commitments (in thousands):

| | Year ended December 31, | | | | | | |
	2012	2013	2014	2015	2016	Thereafter	Total
Inventory purchase obligations (1)	$351,854	$ —	$ —	$ —	$ —	$ —	$351,854
Operating leases (2)	38,773	35,060	29,819	26,892	25,254	94,892	250,690

(1)   See *Inventory Purchase Obligations* in Note 13 of Notes to Consolidated Financial Statements.
(2)   See *Operating Leases* in Note 13 of Notes to Consolidated Financial Statements.

We have recorded liabilities for net unrecognized tax benefits related to income tax uncertainties in our Consolidated Balance Sheet at December 31, 2011 of approximately $15.4 million; however, they have not been included in the table above because we are uncertain about whether or when these amounts may be settled. See Note 10 of Notes to Consolidated Financial Statements.

Quantitative and Qualitative Disclosures About Market Risk

In the normal course of business, our financial position and results of operations are routinely subject to a variety of risks. These risks include risks associated with global financial and capital markets, primarily currency exchange rate risk and, to a lesser extent, interest rate risk and equity market risk. We regularly assess these risks and have established policies and business practices designed to mitigate the effect of these risks. We do not engage in speculative trading in any financial or capital market.

Our primary currency exchange rate risk management objective is to mitigate the uncertainty of anticipated cash flows attributable to changes in exchange rates. We focus on mitigating changes in functional currency equivalent cash flows resulting from anticipated U.S. dollar denominated inventory purchases by subsidiaries that use European euros, Canadian dollars, Japanese yen or Korean won as their functional currency. We manage this risk primarily by using currency forward and option contracts. Additionally, we use foreign currency forward and option contracts to hedge net balance sheet exposures related primarily to intercompany transactions and borrowing arrangements.

The net fair value of our derivative contracts was favorable by approximately $4.5 million at December 31, 2011. A 10% exchange rate change in the euro, Canadian dollar, yen and won against the U.S. dollar would have resulted in the net fair value declining by approximately $17.0 million at December 31, 2011. A 10% exchange rate change in the yen and won against the euro would have resulted in the net fair value declining approximately $4.2 million at December 31, 2011. Changes in fair value resulting from foreign exchange rate fluctuations would be substantially offset by the change in value of the underlying hedged transactions.

Our negotiated credit facilities generally charge interest based on a benchmark rate such as the London Interbank Offered Rate ("LIBOR"). Fluctuations in short-term interest rates cause interest payments on drawn amounts to increase or decrease. At December 31, 2011, our credit facilities did not have an outstanding balance.

Critical Accounting Policies and Estimates

Management's discussion and analysis of our financial condition and results of operations are based on our consolidated financial statements, which have been prepared in accordance with accounting principles generally accepted in the United States of America. The preparation of these financial statements requires us to make various estimates and assumptions that affect reported amounts of assets and liabilities and related disclosure of contingent assets and liabilities at the date of the consolidated financial statements and the reported amounts of revenue and expenses during the reporting period. We believe that the estimates and assumptions involved in the accounting policies described below have the greatest potential impact on our financial statements, so we consider these to be our critical accounting policies and estimates. Because of the uncertainty inherent in these matters, actual results may differ from the estimates we use in applying these critical accounting policies. We base our ongoing estimates on historical experience and various other assumptions that we believe to be important in the circumstances. Many of these critical accounting policies affect working capital account balances, including the policy for revenue recognition, the allowance for doubtful accounts, the provision for potential excess, closeout and slow moving inventory, product warranty, income taxes and stock-based compensation.

Management regularly discusses with our Audit Committee each of our critical accounting estimates, the development and selection of these accounting estimates, and the disclosure about each estimate in Management's Discussion and Analysis of Financial Condition and Results of Operations. These discussions typically occur at our quarterly Audit Committee meetings and include the basis and methodology used in developing and selecting these estimates, the trends in and amounts of these estimates, specific matters affecting the amount of and changes in these estimates, and any other relevant matters related to these estimates, including significant issues concerning accounting principles and financial statement presentation.

Revenue Recognition

We record wholesale, e-commerce and licensed product revenues when title passes and the risks and rewards of ownership have passed to the customer. Title generally passes upon shipment to or upon receipt by the customer depending on the terms of sale with the customer. Retail store revenues are recorded at the time of sale.

Where title passes upon receipt by the customer, predominantly in our European wholesale business, precise information regarding the date of receipt by the customer is not readily available. In these cases, we estimate the date of receipt by the customer based on historical and expected delivery times by geographic location. We periodically test the accuracy of these estimates based on actual transactions. Delivery times vary by geographic location, generally from one to five days. To date, we have found these estimates to be materially accurate.

At the time of revenue recognition, we also provide for estimated sales returns and miscellaneous claims from customers as reductions to revenues. The estimates are based on historical rates of product returns and claims, as well as events and circumstances that indicate changes to historical rates of returns and claims. However, actual returns and claims in any future period are inherently uncertain and thus may differ from the estimates. If actual or expected future returns and claims are significantly greater or lower than the reserves that we have established, we will record a reduction or increase to net revenues in the period in which we make such a determination.

Allowance for Uncollectible Accounts Receivable

We make ongoing estimates of the collectability of our accounts receivable and maintain an allowance for estimated losses resulting from the inability of our customers to make required payments. In determining the amount of the allowance, we consider our historical level of credit losses and we make judgments about the creditworthiness of customers based on ongoing credit evaluations. We analyze specific customer accounts, customer concentrations, credit insurance coverage, standby letters of credit, current economic trends, and changes in customer payment terms. Continued uncertainty in credit and market conditions may slow our collection efforts if customers experience difficulty accessing credit and paying their obligations, leading to higher than normal accounts receivable and increased bad debt expense. Because we cannot predict future changes in the financial stability of our customers, actual future losses from uncollectible accounts may differ from our estimates and may have a material effect on our consolidated financial position, results of operations or cash flows. If the financial condition of our customers deteriorates and results in their inability to make payments, a larger allowance may be required. If we determine that a smaller or larger allowance is appropriate, we will record a credit or a charge to SG&A expense in the period in which we make such a determination.

Excess, Close-Out and Slow Moving Inventory

We make ongoing estimates of potential excess, close-out or slow moving inventory. We evaluate our inventory on hand considering our purchase commitments, sales forecasts, and historical experience to identify excess, close-out or slow moving inventory and make provisions as necessary to properly reflect inventory value at the lower of cost or estimated market value. If we determine that a smaller or larger reserve is appropriate, we will record a credit or a charge to cost of sales in the period in which we make such a determination.

Product Warranty

We make ongoing estimates of potential future product warranty costs. When we evaluate our reserve for warranty costs, we consider our product warranty policies, historical claim rates by season, product category and mix, current economic trends, and the historical cost to repair, replace, or refund the original sale. If we determine that a smaller or larger reserve is appropriate, we will record a credit or a charge to cost of sales in the period in which we make such a determination.

Income Taxes

We use the asset and liability method of accounting for income taxes. Under this method, we recognize income tax expense for the amount of taxes payable or refundable for the current year and for the amount of deferred tax liabilities and assets for the future tax consequences of events that have been recognized in our financial statements or tax returns. We make assumptions, judgments and estimates to determine our current provision for income taxes, our deferred tax assets and liabilities, and our uncertain tax positions. Our judgments, assumptions and estimates relative to the current provision for income tax take into account current tax laws, our interpretation of current tax laws and possible outcomes of current and future audits conducted by foreign and domestic tax authorities. Changes in tax law or our interpretation of tax laws and the resolution of current and future tax audits could significantly affect the amounts provided for income taxes in our consolidated financial statements. Our assumptions, judgments and estimates relative to the value of a deferred tax asset take into account predictions of the amount and category of future taxable income. Actual operating results and the underlying amount and category of income in future years could cause our current assumptions, judgments and estimates of recoverable net deferred taxes to be inaccurate. Changes in any of the assumptions, judgments and estimates mentioned above could cause our actual income tax obligations to differ from our estimates, which could materially affect our financial position and results of operations.

Our tax provision for interim periods is determined using an estimate of our annual effective tax rate, adjusted for discrete items, if any, that are taken into account in the relevant period. As the calendar year progresses, we periodically refine our estimate based on actual events and earnings by jurisdiction. This ongoing estimation process can result in changes to our expected effective tax rate for the full calendar year. When this occurs, we adjust the income tax provision during the quarter in which the change in estimate occurs so that our year-to-date provision equals our expected annual effective tax rate.

Stock-Based Compensation

Stock-based compensation cost is estimated at the grant date based on the award's fair value and is recognized as expense over the requisite service period using the straight-line attribution method. We estimate stock-based compensation for stock awards granted using the Black-Scholes option pricing model, which requires various highly subjective assumptions, including volatility and expected option life. Further, we estimate forfeitures for stock-based awards granted, but which are not expected to vest. If any of these inputs or assumptions changes significantly, stock-based compensation expense may differ materially in the future from that recorded in the current period.

Recent Accounting Pronouncements

See "Recent Accounting Pronouncements" in Note 2 of Notes to Consolidated Financial Statements.

Item 7A. *QUANTITATIVE AND QUALITATIVE DISCLOSURES ABOUT MARKET RISK*

The information required by this item is included in Management's Discussion and Analysis of Financial Condition and Results of Operations and is incorporated herein by this reference.

Item 8. *FINANCI AL STATEMENTS AND SUPPLEMENTARY DATA*

Our management is responsible for the information and representations contained in this report. The financial statements have been prepared in conformity with accounting principles generally accepted in the United States of America, which we consider appropriate in the circumstances and include some amounts based on our best estimates and judgments. Other financial information in this report is consistent with these financial statements.

Our accounting systems include controls designed to reasonably assure that assets are safeguarded from unauthorized use or disposition and which provide for the preparation of financial statements in conformity with accounting principles generally accepted in the United States of America. These systems are supplemented by the selection and training of qualified financial personnel and an organizational structure providing for appropriate segregation of duties.

The Audit Committee is responsible for recommending to the Board of Directors the appointment of the independent registered public accounting firm and reviews with the independent registered public accounting firm and management the scope and the results of the annual examination, the effectiveness of the accounting control system and other matters relating to our financial affairs as they deem appropriate.

REPORT OF INDEPENDENT AUDITORS

Report of Independent Registered Public Accounting Firm

To the Board of Directors and Shareholders
Columbia Sportswear Company
Portland, Oregon

We have audited the accompanying consolidated balance sheets of Columbia Sportswear Company and subsidiaries (the "Company") as of December 31, 2011 and 2010, and the related consolidated statements of operations, shareholders' equity and cash flows for each of the three years in the period ended December 31, 2011. Our audits also included the financial statement schedule listed in the Index at Item 15. These financial statements and the financial statement schedule are the responsibility of the Company's management. Our responsibility is to express an opinion on these financial statements and financial statement schedule based on our audits.

We conducted our audits in accordance with the standards of the Public Company Accounting Oversight Board (United States). Those standards require that we plan and perform the audit to obtain reasonable assurance about whether the financial statements are free of material misstatement. An audit includes examining, on a test basis, evidence supporting the amounts and disclosures in the financial statements. An audit also includes assessing the accounting principles used and significant estimates made by management, as well as evaluating the overall financial statement presentation. We believe that our audits provide a reasonable basis for our opinion.

In our opinion, such consolidated financial statements present fairly, in all material respects, the financial position of Columbia Sportswear Company and subsidiaries as of December 31, 2011 and 2010, and the results of their operations and their cash flows for each of the three years in the period ended December 31, 2011, in conformity with accounting principles generally accepted in the United States of America. Also, in our opinion, such financial statement schedule, when considered in relation to the basic consolidated financial statements taken as a whole, presents fairly, in all material respects, the information set forth therein.

We have also audited, in accordance with the standards of the Public Company Accounting Oversight Board (United States), the Company's internal control over financial reporting as of December 31, 2011, based on the criteria established in *Internal Control—Integrated Framework* issued by the Committee of Sponsoring Organizations of the Treadway Commission, and our report dated February 28, 2012, expressed an unqualified opinion on the Company's internal control over financial reporting.

/s/   DELOITTE & TOUCHE LLP
Portland, Oregon
February 28, 2012

FINANCIAL STATEMENTS

COLUMBIA SPORTSWEAR COMPANY
CONSOLIDATED BALANCE SHEETS
(In thousands)

	December 31,	
	2011	**2010**
ASSETS		
Current Assets:		
Cash and cash equivalents	$ 241,034	$ 234,257
Short-term investments	2,878	68,812
Accounts receivable, net (Note 4)	351,538	300,181
Inventories, net (Note 5)	365,199	314,298
Deferred income taxes (Note 10)	52,485	45,091
Prepaid expenses and other current assets	36,392	28,241
Total current assets	1,049,526	990,880
Property, plant, and equipment, net (Note 6)	250,910	221,813
Intangible assets, net (Note 7)	39,020	40,423
Goodwill (Note 7)	14,438	14,470
Other non-current assets	28,648	27,168
Total assets	$1,382,542	$1,294,754
LIABILITIES AND SHAREHOLDERS' EQUITY		
Current Liabilities:		
Accounts payable	$ 148,973	$ 130,626
Accrued liabilities (Note 9)	104,496	102,810
Income taxes payable (Note 10)	12,579	16,037
Deferred income taxes (Note 10)	954	2,153
Total current liabilities	267,002	251,626
Other long-term liabilities (Note 11)	23,853	21,456
Income taxes payable (Note 10)	15,389	19,698
Deferred income taxes (Note 10)	1,753	—
Total liabilities	307,997	292,780
Commitments and contingencies (Note 13)		
Shareholders' Equity:		
Preferred stock; 10,000 shares authorized; none issued and outstanding	—	—
Common stock (no par value); 125,000 shares authorized; 33,638 and 33,683 issued and outstanding (Note 14)	3,037	5,052
Retained earnings	1,024,611	950,207
Accumulated other comprehensive income (Note 17)	46,897	46,715
Total shareholders' equity	1,074,545	1,001,974
Total liabilities and shareholders' equity	$1,382,542	$1,294,754

See accompanying notes to consolidated financial statements

COLUMBIA SPORTSWEAR COMPANY
CONSOLIDATED STATEMENTS OF OPERATIONS
(In thousands, except per share amounts)

	Year Ended December 31,		
	2011	2010	2009
Net sales	$1,693,985	$1,483,524	$1,244,023
Cost of sales	958,677	854,120	719,945
Gross profit	735,308	629,404	524,078
Selling, general, and administrative expenses	614,658	534,068	444,715
Net licensing income	15,756	7,991	8,399
Income from operations	136,406	103,327	87,762
Interest income, net	1,274	1,564	2,088
Income before income tax	137,680	104,891	89,850
Income tax expense (Note 10)	(34,201)	(27,854)	(22,829)
Net income	$ 103,479	$ 77,037	$ 67,021
Earnings per share (Note 16):			
Basic	$ 3.06	$ 2.28	$ 1.98
Diluted	3.03	2.26	1.97
Cash dividends per share:	$ 0.86	$ 2.24	$ 0.66
Weighted average shares outstanding (Note 16):			
Basic	33,808	33,725	33,846
Diluted	34,204	34,092	33,981

See accompanying notes to consolidated financial statements

COLUMBIA SPORTSWEAR COMPANY
CONSOLIDATED STATEMENTS OF CASH FLOWS
(In thousands)

	Year Ended December 31,		
	2011	2010	2009
Cash flows from operating activities:			
Net income	$ 103,479	$ 77,037	$ 67,021
Adjustments to reconcile net income to net cash provided by operating activities:			
Depreciation and amortization	43,560	38,430	36,253
Loss on disposal or impairment of property, plant, and equipment	6,485	3,331	1,828
Deferred income taxes	(3,582)	(22,610)	55
Stock-based compensation	7,870	6,730	6,353
Excess tax benefit from employee stock plans	(1,828)	(498)	(41)
Changes in operating assets and liabilities:			
Accounts receivable	(54,334)	(69,500)	77,490
Inventories	(55,223)	(87,265)	38,831
Prepaid expenses and other current assets	(10,186)	3,856	(1,695)
Other assets	(4,520)	(1,566)	(5,179)
Accounts payable	19,081	26,028	(16,944)
Accrued liabilities	17,630	34,224	7,563
Income taxes payable	(7,010)	9,018	(1,558)
Other liabilities	2,374	6,302	4,395
Net cash provided by operating activities	63,796	23,517	214,372
Cash flows from investing activities:			
Purchases of short-term investments	(46,349)	(81,671)	(25,305)
Sales of short-term investments	112,070	35,601	25,163
Capital expenditures	(78,404)	(28,838)	(33,074)
Proceeds from sale of property, plant, and equipment	168	42	31
Acquisitions, net of cash acquired	—	(16,315)	—
Net cash used in investing activities	(12,515)	(91,181)	(33,185)
Cash flows from financing activities:			
Proceeds from credit facilities	119,384	31,680	57,588
Repayments on credit facilities	(119,384)	(31,680)	(57,588)
Repayment on other long-term liabilities	—	—	(4)
Proceeds from issuance of common stock under employee stock plans	10,991	7,333	710
Tax payments related to restricted stock unit issuances	(2,974)	(853)	(624)
Excess tax benefit from employee stock plans	1,828	498	41
Repurchase of common stock	(20,000)	(13,838)	(7,399)
Cash dividends paid	(29,075)	(75,439)	(22,331)
Net cash used in financing activities	(39,230)	(82,299)	(29,607)
Net effect of exchange rate changes on cash	(5,274)	(2,444)	4,467
Net increase (decrease) in cash and cash equivalents	6,777	(152,407)	156,047
Cash and cash equivalents, beginning of year	234,257	386,664	230,617
Cash and cash equivalents, end of year	$ 241,034	$ 234,257	$386,664
Supplemental disclosures of cash flow information:			
Cash paid during the year for interest	$ 183	$ 76	$ 35
Cash paid during the year for income taxes	42,405	34,924	31,284
Supplemental disclosures of non-cash investing activities :			
Capital expenditures incurred but not yet paid	952	1,001	7,852

See accompanying notes to consolidated financial statements

COLUMBIA SPORTSWEAR COMPANY
CONSOLIDATED STATEMENTS OF SHAREHOLDERS' EQUITY
(In thousands)

	Common Stock		Retained Earnings	Accumulated Other Comprehensive Income	Comprehensive Income	Total
	Shares Outstanding	Amount				
BALANCE, JANUARY 1, 2009	33,865	$ 1,481	$ 909,443	$ 33,166		$ 944,090
Components of comprehensive income:						
Net income	—	—	67,021	—	$ 67,021	67,021
Cash dividends ($0.66 per share)	—	—	(22,331)	—	—	(22,331)
Unrealized holding gains on available-for-sales securities, net	—	—	—	64	64	64
Foreign currency translation adjustment	—	—	—	13,854	13,854	13,854
Unrealized holding loss on derivative transactions, net	—	—	—	(3,640)	(3,640)	(3,640)
Comprehensive income	—	—	—	—	$ 77,299	
Issuance of common stock under employee stock plans, net	75	86	—	—		86
Tax adjustment from stock plans	—	(870)	—	—		(870)
Stock-based compensation expense	—	6,353	—	—		6,353
Repurchase of common stock	(204)	(6,214)	(1,185)	—		(7,399)
BALANCE, DECEMBER 31, 2009	33,736	836	952,948	43,444		997,228
Components of comprehensive income:						
Net income	—	—	77,037	—	$ 77,037	77,037
Cash dividends ($2.24 per share)	—	—	(75,439)	—	—	(75,439)
Unrealized holding losses on available-for-sales securities, net	—	—	—	(28)	(28)	(28)
Foreign currency translation adjustment	—	—	—	3,812	3,812	3,812
Unrealized holding loss on derivative transactions, net	—	—	—	(513)	(513)	(513)
Comprehensive income	—	—	—	—	$ 80,308	
Issuance of common stock under employee stock plans, net	240	6,480	—	—		6,480
Tax adjustment from stock plans	—	505	—	—		505
Stock-based compensation expense	—	6,730	—	—		6,730
Repurchase of common stock	(293)	(9,499)	(4,339)	—		(13,838)
BALANCE, DECEMBER 31, 2010	33,683	5,052	950,207	46,715		1,001,974
Components of comprehensive income:						
Net income	—	—	103,479	—	$ 103,479	103,479
Cash dividends ($0.86 per share)	—	—	(29,075)	—	—	(29,075)
Unrealized holding losses on available-for-sales securities, net	—	—	—	(38)	(38)	(38)
Foreign currency translation adjustment	—	—	—	(8,701)	(8,701)	(8,701)
Unrealized holding gains on derivative transactions, net	—	—	—	8,921	8,921	8,921
Comprehensive income	—	—	—	—	$ 103,661	
Issuance of common stock under employee stock plans, net	353	8,017	—	—		8,017
Tax adjustment from stock plans	—	2,098	—	—		2,098
Stock-based compensation expense	—	7,870	—	—		7,870
Repurchase of common stock	(398)	(20,000)	—	—		(20,000)
BALANCE, DECEMBER 31, 2011	33,638	$ 3,037	$1,024,611	$ 46,897		$1,074,545

See accompanying notes to consolidated financial statements

NOTES TO FINANCIAL STATEMENTS

COLUMBIA SPORTSWEAR COMPANY

NOTES TO CONSOLIDATED FINANCIAL STATEMENTS — (Continued)

NOTE 1—BASIS OF PRESENTATION AND ORGANIZATION

Nature of the business:

Columbia Sportswear Company is a global leader in the design, development, marketing and distribution of active outdoor apparel, footwear, accessories and equipment.

Principles of consolidation:

The consolidated financial statements include the accounts of Columbia Sportswear Company and its wholly-owned subsidiaries (the "Company"). All significant intercompany balances and transactions have been eliminated in consolidation.

Estimates and assumptions:

The preparation of financial statements in conformity with accounting principles generally accepted in the United States of America requires management to make estimates and assumptions that affect the reported amounts of assets and liabilities and disclosure of contingent assets and liabilities at the date of the consolidated financial statements and the reported amounts of revenues and expenses during the reporting period. Actual results may differ from these estimates and assumptions. Some of these more significant estimates relate to revenue recognition, including sales returns and claims from customers, allowance for doubtful accounts, excess, slow-moving and close-out inventories, product warranty, long-lived and intangible assets, income taxes and stock-based compensation.

NOTE 2—SUMMARY OF SIGNIFICANT ACCOUNTING POLICIES

Cash and cash equivalents:

Cash and cash equivalents are stated at fair value or at cost, which approximates fair value, and include investments with maturities of 90 days or less at the date of acquisition. At December 31, 2011, cash and cash equivalents consisted of cash, money market funds and time deposits with original maturities ranging from overnight to less than 90 days. At December 31, 2010, cash and cash equivalents consisted of cash, money market funds, municipal bonds and time deposits with original maturities ranging from overnight to less than 90 days.

Investments:

At December 31, 2011, short-term investments consisted of time deposits with original maturities greater than 90 days. These investments are considered available for use in current operations. At December 31, 2010, short-term investments consisted of shares in a short-term municipal bond fund and municipal bonds with original maturities greater than 90 days. These investments are considered available for use in current operations. All short-term investments are classified as available-for-sale securities and are recorded at fair value with any unrealized gains and losses reported, net of tax, in other comprehensive income. Realized gains or losses are determined based on the specific identification method.

At December 31, 2011 and 2010, long-term investments included in other non-current assets consisted of mutual fund shares held to offset liabilities to participants in the Company's deferred compensation plan. The investments are classified as long-term because the related deferred compensation liabilities are not expected to be paid within the next year. These investments are classified as trading securities and are recorded at fair value with unrealized gains and losses reported in operating expenses, which are offset against gains and losses resulting from changes in corresponding deferred compensation liabilities to participants.

COLUMBIA SPORTSWEAR COMPANY
NOTES TO CONSOLIDATED FINANCIAL STATEMENTS — (Continued)

Accounts receivable:

Accounts receivable have been reduced by an allowance for doubtful accounts. The Company makes ongoing estimates of the collectability of accounts receivable and maintains an allowance for estimated losses resulting from the inability of the Company's customers to make required payments.

Inventories:

Inventories are carried at the lower of cost or market. Cost is determined using the first-in, first-out method. The Company periodically reviews its inventories for excess, close-out or slow moving items and makes provisions as necessary to properly reflect inventory value.

Property, plant, and equipment:

Property, plant and equipment are stated at cost, net of accumulated depreciation. Depreciation is provided using the straight-line method over the estimated useful lives of the assets. The principal estimated useful lives are: buildings and building improvements, 15-30 years; land improvements, 15 years; furniture and fixtures, 3-10 years; and machinery and equipment, 3-5 years. Leasehold improvements are depreciated over the lesser of the estimated useful life of the improvement, which is most commonly 7 years, or the remaining term of the underlying lease.

Improvements to property, plant and equipment that substantially extend the useful life of the asset are capitalized. Repair and maintenance costs are expensed as incurred. Internal and external costs directly related to the development of internal-use software during the application development stage, including costs incurred for third party contractors and employee compensation, are capitalized and depreciated over a 3-7 year estimated useful life.

Impairment of long-lived assets:

Long-lived assets are amortized over their useful lives and are measured for impairment only when events or circumstances indicate the carrying value may be impaired. In these cases, the Company estimates the future undiscounted cash flows to be derived from the asset or asset group to determine whether a potential impairment exists. When reviewing for retail store impairment, identifiable cash flows are measured at the individual store level. If the sum of the estimated undiscounted cash flows is less than the carrying value of the asset, the Company recognizes an impairment loss, measured as the amount by which the carrying value exceeds the estimated fair value of the asset. Impairment charges for long-lived assets are included in selling, general and administrative ("SG&A") expense and were $6,211,000, $3,003,000 and $1,542,000 for the years ended December 31, 2011, 2010 and 2009, respectively.

Intangible assets and goodwill:

Goodwill and intangible assets with indefinite useful lives are not amortized but are periodically evaluated for impairment. Intangible assets that are determined to have finite lives are amortized using the straight-line method over their useful lives and are measured for impairment only when events or circumstances indicate the carrying value may be impaired.

Impairment of goodwill and intangible assets:

The Company reviews and tests its goodwill and intangible assets with indefinite useful lives for impairment in the fourth quarter of each year and when events or changes in circumstances indicate that the

COLUMBIA SPORTSWEAR COMPANY
NOTES TO CONSOLIDATED FINANCIAL STATEMENTS—(Continued)

carrying amount of such assets may be impaired. The Company's intangible assets with indefinite lives consist of trademarks and tradenames. Substantially all of the Company's goodwill is recorded in the United States segment and impairment testing for goodwill is performed at the reporting unit level. In the impairment test for goodwill, the two-step process first compares the estimated fair value of the reporting unit with the carrying amount of that reporting unit. The Company estimates the fair value of its reporting units using a combination of discounted cash flow analysis, comparisons with the market values of similar publicly traded companies and other operating performance based valuation methods as necessary. If step one indicates impairment, step two compares the estimated fair value of the reporting unit to the estimated fair value of all reporting unit assets and liabilities except goodwill to determine the implied fair value of goodwill. The Company calculates impairment as the excess of carrying amount of goodwill over the implied fair value of goodwill. In the impairment test for trademarks, the Company compares the estimated fair value of the asset to the carrying amount. The fair value of trademarks and tradenames is estimated using the relief from royalty approach, a standard form of discounted cash flow analysis used in the valuation of trademarks. If the carrying amount of trademarks exceeds the estimated fair value, the Company calculates impairment as the excess of carrying amount over the estimate of fair value.

If events or circumstances indicate the carrying value of intangible assets with finite lives may be impaired, the Company estimates the future undiscounted cash flows to be derived from the asset or asset group to determine whether a potential impairment exists. If the sum of the estimated undiscounted cash flows is less than the carrying value of the asset the Company recognizes an impairment loss, measured as the amount by which the carrying value exceeds the estimated fair value of the asset.

Impairment charges are classified as a component of SG&A expense. The fair value estimates are based on a number of factors, including assumptions and estimates for projected sales, income, cash flows, discount rates and other operating performance measures. Changes in estimates or the application of alternative assumptions could produce significantly different results. These assumptions and estimates may change in the future due to changes in economic conditions, changes in the Company's ability to meet sales and profitability objectives or changes in the Company's business operations or strategic direction.

Income taxes:

Income taxes are provided on financial statement earnings for financial reporting purposes. Income taxes are based on amounts of taxes payable or refundable in the current year and on expected future tax consequences of events that are recognized in the financial statements in different periods than they are recognized in tax returns. As a result of timing of recognition and measurement differences between financial accounting standards and income tax laws, temporary differences arise between amounts of pre-tax financial statement income and taxable income and between reported amounts of assets and liabilities in the Consolidated Balance Sheets and their respective tax bases. Deferred income tax assets and liabilities reported in the Consolidated Balance Sheets reflect estimated future tax effects attributable to these temporary differences and to net operating loss and net capital loss carryforwards, based on tax rates expected to be in effect for years in which the differences are expected to be settled or realized. Realization of deferred tax assets is dependent on future taxable income in specific jurisdictions. Valuation allowances are used to reduce deferred tax assets to amounts considered likely to be realized. U.S. deferred income taxes are not provided on undistributed income of foreign subsidiaries, where such earnings are considered to be permanently invested, or to the extent such recognition would result in a deferred tax asset.

Accrued income taxes in the Consolidated Balance Sheets include unrecognized income tax benefits relating to uncertain tax positions, including related interest and penalties, appropriately classified as current or noncurrent. The Company recognizes the tax benefit from an uncertain tax position if it is more likely than not

COLUMBIA SPORTSWEAR COMPANY
NOTES TO CONSOLIDATED FINANCIAL STATEMENTS — (Continued)

that the tax position will be sustained on examination by the relevant taxing authority based on the technical merits of the position. The tax benefits recognized in the financial statements from such positions are then measured based on the largest benefit that has a greater than 50% likelihood of being realized upon ultimate settlement with the relevant tax authority. In making this determination, the Company assumes that the taxing authority will examine the position and that they will have full knowledge of all relevant information. The provision for income taxes also includes estimates of interest and penalties related to uncertain tax positions.

Derivatives:

The effective portion of changes in fair values of outstanding cash flow hedges is recorded in other comprehensive income until earnings are affected by the hedged transaction, and any ineffective portion is included in current income. In most cases amounts recorded in other comprehensive income will be released to earnings some time after maturity of the related derivative. The Consolidated Statements of Operations classification of effective hedge results is the same as that of the underlying exposure. Results of hedges of product costs are recorded in cost of sales when the underlying hedged transaction affects earnings. Unrealized derivative gains and losses, which are recorded in assets and liabilities, respectively, are non-cash items and therefore are taken into account in the preparation of the Consolidated Statements of Cash Flows based on their respective balance sheet classifications. See Note 19 for more information on derivatives and risk management.

Foreign currency translation:

The assets and liabilities of the Company's foreign subsidiaries have been translated into U.S. dollars using the exchange rates in effect at period end, and the net sales and expenses have been translated into U.S. dollars using average exchange rates in effect during the period. The foreign currency translation adjustments are included as a separate component of accumulated other comprehensive income in shareholders' equity and are not currently adjusted for income taxes when they relate to indefinite net investments in non-U.S. operations.

Revenue recognition:

The Company records wholesale, e-commerce and licensed product revenues when title passes and the risks and rewards of ownership have passed to the customer. Title generally passes upon shipment to, or upon receipt by, the customer depending on the terms of sale with the customer. Retail store revenues are recorded at the time of sale.

In some countries outside of the United States where title passes upon receipt by the customer, predominantly in the Company's Western European wholesale business, precise information regarding the date of receipt by the customer is not readily available. In these cases, the Company estimates the date of receipt by the customer based on historical and expected delivery times by geographic location. The Company periodically tests the accuracy of these estimates based on actual transactions. Delivery times vary by geographic location, generally from one to five days. To date, the Company has found these estimates to be materially accurate.

At the time of revenue recognition, the Company also provides for estimated sales returns and miscellaneous claims from customers as reductions to revenues. The estimates are based on historical rates of product returns and claims as well as events and circumstances that indicate changes to historical rates of returns and claims. However, actual returns and claims in any future period are inherently uncertain and thus may differ from the estimates. If actual or expected future returns and claims are significantly greater or lower than the reserves that had been established, the Company would record a reduction or increase to net revenues in the period in which it made such determination.

COLUMBIA SPORTSWEAR COMPANY
NOTES TO CONSOLIDATED FINANCIAL STATEMENTS — (Continued)

Cost of sales:

The expenses that are included in cost of sales include all direct product and conversion-related costs, and costs related to shipping, duties and importation. Specific provisions for excess, close-out or slow moving inventory are also included in cost of sales. In addition, some of the Company's products carry limited warranty provisions for defects in quality and workmanship. A warranty reserve is established at the time of sale to cover estimated costs based on the Company's history of warranty repairs and replacements and is recorded in cost of sales.

Selling, general and administrative expense:

SG&A expense consists of personnel-related costs, advertising, depreciation and other selling and general operating expenses related to the Company's business functions, including planning, receiving finished goods, warehousing, distribution, retail operations and information technology.

Shipping and handling costs:

Shipping and handling fees billed to customers are recorded as revenue. The direct costs associated with shipping goods to customers are recorded as cost of sales. Inventory planning, receiving and handling costs are recorded as a component of SG&A expenses and were $65,290,000, $57,901,000 and $55,867,000 for the years ended December 31, 2011, 2010 and 2009, respectively.

Stock-based compensation:

Stock-based compensation cost is estimated at the grant date based on the award's fair value and is recognized as expense over the requisite service period using the straight-line attribution method. The Company estimates stock-based compensation for stock options granted using the Black-Scholes option pricing model, which requires various highly subjective assumptions, including volatility and expected option life. Further, the Company estimates forfeitures for stock-based awards granted which are not expected to vest. If any of these inputs or assumptions changes significantly, stock-based compensation expense may differ materially in the future from that recorded in the current period. Assumptions are evaluated and revised as necessary to reflect changes in market conditions and the Company's experience. Estimates of fair value are not intended to predict actual future events or the value ultimately realized by people who receive equity awards. The fair value of service-based and performance-based restricted stock units is discounted by the present value of the estimated future stream of dividends over the vesting period using the Black-Scholes model.

Advertising costs:

Advertising costs are expensed in the period incurred and are included in SG&A expenses. Total advertising expense, including cooperative advertising costs, was $85,003,000, $77,978,000 and $65,204,000 for the years ended December 31, 2011, 2010 and 2009, respectively.

Through cooperative advertising programs, the Company reimburses its wholesale customers for some of their costs of advertising the Company's products based on various criteria, including the value of purchases from the Company and various advertising specifications. Cooperative advertising costs are included in expenses because the Company receives an identifiable benefit in exchange for the cost, the advertising may be obtained from a party other than the customer, and the fair value of the advertising benefit can be reasonably estimated. Cooperative advertising costs were $8,554,000, $7,259,000 and $10,978,000 for the years ended December 31, 2011, 2010 and 2009, respectively.

COLUMBIA SPORTSWEAR COMPANY

NOTES TO CONSOLIDATED FINANCIAL STATEMENTS—(Continued)

Recent Accounting Pronouncements:

In May 2011, the Financial Accounting Standards Board ("FASB") issued Accounting Standards Update ("ASU") No. 2011-04, *Fair Value Measurement (Topic 820): Amendments to Achieve Common Fair Value Measurement and Disclosure Requirements in U.S. GAAP and IFRS* . This ASU was issued concurrently with International Financial Reporting Standards ("IFRS") 13 *Fair Value Measurements* , to provide largely identical guidance about fair value measurement and disclosure requirements. The new standards do not extend the use of fair value but, rather, provide guidance about how fair value should be applied where it already is required or permitted under IFRS or U.S. GAAP. This standard is effective prospectively for interim and annual periods beginning after December 15, 2011. The Company does not expect the adoption of this standard to have a material effect on the Company's consolidated financial position, results of operations or cash flows.

In June 2011, the FASB issued ASU No. 2011-05, *Comprehensive Income (Topic 220): Presentation of Comprehensive Income* . This ASU increases the prominence of other comprehensive income in financial statements while eliminating the option in U.S. GAAP to present other comprehensive income in the statement of changes in equity. Under this ASU, an entity will have the option to present the components of net income and comprehensive income in either one or two consecutive financial statements. This ASU is effective for fiscal years, and interim periods within those years, beginning after December 15, 2011. The Company does not expect the adoption of this standard to have a material effect on the Company's consolidated financial position, results of operations or cash flows.

In September 2011, the FASB issued ASU No. 2011-08, *Intangibles—Goodwill and Other (Topic 350): Testing Goodwill for Impairment* . This ASU permits an entity to make a qualitative assessment of whether it is more likely than not that a reporting unit's fair value is less than its carrying amount before applying the two-step goodwill impairment test. Under these requirements, an entity would not be required to calculate the fair value of a reporting unit unless the entity determines, based on the qualitative assessment, that it is more likely than not that its fair value is less than its carrying amount. The ASU is effective for annual and interim goodwill impairment tests performed for fiscal years beginning after December 15, 2011. Early adoption is permitted. The Company does not expect the adoption of this standard to have a material effect on the Company's consolidated financial position, results of operations or cash flows.

NOTE 3—CONCENTRATIONS

Trade Receivables

At December 31, 2011, no single customer accounted for 10% or more of consolidated accounts receivable. At December 31, 2010, the Company had one customer in its Canadian segment that accounted for approximately 11.9% of consolidated accounts receivable. No single customer accounted for 10% or more of consolidated revenues for any of the years ended December 31, 2011, 2010 or 2009.

Derivatives

The Company uses derivative instruments primarily to hedge the currency exchange rate risk of anticipated transactions denominated in non-functional currencies that are designated and qualify as cash flow hedges. The Company also uses derivative instruments to economically hedge the currency exchange rate risk of certain investment positions, to hedge balance sheet re-measurement risk and to hedge other anticipated transactions that do not qualify as cash flow hedges. At December 31, 2011, the Company's derivative contracts had a remaining maturity of approximately two years or less. All the counterparties to these transactions had both long-term and short-term investment grade credit ratings. The maximum net exposure to any single counterparty, which is generally limited to the aggregate unrealized gain of all contracts with that counterparty, was less than

COLUMBIA SPORTSWEAR COMPANY
NOTES TO CONSOLIDATED FINANCIAL STATEMENTS — (Continued)

$3,000,000 at December 31, 2011. The majority of the Company's derivative counterparties have strong credit ratings and as a result, the Company does not require collateral to facilitate transactions. See Note 19 for further disclosures concerning derivatives.

Country and supplier concentrations

The Company's products are produced by independent factories located outside the United States, principally in Southeast Asia. Apparel is manufactured in more than 15 countries, with Vietnam and China accounting for approximately 73% of 2011 global apparel production. Footwear is manufactured in three countries, with China and Vietnam accounting for approximately 92% of 2011 global footwear production. The five largest apparel factory groups accounted for approximately 25% of 2011 global apparel production, with the largest factory group accounting for 9% of 2011 global apparel production. The five largest footwear factory groups accounted for approximately 72% of 2011 global footwear production, with the largest factory group accounting for 25% of 2011 global footwear production. In addition, a single vendor supplies substantially all of the zippers used in the Company's products. These companies, however, have multiple factory locations, many of which are in different countries, thus reducing the risk that unfavorable conditions at a single factory or location will have a material adverse effect on the Company.

NOTE 4—ACCOUNTS RECEIVABLE, NET

Accounts receivable, net, is as follows (in thousands):

	December 31,	
	2011	2010
Trade accounts receivable	$359,083	$307,279
Allowance for doubtful accounts	(7,545)	(7,098)
Accounts receivable, net	$351,538	$300,181

NOTE 5—INVENTORIES, NET

Inventories, net, consisted of the following (in thousands):

	December 31,	
	2011	2010
Raw materials	$ 2,044	$ 1,096
Work in process	1,240	659
Finished goods	361,915	312,543
	$365,199	$314,298

COLUMBIA SPORTSWEAR COMPANY
NOTES TO CONSOLIDATED FINANCIAL STATEMENTS — (Continued)

NOTE 6 — PROPERTY, PLANT, AND EQUIPMENT, NET

Property, plant, and equipment consisted of the following (in thousands):

	December 31,	
	2011	2010
Land and improvements	$ 20,690	$ 16,898
Building and improvements	155,672	144,004
Machinery and equipment	198,387	193,104
Furniture and fixtures	50,108	46,147
Leasehold improvements	65,476	62,884
Construction in progress	36,463	9,775
	526,796	472,812
Less accumulated depreciation	(275,886)	(250,999)
	$ 250,910	$ 221,813

NOTE 7 — INTANGIBLE ASSETS, NET AND GOODWILL

Intangible assets that are determined to have finite lives include patents and purchased technology and are amortized over their estimated useful lives, which is approximately 10 years. Intangible assets with indefinite useful lives include trademarks and tradenames and are not amortized but are periodically evaluated for impairment.

Identifiable intangible assets consisted of the following (in thousands):

	December 31,	
	2011	2010
Intangible assets subject to amortization:		
Gross carrying amount	$14,198	$14,198
Accumulated amortization	(2,599)	(1,196)
Net carrying amount	11,599	13,002
Intangible assets not subject to amortization	27,421	27,421
Intangible assets, net	$39,020	$40,423

Amortization expense for the years ended December 31, 2011, 2010, and 2009 was $1,403,000, $553,000 and $109,000, respectively. Amortization expense for intangible assets subject to amortization is estimated to be $1,402,000 in 2012 and $1,330,000 in 2013 through 2016.

At December 31, 2011, 2010 and 2009, the Company determined that its goodwill and intangible assets were not impaired. The change in goodwill in 2011 resulted from a purchase price adjustment related to an acquisition in 2010.

NOTE 8 — SHORT-TERM BORROWINGS AND CREDIT LINES

The Company has a domestic credit agreement for an unsecured, committed $125,000,000 revolving line of credit. The maturity date of this agreement is July 1, 2016. Interest, payable monthly, is based on the Company's applicable funded debt ratio, ranging from LIBOR plus 100 to 175 basis points. This line of credit requires the

COLUMBIA SPORTSWEAR COMPANY
NOTES TO CONSOLIDATED FINANCIAL STATEMENTS — (Continued)

Company to comply with certain financial covenants covering net income, tangible net worth and borrowing basis. If the Company is in default, it is prohibited from paying dividends or repurchasing common stock. At December 31, 2011, the Company was in compliance with all associated covenants. At December 31, 2011 and 2010, no balance was outstanding under this line of credit.

The Company's Canadian subsidiary has available an unsecured and uncommitted line of credit guaranteed by the parent company providing for borrowing to a maximum of C$30,000,000 (US$29,374,000) at December 31, 2011. The revolving line accrues interest at the bank's Canadian prime rate. There was no balance outstanding under this line at December 31, 2011 and 2010.

The Company's European subsidiary has available two separate unsecured and uncommitted lines of credit guaranteed by the parent company providing for borrowing up to a maximum of €30,000,000 and €5,000,000, respectively (combined US$45,366,000) at December 31, 2011, of which US$3,240,000 of the €5,000,000 line is designated as a European customs guarantee. These lines accrue interest based on the European Central Bank refinancing rate plus 50 basis points and Euro Overnight Index Average plus 75 basis points, respectively. There was no balance outstanding under either line at December 31, 2011 or 2010.

The Company's Japanese subsidiary has an unsecured and uncommitted line of credit guaranteed by the parent company providing for borrowing to a maximum of US$5,000,000 at December 31, 2011. The revolving line accrues interest at LIBOR plus 110 basis points. There was no balance outstanding under this line at December 31, 2011 and 2010.

On August, 31, 2011, the Company's Korean subsidiary entered into an unsecured and uncommitted line of credit agreement guaranteed by the parent company providing for borrowing to a maximum of US$10,000,000. The revolving line accrues interest at the Korean three-month CD rate plus 220 basis points. There was no balance outstanding under this line at December 31, 2011.

Off-Balance Sheet Arrangements

The Company has arrangements in place to facilitate the import and purchase of inventory through import letters of credit. The Company has available unsecured and uncommitted import letters of credit in the aggregate amount of $15,000,000 subject to annual renewal. At December 31, 2011, the Company had outstanding letters of credit of $2,029,000 for purchase orders for inventory under this arrangement.

NOTE 9 — ACCRUED LIABILITIES

Accrued liabilities consisted of the following (in thousands):

	December 31,	
	2011	2010
Accrued salaries, bonus, vacation and other benefits	$ 55,958	$ 49,078
Accrued import duties	11,258	13,443
Product warranties	10,452	10,256
Other	26,828	30,033
	$104,496	$102,810

COLUMBIA SPORTSWEAR COMPANY

NOTES TO CONSOLIDATED FINANCIAL STATEMENTS — (Continued)

A reconciliation of product warranties is as follows (in thousands):

	Year Ended December 31,		
	2011	2010	2009
Balance at beginning of period	$10,256	$12,112	$ 9,746
Provision for warranty claims	4,758	1,371	5,133
Warranty claims	(4,468)	(3,104)	(2,984)
Other	(94)	(123)	217
Balance at end of period	$10,452	$10,256	$12,112

NOTE 10—INCOME TAXES

Consolidated income from continuing operations before income taxes consisted of the following (in thousands):

	Year Ended December 31,		
	2011	2010	2009
U.S. operations	$ 68,412	$ 59,881	$59,629
Foreign operations	69,268	45,010	30,221
Income before income tax	$137,680	$104,891	$89,850

The components of the provision (benefit) for income taxes consisted of the following (in thousands):

	Year Ended December 31,		
	2011	2010	2009
Current:			
Federal	$16,384	$ 24,419	$10,030
State and local	1,995	4,060	2,088
Non-U.S.	19,508	23,253	10,399
	37,887	51,732	22,517
Deferred:			
Federal	407	(18,405)	2,377
State and local	229	(1,223)	12
Non-U.S.	(4,322)	(4,250)	(2,077)
	(3,686)	(23,878)	312
Income tax expense	$34,201	$ 27,854	$22,829

COLUMBIA SPORTSWEAR COMPANY
NOTES TO CONSOLIDATED FINANCIAL STATEMENTS—(Continued)

The following is a reconciliation of the statutory federal income tax rate to the effective rate reported in the financial statements:

	Year Ended December 31,		
	2011	2010	2009
	(percent of income)		
Provision for federal income taxes at the statutory rate	35.0%	35.0%	35.0%
State and local income taxes, net of federal benefit	1.4	2.6	1.9
Non-U.S. income taxed at different rates	(6.5)	(2.3)	0.4
Foreign tax credits	(1.8)	(3.5)	(5.8)
Reduction of accrued income taxes	(3.5)	(4.0)	(4.1)
Tax-exempt interest	(0.1)	(0.2)	(0.5)
Other	0.3	(1.0)	(1.5)
Actual provision for income taxes	24.8%	26.6%	25.4%

Significant components of the Company's deferred taxes consisted of the following (in thousands):

	December 31,	
	2011	2010
Deferred tax assets:		
Non-deductible accruals and allowances	$ 30,307	$26,905
Capitalized inventory costs	25,814	21,065
Stock compensation	6,283	6,157
Net operating loss carryforwards	6,364	6,894
Depreciation and amortization	1,693	1,722
Tax credits	12,702	11,187
Other	1,121	414
Gross deferred tax assets	84,284	74,344
Valuation allowance	(6,690)	(7,261)
Net deferred tax assets	77,594	67,083
Deferred tax liabilities:		
Deductible accruals and allowance	(801)	(593)
Depreciation and amortization	(12,320)	(7,182)
Foreign currency loss	(2,494)	—
Other	(596)	(1,564)
Gross deferred tax liabilities	(16,211)	(9,339)
Total net deferred taxes	$ 61,383	$57,744

We record net deferred tax assets to the extent we believe these assets will more likely than not be realized. In making such a determination, we consider all available positive and negative evidence, including future reversals of existing taxable temporary differences, projected future taxable income, tax-planning strategies, and results of recent operations. The Company had net operating loss carryforwards at December 31, 2011 and 2010 in certain international tax jurisdictions of $58,272,000 and $67,800,000, respectively, which will begin to expire in 2015. The net operating losses result in a deferred tax asset of $6,364,000 and $6,894,000 at December 31, 2011 and 2010, respectively, both of which were subject to a 100% valuation allowance. To the extent that the Company reverses a portion of the valuation allowance, the adjustment would be recorded as a reduction to income tax expense.

COLUMBIA SPORTSWEAR COMPANY
NOTES TO CONSOLIDATED FINANCIAL STATEMENTS — (Continued)

Non-current deferred tax assets of $11,605,000 and $14,806,000 are included as a component of other non-current assets in the consolidated balance sheet at December 31, 2011 and 2010, respectively.

The Company had undistributed earnings of foreign subsidiaries of approximately $218,023,000 at December 31, 2011 for which deferred taxes have not been provided. Such earnings are considered indefinitely invested outside of the United States. If these earnings were repatriated to the United States, the earnings would be subject to U.S. taxation. The amount of the unrecognized deferred tax liability associated with the undistributed earnings was approximately $50,059,000 at December 31, 2011. The unrecognized deferred tax liability approximates the excess of the United States tax liability over the creditable foreign taxes paid that would result from a full remittance of undistributed earnings.

A reconciliation of the beginning and ending amount of gross unrecognized tax benefits is as follows (in thousands):

	December 31,		
	2011	2010	2009
Balance at beginning of period	$18,694	$20,183	$21,839
Increases related to prior year tax positions	43	893	1,346
Decreases related to prior year tax positions	(141)	(27)	(634)
Increases related to current year tax positions	1,388	1,278	1,598
Settlements	(649)	—	(1,194)
Expiration of statute of limitations	(5,019)	(3,633)	(2,772)
Balance at end of period	$14,316	$18,694	$20,183

Unrecognized tax benefits of $12,735,000 and $16,740,000 would affect the effective tax rate if recognized at December 31, 2011 and 2010, respectively.

The Company conducts business globally, and as a result, the Company or one or more of its subsidiaries files income tax returns in the U.S. federal jurisdiction and various state and foreign jurisdictions. The Company is subject to examination by taxing authorities throughout the world, including such major jurisdictions as Canada, China, France, Germany, Hong Kong, Italy, Japan, South Korea, Switzerland, the United Kingdom and the United States. The Company has effectively settled U.S. tax examinations of all years through 2007. Internationally, the Company has effectively settled Canadian tax examinations of all years through 2004, Swiss tax examinations of all years through 2008, French tax examinations of all years through 2008, Japanese tax examinations of all years through 2007 and Korean tax examinations of all years through 2007. The Company is currently under examination in Canada for the tax years 2005 through 2008 and in Japan for the tax years 2008 through 2010. The Company does not anticipate that adjustments relative to these ongoing tax audits will result in a material change to its consolidated financial position, results of operations or cash flows.

Due to the potential for resolution of income tax audits currently in progress, and the expiration of various statutes of limitation, it is reasonably possible that the unrecognized tax benefits balance may change within the twelve months following December 31, 2011 by a range of zero to $10,195,000. Open tax years, including those previously mentioned, contain matters that could be subject to differing interpretations of applicable tax laws and regulations as they relate to the amount, timing, or inclusion of revenue and expenses or the sustainability of income tax credits for a given examination cycle.

The Company recognizes interest expense and penalties related to income tax matters in income tax expense. The Company recognized a net reversal of accrued interest and penalties of $501,000 in 2011, net accrued interest and penalties of $780,000 in 2010 and a net reversal of accrued interest and penalties of $80,000

COLUMBIA SPORTSWEAR COMPANY

NOTES TO CONSOLIDATED FINANCIAL STATEMENTS — (Continued)

in 2009, all related to uncertain tax positions. The Company had $3,434,000 and $3,935,000 of accrued interest and penalties related to uncertain tax positions at December 31, 2011 and 2010, respectively.

NOTE 11—OTHER LONG-TERM LIABILITIES

Other long-term liabilities consisted of the following (in thousands):

	December 31,	
	2011	2010
Straight-line and deferred rent liabilities	$18,028	$16,296
Asset retirement obligations	1,565	1,122
Deferred compensation plan liability	2,521	1,670
Other	1,739	2,368
	$23,853	$21,456

NOTE 12—RETIREMENT SAVINGS PLANS

401(k) Profit-Sharing Plan

The Company has a 401(k) profit-sharing plan, which covers substantially all U.S. employees. Participation begins the first of the quarter following completion of thirty days of service. The Company may elect to make discretionary matching and/or non-matching contributions. All Company contributions to the plan as determined by the Board of Directors totaled $5,223,000, $4,443,000 and $2,610,000 for the years ended December 31, 2011, 2010 and 2009, respectively.

Deferred Compensation Plan

The Company sponsors a nonqualified retirement savings plan for certain senior management employees whose contributions to the tax qualified 401(k) plan would be limited by provisions of the Internal Revenue Code. This plan allows participants to defer receipt of a portion of their salary and incentive compensation and to receive matching contributions for a portion of the deferred amounts. Company contributions to the plan totaled $245,000, $155,000 and $108,000 for the years ended December 31, 2011, 2010 and 2009, respectively. Participants earn a return on their deferred compensation based on investment earnings of participant-selected mutual funds. Changes in the market value of the participants' investment selections are recorded as an adjustment to deferred compensation liabilities, with an offset to compensation expense. Deferred compensation, including accumulated earnings on the participant-directed investment selections, is distributable in cash at participant-specified dates or upon retirement, death, disability or termination of employment. At December 31, 2011 and 2010, the liability to participants under this plan was $2,521,000 and $1,670,000, respectively, and was recorded in other long-term liabilities. The current portion of the participant liability at December 31, 2011 and 2010 was not material.

The Company has purchased specific mutual funds in the same amounts as the participant-directed investment selections underlying the deferred compensation liabilities. These investment securities and earnings thereon, held in an irrevocable trust, are intended to provide a source of funds to meet the deferred compensation obligations, subject to claims of creditors in the event of the Company's insolvency. The mutual funds are recorded at fair value in other non-current assets. At December 31, 2011 and 2010, the fair value of the mutual fund investments was $2,521,000 and $1,670,000, respectively. Realized and unrealized gains and losses on the mutual fund investments are offset against gains and losses resulting from changes in corresponding deferred compensation liabilities to participants.

COLUMBIA SPORTSWEAR COMPANY
NOTES TO CONSOLIDATED FINANCIAL STATEMENTS — (Continued)

NOTE 13—COMMITMENTS AND CONTINGENCIES

Operating Leases

The Company leases, among other things, retail space, office space, warehouse facilities, storage space, vehicles and equipment. Generally, the base lease terms are between 5 and 10 years. Certain lease agreements contain scheduled rent escalation clauses in their future minimum lease payments. Future minimum lease payments are recognized on a straight-line basis over the minimum lease term and the pro rata portion of scheduled rent escalations is included in other long-term liabilities. Certain retail space lease agreements provide for additional rents based on a percentage of annual sales in excess of stipulated minimums ("percentage rent"). Certain lease agreements require the Company to pay real estate taxes, insurance, common area maintenance ("CAM"), and other costs, collectively referred to as operating costs, in addition to base rent. Percentage rent and operating costs are recognized as incurred in SG&A expense in the Consolidated Statements of Operations. Certain lease agreements also contain lease incentives, such as tenant improvement allowances and rent holidays. The Company recognizes the benefits related to the lease incentives on a straight-line basis over the applicable lease term.

Rent expense, including percentage rent but excluding operating costs for which the Company is obligated, consisted of the following (in thousands):

| | Year Ended December 31, | | |
	2011	2010	2009
Rent expense included in SG&A	$46,869	$39,898	$31,140
Rent expense included in cost of sales	1,429	1,351	1,465
	$48,298	$41,249	$32,605

Approximate future minimum payments, including rent escalation clauses and stores that are not yet open, on all lease obligations at December 31, 2011, are as follows (in thousands). Operating lease obligations listed below do not include percentage rent, real estate taxes, insurance, CAM, and other costs for which the Company is obligated. These operating lease commitments are not reflected on the Consolidated Balance Sheet.

2012	$ 38,773
2013	35,060
2014	29,819
2015	26,892
2016	25,254
Thereafter	94,892
	$250,690

Inventory Purchase Obligations

Inventory purchase obligations consist of open production purchase orders for sourced apparel, footwear, accessories and equipment, and raw material commitments not included in open production purchase orders. At December 31, 2011 inventory purchase obligations were $351,854,000. To support certain inventory purchase obligations, the Company maintains unsecured and uncommitted lines of credit available for issuing import letters of credit. At December 31, 2011 the Company had letters of credit of $2,029,000 outstanding for inventory purchase obligations.

COLUMBIA SPORTSWEAR COMPANY
NOTES TO CONSOLIDATED FINANCIAL STATEMENTS — (Continued)

Litigation

The Company is a party to various legal claims, actions and complaints from time to time. Although the ultimate resolution of legal proceedings cannot be predicted with certainty, management believes that disposition of these matters will not have a material adverse effect on the Company's consolidated financial statements.

Indemnities and Guarantees

During its normal course of business, the Company has made certain indemnities, commitments and guarantees under which it may be required to make payments in relation to certain transactions. These include (i) intellectual property indemnities to the Company's customers and licensees in connection with the use, sale and/or license of Company products, (ii) indemnities to various lessors in connection with facility leases for certain claims arising from such facility or lease, (iii) indemnities to customers, vendors and service providers pertaining to claims based on the negligence or willful misconduct of the Company, (iv) executive severance arrangements and (v) indemnities involving the accuracy of representations and warranties in certain contracts. The duration of these indemnities, commitments and guarantees varies, and in certain cases, may be indefinite. The majority of these indemnities, commitments and guarantees do not provide for any limitation of the maximum potential for future payments the Company could be obligated to make. The Company has not recorded any liability for these indemnities, commitments and guarantees in the accompanying Consolidated Balance Sheets.

NOTE 14—SHAREHOLDERS' EQUITY

Since the inception of the Company's stock repurchase plan in 2004 through December 31, 2011, the Company's Board of Directors has authorized the repurchase of $500,000,000 of the Company's common stock. As of December 31, 2011, the Company had repurchased 9,588,798 shares under this program at an aggregate purchase price of approximately $441,237,000. During the year ended December 31, 2011, the Company repurchased an aggregate of $20,000,000 of common stock under the stock repurchase plan. Shares of the Company's common stock may be purchased in the open market or through privately negotiated transactions, subject to market conditions. The repurchase program does not obligate the Company to acquire any specific number of shares or to acquire shares over any specified period of time.

NOTE 15—STOCK-BASED COMPENSATION

The Company's stock incentive plan (the "Plan") provides for issuance of up to 8,900,000 shares of the Company's Common Stock, of which 1,344,342 shares were available for future grants under the Plan at December 31, 2011. The Plan allows for grants of incentive stock options, non-statutory stock options, restricted stock awards, restricted stock units and other stock-based awards. The Company uses original issuance shares to satisfy share-based payments.

Stock-based compensation expense consisted of the following (in thousands):

	Year Ended December 31,		
	2011	2010	2009
Cost of sales	$ 282	$ 286	$ 335
Selling, general, and administrative expense	7,588	6,444	6,018
Pre-tax stock-based compensation expense	7,870	6,730	6,353
Income tax benefits	(2,729)	(2,162)	(2,258)
Total stock-based compensation expense, net of tax	$ 5,141	$ 4,568	$ 4,095

COLUMBIA SPORTSWEAR COMPANY
NOTES TO CONSOLIDATED FINANCIAL STATEMENTS — (Continued)

No stock-based compensation costs were capitalized for the years ended December 31, 2011, 2010 or 2009.

The Company realized a tax benefit for the deduction from stock-based award transactions of $4,702,000, $1,909,000, and $851,000 for the years ended December 31, 2011, 2010 and 2009, respectively.

Stock Options

Options to purchase the Company's common stock are granted at exercise prices equal to or greater than the fair market value of the Company's common stock on the date of grant. Options granted after 2000 and before 2009 generally vest and become exercisable over a period of four years (25 percent on the first anniversary date following the date of grant and monthly thereafter) and expire ten years from the date of the grant, with the exception of most options granted in 2005. Most options granted in 2005 vested and became exercisable one year from the date of grant and expire ten years from the date of grant. Options granted after 2008 generally vest and become exercisable ratably on an annual basis over a period of four years and expire ten years from the date of the grant.

The Company estimates the fair value of stock options using the Black-Scholes model. Key inputs and assumptions used to estimate the fair value of stock options include the exercise price of the award, the expected option term, expected volatility of the Company's stock over the option's expected term, the risk-free interest rate over the option's expected term, and the Company's expected annual dividend yield. Assumptions are evaluated and revised as necessary to reflect changes in market conditions and the Company's experience. Estimates of fair value are not intended to predict actual future events or the value ultimately realized by people who receive equity awards.

The following table presents the weighted average assumptions for the years ended December 31:

	2011(1)	2010	2009
Expected term	5.12 years	4.53 years	4.71 years
Expected stock price volatility	30.76%	28.79%	29.52%
Risk-free interest rate	1.84%	1.91%	1.73%
Expected dividend yield	1.31%	1.64%	2.17%
Weighted average grant date fair value	$ 16.09	$ 10.08	$ 6.55

(1)   During the year ended December 31, 2011, the Company granted two stock option awards totaling 53,720 shares that vest 100% on the fifth anniversary of the grant date. Because the Company did not have sufficient historical exercise data to provide a reasonable basis upon which to estimate the expected term for these grants, the Company utilized the simplified method in developing an estimate of the expected term of these options.

COLUMBIA SPORTSWEAR COMPANY
NOTES TO CONSOLIDATED FINANCIAL STATEMENTS—(Continued)

The following table summarizes stock option activity under the Plan:

	Number of Shares	Weighted Average Exercise Price	Weighted Average Remaining Contractual Life	Aggregate Intrinsic Value (in thousands)
Options outstanding at January 1, 2009	1,653,639	$ 45.10	6.73	$ 1,042
Granted	387,505	29.75		
Cancelled	(252,303)	44.90		
Exercised	(28,668)	24.76		
Options outstanding at December 31, 2009	1,760,173	42.08	6.25	4,599
Granted	385,924	44.11		
Cancelled	(77,481)	46.04		
Exercised	(196,402)	37.34		
Options outstanding at December 31, 2010	1,872,214	42.84	6.33	33,057
Granted	340,973	61.38		
Cancelled	(40,396)	43.68		
Exercised	(253,695)	43.32		
Options outstanding at December 31, 2011	1,919,096	$ 46.05	6.25	$ 9,141
Options vested and expected to vest at December 31, 2011	1,857,797	$ 45.81	6.17	$ 8,994
Options exercisable at December 31, 2011	1,145,763	$ 44.24	4.83	$ 5,716

The aggregate intrinsic value in the table above represents pre-tax intrinsic value that would have been realized if all options had been exercised on the last business day of the period indicated, based on the Company's closing stock price on that day.

Total stock option compensation expense for the years ended December 31, 2011, 2010 and 2009 was $3,550,000, $3,348,000 and $2,861,000, respectively. At December 31, 2011, unrecognized costs related to stock options totaled approximately $6,018,000, before any related tax benefit. The unrecognized costs related to stock options are being amortized over the related vesting period using the straight-line attribution method. Unrecognized costs related to stock options at December 31, 2011 are expected to be recognized over a weighted average period of 2.33 years. The aggregate intrinsic value of stock options exercised was $4,906,000, $2,854,000 and $333,000 for the years ended December 31, 2011, 2010 and 2009, respectively. The total cash received as a result of stock option exercises for the years ended December 31, 2011, 2010 and 2009 was $10,991,000, $7,333,000 and $710,000, respectively.

Restricted Stock Units

Service-based restricted stock units are granted at no cost to key employees, and shares granted prior to 2009 generally vest over three years from the date of grant. Service-based restricted stock units granted after 2008 generally vest over a period of four years. Performance-based restricted stock units are granted at no cost to certain members of the Company's senior executive team, excluding the Chairman and the President and Chief Executive Officer. Performance-based restricted stock units granted prior to 2010 generally vest over a performance period of between two and one-half and three years with an additional required service period of one year. Performance-based restricted stock units granted after 2009 generally vest over a performance period of between two and one-half and three years. Restricted stock units vest in accordance with the terms and conditions established by the Compensation Committee of the Board of Directors, and are based on continued service and,

COLUMBIA SPORTSWEAR COMPANY
NOTES TO CONSOLIDATED FINANCIAL STATEMENTS — (Continued)

in some instances, on individual performance and/or Company performance. For the majority of restricted stock units granted, the number of shares issued on the date the restricted stock units vest is net of the minimum statutory withholding requirements that the Company pays in cash to the appropriate taxing authorities on behalf of its employees. For the years ended December 31, 2011, 2010 and 2009, the Company withheld 48,059, 18,721 and 19,819 shares, respectively, to satisfy $2,974,000, $853,000 and $624,000 of employees' tax obligations, respectively.

The fair value of service-based and performance-based restricted stock units is discounted by the present value of the estimated future stream of dividends over the vesting period using the Black-Scholes model. The relevant inputs and assumptions used in the Black-Scholes model to compute the discount are the vesting period, expected annual dividend yield and closing price of the Company's common stock on the date of grant.

The following table presents the weighted average assumptions for the years ended December 31:

	2011	2010	2009
Vesting period	3.96 years	3.75 years	3.82 years
Expected dividend yield	1.33%	1.56%	2.19%
Estimated average fair value per restricted stock unit granted	$ 58.37	$ 43.95	$ 27.14

The following table summarizes the restricted stock unit activity under the Plan:

	Number of Shares	Weighted Average Grant Date Fair Value Per Share
Restricted stock units outstanding at January 1, 2009	260,509	$ 46.32
Granted	136,327	27.14
Vested	(65,935)	53.41
Forfeited	(44,381)	41.22
Restricted stock units outstanding at December 31, 2009	286,520	36.35
Granted	128,525	43.95
Vested	(62,417)	42.95
Forfeited	(23,833)	42.44
Restricted stock units outstanding at December 31, 2010	328,795	37.63
Granted	145,768	58.37
Vested	(146,951)	38.01
Forfeited	(30,860)	41.79
Restricted stock units outstanding at December 31, 2011	296,752	$ 47.19

Restricted stock unit compensation expense for the years ended December 31, 2011, 2010 and 2009 was $4,320,000, $3,382,000 and $3,492,000, respectively. At December 31, 2011, unrecognized costs related to restricted stock units totaled approximately $8,806,000, before any related tax benefit. The unrecognized costs related to restricted stock units are being amortized over the related vesting period using the straight-line attribution method. These unrecognized costs at December 31, 2011 are expected to be recognized over a weighted average period of 2.34 years. The total grant date fair value of restricted stock units vested during the year ended December 31, 2011, 2010 and 2009 was $5,586,000, $2,681,000 and $3,522,000, respectively.

COLUMBIA SPORTSWEAR COMPANY
NOTES TO CONSOLIDATED FINANCIAL STATEMENTS—(Continued)

NOTE 16—EARNINGS PER SHARE

Earnings per share ("EPS") , is presented on both a basic and diluted basis. Basic EPS is based on the weighted average number of common shares outstanding. Diluted EPS reflects the potential dilution that could occur if outstanding securities or other contracts to issue common stock were exercised or converted into common stock. For the calculation of diluted EPS, the basic weighted average number of shares is increased by the dilutive effect of stock options and restricted stock units determined using the treasury stock method.

A reconciliation of the common shares used in the denominator for computing basic and diluted EPS is as follows (in thousands, except per share amounts):

	Year Ended December 31,		
	2011	2010	2009
Weighted average common shares outstanding, used in computing basic earnings per share	33,808	33,725	33,846
Effect of dilutive stock options and restricted stock units	396	367	135
Weighted-average common shares outstanding, used in computing diluted earnings per share	34,204	34,092	33,981
Earnings per share of common stock:			
Basic	$ 3.06	$ 2.28	$ 1.98
Diluted	3.03	2.26	1.97

Stock options and service-based restricted stock units representing 452,907, 480,707 and 1,562,064 shares of common stock for the years ended December 31, 2011, 2010 and 2009, respectively, were outstanding but were excluded in the computation of diluted EPS because their effect would be anti-dilutive as a result of applying the treasury stock method. In addition, performance-based restricted stock units representing 34,448, 43,323 and 44,043 shares for the years ended December 31, 2011, 2010 and 2009, respectively, were outstanding but were excluded from the computation of diluted EPS because these shares were subject to performance conditions that had not been met.

NOTE 17—COMPREHENSIVE INCOME

Accumulated other comprehensive income, net of applicable taxes, reported on the Company's Consolidated Balance Sheets consists of unrealized gains and losses on available-for-sale securities, unrealized gains and losses on derivative transactions and foreign currency translation adjustments. A summary of comprehensive income, net of related tax effects, for the years ended December 31, is as follows (in thousands):

	2011	2010	2009
Net income	$103,479	$77,037	$67,021
Other comprehensive income:			
Unrealized holding gains (losses) on available-for-sale securities	(38)	(28)	64
Unrealized derivative holding gains (losses) arising during period (net of tax expense (benefit)) of $351, ($725) and ($1,054) in 2011, 2010 and 2009, respectively)	3,489	1,167	(3,024)
Reclassification to net income of previously deferred (gains) losses on derivative transactions (net of tax benefit of $1,507, $269 and $227 in 2011, 2010 and 2009, respectively)	5,432	(1,680)	(616)
Foreign currency translation adjustments	(8,701)	3,812	13,854
Other comprehensive income	182	3,271	10,278
Comprehensive income	$103,661	$80,308	$77,299

COLUMBIA SPORTSWEAR COMPANY

NOTES TO CONSOLIDATED FINANCIAL STATEMENTS — (Continued)

Accumulated other comprehensive income, net of related tax effects, is as follows (in thousands):

	December 31,	
	2011	2010
Unrealized holding gains (losses) on available-for-sale securities	$ (2)	$ 36
Unrealized holding gains (losses) on derivative transactions	7,250	(1,671)
Foreign currency translation adjustments	39,649	48,350
Accumulated other comprehensive income	$46,897	$46,715

NOTE 18—SEGMENT INFORMATION

The Company operates in four geographic segments: (1) the United States, (2) Latin America and Asia Pacific ("LAAP"), (3) Europe, Middle East and Africa ("EMEA"), and (4) Canada, which are reflective of the Company's internal organization, management, and oversight structure. Each geographic segment operates predominantly in one industry: the design, development, marketing and distribution of active outdoor apparel, footwear, accessories and equipment.

COLUMBIA SPORTSWEAR COMPANY
NOTES TO CONSOLIDATED FINANCIAL STATEMENTS—(Continued)

The geographic distribution of the Company's net sales, income before income taxes, interest income (expense), income tax (expense) benefit, and depreciation and amortization expense are summarized in the following tables (in thousands) for the years ended December 31, 2011, 2010 and 2009 and for identifiable assets at December 31, 2011 and 2010. Inter-geographic net sales, which are recorded at a negotiated mark-up and eliminated in consolidation, are not material.

	2011	2010	2009
Net sales to unrelated entities:			
United States	$ 947,970	$ 880,990	$ 736,942
LAAP	340,977	263,429	203,230
EMEA	275,416	222,451	197,357
Canada	129,622	116,654	106,494
	$1,693,985	$1,483,524	$1,244,023
Income before income taxes:			
United States	$ 63,847	$ 53,752	$ 49,660
LAAP	46,214	35,635	27,138
EMEA	13,779	5,817	1,410
Canada	12,566	8,123	9,554
Interest	1,274	1,564	2,088
	$ 137,680	$ 104,891	$ 89,850
Interest income (expense), net:			
United States	$ 4,565	$ 4,664	$ 4,561
LAAP	(666)	500	561
EMEA	648	(717)	(910)
Canada	(3,273)	(2,883)	(2,124)
	$ 1,274	$ 1,564	$ 2,088
Income tax (expense) benefit:			
United States	$ (19,233)	$ (9,938)	$ (13,710)
LAAP	(12,163)	(9,325)	(6,745)
EMEA	(80)	(7,668)	(2,744)
Canada	(2,725)	(923)	370
	$ (34,201)	$ (27,854)	$ (22,829)
Depreciation and amortization expense:			
United States	$ 33,100	$ 28,634	$ 26,850
LAAP	3,241	2,557	2,120
EMEA	6,292	6,410	6,642
Canada	927	829	641
	$ 43,560	$ 38,430	$ 36,253
Assets:			
United States	$ 977,792	$ 941,154	
LAAP	242,124	141,911	
EMEA	281,118	276,136	
Canada	179,851	150,236	
Total identifiable assets	1,680,885	1,509,437	
Eliminations and reclassifications	(298,343)	(214,683)	
	$1,382,542	$1,294,754	
Net sales by product category:			
Apparel, accessories and equipment	$1,334,883	$1,213,301	$1,029,458
Footwear	359,102	270,223	214,565
	$1,693,985	$1,483,524	$1,244,023

COLUMBIA SPORTSWEAR COMPANY
NOTES TO CONSOLIDATED FINANCIAL STATEMENTS — (Continued)

NOTE 19—FINANCIAL INSTRUMENTS AND RISK MANAGEMENT

In the normal course of business, the Company's financial position and results of operations are routinely subject to a variety of risks. These risks include risks associated with financial markets, primarily currency exchange rate risk and, to a lesser extent, interest rate risk and equity market risk. The Company regularly assesses these risks and has established policies and business practices designed to mitigate them. The Company does not engage in speculative trading in any financial market.

The Company actively manages the risk of changes in functional currency equivalent cash flows resulting from anticipated U.S. dollar denominated inventory purchases by subsidiaries that use European euros, Canadian dollars, Japanese yen or Korean won as their functional currency. The Company manages this risk by using currency forward and European-style option contracts formally designated and effective as cash flow hedges. Hedge effectiveness is determined by evaluating the ability of a hedging instrument's cumulative change in fair value to offset the cumulative change in the present value of expected cash flows on the underlying exposures. For forward contracts, the change in fair value attributable to changes in forward points are excluded from the determination of hedge effectiveness and included in current cost of sales. For option contracts, the hedging relationship is assumed to have no ineffectiveness if the critical terms of the option contract match the hedged transaction's terms. Hedge ineffectiveness was not material during the years ended December 31, 2011, 2010 and 2009.

The Company also uses currency forward and option contracts not formally designated as hedges to manage the currency exchange rate risk associated with the remeasurement of non-functional monetary assets and liabilities. Non-functional monetary assets and liabilities consist primarily of cash, intercompany loans and payables.

The following table presents the gross notional amount of outstanding derivative instruments (in thousands):

	December 31,	
	2011	2010
Derivative instruments designated as cash flow hedges:		
Currency forward contracts	$144,000	$ 86,260
Currency option contracts	—	4,500
Derivative instruments not designated as hedges:		
Currency forward contracts	138,807	179,382

At December 31, 2011, approximately $6,074,000 of deferred net gains on both outstanding and matured derivatives accumulated in other comprehensive income are expected to be reclassified to net income during the next twelve months as a result of underlying hedged transactions also being recorded in net income. Actual amounts ultimately reclassified to net income are dependent on U.S. dollar exchange rates in effect against the European euro, Canadian dollar, Japanese yen and Korean won when outstanding derivative contracts mature.

At December 31, 2011 the Company's derivative contracts had a remaining maturity of approximately two years or less. All the counterparties to these transactions had both long-term and short-term investment grade credit ratings. The maximum net exposure to any single counterparty, which is generally limited to the aggregate unrealized gain of all contracts with that counterparty, was less than $3,000,000 at December 31, 2011. The majority of the Company's derivative counterparties have strong credit ratings and, as a result, the Company does not require collateral to facilitate transactions. The Company does not hold derivatives featuring credit-related contingent terms. In addition, the Company is not a party to any derivative master agreement featuring credit-related contingent terms. Finally, the Company has not pledged assets or posted collateral as a requirement for entering into or maintaining derivative positions.

COLUMBIA SPORTSWEAR COMPANY

NOTES TO CONSOLIDATED FINANCIAL STATEMENTS — (Continued)

The following table presents the balance sheet classification and fair value of derivative instruments (in thousands):

	Balance Sheet Classification	December 31, 2011	December 31, 2010
Derivative instruments designated as cash flow hedges:			
Derivative instruments in asset positions:			
Currency forward contracts	Prepaid expenses and other current assets	$6,591	$ 362
Currency forward contracts	Other non-current assets	1,117	—
Currency option contracts	Prepaid expenses and other current assets	—	15
Derivative instruments in liability positions:			
Currency forward contracts	Accrued liabilities	824	2,732
Currency forward contracts	Other long-term liabilities	91	—
Currency option contracts	Accrued liabilities	—	102

	Balance Sheet Classification	December 31, 2011	December 31, 2010
Derivative instruments not designated as hedges:			
Derivative instruments in asset positions:			
Currency forward contracts	Prepaid expenses and other current assets	$ 645	$ 789
Derivative instruments in liability positions:			
Currency forward contracts	Accrued liabilities	2,962	4,169

The following table presents the effect and classification of derivative instruments for the years ended December 31, 2011 and 2010 (in thousands):

	Statement Of Operations Classification	For the Year Ended December 31, 2011	For the Year Ended December 31, 2010	For the Year Ended December 31, 2009
Currency Forward Contracts:				
Derivative instruments designated as cash flow hedges:				
Gain (Loss) recognized in other comprehensive income, net of tax	—	$ 3,489	$1,167	$(3,024)
Gain (Loss) reclassified from accumulated other comprehensive income to income for the effective portion	Cost of sales	(6,862)	1,789	(740)
Loss recognized in income for amount excluded from effectiveness testing and for the ineffective portion	Cost of sales	(1,889)	(230)	(14)
Derivative instruments not designated as hedges:				
Loss recognized in income	Cost of sales	—	(130)	(130)
Gain (Loss) recognized in income	SG&A	1,216	(54)	—

COLUMBIA SPORTSWEAR COMPANY

NOTES TO CONSOLIDATED FINANCIAL STATEMENTS — (Continued)

NOTE 20—FAIR VALUE MEASURES

Certain assets and liabilities are reported at fair value on either a recurring or nonrecurring basis. Fair value is defined as an exit price, representing the amount that would be received to sell an asset or paid to transfer a liability in an orderly transaction between market participants, under a three-tier fair value hierarchy which prioritizes the inputs used in measuring fair value as follows:

Level 1 –   observable inputs such as quoted prices in active liquid markets;

Level 2 –   inputs, other than the quoted market prices in active markets, which are observable, either directly or indirectly; or observable market prices in markets with insufficient volume and/or infrequent transactions; and

Level 3 –   unobservable inputs for which there is little or no market data available, which require the reporting entity to develop its own assumptions.

Assets and liabilities measured at fair value on a recurring basis as of December 31, 2011 are as follows (in thousands):

	Level 1	Level 2	Level 3	Total
Assets:				
Cash equivalents				
Money market funds	$55,542	$ —	$ —	$55,542
Time deposits	10,000	—	—	10,000
Available-for-sale short-term investments				
Time deposits	2,878	—	—	2,878
Other current assets				
Derivative financial instruments (Note 19)	—	7,236	—	7,236
Non-current assets				
Derivative financial instruments (Note 19)	—	1,117	—	1,117
Mutual fund shares	2,521	—	—	2,521
Total assets measured at fair value	$70,941	$8,353	$ —	$79,294
Liabilities:				
Accrued liabilities				
Derivative financial instruments (Note 19)	$ —	$3,786	$ —	$ 3,786
Other long-term liabilities				
Derivative financial instruments (Note 19)	—	91	—	91
Total liabilities measured at fair value	$ —	$3,877	$ —	$ 3,877

COLUMBIA SPORTSWEAR COMPANY

NOTES TO CONSOLIDATED FINANCIAL STATEMENTS — (Continued)

Assets and liabilities measured at fair value on a recurring basis at December 31, 2010 are as follows (in thousands):

	Level 1	Level 2	Level 3	Total
Assets:				
Cash equivalents				
Money market funds	$177,104	$ —	$ —	$177,104
Time deposits	7,510	—	—	7,510
U.S. Government-backed municipal bonds	—	5,560	—	5,560
Available-for-sale short-term investments				
Short-term municipal bond fund	15,624	—	—	15,624
U.S. Government-backed municipal bonds	—	53,188	—	53,188
Other current assets				
Derivative financial instruments (Note 19)	—	1,166	—	1,166
Non-current assets				
Mutual fund shares	1,670	—	—	1,670
Total assets measured at fair value	$201,908	$59,914	$ —	$261,822
Liabilities:				
Accrued liabilities				
Derivative financial instruments (Note 19)	$ —	$ 7,003	$ —	$ 7,003
Total liabilities measured at fair value	$ —	$ 7,003	$ —	$ 7,003

Level 1 instrument valuations are obtained from real-time quotes for transactions in active exchange markets involving identical assets. Level 2 instrument valuations are obtained from inputs, other than quoted market prices in active markets, that are directly or indirectly observable in the marketplace and quoted prices in markets with limited volume or infrequent transactions.

There were no material assets and liabilities measured at fair value on a nonrecurring basis at December 31, 2011 or 2010.

SUPPLEMENTARY DATA—QUARTERLY FINANCIAL DATA (Unaudited)

The following table summarizes the Company's quarterly financial data for the past two years ended December 31, 2011 (in thousands, except per share amounts):

2011	First Quarter	Second Quarter	Third Quarter	Fourth Quarter
Net sales	$333,086	$268,030	$566,791	$526,078
Gross profit	149,536	112,413	249,585	223,774
Net income (loss)	12,770	(13,558)	67,539	36,728
Earnings (loss) per share				
Basic	$ 0.38	$ (0.40)	$ 2.00	$ 1.09
Diluted	0.37	(0.40)	1.98	1.08

2010	First Quarter	Second Quarter	Third Quarter	Fourth Quarter
Net sales	$300,406	$221,831	$504,028	$457,259
Gross profit	127,304	96,922	214,281	190,897
Net income (loss)	9,228	(10,604)	52,205	26,208
Earnings (loss) per share				
Basic	$ 0.27	$ (0.31)	$ 1.55	$ 0.78
Diluted	0.27	(0.31)	1.53	0.77

Item 9.   *CHANGES IN AND DISAGREEMENTS WITH ACCOUNTANTS ON ACCOUNTING AND FINANCIAL DISCLOSURE*

None.

Item 9A.   *CONTROLS AND PROCEDURES*

Evaluation of Disclosure Controls and Procedures

Our management has evaluated, under the supervision and with the participation of our chief executive officer and chief financial officer, the effectiveness of our disclosure controls and procedures as of the end of the period covered by this report pursuant to Rule 13a-15(b) under the Securities Exchange Act of 1934 (the "Exchange Act"). Based on that evaluation, our chief executive officer and chief financial officer have concluded that, as of the end of the period covered by this report, our disclosure controls and procedures were effective in ensuring that information required to be disclosed in our Exchange Act reports is (1) recorded, processed, summarized and reported in a timely manner, and (2) accumulated and communicated to our management, including our chief executive officer and chief financial officer, as appropriate to allow timely decisions regarding required disclosure.

Design and Evaluation of Internal Control Over Financial Reporting

Report of Management

Our management is responsible for establishing and maintaining adequate internal control over financial reporting. All internal control systems, no matter how well designed, have inherent limitations. Therefore, even those systems determined to be effective can provide only reasonable assurance with respect to financial statement preparation and presentation.

Under the supervision and with the participation of our management, we assessed the effectiveness of our internal control over financial reporting as of December 31, 2011. In making this assessment, we used the criteria set forth by the Committee of Sponsoring Organizations of the Treadway Commission in *Internal Control —*

Integrated Framework . Based on our assessment we believe that, as of December 31, 2011, the Company's internal control over financial reporting is effective based on those criteria.

There has been no change in our internal control over financial reporting that occurred during our fiscal quarter ended December 31, 2011 that has materially affected, or is reasonably likely to materially affect, our internal control over financial reporting.

Our independent auditors have issued an audit report on the effectiveness of our internal control over financial reporting as of December 31, 2011, which is included herein.

REPORT ON INTERNAL CONTROL

Report of Independent Registered Public Accounting Firm

To the Board of Directors and Shareholders
Columbia Sportswear Company
Portland, Oregon

We have audited the internal control over financial reporting of Columbia Sportswear Company and subsidiaries (the "Company") as of December 31, 2011, based on criteria established in *Internal Control—Integrated Framework* issued by the Committee of Sponsoring Organizations of the Treadway Commission. The Company's management is responsible for maintaining effective internal control over financial reporting and for its assessment of the effectiveness of internal control over financial reporting, included in the accompanying "Report of Management". Our responsibility is to express an opinion on the Company's internal control over financial reporting based on our audit.

We conducted our audit in accordance with the standards of the Public Company Accounting Oversight Board (United States). Those standards require that we plan and perform the audit to obtain reasonable assurance about whether effective internal control over financial reporting was maintained in all material respects. Our audit included obtaining an understanding of internal control over financial reporting, assessing the risk that a material weakness exists, testing and evaluating the design and operating effectiveness of internal control based on the assessed risk, and performing such other procedures as we considered necessary in the circumstances. We believe that our audit provides a reasonable basis for our opinion.

A company's internal control over financial reporting is a process designed by, or under the supervision of, the company's principal executive and principal financial officers, or persons performing similar functions, and effected by the company's board of directors, management, and other personnel to provide reasonable assurance regarding the reliability of financial reporting and the preparation of financial statements for external purposes in accordance with generally accepted accounting principles. A company's internal control over financial reporting includes those policies and procedures that (1) pertain to the maintenance of records that, in reasonable detail, accurately and fairly reflect the transactions and dispositions of the assets of the company; (2) provide reasonable assurance that transactions are recorded as necessary to permit preparation of financial statements in accordance with generally accepted accounting principles, and that receipts and expenditures of the company are being made only in accordance with authorizations of management and directors of the company; and (3) provide reasonable assurance regarding prevention or timely detection of unauthorized acquisition, use, or disposition of the company's assets that could have a material effect on the financial statements.

Because of the inherent limitations of internal control over financial reporting, including the possibility of collusion or improper management override of controls, material misstatements due to error or fraud may not be prevented or detected on a timely basis. Also, projections of any evaluation of the effectiveness of the internal control over financial reporting to future periods are subject to the risk that the controls may become inadequate because of changes in conditions, or that the degree of compliance with the policies or procedures may deteriorate.

In our opinion, the Company maintained, in all material respects, effective internal control over financial reporting as of December 31, 2011, based on the criteria established in *Internal Control—Integrated Framework* issued by the Committee of Sponsoring Organizations of the Treadway Commission.

We have also audited, in accordance with the standards of the Public Company Accounting Oversight Board (United States), the consolidated financial statements and financial statement schedule as of and for the year ended December 31, 2011 of the Company, and our report dated February 28, 2012, expressed an unqualified opinion on those financial statements and financial statement schedule.

/s/ DELOITTE & TOUCHE LLP
Portland, Oregon
February 28, 2012

I tem 9B.   *OTHER INFORMATION*

None.

MANAGEMENT'S CERTIFICATION OF FINANCIAL STATEMENTS

EXHIBIT 32.1

SECTION 1350 CERTIFICATION

In connection with the Annual Report of Columbia Sportswear Company (the "Company") on Form 10-K for the period ended December 31, 2011 as filed with the Securities and Exchange Commission on the date hereof (the "Form 10-K"), I, Timothy P. Boyle, Chief Executive Officer of the Company, certify, pursuant to 18 U.S.C. Section 1350, as adopted pursuant to Section 906 of the Sarbanes-Oxley Act of 2002, that to my knowledge:

(1) The Form 10-K fully complies with the requirements of Section 13(a) or 15(d), as applicable, of the Securities Exchange Act of 1934 as of, and for, the periods presented in the Form 10-K; and

(2) The information contained in the Form 10-K fairly presents, in all material respects, the financial condition and results of the operation of the Company.

Dated: February 28, 2012

/s/ TIMOTHY P. BOYLE
Timothy P. Boyle
President and Chief Executive Officer

SUPPLEMENTAL INFORMATION

Stock Price Performance Graph

Our current dividend policy is dependent on our earnings, capital requirements, financial condition, restrictions imposed by our credit agreements, and other factors considered relevant by our Board of Directors. For various restrictions on our ability to pay dividends, see Item 7, Management's Discussion and Analysis of Financial Condition and Results of Operations, and Note 8 of Notes to Consolidated Financial Statements.

Performance Graph

The line graph below compares the cumulative total shareholder return of our common stock with the cumulative total return of the Standard & Poor's ("S&P") 400 Mid-Cap Index and the Russell 3000 Textiles Apparel Manufacturers for the period beginning December 31, 2006 and ending December 31, 2011. The graph assumes that $100 was invested on December 31, 2006, and that any dividends were reinvested.

Historical stock price performance should not be relied on as indicative of future stock price performance.

Columbia Sportswear Company
Stock Price Performance
December 31, 2006 — December 31, 2011

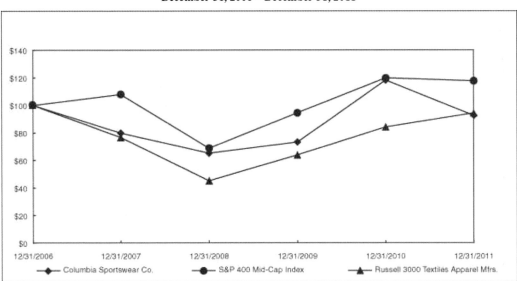

Total Return Analysis

	12/31/2006	12/31/2007	12/31/2008	12/31/2009	12/31/2010	12/31/2011
Columbia Sportswear Co.	$ 100.00	$ 79.94	$ 65.18	$ 73.37	$ 118.19	$ 92.61
S&P 400 Mid-Cap Index	$ 100.00	$ 107.97	$ 68.84	$ 94.57	$ 119.77	$ 117.68
Russell 3000 Textiles Apparel Mfrs.	$ 100.00	$ 76.73	$ 45.15	$ 64.00	$ 84.31	$ 94.38

EARNINGS PER SHARE DATA

Item 6.   *SELECTED FINANCIAL DATA*

Selected Consolidated Financial Data

The selected consolidated financial data presented below for, and as of the end of, each of the years in the five-year period ended December 31, 2011 have been derived from our audited consolidated financial statements. The consolidated financial data should be read in conjunction with the Consolidated Financial Statements and accompanying Notes that appear elsewhere in this annual report and Management's Discussion and Analysis of Financial Condition and Results of Operations set forth in Item 7.

	Year Ended December 31,				
	2011	2010	2009	2008	2007
	(In thousands, except per share amounts)				
Statement of Operations Data:					
Net sales	$1,693,985	$1,483,524	$1,244,023	$1,317,835	$1,356,039
Net income	103,479	77,037	67,021	95,047	144,452
Per Share of Common Stock Data:					
Earnings per share:					
Basic	$ 3.06	$ 2.28	$ 1.98	$ 2.75	$ 4.00
Diluted	3.03	2.26	1.97	2.74	3.96
Cash dividends per share	0.86	2.24	0.66	0.64	0.58
Weighted average shares outstanding:					
Basic	33,808	33,725	33,846	34,610	36,106
Diluted	34,204	34,092	33,981	34,711	36,434

	December 31,				
	2011	2010	2009	2008	2007
Balance Sheet Data:					
Total assets	$1,382,542	$1,294,754	$1,212,883	$1,148,236	$1,166,481
Long-term obligations, net of current maturities	—	—	—	15	61

SOCIAL RESPONSIBILITY[1]

At Columbia we value ethical, sustainable manufacturing practices and are committed to assuring that the partners with whom we do business share these values.

Our Code

At the heart of our Social Responsibility program is our Standards of Manufacturing Practices (SMP). Columbia's products are manufactured at independent factories around the world. We value, expect and promote ethical and fair treatment of people and are committed to assuring that the partners with whom we do business share these values. Each factory producing Columbia Sportswear products is monitored regularly against these Standards in addition to local labor laws and International Labor Organization (ILO) conventions. Our SMP outlines standards in the following areas:

- Forced Labor
- Child Labor
- Harassment or Abuse
- Nondiscrimination
- Freedom of Association
- Wages and Benefits
- Hours of Work
- Health and Safety
- Environment
- Ethical Conduct

Monitoring and Remediation

Columbia employs a team of Specialists who conduct regular, unannounced audits of our suppliers against our SMP. All of our audits are conducted unannounced, which allows our Specialists to see the factory conditions as they are on a typical day.

Our Specialists are not the only internal staff trained on our SMP. We also train our internal supply chain management staff on our SMP, including how to identify and respond to supply chain risk issues. With all supply chain employees working together, we can have greater influence at our contract facilities to alleviate risks and affect change.

Training and Capacity Building

Monitoring alone is not enough. We also support supplier efforts to promote sustainable solutions. Our training and capacity building program encourages suppliers to further develop skills to effectively remediate and enhance overall performance. Our program does this by partnering with training providers to offer consulting and workshops that provide suppliers with tools and techniques to enhance management systems in the areas of:

- Human Resources Management
- Communications
- Production Efficiency
- Environmental Management

In addition to working with consultants and training providers, we leverage industry partnerships to support and capitalize on resources developed by non-governmental and

---

[1]   http://www.columbia.com/Social-Corporate-Responsibility/Corp_Responsibility_Social.default.pg.html, 12/13/12.

non-profit organizations. We are currently participating in Better Work programs in Cambodia and Vietnam.

Better Work is a unique partnership program between the International Labor Organization (ILO) and the International Finance Corporation (IFC). The program aims to improve both compliance with labor standards and competitiveness in global supply chains. Better Work involves the development of both global tools and country-level projects, with a focus on scalable and sustainable solutions that build cooperation between governments, employers' and workers' organizations and international buyers. Read more.

Multi-Stakholder Engagement and Collaboration

Social responsibility is not a statement, it's a conversation. It's about engaging others in the industry for continuous improvement.

We collaborate with other apparel and footwear brands who share our Corporate Responsibility approach and whose products are produced in the same factories as ours. At any given time, a factory could be making shirts for ten different companies in the US and Europe, each with its own code of conduct. By sharing audit findings with other brands, we can reduce redundant auditing and focus on finding solutions.

We also engage the communities in which our manufacturing partners operate. HERproject is an example of one of our long-term projects that focuses on worker wellbeing. HERproject works to change women's lives through workplace programs that provide access to women's health education.

We also participate in industry-wide initiatives and organizations to explore how we can address complex questions around corporate responsibility as an industry.

Fair Labor Association

Columbia is a proud affiliate of the Fair Labor Association (FLA) as a Collegiate Licensee, Category B. The FLA is an independent nonprofit dedicated to improving the lives of factory workers and providing independent monitoring of factory conditions. FLA is governed by a multi-stakeholder board with equal representation of companies, universities, and civil society organizations. The organization provides a forum where companies can exchange ideas with universities and nonprofits that share a commitment to ethical sourcing. For more information about the FLA, click here.

Columbia's collegiate apparel and equipment is subjected to FLA's rigorous Independent External Monitoring (IEM) process and public reporting. Our program is also informed by FLA guidance on challenging issues such as effective grievance systems and migrant labor.

Outdoor Industry Association

Columbia leads the Outdoor Industry Association (OIA)'s Social Responsibility Working Group. This group works to create tools that support the effort of industry partners working conditions.

American Apparel & Footwear Industry

Columbia is a member of the American Apparel & Footwear Association Social Responsibility Committee, though which we learn and share information and best practices with industry peers.

UN International Labor Organization (ILO) Better Work Program

Columbia participates in the Better Work program, which is a unique partnership between the International Labor Organization (ILO) and the International Finance Corporation (IFC). It unites the expertise of the ILO in labor standards with that of the IFC in private sector development. Click here for more information.

Business for Social Responsibility's HERproject

Columbia participates in HERproject with factories in India, China and Vietnam. HERproject works to change women's lives through workplace programs that provide access to women's health education. Partners include eight multinational companies, 30 factories, eight local organizations, and multiple clinics, hospitals, and public-sector population and health departments. Each play a role in making HERproject a success.

Our Position Statements

We value ethical manufacturing practices at every step in the supply chain and work with industry groups, civil society organizations and government organizations to keep educated on ethical standards and practices across the supply chain. Read more about Columbia's specific positions on:

- Natural Goose Down
- Brazilian Leather
- Mulesed Wool
- Uzbek Cotton
- Perflourinated Compounds (PFC)

Appendix

B

Financial Statements for Under Armour

The complete annual report for Under Armour is available on this book's website.

Under Armour, Inc. and Subsidiaries

Consolidated Balance Sheets
(In thousands, except share data)

	December 31, 2011	December 31, 2010
Assets		
Current assets		
Cash and cash equivalents	$175,384	$203,870
Accounts receivable, net	134,043	102,034
Inventories	324,409	215,355
Prepaid expenses and other current assets	39,643	19,326
Deferred income taxes	16,184	15,265
Total current assets	689,663	555,850
Property and equipment, net	159,135	76,127
Intangible assets, net	5,535	3,914
Deferred income taxes	15,885	21,275
Other long term assets	48,992	18,212
Total assets	$919,210	$675,378
Liabilities and Stockholders' Equity		
Current liabilities		
Accounts payable	$100,527	$ 84,679
Accrued expenses	69,285	55,138
Current maturities of long term debt	6,882	6,865
Other current liabilities	6,913	2,465
Total current liabilities	183,607	149,147
Long term debt, net of current maturities	70,842	9,077
Other long term liabilities	28,329	20,188
Total liabilities	282,778	178,412
Commitments and contingencies (see Note 8)		
Stockholders' equity		
Class A Common Stock, $.0003 1/3 par value; 100,000,000 shares authorized as of December 31, 2011 and 2010; 40,496,126 shares issued and outstanding as of December 31, 2011 and 38,660,355 shares issued and outstanding as of December 31, 2010.	13	13
Class B Convertible Common Stock, $.0003 1/3 par value; 11,250,000 shares authorized, issued and outstanding as of December 31, 2011, 12,500,000 shares authorized, issued and outstanding as of December 31, 2010.	4	4
Additional paid-in capital	268,223	224,887
Retained earnings	366,164	270,021
Accumulated other comprehensive income	2,028	2,041
Total stockholders' equity	636,432	496,966
Total liabilities and stockholders' equity	$919,210	$675,378

See accompanying notes.

Under Armour, Inc. and Subsidiaries

Consolidated Statements of Income
(In thousands, except per share amounts)

	Year Ended December 31,		
	2011	**2010**	**2009**
Net revenues	$1,472,684	$1,063,927	$856,411
Cost of goods sold	759,848	533,420	446,286
Gross profit	712,836	530,507	410,125
Selling, general and administrative expenses	550,069	418,152	324,852
Income from operations	162,767	112,355	85,273
Interest expense, net	(3,841)	(2,258)	(2,344)
Other expense, net	(2,064)	(1,178)	(511)
Income before income taxes	156,862	108,919	82,418
Provision for income taxes	59,943	40,442	35,633
Net income	$ 96,919	$ 68,477	$ 46,785
Net income available per common share			
Basic	$ 1.88	$ 1.35	$ 0.94
Diluted	$ 1.85	$ 1.34	$ 0.92
Weighted average common shares outstanding			
Basic	51,570	50,798	49,848
Diluted	52,526	51,282	50,650

See accompanying notes.

Under Armour, Inc. and Subsidiaries

Consolidated Statements of Stockholders' Equity and Comprehensive Income
(In thousands)

	Class A Common Stock		Class B Convertible Common Stock		Additional Paid-In Capital	Retained Earnings	Unearned Compensation	Accumulated Other Comprehensive Income (Loss)	Comprehensive Income	Total Stockholders' Equity
	Shares	Amount	Shares	Amount						
Balance as of December 31, 2008	36,809	$ 12	12,500	$ 4	$174,725	$156,011	$ (60)	$ 405		$331,097
Exercise of stock options	853	1	—	—	4,000	—	—	—		4,001
Shares withheld in consideration of employee tax obligations relative to stock-based compensation arrangements	(26)	—	—	—	—	(608)	—	—		(608)
Issuance of Class A Common Stock, net of forfeitures	112	—	—	—	1,509	—	—	—		1,509
Stock-based compensation expense	—	—	—	—	12,864	—	46	—		12,910
Net excess tax benefits from stock-based compensation arrangements	—	—	—	—	4,244	—	—	—		4,244
Comprehensive income :										
Net income	—	—	—	—	—	46,785	—	—	$46,785	46,785
Foreign currency translation adjustment, net of tax of $101	—	—	—	—	—	—	—	59	59	59
Comprehensive income									46,844	
Balance as of December 31, 2009	37,748	13	12,500	4	197,342	202,188	(14)	464		399,997
Exercise of stock options	799	—	—	—	6,104	—	—	—		6,104
Shares withheld in consideration of employee tax obligations relative to stock-based compensation arrangements	(19)	—	—	—	—	(644)	—	—		(644)
Issuance of Class A Common Stock, net of forfeitures	132	—	—	—	1,788	—	—	—		1,788
Stock-based compensation expense	—	—	—	—	16,170	—	14	—		16,184
Net excess tax benefits from stock-based compensation arrangements	—	—	—	—	3,483	—	—	—		3,483
Comprehensive income :										
Net income	—	—	—	—	—	68,477	—	—	68,477	68,477
Foreign currency translation adjustment	—	—	—	—	—	—	—	1,577	1,577	1,577
Comprehensive income									70,054	
Balance as of December 31, 2010	38,660	13	12,500	4	224,887	270,021	—	2,041		496,966
Exercise of stock options	563	—	—	—	12,853	—	—	—		12,853
Shares withheld in consideration of employee tax obligations relative to stock-based compensation arrangements	(12)	—	—	—	—	(776)	—	—		(776)
Issuance of Class A Common Stock, net of forfeitures	35	—	—	—	2,041	—	—	—		2,041
Class B Convertible Common Stock converted to Class A Common Stock	1,250	—	(1,250)	—	—	—	—	—		—
Stock-based compensation expense	—	—	—	—	18,063	—	—	—		18,063
Net excess tax benefits from stock-based compensation arrangements	—	—	—	—	10,379	—	—	—		10,379
Comprehensive income :										
Net income	—	—	—	—	—	96,919	—	—	96,919	96,919
Foreign currency translation adjustment	—	—	—	—	—	—	—	(13)	(13)	(13)
Comprehensive income									$96,906	
Balance as of December 31, 2011	40,496	$ 13	11,250	$ 4	$268,223	$366,164	$—	$2,028		$636,432

See accompanying notes.

Under Armour, Inc. and Subsidiaries

Consolidated Statements of Cash Flows
(In thousands)

	Year Ended December 31,		
	2011	**2010**	**2009**
Cash flows from operating activities			
Net income	$ 96,919	$ 68,477	$ 46,785
Adjustments to reconcile net income to net cash provided by operating activities			
Depreciation and amortization	36,301	31,321	28,249
Unrealized foreign currency exchange rate (gains) losses	4,027	1,280	(5,222)
Loss on disposal of property and equipment	36	44	37
Stock-based compensation	18,063	16,227	12,910
Gain on bargain purchase of corporate headquarters (excludes transaction costs of $1.9 million)	(3,300)	—	—
Deferred income taxes	3,620	(10,337)	(5,212)
Changes in reserves and allowances	5,536	2,322	1,623
Changes in operating assets and liabilities:			
Accounts receivable	(33,923)	(32,320)	3,792
Inventories	(114,646)	(65,239)	32,998
Prepaid expenses and other assets	(42,633)	(4,099)	1,870
Accounts payable	17,209	16,158	(4,386)
Accrued expenses and other liabilities	23,442	21,330	11,656
Income taxes payable and receivable	4,567	4,950	(6,059)
Net cash provided by operating activities	15,218	50,114	119,041
Cash flows from investing activities			
Purchase of property and equipment	(56,228)	(30,182)	(19,845)
Purchase of corporate headquarters and related expenditures	(23,164)	—	—
Purchase of long term investment	(3,862)	(11,125)	—
Purchases of other assets	(1,153)	(478)	(35)
Change in restricted cash	(5,029)	—	—
Net cash used in investing activities	(89,436)	(41,785)	(19,880)
Cash flows from financing activities			
Proceeds from revolving credit facility	30,000	—	—
Payments on revolving credit facility	(30,000)	—	(25,000)
Proceeds from term loan	25,000	—	—
Proceeds from long term debt	5,644	5,262	7,649
Payments on long term debt	(7,418)	(9,446)	(7,656)
Payments on capital lease obligations	—	(97)	(361)
Excess tax benefits from stock-based compensation arrangements	10,260	4,189	5,127
Proceeds from exercise of stock options and other stock issuances	14,645	7,335	5,128
Payments of debt financing costs	(2,324)	—	(1,354)
Net cash provided by (used in) financing activities	45,807	7,243	(16,467)
Effect of exchange rate changes on cash and cash equivalents	(75)	1,001	2,561
Net increase (decrease) in cash and cash equivalents	(28,486)	16,573	85,255
Cash and cash equivalents			
Beginning of year	203,870	187,297	102,042
End of year	$ 175,384	$203,870	$187,297
Non-cash financing and investing activities			
Debt assumed in connection with purchase of corporate headquarters	$ 38,556	$ —	$ —
Other supplemental information			
Cash paid for income taxes	56,940	38,773	40,834
Cash paid for interest	2,305	992	1,273

See accompanying notes.

Appendix

C

Financial Statements for Tesco PLC

The complete annual report for Tesco PLC is available on this book's website.

FINANCIAL STATEMENTS

Independent auditors' report to the members of Tesco PLC

We have audited the Group financial statements of Tesco PLC for the 52 weeks ended 26 February 2011 which comprise the Group Income Statement, the Group Statement of Comprehensive Income, the Group Balance Sheet, the Group Cash Flow Statement, the Group Statement of Changes in Equity and the related notes. The financial reporting framework that has been applied in their preparation is applicable law and International Financial Reporting Standards (IFRSs) as adopted by the European Union.

Respective responsibilities of directors and auditors

As explained more fully in the Statement of Directors' responsibilities set out on page 92, the Directors are responsible for the preparation of the Group financial statements and for being satisfied that they give a true and fair view. Our responsibility is to audit and express an opinion on the Group financial statements in accordance with applicable law and International Standards on Auditing (UK and Ireland). Those standards require us to comply with the Auditing Practices Board's Ethical Standards for Auditors.

This report, including the opinions, has been prepared for and only for the Company's members as a body in accordance with Chapter 3 of Part 16 of the Companies Act 2006 and for no other purpose. We do not, in giving these opinions, accept or assume responsibility for any other purpose or to any other person to whom this report is shown or into whose hands it may come save where expressly agreed by our prior consent in writing.

Scope of the audit of the financial statements

An audit involves obtaining evidence about the amounts and disclosures in the financial statements sufficient to give reasonable assurance that the financial statements are free from material misstatement, whether caused by fraud or error. This includes an assessment of: whether the accounting policies are appropriate to the Group's circumstances and have been consistently applied and adequately disclosed; the reasonableness of significant accounting estimates made by the Directors; and the overall presentation of the financial statements.

Opinion on financial statements

In our opinion the Group financial statements:

- give a true and fair view of the state of the Group's affairs as at 26 February 2011 and of its profit and cash flows for the 52 weeks then ended;
- have been properly prepared in accordance with IFRSs as adopted by the European Union; and
- have been prepared in accordance with the requirements of the Companies Act 2006 and Article 4 of the IAS Regulation.

Opinion on other matter prescribed by the Companies Act 2006

In our opinion the information given in the Directors' Report for the 52 weeks ended 26 February 2011 for which the Group financial statements are prepared is consistent with the Group financial statements.

Matters on which we are required to report by exception

We have nothing to report in respect of the following:

Under the Companies Act 2006 we are required to report to you if, in our opinion:

- certain disclosures of Directors' remuneration specified by law are not made; or
- we have not received all the information and explanations we require for our audit.

Under the Listing Rules we are required to review:

- the Directors' statement, set out on page 45, in relation to going concern;
- the part of the Corporate Governance Statement relating to the Company's compliance with the nine provisions of the June 2008 Combined Code specified for our review; and
- certain elements of the report to shareholders by the Board on directors' renumeration.

Other matter

We have reported separately on the Parent Company financial statements of Tesco PLC for the 52 weeks ended 26 February 2011 and on the information in the Directors' Remuneration Report that is described as having been audited.

Richard Winter (Senior Statutory Auditor)
for and on behalf of PricewaterhouseCoopers LLP
Chartered Accountants and Statutory Auditors
London
6 May 2011

FINANCIAL STATEMENTS

Group income statement

Year ended 26 February 2011	notes	52 weeks 2011 £m	52 weeks 2010 £m
Continuing operations			
Revenue (sales excluding VAT)	2	60,931	56,910
Cost of sales		(55,871)	(52,303)
Gross profit		5,060	4,607
Administrative expenses		(1,676)	(1,527)
Profit arising on property-related items	3	427	377
Operating profit		3,811	3,457
Share of post-tax profits of joint ventures and associates	13	57	33
Finance income	5	150	265
Finance costs	5	(483)	(579)
Profit before tax	3	3,535	3,176
Taxation	6	(864)	(840)
Profit for the year		2,671	2,336
Attributable to:			
Owners of the parent		2,655	2,327
Non-controlling interests		16	9
		2,671	2,336
Earnings per share			
Basic	9	33.10p	29.33p
Diluted	9	32.94p	29.19p

Non-GAAP measure: underlying profit before tax

	notes	52 weeks 2011 £m	52 weeks 2010 £m
Profit before tax		3,535	3,176
Adjustments for:			
IAS 32 and IAS 39 'Financial Instruments' – fair value remeasurements	1/5	(19)	(151)
IAS 19 'Employee Benefits' – non-cash Group Income Statement charge for pensions	1/28	113	24
IAS 17 'Leases' – impact of annual uplifts in rent and rent-free periods	1	50	41
IFRS 3 'Business Combinations' – intangible asset amortisation charges and costs arising from acquisitions	1	42	127
IFRIC 13 'Customer Loyalty Programmes' – fair value of awards	1	8	14
IAS 36 'Impairment of Assets' – impairment of goodwill arising on acquisitions	1	55	131
Restructuring costs	1	29	33
Underlying profit before tax	1	3,813	3,395

The notes on pages 99 to 145 form part of these financial statements.

FINANCIAL STATEMENTS

Group statement of comprehensive income

Year ended 26 February 2011	notes	52 weeks 2011 £m	52 weeks 2010 £m
Change in fair value of available-for-sale financial assets and investments		2	1
Currency translation differences		(344)	343
Actuarial gains/(losses) on defined benefit pension schemes	28	595	(322)
(Losses)/gains on cash flow hedges:			
Net fair value losses		(22)	(168)
Reclassified and reported in the Group Income Statement		8	5
Tax relating to components of other comprehensive income for the year	6	(153)	54
Total other comprehensive income for the year		86	(87)
Profit for the year		2,671	2,336
Total comprehensive income for the year		2,757	2,249
Attributable to:			
Owners of the parent		2,746	2,222
Non-controlling interests		11	27
		2,757	2,249

The notes on pages 99 to 145 form part of these financial statements.

FINANCIAL STATEMENTS

Group balance sheet

	notes	26 February 2011 £m	27 February 2010 £m
Non-current assets			
Goodwill and other intangible assets	10	4,338	4,177
Property, plant and equipment	11	24,398	24,203
Investment property	12	1,863	1,731
Investments in joint ventures and associates	13	316	152
Other investments	14	1,108	863
Loans and advances to customers	17	2,127	1,844
Derivative financial instruments	22	1,139	1,250
Deferred tax assets	6	48	38
		35,337	34,258
Current assets			
Inventories	15	3,162	2,729
Trade and other receivables	16	2,314	1,888
Loans and advances to customers	17	2,514	2,268
Loans and advances to banks and other financial assets	18	404	144
Derivative financial instruments	22	148	224
Current tax assets		4	6
Short-term investments		1,022	1,314
Cash and cash equivalents	19	1,870	2,819
		11,438	11,392
Non-current assets classified as held for sale	7	431	373
		11,869	11,765
Current liabilities			
Trade and other payables	20	(10,484)	(9,442)
Financial liabilities:			
Borrowings	21	(1,386)	(1,529)
Derivative financial instruments and other liabilities	22	(255)	(146)
Customer deposits	24	(5,074)	(4,357)
Deposits by banks	25	(36)	(30)
Current tax liabilities		(432)	(472)
Provisions	26	(64)	(39)
		(17,731)	(16,015)
Net current liabilities		(5,862)	(4,250)
Non-current liabilities			
Financial liabilities:			
Borrowings	21	(9,689)	(11,744)
Derivative financial instruments and other liabilities	22	(600)	(776)
Post-employment benefit obligations	28	(1,356)	(1,840)
Deferred tax liabilities	6	(1,094)	(795)
Provisions	26	(113)	(172)
		(12,852)	(15,327)
Net assets		16,623	14,681
Equity			
Share capital	29	402	399
Share premium account		4,896	4,801
Other reserves		40	40
Retained earnings		11,197	9,356
Equity attributable to owners of the parent		16,535	14,596
Non-controlling interests		88	85
Total equity		16,623	14,681

The notes on pages 99 to 145 form part of these financial statements.

Philip Clarke
Laurie McIlwee

Directors
The financial statements on pages 94 to 145 were authorised for issue by the Directors on 6 May 2011 and are subject to the approval of the shareholders at the Annual General Meeting on 1 July 2011.

FINANCIAL STATEMENTS

Group statement of changes in equity

	Issued share capital £m	Share premium £m	Other reserves £m	Capital redemption reserve £m	Hedging reserve £m	Translation reserve £m	Treasury shares £m	Retained earnings £m	Total £m	Non-controlling interests £m	Total equity £m
						Attributable to owners of the parent					
At 27 February 2010	399	4,801	40	13	12	463	(180)	9,048	14,596	85	14,681
Profit for the year	–	–	–	–	–	–	–	2,655	2,655	16	2,671
Other comprehensive income											
Change in fair value of available-for-sale financial assets	–	–	–	–	–	–	–	2	2	–	2
Currency translation differences	–	–	–	–	–	(339)	–	–	(339)	(5)	(344)
Actuarial gains on defined benefit pension schemes	–	–	–	–	–	–	–	595	595	–	595
Losses on cash flow hedges	–	–	–	–	(14)	–	–	–	(14)	–	(14)
Tax relating to components of other comprehensive income	–	–	–	–	1	31	–	(185)	(153)	–	(153)
Total other comprehensive income	–	–	–	–	(13)	(308)	–	412	91	(5)	86
Total comprehensive income	–	–	–	–	(13)	(308)	–	3,067	2,746	11	2,757
Transactions with owners											
Purchase of treasury shares	–	–	–	–	–	–	(50)	–	(50)	–	(50)
Share-based payments	–	–	–	–	–	–	89	131	220	–	220
Issue of shares	3	95	–	–	–	–	–	–	98	–	98
Purchase of non-controlling interests	–	–	–	–	–	–	–	6	6	(6)	–
Dividends paid to non-controlling interests	–	–	–	–	–	–	–	–	–	(2)	(2)
Dividends authorised in the year	–	–	–	–	–	–	–	(1,081)	(1,081)	–	(1,081)
Total transactions with owners	3	95	–	–	–	–	39	(944)	(807)	(8)	(815)
At 26 February 2011	402	4,896	40	13	(1)	155	(141)	11,171	16,535	88	16,623

	Issued share capital £m	Share premium £m	Other reserves £m	Capital redemption reserve £m	Hedging reserve £m	Translation reserve £m	Treasury shares £m	Retained earnings £m	Total £m	Non-controlling interests £m	Total equity £m
						Attributable to owners of the parent					
At 28 February 2009	395	4,638	40	13	175	173	(229)	7,644	12,849	57	12,906
Profit for the year	–	–	–	–	–	–	–	2,327	2,327	9	2,336
Other comprehensive income											
Change in fair value of available-for-sale financial assets	–	–	–	–	–	–	–	1	1	–	1
Currency translation differences	–	–	–	–	–	325	–	–	325	18	343
Actuarial losses on defined benefit pension schemes	–	–	–	–	–	(2)	–	(320)	(322)	–	(322)
Losses on cash flow hedges	–	–	–	–	(163)	–	–	–	(163)	–	(163)
Tax relating to components of other comprehensive income	–	–	–	–	–	(33)	–	87	54	–	54
Total other comprehensive income	–	–	–	–	(163)	290	–	(232)	(105)	18	(87)
Total comprehensive income	–	–	–	–	(163)	290	–	2,095	2,222	27	2,249
Transactions with owners											
Purchase of treasury shares	–	–	–	–	–	–	(24)	–	(24)	–	(24)
Share-based payments	–	–	–	–	–	–	73	168	241	–	241
Issue of shares	4	163	–	–	–	–	–	–	167	–	167
Purchase of non-controlling interests	–	–	–	–	–	–	–	91	91	3	94
Dividends paid to non-controlling interests	–	–	–	–	–	–	–	–	–	(2)	(2)
Dividends authorised in the year	–	–	–	–	–	–	–	(968)	(968)	–	(968)
Tax on items charged to equity	–	–	–	–	–	–	–	18	18	–	18
Total transactions with owners	4	163	–	–	–	–	49	(691)	(475)	1	(474)
At 27 February 2010	399	4,801	40	13	12	463	(180)	9,048	14,596	85	14,681

The notes on pages 99 to 145 form part of these financial statements.

FINANCIAL STATEMENTS

Group cash flow statement

Year ended 26 February 2011	notes	52 weeks 2011 £m	52 weeks 2010 £m
Cash flows from operating activities			
Cash generated from operations	31	5,366	5,947
Interest paid		(614)	(690)
Corporation tax paid		(760)	(512)
Net cash from operating activities		3,992	4,745
Cash flows from investing activities			
Acquisition of subsidiaries, net of cash acquired		(89)	(65)
Proceeds from sale of property, plant and equipment		1,906	1,820
Purchase of property, plant and equipment and investment property		(3,178)	(2,855)
Proceeds from sale of intangible assets		3	4
Purchase of intangible assets		(373)	(163)
Increase in loans to joint ventures		(219)	(45)
Decrease in loans to joint ventures		25	–
Investments in joint ventures and associates		(174)	(4)
Investments in short-term and other investments		(1,264)	(1,918)
Proceeds from sale of short-term investments		1,314	1,233
Dividends received		62	35
Interest received		128	81
Net cash used in investing activities		(1,859)	(1,877)
Cash flows from financing activities			
Proceeds from issue of ordinary share capital		98	167
Increase in borrowings		2,175	862
Repayment of borrowings		(4,153)	(3,601)
Repayment of obligations under finance leases		(42)	(41)
Dividends paid to equity owners		(1,081)	(968)
Dividends paid to non-controlling interests		(2)	(2)
Own shares purchased		(31)	(24)
Net cash from refinancing activities		(3,036)	(3,607)
Net decrease in cash and cash equivalents		(903)	(739)
Cash and cash equivalents at beginning of year		2,819	3,509
Effect of foreign exchange rate changes		(46)	49
Cash and cash equivalents at end of year	19	1,870	2,819

Reconciliation of net cash flow to movement in net debt note

Year ended 26 February 2011	note	52 weeks 2011 £m	52 weeks 2010 £m
Net decrease in cash and cash equivalents		(903)	(739)
Investment in Tesco Bank		(446)	(230)
Elimination of net increase in Tesco Bank cash and cash equivalents		56	(167)
Debt acquired on acquisition		(17)	–
Net cash outflow to repay debt and lease financing		2,870	2,780
Dividend received from Tesco Bank		150	150
(Decrease)/increase in short-term investments		(292)	81
Increase in joint venture loan receivables		159	45
Other non-cash movements		(438)	(249)
Decrease in net debt in the year		1,139	1,671
Opening net debt	32	(7,929)	(9,600)
Closing net debt	32	(6,790)	(7,929)

NB. The reconciliation of net cash flow to movement in net debt note is not a primary statement and does not form part of the cash flow statement but forms part of the notes to the financial statements.

The notes on pages 99 to 145 form part of these financial statements.

Appendix

D

Accounting for Investments and Consolidated Financial Statements

LEARNING OBJECTIVES

1. **Identify** and **define** the investment categories for debt and equity securities. *(p. D-2)*

2. **Describe** the accounting for various kinds of debt security investments. *(p. D-3)*

3. **Describe** the accounting for various kinds of equity security investments. *(p. D-8)*

4. **Define** parent-subsidiary relationships and **discuss** how their balance sheet data are consolidated. *(p. D-12)*

INVESTMENTS

<table>
<tr><td>**LO1**</td><td>**Identify** and **define** the investment categories for debt and equity securities.</td></tr>
</table>

Debt and Equity Securities

The assets of a business may include investments in one or more types of debt or equity securities. For some businesses, such as insurance companies, investments in debt and equity securities constitute the major portion of a company's total assets. Investments in various debt and equity securities, for example, represent more than 50 percent of the assets of **Aetna Inc.**, a large diversified insurance company and a member of the Fortune 100 companies.

A **debt security** refers to a financial instrument that creates a creditor relationship for the debtholder. Examples of debt securities include U.S. Treasury bills, notes, and bonds; U.S. government agency bonds, such as Fannie Mae and Ginnie Mae bonds; state and local government bonds; corporate bonds; and commercial paper. *Bonds* are long-term debt securities and are discussed in detail in Chapter 10. Some bonds may not mature for 30 to 40 years, while others may have short maturity periods. *Commercial paper*, on the other hand, refers to very short-term (1 to 180 days), unsecured promissory notes issued by large corporations.

An **equity security** is a financial instrument that represents an ownership interest in a company. Shares of stock represent ownership interests in a corporation and are discussed in detail in Chapter 11. Investors owning a company's *common stock* have the most basic ownership rights, whereas owners of a company's *preferred stock* have some rights that take preference over the common stockholders, such as preferential treatment in the receipt of dividends and the receipt of assets in the event that a company liquidates.

Debt and equity securities may be acquired directly from the entity that issues the securities or through a secondary market. When corporations or government agencies need to borrow, they offer their debt securities for sale to the general public. This process is called *floating an issue*. When a corporation initially issues (sells) stock to the general public to raise money, the process is called an *initial public offering* (IPO). When companies need additional cash to fund their operations after initially going public, they may conduct additional sales of their shares through secondary public offerings.

More frequently, investors acquire debt and equity securities through the secondary capital market. The secondary capital market consists of individual and institutional investors desiring to buy or sell securities. Many debt and equity securities are bought and sold on organized exchanges. Stocks and bonds, for example, may trade on a national exchange such as the New York Stock Exchange or the London Stock Exchange. (Despite their names, both exchanges list both bonds and stocks.) Stocks and bonds may also trade in a less formal market known as the *over-the-counter* market. Both the buyer and seller of a security normally use the services of a brokerage firm, such as **Charles Schwab** or **Fidelity Investments**, to facilitate the acquisition and disposition of their investments.

Investment Categories

For accounting purposes, each debt or equity security is placed in one of five investment categories: **trading securities**, **available-for-sale securities**, **held-to-maturity securities**, **influential securities**, and **controlling securities**. Of these categories, three apply to debt securities and four apply to equity securities. Exhibit D-1 presents the five investment categories.

The placement of an investment in the proper investment category depends on (1) management's intent with respect to selling the security and (2) the ability to influence or control another entity's activities as a result of an equity investment. Typical evidence of the latter factor is the ownership percentage represented by the equity investment. Exhibit D-2 defines and explains the five investment categories.

Notice in Exhibit D-2 that the trading securities and available-for-sale securities categories may include noninfluential equity securities. Noninfluential equity securities refer to stock investments that do not permit the investor to exert significant influence over

EXHIBIT D-1 | Investment Categories for Debt and Equity Securities

the policies of the investee company (the company whose stock is acquired). Accountants consider stock investments noninfluential if the quantity of stock purchased is less than 20 percent of a company's outstanding voting (common) stock.

An entity that owns 20 percent or more of a company's outstanding voting stock may exert a significant influence on the operating or financial decisions of that company. However, if 50 percent or less of the total voting stock is owned, the investment does not represent a controlling interest. Voting stock investments in the 20 to 50 percent ownership range, therefore, compose the influential securities category.

When more than 50 percent of a corporation's voting stock is owned, the investor is a majority owner and is in a position to control the operating and financial policies of the investee company. These majority-ownership stock investments are classified as controlling securities.[1]

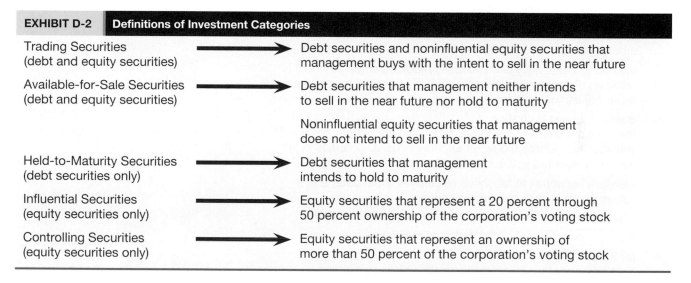

EXHIBIT D-2 | Definitions of Investment Categories

Trading Securities (debt and equity securities)	Debt securities and noninfluential equity securities that management buys with the intent to sell in the near future
Available-for-Sale Securities (debt and equity securities)	Debt securities that management neither intends to sell in the near future nor hold to maturity
	Noninfluential equity securities that management does not intend to sell in the near future
Held-to-Maturity Securities (debt securities only)	Debt securities that management intends to hold to maturity
Influential Securities (equity securities only)	Equity securities that represent a 20 percent through 50 percent ownership of the corporation's voting stock
Controlling Securities (equity securities only)	Equity securities that represent an ownership of more than 50 percent of the corporation's voting stock

Debt and equity investments are placed in one of the five different categories because accounting guidelines differ among the categories. We now review those accounting guidelines, considering debt securities first, followed by equity securities.

Investments in Debt Securities

Investments in debt securities are placed in one of three investment categories: trading securities, available-for-sale securities, or held-to-maturity securities. The major accounting events concerning investments in debt securities are their purchase, the recognition of interest income, their balance sheet

LO2 **Describe** the accounting for various kinds of debt security investments.

---

[1] The ownership percentages are guidelines only and may be overcome by other factors. In some cases, a company may own more than 20 percent of the outstanding voting shares of another company and still not be able to significantly influence its operating and financial activities. Or, effective control of another entity may exist with less than 50 percent ownership of its voting stock. For example, ownership of a large minority interest (such as 45 percent), with other owners widely dispersed and unorganized, may provide effective control. The key to proper accounting classification is the presence of significant influence on, or effective control over, another entity.

valuation, and their sale or redemption at maturity. Exhibit D-3 summarizes the accounting guidelines for these events. We will illustrate these guidelines with examples.

Purchase

Assume that the Warner Company purchases $300,000 face value of Natco Company 8 percent bonds at 98 on July 1, 2010. (Recall from Chapter 10 that bond prices are quoted on a basis of $100 while their base value is actually $1,000. Thus, a bond said to sell for 98 is actually selling for $980. And, for a group of bonds with an aggregate maturity value of $100,000, this would imply a selling price of $98,000.) The bonds pay interest on December 31 and June 30 and mature in 10 years. The brokerage commission is $600. Warner's management considers the bond investment to be divided equally between trading securities, available-for-sale securities, and held-to-maturity securities. Exhibit D-4 shows the entry to record this debt investment. Note that the accounting for the purchase event is the same regardless of the classification of the bond investment.

EXHIBIT D-3	Accounting Guidelines for Investments in Debt Securities			
	Event/Accounting Guideline	Trading Securities	Available-for-Sale Securities	Held-to-Maturity Securities
1.	**Purchase** Record at cost, which includes any broker's fees.	X	X	X
2.	**Recognition of Interest Income** Interest accrues daily and is usually recorded when payment is received. Premium or discount on purchase price is not amortized.	X		
	Interest accrues daily and is usually recorded when payment is received. Premium or discount on purchase price is amortized as an adjustment of interest income.		X	X
3.	**Balance Sheet Valuation** Measure securities at fair value at balance sheet date. No valuation account to the asset account is used. Changes in fair value are reported in the income statement.	X		
	Measure securities at fair value at balance sheet date. Use a valuation account to the asset account. Changes in fair value are reported in stockholders' equity.		X	
	Measure securities at amortized cost at balance sheet date.			X
4.	**(a) Sale** Sale proceeds less investment's book value is a realized gain or loss.	X		
	Sale proceeds less investment's amortized cost is a realized gain or loss.		X	
	(b) Redemption at Maturity At maturity, the investment's book value will equal the redemption proceeds.			X

The Natco Company bonds are purchased the first day after an interest payment date, so there is no unpaid interest related to the bonds. If any more time had elapsed, however, the bond price would include an amount for the accrued but unpaid interest. This occurs because the bond seller is entitled to receive the interest earned up to the date of sale. As a result, the purchase price of a bond that is sold between interest payment dates includes not only the current market price but also any interest accrued since the last interest payment date. (See Chapter 10 for additional discussion regarding the accrual of interest between interest payment dates.) The bond buyer pays the accrued interest amount to the bond seller, debits the amount to the Bond Interest Receivable account, and then collects it as part of the next interest payment received from the bond issuer. Because the accrued interest purchased by the bond buyer is collected with the next interest payment, the accrued interest is not treated as part of the initial cost of the bond investment.

EXHIBIT D-4	Purchase of Debt Securities			

2010

July 1	Bond investment—Trading (Natco)	98,200			A	= L +	SE
	Bond investment—Available-for-sale (Natco)	98,200			+98,200		
	Bond investment—Held-to-maturity (Natco)	98,200			+98,200		
	Cash		294,600		+98,200		
	To record purchase of $300,000 of Natco Company bonds at 98 plus				−294,600		
	$600 commission [($300,000 × 0.98) + $600 = $294,600].						

Recognition of Interest Income

Each $100,000 of Natco Company bonds acquired on July 1, 2010, was purchased at a $1,800 discount ($100,000 − $98,200). This means that the market rate of interest on July 1, 2010 was higher than the 8 percent coupon rate offered on the bonds. For trading securities, any bond discount (or premium) is ignored in accounting for the periodic interest income because management plans to sell the securities in the near future. As such, the effect on net income from ignoring the bond discount (or premium) is immaterial.

Materiality Concept	PRINCIPLE ALERT

Note the role played by the *materiality concept* in determining interest income on trading securities. Because of the short time period that trading securities are held by a company before being resold, accountants do not bother to amortize any discount or premium associated with the debt securities. This simplifies the accounting for these debt securities, yet it causes no significant distortion in the periodic reporting of interest income.

For available-for-sale securities and held-to-maturity securities, any bond discount (or premium) is amortized to interest income. This is done to make periodic interest income more accurately reflect the economic reality of the bond investment. The amortization of bond discount causes the periodic interest income to be higher than the semiannual cash receipt of interest. If the bonds had been purchased at a premium (more than their face value), the premium amortization would cause periodic interest income to be less than the semiannual cash receipt of interest.

Two amortization methods are available for use: the straight-line method and the effective interest method. We use the straight-line method here because the difference in the financial effect between the two methods is immaterial in this case. The *straight-line method* of amortization writes off an equal amount of discount or premium each interest period. The Natco Company bonds, when purchased, had 10 years to maturity, with interest paid semi-annually. Consequently, there are 20 interest periods associated with the bonds. During each interest period, $90 ($1,800/20 periods) of discount will be amortized for the available-for-sale securities and the held-to-maturity securities. Each $100,000 (face value) of Natco bonds pays $4,000 interest semiannually (8 percent × $100,000 × ½ year). The entries to record interest income at December 31, 2010, are shown in Exhibit D-5.

Balance Sheet Valuation

Debt securities are interest rate sensitive; that is, as market interest rates change, the market values of debt securities also change. Debt securities that management intends to sell (trading securities) or may sell (available-for-sale securities) are reported on the balance sheet at their current fair value. If available, quoted market prices from one of

EXHIBIT D-5	Recognition of Interest Income on Debt Securities

2010

Trading Debt Securities

Dec. 31	Cash		4,000	
	Bond interest income			4,000
	To record receipt of semiannual interest on $100,000 of trading bonds.			

A = L + SE
+4,000   +4,000
               Rev

Available-for-Sale Debt Securities

Dec. 31	Cash		4,000	
	Bond investment—Available-for-sale (Natco)		90	
	Bond interest income			4,090
	To record receipt of semiannual interest and discount amortization on $100,000 of available-for-sale bonds.			

A = L + SE
+4,000   +4,090
+90   Rev

Held-to-Maturity Debt Securities

Dec. 31	Cash		4,000	
	Bond investment—Held-to-maturity (Natco)		90	
	Bond Interest Income			4,090
	To record receipt of semiannual interest and discount amortization on $100,000 of held-to-maturity bonds.			

A = L + SE
+4,000   +4,090
+90   Rev

the national bond exchanges provide the best evidence of a bond's fair value. Year-end adjusting entries are made to record these current fair values. Current fair value is not a relevant measure for debt securities that management intends to hold to maturity. Thus, no adjustment to fair value is made for held-to-maturity securities.

Assume that a general decline in market interest rates causes the Natco Company bonds to trade at 99.5 as of December 31, 2010. (Remember that 99.5 means that a bond is actually selling for $995; and, for a group of bonds with a maturity value of $100,000, this equates to an aggregate selling price of $99,500.) Exhibit D-6 shows the adjusting entries made on this date to record the relevant fair values.

EXHIBIT D-6	Balance Sheet Valuation for Debt Securities

2010

Trading Debt Securities

Dec. 31	Bond investment—Trading (Natco)		1,300	
	Unrealized gain on investments (income)			1,300
	To adjust trading debt securities to year-end fair value ($99,500 − $98,200 = $1,300 gain).			

A = L + SE
+1,300   +1,300 Gain

Available-for-Sale Debt Securities

Dec. 31	Fair value adjustment to bond investment		1,210	
	Unrealized gain/loss on investments (equity)			1,210
	To adjust available-for-sale debt securities to year-end fair value ($99,500 − $98,290 = $1,210 gain).			

A = L + SE
+1,210   +1,210
               Comprehensive
               Income

Fair value changes in securities that are still owned are called *unrealized gains and losses*. Unrealized gains and losses that relate to trading securities are reported in the income statement. Thus, the $1,300 unrealized gain shown in Exhibit D-6 is included in Warner's 2010 income statement.

Unrealized gains and losses that relate to available-for-sale securities are excluded from the income statement. Instead, their net amount is reported as a separate component of stockholders' equity called Unrealized Gain/Loss on Investments (Equity). Unrealized Gain/Loss on Investments is included in comprehensive income that was discussed in Chapter 13 (see pages 597–598). Because these unrealized gains and losses are not included in earnings, the investment's cost must be maintained in the accounts so that a total realized gain or loss can be determined when the investment is actually sold. Using the valuation account Fair Value Adjustment to Bond Investment permits the maintenance of the investment's cost in the Bond Investment—Available for Sale account.[2] After the adjustments shown in Exhibit D-6, the December 31, 2010, balance sheet reports the bond investments as follows:

Bond investment—Trading (fair value)		$99,500
Bond investment—Available-for-sale (cost).	$98,290	
Add: Fair value adjustment to bond investment	1,210	99,500
Bond investment—Held-to-maturity (cost)		98,290

Hint: Although the accounting for debt (and equity) trading securities calls for the recognition of any fair value changes as part of a company's current net income, those unrealized gains or losses are not reported as part of a company's net income for income tax purposes. The IRS does not require the reporting of any gains until they are realized and prohibits the reporting of any losses until realized (when a security is sold).

Sale or Redemption at Maturity

To complete our illustration, assume that the trading and available-for-sale bond investments are both sold on July 1, 2011, for $99,800 each (after recognizing interest income on June 30, 2011). The remaining bond investment is held to maturity (June 30, 2020), at which time the issuer redeems the bonds for their maturity value of $100,000. Exhibit D-7 shows the appropriate journal entries related to these events.

EXHIBIT D-7	Sale or Redemption at Maturity of Debt Securities

2011

Trading Debt Securities

July	1	Cash	99,800		A = L + SE
		Bond investment—Trading (Natco)		99,500	+99,800 +300 Gain
		Gain on sale of investments		300	−99,500
		To record sale of trading debt securities for $99,800			
		($99,800 − $99,500 = $300 realized gain).			

Available-for-Sale Debt Securities

July	1	Cash	99,800		A = L + SE
		Bond investment—Available-for-sale (Natco)		98,380	+99,800 +1,420
		Gain on sale of investments		1,420	−98,380 Gain
		To record sale of available-for-sale debt securities for $99,800			
		($99,800 − $98,380 = $1,420 gain).			
Dec.	31	Unrealized gain/loss on investments (equity)	1,210		A = L + SE
		Fair value adjustment to bond investment		1,210	−1,210 −1,210
		To adjust these account balances to zero.			Comprehensive Income

2020

Held-to-Maturity Debt Securities

June	30	Cash	100,000		A = L + SE
		Bond investment—Held-to-maturity (Natco)		100,000	+100,000
		To record redemption of bonds at maturity.			−100,000

    In Exhibit D-7, the $300 gain on the sale of the trading securities is the difference between the $99,800 sales proceeds and the last recorded fair value of $99,500. By July 1, 2011, another $90 of discount amortization would have been recorded on the available-for-sale securities, increasing their amortized cost to $98,380 ($98,290 + $90). The $1,420 gain that is recorded on their sale is the difference between the $99,800 sales proceeds and the amortized cost of $98,380. Because all available-for-sale bonds were

---

[2] The cost of trading securities must be maintained for income tax purposes. A fair value valuation account, therefore, may be used for maintaining the income tax records of trading securities.

sold, the related valuation account and unrealized gain/loss account are adjusted to zero balances at the next financial statement closing date (December 31, 2011). The completion of the discount amortization on the held-to-maturity bonds brings their amortized cost to $100,000 on June 30, 2020. Thus, there is no gain or loss associated with the redemption of the bonds at maturity.

Investments in Equity Securities

LO3 **Describe** the accounting for various kinds of equity security investments.

Equity security investments fit into one of four categories: trading securities, available-for-sale securities, influential securities, and controlling securities. The major accounting events associated with investments in equity securities are their purchase, the recognition of investment income, their balance sheet valuation, and their sale. Exhibit D-8 summarizes the accounting guidelines for these events. We will illustrate these guidelines with examples.

EXHIBIT D-8	Accounting Guidelines for Investments in Equity Securities				
Event/Accounting Guideline		**Trading Securities**	**Available-for-Sale Securities**	**Influential Securities**	**Controlling Securities**
1.	**Purchase** Record at cost, which includes any broker's fees.	X	X	X	X
2.	**Recognition of Investment Income** Record dividend income when dividends are received.	X	X		
	Record equity in investee company's net income as investment income. Decrease investment account for dividends received.			X	X
3.	**Balance Sheet Valuation** Measure securities at fair value at balance sheet date. No valuation account to the investment account is used. Changes in fair value are reported in the income statement.	X			
	Measure securities at fair value at balance sheet date. Use a valuation account to the investment account. Changes in fair value are reported in stockholders' equity.		X		
	Report securities at book value (cost plus share of investee net income less dividends).			X	
	Eliminate investment account as part of consolidation procedures.				X
4.	**Sale** Sale proceeds less investment's book value is a realized gain or loss.	X		X	X
	Sale proceeds less investment's cost is a realized gain or loss.		X		

Purchase

Assume that Warner Company purchases 1,500 shares of common stock in each of four different companies—Ark, Inc.; Bain, Inc.; Carr, Inc.; and Dot, Inc.—on January 1, 2010. Each investment cost $15,000, including broker's fees. The shares acquired represent 10 percent of Ark's voting stock, 10 percent of Bain's voting stock, 25 percent of Carr's voting stock, and 60 percent of Dot's voting stock.[3] Only the Ark investment is considered by management to be a trading security. Thus, each of these stock investments is placed in a different category. Exhibit D-9 presents the journal entry to record the purchase of these investments. Note that each stock investment is recorded at its acquisition cost.

EXHIBIT D-9	Purchase of Equity Securities

2010					
Jan. 1	Stock investment—Trading (Ark)	15,000		A = L + SE	
	Stock investment—Available-for-sale (Bain)	15,000		+15,000	
	Stock investment—Influential (Carr)	15,000		+15,000	
	Stock investment—Controlling (Dot)	15,000		+15,000	
	Cash		60,000	+15,000	
	To record purchase of 1,500 shares each of Ark, Inc., Bain, Inc., Carr,			−60,000	
	Inc., and Dot, Inc., common stock for $60,000 ($15,000 for each				
	investment), including broker's fees.				

Recognition of Investment Income

Now assume that each of the four companies earns net income of $10,000 in 2010; and, that each company also declares a cash dividend of $0.50 per share, which is received by Warner on December 31, 2010. Exhibit D-10 shows the journal entries to record this information.

As shown in Exhibit D-10, the dividends of $750 received on both the Ark and Bain investments are reported as Dividend Income. This is the proper treatment for cash dividends received on trading securities (Ark) and available-for-sale securities (Bain).

When the percentage ownership of voting stock reaches 20 percent or more, as is the case with the investment in Carr stock, the **equity method** of accounting is used. Under the equity method, the investor company records as income or loss its proportionate share of the net income or net loss reported for the period by the investee company (Carr), with an offsetting debit or credit going to the Stock Investment account. In addition, the receipt of any cash dividends from the investee company reduces the Stock Investment account. *The equity method prevents an investor company from manipulating its own income by the influence it can exercise on the dividend policies of the investee company.*

In Exhibit D-10, the equity method is used for the Carr stock investment (25 percent ownership) and Dot stock investment (60 percent ownership). At December 31, 2010, the Income from Stock Investments account and the Carr Stock Investment account are increased by 25 percent of Carr's 2010 net income (25 percent × $10,000 = $2,500). The receipt of the $750 cash dividend from Carr reduces the Carr Stock Investment account. Similarly, the equity method causes a $6,000 increase (60 percent × $10,000 net income) in both the Income from Stock Investments account and the Dot Stock Investment account at December 31, 2010. The $750 cash dividend received from Dot decreases the Dot Stock Investment account.

A.K.A. Stock investments involving ownership interests of 20 to 50 percent of the outstanding voting shares are often referred to as affiliate companies.

Balance Sheet Valuation

The balance sheet valuations for equity trading securities and available-for-sale securities are handled in the same manner as the corresponding debt securities. Year-end adjusting entries are made to record these equity securities at their current fair value, with quoted market prices from established exchanges like the New York and London stock exchanges, being the best evidence of a stock's current fair value.

---

[3] We assume that the cost of the investments in Carr and Dot are equal to the book value of the underlying net assets of the investee company. This assumption permits us to simplify the illustration of the accounting for these two investments.

EXHIBIT D-10	Recognition of Investment Income on Equity Securities

2010

Trading Equity Securities

$A = L + SE$
$+750$ $+750$ Rev

Dec. 31	Cash	750	
	Dividend income		750
	To record receipt of cash dividend from Ark, Inc.		

Available-for-Sale Equity Securities

$A = L + SE$
$+750$ $+750$ Rev

Dec. 31	Cash	750	
	Dividend income		750
	To record receipt of cash dividend from Bain, Inc.		

Influential Equity Securities

$A = L + SE$
$+2,500$ $+2,500$ Rev

Dec. 31	Stock investment—Influential (Carr)	2,500	
	Income from stock investments		2,500
	To record as income 25% of Carr's 2010 net income of $10,000		
	(investment balance = $17,500).		

$A = L + SE$
$+750$
-750

Dec. 31	Cash	750	
	Stock investment—Influential (Carr)		750
	To record receipt of cash dividend from Carr, Inc.		
	(investment balance = $16,750).		

Controlling Equity Securities

$A = L + SE$
$+6,000$ $+6,000$ Rev

Dec. 31	Stock investment—Controlling (Dot)	6,000	
	Income from stock investments		6,000
	To record as income 60% of Dot's 2010 net income of $10,000		
	(investment balance = $21,000).		

$A = L + SE$
$+750$
-750

Dec. 31	Cash	750	
	Stock investment—Controlling (Dot)		750
	To record receipt of cash dividend from Dot, Inc.		
	(investment balance = $20,250).		

PRINCIPLE ALERT	Objectivity Principle

The standard to measure equity trading securities and available-for-sale securities at current fair value applies only to equity securities that have readily determinable fair values. It does not apply to equity investments that would create significant valuation problems, such as equity investments in closely held companies whose shares do not trade on an established stock exchange. This represents an application of the *objectivity principle*, which states that accounting entries should be based on objectively determined evidence.

Assume that at December 31, 2010, the fair values of 1,500 shares of Ark common stock and Bain common stock are each $23,000. Exhibit D-11 shows the adjusting entries made on this date to record the relevant fair values.

As is true with debt securities, the $8,000 unrealized gain shown in Exhibit D-11 on the trading securities (Ark) is reported in Warner's 2010 income statement, whereas the $8,000 unrealized gain on the available-for-sale securities (Bain) is reported in the stockholders' equity section of the balance sheet of the Warner Company. The valuation account for the Bain stock investment plays the same role as discussed earlier in the accounting for debt securities; it permits the security's cost basis to be maintained in the Stock Investment—Available for Sale account.

Stock investments accounted for by the equity method are not measured at year-end fair values. The year-end account balances remain as calculated using the equity method— that is, $16,750 for the Carr investment and $20,250 for the Dot investment. For controlling investments, the financial statements of the investee company are usually consolidated with the statements of the investor company; consequently, the investment account does not appear in the consolidated statements.

EXHIBIT D-11	Balance Sheet Valuation for Equity Securities

2010

Trading Equity Securities

Dec.	31	Stock investment—Trading (Ark)	8,000			
		Unrealized gain on investments (income)		8,000	A = L + SE	+8,000 +8,000 Gain
		To adjust trading stock securities to year-end fair value of $23,000				
		($23,000 − $15,000 = $8,000 gain).				

Available-for-Sale Equity Securities

Dec.	31	Fair value adjustment to stock investment	8,000			
		Unrealized gain/loss on investments (equity)		8,000	A = L + SE	+8,000 +8,000 Comprehensive Income
		To adjust available-for-sale equity securities (Bain) to year-end fair				
		value of $23,000 ($23,000 − $15,000 = $8,000 gain).				

Sale

To complete our illustration, assume that all four stock investments are sold on July 1, 2011. Each of the stock investments is sold for $22,000. Exhibit D-12 shows the journal entries related to these events. As shown in Exhibit D-12, each sale generates a different gain or loss. Even though the basic events relating to each of the stock investments were the same, the accounting guidelines result in quite different analyses.

EXHIBIT D-12	Sale of Equity Securities

2011

Trading Equity Securities

July	1	Cash	22,000			
		Loss on sale of investments	1,000		A = L + SE	+22,000 −1,000 Loss
		Stock investment—Trading (Ark)		23,000	−23,000	
		To record sale of trading equity securities for $22,000				
		($22,000 − $23,000 = $1,000 loss).				

Available-for-Sale Equity Securities

July	1	Cash	22,000			
		Stock investment—Available-for-sale (Bain)		15,000	A = L + SE	+22,000 +7,000 Gain
		Gain on sale of investments		7,000	−15,000	
		To record sale of available-for-sale equity securities for $22,000				
		($22,000 − $15,000 = $7,000 gain).				
Dec.	31	Unrealized gain/loss on investments (equity)	8,000			
		Fair value adjustment to stock investment		8,000	A = L + SE	−8,000 −8,000 Comprehensive Income
		To adjust these account balances to zero.				

Influential Equity Securities

July	1	Cash	22,000			
		Stock investment—Influential (Carr)		16,750	A = L + SE	+22,000 +5,250 Gain
		Gain on sale of investments		5,250	−16,750	
		To record sale of influential equity securities for $22,000				
		($22,000 − $16,750 = $5,250 gain).				

Controlling Equity Securities

July	1	Cash	22,000			
		Stock investment—Controlling (Dot)		20,250	A = L + SE	+22,000 +1,750 Gain
		Gain on sale of investments		1,750	−20,250	
		To record sale of controlling equity securities for $22,000				
		($22,000 − $20,250 = $1,750 gain).				

Because all available-for-sale stock was sold, the second entry in Exhibit D-12 for the Bain stock investment eliminates the balances in the related valuation account and unrealized gain/loss account at the next adjustment date (December 31, 2011).

In some countries where there are not actively traded markets for debt and equity securities, the balance sheet valuation of debt and equity securities is often at the original acquisition cost of an investment. In other countries, where actively traded markets for securities do exist, a variant of the current fair value approach used under U.S. GAAP, called the lower-of-cost-or-market method, may be used. Under the lower-of-cost-or-market method, a debt or equity security is valued at the lower of two values—its current fair value or its original acquisition cost. When a security's current fair value falls below its acquisition cost, the security's carrying value is written down to the lower amount and an unrealized loss is reported as part of the company's current income.

Current and Noncurrent Classifications

Each investment in debt and equity securities must be classified as either a current asset or a noncurrent asset in the balance sheet. Trading securities are always classified as *current assets*. Held-to-maturity securities are classified as *noncurrent assets* until the last year before maturity. Available-for-sale securities may be classified as either *current* or *noncurrent assets*, depending on management's intentions regarding their sale. Influential investments are usually classified as *noncurrent assets*, but a current classification is proper if management intends to sell the investments within the next year or operating cycle, whichever is longer. As mentioned earlier, controlling investments do not appear in consolidated financial statements as a separate account but rather are "consolidated" into the accounts of the parent company.

IN PRACTICE	**Cherry Picking**

The treatment of unrealized gains and losses on available-for-sale investments permits management to engage in a practice known as "cherry picking." Management may select for sale those available-for-sale securities that have unrealized gains, thereby converting the unrealized gains into realized gains that appear in the company's income statement. Similarly, available-for-sale investments having unrealized losses are not sold, thereby keeping the losses out of the income statement and on the company's balance sheet instead. Cherry picking is a management behavior fostered by accounting principles. Many observers believe that it is a practice that gives management too much control over income statement results.

PARENT-SUBSIDIARY RELATIONSHIP

LO4 **Define** parent-subsidiary relationships and **discuss** how their balance sheet data are consolidated.

A corporation that controls another corporation through ownership of a company's voting stock is known as a **holding company**. Control over another corporation is ensured through ownership of all or a majority of the investee's voting stock. Another name for a holding company is **parent company**, and the wholly owned or majority-held investees are called **subsidiaries**. The parent company and each subsidiary company are separate legal entities.

Consolidated Financial Statements

As separate legal entities, a parent company and its subsidiaries maintain their own accounting records and prepare separate financial statements primarily for internal purposes. In the parent company's *separate* financial statements, the ownership of a subsidiary's stock is reported as a stock investment accounted for by the equity method. When the parent company prepares financial statements for its stockholders and creditors, however, the financial statements of the parent company and its subsidiaries are combined and reported as a single set of **consolidated financial statements**.

Under consolidated accounting, the individual line item (stock investment – controlling) used to account for an investment in a subsidiary under the equity method is replaced by all the individual asset and liability accounts of the consolidated subsidiary. In other words, the cash account of the subsidiary is combined with the cash account of the parent, the accounts receivable of the subsidiary is combined with the accounts receivable of the parent, the accounts payable of the subsidiary is combined with the accounts payable of the parent, and so on. The financial statements of a parent company and its various subsidiaries are combined using what is known as the acquisition method. When the financial data of these legal entities are consolidated, the resulting statements represent the group as an *economic entity*, as shown in Exhibit D-13.

Consolidated financial statements are prepared to avoid the problem of information overload in which investors and investment professionals receive more financial data than can be purposely processed. For example, the **General Electric Company** is made up of over 2,000 companies worldwide. A shareholder of General Electric would be overwhelmed to receive 2,000 individual company balance sheets, 2,000 individual company income statements, and 2,000 individual company statements of cash flows. Consolidated financial statements avoid this data problem for financial statement users by providing a single set of financial data for the economic entity.

EXHIBIT D-13	Parent-Subsidiary Relationship: Legal and Economic Entities

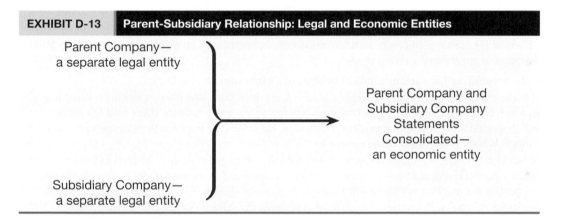

Consolidated financial statements present both the total assets controlled by a parent company and the aggregate results of the group's operations and cash flows. These amounts are difficult to perceive when viewing only the separate reports of the individual companies. Consolidated statements are particularly valuable to the managers and stockholders of the parent company. In addition, creditors, government agencies, and the general public are informed of the magnitude and scope of an economic enterprise through consolidated statements.

	ACCOUNTING ENTITY CONCEPT	PRINCIPLE ALERT

The preparation of consolidated financial statements represents an application of the *accounting entity concept*. By viewing the parent company and its subsidiaries as a single economic entity, accountants ignore the legal boundaries of the separate companies. For consolidated financial statements, the overall economic entity is the accounting entity.

Limitations of Consolidated Statements

Consolidated statements have certain limitations. The status or performance of weak subsidiaries in a group can be "masked" through consolidation with more successful subunits. Rates of return, other ratios, and trend percentages calculated from consolidated statements may sometimes prove deceptive because they are really composite calculations.

Stockholders and creditors of controlled companies who are interested in their legal rights and prerogatives should examine the separate financial statements of the relevant constituent companies.

Supplemental disclosures do improve the quality of consolidated statements, particularly those of *conglomerates – that is,* entities with diversified lines of business. U.S. GAAP stipulates that firms disclose information regarding revenues, income from operations, and identifiable assets for significant business segments.

SUMMARY OF LEARNING OBJECTIVES

LO1   Identify and define the investment categories for debt and equity securities. (p. D-2)
- Debt and equity security investments are placed in one of five investment categories:
  a. *Trading security,* a debt or equity security that management buys with the intent to sell in the near future.
  b. *Held-to-maturity security,* a debt security that management intends to hold to maturity.
  c. *Available-for-sale security,* a debt security that management neither intends to sell in the near future nor hold to maturity or a noninfluential equity security that management does not intend to sell in the near future.
  d. *Influential security,* an equity security investment that represents a 20 to 50 percent ownership of a company's voting stock.
  e. *Controlling security,* an equity security investment that represents an ownership of more than 50 percent of a company's voting stock.

LO2   Describe the accounting for various kinds of debt security investments. (p. D-3)
- Debt trading securities are initially recorded at their acquisition cost, and interest income is recorded when received. The securities are reported at current fair value on the balance sheet with fair value changes reported on the income statement. When sold, the difference between the sales proceeds and the investment's book value is a realized gain or loss.
- Debt available-for-sale securities are initially recorded at their acquisition cost. Interest income is recorded when received, with any premium or discount amortized as an adjustment to interest income. The securities are reported at current fair value on the balance sheet with fair value changes reported in stockholders' equity. When sold, the difference between the sales proceeds and the investment's amortized cost is a realized gain or loss.
- Debt held-to-maturity securities are initially recorded at their acquisition cost. Interest income is recorded when received, with any premium or discount amortized as an adjustment to interest income. At maturity, the investment's book value equals the redemption proceeds.

LO3   Describe the accounting for various kinds of equity security investments. (p. D-8)
- Equity trading securities are initially recorded at their acquisition cost, and dividend income is recorded when received. The securities are reported at current fair value on the balance sheet with fair value changes reported on the income statement. When sold, the difference between the sales proceeds and the investment's book value is a realized gain or loss.
- Equity available-for-sale securities are initially recorded at their acquisition cost. Dividend income is recorded when received. The securities are reported at current fair value on the balance sheet with fair value changes reported in stockholders' equity. When sold, the difference between the sales proceeds and the investment's cost is a realized gain or loss.
- Equity influential securities are initially recorded at their acquisition cost. Subsequent accounting uses the equity method: the investment account is increased by a proportionate share of the investee company's net income and decreased by the amount of any dividends received. When sold, the difference between the sales proceeds and the investment's book value is a realized gain or loss.
- Equity controlling securities are initially recorded at their acquisition cost. Subsequent accounting uses the equity method: the investment account is increased by a proportionate share of the investee company's net income and decreased by the amount of any dividends received. For financial reporting, however, the investment account is replaced by a subsidiary's individual assets and liabilities, producing consolidated financial statements. When sold, the difference between the sales proceeds and the investment's book value is a realized gain or loss.

Define parent-subsidiary relationships and discuss how their balance sheet data are consolidated.   **LO4**
(p. D-12)

- A corporation that controls another corporation (the investee) by virtue of owning all, or a majority, of the investee's common stock is referred to as the parent company. The wholly owned or majority-owned investee is called the subsidiary.

- When a parent company prepares financial statements for its stockholders, the financial statements of the parent and its subsidiaries are combined and reported as a single set of consolidated financial statements.

KEY TERMS

Available-for-sale securities (p. D-2)	Debt security (p. D-2)	Holding company (p. D-12)
Consolidated financial statements (p. D-12)	Equity method (p. D-9)	Influential securities (p. D-2)
	Equity security (p. D-2)	Parent company (p. D-12)
Controlling securities (p. D-2)	Held-to-maturity securities (p. D-2)	Subsidiaries (p. D-12)
		Trading securities (p. D-2)

SELF-STUDY QUESTIONS

(Answers to the Self-Study Questions are at the end of the chapter.)

1. Snyder, Inc., purchased $100,000 of Dane Company's 8 percent, 15 year, bonds for $96,400 on   **LO2**
   January 1. Snyder plans to hold the bonds to maturity. Snyder records interest and straight-line amortization on interest dates (June 30 and December 31). At December 31, the bonds have a market value of $97,200. Snyder's balance sheet at December 31 should report the bonds at:
   a. $96,400.
   b. $96,640.
   c. $97,200.
   d. $96,160.

2. A firm purchased noninfluential and noncontrolling stock investments for $65,000. The firm does   **LO3**
   not intend to sell the investments in the near future. During the year, the firm received dividends totaling $4,000 from these stock investments. At year-end, the stock portfolio had a quoted market value of $68,000. The increase in net income for the year (ignore income taxes) from these stock investments is:
   a. $1,000.
   b. $3,000.
   c. $4,000.
   d. $7,000.

3. Artway Company purchased 30 percent of the voting stock of Barton Company for $60,000 on   **LO3**
   January 1. During the year, Barton Company earned $50,000 net income and paid $15,000 in dividends. At the end of the year, Artway Company's account, Stock Investment—Influential (Barton) should have a balance of:
   a. $110,000.
   b. $70,500.
   c. $95,000.
   d. $60,000.

4. The proper category to classify an investment in equity securities depends on: **LO1**
   a.   management's intentions with regard to when to sell the investment.
   b.   the relative size of the investment to the purchasing company's total assets.
   c.   the ability of the purchasing company to influence the investee company.
   d.   both *a* and *c*.

5. Where would the account unrealized gain/loss on investment appear for trading security   **LO3**
   investment?
   a.   Income Statement
   b.   Equity section of the Balance Sheet
   c.   Statement of Cash Flows
   d.   It does not appear on any statement.

LO3   **6. Where would the account unrealized gain/loss on investment appear for an available-for-sale security investment?**

     a.   Income Statement

     b.   Equity section of the Balance Sheet

     c.   Statement of Cash Flows

     d.   It does not appear on any statement.

LO1   **7. Controlling securities typically require the investor to acquire what percent of the investee company common stock?**

     a.   Under 20 percent

     b.   Between 20 and 50 percent

     c.   Over 50 percent

     d.   100 percent

LO2   **8. Jeffrey Company invested in debt securities. Jeffrey will initially record this investment at:**

     a.   Cost

     b.   Cost plus any accrued interest

     c.   Cost less any accrued interest

     d.   Maturity value

LO3   **9. Franz Co. acquired a 30% interest in Esik for $420,000 and appropriately applied the equity method. During the first year, Esik reported net income of $200,000 and paid cash dividends totaling $50,000. What amount will Franz report as it relates to the investment at the end of the first year on its income statement?**

     a.   Investment earnings totaling $60,000

     b.   Investment earnings totaling $45,000

     c.   Net investment earnings totaling $150,000

     d.   Dividend income totaling $15,000

LO3   **10. Blanc Co. received dividends from its common stock investments during the year ended December 31 as follows:**

     •   A cash dividend totaling $15,000 from its trading security investment in Fisher Corporation, when the market price of Fisher's shares was $20 per share

     •   A cash dividend of $10,000 from Myler Corp. in which Blanc Co. owns a 32% interest

     How much dividend income should Blanc report in its income statement?

     a. $25,000

     b. $15,000

     c. $10,000

     d. $ 0

LO2   **11. At what value are held-to-maturity debt securities reported on the balance sheet?**

     a.   Acquisition cost

     b.   Market value

     c.   Amortized cost

     d.   Historical cost adjusted for a proportionate share of the affiliate's earnings, losses, and dividends

LO4   **12. Norma Travel, Inc., acquired an 80% interest in CruisesByBen on December 31 for $870,000. Norma has the ability to exercise significant influence on management decisions. The CruisesByBen stock is publicly traded. During the year, CruisesByBen reported net income of $160,000 and paid cash dividends of $40,000. How should Norma Travel account for its investment in CruisesByBen?**

     a.   Apply the equity method and report the investment at market value at year end

     b.   Apply the equity method and perform a full consolidation

     c.   Apply mark-to-market accounting and consolidate the statements at year end

     d.   Account for the investment as a trading security

LO1   **13. In classifying investments, how do held-to-maturity securities differ from other marketable securities?**

     a.   The investor plans to hold the securities until they mature.

     b.   The investor has the ability to exercise significant influence over management of the investee.

     c.   The investor has the ability to control the investee.

     d.   These securities have a high degree of liquidity.

QUESTIONS

1. Debt security investments are placed in one of three investment categories. What are these three categories?

2. Equity security investments are placed in one of four investment categories. What are these four categories?

3. Caldwell Company invests in bonds at a premium. Caldwell does not intend to sell the bonds in the near future, nor does it intend to hold the bonds to maturity. Should the bond premium be amortized? What measure should be used to report these bonds on the company's year-end balance sheet?

4. What measure should be used to report trading securities on the balance sheet? Available-for-sale securities? Held-to-maturity securities?

5. What is an unrealized gain? Unrealized loss?

6. Where are unrealized gains and losses related to trading securities reported in the financial statements? Where are unrealized gains and losses related to available-for-sale securities reported in the financial statements?

7. What is an influential stock investment? Describe the accounting procedures used for such investments.

8. On January 1, Mower Company purchased 40 percent of the common stock of Starr Company for $250,000. During the year, Starr reported $80,000 of net income and paid $60,000 in cash dividends. At year-end, what amount should appear on Mower's balance sheet for its investment in Starr?

9. What accounting procedures are used when a stock investment represents more than 50 percent of the investee company's voting stock?

10. What is the purpose of consolidated financial statements?

11. What are the inherent limitations of consolidated financial statements?

EXERCISES—SET A

ED-1A. Accounting for Debt Securities—Trading   Gressens Company had the following transactions and adjustments related to a bond investment: **LO2**

2010
Oct. 1 Purchased $500,000 face value of Skyline, Inc.'s 7 percent bonds at 97 plus a brokerage commission of $1,000. The bonds pay interest on September 30 and March 31 and mature in 20 years. Gressens expects to sell the bonds in the near future.
Dec. 31 Made the adjusting entry to record interest earned on investment in the Skyline bonds.
　　 31 Made the adjusting entry to record the current fair value of the Skyline bonds. At December 31, the market value of the Skyline bonds was $490,000.

2011
Mar. 31 Received the semiannual interest payment on investment in the Skyline bonds.
Apr. 1 Sold the Skyline bond investment for $492,300 cash.

Record the transactions and adjustments of the Gressens Company using journal entries.

ED-2A. Accounting for Debt Securities—Available-for-Sale   Hilyn Company had the following transactions and adjustments related to a bond investment: **LO2**

2010
Jan. 1 Purchased $800,000 face value of Cynad, Inc.'s 9 percent bonds at 99 plus a brokerage commission of $1,400. The bonds pay interest on June 30 and December 31 and mature in 15 years. Hilyn does not expect to sell the bonds in the near future, nor does it intend to hold the bonds to maturity.
June 30 Received the semiannual interest payment on the Cynad bonds and amortized the bond discount for six months. Hilyn uses the straight-line method to amortize bond discounts and premiums.
Dec. 31 Received the semiannual interest payment on the Cynad bonds and amortized the bond discount for six months.
　　 31 Made the adjusting entry to record the current fair value of the Cynad bonds. At December 31, the market value of the Cynad bonds was $790,000.

2011

June   30   Received the semiannual interest payment on the Cynad bonds and amortized the bond discount for six months.

July   1   Sold the Cynad bond investment for $792,500 cash.

Dec.   31   Made the adjusting entry to eliminate balances from the Fair Value Adjustment to Bond Investment account and the Unrealized Gain/Loss on Investments (Equity) account.

Record the transactions and adjustments of Hilyn Company using journal entries.

LO2   **ED-3A.**   **Accounting for Debt Securities—Held-to-Maturity**   Kurl Company had the following transactions and adjustments related to a bond investment:

2010

Jan.   1   Purchased $600,000 face value of Sphere, Inc.'s 9 percent bonds at 102 plus a brokerage commission of $900. The bonds pay interest on June 30 and December 31 and mature in 10 years. Kurl expects to hold the bonds to maturity.

June   30   Received the semiannual interest payment on the Sphere bonds and amortized the bond premium for six months. Kurl uses the straight-line method to amortize bond discounts and premiums.

2019

Dec.   31   Received the semiannual interest payment on the Sphere bonds and amortized the bond premium for six months.

31   Received the principal amount in cash on maturity date of the Sphere bonds.

Record the transactions and adjustments of Kurl Company using journal entries.

LO3   **ED-4A.**   **Accounting for Equity Securities—Trading**   The Glass Company had the following transactions and adjustment related to a stock investment:

2010

Nov.   15   Purchased 6,000 shares of Erie, Inc.'s common stock at $12 per share plus a brokerage commission of $750. Glass expects to sell the stock in the near future.

Dec.   22   Received a cash dividend of $1.10 per share of common stock from Erie.

31   Made the adjusting entry to reflect year-end fair value of the stock investment in Erie. The year-end market price of the Erie common stock is $11.25 per share.

2011

Jan.   20   Sold all 6,000 shares of the Erie common stock for $66,900.

Record the transactions and adjustment of the Glass Company using journal entries.

LO3   **ED-5A.**   **Accounting for Equity Securities—Available-for-Sale**   Refer to the data for the Glass Company in ED-4A. Assume that when the shares were purchased, management did not intend to sell the stock in the near future. Record the transactions and adjustment for Glass Company under this assumption using journal entries. In addition, prepare any adjusting entry needed at December 31, 2011.

LO3   **ED-6A.**   **Accounting for Equity Securities—Influential**   The Dunn Company had the following transactions and adjustment related to a stock investment:

2010

Jan.   15   Purchased 12,000 shares of Van, Inc.'s common stock at $9 per share plus a brokerage commission of $900. These shares represent a 30 percent ownership of Van's common stock.

Dec.   31   Received a cash dividend of $1.25 per share of common stock from Van.

31   Made the adjusting entry to reflect income from the Van stock investment. Van's 2010 net income is $80,000.

2011

Jan.   20   Sold all 12,000 shares of the Van common stock for $120,500.

Record the transactions and adjustment of the Dunn Company using journal entries.

LO3   **ED-7A.**   **Accounting for Equity Securities**   On March 15, Kat Corp. purchased 200 shares of common stock of Scott Company for $15 per share. Kat Corp. is not able to exercise significant influence over Scott.

On December 31, the market value of the Scott stock was $14.00 per share. Kat Corp. plans to hold the stock for the unforeseeable future.

a.   Upon the purchase of the Scott stock, how should Kat Corp. classify the shares on its balance sheet? Justify your answer.

b.   Record all transactions necessary for Kat.

ED-8A   Recording Influential Securities   On January 3, Mahony Farm purchased 20% of the outstanding   **LO3**
stock of Flepo Company for $80,000. The purchase gave Mahony the ability to exercise significant influence over Flepo. During the year, Flepo paid cash dividends totaling $70,000 and reported net income for the year of $90,000.

Record all transactions necessary for Mahony Farm.

ED-9A.   Accounting for Equity Securities   Microsoft, Inc., maintained a large investment in marketable se-   **LO3**
curities valued at approximately $42 billion as of the beginning of the year. During the year, the securities produced investment income (dividends and interest income) totaling $2 billion. At year-end, the portfolio of marketable securities had appreciated to $43.5 billion.

Calculate the income statement effect of the marketable securities if:

1.   The entire portfolio is classified as trading securities.

2.   The entire portfolio is classified as available-for-sale securities.

ED-10A. Consolidation Accounting   Fletcher Company, a manufacturer of precision mining equipment, ac-   **LO4**
quired 100 percent of the outstanding common stock of Denfork Company, a small mining company with several mines that extract rare earth materials.

a.   How should Fletcher account for this acquisition during the year?

b.   What adjustments are needed at year-end?

c.   What limitations are present in this method of accounting?

EXERCISES—SET B

ED-1B.   Accounting for Debt Securities—Trading   Sanders, Inc. had the following transactions and adjust-   **LO2**
ments related to a bond investment:

2010
Nov.   1   Purchased $300,000 face value of Batem, Inc.'s 9 percent bonds at 102 plus a brokerage commission of $900. The bonds pay interest on October 31 and April 30 and mature in 15 years. Sanders expects to sell the bonds in the near future.

Dec.   31   Made the adjusting entry to record interest earned on investment in the Batem bonds.
        31   Made the adjusting entry to record the current fair value of the Batem bonds. At December 31, the market value of the Batem bonds was $301,500.

2011
Apr.   30   Received the semiannual interest payment on investment in the Batem bonds.
May   1   Sold the Batem bond investment for $300,900 cash.

Record the transactions and adjustments of the Sanders Company using journal entries.

ED-2B.   Accounting for Debt Securities—Available-for-Sale   The Witt Company had the following transac-   **LO2**
tions and adjustments related to a bond investment:

2010
Jan.   1   Purchased $600,000 face value of Chevy, Inc.'s 8 percent bonds at 101 plus a brokerage commission of $1,400. The bonds pay interest on June 30 and December 31 and mature in 10 years. Witt does not expect to sell the bonds in the near future, nor does it intend to hold the bonds to maturity.

June   30   Received the semiannual interest payment on the Chevy bonds and amortized the bond premium for six months. Witt uses the straight-line method to amortize bond discounts and premiums.

Dec.   31   Received the semiannual interest payment on the Chevy bonds and amortized the bond premium for six months.

Dec. 31 Made the adjusting entry to record the current fair value of the Chevy bonds. At December 31, the market value of the Chevy bonds was $609,000.

2011

June 30 Received the semiannual interest payment on the Chevy bonds and amortized the bond premium for six months.

July 1 Sold the Chevy bond investment for $608,500 cash.

Dec. 31 Made the adjusting entry to eliminate balances from the Fair Value Adjustment to Bond Investment account and the Unrealized Gain/Loss on Investments (Equity) account.

Record the transactions and adjustments of the Witt Company using journal entries.

LO2 **ED-3B. Accounting for Debt Securities—Held-to-Maturity** The Shepler Company had the following transactions and adjustments related to a bond investment:

2010

Jan. 1 Purchased $250,000 face value of Lowe, Inc.'s 6 percent bonds at 98 plus a brokerage commission of $500. The bonds pay interest on June 30 and December 31 and mature in 15 years. Shepler expects to hold the bonds to maturity.

June 30 Received the semiannual interest payment on the Lowe bonds and amortized the bond discount for six months. Shepler uses the straight-line method to amortize bond discounts and premiums.

2024

Dec. 31 Received the semiannual interest payment on the Lowe bonds and amortized the bond discount for six months.

31 Received the principal amount in cash on maturity date of the Lowe bonds.

Record the transactions and adjustments of the Shepler Company using journal entries.

LO3 **ED-4B. Accounting for Equity Securities—Trading** The Dale Company had the following transactions and adjustment related to a stock investment:

2010

Nov. 15 Purchased 5,000 shares of Lake, Inc.'s common stock at $16 per share plus a brokerage commission of $900. Dale Company expects to sell the stock in the near future.

Dec. 22 Received a cash dividend of $1.25 per share of common stock from Lake.

31 Made the adjusting entry to reflect year-end fair value of the stock investment in Lake. The year-end market price of the Lake common stock is $17.50 per share.

2011

Jan. 20 Sold all 5,000 shares of the Lake common stock for $86,400.

Record the transactions and adjustment of the Dale Company using journal entries.

LO3 **ED-5B. Accounting for Equity Securities—Available-for-Sale** Refer to the data for Dale Company in ED-4B. Assume that when the shares were purchased, management did not intend to sell the stock in the near future. Record the transactions and adjustment for Dale Company under this assumption using journal entries. In addition, prepare any adjusting entry needed at December 31, 2011.

LO3 **ED-6B. Accounting for Equity Securities—Influential** The Prince Company had the following transactions and adjustment related to a stock investment:

2010

Jan. 15 Purchased 15,000 shares of Park, Inc.'s common stock at $8 per share plus a brokerage commission of $1,000. These shares represent a 25 percent ownership of the Park common stock.

Dec. 31 Received a cash dividend of $0.80 per share of common stock from Park.

31 Made the adjusting entry to reflect income from the Park stock investment. Park's 2010 net income is $120,000.

2011

Jan. 20 Sold all 15,000 shares of the Park common stock for $132,000.

Record the above transactions for the Prince Company using journal entries.

ED-7B. Accounting for Equity Securities On March 15, Kit Corp. purchased 400 shares of common stock   LO3
of Murat Company for $25 per share. Kit Corp. is not able to exercise significant influence over Murat. On December 31, the market value of the Murat stock was $27.00 per share. Kat Corp. plans to sell the stock soon.

  a. Upon the purchase of the Murat stock, how should Kit Corp. classify the shares on its balance sheet? Justify your answer.
  b. Record all transactions necessary for Kit.

ED-8B. Recording Influential Securities On January 3, Negrito Farm purchased 25% of the outstanding   LO3
stock of Philip Company for $90,000. The purchase gave Negrito the ability to exercise significant influence over Philip. During the year, Philip paid cash dividends totaling $80,000 and reported net income for the year of $100,000.

   Record all transactions necessary for Negrito Farm.

ED-9B. Accounting for Equity Securities   LO3

   Macroview, Inc., maintained a large investment in marketable securities valued at approximately $60 billion as of the beginning of the year. During the year, the securities produced investment income (dividends and interest income) totaling $3 billion. At year-end, the portfolio of marketable securities had appreciated to $64.5 billion.

   Calculate the income statement effect of the marketable securities if:

  1. The entire portfolio is classified as trading securities
  2. The entire portfolio is classified as available-for-sale securities

ED-10B. Consolidation Accounting Peyton Company, a manufacturer of silicon chips, acquired 100 per-   LO4
cent of the outstanding common stock of Visik Company, a small manufacturer of mobile computing devices.

  a. How should Peyton account for this acquisition during the year?
  b. What adjustments are needed at year-end?
  c. What limitations are present in this method of accounting?

PROBLEMS—SET A

PD-1A. The Analysis of Bond Investments Columbia Company began operations in 2010 and by year-end   LO2
(December 31) had made six bond investments. Year-end information on these bond investments follows:

Company	Face Value	Cost or Amortized Cost	Year-End Market Value	Classification
Ling, Inc.................	$100,000	$102,400	$105,300	Trading
Wren, Inc.................	$250,000	$262,500	$270,000	Trading
Olanamic, Inc.	$200,000	$197,000	$199,000	Available for sale
Fossil, Inc.	$150,000	$154,000	$160,000	Available for sale
Meander, Inc..............	$100,000	$101,200	$102,400	Held to maturity
Resin, Inc................	$140,000	$136,000	$137,000	Held to maturity

Required
  a. At what total amount will the trading bond investments be reported on the December 31 balance sheet?
  b. At what total amount will the available-for-sale bond investments be reported on the December 31 balance sheet?
  c. At what total amount will the held-to-maturity bond investments be reported on the December 31 balance sheet?
  d. What total amount of unrealized holding gains or unrealized holding losses related to bond investments will appear on the income statement?
  e. What total amount of unrealized holding gains or unrealized holding losses related to bond investments will appear in the stockholders' equity section of the December 31 balance sheet?

f.   What total amount of fair value adjustment to bond investments will appear on the December 31 balance sheet? Which category of bond investments does the fair value adjustment relate to? Does the fair value adjustment increase or decrease the financial statement presentation of these bond investments?

LO2   **PD-2A.** **Bond Investment Journal Entries** The following transactions and adjustments relate to bond investments acquired by Bloom Corporation:

2010

June   30   Purchased $200,000 face value of Dynamo, Inc.'s 20-year, 9 percent bonds dated June 30, 2010, for $215,200 cash. Interest is paid December 31 and June 30. The investment is classified as an available-for-sale security.

Dec.   31   Received the semiannual interest payment from Dynamo and amortized the bond premium (straight-line method).

        31   Purchased $300,000 face value of Link, Inc.'s 10-year, 7 percent bonds dated December 31, 2010, for $297,000 cash. Interest is paid June 30 and December 31. The investment is classified as a held-to-maturity security.

        31   Made an adjusting entry to record the current fair value of the Dynamo bonds. At December 31, the market value was $216,000.

2011

June   30   Received the semiannual interest payment from Dynamo and amortized the bond premium.

        30   Received the semiannual interest payment from Link and amortized the bond discount (straight-line method).

July   1   Sold the Dynamo bonds for $216,500.

Oct.   31   Purchased $60,000 face value of Taxco, Inc.'s 5-year, 8 percent bonds dated October 31, 2011, for $60,500. Interest is paid April 30 and October 31. The investment is classified as a trading security.

Dec.   31   Received the semiannual interest payment from Link and amortized the bond discount.

        31   Made an adjusting entry to record interest earned on the investment in Taxco bonds.

        31   Made an adjusting entry to record the current fair value of the Taxco bonds. At December 31, the market value of the bonds was $59,200.

        31   Made an adjusting entry to eliminate balances in the Fair Value Adjustment to Bond Investment account and the Unrealized Gain/Loss on Investments (Equity) account.

Required

Prepare the journal entries to record these transactions and adjustments.

LO3   **PD-3A.** **Stock Investment Journal Entries** The following transactions and adjustments relate to stock investments made by Steen Corporation:

2010

July   1   Purchased 1,000 shares of Polk, Inc.'s common stock for $66,200 cash. The investment is noninfluential and noncontrolling and is classified as a trading security.

Oct.   1   Purchased 3,000 shares of Wynn, Inc.'s common stock for $78,000 cash and 2,000 shares of Maple, Inc.'s common stock for $64,000 cash. These investments are noninfluential and noncontrolling and are classified as available-for-sale securities. (Note: Use two separate investment accounts.)

Nov.   9   Received a cash dividend of 90 cents per share on the Wynn stock.

Dec.   31   Made an adjusting entry to record the current fair value of the Polk stock. At December 31, the stock has a market value of $63.00 per share.

        31   Made an adjusting entry to record the current fair value of the Wynn and Maple stocks. At December 31, the Wynn stock has a market value of $27.50 per share and the Maple stock has a market value of $31.00 per share. (*Note:* Make one adjusting entry for the portfolio of available-for-sale stocks.)

2011

Feb.   1   Sold the Polk stock for $62 per share.

Dec. 31 Made an adjusting entry to record the current fair value of the Wynn and Maple stocks. At December 31, 2011, the per-share market values are Wynn, $30.00, and Maple, $33.00. (*Note:* Be sure to allow for the adjustment made at December 31.)

Required
Prepare the journal entries to record these transactions and adjustments.

PD-4A. Contrasting Journal Entries for Stock Investments: Trading and Equity Methods On January 2, 2010, Trubek Corporation purchased 10,000 shares of Forge Company common stock for $15 per share, including commissions and taxes. On December 31, 2010, Forge announced its net income of $80,000 for the year and paid a dividend of $1.10 per share. At December 31, 2010, the market value of Forge's stock was $19 per share. Trubek received its dividend on December 31, 2010. **LO3**

Required
a. Assume that the stock acquired by Trubek represents 15 percent of Forge's voting stock and is classified as a trading security. Prepare all journal entries appropriate for this investment.
b. Assume that the stock acquired by Trubek represents 25 percent of Forge's voting stock. Prepare all journal entries appropriate for this investment.

PD-5A. Recording Influential Securities At the beginning of the year, the Carlton and United Brewery (CUB) of Melbourne, Australia, purchased a 30 percent ownership interest in Icehouse Brewery of Brisbane, Australia. The investment cost $30 million. At year-end, Icehouse Brewery declared and paid cash dividends to shareholders totaling $800,000, after reporting earnings of $5 million. **LO3**

Required
a. Calculate the income statement effect of CUB's investment in Icehouse Brewery as of year-end.
b. Calculate the book value of CUB's equity investment in Icehouse Brewery at year-end.
c. Calculate the book value of CUB's equity investment in Icehouse Brewery at year-end assuming that Icehouse reported a loss of $3 million instead of a profit of $5 million and still paid its dividend of $800,000.

PD-6A. Accounting for Equity Securities Susan Company has the following securities in its portfolio on December 31, 2011: **LO3**

		Market Values	
	Cost	Dec. 31, 2011	Dec. 31, 2010
5,000 shares of Answa Corp.....................	$60,000	$58,000	$ 0
10,000 shares of Smiler Co.	80,000	85,300	88,400

Additional information:

- Susan is not able to exercise significant influence over either of the investments.
- The Smiler Company securities were purchased at the beginning of 2010 and the appropriate year-end adjustments were made at the end of that year. Susan intends to hold the Smiler stock for long-term growth.
- The investment in Answa Corp. was in anticipation of a quick sale during February of 2012.
- During 2011, Susan received cash dividends of $700 from Smiler Corp.

Required
a. How will each of the two securities be accounted for by Susan Company? Justify your choices.
b. Prepare a partial balance sheet and partial income statement at December 31, 2011, which reflect the transactions provided.

PROBLEMS—SET B

PD-1B. The Analysis of Stock Investments The Discovery Company began operations in 2010, and by year-end (December 31), had made six stock investments. Year-end information on these stock investments follows: **LO3**

Company	Cost or Equity (as appropriate)	Year-End Market Value	Classification
Lisle, Inc.	$ 68,000	$ 65,300	Trading
Owl, Inc.	$162,500	$160,000	Trading
Bionamic, Inc.	$197,000	$192,000	Available for sale
Foote, Inc.	$157,000	$154,700	Available for sale
Buckley, Inc.	$100,000	$102,400	Influential
Riccer, Inc.	$136,000	$133,200	Influential

Required

a. At what total amount will the trading stock investments be reported on the December 31 balance sheet?

b. At what total amount will the available-for-sale stock investments be reported on the December 31 balance sheet?

c. At what total amount will the influential stock investments be reported on the December 31 balance sheet?

d. What total amount of unrealized holding gains or unrealized holding losses related to stock investments will appear on the income statement?

e. What total amount of unrealized holding gains or unrealized holding losses related to stock investments will appear in the stockholders' equity section of the December 31 balance sheet?

f. What total amount of fair value adjustment to stock investments will appear on the December 31 balance sheet? Which category of stock investments does the fair value adjustment relate to? Does the fair value adjustment increase or decrease the financial statement presentation of these stock investments?

LO2   **PD-2B.   Bond Investment Journal Entries** The following transactions and adjustments relate to bond investments acquired by Jackson Corporation:

2010

June   30   Purchased $100,000 face value of Alamo, Inc.'s 20-year, 7 percent bonds dated June 30, 2010, for $97,200 cash. Interest is paid December 31 and June 30. The investment is classified as an available-for-sale security.

Dec.   31   Received the semiannual interest payment from Alamo and amortized the bond discount (straight-line method).

31   Purchased $300,000 face value of Lyme, Inc.'s 10-year, 8 percent bonds dated December 31, 2010, for $304,000 cash. Interest is paid June 30 and December 31. The investment is classified as a held-to-maturity security.

31   Made an adjusting entry to record the current fair value of the Alamo bonds. At December 31, the market value was $96,400.

2011

June   30   Received the semiannual interest payment from Alamo and amortized the bond discount.

30   Received the semiannual interest payment from Lyme and amortized the bond premium (straight-line method).

July   1   Sold the Alamo bonds for $96,500.

Oct.   31   Purchased $80,000 face value of Weir, Inc.'s 5-year, 7.57 percent bonds dated October 31, 2011, for $79,000. Interest is paid April 30 and October 31. The investment is classified as a trading security.

Dec.   31   Received the semiannual interest payment from Lyme and amortized the bond premium.

31   Made an adjusting entry to record interest earned on investment in the Weir bonds.

31   Made an adjusting entry to record the current fair value of Weir bonds. At December 31, the market value of the bonds was $79,900.

31   Made an adjusting entry to eliminate balances in the Fair Value Adjustment to Bond Investment account and the Unrealized Gain/Loss on Investments (Equity) account.

Required

Prepare the journal entries to record these transactions and adjustments.

PD-3B. **Stock Investment Journal Entries** The following transactions and adjustments relate to stock investments made by Kramer Corporation: **LO3**

2010
July	1	Purchased 2,000 shares of Cook, Inc.'s common stock for $96,200 cash. The investment is noninfluential and noncontrolling and is classified as a trading security.
Oct.	1	Purchased 1,000 shares of Fox, Inc.'s common stock for $28,000 cash and 5,000 shares of Dent, Inc.'s common stock for $75,000 cash. These investments are noninfluential and noncontrolling and are classified as available-for-sale securities. (Note: Use two separate investment accounts.)
Nov.	9	Received a cash dividend of 70 cents per share on the Dent stock.
Dec.	31	Made an adjusting entry to record the current fair value of the Cook stock. At December 31, the stock has a market value of $50.50 per share.
	31	Made an adjusting entry to record the current fair values of the Fox and Dent stocks. At December 31, the Fox stock has a market value of $26.25 per share and the Dent stock has a market value of $14.00 per share. (*Note:* Make one adjusting entry for the portfolio of available-for-sale stocks.)

2011
Feb.	1	Sold the Cook stock for $52 per share.
Dec.	31	Made an adjusting entry to record the current fair values of Fox and Dent stocks. At December 31, the per-share market values are Fox, $25.00, and Dent, $12.00. (*Note:* Be sure to allow for the adjustment made at December 31.)

Required
Prepare the journal entries to record these transactions and adjustments.

PD-4B. **Contrasting Journal Entries for Stock Investments: Trading and Equity Methods** On January 2, 2010, Clemens, Inc., purchased 20,000 shares of Baer, Inc.'s common stock for $21 per share, including commissions and taxes. On December 31, 2010, Baer announced its net income of $280,000 for the year and paid a dividend of 80 cents per share. At December 31, 2010, the market value of Baer's stock was $18 per share. Clemens received its dividend on December 31, 2010.   **LO3**

Required
a.   Assume that the stock acquired by Clemens represents 10 percent of Baer's voting stock and is classified as a trading security. Prepare all journal entries appropriate for this investment.
b.   Assume that the stock acquired by Clemens represents 40 percent of Baer's voting stock. Prepare all journal entries appropriate for this investment.

PD-5B. **Recording Influential Securities** At the beginning of the year, the Frederick and Prince Brewery (FPB) of Auckland, New Zealand, purchased a 40 percent ownership interest in Flanagan Brewery of Belfast, Ireland. The investment cost $40 million. At year-end, Flanagan Brewery declared and paid cash dividends to shareholders totaling $1,200,000, after reporting earnings of $7 million.   **LO3**

Required
a.   Calculate the income statement effect of FPB's investment in Flanagan Brewery as of year-end.
b.   Calculate the book value of FPB's equity investment in Flanagan Brewery at year-end.
c.   Calculate the book value of FPB's equity investment in Flanagan Brewery at year-end assuming that Flanagan reported a loss of $4 million instead of a profit of $7 million and still paid its dividend of $1,200,000.

PD-6B. **Accounting for Equity Securities** Sally Company has the following securities in its portfolio on December 31, 2011:   **LO3**

		Market Values	
	Cost	Dec. 31, 2011	Dec. 31, 2010
5,000 shares of Peach Corp.	$ 90,000	$ 85,000	$ 0
10,000 shares of Gordon Co.	120,000	130,300	133,400

Additional information:

- Sally is not able to exercise significant influence over either of the investments.
- The Gordon Company securities were purchased at the beginning of 2010 and the appropriate year-end adjustments were made at the end of that year. Sally intends to hold the Gordon stock for long-term growth.
- The investment in Peach Corp. was in anticipation of a quick sale during February of 2012.
- During 2011, Sally received cash dividends of $900 from Peach Corp.

Required

a. How will each of the two securities be accounted for by Sally Company? Justify your choices.
b. Prepare a balance sheet and partial income statement at December 31, 2011, which reflects the transactions provided.

ANSWERS TO SELF-STUDY QUESTIONS

1. b, (p. D-6) 2. c, (p. D-9) 3. b, (p. D-9) 4. d, (p. D-3) 5. a, (p. D-10) 6. b, (p. D-10)
7. c, (p. D-3) 8. c, (p. D-4) 9. a, (p. D-9) 10. b, (p. D-9) 11. c, (p. D-6) 12. b, (p. D-12)
13. a, (p. D-3)

Appendix

E

Accounting and the Time Value of Money

LEARNING OBJECTIVES

1. **Describe** the nature of interest and **distinguish** between simple and compound interest. *(p. E-2)*

2. **Calculate** future values. *(p. E-3)*

3. **Calculate** present values. *(p. E-6)*

TIME VALUE OF MONEY CONCEPT

LO1 **Describe** the nature of interest and **distinguish** between simple and compound interest.

Would you rather receive a dollar now or a dollar one year from now? Most persons would answer "a dollar now." Intuition tells us that a dollar received now is more valuable than the same amount received sometime in the future. Sound reasons exist, however, for choosing the option of receiving the money sooner rather than later, the most obvious of which concerns risk. Because the future is always uncertain, some event may prevent you from receiving the dollar at a later date. To avoid this risk, we choose the earlier date.

A second reason for choosing the earlier date is that the dollar has a **time value**—that is, the dollar received now could be invested such that one year from now, you could have not only the original dollar but also the interest income on the dollar for the past year. **Interest** is a payment for the use of money, much like a rent payment for the use of an apartment. Interest is calculated by multiplying an interest rate, usually stated as an annual rate, by a principal amount for a period of time. The **principal** amount represents the amount to be repaid. The amount of interest can be computed as either a simple interest amount or a compound interest amount.

Time Value of Money: Simple Interest Model

Simple interest involves calculating interest on only the principal amount owed without considering any interest already earned. Simple interest is calculated using the following well-known formula:

$$\text{Interest} = p \times i \times n$$

where

p = principal (total amount)
i = interest rate for one period
n = time (number of periods)

For example, if you borrow \$3,000 for four years at a simple interest rate of six percent annually, the amount of simple interest would total \$720, calculated as \$3,000 × .06 × 4.

Time Value of Money: Compound Interest Model

Compound interest differs from simple interest because it is calculated on both the principal and any previously earned interest that has not been paid. In other words, compound interest involves computing interest on interest, along with the principal amount.

As we can see in Exhibit E-1, simple interest only uses the original \$3,000 principal to compute the annual interest in each of the four years. In contrast, compound interest uses the entire principal balance, including both the original \$3,000 principal and the accumulated interest to date, to compute the next year's interest. This results in increasing interest each year, with the result in Exhibit E-1 for compound interest yielding a larger ending balance by \$67.43.

Because almost all businesses use compound interest, we will assume the use of compound interest in all of the illustrations in this appendix. Simple interest is generally only used in short-term credit arrangements, typically lasting less than a year.

| Exhibit E-1 | Illustration Comparing Simple Interest to Compound Interest |

	Simple Interest Model			Compound Interest Model		
	Interest Calculation	Simple Interest	Principal Balance	Interest Calculation	Compound Interest	Principal Balance
Year 1..	$3,000.00 × 6%	$180.00	$3,180.00	$3,000.00 × 6%	$180.00	$3,180.00
Year 2..	$3,000.00 × 6%	$180.00	$3,360.00	$3,180.00 × 6%	$190.80	$3,370.80
Year 3..	$3,000.00 × 6%	$180.00	$3,540.00	$3,370.80 × 6%	$202.25	$3,573.05
Year 4..	$3,000.00 × 6%	$180.00	$3,720.00	$3,573.05 × 6%	$214.38	$3,787.43
		$720.00			$787.43	

$720.00 ⟶ $67.43 variance ⟵ $787.43

FUTURE VALUE OF AN AMOUNT

The **future value** of a single sum is the amount that a specified investment will be worth at a future date if invested at a given rate of compound interest. For example, suppose that we decide to invest $6,000 in a savings account that pays six percent annual interest, and that we intend to leave the principal and interest in the account for five years. Assuming that interest is credited to the account at the end of each year, the balance in the account at the end of five years is determined using the following formula:

LO2 Calculate future values.

$$FV = PV \times (1 + i)^n$$

where

FV = future value of an amount
PV = present value (today's value)
i = interest rate for one period
n = number of periods

The future value in this case is $8,028, computed as [$6,000 × (1.06)^5] = ($6,000 × 1.338).

It is often easier to solve time value of money problems with the aid of a time diagram, as illustrated in Exhibit E-2. Time diagrams are drawn to show the timing of the various cash inflows and outflows. Note in Exhibit E-2 that our initial $6,000 cash inflow (the amount deposited in a savings account) allows us to remove $8,028 (a cash outflow) at the end of five years.

| Exhibit E-2 | Solving Future Values with the Aid of a Time Diagram |

Present Value	i = 6%	Future Value
$6,000		($8,028)

```
|-----|-----|-----|-----|-----|
0     1     2     3     4     5
          n = 5 years
```

We can also calculate the future value of a single amount with the use of a table like Table I, which presents the future value of a single dollar after a given number of time periods. Simply stated, future value tables provide a multiplier for many combinations of time periods and interest rates that, when applied to the dollar amount of a present value, determines its future value.

Table I	Future Value of $1											
Period	1%	2%	3%	4%	5%	6%	7%	8%	9%	10%	11%	12%
1	1.010	1.020	1.030	1.040	1.050	1.060	1.070	1.080	1.090	1.100	1.110	1.120
2	1.020	1.040	1.061	1.082	1.103	1.124	1.145	1.166	1.188	1.210	1.232	1.254
3	1.030	1.061	1.093	1.125	1.158	1.191	1.225	1.260	1.295	1.331	1.368	1.405
4	1.041	1.082	1.126	1.170	1.216	1.262	1.311	1.360	1.412	1.464	1.518	1.574
5	1.051	1.104	1.159	1.217	1.276	1.338	1.403	1.469	1.539	1.611	1.685	1.762
6	1.062	1.126	1.194	1.265	1.340	1.419	1.501	1.587	1.677	1.772	1.870	1.974
7	1.072	1.149	1.230	1.316	1.407	1.504	1.606	1.714	1.828	1.949	2.076	2.211
8	1.083	1.172	1.267	1.369	1.477	1.594	1.718	1.851	1.993	2.144	2.305	2.476
9	1.094	1.195	1.305	1.423	1.551	1.689	1.838	1.999	2.172	2.358	2.558	2.773
10	1.105	1.219	1.344	1.480	1.629	1.791	1.967	2.159	2.367	2.594	2.839	3.106
11	1.116	1.243	1.384	1.539	1.710	1.898	2.105	2.332	2.580	2.853	3.152	3.479
12	1.127	1.268	1.426	1.601	1.796	2.012	2.252	2.518	2.813	3.138	3.498	3.896
13	1.138	1.294	1.469	1.665	1.886	2.133	2.410	2.720	3.066	3.452	3.883	4.363
14	1.149	1.319	1.513	1.732	1.980	2.261	2.579	2.937	3.342	3.797	4.310	4.887
15	1.161	1.346	1.558	1.801	2.079	2.397	2.759	3.172	3.642	4.177	4.785	5.474
16	1.173	1.373	1.605	1.873	2.183	2.540	2.952	3.426	3.970	4.595	5.311	6.130
17	1.184	1.400	1.653	1.948	2.292	2.693	3.159	3.700	4.328	5.054	5.895	6.866
18	1.196	1.428	1.702	2.026	2.407	2.854	3.380	3.996	4.717	5.560	6.544	7.690
19	1.208	1.457	1.754	2.107	2.527	3.026	3.617	4.316	5.142	6.116	7.263	8.613
20	1.220	1.486	1.806	2.191	2.653	3.207	3.870	4.661	5.604	6.727	8.062	9.646
25	1.282	1.641	2.094	2.666	3.386	4.292	5.427	6.848	8.623	10.835	13.585	17.000
30	1.348	1.811	2.427	3.243	4.322	5.743	7.612	10.063	13.268	17.449	22.892	29.960
35	1.417	2.000	2.814	3.946	5.516	7.686	10.677	14.785	20.414	28.102	38.575	52.800
40	1.489	2.208	3.262	4.801	7.040	10.286	14.974	21.725	31.409	45.259	65.001	93.051
50	1.645	2.692	4.384	7.107	11.467	18.420	29.457	46.902	74.358	117.391	184.565	289.002

Future value tables are used as follows. First, determine the number of interest compounding periods involved (five years compounded annually are five periods, five years compounded semiannually are ten periods, five years compounded quarterly are 20 periods, and so on). The extreme left-hand column indicates the number of periods covered in the table.

Next, determine the interest rate per compounding period. Note that interest rates are usually quoted on an annual or *per year* basis. Therefore, only in the case of annual compounding is the quoted interest rate the interest rate per compounding period. In other cases, the rate per compounding period is the annual rate divided by the number of compounding periods in a year. For example, an interest rate of ten percent per year would be ten percent for one compounding period if compounded annually, five percent for two compounding periods if compounded semiannually, and 2 ½ percent for four compounding periods if compounded quarterly.

Locate the factor that is to the right of the appropriate number of compounding periods and beneath the appropriate interest rate per compounding period. Multiply this factor by the number of dollars involved.

Note the logical progression among the various multipliers in Table I. All values are 1.0 or greater because the future value is always greater than the $1 present amount if the interest rate is greater than zero. Also, as the interest rate increases (moving from left to right in the table) or the number of periods increases (moving from top to bottom), the multipliers become larger.

Continuing with our example of calculating the future value of a $6,000 savings account deposit earning 6 percent annual compound interest for five years, and using the multipliers from Table I, we solve for the future value of the deposit as follows:

Principal × **Factor** = **Future Value**

$6,000 × **1.338** = **$8,028**

The factor 1.338 is in the row for five periods and the column for six percent.

Suppose, instead, that the interest is credited to the savings account semiannually rather than annually. In this situation, there are ten compounding periods, and we use a three percent rate (one-half the annual rate). The future value calculation using the Table I multipliers is as follows:

Principal × **Factor** = **Future Value**

$6,000 × **1.344** = **$8,064**

FUTURE VALUE OF AN ANNUITY

Using future value tables like Table I, we can calculate the future value of any single future cash flow or series of future cash flows. One frequent pattern of cash flows, however, is subject to a more convenient calculation. This pattern, known as an **annuity**, can be described as *equal amounts equally spaced over a period.*

For example, assume that $100 is to be deposited at the end of each of the next three years as an annuity into a savings account. When annuity cash flows occur at the end of each period, the annuity is called an **ordinary annuity**. As shown below in Exhibit E-3, the future value of this ordinary annuity can be calculated from Table I by calculating the future value of each of the three individual deposits and summing them (assuming eight percent annual interest).

Exhibit E-3	Future Value of an Ordinary Annuity					
Future Deposits (ordinary annuity)				**PV Multiplier (Table I)**		**Future Value**
Year 1	**Year 2**	**Year 3**				
$100			×	1.166	=	$116.60
	$100		×	1.080	=	108.00
		$100	×	1.000	=	100.00
				Total future value		$324.60

Present Value				**Future Value**
	$100		$100	$100
0	1		2	3

Table II, on the other hand, provides a single multiplier for calculating the future value of a series of future cash flows that reflect an ordinary annuity. Referring to Table II in the three periods row and the eight percent interest column, we see that the multiplier is 3.246. When applied to the $100 annuity amount, the multiplier gives a future value of $324.60, or $100 × 3.246. As shown above, the same future value is derived from the several multipliers of Table I. For annuities of 5, 10, or 20 years, numerous calculations are avoided by using annuity tables like Table II.

Table II	Future Value of an Ordinary Annuity of $1 per period											
Period	**1%**	**2%**	**3%**	**4%**	**5%**	**6%**	**7%**	**8%**	**9%**	**10%**	**11%**	**12%**
1	1.000	1.000	1.000	1.000	1.000	1.000	1.000	1.000	1.000	1.000	1.000	1.000
2	2.010	2.020	2.030	2.040	2.050	2.060	2.070	2.080	2.090	2.100	2.110	2.120
3	3.030	3.060	3.091	3.122	3.153	3.184	3.215	3.246	3.278	3.310	3.342	3.374
4	4.060	4.122	4.184	4.246	4.310	4.375	4.440	4.506	4.573	4.641	4.710	4.779
5	5.101	5.204	5.309	5.416	5.526	5.637	5.751	5.867	5.985	6.105	6.228	6.353
6	6.152	6.308	6.468	6.633	6.802	6.975	7.153	7.336	7.523	7.716	7.913	8.115
7	7.214	7.434	7.662	7.898	8.142	8.394	8.654	8.923	9.200	9.487	9.783	10.089
8	8.286	8.583	8.892	9.214	9.549	9.897	10.260	10.637	11.028	11.436	11.859	12.300
9	9.369	9.755	10.159	10.583	11.027	11.491	11.978	12.488	13.021	13.579	14.164	14.776
10	10.462	10.950	11.464	12.006	12.578	13.181	13.816	14.487	15.193	15.937	16.722	17.549
11	11.567	12.169	12.808	13.486	14.207	14.972	15.784	16.645	17.560	18.531	19.561	20.655
12	12.683	13.412	14.192	15.026	15.917	16.870	17.888	18.977	20.141	21.384	22.713	24.133
13	13.809	14.680	15.618	16.627	17.713	18.882	20.141	21.495	22.953	24.523	26.212	28.029
14	14.947	15.974	17.086	18.292	19.599	21.015	22.550	24.215	26.019	27.975	30.095	32.393
15	16.097	17.293	18.599	20.024	21.579	23.276	25.129	27.152	29.361	31.772	34.405	37.280
16	17.258	18.639	20.157	21.825	23.657	25.673	27.888	30.324	33.003	35.950	39.190	42.753
17	18.430	20.012	21.762	23.698	25.840	28.213	30.840	33.750	36.974	40.545	44.501	48.884
18	19.615	21.412	23.414	25.645	28.132	30.906	33.999	37.450	41.301	45.599	50.396	55.750
19	20.811	22.841	25.117	27.671	30.539	33.760	37.379	41.446	46.018	51.159	56.939	63.440
20	22.019	24.297	26.870	29.778	33.066	36.786	40.995	45.762	51.160	57.275	64.203	72.052
25	28.243	32.030	36.459	41.646	47.727	54.865	63.249	73.106	84.701	98.347	114.41	133.33
30	34.785	40.568	47.575	56.085	66.439	79.058	94.461	113.28	136.31	164.49	199.02	241.33
35	41.660	49.994	60.462	73.652	90.320	111.43	138.24	172.32	215.71	271.02	341.59	431.66
40	48.886	60.402	75.401	95.026	120.80	154.76	199.64	259.06	337.88	442.59	581.83	767.09
50	64.463	84.579	112.80	152.67	209.35	290.34	406.53	573.77	815.08	1,163.9	1,668.8	2,400.0

If we decide to invest $50 at the end of each six months for three years at an eight percent annual rate of return, we would use the factor for 6 periods at four percent, as follows:

$$\text{Periodic Payment} \times \text{Factor} = \text{Future Value}$$
$$\$50 \times 6.633 = \$331.65$$

PRESENT VALUE OF AN AMOUNT

LO3 Calculate present values.

We can generalize that (1) the right to receive an amount of money now—its **present value**—is normally worth more than the right to receive the same amount later—its future value; (2) the longer we must wait to receive an amount, the less attractive the receipt is; and (3) the difference between the present value of an amount and its future value is a function of interest (Principal × Interest Rate × Interest Time). Further, the more risk associated with any situation, the higher the appropriate interest rate.

We support these generalizations with an illustration. What amount should we accept now that would be as valuable as receiving $100 one year from now ($100 represents the future value) if the appropriate interest rate is ten percent? We recognize intuitively that with a ten percent interest rate, we should accept less than $100, or approximately $91. We base this estimate on the realization that the $100 received in the future must equal the present value (100 percent) plus ten percent interest on the present value. Thus, in our example, the $100 future receipt must be 1.10 times the present value. Dividing $100 by 1.10, we obtain a present value of $90.91. In other words, under the given conditions, we would do as well to accept $90.91 now as to wait one year and receive $100. To confirm the equality of a $90.91 payment now with a $100 payment one year later, we calculate the future value of $90.91 at ten percent for one year as follows:

$$\$90.91 \times 1.10 \times 1 \text{ year} = \$100 \text{ (rounded)}$$

Thus, we calculate the present value of a future receipt by discounting (deducting an interest factor) the future receipt back to the present at an appropriate interest rate. We present this schematically below:

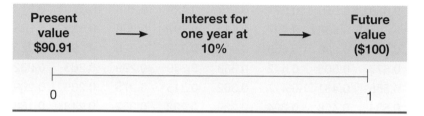

The formula for calculating the present value of a single amount is determined using the following formula:

$$PV = FV \times [1 \div (1 + i)^n]$$

where

    PV = present value of an amount
    FV = future value
      i = interest rate for one period
     n = number of periods

As can be seen from this formula, if either the time period or the interest rate is increased, the resulting present value would decrease. If more than one time period is involved, compound interest calculations are appropriate.

Exhibit E-4	Present Value of a Single Amount

How much must be deposited in a savings account today in order to have $1,000 in four years if the savings account pays 12 percent annual interest?

$$PV = \$1,000 \times [1 \div (1.12)^4] = (\$1,000 \times 0.636) = \$636$$

Present Value	←	Discounted for 4 years at 6%	←	Future Value

| $636 | | | | ($1,000) |
| 0 | 1 | 2 | 3 | 4 |

Tables III and IV can be used to calculate the present value amounts in a manner similar to the way we previously calculated future values using Tables I and II. As with the future value tables, present value tables provide a multiplier for many combinations of time periods and interest rates that, when applied to the dollar amount of a future cash flow or annuity, determines its present value.

Table III	Present Value of $1											
Period	**1%**	**2%**	**3%**	**4%**	**5%**	**6%**	**7%**	**8%**	**9%**	**10%**	**11%**	**12%**
1	0.990	0.980	0.971	0.962	0.952	0.943	0.935	0.926	0.917	0.909	0.901	0.893
2	0.980	0.961	0.943	0.925	0.907	0.890	0.873	0.857	0.842	0.826	0.812	0.797
3	0.971	0.942	0.915	0.889	0.864	0.840	0.816	0.794	0.772	0.751	0.731	0.712
4	0.961	0.924	0.888	0.855	0.823	0.792	0.763	0.735	0.708	0.683	0.659	0.636
5	0.951	0.906	0.863	0.822	0.784	0.747	0.713	0.681	0.650	0.621	0.593	0.567
6	0.942	0.888	0.837	0.790	0.746	0.705	0.666	0.630	0.596	0.564	0.535	0.507
7	0.933	0.871	0.813	0.760	0.711	0.665	0.623	0.583	0.547	0.513	0.482	0.452
8	0.923	0.853	0.789	0.731	0.677	0.627	0.582	0.540	0.502	0.467	0.434	0.404
9	0.914	0.837	0.766	0.703	0.645	0.592	0.544	0.500	0.460	0.424	0.391	0.361
10	0.905	0.820	0.744	0.676	0.614	0.558	0.508	0.463	0.422	0.386	0.352	0.322
11	0.896	0.804	0.722	0.650	0.585	0.527	0.475	0.429	0.388	0.350	0.317	0.287
12	0.887	0.788	0.701	0.625	0.557	0.497	0.444	0.397	0.356	0.319	0.286	0.257
13	0.879	0.773	0.681	0.601	0.530	0.469	0.415	0.368	0.326	0.290	0.258	0.229
14	0.870	0.758	0.661	0.577	0.505	0.442	0.388	0.340	0.299	0.263	0.232	0.205
15	0.861	0.743	0.642	0.555	0.481	0.417	0.362	0.315	0.275	0.239	0.209	0.183
16	0.853	0.728	0.623	0.534	0.458	0.394	0.339	0.292	0.252	0.218	0.188	0.163
17	0.844	0.714	0.605	0.513	0.436	0.371	0.317	0.270	0.231	0.198	0.170	0.146
18	0.836	0.700	0.587	0.494	0.416	0.350	0.296	0.250	0.212	0.180	0.153	0.130
19	0.828	0.686	0.570	0.475	0.396	0.331	0.277	0.232	0.194	0.164	0.138	0.116
20	0.820	0.673	0.554	0.456	0.377	0.312	0.258	0.215	0.178	0.149	0.124	0.104
25	0.780	0.610	0.478	0.375	0.295	0.233	0.184	0.146	0.116	0.092	0.074	0.059
30	0.742	0.552	0.412	0.308	0.231	0.174	0.131	0.099	0.075	0.057	0.044	0.033
35	0.706	0.500	0.355	0.253	0.181	0.130	0.094	0.068	0.049	0.036	0.026	0.019
40	0.672	0.453	0.307	0.208	0.142	0.097	0.067	0.046	0.032	0.022	0.015	0.011
50	0.608	0.372	0.228	0.141	0.087	0.054	0.034	0.021	0.013	0.009	0.005	0.003

Exhibit E-5	Present Value of a Single Amount Using Present Value Tables

Calculate the present value of $1,000 four years hence, at twelve percent interest compounded annually:

   Number of periods (one year, annually) = 4
   Interest rate per period (12%/1) = 12%
   Multiplier = 0.636
   Present value = $1,000 × 0.636 = $636
   (This result agrees with our earlier illustration.)

Calculate the present value of $116.99 two years hence, at eight percent compounded semiannually:

   Number of periods (two years, semiannually) = 4
   Interest rate per period (8%/2) = 4%
   Multiplier = 0.855
   Present value = $116.99 × 0.855 = $100 (rounded)

PRESENT VALUE OF AN ANNUITY

We can also use present value tables like Table III to calculate the present value of any single future cash flow or series of future cash flows. For example, assume $100 is to be received at the end of each of the next three years as an annuity. As shown below, the present value of this ordinary annuity can be calculated from Table III by calculating the present value of each of the three individual receipts and summing them (assuming five percent annual interest).

Future Receipts (ordinary annuity)				PV Multiplier (Table I)		Future Value
Year 1	Year 2	Year 3				
$100			×	0.952	=	$ 95.20
	$100		×	0.907	=	90.70
		$100	×	0.864	=	86.40
				Total present value . . .		$272.30

Table IV, on the other hand, provides a single multiplier for calculating the present value of a series of future cash flows that represent an ordinary annuity. Referring to Table IV in the three periods row and the five percent interest column, we see that the multiplier is 2.723. When applied to the $100 annuity amount, the multiplier gives a present value of $272.30.

Table IV	Present Value of an Ordinary Annuity of $1 per period											
Period	1%	2%	3%	4%	5%	6%	7%	8%	9%	10%	11%	12%
1	0.990	0.980	0.971	0.962	0.952	0.943	0.935	0.926	0.917	0.909	0.901	0.893
2	1.970	1.942	1.913	1.886	1.859	1.833	1.808	1.783	1.759	1.736	1.713	1.690
3	2.941	2.884	2.829	2.775	2.723	2.673	2.624	2.577	2.531	2.487	2.444	2.402
4	3.902	3.808	3.717	3.630	3.546	3.465	3.387	3.312	3.240	3.170	3.102	3.037
5	4.853	4.713	4.580	4.452	4.329	4.212	4.100	3.993	3.890	3.791	3.696	3.605
6	5.795	5.601	5.417	5.242	5.076	4.917	4.767	4.623	4.486	4.355	4.231	4.111
7	6.728	6.472	6.230	6.002	5.786	5.582	5.389	5.206	5.033	4.868	4.712	4.564
8	7.652	7.325	7.020	6.733	6.463	6.210	5.971	5.747	5.535	5.335	5.146	4.968
9	8.566	8.162	7.786	7.435	7.108	6.802	6.515	6.247	5.995	5.759	5.537	5.328
10	9.471	8.983	8.530	8.111	7.722	7.360	7.024	6.710	6.418	6.145	5.889	5.650
11	10.368	9.787	9.253	8.760	8.306	7.887	7.499	7.139	6.805	6.495	6.207	5.938
12	11.255	10.575	9.954	9.385	8.863	8.384	7.943	7.536	7.161	6.814	6.492	6.194
13	12.134	11.348	10.635	9.986	9.394	8.853	8.358	7.904	7.487	7.103	6.750	6.424
14	13.004	12.106	11.296	10.563	9.899	9.295	8.745	8.244	7.786	7.367	6.982	6.628
15	13.865	12.849	11.938	11.118	10.380	9.712	9.108	8.559	8.061	7.606	7.191	6.811
16	14.718	13.578	12.561	11.652	10.838	10.106	9.447	8.851	8.313	7.824	7.379	6.974
17	15.562	14.292	13.166	12.166	11.274	10.477	9.763	9.122	8.544	8.022	7.549	7.120
18	16.398	14.992	13.754	12.659	11.690	10.828	10.059	9.372	8.756	8.201	7.702	7.250
19	17.226	15.678	14.324	13.134	12.085	11.158	10.336	9.604	8.950	8.365	7.839	7.366
20	18.046	16.351	14.877	13.590	12.462	11.470	10.594	9.818	9.129	8.514	7.963	7.469
25	22.023	19.523	17.413	15.622	14.094	12.783	11.654	10.675	9.823	9.077	8.422	7.843
30	25.808	22.396	19.600	17.292	15.372	13.765	12.409	11.258	10.274	9.427	8.694	8.055
35	29.409	24.999	21.487	18.665	16.374	14.498	12.948	11.655	10.567	9.644	8.855	8.176
40	32.835	27.355	23.115	19.793	17.159	15.046	13.332	11.925	10.757	9.779	8.951	8.244
50	39.196	31.424	25.730	21.482	18.256	15.762	13.801	12.233	10.962	9.915	9.042	8.304

CALCULATIONS USING A CALCULATOR AND A SPREADSHEET

While present value tables can provide a handy method to solve some time value of money problems, they are not suitable for many real world situations. For example, many real world interest rates are not even integers like those appearing in Table I through Table IV, nor are many problems limited to the number of time periods appearing in the tables. While it is still possible to solve these problems with the provided formulas, financial calculators and spreadsheet programs provide a much quicker solution. Financial calculators can be distinguished from other calculators by the presence of dedicated keys for present and future values, along with keys for the number of periods, interest rates, and annuity payments. There exists many brands of financial calculators; however, all of them work in much the same way.[1] We illustrate the calculation of bond issuance prices using a calculator and a spreadsheet in Appendix 10A at the end of Chapter 10.

---

[1] It is usually necessary to do some preliminary setup on a financial calculator before performing time value of money calculations. For example, the HP 10BII calculator has a default setting of monthly compounding. This may need to be changed if the problem calls for a different number of compounding periods, such as annual. In addition, the calculator assumes annuity payments occur at the end of each period. This will need to be changed if the problem requires beginning of period payments. See your calculator manual to determine how to make these setting changes.

SUMMARY OF LEARNING OBJECTIVES

LO1 **Describe the nature of interest and distinguish between simple and compound interest. (p. E-2)**
- Interest is payment for the use of money over time.
- Simple interest is computed only on the principal.
- Compound interest is computed on the accumulated principal including any earned interest that has not been paid.

LO2 **Calculate future values. (p. E-3)**
- The future value of a single sum is the amount that a specified investment will be worth at a future date if invested at a given rate of compound interest.
- The formula for calculating the future value of a single amount is $PV = FV \times (1 + i)^n$.
- Future value tables provide a multiplier for many combinations of time periods and interest rates that, when applied to the dollar amount of a present value, determines its future value.
- An annuity represents a special case of a pattern of cash flows where the cash flow amounts are of equal amounts and equally spaced over time.
- A separate table is available that provides a multiplier for the future value of an annuity rather than using separate multipliers from the future value of $1 table.

LO3 **Calculate present values. (p. E-6)**
- The right to receive an amount of money now—its present value—is normally worth more than the right to receive the same amount later—its future value.
- The formula for calculating the present value of a single amount is $PV = FV \times [1 \div (1 + i)^n]$.
- A separate table is available that provides a multiplier for the present value of an annuity rather than using separate multipliers from the present value of $1 table.

GLOSSARY OF KEY TERMS

Annuity (p. E-5)

Compound interest (p. E-2)

Future value (p. E-3)

Interest (p. E-2)

Ordinary annuity (p. E-5)

Present value (p. E-6)

Principal (p. E-2)

Simple interest (p. E-2)

Time value (p. E-2)

SELF-STUDY QUESTIONS

(Answers to Self-Study Questions are at the end of this appendix.)

1. **Calculate the future value of each of the following items.**   **LO2**
   a. $50,000 deposited in a savings account for ten years if the annual interest rate is
      1. Twelve percent compounded annually.
      2. Twelve percent compounded semiannually.
      3. Twelve percent compounded quarterly.
   b. $5,000 received at the end of each year for the next ten years if the money earns interest at the rate of four percent compounded annually.
   c. $3,000 received semiannually for the next five years if the money earns interest at the rate of eight percent compounded semiannually.
   d. $1,000 deposited each year for the next ten years plus a single sum of $15,000 deposited today if the interest rate is ten percent per year compounded annually.

2. **Calculate the present value of each of the following items.**   **LO3**
   a. $90,000 ten years hence if the annual interest rate is
      1. Eight percent compounded annually.
      2. Eight percent compounded semiannually.
      3. Eight percent compounded quarterly.
   b. $1,000 received at the end of each year for the next eight years if money is worth ten percent per year compounded annually.
   c. $600 received at the end of each six months for the next fifteen years if the interest rate is eight percent per year compounded semiannually.
   d. $500,000 inheritance ten years hence if money is worth ten percent per year compounded annually.
   e. $2,500 received each half year for the next ten years plus a single sum of $85,000 at the end of ten years if the interest rate is twelve percent per year compounded semiannually.

Assignments with the ✔ logo in the margin are available in BusinessCourse.
See the Preface of the book for details.

EXERCISES—SET A

EE-1A. Simple and Compound Interest   **LO1** ✔
   a. For each of the following notes, calculate the simple interest due at the end of the term.

Note	Principal	Rate	Term
1	$10,000	4%	6 years
2	$10,000	6%	4 years
3	$10,000	8%	3 years

   b. Compute the amount of interest due at the end of the term for each of the above notes assuming interest is compounded annually.

EE-2A. Future Value Computation At the beginning of the year you deposit $2,500 in a savings account. How much will accumulate in three years if you earn 8% compounded annually?   **LO2** ✔

EE-3A. Future Value Computation You deposit $2,500 at the end of every year for three years. How much will accumulate in three years if you earn 8% compounded annually?   **LO2** ✔

EE-4A. Present Value Computation You will receive $2,500 in three years. What is the present value if you can earn 8% interest compounded annually?   **LO3** ✔

EE-5A. Present Value Computation You receive $2,500 at the end of every year for three years. What is the present value of these receipts if you earn 8% compounded annually?   **LO3** ✔

EE-6A. Future Value Computation What amount will be accumulated in four years if $10,000 is invested today at 6% interest compounded annually?   **LO2** ✔

LO3 ✓   **EE-7A. Present Value Computation** You are scheduled to be paid $10,000 in four years. What amount today is equivalent to the $10,000 to be received in four years assuming interest is compounded annually at 6%?

LO2 ✓   **EE-8A. Future Value Computation** What amount will be accumulated in four years if $10,000 is invested every six months beginning in six months and ending four years from today? Interest will accumulate at an annual rate of 10% compounded semiannually.

LO2 ✓   **EE-9A. Future Value Computation** You are scheduled to receive $10,000 every six months for ten periods beginning in six months. What amount in five years is equivalent to the future series of payments assuming interest compounds at the annual rate of 10% compounded semiannually?

LO3 ✓   **EE-10A. Present Value Computation** Zazzi, Inc., believes it will need $200,000 in seven years to expand its operations. Zazzi can earn 6%, compounded annually, if it deposits its money right now. How large of a deposit must Zazzi make in order to have the necessary $200,000 in seven years?

LO2 ✓   **EE-11A. Future Value Computation** Peyton Company deposited $10,000 in the bank today, earning 12% interest. Peyton plans to withdraw the money in five years. How much money will be available to withdraw assuming that interest is compounded (a) annually, (b) semiannually, and (c) quarterly?

LO2 ✓   **EE-12A. Future Value Computation** Sam Smith deposited $6,000 in a savings account today. The deposit will earn interest at the rate of 8%. How much will be available for Sam to withdraw in three years, assuming interest is compounded (a) annually, (b) semiannually, and (c) quarterly?

LO3 ✓   **EE-13A. Present Value Computation** Pete Frost made a deposit into his savings account three years ago, and earned interest at an annual rate of 8%. The deposit accumulated to $20,000. How much was initially deposited assuming that the interest was compounded (a) annually, (b) semiannually, and (c) quarterly?

LO2 ✓   **EE-14A. Future Value Computation** Kumari Jennings has decided to start saving for his daughter's college education by depositing $2,500 at the end of every year for 18 years. He has determined that he will be able to earn 5% interest compounded annually. He hopes to have at least $70,000 when his daughter starts college in eighteen years. Will his savings plan be successful?

LO3 ✓   **EE-15A. Present Value Computation** Kerry Bales won the state lottery and was given four choices for receiving her winnings.

1. Receive $200,000 right now.
2. Receive $216,000 in one year.
3. Receive $40,000 at the end of each year for eight years.
4. Receive $20,000 at the end of each year for 30 years.

Assuming Kerry can earn interest of 8% compounded annually, which option should Kerry choose?

EXERCISES—SET B

LO1 ✓   **EE-1B. Simple and Compound Interest**

a. For each of the following notes, calculate the simple interest due at the end of the term.

Note	Principal	Rate	Term
1	$5,000	8%	8 years
2	$5,000	12%	5 years
3	$5,000	4%	2 years

b. Compute the amount of interest due at the end of the term for each of the above notes assuming interest is compounded annually.

EE-2B. **Future Value Computation** At the beginning of the year you deposit $3,500 in a savings account. How much will accumulate in four years if you earn 6% compounded annually? **LO2** ✓

EE-3B. **Future Value Computation** You deposit $3,500 at the end of every year for four years. How much will accumulate in four years if you earn 6% compounded annually? **LO2** ✓

EE-4B. **Present Value Computation** You will receive $3,500 in four years. What is the present value if you can earn 6% interest compounded annually? **LO3** ✓

EE-5B. **Present Value Computation** You receive $3,500 at the end of every year for four years. What is the present value of these receipts if you earn 6% compounded annually? **LO3** ✓

EE-6B. **Future Value Computation** What amount will be accumulated in five years if $5,000 is invested today at 4% interest compounded annually? **LO2** ✓

EE-7B. **Present Value Computation** You are scheduled to be paid $5,000 in five years. What amount today is equivalent to the $5,000 to be received in five years assuming interest is compounded annually at 4%? **LO3** ✓

EE-8B. **Future Value Computation** What amount will be accumulated in five years if $5,000 is invested every six months beginning in six months and ending five years from today? Interest will accumulate at an annual rate of 4% compounded semiannually. **LO2** ✓

EE-9B. **Future Value Computation** You are scheduled to receive $5,000 every six months for six periods beginning in six months. What amount in three years is equivalent to the future series of payments assuming interest compounds at the annual rate of 8% compounded semiannually? **LO2** ✓

EE-10B. **Present Value Computation** Zumi, Inc., believes it will need $150,000 in nine years to expand its operations. Zumi can earn 5%, compounded annually, if it deposits its money right now. How large of a deposit must Zumi make in order to have the necessary $150,000 in nine years? **LO3** ✓

EE-11B. **Future Value Computation** Triton Company deposited $7,500 in the bank today, earning 8% interest. Triton plans to withdraw the money in five years. How much money will be available to withdraw assuming that interest is compounded (a) annually, (b) semiannually, and (c) quarterly? **LO2** ✓

EE-12B. **Future Value Computation** Sally Smithton deposited $4,000 in a savings account today. The deposit will earn interest at the rate of 12%. How much will be available for Sally to withdraw in three years, assuming interest is compounded (a) annually, (b) semiannually, and (c) quarterly? **LO2** ✓

EE-13B. **Present Value Computation** Raul Gomez made a deposit into his savings account four years ago, and earned interest at an annual rate of 12%. The deposit accumulated to $30,000. How much was initially deposited assuming that the interest was compounded (a) annually, (b) semiannually, and (c) quarterly? **LO3** ✓

EE-14B. **Future Value Computation** Herman Lee has decided to start saving for his daughter's college education by depositing $4,000 at the end of every year for 15 years. He has determined that he will be able to earn 6% interest compounded annually. He hopes to have at least $90,000 when his daughter starts college in fifteen years. Will his savings plan be successful? **LO2** ✓

EE-15B. **Present Value Computation** Kelly Zales won the state lottery and was given four choices for receiving her winnings. **LO3** ✓

1. Receive $100,000 right now.
2. Receive $104,000 in one year.
3. Receive $15,000 at the end of each year for eight years.
4. Receive $6,000 at the end of each year for 30 years.

Assuming Kelly can earn interest of 4% compounded annually, which option should Kelly choose?

ANSWERS TO SELF-STUDY QUESTIONS

1. *a.* 1. $50,000 × 3.106 = $155,300
   2. $50,000 × 3.207 = $160,350
   3. $50,000 × 3.262 = $163,100
 b. $5,000 × 12.006 = $60,030
 c. $3,000 × 12.006 = $36,018
 d. $1,000 × 15.937 = $15,937
  $15,000 × 2.594 = $38,910
         $54,847

2. *a.* 1. $90,000 × 0.463 = $41,670
   2. $90,000 × 0.456 = $41,040
   3. $90,000 × 0.453 = $40,770
 b. $1,000 × 5.335 = $5,335
 c. $600 × 17.292 = $10,375.20
 d. $500,000 × 0.386 = $193,000
 e. $2,500 × 11.470 = $28,675
  $85,000 × 0.312 = $26,520
        $55,195

10-K The report filed annually with the U.S. Securities and Exchange Commission by publicly held companies that reports the financial position and operating performance of the company (p. 19).

A

Accelerated depreciation method A depreciation method in which the amounts of depreciation expense taken in the early years of an asset's life are greater than the amounts expensed in later years (p. 413).

Account A record of the additions, deductions, and balances of individual assets, liabilities, stockholders' equity, dividends, revenues, and expenses (p. 65).

Account form A format of the classified balance sheet in which assets are displayed on the left side and liabilities and stockholders' equity are displayed on the right side (p. 183).

Accounting cycle A sequence of activities undertaken by company accountants to accumulate and report the financial information of a business (p. 58).

Accounting entity An economic unit with identifiable boundaries that is the focus for the accumulation and reporting of financial information (p. 26).

Accounting equation An expression of the equivalency of the economic resources and the claims upon those resources of a business, often stated as Assets = Liabilities + Stockholders' Equity (p. 13).

Accounting period The time period, usually one year, to which periodic accounting reports are related; also known as the fiscal period (p. 27).

Accounting The process of measuring the economic activity of a business in money terms and communicating those financial results to interested parties. The purpose of accounting is to provide financial information that is useful in economic decision making (p. 10).

Accounting transaction An economic event that requires accounting recognition; an event that affects any of the elements of the accounting equation—assets, liabilities, or stockholders' equity (p. 59).

Accounts receivable A current asset that is created by a sale of merchandise or the provision of a service on a credit basis. It represents the amount owed the seller by a customer (p. 362).

Accounts receivable aging method A procedure that uses an aging schedule to determine the year-end balance needed in the Allowance for Doubtful Accounts account (p. 368).

Accounts receivable turnover A ratio calculated as annual net sales divided by the average balance of accounts receivable (pp. 376, 619).

Accounts receivable turnover Annual net sales divided by average accounts receivable (net) (p. 610).

Accrual basis of accounting Accounting procedures whereby sales revenue is recorded when earned and realized and expenses are recorded in the period in which they help to generate the sales revenue (p. 27).

Accruals Adjustments that reflect revenues earned but not received or recorded and expenses incurred but not paid or recorded (p. 121).

Accrued expense An expense incurred but not yet paid; recognized with an adjusting entry (p. 124).

Accrued revenue Revenue earned but not yet billed or received; recognized with an adjusting entry (p. 125).

Accumulated depreciation The cumulative amount of depreciation expense taken in prior periods; subtracted from the related asset account (p. 123).

Adjusted trial balance A list of general ledger accounts and their balances prepared after all adjustments have been made (p. 128).

Adjusting entries Entries made at the end of an accounting period under accrual accounting to ensure the proper matching of expenses incurred with revenues earned for the period (p. 121).

Aging schedule An analysis that shows how long a business's accounts receivable balances have remained unpaid (p. 368).

Allowance for doubtful accounts A contra-asset account with a normal credit balance shown on the balance sheet as a deduction from accounts receivable to reflect the expected uncollectible amount of accounts receivable (p. 365).

Allowance method An accounting procedure whereby the amount of bad debts expense is estimated and recorded in the period in which the related credit sales occur (p. 364).

American Institute of Certified Public Accountants (AICPA) (p. 9)

Amortization The periodic write-off of an intangible asset to expense on a company's income statement (p. 423).

Annual report A report filed with the U.S. Securities and Exchange Commission by publicly held companies that reports the financial position and operating performance of the company. A less detailed version is mailed to the company's stockholders (p. 19).

Annuity A pattern of cash flows in which equal amounts are spaced equally over a number of periods (p. E-5).

Articles of incorporation A document prepared by the founders of a corporation that sets forth the structure and purpose of the corporation and specifics regarding the type and quantity of capital stock to be issued (p. 504).

Asset turnover Net sales divided by average total assets; it represents a measure of a firm's efficiency in producing sales revenue using its total assets (p. 426).

Asset turnover ratio Net sales divided by average total assets (p.615).

Assets The economic resources of a business that can be expressed in money terms (p. 13).

Audit report A report issued by an independent auditor that reports the auditor's opinion regarding a company's financial statements (p. 338).

Auditor's report The report of the independent auditor that describes the activities undertaken by a company's outside auditor and reports the auditor's opinion regarding whether the financial statements fairly present the results of the company's operations and financial health (p. 21).

Authorized shares The maximum number of shares in a class of stock that a corporation may issue (p. 508).

Available-for-sale securities Debt securities and noninfluential equity securities that management does not intend to sell in the near future or hold to maturity (p. D-2).

Average collection period 365 days divided by accounts receivable turnover (pp. 376, 620).

Average collection period A ratio calculated by dividing 365 days by the accounts receivable turnover ratio (p. 378).

B

Bad debts expense The expense stemming from the inability of a business to collect an amount previously recorded as receivable. It is normally classified as a selling or administrative expense (p. 364).

Balance sheet A financial statement showing a business's assets, liabilities, and stockholders' equity as of a specific date (p. 13).

Bank reconciliation A procedure explaining the various items—such as deposits in transit, checks outstanding, bank charges, and errors—that lead to differences between the balance shown on a bank statement and the related Cash account in a company's general ledger (p. 329).

Bearer One of the terms that may be used to designate the payee on a promissory note; it means that a note is payable to whoever holds the note (p. 372).

Benchmarking analysis A technique where the analyst or investor compares a firm's performance, or a ratio like the ROA, to that of the firm's principal competitors or to an industry average (p. 188).

Betterments Capital expenditures that improve the quality of services rendered by a plant asset or extend the asset's useful life (p. 419).

Bond A long-term debt instrument that promises to pay interest periodically and a principal amount at maturity. Bonds may incorporate a variety of provisions relating to security for the debt involved, methods of paying the periodic interest, and retirement provisions (p. 457).

Book value The dollar amount carried in the accounts for a particular asset. The book value of a depreciable asset is derived by deducting the contra account Accumulated Depreciation from the balance in the depreciable asset account (p. 123).

Budget A planning device that forecasts a business's future operating activities using financial data. The budget serves as an internal control device by providing a benchmark to compare actual performance against so that material deviations can be investigated (p. 318).

C

Calendar year A fiscal year that ends on December 31 (p. 59).

Call provision A bond feature that allows the borrower to retire (call in) the bonds after a stated date (p. 459).

Callable A feature associated with preferred stock whereby the preferred stock can be redeemed by the issuing corporation at a price specified in the stock contract (p. 511).

Capital expenditures An expenditure that increases the book value of long-term assets (p. 419).

Capital lease A lease that transfers to the lessee substantially all of the usual benefits and risks related to ownership of the property. The lessee records the leased property as an asset and establishes a liability for the lease obligation (p. 478).

Cash An asset category representing the amount of a firm's paper money, coins, checks, money orders, traveler's checks, and funds on deposit at a bank in a company's checking accounts and savings accounts (p. 321).

Cash and cash equivalents The sum of cash plus short-term, highly liquid investments such as U.S. Treasury bills and money market funds (p. 323).

Cash basis of accounting Accounting procedures whereby sales revenue is recorded when cash is received from operating activities and expenses are recorded when cash payments related to operating activities are made (p. 27).

Cash discount An amount that a purchaser of merchandise may deduct from the purchase price for paying within the allowed discount period (p. 227).

Cash equivalents Short-term, highly liquid investments that firms acquire with temporarily idle cash to earn interest on these funds. To qualify as a cash equivalent, an investment must be readily convertible into cash and be close enough to maturity so that its market value is not sensitive to interest rate changes (p. 550).

Cash management Management's efforts to determine cash needs and maintain the proper amount of cash for the company's needs (p. 550).

Certificate of deposit (CD) An investment security offering a fixed rate of return for a specified period of time (p. 321).

Certified public accountant (CPA) A professional designation given to an accountant who has fulfilled stringent licensing requirements (p. 7).

Change in accounting principle A switch from one generally accepted accounting method to another generally accepted method, such as changing depreciation methods (p. 603).

Chart of accounts A list of all of the general ledger account titles and their numerical code (p. 68).

Check A written order signed by a checking account owner directing the bank to pay a specified amount of money to the person or company named on the check (p. 327).

Classified balance sheet A balance sheet in which items are classified into subgroups to facilitate financial analysis and management decision making (p. 180).

Classified income statement An income statement in which items are classified into subgroups to facilitate financial analysis and management decision making (p. 233).

Closing process A step in the accounting cycle in which the balances of all temporary accounts are transferred to the Retained Earnings account, leaving the temporary accounts with zero balances (pp. 131, 137).

Commitments A contractual arrangement in which both parties to the contract still have acts yet to perform (p. 630).

Common stock The basic ownership class of capital stock, carrying the right to vote, share in earnings, participate in future share issues, and share in any liquidation proceeds after all more senior claims have been settled (p. 508).

Common-size financial statement A financial statement in which each item is presented as a percentage of a key statement item (p. 611).

Comparability The qualitative characteristic that enables users to determine similarities and differences among items. (p. 26)

Comparative financial statement analysis A form of horizontal analysis involving a comparison of two or more periods of financial statement data showing dollar and/or percentage changes (p. 606).

Compensating balance A minimum amount that a financial institution requires a firm to maintain in its bank account as a condition of a borrowing arrangement (p. 322).

Compound interest Interest that is computed on the accumulated principal balance plus any interest that has been earned but not yet paid (p. E-2).

Compound journal entry A journal entry containing more than one debit and one credit (p. 69).

Comprehensive income A broader definition of a company's income that includes net income plus any changes in the market value of certain marketable securities and any unrealized gains and losses from translating foreign currency denominated financial statements into U.S. dollars (p. 604).

Conceptual framework A cohesive set of interrelated objectives, elements, and recognition and measurement criteria for the GAAP developed by the FASB (p. 24).

Conservatism principle An accounting principle stating that judgmental determinations should tend toward understatement rather than overstatement of assets and net income (p. 27).

Consignment goods Items held for sale by parties other than the item's owner (p. 264).

Consistency An accounting principle stating that accounting reports should be prepared on a basis consistent with the prior periods (p. 26).

Consolidated financial statements Financial statements prepared to portray the financial position, results of operations, and cash flows of two or more affiliated companies as a single economic entity (p. D-12).

Contingency A possible future event; significant contingent liabilities must be disclosed in the notes to the financial statements (p. 631).

Contingent liabilities A potential obligation, the eventual occurrence of which usually depends on some future event beyond the control of the firm. Contingent liabilities may originate from such things as lawsuits, credit guarantees, and contested income tax assessments (p. 466).

Contra account An account related to, and deducted from, another account when financial statements are prepared or when book values are computed (p. 123).

Contributed capital The capital contributed to a company by stockholders when they purchase shares of stock from the company (pp. 16, 192).

Control numbers Preprinted numbers on documents such as purchase orders, invoices, credit memos, and checks used to provide an internal control that all documents are accounted for (p. 318).

Controlling securities Equity securities that represent an ownership of more than 50 percent of a corporation's voting stock (p. D-2).

Convertible A feature associated with preferred stock whereby the preferred stock can be converted into common stock at a specified conversion rate (p. 511).

Convertible bond A bond incorporating the holder's right to convert the bond into common stock under prescribed terms (p. 458).

Copyright An exclusive right that protects an owner against the unauthorized reproduction of a specific written work or artwork (p. 423).

Corporate social responsibility The practice that considers how a corporation's behavior affects its various stakeholders to ensure an adherence to ethical standards (p. 15).

Corporation A legal entity created under the laws of a state or the federal government. The owners of a corporation receive shares of stock as evidence of their ownership interest in the company (pp. 4, 504).

Cost flow The actual or assumed assignment of costs to goods sold and to ending inventory (p. 267).

Cost of goods available for sale An amount that represents the inventory available to be sold, consisting of the beginning inventory plus purchases during the period (p. 239).

Cost of goods sold percentage The ratio of cost of goods sold divided by net sales (p. 238).

Cost of goods sold The total cost of merchandise sold to customers during the accounting period; often abbreviated as COGS (p. 229).

Cost principle An accounting principle stating that asset measures should be based on the price paid to acquire an asset (p. 27).

Cost-benefit constraint Requires that the benefits derived from accounting information are greater than the cost of providing the information. (p. 27)

Coupon rate The rate of interest stated on a bond certificate (p. 460).

Credit (entry) An entry on the right side (or in the credit column) of an account (p. 66).

Credit card fee A fee charged to retailers for credit card services provided by a financial institution. The fee is usually stated as a percentage of credit card sales (p. 371).

Credit guarantee A guarantee of another company's debt by cosigning a note payable; a guarantor's contingent liability must be disclosed in a balance sheet footnote (p. 467).

Credit period The maximum time period, stated in days, that a purchaser of merchandise has to pay a seller (p. 227).

Credit-collection policy A policy establishing the amount of time that customers are allowed before they must pay their outstanding accounts receivable (p. 363).

Credit-granting policy A policy to determine which customers to grant credit and how much credit to grant those customers (p. 363).

Creditor An individual or financial institution that lends money or services to a company with the expectation of receiving repayment in the future (p. 5).

Cumulative A feature associated with preferred stock whereby any dividends-in-arrears must be paid before any dividends may be paid on common stock (p. 510).

Current assets Cash and other assets that will be converted to cash or used up during the normal operating cycle of a business or one year, whichever is longer (p. 180).

Current liabilities Liabilities that must be settled within the normal operating cycle or one year, whichever is longer (pp. 182, 450).

Current liabilities Obligations that will require within the coming year or operating cycle, whichever is longer, (1) the use of existing current assets or (2) the creation of other current liabilities (p. 450).

Current ratio A measure of a firm's liquidity, calculated as current assets divided by current liabilities (pp. 189, 469, 617).

D

Days' sales in inventory A ratio computed by dividing 365 by Inventory Turnover; this ratio indicates the number of days it takes, on average, for a company to sell its inventory (pp. 279, 621).

Debenture bond A bond that has no specific property pledged as security (or collateral) for the repayment of the borrowed funds (p. 457).

Debit (entry) An entry on the left side (or in the debit column) of an account (p. 66).

Debt financing A source of financing for a company involving the use of debt, such as a bank loan or the issuance of bonds (p. 5).

Debt security A security that creates, for the holder, a creditor relationship with an entity (p. D-2).

Debt-to-total-assets ratio A measure of a firm's solvency, calculated as total liabilities divided by total assets (p. 190).

Debt-to-equity ratio A firm's total liabilities divided by its total stockholders' equity (p. 622).

Declining-balance method An accelerated depreciation method that allocates depreciation expense to each year by applying a constant depreciation percentage to the declining book value of a long-lived asset (p. 413).

Deferrals Adjustments that allocate various assets and revenues received in advance to the proper accounting periods as expenses and revenues (p. 121).

Deferred revenue A liability representing revenues received in advance; also called *unearned revenue* (p. 124).

Deposits in transit Cash deposits made to a bank account near the end of a month that do not appear on that month's bank statement (p. 331).

Depreciation accounting The process of allocating the cost of long-lived assets (less salvage value) to expense in a systematic and rational manner over the time period benefitting from their use (p. 410).

Depreciation The process of allocating the cost of buildings, equipment, and vehicles to expense over the time periods benefiting from their use (pp. 123, 410).

Detection control An internal control designed to discover problems soon after they arise (p. 316).

Direct method A presentation of the cash flow from operating activities in a statement of cash flows that shows the major categories of operating cash receipts and payments (p. 555).

Direct write-off method An accounting procedure whereby the amount of bad debts expense is not recorded until specific uncollectible customer accounts are identified (p. 379).

Discontinued operations Operating segments of a company that have been sold, abandoned, or disposed of during the accounting period. Related operating income (or loss) and related gains and losses on disposal are reported separately on the income statement (p. 602).

Discount period The maximum amount of time, stated in days, that a purchaser of merchandise has to pay a seller if the purchaser wants to claim any available cash discount (p. 227).

Discounting Selling a note receivable for cash at a financial institution (p. 377).

Dividend payout ratio A financial ratio showing the percentage of net income available to common stockholders that is paid out as dividends; calculated as the annual dividend per share divided by earnings per share (pp. 523, 626).

Dividend yield Annual dividend per share divided by the market price per share (pp. 522, 625).

Dividends Distributions of assets (usually cash) or stock from a corporation to its stockholders (p. 516).

Double-entry accounting A method of accounting that results in the recording of equal amounts of debits and credits (p. 59).

E

Earned capital Capital that is earned by a company and not distributed to its stockholders as a dividend; referred to as retained earnings (pp. 16, 192).

Earnings per share (EPS) A financial ratio computed as net income less preferred stock dividends divided by the weighted average number of common shares outstanding for the period (p. 624).

Earnings quality The degree to which reported financial results reflect the actual financial condition and performance of the reporting company (p. 135).

Effective interest method A method of interest amortization that recognizes a constant percentage of the book value of a bond as interest expense for each interest payment period. (p. 473)

Effective interest rate The current rate of interest in the market for a bond or other debt instrument. When issued, a bond is priced to yield the market rate of interest at the date of issuance (pp. 463, 473).

Electronic funds transfer Sending an electronic message from one computer to another to cause a transfer of money from one financial institution to another (p. 328).

Employee collusion When one or more employees work together to circumvent an internal control (p. 320).

Equity financing A source of financing for a company involving the sale of shares of common stock (p. 5).

Equity method A method of accounting by a parent company for investments in affiliate companies by which the parent's share of subsidiary income or loss is periodically recorded in the parent company's investment account (p. D-9).

Equity security A security that represents an ownership interest in an entity (p. D-2).

Ethics An area of inquiry dealing with the values, rules, and justifications that govern an individual's way of life or a corporation's behavior (p. 8).

Expense recognition (matching) principle An accounting guideline that states that net income is determined by relating expenses to the sales revenues generated by the expenses (p. 27).

Expenses Decreases in stockholders' equity incurred by a firm during the process of generating its sales revenues (p. 14).

Extraordinary items Transactions and events that are unusual in nature and occur infrequently. Gains and losses on such items are shown separately, net of tax effects, on the income statement (p. 602).

F

F.O.B. destination Free-on-board destination indicates that the items being shipped are owned by the seller while the items are in transit (p. 264).

F.O.B. shipping point Free-on-board shipping point indicates that the items being shipped are owned by the buyer while the items are in transit (p. 264).

Factoring Selling an account receivable for cash to a financial institution (p. 377).

Factors Finance companies and financial institutions that buy receivables (p. 377).

Faithful representation The fundamental qualitative characteristic that requires a depiction to be complete, neutral, and free from error such that it depicts the phenomena it purports to represent. (p. 25)

Federal Insurance Contributions Act (FICA) Under this act, the income of an individual is taxed to support the national social security program providing retirement income, medical care, and death benefits. Employers pay a matching amount of tax on their eligible employees (p. 453).

Fidelity bond An insurance policy that provides financial compensation for theft by employees specifically covered by the insurance (p. 320).

Financial Accounting Standards Board (FASB) A private, not-for-profit organization whose task is to develop generally accepted accounting principles in the United States (p. 11).

Financial accounting The area of accounting dealing with the preparation of financial statements showing a business's results of operations, financial position, and cash flow (p. 7).

Financial flexibility A firm's ability to generate sufficient amounts of cash to respond to unanticipated business needs and opportunities (p. 555).

Financial reporting objectives A component of the conceptual framework which specifies that financial statements should provide information that is (1) useful for investment and credit decisions, (2) helpful in assessing an entity's ability to generate future cash flows, and (3) about an entity's resources, claims on those resources, and the effects of events causing changes in these items (p. 25).

Financial statement audit An examination of a company's financial statements by a firm of independent certified public accountants (p. 337).

Financial statement elements A component of the conceptual framework that identifies the significant components—assets, liabilities, stockholders' equity, revenues, and expenses—used to prepare financial statements (p. 25).

Financing activities A section in the statement of cash flows that reports cash flows associated with obtaining cash from owners and creditors, returning cash to owners, and repaying amounts borrowed (pp. 5, 552).

Finished goods inventory A manufacturer's inventory that includes all products that have been completed and are ready for sale to customers (p. 263).

First-in, first-out (FIFO) method An inventory costing method that assumes that the oldest (earliest purchased) goods are sold first (pp. 268, 282).

Fiscal year The annual accounting period used by a business (p. 59).

FOB destination Free on board destination indicates that the items being shipped are owned by the seller while the items are in transit (p. 226).

FOB shipping point Free on board shipping point indicates that the items being shipped are owned by the buyer while the items are in transit (p. 225).

Forensic accounting A branch of accounting that involves investigations that result from actual or anticipated disputes such as criminal activity (p. 9).

Forward stock split Additional shares of capital stock issued by a corporation to its current stockholders in proportion to their current ownership interests without changing the balances in the related stockholders' equity accounts. A forward stock split increases the number of shares outstanding and reduces proportionately the stock's par value per share (p. 514).

Franchise An exclusive right to operate or sell a specific brand of products in a given geographic area (p. 424).

Fraud Any act by the management or employees of a business involving an intentional deception for personal gain (p. 314).

Fraud triangle The three elements of fraud, consisting of (1) pressure, (2) rationalization, and (3) opportunity (p. 314).

Free cash flow (FCF) A measure of a firm's cash flow health, calculated as cash provided by operating activities less cash expenditures for property, plant, and equipment. Free cash flow is a measure of a firm's operating cash flow available for general corporate purposes such as debt retirement or dividend payment (pp. 194, 564).

Free on board A term for determining ownership for items in transit (p. 226).

Full disclosure principle An accounting principle stipulating that all facts necessary to make financial statements useful should be disclosed in a firm's annual report (p. 27).

Future value The amount that a specified investment (or series of investments) will be worth at a future date if invested at a given rate of compound interest (p. E-3).

G

General journal An accounting record with enough flexibility so that any type of business transaction may be recorded in it; a diary of a business's accounting transactions (p. 68).

General ledger A grouping of all of a business's accounts that are used to prepare the basic financial statements (p. 70).

Generally accepted accounting principles (GAAP) A set of standards and procedures that guide the preparation of financial statements (p. 10).

Going concern concept An accounting principle that assumes that, in the absence of evidence to the contrary, a business enterprise will have an indefinite life (p. 27).

Goods flow The actual physical movement of inventory through a business (p. 267).

Goods in transit Items that are being shipped by a common carrier (p. 264).

Goodwill The value of all attributes acquired in an acquisition that are not otherwise associated with other specific assets; calculated as the purchase price of the acquired company less the fair market value of the identifiable net assets (p. 424).

Gross pay The amount an employee earns before any withholdings or deductions (p. 453).

Gross profit percentage Gross profit on sales divided by net sales (pp. 232, 612).

Gross profit The difference between net sales and cost of goods sold; also called gross margin (pp. 185, 614).

H

Held-to-maturity securities Debt securities that management intends to hold to maturity (p. D-2).

Holding company A corporation that controls another corporation through ownership of the latter's stock (p. D-12).

Horizontal analysis The analysis of a firm's financial statements that covers two or more years (p. 605).

I

Impairment loss A loss recognized on an impaired asset equal to the difference between its book value and its current fair value (p. 416).

Income statement A financial statement reporting a business's sales revenue and expenses for a given period of time (p. 14).

Indirect method A presentation of cash flow from operating activities in a statement of cash flows that begins with net income and applies a series of adjustments to convert the net income to a cash basis amount (p. 555).

Influential securities Equity securities that represent a 20 to 50 percent ownership of a corporation's voting stock (p. D-2).

Institute of Management Accountants (p. 9).

Intangible asset An asset lacking a physical presence; examples of intangible assets include patents, copyrights, and brand names (pp. 181, 421).

Interest A payment for the use of money (p. E-2).

Internal auditing A company function that provides independent appraisals of the company's financial statements, its internal control, and its operations (p. 319).

Internal controls The measures undertaken by a company to ensure the reliability of its accounting data, protect its assets from theft or unauthorized use, insure that employees follow the company's policies and procedures, and evaluate the performance of employees, departments, divisions, and the company as a whole (p. 315).

International accounting principles A set of accounting guidelines that are acceptable for the preparation of financial statements worldwide (p. 23).

International Accounting Standards Board (IASB) An independent accounting standard-setting agency whose purpose is to develop international financial accounting standards (p. 12).

International Financial Reporting Standards (IFRS) An international set of accounting standards, interpretations, and the framework for the preparation and presentation of financial statements used in many countries (p. 12).

Inventory carrying costs Costs created by just-in-case inventories, including casualty insurance, building usage costs, and the cost of capital invested in the inventory (p. 263).

Inventory overage The increase in the inventory account that occurs when the physical inventory count is greater than the inventory account balance (p. 265).

Inventory shrinkage The decrease in the inventory account that occurs when the physical inventory count is less than the inventory account balance (p. 265).

Inventory turnover Cost of goods sold divided by average inventory (p. 620).

Inventory turnover ratio A ratio computed by dividing cost of goods sold by the average ending inventory (p. 278).

Investing activities A section in the statement of cash flows that reports cash flows involving (1) the purchase and sale of plant assets and intangible assets, (2) the purchase and sale of stocks, bonds, and other securities (other than cash equivalents), and (3) the lending and subsequent collection of money (pp. 6, 552).

Invoice price The price that a seller charges a purchaser for merchandise (p. 226).

Issued shares Shares of stock that have been sold and issued to stockholders; issued stock may be either outstanding or held in the treasury (p. 508).

J

Journal A tabular record in which business transactions are analyzed in debit and credit terms and recorded in chronological order (p. 68).

Journal entry An entry of accounting information into a journal (p. 68).

Just-in-case inventory The extra quantity of inventory that a firm carries just in case suppliers do not deliver when scheduled or just in case the company decides to make previously unplanned quantities of product for sale to customers (p. 263).

Just-in-time (JIT) manufacturing A manufacturing philosophy that seeks to minimize or eliminate just-in-case inventory quantities through careful planning of raw material purchases and manufacturing management (p. 263).

L

Land improvements Improvements with limited useful lives made to land sites, such as paved parking lots and driveways (p. 409).

Last-in, first-out (LIFO) method An inventory costing method that assumes that the newest (most recently purchased) goods are sold first (p. 269, 283).

Lawsuit A prosecution of a claim in a court of law; may lead to a financial statement footnote disclosure by the defendant as a contingent liability (p. 467).

Lease A contract between a lessor (owner) and lessee (tenant) for the rental of property (p. 478).

Leasehold improvements Expenditures made by a lessee to alter or improve leased property (p. 409).

Leasehold The rights transferred from the lessor to the lessee by a lease (p. 478).

Lessee The party acquiring the right to the use of property by a lease (p. 478).

Lessor The owner of property who transfers the right to use the property to another party by a lease (p. 478).

Leverage The use of borrowed funds to finance the assets or operations of a firm (p. 468).

Liabilities The obligations or debts that a business must pay in money or services at some time in the future as a consequence of past transactions or events (pp. 13, 450).

LIFO conformity rule A section of the Internal Revenue Code requiring that any company that selects LIFO for income tax reporting must also use LIFO for financial reporting to stockholders (p. 274).

LIFO inventory reserve The difference between the value of ending inventory reported under LIFO and what the inventory would have been valued at under FIFO (p. 287).

Liquidity A measure of a company's ability to pay its obligations expected to come due in the next year (pp. 181, 189).

List price The suggested price or reference price of merchandise in a catalog or price list (p. 232).

Long-term liabilities Debt obligations not due to be repaid within the normal operating cycle or one year, whichever is longer (p. 183).

Lower-of-cost-or-market (LCM) A measurement method that, when applied to inventory, provides for ending inventory to be valued on the balance sheet at the lower of its acquisition cost or current replacement cost (p. 276).

M

Maker The signer of a promissory note (p. 372).

Management Discussion and Analysis (MD&A) Part of the annual report that contains management's interpretation of the company's recent past performance along with discussion of possible future opportunities and risks (p. 20).

Managerial accounting The accounting activities carried out by a firm's accounting staff primarily to provide management with accounting data for decisions related to a firm's operations (p. 8).

Manufacturer A company that converts raw materials and components into finished goods through the application of skilled labor and machine operations (p. 222).

Market rate of interest The rate of interest in the market for a bond or other debt instrument (p. 460).

Materiality An accounting guideline that states that insignificant data that would not affect a financial statement user's decisions may be recorded in the most expedient manner (p. 27).

Maturity date The date on which a note or bond matures (pp. 373, 451).

Merchandise inventory A stock of goods that a company buys from another company and makes available for sale to its customers (p. 224).

Merchandising firm A company that buys finished goods, stores the goods for varying periods of time, and then resells the goods (p. 222).

Modified accelerated cost recovery system (MACRS) A system of accelerated depreciation for U.S. income tax purposes; it prescribes depreciation rates by asset-life classification (p. 417).

Monetary unit concept An accounting guideline that reports assets, liabilities and stockholders' equity in the basic unit of money (p. 27).

Multi-step income statement An income statement in which items are classified into subgroups to facilitate financial analysis and management decision making (p. 185).

Multiple-step income statement An income statement in which one or more intermediate performance measures, such as gross profit on sales, are derived before the continuing income is reported (p. 600).

N

Net assets The difference between a business's assets and liabilities. Net assets are equal to stockholders' equity (p. 13).

Net income The excess of a business's sales revenues over its expenses (p. 15).

Net pay The amount of an employee's paycheck, after subtracting withheld amounts (p. 453).

Net realizable value An asset measure calculated by subtracting the expected disposal cost from an asset's expected selling price (p. 276).

Net sales The total revenue generated by a company through merchandise sales less the revenue given up through sales returns and allowances and less the revenue given up through sales discounts (pp. 185, 232).

New York Stock Exchange (NYSE) A marketplace, located in New York City, for the buying and selling of corporate shares (p. 5).

No-par value stock Stock that does not have a par value (p. 508).

Noncash expenses Expenses that do not involve any current period cash outflows and that are deducted in the process of calculating a company's accrual basis net income (p. 560).

Noncash investing and financing activities Investing activities and financing activities that do not affect current cash flows; information about these events must be reported as a supplement to the statement of cash flows (p. 554).

Normal balance The side on which increases to the account are recorded. (p. 67)

Normal operating cycle The average period of time between the use of cash to buy goods for resale or to provide services and the subsequent collection of cash from customers (p. 180).

Not-sufficient-funds check A check from an individual or company that had an insufficient cash balance in the bank when the holder of the check presented it to the bank for payment (p. 322).

Note receivable A promissory note held by the note's payee (p. 372).

Notes to the financial statements The annual report section following the four financial statements that includes a description of the assumptions and estimates that were used in preparing the statements, the measurement procedures that were followed, and the details behind the summary numbers (p. 20).

O

Objectivity An accounting notion requiring that, whenever possible, accounting data should be based on objectively determined evidence (p. 7).

Off-balance-sheet financing The structuring of a financing arrangement such that no liability is recorded on the borrower's balance sheet (p. 478).

Open account A charge account provided by a retailer for its customers (p. 224).

Operating activities A section in the statement of cash flows that reports cash flows from all activities that are not classified as investing or financing activities (pp. 6, 552).

Operating cycle For a particular business, the average period of time between the use of cash in its typical operating activity and the subsequent collection of cash from customers (p. 223).

Operating lease A lease by which the lessor retains the usual risks and rewards of owning the property (p. 478).

Operating-cash-flow-to-capital-expenditures ratio A financial ratio calculated by dividing a firm's cash flow from operating activities by its annual capital expenditures (pp. 565, 623).

Operating-cash-flow-to-current-liabilities ratio A financial ratio calculated by dividing cash flow from operating activities by the average current liabilities for the year (pp. 564, 619).

Operational audit An evaluation of activities, systems, and internal controls within a company to determine their efficiency, effectiveness, and economy (p. 338).

Ordinary annuity An annuity where the payments occur at the end of each period (p. E-5).

Outstanding checks Checks issued by a firm that have not yet been presented to its bank for payment (p. 331).

Outstanding shares Shares of stock that are currently held by stockholders (p. 508).

P

Paid-in capital The amount of capital contributed to a corporation by its stockholders in excess of its par value or stated value (p. 513).

Par value An amount specified in the corporate charter for each class of stock and imprinted on the face of each stock certificate; often determines the legal capital of a corporation (p. 507).

Parent company A company holding all, or a majority, of the voting stock of another company, called a subsidiary (p. D-12).

Participating A feature associated with preferred stock whereby the preferred stock can share any special dividend distribution with common stock beyond the regular preferred stock divid*end rate (*p. 511).

Partnership A voluntary association of two or more persons for the purpose of conducting a business (p. 4).

Password A string of characters that a user enters into a device to prove that the user is actually the user that is allowed to use the device (p. 325).

Patent An exclusive privilege granted for 20 years to an inventor that gives the patent holder the right to exclude others from making, using, or selling the invention (p. 423).

Payee The company or individual to whom a promissory note is made payable (p. 372).

Percentage of net sales method A procedure that determines the bad debts expense for the year by multiplying net credit sales by an estimated uncollectible percentage (p. 367).

Period-in-time statement A financial statement accumulating information for a specific period of time; examples include the income statement, the statement of stockholders' equity, the statement of retained earnings, and the statement of cash flows (p. 18).

Periodic inventory system A system that records merchandise transactions in a variety of accounts; the Inventory account and Cost of Goods Sold account are not updated until the end of the period when a physical count of the inventory is taken (p. 224).

Permanent account An account used to prepare the balance sheet—that is, an asset, liability, or stockholders' equity account; any balance in a permanent account at the end of an accounting period is carried forward to the following accounting period (pp. 131, 137).

Perpetual inventory system A system that records the cost of merchandise inventory in the Inventory account at the time of purchase and updates the Inventory account for subsequent purchases and sales of merchandise as they occur (p. 224).

Persistent earnings Earnings that are expected to recur over time. Also known as *sustainable earnings* or *permanent earnings* (p. 600).

Petty cash fund A special, relatively small cash fund established for making minor cash disbursements in the operation of a business (p. 329).

Physical count of inventory A year-end procedure that involves counting the quantity of each inventory item, determining the unit cost of each item, multiplying the unit cost times the quantity on hand, and summing the costs of all the items to determine the total inventory at cost (p. 265).

Physical count of inventory The counting of inventory used to verify the balance of inventory (p. 270).

Plant assets A firm's property, plant, and equipment; also called fixed assets (p. 406).

Point-in-time statement A financial statement presenting information as of a particular date; the balance sheet is a point-in-time statement (p. 18).

Post-closing trial balance A list of general ledger accounts and their balances after closing entries have been recorded and posted (pp. 133, 139).

Postdated check A check from another person or company with a calendar date that is later than the current date. A postdated check does not become cash until the calendar date of the check (p. 321).

Posting references A series of abbreviations used in posting to indicate to where or from where a journal entry is posted (p. 70).

Posting The transfer of information from the journal to the general ledger accounts (p. 70).

Preemptive right The right of a stockholder to maintain his or her proportionate ownership interest in a corporation by having the right to purchase an appropriate quantity of shares in any new share issue (p. 509).

Preferred stock A class of capital stock with priority over common stock in dividend payments and in the distribution of assets in the event of a corporation liquidation (p. 509).

Present value The current worth of amounts to be paid (or received) in the future; calculated by discounting the future payments (or receipts) at a specified interest rate (p. E-6).

Prevention control An internal control designed to discover problems before they arise (p. 316).

Price-earnings ratio The current market price per common share divided by a company's earnings per share (p. 625).

Principal As it relates to debt financing, the amount initially borrowed from the creditor (pp. 5, E-2).

Product warranties Guarantees against product defects for a designated period of time following product sale (p. 456).

Promissory note A written promise to pay a certain sum of money on demand or at a determinable future time (p. 372).

Property, plant, and equipment The land, buildings, equipment, vehicles, furniture, and fixtures that a firm uses in its operations; often referred to as PP&E (p. 181).

Public Company Accounting Oversight Board (PCAOB) A quasi-governmental agency established by the Sarbanes-Oxley Act to overhaul auditing standards, inspect the work of accounting firms, and discipline independent auditors that fail to meet and maintain acceptable standards of audit performance (pp. 11, 337).

Purchase allowance A reduction in the selling price of merchandise granted by a seller due to dissatisfaction by the purchaser (p. 226).

Purchase return Shipping unsatisfactory merchandise from a purchaser back to the seller for a purchase allowance (p. 226).

Q

Qualitative characteristics of accounting information The characteristics of accounting information that contribute to decision usefulness; the primary qualities are relevance and faithful representation. (p. 25)

Qualitative characteristics of accounting information The characteristics of accounting information that contribute to decision usefulness; the primary qualities are relevance and reliability (p. 25).

Quarterly data Selected quarterly financial information that is reported in the annual report to stockholders (p. 631).

Quick ratio Quick assets (that is, cash and cash equivalents, short-term investments, and accounts receivable) divided by current liabilities (pp. 470, 618).

Quick ratio The sum of (1) cash and cash equivalents, (2) short-term investments, and (3) accounts receivables divided by current liabilities (pp. 470, 618).

Quick response system A system used with a point-of-sale system that is designed to insure that a retailer quickly orders more of the items that are selling and quickly eliminates those items that are not selling (p. 263).

R

Ratio analysis The process of expressing the relationship of one accounting number to another accounting number through the process of division (p. 188).

Raw materials inventory A manufacturer's inventory that includes raw materials and components that have been purchased for use in the factory but have not yet been placed into production (p. 262).

Recognition and measurement criteria The criteria that must be met before a financial statement element may be recorded in the accounts. Essentially, the item must meet the definition of an element and must be measurable, and the resultant information about the item must be relevant and reliable (p. 26).

Relevance A qualitative characteristic of accounting information; relevant information contributes to the predictive and evaluative decisions made by financial statement users (p. 25).

Reliability A qualitative characteristic of accounting information; reliable information contains no bias or error and faithfully portrays what it intends to represent (p. 25).

Remittance advice A form that accompanies a check to inform the person receiving the check about the purpose of the check (p. 323).

Remittance list A list of the checks received from customers to pay their accounts receivable (p. 324).

Report form A format of the classified balance sheet where assets are displayed on the top and liabilities and stockholders' equity are displayed below the assets (p. 183).

Research and development costs Expenditures for the research and development of products or processes. These costs are almost always expensed rather than capitalized (p. 422).

Restricted cash Cash that is restricted for a specific use and not available for general use (p. 322).

Retailer A company that buys goods from wholesale distributors and sells the goods to individual customers (p. 223).

Retained earnings The earnings of a corporation that have been retained in the corporation (have not been paid out as a dividend) for future corporate use (p. 16, 513).

Return on assets (ROA) A measure of profitability; defined as net income divided by average total assets (or period-end assets). (pp. 188, 426, 615).

Return on common stockholders' equity A financial ratio computed as (net income - preferred stock dividends) divided by average common stockholders' equity (pp. 522, 616).

Return on sales (profit margin) Net income divided by net sales (p. 614).

Return on sales (ROS) ratio A measure of a firm's profitability, calculated as net income divided by net sales (p. 191).

Return on sales ratio (profit margin) The ratio of net income divided by net sales, representing the net profit earned on each dollar of net sales (p. 233).

Revenue expenditures An expenditure related to plant assets that is expensed when incurred (p. 418).

Revenue recognition principle An accounting principle requiring that sales revenues be recognized when services are performed or goods are sold (p. 27).

S

Sale on account A sale of merchandise made on a credit basis (p. 224).

Sale on credit See sale on account (p. 224).

Sales discounts An account used by a seller to record cash discounts taken by a buyer when payment is made during the allowed discount period (pp. 186, 227).

Sales returns and allowances An account used by a seller to record either the return of merchandise by a buyer or an allowance given to the buyer in lieu of a return (p. 186, 230).

Sales revenue Increases in stockholders' equity that result when a firm provides goods or services to its customers (p. 14).

Salvage value The expected net recovery when a plant asset is sold or removed from service; also called *residual value* (p. 410).

Sarbanes-Oxley Act (SOX) A set of legislative rules enacted in 2002 to provide stricter guidance over corporate behavior. The legislation was a reaction to the infamous accounting scandals at Enron and WorldCom (p. 9).

Secured bond A bond that pledges specific property as security (or collateral) for meeting the terms of a bond agreement (p. 457).

Segment A subdivision of a firm for which supplemental financial information is disclosed (p. 631).

Segregation of duties An internal control principle that requires that duties should be allocated to separate individuals (p. 317).

Serial bond A bond issue that staggers the bond maturity dates over a series of years (p. 458).

Service company A firm whose primary revenue source is from providing services to a customer rather than manufacturing or selling a physical product. (p. 222)

Simple interest Interest that is calculated only on the initial principal and not on any unpaid interest (p. E-2).

Single-step income statement A simple format of the income statement where net income is computed in a single step; subtracting total expenses from total revenues. (p. 185)

Single-step income statement An income statement in which the continuing income is derived in one step by subtracting total expenses from total sales revenues (p. 600).

Sinking fund provision A bond feature that requires the borrower to retire a portion of the outstanding bonds each year or, in some cases, to make payments each year to a trustee who is responsible for managing the resources needed to retire the bonds at maturity (p. 459).

Socially responsible investing (SRI) An investment strategy that considers not just financial performance but also the social concepts of environmental stewardship, consumer protection, human rights, and diversity (p. 193).

Sole proprietorship A form of business organization in which one person owns the business (p. 4).

Solvency A measure of a company's ability to repay its debts in the long term (p. 190).

Source document Any written document or computer record evidencing an accounting transaction, such as a bank check, deposit slip, sales invoice, or cash register tape (p. 67).

Specific identification method An inventory costing method involving the physical identification of goods sold and goods remaining and costing these amounts at their actual costs (pp. 268, 282).

Stated value A nominal amount that may be assigned to each share of no-par value stock and accounted for much as if it were a par value (p. 508).

Statement of cash flows A financial statement showing a firm's cash inflows and cash outflows for a specific period, classified into operating, investing, and financing activity categories (pp. 17, 544).

Statement of retained earnings A financial statement showing the financial changes that occurred in retained earnings during the accounting period (p. 520).

Statement of stockholders' equity A financial statement presenting information regarding the events that cause a change in stockholders' equity during a period. The statement presents the beginning balance, additions to, deductions from, and the ending balance of stockholders' equity for the period (pp. 15, 520).

Stock dividends Additional shares of capital stock issued by a corporation to its current stockholders in proportion to their existing ownership interest (p. 518).

Stockholder An owner of a corporation as a result of the purchase of the corporation's shares of stock; also known as a shareholder (p. 4).

Stockholders' equity The residual interest in the assets of a business after all liabilities have been paid off; stockholders' equity is equal to a firm's net assets, or total assets less total liabilities (pp. 13, 183).

Straight-line depreciation A depreciation procedure that allocates uniform amounts of depreciation expense to each period of an asset's useful life (p. 123).

Straight-line method A depreciation method that allocates equal amounts of depreciation expense to each period of an asset's expected useful life (p. 411).

Subsequent events Events occurring shortly after a fiscal year-end that are reported as supplemental information to the financial statements of the year just ended (p. 631).

Subsidiaries Corporations that have at least a majority of their voting stock owned by another company (p. D-12).

Summary of significant accounting policies A financial statement disclosure, usually the initial note to the financial statements, which identifies the major accounting policies and procedures used by a firm (p. 630).

T

T-account An abbreviated form of the formal account in the shape of a T (p. 65).

Temporary account An account used to gather information for an accounting period; revenue, expense, and dividend accounts are temporary accounts (pp. 131, 137).

Term loan A long-term borrowing, evidenced by a note payable, that is arranged with a single lender (pp. 457, 465).

Time value of money The concept that money can be invested at a positive interest rate and grow to a larger sum in the future (p. E-2).

Timeliness Having information available in time to be capable of influencing a decision. (p. 26)

Times-interest-earned ratio Income before interest expense and income taxes divided by interest expense (pp. 471, 623).

Trade name An exclusive and continuing right to use a certain term or name to identify a brand or family of products (p. 425).

Trademark An exclusive and continuing right to use a certain symbol to identify a brand or family of products (p. 424).

Trading securities Debt securities and noninfluential equity securities that management buys with the intent to sell in the near future (p. D-2).

Transitory earnings Single-period events such as extraordinary gains/losses, special items, restructuring charges, changes in accounting principle, and discontinued operations (p. 600).

Treasury stock Shares of a corporation that have been acquired for purposes other than retiring (cancelling) the stock. Treasury stock is recorded at cost and is deducted from stockholders' equity on the balance sheet (p. 515).

Trend analysis A process in which an analyst or investor compares a company's results, or the results of a ratio, over time (p. 188).

Trend percentages A comparison of the same financial item over two or more years stated as a percentage of a base-year amount (p. 609).

Trial balance A list of the account titles in the general ledger, their respective debit or credit balances, and the totals of the debit and credit balances (p. 75).

Triple bottom line A form of reporting that captures an expanded set of measures in addition to traditional financial reporting. The three bottom lines include economic, ecological, and social (p. 15).

U

U.S. Securities and Exchange Commission (SEC) (p. 11)

Unadjusted trial balance A list of general ledger accounts and their balances taken before adjustments have been made (p. 120).

Unearned revenue A liability representing revenues received in advance; also called *deferred revenue* (pp. 62, 124).

Units-of-production method A depreciation method that allocates depreciation expense to each operating period in proportion to the amount of the asset's total expected productive capacity used each period (p. 414).

Unusual items Items that display a high degree of abnormality and/or are unrelated, or only incidentally related, to the normal activities of a business (p. 601).

Useful life The period of time that an asset is used by a business, running from the date of acquisition to the date of disposal (or removal from service) (p. 410).

V

Verifiability Different individuals can independently reach a consensus that the reported amounts represent a faithful representation. (p. 26)

Vertical analysis Analysis of a firm's financial statements that focuses on the statements of a single year (p. 606).

W

Weighted-average cost method An inventory costing method that calculates an average unit purchase cost, weighted by the number of units purchased at each price, and uses that weighted-average unit cost to determine the cost of goods sold for all sales (pp. 270, 284).

Wholesaler A company that buys finished products from manufacturing firms in large quantities and resells the products to retailers (p. 223).

Work-in-process inventory A manufacturer's inventory that consists of units of product that have been entered into production in the factory but have not yet been completed (p. 262).

Working capital The difference between a firm's current assets and current liabilities (pp. 469, 617).

Working capital The difference between current assets and current liabilities (p. 470).

Worksheet An informal accounting document used to facilitate the preparation of financial statements (p. 140).

Z

Zero-coupon bond A bond that offers no periodic interest payments and that is issued at a substantial discount from its face value (p. 458).